W9-AQV-341

What Is Psychology?

Foundations, Applications, and Integration

Ellen Pastorino | Valencia College

Susann Doyle-Portillo | University of North Georgia

CENGAGE Learning®

Australia • Brazil • Japan • Korea • Mexico • Singapore • Spain • United Kingdom • United States

CENGAGE Learning®

What Is Psychology? Foundations, Applications, and Integration
Ellen Pastorino and Susann Doyle-Portillo

Product Director: Jon-David Hague

Senior Product Manager: Clay Austin

Content Developers: Michelle Newhart and Mary Noel

Product Assistant: Kimiya Hojjat

Managing Media Developer: Mary Noel

Marketing Director: Jennifer Levanduski

Senior Content Project Manager: Christy Frame

Senior Art Director: Vernon Boes

Senior Manufacturing Planner: Karen Hunt

Production and Composition: Jill Traut, MPS Limited

Photo Researcher: Priya Subrayal, Lumina Datamatics

Text Researcher: Kavitha Balasundaram, Lumina Datamatics

Copy Editor: Laura Larson

Text Designer: Marsha Cohen

Cover Designer: Jeff Bane

Cover Image: Sergey Chernov/iStock/Thinkstock

© 2016 Cengage Learning.

Unless otherwise noted all items are © Cengage Learning®

WCN: 01-100-101

ALL RIGHTS RESERVED. No part of this work covered by the copyright herein may be reproduced, transmitted, stored, or used in any form or by any means graphic, electronic, or mechanical, including but not limited to photocopying, recording, scanning, digitizing, taping, Web distribution, information networks, or information storage and retrieval systems, except as permitted under Section 107 or 108 of the 1976 United States Copyright Act, without the prior written permission of the publisher.

For product information and technology assistance, contact us at
Cengage Learning Customer & Sales Support, 1-800-354-9706

For permission to use material from this text or product, submit all requests online at **www.cengage.com/permissions**
Further permissions questions can be e-mailed to
permissionrequest@cengage.com

Library of Congress Control Number: 2014942023

ISBN: 978-1-305-08874-0

Cengage Learning
20 Channel Center Street
Boston, MA 02210
USA

Cengage Learning is a leading provider of customized learning solutions with office locations around the globe, including Singapore, the United Kingdom, Australia, Mexico, Brazil, and Japan. Locate your local office at **www.cengage.com/global**

Cengage Learning products are represented in Canada by Nelson Education, Ltd.

To learn more about Cengage Learning Solutions, visit **www.cengage.com**

Purchase any of our products at your local college store or at our preferred online store **www.cengagebrain.com**

Printed in Canada
Print Number: 01 Print Year: 2014

To my students. You have motivated me to be a better teacher, but more importantly a better person. Thank you.

—Ellen Pastorino

For E. Portillo, John Busby, Larry Toothaker, and E. J. Doyle—knowledge comes from many places. You are my greatest teachers.

—Susann Doyle-Portillo

About the Authors

Ellen E. Pastorino (Ph.D., Florida State University, 1990) is a developmental psychologist who established her teaching career at Gainesville State College in Georgia. As a tenured professor, she created and developed the college's Teaching and Learning Center, working with faculty to promote student learning. For the past 16 years, she has been teaching at Valencia College in Orlando, Florida. Here, too, she has worked with faculty in designing learning-centered classroom practices. Ellen has won numerous teaching awards, including the University of Georgia Board of Regents Distinguished Professor, the NISOD Excellence in Teaching Award, and Valencia's Teaching and Learning Excellence Award. Ellen has published articles in the *Journal of Adolescent Research* and *Adolescence* and actively participates in many regional and national teaching conferences. However, her main passion has always been to get students excited about the field of psychology. Ellen is a member of the Association for Psychological Science (APS) and currently serves as the Discipline Coordinator of Psychological Sciences at Valencia's Osceola campus. Ellen has authored test banks, instructor manuals, and student study guides. While working as a consultant for IBM Corporation, she developed numerous educational materials for teachers and students. Her current interests include assessment, inclusion, service learning, and reaching underprepared students. Ellen strives to balance her professional responsibilities with her love of physical fitness and family life.

Susann M. Doyle-Portillo is a professor of psychological science at the University of North Georgia. Prior to the University of North Georgia, she taught at Gainesville State College for close to 19 years. Susann earned her Ph.D. in social cognition in 1994 from the University of Oklahoma. Prior to her doctoral program, Susann earned bachelor's degrees in engineering and psychology. This exposure to both the hard sciences and the social sciences helped to ground her firmly in the experimental tradition of psychology. She has published articles in *Social Cognition* and *Contemporary Social Psychology*, but the main focus of her career has been and will always be teaching. During her career, Susann has earned a reputation as an excellent but challenging instructor. In 2010, she was awarded the Gainesville State College Best Practices Award for her teaching, and in 2011 she was a recipient of a Gainesville State College Foundation Innovative Teaching Grant Award. In addition, she has three times been listed in *Who's Who Among America's Teachers*. Susann is also actively engaged in student learning outside the classroom. One of her major goals is to help students learn by getting them involved in conducting original research. Susann and her research team are currently investigating the connection between individual difference variables and online behavior, factors affecting eyewitness testimony, and griefing among gamers.

Brief Contents

1 The Science of Psychology | 2

Part 1 Foundations in Biological Psychology 40

2 Neuroscience | 44

3 Sensation and Perception | 84

4 Consciousness | 128

5 Motivation and Emotion | 172

Part 2 Foundations in Cognitive Psychology 220

6 Learning | 224

7 Memory | 268

8 Cognition, Language, and Intelligence | 306

Part 3 Foundations in Developmental and Social Psychology 350

9 Human Development | 354

10 Social Psychology | 410

11 Personality | 462

Part 4 Foundations in Physical and Mental Health 498

12 Health, Stress, and Coping | 502

13 Mental Health Disorders | 544

14 Mental Health Therapies | 590

A Statistics in Psychology | 633

B Applying Psychology in the Workplace | 649

Contents

1 The Science of Psychology 2

1-1 What Is Psychology? 4

Correcting Common Misconceptions About the Field of Psychology 4
Psychology Will Teach You About Critical Thinking 6

1-2 The Science of Psychology: Goals, Hypotheses, and Methods 7

Psychologists Are Scientists: The Scientific Method 8
Psychologists Ask Questions: Hypotheses 10
Psychologists Strategize: Sampling and Research Methods 10

1-3 Ethical Principles of Psychological Research 20

Ethical Guidelines for Participants 20
Ethical Guidelines for Animal Research 22

1-4 Psychology in the Modern World: Foundations and Growth 23

Psychology's Roots and Modern Perspectives 23
Specialty Areas in Psychology 29
Gender, Ethnicity, and the Field of Psychology 30

PSYCHOLOGY APPLIES TO YOUR WORLD: Training to Be a Psychologist 32

1-5 Integrating Psychology: The Big Picture 34

Studying the Chapter 35
Are You Getting the Big Picture? 38

Part 1

Foundations in Biological Psychology 40

2 Neuroscience 44

2-1 Billions of Neurons: Communication in the Brain 46

The Anatomy of the Neuron 47
Signals in the Brain: How Neurons Fire Up 49
Jumping the Synapse: Synaptic Transmission 51
Cleaning Up the Synapse: Reuptake 52

2-2 **Neurotransmitters: Chemical Messengers in the Brain** 53

Acetylcholine: Memory and Memory Loss 54
Dopamine, Serotonin, and Norepinephrine: Deepening Our Understanding of Mental Illness 54
GABA and Glutamate: Regulating Brain Activity 55
Endorphins: Pain and Pleasure in the Brain 56

2-3 **The Structure of the Nervous System** 57

Sensing and Reacting: The Peripheral Nervous System 58
Voluntary Action: The Somatic Nervous System 59
Involuntary Actions: The Autonomic Nervous System 59

2-4 **The Brain and Spine: The Central Nervous System** 61

The Hindbrain 62
The Midbrain 63
The Forebrain 63
The Cortex 67
The Specialization of Function in the Lobes of the Cortex 71

PSYCHOLOGY APPLIES TO YOUR WORLD: Technologies for Studying the Brain 74

2-5 **The Endocrine System: Hormones and Behavior** 76

2-6 **Integrating Psychology: The Big Picture** 78

Studying the Chapter 79
Are You Getting the Big Picture? 82

3 Sensation and Perception 84

3-1 **Measuring Sensation and Perception: Psychophysics** 86

The Limits of Sensation: Absolute Thresholds 86
The Just Noticeable Difference and Weber's Law 86
Processing Without Awareness: Subliminal Stimulation of the Senses 87
Extrasensory Perception: Can Perception Occur Without Our Five Senses? 87

3-2 **Vision: Seeing the World** 88

How Vision Works: Light Waves and Energy 88
The Anatomy of the Outer Eye 90
The Retina: Light Energy to Neural Messages 91
Adapting to Light and Darkness 93
How We See Color 94
The Visual Pathways of the Brain 96

3-3 **Hearing: Listening to the World** 98

Environmental Noise and Hearing Loss 99
The Anatomy and Function of the Ear 99
The Auditory Pathways of the Brain 100

3-4 **The Other Senses: Taste, Smell, Touch, and the Body Senses** 103

Taste: Information from the Tongue 103

PSYCHOLOGY APPLIES TO YOUR WORLD: Why Don't We All Like the Same Foods? 104

Smell: Aromas, Odors, and a Warning System 106
Touch: The Skin Sense 108
The Body Senses: Experiencing the Physical Body in Space 109

3-5 **Perception: The Interpretation of Sensory Information** 110

Using What We Know: Top-Down Perceptual Processing 110
Building a Perception "from Scratch": Bottom-Up Perceptual Processing 111
Understanding What We Sense: Perceiving Size, Shape, and Brightness 112
Depth Perception: Sensing Our 3-D World with 2-D Eyes 112
Perceiving Form: The Gestalt Approach 115
Perceiving Form: Feature Detection Theory 116

3-6 **The Accuracy of Perception** 118

Errors Due to Top-Down Processing: Seeing What We Expect to See 118
Errors Due to Perceptual Constancy: Tricks of the Brain 118
Cultural Factors in Perception 120

3-7 **Integrating Psychology: The Big Picture** 121

Studying the Chapter 123
Are You Getting the Big Picture? 126

4 Consciousness 128

4-1 **Sleep, Dreaming, and Circadian Rhythm** 130

Functions of Sleep: Why Do We Sleep, and What If We Don't? 130
Variations in How Much Sleep We Need 131
Circadian Rhythm and Its Application to Our Lives 134
Stages of Sleep: What Research Tells Us 136
Dreaming: The Night's Work 139
Sleep Disorders: Tossing and Turning—and More 140
Gender, Ethnic, and Cultural Variations in Sleep 143

4-2 Hypnosis 145

The Experience of Hypnosis 145
Variations in Hypnotic Susceptibility 145
Explaining Hypnosis: Applying Neodissociation and Response Set Theories 146
Evaluating the Research: What Hypnosis Can and Cannot Do 147

4-3 Psychoactive Drugs 148

Variations in Drug Use 149
Drug Tolerance and Substance Dependence 150
How Drugs Work: Biology, Expectations, and Culture 151
Alcohol and Other Depressants 151
Opiates (Narcotics): The Painkillers 157
Stimulants: Legal and Otherwise 158

PSYCHOLOGY APPLIES TO YOUR WORLD: The Mystery of Bath Salts 162

Hallucinogens: Distorting Reality 163

4-4 Integrating Psychology: The Big Picture 166

Studying the Chapter 167
Are You Getting the Big Picture? 170

5 Motivation and Emotion 172

5-1 Theories of Motivation 174

Motivation as Instinct 174
Motivation as a Drive 174
Arousal Theories of Motivation 176
Self-Determination Theory of Motivation 177
Maslow's Hierarchy of Needs 178

5-2 Hunger and Eating 180

The Origins of Hunger 180

PSYCHOLOGY APPLIES TO YOUR WORLD: The Obesity Epidemic 186

The Battle of the Bulge: Why Is Losing Weight So Hard? 188
Culture and Weight-Based Prejudice 189
Eating Disorders: Bulimia Nervosa, Anorexia Nervosa, and Binge Eating Disorder 190

5-3 Sexual Motivation 195

Sexual Desire: A Mixture of Chemicals, Thoughts, and Culture 195
The Sexual Response Cycle 197

Variations in Sexuality: Generational, Age, Gender and Sexual Orientation Differences 199
Whom Do We Desire? Sexual Orientation 200

5-4 **Theories and Expression of Emotion** 205
The James-Lange Theory of Emotion 206
The Facial Feedback Hypothesis 207
The Schachter-Singer Two-Factor Theory of Emotion 208
Lazarus's Cognitive-Mediational Theory of Emotion 209
Communicating Emotions: Culture, Gender, and Facial Expressions 211

5-5 **Integrating Psychology: The Big Picture** 213
Studying the Chapter 215
Are You Getting the Big Picture? 218

Part 2
Foundations in Cognitive Psychology 220

6 **Learning** 224

6-1 **Learning from the First Days of Life: Habituation** 226
Paying Attention and Learning to Ignore: Orienting Reflexes and Habituation 226
Possible Benefits of Habituation: Protecting the Brain 227
Dishabituation 228
Practical Applications of Habituation 228

6-2 **Classical Conditioning: Learning Through the Association of Stimuli** 229
The Elements of Classical Conditioning 230
Factors Affecting Classical Conditioning 233
Real-World Applications of Classical Conditioning 234
Extinction of Classically Conditioned Responses 238
PSYCHOLOGY APPLIES TO YOUR WORLD: Using Taste Aversion to Help People 239

6-3 **Operant Conditioning: Learning from the Consequences of Our Actions** 241
E. L. Thorndike's Law of Effect 241
B. F. Skinner and the Experimental Study of Operant Conditioning 244
Acquisition and Extinction 246
Schedules of Reinforcement 247

Discrimination and Generalization 250
Shaping New Behaviors 251
Decisions That Must Be Made When Using Operant Conditioning 252
The Role of Cognition in Learning 256

6-4 Observational Learning or Modeling: Learning by Watching Others 258

Albert Bandura and the Bobo Doll Experiments 259
Observational Learning and Cognition 260

6-5 Integrating Psychology: The Big Picture 262

Studying the Chapter 263
Are You Getting the Big Picture? 266

7 Memory 268

7-1 The Functions of Memory: Encoding, Storing, and Retrieving 270

Explicit and Implicit Memory 270

7-2 The Development of New Memories 271

The Traditional Three-Stages Model of Memory 271
The Capacity of Short-Term Memory: Seven (Plus or Minus Two) 274
The Duration of Short-Term Memory: It's Yours for 30 Seconds 275
Elaborative Rehearsal: Making Memories Stick 276
Levels of Processing 277
The Serial-Position Curve and Age-related Changes in Memory 278
The Working Memory Model: Parallel Memory 279

7-3 Long-Term Memory: Permanent Storage 283

The Capacity of Long-Term Memory 283
Encoding in Long-Term Memory 283
Organization in Long-Term Memory 284
Declarative and Procedural Long-Term Memories 284
Amnesia: What Forgetting Can Teach Us About Memory 287

7-4 Retrieval and Forgetting in Long-Term Memory 289

PSYCHOLOGY APPLIES TO YOUR WORLD: Tips for Improving Your Memory 290

Recognition and Recall 290
Forgetting: Why Can't I Remember That? 292

7-5 **The Accuracy of Memory** 295

Memory Is Not Like a Video Camera 295
Eyewitness Memory 296

7-6 **The Biology of Memory** 297

7-7 **Integrating Psychology: The Big Picture** 300

Studying the Chapter 301
Are You Getting the Big Picture? 304

8 Cognition, Language, and Intelligence 306

8-1 **Thinking: How We Use What We Know** 308

Visual Images: How Good Is the Mental Picture? 308
Concepts: How We Organize What We Know 310

8-2 **Problem Solving: Putting Our Thinking to Good Use** 314

Well-Structured and Ill-Structured Problems 315
Creativity: Overcoming Obstacles to Problem Solving 316

8-3 **Reasoning, Decision Making, and Judgment** 318

Deductive and Inductive Reasoning 318
Decision Making: Outcomes and Probabilities 319
Judgments: Estimating the Likelihood of Events 319

8-4 **Language: Communication, Thought, and Culture** 322

How Humans Acquire Language 322
The Function of Language in Culture and Perception 325

PSYCHOLOGY APPLIES TO YOUR WORLD: Are Humans the Only Animals to Use Language? 326

8-5 **Defining and Measuring Intelligence** 328

Measuring Intelligence by Abilities and IQs 328
The Nature of Intelligence: The Search Continues 333
Nature, Nurture, and IQ: Are We Born Intelligent, or Do We Learn to Be? 337
Diversity in Intelligence: Race, Gender, and Age 339

8-6 **Integrating Psychology: The Big Picture** 344

Studying the Chapter 345
Are You Getting the Big Picture? 348

Part 3

Foundations in Developmental and Social Psychology 350

9 Human Development 354

9-1 Human Development: How Does It All Begin? 356

Nature–Nurture Revisited: How Biology and Culture Lead to Diversity 356
Prenatal Development 357
Application: The Importance of a Positive Prenatal Environment 358

9-2 Physical Development in Infancy and Childhood 360

Brain Development 360
Reflexes and Motor Development 361

9-3 Cognitive Development in Infancy and Childhood 363

Perceptual Development: Gathering Information from the Environment 363
Piaget's Theory of Cognitive Development 365
Vygotsky's Theory of Cognitive Development: Culture and Thinking 370
Moral Reasoning: How We Think About Right and Wrong 372

9-4 Psychosocial Development in Infancy and Childhood 374

Temperament: The Influence of Biology 374
Attachment: Learning About Relationships 375
Variations in Parenting Styles 377
Erikson's Stages of Psychosocial Development: The Influence of Culture 378
Gender-Role Development 380

9-5 Physical Changes in Adolescence and Adulthood 383

Puberty: Big Changes, Rapid Growth, and Impact on Behavior 384
Brain Changes in Adolescence and Adulthood 385
Physical Changes from Early to Later Adulthood 387
Gender and Reproductive Capacity 388

9-6 Cognitive Changes in Adolescence and Adulthood 389

Formal Operations Revisited: Applying Cognition to Adolescent Behavior 389
Postformal Thought: Developing Adult Reasoning 391
Changes in Mental Abilities 391

9-7 Psychosocial Changes in Adolescence and Adulthood 393

Erikson's Psychosocial Stages of Adolescence and Adulthood 393
Emerging Adulthood 395

Variations in Social Relations in Adolescence and Adulthood 395
Parenting 398
PSYCHOLOGY APPLIES TO YOUR WORLD: Career Development 400

9-8 Death and Dying 402
Emotional Reactions to Death: Kübler-Ross's Stages 402
Bereavement and Grief: How We Respond to Death 403

9-9 Integrating Psychology: The Big Picture 404
Studying the Chapter 405
Are You Getting the Big Picture? 408

10 Social Psychology 410

10-1 Evaluating the World: Attitudes 412
Acquiring Attitudes Through Learning 412
Attitude–Behavior Consistency 413
Cognitive Consistency and Attitude Change 414
Persuasion and Attitude Change 415

10-2 Forming Impressions of Others 417
The Attribution Process 417
Heuristics and Biases in Attribution 418

10-3 Prejudice: Why Can't We All Just Get Along? 421
Stereotypes, Prejudice, and Discrimination 422
Stereotype Threat: Prejudice Can Be a Self-Fulfilling Prophecy 423
Social Transmission of Prejudice 424
Intergroup Dynamics and Prejudice 425
Reducing Prejudice in the Real World 427

10-4 Being Drawn to Others: The Nature of Attraction 429
Proximity and Exposure: Attraction to Those That Are Nearby 430
Similarity: Having Things in Common 430
The Importance of Physical Attractiveness 431
The "Chemistry" of Lust, Love, and Romance 432

10-5 Group Influence 433
Social Forces Within Groups: Norms and Cohesiveness 434
Conformity Within a Group 435
Is Working in a Group Better Than Working Alone? 437

10-6 Requests and Demands: Compliance and Obedience 439

Compliance Techniques: Getting People to Say "Yes" 440
Obedience: Doing What We Are Told to Do 442

10-7 Aggression: Hurting Others 447

Biological Theories of Aggression 448
Learning Theories of Aggression 449
PSYCHOLOGY APPLIES TO YOUR WORLD: Does Television Portray Violence Accurately? 450
Situations That Promote Aggressive Behavior 451

10-8 Choosing to Help Others: Prosocial Behavior 451

The Murder of Kitty Genovese 452
The Bystander Effect 453
When People Choose to Help 453

10-9 Integrating Psychology: The Big Picture 455

Studying the Chapter 457
Are You Getting the Big Picture? 460

11 Personality 462

11-1 The Psychoanalytic Approach: Sigmund Freud and the Neo-Freudians 464

Freud's Levels of Awareness 464
Freud's Structure of Personality 464
Freud's Psychosexual Stages of Development 467
Neo-Freudian Theories Explaining Variations in Personality: Carl Jung, Alfred Adler, and Karen Horney 469
Contributions and Criticisms of the Psychoanalytic Approach 471

11-2 The Trait Approach: Consistency and Stability in Personality 472

Gordon Allport's Trait Theory 472
Raymond Cattell's Factor Analytic Trait Theory 473
Hans Eysenck Narrows the Traits: The PEN Model 473
PSYCHOLOGY APPLIES TO YOUR WORLD: Are You a Sensation Seeker? 474
The Five Factor Trait Theory 477
Genetic Contributions to Personality 478
Stability and Change in Personality 479
Contributions and Criticisms of the Trait Approach 481

11-3 The Social Cognitive Approach: The Environment and Patterns of Thought 482

Reciprocal Determinism: Albert Bandura's Interacting Forces 482
Julian Rotter's Locus of Control: Internal and External Expectations 483
Contributions and Criticisms of the Social Cognitive Approach 484

11-4 The Humanistic Approach: Free Will and Self-Actualization 485

Abraham Maslow and the Hierarchy of Needs Theory 485
Carl Rogers and Self Theory 485
Contributions and Criticisms of the Humanistic Approach 487

11-5 Scientifically Measuring Personality 488

Personality Inventories: Mark Which One Best Describes You 488
Projective Tests: Tell Me What You See 490
Rating Scales and Direct Observation 490
Clinical Interviews 491

11-6 Integrating Psychology: The Big Picture 492

Studying the Chapter 493
Are You Getting the Big Picture? 496

Part 4

Foundations in Physical and Mental Health 498

12 Health, Stress, and Coping 502

12-1 What Is Stress? Stress and Stressors 504

Life Events: Change Is Stressful 504
Catastrophes: Natural Disasters and Wars 508
Daily Hassles: Little Things Add Up! 508
Conflict: Approach and Avoidance 510

12-2 The Stress Response 512

Cognitive Appraisal: Assessing Stress 513
Selye's General Adaptation Syndrome: The Body's Response to Stress 514
Gender and the Stress Response 516
Stress and the Immune System: Resistance to Disease 516

12-3 **Coping with Stress** 518

Problem-Focused Coping: Change the Situation 519
Emotion-Focused Coping: Change Your Reaction 519
Managing Stress: Applying the Research 522

12-4 **Personality and Health** 525

Type A Personality: Ambition, Drive, and Competitiveness 525
Learned Helplessness: I Can't Do It 527
The Hardy Personality: Control, Commitment, and Challenge 528

12-5 **Lifestyle, Health, and Well-Being** 529

Health-Defeating Behaviors 529
PSYCHOLOGY APPLIES TO YOUR WORLD: Technology's Health Effects 531
Health-Promoting Behaviors 534
Happiness and Well-Being 536

12-6 **Integrating Psychology: The Big Picture** 537

Studying the Chapter 539
Are You Getting the Big Picture? 542

13 Mental Health Disorders 544

13-1 **What Is Abnormal Behavior?** 546

Prevalence of Mental Health Disorders 546
Explaining Abnormal Behavior: Perspectives Revisited 547

13-2 **The *DSM* Model for Classifying Abnormal Behavior** 549

The Structure of the *DSM* 550
How Good Is the *DSM* Model? 552

13-3 **Anxiety, Trauma-, Obsessive-Compulsive and Related Disorders: It's Not Just "Nerves"** 553

Components of Excessive Anxiety 553
Types of Excessive Anxiety Disorders 554
Research Explaining Anxiety, Trauma-, Obsessive-Compulsive and Related Disorders 558

13-4 **Dissociative and Somatic Symptom Disorders: Other Forms of Anxiety?** 562

Dissociative Disorders: Multiple Personalities 562
Somatic Symptom Disorders: "Doctor, I'm Sure I'm Sick" 564

13-5 **Mood Disorders: Beyond the Blues** 565

Depressive Disorders: A Change to Sadness 566
Bipolar-Related Disorders: The Presence of Mania 567

PSYCHOLOGY APPLIES TO YOUR WORLD: Suicide Facts and Misconceptions 568

Research Explaining Mood Disorders 570
Gender and Depression 573

13-6 **Schizophrenia: Disintegration** 575

Individual Variations: Onset, Gender, Ethnicity, and Prognosis 576
Symptoms of Schizophrenia 576
Research Explaining Schizophrenia: Genetics, the Brain, and the Environment 578

13-7 **Personality Disorders: Maladaptive Patterns of Behavior** 581

Antisocial Personality Disorder: Impulsive and Dangerous 581
Borderline Personality Disorder: Living on Your Fault Line 583

13-8 **Integrating Psychology: The Big Picture** 584

Studying the Chapter 585
Are You Getting the Big Picture? 588

14 Mental Health Therapies 590

14-1 **Providing Psychological Assistance** 592

Psychotherapy Versus Biomedical Therapy 592
Who Is Qualified to Give Therapy? 592
Ethical Standards for Psychotherapists 593

PSYCHOLOGY APPLIES TO YOUR WORLD: When Does One Need to Consider Psychotherapy? 595

Seeking Therapy 596

14-2 **Psychoanalytic Therapies: Uncovering Unconscious Conflicts** 596

Traditional Psychoanalysis 597
Modern Psychoanalysis 598

14-3 **Humanistic Therapy: Facilitating Self-Actualization** 599

The Aim of Humanistic Therapy Approaches 599
Client-Centered Therapy: Three Key Ingredients 599

14-4 **Behavior Therapies: Learning Healthier Behaviors** 601

Applying Classical Conditioning Techniques in Therapy 602
Applying Operant Conditioning Techniques in Therapy 605

14-5 **Cognitive Therapies: Changing Thoughts** 607

Ellis's Rational-Emotive Therapy: Reinterpret One's Viewpoint 607
Beck's Cognitive Therapy: Replace Negative Thoughts 608

14-6 **Group Therapy Approaches: Strength in Numbers** 611

The Benefits of Group Therapy 611
The Nature and Types of Group Therapy 612

14-7 **Effective Psychotherapy: Do Treatments Work?** 614

Conducting Research on Therapy's Effectiveness 614
Factors That Contribute to Effective Psychotherapy 616
The Effectiveness and Ethics of Technology in the Delivery of Psychotherapy 617

14-8 **Biomedical Therapies: Applying Neuroscience** 618

Drug Therapies: Chemically Altering the Brain 618
Noninvasive Brain Stimulation Procedures: TMS and ECT 624
Psychosurgery: Deep Brain Stimulators and Targeted Brain Lesions 625

14-9 **Integrating Psychology: The Big Picture** 626

Studying the Chapter 627
Are You Getting the Big Picture? 630

A Statistics in Psychology 633

A-1 **Using Statistics to Describe Data 633**

Graphs: Depicting Data Visually 634
Measures of Central Tendency: Means, Medians, and Modes 636
Measures of Variability: Analyzing the Distribution of Data 638
Normal and Standard Normal Distributions 639
The Correlation Coefficient: Measuring Relationships 640

A-2 **Using Statistics to Draw Conclusions** 643

A-3 **Summary** 644

Studying the Appendix 646

B Applying Psychology in the Workplace 649

B-1 Industrial and Organizational Psychology 649

Work in Our Lives 651
Types of Jobs 652

B-2 Selecting Employees: The Hiring Process 652

Job Analysis 653
Testing 653
Legal Issues 654
Recruitment 655
Making the Decision 656

B-3 Socializing Employees: Culture, Groups, Leadership, and Performance Appraisal 657

Organizational Culture and Climate 658
Groups and Teams 658
Leadership 659
Performance Appraisal 660

B-4 Employee Satisfaction: Attitudes and Behaviors at Work 661

Attitudes at Work 661
Behaviors at Work 663
Relation Between Attitude and Behavior 664

B-5 Summary 665

Studying the Appendix 667

Glossary 669

References 679

Name Index 741

Subject Index 750

Preface

Together, we have almost 45 years of experience teaching Introductory Psychology. We have each spent the bulk of our careers teaching multiple sections of Introductory Psychology each semester—it is our bread and butter, so to speak. So, it's a good thing that Introductory Psychology is also our favorite course. Contrary to what many may think of professors teaching the same course over and over, it never grows old for us. Teaching Introductory Psychology allows us to touch on many different aspects of our fascinating field and to work with diverse students from all walks of life, such that no two classes are ever alike.

The uniqueness of each class is just one of the challenges that keeps us excited about teaching this course. There are others. Introductory Psychology classes are often full of students who are just beginning their academic careers—some are fresh from high school; others are returning, nontraditional students who've been out of the classroom for several years. They come to us with the desire to learn about psychology, but often they face serious obstacles. Some are overworked in their personal lives. Some have lingering academic challenges. And most expect learning to be easier than we know it to be. As such, a big part of our mission is to help students overcome these obstacles and obtain success.

Our Mission: Motivating Students to Read

Getting students to read their textbook in preparation for lectures and exams is one of the biggest problems we face as instructors. Like many professors, our experience has been that few students read assigned chapters prior to lecture, and some even fail to read the chapters by the time they take exams. For years, we have tried various methods of motivating students to read—pop quizzes, reading quizzes, test questions from material in the book but not covered in lecture, and so on. None of these methods seemed to have much of an impact on students.

Students' free time is, of course, in short supply. And when they do have free time, reading a textbook doesn't always seem like an attractive option. Students often find their texts difficult to read, boring, and full of content that is far removed from the concerns of their daily lives. One of us overheard students speaking before class the second week of the semester. One student asked those sitting around him if they had read the reading assignment—most replied they had not. He then said, "I read it, but man, I have no idea what they were saying in that chapter!" If we want students to read their textbooks, we will have to give them books that they will want to read, and that means giving them a book that they can understand and one that they find relevant enough to be worth the time it takes to read. Motivating students to read is our primary mission, and we wrote our original texts, *What Is Psychology?* and *What Is Psychology? Essentials,* to give students textbooks that they would find interesting to read, easy to read, and memorable.

Our Mission: Giving Students an Integrated View of Psychology that Aligns with APA Guidelines

Getting students to read their textbook is a primary goal of all instructors. Another important goal is providing students with a comprehensive and integrated view of the field of psychology. We have long advocated for a "Big Picture" approach to the teaching of psychology, and our previous editions of *What Is Psychology?* emphasized the integrated nature of psychology as a field. Through the use of case studies that were woven throughout the chapters and through constantly drawing cross-references to material in other chapters, *What Is Psychology?* encouraged students to see psychology as a whole rather than as a sum of many parts.

The need to provide Introductory Psychology students with an integrated view of psychology has also been recognized by the American Psychological Association (APA). In March 2014, the APA released guidelines for strengthening the Common Core in the Introductory Psychology course. A prominent theme in these guidelines is that all Introductory Psychology courses should present students with a "big picture" view of psychology that integrates the different perspectives that psychologists take in examining mental processes and behavior. Furthermore, in presenting this integrated view of psychology, Introductory Psychology courses should highlight the common themes that tie the different perspectives or areas of psychology together—themes that include the scientific method of research, diversity and variations seen in human behavior, the applicability of psychology to real life, and the ethics that guide psychological research and practice.

This call for a Common Core in introductory courses places the Introductory Psychology course in line with the broader *APA Guidelines for the Undergraduate Psychology Major* (APA, 2013a). These new guidelines for the major contain the learning goals that students should attain by the time they complete an undergraduate degree in psychology. Each of these goals is broken down into a series of specific learning outcomes that are divided into two levels. The first level defines goals that students should attain during their first three or four "foundational" psychology courses, while the second level defines goals for what students should achieve by the completion of their degree program. Introductory psychology is clearly often the first foundation course taken by students who may take a few psychology classes, or decide to major in the field. These goals are numerically indexed; for example the first learning outcome under Goal 1 is Learning Outcome 1.1.

A Summary of the New APA Learning Goals

Goal 1: Knowledge Base in Psychology

Learning Outcomes 1.1–1.3 pertain to students' acquisition of the key concepts, domains, and applications of psychology.

1.1 Describe key concepts, principles and overarching themes in psychology
1.2 Develop a working knowledge of psychology's content domains
1.3 Describe applications of psychology

Goal 2: Scientific Inquiry and Critical Thinking

Learning Outcomes 2.1–2.5 pertain to students' understanding and use of the scientific method, information literacy, integrative thinking, and use of sociocultural factors in scientific inquiry.

2.1 Use scientific reasoning to interpret psychological phenomena
2.2 Demonstrate psychology information literacy
2.3 Engage in innovative and integrative thinking and problem solving
2.4 Interpret, design, and conduct basic psychological research
2.5 Incorporate sociocultural factors in scientific inquiry

Goal 3: Ethical and Social Responsibility in a Diverse World

Learning Outcomes 3.1–3.3 pertain to students' understanding and use of ethical standards to build interpersonal relationships and communities.

3.1 Apply ethical standards to evaluate psychological science and practice
3.2 Build and enhance interpersonal relationships
3.3 Adopt values that build community at local, national, and global levels

Goal 4: Communication

Learning Outcomes 4.1–4.3 pertain to students' demonstration of effective writing, presentation, and interpersonal communication skills.

4.1 Demonstrate effective writing for different purposes
4.2 Exhibit effective presentation skills for different purposes
4.3 Interact effectively with others

Goal 5: Professional Development

Learning Outcomes 5.1–5.5 pertain to students' demonstration of the skills and knowledge necessary to meet their career goals in psychology, including self-management skills, project management skills, and the applicability of psychology to various professional pursuits.

5.1 Apply psychological content and skills to career goals
5.2 Exhibit self-efficacy and self-regulation
5.3 Refine project-management skills
5.4 Enhance teamwork capacity
5.5 Develop meaningful professional direction for life after graduation

As professors of psychology, we firmly agree with the APA that students should be taught to see psychology as a unified whole rather than as a series of discrete areas of study. For this reason, we are very excited to introduce the current text, *What Is Psychology? Foundations, Applications, and Integration.* This new text retains the very best features from our previous two texts that motivated students to actually read and learn psychology, while strengthening the three themes now represented in the subtitle: foundations, applications, and integration. These themes align with the *APA Guidelines for the Undergraduate Psychology Major Version 2.0*, and the text's organization follows recommendations made by the APA's Board of Educational Affairs (BEA) Working Group to Strengthen the Common Core. While the APA 2.0 guidelines suggest learning outcomes for college psychology courses, the Common Core proposes an optimal course structure to provide the best introduction to the field of psychology (APA, 2014).

What Is Psychology? Foundations, Applications, and Integration

What Is Psychology? Foundations, Applications, and Integration utilizes some of the most effective features from each of our previous two texts, as well as several new and innovative features to excite students about the field of psychology.

Foundations: Content Organized Around the Foundational Areas of Psychological Research

What Is Psychology? Foundations, Applications, and Integration is organized around the foundational areas of psychology emphasized by the APA in the Common Core discussions. The text opens with the ultimate foundation of psychology, the scientific research methods that inform all study of mental processes and behavior. The remaining chapters are organized around four foundational areas: the *biological, cognitive, developmental and social,* and *physical and mental health* areas of psychology. Content is divided to follow these topical sections of psychology while creating manageable chunks of related material, allowing professors to easily align their content with testing during the semester or quarter:

Chapter 1: The Science of Psychology

Part 1: Foundations in Biological Psychology:
Chapter 2: Neuroscience
Chapter 3: Sensation and Perception
Chapter 4: Consciousness
Chapter 5: Motivation and Emotion

Part 2: Foundations in Cognitive Psychology
Chapter 6: Learning
Chapter 7: Memory
Chapter 8: Cognition, Language, and Intelligence

Part 3: Foundations in Developmental and Social Psychology
Chapter 9: Human Development
Chapter 10: Social Psychology
Chapter 11: Personality

Part 4: Foundations in Physical and Mental Health
Chapter 12: Health, Stress, and Coping
Chapter 13: Mental Health Disorders
Chapter 14: Mental Health Therapies

Applications: Integrating Psychology Through the Use of Case Studies

One of the best ways to motivate students to read is to capture their curiosity from the very beginning. If psychology is interesting for students, they will read. Each of our previous texts drew rave reviews from students for the use of attention-grabbing case studies at the opening of each chapter. In *Foundations, Applications, and Integration,* we continue this tradition. Each of the four foundational sections of the text opens with a case study that illustrates how the content covered in the chapters of that section helps us understand the behavior and mental processes of a real-life person. The case studies are compelling stories of people who have faced life's challenges with courage and grace. For example, the biological section opens with the case study of Jean-Dominique Bauby, a man who wrote a moving book that was later turned into a movie, *The Diving Bell and the Butterfly,* while in a state of locked-in syndrome that left him completely paralyzed save the ability to blink his left eye. The developmental and social psychology section begins with the story of Hongyong Baek, a woman who survived many challenges, including the Korean War and devastating personal losses, but still managed many triumphs in her lifetime. Each of the case studies is woven throughout all of the chapters of that section, providing students with a view of the content that is both integrated and applied to real life. By using one case study to tie all of the chapters of the section together, students are encouraged to see the material as a whole rather than as a series of disparate parts; and in doing so, they begin forming an integrated "big picture" of psychology.

Integration: The Big Picture

To further facilitate the development of an integrated, "big picture" view of psychology in students, each chapter closes with a section called Integrating Psychology: The Big Picture. In this section, we revisit the section case study and use it as a vehicle for both reviewing the content of the chapter(s) of the section and previewing the content of the coming chapter(s). Through Integrating Psychology: The Big Picture, students begin to see that all of the material fits together—what has been learned informs what is yet to be learned.

Numerical Indexing and Color-Coding Allow for Easy Cross-Referencing

Throughout the text, numeric indexing and color-coding are used to help students quickly locate relevant information. Each primary or main section of a chapter has been assigned a specific color and all learning objectives and subordinate headings that relate to that primary head are coded with the same color. This coding scheme allows students to quickly and visually relate objectives and content to the relevant section of the text.

All primary and secondary heads for the chapter are also numerically indexed with a sequential code. For example, here is the indexing for a portion of Chapter 2 content:

2.1 Billions of Neurons: Communication in the Brain
  2.1.1 The Anatomy of the Neuron
  2.1.2 Signals in the Brain: How Neurons Fire Up
  2.1.3 Jumping the Synapse: Synaptic Transmission

This numeric coding scheme allows for relevant material to be indexed back to the applicable section of the text, tying content to each section heading. Through coloring and numbering, the learning objectives, quizzes, review summaries, and visual summaries at the ends of each chapter are easy to reference to a specific location within the text. Numeric coding also makes it easy for instructors to assign specific portions of chapters, and for students to find that material across mediums. Online quizzes and review materials are indexed back to the appropriate numeric sections of the text, creating a smoother experience when moving around in the physical text or between the text and digital formats. Through the use of these colors and codes, students can quickly tie content from a variety of sources back to specific sections of the text.

Learning Objectives That Are Aligned with the APA Learning Goals and Outcomes

Each chapter opens with the Learning Objectives that are numerically indexed to the appropriate Learning Goal and Learning Outcome in the new *APA Guidelines for the Undergraduate Psychology Major Version 2.0* (APA, 2013). Learning Objectives are also numerically indexed and color coded to the section heading of the chapter in which the relevant material is covered. This allows both the instructor and the student to quickly assess which objectives are covered in each discrete section of the text, and which APA program outcomes are being addressed in that section. For example, here is a sample of the learning objectives for Chapter 8. The index numbers on the left refer to the relevant sections of the chapter. The codes on the right relate the learning objectives to the specific APA Goal learning outcomes.

8.1 Describe how we represent knowledge in our memory. (APA 1.1, 1.2, 1.3)
8.1 Describe how we organize knowledge in our memory. (APA 1.1, 1.2, 1.3)
8.2 Describe the different types of problems we face in life and the ways in which we may try to solve them. (APA 1.1, 1.2, 1.3)
8.2 Describe common obstacles to problem solving. (APA 1.1, 1.2, 1.3)
8.3 Describe the processes of deductive and inductive reasoning. (APA 1.1, 1.2, 1.3, 2.1)
8.3 Describe the factors that affect decision making. (APA 1.1, 1.2, 1.3)
8.3 Describe the process of judgment, and heuristics that bias our judgments. (APA 1.1, 1.2, 1.3, 3.3)

Diversity: Making Psychology Relevant for All People

There is little doubt that students learn best when they become personally invested in the material they are reading and studying. However, for this to occur, students must actually find the material to be applicable to their lives. Given that today's college students are a diverse group of people, writing a text that is relevant to today's students means writing a text that embraces their diversity. Diversity and variations in human behavior are also themes that are emphasized in the APA Common Core guidelines and the *APA Guidelines for the Undergraduate Psychology Major.* Understanding psychology means understanding the behavior and mental processes of *all* people.

Appropriately, we wrote our book with inclusion in mind. Throughout the text we use examples of real people (such as those whose stories open each foundational section) who reflect the diversity seen in our classrooms. Where applicable, we have cited and highlighted research that reflects many aspects of diversity, including gender, racial diversity, sexual orientation, cultural diversity, age and generational differences, socioeconomic levels, and physical and/or mental health challenges. In all, we reference people from over 120 countries and/or cultural groups.

An Engaging Narrative Writing Style Makes Difficult Material Easier to Understand

Motivating a student to read the text is, of course, a primary concern of professors. But reading the text does no good if the student does not understand what he or she has read. The student comment we mentioned previously is very telling: he read the assignment, but he did not understand it. We doubt this did much to encourage him to approach his next reading assignment! A major goal of this text is to bring psychology to the student by making it understandable, and to do so without sacrificing content. We believe that it is not necessary to condescend to students to get them to understand. Rather, you just have to explain difficult concepts thoroughly and clearly.

Throughout the text, we have adopted an engaging narrative writing style that will not intimidate students. Difficult concepts (such as neural transmission and classical conditioning) are given extended description, and many real-life examples are used to illustrate and clarify our points. The language we use in the text strongly reflects the way we speak to our students during class. We also include a pronunciation glossary so students will know how to correctly pronounce the more difficult, unfamiliar terms.

We attempted to use our prose to tell students the story of psychology, as opposed to a mere litany of theories and research findings. Throughout the text, we directly address students as "you" and refer to ourselves as "we" to help draw students into a conversation about psychology. And through that conversation, we provide students with an accessible and engaging story of psychology. Throughout the process of writing this text, many faculty reviewers and students have consistently praised our writing style for its clarity and accessibility. One reviewer commented that it was obvious that this text was written by authors who have spent much time in the classroom in front of students.

Enhancing Motivation and Learning by Making Psychology Practical

A key point in getting students to read a text and retain what they've read is making the material applicable to their lives. When information is associated with the self, it becomes more easily retrieved from memory. So, when students can see how psychology relates to their personal lives, they are much more likely to find it interesting and a lot less likely to forget it. Throughout the text, we have made a concerted effort to use practical, everyday examples to illustrate the concepts of psychology.

What Is Psychology? Foundations, Applications, and Integration includes Psychology Applies to Your World, a feature that emphasizes the personal relevance of psychology by showing students that an understanding of psychology can help them to better understand their world. Psychology Applies to Your World topics include the dangers of bath salts (Chapter 4), the obesity epidemic (Chapter 5), televised violence (Chapter 10), and the use of taste aversion to help people cope with chemotherapy and alcoholism (Chapter 6).

Enhancing Student Learning by Encouraging Active Learning and Self-Assessment

Many of our students learn best when they engage in active rather than passive learning. We have made a concerted effort to get students involved with the material as they read. By remaining engaged, students will be more motivated to read, and they will likely retain the information in memory much better.

Engage Yourself!

The Engage Yourself! active learning feature asks students to do hands-on activities to illustrate important chapter concepts. Active learning not only encourages students to see the personal relevance of the material, it also helps students elaborate the material in memory by connecting it to personal experience. Examples of Engage Yourself! activities include having students examine their attributional biases when making judgments about celebrities (Chapter 10), illustrating the effects of elaborative rehearsal on memory for song lyrics (Chapter 7), and an activity that demonstrates the brain's predisposition to perceive faces (Chapter 9).

Quiz Yourself

Another feature, Quiz Yourself, appears after each major section of the chapter. Quiz Yourself allows students to actively assess their learning by asking them to apply the material of the preceding section to answer several multiple choice questions. Most of the Quiz Yourself questions are application questions that apply the material to practical situations. For example, in Chapter 10, Social Psychology, we use the following question to test the student's understanding of attribution theory:

> Jasper was quick to assume that Susan was intelligent when he saw that she earned an "A" on her last psychology exam. However, when Jasper earned an "A" on his history test, he was not so quick to assume that he was intelligent. Which of the following biases in social cognition best explains Jasper's behavior?
>
> **a.** The fundamental attribution error
> **b.** The self-serving bias
> **c.** The social desirability bias
> **d.** The actor-observer bias

To answer this question, the student must not only understand the different attribution biases, but he or she must also be able to think analytically about them in applying these concepts to a very common student-oriented scenario.

You Review

Each chapter features a You Review table that summarizes key points of a particular topic. For example, in Chapter 12, the transmission modes, symptoms, and treatments of sexually transmitted infections are summarized. In Chapter 8, gender differences on some cognitive tasks are highlighted.

What Do You Know? Assess Your Understanding

In addition to the Quiz Yourself questions at the end of each major section of the chapter, we have included a more extensive self-assessment for students at the end of each chapter. This assessment, What Do You Know? Assess Your Understanding, includes a 20-question multiple choice practice test (with the answers provided) that allows students to evaluate their retention and understanding of the entire chapter. By self-assessing, students can better judge which concepts and/or sections of the chapter they should target for further study.

Use It or Lose It: Applying Psychology Questions

In addition to the multiple-choice section, the end-of-chapter assessments also include Use It or Lose It: Applying Psychology, a series of essay or short-answer questions that require students to further elaborate and integrate their knowledge by applying what they have learned to a real-world problem or question. An example question from Chapter 2 reads:

1. Jean-Dominique Bauby was still able to think, feel, and remember the events of his life after a stroke left him in a permanent state of locked-in syndrome. Now that you know something about the brain, can you explain why he retained these abilities?

Critical Thinking for Integration Questions

Also included in the end-of-chapter assessments are Critical Thinking for Integration questions. These essay or short-answer questions tap into the need to get students to integrate their learning by specifically asking them to use information from different chapters to solve problems and answer questions. An example question from Chapter 5 reads:

3. How might learning theories (Chapter 6) be used to design a therapy aimed at helping people to overcome obesity?

Visual Summary: Are You Getting the Big Picture?

A Visual Summary of the chapter, entitled "Are You Getting the Big Picture?" is also included in the end-of-chapter material to allow students to truly see the big picture of the chapter. All of the major concepts and theories of the chapter are brought together in a graphical format in the Visual Summary that is also color coded to the section headers. This tool will be especially helpful to students who prefer to learn through visual means.

Chapter-by-Chapter Changes to Content

In addition to the new pedagogical features of *What Is Psychology? Foundations, Applications, and Integration,* the current text also represents a thorough updating of the ongoing research in all the areas of psychology. Here is a chapter-by-chapter summary of some of the important changes in this new text.

All Chapters

- All chapters were retitled with more concise titles.
- All learning objectives are cross-referenced to the APA Learning Goal Outcomes.
- A new Integrating Psychology: The Big Picture section concludes each chapter.
- A numerical and color-based indexing system was added to all chapter primary and secondary heads.
- APA Common Core themes such as scientific research, variations, diversity, and application are reinforced in headings within the chapters.
- Application and Critical Thinking for Integration questions have been added at the end of each chapter.

Chapter 1: The Science of Psychology

- Reorganized chapter to emphasize the scientific foundations of psychology as a field
- Historical figures and theories incorporated into modern perspectives on psychology to make clearer the connections between past and present-day psychology
- New coverage of issues in conducting research online
- Replication included as part of the scientific method
- New definitions and examples of perfect and zero correlations
- More extended explanations of independent and dependent variables
- A new You Review table on research methods
- Added coverage of Hippocrates, ancient Indian text and chakras, along with the influence of medicine to the history of psychology section
- A new Engage Yourself! Activity on misconceptions about behavior

Chapter 2: Neuroscience

- New information on meditation and the hippocampus
- A thorough updating of all content, including 30 new references

Chapter 3: Sensation and Perception

- Information on personal listening devices and hearing loss incorporated into the body of the chapter text
- Expanded section on chemo-signaling in humans

Chapter 4: Consciousness

- An extensive updating of the research, including more than 80 new references
- The association among cell phone, computer use and insomnia is discussed
- Addition of sleep apnea's association with heart disease
- Coverage of cultural variations in sleep habits
- Coverage of restless legs syndrome added to sleep disorders
- Detailed discussion added on abuse of prescription drugs
- Background information on Ecstasy, molly, and PCP provided
- The research on the therapeutic use of MDMA for PTSD introduced
- All graphs updated with the most recent data

- Review questions added to sleep and drug sections
- New Psychology Applies to Your World topic that focuses on bath salts

Chapter 5: Motivation and Emotion

- Addition of more than 50 new references
- Expanded coverage of arousal theory of motivation to include task complexity issues
- Expanded coverage of self-determination theory in the real world
- Updated research on Maslow's hierarchy of needs
- Expanded coverage of hunger feedback mechanisms in the body
- Updated coverage of hunger regulation in the brain
- Updated information on global rates of obesity
- Expanded coverage of circadian rhythms and obesity
- Added coverage of personality factors and weight-based prejudice
- *DSM-5* updates for eating disorders
- Updated information on laws pertaining to same-sex marriage and sexual orientation-based discrimination in the United States and globally
- Updated information on trends in sexual behavior
- Updated coverage of emotion

Chapter 6: Learning

- Expanded coverage of the cultural debate over the use of physical punishment in children
- Updated research on habituation and migraines
- Expanded Review questions

Chapter 7: Memory

- A thorough updating of the content with 32 new references
- Included coverage of technology and distraction in the classroom into the text
- Updated the coverage of memory in older people and people with Alzheimer's disease

Chapter 8: Cognition, Language, and Intelligence

- Added information on the affective heuristic
- Enhanced the section on creativity with new research on characteristics of creative people
- Added new research on animal language being influenced by social context
- Expanded coverage of genetics and intelligence
- Expanded coverage of diversity in intelligence and intellectual abilities

Chapter 9: Human Development

- Thoroughly updated the chapter with more than 60 new references
- Added new research on analysis of gender stereotypes in films
- Added cross-cultural variations in motor development
- Added a discussion of motherese
- Added a discussion of neuroimaging of adolescent social evaluation
- New discussion of the influence of private speech on sports performance
- Added coverage of the evolution of moral sense
- Added additional information on emerging adulthood
- New information on the cost of raising a child
- New research on higher levels of well-being in parents
- Added information on the influence of culture on grief
- New research on mother's prenatal stress and its influence on child's health
- Added pareidolia (seeing faces in inanimate objects) and the evolutionary advantage of face perception
- Added review questions to 3 main sections of the chapter

Chapter 10: Social Psychology

- Thoroughly updated the text with more than 50 new references
- Added several new pieces of cross cultural research
- Added the variable of task difficulty to the discussion of stereotype threat and tied this concept back to the Yerkes-Dodson law in Chapter 5
- Added additional information on characteristics of attractive faces
- Added additional information on the role of oxytocin on the romantic behavior of men
- Added information on the lack of cultural differences in conformity rates in an online environment
- Updated Jerry Burger's new work on replication of Milgram's study of obedience
- Expanded summary tables with reference citations

Chapter 11: Personality

- Research on arousal theory and reward-processing theory included in discussion of introversion/extraversion

Chapter 12: Health, Stress, and Coping

- Thoroughly updated the chapter with more than 70 new references
- Added research on influence of prejudice and discrimination as stressors
- Expanded Psychology Applies to Your World to include research on the health effects of more technologies
- Added more review questions to 3 sections of the chapter
- New coverage of research on resilience
- The relationship between optimism and morning cortisol levels discussed
- New research on person-situation effect on emotion-focused coping

- Mindfulness added to meditation section
- Added influence of smiling through stress on stress response
- Updated research on income level and well-being
- Men who have sex with men added in STI section

Chapter 13: Mental Health Disorders

- Thoroughly updated the chapter with more than 75 new references
- Mental health disorder, psychopathology, and hoarding disorder added as key terms
- Chapter updated in accord with changes in the *DSM-5*.
- Tables updated to reflect new data and *DSM*-5.
- Hypochondriasis renamed illness anxiety disorder; social phobia renamed social anxiety disorder; dysthymia now called persistent depressive disorder
- Dissociative fugue removed as no longer a separate disorder (considered a subtype of dissociative amnesia)
- Social expectancy theory added as an explanation for dissociative identity disorder
- Anxiety disorders broken out into anxiety, trauma, and obsessive-compulsive disorders
- Updated information included on brain areas in depression
- Cultural expectedness emphasized in definition of abnormality
- Rates of mental illness among high school and college students discussed
- New discussion on the influence of hormonal and sociocultural factors and their relationship to gender differences in schizophrenia prognosis

Chapter 14: Mental Health Therapies

- Thoroughly updated the chapter with more than 70 new references
- More attention to culturally sensitive therapy in ethics
- Expanded discussion on technology and therapies to include behavioral intervention technologies and e-health interventions
- Emotionally focused couple therapy included as a group therapy approach
- Transcranial magnetic stimulation (TMS) included as a noninvasive brain stimulation therapy technique
- TMS, CBT, and EMDR added as key terms

MindTap Psychology for *What Is Psychology?*

MindTap is a personalized teaching experience with relevant assignments that guide students to analyze, apply, and improve thinking, allowing you to measure skills and outcomes with ease.

Available Supplements

Cengage Learning Testing, powered by Cognero

Cengage Learning Testing Powered by Cognero® is a flexible, online system that allows you to: import, edit, and manipulate content from the text's test bank or elsewhere, including your own favorite test questions; create multiple test versions in an instant; and deliver tests from your LMS, your classroom, or wherever you want.

Online Instructor's Manual

The instructor's manual (IM) contains a variety of resources to aid instructors in preparing and presenting text material in a manner that meets their personal preferences and course needs. It presents suggestions and resources to enhance and facilitate learning.

Online PowerPoints

These vibrant, Microsoft PowerPoint lecture slides provide concept coverage to assist you with your lecture.

Acknowledgments

Writing a college textbook has been an exhausting yet rewarding experience. We are ordinary college professors who teach four to six classes every semester, so we are often writing in whatever free time we have—weekends, nights, and holidays. We are valued for our contributions to student learning and service to our institutions. And we have grown so much as educators and psychologists in tackling this project. This would not have been possible without the support of many people who deserve our acknowledgment.

We would like to thank Thomas Takayama at Valencia College and Steve Lloyd and Diane Cook at the University of North Georgia for their administrative support. Our deepest gratitude and thanks also go out to the great people who have helped with the development of *What Is Psychology?* in its prior standard and *Essentials* editions: Jaime Perkins, Kristin Makarewycz, Shannon LeMay-Finn, Kim Russell, Liz Rhoden, Nicole Lee Petel, Mary Noel, Christy Frame, Vernon Boes, Paige Leeds, Jessica Alderman, Roman Barnes, and everyone else at Cengage and MPS Limited who helped make these texts the best possible learning tools for students everywhere.

For this new edition we are grateful for the invaluable contributions made by Clayton Austin, Shelli Newhart, Jill Traut, Priya Subbrayal, Christy Frame, Mary Noel, Jennifer Levanduski, and Vernon Boes.

We also would like to thank the following reviewers for their insightful comments and expert guidance in developing this text:

David Baskind
Delta College

Brenda J. Beagle
John Tyler Community College

Amy A. Bradshaw
Embry-Riddle Aeronautical University

Wendy Brooks
College of the Desert

Mary Cordell
Hills College

Adria DiBenedetto
Quinnipiac University

Kimberley Duff
Cerritos College

Jean M. Egan
Asnuntuck Community College

Kimberly Fairchild
Manhattan College

Keith D. Foust
Shasta College

Laura Fry
Coconino Community College

Terry Lyn Funston
Sauk Valley Community College

Andrea Goldstein
Keiser University

Pete Gram
Pensacola Junior College

Julie A. Gurner
Community College of Philadelphia

Jill Haasch
Glenville State College

Sean C. Hill
Lewis and Clark Community College

Bobby Hutchison
Modesto Junior College

Joni Jecklin
Heartland Community College

Michael Leffingwell
Tarrant County College, Northeast Campus

John Lu
Concordia University–Irvine

George Martinez
Somerset Community College

Cheryl McGill
Florence Darlington Technical College

Robin P. McHaelen
University of Connecticut, School of Social Work

Yvonne Kim McKeithen-Franks
Massasoit Community College

Antoinette R. Miller
Clayton State University

Nancy Murray
Vermont Technical College

Linda Petroff
Central Community College

Andrea Rashtian
California State University–Northridge

Illeana P. Rodriguez
Triton College

Gwendolyn Scott
University of Houston–Downtown

Jason S. Spiegelman
College of Baltimore County

Ronald W. Stoffey
Kutztown University of Pennsylvania

Eva Szeli
Arizona State University

Christopher C. Thomas
Florence Darlington Technical College

Jeff Wachsmuth
Napa Valley College

We would also like to thank our friends and colleagues at the University of North Georgia and Valencia College for their support and latitude over the past 15 years. We would also like to thank the thousands of students we have worked with over the years. In your own way, each of you has helped us to become better teachers and better people. Our hope is that this book will touch many other students and foster an interest in and passion for psychology.

Finally, we would like to thank our families. Susann would like to thank her husband Eddie for his loving support and for enduring far too many nights of watching TV alone while his wife was writing. Ellen would like to thank her husband Dave for his technical assistance, his tireless rereading of material, and his patience and support through all the frustration, deadlines, and apprehension.

The Science of Psychology

Learning Objectives

1.1 Define psychology. (APA 1.1)

1.1 Identify common misconceptions about the field of psychology. (APA 2.1)

1.2 Identify the four goals of psychological research. (APA 1.1, 2.1)

1.2 Outline the steps of the scientific method, and distinguish between predictive and causal hypotheses. (APA 2.1, 2.4)

1.2 Describe the advantages and disadvantages of observational, survey, correlational, and experimental research methods and the types of conclusions that can be drawn about behavior from each method. (APA 2.1, 2.2, 2.4, 2.5, 5.1)

1.3 Describe the main ethical principles that guide psychologists as they conduct research. (APA 3.1)

1.4 Distinguish among the seven modern perspectives of psychology and the eclectic approach, and identify the major historical figures that influenced psychology's development. (APA 1.1, 1.2, 2.1, 2.5, 5.1)

1.4 Describe the training of a psychologist, and compare and contrast the different specialty areas of the profession. (APA 1.3, 5.1, 5.5)

1.4 Describe how women and minorities have contributed to the field of psychology. (APA 1.2, 3.3)

It was the first day of the semester. Parking, as usual, was a challenge. Christian finally found a spot, parked his car, and headed toward campus. While grabbing a coffee at the college café, he ran into his friend Andrew. "Hey, man, what's up?" he asked. "Not much," Andrew replied. "Just getting coffee before I head to class." "What are you taking?" Christian asked. "Well, I've got math and music appreciation tomorrow. Today, I've got oceanography and general psychology. I'm heading to the psych class now." Christian smiled and said, "Cool, I've got that psych class now, too." The two students grabbed their coffees and headed toward the psychology building, continuing their conversation. "What do you think the course will be about?" Andrew asked. "Probably how you feel about things. Ought to be an easy A—like being with Dr. Phil all semester," Christian joked. Andrew laughed. "Yeah, I guess we'll see how screwed up we are and get a lot of therapy." "Speak for yourself," Christian kidded. "I figure it's just commonsense stuff, things your parents have been telling you since you were a kid. Shouldn't be too hard." Andrew nodded in agreement as they arrived at the classroom. "Let's take a seat in the back so we don't have to share our feelings too much," Christian whispered. The two found a seat in the back and waited for class to begin.

© Ellen Pastorino

Many students hold misconceptions about the field of psychology.

1

Greg Hinsdale/Corbis

Chapter Outline

1.1 What Is Psychology? / 4

1.2 The Science of Psychology: Goals, Hypotheses, and Methods / 7

1.3 Ethical Principles of Psychological Research / 20

1.4 Psychology in the Modern World: Foundations and Growth / 23

PSYCHOLOGY APPLIES TO YOUR WORLD: Training to Be a Psychologist / 32

1.5 Integrating Psychology: The Big Picture / 34

1.1 What Is Psychology?

psychology the scientific study of behavior and mental processes

scientific method a systematic process used by psychologists for testing hypotheses about behavior

Welcome to the world of **psychology**, the scientific study of behavior and mental processes. But what exactly does that include? Behavior includes actions, feelings, and biological states such as sleeping. Mental processes include problem solving, intelligence, and memory, to name just a few. Psychology is a science because psychologists conduct research in accord with the **scientific method**—a systematic process used to test ideas about behavior. Psychologists analyze the behavior of humans as well as other species.

Psychology is probably one of the few disciplines in which students come to the first class believing they already know much about the topic. We see psychologists and psychiatrists on talk shows (Dr. Phil, Dr. Drew) and listen to them on the radio. We frequently see them depicted on television (*Criminal Minds, Bones*) and in the movies (*Side Effects, The Departed, Man on a Ledge, A Beautiful Mind*). Many of these portrayals are quite entertaining, but they do not always represent psychology accurately. As a result, the public image of the discipline tends to be distorted.

The purpose of this textbook is to help you develop a deeper understanding of psychology. In this chapter, we explain what psychologists do, how they think, and where they work. It is a general overview of the field of psychology, an introduction to the more specific areas of psychology discussed in subsequent chapters. We describe how psychology is a science, the goals of psychological research, how psychologists study behavior, and what the field is like today.

This textbook follows the recommendations and guidelines of the American Psychological Association (2014) by emphasizing a common core structure of contemporary psychology. The chapters are arranged into four main sections representing foundational areas in the field of psychology: *biological, cognitive, developmental and social psychology,* and *physical and mental health*. Each section begins with a real-life story of a person whose life and experiences illustrate the concepts of the chapters that follow. Each chapter ends with an *Integrating Psychology: The Big Picture* section that ties together the person's story, the contents of the chapter, and the broader core of psychology. We hope that by reading these real-life stories, you will find psychological topics easier to understand and will be better able to apply psychological principles and concepts to your own life. We also hope you will come to appreciate that understanding the mind and behavior is not a simple process but requires the integration of a multitude of perspectives to more fully comprehend humans' experiences.

1.1.1 • Correcting Common Misconceptions About the Field of Psychology

You are probably reading this book because you have enrolled in a general psychology course. Your expectations of what you will learn have been influenced by your general impressions of psychology. Much of the psychological information presented in the media focuses on practitioners, therapy, and helping others, and you—like the students in the opening section—may have the impression that psychology is all about how you feel and how you can feel better. Although a large proportion of psychologists counsel or otherwise treat clients, most of these professionals hold a doctorate degree in psychology, which required that they study scientific methodology and complete a considerable amount of research (Wicherski, Michalski, & Kohout, 2009).

Psychology is rooted in scientific research. The information in this book is research based. Every idea put forward in the field is subject to scientific study. You will notice that many statements in this text are followed by names and years in parentheses—for example, (Pastorino, 2014). These text citations refer to the scientific studies on which the stated conclusions are based, with the researcher name(s) and date of the study. The complete research citations can be found in the References section at the end of this book. An example of a complete research citation is shown in • FIGURE 1.1.

APA Style:

Author, A. A., Author, B. B., & Author, C. C. (Year). Title of article: Subtitle of article. *Title of Periodical or Journal, Vol #*, pages.

Example:

Whitton, S. W., & Whisman, M. A. (2010). Relationship satisfaction instability and depression. *Journal of Family Psychology, 24*, 791–794.

FIGURE 1.1

Reference Citations in Psychology

The References section at the end of this book lists the complete source for each citation. Here is the APA style format for psychological references. The citation for this particular reference would appear in the text as (Whitton & Whisman, 2010).

A psychologist's explanation of a particular behavior is generally presented as a theory. A **theory** is an explanation of why and how a behavior occurs. It does not explain a particular behavior for all people, but it provides general guidelines that summarize facts and help us organize research on a particular subject.

theory an explanation of why and how a behavior occurs

We all, at times, fancy ourselves as psychologists. We interact with people all the time, we observe others' behaviors, and we have our own personal experiences. Therefore, we might naturally think that we already know a lot about psychology. People often behave the way we think they will behave, so psychology seems as though it is just common sense. However, we often overlook the examples of behavior that don't confirm our expectations or support our preexisting beliefs. Psychologists systematically test their ideas about behavior using the prescribed methods and procedures we will describe in the next section of this chapter.

ENGAGE YOURSELF Take a look at • TABLE 1.1 and answer the questions about behavior.

TABLE 1.1

How Much Do You Know About Behavior?

Indicate whether you believe each statement is true (T) or false (F).	
1. We are either left-brain or right-brain thinkers.	T F
2. Genes work only during prenatal development.	T F
3. No new neurons develop after infancy.	T F
4. Brain injury in children is always worse than brain injury in adults.	T F
5. Stress is caused by bad things that happen to you.	T F
6. During sleep, the brain rests.	T F
7. There are female brains and male brains.	T F
8. Males are better than females at math.	T F
9. We have only five senses.	T F
10. Legal drugs don't hurt the brain, but illegal ones do.	T F
11. Our memory works like a video recorder.	T F
12. Schizophrenia means you have multiple personalities.	T F

How many of the items did you mark as true? All the statements are false, yet many students have such misconceptions or believe such myths about human behavior. Psychological findings do *not* always confirm our everyday observations about behavior. Only by objectively measuring and testing our ideas and observations about behavior can we determine which ideas are more likely to stand up to scientific scrutiny. Behavior is much more complex than the simple statements in Table 1.1 suggest.

Most students entering a general psychology class, like Christian and Andrew, expect to focus on diagnosing and treating mental disorders. Although some psychologists specialize in mental illness, many others work in academic settings, in the business world, in education, or in government agencies. Psychology is an extremely diverse field, and new specialties are appearing each year. Psychologists are interested in numerous topics, including neuroscience, learning, memory, aging, development, gender, motivation, emotion, sports, criminal behavior, and many other subjects. We cannot cover every area of psychology in this textbook, but we will give you an overview of the main areas of psychological research.

1.1.2 • Psychology Will Teach You About Critical Thinking

pseudopsychology psychological information or conclusions that sound scientific but that have not been systematically tested using the scientific method

critical thinking thought processes used to evaluate and analyze information and apply it to other situations

Because behavior is so complex, psychological theories generally don't definitively explain the behavior of all people. To think like a psychologist, you must think critically, analyzing and evaluating information. You must be able to distinguish true psychological information from **pseudopsychology**. Pseudopsychological findings sound persuasive, but they are not necessarily based on scientific procedures. Their conclusions may go far beyond the scope of their actual data. For example, have you ever heard that people use only 10% of their brains? Many college students believe this false statement despite evidence that shows it is not true (Higbee & Clay, 1998). To think like a psychologist, you must be skeptical rather than accepting about explanations of behavior.

Critical thinking involves analyzing and evaluating information and applying it to other situations. Critical thinking also makes you an intelligent consumer of information. You will be encouraged to practice this skill throughout the book as you read the chapter and test your mastery of the material in the *Quiz Yourself* sections at the end of each main topic and in the *What Do You Know? Assess Your Understanding* questions at the end of each chapter. In the end-of-chapter material, we have also included *Use It or Lose It* questions. These short answer questions ask you to apply your knowledge to solve a problem or situation. Immediately following are *Critical Thinking for Integration* questions that require you to analyze and synthesize concepts from several chapters in order to solve a problem or situation.

Because we all engage in behavior, much of the information in this text will apply to your life. We all dream, remember, like or dislike others, are motivated, have high or low self-esteem, experience sadness, behave aggressively, help others, learn, perceive, and use our senses. Consequently, we recommend that you apply the material in this text to your own behavior as much as possible. This connection will increase your interest in the text, and you will study more effectively.

1.1

Quiz Yourself

1. **Which of the following statements is *true*?**
   a. Psychology is just common sense.
   b. Psychologists study only abnormal behavior.
   c. Psychologists know why people behave the way that they do.
   d. Psychologists test ideas about behavior according to the scientific method.

2. **Which of the following topics would a psychologist most likely study?**
   a. Weather patterns in Africa
   b. Memory changes in adults
   c. Causes of the Vietnam War
   d. All of the above

3. **Which of the following statements is *not* a pseudopsychology claim?**
   a. Transplant organs carry personality traits that are always transferred from donors to receivers.
   b. Walking on hot coals without burning one's feet requires paranormal abilities.
   c. You can make a blood clot in your brain disappear by humming.
   d. Several studies show a relationship between academic achievement and self-esteem.

Answers 1. d; 2. b; 3. d

1.2 The Science of Psychology: Goals, Hypotheses, and Methods

Though psychologists study and emphasize different aspects of behavior, they all share similar goals. The main goals of psychology and psychological research are as follows:

- To describe behavior
- To predict behavior
- To explain behavior
- To control or change behavior

Description involves observing events and describing them. Typically, description is used to understand how events are related to one another. For example, you may notice that your health club tends to get more crowded in the months of January, February, and March. It seems you have to wait longer to use the weight machines or there are more people in the yoga classes. This observation describes an event.

If you observe that two events occur together rather reliably or with a general frequency or regularity, you can make *predictions* about or anticipate what events may occur. From your observations, you may predict that the health club will be more crowded in January. You may arrive earlier to make sure you get a parking spot or a place in the spinning class.

Although it may be known that two events regularly occur together, that doesn't tell us what *caused* a particular behavior to occur. Winter months do not cause health clubs to become crowded. These two events are related, but one event does not cause the other. Therefore, an additional goal of psychology is to *explain* or understand the causes of behavior. As stated previously, psychologists usually put forth explanations of behavior in the form of theories. A *theory* is an explanation of why and how a particular behavior occurs. We will detail seven types of explanations, or perspectives, later in the chapter. For example, how do we explain higher health club attendance in the winter months? Is it a behavior that is

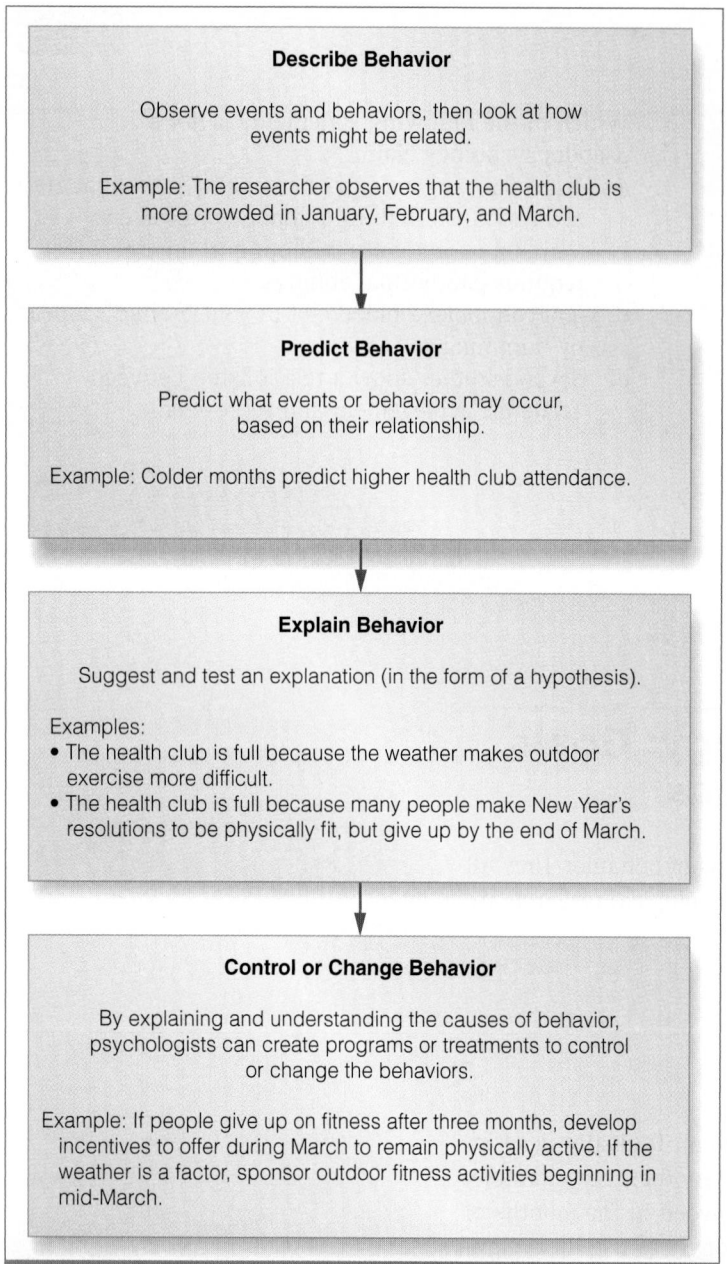

FIGURE 1.2

Goals of Psychology

Psychologists attempt to describe, predict, explain, and ultimately control or change behavior.

influenced by the environment? Perhaps health clubs are more crowded because the weather makes outdoor exercise more difficult. Perhaps it is more influenced by motivation as many people at the start of a new year resolve to work out more. As these ideas are tested, more and more causes and predictors of behavior are discovered. Some of these explanations or theories will be modified, some will be discarded, and new ones will be developed.

The purpose behind explaining and understanding the causes of behavior is the final goal of psychology, *controlling* or *changing* behavior. It relates to the goal of explanation because one needs to understand what is causing a behavior in order to change or modify it. For example, let's say that the weather is a factor in health club attendance. Health clubs could offer outdoor fitness activities beginning in mid-March to prevent declining enrollment. Many psychologists go into the field in the hope of improving society. They may want to improve child care, create healthier work environments, or reduce discrimination in society. Such sentiments reflect the goal of control and underscore the potential impact of good research. • FIGURE 1.2 summarizes the goals of psychology.

1.2.1 • Psychologists Are Scientists: The Scientific Method

The purpose of psychological research is to test ideas about behavior. As previously stated, researchers use the *scientific method* when testing ideas about behavior. The scientific method is a set of rules for gathering and analyzing information that enables you to test an idea or hypothesis. All scientists adhere to these same steps even though they may use different techniques within each step. The decisions that scientists make at each step of the scientific method will ultimately affect the types of conclusions they can draw about behavior.

How can the scientific method be used to meet the goals of psychology? Let's say that you have an interest in understanding beer drinking among college students. You want to make some predictions (a goal of psychology) about beer drinking. You use the scientific method to test this idea, as outlined in • FIGURE 1.3.

1. *Define and describe the issue to be studied.* You might hypothesize that college students who buy pitchers of beer tend to drink more than college students who purchase bottles of beer (a **prediction**). You study previous research in scientific journals on alcohol consumption.
2. *Form a testable hypothesis.* Students who buy pitchers of beer tend to drink more than students who buy beer in bottles. This **hypothesis** must be phrased in a way that can be objectively measured—that is, in such a way that another person can test the same hypothesis to verify or replicate your results.

prediction an expected outcome of how variables will relate

hypothesis an educated guess

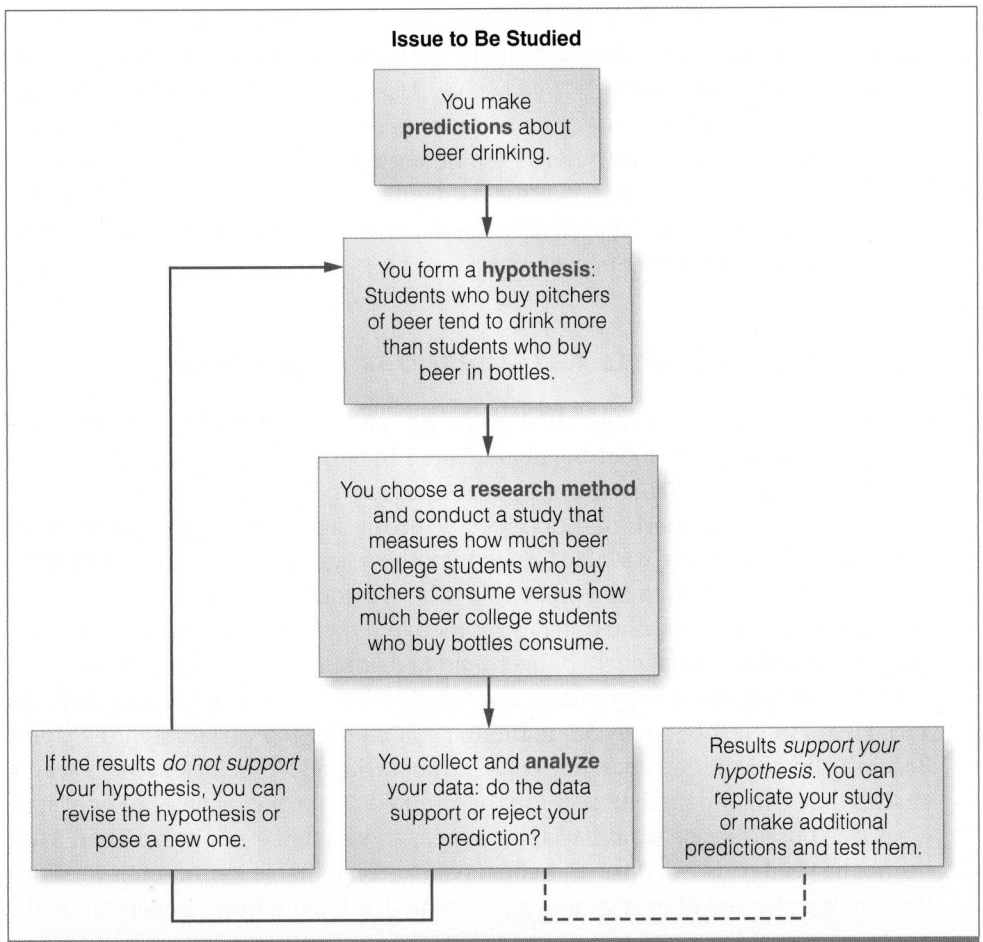

FIGURE 1.3

The Scientific Method

The scientific method enables researchers to test ideas about behavior.

3. *Choose an appropriate research strategy.* You choose a group of people to observe (college students) and a research method that allows you to measure objectively how much beer students who buy pitchers drink versus how much beer students who buy bottles drink. You decide where your study will be conducted. Will it be in the environment where the behavior naturally occurs (such as the local college bar) or in a laboratory (a more controlled setting)? You decide who you will use as *participants.* Will you use animals or humans? If using humans, how will they be selected? If using animals, what species will you use?
4. *Conduct the study to test your hypothesis.* Run the study and collect the data based on the decisions in steps 1–3.
5. *Analyze the data to support or reject your hypothesis.* Researchers usually analyze their data using statistics. If the results do not support your hypothesis, you can revise the hypothesis or pose a new one. If the results do support your hypothesis, you can *replicate* your study (do the same one again) to increase your confidence that your findings support your hypothesis or make additional predictions and test them. Geller, Russ, and Altomari (1986) actually included this prediction in a larger study on beer drinking among college students and found support for the hypothesis that buying pitchers was associated with consuming larger amounts of beer.

No matter which goal of psychology you are addressing, the process is the same. The goal merely influences the decisions you make when testing an idea through the scientific method. If your goal is description or prediction, your hypothesis will state what you expect to observe or what relationships you expect to find. Your research strategy will then be designed to measure observations or relationships, and your analysis of the data will employ statistics that enable you to support or refute your hypothesis. It is in this way that the scientific method allows us to test the ideas of psychology.

1.2.2 • Psychologists Ask Questions: Hypotheses

As you have seen, one of the first steps of the scientific method is to formulate a question or hypothesis about behavior. These hypotheses generally fall into one of two categories: *predictive hypotheses* and *causal hypotheses*.

predictive hypothesis an educated guess about the relationships among variables

causal hypothesis an educated guess about how one variable will influence another variable

A **predictive hypothesis** makes a specific prediction or set of predictions about the relationships among variables. Such hypotheses are used to address two goals of psychology: description and prediction. The previous example on beer drinking among college students illustrated a predictive hypothesis: The study predicted that students who buy pitchers of beer tend to drink more than students who buy beer in bottles. Predictive hypotheses are made when the researcher measures the variables of interest but does not manipulate or control the variables in the study. Because the researcher does not control the variables, conclusions of research studies that test predictive hypotheses are limited. The conclusions can only state what was observed, or what variables appear to be related to one another. They cannot be used to draw cause-and-effect conclusions; that is, one cannot conclude that buying pitchers of beer causes a person to drink more beer. To determine the cause, you must form and test a *causal hypothesis*.

A **causal hypothesis** specifically states how one variable will influence another variable. Causal hypotheses can be tested only when the researcher is able to control or manipulate the main variables in a study. The researcher sets up different conditions in a study and then observes whether there is a change in behavior because of the different conditions. For example, suppose a researcher has developed a new strategy to teach children how to read. The researcher hypothesizes that this program will cause greater gains in reading than the standard method for teaching reading. This is a causal hypothesis. Some students are assigned to the new reading program, and others are assigned to the standard program. The researcher then measures the children's gains in reading at the end of the year to see whether there is a difference. As you will soon see, causal hypotheses can only be tested by means of an experiment. To test a causal hypothesis, a researcher must be able to conclude how one variable affects or causes a change in another variable.

1.2.3 • Psychologists Strategize: Sampling and Research Methods

Once you have stated a hypothesis, the next step in the research process is to decide on a research strategy and a way of selecting participants. The type of hypothesis you make (predictive or causal) typically determines which research methods you can employ. You are more likely to use some research methods to test predictive hypotheses and other methods to test causal hypotheses.

Naturalistic observations, case studies, surveys, and *correlational research* are used to test predictive hypotheses. All of these methods are used when the researcher cannot control or manipulate the main variables in the study. Each method has its advantages and disadvantages, which we will discuss in a moment.

SELECTING PARTICIPANTS

In a perfect world, researchers would include every person they are interested in studying. This is termed the **population of interest**. For example, for a developmental psychologist who specializes in infant development, all infants would be the population of interest. It is impossible to test everyone, however, so researchers select a portion, or subset, of the population of interest called a **sample**. Because the sample will be used to make inferences or judgments about the entire population, the sample should reflect the whole population as much as possible; that is, it should be a *representative sample*. Random sampling of participants ensures a representative sample. In a *random sample,* every member of the population has an equal chance of being selected to participate in the study; this avoids introducing *sampling bias* into the research.

population of interest the entire universe of animals or people that could be studied

sample the portion of the population of interest that is selected for a study

naturalistic observation observing behavior in the environment in which the behavior typically occurs

The more representative the sample is, the more the results will generalize (or apply) to the population of interest. But random sampling is not always possible. Instead, psychological research often uses *samples of convenience,* or groups of people who are easily accessible to the researcher. The students in your psychology course are a sample of convenience. In fact, much psychological research relies on using college students as the sample of convenience! Only 28.5% of people in the United States over the age of 25 have a college degree or higher, so samples of college students probably do not represent all types of people and groups (U.S. Census Bureau, 2012a).

In addition, online psychology labs at well-known universities across the United States are now much more common. On the plus side, researchers conducting online research have the distinct advantage of soliciting a larger and more diverse sample at a fraction of the cost, with improved efficiency and data storage (Gosling & Johnson, 2010). Thousands of participants from all over the world may be gathered over the Internet as opposed to a few hundred that can be collected on-site. However, recall that the people you get to participate in your study are very important to the conclusions of your study. Internet research does not ensure a representative sample. Some people do not have access to a computer or may not know how to use the Internet. Web surveys often produce a lower response rate than traditional formats (Fan & Yan, 2010), and people who complete online research may be different in some way from people who are less willing to complete online research that presents an alternative explanation for one's results. Moreover, researchers may not be able to ensure that participants are who they say they are. People can more easily falsify their identity on the Internet than they can in person, calling into question the "true" characteristics of the sample that is generated.

NATURALISTIC OBSERVATIONS

Naturalistic observations are research studies that are conducted in the environment in which the behavior typically occurs. For example, Campos, Graesch, Repetti, and others (2009) wanted to investigate when and in what manner dual-earner families interact after work. The researchers measured interaction by observing and video-recording dual-earner couples and their children in their homes throughout two weekday afternoons and evenings. The researcher in a naturalistic study is a recorder or observer of behavior who then describes or makes predictions about behavior based on what he or she has observed.

© Ariel Skelley/Corbis

A school playground could be an environment for naturally observing children's behaviors.

Because the researcher does not control events in a naturalistic study, it is not possible to pinpoint the causes of behavior. Therefore, naturalistic studies are predominately used to achieve the goals of description and prediction. In their observational study, Campos et al. found that although both mothers and fathers were likely to be greeted with positive behavior from family members, mothers spent more time with children whereas fathers spent more time alone.

While naturalistic observation can provide a picture of behavior as it normally occurs, researchers need to consider the influence of *reactivity*. Suppose you want to study childhood aggression by observing students on a school playground. What might happen if you were to simply enter the playground, sit down, and start writing about what you saw? The children might behave differently because of your presence and/or their awareness that they are being observed; as a result, your observations of aggression might not be reliable or true. When conducting a naturalistic observation, researchers attempt to minimize reactivity to ensure that they are observing the true behavior of their participants.

CASE STUDIES

case study an in-depth observation of one participant

generalizability [jen-er-uh-lies-uh-BILL-uh-tee] how well a researcher's findings apply to other individuals and situations

survey a research method that asks a large group of people about their attitudes, beliefs, and/or behaviors

A **case study** is an in-depth observation of one participant. The participant may be a person, an animal, or even a setting such as a business or a school. As with naturalistic observation, in case studies researchers do not control any variables but merely record or relate their observations. Case studies provide in-depth information on rare and unusual conditions that we might not otherwise be able to study. However, the main disadvantage of the case study method is its limited applicability to other situations. It is very difficult to take one case, especially a rare case, and say that it applies to everyone. In other words, case studies lack **generalizability**; therefore, the conclusions that are drawn from case studies are limited to the participant being studied.

SURVEYS

Often, psychologists want to study a whole group of people but in less depth. **Surveys** can accomplish this task by asking a large group of people about their attitudes, beliefs, and/or behaviors. A large group of people can quickly respond to questions or statements in their homes, online, over the phone, or out in public.

Survey data are used to make predictions and test predictive hypotheses. For example, knowing which people are more likely to buy a product enables a company to market its products more effectively and perhaps devise new strategies to target individuals who are not buying them. Similarly, knowing which behaviors are related to a higher frequency of illness enables a psychologist to predict who is more at risk for physical or mental illness. However, *who* you ask to complete a survey and *how* you ask them are critical elements in distinguishing good survey research from biased research. Recall that a random sampling of participants minimizes sampling bias. The more representative the sample is, the more the results will generalize to the population of interest.

A second critical element of the survey method is how the questions are worded. A respondent has to be able to understand the question and interpret it in the way the researcher intended. It is important to make questions clear and precise to obtain accurate estimates of people's feelings, beliefs, and behavior. For example, differences in survey question wording have been found to have an influence on rape estimates (Fisher, 2009) and estimates of adolescent sexual behaviors (Santelli et al., 2000).

In summary, surveys are advantageous in that they allow psychologists to pose a lot of questions to a large sample of people. Accurate information can be gathered in a relatively short period of time. Yet the survey's wording, the representativeness of the sample, and whether people choose to answer the questions honestly can bias the results.

For example, the Pew Research Center (2010) set out to compare the values, attitudes, and behaviors of Millennials (adults born after 1980) with those of today's older adults as well as with older adults back when they were the age that Millennials are now by using the survey method, with a nationally representative sample of 2,020 adults, including 830 participants between the ages of 18 and 29. Not surprisingly, they reported differences among the groups in behaviors associated with the use of technology. For example, 83% of Millennials reported sleeping with a cell phone by their bed, compared to 68% of Generation Xers (those born between 1965 and 1980), 50% of Baby Boomers (those born between 1946 and 1964), and 20% of the Silent generation (those born before 1946). Nearly two-thirds of Millennials also admitted to texting while driving. Seventy-five percent of Millennials have created a profile on a social networking site such as Facebook, compared with 50% of Generation Xers, 30% of Baby Boomers, and 6% of the Silent generation.

Interestingly, the Millennials appear to be the least overtly religious American generation since survey research began measuring it. Fewer Millennials reported belonging to any particular faith than older people do today, and they were less likely to be affiliated with a particular religion than previous generations were when they were 18–29 years of age. Millennials also reported attending religious services less often than older adults today. However, Millennials reported praying about as often as older adults did when they were 18–29 years old.

What accounts for these reported differences? Survey research cannot explain the differences; it can be used only to describe and predict behavior. However, we can generate multiple hypotheses as to why these generational differences occur. They could be due to the unique historical circumstances or social movements experienced by each generation, such as wars or technological advances. They could be due to changing social roles, longer life expectancies, or varying economic factors, or to some combination of these factors. Also keep in mind that there are as many differences within generations as there are among them. Yet, from this survey research, we get a glimpse of the attitudes, values, and behaviors of the Millennial generation as they move into adulthood.

CORRELATIONAL STUDIES

Correlational studies test the relationship, or **correlation**, between two or more variables—television watching and violent behavior, or depression and gender, for example. The researcher does not control variables but rather measures them to see whether any reliable relationship exists between them. For example, if we were to measure your weight (one variable), what other variable might show a relationship to your weight? Your height? Your calorie consumption? Your gender? Your age? Your life expectancy? If you were to measure all these variables,

correlation [cor-ruh-LAY-shun] the relationship between two or more variables you might find that all of them vary in relation to weight. These relationships are correlations.

The strength of a correlation is measured in terms of a *correlation coefficient*—a statistic that tells us how strong the relationship between two factors is. Correlation coefficients range from –1.00 to +1.00. The closer the correlation coefficient is to –1.00 or +1.00, the stronger the correlation, or the more related the two variables are. A –1.00 or a +1.00 is a *perfect correlation;* the value of one variable always exactly predicts the value of the other variable. For example, every time people get angry, they hit something. The closer the correlation coefficient is to 0, the weaker the correlation—that is, one variable does not reliably predict the other. A *zero correlation* coefficient means that there is no linear relationship between the two variables—for example, how many movies you watch in a month and the color that your walls are painted. To illustrate correlation, let's look at a study by Hays and Robert (2008) on eating behaviors and weight gain in older women. They found a +.25 correlation between weight gain and overeating in response to daily life circumstances. The correlation between weight gain and overeating in response to emotional states such as anxiety and depression was +.17. The higher correlation between weight gain and daily overeating opportunities suggests that ordinary environmental food cues such as television commercials, billboards, or sweets on one's food counter are a better predictor of weight gain in older women than is "emotional eating." Generally, the stronger the correlation between two variables, the more accurate our predictions are, but perfect (+1.00 or –1.00) correlations rarely happen in psychology. Human behavior is too complex for such perfect relationships to occur.

positive correlation a relationship in which increases in one variable correspond to increases in the other variable

negative correlation a relationship in which increases in one variable correspond to decreases in the other variable

The sign before the correlation coefficient tells us how the variables relate to one another (• FIGURE 1.4). A **positive correlation** means that as one variable increases, the other variable also tends to increase; or as one variable decreases, the other variable tends to decrease. In both cases, the variables are changing in the *same* direction. An example of a positive correlation is perceived stress and blood pressure. As perceived stress increases, so does one's blood pressure.

In a **negative correlation**, as one variable increases, the other variable tends to decrease in what is referred to as an *inverse* relationship. Notice that the variables are changing in *opposite* directions. An example of a negative correlation

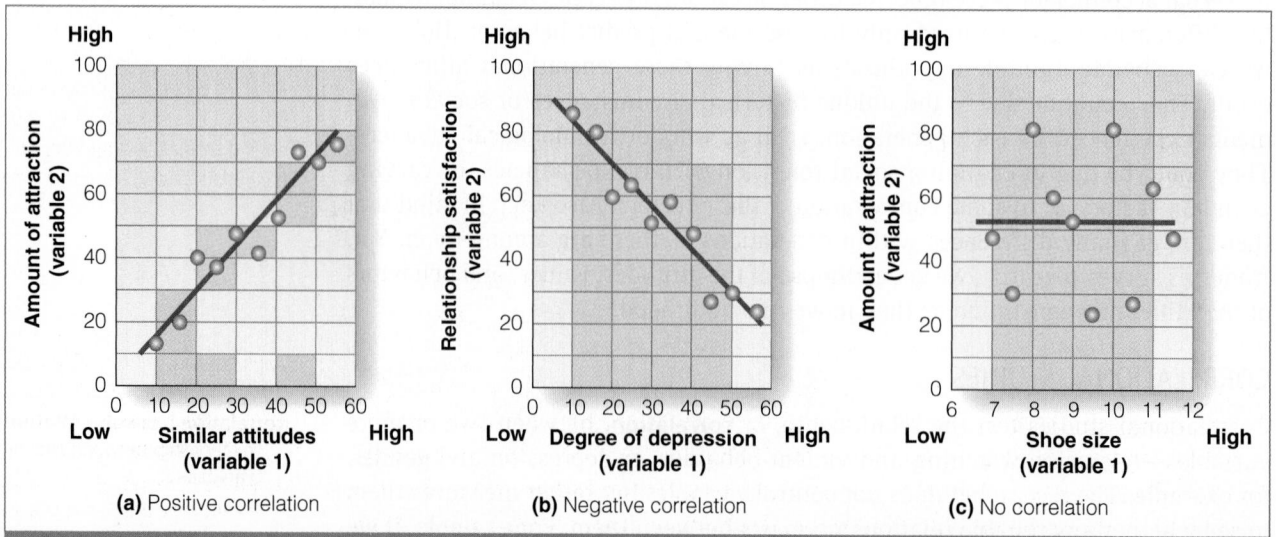

FIGURE 1.4

Correlation

Correlation, a research method used for description and prediction, shows how two variables are related.

is video game playing and school competence. The more time children spend playing video games, the poorer their competence is at school (Hastings et al., 2009). Or consider the negative correlation between relationship satisfaction and depression. As relationship satisfaction increases, feelings of depression decrease (Whitton & Whisman, 2010).

Correlational studies enable researchers to make predictions about behavior, but they do *not* allow us to draw cause-and-effect conclusions (● FIGURE 1.5). For example, there is a positive correlation between academic achievement and self-esteem. Students who have high academic achievement also tend to have high self-esteem. Similarly, students who have low academic achievement tend to have low self-esteem. High academic achievement may cause an increase in self-esteem. However, it is just as likely that having high self-esteem causes one to do better academically. There may be a third variable, such as the parents' educational level or genetics, which actually causes the relationship between academic achievement and self-esteem. A correlational study does not tell us which of these explanations is correct. The only research method that permits us to draw cause-and-effect conclusions is the experiment.

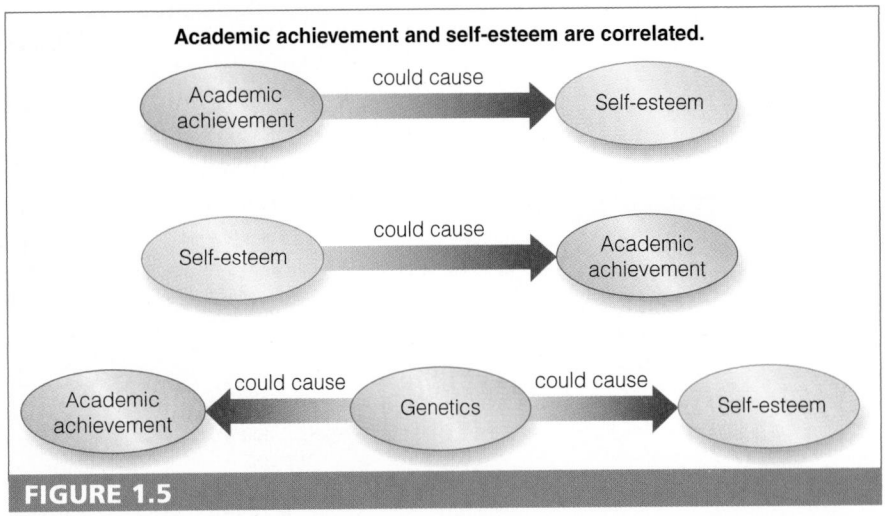

FIGURE 1.5

Correlation Does Not Mean Causation

When two variables are correlated or related, it does not mean that we know why they are related. It is possible that a third variable, not measured in the study, is the real cause of the relationship between the two measured variables. Correlation can only be used for making predictions, not for making cause-and-effect statements.

EXPERIMENTS

Although several types of research methods are used to test predictive hypotheses, only one research method can test a causal hypothesis: the **experiment**. We will discuss several features of the experiment, including its advantages and disadvantages.

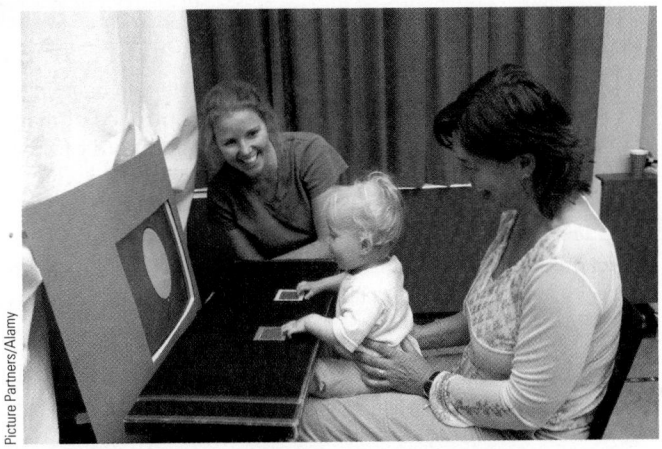
Picture Partners/Alamy

By studying behavior in a lab environment, researchers are better able to control the variables in an experiment.

Necessary Conditions for an Experiment

Two main features characterize an experiment. First, the variables in the study are controlled or manipulated. Second, participants are randomly assigned to the conditions of the study. When these two conditions have been met, causal conclusions *may* be drawn. Let's first turn our attention to the issue of experimenter control.

The point of the experiment is to manipulate one variable and see what effect this manipulation has on another variable (● FIGURE 1.6). These variables are termed the independent and dependent variables, respectively. The **independent variable** is the variable that the experimenter manipulates; it is the *cause* in the experiment, what the researcher is testing. It is independent of or not being affected by the other variables in the study. The **dependent variable** measures any result of manipulating the independent variable; it is the *effect* in the experiment. It is dependent on or influenced by the other variables in the study.

The typical experiment divides participants into two types of groups: the *experimental group* and the *control group*. The **experimental group** includes those

experiment a research method that is used to test causal hypotheses

independent variable the variable in an experiment that is manipulated

dependent variable the variable in an experiment that measures any effect of the manipulation

experimental group the group of participants who receive the manipulation that is being tested

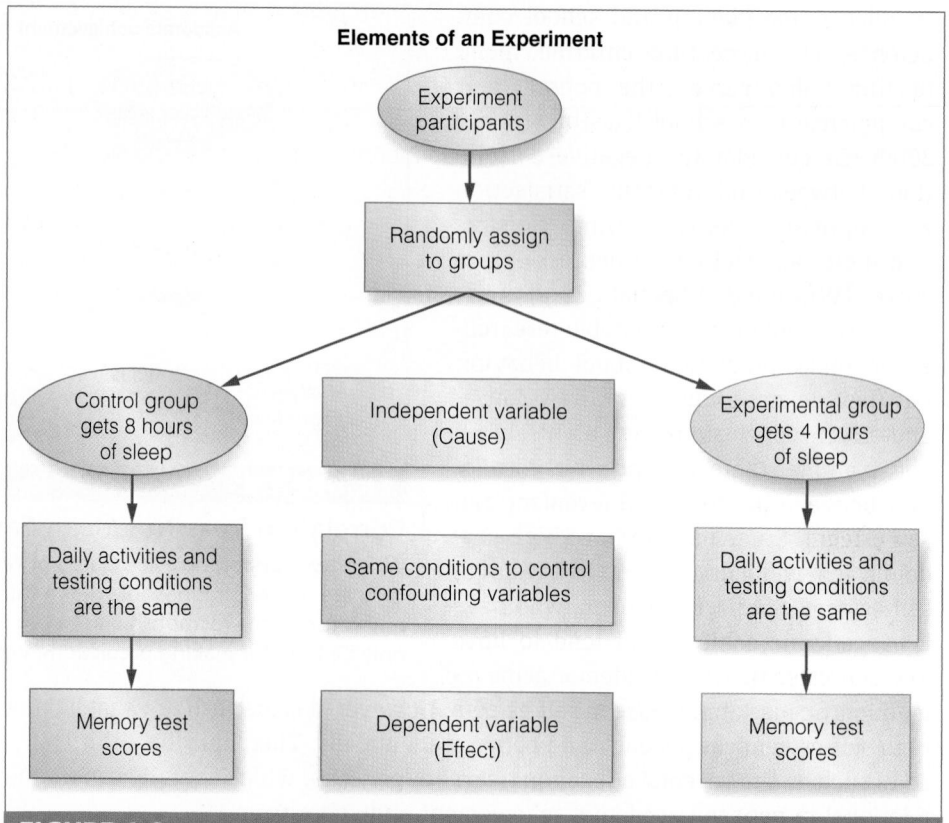

FIGURE 1.6

Elements of an Experiment

The two main ingredients of an experiment are (1) that the variables in the study are controlled or manipulated and (2) that participants are randomly assigned to the conditions of the study. When these two conditions have been met, causal conclusions *may* be drawn.

control group the group of participants who do not receive the manipulation that is being tested

placebo effect a measurable change in participants' behavior due to the expectation or belief that a treatment will have certain effects

double-blind study an experiment in which neither the experimenters nor the participants know to which group (experimental or control) participants have been assigned

participants who receive the manipulation that is being tested. The **control group** includes those participants who do not receive the manipulation that is being tested; they serve as a baseline comparison for the experimental group. Both groups are then measured on the dependent variable to see whether there is a difference between the groups.

In some experiments, the control group receives a *placebo,* or inactive substance such as a sugar pill, rather than being given nothing. This procedure is to control for the *placebo effect*. The **placebo effect** occurs when participants show changes simply because they believe or expect a treatment to have certain effects. In **double-blind studies**, neither experimenters nor participants know who is receiving a placebo and who is receiving the actual treatment; they are *blind* to which group (experimental or control) a person has been assigned. In this way, neither the participant's nor the experimenter's expectations will bias the results.

Suppose, for example, that we want to study the effects of sleep deprivation. Specifically, we hypothesize that sleep deprivation causes deficits in memory. This is a causal hypothesis that can be tested with an experiment. We decide to manipulate the amount of sleep participants receive to see whether it has any effect on memory. In this experiment, we are interested in one's amount of sleep. Other variables do not influence the amount of sleep because we are going to control the amount of sleep to see whether one's memory depends on how much sleep one receives. Therefore, memory is "dependent" and sleep is "independent" for the purposes of this experiment. Some participants (the control group) will be allowed to sleep 8 hours per night for the week of our study. Others (the experimental group) will be allowed to sleep only 4 hours each night. The experimenter has set, or controlled, the amount of sleep (the independent variable) at two levels: 8 hours and 4 hours. Each day of our study, we measure the participants' memory (the dependent variable) by having them complete several memory tasks. At the end of the study, we compare the memory scores of those participants who received 8 hours of sleep (the control group) with those who received only 4 hours of sleep (the experimental group).

To be sure that it is the amount of sleep affecting memory and not something else, we need to be sure that we have controlled any variable (other than the independent variable) that may influence this relationship. These potentially problematic variables are called **confounding variables**. What confounding variables might we need to control? Maybe age influences one's memory or how one handles sleep deprivation. If either of these is true, we would want to control the age of our participants. We also would want to make sure that participants had not used any substances known to affect memory or the sleep cycle prior to their participation in the experiment. Consequently, we would control for this variable, too. Whereas independent variables are controlled by manipulating them to vary with at least two values, confounding variables are controlled by trying to hold them at a constant value so the outcomes of the study cannot be attributed to them.

confounding variable any factor other than the independent variable that affects the dependent measure

random assignment a method of assigning participants in which they have an equal chance of being placed in any group or condition of the study

Both groups must be treated the same except for the amount of sleep they receive, so the researcher sets the conditions of the experiment to be the same for both groups. For example, every participant should complete the memory tasks at the same time of day, and every participant should complete the same memory tasks. The criteria for scoring the memory tasks must be the same as well. The instructions for completing the tasks must be the same. The lighting, temperature, and other physical features of the room in which the participants sleep and complete the memory tasks should be the same for all participants. Our purpose is to design a study in which we manipulate the independent variable to see its effect on the dependent variable. If we control any potentially confounding variables that might influence this relationship and we find a difference between our groups on the dependent variable, that difference is most likely due to the independent variable, and we have established a cause-and-effect relationship.

If the experimenter does not control a confounding variable, we now have more than one variable that could be responsible for the change in the dependent variable: the independent variable and the confounding variable. When this occurs, the researcher is left with an alternative explanation for the results. The change in the dependent variable could have been caused by the independent variable, but it also could have been caused by the confounding variable. Consequently, causal conclusions are limited.

Let's not forget the second condition necessary for an experiment—how participants are assigned to the conditions of the independent variable. We must be sure that there are no differences in the composition of our groups of participants. Psychologists eliminate this problem through **random assignment** of participants to the conditions of the study. In our example on sleep and memory, assigning all the males in the sample to the 4-hour sleep condition and all the females to the 8-hour sleep condition would create a confounding variable. Gender differences might have an effect on memory scores. It may be that gender (the confounding variable) rather than sleep deprivation (the independent variable) is the cause of a difference in memory. To eliminate the influence of such confounding variables, experimenters randomly assign participants to conditions. Each participant has an equal chance of being placed in either condition. Male participants are just as likely to be assigned to the 4-hour condition as they are to the 8-hour condition, and the same is true for female participants. In this way, any participant variable that has the potential to influence the research results is just as likely to affect one group as it is the other. Without random assignment, confounding variables could affect the dependent variable. This is typically what occurs in *quasi-experiments*.

quasi-experiment a research study that is not a true experiment because participants are not randomly assigned to the different conditions

A **quasi-experiment** is in some ways like an experiment. The researcher manipulates the independent variable and sets the other conditions to be the same for both groups. However, the second requirement for an experiment—randomly assigning participants to conditions—has not been met. Quasi-experiments use existing groups of people who differ on some variable. For example, suppose you want to see if smoking cigarettes during pregnancy causes lower-birth-weight babies. For ethical reasons, you cannot assign some pregnant women to smoke and prevent others from smoking. Instead, for your smoking condition, you must select pregnant women who already smoke. These women may differ on other variables when compared to pregnant women who do not smoke. For example, their eating habits may differ. As a result, a confounding variable (the diet of the mothers) rather than smoking could cause a difference in the dependent variable (the birth weight of the offspring). Because quasi-experiments do not meet the conditions necessary for a "true" experiment, causal conclusions based on these designs should be made cautiously (Shadish, Cook, & Campbell, 2002; West, 2009).

Advantages and Disadvantages of Using Experiments Experiments have several advantages. First, it is only through experimentation that we can approach two of the goals of psychology: explaining and changing behavior. An experiment is the only research method that enables us to determine cause-and-effect relationships. This advantage makes interpreting research results less ambiguous. In an experiment, we attempt to eliminate any confounding variables through experimenter control and random assignment of participants to groups. These techniques enable us to draw clearer conclusions from research results.

Experiments also have disadvantages. First, experiments do not address the first two goals of psychology: describing and predicting behavior. These are often the first steps in understanding behavior, and naturalistic observation, surveys, and correlational studies are quite useful for doing this. Second, in an attempt to control confounding variables, experiments conducted in laboratory settings may create an artificial atmosphere. It is then difficult to know whether the same result would occur in a more natural setting. This may be another reason to conduct naturalistic observations or correlational studies. Third, sometimes employing the experimental method is simply not possible for ethical or practical reasons. As we mentioned in the case of quasi-experimental designs, we cannot force people to be randomly assigned to a condition that would harm them (such as smoking) or that does not pertain to them (such as having high blood pressure). Psychologists must follow certain ethical guidelines and practices when conducting research. We turn our attention to this topic next. You Review: Scientific Research Methods summarizes the strengths and weaknesses of the various research methods.

You Review **Scientific Research Methods**

Method	Strengths	Weaknesses
Naturalistic Observation Observing behavior in the environment in which it typically occurs	Describes behavior as it typically occurs in the real world. May test predictive hypotheses.	Little control of variables. Reactivity can influence results. Cannot show cause and effect.
Case Study In-depth observation of one or a few participants or settings	Detailed information on one person or setting. May describe people or settings with special or rare abilities, qualities, or characteristics.	May not generalize to other people or settings. Cannot show cause and effect. Difficult to replicate.
Survey Asks a large group of people about their attitudes, beliefs, and/or behavior	Efficient collection of data with large samples. Can ask a lot of questions at once. Can test predictive hypotheses.	Participants may not answer truthfully. Question wording can bias results. Cannot show cause and effect.
Correlation Measures the relationship between two or more variables	Can measure the strength and direction of relationships between variables. Can test predictive hypotheses.	Does not randomly assign participants to conditions. Cannot show cause and effect.
Quasi-experiment Compare participants who are not randomly assigned on the manipulation of an independent variable	Allows comparisons of treatments. Can control some conditions of study. May test causal hypotheses.	Does not randomly assign participants to conditions. Causal conclusions are difficult to make.
Experiment Manipulate an independent variable to see changes in a dependent measure under controlled conditions.	Allows random assignment of participants to conditions. May eliminate confounding variables. Can show cause and effect.	For ethical and practical reasons, may not be able to test some variables. Results may not apply to real-world settings.

Quiz Yourself 1.2

1. When we know that two events regularly occur together, which goal of psychology can be met?
   a. Predicting behavior
   b. Changing behavior
   c. Understanding behavior
   d. Explaining behavior

2. Dr. Hincapie wants to test the hypothesis that stress increases one's blood pressure. What type of hypothesis is Dr. Hincapie interested in testing?
   a. Predictive
   b. Causal
   c. Correlational
   d. Biological

3. In an experiment on attitudes, participants are given either positive or negative information about a speaker and then asked to evaluate the effectiveness of the speaker. In this experiment, which is the independent variable?
   a. The effectiveness of the speaker
   b. The type of information the participant is given
   c. Attitude change
   d. The speaker

4. The more hours that students work, the less successful they are academically. This is an example of what type of correlation?
   a. zero
   b. positive
   c. perfect
   d. negative
5. Dr. Duarte is studying bullying behavior in children. Every day, he goes to the local playground at 3 P.M., sits on the sidelines, and records the number of times one child bullies another, the sex of the children involved in the bullying, and the duration of the bullying. Dr. Duarte is using which research method in his study?
   a. An experiment
   b. A case study
   c. A naturalistic observation
   d. A quasi-experiment

Answers 1. a; 2. b; 3. b; 4. d; 5. c

1.3 Ethical Principles of Psychological Research

Institutional Review Board (IRB) a committee that reviews research proposals to ensure that ethical standards have been met

informed consent the ethical principle that research participants be told about various aspects of the study, including any risks, before agreeing to participate

Generally, psychologists affiliated with universities and colleges cannot conduct research unless their research proposal has passed review by an **Institutional Review Board (IRB)**. The function of the IRB is to ensure that the research study being proposed conforms to a set of ethical standards or guidelines.

1.3.1 • Ethical Guidelines for Participants

The American Psychological Association (APA), one of the main professional organizations for psychologists, has taken the lead in establishing ethical guidelines, or professional behaviors that psychologists must follow. These guidelines, the "Ethical Principles of Psychologists and Code of Conduct" (APA, 2002), address a variety of issues, including general professional responsibility, clinical practice, psychological testing, and research. Here, we look at the guidelines psychologists must follow when conducting research with humans and animals. The ethical duties of psychologists who treat clients are discussed in Chapter 14.

One of the main concerns of the IRB is to ensure that the proposed research has met the ethical guideline of respect and concern for the dignity and welfare of the people who participate (APA, 2002). Researchers must protect participants from any potential harm, risk, or danger as a result of their participation in a psychological study. If such effects occur, the researcher has the responsibility to remove or correct these effects.

Another fundamental principle of ethical practice in research is **informed consent**. Researchers inform potential participants of any risks during the informed consent process, wherein the researcher establishes a clear and fair agreement with research participants prior to their participation in the research study (APA, 2002). This agreement clarifies the obligations and responsibilities of the participants and the researchers and includes the following information:

- The general purpose of the research study, including the experimental nature of any treatment
- Services that will or will not be available to the control group
- The method by which participants will be assigned to experimental and control groups
- Any aspect of the research that may influence a person's willingness to participate in the research

- Compensation for or monetary costs of participating
- Any risks or side effects that may be experienced as a result of participation in the study

Prospective participants are also informed that they may withdraw from participation in the study at any time, and they are informed of any available treatment alternatives. In addition, the researcher agrees to maintain **confidentiality**. Personal information about participants obtained by the researcher during the course of the investigation cannot be shared with others unless explicitly agreed to in advance by the participant or as required by law or court order.

confidentiality the ethical principle that researchers do not reveal which data were collected from which participant

debriefing the ethical principle that participants be fully informed of the nature of the study after participating in an experiment involving deception

Online research presents unique ethical challenges (Eynon, Schroeder, & Fry, 2009; Solberg, 2010). Psychologists have a duty to maintain confidentiality and privacy of participants' data and personal information. When researchers collect information about users without their active participation (such as from Facebook profiles), users must be adequately informed and give consent. Researchers may or may not consider security as part of their data collection plan or may not have the necessary training to implement electronic security. In such cases, researchers may need to consult technical experts to ensure the security of online information. Even with the best security, databases may still be compromised. Many universities and professional organizations are developing policies and procedures to address these issues.

It is not always possible to fully inform participants of the details of the research, as it may change their behavior. For this reason, psychologists sometimes use *deception* in their research. For example, suppose we wanted to research student cheating. If we tell participants we are studying cheating behavior, it will likely influence their behavior. If we tell participants we are investigating student–teacher behavior, we can measure student cheating more objectively. However, the use of deception must be justified by the potential value of the research results. Moreover, deception can be used only when alternative procedures that do not use deception are unavailable.

If participants have been deceived in any way during the course of a study, the researcher is obligated to *debrief* participants after the experiment ends. **Debriefing** consists of full disclosure by the researcher to inform participants of the true purpose of the research. Any misconceptions that the participant may hold about the nature of the research must be removed at this time.

Consider the following classic research study. In the 1960s, Stanley Milgram (1963) set out to determine whether the average person could be induced to hurt others in response to orders from an authority figure. (You will read more about Milgram's research in Chapter 10.) Participants were deceived into believing that they were participating in a research study on learning rather than on obedience. Participants were told that they would be playing the role of a "teacher" in the experiment. Participants were introduced to a "learner" who was then led to a separate room. The teacher's job was to administer electric shocks to the learner every time the learner made a mistake in an effort to help the learner better learn a list of words. In reality, the participant was not actually shocking the learner. The learner's responses were prerecorded on a tape, but the participants did not know this and believed that they were, indeed, shocking the learner.

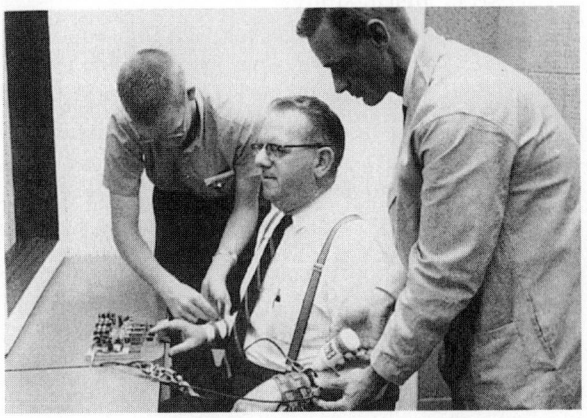

From the film Obedience ©1965 by Stanley Milgram and distributed by Alexander Street Press. Reprinted by permission of Alexandra Milgram

Although Stanley Milgram debriefed his participants, he still caused them psychological harm. Such a study would violate current ethical standards of psychological research.

Despite the fact that participants believed the learner to be ill or worse, most of them continued to follow the experimenter's orders. A full 65% of the participants shocked the learner all the way up to the highest shock level! During the procedure, Milgram's participants exhibited emotional distress. Although Milgram debriefed his participants after the study, he still violated the ethical principle of psychological harm. He was criticized for exposing participants to the trauma of the procedure itself and for not leaving the participants in at least as good a condition as they were prior to the experiment (Baumrind, 1964). Because of these ethical problems, a study such as this would not be approved today.

We should also note that for years the primary focus in research was on White males. Women and minorities were not only discouraged from becoming professionals in psychology but also were largely ignored or neglected when studying psychological issues. Many minority and female as well as male psychologists have contributed to the field of psychology by addressing these shortcomings and designing research that looks specifically at the behaviors of minorities and women.

1.3.2 • Ethical Guidelines for Animal Research

Animal studies have advanced our understanding of many psychological issues, including the importance of prenatal nutrition, our treatment of brain injuries, and our understanding of mental health disorders (Domjan & Purdy, 1995). Psychologists must meet certain standards and follow ethical guidelines when conducting research with animals. Psychological research using animal subjects must also be approved by an IRB. Animals must be treated humanely and in accord with all federal, state, and local laws and regulations. Researchers are responsible for the daily comfort, housing, cleaning, feeding, and health of animal subjects. Discomfort, illness, and pain must be kept at a minimum, and such procedures can only be used if alternative procedures are not available. Moreover, harmful or painful procedures used on animals must be justified in terms of the knowledge that is expected to be gained from the study. Researchers must also promote the psychological well-being of some animals that are used in research, most notably primates (APA, 2002).

Quiz Yourself 1.3

1. **What is the rule for deceiving participants in a psychological study?**
   a. Deception is never allowed in psychological research. It is against the law in every state.
   b. Deception is allowed only when using animals.
   c. Deception is allowed when alternative procedures are unavailable and when participants are debriefed at the end of the study.
   d. Deception can be used under any circumstances.

2. **Dr. Kwan is performing case study research. She should be most concerned with which of the following ethical principles?**
   a. Deception
   b. Physical harm
   c. Debriefing
   d. Confidentiality

3. **Which of the following is *not* an ethical guideline that psychologists must follow when conducting research?**
   a. Paying participants for their participation
   b. Informed consent
   c. Freedom from harm
   d. Confidentiality

Answers 1. c; 2. d; 3. a

1.4 Psychology in the Modern World: Foundations and Growth

Psychology has been described as having "a long past but only a short history" (Ebbinghaus, 1910, p. 9). Traditionally, psychology's birth is linked with the first psychology laboratory, which was established by Wilhelm Wundt in 1879 at the University of Leipzig, in Germany. Wundt (1832–1920), wanted to know what conscious thought processes enable us to experience the external world. In particular, Wundt attempted to detail the *structure* of our mental experiences. Wundt's view that mental experiences were created by different elements is referred to as **structuralism**, a term coined not by Wundt but by his student Edward Titchener.

To identify the structure of thought, British psychologist Titchener (1867–1927) used a process known as **introspection**, a self-observation technique. Trained observers were presented with an event and asked to describe their mental processes. The observations were repeated many times. From these introspections, Titchener identified three basic elements of all conscious experiences: sensations, images, and feelings.

Wundt's and Titchener's research went beyond introspection and structuralism to encompass a very broad view of psychology. They also conducted detailed studies on color vision, visual illusions, attention, and feelings, and influenced the field of psychology through their students, many of whom went on to establish psychology departments and laboratories in the United States. For example, Titchener's first graduate student, American Margaret Washburn (1871–1939), became the first woman to earn a doctorate in psychology. Washburn did not share Titchener's emphasis on structuralism, but she instead investigated the connection between motor movement and the mind and conducted extensive research on animal behavior.

structuralism an early psychological perspective concerned with identifying the basic elements of experience

introspection observing one's own thoughts, feelings, or sensations

Archives of the History of American Psychology, University of Akron, Akron, Ohio

The first woman to be awarded a doctorate in psychology was Margaret Washburn (1871–1939).

1.4.1 • Psychology's Roots and Modern Perspectives

Like Washburn, other psychologists soon reacted against the limited view of the mind that structuralism presented. Such disagreement gave rise to other ways to explain behavior, which resulted in a very broad profession. Here we discuss seven orientations or perspectives on behavior and the historical figures that influenced their development (● FIGURE 1.7): *biological, evolutionary, psychodynamic, behavioral, sociocultural, humanistic,* and *cognitive.* We will also look at a combined perspective referred to as an *eclectic approach.*

THE INFLUENCE OF MEDICINE

Because of the mind's association with the body, much of what we consider psychology today was at times part of the field of medicine. Hippocrates (460–377 BCE), the father of medicine, believed that personality was in part a reflection of the mix of chemicals in the body, and abnormal behavior was typically treated with medical procedures. The ancient Indian texts of knowledge, *The Vedas* (2000–600 BCE), describe *chakras* or energy

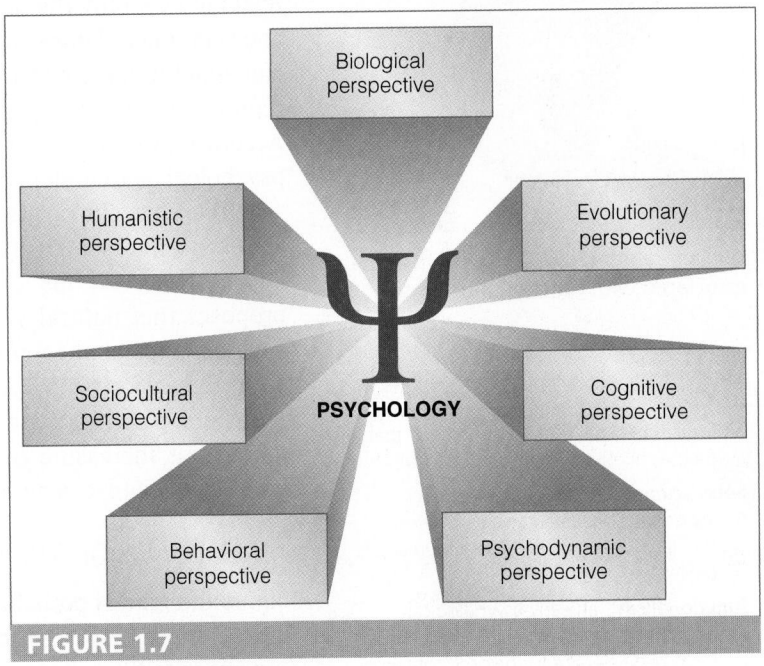

FIGURE 1.7

Psychological Perspectives

Just as a photograph or a piece of art can be examined from many different angles, so, too, can mental processes and behavior. We call these angles *perspectives.* Each offers a somewhat different picture of why people behave as they do. Taken as a whole, these perspectives underscore the complex nature of behavior.

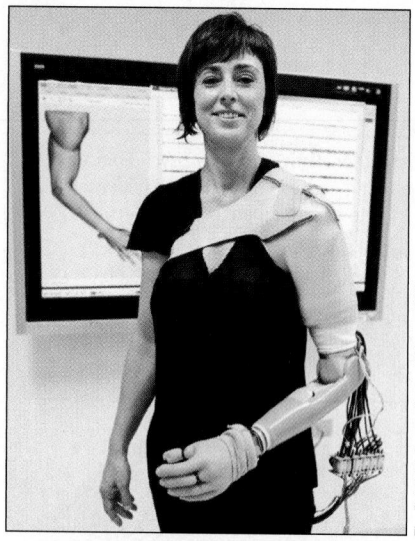

The Rehabilitation Institute of Chicago (RIC)

By studying biological processes, neuroscientists can design neuromotor prosthetic devices such as robotic arms to help restore lost motor functioning.

processing centers within the body that govern physical, mental, emotional, and spiritual health.

Today, psychologists who adopt a **biological perspective** look for a physical cause for a particular behavior. Such psychologists examine genetic, biochemical, and nervous system (brain functioning) relationships to behavior and mental processes. The biological perspective is also a branch of science referred to as **neuroscience**. (We discuss the physical processes of the nervous system in Chapter 2.) For example, electroencephalographs (EEGs) and other brain imaging and computer technology have enabled neuroscientists to measure how a person's body movements cause nerve cells in the brain to fire. They can then use this information to design neuromotor prosthetic devices, such as robotic arms, that work in much the same way. These appliances can help replace or restore lost motor functioning in people with spinal cord injuries and other severe motor deficits (Hochberg et al., 2006; Srinivasan et al., 2007).

FROM FUNCTIONALISM TO EVOLUTION

American psychologist and philosopher William James (1842–1910) had visited Wundt's laboratory in Germany but did not share Wundt's focus on breaking down mental events into their smallest elements. Rather, James proposed a focus on the wholeness of an event and the impact of the environment on behavior. He emphasized *how* a mental process operates as opposed to the *structure* of a mental process. He came to believe that consciousness and thought evolved through the process of natural selection, to help the organism adapt to its environment (Nielsen & Day, 1999). *Evolution* and *natural selection* were ideas that were quite new at the time. Evolution refers to the development of a species—the process by which, through a series of changes over time, humans have acquired behaviors and characteristics that distinguish them from other species. Natural selection refers to how only the organisms best suited to their environment tend to survive and reproduce. James wanted to know how a particular behavior helps an organism adapt to its environment and thereby increases its chances of surviving and reproducing. James's perspective on psychology became known as **functionalism**. According to James, if human behavior is naturally selected, it is important for psychologists to understand the *function,* or survival value, of a behavior.

© Bettmann/Corbis

William James (1842–1910) is associated with functionalism.

Today, psychologists may adopt an **evolutionary perspective**. This approach is similar to the biological approach in that both see the cause of behavior as biological. However, this is where the similarity ends. The evolutionary perspective proposes that natural selection is the process at work. Behaviors that increase your chances of surviving are favored or selected over behaviors that decrease your chances of surviving. Like James's functionalism, this approach analyzes whether a particular behavior increases a person's ability to adapt to the environment, thus increasing the chances of surviving, reproducing, and passing one's genes on to future generations (Buss, 2009).

AN EMPHASIS ON THE UNCONSCIOUS

Sigmund Freud is probably the best-known historical figure in psychology, and his ideas permeate Western culture in music, media, advertising, art, and humor—a testament to his influence and importance. Before creating theories of psychology, however, Freud (1856–1939) studied medicine, focusing on neurology and disorders of the nervous system. He began studying people with all kinds of "nervous" disorders, such as an intense fear of horses or heights or the sudden paralysis of an arm. He began asking patients to express any and every thought that occurred to them, no matter how trivial or unpleasant. Freud theorized that encouraging patients to

biological perspective an approach that focuses on physical causes of behavior

neuroscience a field of science that investigates the relationships between the nervous system and behavior/mental processes

functionalism an early psychological perspective concerned with how behavior helps people adapt to their environment

evolutionary perspective an approach that focuses on how evolution and natural selection influence behavior say whatever came to mind allowed them to recall forgotten memories that seemed to underlie their problems. This process, known today as *free association*, is one element of *psychoanalysis*, a therapy that Freud developed.

From these experiences, Freud came to believe that the unconscious plays a crucial role in human behavior. For Freud, the unconscious was that part of the mind that includes impulses, behaviors, and desires that we are unaware of but that influence our behavior. Until this time, much of psychology had focused on conscious mental processes. Freud's focus on the unconscious was unique and led to his formulation of **psychoanalytic theory**. According to this theory, humans are similar to animals in that they possess basic sexual and aggressive instincts that motivate behavior. However, unlike animals, humans can reason and think, especially as they mature. In childhood we learn to use these conscious reasoning abilities to deal with and to suppress our basic sexual and aggressive desires so that we can be viewed approvingly by others. For Freud, the conflict between the conscious reasoning part of the mind and the unconscious instinctual one was key to understanding human behavior.

Today, psychologists may adopt a **psychodynamic perspective**, a collective term that refers to those assumptions about behavior originally conceived by Freud, which have been modified by his followers. The psychodynamic view focuses on internal, often unconscious mental processes, motives, and desires or childhood conflicts to explain behavior. For example, many children lie to or manipulate parents to get what they want. The psychodynamic view might suggest that such behavior is an unconscious expression of feelings of powerlessness and lack of control that all children face from time to time.

Topham/The Image Works

Sigmund Freud's (1856–1939) focus on the unconscious was unique and led to his formulation of psychoanalytic theory.

psychoanalytic theory Sigmund Freud's view that emphasizes the influence of unconscious desires and conflicts on behavior

psychodynamic perspective an approach that focuses on internal unconscious mental processes, motives, and desires that may explain behavior

behaviorism a psychological perspective that emphasizes the study of observable responses and behavior

stimulus any object or event that is perceived by our senses

response an organism's reaction to a stimulus

A FOCUS ON THE ENVIRONMENT

In the 1920s, in the United States, a growing number of psychologists believed that in order for psychology to be taken seriously as a "true" science, it must focus on observable behavior and not on the mind, a school of thought referred to as **behaviorism**. You can't see the mind or what a person thinks; you can only see what a person does. Behaviorists believed that only overt, observable behaviors could truly be measured consistently from person to person. One of the most vocal proponents of this school of thought was American psychologist John B. Watson (1878–1958).

Watson was influenced by Russian physiologist Ivan Pavlov's studies of digestion in dogs. While measuring and analyzing the first process of digestion (salivation), Pavlov (1849–1936) noticed that his dogs started to salivate *before* he gave them meat powder. When the experiments first started, the salivation had occurred only *after* the dogs were given the meat powder. To further study this curious change in response, Pavlov performed experiments to train the dogs to salivate to other nonfood stimuli. (You will learn more about Pavlov's classic experiments in Chapter 6.)

Pavlov's experiments were important to Watson as examples of how behavior is the product of *stimuli* and *responses*. A **stimulus** is any object or event that is perceived by our senses. A **response** is an organism's reaction to a stimulus. To further his point, Watson and his associate, Rosalie Rayner, performed an experiment on a 9-month-old infant named Albert. Watson first presented "Little Albert" with the stimulus of a white rat. Albert played with the white rat and showed no fear of it (response). Knowing that infants fear loud noises, Watson paired the two stimuli, first presenting the rat to Albert and then presenting a loud gong sound behind Albert's head. Little Albert reacted to the loud noise with the startle, or fear, response. Over and over again, Watson repeated the procedure of pairing the

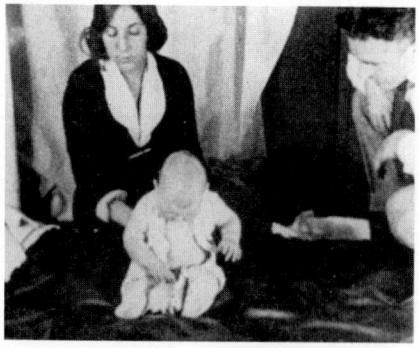

Archives of the History of American Psychology, University of Akron, Akron, Ohio

John B. Watson and Rosalie Rayner showed how stimuli and responses could be studied in their experiment on Little Albert.

two stimuli—presenting the rat followed by the loud gong. Then, when Watson presented the rat to Albert with no gong, the infant responded with the startle response. Watson had conditioned Little Albert to fear a white rat, a rat that Albert had played with earlier without fear. This demonstrated for Watson that observable stimuli and responses should be the focus of psychology. Unfortunately for Watson, a personal scandal resulted in his dismissal as the chair of the psychology department at Johns Hopkins University (Buckley, 1989).

Although Watson was no longer operating within mainstream psychology, behaviorism remained strong in the United States, partially due to the work of B. F. Skinner (1904–1990). Skinner, like Watson, believed that psychology should focus on observable behavior. But Skinner added a dimension to Watson's framework: *consequences*. Skinner believed that psychologists should look not only at the stimuli in the environment that cause a particular response but also at what happens to a person or animal after the response—what Skinner called the consequences of a behavior. To illustrate consequences, let's look at Little Albert's behavior from Skinner's perspective. Once Albert was afraid of the rat, how would he act when he saw it? If Albert moved away from the rat, his behavior effectively reduced his fear. Feeling less fear or anxiety is a good (positive) consequence, or outcome. Whenever Albert saw the rat again, he probably moved away even faster. Skinner asserted that positive consequences, such as the reduction of Albert's anxiety, would lead him to engage in the same behavior again. Negative consequences, or outcomes that are not liked, would lessen Albert's desire to engage in the behavior again. We know these processes as *reinforcement* and *punishment*, topics that are explored further in Chapter 6.

behavioral perspective an approach that focuses on external, environmental influences on behavior

sociocultural perspective an approach that focuses on societal and cultural factors that may influence behavior

Today, psychologists may adopt a **behavioral perspective** that focuses on external causes of behavior. It looks at how stimuli in our environment and/or the rewards and punishments we receive influence our behavior and mental processes. This approach suggests that behavior is learned and is influenced by other people and events. For example, if a student studies and then aces an exam, that reward may encourage her to study again the next time. If she only gets an average score, merely passing the test may not be rewarding enough to encourage the student to study for future exams.

The **sociocultural perspective** adopts a wider view of the impact of the environment on behavior and mental processes. It suggests that your society or culture influences your actions. Like the behavioral perspective, it assumes that much of behavior is learned. However, it goes further to state that one cannot fully explain a person's behavior without understanding his or her culture, gender identity, ethnic identity and other important cultural factors. Consider, for example, that from 1996 to 2006 the United States had a higher teen birth and abortion rate than Canada, Sweden, and England/Wales (McKay & Barrett, 2010). The sociocultural perspective would attribute this phenomenon to aspects of society that may differ in these countries, such as sexual values, contraceptive availability and use, and exposure to sex education. Sociocultural views will be evident throughout this textbook when differences due to culture, age, income level, race, ethnicity, gender, and sexual orientation are highlighted.

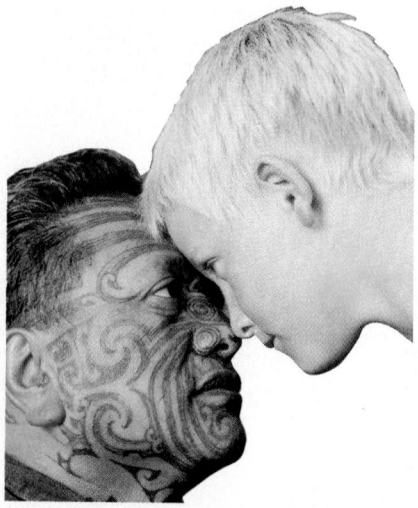

Wilfried Krecichwost/The Image Bank/Getty Images

The sociocultural perspective suggests that one's culture influences behavior.

BEYOND BEHAVIORISM: HUMANISM, COGNITIVE PSYCHOLOGY, AND THE BIRTH OF POSITIVE PSYCHOLOGY

Behaviorism was a dominant force in American psychology until the 1960s. By that time, it became evident that this one theory could not account for all responses. For example, feelings and thoughts could not easily be reduced to stimuli and responses. This criticism, combined with the social climate of the time, led to a growing interest in an approach toward treatment called **humanism**. Many psychologists did not accept the behaviorists' view that humans were governed by stimuli and responses, with no will of their own to change their behavior. In the 1960s, societal values were rapidly changing, and the civil rights movement and the Vietnam War sparked widespread civil disobedience. Many young Americans were endorsing women's rights, free love, and free will. Psychology was changing too, and humanists emphasized that everyone possesses inner resources for personal growth and development. The goal of humanistic therapy, therefore, would be to help people use these inner resources to make healthier choices and thus lead better lives. Humanism stressed the free will of individuals to choose their own patterns of behavior. Two well-known humanists are Abraham Maslow and Carl Rogers.

Today, psychologists who adopt a **humanistic perspective** explain behavior as stemming from your choices and free will. These choices are influenced by your self-concept (how you think of yourself) and by your self-esteem (how you feel about yourself). This view of the self and these feelings toward the self will lead you to choose certain behaviors over others. For example, if you see yourself as a low achiever in school, you may be less likely to take challenging courses or to apply yourself in the courses that you do take. Humanistic views of behavior are explored in Chapters 5, 12, and 14.

While humanism was changing how psychologists were treating clients, changes were also occurring in research psychology. Researchers were becoming disenchanted with the limits of testing stimuli, responses, and consequences in the laboratory, and there was renewed interest in the study of mental processes. Research expanded to subjects such as memory, problem solving, and decision making. However, unlike the earlier functionalism and structuralism, this new study of mental processes was based on more objective experimental methods. Acknowledging that mental processes are not directly observable to the eye, scientists believed that reasonable inferences about mental processes could be made from performance data.

For example, in studying memory processes in children, a researcher can ask children what strategies or techniques they use to remember a list of items. If children using a particular strategy (Strategy A) remember more compared to children using a different strategy (Strategy B), then one can infer that there must be something about Strategy A that facilitates memory. This conclusion is reasonable even though we can't directly see the children use the techniques. Such reasoning led to much experimental research on mental processes, or **cognition**.

Today a **cognitive perspective** explains behavior with an emphasis on thoughts and interpretations based on memory, expectations, beliefs, problem solving, or decision making. A cognitive view focuses on how people process information and on how that process may influence behavior. For example, in explaining depression, a cognitive approach focuses on how people who are depressed think and perceive the world differently from people who are not depressed. You will learn more about cognitive processes in Chapters 7 and 8, when we discuss such topics as memory, problem solving, thinking, decision making, intelligence, and language.

Focusing on *how* we think, particularly whether our thoughts are pessimistic or optimistic in nature, soon led to a growing emphasis on human strengths and on how humans attain happiness, called **positive psychology**. Led by American psychologists Martin

humanism a psychological perspective that emphasizes the personal growth and potential of humans

humanistic perspective an approach that focuses on how an individual's view of him- or herself and the world influences behavior

cognition mental processes such as reasoning and problem solving

cognitive perspective an approach that focuses on how mental processes influence behavior

positive psychology the study of factors that contribute to happiness, positive emotions, and well-being

Positive psychology investigates those factors that contribute to happiness, positive emotions, and well-being.

Anne Ackermann/The Image Bank/Getty Images

Seligman (1942–) (Seligman & Csikszentmihalyi, 2000) and Ed Diener (1946–), positive psychology has produced an explosion of research over the past decade describing the factors that contribute to happiness, positive emotions, and well-being (Ruark, 2009; Wallis, 2005). By scientifically studying positive aspects of human behavior, the goal of positive psychology is to enable individuals, families, and communities to thrive.

eclectic [ee-KLECK-tic] approach an approach that integrates and combines several perspectives when explaining behavior

Today, most psychologists do not rigidly adhere to just one of these perspectives but are likely to take what is referred to as an **eclectic approach** when explaining behavior. An eclectic approach integrates or combines several perspectives to provide a more complete and complex picture of behavior. You Review: Anxiety from Modern Perspectives illustrates these approaches and shows how a combined approach provides a more expansive understanding of behavior than any single approach could, using anxiety as an example.

You Review **Anxiety from Modern Perspectives**

Perspective	Explanation
Biological	Anxiety is related to chemicals in the body or to genetics (heredity).
Evolutionary	Anxiety is an adaptive response that prepares one to respond to potential threats in the environment. This response helps humans survive because it warns them of danger and thereby helps them avoid situations or people that may harm them. However, in modern times, these threats tend to be ongoing: traffic jams, crowding, and the hectic pace of consumerism.
Psychodynamic	Anxiety is the product of unresolved feelings of hostility, guilt, anger, or sexual attraction experienced in childhood.
Behavioral	Anxiety is a learned behavior much like Albert's fear of the white rat. It is a response that is associated with a specific stimulus or a response that has been rewarded.
Sociocultural	Anxiety is a product of a person's culture. In the United States, more women than men report being anxious and fearful, and this gender difference results from different socialization experiences. Men in the United States are raised to believe that they must not be afraid, so they are less likely to acknowledge or report anxiety. Women do not experience this pressure to hide their fears, so they are more likely to tell others that they are anxious and to seek treatment.
Humanistic	Anxiety is rooted in people's dissatisfaction with their real self (how they perceive themselves) as compared to their ideal self (how they want to be).
Cognitive	Anxious people think differently than nonanxious people. Anxious people may engage in more pessimistic thinking or worry that everything will go wrong.
Eclectic	Anxiety stems from various sources depending on the individual. One person may be prone to anxiety because many people in his family are anxious and he has learned to be anxious from several experiences. Another person may be anxious because she is dissatisfied with herself and believes that everything always goes wrong in her life.

1.4.2 • Specialty Areas in Psychology

In addition to the various approaches or perspectives psychologists take, they also study different aspects of behavior, which correspond to specialty areas of psychology. A number of these specialty areas are depicted in • TABLE 1.2, but keep in mind that there are many more. This diversity stems from the complexity of behavior and the interrelatedness of different areas. What a developmental psychologist studies, for example, is connected to and may have an impact on the work of social, clinical, and educational psychologists.

TABLE 1.2

Specialty Areas in Psychology

SPECIALTY AREA	TOPICS OF INTEREST
Biopsychology	Researches the biological processes that underlie behavior, including genetic, biochemical, and nervous system functioning.
Clinical psychology	Researches, assesses, and treats children, adolescents, and adults who are experiencing difficulty in functioning or who have a serious mental health disorder such as schizophrenia.
Cognitive psychology	Studies mental processes such as decision making, problem solving, language, and memory.
Community psychology	Seeks to understand and enhance the quality of life for individuals, communities, and society. Focuses on early intervention in and prevention of individual and community problems.
Counseling psychology	Researches, assesses, and treats children, adolescents, and adults who are experiencing adjustment difficulties.
Cross-cultural psychology	Investigates cultural similarities and differences in psychological traits and behaviors.
Developmental psychology	Researches how we develop physically, cognitively, socially, and emotionally over the life span.
Educational psychology	Researches how people learn and how variables in an educational environment influence learning. May develop materials and strategies to enhance learning.
Environmental psychology	Examines the relationship between environments and human behavior. Focuses on designing, managing, protecting, and/or restoring the environment to enhance behavior. Also studies environmental attitudes, perceptions, and values to promote environmentally appropriate behavior.
Experimental psychology	Conducts research on sensation, perception, learning, motivation, and emotion.
Forensic psychology	Works with mental health issues within the context of the legal system. May study a certain type of criminal behavior such as rape or murder, or may be asked to determine a person's competence to stand trial.
Health psychology	Researches ways to promote health and prevent illness. May be concerned with issues such as diet and nutrition, exercise, and lifestyle choices that influence health.

(continued)

TABLE 1.2—CONTINUED

Specialty Areas in Psychology

SPECIALTY AREA	TOPICS OF INTEREST
Human factors psychology	Researches human capabilities as they apply to the design, operation, and maintenance of machines, systems, and environments to achieve optimal performance (for example, designing the most effective configuration of control knobs in airplane cockpits for pilots).
Industrial/ organizational (I/O) psychology	Examines the relationship between people and their work environments. May study issues such as increasing job satisfaction or decreasing employee absenteeism, or focus on understanding the dynamics of workplace behavior, such as leadership styles or gender differences in management styles.
Personality psychology	Researches how people differ in their individual traits, how people develop personality, whether personality traits can be changed, and how these qualities can be measured.
Positive psychology	Seeks to discover and promote those factors that contribute to happiness, positive emotions, and well-being.
School psychology	Assesses students' psychoeducational abilities (academic achievement, intelligence, cognitive processing) and shares test results with teachers and parents to help them make decisions regarding the best educational placement for students.
Social psychology	Researches how our beliefs, feelings, and behaviors are influenced by others, whether in the classroom, on an elevator, on the beach, on a jury, or at a football game.
Sports psychology	Investigates the mental and emotional aspects of physical performance.

1.4.3 • Gender, Ethnicity, and the Field of Psychology

In the early development of psychology, women and minorities were not allowed in many instances to receive graduate degrees despite completing all the requirements for such degrees. Despite these constraints and many other societal hurdles, several women and minority individuals contributed significantly to the field. As previously mentioned, Margaret Washburn became the first woman to be awarded a doctorate in psychology in 1894 (Furumoto, 1989). Mary Calkins (1863–1930) became the first female president of the American Psychological Association in 1905. She studied at Harvard University with William James and performed several studies on the nature of memory. Christine Ladd-Franklin (1847–1930) studied color vision in the early 1900s. Karen Horney (1885–1952) focused on environmental and cultural factors that influence personality development (see Chapter 11).

Few degrees were awarded to minority students in the early 1900s. Gilbert Haven Jones (1883–1966) was the first African American to earn a doctorate in psychology—in Germany in 1909. Francis Sumner (1895–1954) was the first African American to receive a doctorate in psychology from a university in the United States (in 1920) and is known as the father of African American psychology for his many contributions to the education of Black people. His research focused on equality between Blacks and Whites, refuting the idea that African Americans were inferior. He also helped establish an independent psychology department at Howard University, a historically Black college.

Two of Sumner's students, Kenneth Clark (1914–2005) and Mamie Phipps Clark (1917–1983), conducted research on the self-perceptions of Black children. The Clarks' experiments (Clark, 1950; Clark & Clark, 1950) found that Black children often preferred to play with White dolls over Black dolls and attributed positive descriptors such as *good* and *pretty* to the color white and negative descriptors such as *bad* and *ugly* to the color black. The Clarks' findings were noted in the landmark 1954 case, *Brown v. Board of Education of Topeka,* in which the Supreme Court ruled that segregation of public schools was unconstitutional.

Inez Prosser was the first African American woman to be awarded a doctorate in psychology, in 1933 (Benjamin, Henry, & McMahon, 2005). Her doctoral dissertation (Prosser, 1933) studied the self-perceptions of Black children. She compared the self-esteem of Black children attending a segregated school to that of Black children attending an integrated school. She found that the Black children at the segregated school fared better. The Black children at the integrated school were more likely to feel inferior and report less satisfactory school relations. Given the probable prejudicial attitudes of White people at the integrated school, it is not surprising that the Black children at that school did not have positive experiences.

© History of American Psychology, U. of Akron, Akron, Ohio

Known as the father of African American psychology, Francis Sumner (1895–1954) was the first African American to receive a doctorate from a U.S. university, in 1920.

Have times changed for women and minorities in psychology? Women have indeed made great progress in the field of psychology. From 1920 to 1974, 23% of doctorates in psychology went to women (APA, 2000). Today, far more women than men earn psychology degrees. In 2009, nearly 79% of master's degrees and 72% of doctorate degrees in psychology were awarded to women (National Science Foundation [NSF], 2012). Educational gains have to some extent been followed by progress in the careers of women in psychology. In 2010–2011, 45% of full-time faculty in graduate psychology departments in the United States were women (Hart, Wicherski, & Kohout, 2011). However, female psychology faculty members are less likely than males to attain tenured faculty positions. In 2009, women represented only 39% of tenured faculty members in U.S. psychology graduate departments (Willyard, 2011). Thus, although psychology has become more fully open to both men and women at the educational level, inequities at the professional level still exist.

Likewise, progress has also been made in the numbers of racial and ethnic minorities in psychology. While minorities make up approximately 37% of the U.S. population (U.S. Census Bureau, 2012c), nearly 25% of students in graduate schools in psychology were minorities in 2010 (NSF, 2013). Between 1976 and 1993, about 8% of all doctorates in psychology were awarded to minorities (APA, 1997); by 2010, that number had increased to almost 20% (NSF, 2013).

Despite the increase in the number of advanced degrees awarded to minorities, they are still underrepresented among college faculty. In 2008–2009, minorities represented nearly 13% of total faculty members in psychology graduate departments (Kohout & Wicherski, 2010). To address this lack of minority representation, the APA has established several programs to attract more minorities to the field of psychology.

Psychology Applies to Your World

Training to Be a Psychologist

The majority of psychologists hold a doctorate in psychology—usually a Ph.D. (Doctor of Philosophy) or a Psy.D. (Doctor of Psychology). A Ph.D. program focuses more on research, whereas the Psy.D. focuses more on clinical training. To obtain either doctorate, psychologists must first complete a bachelor's and a master's degree. The road to a doctoral degree is long, usually 4–7 years after the undergraduate degree. Most doctoral programs require extensive study of research methods and statistics, and most require that students do some form of research.

Those who study psychology to the point of a bachelor's or master's degree aren't excluded from the profession. As you can see in ● FIGURE 1.8, psychology is a popular degree among undergraduate students. A bachelor's degree in psychology may qualify you to assist psychologists in mental health centers or rehabilitation and correctional programs or to serve as a research assistant. However, without additional academic training, the opportunities for advancement in the profession are limited (Appleby, 1997). Median starting and midcareer salaries for people with just a bachelor's degree are below average when compared to other liberal arts majors (Rajecki, 2012; Rajecki & Borden, 2011).

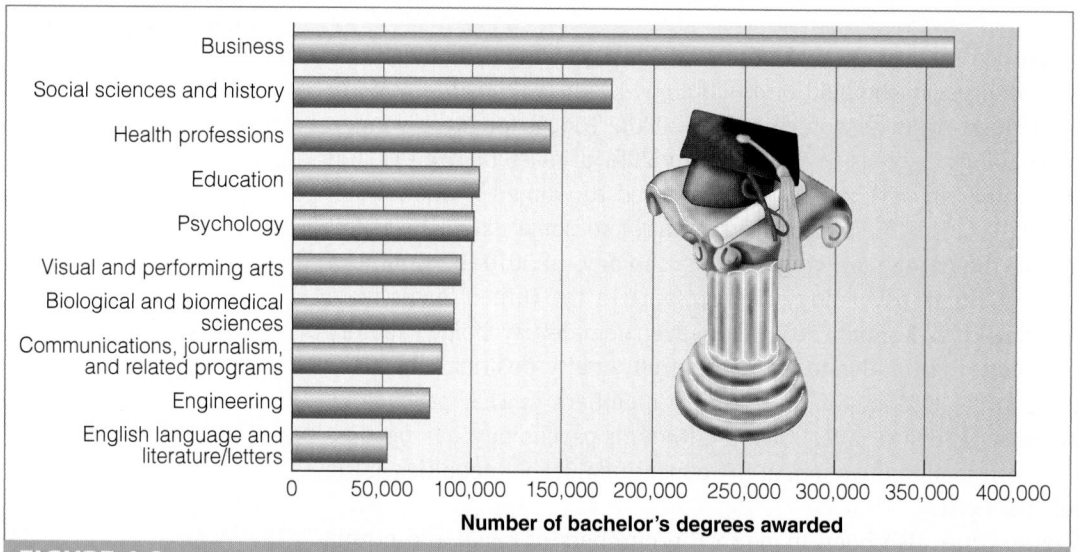

Chuck Karcher/Jupiter Images

FIGURE 1.8

Undergraduate Degrees in Psychology

Psychology is a popular undergraduate degree. It ranked fifth following business, social sciences and history, health professions, and education in number of degrees awarded in 2010–2011.

Source: Data from U.S. Department of Education, National Center for Education Statistics, 2012.

A master's degree typically requires 2–3 years of graduate work. Master's-level psychologists may administer tests, conduct research, or counsel patients under the supervision of a doctoral-level psychologist. In a few states, they may be able to practice independently. They may teach in high schools or community colleges, work in corporate human resource departments, or work as school psychologists.

A large percentage of psychologists affiliated with colleges and universities teach and do research. Psychologists also work in school systems, hospitals, business, government, and other human services settings (Michalski et al., 2011; ● FIGURE 1.9). Psychologists perform many functions in many different roles at varying institutions. Their job descriptions may include conducting research, counseling clients, and teaching college courses.

A related profession is *psychiatry*. A psychiatrist holds a medical degree (M.D.) and then specializes in mental health. A psychiatrist's graduate work includes a medical internship and residency, followed by training in the treatment of mental health disorders. As medical practitioners, psychiatrists have extensive training in the use of therapeutic drugs; they may dispense or prescribe medication and order medical procedures such as brain scans.

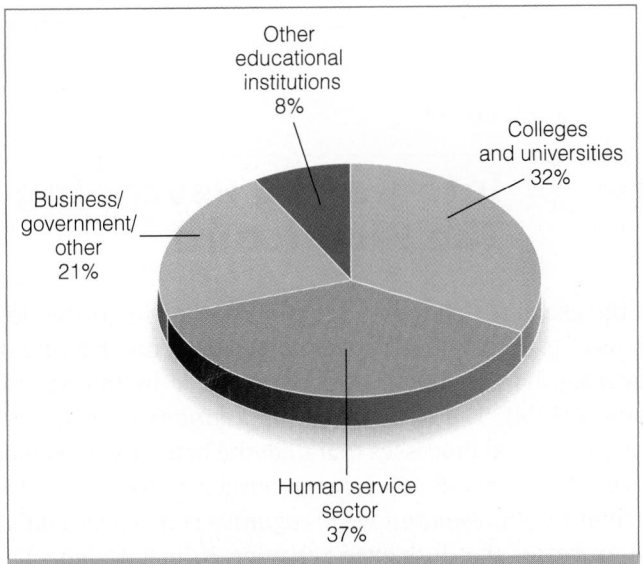

FIGURE 1.9

Work Settings of Psychologists

A large percentage of psychologists affiliated with colleges and universities teach and do research. Psychologists also work in school systems, business and government, or are employed in health-related or other human services settings.

Source: 2009 Doctorate Employment Survey, APA Center for Workforce Studies.

Quiz Yourself 1.4

1. Javier wants to know how aggression helps a person adapt to the environment. Which historical approach is Javier emphasizing?
   a. Structuralism
   b. Psychoanalysis
   c. Functionalism
   d. Humanism
2. Which of the following persons would be *least* likely to emphasize the influence of stimuli and responses on behavior?
   a. John Watson
   b. Carl Rogers
   c. Rosalie Rayner
   d. B. F. Skinner
3. Which modern psychological perspective emphasizes the importance of thought processes for understanding behavior?
   a. Behavioral
   b. Humanistic
   c. Sociocultural
   d. Cognitive
4. Which of the following professionals is most likely to prescribe medication for a mental health disorder?
   a. A clinical psychologist
   b. A psychiatrist
   c. A biopsychologist
   d. An experimental psychologist
5. A psychologist who studies individual differences in shyness is probably from which specialty area?
   a. Cognitive
   b. Social
   c. Developmental
   d. Personality

Answers 1. c; 2. b; 3. d; 4. b; 5. d

1.5 Integrating Psychology: The Big Picture

In the chapters that follow, we will describe in greater detail research in the main areas of psychology. The material has been divided into four roughly equal parts, covering the Common Core recommended by the American Psychological Association (2014). The first section, *foundations in biological psychology,* details the basic biological processes that underlie behavior. It includes chapters on neuroscience, sensation and perception, consciousness, and motivation and emotion. The second section, *foundations in cognitive psychology,* contains research on the mental processes that influence behavior. It includes chapters on learning, memory, and cognition and intelligence. The third section, *foundations in developmental and social psychology,* examines how behavior varies across the life span, individuals, and social contexts. It includes chapters on human development, social psychology, and personality. The last section, *foundations in physical and mental health,* emphasizes those factors that influence our success or failure at achieving healthy behavior. It includes chapters on stress and health, mental health disorders, and mental health therapies. Each chapter will prepare you for mastering the concepts of the next chapter, and we frequently remind you of concepts presented in earlier chapters to help you connect and integrate the information.

Two features to help you study and master the material conclude each chapter: a 20-item quiz called *What Do You Know? Assess Your Understanding* and a visual summary, entitled *Are You Getting the Big Picture?* The former will help you assess your mastery and application of the material, and the latter will help you remember the topics and concepts that have been introduced and further your understanding of how these concepts relate to one another. Psychology is an integrated field. It is important not only to master the basic concepts of each chapter but also to understand how the information from the chapters ties together and applies to your life. It is in this way that a comprehensive explanation of behavior can be realized and that psychological knowledge can be used in practical ways to improve your daily life.

Studying the Chapter

Key Terms

behavioral perspective (26)
behaviorism (25)
biological perspective (24)
case study (12)
causal hypothesis (10)
cognition (27)
cognitive perspective (27)
confidentiality (21)
confounding variables (17)
control group (16)
correlation (13)
critical thinking (6)
debriefing (21)
dependent variable (15)
double-blind studies (16)
eclectic approach (28)
evolutionary perspective (24)
experiment (15)
experimental group (15)
functionalism (24)
generalizability (12)
humanism (27)
humanistic perspective (27)
hypothesis (8)
independent variable (15)
informed consent (20)
Institutional Review Board (IRB) (20)
introspection (23)
naturalistic observations (11)
negative correlation (14)
neuroscience (24)
placebo effect (16)
population of interest (11)
positive correlation (14)
positive psychology (27)
prediction (8)
predictive hypothesis (10)
pseudopsychology (6)
psychoanalytic theory (25)
psychodynamic perspective (25)
psychology (4)
quasi-experiment (18)
random assignment (17)
response (25)
sample (11)
scientific method (4)
sociocultural perspective (26)
stimulus (25)
structuralism (23)
surveys (12)
theory (5)

What Do You Know? Assess Your Understanding

Test your retention and understanding of the material by answering the following questions.

1. Which of the following is *not* true about psychology?

a. Psychology is just common sense.
b. Psychology is just the study of mental illness.
c. Psychology has no connection with everyday life.
d. All of the above are not true.

2. Which of the following topics would a psychologist have the least interest in?

a. Learning
b. Sexuality
c. Employment trends
d. Color perception

3. Which of the following is *not* a goal of psychology?

a. To describe behavior
b. To change behavior
c. To explain behavior
d. To practice behavior

4. Which of the following best defines the nature of a theory?

a. An explanation of why a behavior occurs
b. A statement of fact
c. An untestable assumption
d. A prediction

5. The hypothesis that the number of rapes will increase during the summer months is an example of a(n) _____ hypothesis.

a. causal
b. predictive
c. untestable
d. nonscientific

6. Dr. Vaz conducted an experiment in which she randomly assigned her participants to one of two conditions. In the first condition, the participants were shown visual images of common objects and then 1 hour later asked to recall as many of the objects as they could remember. In the second condition, the participants heard the names of the same objects and then 1 hour later were asked to recall as many of the objects as they could. Dr. Vaz then compared the number of items recalled for these two groups of participants. In this experiment, the independent variable is _____.

a. the number of items recalled
b. whether the participants saw or heard the objects
c. the sex of the participants
d. the room in which the participants were tested

7. Dr. Pi wants to test the hypothesis that smoking marijuana impairs one's ability to remember information. What type of hypothesis is Dr. Pi interested in testing?

a. Predictive
b. Causal
c. Correlational
d. Biological

8. Dr. Ling is studying helping behavior in children. Every day, he goes to the local playground at 3 P.M., sits on the sidelines, and records the number of times one child helps another, the sex of the child who helps, and the sex of the child who is helped. Dr. Ling is using which research method in his study?

a. An experiment
b. A case study
c. A naturalistic observation
d. A quasi-experiment

9. A confounding variable _____.

a. measures the effect of the independent variable
b. is the variable that is manipulated by the experimenter
c. has no effect on the dependent variable
d. is any factor other than the independent variable that affects the dependent variable

10. The longer the commute for a student to a college campus, the less likely he or she is to complete a degree. This is an example of a _____.

a. positive correlation
b. negative correlation
c. zero correlation
d. case study

11. Dr. Eden tells potential participants of any risks they may experience prior to their participation in his research study. He is following the ethical guideline of _____.

a. deception
b. confidentiality
c. informed consent
d. debriefing

12. The _____ perspective in psychology stresses the importance of looking at the influence of unconscious drives and motives on behavior and mental processes.

a. functionalism
b. cognitive
c. psychodynamic
d. behavioral

13. Dr. Babar is a psychologist who studies how people's eating habits help them adapt to and survive in their environments. Dr. Babar is emphasizing which psychological perspective?

a. Evolutionary
b. Biological
c. Humanistic
d. Behavioral

14. Many modern psychologists follow the _____ approach to psychology, in that they do not adhere strictly to any one psychological perspective.

a. pragmatic
b. functional
c. common sense
d. eclectic

15. Which of the following is the most likely educational attainment of the majority of psychologists?

a. Doctorate degree
b. Master's degree
c. Bachelor's degree
d. Associate's degree

16. Dr. Warren is a psychologist who studies chemicals in the brain. Dr. Warren is approaching psychology from the _____ perspective.

a. cognitive
b. eclectic
c. biological
d. sociocultural

17. Dr. Barrios is a psychologist who studies how people change over time. Dr. Barrios is most likely a _____ psychologist.

a. cognitive
b. biological
c. social
d. developmental

18. Dr. Grogan studies how psychological principles can be applied in the workplace. Dr. Grogan is most likely a(n) _____ psychologist.

a. industrial/organizational
b. clinical
c. social
d. health

19. The first African American to earn a doctorate in psychology was _____.

a. Karen Horney
b. Mary Calkins
c. Gilbert Haven Jones
d. Sidney Beckham

20. Today, who earns most of the doctorates in psychology?

a. Men
b. Women
c. African Americans
d. Asian Americans

Answers: 1. d; 2. c; 3. d; 4. a; 5. b; 6. b; 7. b; 8. c; 9. d; 10. b; 11. c; 12. c; 13. a; 14. d; 15. a; 16. c; 17. d; 18. a; 19. c; 20. b

Use It or Lose It: Applying Psychology

1. Explain how you can apply the scientific method to decide on a college major or a career choice. Could this method also be used as part of your decision-making process when purchasing a large item such as a car or a house? Explain how it could be used for these major purchases.
2. Design a research study to test the idea that listening to rock music while studying facilitates learning. What type of hypothesis would you make? Could this idea be tested by naturalistic observation? How could you set up a correlational study to test this idea? Could an experiment be designed to address this issue? What types of conclusions could you reach from these different research methods? What ethical considerations would you follow when conducting this study?
3. Suppose William James, Sigmund Freud, and John Watson had the opportunity to sit down and discuss the causes of behavior. What might this conversation sound like? On what issues might they agree? On what issues might they disagree?
4. Explain depression from each of the modern perspectives and using the eclectic approach. Use You Review: Anxiety from Modern Perspectives as a guide if you need help.

Greg Hinsdale/Corbis

Are You Getting the Big Picture? The Science of Psychology

1.1 What Is Psychology?

To think like a psychologist, you must be skeptical about explanations of behavior, rather than accepting of them. **Psychology** is

- NOT simply giving advice
- NOT just "common sense"
- NOT limited to studying mental illness

1.2 The Science of Psychology: Goals, Hypotheses, and Methods

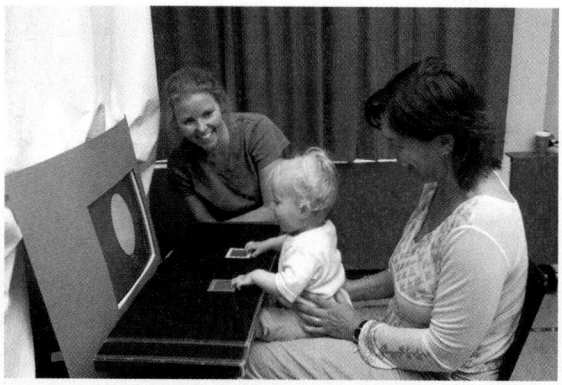

Picture Partners/Alamy

- The goals of psychological research are to:
  - describe behavior
  - predict behavior
  - explain behavior
  - control or change behavior
- Psychologists form **predictive** and **causal hypotheses** and then conduct research using the **scientific method**.
- Predictive hypotheses are tested by **naturalistic observation**, **case studies**, **surveys**, and **correlational studies**.
- Causal hypotheses are tested by **experiments** in which variables are controlled and care is taken to test a **random sample** of a **population of interest**. The **experimental group** is compared to the **control group** on the **dependent variable** to see whether the **independent variable** had an effect.

1.3 Ethical Principles of Psychological Research

- To ensure humane conduct of experiments, the American Psychological Association has established a set of strict ethical guidelines that must be followed when researchers study animals and humans.
- Key ethical guidelines for humans include **informed consent**, **confidentiality**, protecting the participant from harm, and **debriefing** to explain any deceptions used in research.

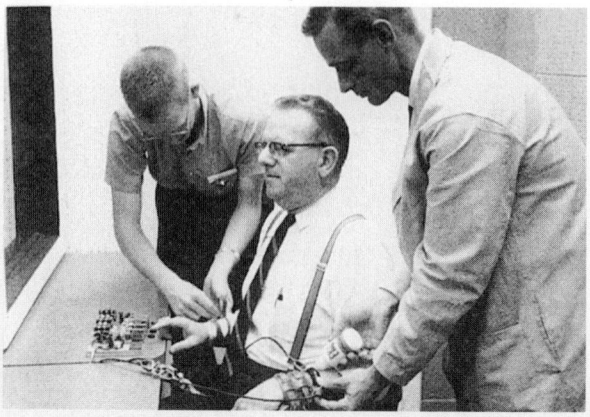

From the film Obedience ©1965 by Stanley Milgram and distributed by Alexander Street Press. Reprinted by permission of Alexandra Milgram

1.4 Psychology in the Modern World: Foundations and Growth

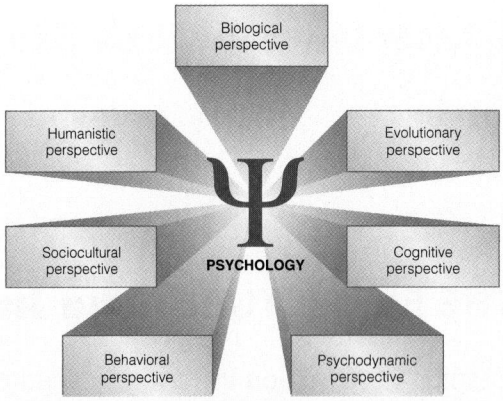

- Psychology became a distinct field of scientific study when Wilhelm Wundt established the first psychology laboratory, in Germany, in 1879.
- A **biological perspective**, stemming from the field of medicine, examines the physiological contributions to behavior.
- William James's focus was on how particular behaviors helped people adapt to their environment (**functionalism**). Today, an **evolutionary perspective** looks at how behaviors may be genetically programmed to help us adapt better for survival.
- Sigmund Freud, one of the most famous people to influence psychology, believed the key to understanding behavior was uncovering unconscious motivations (**psychoanalytic theory**). Today, the **psychodynamic perspective** focuses on internal, often unconscious, mental processes, motives, and desires or childhood conflicts to explain behavior.
- John B. Watson and B. F. Skinner emphasized the need to study observable behavior and the influence of the environment on behavior. Their research led to the **behavioral perspective**, which focuses on external causes of behavior, such as how **stimuli** in the environment and/or rewards and punishments influence our **responses**.
- The **sociocultural perspective** researches behaviors across societal groups and cultures (such as ethnicity, social class, or gender).
- The **humanistic perspective** explains behavior as stemming from choices and free will.
- The **cognitive perspective** focuses on how people process information and on how that process may influence behavior. Focusing on how we think led to the birth of **positive psychology**, which describes the factors that contribute to happiness, positive emotions, and well-being.
- Psychologists today embrace an **eclectic approach,** which integrates several perspectives when studying and explaining behavior.

Careers in Psychology

- Psychologists typically have a doctorate in psychology, which usually involves 4–7 years of postgraduate study and research beyond the undergraduate (bachelor's) degree.
- Psychology has numerous specialty areas, including these:
  - Developmental psychology (which studies child and adult development)
  - Social psychology (which examines ways in which we are influenced by others)
  - Industrial/organizational psychology (which looks at behavior in the workplace)
  - Experimental psychology (which performs research on sensation, perception, and learning)
  - Clinical or counseling psychology (which researches and treats people who are experiencing difficulty in functioning or who have a serious mental health disorder)
- Although the numbers of women and ethnic minorities in psychology have increased, they are still underrepresented as faculty in colleges.

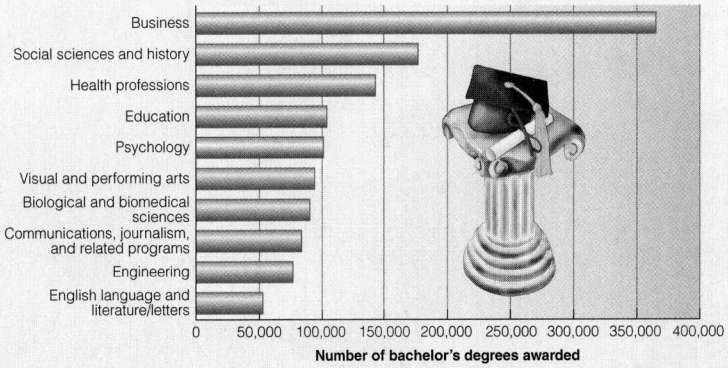

Part 1
Foundations in Biological Psychology

THE BIG PICTURE **The Importance of a Healthy Brain**

Chapter 1 focused on the scientific method that forms the foundation of all areas of psychology. In this next part, we will discuss the biological foundations of psychology—the nervous and endocrine system functions (Chapter 2), sensation and perceptual processes (Chapter 3), states of consciousness (Chapter 4), and motivational and emotional functions (Chapter 5) that influence our mental processes and behavior. The fields of psychology and biology are intimately intertwined. Biology focuses on the body, its structures and physiological functions. Our knowledge about the body helps to inform psychology's study of mental processes and behavior. Without biological functioning, there would be no mental processes or behavior for psychologists to study. And changes in biological functioning, through taking drugs, injury, or illness, have the potential to affect our thoughts and behavior.

Despite its importance in our lives, we often pay little attention to our biological functioning. For example, when did you last stop to wonder how your brain works? For most of us, the answer to that question is probably never! Most of us lead our lives without giving our brain much thought. Every day we go about our business, taking for granted our ability to move, speak, feel, and breathe. We seldom, if ever, stop to think about the amazing internal systems that allow us to accomplish these tasks. Sometimes the best way to gain an appreciation for things we take for granted is to see what life would be like without them. In the case study for this section, we see what life was like

AP Images/Andre Rau/Elle/File

Jean-Dominique Bauby

for Jean-Dominique Bauby when he suddenly lost certain aspects of his brain function. After reading his story, you might just find yourself with increased respect for your own brain and the abilities that it gives you.

When Jean-Dominique Bauby began his day on December 8, 1995, his life was the essence of success. At age 43 he was editor-in-chief of the French fashion magazine *Elle*, the father of two loving children, a world traveler—a man who seemed to have everything. But all of this was about to change. As Bauby was driving that afternoon, he suddenly began to experience unusual neurological problems. As he drove along, Bauby began to feel as if he were moving in slow motion. His vision began to blur and double, and familiar landmarks along the road seemed only vaguely recognizable. Realizing that he was in trouble, Bauby pulled off the road and attempted to get out of the car, only to find that he was unable to walk. He collapsed and was rushed to a nearby hospital where he lapsed into a coma that lasted nearly 3 weeks.

As you may have guessed, Bauby experienced a stroke on that December afternoon. Blood flow to the brainstem was disrupted, leaving Bauby with what physicians call "locked-in syndrome." People with locked-in syndrome remain conscious but are almost completely unable to move or speak. They are essentially trapped or "locked" inside their bodies. When Bauby awoke from his coma, he was aware of his surroundings but unable to move any part of his body except for his left eyelid. He was also completely mute and half deaf; and because he was unable to blink his right eye, it had to be sewn shut to protect his cornea. For the remaining 15 months of his life, Bauby lived in this locked-in state, unable to move or speak but very aware of his surroundings and able to think, feel pain, and experience normal emotions and desires.

In This Part:

CHAPTER 2 **Neuroscience**

CHAPTER 3 **Sensation and Perception**

CHAPTER 4 **Consciousness**

CHAPTER 5 **Motivation and Emotion**

If Bauby's story were simply the tale of a man cut down in the prime of life, it would certainly be a sad one. However, even as he lay locked inside his own body and fighting a losing battle, there was more to Bauby's life than tragedy. There was also the remarkable triumph of an intelligent and resourceful man. From his hospital bed, Bauby gradually learned to communicate with others by doing the only thing he could—blinking his left eye. Using an ingenious system, an assistant would read off the letters of the alphabet one at a time. When the assistant read the appropriate letter, Bauby would blink and the assistant would gradually compile the words and phrases that Bauby spelled out. Although it was painstaking, this system allowed Bauby to communicate with those who were patient enough to go through the process. Through blinking, Bauby was able to free himself to a small but meaningful degree from the prison of locked-in syndrome.

Not only did Bauby communicate with his family and friends, he also dictated a best-selling book that was later made into a major motion picture in 2007. It is estimated that Bauby had to blink his eye more than 200,000 times to dictate the manuscript (MacIntyre, 1998). *The Diving Bell and the Butterfly* (Bauby, 1997), published in France just days after his death on March 9, 1997, recounts Bauby's struggle to cope with the infirmities he suffered as a result of his devastating stroke, as well as his musings on the life he lost that December day. It also serves as a testament to the awesome complexity and power of the human brain.

Although it took a life-changing illness to make Bauby aware of his amazing biology, the same does not have to be true for us. In the chapters of this section, you will learn about the biological processes of the nervous and endocrine systems that underlie your thoughts and behavior (Chapter 2), the way you sense and perceive the world (Chapter 3), your awareness of the outside world and your own mind (Chapter 4), and the motivation and emotion that guide your behavior (Chapter 5). As you read these chapters, we hope that you will begin to recognize the amazing intricacy and precision with which the systems within our bodies influence even our simplest behaviors. For as Jean-Dominique Bauby showed us, a glitch in our biological functioning can change our lives in profound ways. Keep in mind that as you read this page, *everything* you are doing—perceiving these words on the page, being conscious of the meaning of the words, being motivated to continue reading, and so on—originates in your wonderfully complex biology.

© Miramax/Courtesy Everett Collection

Jean-Dominique Bauby blinked more than 200,000 times to write the Diving Bell and the Butterfly after having a stroke and ending up in a locked-in state. This book was later turned into a major motion picture.

Neuroscience

Learning Objectives

2.1 Describe the basic structure of a neuron, including the axon, dendrites, and synapse. (APA 1.1, 1.2)

2.1 Explain what an action potential is and how it moves down the axon and across the synapse. (APA 1.1, 1.2)

2.1 Explain the processes of excitation and inhibition at the synapse. (APA 1.1, 1.2, 1.3)

2.2 List the major neurotransmitters, and describe the functions they may influence. (APA 1.1, 1.2, 1.3)

2.3 Describe the major parts of the nervous system and the types of information they process. (APA 1.1, 1.2, 1.3)

2.4 Be able to locate the hindbrain, midbrain, and forebrain; list their parts; and explain what they do. (APA 1.1, 1.2, 1.3)

2.4 Describe brain-imaging techniques and other ways we can study the brain, and explain their advantages and limitations. (APA 1.1, 1.2, 1.3)

2.4 Describe changes in the aging brain and what is known about protecting the brain as we age. (APA 1.1, 1.2, 1.3)

2.5 Explain how the endocrine system works and describe the function of the endocrine glands. (APA 1.1, 1.2, 1.3)

As you read at the beginning of this part on foundations in biological psychology, the case of Jean-Dominique Bauby clearly highlights the importance of the brain and nervous system to our ability to control our bodies. When Jean-Dominique had his stroke, the lines of communication between his brain and body were severely damaged, resulting in *locked-in syndrome.* This left Jean a prisoner inside his own body. Modern psychologists are very interested in **neuroscience**—the study of how the brain and nervous system affect our mental processes and our behavior. This interest is well placed because we rely on our brains and nervous systems to enable us to perform all the tasks of daily life. Prior to his illness, Jean-Dominque took for granted the amazing things his nervous

2

system did for him. Similarly, most of us do not question that our brain will somehow store the information we just learned in psychology class, and that on exam day it will retrieve that information. We take for granted that we will be able to walk, to talk, to write, and to maintain a constant body temperature and a steady heart rate. But psychologists want to know how such everyday miracles are accomplished. How does your brain know when you need to eat or sleep? How does your brain tell the muscles of your arm to contract so you can hold a pencil? In short, how does the brain communicate? This is one of the main questions we will examine in this chapter on *neuroscience.*

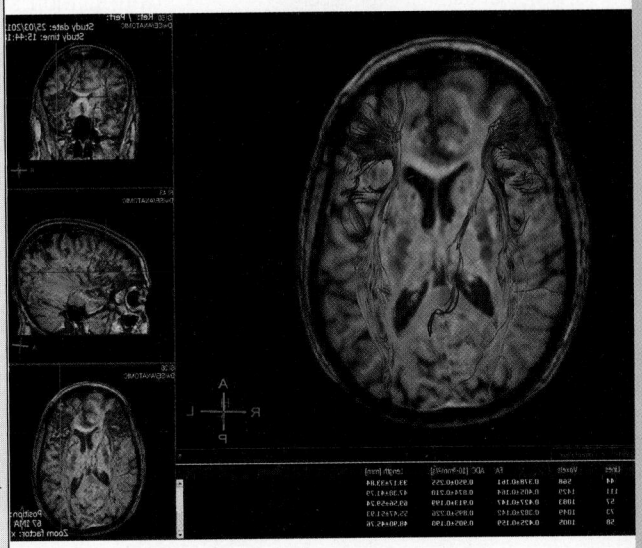

© iStockphoto.com/wenht

Chapter Outline

2.1 Billions of Neurons: Communication in the Brain / 46

2.2 Neurotransmitters: Chemical Messengers in the Brain / 53

2.3 The Structure of the Nervous System / 57

2.4 The Brain and Spine: The Central Nervous System / 61

PSYCHOLOGY APPLIES TO YOUR WORLD: Technologies for Studying the Brain / 74

2.5 The Endocrine System: Hormones and Behavior / 76

2.6 Integrating Psychology: The Big Picture / 78

2.1 Billions of Neurons: Communication in the Brain

neuroscience [NUR-o-SCI-ence] the study of how the brain and nervous system affect mental processes and behavior

neurons [NUR-ons] cells in the nervous system that transmit information

glia [GLEE-uh] cells brain cells that provide important support functions for the neurons and are involved in the formation of myelin

myelin [MY-eh-lynn] a fatty, waxy substance that insulates portions of some neurons in the nervous system

cell body the part of the neuron that contains the nucleus and DNA

DNA the chemical found in the nuclei of cells that contains the genetic blueprint that guides development in the organism

dendrites [DEN-drights] branchlike structures on the head of the neuron that receive incoming signals from other neurons in the nervous system

The brain communicates with itself and the rest of the body over networks of specialized information-carrying cells called **neurons**. Neurons use a sophisticated communication system to conduct signals across these neural networks, enabling us to control our bodies. For example, when you touch a hot stove, neurons in your fingertips send information up your arm to your spinal column. In response to this possible threat, signals are sent back out from the spine to the muscles of your arm. The result is a quick, reflexive jerking of your arm away from the hot stove (• FIGURE 2.1).

Researchers have long believed that the average adult brain contains around 100 billion neurons. However, newly developed estimation techniques now suggest that the brain may contain roughly 86 billion neurons and similar numbers of another type of cell called **glia cells** (Azvedo et al., 2009; see also Herculano-Houzel, 2011). Glia cells were once thought to provide only support functions, such as providing nutrients and removing wastes, for the neurons of the brain. However, it is more likely that glia cells also play a critical role in both neural signaling and the formation of neural networks in the brain (Eroglu & Barres, 2010; Volterra & Steinhauser, 2004).

Although scientists do not yet understand the full role of glia cells, we have abundant evidence of the importance of glia cells to normal brain functioning (Coutinho-Budd & Freeman, 2013; Nave, 2010). For starters, glia cells help maintain the chemical environment of the neuron, and they help repair neural damage after injuries. However, one of their most important functions is the formation of **myelin**. Myelin is a whitish, fatty, waxy substance that coats many neurons. This protective coating insulates and speeds up neural signals. Much like rubber or plastic insulation on an electrical cord, myelin helps the signal get where it is going quickly. Myelinated neurons can conduct signals much faster than unmyelinated neurons. To appreciate what myelin does for neural communication, let's look at what happens when myelin is lost due to illness.

Multiple sclerosis (MS) is one disease that attacks and destroys the myelin insulation on neurons (Blanchard et al., 2013; Junker, Hohlfeld, & Meinl, 2010). People with MS have difficulty controlling the actions of their body and have sensory problems, including numbness and vision loss. When myelin breaks down, neural signals are greatly slowed or halted altogether.

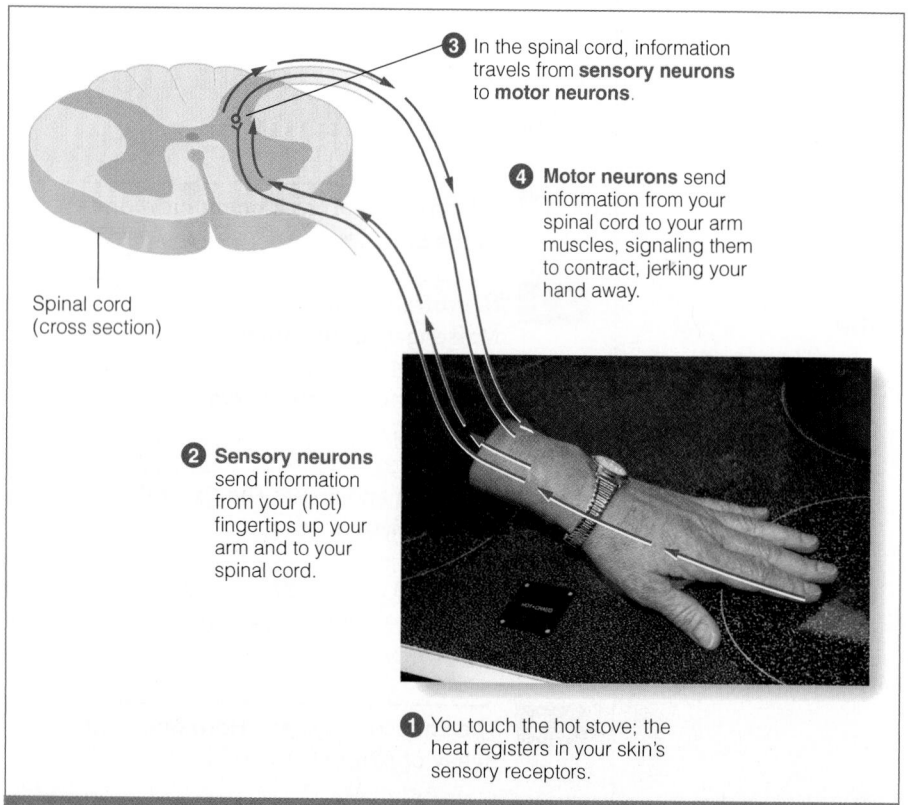

Courtesy of William L. Breneman

FIGURE 2.1

The Neurons Involved in a Reflex

When you touch a hot stove, neurons in your fingertips send information up your arm to your spinal column. In response to this possible threat, signals are sent out from the spine to the muscles of your arm. The result is a quick, reflexive jerking of your arm away from the hot stove.

Initially, movement becomes difficult; as the disease progresses, voluntary movement of some muscles may become impossible. Sensory systems such as vision may also fail because incoming signals from the eye do not reach the vision-processing parts of the brain. Life often becomes very challenging for people with MS as the "orders" sent to and from the brain are delayed or lost along the way.

Without myelin, our nervous system cannot function properly—our neurons cannot carry information efficiently from one point to another. As psychologists, we are particularly interested in understanding how healthy neurons send signals throughout the nervous system. Before we can examine how neurons transmit signals, however, we must first examine the anatomy of neural cells and how they connect with one another in the nervous system.

Alberto E. Rodriguez/WireImage/Getty Images

Television personality Montel Williams has multiple sclerosis, a disease that results in the destruction of myelin. As the myelin is destroyed, patients may experience a variety of neurological symptoms, including difficulty moving and sensory loss.

2.1.1 • The Anatomy of the Neuron

Like any cell in the body, the neuron has a **cell body** that contains a nucleus (• FIGURE 2.2). The cell body is somewhat similar in shape to a fried egg, with the nucleus being the yolk. Like the nucleus of any cell, the nucleus of the neuron contains **DNA** (deoxyribonucleic acid), the chemical that contains the genetic blueprint that directs the development of the neuron. Growing out of the cell body are branchlike structures called **dendrites** (from the Greek word for tree branch). The dendrites receive incoming signals from other neurons. For ease of understanding, we will refer to the dendrite end of the neuron as the *head* of the cell.

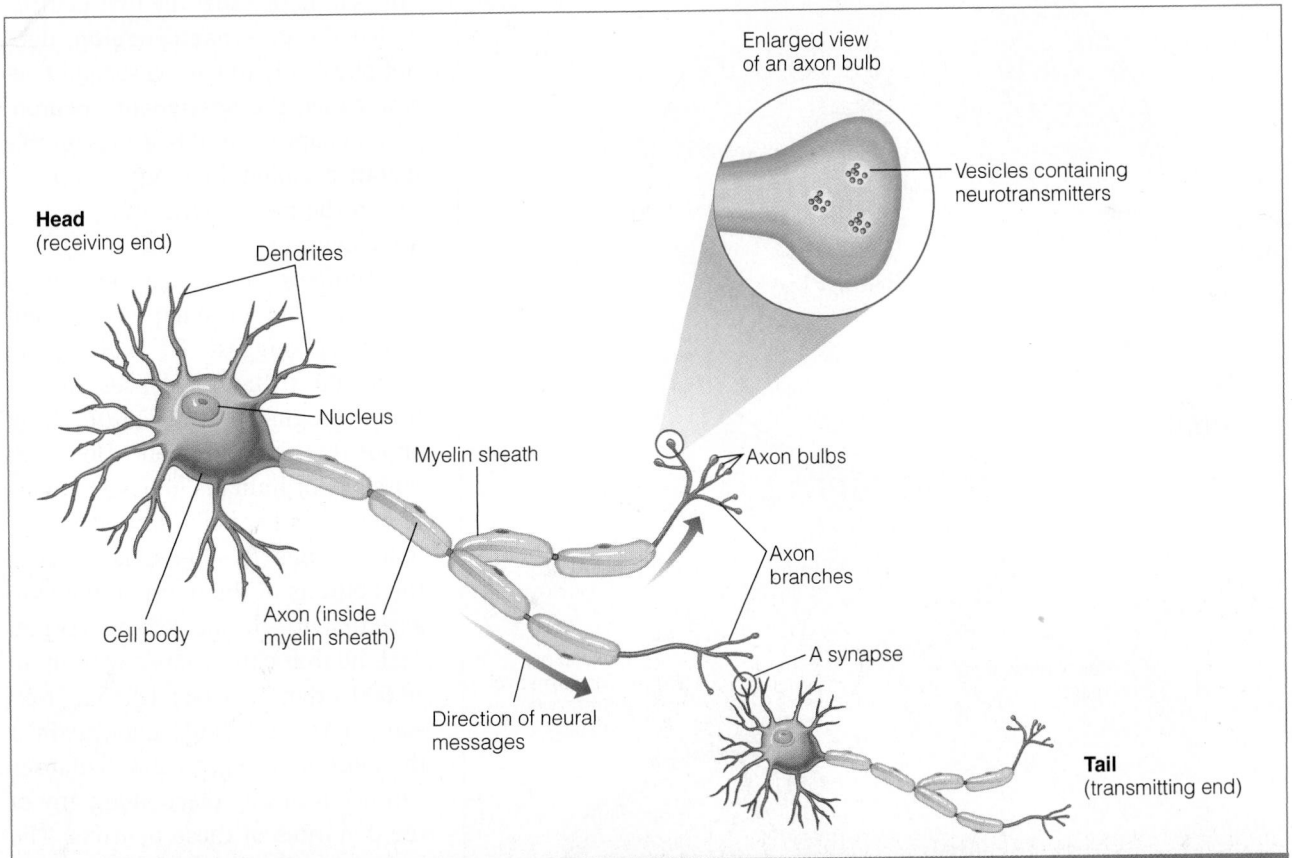

FIGURE 2.2

A Typical Neuron

The arrows indicate the flow of information from the dendrites on the head of the neuron to the axon bulbs at the tail of the neuron. Neurons may have many dendrites and axon branches, and some neurons are insulated with myelin, which helps speed up neural signals in the neuron.

axon [AXE-on] a long tail-like structure growing out of the cell body of a neuron that carries action potentials that convey information from the cell body to the synapse

myelin sheath [MY-eh-lynn SHEE-th] the discontinuous segments of myelin that cover the outside of some axons in the nervous system

neurotransmitters [NUR-oh-TRANS-mitt-ers] chemical messengers that carry neural signals across the synapse

synapse [SIN-aps] the connection formed between two neurons when the axon bulb of one neuron comes into close proximity with the dendrite of another neuron

presynaptic neuron [pre-sin-AP-tic NUR-on] the neuron that is sending the signal at a synapse in the nervous system

postsynaptic neuron [post-sin-AP-tic NUR-on] the neuron that is receiving the signal at a synapse in the nervous system

Growing out of the other end of the cell body is a long tail-like structure called an **axon**, which carries signals away from the cell body. We will refer to the axon end of the neuron as the *tail* end of the cell. When a neuron is insulated with myelin, it is the axon that is covered, or myelinated. As you can see in Figure 2.2, myelin does not continuously cover the entire length of a neuron's axon. Rather, the myelin covers segments of the axon with a **myelin sheath**. Axons vary in length from a few hundred micrometers to many centimeters, depending on where in the nervous system they are located. Axons in the brain are typically very short (1 millimeter or less), whereas other axons in the body, such as those that extend down the legs, can be almost a meter in length (Purves et al., 1997).

The tail end of the axon splits into separate branches (Figure 2.2). At the end of each branch is an *axon bulb* that contains small storage pouches called *vesicles* that hold **neurotransmitters**, the chemical messengers that carry signals across the synapse. A **synapse** is the junction between two neurons where the axon bulb of one neuron comes into close proximity with specialized receptor sites on another neuron.

The neural structure of the brain is extremely complex, and synapses can occur at several places along a neuron (e.g., dendrites, axon, or cell body). However, for simplicity's sake we will discuss only a simple head-to-tail synapse. In this type of synapse, the axon bulb on the tail end of the first neuron is in close proximity to specialized *receptor sites* on the dendrites on the head of a second neuron (• FIGURE 2.3). You will notice that the first neuron, called the **presynaptic neuron**, does not physically touch the second neuron, called the **postsynaptic neuron**. At a synapse, there is a measurable distance, called the *synaptic gap*, between the presynaptic and postsynaptic neurons.

Humans have an extremely large number of synapses. Current estimates suggest we have more than 100 trillion synapses in our brain (Eroglu & Barres, 2010). Think about this for a moment. How is it possible for humans to have trillions of synapses but only around 86 billion neurons? It's possible because the neurons of the brain do not synapse in a one-to-one fashion. Rather, each neuron can synapse with up to 10,000 other neurons (Bloom, Nelson, & Lazerson, 2001). Look again at the neurons in Figure 2.3. Synapses can occur at any place along any of the dendrites of these neurons. The vast network of neurons that results from all of these synapses gives our nervous system the ability to generate and send the messages that are necessary to govern our bodies. Let's

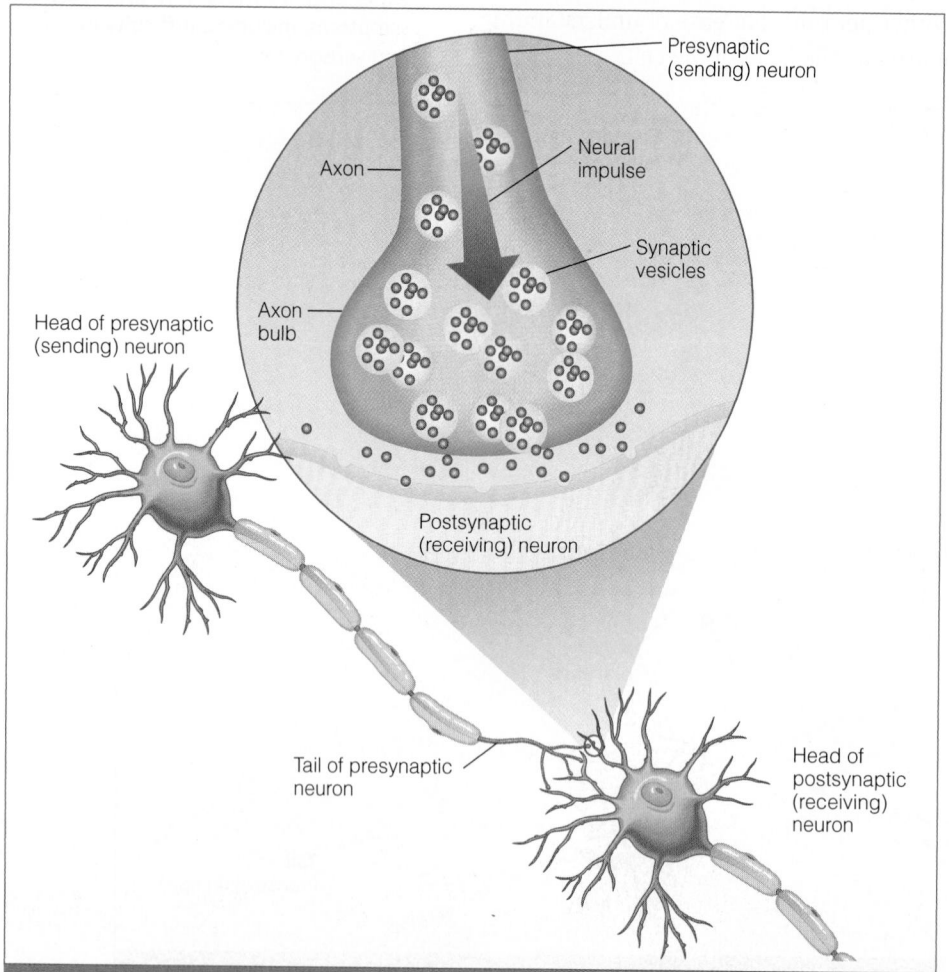

FIGURE 2.3

Detail of a Synapse

A synapse is formed when the axon bulb of one neuron comes in close proximity to the receptors on the dendrites of the postsynaptic neuron.

take a closer look at how these signals are generated within the neuron and how the signals jump across the synapse as they travel through the nervous system.

2.1.2 • Signals in the Brain: How Neurons Fire Up

Neural signals underlie much of the action in our bodies—breathing, movement, using our senses, and so on. To understand how these neural signals are generated within a neuron, we must first understand the chemical environment of the neuron.

Understanding brain chemistry is important because the brain uses *electrochemical* energy that is produced by charged particles called **ions** to send neural signals. Brain tissue is made up largely of densely packed neurons and glia cells. Brain tissue is surrounded by a constant bath of body fluid that contains many different ions. Some of these ions are positively charged, whereas others carry negative charges. Of all the different ions found in our body fluids, sodium (Na+) and potassium (K+) play a particularly important role in allowing our neurons to send signals.

ions [EYE-ons] charged particles that play an important role in the firing of action potentials in the nervous system

resting potential the potential difference that exists in the neuron when it is resting (approximately –70 mv in mammals)

threshold of excitation the potential difference at which a neuron will fire an action potential (–55 mv in mammals)

THE NEURON AT REST: THE RESTING POTENTIAL

When a neuron is at rest, meaning it is not actively conducting a signal, there is an imbalance in the types of ions found inside and outside the cell walls of the neuron. This imbalance exists because openings in the axon, called ion channels, allow only some ions to pass into and out of the neuron. At rest, these ion channels will not allow sodium (Na+) to enter the neuron, which results in an imbalance in the type of charge that is found inside and outside of the neuron. If you look at • FIGURE 2.4, you'll see that at rest, the charge inside the neuron is more negative than the charge outside of the neuron.

This difference in the charges found inside and outside the neuron is referred to as the neuron's **resting potential**. In mammals, the resting potential is about –70 millivolts (a millivolt, mv, is 1/1000 of a volt). This means that when resting, the inside of the neuron is about 70 mv more *negative* than the outside of the neuron. Although it is far less than 1 volt in magnitude, the resting potential is an important driving force in creating neural signals.

THE NEURON IN ACTION: FIRING AN ACTION POTENTIAL

When a neuron receives input from other neurons, these incoming signals enter at the dendrites and travel across the cell body to the axon. These signals can make the inside of the cell more positive or more negative. If the incoming signals make the inside of the neuron more positive, the inside of the neuron may become positive enough to reach the neuron's **threshold of excitation** (about –55 mv in mammals). When the threshold of excitation is reached, the ion channels along the axon suddenly open and allow Na+ ions to enter the cell. As Na+ ions flood

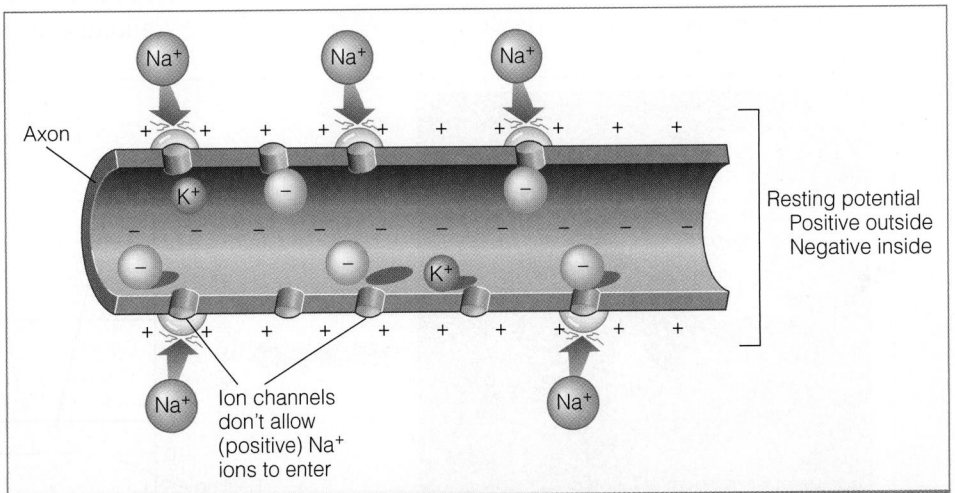

FIGURE 2.4

Resting Potential

When a neuron is at rest, the ion channels do not allow large sodium ions (Na+) to enter the cell. As a result of the high concentration of Na+, the predominant charge on the outside of the neuron is positive. The predominant charge inside the neuron is negative because of the high concentration of negatively charged ions found there. This difference in charge between the inside and the outside of the cell is called the resting potential.

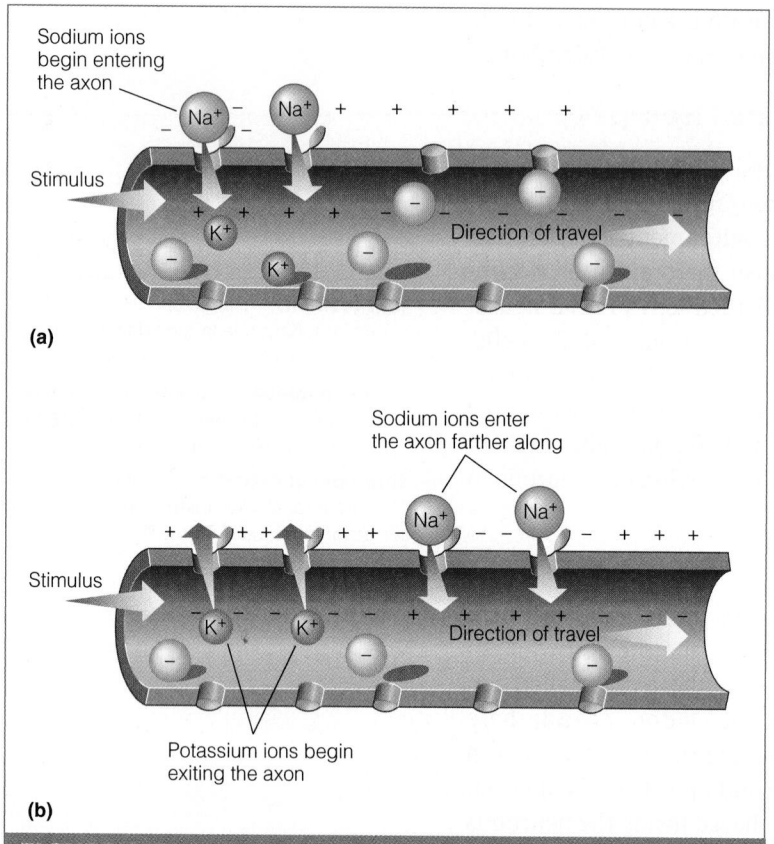

FIGURE 2.5

Action Potential

The action potential shown here (a) occurs all the way down the axon and is how we send neural signals in our nervous system. As the action potential travels down the axon (b), the sodium channels close and potassium (K+) channels open, allowing potassium to leave the cell. As the K+ leaves the cell, the inside of the cell becomes more negative. Potassium will continue to leave the cell until the neuron has returned to its resting potential.

Source: Modified from Starr & Taggart (1989).

into the cell, the inside of the neuron rapidly becomes more and more positive. This is how a neuron fires. These "firings" or neural impulses within the neuron are called **action potentials** (• FIGURE 2.5a).

All neural impulses are equally strong: If a neuron reaches threshold and fires an action potential, the neural signal will reach the synapse. A neuron firing an action potential is like firing a gun. You either shoot or you don't; and once the shot is fired, it's not going to stop in midair! Because all action potentials are equally strong and because, once fired, they will reach the synapse, action potentials are said to fire in an **all-or-none fashion**.

RETURNING TO THE RESTING POTENTIAL: THE REFRACTORY PERIOD

As the action potential travels to the end of the axon, Na+ floods into the neuron and the inside of the axon becomes more and more positive. As the inside of the neuron becomes increasingly positive, additional ion channels open along the axon and begin to pump positive potassium ions (K+) *out* of the cell. This removal of potassium (K+) from the neuron works to once again make the inside of the neuron more negatively charged (because *positive* ions are leaving the cell). Potassium will continue to leave the neuron until the neuron's original resting potential (−70 mv) is restored (Figure 2.5b). As the neuron is returning to its resting potential, it will experience a very brief (a few milliseconds) **refractory period** during which it is unable to fire another action potential (• FIGURE 2.6).

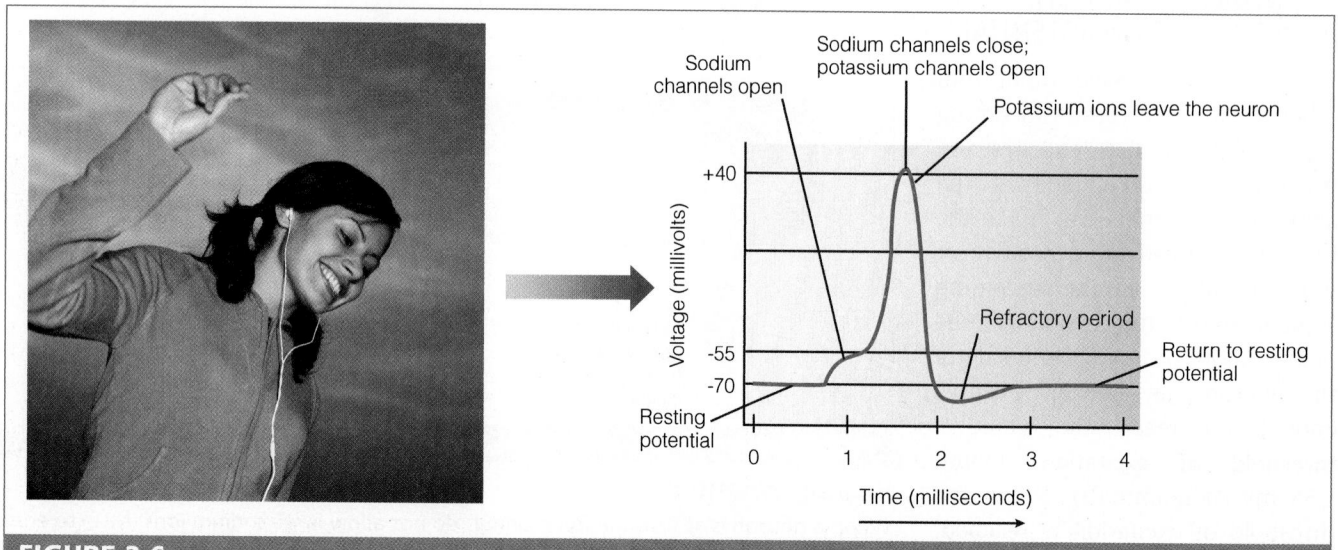

Ocean/Corbis

FIGURE 2.6

Electrical Changes in the Neuron As It Fires an Action Potential

Actions, such as snapping your fingers, require action potentials to be sent from your brain to your arms and hands. As each neuron fires, it will experience changes in the electrical charges inside its axon, as depicted in the graph to the right.

So far, we've looked at how a neural signal travels down the axon, but what happens when the action potential hits the axon bulb at the end of the axon? How does the signal get across the synapse?

2.1.3 • Jumping the Synapse: Synaptic Transmission

When the action potential reaches the axon bulb of the presynaptic (sending) neuron, it causes the release of neurotransmitters into the synapse. The neurotransmitter molecules float in the fluid-filled synapse (●FIGURE 2.7). Some of them will quickly drift across the synapse and come into contact with the tulip-shaped receptor sites lined up on the dendrites of the postsynaptic (receiving) neuron.

Each type of neurotransmitter has a specific molecular shape, and each type of receptor site has a specific configuration. Only certain types of neurotransmitters open specific receptor sites. Just as you must have the correct key to open a lock, a particular receptor site will be activated only by a specific neurotransmitter. When a neurotransmitter finds the correct receptor site on the postsynaptic neuron, it binds with the receptor site and causes a change in the electrical potential inside the postsynaptic neuron (Figure 2.7).

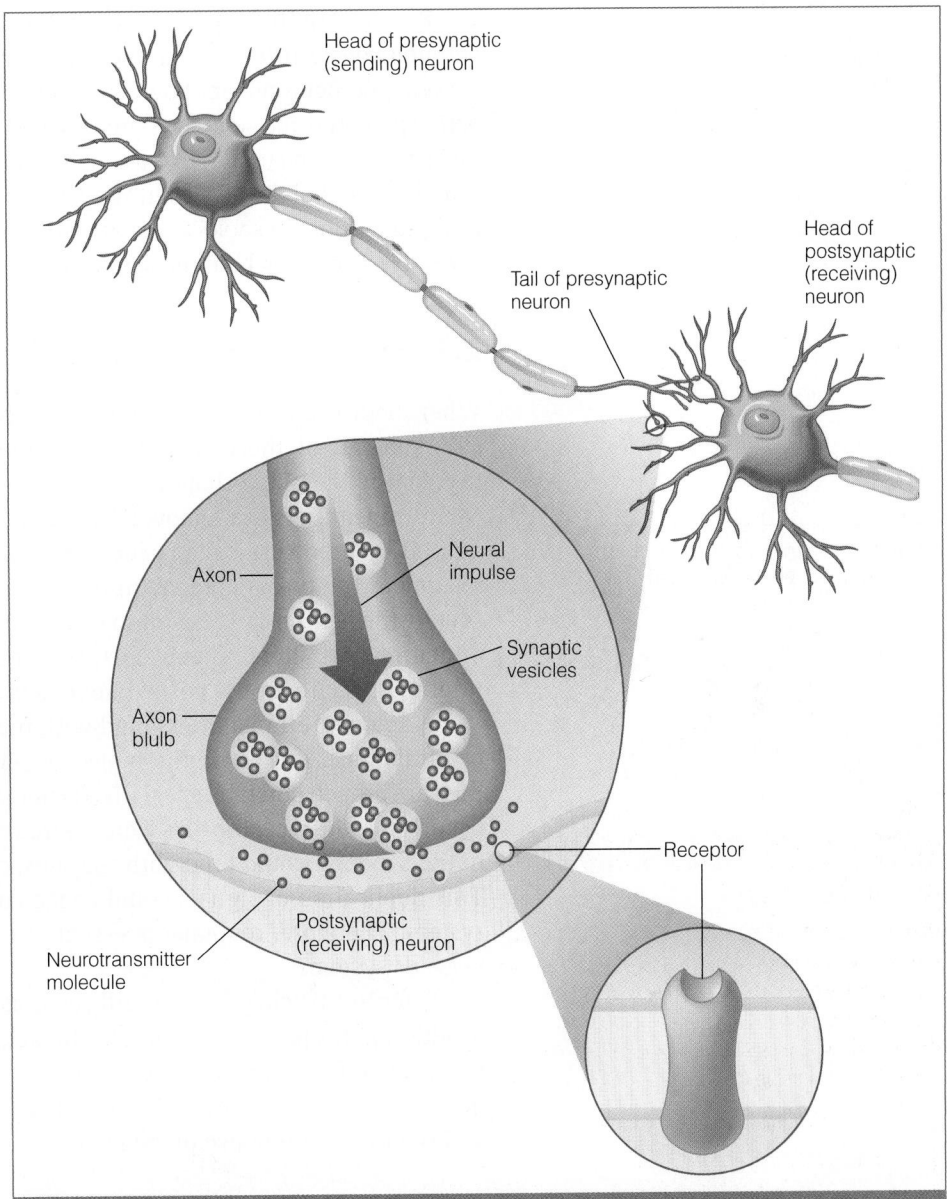

FIGURE 2.7

Neurotransmitters Carry the Signal Across the Synapse

The neurotransmitter is released in the synapse from the axon bulb of the presynaptic neuron. The neurotransmitters travel across the synapse and bind with receptor sites on the postsynaptic neuron.

EXCITATION AND INHIBITION

In some instances, the neurotransmitter will cause **excitation** in the postsynaptic cell. Excitation occurs when the neurotransmitter makes the postsynaptic cell more likely to fire an action potential. Excitatory neurotransmitters move the postsynaptic neuron closer to its threshold of excitation by causing the postsynaptic neuron to become more positive on the inside. Excitation is very important because it ensures that messages will continue onward through the nervous system after they cross the synapse.

However, sometimes we need to stop the message from continuing onward. This process is called **inhibition**. Inhibition occurs when the neurotransmitter makes the postsynaptic cell less likely to fire an action potential. As you may have guessed, inhibitory neurotransmitters cause the inside of the postsynaptic cell to become more negative, moving it away from its threshold of excitation.

action potential a neural impulse fired by a neuron when it reaches –55 mv

all-or-none fashion all action potentials are equal in strength; once a neuron begins to fire an action potential, it fires all the way down the axon

refractory period a brief period of time after a neuron has fired an action potential during which the neuron is inhibited and unlikely to fire another action potential

excitation when a neurotransmitter makes the postsynaptic cell more positive inside, it becomes more likely to fire an action potential

inhibition when a neurotransmitter makes the postsynaptic cell more negative inside, it becomes less likely to fire an action potential

Because of the complexity of the brain, a single postsynaptic cell can simultaneously receive excitatory and inhibitory signals from a great number of presynaptic neurons. So, how does the postsynaptic cell know whether to fire an action potential and send the signal down the line? All the incoming signals converge on the axon, which acts like an adding machine, summing up the excitatory and inhibitory signals. Only when the sum of the signals moves the resting potential at the axon to threshold (–55 mv) will the neuron fire an action potential. If the threshold is not reached, the signal simply does not go any farther at this time.

2.1.4 • Cleaning Up the Synapse: Reuptake

When neurotransmitters cross the synapse to bind with postsynaptic receptor sites, not all of these floating neurotransmitters will find available receptors to bind with. What happens to the neurotransmitters left in the synapse? Neurotransmitters are removed from the synapse and returned to the presynaptic neuron by a process called **reuptake**. Reuptake accomplishes two goals. First, it resupplies the presynaptic neuron with neurotransmitters so that the next signal sent by the neuron can also jump the synapse. Second, reuptake clears the synapse of neurotransmitters, thereby ensuring that just the right amount of excitation or inhibition occurs in the postsynaptic neuron.

reuptake the process through which neurotransmitters are recycled back into the presynaptic neuron

When neurotransmitters bind with receptor sites, they cause either excitation or inhibition. Afterward, the molecules either dislodge from the receptor site or they are broken down by specialized chemicals called *enzymes*. If reuptake did not occur, once the receptor sites were cleared out, other unattached neurotransmitters in the synapse would bind with the sites, causing further excitation or inhibition. This duplication of signals could cause confusion or dysfunction in the nervous system. Therefore, reuptake is essential to healthy functioning of our brain and nervous system.

Later in this chapter, you will see that some beneficial drugs act on the body by altering this process of reuptake. In fact, as we will see in Chapter 4, most drugs have their effect in the body by altering the functioning of neurotransmitters in the nervous system. For now, let's turn our attention to the types of neurotransmitters and their basic influence on behavior.

ENGAGE YOURSELF! The function of excitation in the nervous system is pretty clear. Excitation starts actions in the nervous system. But why do we need inhibition in the nervous system? Simply put, inhibition is required to slow down and shut off certain processes in the nervous system. Try this demonstration: Sit on the edge of a bed or table with both legs dangling freely. Reach down with the edge of your hand and strike your left leg just below the kneecap with moderate force. If done correctly, your leg should kick forward in what's called the patellar reflex. This reflex results in excitatory signals being sent to contract your quadriceps muscles (top of thigh) and inhibitory signals being sent to relax your hamstring muscles (back of thigh), causing your leg to kick. If you only had the capacity for excitation, your leg would tense but not kick. The interacting inhibition and excitation seen in this reflex are also at work when we walk, helping us balance and maintain posture.

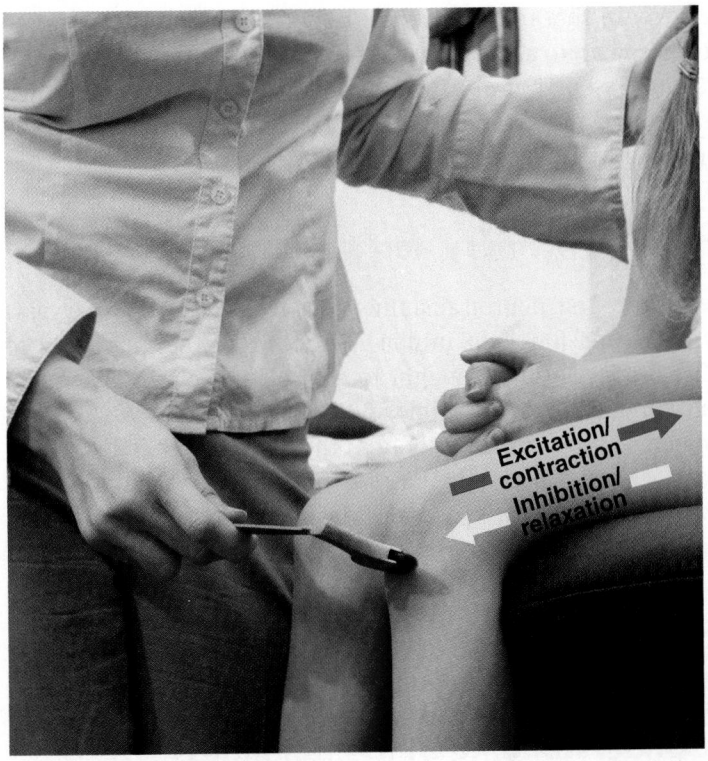

Junophoto/fStop/Alamy

When your knee is hit just below the kneecap, the quadriceps muscles on the top of the thigh are stretched. This stretching sets off a reflex in which the quadriceps receive excitatory impulses that contract them. At the same time, the hamstring muscles on the back of the thigh receive inhibitory impulses that cause them to relax. The result is the patellar reflex, and the leg kicks forward. This reflex, with its combination of inhibitory and excitatory impulses, helps us walk smoothly by automatically coordinating the contraction and relaxation of our thigh muscles.

Quiz Yourself

2.1

1. **Suki's dentist gave her a drug that froze the sodium ion channels along Suki's neural axons. What is the likely effect of this drug?**
   a. Suki's neurons will fire more action potentials than normal.
   b. Suki's neurons will fire stronger action potentials.
   c. Suki's neurons will fire weaker action potentials.
   d. Suki's neurons will fail to fire action potentials.

2. **Sabrina has contracted a disease that is destroying her myelin sheath. What effect would you expect this disease to have on the functioning of Sabrina's nervous system?**
   a. It will speed up the neural signals traveling through her nervous system.
   b. It will slow down the neural signals traveling through her nervous system.
   c. It won't affect the functioning of her nervous system in any measurable way.
   d. Her nervous system will speed up and slow down in a random fashion.

3. **A drug that causes potassium ions to leave one's neurons is likely to produce what type of effect on the neuron?**
   a. Depolarization
   b. Excitation
   c. Inhibition
   d. Both excitation and inhibition

Answers 1. d; 2. b; 3. c

2.2 Neurotransmitters: Chemical Messengers in the Brain

Well over 100 different chemical compounds have been identified as neurotransmitters (Morrow et al., 2008), and researchers continue to investigate more substances that may affect neural signaling. For example, some forms of the female sex hormone *estrogen* that regulate certain aspects of reproduction in the body have recently been shown to also behave like neurotransmitters in the brain (Balthazart & Ball, 2006; Gasbarri et al., 2012). A complete review of all known neurotransmitters is well beyond the scope of this text, but we will look at the ones that most influence our moods and behavior.

2.2.1 • Acetylcholine: Memory and Memory Loss

acetylcholine [uh-see-til-COE-leen] (ACh) a neurotransmitter related to muscle movement and perhaps consciousness, learning, and memory

dopamine [DOPE-uh-mean] a neurotransmitter that plays a role in movement, motivation, learning, and attention

Acetylcholine (ACh) was the first neurotransmitter discovered. In the early part of the 20th century, ACh was found to inhibit the action of the heart and to excite skeletal muscles. Today, ACh is thought to also play a role in awareness or consciousness and in memory (Hasselmo, 2010; Perry et al., 1999). This hypothesized role in memory comes primarily from the discovery that during the course of their disease, people with Alzheimer's experience loss of functioning in neurons that release ACh into their synapses (Martorana et al., 2009; Murray et al., 2013). Because Alzheimer's disease is associated with both memory loss and the loss of ACh action in the brain, it appears that ACh may help the brain store and/or process memories.

2.2.2 • Dopamine, Serotonin, and Norepinephrine: Deepening Our Understanding of Mental Illness

One group of neurotransmitters in particular, *dopamine, serotonin,* and *norepinephrine,* has proven to be very important to our understanding of a wide range of normal behaviors and mental illnesses. **Dopamine** appears to influence processes such as movement, learning, attention, and motivation. Dopamine may influence motivation by making some activities, such as sex and eating, very pleasurable or rewarding. The reward produced by dopamine may even play a role in the development of certain types of substance abuse (see Chapter 4; Neisewander, Cheung, & Pentkowski, 2014; Peng et al., 2013).

Parkinson's disease is associated with the loss of neurons in an area of the brain richest in dopamine. Drugs used to treat Parkinsonian symptoms work to indirectly increase the amount of dopamine in the brain. Care must be used in administering such drugs, though, because too much dopamine action in the brain produces some very troubling symptoms—in particular, symptoms similar to those of the psychiatric disorder schizophrenia (see Chapter 13), which is associated with too much dopamine action in the brain (Seeman, 2010). Drugs used to treat schizophrenia often block the action of dopamine at the synapse. Regulating brain chemistry is not simple.

© Stephen Jaffe/AFP/Getty Images

Actor Michael J. Fox has Parkinson's disease, and former boxer Mohammed Ali has a related condition called Parkinsonianism. Parkinson's is a degenerative disease that results in decreased dopamine action in the brain, which causes tremors and other neurological symptoms.

As you might imagine, prolonged use of dopamine-blocking drugs can cause Parkinsonian-like side effects. Think about it. Too little dopamine, and one has the symptoms of Parkinson's disease; too much dopamine, and the result is schizophrenic symptoms. It appears that healthy functioning requires just the right amount of dopamine in the brain.

Mental health may depend on having proper levels of other neurotransmitters as well. The neurotransmitter **serotonin** is thought to play a role in many different behaviors, including sleep, arousal, mood, eating, and pain perception. A lack of serotonin in the brain has been linked to several mental and behavioral disorders (e.g., depression). Drugs that increase the action of serotonin at the synapse by preventing its reuptake are called *selective serotonin reuptake inhibitors (SSRIs).* Prozac and other SSRIs have been used to successfully treat depression, eating disorders, compulsive behavior, and pain. However, not all drugs that act on serotonin are therapeutic. The illegal drug *MDMA* (or *ecstasy,* as it is commonly known) may actually reduce serotonin action in the brain (Do & Schenk, 2013; Xie et al., 2006). This loss of serotonin action may account for reports of depression following ecstasy highs in some users (see Chapter 4).

serotonin [ser-uh-TOE-nin] a neurotransmitter that plays a role in many different behaviors, including sleep, arousal, mood, eating, and pain perception

norepinephrine [nor-ep-in-EF-rin] (NOR) a neurotransmitter that plays a role in regulating sleep, arousal, and mood

gamma amino butyric [GAM-ma uh-MEAN-oh bee-you-TREE-ick] acid (GABA) the body's chief inhibitory neurotransmitter, which plays a role in regulating arousal

Jose Luis Pelaez Inc/Blend Images/Getty Images

Joe Raedle/Getty Images

By inhibiting the reuptake of serotonin, Paxil increases the amount of serotonin activity in the synapse, which may reduce depressive symptoms in some patients and allow them to once again enjoy pleasurable moments of their lives.

Also related to mental health is **norepinephrine (NOR),** a neurotransmitter thought to play a role in regulating sleep, arousal, and mood. Some drugs that alleviate depression have an effect on NOR as well as on serotonin. NOR may also play a role in the development of synapses during childhood (Sanders et al., 2005) and recovery of functioning after brain injury (Bueno-Nava et al., 2008). In addition to its function in the brain, NOR also plays a role in the functioning of the *endocrine system,* which we will discuss later in this chapter (see Section 2.5).

2.2.3 • GABA and Glutamate: Regulating Brain Activity

Gamma amino butyric acid (GABA) is thought to regulate arousal, our general level of energy and alertness. GABA is the main inhibitory neurotransmitter in the brain (Augustine, 2012). It is estimated that one-third of all synapses, including most inhibitory synapses, in the brain use GABA as their neurotransmitter. Therefore, it appears that GABA plays an essential role in normal brain function. Loss of GABA in the brain can produce seizures, because without GABA's inhibitory effects, arousal levels become too high. Some anticonvulsant drugs work by lessening the effects of enzymes that destroy GABA molecules (Rowlett et al., 2005). GABA may also play a role in mediating anxiety. Rats injected with drugs that increase GABA action in certain parts of the brain demonstrate fewer anxiety-related behaviors (e.g., Degroot, 2004), and drugs that increase GABA action in the brain are often used to calm and sedate humans. These drugs include benzodiazepines such as Valium, barbiturates (Phenobarbital), and alcohol (see Chapter 4). We will discuss treatment of anxiety again in Chapter 14.

glutamate [GLUE-tuh-mate] the chief excitatory neurotransmitter in the brain, found at more than 50% of the synapses in the brain

endorphins [in-DOOR-fins] neurotransmitters that act as natural painkillers

Whereas GABA is the chief inhibitory neurotransmitter, **glutamate** is the chief excitatory neurotransmitter in the brain (Augustine, 2012). More than 50% of all synapses in the brain use glutamate as a neurotransmitter, and without it many brain processes would not take place. Ironically, glutamate can also be a deadly force in the brain. When physical brain damage affects glutamate-bearing neurons, glutamate molecules may be released in large quantities from the damaged neuron. Large amounts of extracellular glutamate can cause brain cell death as the neurons literally become excited to death when the glutamate spreads to neighboring neurons and causes them to fire a frenzy of action potentials. It appears that in the brain too much excitation is a very bad thing!

2.2.4 • Endorphins: Pain and Pleasure in the Brain

Have you ever heard the term *endorphin*? If you have, what was the context? If you are like most people, your first exposure to endorphins was probably in the context of exercise or physical injuries. **Endorphins** are neurotransmitters that are chemically very similar to the class of narcotic drugs called *opiates* (e.g., opium, heroin, morphine, and codeine). Endorphins are released in the central nervous system during times of stress, such as physical exertion or physical injury, to protect us from pain (Kavushansky et al., 2013). Because endorphins block pain messages in the central nervous system, we feel less pain and a mild sense of euphoria when they are released. Endorphins may be one of the reasons that physical activity makes us feel physically and mentally better (Fichna et al., 2007).

Exercise can lead to the release of endorphins, producing feelings of pleasure and well-being that are sometimes called a "runner's high."

© TMI/Alamy

Endorphins may also play a role in making other activities, such as eating, pleasurable (Hayward et al., 2006). For example, research indicates that endorphins are released about 15 minutes after eating fat. The reward from endorphin may be one reason for the appeal of fatty foods (Mizushige, Inoue, & Fushiki, 2007).

We hope that you now have a basic understanding of the role that neurotransmitters play in allowing our neurons to communicate with one another (see You Review: Neurotransmitters). Our next step is to take a look at how this neural signaling fits into the structure of the nervous system.

You Review **Neurotransmitters**

Neurotransmitter	Functions	Related Diseases and Clinical Conditions
Acetylcholine	Excites skeletal muscles; inhibits heart action; memory	Alzheimer's disease
Dopamine	Movement; learning; attention; motivation and reward	Parkinson's disease; schizophrenia; substance abuse
Serotonin	Sleep; arousal; mood; eating; pain perception	Depression; obsessive compulsive disorder and other anxiety disorders; eating disorders; chronic pain
Norepinephrine	Sleep; arousal; mood	Depression and other mood disorders
GABA	Chief inhibitor; regulates arousal	Some anxiety disorders; some seizure disorders
Glutamate	Chief excitatory neurotransmitter; many diverse functions	Neural death following head injuries
Endorphins	Suppression of pain; eating; cardiovascular functioning	Depression

Quiz Yourself

2.2

1. Lamont developed a disease that reduces the amount of serotonin in his brain. What symptoms would you expect Lamont to have?
   a. Hallucinations
   b. Trouble with his motor skills
   c. Symptoms of depression
   d. Seizures
2. Jackson is a normal, healthy adult man. Jackson's brain likely contains more _____ than any other neurotransmitter.
   a. glutamate
   b. GABA
   c. dopamine
   d. acetylcholine
3. Sasha has been drinking an herbal tea that she believes boosts her body's ability to manufacture acetylcholine. Why do you suppose Sasha is so interested in drinking this tea?
   a. She is trying to improve her memory.
   b. She is trying to treat her depression.
   c. She is hoping it will help her have more energy.
   d. She is hoping it will help her sleep better.

Answers 1. c; 2. a; 3. a

2.3 The Structure of the Nervous System

Our **nervous system** is the vast, interconnected network of all the neurons in our body. Every single facet of our body's functioning and our behavior is monitored and influenced by the nervous system. The nervous system is arranged in a series of interconnected subsystems, each with its own specialized tasks. At the broadest level, the nervous system is divided into the brain and spinal cord, known as the

nervous system an electrochemical system of communication within the body that uses cells called neurons to convey information

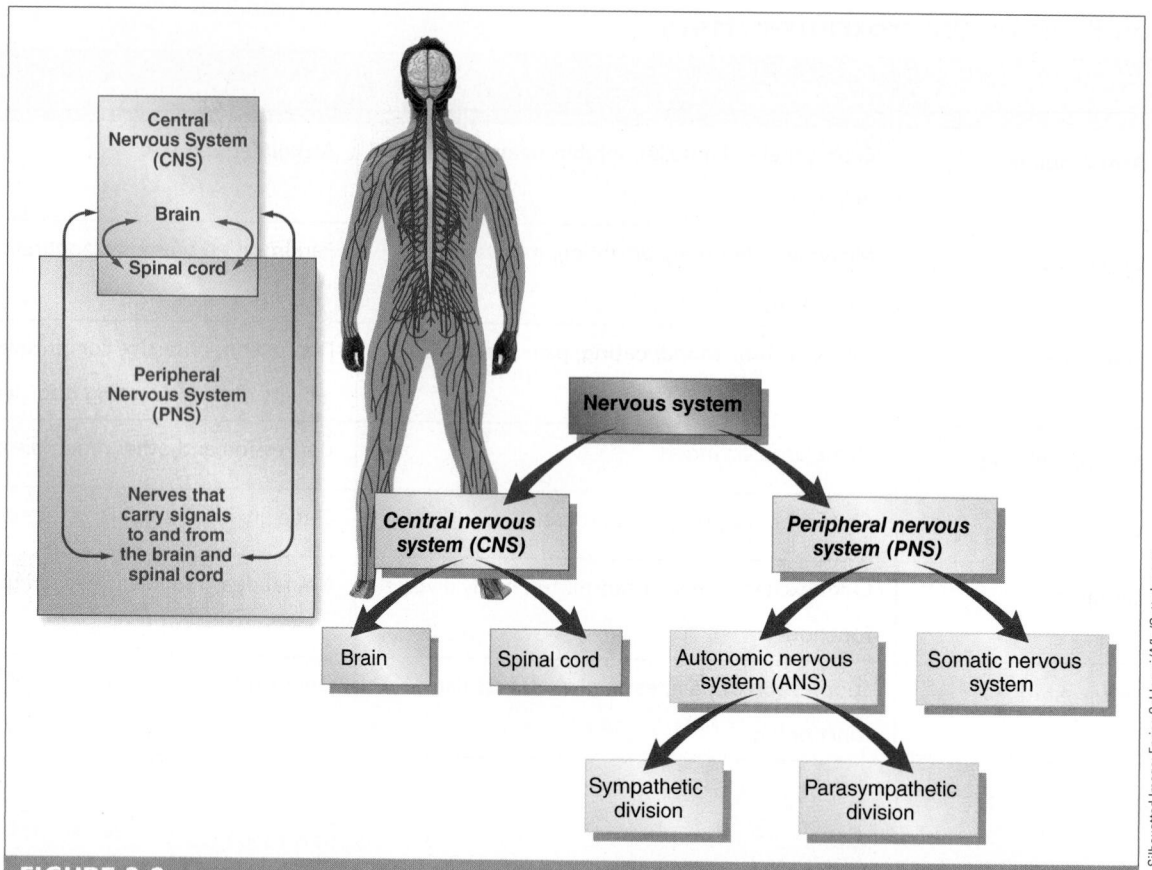

Silhouetted Image: Enrico Calderoni/Afflo/Getty Images

FIGURE 2.8

The Human Nervous System

The nervous system is divided into the central nervous system (CNS, shown in blue) and the peripheral nervous system (PNS, shown in red). Together the central and peripheral nervous systems affect virtually all of our bodily functions. The PNS can be further subdivided into the somatic nervous system (governs voluntary action and sensory functioning) and the autonomic nervous system (governs involuntary organ functioning). The autonomic nervous system can be further subdivided into the parasympathetic nervous system (governs organs in calm situations) and the sympathetic nervous system (governs organs during times of stress).

central nervous system (CNS), and the remaining components of the nervous system, referred to collectively as the **peripheral nervous system (PNS)** (•FIGURE 2.8). We will discuss the function of the CNS later when we discuss the brain, but first let's take a closer look at the PNS.

2.3.1 • Sensing and Reacting: The Peripheral Nervous System

The functions of the PNS are twofold. First, the PNS must ensure that the CNS is informed about what is happening inside and outside our body. To this end, the PNS is equipped with **sensory neurons** that convey information to the CNS from the outside world, such as sights and sounds, as well as information from our internal world, such as aches and pains. Once the information has reached the CNS, it is carried across *interneurons* as the brain processes the information. Then the second function of the PNS takes over as it acts out the directives of the CNS. The PNS is equipped with **motor neurons** that carry signals from the CNS to our muscles. For example, when you see a juicy apple, the sensory neurons

central nervous system (CNS) the brain and the spinal cord

peripheral nervous system (PNS) all of the nervous system except the brain and the spinal cord

sensory neurons neurons that transmit information from the sense organs to the central nervous system

motor neurons neurons that transmit commands from the brain to the muscles of the body of your eye send this information upward to the part of the brain that processes visual information. Here the brain recognizes the apple, and you decide to eat the apple. The brain then sends signals downward to the motor neurons of your hand and arm, which, in turn, direct you to reach out and grasp the apple with your hand (• FIGURE 2.9). In this fashion, the sensory pathways send sensory information to the spinal cord and brain, and the motor pathways carry "orders" away from the brain and spinal cord to the rest of the body.

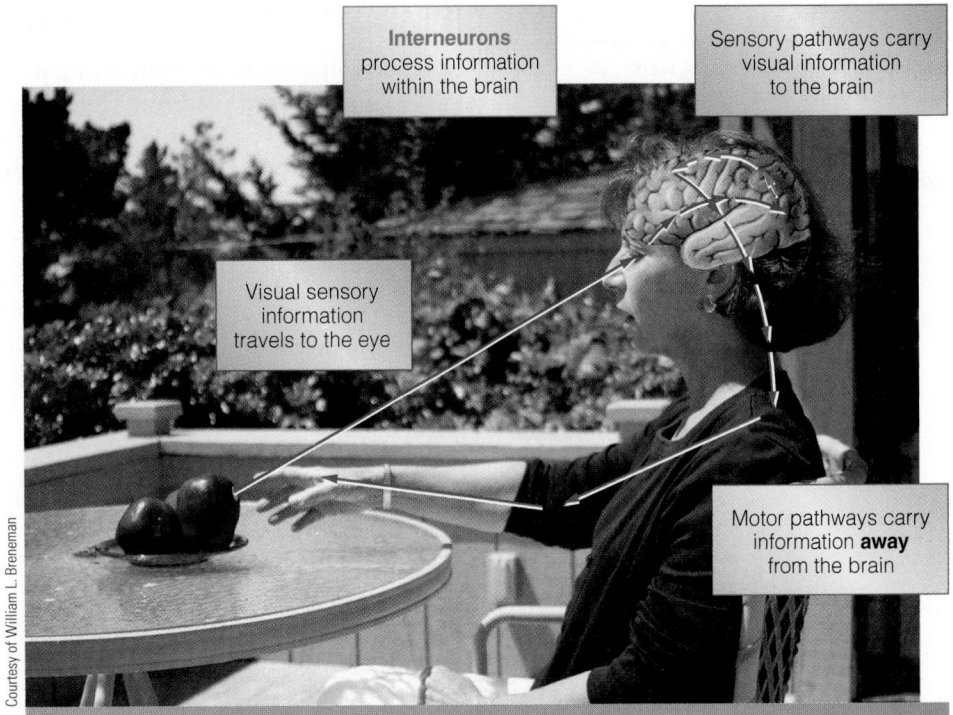

FIGURE 2.9

Sensory and Motor Pathways

Reaching for an apple involves sensory pathways (shown in red), motor pathways (shown in blue), and interneuron pathways (shown in green).

2.3.2 • Voluntary Action: The Somatic Nervous System

Traditionally, psychologists and physiologists have further subdivided the neurons of the PNS into two subsystems: the *somatic nervous system* and the *autonomic nervous system*. The **somatic nervous system** includes those neurons that control the skeletal muscles of the body that allow us to engage in voluntary actions. For example, reaching for an apple requires the activation of the somatic nervous system. The brain makes the decision to reach for the apple; then this "order" is sent downward, across the motor neurons of the somatic nervous system that control the muscles of the arm. The arm muscles react to the orders from the CNS, and you reach for the apple. The functioning of the somatic nervous system enables us to control our bodies in a deliberate and flexible manner.

somatic nervous system the branch of the peripheral nervous system that governs sensory and voluntary motor action in the body

autonomic nervous system the branch of the peripheral nervous system that primarily governs involuntary organ functioning and actions in the body

2.3.3 • Involuntary Actions: The Autonomic Nervous System

Although controlling body movements is important, it is equally advantageous to have some processes in the body controlled automatically and involuntarily. The neurons of the **autonomic nervous system** control the smooth muscles of the internal organs, the muscles of the heart, and the glands. By automatically regulating organ functions, the autonomic nervous system frees up our conscious resources and enables us to respond quickly and efficiently to the demands placed on us by the environment. Imagine how hard life would be if you had to remember to breathe, tell your heart to beat, and remind your liver to do its job! You would have little energy and attention left for thinking and learning, let alone responding quickly to threatening situations. Thankfully, we have the autonomic nervous system to regulate our organ functions, and it is equipped with separate divisions to help us survive in an ever-changing and sometimes dangerous world.

parasympathetic nervous system the branch of the autonomic nervous system most active during times of normal functioning

sympathetic nervous system the branch of the autonomic nervous system most active during times of danger or stress

THE PARASYMPATHETIC NERVOUS SYSTEM

The **parasympathetic nervous system** operates mainly under conditions of relative calm. As you read this page, it is very likely that your parasympathetic nervous system is primarily responsible for regulating the functions of your internal organs. When the parasympathetic nervous system is active, heart rate, blood pressure, and respiration are kept at normal levels. Blood is circulated to the digestive tract and other internal organs so that they can function properly, and your pupils are not overly dilated. Your body is calm, and everything is running smoothly. But if threat arises in the environment, this will quickly change. During times of stress, the sympathetic system takes over primary regulation of our organ functions from the parasympathetic system.

THE SYMPATHETIC NERVOUS SYSTEM

The **sympathetic nervous system** springs into action under conditions of threat or stress. The sympathetic nervous system evolved to protect us from danger. When it is activated, heart rate increases, breathing becomes more rapid, blood pressure increases, digestion slows, muscle tissue becomes engorged with blood, the pupils dilate, and the hair on the back of the neck stands up. All of these changes help to prepare us to defend our body from threat. For this reason, the actions of the sympathetic nervous system are often referred to as the *fight-or-flight response*. The increased cardiovascular activity quickly pumps oxygenated blood away from internal organs and to the muscles of the arms and legs so that the animal or person can swiftly attack, defend itself, or run away. Once the danger is past, the parasympathetic system resumes control, and heart rate, respiration, blood pressure, and pupil dilation return to normal. Because the sympathetic nervous system plays an important role in our response to stress, it also plays an important role in our health. We explore this connection in Chapter 12.

Quiz Yourself 2.3

1. Juanita was hiking in the woods when she stumbled upon a rattlesnake. Immediately *after* she saw the snake, which division of the nervous system was most likely in control of Juanita's internal organ functions?
   a. Parasympathetic
   b. Sympathetic
   c. Endocrine
   d. Spinal

2. Moving your arm is an example of a behavior that is governed by which branch of the nervous system?
   a. Somatic nervous system
   b. Autonomic nervous system
   c. Sympathetic nervous system
   d. Parasympathetic nervous system

3. The sensory neurons in your fingertips are part of the _____ nervous system.
   a. central
   b. peripheral
   c. autonomic
   d. sympathetic

Answers 1. b; 2. a; 3. b

2.4 The Brain and Spine: The Central Nervous System

As we have discussed, the structures of the brain are composed largely of neurons and glia cells. These structures are organized into three regions: the *hindbrain*, the *midbrain*, and the *forebrain*. The **hindbrain** sits directly above the spinal cord and is named for its position at the bottom of the brain (●FIGURE 2.10). The hindbrain is the most "primitive" part of the brain, involved in the most basic life-sustaining functions. The hindbrain makes up a good portion of the *brainstem*, a series of brain structures that are essential for life. Even small amounts of damage to the brainstem can be life threatening.

The **forebrain** resides in the top part of the skull and regulates complex mental processes such as thinking and emotional control. It is the largest region of the brain and includes structures that regulate many emotional, motivational, and cognitive processes. Without this well-developed forebrain, humans would not have the mental abilities such as problem solving, thinking, remembering, and using language.

Between the hindbrain and the forebrain is the **midbrain**, which acts as a connection between the more basic functions of the hindbrain and the complex mental

hindbrain a primitive part of the brain that comprises the medulla, pons, and cerebellum

forebrain the brain structures, including the limbic system, thalamus, hypothalamus, and cortex, that govern higher-order mental processes

midbrain the brain structure that connects the hindbrain with the forebrain

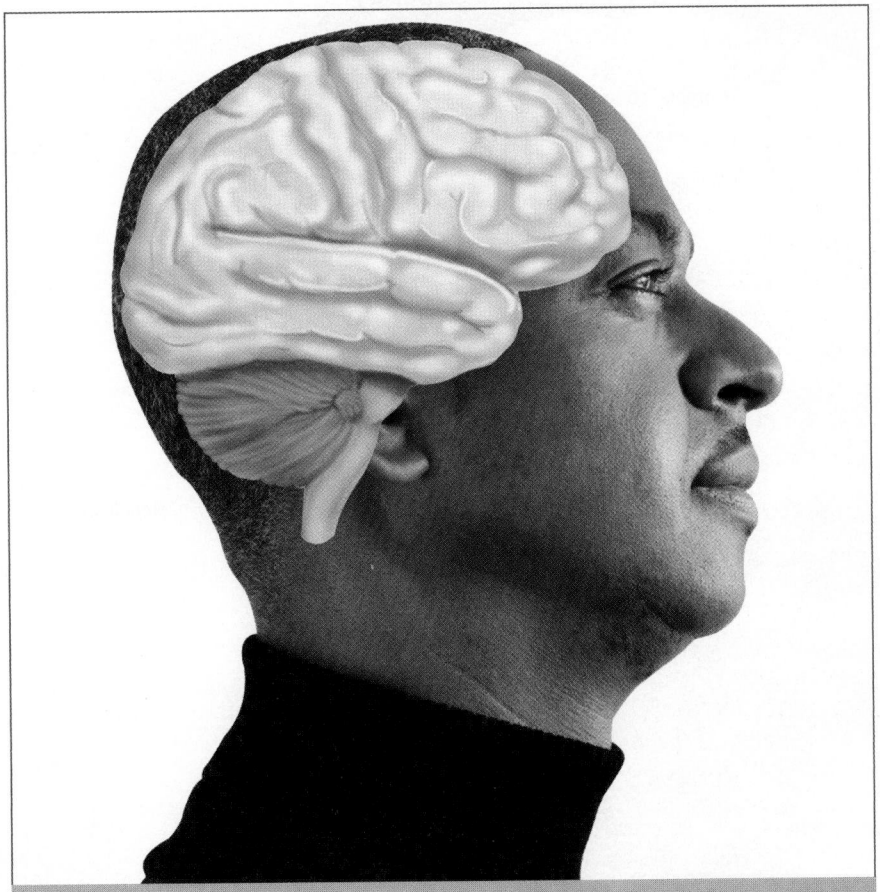

Image Source/Getty Images

FIGURE 2.10

The Human Hindbrain, Midbrain, and Forebrain

The human hindbrain (shown in blue) governs basic and life-sustaining functions. The midbrain (shown in red) connects the lower structures of the hindbrain with the higher structures of the forebrain. The forebrain (shown in tan) governs complex processes such as cognition, sensory processing, and the planning and execution of behaviors.

medulla [meh-DOO-luh] a part of the hindbrain that controls basic, life-sustaining functions such as respiration, heart rate, and blood pressure

pons a hindbrain structure that plays a role in respiration, consciousness, sleep, dreaming, facial movement, sensory processes, and the transmission of neural signals from one part of the brain to another

cerebellum a hindbrain structure that plays a role in balance, muscle tone, and coordination of motor movements

reticular formation a part of the midbrain that regulates arousal and plays an important role in attention, sleep, and consciousness

processes of the forebrain. Without the midbrain, the hindbrain could not supply the forebrain with the neural impulses it needs to remain active and to keep us conscious.

Now that we have a feel for the overall organization of the brain, let's examine the components and functions of these structures.

2.4.1 • The Hindbrain

Simply put, without the functioning of the hindbrain, we would die (Wijdicks, Atkinson, & Okazaki, 2001). The hindbrain consists of three structures: the *medulla*, the *pons*, and the *cerebellum*. The **medulla** sits at the top of the spinal column at the point where the spinal cord enters the base of the skull (•FIGURE 2.11). The medulla regulates heartbeat and respiration, and even minor damage to the medulla can result in death from heart or respiratory failure. It also plays a role in sneezing, coughing, vomiting, swallowing, and digestion.

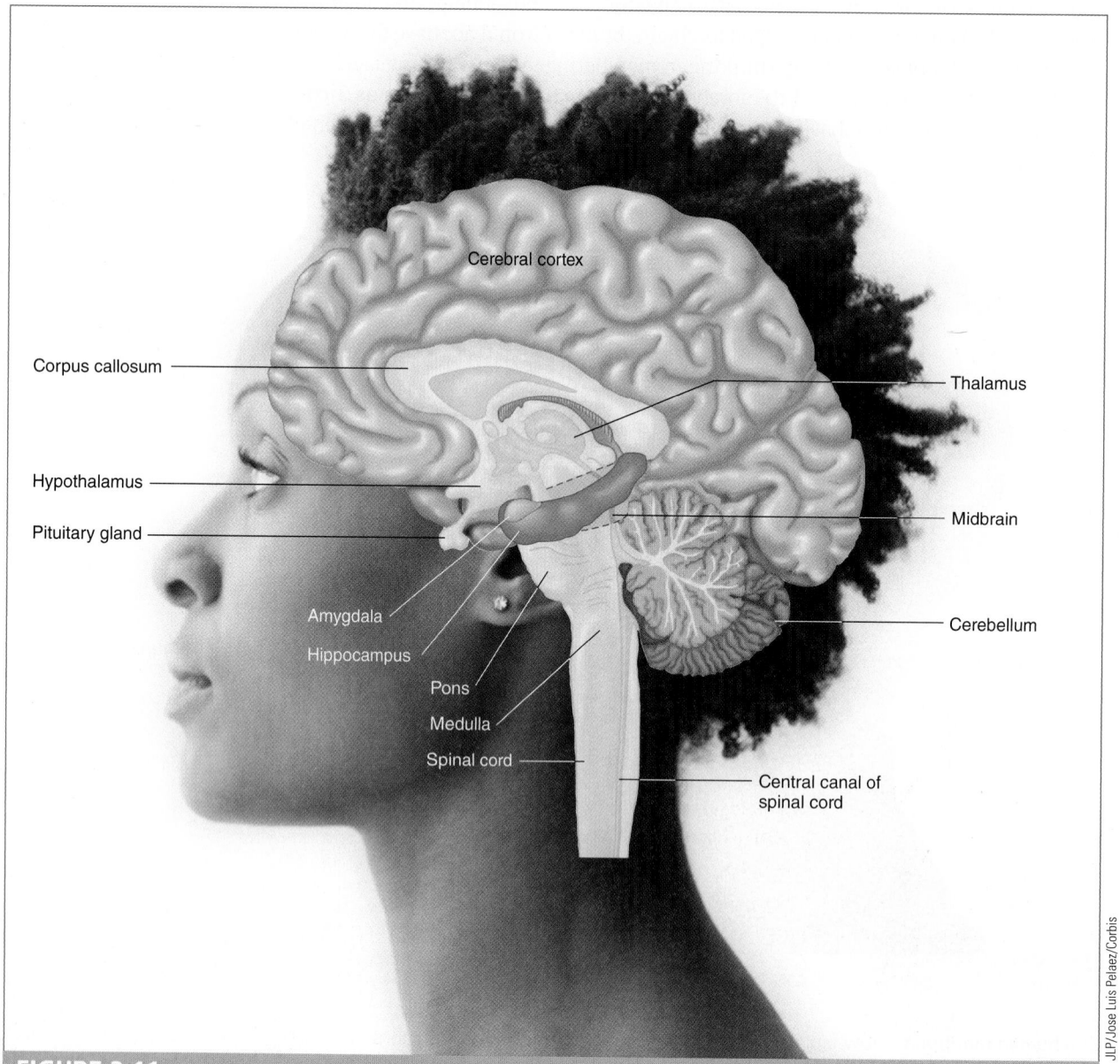

JLP/Jose Luis Pelaez/Corbis

FIGURE 2.11

The Brain and Its Structures

This figure shows the cortex and the subcortical structures of the brain.

The **pons** sits above the medulla, where the brainstem bulges inside the skull (Figure 2.11). Like the medulla, the pons is crucial to life. The pons plays a role in respiration, consciousness, sleep, dreaming, facial movement, sensory processes, and the transmission of neural signals from one part of the brain to another. The pons acts as a "bridge" for neural signals; in particular, sensory information coming from the right and left sides of the body crosses through the pons before moving on to other parts of the brain. If the pons becomes damaged, the "bridge" is out, and serious motor sensory impairments can result.

The final part of the hindbrain is the **cerebellum**. The cerebellum is the large, deeply grooved structure at the base of the brain (Figure 2.11). The cerebellum is necessary for balance, muscle tone, and the performance of motor skills (Pool et al., 2013; Seidler et al., 2002). It may also play a critical role in the learning of motor skills (Ferrucci et al., 2013; Hikosaka et al., 2002) and the execution of certain behaviors (Walker, Diefenbach, & Parikh, 2007). Damage to the cerebellum leads to loss of balance and coordination. Alcohol impairs the functioning of the cerebellum (and some forebrain structures), producing the familiar symptoms of staggering, clumsiness, and slowed reaction time that make driving dangerous. Studies also suggest that fetal exposure to alcohol during pregnancy may lead to death of cerebellar neurons, perhaps contributing to birth defects such as *fetal alcohol spectrum disorders* (Luo, 2012). For this reason, alcohol should be avoided during pregnancy.

© Peter Hvizdak/The Image Works

Without the cerebellum, we would not be able to accomplish tasks such as learning to ride a bicycle.

limbic system a system of structures, including the amygdala and hippocampus, that govern certain aspects of emotion, motivation, and memory

cerebral cortex the thin, wrinkled outer covering of the brain in which high-level processes such as thinking, planning, language, interpretation of sensory data, and coordination of sensory and motor information take place

cerebral hemispheres the right and left sides of the brain that to some degree govern different functions in the body

2.4.2 • The Midbrain

The midbrain structures connect the hindbrain with the more sophisticated forebrain. For psychologists, one of the most interesting midbrain structures is the **reticular formation**. The reticular formation, located near the pons, is a network of neurons that extends from the hindbrain region into the midbrain. The reticular formation serves primarily to regulate arousal levels (Kinomura et al., 1996), thereby playing an important role in attention, sleep, and consciousness (Hudson, 2009; Izac, 2006; Vanini & Baghdoyan, 2013). The reticular formation functions as a type of "on switch" for the high-level thinking centers of the forebrain. Additionally, the reticular formation appears to play a role in regulating cardiovascular activity, respiratory functioning, and body movement.

2.4.3 • The Forebrain

The forebrain contains several groups of structures that function as subsystems. The structures of the **limbic system** govern emotional and motivational processes, and other forebrain structures govern sensory processing and motivation. The wrinkled and folded external surface of the brain, the **cerebral cortex**, governs high-level processes such as cognition and language. In • FIGURE 2.12 you can see that the forebrain is divided into right and left **cerebral hemispheres**. For the most part,

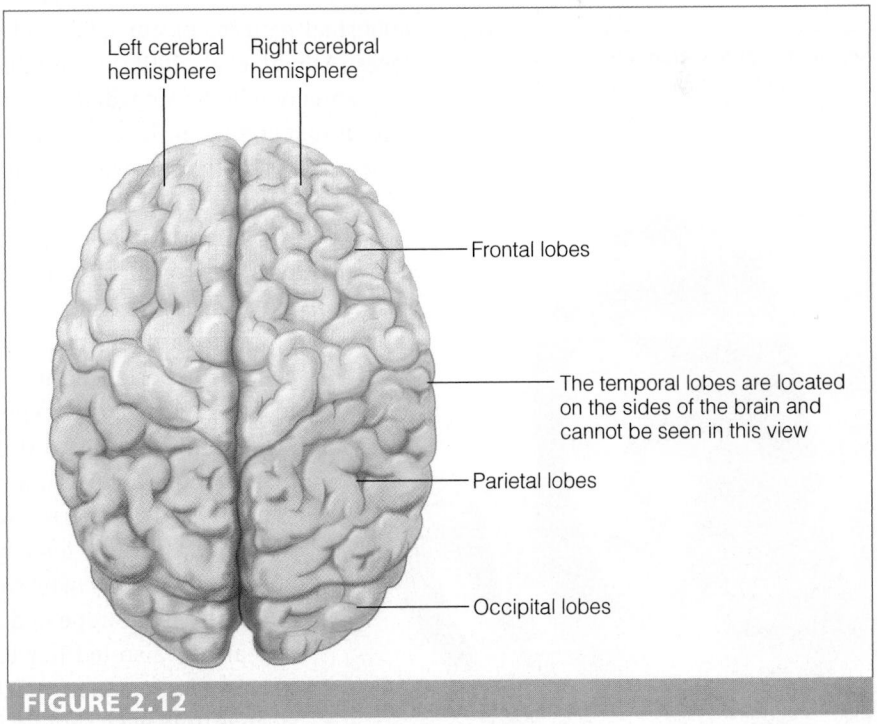

FIGURE 2.12

The Cerebral Hemispheres

The brain is divided into right and left hemispheres. The outside covering of the hemispheres, the cortex, is where the higher-order processing in the brain takes place.

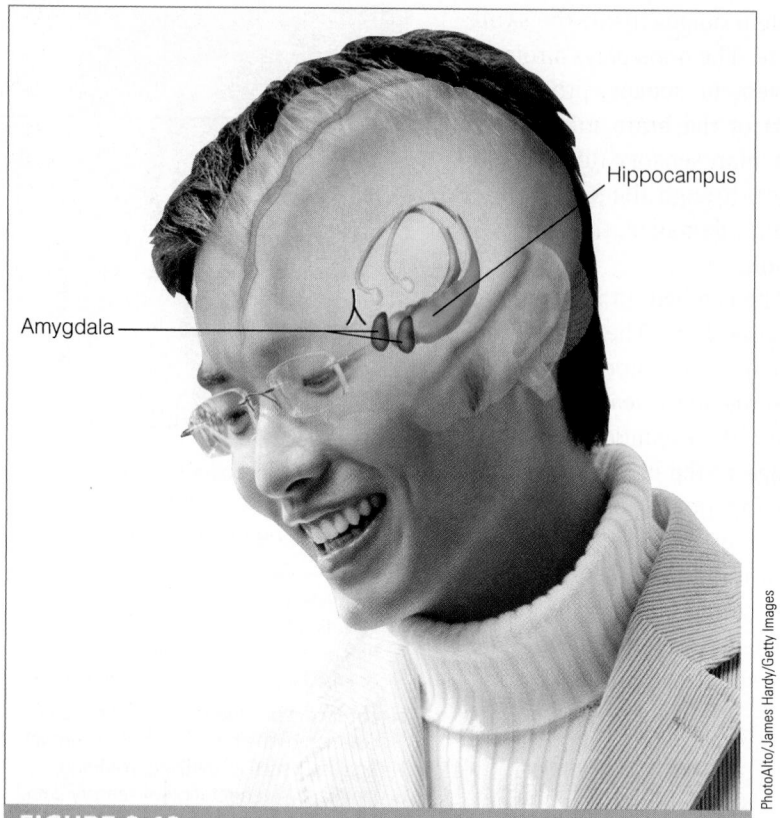

PhotoAlto/James Hardy/Getty Images

FIGURE 2.13

The Limbic System

Limbic system structures, including the amygdala and the hippocampus, process specific aspects of emotion and memory.

forebrain structures are duplicated in the right and left hemispheres.

THE LIMBIC SYSTEM

The series of forebrain structures collectively called the limbic system regulate some of our basic emotional reactions. Two limbic structures are located deep in the central region of the brain, above the hindbrain and beneath the cerebral cortex: the *amygdala* and the *hippocampus* (• FIGURE 2.13).

The **amygdala** is an almond-shaped structure located almost directly behind the temples. The amygdala governs the emotions of fear and aggression (Sah et al., 2003). More specifically, the amygdala may play a role in the way we perceive and respond to emotion-evoking stimuli (Adolphs, 2002; Isenberg et al., 1999). For example, how we process fearful expressions in others (see Hornboll et al., 2013). Studies have found that participants with damage to their amygdala have a difficult time making accurate judgments about others' mood states by looking at their facial expressions. This is especially true when participants are making judgments about other people's level of fear and anger (Adolphs, Tranel, & Damasio, 1998; Graham, Devinsky, & LaBar, 2007). Researchers have shown that persons with *autism spectrum disorders,* mental health disorders characterized by deficits in social behavior, experience abnormal patterns of amygdala activation when perceiving fear in other people's faces (Ashwin et al., 2006). The inability to correctly perceive people's emotions due to dysfunction in the amygdala may lead to awkward social interactions. A complete lack of functioning in the amygdala can lead to even bigger problems.

amygdala [uh-MIG-duh-luh] a part of the limbic system that plays a role in the emotions of fear and aggression

Although we may admire people for being "fearless," the recent case of a woman known as S.M. (Feinstein et al., 2011) illustrates the important role that fear can play in our lives. S.M.'s amygdala was destroyed by a brain disease, leaving her completely unable to experience the emotion of fear. In more than two decades of studying S.M., researchers have never documented a single instance in which she has experienced fear as an adult. She is also unable to recognize fear in others' facial expressions.

© Masterfile

The amygdala plays a role in emotions such as fear and anger.

On the surface, you might think that living a fear-free life would be great, but a closer look at S.M. shows the dark side of fearlessness. When researchers tried to scare her with snakes and tarantulas, she was unafraid and intensely curious about them. She wanted to approach animals that many of us would avoid. She even tried to handle dangerous animals despite repeated warnings (Feinstein et al., 2011). S.M.'s lack of fear has also led her to approach dangerous situations in everyday life. In one instance, while walking alone at night, she approached a strange man even though he looked suspicious to her. The man grabbed her and held a knife to her throat—yet she felt no fear. Luckily he let her go unharmed, but without fear, S.M. will likely find herself in harm's way again and again. S.M.'s case shows us that although fear may be unpleasant, it can also be protective. The amygdala functions as part of an emotional early warning system that helps us avoid danger. Studies like these suggest that the amygdala may play an essential role in helping us size up social situations and, in turn, regulate our emotional reactions to these situations.

The **hippocampus**, a structure related to learning and memory, is the final structure of the limbic system that we will describe (Figure 2.13). Much of what we know about the function of the hippocampus comes from case studies of people who have had damage to their hippocampus. One of the first of these studies dates from the early 1950s. Scoville and Milner (1957) reported the case of H.M., a young man with severe, uncontrollable epilepsy. H.M.'s epilepsy did not respond to medication and threatened his health as well as his lifestyle. In a last-ditch effort to reduce the severity of his seizures, doctors decided to take the drastic measure of destroying part of H.M.'s brain with surgically produced lesions. The doctors cut neurons in the limbic system, hoping to check the uncontrolled electrical current that occurs when an epileptic has a seizure. The surgery performed on H.M. destroyed his hippocampus.

The surgery did reduce the intensity of H.M.'s seizures, but it also produced some unexpected and devastating side effects. Shortly after the surgery, it became apparent that H.M. had *anterograde amnesia,* the inability to store *new* memories (Chapter 7). He could hold information in consciousness the way we briefly hold a phone number in mind while we dial, and his memory for events that occurred prior to the surgery remained intact, but H.M. was unable to form new memories for concepts and events. He would forget conversations seconds after they occurred. He was unable to learn new facts. Oddly, though, H.M. could store new motor skills (for example, he could learn new dance steps), but later he would have no recollection of having ever executed the new skill. Imagine waking up one day and knowing how to do a dance that you don't remember ever having danced!

Since H.M.'s surgery, a large number of subsequent case studies and controlled animal experiments have supported the hypothesis that the hippocampus is important to learning and memory, including tasks that relate to *episodic memory* (Chapter 7), imagining the future, and spatial navigation (Maguire & Mullally, 2013). In one important study, researchers used brain-imaging techniques to compare the hippocampi of London taxi drivers with those of London bus drivers. They found that certain areas of the hippocampus were enlarged in the taxi drivers but not in the bus drivers. Furthermore, the number of years a participant had been driving a taxi was positively correlated with the size of certain hippocampal areas. These data suggest that portions of the hippocampus enlarged as the taxi drivers memorized complicated maps of the entire city. For bus drivers, who only had to memorize a small number of bus routes, length of time driving did not correlate with the size of their hippocampus (Maguire, Woollett, & Spiers, 2006).

Researchers then compared the hippocampi of medical doctors, who also have to learn vast amounts of information, with those of people of similar intelligence who were not doctors. They found no difference in the size of the hippocampus between these two groups. It appears that having a larger hippocampus is only associated with performing tasks that specifically involve spatial memory (Woollet, Glensman, & Maguire, 2008).

These studies suggest that the hippocampus exhibits **neuroplasticity**—the brain's ability to rewire its structures as a result of experience (see also Woollett & Maguire, 2012). Keep in mind, however, that the research you just read is merely correlational in nature. For example, it is impossible to tell if the differences

© Image Source/Alamy

The amygdala plays a role in the experience of fear. Without a functioning amygdala, S.M. was unable to experience fear. Fear acts as an early warning system that steers us clear of danger. Without it, S.M. repeatedly finds herself in harm's way.

hippocampus [HIP-po-CAM-puss] a part of the brain that plays a role in the transfer of information from short- to long-term memory

neuroplasticity [NUR-o-plas-TI-city] the nervous system's ability to rewire its structures as a result of experience

© Peter Turnley/Corbis

Researchers (Maguire, Woolett, & Spiers, 2006) found that some regions of the hippocampus in London taxi drivers were larger than the same hippocampal regions in the brains of London bus drivers. These results suggest that certain regions of the hippocampus may enlarge as a cab driver uses his or her brain to memorize complicated street maps of an entire city such as London.

seen in the taxi drivers' hippocampi were directly caused by memorizing the maps or by some other activity. Perhaps taxi drivers spend more time talking to passengers than bus drivers and this influenced their hippocampal development. This is just one of the many possibilities that need further investigation.

A similar debate concerns the relationship between the amount of stress we experience and hippocampal size. Studies have shown that certain hormones released during times of stress can damage hippocampal tissue (Hawley & Leasure, 2012; Tata & Anderson, 2009) and that people who have experienced prolonged stress (such as combat or childhood abuse) have smaller hippocampi (Sapolsky, 2002). At first glance, the conclusion looked simple—stress shrinks the hippocampus. However, it's not that simple. One study found that combat veterans with *posttraumatic stress disorder* (Chapter 13) had smaller hippocampi—but so did their identical twin brothers who had never faced combat. This finding suggests that having a smaller hippocampus to begin with may predispose one to developing posttraumatic stress (Bonne et al., 2008; Childress et al., 2013; Gilbertson et al., 2002). Further studies are being conducted to try to isolate exactly how stress affects the structure of the hippocampus and how the hippocampus affects our reaction to stress (e.g., Weidenmayer et al., 2006). In one recent study, researchers found that people who practice meditation tend to have larger hippocampi than those of nonmeditators. Because meditation is effective in relieving stress and having a small hippocampus is associated with posttraumatic stress disorder, this study brings up the question of whether meditation may protect us via its effects on the hippocampus (Luders et al., 2013). Clearly, more research is needed to answer this question.

The broader question of whether the brain exhibits neuroplasticity also needs more study. Is there any direct evidence to support the notion of neuroplasticity in humans? There is some. Recently, researchers used brain-scanning technologies to look at activity in the brain as participants learned new words. They found that as the participants learned the words, their brain began to react in a fashion that was similar to its reaction to already known words. The researchers interpreted this finding as evidence of neuroplasticity in action—the brain forming new circuits in response to being exposed to new words (Shtyrov, Nikulin, & Pulvermüller, 2010). The study of how brain structures, including the hippocampus, may be affected by experience is likely to be an exciting area of study for some time to come.

THE THALAMUS AND HYPOTHALAMUS

The *thalamus* and the *hypothalamus* of the forebrain may have similar names, but they have distinctly different functions. The **thalamus** plays a role in the attention we pay to things that stimulate our senses (Michael et al., 2001; Saalmann & Kastner, 2009), and it functions as a relay station for information coming from our senses to the brain (see Chapter 3).

The thalamus also plays a role in keeping specific areas of the cortex activated during rapid eye movement or REM sleep, when much of our dreaming occurs (Miyauchi et al., 2009; Murillo-Rodriguez et al., 2009). The thalamus has also been shown to affect slow wave activity during non-REM sleep (Connelly & Errington, 2012). We will discuss the process of sleep more fully in Chapter 4.

Nestled below the thalamus is the **hypothalamus** (the prefix *hypo* means "below"). The hypothalamus maintains **homeostasis** in the body, a state of internal equilibrium across a variety of bodily systems (see Makris et al., 2013). In maintaining homeostasis, the hypothalamus is responsible for monitoring and regulating body temperature, thirst, hunger, sleep, autonomic nervous system functioning, and some sexual and reproductive functions, and can change

thalamus [THAL-uh-muss] a part of the forebrain that functions as a sensory relay station

hypothalamus [high-poe-THAL-uh-muss] a part of the forebrain that plays a role in maintaining homeostasis in the body, involving sleep, body temperature, sexual behavior, thirst, and hunger; also the point where the nervous system intersects with the endocrine system

homeostasis [hoe-mee-oh-STAY-suss] an internal state of equilibrium in the body hormone levels in the bloodstream. To maintain homeostasis, the hypothalamus must ultimately motivate us to engage in certain behaviors. For example, when our body needs fuel, the hypothalamus motivates us with hunger. When we need sleep, the hypothalamus makes us sleepy, and we are motivated to go to bed. No other part of the nervous system plays a more central role in physiological motivation, a topic we will return to in Chapters 4 and 5. Without the hypothalamus, we would not know when to engage in the behaviors that keep our bodily systems in balance.

2.4.4 • The Cortex

The most noticeable structure on the external surface of the brain is the *cerebral cortex*, or simply the cortex. The cortex is the thin (approximately 2 millimeters thick), wrinkled layer of tissue that covers the outside of the cerebral hemispheres, or the two sides of the brain (•FIGURE 2.14). The cortex is arguably the most sophisticated part of the brain and is responsible for the highest levels of processing: cognition and mental processes such as planning, decision making, perception, and language. It is the cortex that gives us our humanness. It is no coincidence that the human cortex is the most developed of all known creatures and that humans also have the most highly developed cognitive skills of all known species. Compare the photographs in Figure 2.14. Notice that the human cortex is very folded and convoluted, whereas the cat's cortex is much less so. The folds allow for more cortical surface area within the confines of the skull cavity. A cat has proportionately less cortical area than a human does, and this smaller cortex translates into fewer cognitive abilities for the cat.

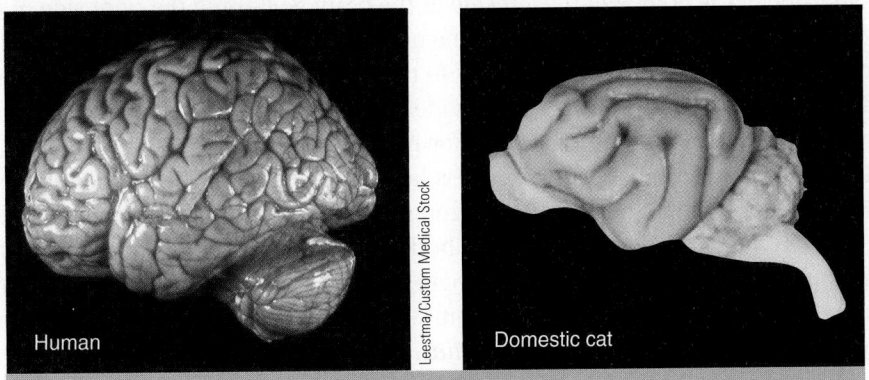

Leestma/Custom Medical Stock

Reproduced with permission from an image(s) by Wally Welker (University of Wisconsin-Madison) at http://www.brainmuseum.org, supported by the US National Science Foundation Division of Integrative Biology and Neuroscience.

FIGURE 2.14

Cortex of a Human Brain and a Cat Brain

Note how much more convoluted, or folded, the human brain is compared to the cat brain. Many of the higher-order processes that humans engage in, such as language and thinking, are processed in the cortex.

THE LOBES OF THE CORTEX AND LATERALIZATION IN THE BRAIN

The human cortex is divided into four distinct physical regions called *lobes*. These are the **frontal lobe**, the **parietal lobe**, the **occipital lobe**, and the **temporal lobe** (•FIGURE 2.15a). The lobes of the cortex are structurally symmetrical in the two hemispheres of the brain, meaning that the brain has both right and left frontal lobes, right and left temporal lobes, and so on. However, the functions of the right and left lobes are often somewhat different. Functions are lateralized, or found in only one hemisphere of the brain, for a couple of reasons. First, the lobes of the brain

frontal lobe the cortical area directly behind the forehead that plays a role in thinking, planning, decision making, language, and motor movement

parietal [puh-RYE-it-ull] lobe the cortical area on the top sides of the brain that play a role in touch and certain cognitive processes

occipital [ox-SIP-it-ull] lobe the cortical area at the back of the brain that plays a role in visual processing

temporal [TEM-por-ull] lobe the cortical area directly below the ears that play a role in auditory processing and language

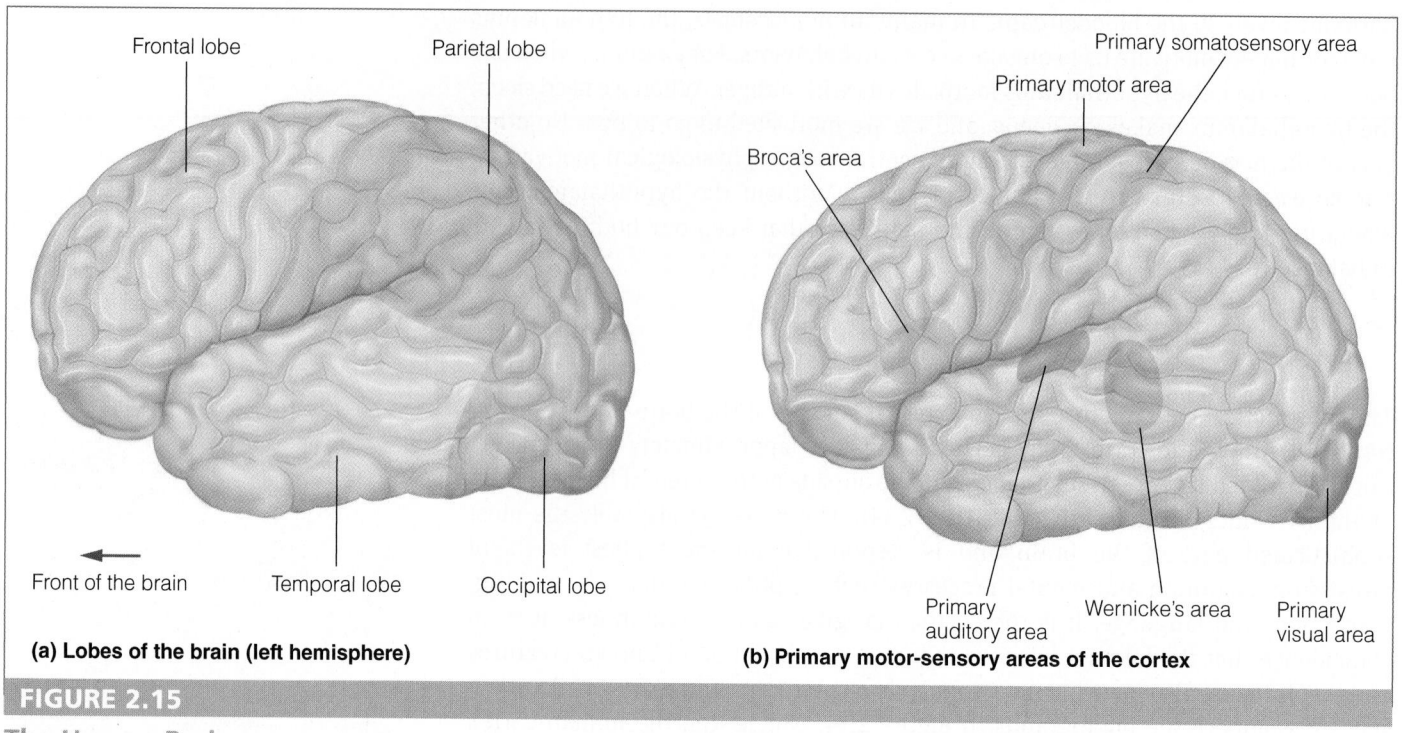

FIGURE 2.15

The Human Brain

(a) The lobes of the brain. (b) The language centers of the brain are generally found in the left hemisphere. Wernicke's area in the left temporal lobe allows us to comprehend speech. Broca's area in the left frontal lobe allows us to produce speech.

tend to be wired in a *contralateral* fashion, with the right side of the brain governing the left side of the body and the left side of the brain governing the right side of the body. Although contralateral wiring is the norm in the brain, some neural pathways carry information to and from the body to the same hemisphere of the brain.

Lateralization in the brain is also evident in that the right and left hemispheres process somewhat different types of information (Gotts et al., 2013; Stephan et al., 2003). For example, most people process language largely in the left hemisphere. Although some people have major language centers in the right hemisphere, and some have major language centers in both hemispheres, for the average person language is located in the left hemisphere. As a result, when people incur major damage to the left hemisphere (as from a stroke), their ability to use language often suffers, a condition known as *aphasia*.

Two examples illustrate this hemispheric specialization of language. When damage is severe in **Broca's area** in the left frontal lobe (Figure 2.15b), people are unable to produce understandable speech, a condition known as **Broca's aphasia** (Geschwind, 1975; Geschwind & Levitsky, 1968). When people have damage to **Wernicke's area** in the left temporal lobe (Figure 2.15b), the resulting **Wernicke's aphasia** leaves them unable to understand spoken language. When the damage is confined to the right side of the brain, people usually remain able to understand and produce speech, but they have some difficulty processing certain types of spatial information such as visually searching for a target stimulus on a computer screen (Rastelli et al., 2013).

Differences in the linguistic and spatial processing of the left and right hemispheres once led scientists to conclude broadly that the hemispheres of the brain processed very different categories of information: they surmised that the left hemisphere processed verbal information and the right hemisphere processed spatial information. However, more recent studies have suggested that the left

Broca's [BRO-kuz] area a region in the left frontal lobe that plays a role in the production of speech

Broca's aphasia [ah-FAYZ-yah] a condition resulting from damage to Broca's area of the brain that leaves the person unable to produce speech.

Wernicke's [WURR-neh-kees] area a region of the left temporal lobe that plays a role in the comprehension of speech

Wernicke's aphasia [ah-FAYZ-yah] a condition resulting from damage to Wernicke's area of the brain that leaves a person unable to comprehend speech and right hemispheres of the brain may not divide up their functions as neatly as once thought. For example, the right hemisphere also seems to process some of the more subtle aspects of language, such as the processing of novel metaphors (Mashal & Faust, 2008). Newer research also indicates that both hemispheres process different aspects of spatial information (Amorapanth, Widick, & Chatterjee, 2009; Suegami & Laeng, 2013). To sum up, we are coming to understand that the two hemispheres accomplish tasks, such as processing language and spatial information, by working together and performing complementary functions.

VARIATIONS: ARE WOMEN'S BRAINS LESS LATERALIZED THAN MEN'S ARE?

Whether the hemispheres process different information or merely different aspects of the same information, they must have some means of coordinating the information they process. The **corpus callosum** is a dense band of neurons that sits just below the cortex along the midline of the brain (Banich & Heller, 1998; Figure 2.11). This band physically connects the right and left cortical areas and ensures that each hemisphere "knows" what the other hemisphere is doing. The corpus callosum passes information back and forth between the right and left hemispheres, allowing us to integrate these somewhat independent functions. Without the corpus callosum, the right and left cortices would function independently and in ignorance of each other.

corpus callosum [COR-puss cal-OH-sum] a thick band of neurons that connects the right and left hemispheres of the brain

split brain a brain with its corpus callosum severed; sometimes done to control the effects of epilepsy in people who do not respond to other therapies

Early studies suggested that certain areas of the corpus callosum may be larger in women than in men (DeLacoste-Utamsing & Holloway, 1982; Halloway et al., 2007). Having a larger corpus callosum may allow for more connections between hemispheres, resulting in a brain that is less lateralized and more integrated (Reite et al., 1995). This interpretation is supported by the finding that the pattern of electrical activity in male brains tends to be more confined to one hemisphere than it is in female brains (Koles, Lind, & Flor-Henry, 2010; Tomasi & Volkow, 2012).

Yet the idea that women have larger corpora callosa (the plural of *corpus callosum*) is controversial. Some researchers suggest that the differences seen may have less to do with gender than with brain size; that is, people with smaller brains may have larger corpora callosa, regardless of gender (Jäncke & Steinmetz, 2003). Furthermore, the implications of callosal size on brain lateralization are still being debated (for review, see Nowicka & Tacikowski, 2011). For example, some have argued that increased communication between hemispheres, such as would be facilitated by a larger corpus callosum, may actually increase lateralization in the brain (Kimura, 2000). Although a clear picture of sex differences in the corpus callosum and brain lateralization has not yet emerged, psychologists do have a much clearer understanding of what happens to the brain when the corpus callosum fails to do its job.

THE SPLIT BRAIN

Physicians have at times willfully disrupted communication between the hemispheres by destroying the corpus callosum in the human brain. Such a drastic measure is taken in cases where people have severe, uncontrollable epilepsy. In severe epilepsy, abnormal electrical activity can build up in one hemisphere and spread across the corpus callosum to engulf the opposite hemisphere. This short-circuiting of both hemispheres produces a severe, life-threatening seizure called a *grand mal seizure*. If drugs cannot control the seizures, surgery may be performed to cut the corpus callosum and thereby contain the short-circuiting to one hemisphere only. The person still has seizures, but they are not as severe. People who have had this surgery are referred to as having **split brains** because their hemispheres are no longer connected by neural pathways. People with split brains provide scientists with an opportunity to study the lateralization of the brain.

Working with split-brain people, researchers have a chance to study the functioning of each hemisphere independent of the other. For example, split-brain research helped researchers conclude that the left hemisphere enables us to produce speech. Researcher Michael Gazzaniga (1967) briefly flashed pictures of familiar objects to the right and left visual fields of split-brain people and asked them to identify the objects (• FIGURE 2.16). When an object is briefly presented to the right peripheral field of vision, the resulting visual information is sent directly to the left hemisphere of the brain. Because Broca's area is in the left hemisphere for most people, Gazzaniga found that the average split-brain person could verbally identify the object.

But what about an object presented to the person's left peripheral field of vision? When an object is briefly shown on the far left side, the resulting visual information is sent directly to the right hemisphere of the brain. Recall that most people do not have a Broca's area in their right hemisphere. In a normal brain, the information travels from the right hemisphere across the corpus callosum to the language centers in the left hemisphere. However, in split-brain individuals, this cannot happen. Without the corpus callosum, Gazzaniga's split-brains could not transmit the knowledge of what they were seeing to the language centers in their left hemisphere. The right brain knew what the objects were, but it could not inform the "speaking" left brain! Predictably, the split-brain people were unable to name the objects they saw in their left visual fields. Interestingly, in this situation, split-brain people were able to point to the objects in a drawing—provided they used their left hand (which is controlled by the right brain). Split-brain research has helped us begin to sort out the relative contributions that the right and left hemispheres make to everyday cognitive processes.

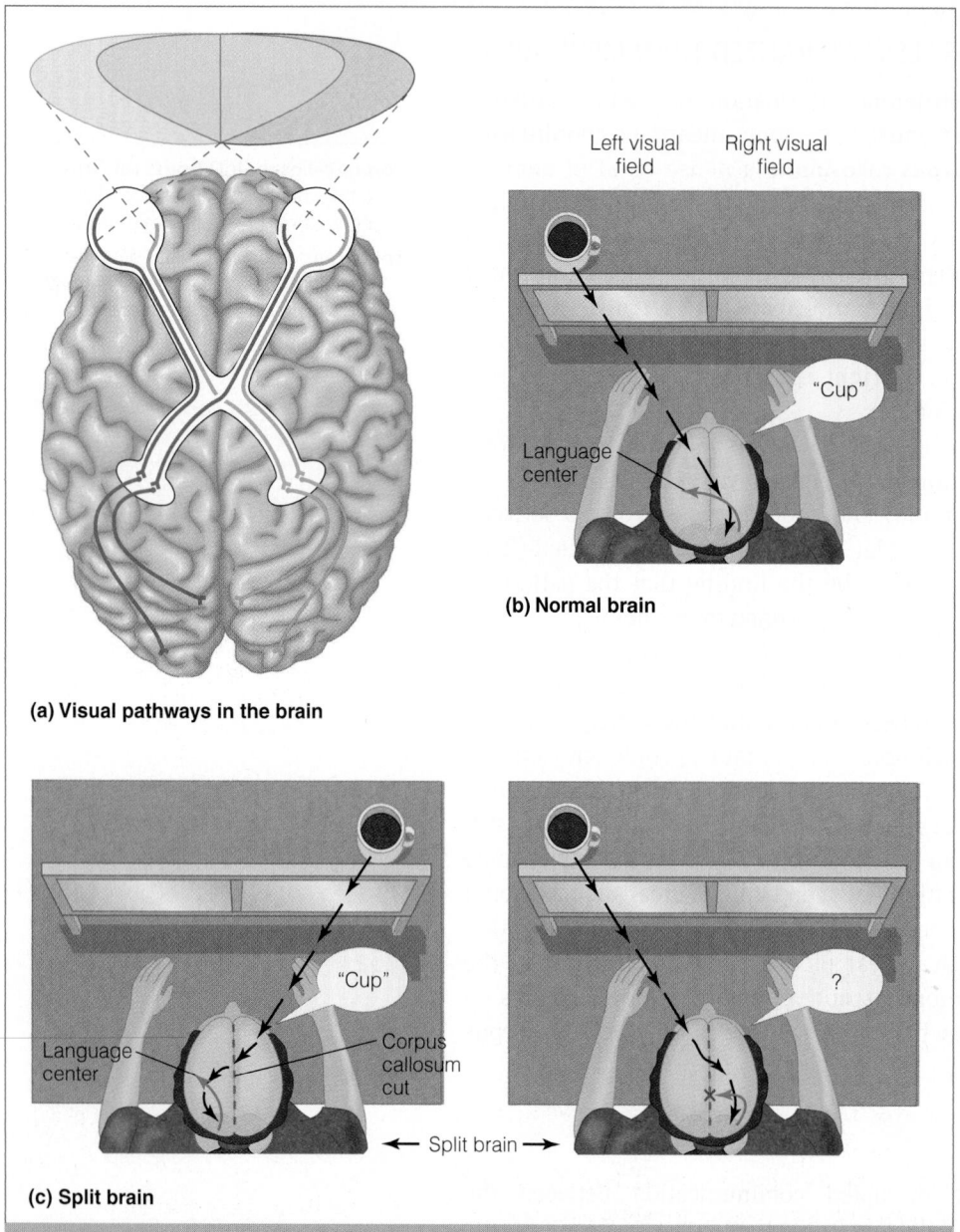

FIGURE 2.16

A Typical Split-Brain Study

Visual pathways in the intact brain (a) send information to both hemispheres. As a result, when a person with an intact brain sees an object in either his right or left visual field, he will be able to name it (b). However, this is not true for people with split brains. In a typical split-brain experiment (c), an image is flashed to a split-brain person's right or left visual field, and he is asked to identify the object in the image. When the image is flashed to the person's right visual field, he is able to name it; but when it is flashed to his left visual field, he is unable to name it because the information cannot travel to the language centers in the left hemisphere.

2.4.5 • The Specialization of Function in the Lobes of the Cortex

Just as there is specialization in the hemispheres of the brain, there is also specialization within the different lobes of the brain. About 25% of the total surface area of the cortex is dedicated to motor and sensory functions such as vision, hearing, movement, and tactile sensation. Specific motor-sensory areas can be found in all the lobes of the brain (frontal, parietal, occipital, and temporal). The remaining 75% of the cortical area is thought to be devoted to higher-order processes that involve the integration of information, such as thinking, planning, decision making, and language. Collectively, this 75% is referred to as the **association cortex** because these areas are presumed to involve the association of information from the motor-sensory areas of the cortex.

We do not yet have a complete understanding of the functions of specific areas of the association cortex. Often, damage to the association areas produces general changes and deficits in behavior. However, stimulation of specific areas of the association cortex does not usually lead to specific, predictable physical reactions. It is thought that the association cortex plays a role in general cognition, such as planning and decision making. Where applicable, we will discuss the known functions of the association areas for the specific lobes of the brain.

association cortex areas of the cortex involved in the association or integration of information from the motor-sensory areas of the cortex

motor cortex a strip of cortex at the back of the frontal lobe that governs the execution of motor movement in the body

THE FRONTAL LOBE

The frontal lobe is the area of the cortex that lies closest to the forehead (refer back to Figure 2.15a, p. 68). Much of the frontal lobe is association cortex. We know more about the association areas of the frontal lobe than any other lobes. Broca's area in the association area of the left frontal lobe is, as previously mentioned, involved in the production of speech. It also appears that the frontal lobe association areas play a role in cognitive processes such as attention, problem solving, judgment, the planning and executing of behavior, and certain aspects of personality.

These cognitive functions are illustrated in a famous case study from the history of psychology. In 1848, a railway worker named Phineas Gage suffered severe trauma to his prefrontal cortex (the association area in the very front part of the frontal lobe) when a metal rod was shot through his head in an explosion. The rod entered his left cheek and shot out of the top of his head. Although he survived his injuries, they resulted in some dramatic personality changes. Whereas Gage had been a calm, responsible man prior to his injuries, he became impulsive, emotionally volatile, and irresponsible afterward. Because the prefrontal cortex is important for the regulation of emotion (Davidson, Putman, & Larson, 2000), the damage to Gage's brain robbed him of his ability to control his emotions, make good judgments, and execute planned behaviors (Damasio et al., 1994). Phineas Gage was no longer himself, but he could still move and speak because the motor-sensory areas of his frontal lobe were undamaged.

At the back of the frontal lobe (behind the prefrontal cortex) lies the **motor cortex** or *primary motor area,* a narrow band of cortex that allows us to execute motor movements. The motor cortex on the right side of the brain affects movement on the left side of the body, and vice versa. Additionally, specific points along the motor cortex correspond to particular points on the body. ●FIGURE 2.17a is a rendering of a *homunculus,* a humorous mapping of body parts onto their appropriate motor cortical points. If stimulation were applied to these points along the motor cortex, the result would be movement of the corresponding body part.

As you can see, the frontal lobe plays several roles in our daily functioning. Curiously, the frontal lobe is also an area of the brain that experiences changes across adulthood. We will discuss changes in the aging brain later in this section.

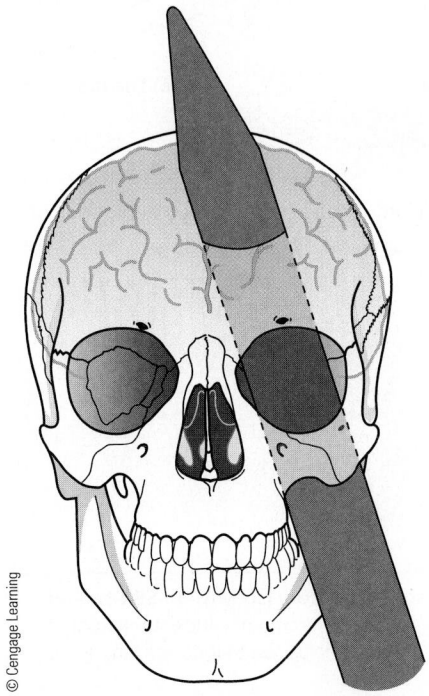

© Cengage Learning

Phineas Gage was a responsible, mild-mannered worker on a railway construction crew until a rod like this one was shot through his head in a freak accident. Gage survived, but he was never the same. The damage to Gage's prefrontal cortex coincided with dramatic changes in his personality. The once calm Gage became emotionally volatile and difficult. As a result, he was unable to perform his former job with the railroad.

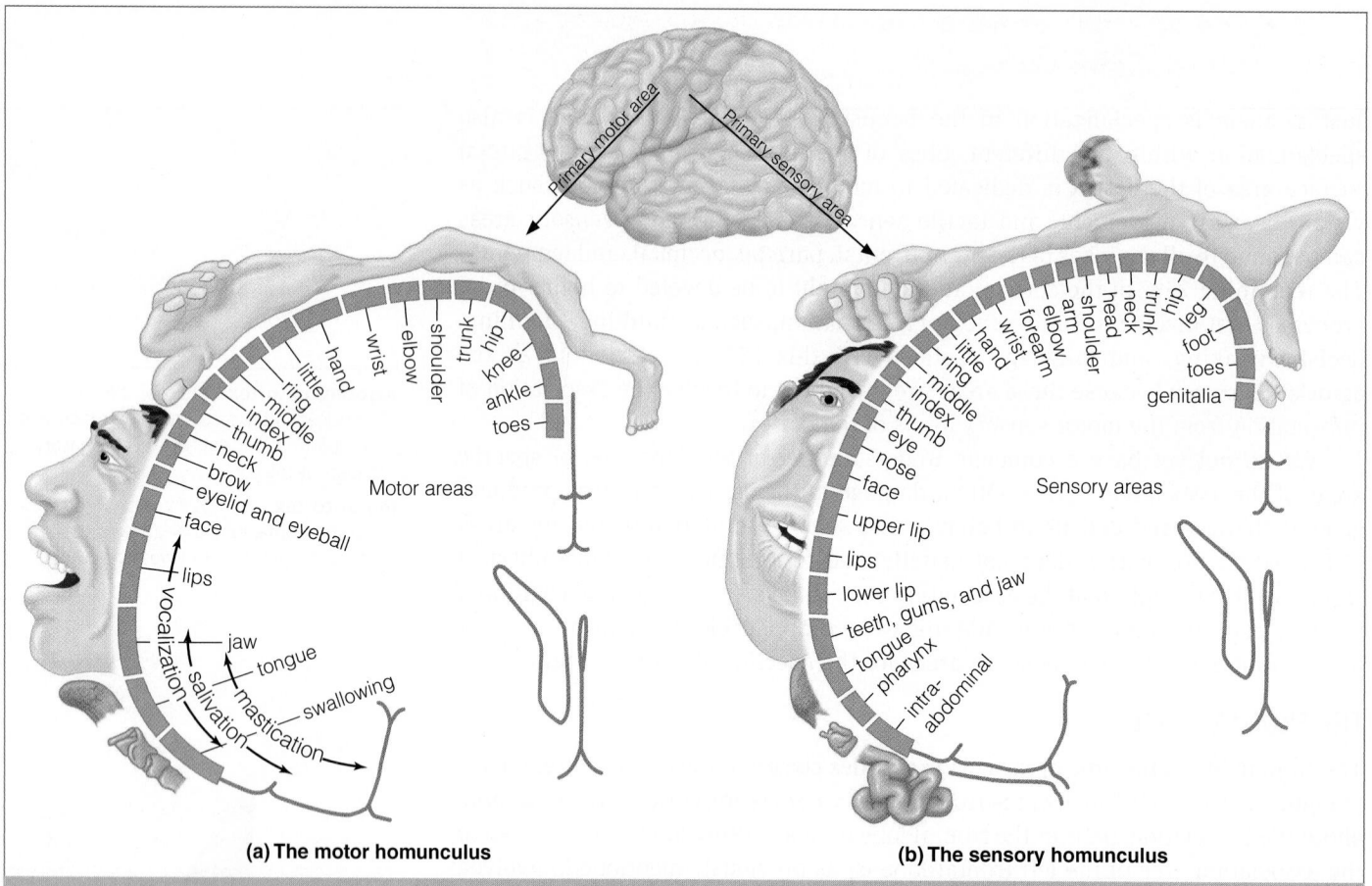

FIGURE 2.17

Motor and Sensory Homunculi

Homunculi are humorous depictions of the localization of function on the cortex.

From Penfield and Rasmussen, *The Cerebral Cortex of Man,* © 1950 Macmillan Library Reference. Renewed 1978 by Theodore Rasmussen. Reprinted by permission of The Gale Group.

THE PARIETAL LOBE

As with the frontal lobe, much of the parietal lobe is association cortex, but we know much less about the specific functions of these association areas. We do know that the motor-sensory areas of the parietal lobe play a role in sensation. A thin strip of the parietal lobe affects our sense of touch, pressure, and pain. This strip, called the **somatosensory cortex**, or *primary somatosensory area*, lies directly behind the motor cortex, along the leading edge of the parietal lobe (Figure 2.15b). The somatosensory cortex is wired much like the motor cortex, and specific points along the somatosensory cortex correspond to particular points on the body (Figure 2.17b). Damage to the somatosensory cortex often results in numbness of the corresponding body part.

somatosensory [so-MAT-oh-SEN-sor-ee] cortex a strip of cortex at the front of the parietal lobe that governs the sense of touch

visual cortex a region of cortex found at the back of the occipital lobe that processes visual information in the brain

THE OCCIPITAL LOBE

The occipital lobe of the brain is located at the very back of the skull, above the cerebellum. Much of the occipital lobe is dedicated to processing visual information. The **visual cortex**, or *primary visual area* (Figure 2.15b, p. 68), of the occipital lobe is composed of layers of tissue that contain long axonal fibers. An action potential is stimulated in specialized cells of the visual cortex when our eyes receive specific types of visual stimuli from the outside world. For instance, some cells begin to fire only when we see lines, and other cells fire only when we see circular shapes. Like a computer, our brain integrates all the incoming neural impulses from these specialized cells in the visual cortex to enable us to perceive what we are viewing. Without the operation of the visual cortex, our brain could not make sense of what our eyes see and we would be functionally blind.

THE TEMPORAL LOBE

The temporal lobe is in front of the occipital lobe and just below the parietal and frontal lobes—roughly behind our ears inside the skull. Not surprisingly, one of the major functions of the temporal lobe is the processing of auditory information, or hearing. The temporal lobe area devoted to hearing is the **auditory cortex**, or *primary auditory area,* located on the upper edge of the temporal lobe (Figure 2.15b, p. 68). In addition to the auditory cortex, the left temporal lobe of most people contains Wernicke's area. As we've already seen, Wernicke's area is responsible for the comprehension of speech. Persons who have major damage to Wernicke's area often cannot understand the meaning of spoken words. They hear the words, but they can't make sense of them.

auditory cortex a region of cortex found in the temporal lobe that governs the processing of auditory information in the brain

VARIATIONS: THE AGING BRAIN

As you just learned, the cortex of the brain is where some of our most important mental functioning takes place. Our ability to think, remember, and make sense of the world is due, in large part, to the cortex. However, many studies suggest that as we age, we tend to experience specific declines in our ability to do some mental or cognitive tasks (see Chapters 7, 8, and 9). For example, when compared to young adults, older adults tend to score lower on tests of *fluid intelligence,* the ability to process information rapidly and efficiently (see, e.g., Yu et al., 2009). Some capacities, such as the ability to learn new faces, can peak as early as our 30s (Germine, Duchaine, & Nakayama, 2010). But why do we perform more poorly as we age? What's happening in our brains?

A number of changes occur in our brains as we age. For example, certain brain structures shrink (Raz & Kennedy, 2009), lesions develop (Bohnen et al. 2009), and changes in neuronal functioning occur (Andrews-Hanna et al., 2007). Blood flow in the brain also changes as we age. Recently, researchers compared the brains of healthy people aged 20–80 and found that blood flow to the brain diminished about 1.38% per decade. The amount of oxygen carried in the blood also declined by about 1.4% per decade. Interestingly, some areas of the brain experienced more loss of blood flow than others did. Especially hard hit were the right frontal regions of the brain, including the prefrontal cortex (Lu et al., 2010). Unfortunately, the researchers also found that although the aging brain receives less blood flow and less oxygen, its need for oxygen actually increases, presenting something of a double whammy for the brain (Lu et al., 2010).

Given that blood flow to the brain is fed by the same circulatory system that feeds the body, it is reasonable to expect that keeping our cardiovascular system in good shape may also help our brain. Therefore, regular exercise may be one of our most powerful tools for protecting

Exercise helps to maintain blood flow in the brain, and it may be one way to help us retain as many of our cognitive abilities as we can in the future.

© moodboard/Alamy

Psychology Applies to Your World:

Technologies for Studying the Brain

Recently, a friend of ours hit her head in a car accident. As a precaution, doctors ordered an MRI of her brain. An MRI, or magnetic resonance imaging scan, allows doctors to see a detailed picture of the brain. If our friend had serious damage from the injury, it would have shown up on the MRI. Luckily, the MRI showed no serious damage from the accident, but it did produce another surprise: It showed that despite having no troubling symptoms, she had a very large tumor growing in her brain. Without the MRI, the tumor would have gone undiagnosed until she began having serious symptoms; at that point, it might have been too late to do much

Common Techniques for Studying the Brain and Examples of Their Usage

TECHNIQUE FOR STUDYING THE BRAIN	DESCRIPTION	ASPECT MEASURED
Computerized Axial Tomography (CAT Scan) 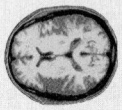 © Custom Medical Stock Photo	Multiple X-ray beams are passed through the brain from different angles. A computer then analyzes the X-rays that exit the head and uses this information to build a very detailed picture of the brain and its structures. CAT scans can be used to diagnose tumors, strokes, certain diseases, and the structural features of the brain.	Brain structures
Magnetic Resonance Imaging (MRI) 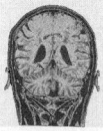 S&I/Science Source	A magnetic field is used to excite the atoms in the body, and the energy emitted by these atoms is used to construct a highly detailed computer-generated picture of the brain's structure.	Brain structures
Positron Emission Tomography (PET Scan) 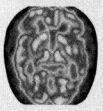 Tim Beddow/ Science Source	Radioactive glucose (the brain's fuel source) is injected into the bloodstream. The computer measures which areas of the brain are consuming the most glucose, meaning that they are most active.	Areas of activity in the brain

the aging brain (Anderson, Greenwood, & McCloskey, 2010) and maintaining our cognitive abilities (Jedrziewski et al., 2010). So, if you haven't already done so, perhaps now would be a good time to develop an exercise program. Your physician can evaluate your situation and suggest an appropriate level of activity for your age and physical condition.

Now that you have learned about the structure and function of the brain, we hope that you are suitably impressed. In this chapter we have merely begun to explore the functioning of our nervous system, and scientists are far from a complete understanding of this amazing system. As research continues, scientists for her. We are happy to report that shortly after discovering the tumor doctors were able to quickly remove most of it, and she is now recovering nicely.

Both doctors and psychologists use technologies like MRIs for studying the brain. Some of these procedures allow researchers to examine only the structure of the brain, whereas others indicate which areas of the brain are most active at a given moment. Because these techniques can be used on living brain tissue, they can give researchers important information about the specific behavioral functions that are governed by particular areas of the brain. The table below summarizes some of the most useful technologies available for helping us to better understand the inner workings of the brain: CAT scans, MRIs, PET scans, fMRIs, EEGs, and brain stimulation.

TECHNIQUE FOR STUDYING THE BRAIN	DESCRIPTION	ASPECT MEASURED
Functional MRI (fMRI) 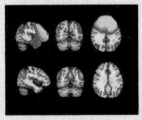 James King-Holmes/Henry Luckhoo/Science Source	Uses MRI technology to track which neurons in the brain are most active at a given moment by examining the energy released by hemoglobin molecules in the bloodstream.	Areas of activity in the brain; brain structures
Electroencephalography (EEG)  CC Studio/Science Source	Measures changes in electrical voltage at points along the scalp and yields information on gross patterns of brain activation.	Patterns of electrical activity in the lobes of the brain
Brain Stimulation  NASA/Hulton Archive/Getty Images	By stimulating specific areas of the brain, researchers can see what effect this stimulation has on behavior. Doctors also use this technology to treat conditions such as depression. By implanting brain "pacemakers," doctors can stimulate areas of the brain that are not functioning properly.	Cognitive and behavioral reactions to stimulation of brain locations

learn more about how our physiology influences our thoughts and behaviors. Luckily, researchers have a great deal of modern technology to help them learn about the brain (see Psychology Applies to Your World). These technologies have helped doctors and psychologists gain a better understanding of how the brain works to regulate and control our mental processes and behavior. Through the use of these technologies, we have learned that the human nervous system is an extremely impressive and important network. However, the nervous system is not the only communication system within the body. We turn now to the other major communication network, the *endocrine system*.

Quiz Yourself

2.4

1. **Damage to which of the following brain structures would be most likely to cause locked-in syndrome, such as seen in the case of Jean-Dominique Bauby?**
   a. Frontal lobe
   b. Amygdala
   c. Pons
   d. Hippocampus
2. **Billy had a stroke on the left side of his brain. Most of his left frontal lobe was destroyed. What symptoms would you most expect to see in Billy as a result of this damage?**
   a. Paralysis on the right side of his body and an inability to speak
   b. Paralysis on the right side of his body and an inability to understand speech
   c. Paralysis of his left leg, partial deafness, and stuttering
   d. Paralysis on the left side of his body and an inability to understand speech
3. **Juanita experienced a brain injury that left her with an inability to store new memories for events and concepts. Which part of Juanita's brain was most likely damaged?**
   a. Hippocampus
   b. Hypothalamus
   c. Thalamus
   d. Midbrain

Answers 1. c; 2. a; 3. a

2.5 The Endocrine System: Hormones and Behavior

We have seen that because of its electrochemical nature, the nervous system is especially good at quickly conveying information within the body. It is the speed of the nervous system that enables us to react quickly to changes in our environment. Messages are sent, decisions are made, and actions are taken—all accomplished with the speed of firing action potentials. At times, however, we require communication within the body that is slower and produces more long-lasting effects. In these circumstances, the **endocrine system** is called into action.

The endocrine system is a chemical system of communication that relies on the action of specialized organs called **endocrine glands** that are located throughout the body (• FIGURE 2.18). When stimulated, endocrine glands release chemicals called **hormones** into the bloodstream. These hormones circulate through the bloodstream until they reach other organs in the body. Our internal organs are equipped with special receptor sites to accept these hormones.

The endocrine system is considerably slower than the nervous system in relaying messages because it relies on blood circulating through the veins and arteries of the cardiovascular system to transport hormones throughout the body. The stimulation created by hormones, however, tends to last longer than the stimulation caused by action potentials at the synapse. Some of the bodily processes that are heavily influenced by hormonal activity include sexual activity, eating, sleeping, general physiological arousal, and growth.

Communication between the nervous and endocrine systems takes place through the hypothalamus and its connection with the **pituitary gland**. The

endocrine [EN-doe-crin] system a chemical system of communication in the body that uses chemical messengers, called hormones, to affect organ function and behavior

endocrine [EN-doe-crin] glands the organs of the endocrine system that produce and release hormones into the blood

hormones the chemical messengers of the endocrine system

pituitary [peh-TOO-uh-tare-ee] gland the master gland of the endocrine system that controls the action of all other glands in the body pituitary gland, situated in the vicinity of the limbic system under the hypothalamus (Figure 2.18), is responsible for regulating hormone release in all the other endocrine glands. When the endocrine system is called into action, the hypothalamus sends a signal to the pituitary gland. The pituitary gland then releases hormones that travel through the bloodstream to the other endocrine glands, stimulating them to release the hormones they produce into the bloodstream. These hormones circulate to their target organs, where they bring about specific changes in the functioning of these organs.

Our bodies are equipped with a great number of peripheral endocrine glands (see Figure 2.18). Probably the best known endocrine glands are the **gonads**, which are necessary for sexuality and reproduction. *Ovaries* are the female gonads, located in the abdominal cavity. Ovaries are directly responsible for the production of female eggs (ova) and the release of female sex hormones, or **estrogens**. *Testes* are the male gonads, located in the testicles. Testes produce male sex cells (sperm) and male hormones, or **androgens**.

The *adrenal glands* sit just above the kidneys in both males and females and are important for regulating arousal and sexual behavior, among many things. When the sympathetic nervous system becomes active during times of stress, the inside of the adrenal glands, or the **adrenal medulla**, releases norepinephrine and epinephrine (also known as *adrenaline*) into the body's bloodstream, where they function as hormones. The sudden flooding of the bloodstream with these hormones causes the familiar sympathetic reactions of increased heart rate, blood pressure, and respiration.

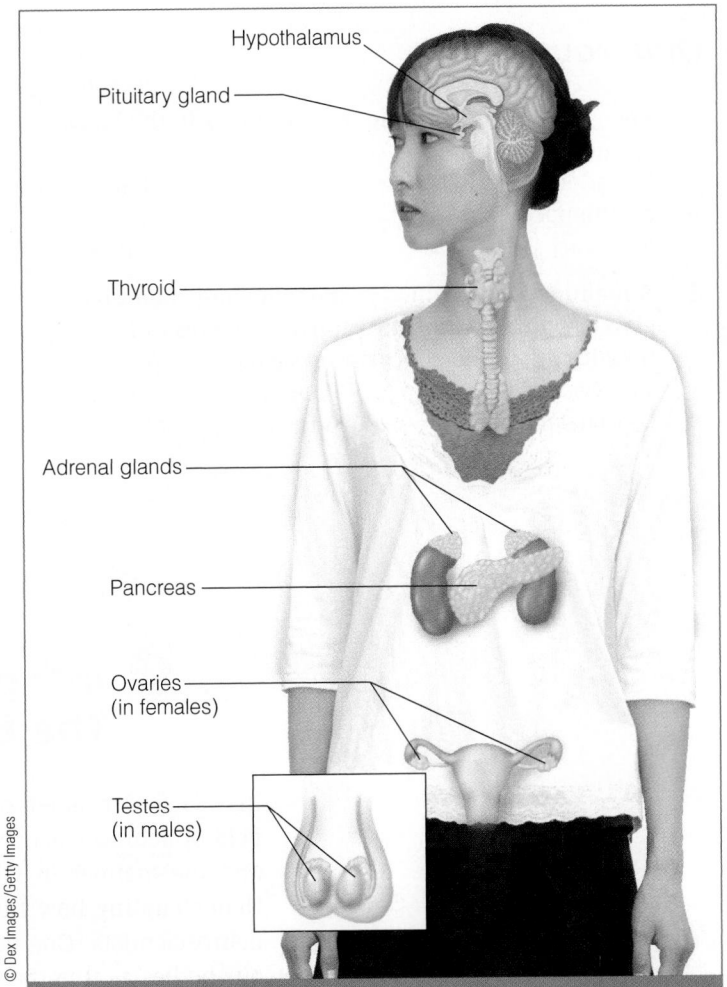

© Dex Images/Getty Images

FIGURE 2.18

Major Endocrine Glands of the Body

The glands of the endocrine system make and release hormones into the bloodstream.

The outside of the adrenal glands, or the **adrenal cortex**, produces *adrenal androgens*, which are male sex hormones found in both males and females. These androgens control many aspects of our sexual characteristics and basic physiological functioning. The adrenal cortex also interacts with the immune system to help protect us from infection and disease.

Other important endocrine glands include the *thyroid,* which regulates how energy is used in our bodies; the *pancreas,* which regulates blood sugar levels in the body (see also Chapter 5); and the *pineal gland,* located in the brain, which may play a role in sexual maturation.

The nervous and endocrine systems are nothing short of amazing in their intricate structure and function. Without these systems we would not be able to control our bodies, think, feel, and interact with our environment. After studying this chapter, we hope you are impressed with the wonder of your own biology. In the next chapter, we will explore the areas of sensation and perception, the study of how we sense and perceive information from the outside world.

gonads [go-NADS] endocrine glands that directly affect sexual reproduction by producing sperm (testes) or eggs (ovaries)

estrogens [ESS-tro-jens] a class of female sex hormones that regulate many aspects of sexuality and are found in both males and females

androgens [ANN-dro-jens] a class of male hormones that regulate many aspects of sexuality and are found in both males and females

adrenal [uh-DREEN-ull] medulla the center part of the adrenal gland that plays a crucial role in the functioning of the sympathetic nervous system

adrenal cortex the outside part of the adrenal gland that plays a role in the manufacture and release of androgens, and therefore influences sexual characteristics

Quiz Yourself

2.5

1. The _____ releases male sex hormones in the body.
   a. adrenal cortex
   b. adrenal medulla
   c. hippocampus
   d. ovary

2. A malfunction in which of the following endocrine glands would be most disruptive to the overall functioning of the endocrine system?
   a. Ovaries/testes
   b. Thalamus
   c. Pituitary
   d. Adrenal

3. Juanita was just frightened by a snake. Which of the following endocrine glands most likely played the biggest role in her response to stress?
   a. Testes
   b. Adrenal cortex
   c. Ovaries
   d. Adrenal medulla

Answers Answers 1. a; 2. c; 3. d

2.6 Integrating Psychology: The Big Picture

In this first chapter on foundations in biological psychology, we covered the field of neuroscience. Neuroscience is the study of the brain and nervous system and the manner in which they influence our mental processes and behavior. Understanding how the brain functions is one of the chief concerns of modern neuroscientists. One could argue that the brain is the most important organ in our bodies as it is the organ that ultimately controls communication within our bodies via the nervous and endocrine systems. The case study of Jean-Dominique Bauby highlights just how important our brains are to our ability to function. When his brainstem was affected by a stroke, Jean-Dominique lost the ability to move most of his body at will. The only part he could still control was his left eye. Yet, he managed to communicate with the outside world and to write a bestselling book—all by blinking his left eye.

The locked-in syndrome that Jean-Dominque endured for the rest of his life left him a prisoner in his own body. But, it did not rob him of his ability to take in the world around him, his mind, the motivation to accomplish great things in life, or his ability to feel emotion. In the coming chapters of this section on foundations in biological psychology, we will continue to explore the biological processes that still allowed Jean these pleasures in life. In Chapter 3, we will examine how sensation and perception allow us to interact with the world outside our bodies. In Chapter 4, we will look at consciousness, our awareness of our world and our own internal mental processes. And, in Chapter 5, we will examine what motivates our behavior and makes us feel the emotions we all feel. As you read these chapters, think about your own life and the place these abilities play in it. And, think of Jean-Dominique and how, even with the hand life dealt him, he still lived life to its fullest.

Studying the Chapter

Key Terms

acetylcholine (ACh) (54)
action potentials (50)
adrenal cortex (77)
adrenal medulla (77)
all-or-none fashion (50)
amygdala (64)
androgens (77)
association cortex (71)
auditory cortex (73)
autonomic nervous system (59)
axon (48)
Broca's aphasia (68)
Broca's area (68)
cell body (47)
central nervous system (CNS) (58)
cerebellum (63)
cerebral cortex (63)
cerebral hemispheres (63)
corpus callosum (69)
dendrites (47)
DNA (47)
dopamine (54)
endocrine glands (76)
endocrine system (76)
endorphins (56)
estrogens (77)
excitation (51)
forebrain (61)
frontal lobe (67)
gamma amino butyric acid (GABA) (55)
glia cells (46)
glutamate (56)
gonads (77)
hindbrain (60)
hippocampus (65)
homeostasis (66)
hormones (76)
hypothalamus (66)
inhibition (51)
ions (49)
limbic system (63)
medulla (62)
midbrain (61)
motor cortex (71)
motor neurons (58)
myelin (46)
myelin sheath (48)
nervous system (57)
neurons (46)
neuroplasticity (65)
neuroscience (44)
neurotransmitters (48)
norepinephrine (NOR), (55)
occipital lobe (67)
parasympathetic nervous system (60)
parietal lobe (67)
peripheral nervous system (PNS) (58)
pituitary gland (76)
pons (63)
postsynaptic neuron (48)
presynaptic neuron (48)
refractory period (50)
resting potential (49)
reticular formation (63)
reuptake (52)
sensory neurons (58)
serotonin (55)
somatic nervous system (59)
somatosensory cortex (72)
split brain (69)
sympathetic nervous system (60)
synapse (48)
temporal lobe (67)
thalamus (66)
threshold of excitation (49)
visual cortex (72)
Wernicke's aphasia (68)
Wernicke's area (68)

What Do You Know? Assess Your Understanding

Test your retention and understanding of the material by answering the following questions.

1. The _____ system is an electrochemical system of communication in the body.

a. nervous
b. endocrine
c. hormonal
d. All of the above

2. When the potential of a neuron hits its threshold of excitation at _____, it will fire an action potential.

a. –55 mv
b. +55 mv
c. –70 mv
d. +70 mv

3. Neurotransmitters can be found in the _____ of the neuron.

a. axon
b. myelin
c. axon bulb
d. dendrites

4. Sara slipped and nearly fell while walking down the stairs. The increased heart rate and blood pressure that accompanied Sara's fear at almost falling were most likely due to activation of Sara's _____ nervous system.

a. sympathetic
b. parasympathetic
c. somatic
d. voluntary

5. There tends to be a(n) _____ of _____ in the brains of people with Alzheimer's disease.

a. excess; dopamine
b. lack; dopamine
c. excess; acetylcholine
d. lack; acetylcholine

6. Drugs that are used to treat depression often _____ the action of _____ in the brain.

a. increase; serotonin
b. decrease; serotonin
c. increase; GABA
d. decrease; GABA

7. The chief excitatory neurotransmitter in the brain is _____.

a. acetylcholine
b. dopamine
c. GABA
d. glutamate

8. An inhibitory neurotransmitter makes the postsynaptic neuron _____ likely to fire an action potential by making the inside of the postsynaptic neuron more _____.

a. more; positive
b. less; positive
c. more; negative
d. less; negative

9. Rashid cut his finger while cooking. Which neurotransmitter would be most useful in alleviating his pain?

a. Dopamine
b. Endorphin
c. Norepinephrine
d. GABA

10. The frontal lobe of the brain contains the _____ cortex.

a. somatosensory
b. auditory
c. motor
d. visual

11. Our ability to detect anger and fear in others is likely influenced by which part of the brain?

a. Hippocampus
b. Amygdala
c. Thalamus
d. Hypothalamus

12. Loss of balance and coordination when drunk is most likely due to alcohol's effects on which part of the brain?

a. Thalamus
b. Hippocampus
c. Cerebellum
d. Broca's area

13. The _____ allows the right and left hemispheres of the brain to communicate.

a. pons
b. medulla
c. corpus callosum
d. limbic system

14. Yumiko was in a car accident in which she incurred massive damage to her left frontal lobe. What types of impairments would you most expect to see in Yumiko as a result of this damage?

a. Paralysis on her right side
b. Numbness on her right side
c. An inability to comprehend speech
d. Blindness in her right visual field

15. Damage to the left temporal lobe would likely produce what effect?

a. An inability to produce speech
b. Paralysis on the right side of the body
c. Broca's aphasia
d. Wernicke's aphasia

16. The master gland of the endocrine system is the _____ gland.

a. hippocampus
b. pituitary
c. adrenal medulla
d. adrenal cortex

17. During times of stress, the endocrine system is most likely to release _____.

a. GABA
b. estrogens
c. adrenaline
d. dopamine

18. Male sex hormones are called _____.

a. estrogens
b. androgens
c. endorphins
d. adrenalines

19. A split-brain operation is done to control _____.

a. seizures
b. depression
c. schizophrenia
d. pain

20. Auditory information is processed in the _____ lobe of the brain.

a. temporal
b. occipital
c. parietal
d. frontal

Answers: 1. a; 2. a; 3. c; 4. a; 5. d; 6. a; 7. d; 8. d; 9. b; 10. c; 11. b; 12. c; 13. c; 14. a; 15. d; 16. b; 17. c; 18. b; 19. a; 20. a.

Use It or Lose It: Applying Psychology

1. Jean-Dominique Bauby was still able to think, feel, and remember the events of his life after a stroke left him in a permanent state of locked-in syndrome. Now that you know something about the brain, can you explain why he retained these abilities?

2. If a person were injected with a drug that blocked the action of acetylcholine in the brain, what would you expect to happen?

3. Your best friend is interested in what you are learning in your psychology class. He asks you to explain how the endocrine system differs from the nervous system. What would you tell him?

4. Your best friend's grandmother has just suffered a stroke. This stroke has left her with an inability to speak, but she can still understand what others say to her. She also has paralysis on the right side of her body. Your friend wants to know what part of her grandmother's brain was likely damaged by the stroke. Based on your understanding of the brain, what would you tell your friend?

Critical Thinking for Integration

1. Design an *experiment* to test the hypothesis that the amygdala plays a role in the processing of emotional memories.

2. You want to test the hypothesis that low levels of serotonin are related to obesity in humans. Which type(s) of research design(s) would you *not* want to use? Why?

3. Discuss the ethical considerations involved in using invasive techniques for studying the brains of animals.

4. What questions would a developmental psychologist be *most* interested in asking about the nervous system?

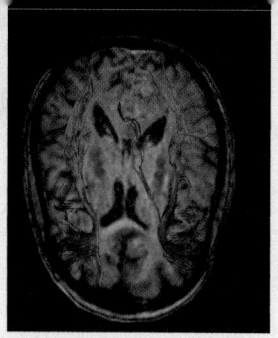

Are You Getting the Big Picture? Neuroscience

2.1 Communication in the Brain

- **Neurons** use electrochemical energy to generate **action potentials** that travel to the end of the neuron and cause the release of **neurotransmitters**.
- Action potentials or neural signals are fired when a neuron is depolarized enough to reach its **threshold of excitation** (–55 mv).

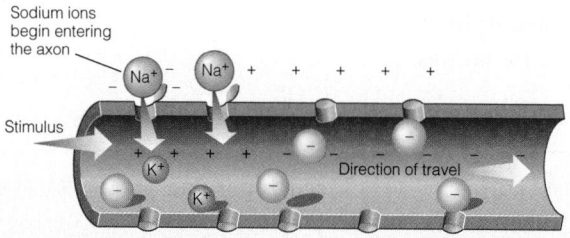

(a)

2.2 Neurotransmitters in the Brain

- Neurotransmitters are chemical compounds that carry signals across neurons. Some of the key neurotransmitters are **acetylcholine**, **dopamine**, **serotonin**, **norepinephrine**, **endorphin**, **GABA**, and **glutamate**.
- Neurotransmitters play significant roles in regulating behavior and mood.

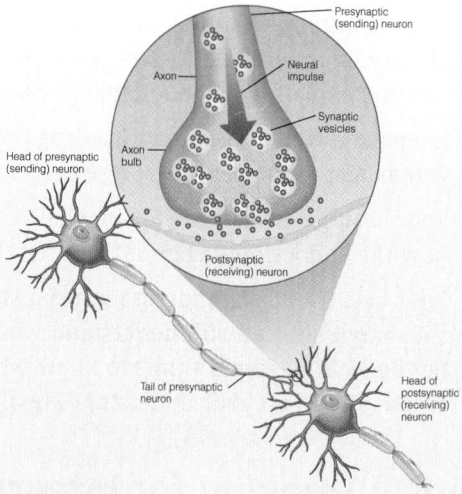

2.3 The Structure of the Nervous System

- The **nervous system** is arranged into a hierarchy of subsystems.

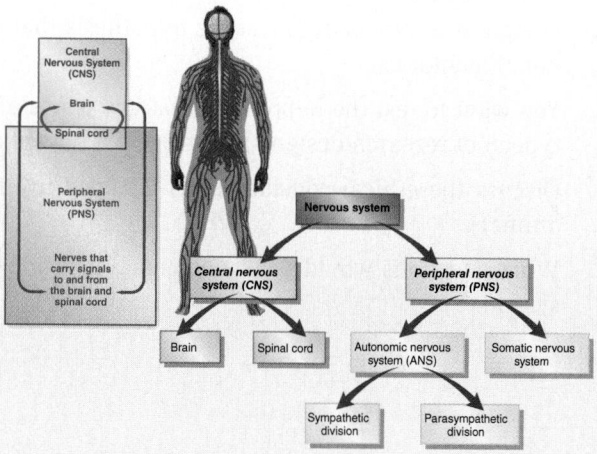

2.4 The Structure and Function of the Brain

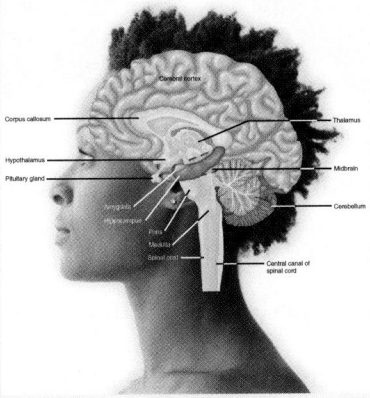

- The brain is divided into three key regions. The **hindbrain** governs basic and life-sustaining functions in the body. The **midbrain** connects the lower structures of the hindbrain with the more sophisticated structures of the **forebrain** that regulate higher-order processes such as thinking and emotional control.
- The brain regulates motor activity, sensation and perception, emotions, our ability to learn and remember, and all the other elements of human behavior.

NASA/Hulton Archive/Getty Images

- The **cerebral cortex** is a thin layer of wrinkled tissue that covers the outside of the brain and is most responsible for the cognition, decision making, and language capabilities that are unique to humans.
- The brain is divided into right and left hemispheres. The left hemisphere generally governs the right side of the body, whereas the right hemisphere governs the left side of the body.
- To assist in studying the brain and its functioning, technology such as CAT scans, MRIs, fMRIs, PET scans, EEGs, and brain stimulation are all important tools.

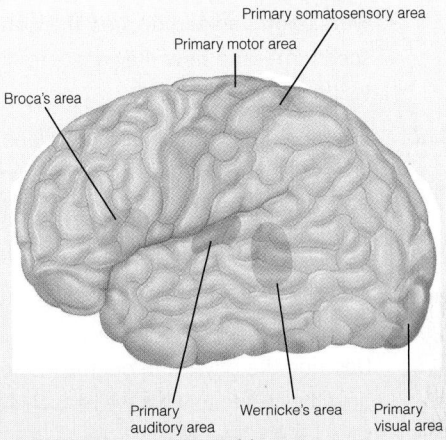

(b) Primary motor-sensory areas of the cortex

2.5 The Endocrine System

- The **endocrine system** contains glands that release chemical messengers—**hormones**—into the bloodstream. Compared to the nervous system, the endocrine system is slower and more long-lasting in its effects.

Leland Bobby/Getty Images

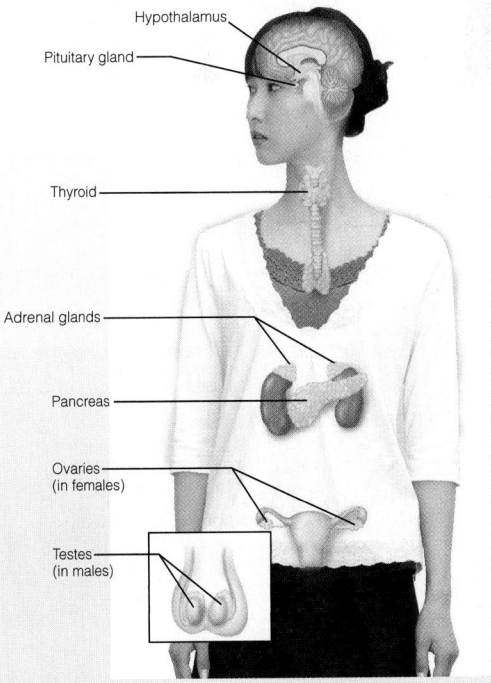

Sensation and Perception

Learning Objectives

3.1 Explain the concepts of absolute threshold, just noticeable difference (jnd), subliminal perception, and extrasensory perception. (APA 1.1, 2.1)

3.2 Describe the physical properties of light—wavelength, amplitude, and the visible spectrum—and how they relate to human vision. (APA 1.1, 1.2)

3.2 Describe the anatomy of the eye and the layers of the retina and how they function. (APA 1.1, 1.2)

3.2 Explain how we adapt to light and dark, how we see color, and how the brain processes what we see. (APA 1.1, 1.2)

3.3 Describe the physical properties of sound and how they relate to what we hear. (APA 1.1, 1.2)

3.3 Be able to locate the outer, middle, and inner ear; list their major structures; and describe their roles in hearing. (APA 1.1, 1.2)

3.4 Explain the processes involved in taste, smell, touch, and the body senses. (APA 1.1, 1.2)

3.5 Describe top-down and bottom-up perceptual processing, and explain the differences between them. (APA 1.1, 1.2, 2.1)

3.5 Give an overview of perceptual constancy theories and how we perceive depth. (APA 1.1, 1.2)

3.5 Describe the process of shape and form perception. (APA 1.1, 1.2)

3.6 Describe some of the common perceptual errors and illusions we experience, and explain their causes. (APA 1.1, 1.2, 2.1)

3.6 Explain how culture affects perception. (APA 1.1, 1.2, 2.5)

When Jean-Dominique Bauby awoke from his coma following his stroke, he once again became aware of the world around him. He was able to focus his conscious awareness or **attention** on the people and equipment in his hospital room. He could feel pain in his body, and he was able to hear some of what was going on around him. Seeing, hearing, and feeling are examples of what psychologists call **sensation**. In sensation, sense organs of the body (for example, the eyes) convert environmental energy, such as the light that is bouncing off of objects, into neural signals that the brain can then process. Sensation—in this case, seeing—is the first step to getting information into our minds. After

3

sensation, you must understand the meaning of what you are seeing. **Perception** occurs when you interpret the meaning of the information gathered through your senses. Although Bauby's stroke did damage part of his hearing, Bauby's book documents, in part, his continued ability to sense and perceive the world. Although he lay motionless in bed, Bauby was just as aware of what was going on as you are aware right now that you are sensing and perceiving these words on this page. In this chapter, we will explore how sensation and perception take place in our bodies and the role that they play in our everyday lives.

© Peter Nadolski/Shutterstock.com

Chapter Outline

3.1 Measuring Sensation and Perception: Psychophysics / 86

3.2 Vision: Seeing the World / 88

3.3 Hearing: Listening to the World / 98

3.4 The Other Senses: Taste, Smell, Touch, and the Body Senses / 103

PSYCHOLOGY APPLIES TO YOUR WORLD: Why Don't We All Like the Same Foods? / 104

3.5 Perception: The Interpretation of Sensory Information / 110

3.6 The Accuracy of Perception / 118

3.7 Integrating Psychology: The Big Picture / 121

attention conscious awareness; can be focused on events that are taking place in the environment or inside our minds

sensation the process through which our sense organs convert environmental energy such as light and sound into neural impulses

perception the process through which we interpret sensory information

psychophysics the study of how the mind interprets the physical properties of stimuli

absolute threshold the minimum intensity of a stimulus at which participants can identify its presence 50% of the time

3.1 Measuring Sensation and Perception: Psychophysics

Psychologists who study sensation and perception are most interested in understanding how we process sensory stimuli such as sights, sounds, and smells. How does your mind interpret the color of light bouncing off the surface of an apple? What physical properties of a food make it taste sweet or bitter? Questions like these are the focus of the branch of psychology called **psychophysics**.

3.1.1 • The Limits of Sensation: Absolute Thresholds

One of the fundamental questions psychophysicists have sought to answer concerns the limits of human sensory capabilities. How faint a light can humans see? How soft a tone can we hear? Psychophysicists have conducted many experiments to answer these questions. These experiments typically involve presenting stimuli of gradually increasing or decreasing intensity (along with some trials on which the stimulus is not presented at all). Participants are asked to report whether they can detect the presence of the stimulus. In this way, psychophysicists establish an *absolute threshold*. **Absolute threshold** is defined as the minimum intensity of a stimulus that can be detected 50% of the time. This 50% mark is used because the level of the stimulus required for it to *just* be perceived varies from trial to trial and from person to person during an experiment. • TABLE 3.1 lists the approximate established absolute thresholds for our five senses, described in familiar descriptive terms.

TABLE 3.1

Descriptions of the Absolute Thresholds for Our Five Senses

SENSE	ABSOLUTE THRESHOLD
Vision 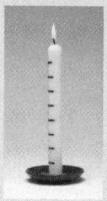 Paul Bricknell/Dorling Kindersley/Getty Images	A candle seen from 30 miles away on a clear, dark night.
Hearing  © Peter Baxter/Shutterstock.com	A ticking watch that is 20 feet away in an otherwise quiet room.
Smell  Image Source/Photodisc/Getty Images	One drop of perfume diffused in a three-room apartment.
Taste  Digital Light Source/Getty Images	One teaspoon of sugar dissolved in 2 gallons of water.
Touch  tanjica perovic photography/Getty Images	The wing of a bumblebee falling on one's cheek from a distance of 1 centimeter.

3.1.2 • The Just Noticeable Difference and Weber's Law

In addition to establishing absolute thresholds for the senses, psychophysicists have tried to establish the minimum change in the intensity of a stimulus that can be detected 50% of the time. This barely noticeable change in the stimulus is referred to as the *difference threshold* or the **just noticeable difference (jnd)**. In the early 1800s, psychophysicist Ernst Weber (1795–1878) discovered an interesting characteristic of the jnd, known as **Weber's law**. According to this law, for each of our five senses, the amount of change in the stimulus that is necessary to produce a jnd depends on the intensity at which the stimulus is first presented. For example, if you add one additional teaspoon of salt to a very salty pot of soup, it will probably not be noticeable. But that same teaspoon of salt added to a less salty pot of soup may be very noticeable. Weber's law helps explain some of the subjectivity we experience in sensation. Under some conditions, 1 teaspoon of salt won't make a difference to our enjoyment of a recipe. Under other conditions, it might.

just noticeable difference (jnd) the minimum change in intensity of a stimulus that participants can detect 50% of the time

Weber's [VAY-bers] law a psychological principle that states that for each of our five senses, the amount of change in the stimulus that is necessary to produce a jnd depends on the intensity at which the stimulus is first presented

subliminal perception when the intensity of a stimulus is below the participant's absolute threshold and the participant is not consciously aware of the stimulus

extrasensory perception (ESP) also known as *psi*, the purported ability to acquire information about the world without using the known senses

3.1.3 • Processing Without Awareness: Subliminal Stimulation of the Senses

Absolute thresholds and just noticeable differences describe the limits of our conscious awareness of sensations. But is sensation always a conscious experience? Or is it possible that we might be affected by sensory stimuli even when we are unaware of sensing them? **Subliminal perception**, the unconscious perception of stimuli, became a topic of many debates in the late 1950s when a man named James Vicary attempted to use subliminal messages to entice moviegoers at a public theater to buy more popcorn and soda without them knowing that they were being persuaded. Vicary flashed messages such as "Eat popcorn" and "Drink Coca-Cola" between the frames of a movie at a speed so fast that moviegoers did not have time to consciously perceive the messages. Because the messages were flashed so briefly, the moviegoers never consciously saw anything other than the movie.

Vicary reported that as a result of his "experiment," concession sales rose 18%. As it turns out, Vicary admitted in 1962 that he had not conducted a true experiment. The data that he collected were so few that they could not be used for scientific purposes (Epley, Savitsy, & Kachelski, 1999; Pratkanis, 1992). After Vicary's attempts at subliminal persuasion, researchers began to carefully examine the effects of subliminal perception both in the real world and in the laboratory. Many studies have failed to yield convincing evidence for the effectiveness of persuasive subliminal messages (see Pratkanis et al., 2007). However, newer studies suggest that when certain criteria are met, subliminal persuasion can occur. For example, when subliminal messages specifically address the dimensions we are evaluating about the product, they may be effective (Loersch, Durso, & Petty, 2013).

3.1.4 • Extrasensory Perception: Can Perception Occur Without Our Five Senses?

As with subliminal persuasion, scientific research casts serious doubts on the existence of **extrasensory perception (ESP)**, sometimes also referred to as *psi*. ESP is the purported ability to acquire information about the world without using the known senses—for example, the ability to read people's minds or see the future. Most of the scientific tests of ESP involve the *Ganzfeld procedure*, in which one participant acts as a *sender* who tries to send a message to another participant acting as a *receiver* in another room. Although a few of these studies have suggested that some people may be better at sending and receiving such telepathic messages, the vast majority fail to support the existence of ESP (Milton & Wiseman, 2001).

Recently, researchers have used neuroimaging to investigate whether ESP exists. Researchers Samuel Moulton and Steven Kosslyn (2008) had participants engage in a modified version of the Ganzfeld procedure. During the experiment, the receiver had to guess which of two images on a computer screen was being sent by the sender in another room. As the receivers made these judgments, their brains were scanned using fMRI technology. Moulton and Kosslyn found

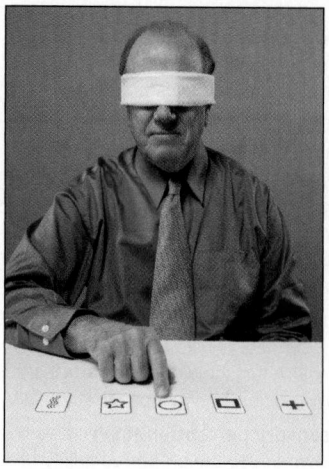

PM Images/The Image Bank/Getty Images

Although researchers have been searching for evidence of ESP for a century, to date compelling evidence of its existence has not been found.

that the receivers guessed the correct image only about 50% of the time (no better than chance alone). Furthermore, the fMRIs showed no differences in brain functioning between the trials resulting in correct and incorrect responses. Moulton and Kosslyn interpret these results as powerful evidence against the existence of ESP.

But not everyone agrees. In 2011, one of psychology's most prestigious journals, the *Journal of Personality and Social Psychology*, published a paper by psychologist Daryl Bem (2011) in which he claims to have experimental evidence for the existence of ESP. Bem contends that his data show that his participants were able to predict events before they happened at a rate better than chance guessing. Critics contend that Bem's studies are methodologically flawed and that the statistical analyses of the data were not performed correctly (Fiedler, 2013). The debate over the existence of ESP seems destined to continue into the foreseeable future (see also Carpenter, 2012).

Now that we have a basic understanding of how psychologists measure the limits of our sensory abilities, we will examine how our bodies accomplish the process of sensation, starting with vision.

Quiz Yourself 3.1

1. Jerry wants to sweeten his iced tea. He adds 1 teaspoon of sugar, but the tea does not taste sweet to him. When Jerry adds one more teaspoon of sugar, he finds that the tea now tastes sweet—but just barely. Two teaspoons of sugar seem to correspond to Jerry's _____.
   a. just noticeable difference
   b. absolute threshold
   c. *k* value
   d. stimulus threshold
2. If your tea already tastes sweet to you, the minimum amount of sugar that you would have to add to your tea to make it taste sweeter corresponds to your _____.
   a. just noticeable difference
   b. absolute threshold
   c. *k* value
   d. stimulus threshold
3. According to Weber's law, who will most likely notice the addition of one more teaspoon of sugar in a glass of iced tea?
   a. Joni, whose tea has no sugar in it
   b. Bill, who has 2 teaspoons of sugar in his tea
   c. Sarafina, who has 3 teaspoons of sugar in her tea
   d. All of these people will be equally likely to notice the difference.

Answers 1. b; 2. a; 3. a

3.2 Vision: Seeing the World

Our eyes are at the front of our skulls, so you might assume that vision is a direct transfer from object to eye to brain. Vision is more complicated than that, however, and researchers have studied vision more than the other senses. To understand vision, we'll look at the properties of light that apply to vision, the anatomy of the eye, the layers of the retina, and how we process visual information in the brain.

3.2.1 • How Vision Works: Light Waves and Energy

When we see an object, what we really see are the light waves that are reflected off the surface of the object. Thus, a blue shirt appears blue because blue is the only color of light that the shirt reflects. The shirt absorbs all other colors of light.

As we'll see, the specific characteristics of the shirt's color and brightness are all determined by the physical characteristics of the particular light energy that is bouncing off the shirt.

MEASURING LIGHT: WAVELENGTH AND AMPLITUDE

• FIGURE 3.1 depicts the *electromagnetic spectrum,* which includes visible light. Electromagnetic energies, including light, result from disturbances in the electrical and magnetic fields that exist in the universe. Like all electromagnetic energies, light waves are characterized by their *wavelength* and *amplitude.* The **wavelength** of light is the distance between the peaks of consecutive waves. The **amplitude** of the light wave is the height of each wave peak. These distances are typically measured in nanometers (nm).

wavelength a physical property of some energies that corresponds to the distance between wave peaks

amplitude a physical property of some energies that corresponds to the height of wave peaks

visible spectrum the spectrum of light that humans can see

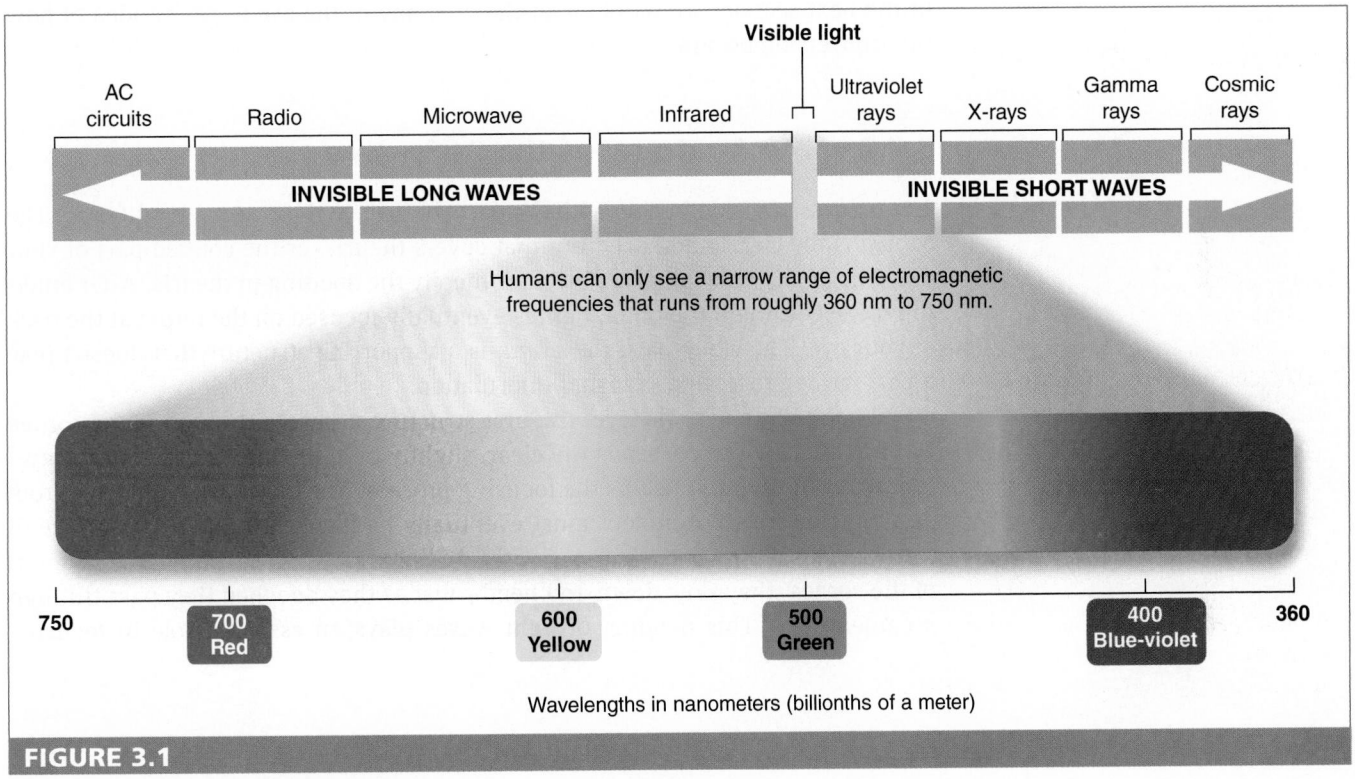

FIGURE 3.1

The Visible Spectrum of Light

The human visible spectrum comprises a narrow range of electromagnetic energies.

The human eye cannot sense all electromagnetic energy. In fact, the **visible spectrum** for humans is only a very narrow band of the electromagnetic spectrum that spans from about 360 nm to 750 nm (Figure 3.1). Other species can sense electromagnetic wavelengths that are beyond the human visible spectrum. Some snakes sense infrared rays, allowing them to sense other animals' body heat (Sinclair, 1985). Other animals, such as spiders and rats, use their ability to sense ultraviolet (UV) light during hunting (Bhaskara et al., 2009). If you are hiking through the woods, keep in mind that certain animals may be able to see you before you see them!

PROPERTIES OF LIGHT: HUE, BRIGHTNESS, AND SATURATION

Although our eyes cannot sense much of the electromagnetic spectrum, we are capable of seeing millions of different combinations of color, richness, and

hue the color of light; it corresponds to the light's wavelength

brightness the intensity of light; it corresponds to the amplitude of the light waves

saturation the purity of light; light that consists of a single wavelength produces the richest or most saturated color

cornea [COR-nee-ah] the clear, slightly bulging outer surface of the eye that both protects the eye and begins the focusing process

brightness of light (Linhares, Pinto, & Nascimento, 2008). The wavelength of the light wave corresponds to the color or **hue** of the light we see. Shorter wavelengths correspond to cool colors such as blues and purples; longer wavelengths correspond to warmer colors such as yellows and reds (Figure 3.1). The amplitude of the light wave corresponds to its **brightness**. The higher the amplitude of the light wave, the brighter the color we perceive. One other characteristic of light, **saturation**, corresponds to the purity of the light. Light that consists of a single wavelength will produce the most saturated, or richest, color. Light that is a mixture of wavelengths produces less saturated colors. For example, pure blue light is high in saturation, but a mixture of blue and white light produces a less saturated blue light.

For vision to occur, our eyes must be able to convert the electromagnetic waves of the visible spectrum into action potentials that our brains can process. In the next section, we will look at the anatomy of the eye to get an idea of how this conversion occurs.

3.2.2 • The Anatomy of the Outer Eye

The process of vision begins with the parts of the eye that we can readily see. The *cornea* is the clear outer structure that covers the *iris,* or the colored part of your eye. The *pupil,* which appears black, is merely the opening in the iris. After entering the eye through the pupil, light is eventually focused on the retina at the back of your eye. The white part, the *sclera,* is a supporting structure that doesn't play a part in the processing of visual information.

When light enters the eye, the first structure it passes through is the **cornea** (• FIGURE 3.2). The cornea is the clear, slightly bulging outer surface of the eye. It protects the eye and begins the focusing process. The light that is reflected from an object in the environment must eventually be focused on the rear surface of the eye if we are to see the object clearly. As light waves pass through the material of the cornea, they slow down and bend—just as they do when they pass through a camera lens. This bending of light waves plays an essential role in focusing

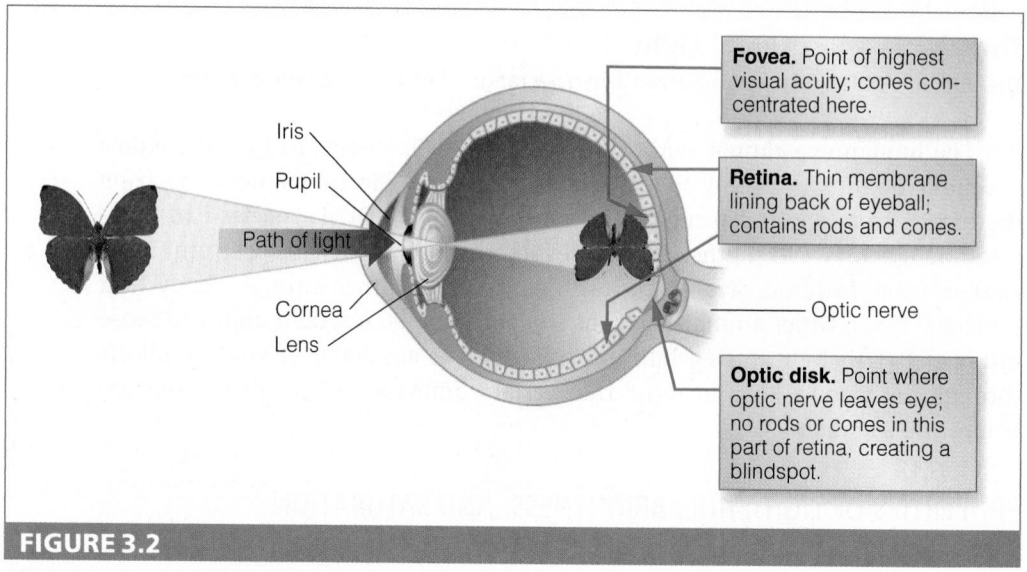

FIGURE 3.2
The Anatomy of the Eye

images on the back of your eye. A damaged cornea can make it impossible for a person to see clearly.

Directly behind the cornea is the **pupil**. This black opening in the center of your eye is not really a structure. Rather, it is an opening, or aperture, through which light passes into the center of the eye. Light cannot pass through the white part of the eye, the sclera. Therefore, it must pass through the cornea and pupil to enter the eye. The iris, the colored part of the eye surrounding the pupil, is constructed of rings of muscles that control the size of the pupil. In dimly lit conditions, muscles in the iris pull outward to dilate the pupil, allowing the maximum amount of light into the eye. In brightly lit conditions, the iris constricts to close the pupil, thus reducing the amount of light entering the eye so as not to overwhelm the light-sensitive cells in the eye.

Directly behind the iris and the pupil is the **lens** of the eye. The lens is a clear structure that is attached to the eye with strong ciliary muscles. The lens of the eye is rather like the lens of a camera—its job is to bring the light waves entering the eye into sharp focus on the back of the eye. The lens of the eye is somewhat soft and flexible. As the ciliary muscles stretch the lens, it changes shape, or undergoes **accommodation**, so that the image passing through it is focused properly.

pupil the hole in the iris through which light enters the eye

lens the part of the eye that lies behind the pupil and focuses light rays on the retina

accommodation the process through which the lens is stretched or squeezed to focus light on the retina

retina the structure at the back of the eye that contains cells that convert light into neural signals

optic nerve the structure that conveys visual information away from the retina to the brain

blindspot the point where the optic nerve leaves the retina (the optic disk) where there are no rods or cones

3.2.3 • The Retina: Light Energy to Neural Messages

Once the light waves have been focused on the back of the eye, conversion of light waves into neural impulses occurs in the retina, the surface that lines the inside of the back of the eyeball. In the **retina**, specialized cells called *rods* and *cones* convert light into neural signals. Without these cells, vision would not be possible.

THE ANATOMY OF THE RETINA

The diagram in • FIGURE 3.3 shows a cross-section of the layers in the human retina. The *ganglion cells* are on the surface of the retina, followed by successive layers of *amacrine, bipolar,* and *horizontal cells* and, finally, the light-sensitive rods and cones. Look closely at Figure 3.3 and you will see that the light entering the eye must filter through all the layers of the retina before finally striking the rods and cones.

Incoming light passes unimpeded through the transparent layers of the retina to reach the rods and cones, which convert the light energy into neural impulses. These signals travel back out to the ganglion cells on the surface of the retina. Along the way, the horizontal, bipolar, and amacrine cells funnel and consolidate the neural information from the rods and cones so that we can see a unified, coherent image. The signals that reach the ganglion cells in the top layer of the retina are to some degree summaries of the visual information from the rods and cones.

LWA/Stone/Getty Images

Vision problems can strike at any age. Nearsightedness, or not seeing distant objects well, is common at all ages. Another condition, presbyopia, is more common after middle age. Presbyopia occurs when, as we age, the lens of the eye becomes more rigid and the eye is less able to accommodate to close objects. Because of presbyopia, many middle-aged and older adults need reading glasses or bifocals.

THE OPTIC NERVE AND THE BLINDSPOT

Once the neural impulses reach the ganglion cells, they exit the retina and travel to the brain via the **optic nerve**, which is composed of the axons of the ganglion cells (see Figures 3.2 and 3.3). The optic nerve actually exits the retina on the *surface* of the retina; there are no light-sensitive rods or cones at the point where the optic nerve leaves the retina. With no rods or cones at this spot, each of our eyes has a **blindspot**, which is a point in our visual field that we cannot see.

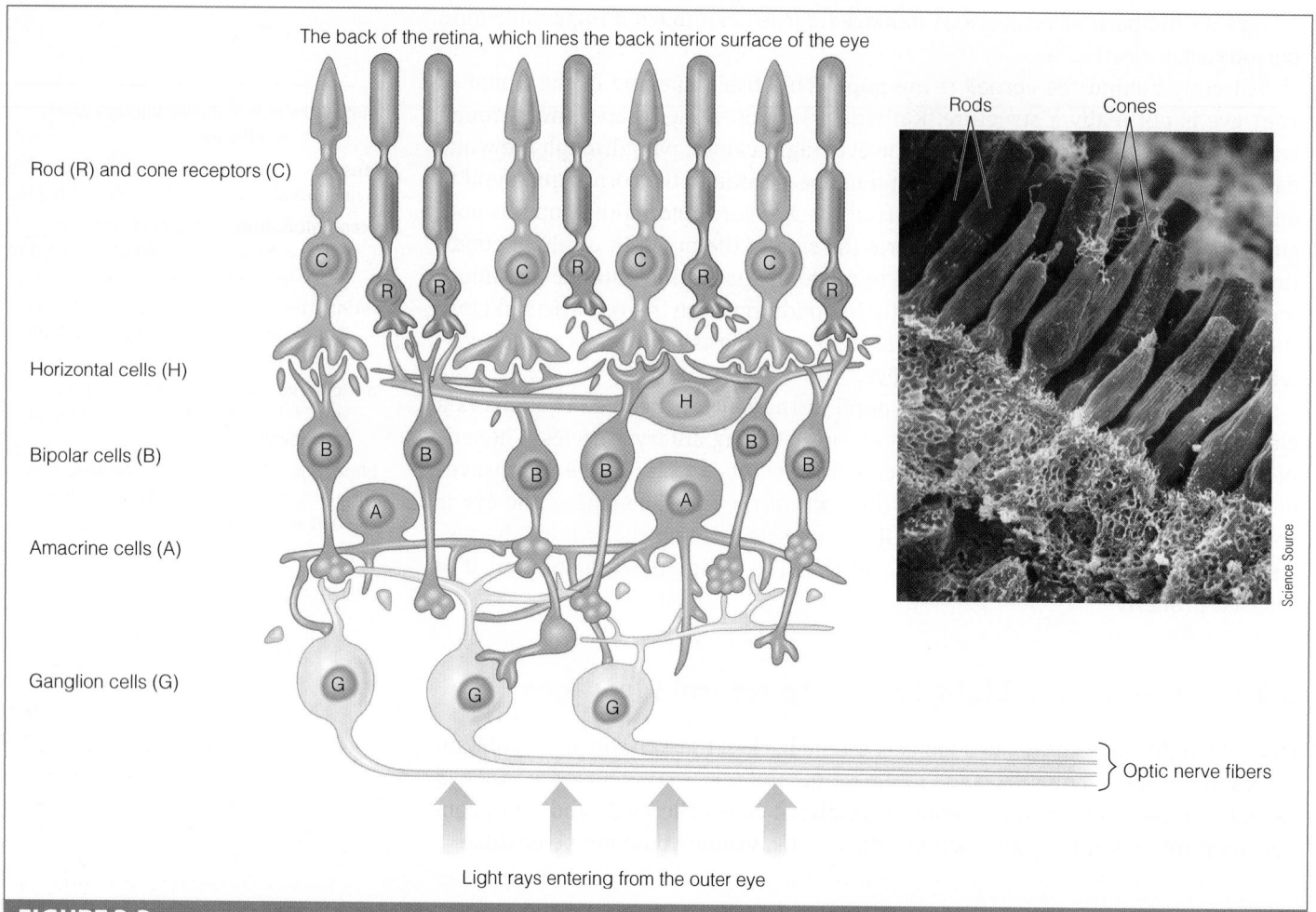

FIGURE 3.3

A Cross-section of the Retina

Above is a schematic of the retina with the rods shown in purple and the cones in pink. To the right is an electron micrograph of the retina showing the rods and cones.

From "Organization of the Primate Retina," by J. E. Dowling and B. B. Boycott, in *Proceedings of the Royal Society of London, 16,* Series B, 80–111. Copyright © 1966 by the Royal Society.

Luckily, however, our blindspots do not pose much of a problem. For one thing, the blindspot is at the side of our visual field, where we normally do not bring objects into focus in the first place (see Figure 3.2). If the blindspot were located at the *fovea* (the point directly behind the pupil), we might be much more aware of it. Another reason is that we have two eyes. Whatever part of the world we miss seeing because of the blindspot in our left eye we see with our right eye, and vice versa.

THE RODS AND CONES

The rods and cones that line the inside layer of the retina play different roles in the process of vision. The **rods**, which are long and skinny, are sensitive to all colors of light, but they do not transmit information about color to the brain (see Figure 3.3). You can think of the rods as being black-and-white receptors. If you had only rods in your retina, you'd see everything in black and white. We see the world in color because of the cone cells in the retina. The **cones**, which are shorter and fatter than the rods, are responsible for transmitting information about color to the brain.

rods the light-sensitive cells of the retina that pick up any type of light energy and convert it to neural signals

cones the cells of the retina that are sensitive to specific colors of light and send information to the brain concerning the colors we are seeing

Relative to rods, the cones of the eye require a higher intensity of light to become activated. Because of this, we do not have good color vision in dimly lit situations. Think about driving at night. When light levels are not very intense, it may be possible to see objects in the distance, but impossible to discern their color. In each eye you have about 100 million rods but only about 5 million cones (Matlin & Foley, 1997). Having so many rods and so few cones in the retina indicates that perceiving shape and form takes precedence over perception of color. If you think about it for a minute, this arrangement makes sense. Which information would you need first: to see the shape of a car speeding toward you in the dark, or to see the color of the car? Your first concern would be seeing the car to avoid a collision!

In addition to being differentially sensitive to light energy, the rods and cones are not distributed evenly across the surface of the retina. The highest concentration of cones is at the fovea, with fewer and fewer cones toward the peripheral edges of the retina. The density of rods follows the opposite pattern, with the highest concentration at the peripheral edges of the retina and fewer and fewer rods as you move toward the fovea. This arrangement means that our best color vision is for objects placed directly in front of us, whereas our color vision for objects seen out of the corners of our eyes (in our peripheral vision) is very poor.

TURNING LIGHT ENERGY INTO NEURAL MESSAGES

The rods and cones of the eye are able to convert light into neural impulses because they contain light-sensitive **photopigments**, chemicals that are activated by light energy (Fitzpatrick & Mooney, 2012). When a rod is not receiving light input, its photopigment molecules are stable. However, when light strikes the rod, this incoming light energy splits the photopigments apart (Yau & Hardie, 2009). As the photopigments break up, they set off a complex chain of chemical reactions that change the rate at which the neurons of the visual system fire action potentials. The brain uses the pattern of these action potentials to interpret what we are seeing.

photopigments light-sensitive chemicals that create electrical charges when they come into contact with light

dark adaptation the process through which our eyes adjust to dark conditions after having been exposed to bright light

light adaptation the process through which our eyes adjust to bright light after having been exposed to darkness

3.2.4 • Adapting to Light and Darkness

Have you ever had to wait at the back of a dark movie theater for your eyes to adjust before you could find your seat? This type of adjustment is referred to as **dark adaptation**. It also takes our eyes a while to adapt to sudden increases in brightness, or undergo **light adaptation**.

Dark and light adaptation are accomplished, in part, by changes in pupil size. Unfortunately, the amount of dilation and constriction that our pupils can provide is limited, and they alone cannot fully account for the adaptations we experience. Another mechanism of adaptation is found in the photopigments themselves. If you were to enter a completely darkened room, no light would enter your eyes and no photopigments would break down. After remaining in these darkened conditions for a period of time, the photopigment levels in your eyes would build up because they are not being broken down by light. This is what occurs when we sleep at night. With a large store of photopigments, your eyes are very sensitive to light. If someone were to suddenly turn on the lights in the bedroom, you would experience a bright flash of light and perhaps even pain as the large number of available photopigments makes your eyes very sensitive to the light. It would take about 1 minute for your eyes to adjust to the light (Hood & Finkelstein, 1986).

Jack Wild/The Image Bank/Getty Images

When you step out of the darkness into bright light, you may experience a flash of pain as the built-up photopigment in your eyes reacts all at once to the bright light.

© Ocean/Corbis

When suddenly entering dim conditions after leaving a brightly environment, such as occurs when you enter a darkened theater, it will take more than 30 minutes for your eyes to fully adjust to the darkness. In addition, because cones require more light energy than rods, it can be difficult to discriminate among colors in dim conditions.

The process of dark adaptation is the opposite of what occurs during light adaptation. Under normal daytime lighting conditions, we constantly use our photopigments to see our surroundings. So, at any given moment during the day, a certain percentage of our photopigments is broken down. If you suddenly enter a darkened theater after being in bright daylight, you will not have enough photopigments to be able to see well. It will take approximately 30–45 minutes for your photopigment levels to build up completely (Poelman & Smet, 2010). This is why you may have to stand, popcorn in hand, at the back of the darkened theater for several minutes before you can find your seat.

3.2.5 • How We See Color

Like the rods, the cones of the retina also contain photopigments. However, there is an important distinction between the photopigments in the rods and cones. All rods contain the same photopigment. In contrast, there are three different types of cones, each containing a slightly different photopigment. Having different types of photopigments in our cones is one reason we see color.

THE COLORS OF LIGHT

You may have learned in elementary school about three primary colors (red, yellow, and blue) from which all other colors can be made. This is true when you are talking about paint or crayons that actually reflect the color of light that we see. However, mixing colored light is different from mixing colors of paints or crayons. The primary colors of light are red, green, and blue. All other colors of light can be made from these three colors. If you mix all the primary colors of light together, you get white light. In contrast, if you mixed red, blue, and yellow paint together, you would get black paint (• FIGURE 3.4). When we describe color vision and combinations of colors, remember to think in terms of light, and not in terms of paint.

trichromatic [try-crow-MAT-ick] theory of color vision the idea that color vision is made possible by the presence of three different types of cones in the retina that react respectively to red, green, or blue light

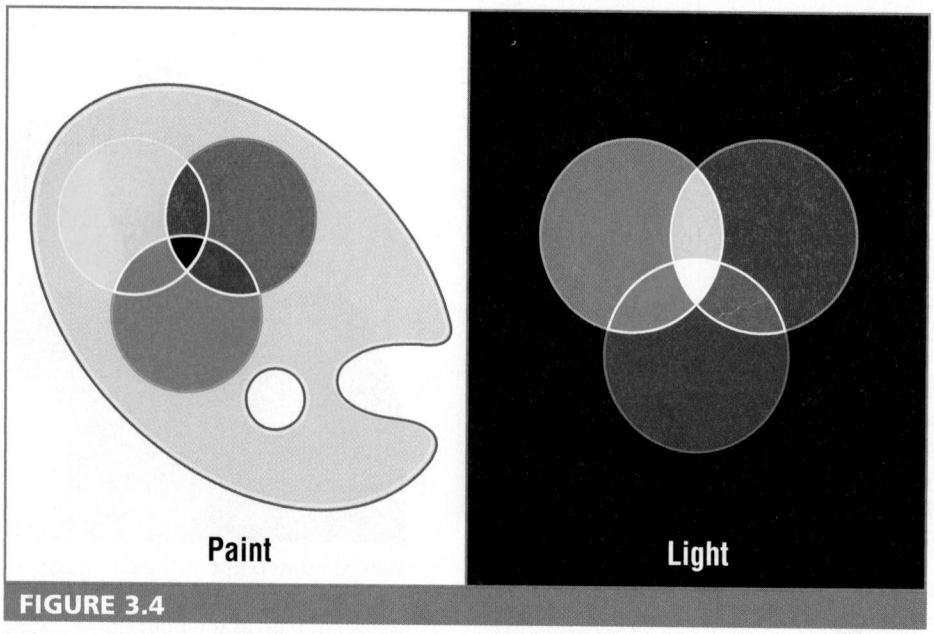

FIGURE 3.4

Primary Colors of Paint and Light

Mixing paint is not the same as combining colors of light.

THE TRICHROMATIC THEORY OF COLOR VISION

By now, we hope that some of you have made the connection between the three primary colors of light and the three different types of cones in our retinas. Could it be that each type of cone detects the presence of a different primary color of light? This is the central assumption of the **trichromatic theory of color vision**.

The exact origin of the trichromatic theory of color vision is not really known (Rushton, 1975; Wasserman, 1978). Most psychologists credit Hermann von Helmholtz (1821–1894) with proposing this theory in the mid-1800s. According to the trichromatic theory, we have three different types of cones, each of which contains a slightly different photopigment that makes the cell particularly sensitive to a certain wavelength of light. One type of cone is particularly sensitive to long wavelengths (red), another is very sensitive to medium wavelengths (green), and the third is most sensitive to short wavelengths (blue). Notice that these colors correspond to the primary colors of light.

These differentially sensitive cones give our brain a means of knowing what color of light we are seeing at any particular moment (Conway, 2009). For example, if the brain receives input that the red cones are very active and the green and blue are not very active, the brain knows you are seeing the color red. This same logic can be applied to seeing the colors green and blue, but how does it apply to seeing nonprimary colors? All colors of light are some combination of red, green, and blue light (see Figure 3.4). So, the brain processes the proportions of red, green, and blue cones that are firing intensely to know what color you are seeing.

COLOR BLINDNESS: DO WE ALL SEE THE SAME COLORS?

Color blindness, or the inability to see one or more colors, results from altered cone activity in the retina. A particularly common type is red–green color blindness, a disorder that occurs in approximately 8% of males in the United States. Similar levels of color blindness have been seen in specific populations of males in Turkey and Greenland, whereas lower levels of color blindness have been found among males in Colombia, Spain, and Italy. The fact that rates of color blindness vary across genetically disparate populations suggests a genetic basis to the disorder (see Citirik et al., 2005). Furthermore, the fact that the condition is seen much more often in men suggests a sex-linked genetic condition.

Red–green color blindness can result from a lack of red or green cones in the retina. Without one of these types of cones, a person is unable to discriminate between red and green. At a stoplight, a person with such red–green color blindness must look at the position of the red and green lights because the lights appear to be the same color.

Yet some people who have all three types of cones also experience red–green color vision deficiencies. For these people (again mostly men), the issue is that the red or green cones are not sensitive to exactly the same ranges of wavelengths as the cones found in the average person. Therefore, these men experience difficulties in distinguishing among certain hues (e.g., Baraas et al., 2006). For example, a man with abnormally insensitive green cones may have trouble distinguishing small changes in color among orange hues. These deficiencies are sometimes more detectable in a laboratory where participants are asked to view samples of color under tightly controlled conditions than they are in the real world. In the natural environment, where colors and light levels are varied and mixed, some of these color deficiencies do not seem to be as problematic (Baraas et al., 2006).

Although trichromatic theory explains certain aspects of color vision, it does not explain all aspects of vision (see Horiguchi, et al. 2013). For example, trichromatic theory cannot explain *negative afterimages*. To understand what an afterimage is, try this demonstration.

ENGAGE YOURSELF! Get a blank sheet of paper and set it aside. Stare at the black dot in the center of • FIGURE 3.5 without blinking or moving your eyes. Continue staring for 60–90 seconds. Then quickly move your gaze to the blank sheet of white paper. What do you see? You should see the image of a green shamrock with a yellow border on the blank sheet of white paper. The shamrock is a negative afterimage. Notice that the colors you see in the

Barbara Eberhart/Perspectives/Getty Images

If you were missing all of your cones, this piece of art would be perceived in grayscale instead of color.

color blindness a condition in which a person cannot perceive one or more colors because of altered cone activity in the retina

FIGURE 3.5
Negative Afterimages
See text for instructions.

afterimage are different from the colors in the original. Why would you see different colors in your afterimage? Simply having different types of cones cannot explain this phenomenon. So, what does explain afterimages?

THE OPPONENT-PROCESS THEORY OF COLOR VISION

opponent-process theory the idea that we have dual-action cells beyond the level of the retina that signal the brain when we see one of a pair of colors

The **opponent-process theory** proposes a different type of color-sensitive cell in the visual system, a cell that is sensitive to two colors of light. There are thought to be three types of opponent-process cells in our visual system: red/green, yellow/blue, and black/white. The key to opponent-process theory is that these cells can detect the presence of only one color at a time. The colors *oppose* each other so that the opponent-process cell cannot detect the presence of both colors at the same time. For example, a red/green cell can detect either red or green light at any one time. If you shine a red light in the eye, the red/green cells tell our brain that we are seeing red. If you shine a green light in the eye, the red/green cells tell our brain that we are seeing green. But these red/green cells cannot detect red and green at the same time. Opponent-process theory is consistent with the finding that if we simultaneously shine red and green lights into your eye, you will likely see a neutral shade that is neither red nor green (Hurvich & Jameson, 1957/2000).

Opponent-process theory can explain the phenomenon of negative afterimages. Recall the demonstration you tried with Figure 3.5. After staring at the red and blue shamrock, you saw a green and yellow afterimage. Opponent-process theory proposes that as you stared at the red and blue shamrock, you were using the red and blue portions of the opponent-process cells. After a period of 60–90 seconds of continuous staring, you expended these cells' capacity to fire action potentials. In a sense, you temporarily "wore out" the red and blue portions of these cells. Then you looked at a blank sheet of white paper. Under normal conditions, the white light would excite *all* of the opponent-process cells. Recall that white light contains all colors of light. But, given the exhausted state of your opponent-process cells, only parts of them were capable of firing action potentials.

In this example, the green and yellow parts of the cells were ready to fire. The light reflected off the white paper could excite only the yellow and green parts of the cells, so you saw a green and yellow shamrock.

TRICHROMATIC THEORY OR OPPONENT-PROCESS THEORY?

We've seen that trichromatic theory and opponent-process theory each explain certain aspects of color vision. So, which theory is correct? Both theories seem to have merit. It is generally believed that these two theories describe processes that operate at different places in the visual system (Hubel, 1995; Wade, 2010).

Trichromatic theory does a good job of explaining color vision at the level of the rods and cones. Opponent-process theory best explains the processing of color vision beyond the level of the rods and cones. Evidence suggests that opponent processing may occur at the level of the ganglion cells (Conway, 2009; DeValois & DeValois, 1975); the amacrine, horizontal, and bipolar cells of the retina; or even in the visual cortex (see Conway & Livingstone, 2005). In the next section, we will trace the path that visual information takes as it leaves the retina and enters the brain.

3.2.6 • The Visual Pathways of the Brain

Once the rods and cones of the retina convert light into neural signals, this information begins its journey into the visual cortex of the brain. Along the way, visual information is continually processed and combined to ultimately give us a coherent perception of what we see in the environment. The bipolar, horizontal, and amacrine cells gather the information from the rods and cones and funnel it to the ganglion cells. The ganglion cells join together to form the optic nerve, which carries visual information into the brain.

Visual information from the right side of the body travels to the left hemisphere, and information from the left side travels to the right hemisphere. The point at which the optic nerve from the left eye and the optic nerve from the right eye cross over is called the **optic chiasm**. From the optic chiasm, most visual information travels to the thalamus before traveling to the visual cortex, where the meaning of the visual input is interpreted. We will discuss this interpretive process when we discuss perception later in the chapter (see ● FIGURE 3.6).

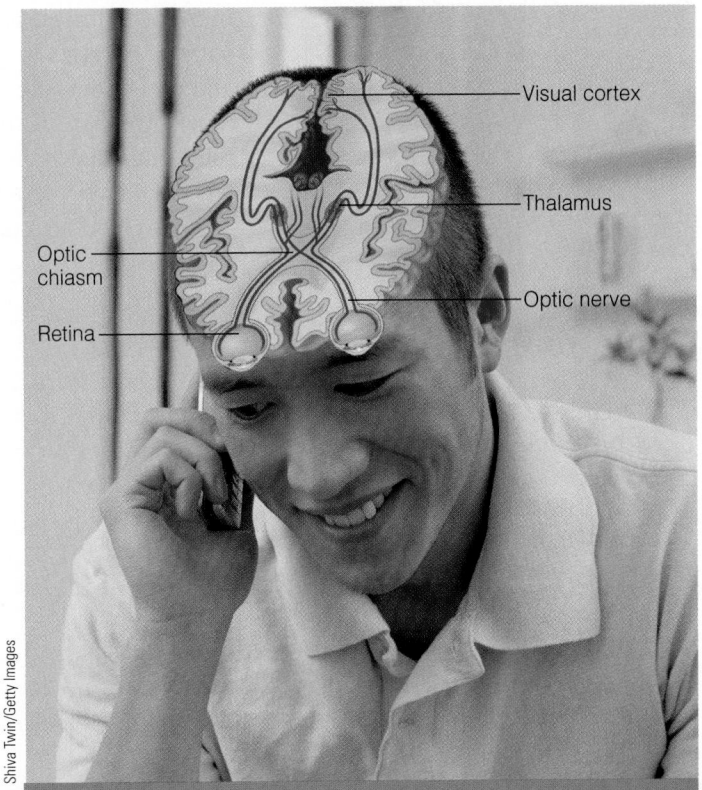

Shiva Twin/Getty Images

FIGURE 3.6

The Visual Pathways in the Brain

Visual information from your right side travels to the visual cortex on the left side of the brain, and information from your left side travels to the visual cortex on the right side.

DO MEN AND WOMEN SEE THE WORLD DIFFERENTLY?

Evidence suggests that when it comes to processing visual information, men and women see things differently. Females tend to be better at discriminating one object from another (Overman et al., 1996), naming colors (Bornstein, 1985), processing facial expressions accurately (Vassallo, Cooper, & Douglas, 2009), and perceiving colors (Jaint et al., 2010). In addition to having better color vision in general, females also tend to show a preference for using many colors and seem to prefer warm colors to cool ones. Males tend to be better at processing moving objects and the spatial aspects of objects (Alexander, 2003). Differences appear at a very early age: female infants aged 3–8 months prefer to look at dolls, whereas male infants of the same age prefer to look at trucks (Alexander, Wilcox, & Woods, 2009).

Researcher Gerianne Alexander (2003) has argued that such gender differences in visual processing are neurological and that they have evolved to facilitate the performance of traditional male/female roles. In many societies, males have historically hunted for food, whereas women have gathered crops and nurtured children. On the one hand, by being able to discriminate among objects and colors well, females are well suited to gathering food. For example, good color vision allows you to see a ripe fig among the green leaves of a tree. A preference for warm colors (skin tones of all races tend to be warm) and faces may also predispose women to care for their young. On the other hand, male facility in processing movement and spatial information may have helped them perform hunting duties.

Recently, researchers have been intrigued by the finding that roughly 12% of women have a genetic condition that causes them to have four types of cones in their retinas rather than three. Does this provide evidence that at least some women have genetically superior color vision? When put to the test, color vision in these women was no better than in women with the usual three cone types (Jordan et al., 2010). So, direct evidence of Alexander's ideas on innate gender differences in color vision still awaits us.

Keep in mind that both color preference and gender roles may also be highly influenced by the particular culture in which a boy or girl is raised. For example,

optic chiasm the point in the brain where the optic nerve from the left eye crosses over the optic nerve from the right eye in many cultures, products marketed to girls are often colored with bright, warm colors. Worldwide, girls' toys often involve babies, fashion, cooking, nurturing, and other domestic themes, whereas toys marketed to boys frequently involve vehicles, weaponry, and darker, cooler colors. Thus, observed differences in gender roles and color preferences may simply reflect what we teach our children to prefer. We'll have more to say about gender roles and gender differences in Chapter 9. For now, let's turn our attention to our other senses.

Quiz Yourself

3.2

1. **Juan was born with no cones in his retina. How will this condition affect Juan?**
   a. He will be blind.
   b. He will not be able to see black or white.
   c. He will see the world in shades of black and white.
   d. His vision will be blurry.
2. **Which theory best explains why Sara would see flashes of red light after 8 hours of working on a computer monitor that has a green and black screen?**
   a. The opponent-process theory
   b. The trichromatic theory
   c. The rod-and-cone theory
   d. The theory of red–green color blindness
3. **You have just returned to a darkened theater after a trip to the concession stand. Now you have a problem—you can't find your seat in the dark. Knowing what you do about vision, which of the following would most likely help you find your seat?**
   a. Stare straight ahead at the seats.
   b. Search for your seat out of the corner of your eye.
   c. Go back out into the bright light and allow your eyes to deplete their photopigments.
   d. Cross your eyes and search for your seat.

Answers 1. c; 2. a; 3. b

3.3 Hearing: Listening to the World

Like vision, hearing is one of our most important senses; much of what we learn in life depends on these two senses. Additionally, hearing plays an important role in our ability to communicate with others. Sounds, such as a human voice, produce waves of compressed air that our ears convert to neural impulses. Like light waves, sound waves have their own psychophysical properties. A sound wave has both peaks and valleys (see • FIGURE 3.7).

A **cycle** includes the peak of the wave and the valley that immediately follows it (Figure 3.7a). Counting the number of cycles in a given time frame allows us to determine the **frequency** of a sound wave. Traditionally, the frequency of sound waves is measured in hertz (Hz), or the number of cycles completed per second. A sound wave with a frequency of 1,000 Hz would complete 1,000 cycles per second. The **loudness** of the sound we hear, measured in **decibels (dB),** corresponds to the amplitude of a sound wave (Figure 3.7b). The higher the amplitude, the more pressure is exerted on the eardrum, and the louder the sound is.

The frequency of a sound wave corresponds to the **pitch** of the sound we perceive: the higher the frequency, the higher the pitch. The average young adult can perceive sounds that range from a low of 20 Hz to a high of 20,000 Hz (Gelfand, 1981). For example, we can hear the low pitch of a foghorn and the high pitch of a mosquito's wings. We lose some of this range as we age, however, particularly our ability to hear high pitches. Some young people have capitalized on this by downloading ultra-high-pitched "mosquito" ringtones for their

cycle a physical characteristic of energy defined as a wave peak and the valley that immediately follows it

frequency a physical characteristic of energy defined as the number of cycles that occur in a given unit of time

loudness the psychophysical property of sound that corresponds to the amplitude of a sound wave

decibels [DESS-uh-bells] (dB) the unit of measurement used to describe the loudness of a sound

pitch the psychophysical property of sound that corresponds to the frequency of a sound wave cell phones so that parents and other adults will be unaware of incoming calls and text messages. Tones above 16,000 Hz go unheard by people as young as 24! Luckily, most of the everyday sounds we hear fall well below the 20,000-Hz level. In fact, unless the gradual deterioration impairs our ability to hear sounds at 1,800 Hz and below, our ability to comprehend speech should remain pretty much intact (Welford, 1987). Yet all of us would do well to protect our hearing. Threats to our hearing are all around us, and if we experience too much damage, we may find our hearing loss to be problematic.

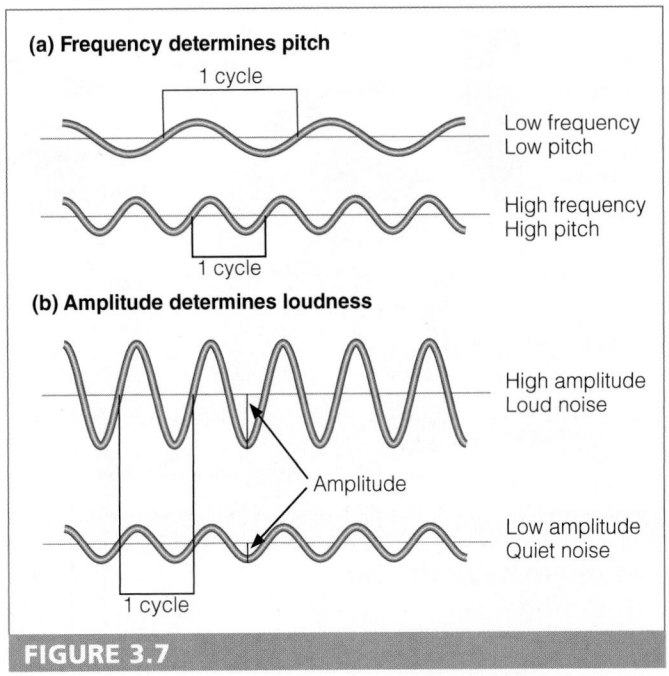

FIGURE 3.7

The Amplitude and Frequency of Sound Waves

The frequency, or number of cycles per second, determines the sound's pitch. The higher the wave's frequency, the higher the sound's pitch will be (a). The height, or amplitude, of a sound wave determines its loudness. Higher amplitudes correspond to louder sounds (b).

3.3.1 • Environmental Noise and Hearing Loss

Living and working in noisy environments increase the likelihood of experiencing hearing loss as we age. For example, people living in North American urban areas experience greater age-related hearing loss than do people living in quiet rural areas of Africa (Bennett, 1990). In fact, roughly 10% of Americans between 20 and 69 have already experienced some level of permanent damage to their hearing as a result of overexposure to noise (Griest, Folmer, & Martin, 2007).

These numbers are not too surprising because today's world is full of noise-producing technologies (lawn mowers, power tools, MP3 players, and so on) that can be damaging to our hearing. For example, typical rock concert amplifier volumes of 120 dB can damage your hearing in as little as 15 minutes. A lawnmower can put out 90 dB, as can a noisy restaurant. Any sound over 85 dB has the potential to damage your hearing with prolonged exposure. Of particular concern today is that so many people listen to loud music on MP3 or personal listening devices (PLDs), some of which are capable of outputting more than 130 dB! Studies indicate that up to 25% of college students listen to their PLDs in violation of the so-called *60–60 rule*, which states that to avoid hearing damage, one should listen to a PLD for no more than 60 minutes a day at 60% of its maximum volume (Danhauer et al., 2009). So, think about turning down the volume and wearing ear protection when using any noisy machinery. You might just thank yourself later in life!

© Blend Images/MasterFile

Listening to personal listening devices (PLDs) at too high a volume and for too long a time can permanently damage your hearing. To protect your hearing, follow the 60–60 rule: listen to your PLD at no more than 60% of its maximum volume for no more than 60 minutes.

3.3.2 • The Anatomy and Function of the Ear

The very outside of the **outer ear** is called the *pinna* (●FIGURE 3.8). This is the part of the body normally referred to as the ear and earlobe. The pinna acts as a funnel to gather sound waves. After being gathered by the pinna, sound waves are channeled through the *auditory canal,* where the sounds are amplified and then strike the membrane at the end of the auditory canal, the *eardrum.*

The eardrum, or *tympanic membrane,* is a very thin membrane that vibrates as the incoming sound waves strike it, much as the head of a drum vibrates when a drumstick strikes it. The three bones of the **middle ear** that are directly behind the eardrum are the *hammer, anvil,* and *stirrup* (Figure 3.8). These very small bones mechanically amplify the vibrations coming from the eardrum and transmit them to the **inner ear.** The middle ear connects to the inner ear at the point where the stirrup rests against the *oval window* (Figure 3.8). The oval window

outer ear the outermost parts of the ear, including the pinna, auditory canal, and surface of the ear drum

middle ear the part of the ear behind the ear drum and in front of the oval window, including the hammer, anvil, and stirrup

inner ear the innermost portion of the ear that includes the cochlea

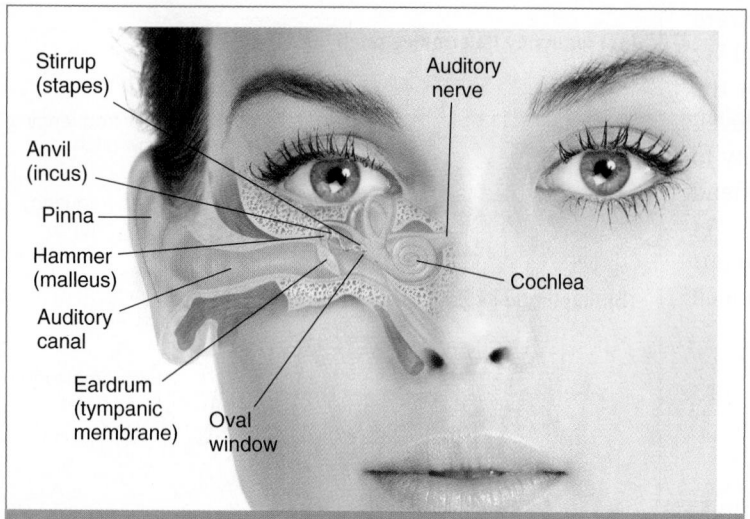

© iStockphoto.com/iconogenic

FIGURE 3.8

The Anatomy of the Ear

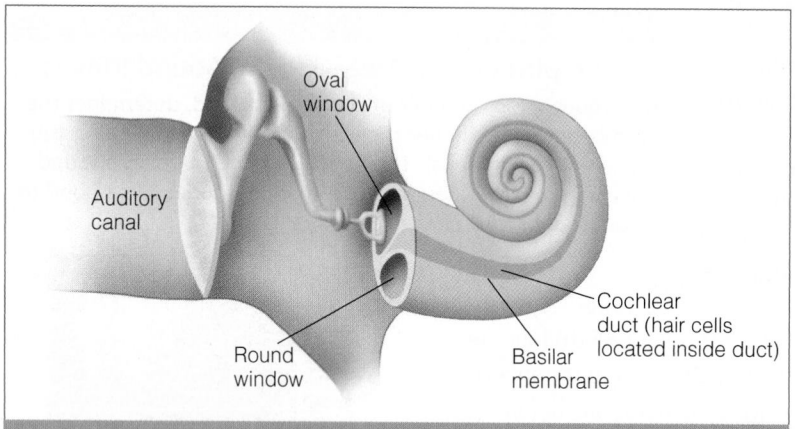

FIGURE 3.9

Enlarged Detail of the Inner Ear

is found on the outer end of the **cochlea**, one of the major components of the inner ear. The cochlea is a coiled, fluid-filled tube about 1.4 inches long that resembles a snail (Matlin & Foley, 1997). It is here that sound waves are turned into neural impulses.

If you were to uncoil the cochlea, you would see that it resembles a flexible tube that is closed off at the end. The inside of the tube contains a fluid-filled canal called the *cochlear duct* (• FIGURE 3.9). The floor of the cochlear duct is lined with the **basilar membrane**. Growing out of the basilar membrane are specialized **hair cells** that convert sound wave energy into neural impulses.

Incoming sound waves cause the bones of the middle ear to vibrate (Figures 3.8 and 3.9). The vibration of the stirrup against the oval window sets up a pressure wave inside the fluid-filled cochlea. As this wave travels through the cochlea, the cochlear duct begins to ripple. Inside the cochlear duct, the traveling wave ripples across the hair cells, causing them to begin sending neural impulses.

3.3.3 • The Auditory Pathways of the Brain

Once the hair cells convert sound into neural impulses, these impulses must be sent to the brain for further processing. Attached to the end of the cochlea is the **auditory nerve** (Figure 3.8). The bundled neurons of the auditory nerve gather the information from the hair cells to relay it to the brain. • FIGURE 3.10 shows the path that auditory information takes from the ears to the brain. Notice that auditory information from each ear reaches both hemispheres of the cortex, after leaving the brainstem. It was in the brainstem that Jean-Dominique Bauby lost part of his hearing after the stroke damaged portions of his brainstem, including the *pons* (see Chapter 2).

The auditory cortex has the capacity to decode the meanings of the sounds we hear. Our next task is to examine how the brain perceives, or makes sense of, the auditory information it receives from the ears. We will begin by looking at several theories that explain our ability to perceive pitch.

cochlea [COCK-lee-uh] the curled, fluid-filled tube in the inner ear that contains the basilar membrane

basilar membrane the structure in the cochlear duct that contains the hair cells, which convert sound waves into action potentials

hair cells neurons that grow out of the basilar membrane and convert sound waves into action potentials

auditory nerve the nerve that carries information from the inner ear to the brain

place theory a theory that proposes that our brain decodes pitch by noticing which region of the basilar membrane is most active

PLACE THEORY OF PITCH PERCEPTION

Hermann von Helmholtz, who is credited by many with the trichromatic theory of color vision, also studied pitch perception. His **place theory** of pitch perception (Helmholtz, 1863/1930) proposes that sounds of different frequencies excite different hair cells at particular points along the basilar membrane. According to place theory, the brain receives information on pitch from the location, or place, on the basilar membrane that is being most excited by incoming sound waves. Evidence suggests that place theory may indeed explain some of our ability to perceive pitch.

In the late 1950s, Georg von Békésy conducted some important studies using pure tones, made up of single sound waves, which revealed that different pitches caused the most vibration at different points along the basilar membrane (Békésy, 1960). Low-frequency sounds activate the far end of the basilar membrane the most. High-frequency sounds cause the most activation at the front part of the basilar membrane, near the oval window. Hair cells at the front of the basilar membrane are most vulnerable to damage, explaining why age-related hearing loss occurs first for high pitches.

Although Békésy's research on place theory does describe some of our ability to perceive pitch, he only tested pure tones composed of a single frequency. He did not test tones of other *timbres,* meaning tones made up of multiple frequencies. This is important because most of the sounds we hear in life are a mixture of frequencies. When place theory is tested using complex sounds rather than pure tones, it does not fare as well as it does in explaining perception of pure tones (Matlin & Foley, 1997).

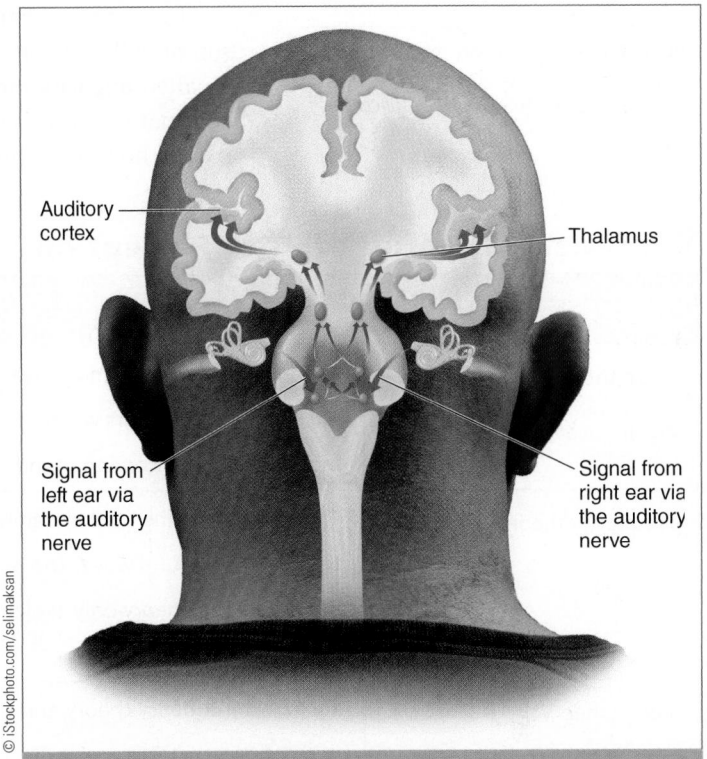

© iStockphoto.com/selimaksan

FIGURE 3.10
The Auditory Pathways in the Brain

FREQUENCY THEORY OF PITCH PERCEPTION

Frequency theory proposes that our brain receives information about pitch directly from the frequency at which the hair cells are firing (Rutherford, 1886; Wever, 1949/1970). An incoming sound wave will cause the hair cells to fire action potentials at a frequency that is equal to the frequency of the sound wave. For example, a sound wave at 500 Hz would cause the hair cells to fire 500 action potentials per second; a sound wave at 750 Hz would produce 750 action potentials per second.

Frequency theory is a very simple concept, but it has a severe limitation. Hair cells can fire only at a maximum rate of 1,000 action potentials per second (1,000 Hz), yet we can hear sounds in the range of 20–20,000 Hz. Frequency theory obviously falls short in explaining perception of pitches over 1,000 Hz.

frequency theory a theory that proposes that our brain decodes pitch directly from the frequency at which the hair cells of the basilar membrane are firing

volley theory a theory that proposes that our brain decodes pitch by noticing the frequency at which groups of hair cells on the basilar membrane are firing

VOLLEY THEORY OF PITCH PERCEPTION

Volley theory is an updated version of frequency theory that seeks to explain perception of sounds over 1,000 Hz (Wever, 1949/1970). According to volley theory, "teams" of hair cells work together to give us the perception of sounds over 1,000 Hz. For example, let's say you hear a tone of 3,000 Hz (a pitch higher than human speech). No single hair cell can fire at 3,000 Hz, but three hair cells, each firing at 1,000 Hz, can work together as a group to tell your brain that you are hearing a 3,000-Hz tone.

DUPLICITY THEORY: AN INTEGRATION

Volley theory seems adequate to explain pitch perception, but we still have to deal with place theory, which also seems to explain some aspects of our perception. Recall that Georg von Békésy (1960) found that different pitches excite different parts of the basilar membrane. Volley theory cannot explain why this would be the case. So, what is going on in our ears? Is it the place or the frequency of the excited hair cells that tells us what pitch we are hearing? It may well be *both*.

duplicity theory a theory that proposes that a combination of volley and place theory explains how our brain decodes pitch

Today researchers widely believe that we perceive pitch through a combination of volley theory and place theory. This combination of perceptual processes is called **duplicity theory**. Researchers strongly suspect that frequency and place information work together to give us pitch perception, but we don't yet understand exactly how these two mechanisms work together.

You Review **Theories of Pitch Perception**

Theory	Description
Place theory	Different pitches of sound activate specific regions of the basilar membrane more than others. Pitch perception occurs when the brain notices which portions of the basilar membrane are being most excited by incoming sound waves.
Frequency theory	The hair cells of the basilar membrane fire action potentials at a rate equal to the frequency of the incoming sound wave. The brain determines pitch by noticing the rate at which the hair cells are firing. This theory only explains perception of pitches up to 1,000 Hz, the maximum firing rate of a hair cell.
Volley theory	Similar to frequency theory, this theory states that groups of hair cells fire as teams to give us the perception of pitches over 1,000 Hz. For example, three hair cells each firing at 1,000 Hz together yield the perception of a 3,000-Hz tone.
Duplicity theory	This theory states that a combination of frequency and place information is used in pitch perception. Exactly how these sources of information are integrated in the brain is still being investigated.

Quiz Yourself 3.3

1. Jack is 58 years old and having trouble with his hearing. He has spent his life working around noisy machinery without any ear protection. Knowing what you do about hearing, what type of hearing loss is Jack most likely experiencing?
   a. Total deafness
   b. Deafness for low pitches
   c. Deafness for medium pitches
   d. Deafness for high pitches

2. By turning up the volume on your stereo, you are changing the _____ of the sound waves being emitted by the stereo.
   a. amplitude
   b. wavelength
   c. pitch
   d. width

3. _____ theory proposes that pitch is perceived when the brain locates the region of the basilar membrane that is firing the most action potentials.
   a. Frequency
   b. Basilar
   c. Place
   d. Volley

Answers 1. d; 2. a; 3. c

3.4 The Other Senses: Taste, Smell, Touch, and the Body Senses

3.4.1 • Taste: Information from the Tongue

For most of us, the senses of taste and smell are interconnected. These two senses are called *chemical senses* because they require that certain chemicals come into direct contact with our sense organs. Vision and hearing don't require such direct contact; we can perceive visual and auditory stimuli at a distance. But for taste, or **gustation**, to occur, certain chemicals in foods and other substances must be dissolved in our saliva and come into direct contact with the sense organ commonly known as the tongue. For smell, chemicals in the nearby air—from food or other substances—must come into contact with cells in the nasal cavity.

gustation [gus-TAY-shun] the sense of taste

papillae [puh-PILL-ee] bumps on the tongue that many people mistake for taste buds

taste buds the sense organs for taste that are found between the papillae on the tongue

Jack Louth/Getty Images

If you burn your taste buds, you will experience temporary loss of taste sensation until the taste buds grow back.

SENSING FLAVOR: THE FIVE BASIC TASTES

Traditionally, it was believed that humans could sense only four different types of tastes: *bitter, sweet, salty,* and *sour* (Bartoshuk & Beauchamp, 1994). However, it now appears that humans are also sensitive to a fifth taste called *umami,* or glutamate (Rolls, 2000). Umami is a meaty, brothy flavor that is more common in Asian foods than it is in Western cuisine (MSG, or monosodium glutamate, is a common ingredient in Asian dishes), so Westerners are not likely to be as familiar with umami's flavor as they are with the other basic tastes. Nonetheless, studies indicate that the ability to taste umami exists (Damak et al., 2003; Hodson & Linden, 2006) and that umami receptors are activated by glutamate (Lopez Cascales et al., 2010).

It makes good sense that our tongues can detect these five tastes, because they are associated with certain types of foods that have implications for our survival (Scott & Plata-Salaman, 1991). For example, sweet flavors are associated with edible foods and bitter tastes with poisons. It is likely that our sense of taste helps us meet our nutritional needs and avoid the numerous poisons that exist around us.

FROM TONGUE TO TASTE: HOW DO WE EXPERIENCE FLAVOR?

When you look at your tongue in the mirror, you normally see a bunch of little bumps lining its surface. We'll guess that you were taught to refer to these visible bumps as taste buds. This is incorrect—the bumps you see are the **papillae** of the tongue. Your **taste buds** actually reside in the pits between the papillae (• FIGURE 3.11). Your taste buds are what convert the chemicals in the foods you eat into the neural impulses that convey taste information to your brain. Most people have between 2,000 and 5,000 taste buds on their tongue (I. J. Miller & Bartoshuk, 1991). Unlike some types of sensory cells, taste buds can regenerate. This is important

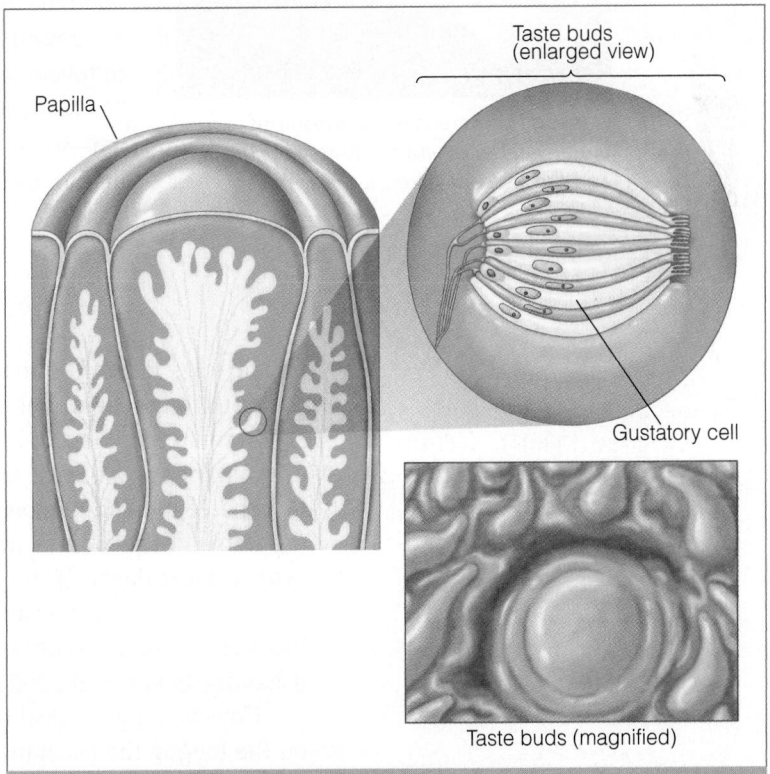

FIGURE 3.11

Papilla and Taste Buds

Taste buds are the sensory receptors for taste. Contrary to popular belief, the bumps on our tongues are not taste buds—they are papillae. Our taste buds are located next to the papillae on the tongue.

Psychology Applies to Your World:

Why Don't We All Like the Same Foods?

Have you ever found yourself discussing where to go for dinner with your friends, only to find that everyone has a different opinion on which type of food you should have? What accounts for the wide variation in taste preferences that humans experience?

As it turns out, several factors affect our taste preferences. One of these is age. We lose some of our taste buds permanently with age. This may contribute to the diminished sense of taste that older adults often experience (Nordin et al., 2003). With fewer active taste buds, it might seem that older people would tend to prefer richly flavored foods. In fact, some people have proposed that diets enriched with intensely flavored foods may help maintain elders' appetites. However, studies have shown that this strategy may not always work (Essed et al., 2007).

Culture is another factor in taste preferences. For example, the spouse of one of your authors is from El Salvador, where iguana meat is considered a treat enjoyed mostly by the wealthy. In the United States, iguanas are more likely to be kept as pets than eaten. Why do food preferences vary across cultures? One reason is that the availability of food sources dictates what a particular people can eat. Central Americans eat iguana meat today partly because their ancestors once ate the wild iguanas that roamed there. Every culture must take advantage of the food sources at its disposal, and hunger can make foods taste better, especially when those foods provide needed nutrients (Mobini, Chambers, & Yeomans, 2007).

Catherine Karnow/Terra/Corbis

Our food preferences are a result of biological factors, our cultural background, and our personal experience with food.

Religious values and traditions also shape cultural food preferences. For example, observant Jews and Muslims will not eat pork, Hindus often do not eat beef, and Seventh Day Adventists frown upon the use of certain spices (Grivetti, 2000). These taste preferences are passed from generation to generation as parents teach children to follow their religious values.

Many of our individual food preferences develop through learning—some of it very early in life. Research shows that the foods a mother eats can affect the flavor of her breast milk, and exposure to

because we damage our taste buds on a regular basis—for example, when we burn our tongue with hot food.

Many researchers believe that, like the cones of the eye, different taste buds are maximally sensitive to one of the basic flavors (Shallenberger, 1993). Thus, taste perception on the tongue appears to work very much like color perception in the retina. If the brain is informed that the "sweet taste buds" are very active, we taste a sweet flavor. If the "sour taste buds" are most active, we taste something sour. If all flavors are some combination of sweet, salty, sour, bitter, and umami, the presence of five types of taste buds is sufficient to explain our taste perception (Chandrashekar et al., 2006).

However, a good deal of our ability to taste certain flavors depends on where on the tongue the substance is placed. The different types of taste buds are concentrated in certain locations. Over the years, there has been significant disagreement as to exactly where these areas of sensitivity are located, although there is more agreement on the sweet and sour tastes. Sweet tastes are best detected at the front of the tongue and sour tastes on the sides; salty tastes are thought to be detected best near the front of the tongue (Shallenberg, 1993).

these flavors during breast-feeding can affect her child's later taste preferences (Mennella & Beauchamp, 1991). Being exposed to a variety of flavors in infancy tends to make infants more open to new and novel foods (Hausner et al., 2010).

Although the influence of learning on food preferences is strong, evidence also suggests that biological factors can affect our sense of taste. Prior to menopause, women's ability to taste fluctuates with hormone levels; and after menopause, the ability to taste declines (Prutkin et al., 2000). There are also some genetic variations in the ability to taste. Some people, called *supertasters,* have a higher-than-average number of taste buds and are able to strongly taste a bitter compound called *6-n-propylthiocuracil* (PROP). In contrast, *nontasters* perceive very little or no bitterness from PROP (Bartoshuk, 2000). Nontasters have been shown to eat a wider variety of foods (Azar, 1998; Pasquet et al., 2002) and have higher body mass indexes (BMIs; Feeney et al., 2011) than supertasters do. Compared to nontasters, female PROP tasters tend to eat more fat and less fruit in their diets (Yackinous & Guinard, 2002). Supertasters may avoid some foods that are rich in cancer-fighting compounds but also have bitter flavors (such as Brussels sprouts). Being a supertaster may also allow a person to make finer discriminations among flavors. Connoisseurs of wine have been shown to be more likely to be supertasters or at least "medium" tasters. Their increased ability to perceive PROP may allow them to perceive nuanced flavors in the wine (Pickering, Jain, & Bezawada, 2013).

Finally, our sense of taste is not influenced solely by our culture, early learning, or taste buds. Our sense of taste is also heavily dependent on our sense of smell (Shepard, 2006). If you've ever tried to taste food when you've had a bad cold, you know that your sense of smell makes a significant contribution to taste and that clogged nasal passages tend to make food taste bland. Our food preferences are a result of biological factors, our cultural background, and our personal experience with food.

Bill Losh/The Image Bank/Getty Images

The inability to smell also limits the ability to taste.

You may be surprised to learn that the center of the tongue lacks taste buds. You won't taste flavors that are placed directly in the center of your tongue. In a sense, this region of the tongue is like the blindspot in the eye—no taste sensation can occur here (Matlin & Foley, 1997). Despite this taste blindspot, we still manage to taste the foods we eat because chewing distributes food across the tongue.

Of course, only after your brain has done its part can you become consciously aware of the flavor of your food. Each taste bud is connected to neurons that receive input from that taste bud. These neurons join together to form three nerves. One nerve gathers input from the front of the tongue, another from the back of the tongue, and a third from the throat. These nerves travel to the medulla and the pons of the brainstem before conveying the taste information to the thalamus. Like most sensory information, taste information travels from the thalamus to the "thinking" part of the brain, the cortex. Most of the taste information ends up in the somatosensory cortex of the parietal lobe, but some of the information is diverted to the limbic system before reaching the cortex. It's here in the cortex that we perceive the flavor of our food.

3.4.2 • Smell: Aromas, Odors, and a Warning System

olfaction the sense of smell

olfactory epithelium [ole-FACT-uh-ree epp-ith-THEEL-ee-um] a special piece of skin at the top of the nasal cavity that contains the olfactory receptors

Olfaction, our sense of smell, has adaptive value. Smells can alert us to danger. The ability to smell smoke enables us to detect a fire long before we see flames. The rotten smell of spoiled food warns us not to eat it. Without such odoriferous warnings, we could easily find ourselves in harm's way.

Like the sense of taste, the sense of smell is a chemical sense. Odors come from airborne chemicals that are diffused in the air. When we inhale these molecules into our nose, we may experience smelling the substance. Compared with our other senses, our sense of smell is quite sensitive. Recall from our earlier discussion of sensory thresholds that we can detect the presence of a single drop of perfume in a three-room apartment (see Table 3.1). When it comes to discriminating between odors, we can detect roughly 500,000 different scents (Cain, 1988), and we can identify by name about 10,000 different smells (Lancet et al., 1993). Yet, despite these impressive abilities, in daily life we typically pay attention only to odors that are quite strong (Sela & Sobel, 2010). For example, we are frequently unaware of the detectable smells of other people unless they are strong (for example, heavy cologne or strong body odor). In other words, smells have to make a big impact on us to capture our attention.

THE MYSTERY OF SMELL

Researchers have not been able to determine precisely how our sense of smell works. Of the senses we have described to this point, smell is by far the least understood. What we do know is that we are able to smell because of a special piece of skin that lines the top of the nasal cavity (• FIGURE 3.12). This special piece of skin, the **olfactory epithelium**, probably contains only a few hundred

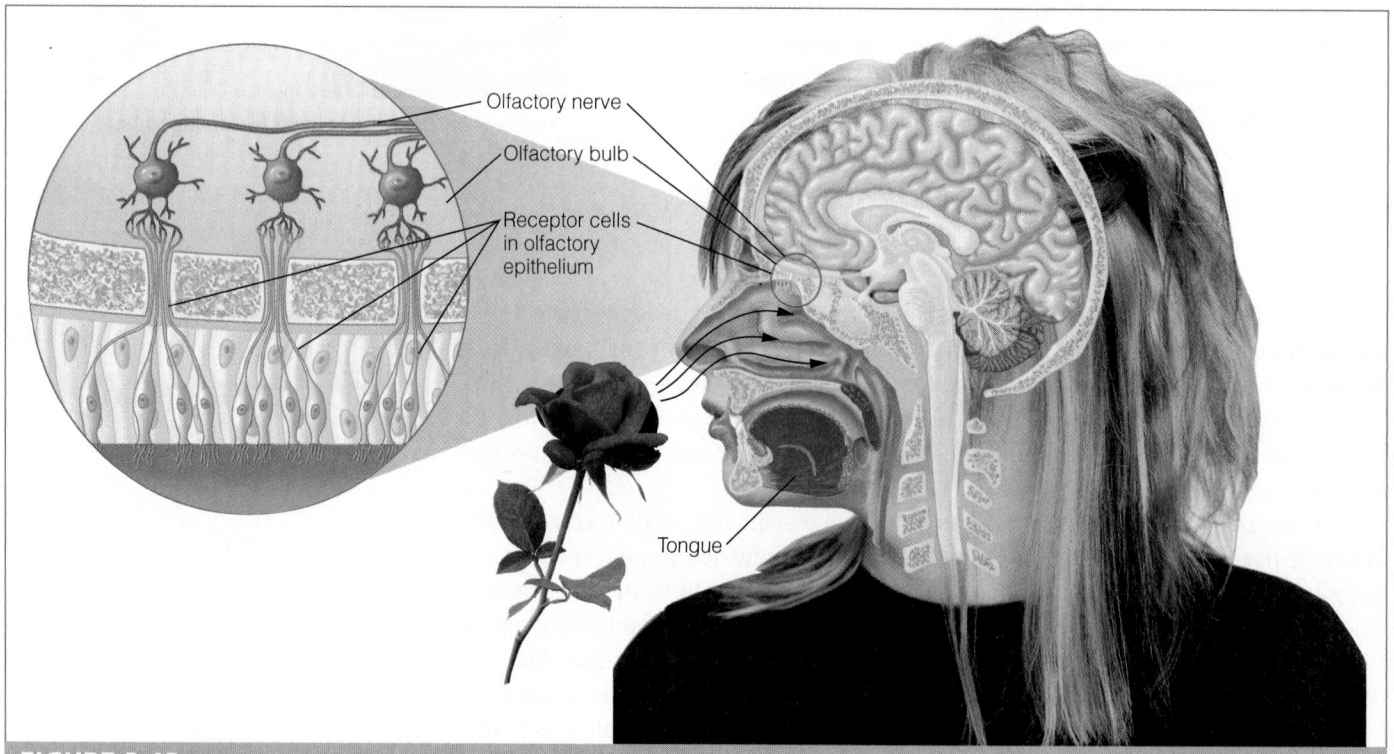

Woman: © Wayne Eardley/Masterfile; Rose: © Margo Harrison/Shutterstock.com

FIGURE 3.12

The Anatomy of the Nose

Odors in the form of airborne chemicals are inhaled into the nasal cavity, where sensory cells in the olfactory epithelium convert them into neural signals.

different types of odor receptors (Lancet et al., 1993). When we breathe in odor-laden air, the odor molecules reach the receptors in the olfactory epithelium and stimulate these cells. This stimulation accomplishes the conversion of odor into smell, but just how our brain understands what we smell is not well understood at this time (Matlin & Foley, 1997). One theory, **lock-and-key theory**, proposes that olfactory receptors are excited by odor molecules in much the same way that neurotransmitters excite receptor sites on the postsynaptic neuron (Amoore, 1970). According to lock-and-key theory, specific odor molecules have the power to "unlock" or excite certain olfactory receptors in the olfactory epithelium.

lock-and-key theory a theory that proposes that olfactory receptors are excited by odor molecules in a way that is similar to the way in which neurotransmitters excite receptor sites

pheromones [FAIR-uh-moans] airborne chemicals that are released from glands and detected by the vomeronasal organs in some animals and perhaps humans

Once the cells of the epithelium have converted odor into neural impulses, these signals travel across the *olfactory nerve* to the *olfactory bulb* of the brain. The olfactory bulb is located just below the bottom edge of the frontal lobe of the brain (see Figure 3.12). The olfactory bulb processes incoming information before sending it on to other parts of the brain. Some olfactory information goes directly to the primary smell cortex, in the temporal lobes of the brain.

Other olfactory information is sent to both the cortex and the limbic system. Recall from Chapter 2 that the limbic system regulates emotional and motivational activity. The limbic system seems to be heavily involved in the processing of olfactory information. This may explain the strong emotional reactions we often have to certain smells. For example, the smell of one of your favorite childhood meals may conjure up beloved memories of your childhood. Are there particular smells that bring back emotionally charged memories for you?

CHEMOSIGNALS: PHEROMONES AND THE VOMERONASAL SENSE

Some researchers believe that humans have yet another sense somewhat related to smell. This sense, the *vomeronasal sense*, is well documented in animals (Doty, 2001). Many animals communicate with each other via airborne *chemosignals* called **pheromones**. Pheromones are produced by glands in the animal's body and dispersed into the air, where other animals then inhale them. Such animals are equipped with vomeronasal organs that can detect the presence of inhaled pheromones. Perhaps you have seen a cat inhale deeply through its open mouth—a process called cat's *flehmen*. The cat is passing pheromone-laden air over special organs, called Jacobson's organs, in the roof of its mouth. These organs can detect the presence of pheromones. The presence of such an organ in humans has been the subject of controversy, but at least one study has found evidence that some people have vomeronasal organs in their nasal cavities (Won et al., 2000). There is also some suggestion that a little-known cranial nerve (cranial nerve 0, or CN0), found in humans and many other vertebrates, may play a role in the detection of pheromones. CN0 travels from the nasal cavity to the brain, including areas of the brain known to be involved in sexual behavior (see Fields, 2007).

Although the existence of human vomeronasal organs is controversial, it does seem that pheromones affect certain aspects of our behavior, particularly those related to sexuality. For example, when women are exposed to pheromones in the underarm secretions of another woman, their menstrual cycle tends to synchronize with the other woman's cycle (Larkin, 1998; Stern & McClintock, 1998). And after exposure to a pheromone that is released from men's hair follicles, women increase their social interactions with males (E. Miller, 1999). Other pheromones found in men's sweat tend to improve a woman's mood state (Monti-Bloch et al., 1998).

It also appears that when women cry, their tears contain chemosignals that may affect men's behavior. Recently, Shani Gelstein and colleagues (2011) collected women's tears in a vial as they watched a sad movie and later had men smell the tears without the women present. Compared to a control group that

© NaturePL/SuperStock

Many mammals use pheromones to communicate with each other. This cat is passing pheromone-laden air over vomeronasal organs in the roof of its mouth.

© Alena Ozerova/Shutterstock.com

Research suggests that the tears of women contain chemosignals that impact men by reducing their level of testosterone production.

sniffed pure saline, the men who sniffed tears experienced decreased levels of testosterone (male sex hormones, see Chapter 2), and they reported lowered sexual arousal. fMRI scans of the men's brains also showed reduced brain activity in areas of the brain related to sexual arousal, such as the hypothalamus and the left *fusiform gyrus* (Gelstein et al., 2011). These findings suggest that men may be biologically programmed to lose interest in sex when they encounter a crying woman. More research is needed to determine the significance of this effect. Also unclear is whether chemosignals are found in the tears of men and children and what, if any, effect they may have on others.

Whether or not a vomeronasal sense exists separately from our olfactory sense, it is clear that chemosignals affect our social behavior. For example, people born without a sense of smell have been shown to experience specific relationship difficulties. Specifically, males without a sense of smell exhibit fewer sexual relationships and females without the ability to smell exhibit a weaker sense of security with their partners (Croy, Bojanowski, & Hummel, 2013). Odd as it may sound, our sense of smell appears to facilitate our social interactions with others.

3.4.3 • Touch: The Skin Sense

Touch is another sense that is important to social relationships. Touch is associated with many of life's pleasurable experiences. Feeling a friendly pat on the back can certainly enhance our social interactions. Sexual activity depends heavily on our ability to feel touch. But our ability to sense with our skin also affects our survival. Through our skin we feel touch, temperature, and pain.

dermis the inner layer of the skin

epidermis the outer layer of the skin

Our keen sense of touch originates in our skin. The skin is composed of several layers that contain touch receptors. The inner layer, the **dermis**, contains most of the touch receptors (• FIGURE 3.13). The skin's outer layer is the **epidermis**, which consists of several layers of dead skin cells. The epidermis also contains touch receptors, especially in areas of the skin that do not have hair, such as

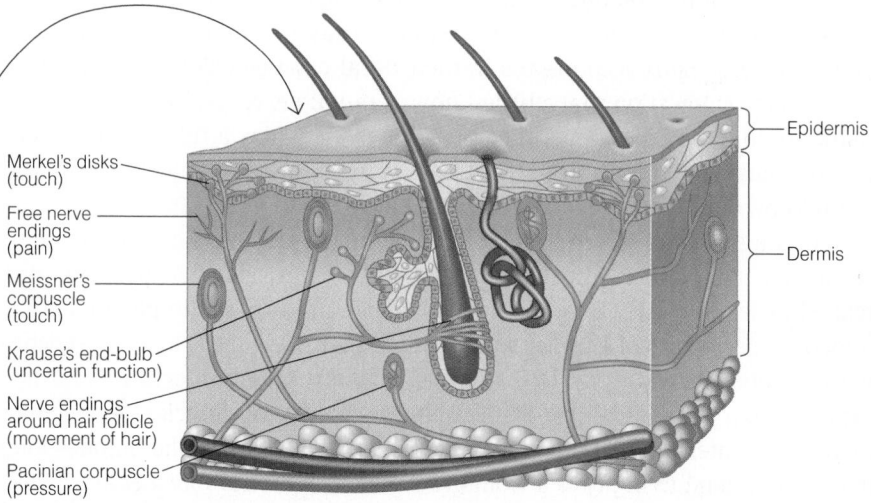

© Jose Luis Palaez/Blend Images/Corbis

FIGURE 3.13

Anatomy of the Skin and Its Receptors

Different types of skin receptors pick up different types of stimulation.

the fingertips. Receptors in our fingertips are arguably the most important touch receptors in the body because we use our hands so much in interacting with the world (Martuzzi et al., 2013).

We have different types of receptors for touch, temperature, and pain (Figure 3.13). We know more about the function of the touch receptors than we do about the pain and temperature receptors. Pressure on the skin pushes against the axons of the touch receptors. This causes a change in the axonal membrane's permeability to positive ions, allowing them to enter the cell (Hu et al., 2010; Loewenstein, 1960). As you recall from Chapter 2, as positive ions enter a cell, the cell becomes more likely to fire an action potential. If the touch is intense enough to allow the receptors to reach threshold, neural impulses will be fired. These impulses travel to the spinal cord, and then to the brain. In the brain, the signals enter the thalamus and then go on to the somatosensory cortex of the parietal lobe. Some signals, particularly those indicating the presence of threatening stimuli, go to the limbic system as well as the somatosensory cortex (Coren, Ward, & Enns, 1999). Once the signals reach the somatosensory cortex, our brain interprets the sensation and directs us to take the appropriate action.

3.4.4 • The Body Senses: Experiencing the Physical Body in Space

So far, we have covered what are referred to as the five senses: vision, hearing, taste, smell, and touch. Do we possess other senses? The answer is yes, but this time, we're not talking about ESP. We are referring to the body senses, the senses that help us experience our physical bodies in space: *kinesthesis* and the *vestibular sense*.

kinesthesis [kin-ess-THEE-sis] the ability to sense the position of our body parts in relation to one another and in relation to space

vestibular [ves-STIB-you-lar] sense the sense of balance

KINESTHESIS

Kinesthesis is the ability to sense the position of our body parts in space and in relation to one another. As you walk, you are aware of where your arms, legs, and head are in relation to the ground. Kinesthetic sense is important to athletes, especially to gymnasts and high divers. It allows them to know where their bodies are as they execute their routines and dives. Our kinesthetic sense uses information from the muscles, tendons, skin, and joints to keep us oriented at all times. The information from these sources is processed in the somatosensory cortex and the cerebellum of the brain (see Chapter 2).

THE VESTIBULAR SENSE

Another important body sense is our sense of balance, or **vestibular sense**. The vestibular system uses input from the semicircular canals and the vestibular sacs of the inner ear to keep us balanced (• FIGURE 3.14). These structures are filled with a fluid gel that surrounds hair cells much like those in the cochlea. When your head moves in any direction, the gel inside these structures moves in the opposite direction. The movement of the gel bends the

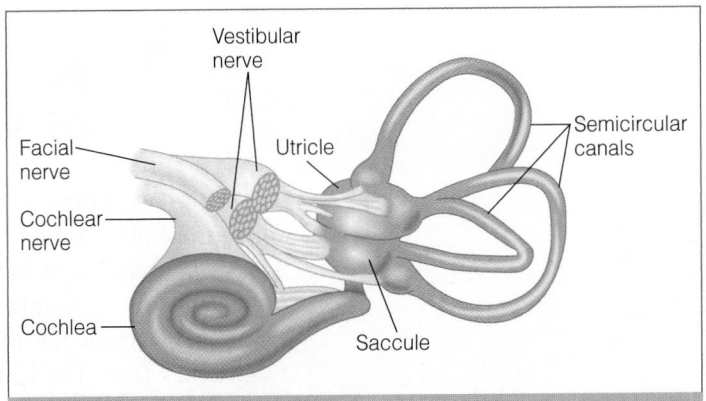

FIGURE 3.14

The Vestibular Organs

The vestibular system helps us balance our body by monitoring the position and acceleration of our head as we move. To accomplish this, a gel-like fluid in the semicircular canals, saccule, and utricle presses against hair cells much like those found in the cochlea of the inner ear. When the hair cells of the vestibular system are moved, they signal the brain with information about the orientation of our head in three-dimensional space.

Nick Laham/Getty Images Sport/Getty Images

Our vestibular sense keeps us balanced, and the kinesthetic sense allows this skateboarder to perform intricate moves without falling.

hair cells and stimulates them to send neural impulses to the brain, which then uses these signals to determine the orientation of your head. Our vestibular system allows us to do such everyday tasks as walking, driving a car, and bending over to pick up a pencil from the floor. Without our vestibular sense, we would simply topple over.

Rapid movements of your head, such as those you experience on spinning carnival rides, can overstimulate the vestibular system. Such movements can cause a violent wave action in the fluid gel of the vestibular system. When the gel crashes against the sensory cells, the result can be dizziness and nausea. People vary with respect to the degree of vestibular stimulation that they can comfortably tolerate.

You now have a working knowledge of how our sensory organs convert environmental energies into neural impulses. Our next topic is perception, or how we make sense of all of this sensory information.

Quiz Yourself

3.4

1. Which of the following is *not* thought to be a taste for which your tongue has receptors?
   a. Salty
   b. Sour
   c. Spicy
   d. Bitter
2. Spinning around and around on a carnival ride is most likely to affect which of your senses?
   a. Taste
   b. Hearing
   c. Smell
   d. Vestibular sense
3. Which of your senses would be *least* likely to be affected when you have a bad head cold?
   a. Taste
   b. Touch
   c. Smell
   d. Vestibular sense

Answers 1. c; 2. d; 3. b

3.5 Perception: The Interpretation of Sensory Information

At the beginning of this chapter, we defined perception as the *interpretation of sensory information*. That's it in a nutshell. When you look at your friend, light bounces off his or her face. This light strikes your retina, and the rods and cones convert the light into neural impulses. Sensation is complete. But now your brain must interpret the meaning of the neural impulses so you will recognize your friend's face. The fact that you believe you are seeing your friend and not, say, a dog or your psychology instructor is the result of perceptual processes in your brain. But how does your brain know that you are seeing your friend's face?

3.5.1 • Using What We Know: Top-Down Perceptual Processing

top-down perceptual processing perception that is guided by prior knowledge or expectations

Top-down perceptual processing occurs when we use previously gained knowledge to help us interpret a stimulus. Let's go back to the example of perceiving your friend's face. When you see a face that you recognize, what leads you to this recognition? Your memory helps you understand the "meaning" of the face you see. You know that faces usually contain two eyes, a nose, a mouth, and so on. Furthermore, you know how your friend's particular eyes, nose, and other features look. This stored knowledge allows you to quickly perceive the face of a friend.

Top-down perceptual processing can also fill in parts of a stimulus that are missing from our actual sensation of it. For example, look at • FIGURE 3.15. You cannot see this man's left leg or his feet, but you probably assume that they are there. Your knowledge of the human body tells you that the odds are slim that he is actually missing the limbs you cannot see. Consequently, in perceiving this picture, you implicitly assume that the "missing" leg and feet do, in fact, exist. This effect is so strong that later when you recall this picture, you might even remember having seen the missing limbs—right down to the type of shoes the man was "wearing."

Unfortunately, this "filling-in" of missing details can sometimes lead to mistakes in perception. Because people have different knowledge and expectations about the world, two people can witness the same event and yet perceive it differently. For example, what if the correct identification of a suspect depended on accurately remembering what he was wearing? Or recalling the color of her eyes? This can be a real problem in eyewitness accounts of crimes (see also Chapter 7). In fact, one study showed that a majority of the falsely convicted people being studied had been mistakenly identified by eyewitnesses (Wells & Olson, 2003). Curiously, research suggests that compared to simply warning prospective jurors about the weaknesses of eyewitness testimony, actually demonstrating the limitations of eyewitness testimony by having prospective jurors experience firsthand an eyewitness identification procedure can make jurors place less faith in eyewitness testimony when making decisions (Duckworth et al., 2011). The hope is that such interventions may prove useful in reducing false convictions.

PM Images/Iconica/Getty Images

FIGURE 3.15

Top-Down Perceptual Processing

When you perceive the image in this photograph, your knowledge of the human body leads you to have certain expectations about the man in this picture. Because of top-down processing, you do not perceive that this man is missing his feet or parts of his legs.

3.5.2 • Building a Perception "from Scratch": Bottom-Up Perceptual Processing

What do we do when we have very little or no stored knowledge to help us perceive a stimulus? We use a different perceptual process, one that does not rely on stored knowledge or expectations of the stimulus. In **bottom-up perceptual processing**, the properties of the stimulus itself are what we use to build our perception of that stimulus.

bottom-up perceptual processing perception that is not guided by prior knowledge or expectations

ENGAGE YOURSELF! Look at • FIGURE 3.16. What do you see? With few clues about what this stimulus is, you cannot easily use your knowledge to help you perceive it. The stimulus is too ambiguous. Without top-down processing, you are forced to use bottom-up processes to perceive the stimulus. You build your perception of the picture by piecing together your perceptions of the many different components that make up this stimulus. You perceive the lines, curves, dots, shaded areas, and shapes. You then try to fit these

FIGURE 3.16

Top-Down Versus Bottom-Up Processing

What is this picture? With no expectations to guide your perception, you are forced to rely mainly on bottom-up processes. Because the picture is ambiguous, bottom-up processes do not lead to a quick recognition of the stimulus. Now turn to Figure 3.19 (p. 114), which will enable you to engage your top-down perceptual processes. After looking at Figure 3.19, you should be able to quickly recognize the figure in this picture because you now have expectations to guide your perception.

components together to figure out what the drawing means. Most people find it very difficult to figure out what Figure 3.16 is using only bottom-up perceptual processes!

If you are ready to give up and try top-down perceptual processing, look at • FIGURE 3.19 (p. 114). Now turn back to Figure 3.16. You will likely find that you can now readily perceive the image in Figure 3.16. You now have knowledge of what to look for, so perception becomes much easier. Your knowledge of what the picture is guides the way you piece together the components of the stimulus. When you switch to top-down processing, the picture becomes almost obvious.

In the course of a typical day, we probably use both top-down and bottom-up perceptual processes continually. We use bottom-up processes to piece together perceptions of ambiguous stimuli and top-down processes to tell us what we can expect to perceive in certain situations. Perception can be complicated in a three-dimensional world that is full of shapes and forms. To make perception even more complicated, our bodies do not remain stationary during perception. We move. The objects we perceive sometimes move. As a result, the information our senses receive from our world is highly variable. Our perceptual processes must be able to deal with these dynamic conditions. So how do we organize and make sense of our perceptions?

3.5.3 • Understanding What We Sense: Perceiving Size, Shape, and Brightness

One of the phenomena encountered in interpreting sensory data is *perceptual constancy* (see Hatfield & Allred, 2012). When you look at a visual stimulus, the image it projects on your retina is highly influenced by the perspective from which you view the object. Yet your perception of the object is not as dependent on perspective as your sensation is. For example, if you view a friend from a distance of 3 feet, an image of a certain size is projected onto your retina. If you move away and view the same friend from a distance of 6 feet, a smaller image is projected on your retina. Your sensation has changed, but you will not perceive that your friend has shrunk. In this case, your brain appears to step in to correct your perception, to give you a constant perception of the objects that you see in the world. There is evidence that our brains correct not only for size constancy, but also for *shape constancy, brightness constancy,* and *color constancy* (• FIGURE 3.17).

3.5.4 • Depth Perception: Sensing Our 3-D World with 2-D Eyes

Another perceptual challenge is *depth perception*. The world we view is three-dimensional, but the image it projects onto our retina is two-dimensional, like a photograph. Somehow our brains must be able to determine depth from the information our eyes receive from the outside world. What makes this possible?

BINOCULAR DEPTH PERCEPTION

One way that we perceive depth is through binocular depth cues. The term *binocular* means "two-eyed." **Binocular depth cues** rely on information from both eyes—specifically, information based on *retinal disparity*. **Retinal disparity** refers to the

binocular [bye-NOCK-you-lar] depth cues depth cues that utilize information from both eyes

retinal disparity a binocular depth cue that uses the difference in the images projected on the right and left retinas to inform the brain about the distance of a stimulus

Matthias Clamer/The Image Bank/Getty Images

(a) (b) (c) (d)

FIGURE 3.17

Perceptual Constancies

(a) The shape of the image this door projects onto the retina changes dramatically as the orientation of the door changes. Yet we still perceive that the door is rectangular because of shape constancy. (b) Even though the size of the image this person projects onto the retina shrinks as he walks away, because of size constancy, we do not perceive that he is shrinking. (c) The coal may reflect more light in the sun than the paper does in the shade, yet we still perceive that the paper is brighter than the coal because of brightness constancy. (d) Even though this apple is in the shade, we still perceive it as being red because of color constancy.

fact that, because our eyes are set a few centimeters apart, each eye sees a slightly different view of the world. Retinal disparity is greatest for objects that are close to us and less for objects that are distant (● FIGURE 3.18). Thus, the amount of retinal disparity we experience is a function of the distance from which we view an object.

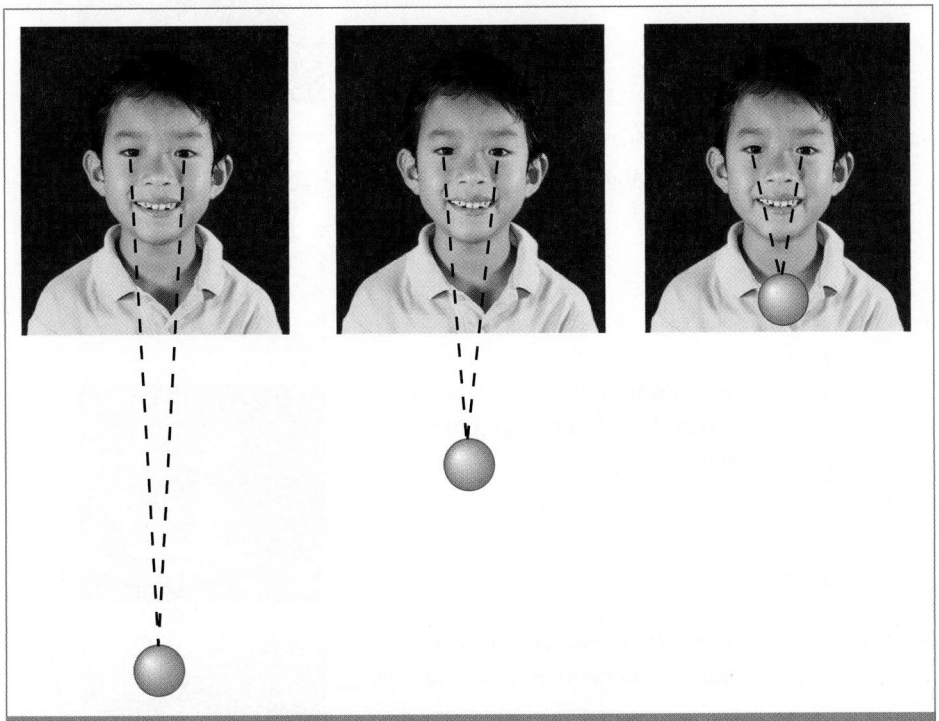

© iStockphoto.com/Byteandpixel

FIGURE 3.18

Binocular Depth Cues

The brain uses retinal disparity, or the degree to which the images projected on the right and left retinas differ from each other, to calculate how far away an object is. The farther away the object, the smaller the degree of retinal disparity.

monocular depth cues depth cues that require information from only one eye

Our brain uses the amount of retinal disparity we experience to calculate how far the object is from us, enabling us to perceive depth in the world.

MONOCULAR DEPTH CUES

Binocular disparity is an important depth cue, but it is not the only way we perceive depth. If it were, we would be in serious trouble if we lost the use of one eye. We also would not be able to perceive depth in paintings or photographs. Luckily, we have other means of depth perception that require the use of only one eye: **monocular depth cues**.

Many of you may have learned about monocular depth cues when you began drawing and painting as a child. Because a canvas has no depth, all parts of the painting are the same distance from the viewer's eyes, and retinal disparity does not help us perceive depth. So how do we perceive depth in paintings and photographs? We use cues such as the *relative size* of objects and *interposition* to tell us which objects are farther away. In fact, some people now believe that the famous Dutch painter Rembrandt had a visual problem that forced him to see the world using only monocular depth cues. Perhaps this helped him use monocular depth cues so effectively in his paintings (Dingfelder, 2010). In fact, one of your authors paints as a hobby, and she often closes one eye when trying to depict a three-dimensional real-world scene on the canvas. • TABLE 3.2 describes some of the most useful monocular depth cues.

FIGURE 3.19

Solution to the Problem in Figure 3.16

After looking at this picture, can you easily find the cow in Figure 3.16?

TABLE 3.2

Monocular Depth Cues

MONOCULAR DEPTH CUE	DESCRIPTION	EXAMPLE
Interposition	More distant objects are partially hidden by closer objects.	 Robert Estall/Encyclopedia/Corbis
Height on the horizon	More distant objects are placed higher on the horizon than closer objects.	 © Perati Komson/Shutterstock.com
Relative size	More distant objects are seen as smaller than closer objects of the same size.	 W. Cody/Flirt/Corbis
Texture gradient	More distant objects have less texture or detail than closer objects.	 68/Ocean/Corbis

TABLE 3.2

Monocular Depth Cues (*continued*)

MONOCULAR DEPTH CUE	DESCRIPTION	EXAMPLE
Aerial perspective	More distant objects are hazier and blurrier than closer objects.	 Sylvain Grandadam/The Image Bank/Getty Images
Linear perspective	Converging lines indicate distance or depth.	 Robert Glusic/keepsake RF/Corbis
Motion parallax	More distant objects appear to move more slowly than closer objects as we pass by them.	 Robert Glusic/keepsake RF/Corbis

Perceptual constancy and depth perception are both important components of our perceptual processing. But how do we perceive the cylindrical shape of a soda can or the rectangular shape of a shoebox? To understand this level of perceptual processing, we will examine theories of *form perception.*

3.5.5 • Perceiving Form: The Gestalt Approach

One influential approach to understanding form perception is the **Gestalt approach**. According to the Gestalt approach, the whole of a perception is greater than the sum of its parts. In fact, the word *Gestalt* is German for "whole form." According to the Gestaltists, when you look at your friend's face, the resulting perception is not merely a sum of the angles, curves, shapes, and lines that make up the face; rather, you perceive the stimulus *as a whole.* In this case, you perceive a face because your mind has implicitly grouped all of the stimuli that make up that face into a coherent whole.

One of the major contributions of Gestalt theory is a series of perceptual laws that attempt to explain how our minds automatically organize perceptual stimuli together to produce the perception of a whole form (Wertheimer, 1923). One of the most important Gestalt concepts of perceptual organization is **figure–ground.**

When you look at your world, you see a multitude of objects or figures that seem to stand away from the background. For instance, your professor standing at the blackboard is a *figure* against the blackboard or *ground.* ● FIGURE 3.20 shows figure–ground in action. You should have two different perceptions of this picture, depending on what you visually pull forward as the figure and what you push back as the ground. For example, if you pull certain darker-colored parts forward, you will see a man's face rather than the pupil of the eye.

Gestalt [gush-TALLT] approach a psychological school of thought originating in Germany that proposed that the whole of a perception must be understood rather than trying to deconstruct perception into its parts

figure–ground a Gestalt principle of perception that states that when we perceive a stimulus, we visually pull the figure part of the stimulus forward while visually pushing backward the background, or ground, part of the stimulus

Patricia Aranda/Moment/Flickr Vision/Getty Images

FIGURE 3.20

Figure–Ground

What do you see when you look at this picture? Depending on how you use the perceptual rule of figure–ground, you will see different things in this work by Octavio Campo. Do you see horses? Trees? Men's faces?

FIGURE 3.21

Closure

According to the Gestaltists, we tend to mentally fill in, or close, solid forms during perception.

closure a Gestalt principle of perception that states that when we look at a stimulus, we tend to see it as a closed shape rather than lines

proximity a Gestalt principle of perception that states that we tend to group close objects together during perception

similarity a Gestalt principle of perception that states that we tend to group like objects together during perception

Another Gestalt principle is **closure**. When we perceive a stimulus such as the one in • FIGURE 3.21, we tend to mentally fill in, or close, the object. The stimulus is not a complete triangle, but nearly everyone will perceive it as complete. According to the principle of closure, we have a preference for viewing solid shapes as opposed to lines.

The Gestalt principles of **proximity** and **similarity** help explain how we group objects together. These rules state that we group together stimuli that are close to each other, or proximal, and also stimuli that are similar (• FIGURE 3.22). As you read this page, you are continually using proximity to discriminate between the words that make up the sentences. Without proximity, you would see a mass of letters, but you would not know where one word ends and another begins.

The final Gestalt principle that we will look at is **good continuation**. The principle of good continuation states that we prefer to perceive stimuli that seem to follow one another as part of a continuing pattern (• FIGURE 3.23). Camouflage works on the principle of good continuation. Can you see the hidden animal in Figure 3.23b? This animal's survival depends on its predator's use of good continuation!

3.5.6 • Perceiving Form: Feature Detection Theory

Feature detection theory states that we have cells in our visual cortex that fire only in response to certain stimuli. These *feature detectors* fire

(a) Grouping based on proximity

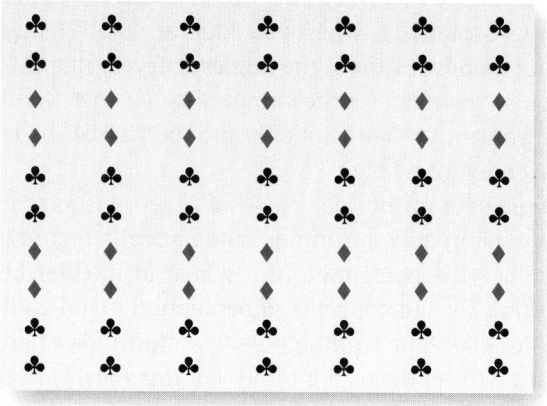

(b) Grouping based on similarity

FIGURE 3.22

The Gestalt Rules of Similarity and Proximity

FIGURE 3.23

Two Instances of Good Continuation

Good continuation ensures that we perceive continuous patterns in the world. This perceptual principle is vital to the survival of the animal in (b).

only when they receive input that indicates we are looking at a particular shape, color, angle, or other visual feature. We have feature detectors for many different specific features of visual stimuli (Conway, 2003; Hulbert, 2003; Seiffert et al., 2003; Xiao, Wang, & Felleman, 2003). The visual cortex and other parts of the brain gather information from our various feature detectors and combine it to help give us a coherent picture of whatever it is we are seeing (Jackson & Blake, 2010; Lumer, Friston, & Rees, 1998; Murray, Olshausen, & Woods, 2003).

The world is a complex place full of rich visual detail. Is it possible that all of our visual perception of the world results from feature detectors that respond to simple geometric shapes? Maybe not. Evidence is mounting to suggest that other areas of the brain may be organized to further process certain complex stimuli. For example, we have a region in the temporal lobe called the *fusiform face* area, which enlarges and specializes during childhood to selectively process the faces we see (Peelen et al., 2010). Likewise, other areas have been shown to selectively process body parts (Cross et al., 2009) and pictures of indoor and outdoor scenes (Kanwisher, 2003). At the moment, it seems that a simple feature detector explanation does not fully account for the complexity of human visual perception (Egner, Monti, & Summerfield, 2010; Jiang, Schmajuk, & Egner, 2012).

good continuation a Gestalt principle of perception that states that we have a preference for perceiving stimuli that seem to follow one another as part of a continuing pattern

feature detection theory a theory of perception that proposes that we have specialized cells in the visual cortex, feature detectors, that fire only when they receive input that indicates we are looking at a particular shape, color, angle, or other visual feature

Quiz Yourself

3.5

1. Jamal was a witness to a bank robbery. Although he did not clearly see the robber's face, Jamal assumed that the robber was a man. What is the most likely reason for Jamal's assumption?
   a. Bottom-up perceptual processing
   b. Top-down perceptual processing
   c. Gestalt perceptual processing
   d. Feature detection processing

2. If you went blind in one eye, which depth cue would you lose?
   a. Motion parallax
   b. Interposition
   c. Retinal disparity
   d. Texture gradient

3. A brain tumor in your occipital lobe might result in distorted visual perception. This result is most consistent with which theory of perception?
   a. Feature detection theory
   b. Gestalt theory of perceptual organization
   c. Top-down perceptual processing theory
   d. Bottom-up perceptual processing theory

Answers 1. b; 2. c; 3. a

3.6 The Accuracy of Perception

Thinkstock/Stockbyte/Getty Images

Because of top-down processing, it would take a long time to accurately perceive this laptop computer in the road. We simply don't expect to see laptop computers in the middle of the highway; therefore, our perception is slowed down.

One of our students once had a frightening experience in which he misinterpreted a visual stimulus. He was driving in the mountains of northern Georgia when he passed a bear on a distant hillside. The bear was standing on its hind legs, towering over the 20-foot-tall pine trees that surrounded it. The student knew this was very unlikely, so he turned his car around and went back for another look. On closer inspection of the scene, he saw that all of the pine trees on the mountainside were newly planted saplings, about 3 feet high. The bear that towered over them was only an average-sized Georgia black bear! Our student was able to go back and correct his perception, but this is not always the case. We may never discover that we have misperceived a situation. Why do we sometimes misperceive our world?

3.6.1 • Errors Due to Top-Down Processing: Seeing What We Expect to See

Why do you think the student misperceived the size of the black bear? The key to his misperception of the bear was in his misperception of the size of the pine trees. We would explain this in terms of top-down processing. When driving through the mountains, most Georgians do not expect to see hillsides of baby trees. It's more typical to see mountainsides covered with mature pine trees that can be well over 20 feet tall. Because this is the normal expectation, the student simply took for granted that the trees were a mature height. It wasn't until he saw the pine trees up close that he realized that his top-down processing had failed him. Because he misperceived the trees, he also misperceived the height of the bear.

3.6.2 • Errors Due to Perceptual Constancy: Tricks of the Brain

Errors that are caused by top-down processing relate to the knowledge and the expectations we have of our world. Misperceptions occur for other reasons, too. Sometimes we misperceive things when our brain's attempts to give us perceptual constancy go awry.

Johnny Stockshooter/Alamy

One explanation for the moon illusion is that it occurs when our brain corrects for what it thinks is a perceptual error.

THE MOON ILLUSION

Have you ever noticed that the moon appears to be much larger as it rises over the horizon than when it is directly overhead? Many people think it is because the Earth is closer to the moon when it is at the horizon, but this is not true. Scientists are still trying to determine the exact cause of the moon illusion (see Kim, 2012). A leading theory, *the apparent distance theory,* argues that the answer lies in our brain's attempt to correct for what it thinks is a mistake in perception. The moon projects the same size image on our retina when it is on the horizon as it does when it is directly overhead. But when the moon is on the horizon, many interposition cues, such as trees and buildings that stand between the moon and us, indicate distance to our brain. When we view the moon directly overhead, however, there are no interposition cues to indicate distance (Jones & Wilson, 2009). Consequently, our brain thinks the moon is farther away when it is on the horizon. The logic involved is this: If the moon is farther away on the horizon, but it still projects the same size image on the retina as the moon overhead, then the moon on the horizon must actually be bigger than the moon overhead. The brain tries to "fix" the inconsistency by inflating our perception of the size of the moon on the horizon (Kaufman & Rock, 1989). Curiously, you can undo the *moon illusion* by facing away from the moon, bending over, and looking at the moon from between your legs. In this position, the brain does not try to fix the inconsistency, and the illusion disappears.

THE PONZO ILLUSION

This same logic underlies one explanation of the *Ponzo illusion,* in which lines of equal length that lie across converging lines appear to be unequal in length (• FIGURE 3.24). Although, the exact cause of the Ponzo illusion is not yet known (see Prinzmetal & Beck, 2001), some suggest that in the Ponzo illusion, linear perspective and height on the horizon cues tell the brain that the top line is farther away than the bottom one. Yet both lines project the same size image on the retina. In an attempt to maintain size constancy, the brain inflates our perception of the top line's length, thus causing the illusion that the top line is longer than the bottom line. This illusion occurs even though we do not consciously perceive the line on top as farther away (Gillam, 1980).

The Ponzo Illusion

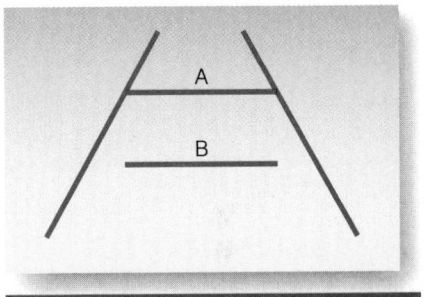

FIGURE 3.24

The Ponzo Illusion

Line segments A and B are both the same length, but we perceive that A is longer than B.

THE MÜLLER-LYER ILLUSION

Size constancy probably also plays a role in the *Müller-Lyer illusion* (• FIGURE 3.25; Coren et al., 1988). In this illusion, our perception of the length of the vertical line segments changes, depending on the direction of the arrows at either end of the line. When the arrows extend away, the line looks longer (Figure 3.25b).

Although researchers are not quite sure why the Müller-Lyer illusion occurs, it is thought that the arrows serve as depth cues, much as we might find in the inside and outside corners of a building. If you look at Figure 3.25c, you can see that this type of corner produces a surface that is closer to the viewer than the recessed corner in Figure 3.25d. These depth cues may set off a process of compensation for size consistency that is similar to those found in the moon illusion and the Ponzo illusion.

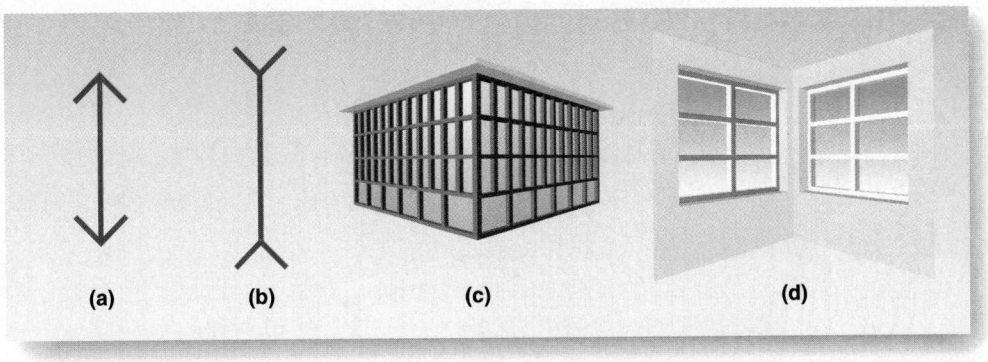

FIGURE 3.25

The Müller-Lyer Illusion

In the Müller-Lyer illusion, the line in (a) is perceived as being shorter than the line in (b), even though they are of equal length. The Müller-Lyer illusion is often seen in rectangular, "carpentered" buildings. The vertical line in the outside corner (c) looks shorter than the vertical line in the inside corner (d)—yet they are the same length. Architects use the Müller-Lyer illusion to create certain perceptions of their buildings.

3.6.3 • Cultural Factors in Perception

As we've discussed, your beliefs and expectations of the world can influence your top-down perceptual processing. Given that culture and environment influence many of our beliefs and expectations (remember our student and the Georgia bear?), it stands to reason that culture and environment also affect perception. The Müller-Lyer illusion is a good example of this type of influence.

People who live in "carpentered" environments, where many of the buildings are wood-framed rectangular structures, have much experience with the architectural angles that produce the Müller-Lyer illusion. Is it possible that these people also experience the Müller-Lyer illusion to a greater degree than those who have lived their lives in "noncarpentered" worlds (where rectangular structures are rare)? This seems to be the case. The Bashi people of Africa traditionally live in round dwellings. When compared to Europeans, the Bashi are often found to be less susceptible to the Müller-Lyer illusion (Bonte, 1962). A similar effect has been found among American Navajos. When traditional Navajos who live in round homes called *hogans* were compared to Navajos who grew up in rectangular buildings, the former were found to be less likely to experience the Müller-Lyer illusion (Pedersen & Wheeler, 1983). These studies suggest that our perceptions are influenced by elements in our culture that prepare us to see the world in a particular way.

People who grow up in noncarpentered environments, where structures tend to be like this round hogan, are less likely to experience the Müller-Lyer illusion.

Rob Crandall/The Image Works

3.6

Quiz Yourself

1. **Leahannaba grew up in a culture where most of the structures were dome-shaped huts. Compared to someone from New York City, which optical illusion is Leahannaba less likely to experience?**
   a. Ponzo illusion
   b. Müller-Lyer illusion
   c. Moon illusion
   d. All of the above
2. **Last night, Samantha noticed that the moon looked huge as it rose above the horizon. Later, when the moon was overhead, it did not look nearly as large to her. Which of the following is thought to be a primary cause of this illusion?**
   a. Perceptual constancies
   b. Top-down processing
   c. Bottom-up processing
   d. Binocular depth cues
3. **When you look down the railroad tracks, the tracks appear to converge even though they are parallel. This illusion is the result of which perceptual process?**
   a. Monocular depth cues
   b. Binocular depth cues
   c. Top-down processing
   d. Subliminal perception

Answers 1. b; 2. a; 3. a

3.7 Integrating Psychology: The Big Picture

In the last chapter, we learned about our nervous and endocrine systems and how they influence our day-to-day functioning. In this chapter, we focused on the biological processes that underlie our ability to sense and perceive. After his stroke, Jean-Dominique Bauby's senses continued to give him a window through which to experience the world. For most of us, they do the same. Our senses are our connection with the outside world—for it is through our senses that environmental stimuli are converted into the neural language of our nervous system. If Bauby had lost his ability to sense and perceive, not only would he have been locked inside his own body, he would also have been completely alone. Take a moment to think about what life would be like if one or more of your senses failed to function. Would losing your sight or hearing affect your ability to learn, to interact with others, or even to survive? In what ways could you adapt, as Bauby did, if you lost one or more of your senses?

After our sense organs do their jobs, we must then make sense of what we are seeing, hearing, tasting, and so on. We accomplish this using a combination of top-down and bottom-up perceptual processes. Bottom-up processes help us piece together what we are sensing. Top-down processes use what we know about the world to help us create coherent perceptions of it. However, sometimes our attempts can lead to perceptual errors, such as those seen in perceptual illusions.

As for Jean-Dominique Bauby, our ability to sense and perceive is a crucial part of our lives. When we focus our attention on what we are sensing, we bring that information into our conscious awareness or *consciousness*. In our consciousness, this information is useful to us in a variety of ways, such as for problem solving, learning, and so on. In Chapter 4, we will take a closer look our consciousness and the role it plays in our lives.

The information we acquire through sensation and perception can also help guide our behavior. We react to what our senses tell us about our bodies and the world. For example, if you saw the sky turning cloudy, you might be inspired to pack an umbrella in your backpack or book bag. If you sensed a rumbling in your stomach, you might be driven to find food to eat. Similarly, Bauby's perceptions of his life after the stroke led him to achieve his desire to write a book. In this manner, sensation and perception play a role in the *motivation* that guides our daily behavior. In Chapter 5, we will look at the motivational processes that drive our behavior and help us achieve our goals. As you read these coming chapters, keep in mind that much of life as you know it wouldn't be possible without the sensory, perceptual, and other biological processes at work inside your body.

Studying the Chapter

Key Terms

absolute threshold (86)
accommodation (91)
amplitude (89)
attention (84)
auditory nerve (100)
basilar membrane (100)
binocular depth cues (112)
blindspot (91)
bottom-up perceptual processing (111)
brightness (90)
closure (116)
cochlea (100)
color blindness (95)
cones (92)
cornea (90)
cycle (98)
dark adaptation (93)
decibels (dB) (98)
dermis (108)
duplicity theory (102)
epidermis (108)
extrasensory perception (ESP), (87)
feature detection theory (116)
figure–ground. (115)
frequency (98)
frequency theory (101)
Gestalt approach (115)
good continuation (116)
gustation (103)
hair cells (100)
hue (90)
inner ear (99)
just noticeable difference (jnd) (86)
kinesthesis (109)
lens (91)
light adaptation (93)
lock-and-key theory (107)
loudness (98)
middle ear (99)
monocular depth cues (114)
olfaction (106)
olfactory epithelium (106)
opponent-process theory (96)
optic chiasm (97)
optic nerve (91)
outer ear (99)
papillae (103)
perception (85)
pheromones (107)
photopigments (93)
pitch (98)
place theory (100)
proximity (116)
psychophysics (86)
pupil (91)
retina (91)
retinal disparity (112)
rods (92)
saturation (90)
sensation (84)
similarity (116)
subliminal perception (87)
taste buds (103)
top-down perceptual processing (110)
trichromatic theory of color vision (94)
vestibular sense (109)
visible spectrum (89)
visible spectrum (89)
volley theory (101)
wavelength (89)
Weber's law (86)

What Do You Know? Assess Your Understanding

Test your retention and understanding of the material by answering the following questions.

1. _____ is the conversion of environmental energies into neural impulses.

a. Sensation
b. Perception
c. Absolute threshold
d. The jnd

2. Determining the qualities of light energy that are related to color would be most central to which of the following areas of psychology?

a. Physiological psychology
b. Perception psychology
c. Psychophysics
d. Psychodynamics

3. According to Weber's law, a teaspoon of sugar added to an already sweet glass of tea will be _____ noticeable than a teaspoon of sugar added to a glass of tea that has no sugar to begin with.

a. less
b. more
c. equally
d. Weber's law does not tell us what to expect in this situation.

4. The average human would be able to see which of the following wavelengths?

a. 950 nm
b. 850 nm
c. 789 nm
d. 550 nm

5. The hue or color of a light we perceive corresponds to the _____ of the light wave.

a. purity
b. wavelength
c. amplitude
d. frequency

6. The eye's _____ undergoes _____ to focus an image of what we see on our retina.

a. iris; constriction
b. pupil; constriction
c. lens; accommodation
d. sclera; accommodation

7. _____ in the _____ of the retina allow us to see color.

a. Neurotransmitters; cones
b. Photopigments; cones
c. Neurotransmitters; rods
d. Photopigments; rods

8. According to the trichromatic theory of color vision, we have _____ for _____, _____, and _____ light.

a. cones; red; green; blue
b. cones; red; green; yellow
c. rods; red; green; blue
d. rods; red; green; yellow

9. The _____ of a sound corresponds to the _____ of a sound wave.

a. loudness; frequency
b. pitch; frequency
c. loudness; cycle
d. pitch; amplitude

10. When we hear a sound, _____ cells on the _____ _____ convert sound waves into neural signals.

a. cone; tympanic membrane
b. rod; cochlear duct
c. hair; basilar membrane
d. hair; tympanic membrane

11. The _____ of the brain processes visual information before it travels to the cortex.

a. thalamus
b. hypothalamus
c. olfactory bulb
d. cerebellum

12. Jonas, a retired jet engine mechanic, is 65 years old. Lately he's been experiencing some hearing loss. From what you know about hearing and exposure to loud sounds, what would you predict about Jonas's hearing loss?

a. He will have the most trouble hearing low-pitched sounds.
b. He will have the most trouble hearing medium-pitched sounds.
c. He will have the most trouble hearing high-pitched sounds.
d. He will most likely be completely deaf.

13. To date, the most widely accepted theory of pitch perception is _____ theory.

a. place
b. volley
c. frequency
d. duplicity

14. If you want to be sure to taste the full flavor of a piece of chocolate, where should you avoid placing the chocolate as you taste it?

a. The front of the tongue
b. The center of the tongue
c. The right side of the tongue
d. The back of the tongue

15. Ultimately, most taste information is processed in the _____ cortex of the brain.

a. somatosenosory
b. occipital
c. temporal
d. motor

16. The fact that women who are exposed to the underarm secretions of other women tend to synchronize their menstrual cycles is most consistent with the notion that humans possess a(n) _____ sense.

a. vomeronasal
b. olfactory
c. vestibular
d. kinesthetic

17. Karina goes to a Halloween party where she meets a man who is wearing a monster mask that covers his entire face. Later, when her best friend asks her to describe the man, she describes him as being "good-looking" even though she never actually saw his face. Which of the following best explains Karina's perception of the man?

a. Good continuation
b. Closure
c. Bottom-up perceptual processing
d. Top-down perceptual processing

18. Mike was in an accident that injured his right eye. Although he'll recover, he must wear an eye patch for the next 2 weeks. During this time, Mike's doctor will not allow him to drive a car. Mike's doctor is most likely concerned with disturbances to Mike's _____.

a. vestibular system
b. binocular depth cues
c. monocular depth cues
d. kinesthetic system

19. In which of the following situations, would you be most likely to use bottom-up perceptual processing?

a. When viewing a piece of abstract art composed of nothing but paint splatters on a canvas
b. When reading your best friend's bad handwriting
c. When trying to watch a movie in a crowded theater where your view of the screen is obstructed by the people sitting in front of you
d. When reading the daily news on the Internet

20. According to your text, we experience perceptual constancies for all of the following except which one?

a. Size
b. Texture
c. Shape
d. Brightness

Answers: 1. a; 2. c; 3. a; 4. d; 5. b; 6. c; 7. b; 8. a; 9. b; 10. c; 11. a; 12. c; 13. d; 14. b; 15. a; 16. a; 17. d; 18. b; 19. a; 20. b.

Use It or Lose It: Applying Psychology

1. Your younger sister listens to music at a very loud level on her iPod nearly every day. What would you tell her to convince her to turn down the volume?

2. Because you are studying sensation in psychology, your uncle asks you to explain why he cannot distinguish red objects from green objects. What would you tell him?

3. Assume you work on the staff of a nursing home. Most of your clients are people in their 80s and 90s. How can you use your knowledge of sensation and perception to do your job better? In other words, what changes can you expect to see in your clients' sensory and perceptual abilities, and how can you accommodate those changes?

4. You have been charged with determining the additional amount of sugar one would have to add to a cup of coffee that already contained 2 teaspoons of sugar to produce a jnd. How would you go about determining this?

5. Find a picture of Vincent Van Gogh's painting *Starry Night*. What monocular depth cues are used in this painting? Provide specific examples of your choices.

6. Can you identify specific examples of how your cultural background has affected your perception?

Critical Thinking for Integration

1. Explain how top-down perceptual processing may affect the testimony (Chapter 7) of a person who has witnessed an armed robbery.

2. If Ali has a brain tumor in his occipital lobe (Chapter 2), how might this affect his sensory and perceptual processes?

3. How might strongly held beliefs, such as racial prejudices (Chapter 10), affect perception?

4. Design a research study to test the hypothesis that males and females have different food preferences (Chapter 1).

© Peter Nadolski/Shutterstock.com

Are You Getting the Big Picture? Sensation and Perception

3.1 Measuring Sensation and Perception

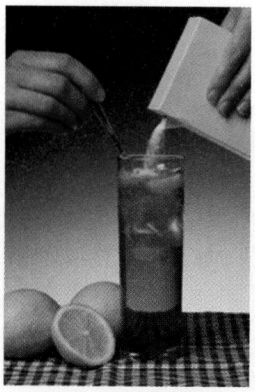

Digital Light Source/Getty Images

- **Psychophysics** is the branch of psychology that studies how we process sensory stimuli.
- Psychophysicists conduct experiments to determine the **absolute threshold** and **just noticeable difference (jnd)** of each of the five senses.
- **Weber's law** is the relationship between the original intensity of a stimulus and the amount of change that is required to produce a jnd.
- When sensory stimuli are too weak in intensity to reach absolute threshold, the stimuli are said to be **subliminal**.
- The existence of **ESP** remains a controversial subject; however, to date there has not been convincing evidence of its existence.

3.2 Vision: Seeing the World

- Light is electromagnetic energy, measured primarily by **wavelength** and **amplitude**. Wavelength = **hue**; amplitude = **brightness**.
- The **visible spectrum** of light is the narrow band we are able to see. Some animals are able to see a much broader spectrum.
- In the **retina** of the eye, specialized cells known as **rods** and **cones** convert light into neural impulses, which eventually travel to the brain via the **optic nerve**.
- The **trichromatic theory of color vision** and the **opponent-process theory** are both used to explain how we process color.

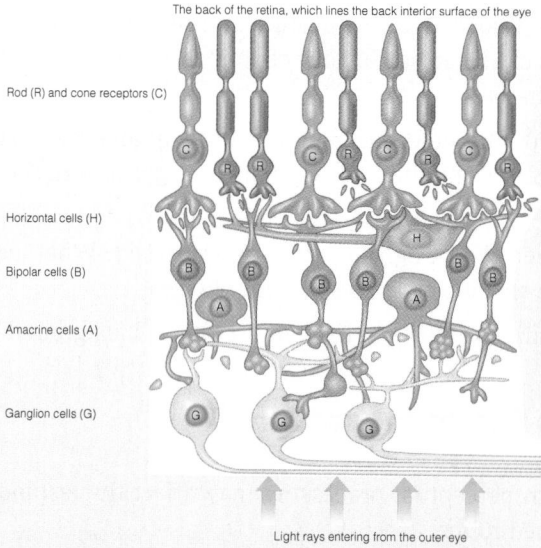

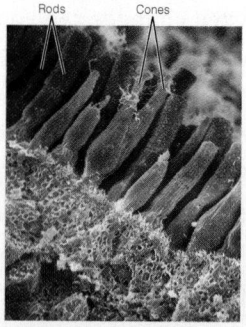

Science Source

- **Color blindness** is the inability to see certain colors and is the result of missing cones in the retina or having cones that are sensitive to atypical ranges of light wave frequencies.

3.3 Hearing: Listening to the World

- Sounds are produced by waves of compressed air.
- **Frequency** = **pitch**; **amplitude** = **loudness**.
- The eardrum, or tympanic membrane, is a very thin membrane in the **middle ear** that vibrates to incoming sounds. It begins transmitting those sounds through the small bones to the **hair cells** of the fluid-filled **cochlea**, where neural impulses are generated.
- The **auditory nerve** carries the sounds we hear into the brain.

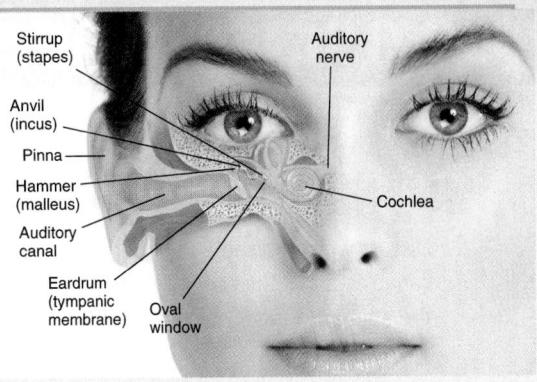

© iStockphoto.com/iconogenic

3.4 The Other Senses: Taste, Smell, Touch, and the Body Senses

- Humans are sensitive to five tastes: bitter, sweet, sour, salty, and umami.
- The **taste buds**, which reside in the pits between the **papillae** on your tongue, convert the chemicals in the foods you eat into neural impulses.
- The sense of smell operates by converting odors captured by a special piece of skin, the **olfactory epithelium**, which lines the top of the nasal cavity, to neural impulses that travel via the olfactory nerve to the olfactory bulb in the brain.

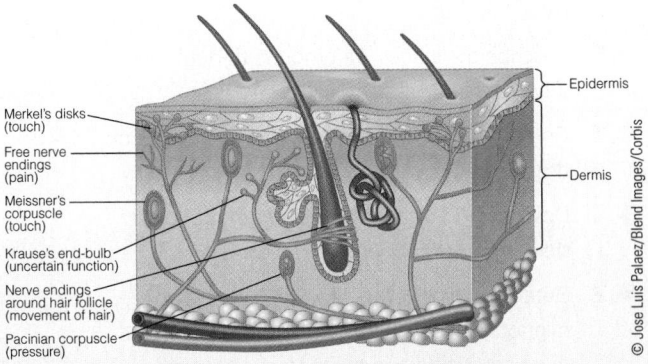

© Jose Luis Palaez/Blend Images/Corbis

- Many animals (and perhaps humans) have a vomeronasal system that allows them to communicate with other animals via airborne chemosignals known as **pheromones**. Chemosignals may impact some aspects of human social interaction and sexuality.
- The sense of touch originates in the skin, with the inner layer—the **dermis**—containing most of the touch receptors.
- **Kinesthesis** is our ability to sense the position of our body parts in space and in relation to one another.
- **Vestibular sense** monitors the position of our head in space and helps us stay balanced.

3.5 Perception: The Interpretation of Sensory Information

- **Top-down perceptual processing** refers to using previously gained knowledge to interpret a sensory stimulus.
- **Bottom-up perceptual processing** refers to using properties of the stimulus itself to form our perception of a stimulus.
- Perceptual constancies, depth cues, and **feature detection** are among the mental shortcuts we automatically employ to assist in perceiving stimuli.

Frank Burek/Spirit/Corbis

(b)

3.6 The Accuracy of Perception

- Perceptual errors can occur for a variety of reasons. They are often due to misapplied expectations that lead us to think we have seen or heard something that we have not.

The Ponzo Illusion

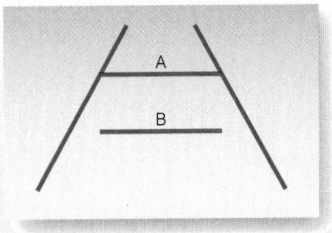

Consciousness

Learning Objectives

4.1 Discuss why we sleep and understand the variables that influence individual variations in the amount of sleep we need. (APA 1.1, 1.2, 1.3, 2.1, 2.5)

4.1 Describe how our circadian rhythm of sleep operates, and apply how disruptions in circadian rhythm influence our behavior. (APA 1.1, 1.3)

4.1 Describe the stages we progress through during a typical night of sleep. (APA 1.1, 2.2)

4.1 Compare and contrast the different theories on dreaming. (APA 1.1, 1.2)

4.1 Describe and distinguish among the various sleep disorders. (APA 1.1, 1.3)

4.2 Detail the experience of hypnosis, describe hypnotic susceptibility, and apply the neodissociation and response set theories to how hypnosis occurs. (APA 1.1, 1.2)

4.2 Examine the scientific research to critically evaluate what hypnosis can and cannot do for you. (APA 2.1, 2.2, 5.1)

4.3 Define tolerance and substance dependence, and explain how one's biology, expectations, and culture influence how psychoactive drugs work. (APA 1.1, 1.2, 1.3, 2.2, 2.5, 3.2)

4.3 Identify depressants, opiates, stimulants, and hallucinogens, and describe the effects these types of drugs have on our health, cognitions, and behavior. (APA 1.1, 1.3, 2.2, 3.3)

Consciousness, in psychological terms, includes the feelings, thoughts, and aroused states of which we are aware. This chapter examines the levels or gradations of consciousness—when you are not fully awake, alert, aware, or perhaps of sound mind. Recall in the Part I case study how Jean-Dominique Bauby, after his stroke, went into a coma, a unique altered state that not many people experience. Yet, even during this state, Bauby still had some awareness of his surroundings. When he awoke from the coma, he was in a locked-in state. Although this dramatically affected his day-to-day living, Bauby's consciousness still functioned much like yours and mine. Psychologists have done quite a bit of research on three particular states of consciousness: sleep, hypnosis, and the effects of various psychoactive drugs. By closely examining these states, we may better understand our behavior and the behavior of those around us. We will start with an altered state we all experience—sleep.

4

caia image/Alamy

Chapter Outline

4.1 Sleep, Dreaming, and Circadian Rhythm / 130

4.2 Hypnosis / 145

4.3 Psychoactive Drugs / 148

PSYCHOLOGY APPLIES TO YOUR WORLD: The Mystery of Bath Salts / 162

4.4 Integrating Psychology: The Big Picture / 166

consciousness [CON-shis-nus] feelings, thoughts, and aroused states of which we are aware

microsleep a brief episode of sleep that occurs in the midst of a wakeful activity

4.1 Sleep, Dreaming, and Circadian Rhythm

Many of us never question what goes on in our bodies and minds as we sleep. But sleep offers plenty of behaviors for psychologists to explore. First, we will look at why we sleep and what occurs in our brains and bodies as we sleep. We will then explore the purpose of dreams and whether dreams have meaning. We will conclude by describing different types of sleep disorders. We caution you that just reading about sleep can make you drowsy!

4.1.1 • Functions of Sleep: Why Do We Sleep, and What If We Don't?

What would happen if you tried to stay awake indefinitely? William C. Dement, a pioneer in sleep research, actually tried this experiment on himself. Although Dement's lack of sleep made him a danger to himself and others, he was not in danger of dying from lack of sleep. Eventually, he fell asleep. In the same way that you cannot hold your breath until you die, you cannot deprive yourself of all sleep. Sleep always wins. This is because we drift into repeated *microsleeps* (Goleman, 1982; Innes, Poudel, & Jones, 2013). A **microsleep** is a brief (3- to 15-second) episode of sleep that occurs in the midst of a wakeful activity. We are typically unaware of its occurrence unless we are behind the wheel of a car, steering a ship, or flying a plane. In such circumstances, microsleeps could cause a disaster. In general, though, microsleeps appear to help us survive by preventing total sleep deprivation.

Sleep ensures our continued physical and mental health in several ways:

- *Sleep restores body tissues and facilitates body growth.* Sleep allows your immune system, nervous system, and organs time to replenish lost reserves and energy and to repair any cellular damage. This prepares the body for action the next day and ensures the continued health of the body. Lack of adequate sleep can affect energy levels, often making us feel drowsy and fatigued (Lekander et al., 2013; Murphy & Delanty, 2007; Oginska & Pokorski, 2006). Sleep also activates growth hormone, which facilitates physical growth during infancy, childhood, and the teen years (Gais, Lucas, & Born, 2006; Szentirmai et al., 2007).
- *Sleep increases immunity to disease.* During sleep, the production of immune cells that fight off infection increases. Therefore, your immune system is stronger when you receive the appropriate amount of sleep (Lange et al., 2006; Motivala & Irwin, 2007). When you deprive your body of sleep, your natural immune responses are reduced (Irwin et al., 2003; Murphy & Delanty, 2007; Ruiz et al., 2012). This is in part why you are encouraged to sleep and rest when you are ill. This effect on immunity occurs after as few as two days of total sleep deprivation or several days of partial sleep deprivation (Heiser et al., 2000; Rogers et al., 2001; Ruiz et al., 2012). For college students, this may mean you are more susceptible to colds and flu at midterm and final exam time. You are likely to sleep less

It is estimated that more than 24,000 deaths occur annually in accidents caused directly or in part by drowsy drivers.

©iStockphoto.com/Manu1174

at these times, thereby decreasing your immune system's ability to combat illnesses. Sleeping truly is good medicine.

- *Sleep keeps your mind alert.* When people do not get enough sleep, they are more likely to be inattentive and easily distracted (Jennings, Monk, & van der Molen, 2003; Kahol et al., 2008; Murphy & Delanty, 2007; Short et al., 2013). Sleep makes your body more sensitive to norepinephrine—the neurotransmitter that keeps you alert during the day (Chapter 2; Steriade & McCarley, 1990).
- *Sleep enhances your mood.* Sleep activates many chemicals that influence your emotions and mood. Consequently, if you are deprived of sleep, you are more likely to be irritable, cranky, and unhappy, in addition to being tired (Durmer & Dinges, 2005; Lemola, Ledermann & Friedman, 2013; Murphy & Delanty, 2007; Short et al., 2013).
- *Sleep is intimately connected to learning and memory.* When you sleep, emotional experiences as well as information that you have reviewed or rehearsed are more likely to be remembered (Fogel, Smith, & Cote, 2007; Payne & Kensinger, 2010; Payne et al., 2008; Poe, Walsh, & Bjorness, 2010; Racsmany, Conway, & Demeter, 2010; Rasch & Born, 2008; Scullin & McDaniel, 2010; Stickgold & Walker, 2007; M. P. Walker, 2009). Chapter 7 offers an in-depth look at memory processing, but a few simple statements here will help you understand the connection between sleep and memory.

  In order to get information into your memory, you must *encode* it, or do something to remember the information. This may mean repeating the information over and over again, visualizing the information, or associating it with a personal experience. When information is thoroughly encoded, it can be more easily transferred to long-term memory so that we can retrieve it later.

  Sleep allows you to better store material that was actually processed (that is, encoded well enough) during studying. Information that you can't readily retrieve in the morning probably wasn't encoded well enough, and you will need to study it again. You can see the advantage of a good night's sleep before an exam.

  Sleep's connection to memory processing may also explain why problem solving seems to improve after a night's sleep (Ellenbogen et al., 2007). You may think about a problem repeatedly during the day, frustrated by your inability to find a solution. The next day you awaken with a solution in mind. This suggests that pertinent details about the problem are processed during sleep. The phrase "sleep on it" really does have merit.

Research suggests that sleep may have evolved as a necessary behavior for humans (Hirshkowitz, Moore, & Minhoto, 1997; Webb, 1983). When humans lived in caves, it was dangerous for them to go out at night to hunt for food because they had very little night vision and were relatively small compared to other species. If they did go outside at night, they were likely to be the food for larger predators. Humans who stayed inside the cave at night were more likely to survive and produce offspring. Over time, these offspring may have adapted to the pattern of nighttime sleeping and daytime hunting and gathering.

As you can see, sleep is a necessity, not a luxury. Sleep offers many benefits to our functioning and ensures that we will be healthy, alert, and happy.

4.1.2 • Variations in How Much Sleep We Need

Some people brag about how little sleep they need. Yet research shows that although the amount of sleep we need varies from person to person and depends on several

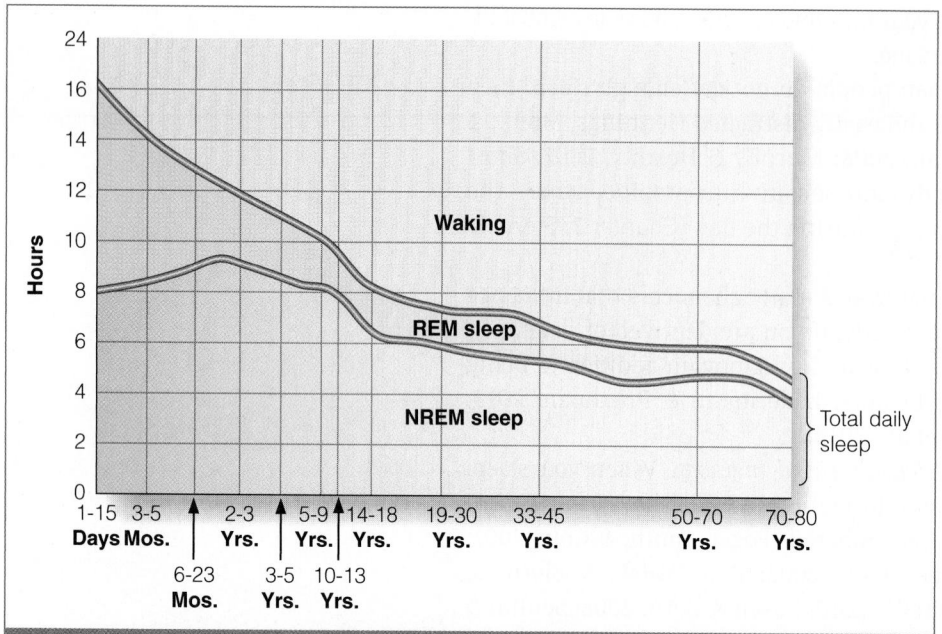

FIGURE 4.1

Age Differences in Sleep Needs

Newborns sleep an average of 16 hours a day. Preschoolers require less sleep, about 10 to 12 hours. Most teenagers and adults require 8 hours.

From "Ontogenetic Development of Human Sleep-Dream Cycle," by H. P. Roffwarg, J. N. Muzino, and W. C. Dement, *Science*, 1966, 152:604–609. Copyright 1966 by the AAAS. Reprinted with permission from AAAS.

factors, many of us are not getting enough. Here are some sleep factors and facts:

- *Age.* The older we get, the less sleep we need (● FIGURE 4.1). Babies require a lot of sleep, between 16 and 18 hours a day. Preschoolers require less sleep, about 10–12 hours a day, typically including a midday nap. Teenagers and young adults need less sleep than children, but they still require 8–10 hours of sleep a night (McLaughlin Crabtree & Williams, 2009). While U.S. children may be getting the recommended amount of sleep, 61% of teenagers get less than 8 hours of sleep on school nights (National Sleep Foundation, 2011; Williams, Zimmerman, & Bell, 2012). People between the ages of 25 and 34 are more likely to report insufficient rest or sleep than are people over the age of 65 (McKnight-Eily et al., 2009). Adults, on average, sleep 6.8 hours a night on weekdays (National Sleep Foundation, 2011). According to sleep experts, most adults require at least 8 hours of sleep a night.
- *Lifestyle (environment).* Our cultural beliefs, lifestyle habits, and bedroom environment also influence the amount of sleep that we need or get (Giannotti & Cortesi, 2009). If you were raised in a home in which everyone was up early on the weekends to do chores, you adapted to a different sleep schedule than someone who slept until 10 A.M. or noon on weekends. In one study of college students, good sleepers were more likely to have regular bedtime and rise time schedules than poorer sleepers (Carney et al., 2006). Sleeping with a light on in the bedroom or one's activities an hour before bedtime (such as watching television, reading, using a laptop or cell phone, or playing video games) also influence one's sleep quality and duration (National Sleep Foundation, 2011). In Jean-Dominique's case, noise and lights within the hospital setting, in addition to his brain injury, probably changed his sleep. Keep in mind, too, that stressors and responsibilities change as we get older. Living on one's own, parenting, and job responsibilities also bring about changes in our sleep schedule.
- *Genetics.* Genes may play a role in the amount of sleep that each of us requires. For example, studies that measured the sleep patterns of identical twins compared to fraternal twins found more similar sleep needs and sleep behaviors among identical twins (de Castro, 2002; Webb & Campbell, 1983). Additional research also suggests that genes may influence our propensity to be either "night owls" or "early birds." Some people may be genetically predisposed to get up early in the morning and go to bed earlier, whereas others may prefer getting up later and going to bed later (Mongrain et al., 2004; Novakova, Sladek, & Sumova, 2013). Learn your propensity toward morningness or eveningness by completing the brief scale in Engage Yourself!

ENGAGE YOURSELF! Answer the questions in the following table, and then add up the values to get your total score. Compare your total score with the key at the end to get an idea of your *chronotype*, or your propensity toward morningness or eveningness.

Morningness–Eveningness Scale

QUESTION	ANSWER	VALUE
If you were entirely free to plan your evening and had no commitments the next day, at what time would you choose to go to bed?	8 P.M.–9 P.M.	5
	9 P.M.–10:15 P.M.	4
	10:15 P.M.–12:30 A.M.	3
	12:30 A.M.–1:45 A.M.	2
	1:45 A.M.–3 A.M.	1
You have to do 2 hours of physically hard work. If you were entirely free to plan your day, in which of the following periods would you choose to do the work?	8 A.M.–10 A.M.	4
	11 A.M.–1 P.M.	3
	3 P.M.–5 P.M.	2
	7 P.M.–9 P.M.	1
For some reason you have gone to bed several hours later than normal, but there is no need to get up at a particular time the next morning. Which of the following is most likely to occur?	Will wake up at the usual time and not fall asleep again	4
	Will wake up at the usual time and doze thereafter	3
	Will wake up at the usual time but will fall asleep again	2
	Will not wake up until later than usual	1
You have a 2-hour test to take that you know will be mentally exhausting. If you were entirely free to choose, in which of the following periods would you choose to take the test?	8 A.M.–10 A.M.	4
	11 A.M.–1 P.M.	3
	3 P.M.–5 P.M.	2
	7 P.M.–9 P.M.	1
If you had no commitments the next day and were entirely free to plan your own day, what time would you get up?	5 A.M.–6:30 A.M.	5
	6:30 A.M.–7:45 A.M.	4
	7:45 A.M.–9:45 A.M.	3
	9:45 A.M.–11 A.M.	2
	11 A.M.–12 P.M.	1
A friend has asked you to join him twice a week for a workout in the gym. The best time for him is between 10 P.M. and 11 P.M. Bearing nothing else in mind other than how you normally feel in the evening, how do you think you would perform?	Very well	1
	Reasonably well	2
	Poorly	3
	Very poorly	4
One hears about "morning" and "evening" types of people. Which of these types do you consider yourself to be?	Definitely a morning type	6
	More a morning than an evening type	4
	More an evening than a morning type	2
	Definitely an evening type	0

MORNINGNESS–EVENINGNESS SCALE	
Definitely morning type	32–28
Moderately morning type	27–23
Neither type	22–16
Moderately evening type	15–11
Definitely evening type	10–6

Adapted from "A Self-Assessment Questionnaire to Determine Morningness–Eveningness in Human Circadian Rhythms," by J. A. Horne and O. Ostberg, *International Journal of Chronobiology,* 1976, Vol. 4, 97–110.

Reproduced with permission of Taylor & Francis UK LTD; permission conveyed through Copyright Clearance Center, Inc.

4.1.3 • Circadian Rhythm and Its Application to Our Lives

circadian rhythm [sir-KAY-dee-un RI-thum] changes in bodily processes that occur repeatedly on approximately a 24- to 25-hour cycle

suprachiasmatic [sue-pra-kigh-as-MAT-ick] nucleus (SCN) a group of brain cells located in the hypothalamus that signal other brain areas when to be aroused and when to shut down

melatonin [mel-uh-TONE-in] a hormone in the body that facilitates sleep

A **circadian rhythm** is a built-in cycle of physical processes in living beings. In humans, circadian rhythms include core body temperature, alertness, hormone productions and other biological processes. Our cycle of sleep is also greatly influenced by our biology. For example, if you were put in a cave and had no cues as to time—no watches, light, or clocks—your body would exhibit a natural rhythm of sleeping and waking that closely resembles a 24- to 25-hour cycle. This sleep circadian rhythm is programmed by a group of brain cells in the hypothalamus called the **suprachiasmatic nucleus (SCN)** (Zee & Manthena, 2007). The SCN works very much like an internal clock, signaling other brain areas when to be aroused (awake) to start the day and when to shut down (sleep) for the day. For Jean-Dominique, it is difficult to know if his SCN operated in this way as circadian rhythms can vary in individuals with brain damage.

How does the SCN know when it's time to be awake or asleep? The SCN is very responsive to light changes and takes its cues from your eyes. When your eyes transmit light information to the SCN, they are in essence telling it whether it is light or dark outside (• FIGURE 4.2). The light information helps the SCN direct the release of **melatonin**, the hormone that facilitates sleep. Hence, light information and melatonin regulate your sleep circadian rhythm and help you get to sleep or awaken (Burke et al., 2013). As darkness increases, so does the production of melatonin in your body (Arendt, 2006; Brzezinski, 1997). For this reason, it is called the "Dracula hormone" because it comes out at night.

A significant amount of research now suggests that a developmental change in our intrinsic sleep–wake cycle occurs during puberty, a phenomenon not

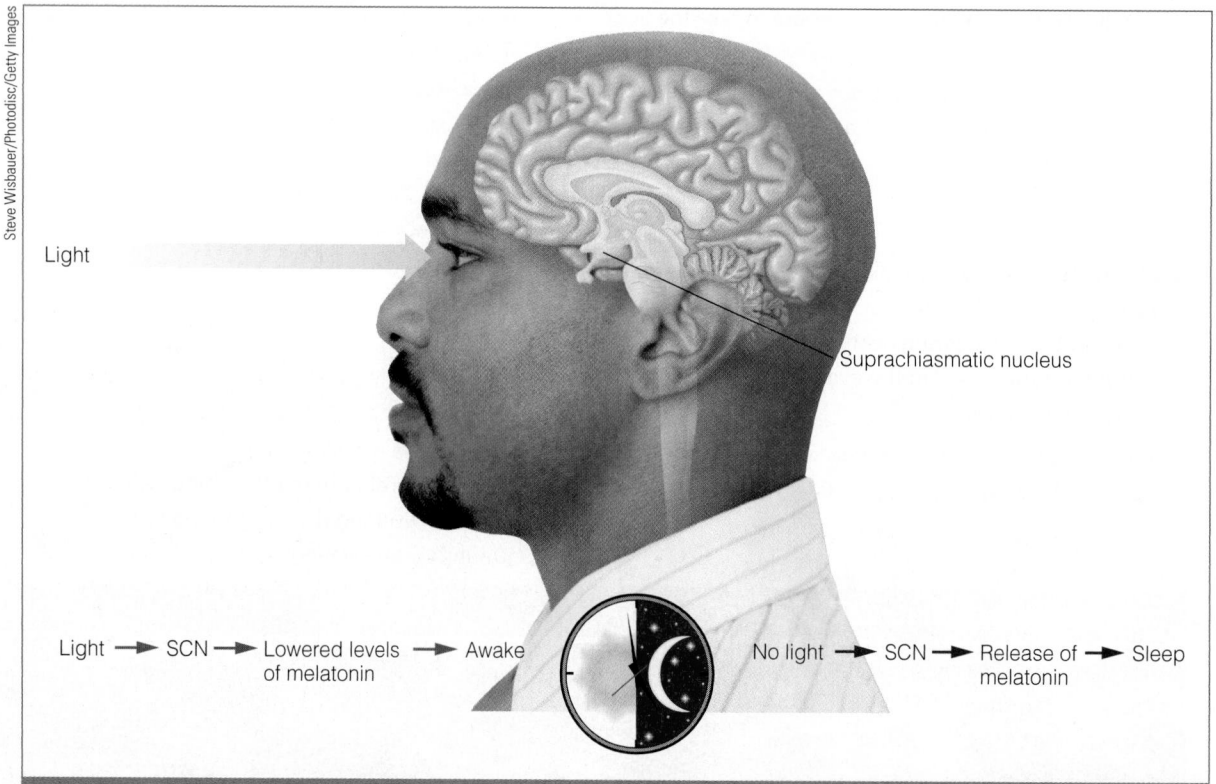

Steve Wisbauer/Photodisc/Getty Images

FIGURE 4.2

Circadian Rhythm, Sleep, and the Brain

The suprachiasmatic nucleus (SCN) takes its cues from the light that is transmitted to your eyes. The light information helps the SCN direct the release of melatonin, the "Dracula hormone" that helps you to get to sleep.

Adapted from Starr and McMillan, *Human Biology* (2nd ed.), p. 271, © 1997 Wadsworth.

specific to human adolescents, but perhaps common in mammals (Crowley, Acebo, & Carskadon, 2007; Hagenauer & Lee, 2012; Hagenauer et al., 2009; Jenni, Achermann, & Carskadon, 2005; Munch et al., 2005; Taylor et al., 2005). Changes in melatonin secretion and light sensitivity alter the timing of our sleep–wake cycle. We are more likely to want to stay up later in the evening and sleep longer in the morning. Although teenagers' social calendars often strengthen this tendency, the finding that part of this change is developmental has serious implications for high school starting times and adolescent academic performance.

Paula Bronstein/Getty Images News/Getty Images

Sleeping on the plane may help reduce jet lag when traveling to other time zones.

"WEEKEND LAG" AND JET LAG

Many of us disrupt our sleep circadian rhythm on a weekly basis. We attempt to maintain a routine sleep schedule on weekdays, going to bed around the same time every night so that we can get up in the morning for work or school. Then the weekend comes, and many of us stay up later at night and "sleep in" the next morning, forcing our SCN to reset its cycle. Then Sunday night arrives. We may have the best intentions—getting to bed at a decent hour so that we'll get enough sleep to meet the demands of our Monday schedules. But instead, we toss and turn, look at the clock, and wonder when we are going to fall asleep. When Monday morning comes, we feel tired. We may hit the snooze button several times, oversleep, or take a long shower to help us wake up. Why? Because we just asked our internal clock to reset itself by 3, 4, or more hours! Disrupting our sleep circadian rhythm to this extent makes us irritable, tired, less attentive, and moody.

Our sleep circadian rhythm must also be reset to adapt to the 1-hour time change that takes place in the fall and spring in most parts of the United States and in many other countries. It must also be reset when we travel to different time zones, and we may experience *jet lag* as we adjust. On average, for each hour of time change, it takes 1 day to reset our sleep circadian rhythm.

Shift work may interfere with normal sleep patterns, affecting job performance.

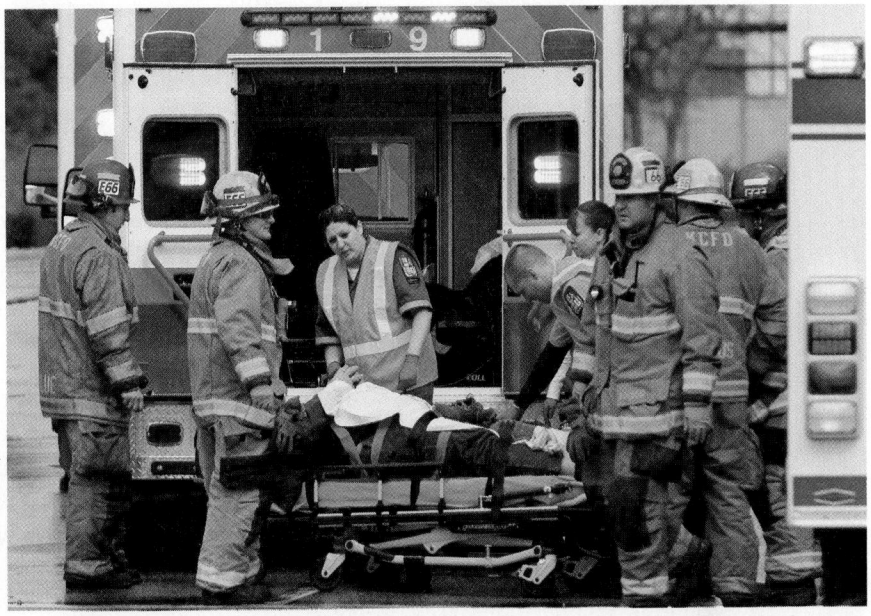

© ZUMA Press, Inc/Alamy

WORKING THE NIGHT SHIFT

Our body's sleep circadian rhythm also has implications for the roughly 15% of full-time workers in the United States who do shift work. In many professions (police work, firefighting, airline flight crew, medical care, and the military), people may be assigned to work 8-, 12-, or even 24-hour shifts, at varying times on different days. When you work Sunday and Monday nights, but Tuesday through Thursday mornings, it is more difficult for your body to reset its sleep circadian rhythm. This disruption can impair your thinking and your health. Shift workers in general report more sleep disturbances; more hormonal irregularities (for women); more accidents, injuries, and illnesses; and decreased cognitive performance (Barger et al., 2009; Berger & Hobbs, 2006; Caldwell, 2012; Haus & Smolensky, 2006; Kahol et al., 2008; Pirrallo et al., 2012; Sharma, 2007; Swanson et al., 2010). If late-night or early-morning shifts are regular, then your body can adapt to the new rhythm. However, if the shift hours are constantly changing, your sleep circadian rhythm is disrupted, and your sleep benefits diminish. Hence, you may be less alert, more easily distracted, and more prone to mental errors.

4.1.4 • Stages of Sleep: What Research Tells Us

Using *electroencephalogram* (EEG) technology, sleep researchers have identified five stages of sleep. Recall from Chapter 2 that EEGs examine the electrical activity of relatively large areas of the brain. These brain waves are then plotted on graph paper or a computer screen. The patterns the brain waves create give researchers an image of our brain activity when we are awake and when we are asleep (• FIGURE 4.3). EEG technology also is often used in comatose patients like Jean-Dominique.

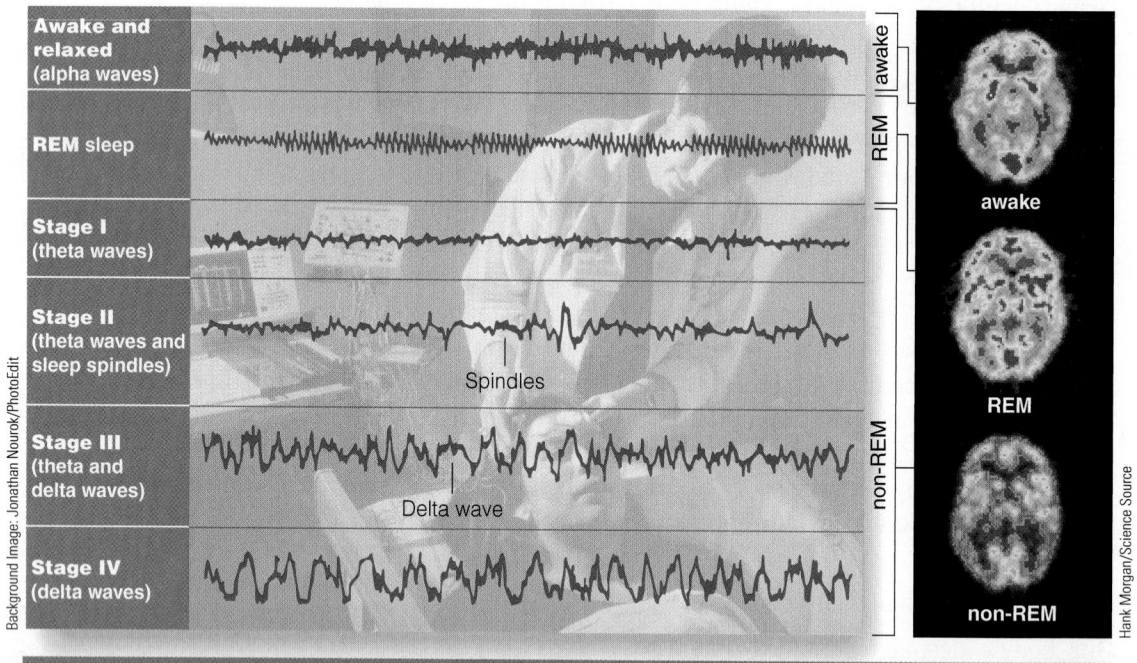

FIGURE 4.3

Brain Activity During Wakefulness and the Various Stages of Sleep

Electroencephalogram technology records brain-wave activity during wakefulness and the various stages of sleep. When awake but relaxed, the brain emits alpha waves. Brain activity during non-REM sleep progressively slows from theta waves (stage I) to delta waves (stage IV). REM sleep is characterized by rapid brain waves. The brain slides also differentiate non-REM sleep, REM sleep, and wakefulness. Notice that your brain looks as though it is awake while you are in REM sleep. The brain slides labeled "awake" and "REM" look very similar, whereas the portion labeled "non-REM" looks quite different.

When we are awake and alert, our brain (as measured by an EEG) emits *beta* waves. Beta brain waves are rapid, with a high number of cycles per second. This indicates frequent impulses of electrical activity in the brain. When we are awake yet relaxed, our brain emits *alpha* waves. Alpha waves are somewhat slower and less frequent than beta waves. As we sleep, our brain-wave patterns change in a predictable sequence.

If you watch someone sleep, you will notice that at times the person's eyes move under the eyelids, showing rapid eye movement (REM). At other times during sleep, such eye movement is absent. From such observations, researchers have identified two distinct sleep patterns: **non-REM sleep** and **REM sleep**. When your eyes do not move during sleep, it is referred to as non-rapid-eye-movement, or non-REM sleep. The state in which our eyes do move is called rapid-eye-movement, or REM sleep. During these two states of sleep, our bodies and brains are experiencing very different activities.

non-REM sleep the relaxing state of sleep in which the person's eyes do not move

REM sleep the active state of sleep in which the person's eyes move

Non-REM sleep is a progressively relaxed state. In contrast, REM sleep is very active. During a night of sleep, our bodies and brains move back and forth between states of relaxation and activity until we wake up in the morning (Armitage, 1995; Dement & Kleitman, 1957). The sleep cycle begins with non-REM sleep.

THE FOUR STAGES OF NON-REM SLEEP

When we fall asleep, our bodies and brains progress through a series of four non-REM sleep stages:

- *Stage I sleep* is a light sleep and is characterized by *theta* waves. Notice in Figure 4.3 that theta waves are slower and less frequent than beta or alpha waves. During this stage, your breathing and heart rate slow down. You may experience sensations such as falling or floating. You can easily awaken from stage I sleep, which typically lasts from 1 to 7 minutes.
- *Stage II sleep* is characterized by *sleep spindles* and lasts approximately 20 minutes. Sleep spindles (see Figure 4.3) are a pattern of slower theta waves sporadically disrupted by bursts of electrical activity. During stage II sleep, breathing, muscle tension, heart rate, and body temperature continue to decrease. You are clearly asleep and not easily awakened. Research suggests that stage II sleep spindles help us process both simple and complex motor skills that we have learned (Barakat et al., 2013; Fogel & Smith, 2006, 2011; Fogel et al., 2007; Tucker & Fishbein, 2009).
- *Stages III and IV* sleep are referred to as *slow-wave sleep*. In stage III sleep, you begin showing *delta* brain-wave patterns. Delta waves are large, slow brain waves. When a consistent pattern of delta waves emerges, you have entered stage IV sleep. Stage IV sleep is referred to as *deep sleep*. The body is extremely relaxed. Heart rate, respiration, body temperature, and blood flow to the brain are reduced. Growth hormone is secreted. It is difficult to awaken people from deep sleep. When they are awakened, they may be disoriented or confused. It is believed that during this deep sleep, body maintenance and restoration occur (Dang-Vu et al., 2010; Porkka-Heiskanen et al., 1997). For example, exercise increases the amount of slow-wave sleep (Driver & Taylor, 2000; Horne & Staff, 1983). Recent findings also indicate a major role of slow-wave sleep for strengthening the long-term storage of specific events and experiences called *episodic memory* (Aly & Moscovitch, 2010; Inostroza & Born, 2013; Scullin, 2013). Your first hour of sleep is predominately slow-wave sleep. Slow-wave sleep then progressively gets shorter the longer you sleep.

REM SLEEP: DREAM ON

After approximately 30–40 minutes of slow-wave sleep, your brain and body start to speed up again. You cycle back through stage II of non-REM sleep and then enter REM (rapid-eye-movement) sleep. REM sleep is a very active stage. Your breathing rate increases, and your heart beats irregularly. Blood flow increases to the genital area and may cause erections in males (Somers et al., 1993). However, your muscle tone significantly decreases, leaving the muscles extremely relaxed and essentially paralyzed. Figure 4.3 shows that your REM brain-wave patterns are similar to your brain-wave patterns when you are awake. The brain slides labeled "awake" and "REM sleep" look almost exactly alike! You can see that the portion labeled "non-REM sleep" looks quite different.

REM sleep is intimately connected to dreaming. Although you can dream in some form in all sleep stages, dreams during REM sleep are more easily recalled. More than 80% of people awakened from REM sleep report dreaming (Hirshkowitz et al., 1997). The body paralysis that occurs during REM prevents you from acting out your dreams. However, in rare instances, people do not experience the paralysis that normally accompanies REM sleep. This condition, which mainly affects older men, is referred to as **REM behavior disorder**. People with REM behavior disorder may thrash about while in REM sleep, causing harm to themselves or others (Gugger & Wagner, 2007; Plazzi et al., 1997).

REM behavior disorder a condition in which normal muscle paralysis does not occur, leading to violent movements during REM sleep

REM rebound the loss of REM sleep is recouped by spending more time in REM on subsequent nights

Researchers are continuously questioning the purpose of REM sleep. Some studies indicate a connection between REM sleep and memory processing. People who are deprived of REM sleep and dreaming are less likely to recall complex information learned earlier in the day than are people who were not deprived of REM sleep (Chollar, 1989; Karni et al., 1994). REM-deprived people also report having difficulty concentrating when they awaken. These findings have led researchers to speculate that REM sleep—and perhaps dreaming—facilitates the storage of memories as well as mental strategies (Diekelmann & Born, 2010; Rauchs et al., 2004). At the same time, REM appears to help us process recent emotional experiences (Desseilles et al., 2011; Menz et al., 2013; Walker & van der Helm, 2009) and to "discard" information that is trivial or less important to us (Crick & Mitchison, 1995; Smith, 1995). Other research shows no relationship between time spent in REM sleep and memory problems (J. M. Siegel, 2001). Scientists continue to explore the exact connection between the various sleep stages and different memory processes (Poe et al., 2010).

Another curiosity of REM sleep is referred to as **REM rebound**. When people lose REM sleep because of medications, drugs, or sleep deprivation, they make up for it on subsequent nights by spending more time dreaming (Dement, 1960). Before we look at research on dreaming, let's review what happens during a typical night of sleep.

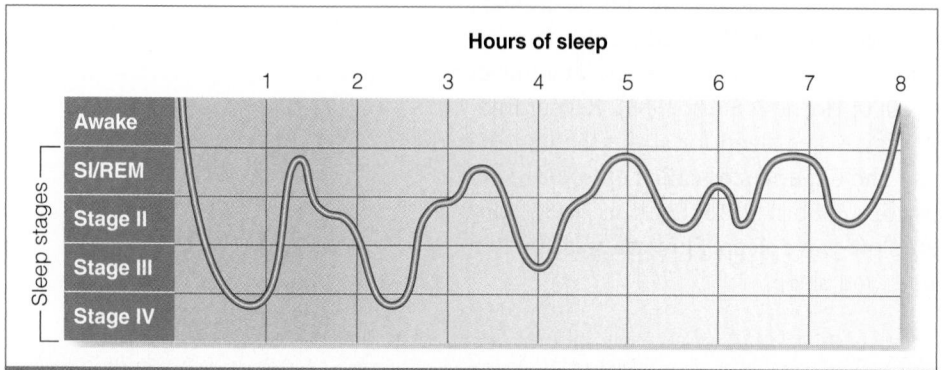

FIGURE 4.4

A Typical Night of Sleep

As the night progresses, we spend less time in slow-wave sleep (stages III and IV) and more time in REM sleep.

A TYPICAL NIGHT'S SLEEP

A typical night of sleep consists of cycling through non-REM stages and REM sleep. We progress through stages I, II, III, and IV of non-REM sleep. We revisit stages III and II of non-REM sleep. We then enter REM sleep. After a brief period in REM sleep, we begin the cycle again, starting with the non-REM stages. The pattern repeats throughout the night. One complete cycle of non-REM and REM sleep takes about 90 minutes. But notice from • FIGURE 4.4 that as the night progresses we spend less time in slow-wave sleep and more time in REM sleep. This means that the body-restoring functions of slow-wave sleep take place early on, during the first few cycles of sleep. After these early cycles, we spend longer in REM sleep. So if you are not getting enough sleep, you will miss out on the longest period of REM sleep. On average, we spend about 20% of our total sleep time in REM sleep. If you sleep 8 hours a night, you spend roughly 90 minutes of that time in REM sleep. That means each night you spend approximately 90 minutes having REM dreams. For Jean-Dominique, this typical pattern of sleep was likely altered. Studies on sleep in locked-in syndrome indicate disturbances in slow-wave sleep and a significant reduction in the amount of REM sleep (Cologan et al., 2010).

4.1.5 • Dreaming: The Night's Work

Although not everyone reports remembering their dreams when they awaken, everyone, regardless of culture, progresses through dream states during sleep. When Jean-Dominique Bauby came out of his coma, he actually thought he was having a bad dream. Dreams do show some similarities in content from one culture to another. For example, dream themes that focus on basic needs or fears (sex, aggression, and death) seem to be universal. Other content seems to be specific to its presence in a culture. For instance, today's Alaskan natives may have dreams that include snowmobiles, but their ancestors of 100 years ago obviously did not. People dream about what they know, which is influenced by the culture in which they live (Price & Crapo, 2002).

SIGMUND FREUD'S INTERPRETATION OF DREAMS

One of the most controversial and best-known theories of dreaming is Sigmund Freud's. In his *Interpretation of Dreams* (1900/1980), Freud called dreams "the royal road to the unconscious." According to Freud, dreams allow us to express fears and sexual and aggressive desires without the censorship of our conscious thought processes. Having straightforward dreams about these "unacceptable" desires would cause us anxiety. Instead, we dream in symbols that represent our unconscious desires. For Freud, dreams contained both **manifest content** and **latent content**. The manifest content of a dream is what you recall when you awaken. The latent, or hidden, content of the dream is the symbolic interpretation. For example, a young girl may dream of coming home from school one day to find the house deserted. She runs from room to room, looking for her parents or some sign that they will be returning soon (manifest content). Such a dream among children may signify the anxiety of being left alone, deserted, uncared for, or unprotected (latent content).

manifest content according to Freud, what the dreamer recalls on awakening

latent content according to Freud, the symbolic meaning of a dream

threat simulation theory (TST) suggests that dreaming is an ancient biological defense mechanism that allows us to repeatedly simulate potentially threatening situations so that we can rehearse our responses to these events

DREAMS AS COPING, EVOLUTIONARY DEFENSE, OR JUST BIOLOGY AT WORK?

Many psychologists and psychiatrists have challenged Freud's theory of dreaming and have proposed alternative explanations for why we dream. For example, the *continuity hypothesis* suggests that dreaming is a way of coping with daily problems and issues. We dream about everyday experiences and current concerns in an effort to resolve these issues (Cartwright, 1993; Pesant & Zadra, 2006; Schredl, 2009; Schredl & Erlacher, 2008). In this view, dreams are not as symbolic as Freud suggested. *Memory theory* suggests that dreams are a way to consolidate information and to get rid of trivial details in our memories (Eiser, 2005; Porte & Hobson, 1996). From this viewpoint, dreams represent a function of memory.

The **threat simulation theory (TST)** suggests an evolutionary function of dreams. TST proposes that dreaming is essentially an ancient biological defense mechanism that allows us to experience potentially threatening situations so that we can rehearse our responses to these events. Although studies do show that childhood trauma or recurrent dreams are associated with a greater number of threatening dream events, not all of our dreams involve themes of survival (Valli & Revonsuo, 2009; Valli et al., 2005; Zadra, Desjardins, & Marcotte, 2006).

activation-synthesis theory suggests that dreams do not have symbolic meaning but are the by-product of the brain's random firing of neural impulses during REM sleep

sleep disorder a disturbance in the normal pattern of sleeping

insomnia a sleep disorder in which a person cannot get to sleep and/or stay asleep

A biologically based theory is the **activation-synthesis theory** (Hobson & McCarley, 1977), which suggests that dreaming is just a consequence of the highly aroused brain during REM sleep, when the brain shows activation of millions of random neural impulses. The cortex of the brain attempts to create meaning out of these neural impulses by synthesizing them into familiar images or stories based on our stored memories. These images and stories may reflect our past, our emotions, our personal perspectives, and information accessed during waking, but they have no hidden "Freudian" meaning. However, because we are the ones who integrate these images into a plot, the storyline may provide us with insights about ourselves (Hobson, Pace-Schott, & Stickgold, 2000; McCarley, 1998).

Obviously, our understanding of the purpose and meaning of dreaming is incomplete. Dreams aside, sleep research indicates that not everyone always gets a good night's sleep. Some of us exhibit sleep disturbances, our next topic of discussion.

4.1.6 • Sleep Disorders: Tossing and Turning—and More

Not everyone sleeps soundly. An estimated 50–70 million adults in the United States experience a **sleep disorder**, or a disturbance in the normal pattern of sleep (Centers for Disease Control, 2011a). Sleep disorders also affect approximately 25% to 40% of children and adolescents (Meltzer & Mindell, 2006). Jean-Dominique and others in intensive care units often can experience sleep disruption due to noise from ventilators, activity from medical personnel, and exposure to light. Here, we will discuss several sleep disorders that influence behavior: *insomnia, narcolepsy, sleep apnea, restless legs syndrome, sleepwalking, night terrors,* and *enuresis.*

INSOMNIA: THERE IS HELP!

Insomnia, the most commonly reported sleep disorder, is the inability to get to sleep and/or stay asleep. Occasional insomnia is quite common, with more than a third of American adults reporting insomnia in the last year (Roth, 2005). Insomnia is associated with a multitude of factors, including stress, coping with the loss of a loved one, a change in sleep schedule, obesity, chronic pain, drug abuse, anxiety, or depression (Roth, Krystal, & Lieberman, 2007).

Insomnia can be treated medically using antianxiety or sedative medications such as Xanax or Ambien, or by taking over-the-counter medications such as Sominex and Nytol that contain antihistamines and pain relievers to induce sleepiness. However, long-term use of these drugs may lead to dependence and serious side effects, including memory loss, fatigue, and increased sleepiness. Chronic insomnia is best treated with a combination of taking medication for a limited time, cognitive-behavioral therapy (which focuses on changing thoughts and behaviors that interfere with restful sleep—discussed more in Chapter 14), and following several sleep guidelines that have evolved from our study of how we sleep (Morin et al., 2009; Riemann & Perlis, 2009; Roth, Krystal, & Lieberman, 2007):

- Establish a regular sleep–wake cycle to work with your body's natural sleep rhythm. Go to bed at the same time every evening and wake up at the same time every morning. Even if you have difficulty falling asleep at night, continue to get up at the same time each morning.

- Avoid long naps during waking hours. Naps can disrupt your sleep circadian rhythm. What about children who take daily naps and adults who take a "power nap" or siesta? Children's naps and siestas typically occur at the same time every day and thereby work with, rather than against, the sleep circadian rhythm. Power naps are short periods of rest (15–20 minutes) that are relaxing and that can reenergize the body and mind; because they are short, they generally do not interfere with our sleep cycles (Milner & Cote, 2009).
- Don't use your bed for anything other than sleeping. For example, people with insomnia should not eat, study, work, or watch television in bed. The bed should be associated only with sleeping.
- If you can't get to sleep after 15 minutes, get up and do something that you think will make you tired enough to get to sleep, such as reading (but not in your bed). Then try again to fall asleep.
- Avoid sleeping pills, alcohol, cigarettes, and caffeine. These are all drugs that can interfere with your natural sleep cycle and disrupt REM sleep.
- Exercise during the day can promote good sleep (Reid et al., 2010; Yang et al., 2012). However, avoid physical workouts within an hour of bedtime. Your body should be relaxed prior to sleeping.
- Turn off your cell phone and computer prior to sleeping. Anticipating incoming text messages or calls, as well as the vibration or sound that occurs when a message or call is received, interrupts the natural sleep cycle and makes deep sleep less likely (Van den Bulck, 2003, 2007). In one study, both cell phone usage and computer usage were positively correlated with insomnia (Fossum et al., 2014).
- Turn off the lights. Unnecessary light exposure, from the television, cell phone, LCD clock display, or a night light affects sleep quality. It increases stage 1 sleep and decreases slow-wave or deeper sleep (Cho, et al., 2013).

NARCOLEPSY AND CATAPLEXY

Narcolepsy, a rare sleep disorder that affects approximately 56 out of every 100,000 Americans, occurs when a person falls asleep during alert times of the day (Longstreth et al., 2007). This condition is not the same as a microsleep, though. Narcolepsy is thought to stem from a loss of neurons in the hypothalamus of the brain. These neurons are responsible for producing a chemical, called *hypocretin*, that helps to control the sleep–wake cycle (J. M. Siegel & Boehmer, 2006; Nishino, 2007; Zeitzer, Nishino, & Mignot, 2006). The person with narcolepsy experiences brief periods of REM sleep that may be accompanied by muscle paralysis, a condition called *cataplexy*. Narcolepsy with cataplexy occurs in roughly 25–50 of every 100,000 persons (Longstreth et al., 2007). People with narcolepsy may fall down or otherwise injure themselves during these episodes. Those with the condition typically take *modafinil* to improve wakefulness (Nishino & Okuro, 2010; Roth, Schwartz et al., 2007) and *sodium oxybate*, the only FDA-approved medication for cataplexy (Thorpy, 2007).

narcolepsy [NAR-co-lep-see] a rare sleep disorder in which a person falls asleep during alert activities during the day

sleep apnea [APP-nee-uh] a sleep disorder in which a person stops breathing during sleep

SLEEP APNEA AND SIDS

Sleep apnea is a disorder in which a person stops breathing while sleeping. In an attempt to get air, people with sleep apnea often emit loud snores or snorts that may awaken them or their partners. This pattern may occur hundreds of times during the night. People afflicted may feel sluggish, tired, irritable, or unable to concentrate the next day because of the nighttime sleep disruption (Naegele et al., 1995).

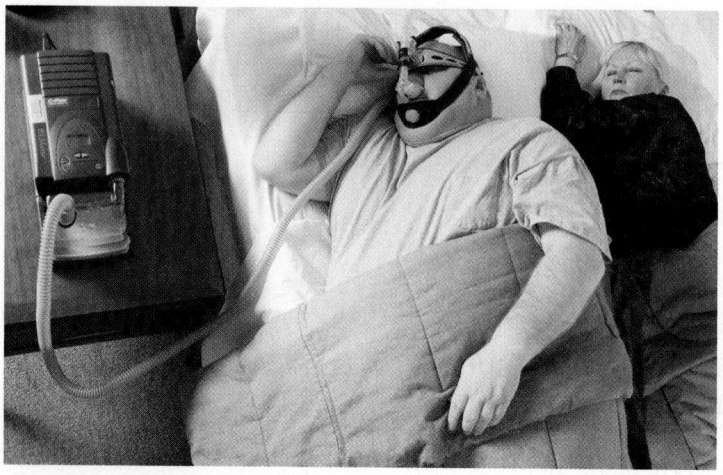

© Custom Medical Stock Photo

A continuous positive airway pressure, or CPAP, device blows air into the nose to facilitate continuous breathing for people who have sleep apnea.

Obesity, being overweight, and the use of alcohol or sedatives increase one's chances of developing sleep apnea (Pillar & Lavie, 2011; Resta et al., 2001). Sleep apnea is a risk factor for heart failure and stroke and is highly associated with heart disease, especially for middle-aged men (Butt et al., 2010; Chen et al., 2014; Sanchez-de-la-Torre, Campos-Rodriguez, & Barbe, 2013). Once diagnosed, sleep apnea may be treated in various ways. If obesity is a factor, a weight-loss program is the first treatment. In addition, a nasal mask (called a continuous positive airway pressure, or CPAP, device) that blows air into the nose to facilitate continuous breathing can be worn at night. Wearing mouth retainers can help in some cases. In severe cases, removing the tonsils or surgery to alter the position of the jaw can be performed (Saskin, 1997). Considerable evidence suggests a genetic basis for sleep apnea (Chiang, 2006; Polotsky & O'Donnell, 2007). Estimates of sleep apnea in the general population range from 4% to 20% (Finkel et al., 2009; Ram et al., 2010).

Sleep apnea has been suggested as one cause of *sudden infant death syndrome* (*SIDS*), or "crib death," when apparently healthy babies die while they are sleeping. They stop breathing for reasons that are not yet understood. SIDS affects babies at an average age of 4 months. African American and American Indian babies are at greater risk than White or Hispanic babies, and the risk is higher for males than for females (Lipsitt, 2003).

RESTLESS LEGS SYNDROME (RLS)

restless legs syndrome (RLS) a neurological movement disorder occurring primarily at night in which a person has unpleasant sensations in the legs and an irresistible urge to move them to relieve the pain

sleepwalking a sleep disorder in which a person is mobile and may perform actions during stage IV sleep

Restless legs syndrome (RLS) is a common sleep movement disorder in which a person has unpleasant sensations in the legs and an irresistible urge to move them to relieve the pain. Symptoms occur primarily at night. Estimates of RLS in the general population range from 5% to 25%, although the incidence is higher in women (Nagandia & De, 2013).

Many people with RLS also experience *periodic limb movement in sleep* (*PLMS*). PLMS includes involuntary leg twitches or jerking movements during sleep that occur roughly every 15–40 seconds, sometimes throughout the night. The symptoms severely disrupt sleep. Although some people with RLS may develop PLMS, most people with PLMS do not experience RLS. PLMS also can occur in people with narcolepsy, sleep apnea, REM sleep behavior disorder, and in those with no sleep disturbances (Hornyak et al., 2006).

The cause of RLS is unknown. Current hypotheses focus on a genetic component, low levels of iron in the brain, and the role of the neurotransmitter dopamine, as dopamine is needed to produce smooth, muscle activity and movement (Nagandia & De, 2013). Medications that influence dopamine functioning can lessen the discomfort and facilitate restful sleep (Rios Romenets & Postuma, 2013). People with Parkinson's disease, another movement disorder of the dopamine pathways, often have RLS as well (Rijsman et al., 2014).

SLEEPWALKING: WAKE ME UP!

Sleepwalking, or *somnambulism*, occurs during non-REM slow-wave sleep. People with this disorder get up and walk around during deep sleep, sometimes performing actions that make them appear to be awake. They may cook, eat, open doors, or engage in minimal conversation. Because sleepwalkers are asleep, they may injure themselves or others. What should you do if you come across a sleepwalker?

Wake them up or guide them back to bed. They may be initially disoriented or confused, but you will not do harm by awakening them. It is estimated that between 1% and 15% of the general population sleepwalk. It is more common in children than in adults (National Sleep Foundation, 2004).

NIGHT TERRORS AND ENURESIS

During **night terrors**, people awaken in an apparent state of fear. Their heart rates and breathing are rapid, and they may scream loudly and sit up in bed, wide-eyed with terror. People rarely recall the incident in the morning (Hartmann, 1981; Llorente, et al., 1992). Night terrors occur during non-REM slow-wave sleep, and an attack may last 5–20 minutes. Although they can occur any time in one's life, night terrors are more commonly reported in children between the ages of 4 and 12, and in older adults with various neurological and cognitive disorders such as Parkinson's disease and elderly dementia (Abad & Guilleminault, 2004). In the United States, an estimated 1% to 6% of children experience night terror episodes. For adults, estimates are less than 1% (Owens, 2007).

Why night terrors occur is still a mystery, although the disorder does tend to run in families (Guilleminault et al., 2003; Owens, 2007). Keep in mind that people who are having night terrors do not know what is occurring. To help a person experiencing a night terror, simply reassure the person that everything is all right and to go back to sleep. Night terrors are different from *nightmares*. **Nightmares** are brief scary dreams that typically occur during REM sleep and are often recalled in vivid detail in the morning.

Enuresis is bedwetting, but it does not refer to the occasional nighttime bedwetting that is common among young children. Enuresis is diagnosed when a child who is at least 5 years old wets his or her bed or pajamas at least twice a week over a 3-month period. It is estimated that 5% to 10% of 5-year-olds are diagnosed with enuresis, but by adolescence the prevalence of enuresis decreases to about 1% (American Psychiatric Association, 2013). It is more common at younger ages, in males, and among African American youth (Shreeram et al., 2009). Enuresis tends to run in families, suggesting that it may be inherited (Ondersma & Walker, 1998; von Gontard et al., 2001). However, the behavior may also occur during times of stress, such as when a new sibling is born or familial conflict is high, and may accompany night terrors. Scolding or punishing a child seldom has any effect on the bedwetting. In fact, scolding can potentially damage the child's self-esteem and the parent–child relationship. Several treatment methods are available, and most children outgrow the behavior (Berry, 2006).

night terrors very frightening non-REM sleep episodes

nightmare a brief scary REM dream that is often remembered

enuresis [en-your-REE-sus] a condition in which a person over the age of 5 shows an inability to control urination during sleep

4.1.7 • Gender, Ethnic, and Cultural Variations in Sleep

Sleep research has also investigated the degree to which gender, ethnicity, and culture influence sleep. Several studies have found that men report needing less sleep than women to function at their best, and that women are more likely than men to sleep 8 hours or more. Women are also more likely than men to report insufficient rest or sleep (McKnight-Eily et al., 2009), daytime sleepiness, and needing 30 minutes or more to fall asleep (National Sleep Foundation, 2005; Oginska & Pokorski, 2006). Working mothers also are two and a half times more likely than working fathers to interrupt their sleep to take care of babies and small children (Burgard, 2011). In the area of sleep disorders, two consistent gender differences have emerged. Insomnia tends to be more frequent in women (Morlock, Tan, & Mitchell, 2006; Roberts, Roberts, & Chan, 2006; Zhang & Wing, 2006), and snoring and sleep apnea are more common in men (Jordan & McEvoy, 2003).

Only a limited number of studies have compared sleep variables across ethnic groups. Those that have suggest that African Americans sleep worse than European Americans. They report poorer sleep quality, more variation in sleep time, and taking longer to fall asleep (McKnight-Eily et al., 2009; National Sleep Foundation, 2010, Nunes et al., 2008). However, African Americans are more likely to live in urban areas, a variable that is also associated with poorer sleep quality (Haie & Do, 2007). Asian Americans were most likely of any ethnic group to say they get a good night's sleep (National Sleep Foundation, 2010). European Americans report the highest rate of insomnia, whereas African Americans, American Indians, and Hispanic adults are also at higher risk for sleep apnea, although these observed ethnic differences are mainly explained by higher rates of obesity among these groups (Fiorentino et al., 2006; National Sleep Foundation, 2010).

Cultural variations in sleep habits also have been investigated. Japanese and U.S. adults report the least amount of sleep when compared to respondents from Canada, Germany, Mexico, and the United Kingdom. Meditation and prayer before sleep are reported by nearly half of U.S. adults and 62% of Mexican adults. The most common sleep ritual reported across the six countries was television. Two-thirds of the adults in all countries surveyed watched television in the hour before bed (National Sleep Foundation, 2013).

In summary, sleep is as necessary to our survival as food and shelter. Sleep refuels our bodies and minds, preparing us for the challenges of the next day. When we skip sleep, change our sleep cycle, or experience disturbances in our sleep, we may feel irritable, tired, and less alert the next day.

Quiz Yourself

4.1

1. Ronnie has a dream that he is being chased by a golden goose. He is told that this reflects his anxiety about impregnating women. This analysis represents the _____ of his dream.
   a. manifest content
   b. latent content
   c. activation synthesis
   d. consolidation

2. Hap is at a workshop and falls asleep. He is relaxed and his brain-wave pattern shows long waves but not delta waves interrupted by short bursts of electrical activity. Hap is in what stage of sleep?
   a. Stage I
   b. Stage II
   c. Stage IV
   d. REM

3. Which of the following statements about sleep is *false*?
   a. Sleep patterns change with age.
   b. Everyone needs at least 8 hours of sleep a night.
   c. Some people are night owls, whereas others are early birds.
   d. Circadian rhythms influence the sleep cycle.

4. Which of the following statements about the biology of sleep is *true*?
   a. In dark conditions, the suprachiasmatic nucleus increases the release of melatonin.
   b. In bright light, the suprachiasmatic nucleus increases the release of melatonin.
   c. In bright light, the suprachiasmatic nucleus increases the release of hypocretin.
   d. In dark conditions, the suprachiasmatic nucleus increases the release of hypocretin.

5. Which of the following is poor advice to give to someone who is experiencing insomnia?
   a. Avoid naps
   b. Exercise during the day.
   c. Go to bed when you feel tired and wake up when you feel rested.
   d. Do not watch television in bed.

Answers 1. b; 2. b; 3. b; 4. a; 5. c

4.2 Hypnosis

Hypnosis is a method occasionally used by researchers and psychologists (and frequently by hypnotists) to create a state of heightened suggestibility in others. This section describes the experience of hypnosis, explains several theories about how hypnosis occurs, and explains what hypnosis can and cannot do for you. Note that not all psychologists are hypnotists, and not all hypnotists are psychologists.

hypnosis a state of heightened suggestibility

4.2.1 • The Experience of Hypnosis

Typically, if you are undergoing hypnosis, you are asked to focus on an object, an image, or the hypnotist's voice. For several minutes, you are told that you are getting sleepy and becoming more relaxed (Druckman & Bjork, 1994). You don't fall asleep—though EEG brain-wave patterns of hypnotized people show an increase in alpha waves—and this condition isn't followed by the non-REM pattern of sleep stages discussed earlier (Graffin, Ray, & Lundy, 1995). After inducing you into this relaxed hypnotic state, the hypnotist makes suggestions about what you are seeing, feeling, or perceiving. For example, one suggestion might be to lift your left arm over your head. A more complex suggestion might be that your eyelids feel as though they are glued shut and you cannot open them. Although accounts vary widely, many hypnotized people report that they feel as though they are floating or that their bodies are sinking. Under hypnosis, they remain in control of their bodies and are aware of their surroundings (Kirsch & Lynn, 1995).

4.2.2 • Variations in Hypnotic Susceptibility

Hypnotic susceptibility is the ability to become hypnotized. Some people have a low degree of susceptibility—they cannot easily be hypnotized. Others have a high susceptibility, meaning that they can be easily hypnotized. One well-known standard test for measuring the degree to which people respond to hypnotic suggestions is the *Stanford Hypnotic Susceptibility Scale.* The scale assesses your suggestibility to certain tasks while in a state of hypnosis with a trained hypnotist. The tasks range from pulling apart your interlocked fingers to hallucinating the presence of a buzzing fly.

Contrary to what you may see on television or in the movies, research using such measures has found that not everyone can be hypnotized. About 25% of adults are difficult to hypnotize (Hoeft et al., 2012).

©iStockphoto.com/PaulaConnelly

Not everyone can be hypnotized. You have to want to be hypnotized and believe it will work for you.

People who are easily hypnotized tend to be better able to focus their attention (Egner, Jamieson, & Gruzelier, 2005; Raz, 2005), have vivid imaginations (Silva & Kirsch, 1992; Spanos, Burnley, & Cross, 1993; Terhune, Cardena, & Lindgren, 2010), and have positive expectations about hypnosis (Barber, 2000). Neuroimaging studies even document differences in brain activation between people who are highly hypnotizable and those who are low in hypnotic susceptibility (Hoeft et al., 2012; Naish, 2010; Nash, 2005; Raz, Fan, & Posner, 2006). Hypnotic suggestibility does not appear to be related to such factors as intelligence, gender, sociability, or gullibility (Kirsch & Lynn, 1995), although in one study (Page & Green, 2007), female undergraduates did score higher than males on the Harvard Group Scale of Hypnotic Susceptibility.

4.2.3 • Explaining Hypnosis: Applying Neodissociation and Response Set Theories

neodissociation [knee o dis-so-see-AYE-shun] theory Hilgard's proposal that hypnosis involves two simultaneous states: a hypnotic state and a hidden observer

response set theory of hypnosis asserts that hypnosis is not an altered state of consciousness, but a cognitive set to respond appropriately to suggestions

Currently, two theories seek to explain hypnosis: *neodissociation theory* and the *response set theory*. Ernest Hilgard's (1977, 1992) **neodissociation theory** suggests that hypnosis is truly an altered state of consciousness: a person feels, perceives, and behaves differently than in a conscious state. To dissociate means to split or break apart. Hilgard maintains that under hypnosis, your consciousness divides into two states. One level of your consciousness voluntarily agrees to behave according to the suggestions of the hypnotist. However, at the same time, a *hidden observer* state exists. This hidden observer is aware of all that is happening.

We all engage in dissociation at times. Have you ever driven to a familiar location and realized when you arrived that you couldn't consciously remember driving there? Have you ever dissociated in a class—paying attention to the lesson while at the same time doodling or mentally organizing the rest of your day? If you have experienced any of these behaviors, then you are familiar with the concept of dissociation. Hilgard believes that hypnosis works in much the same way, allowing the person to attend to the hypnotist's suggestions while still being aware of what is happening through the hidden observer.

In a classic demonstration, Hilgard hypnotized participants and suggested that they would feel no pain. The participants were then instructed to submerge one arm in ice-cold water. When Hilgard asked them whether they felt pain, the participants replied, "No." However, when they were asked to press a key with their other hand if they felt pain, the participants did so. On one level, they agreed with the hypnotist that there was no pain, while at the same time a part of them—a "hidden observer"—indicated that there was pain (Hilgard, Morgan, & MacDonald, 1975).

Another view, the **response set theory of hypnosis** (Kirsch, 2000; Kirsch & Lynn, 1997; Lynn, 1997), asserts that hypnosis is *not* an altered state of consciousness. Rather, hypnosis is merely a willingness to respond appropriately to suggestions. Several studies do support that people's response expectancies influence their responsiveness to hypnosis (Benham et al., 2006; Milling, Reardon, & Carosella, 2006). Highly hypnotizable people enter hypnosis with the intention of behaving as a "hypnotized person" and hold the expectation that they will succeed in following the hypnotist's suggestions. Their intentions and expectations trigger their positive response to being hypnotized. Nonhypnotized participants show behaviors similar to those of hypnotized people, such as behaving in strange ways or acting like a young child, simply because they are willing to do what the hypnotist asks them to do (Dasgupta et al., 1995; Kirsch, 1994).

Currently, theorists suggest that both perspectives can be accommodated by recognizing that some motivated behavior may occur outside awareness, an idea consistent with unconscious processing (Lynn & Green, 2011). Unfortunately, hypnosis has acquired a reputation for doing some things that it cannot do. Let's look at these myths and realities of hypnosis.

4.2.4 • Evaluating the Research: What Hypnosis Can and Cannot Do

In an attempt to separate fact from fiction, psychologists have researched the effects of hypnosis. To date, research reveals the following:

- *Relieving pain.* One of the best documented uses for hypnosis is pain relief (Adachi et al., 2014; Wiechman Askay & Patterson, 2007). Under hypnosis, clients relax, which reduces pain, and/or distract themselves from the pain by focusing on more pleasing and pain-free scenarios. Hypnosis has been used to minimize pain in childbirth, to block pain during medical or dental treatments, and to relieve chronic pain stemming from various health conditions (Adachi et al., 2014; Jensen et al., 2011; Liossi, White, & Hatira, 2006; VandeVusse et al., 2007). This pain relief is more pronounced for people who have a high susceptibility to hypnosis (Bates, 1994). Hypnosis does not reduce the sensation of pain. The pain is still there, but hypnosis changes a person's subjective experience of pain so that it is more bearable (Rainville et al., 1997).
- *Curing addictions.* Posthypnotic suggestions have proven less successful for treating addictions or self-control behaviors, even in people with a high susceptibility to hypnosis. Although hypnosis has been used as a treatment to stop smoking, nail biting, overeating, gambling, alcoholism, and other addictions, it has proven no more successful than other treatments at controlling these behaviors (Barnes et al., 2010; Bates, 1994; Green & Lynn, 2000). Self-control behaviors such as smoking and alcoholism are some of the most difficult behaviors to change, and hypnosis doesn't appear to have an advantage over other types of treatment (Rabkin et al., 1984).
- *Enhancing physical performance.* Hypnosis does not create superhuman capacities. However, being in a relaxed state such as hypnosis can enhance physical performance (Barker, Jones, & Greenlees, 2010). The person can more readily visualize optimal performance and reduce self-doubt or nerves. This enhancement can also be achieved through other techniques, such as deep muscle relaxation and guided imagery (see Chapter 12; Druckman & Bjork, 1994; Newmark & Bogacki, 2005).
- *Decreasing anxiety and enhancing psychotherapy.* Hypnosis has proven useful in decreasing fears and anxieties for people with a high susceptibility to hypnosis (Saadat et al., 2006). Clinicians sometimes use hypnosis in therapy to help their clients solve problems or cope with bodily symptoms such as headaches or stomach pains that appear to be related to psychological stress. Hypnosis has been helpful in reducing pain and tension. Again, it is most effective for clients who have a high susceptibility to hypnosis (Kirsch, Montgomery, & Sapirstein, 1995; Pyun, 2013).
- *Enhancing or recovering memory.* One of the most controversial applications of hypnosis has been in the area of memory enhancement. Research in this area has focused on two key issues: age regression and recovered memories.
  - *Age regression* refers to a person's reliving earlier childhood experiences. Numerous studies on age regression demonstrate that under hypnosis,

adults act the way they *expect* children to behave (Spanos, 1996). They may write, sing, or behave like a child, but it is more like an adult playing the role of a child. Their behavior is not different from that of nonhypnotized people who are asked to behave like a child (Nash, 1987).

- A *recovered memory* is one in which a person recalls forgotten traumatic events or information, such as events from a crime scene or from one's childhood. Being in a relaxed state may facilitate recall under certain circumstances. However, research reveals that hypnotized people may also recall untrue events. For this reason, information gathered under hypnosis is not permissible in a court of law in the United States, Canada, Australia, or Great Britain. People are more suggestible under hypnosis, and consequently their memories are more likely to be influenced by the suggestions, tone, hints, questions, and remarks of the hypnotist. They may recall just as many events that did not occur as events that did, and they may also be more prone to distort information (Geraerts et al., 2009; Scoboria, Mazzoni, & Kirsch, 2006; Scoboria et al., 2002). For these reasons, the use of hypnosis in the area of memory enhancement should be viewed with skepticism.

To summarize, hypnosis does not endow us with superhuman strength, allow us to reexperience childhood events, or improve the accuracy of our memories. However, hypnosis may be of some benefit in decreasing pain, promoting relaxation, and perhaps enhancing therapy for *some* people. These benefits are not universal. The person must want to be hypnotized and have positive beliefs about hypnosis.

Quiz Yourself 4.2

1. **Research on hypnosis suggests that it is *least* helpful for which of the following?**
   a. Relieving pain
   b. Decreasing anxiety
   c. Curing addictions
   d. Enhancing physical performance

2. **Which of the following statements about hypnosis is *false*?**
   a. Everyone can be hypnotized.
   b. Hypnosis can promote relaxation.
   c. Memories recalled under hypnosis are not always accurate.
   d. Not all psychologists agree as to whether hypnosis is an altered state of consciousness.

3. **Cecilia has been hypnotized and told that she will not feel pain in her right hand. Her right hand is then immersed in freezing cold water. According to the dissociation theory of hypnosis, what part of Cecilia will report feeling pain?**
   a. The secret hypnotist
   b. The posthypnotic suggester
   c. The conscious self
   d. The hidden observer

Answers 1. c; 2. a; 3. d

4.3 Psychoactive Drugs

psychoactive drugs substances that influence the brain and thereby the individual's behavior

Psychoactive drugs are substances that influence the brain and thereby a person's behavior. Over the past 25 years, millions of teenagers and children in the United States have routinely been educated about the effects of drugs. The most popular of these programs, Drug Abuse Resistance Education, or DARE, began in 1983. Yet despite widespread education programs, many misperceptions about drugs still exist. For example, can you name the three most widely used psychoactive drugs in American society? The three drugs most commonly used by Americans over the age of 12 are alcohol, nicotine, and caffeine (see • FIGURE 4.5)—substances that are all legal for adults to use (SAMHSA, 2013).

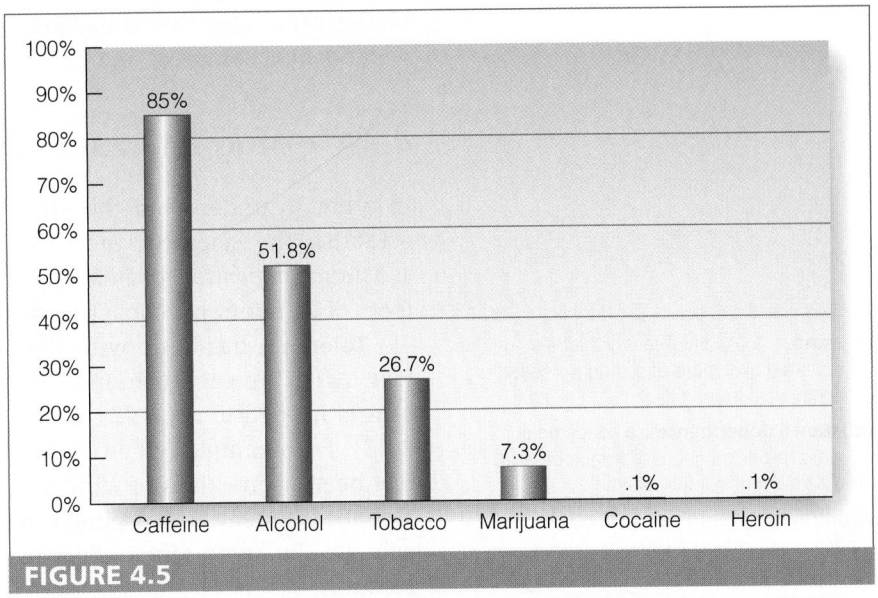

FIGURE 4.5

Current Drug Use in the United States, Ages 12 and Over, 2012

Caffeine, alcohol, and nicotine (the active ingredient in tobacco) are the three most commonly used psychoactive drugs in the United States.

Data from SAMHSA, 2013, *Results from the 2012 National Survey on Drug Use and Health.*

4.3.1 • Variations in Drug Use

In 2012, an estimated 23.9 million people (9.2%) in the United States aged 12 or older admitted to using an illegal substance in the past month (SAMHSA, 2013). Illicit drug use is highest among young adults between the ages of 18 and 25, and is higher in males than in females (SAMHSA, 2013). Substance use in the United States also varies considerably by ethnic group (• FIGURE 4.6; SAMHSA, 2013). Multiracial and American Indian/Alaska Native groups have the highest rates of current illegal drug use, and Asians have the lowest.

Increasingly, young people are also engaging in nonmedical use of prescription drugs. Intentional abuse of prescription drugs is the second most common type of illegal drug use by young people (marijuana ranks first) (Lessenger & Feinberg 2008; SAMHSA, 2013). Many young people hold incorrect assumptions about the nonmedical use of prescription drugs. According to the 2012 Partnership Attitude Tracking Study (PATS, 2013), 27% of teens believe that using prescription drugs is safer than using illegal drugs, 33% believe that there is "nothing wrong" with using prescription drugs without a prescription once in a while, 20% mistakenly believe that prescription pain relievers are not addictive, and almost a third believe that prescription medications have fewer side effects than street drugs. Sadly, the nonmedical use of prescription medication may result

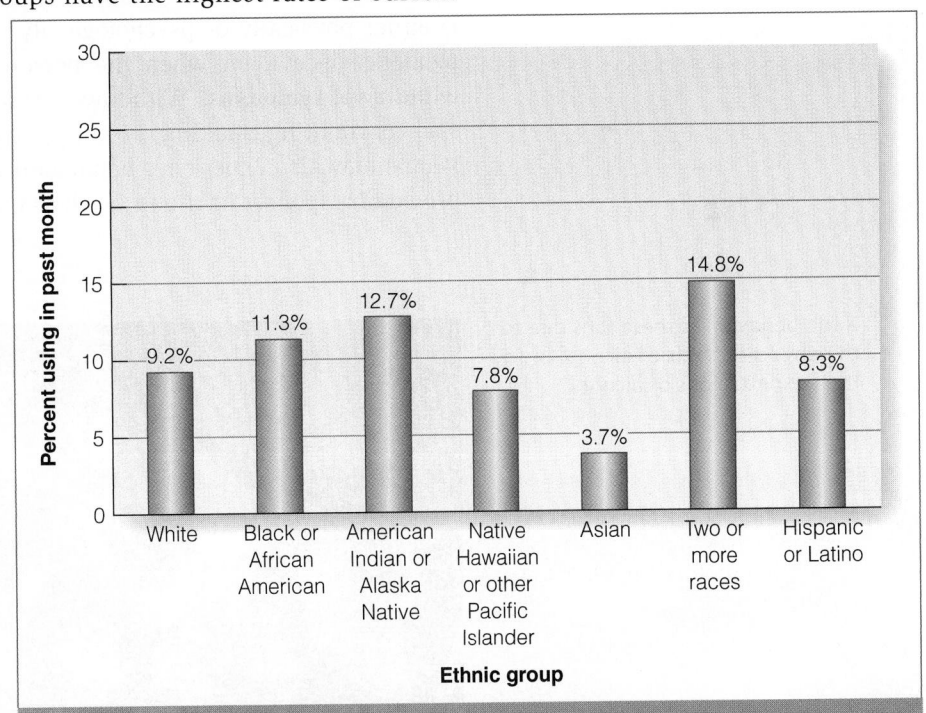

FIGURE 4.6

Ethnicity and Illicit Drug Use

Substance use in the United States varies considerably by ethnic group. Multiracial and American Indian/Alaska Native groups have the highest rates of current illegal drug use; Asians have the lowest incidence.

Data from SAMHSA, 2013, *Results from the 2012 National Survey on Drug Use and Health.*

in the same negative consequences as abuse of other drugs—most notably, dependence, seizures, and death.

4.3.2 • Drug Tolerance and Substance Dependence

In order to understand the effects of psychoactive drugs, it is important to establish the scientific meaning of two specific drug terms: *tolerance* and *substance dependence*. Defining these terms will help you understand the effects of different psychoactive drugs.

tolerance a condition in which after repeated use, more of a drug is needed to achieve the same effect

substance dependence a condition in which a person needs a drug in order to maintain normal functioning

withdrawal symptoms physical or behavioral effects that occur after a person stops using a drug

Tolerance has to do with the amount of a drug required to produce its effect. After repeated use of a drug, it is usually the case that more and more of it is needed to achieve the same effect (American Psychiatric Association, 2013). For example, when someone first drinks alcohol, he or she may have one beer or one glass of wine and get a buzz from it. However, after drinking alcohol frequently, this person will require more beers or glasses of wine to achieve the same effect. This person has increased his or her tolerance for alcohol.

However, as tolerance develops, the difference between a safe dose and a potentially harmful dose, called the *margin of safety,* narrows. Some drugs (like barbiturates) have a very narrow, or small, margin of safety; that is, their too-high, toxic dose differs only slightly from their too-low, ineffectual dose. In order to obtain the same level of intoxication, a user who has developed tolerance may raise his or her dose to a level that may result in coma or death—the too-high, toxic dose.

Related to tolerance is **substance dependence**, which occurs when someone is either physically or psychologically reliant on a drug's effects. Typically, dependence is evident when the person stops using the drug and experiences **withdrawal symptoms**. Withdrawal symptoms may include physical symptoms such as vomiting, shaking, sweating, physical pain, hallucinations, or headaches. People may also experience behavioral withdrawal symptoms when they are deprived of responses or rituals, such as injecting a drug or lighting a cigarette, that

Jon Feingersh/Blend Images/Alamy

Is the behavior of these fans due to the physical effects of alcohol or to their expectations of alcohol?

help them cope with negative emotions (Baker et al., 2006; S. Siegel, 2005). Not all drugs produce the same withdrawal symptoms. In many cases, people continue to use a drug just to ward off the unpleasantness of the withdrawal effects or emotional distress. We often hear the term *addiction* used to indicate that someone has lost control over his or her drug use.

4.3.3 • How Drugs Work: Biology, Expectations, and Culture

Psychoactive drugs alter your state of functioning by interfering with the normal workings of the nervous system. Some drugs slow down normal brain activity, whereas others speed it up. Typically, drugs achieve these effects by interfering with or mimicking neurotransmitters in the brain (Chapter 2).

Psychological factors also influence a drug's effect. Exposure to stress or trauma increases a person's vulnerability to drug dependence (Goeders, 2004; Rohrbach et al., 2009). Learning, specifically classical conditioning (Chapter 6) can also play a role. Environmental stimuli such as where a drug is taken or whether drug paraphernalia are present become associated with drug taking and later trigger the craving for the drug sensation (Crombag & Robinson, 2004; S. Siegel, 2005). Even cognitions play a role in a drug's effects. If you expect a drug to alter your behavior in a particular way, you are more likely to change your behavior to fit your expectations. For example, in several studies people who believed they had consumed a specific drug behaved in accord with the drug's effect, regardless of whether they had actually consumed the drug. Their behavior was influenced by their *expectations* about the effects of the drug (Fillmore, Roach, & Rice, 2002; McMillen, Smith, & Wells-Parker, 1989).

One's culture also influences drug use. For example, rates of alcohol abuse are very low in China, where traditional beliefs scorn alcohol use or being under the influence of alcohol. People in China are not only less likely to drink alcohol but also less likely to advertise the fact that they have been drinking. In contrast, Korean men have a high rate of alcohol abuse, and Korean Americans have higher rates of alcohol use than other Asian American subgroups (SAMHSA, 2006). Their culture encourages drinking in social situations (Helzer & Canino, 1992). As a Frenchman, Jean-Dominique Bauby often drank wine on a daily basis at mealtimes, prior to his stroke.

The variety of psychoactive drugs in use today can be classified into four main groups: *depressants*, *opiates*, *stimulants*, and *hallucinogens*. You Review: Psychoactive Drugs and Their Effects provides a summary comparing the effects of these drugs. We'll begin with depressants.

4.3.4 • Alcohol and Other Depressants

depressants drugs that inhibit or slow down normal neural functioning

Depressants interfere with brain functioning by inhibiting or slowing normal neural functioning. In *low* doses, depressant drugs often cause a feeling of well-being, or a "nice buzz." Anxiety is reduced when the nervous system slows down. This may be why many people mistakenly believe that alcohol is an "upper." In *high* dosages, depressants can cause blackouts, coma, or death. The deaths of Anna Nicole Smith, Heath Ledger, and Michael Jackson were attributed in part to overdoses of depressants. Depressants are usually grouped into *alcohol, barbiturates,* and *sedatives*.

You Review **Psychoactive Drugs and Their Effects**

The four groups of substances most often leading to substance dependence are (1) depressants, (2) opiates, (3) stimulants, and (4) hallucinogens.

Substance	Trade Names; *Street Names*	Medical Uses	Routes of Administration	Main Effects
Depressants				
Alcohol	Beer, wine, liquor	Antidote for methanol poisoning, antiseptic	Oral, topical	Relaxation; lowered inhibitions; impaired reflexes, motor coordination, and memory
Barbiturates	Nembutal, Seconal, Phenobarbital; *barbs*	Anesthetic, anticonvulsant, sedative, relief of high blood pressure	Injected, oral	Anxiety relief, euphoria, severe withdrawal symptoms
Benzodiazepines	Librium, Rohypnol, Valium, Xanax; *roofies, tranks, bars, ladders*	Antianxiety, sedative, sleeping disorders	Injected, oral	Anxiety relief, irritability, confusion, depression, sleep problems
Opiates				
Codeine	Tylenol with codeine, Fiorinal with codeine	Pain relief, antitussive	Injected, oral	Euphoria, constipation, loss of appetite
Heroin	*Horse, smack*	None	Injected, smoked, sniffed	Euphoria, pain control, constipation, loss of appetite
Methadone	Amidone, Methadose	Pain relief, treatment for opiate dependence	Injected, oral	Relief from withdrawal symptoms, constipation, loss of appetite
Morphine	Roxanol	Pain relief	Injected, oral, smoked	Euphoria, pain control
Opium	*Dover's powder, Aunti Emma, Dreams*	Pain relief, antidiarrheal	Oral, smoked	Euphoria, pain control
Stimulants				
Caffeine	Coffee, tea, soda, chocolate, energy drink	Treatment for migraine headaches	Oral	Alertness, insomnia, loss of appetite, high blood pressure

(continued)

Nicotine	Nicorette gum, Nicotrol; *cigars, cigarettes, snuff*	Treatment for nicotine dependence	Smoked, sniffed, oral, transdermal	Alertness, calmness, loss of appetite
Cocaine	*Coke, crack, rock, snow, blow*	Local anesthetic; vasoconstrictor in Europe	Injected, smoked, sniffed	Increased energy, excitation, insomnia, loss of appetite, mood swings, delusions, paranoia, heart problems
Amphetamine	Dexedrine; Adderall; *black beauties, crosses, study buddies*	ADHD, obesity, narcolepsy	Injected, oral, smoked, sniffed	Increased alertness and energy, insomnia, loss of appetite, delusions, paranoia
Methamphetamine	*Crank, crystal, ice, meth*	ADHD, short-term aid to weight loss	Injected, oral, smoked, sniffed	Mood elevation, alertness, insomnia, loss of appetite, anxiety, paranoia
MDMA	*Adam, Ecstasy, XTC, molly*	Trial treatment for PTSD	Oral, sniffed	Increased insight and emotion, muscle tension, sleep problems, anxiety, paranoia
Hallucinogens				
Marijuana/ Cannabis	*Grass, herb, pot, reefer, weed, sinsemilla*	Glaucoma, nausea from chemotherapy, pain relief, muscle spasms, seizure disorders	Oral, smoked	Relaxation, altered perceptions, sleep problems, paranoia, amotivation
Phencyclidine	PCP; *angel dust, hog*	Anesthetic (veterinary)	Injected, oral, smoked	Euphoria, unpredictable moods, hostility
Lysergic acid diethylamide (LSD)	*Acid, microdot*	None	Oral	Altered perceptions, distortion of senses, panic reactions, flashback effects

© Corbis

Alcohol's effect on motor coordination can be seen in a police sobriety test.

HEALTH EFFECTS OF ALCOHOL

Alcohol affects the neurotransmitter GABA, which is related to anxiety levels. As noted earlier, in low dosages, alcohol may make one feel more sociable and relaxed. Alcohol also depresses the functioning of the cerebral cortex. So, in addition to feeling calm and relaxed, we are more likely to shed our inhibitions in regard to our thoughts and behaviors (Giancola et al., 2010; Stahl, 1996). We are more likely to bond with unknown group members in a social setting (Sayette et al., 2012). When we drink alcohol, we are more willing to be silly or aggressive, share our emotions, or engage in behaviors that we would think twice about if we were sober.

Alcohol also inhibits the functioning of the brain stem, impairing motor functioning and coordination. Reaction time and reflexes are slowed. When your tolerance is exceeded, your speech becomes slurred and your judgment is impaired. It is also harder for your brain to sustain attention, process information, and form new memories (Givens, 1995; Sayette, Reichle, & Schooler, 2009).

Heavy drinking on college campuses across Europe and the United States has led to a growing concern about the effects of binge drinking. *Binge drinking* is excessive alcohol use over a short period of time that brings a person's blood alcohol concentration (BAC) to 0.08% or above. This often happens when males consume five or more drinks and when females consume four or more drinks in 2 hours (National Institute of Alcohol Abuse and Alcoholism, 2004). Binge drinking is two times higher among males than females (Kanny, Liu, & Brewer, 2011) and puts one at risk for later developing an alcohol use disorder (Crabbe, Harris, & Koob, 2011). Binge drinking and alcohol use may cause *memory blackouts*—after a heavy night of drinking, you may not remember the events of the night before. Chronic alcohol use can lead to *Korsakoff's syndrome,* a memory disorder caused by a deficiency of vitamin B (thiamine). A person who is an alcoholic often substitutes alcohol for more nutritious foods, which results in numerous vitamin deficiencies. Unfortunately, these memory deficits tend to be irreversible.

fetal alcohol syndrome (FAS) a birth condition resulting from the mother's chronic use of alcohol during pregnancy; characterized by facial and limb deformities and intellectual impairment

Because drinking alcohol results in reduced inhibitions, people are more likely to engage in sexual activity (Davis et al., 2009; Patrick & Maggs, 2009). However, alcohol impairs sexual performance. It makes it more difficult for a male to get and maintain an erection. The ability to achieve orgasm is also hampered by the effects of alcohol. We may think and feel that we are better lovers when under the influence of alcohol, but in reality we are not.

Because ingested alcohol crosses the placenta, women who drink alcohol heavily during pregnancy put their unborn child at risk for **fetal alcohol syndrome (FAS)**. Children born with FAS tend to have low birth weight; exhibit limb, head, and facial deformities; and suffer brain abnormalities that retard intellectual functioning and cause difficulties in learning, memory, problem solving, and attention (Ikonomidou et al., 2000; Kumada et al., 2007). Because of the negative effects of alcohol on prenatal development, even moderate drinking during pregnancy is not recommended.

INDIVIDUAL VARIATIONS IN ALCOHOL'S EFFECT

Does everyone experience the same effects from alcohol? No. The degree to which each of us experiences these effects depends on several factors. For example, alcohol has either more or less effect depending on your tolerance level: The higher your tolerance, the more alcohol you can consume before feeling its effects. Another factor is the rate of consumption. The faster you drink, the faster the alcohol is absorbed into the blood, increasing the alcohol's effect. Gender influences alcohol's effect as well. Metabolic and weight differences between males and females make it easier for male bodies to tolerate higher levels of alcohol (York & Welte, 1994). ●TABLE 4.1 describes the typical effects of alcohol at increasingly higher blood concentrations.

TABLE 4.1

Typical Effects of Blood Alcohol Concentrations (BAC)

Alcohol intoxication varies greatly among individuals. Some people become intoxicated at lower blood alcohol concentration levels.

BAC	TYPICAL EFFECTS
.02–.03	Slight euphoria and loss of shyness; light-headedness. Depressant effects of alcohol are not yet apparent.
.04–.06	Feelings of well-being, relaxation, and lowered inhibitions; minor impairment of reasoning and memory; lowered alertness
.07–.09	Feelings of well-being; slight impairment of balance, speech, vision, reaction time, and hearing; reduced judgment and self-control; impaired reasoning and memory
.10–.125	Significant impairment of motor coordination; loss of judgment; slowed thinking; slurred speech; impairment of balance, vision, reaction time, and hearing
.13–.15	Gross motor impairment and lack of physical control; blurred vision and major loss of balance; severely impaired judgment. Feelings of well-being are reduced.
.16–.20	Anxiety, restlessness, sadness; nausea and vomiting; feeling dazed and confused; blackouts
.25	Severely impaired physical and mental abilities; increased risk of injury by falls or accidents
.30	Stupor; little comprehension of whereabouts; loss of consciousness
.35	Possible coma
.40+	Onset of coma; possible death due to respiratory arrest

ALCOHOL: GENETICS, CULTURE, AND LEARNING

Research suggests a possible genetic factor in alcohol's effect (Stacey, Clarke, & Schumann, 2009). Studies of twins show that if one identical twin is an alcoholic, the other twin has almost a 40% chance of developing a drinking problem. Rates for fraternal twins are much lower (Prescott et al., 1994). Research on sons of alcoholic fathers also suggests a possible genetic predisposition to alcohol dependence. The sons are likely to have an overall higher tolerance for alcohol, requiring more alcohol before feeling its effects, and are therefore at greater risk for abusing alcohol (Schuckit & Smith, 1997). More recently, researchers have located specific strands of genes that regulate the function of GABA. These genes vary across families with multiple members who have alcohol problems and may contribute to a person's vulnerability to alcoholism (Edenberg & Foroud, 2006; Krystal et al., 2006; Soyka et al., 2008).

Cultural studies also support a possible genetic link. In some ethnic groups, such as Japanese and Chinese, drinking alcohol can cause facial flushing. This sudden reddening of the face is a genetic trait that rarely occurs in Europeans. The physical and social discomfort of facial flushing tends to reduce the rate of alcohol consumption and alcoholism in these groups. People in ethnic groups that do not experience facial flushing are more likely to become alcoholics (Helzer & Canino, 1992).

However, environmental factors such as learning also play a role. Children of alcoholics have an increased risk of developing alcoholism that cannot be attributed solely to genetics. As adults, they are more likely to cope with personal or work-related stress by imitating the behavior of an alcoholic parent (Blane, 1988; Rivers, 1994). Similarly, the nature and quality (positive or negative) of an adolescent's environment influences alcohol dependence in teens that are genetically at risk for alcohol dependence (Dick et al., 2011). Clearly, the effects of alcohol and whether one becomes an abuser of alcohol depend on the interaction among genetic, cultural, individual, and environmental factors.

SOCIAL COSTS OF ALCOHOL USE

Alcohol dependence is devastating to individuals, families, and society in general. According to the National Highway Transportation Safety Administration, nearly 31% of all traffic deaths in the United States are alcohol-related (NHTSA, 2012). Alcohol-impaired driving is highest for people between the ages of 16 and 25 and more common for males than for females (Chou et al., 2006; SAMHSA, 2012a). More than half of rapists report that they drank alcohol before committing their crime. In college campus surveys, alcohol plays a role in the majority of sexual assaults and rapes. There is a strong correlation between alcohol and domestic violence (Brookoff et al., 1997; Quigley & Leonard, 2000; Seto & Barbaree, 1995). Millions of children who live with alcoholic parents are also seriously affected. High levels of conflict—as well as physical, emotional, and sexual abuse—are likely in these households (Mathew et al., 1993).

AP Images/Jack Kustron

Alcohol-impaired driving tragically affects families and friends.

Alcohol abuse also has economic costs. Alcohol abuse is associated with excessive absenteeism, lost productivity at work, and higher rates of on-the-job injury. These costs tend to be significantly higher for heavy drinkers (Fisher et al., 2000; Jones, Casswell, & Zhang, 1995). Alcohol-related car accidents cost about $51 billion each year in the United States (Blincoe et al., 2002). Alcohol, contrary to the beer commercials, is indeed dangerous to our health and our society.

John G. Mabanglo/epa/Corbis Wire/Corbis

The combined effects of pain medications and depressant drugs were a major factor in the death of Michael Jackson.

BARBITURATES AND SEDATIVES

Barbiturates, commonly called "downers," are a category of depressants that are typically prescribed to reduce anxiety or to induce sleep. Well-known barbiturate drugs include Nembutal and Seconal. Sedatives or tranquilizers are also prescribed to reduce anxiety. They include a class of drugs called the *benzodiazepines,* including Valium and Xanax. Both types of depressants have effects similar to alcohol. In small dosages, they slow the nervous system, promoting relaxation. In high dosages, though, they severely impair motor functioning, memory, and judgment. Like alcohol, these drugs influence the functioning of the neurotransmitter GABA (Barbee, 1993). When these drugs are taken in combination with alcohol, they are potentially lethal because they can cause suppression of those brain areas that control breathing and heart rate, which can lead to unconsciousness, coma, or death.

You may have heard of the tranquilizer called Rohypnol ("roofies"), commonly known and used as a *date rape drug.* It is placed in a woman's drink at a party or club without her knowledge or consent, and the combined effect of alcohol and Rohypnol renders her unconscious. In this state she is then sexually assaulted or raped. In the morning, because of the drug's effects on memory, she may not recall the event (Britt & McCance-Katz, 2005).

When used as prescribed, barbiturates and sedatives can be helpful in the short-term treatment of anxiety disorders and sleeping problems such as insomnia. However, over the long term, there is a risk of dependence. Long-term use of tranquilizers leads to memory loss and actually heightens anxiety. When the effect of the drug has worn off, the body goes into "overdrive" to overcome its depressing effects (McKim, 1997). Withdrawal from these drugs can be brutal and includes convulsions, hallucinations, and intense anxiety.

4.3.5 • Opiates (Narcotics): The Painkillers

The **opiates**, or narcotics, are drugs that are used to treat pain by mimicking pain-inhibiting neurotransmitters in the body such as endorphins. Opiates include morphine, codeine, Vicodin, hydrocodone, oxycodone, opium, and heroin, although heroin and opium are no longer prescribed as a medicine. In cases of locked-in syndrome, such as we saw in the case of Jean-Dominique Bauby, doctors frequently use opiates to manage pain from still active sensory neurons. The doctors may routinely prescribe them as the patients are unable to express their discomfort to others. While depressing some brain areas, these drugs create excitation in other brain areas. In addition to blocking pain, they produce an intense "rush" of pleasure that is almost like floating on a cloud or being in a dreamlike state (Bozarth & Wise, 1984). The opiates are extremely addictive, causing dependence within a few weeks. When you take opiates, your brain recognizes an abundance of pain inhibitors in the body and decreases its own production of endorphins. So when the effect of the opiate wears off, you feel your earlier pain and the absence of pleasure, and you will want another, larger dose (Hughes et al., 1975; Zadina et al., 1997). It is for this reason that health professionals monitor narcotic administration so closely.

opiates [OH-pee-ates] painkilling drugs that depress some brain areas and excite others

Physical withdrawal symptoms related to opiate use include hot and cold flashes, cramps, sweating, and shaking. These symptoms typically last from 4 to 7 days, but they are not life-threatening. What *is* life-threatening is the risk of overdose. Street concentrations of narcotic drugs such as heroin and opium can vary widely. In addition, a person's sensitivity to opiates may fluctuate on a daily basis (Gallerani et al., 2001). The user never knows, therefore, if the concentration of drug he or she is taking will exceed the body's ability to handle it. There is an added risk of contracting HIV/AIDS and hepatitis C from using contaminated needles because opiates are often injected into a vein.

Currently, many heroin addicts are treated with the chemical *methadone* or buprenorphine. Each reduces the unpleasantness of the withdrawal symptoms yet does not produce the intense high of heroin. They are both equally effective in treating heroin dependence (Fiellin, Friedland, & Gourevitch, 2006; Thomas et al., 2014; Vigezzi et al., 2006).

4.3.6 • Stimulants: Legal and Otherwise

stimulants drugs that speed up normal brain functioning

The **stimulants** include drugs that interfere with brain functioning by speeding up normal brain activity. Five stimulant substances we will review are *caffeine, nicotine, cocaine, amphetamines,* and *MDMA* (*Ecstasy/Molly*).

CAFFEINE: JAVA JITTERS

Because many of us wake up each morning reaching for that cup of coffee or that can of Monster® or Red Bull® to get us going, we may not even consider caffeine a mind-altering drug. Yet caffeine is a psychoactive drug because of its effects on the brain. It is perhaps the most frequently used psychoactive drug in the world. Caffeine is an active ingredient in coffee, tea, sodas, some energy drinks, chocolate, migraine headache medications, and some diet pills. It stimulates the brain by blocking neurotransmitters (primarily adenosine) that slow down our nervous system and cause sleep (Julien, 1995). In small doses, caffeine gives us a boost, keeping us more alert and helping us focus. It helps problem solving and decreases reaction time (Warburton, 1995). However, in large doses, caffeine can "wire" you, causing insomnia, upset stomach, racing heartbeat, nervousness, and irritability.

Regular caffeine use can lead to dependence. If you suddenly stop drinking coffee or kick your cola habit, you will likely experience headaches, irritability, tiredness, and flu-like symptoms (Schuh & Griffiths, 1997). These withdrawal symptoms, even if they aren't severe, can last a week. Excessive caffeine use increases the risk of high blood pressure and encourages the development of fibroid cysts in women's breasts. Pregnant women in particular should reduce caffeine intake because high amounts of caffeine are associated with an increased risk of miscarriage and have been linked with birth defects (Infante-Rivard et al., 1993).

Young people today often mix energy drinks with alcohol. Energy drinks have about two to three times as much caffeine as a cola and include other energy-boosting ingredients such as guarana or taurine. Mixing energy drinks with alcohol (such as a Red Bull and vodka) is becoming increasingly popular among college students (M. C. O'Brien et al., 2008; Oteri et al., 2007). So what happens to our behavior when energy drinks are combined with alcohol?

Ingesting alcohol and energy drinks together decreases one's awareness of alcohol's impairment. In other words, people are more likely to perceive that they are not as intoxicated as they are. Yet motor coordination, reaction time, and driving performance are still impaired (Ferreira et al., 2006; Howland et al., 2011).

Consuming energy drinks and alcohol also negatively influences cognitive functioning (Curry & Stasio, 2009). Moreover, the stimulant effects of the caffeine keep the person awake longer—a "wide-awake" drunk—which may allow him or her to consume even greater quantities of alcohol, increasing the chances of alcohol-related accidents, injuries, risk-taking behavior, and alcohol dependence (M. C. O'Brien et al., 2008; Patrick & Maggs, 2014; Thombs et al., 2010). Yet, caffeine may not be the sole reason for the excessive intoxication. It is possible that energy drinks and alcohol provide a novel context and unusual cues for drinking that enhances the alcohol's effect (Siegel, 2011).

Penny Tweedie/The Image Bank/Getty Images

Nicotine is an addictive substance that makes it difficult for people to quit smoking once they have started.

NICOTINE: A REALLY BAD HABIT

Nicotine, the active ingredient in tobacco and the source of a smoker's craving for cigarettes, is a powerful stimulant. Tobacco use is the most preventable cause of death in the United States. More than 440,000 deaths result each year from tobacco use, at an annual price tag of more than $193 billion in health-related economic costs (Centers for Disease Control and Prevention, 2011b). Tobacco use has been linked to lung cancer, throat cancer, emphysema, and heart disease (Noah & Robinson, 1997).

Most adult smokers started smoking before the age of 18, and every day more people under the age of 18 become regular smokers (● FIGURE 4.7) (Johnston et al., 2013). Although the percentage of people in the United States who smoke has decreased considerably over the last 50 years, 21.5% of adult men and 17.3% of adult women continue to smoke regularly (Schiller et al., 2012). The percentages are significantly higher for adults 21–29 years old (37%) (SAMHSA, 2009a). American Indian/Alaska Native and multiracial adults have the highest rates of tobacco use. Asian American and Hispanic women have the lowest rates (Centers for Disease Control and Prevention, 2006; Schiller et al., 2012).

Nicotine affects several neurotransmitters. It influences acetylcholine and glutamate such that in low doses, nicotine improves attention and memory (McGehee et al., 1995). Nicotine also elevates dopamine levels, leading to feelings of pleasure and reward (Pidoplichko et al., 1997). In high doses, nicotine causes vomiting, diarrhea, sweating, and dizziness. Yet users quickly develop a tolerance to nicotine.

Withdrawal from chronic nicotine use rivals withdrawal from other abused drugs such as cocaine, morphine, and alcohol (Epping-Jordan et al., 1998). Withdrawal symptoms, lasting anywhere from 2 to 6 weeks, include headaches, irritability, stomach upset, difficulty sleeping, and an intense craving for the drug. This indeed illustrates the power of dependence.

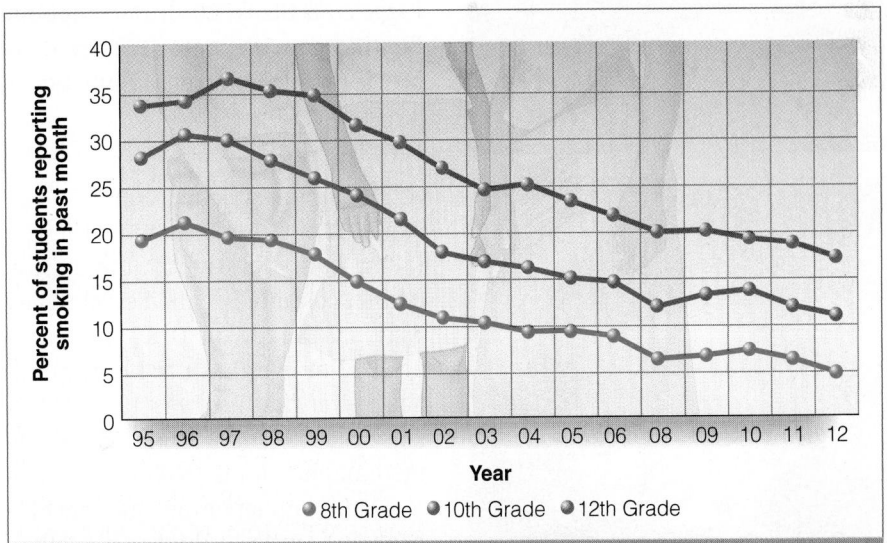

FIGURE 4.7

Cigarette Smoking Among High School Students

In the last decade, cigarette smoking has decreased among high school students. However, in 2012, approximately 17% of high school seniors reported smoking cigarettes in the past month.

From Johnston, L. D., O'Malley, P. M., Bachman, J. G., & Schulenberg, J. E. (2013). Monitoring the future: National results on drug use; 2012 overview, key findings on adolescent drug use. *Ann Arbor: Institute for Social Research, University of Michigan.*

COCAINE AND CRACK

Cocaine and its derivative, crack, are powerful and dangerous stimulant drugs. Snorted, smoked, or injected, cocaine is quickly absorbed into the body and thus reaches the brain rapidly. Crack is powdered cocaine mixed with water and other additives that is then boiled until a solid mass forms. It is broken into rocks and smoked with a long glass tube called a *crack pipe*. Inhaling the smoke delivers large quantities of the drug to the lungs and produces an intense and immediate high.

Cocaine, in all its forms, blocks a protein called the dopamine transporter (DAT), which helps the reuptake of dopamine into the neuron (Chapter 2). Because reuptake is blocked, free dopamine in the brain increases (Hummel & Unterwald, 2002; Nestler, 2006; Williams & Galli, 2006). The buildup of dopamine produces an instant surge of arousal, a feeling of pleasure and optimism. Appetite decreases, but heart rate, blood pressure, and alertness increase. When the effect of the cocaine wears off, the person "crashes," showing decreased energy and depressed mood. This low creates an intense craving for the drug that sets up a cycle of continued use and dependence (Gawin, 1991). High doses of cocaine (relative to one's tolerance) can cause paranoia, sleeplessness, delusions, seizures, strokes, and potentially cardiac arrest (Lacayo, 1995). Users who are dependent on cocaine may lose interest in their usual friends and activities, lose weight, and have chronic sore throats and difficulty sleeping; their finances may also undergo a noticeable change.

Health effects of repeated use of cocaine include chronic nosebleeds, damage to nasal cartilage (from snorting), and respiratory and heart problems. Miscarriages are common for pregnant women who use cocaine. If the pregnancy continues, the infant is more likely to be born premature and, as a newborn, must be weaned from the effects of the drug. The long-term impact of prenatal exposure to cocaine shows a small but less favorable effect on language, cognitive ability, and academic functioning into adolescence. However, a poorer home environment and exposure to violence also played a role in the child's development (Ackerman, Riggins, & Black, 2010; Buckingham-Howes et al., 2013; Lewis et al., 2013). That is, children with poorer academic functioning were more likely to have come from less favorable home environments, regardless of prenatal cocaine exposure.

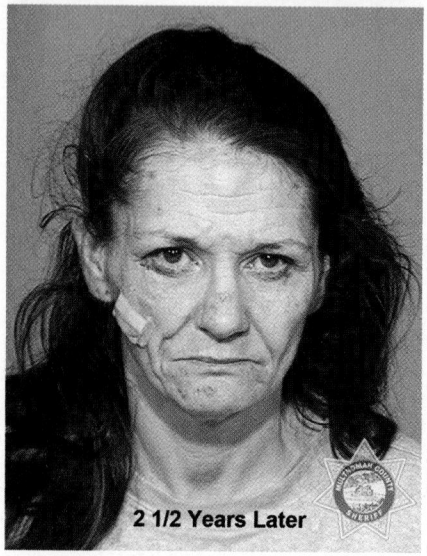

Courtesy of the Multnomah County Sheriff's Office, "Faces of Meth" Program

Methamphetamine abuse can radically alter one's physical appearance as it causes skin lesions and tooth decay.

AMPHETAMINES

Amphetamines, called "uppers" or "speed," have effects similar to those of cocaine. The high produced by these drugs is less intense but generally lasts longer (a few hours). Currently, the most abused form of amphetamine is *methamphetamine,* commonly called crystal meth, ice, chalk, or crank. According to the 2009 National Survey on Drug Use and Health (NSDUH), 5% of the U.S. population aged 12 or over has used crystal meth at least once (SAMHSA, 2010a). The average age at first use was 19.7 years (SAMHSA, 2013). Approximately 4.1% of college students and 8.3% of young adults between the ages of 19 and 28 have tried methamphetamine (NIDA & University of Michigan, 2006).

Methamphetamine, like cocaine, affects dopamine, serotonin, and norepinephrine levels in the brain (Volkow et al., 2001). The result is enhanced mood and pleasure, energy, alertness, and reduced appetite. Heart rate and blood pressure also increase. Like cocaine, methamphetamine leads to a crash to low energy levels, paranoia, and depressed mood when the effects of the drug have subsided. However, methamphetamine remains present in the brain longer than cocaine. It not only blocks the reuptake of dopamine but also increases the release of dopamine, leading to a more toxic effect on the central nervous system (NIDA, 2006b). Continued use results in insomnia, paranoia, agitation, confusion, violent behavior, memory loss, and dependence. Methamphetamine use can also cause strokes, cardiovascular problems, and extreme anorexia. An overdose can cause coma and death. Users who inject the drug and share needles are also at risk for acquiring HIV/AIDS and hepatitis C (Bezchlibnyk-Butler & Jeffries, 1998).

MDMA (ECSTASY/MOLLY)

MDMA has become widely known as Ecstasy, referring to its pill form, but street Ecstasy, Adam, or XTC typically contains other drugs such as amphetamine, ketamine, caffeine, and ephedrine (Walters, Foy, & Castro, 2003). The term *molly* typically refers to a purer MDMA in powder or crystal form. MDMA was originally developed as an antibleeding medication in 1912 by a German pharmaceutical company (Freudenmann, Oxler, & Bernschneider-Reif, 2006). Before it was classified as a controlled substance in 1985, MDMA was used by some psychiatrists in the United States and Europe to enhance psychotherapy and couples counseling (Greer & Tolbert, 1998).

MDMA's use dramatically increased as a "club drug" in the 1990s and early 2000s, particularly among college students and young adults. In 2009, 5.7% of people in the United States over the age of 12 reported having used Ecstasy at some point in their lives (SAMHSA, 2010a), including 4.3% of U.S. high school seniors (SAMHSA, 2012c). The average age at first use was 19.6 years (SAMHSA, 2013). Use has been spreading beyond predominately European American youth to African American and Hispanic populations (Boeri, Sterk, & Elifson, 2004; Maxwell & Spence, 2003), and Ecstasy has become a popular drug among urban gay males (NIDA, 2006a).

Ecstasy and Molly enhance mood and energy levels and heightens users' sensations. Users report increased self-confidence, increased feelings of love and warmth toward others, emotional openness, and lack of inhibition (Fry & Miller, 2002). The effect begins within half an hour of consumption, and lasts approximately 3–6 hours. Negative effects of MDMA use are insomnia, teeth clenching, nausea, increase in heart rate and blood pressure, fatigue, and blurred vision. Most of these negative effects subside within 24 hours. Paranoia, depression, drug craving, overheating, cardiac problems, kidney failure, seizures, strokes, and/or loss of touch with reality may also occur (Bezchlibnyk-Butler & Jeffries, 1998).

Although MDMA increases the activity of several neurotransmitters in the brain, it is the serotonin pathway that has received the most attention. MDMA binds to the serotonin transport protein so that the availability of free serotonin increases (Britt & McCance-Katz, 2005; Colado, O'Shea, & Green, 2004). The long-term effects of MDMA on the human brain have not yet been determined. Some research suggests that it causes long-term (2 years or more) permanent alteration in serotonin receptors, but this claim remains controversial (Di lorio et al., 2012). However, disrupted sleep patterns and subtle, persistent deficits in memory have been documented for both former and current users (Kuypers, Wingen, & Ramaekers, 2008; McCann et al., 2009; Randall et al., 2009; Taurah, Chandler, & Sanders, 2014). It also is unclear whether Ecstasy shares properties with the hallucinogens. Users regularly report hallucinations, but it is impossible to know whether they have really been using pure MDMA or have bought low doses of LSD instead.

Recently, therapeutic use of MDMA, particularly for the treatment of post-traumatic stress disorder (PTSD), has been investigated with promising results (Mithoefer et al., 2011; Oehen et al., 2013). Although the research samples were small, patients treated with MDMA-psychotherapy showed a greater decrease in PTSD symptoms compared to placebo–psychotherapy control groups. In one study, the majority of MDMA-treated patients maintained symptom relief 17–74 months after the original study (Mithoefer et al., 2013). Replication of these results with larger samples will be needed to substantiate the efficacy of these results.

Psychology Applies to Your World:

The Mystery of Bath Salts

In a widely publicized news event from Miami, Florida, Rudy Eugene was shown on video naked and jumping on a sleeping homeless man, devouring the man's face, earning him the nickname "Causeway Cannibal." Many believed Eugene had taken "bath salts," but toxicology reports indicated only the presence of marijuana. Perhaps you have seen other Internet videos of young adults seemingly "out of their minds" behaving in strange and unusual ways. "Bath salts" is the street name for a family of synthetic substances that are becoming increasingly popular as recreational drugs used for a "legal high." Marketed under such names as *Vanilla Sky, Bliss,* and *Ivory Wave* and labeled as "not intended for human consumption" to circumvent drug legislation, these drugs are readily available on the Internet (Prosser & Nelson, 2012). The 2012 Synthetic Drug Abuse Prevention Act banned some but not all of the chemicals used to make these designer drugs.

Bath salts contain synthetic chemicals called *cathinones* that mimic the effects of cocaine, MDMA, and other amphetamines, and they are highly hallucinogenic. They often are in a form of a white or colored crystalline powder that can be snorted, injected, or mixed with food and drinks. Their effects are unpredictable because there is no consistency in the substances that are used in the products, so their content from product to product is often unknown. As a result, they can produce different neurological and behavioral effects (Gregg & Rawls, 2014; Simmler et al., 2013).

Typical positive effects of bath salts include increased energy, empathy, and sex drive. However, adverse effects may include agitation, paranoia, hallucinations, chest pain, high blood pressure, aggression, suicidal thoughts and/or behavior, and, in some cases, death (German, Fleckenstein, & Hanson, 2014; Prosser & Nelson, 2012). Many still believe Rudy Eugene had taken some type of synthetic drug. Unfortunately, drug labs across the country cannot test for the infinite number of synthetic chemicals that are out there. These designer drugs truly are dangerous and should not be consumed. Further research will hopefully provide insight into the danger that bath salts pose to the individual and society as a whole.

© FomaA/Shutterstock.com

4.3.7 • Hallucinogens: Distorting Reality

Hallucinogens are drugs that interfere with brain functioning by simultaneously exciting and inhibiting the nervous system. These contrasting effects often cause distortions in perception, or *hallucinations*. Hallucinogenic substances include *marijuana, synthetic marijuana, PCP,* and *LSD.*

Uriel Sinai/Getty Images News/Getty Images

Although controversy continues over the medicinal and recreational use of marijuana, smoking pot increases one's chances of respiratory problems and lung damage.

MARIJUANA

Marijuana, also known formally as *cannabis* or informally as *pot* or *weed,* is a mild hallucinogen. Twenty states and the District of Columbia currently allow for its medicinal use, with other states pending legislation. Recently, Washington and Colorado legalized recreational use of marijuana for adults over the age of 21. It has been recommended for medical conditions such as glaucoma, chronic pain, and nausea from cancer chemotherapy and has been found moderately effective in clinical trials for muscle spasms and multiple sclerosis (Croxford, 2003; Iverson, 2003; Klein & Newton, 2007). It is also the most widely used illegal substance in the United States, with 41.5% of people over the age of 12 reporting having tried the drug. Past-year usage is highest among 17- to 24-year-olds, and males report higher usage than females. American Indian and multiracial groups report the highest use and Asian Americans the lowest (SAMHSA, 2010a).

The main psychoactive ingredient in marijuana is **THC (tetrahydrocannabinol)**. THC is absorbed by the lungs and produces a high that lasts for several hours. THC binds to a neurotransmitter called *anandamide* that influences learning, short-term memory, motor coordination, emotions, and appetite—behaviors that are all affected when people are high on marijuana (Matsuda et al., 1990). In low doses, cannabis makes users feel good and experience vivid sensations. Cannabis affects cognition and motor coordination in ways that slow reaction time and increase risks of injury when driving a car or operating machinery. Marijuana use also interferes with memory, disrupting both the formation of memories and the recall of information (Nestor et al., 2008; Pope & Yurgelun-Todd, 1996; Ranganathan & D'Souza, 2006). Its stimulation of appetite and increased sensitivity to taste may result in an attack of the "munchies." In high doses, marijuana may produce hallucinations, delusions, paranoia, and distortions in time and body image (Hanson & Venturelli, 1998; Morrison et al., 2009). Long-term marijuana use can lead to psychological dependence. Many people report mild withdrawal symptoms when marijuana use is stopped, including irritability, sleeplessness, decreased appetite, anxiety, and drug cravings (Z. D. Cooper & Haney, 2008; de Fonseca et al., 1997; Grinspoon et al., 1997; Vandrey et al., 2008; Wickelgren, 1997).

Studies on long-term users of marijuana have shown long-lasting cognitive effects including impaired attention, learning, and motor coordination (Pope & Yurgelun-Todd, 1996; Volkow et al., 1996). However, permanent structural changes in the brain have not been identified with chronic use (Quickfall & Crockford, 2006). When smoked, marijuana users may experience respiratory problems such as bronchitis and lung damage (Tashkin, 2005).

hallucinogens [huh-LOO-sin-no-gens] drugs that simultaneously excite and inhibit normal neural activity, thereby causing distortions in perception

THC (tetrahydrocannabinol) [tet-rah-high-dro-can-NAH-bin-all] the active ingredient in marijuana that affects learning, short-term memory, coordination, emotion, and appetite

SYNTHETIC MARIJUANA: K2 AND SPICE

An increasing number of young people are turning to unregulated herbal smoking mixtures labeled as *K2* or *Spice* to get high. These products are sprayed with synthetic substances that attempt to mimic THC, and claim to produce a marijuana-like high. Adverse side effects of synthetic THC include extreme paranoia, hallucinations, heart palpitations, racing thoughts, and seizures (Fattore & Fratta, 2011; Hudson & Ramsey, 2011; Wells & Ott, 2011). Citing these products as a threat to public health, many countries (including the United States) have banned the sale of these herbs and screen for synthetic THC during drug testing, yet new products can easily be accessed from online markets (Fattore & Fratta, 2011).

PHENCYCLIDINE (PCP)

In the 1950s, Parke, Davis and Company developed PCP (phencyclidine) as an anesthetic for surgery. However, following surgery, individuals showed worrisome side effects including hallucinations, delirium, and disorientation. Consequently, it was removed from the market (for humans) in 1965 and sold to veterinarians for use in animal surgery. Its use as a street drug spread significantly until 1978, when it was taken off the market completely (Rudgley, 1998). Today, PCP is manufactured illegally and sold on the street by such names as "angel dust" and "lovely." PCP also may be poured over cigarettes or marijuana joints. PCP can be eaten, snorted, smoked, or injected. Although the use of PCP has declined steadily since 1979, in 2009, 2.5% of people over the age of 12 reported having tried PCP, with males again outnumbering females (SAMHSA, 2010a).

PCP has hallucinogenic properties as well as stimulant and depressant effects. These unpredictable effects often lead to distress, mood swings, and confusion. PCP inhibits the neurotransmitter *glutamate,* which is involved in the perception of pain, responses to the environment, and memory. In low doses, PCP produces a sudden increase in blood pressure, pulse rate, and breathing. Flushing, profuse sweating, and numbness of the limbs may also occur. Out-of-body experiences and the sensation of walking on a spongy surface are also reported. In higher doses, PCP causes a drop in blood pressure, pulse rate, and respiration. This reaction may be accompanied by nausea, vomiting, blurred vision, drooling, loss of balance, and dizziness. Hallucinations, confusion, paranoia, and garbled speech also result. Users may become severely disoriented or suicidal and may therefore be a danger to themselves or others. Seizures, coma, or death may also occur (Rudgley, 1998).

Using PCP can lead to dependence. Users often crave the feelings of strength, power, and invulnerability and the escape from real life that PCP brings. Long-term use of PCP is associated with memory loss and difficulty in speaking and thinking, and may lead to permanent changes in fine motor abilities (NIDA, 2001).

LYSERGIC ACID DIETHYLAMIDE (LSD)

LSD, more commonly referred to as *acid,* is a potent perception-altering drug. First synthesized in 1938 and used in the 1950s and 1960s in psychiatric research, it became an illegal drug of abuse (Passie et al., 2008). In 2009, 9.4% of people over the age of 12 reported having tried LSD at some time in their lives; males were more likely to have tried the drug than females (SAMHSA, 2010a). LSD's effects typically begin 30–90 minutes after ingestion and can last from 6 to 12 hours.

Users of LSD may experience increased blood pressure and heart rate, dizziness, loss of appetite, and nausea, but the drug's main effects appear to be emotional and sensory. Even at very low doses, LSD causes bizarre hallucinations, distortions in time and body image, and intense emotions that together are often referred to as "tripping." Emotions may shift rapidly from fear to happiness, and the user may seem to experience several emotions at once. Colors, smells, sounds, and other sensory stimuli seem highly intensified and may even blend in what is known as *synesthesia,* in which a person seems to hear or feel colors and see sounds (NIDA, 2001). These effects are due to LSD's influence on the neurotransmitter serotonin (Aghajanian, 1994). LSD stimulates serotonin receptors, influencing perceptions, emotions, and sleep. However, whether one's "trip" is pleasant or unpleasant is unpredictable and depends on the user's expectations and mood. On good trips, users experience enjoyable sensations, but bad trips produce terrifying thoughts and feelings, including fears of insanity, death, or losing control. Although withdrawal symptoms from LSD have not been documented, users quickly develop tolerance, requiring a higher dosage to experience the mind-altering effects (Miller & Gold, 1994; NIDA, 2001).

There have been no documented human deaths from LSD overdose, but two rare yet serious documented long-term effects of LSD are *persistent psychosis* and *hallucinogen persisting perception disorder* (*HPPD*). Persistent psychosis is a long-lasting psychotic-like state after the trip has ended. It may include dramatic mood swings, visual disturbances, and hallucinations. These effects may last for years and can affect people who have no history or other symptoms of a mental health disorder. HPPD is a reexperiencing of the sensations originally produced by the LSD hours, weeks, or even years after its initial use that causes distress. It typically consists of visual disturbances, such as seeing bright or colored flashes and trails attached to moving objects (NIDA, 2001). Our knowledge of the causes and treatment for persistent psychosis and HPPD is very limited; further studies are needed (Halpern & Pope, 2003). Additional lasting side effects of LSD use may include short-term memory loss, paranoia, nightmares, and panic attacks (Gold, 1994).

Quiz Yourself

4.3

1. Which category of drugs has its main effects by reducing activity in the nervous system?
   a. Stimulants
   b. Hallucinogens
   c. Depressants
   d. Opiates

2. Rolanda takes a drug that raises her blood pressure and heart rate, makes her feel euphoric and excited, and suppresses her appetite. She in all likelihood has *not* taken _____.
   a. cocaine
   b. alcohol
   c. methamphetamine
   d. crack

3. The designer drug Ecstasy, or MDMA, produces effects similar to what two categories of drugs?
   a. Stimulants and depressants
   b. Hallucinogens and depressants
   c. Stimulants and hallucinogens
   d. Opiates and depressants

4. Mick, a successful author, has been drinking alcohol for 10 years. He feels that alcohol relaxes him and expands his mind, which makes him a more creative writer. In fact, he never attempts to write unless he has first had a drink. Mick has tried to stop drinking in the past, but he has always returned to it because he fears losing his creativity. Mick's behavior is *best* explained by _____.
   a. substance dependence
   b. withdrawal symptoms
   c. the margin of safety
   d. tolerance

5. Deana takes a drug that blocks adenosine in her brain. This drug causes her to be more alert and enhances her ability to focus. If she takes too much, it causes irritability, nausea, and a racing heartbeat. Deanna is most likely taking _____.
   a. nicotine
   b. cocaine
   c. methamphetamine
   d. caffeine

Answers 1. c; 2. b; 3. c; 4. a; 5. d

4.4 Integrating Psychology: The Big Picture

This chapter examined three altered states of consciousness—when you are not fully awake, alert, aware, or perhaps of sound mind. We saw that sleep is a necessity, providing many benefits to our functioning and ensuring that we will be healthy, alert, and happy. Hypnosis is a state of heightened suggestibility that may help *some* people decrease anxiety and manage pain. Psychoactive drugs alter our state of consciousness—in sometimes unpredictable and occasionally tragic ways. Although much is still unknown about many of these drugs, it is clear from the research cited here that the long-term negative effects outweigh the short-term high and feelings of well-being that they produce.

Our state of consciousness cannot easily be divorced from our general behavior as the section case study on Jean-Dominique Bauby clearly illustrated. Despite Bauby's severely limited physical abilities, he found a way to communicate his thoughts and awareness of his surroundings to others through the blinking of his one eye. These communications also allowed him to continue his social interactions with his family and medical staff. Jean-Dominique's case represents an extreme variation of human behavior, yet it still demonstrates how our biology, cognitions, and social interactions intertwine with our states of consciousness. His story also beautifully exemplifies the resilience of the human spirit and the need or *motivation* humans have to find purpose in our lives—our next chapter of study.

Studying the Chapter

Key Terms

activation-synthesis theory (140)
circadian rhythm (134)
consciousness (128)
depressants (151)
enuresis (143)
fetal alcohol syndrome (FAS) (154)
hallucinogens (163)
hypnosis (145)
insomnia (140)
latent content (139)
manifest content (139)
melatonin (134)
microsleep (130)
narcolepsy (141)
neodissociation theory (146)
night terrors (143)
nightmares (143)
non-REM sleep (137)
opiates (157)
psychoactive drugs (148)
REM behavior disorder (138)
REM rebound (138)
REM sleep (137)
restless legs syndrome (RLS) (142)
response set theory of hypnosis (146)
sleep apnea (141)
sleep disorder (140)
sleepwalking (142)
stimulants (158)
substance dependence (150)
suprachiasmatic nucleus (SCN) (134)
THC (tetrahydrocannabinol) (163)
threat simulation theory (TST) (139)
tolerance (150)
withdrawal symptoms (150)

What Do You Know? Assess Your Understanding

Test your retention and understanding of the material by answering the following questions.

1. Which of the following is *not* a benefit of sleep?

a. Increased alertness
b. Memory processing
c. Decreased immunity to disease
d. Enhanced mood

2. Marco is 62 and Isaac is 22. Which of these men requires more sleep at night?

a. Marco
b. Isaac
c. Both men require the same amount of sleep.
d. Marco needs more non-REM sleep, and Isaac needs more REM sleep.

3. Alfred is just falling asleep. An EEG would most likely show Alfred exhibiting _____ brain waves.

a. beta
b. delta
c. sleep spindle
d. theta

4. Which of the following brain waves is most likely to occur during slow-wave sleep?

a. Beta
b. Alpha
c. Delta
d. Theta

5. Benita often wakes up in the morning feeling very tired, despite sleeping 9–10 hours. Her partner has noticed that she often emits loud snores and seems to have erratic breathing while she is sleeping. Benita most likely has which sleep disorder?

a. Narcolepsy
b. Sleep apnea
c. Night terrors
d. Enuresis

6. Recent research suggests a relationship between the sleep spindles of stage II sleep and _____.

a. processing of motor skills
b. body restoration
c. storage of memories
d. growth hormone

7. Dr. Surrell believes that dreaming evolved to help us rehearse potentially harmful events. Dr. Surrell is endorsing which dream theory?

a. Freudian theory
b. Activation-synthesis theory
c. Continuity hypothesis
d. Threat simulation theory

8. When Kaitlin wakes up in the morning, she recalls having a dream that toads were invading her room. According to Freud, Kaitlin's recall is an example of _____.

a. latent content
b. manifest content
c. activation-synthesis
d. the continuity hypothesis

9. Why is melatonin referred to as the "Dracula hormone"?

a. Because it increases during the day
b. Because it increases at night
c. Because it is in the blood
d. Because it was first found in bats

10. EEG brain-wave patterns of people who are hypnotized show an increase in _____ waves.

a. theta
b. delta
c. beta
d. alpha

11. Which of the following is *not* a well-documented use of hypnosis?

a. Decreasing anxiety
b. Relieving pain
c. Recovering memories
d. Enhancing therapy

12. People who are easily hypnotized tend to have which of the following traits?

a. Positive expectations about hypnosis
b. Higher intelligence
c. Higher sociability
d. All of the above

13. Which of the following drugs is a depressant?

a. Ecstasy
b. Nicotine
c. PCP
d. Alcohol

14. Paz now needs more alcohol to get high than she did when she first started drinking. Paz has developed _____ alcohol.

a. an addiction to
b. tolerance to
c. a withdrawal from
d. a dependence for

15. Howe has been using methamphetamine for several months now. If he stops taking the drug, which of the following is he most likely to experience?

a. Paranoia
b. Enhanced mood
c. Reduced appetite
d. High energy

16. Which of the following variables influences a drug's effects?

a. How much of the drug is taken
b. Your tolerance to the drug
c. Your expectations about the drug's effects
d. All of the above

17. The feeling of well-being that results from nicotine or cocaine use is due to the activity of which of the following neurotransmitters?

a. Dopamine
b. Serotonin
c. Acetylcholine
d. Endorphins

18. Sven still experiences visual disturbances and dramatic mood swings after taking LSD several months ago. Sven is most likely experiencing _____.

a. HPPD
b. PTSD
c. persistent psychosis
d. tweaking

19. While at a nightclub one weekend, Aoki had a drug slipped into her drink that made her "pass out" and have no recall of the events of the evening. What type of drug was most likely put in Aoki's drink?

a. Hallucinogen
b. Sedative
c. Stimulant
d. Opiate

20. Which of the following drugs is most likely to be prescribed to reduce pain?

a. Stimulant
b. Depressant
c. Hallucinogen
d. Opiate

Answers: 1. c; 2. b; 3. d; 4. c; 5. b; 6. a; 7. d; 8. b; 9. b; 10. d; 11. c; 12. a; 13. d; 14. b; 15. a; 16. d; 17. a; 18. c; 19. b; 20. d.

Use It or Lose It: Applying Psychology

1. How would you rate your hypnotic susceptibility? Indicate under what circumstances you would consider using hypnosis as a therapy or treatment, and why.
2. Apply the theories on hypnosis to explain how stage hypnotists alter the behavior of their audience volunteers.
3. How prevalent is drug use at your campus? Design a research survey to assess this issue at your school. Administer the survey to student volunteers following the ethical procedures for participants, and tabulate the results. What conclusions can you draw from your results? What factors may have influenced your results?
4. Given the numerous factors, such as age and lifestyle, that influence the amount of sleep a person needs, apply each of these factors to the amount of sleep that you get. How can you improve the quality of your sleep? What benefits might this change bring you?
5. Keep a dream log for a week. Applying the different theories on dreaming, interpret what your dreams mean. Which of these interpretations seems the most plausible, and why?

Critical Thinking for Integration

1. Applying the information from Chapter 1 on research methods, design a study that will test the hypothesis that sleep changes as we age. (You are not implementing a study, just detailing how it would be conducted.)
2. Using Chapter 2 as a guide, draw a model of the brain and graphically represent where in the brain various psychoactive drugs have their effects. Also integrate on this visual schematic the neurotransmitters that affect these areas of the brain.
3. Explain individual differences in hypnotic suggestibility as a result of variations in sensation, expectations, and perceptual errors. Integrate the information from Chapter 3 as a guide in formulating your answer.

caia image/Alamy

Are You Getting the Big Picture? Consciousness

Consciousness includes the feelings, thoughts, and aroused states of which we are aware. Altered states of consciousness occur when we sleep, are hypnotized, or take any psychoactive drug.

4.1 Sleep, Dreaming, and Circadian Rhythm

- When teenagers and adults get at least 8 hours of sleep, the benefits include restored body tissues, body growth, immunity to disease, an alert mind, processing of memories, and enhanced mood.
- The **circadian rhythm** of sleep is a natural rhythm of sleep and waking programmed by a group of brain cells in the hypothalamus called the **suprachiasmatic nucleus**.
- A typical night of sleep involves cycling through two states of sleep: **non-REM sleep**, which progressively relaxes the person; and **REM** (rapid-eye-movement) **sleep**, which is very active.
- Freud believed that dreams allow us to express fears and desires without conscious censorship. Many psychologists and psychiatrists dispute Freud's emphasis on sex and aggression in interpreting dreams.
- **Threat simulation theory** proposes that dreaming is an evolved defense mechanism that allows us to rehearse our responses to threatening situations.
- **Activation-synthesis theory** suggests that dreaming is just a consequence of the highly aroused brain during REM sleep.
- **Insomnia** is the inability to get to sleep or to stay asleep. It is the most common sleep disorder.
- Other sleep disorders include **sleep apnea**, in which a person stops breathing while asleep, and a rarer condition called **narcolepsy**, in which a person falls asleep during alert times of the day.

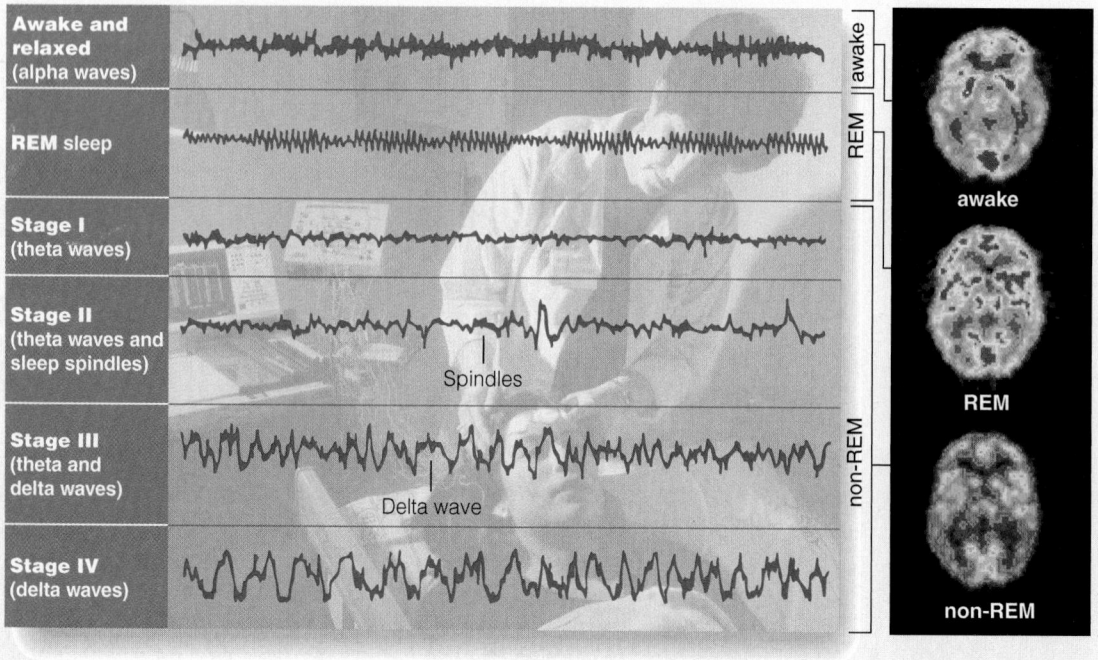

Hank Morgan/Science Source

4.2 Hypnosis

© AP Photo/News Tribune/Stephen Brooks

- **Hypnosis** is a technique used to create a state of heightened suggestibility. Hypnosis usually involves being asked to mentally focus on an object, image, or the hypnotist's voice, thus inducing a deeply relaxed state.
- Hypnotic susceptibility varies greatly and does not seem to be related to intelligence, gender, or sociability. People who are easily hypnotized tend to be better able to focus their attention, have vivid imaginations, and have positive expectations about hypnosis.
- Hypnosis has been shown to be effective for *some* people in providing pain relief and decreasing anxiety. It has not been shown to be as effective in curing addictions or recovering accurate memories.

4.3 Psychoactive Drugs

- **Psychoactive drugs** are substances that influence the brain and therefore the behavior of a person.
- Drug **tolerance** refers to the amount of a drug required to produce its effects. After repeated use of a drug, more of it is usually needed to achieve its initial effect.
- **Substance dependence** refers to a person's need of a drug in order to function emotionally and/or physically.
- **Depressants** such as alcohol, sedatives, and barbiturate drugs interfere with brain functions by inhibiting or slowing normal neural function.

- **Opiates** such as morphine, codeine, and opium are used to treat pain by mimicking the effects of neurotransmitters such as endorphins.
- **Stimulants** are drugs such as caffeine, nicotine, cocaine, and amphetamines that interfere with brain functioning by speeding up normal brain activity.

- **Hallucinogens**, including marijuana and LSD, are drugs that interfere with brain functioning by simultaneously exciting and inhibiting normal neural activity. These contrasting effects often cause disruptions in perception or hallucinations.

© Corbis

Motivation and Emotion

Learning Objectives

5.1 Describe how psychologists define motivation. (APA 1.1)

5.1 Describe the different theoretical ways of conceptualizing motivation. (APA 1.1, 1.2)

5.2 Describe the feedback our bodies use to regulate hunger. (APA 1.1, 1.3, 2.1)

5.2 Explain what is known about why some people become obese. (APA 1.1, 1.3)

5.2 Describe the prevalence of weight-based prejudice and the factors that affect it. (APA 1.1, 1.3, 3.3)

5.2 Describe bulimia, anorexia, and binge eating disorder and explain their possible causes. (APA 1.1, 1.3)

5.3 Explain the biological and psychological components of sexual desire. (APA 1.1, 1.3)

5.3 Describe the phases of the sexual response cycle in men and women. (APA 1.1, 1.3, 2.1)

5.3 Distinguish between sexual orientation and sexual behavior, and describe the research investigating the causes of sexual orientation. (APA 1.1, 1.3, 2.4, 3.3)

5.4 Describe the various theoretical perspectives on emotion. (APA 1.1, 1.3)

5.4 Describe how we express our emotional states through facial expressions. (APA 1.1, 1.3, 4.3)

When Jean-Dominique Bauby awoke from his coma, his first reactions were predictable and understandable—he felt terror. *Emotions,* such as terror, can act as an early warning system, alerting us to danger, sometimes before we even become aware of what the danger is. Bauby's terror signaled that something was very wrong. During the 15 months that Bauby lived in a locked-in state, many more emotions followed. Sadness and fear—but also joy and contentment—punctuated his days. Bauby's emotions connected him to both his current and past life. They allowed him to feel human. Perhaps this is why Bauby was so *motivated* to capture his feelings in print—maybe he needed to let the world know that he was still a living human being despite the unresponsiveness of his body. Think about your own motivations and emotions. What goals do you want to accomplish? What emotions make you feel alive? In this chapter, we will examine the important roles that motivation and emotion play in our lives as they direct our behavior and signal our reactions to everyday experiences.

5

© Kzenon/Shutterstock.com

Chapter Outline

5.1 Theories of Motivation / 174

5.2 Hunger and Eating / 180

PSYCHOLOGY APPLIES TO YOUR WORLD: The Obesity Epidemic / 186

5.3 Sexual Motivation / 195

5.4 Theories and Expression of Emotion / 205

5.5 Integrating Psychology: The Big Picture / 213

5.1 Theories of Motivation

When we are motivated, we are driven to engage in some form of behavior. Just as something motivated you to start reading this chapter, every day we are motivated to do many different things. For example, we are motivated to eat, drink, attend school, go to work, interact with family and friends, and so on. In psychological terms, a **motive** is the tendency to desire and seek out positive incentives or rewards and to avoid negative outcomes (Atkinson, 1955/1983; McClelland, 1987). This means that we are motivated to avoid aversive states and to seek more pleasant states. When we experience the motive of hunger, we eat to avoid this aversive feeling. We are motivated to study because we want the feelings of pride and the opportunities for advancement that accompany academic success. Because we are generally motivated to avoid pain and other aversive states, our motives often serve to protect us. Without the motivation to eat, we could experience malnutrition or even starvation. As you can see, without motivation we would not engage in many behaviors that are necessary for good health and survival.

In an attempt to better understand what motivates us, psychologists have historically viewed motivation in several different ways: as *instincts* that direct our behavior; as uncomfortable biological states called *drives* that motivate us to find ways to feel better; as the desire to maintain an optimal level of *arousal* in our body; or as *incentives* that guide us to seek reward from the world. However, none of these theories seems to fully explain all aspects of motivation. Today psychologists do not expect any single theory to explain all our motivations. Instead, we recognize that each of these theories has its strengths and weaknesses. Let's take a closer look at these different theories of motivation.

5.1.1 • Motivation as Instinct

One of the earliest views on motivation was one that was heavily influenced by the work of Charles Darwin and the theory of natural selection (see Chapter 8; Darwin, 1859/1936). Back in the 1800s, American psychologist William James proposed that motives are, in fact, genetically determined **instincts** that have evolved in humans because they support survival and procreation. According to James, instincts are impulses from within a person that direct or motivate that person's behavior. James proposed that we are motivated by more than 35 different innate instincts, including the impulse to love, fight, imitate, talk, and acquire things (James, 1890).

Over time, the idea that motives are inborn instincts gradually fell out of favor with psychologists. One problem with James's view was that the list of proposed instincts kept getting longer and longer, and it seemed unrealistic to argue that all behavior is due to instinct. Furthermore, it is impossible to determine whether many of the proposed instincts are truly inborn. Many of James's so-called instincts, such as being sympathetic or being secretive, may result from learning.

motive a tendency to desire and seek out positive incentives or rewards and to avoid negative outcomes

instinct an innate impulse from within a person that directs or motivates behavior

drive reduction theory a theory of motivation that proposes that people seek to reduce internal levels of drive

drive an uncomfortable internal state that motivates us to reduce this discomfort through our behavior

5.1.2 • Motivation as a Drive

Instinct theory was followed by **drive reduction theories** of motivation. According to the drive reduction approach, motivation stems from the desire to reduce an uncomfortable, internal state, called a **drive**, that results when our needs are not fulfilled (Hull, 1943). For instance, when we do not have enough food in our system, we feel the uncomfortable state of hunger, which drives us to eat until we have taken in the food that our bodies require. Then, when we have taken in enough food, the hunger drive dissipates, and we stop eating. In this fashion, our drives can help us survive by creating what psychologists call a drive state, which ensures that we will be motivated to meet our biological needs.

Primary drives, such as needing food, water, and warmth, motivate us to maintain certain bodily processes at an internal state of equilibrium, or **homeostasis**. Obviously, it would be desirable for us to take in just the right amount of food and water, to sleep just enough, and to maintain our body temperature at 98.6 degrees. Without the motivation from drives, we would not keep our bodies at homeostasis because we would not know when to eat, sleep, drink, and so on. But what causes a drive state in the first place?

Primary drives begin in the body when the brain recognizes that we are lacking in some biological need. The brain recognizes need based on the *feedback* that it receives from the body's systems and organs. One type of feedback system is called a **negative feedback loop** (● FIGURE 5.1). Negative feedback loops are information systems in the body that monitor the level of a bodily process and adjust it up or down accordingly. A good analogy for a negative feedback loop is a thermostat. In your home, you set the thermostat at a desired level. The thermostat monitors the air temperature and compares it to that set level. If the room gets too cold, the heater turns on; if the room gets too warm, the heater turns off. Many primary drives in the body work in the same fashion.

primary drive a drive that motivates us to maintain homeostasis in certain biological processes within the body

homeostasis [hoe-mee-oh-STAY-suss] an internal state of equilibrium in the body

negative feedback loop a system of feedback in the body that monitors and adjusts our motivation level so as to maintain homeostasis

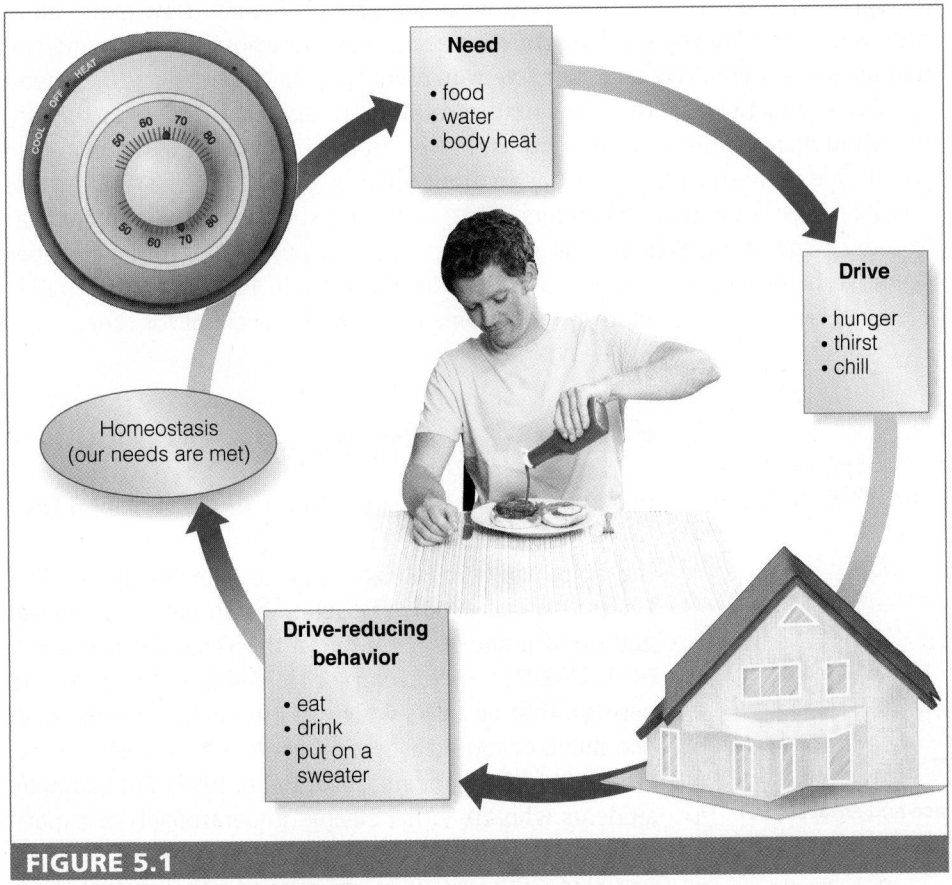

Frank and Helena/Alamy

FIGURE 5.1

Negative Feedback Loops

Negative feedback loops maintain homeostasis in our bodies by monitoring certain physiological conditions (such as glucose levels and fluid levels). When levels drop too low, feedback from the body tells the brain to increase motivation (for example, hunger or thirst). When levels are too high, feedback from the body tells the brain to decrease motivation.

Ashley Cooper/Encyclopedia/Corbis

According to drive reduction theory, we are motivated to eat when our body sends feedback to the brain indicating that our energy supplies are running low. This need for fuel sets up a primary drive state, which motivates us to eat so that we can reduce our hunger.

The idea that motivation in the form of primary drives serves to maintain homeostasis makes a great deal of sense. Without primary drives, our biological needs would likely not be met, and we might not survive. But how well does the idea of drives explain some of our other motivations? For example, does drive reduction theory explain academic achievement motivation, or motivation to be loved? To help explain what motivates these kinds of behaviors, drive reduction theorists developed the notion of **secondary drives**—drives that motivate us to perform behaviors that are not directly related to biological needs.

Secondary drives are presumed to have developed through learning and experience. Back in the 1930s, Henry Murray proposed that human behavior is motivated by a host of secondary motives such as *need for achievement, need for affiliation* (the need to be close to others), and *need for understanding* (the need to understand one's world) (Murray, 1938). According to some psychologists, the need to fulfill certain secondary drives differs from person to person, like any other personality characteristic. For example, some people have a higher need for achievement than others do.

The concept of motivation as a means of reducing drives seems to make more sense for primary drives than for secondary drives, but even here it is not without its faults. There are times when drive reduction theory cannot explain certain aspects of our biological motives. For example, what about overeating? Think about a typical holiday meal in your family. At holiday dinners, do you eat only enough food to satisfy your primary drive of hunger? We bet not. How many times have you eaten until you felt ill because it was a special occasion? If our sole motivation for eating were drive reduction, we would not "pig out" in instances like these.

secondary drive a learned drive that is not directly related to biological needs

Drive reduction theories also fail to account for times when we seem to be motivated to *increase* the tension or arousal levels in our bodies. For instance, when you decide to ride a roller coaster at an amusement park or to try skydiving, what possible drive could these behaviors lower? Activities such as these do not appear to reduce any of our primary drives. Rather, the sole purpose of these activities seems to be to *arouse* us physiologically. Clearly, we will have to conceptualize motivation in some other way to account for these types of behavior.

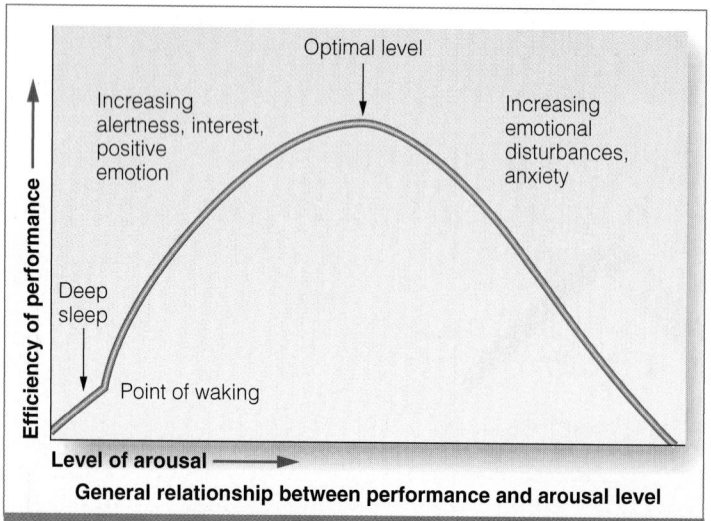

FIGURE 5.2

The Yerkes-Dodson Curve: Performance as a Function of Arousal

Our best performance often occurs at moderate levels of arousal. You would likely do your best on an exam if you were neither too sleepy nor too anxious.

5.1.3 • Arousal Theories of Motivation

In 1908, arousal theorists Richard Yerkes and John Dodson proposed that performance on a task is affected by the amount of physiological arousal in the body (Yerkes & Dodson, 1908). The relationship between arousal and performance is captured in the *Yerkes-Dodson curve* (• FIGURE 5.2). As you can see from Figure 5.2, we tend to perform best on tasks when we are moderately aroused. Too much or too little arousal generally weakens performance (Arent & Landers, 2003; Hebb, 1955). For example, students who are either sleepy (underarousal) or experiencing test anxiety (overarousal) tend to perform poorly on exams. Students who are relaxed yet alert (moderate arousal) tend to perform better.

According to arousal theories of motivation, each of us is motivated to seek out arousal when we find ourselves underaroused and to reduce our arousal level when we are overaroused. This doesn't mean, however, that there is a single level of arousal that is optimal for everyone. Just as we saw with secondary drives, individuals differ in how much arousal is optimal or right for them. Some people are motivated to seek out situations that elicit low arousal (such as going to the bookstore), whereas others tend to crave the excitement of more arousing activities (such as riding a roller coaster). In fact, some people can be classified as *sensation seekers*—people who routinely seek out extremely arousing activities (Zuckerman & Kuhlman, 2000). Sensation seekers may be motivated to skydive, participate in extreme sports, experiment with drugs, and engage in other risky behaviors.

Although people differ with respect to their preferred levels of arousal, situational factors also play a role in determining our performance levels. For example, performance on low-complexity tasks, such as driving in light traffic, might be improved at higher levels of arousal (Ünal et al., 2013). By contrast, performance on tasks of high complexity—such as those involving memorization and recall of new information—might suffer when we are aroused (Martinie, Olive, & Milland, 2010).

5.1.4 • Self-Determination Theory of Motivation

The idea that humans are motivated by different things is part of a broad theory of motivation called *self-determination theory* (Deci & Ryan, 2008). According to **self-determination theory**, humans need to feel competent (skilled), autonomous (in control of our own behavior), and related (or connected) to others. As we try to meet these needs, we will at times experience *autonomous motivation* or *controlled motivation*. When we are autonomously motivated, we are self-motivated to engage in a behavior. For example, you might study for an exam because you want to do well on it. When we experience controlled motivation, we feel more compelled to engage in certain behaviors. For example, you may study for an exam because you want to please your parents or because you feel that you should work hard in school.

self-determination theory a theory of motivation that proposes that as we pursue the fulfillment of basic needs, we experience different types of motivation that come from both the self and the outside world

incentive a goal or desire that we are motivated to fulfill

intrinsic motivation motivation that comes from within the person

extrinsic motivation motivation that comes from outside the person

These examples show the power that **incentives** have to motivate us into action (Atkinson, 1958/1983). You can think of incentives as goals or desires that you wish to satisfy or fulfill. For example, someone who desires money will be motivated to engage in behaviors that will likely lead to obtaining money, such as taking a job or buying lottery tickets. Incentives can be either *intrinsic* (coming from within us) or *extrinsic* (coming from outside us). Intrinsic incentives, such as wanting to make a good grade to please yourself, provide **intrinsic motivation** for behavior. Extrinsic incentives, such as wanting to please others or desiring monetary rewards, provide **extrinsic motivation** for behavior (Deci & Ryan, 1985).

All of us are motivated at times by both intrinsic and extrinsic rewards. For example, in a recent study of firefighters, researchers found that a combination of intrinsic (e.g., wanting to be fit) and extrinsic (e.g., not wanting to let down fellow firefighters by not being fit enough to do the job) motives pushed the firefighters to engage in regular physical exercise (Long, Readdy, & Raabe, 2013).

© Thomas Imo/Alamy

The self-determination theory of motivation states that many of us are motivated by extrinsic rewards such as money, material goods (such as cell phones), and praise from others.

Although all of us can be either intrinsically or extrinsically motivated, we do differ with respect to what types of motives tend to motivate us the most. Some of us tend to be more motivated by intrinsic rewards, such as a sense of accomplishment and pride. Others tend to be more motivated by extrinsic rewards, such as grades and money. Which motivates you more? Some studies suggest an advantage for having more of an intrinsic orientation. For example, studies have found that intrinsically motivated college students are less likely to use drugs and alcohol (Rockafellow & Saules, 2006; Shamloo & Cox, 2010). Intrinsic motivation has also been shown to predict success in sticking to an exercise program (Teixeira et al., 2010) and doing well in school (Lepper, Corpus, & Iyengar, 2005). It appears that intrinsic rewards, such as a sense of accomplishment, are more likely to keep us working hard for success.

5.1.5 • Maslow's Hierarchy of Needs

hierarchy of needs Maslow's theory that humans are motivated by different needs, some of which take precedence over others

Imagine that you have to miss lunch because you don't have time to stop and eat. On this particular day, you have a paper to write, an exam to study for, and a long list of algebra problems to finish. As you sit down to study, you find that several different motives are all trying to direct your behavior at the same time. You need to study, you are hungry, you are sleepy because you did not sleep well last night, and you really want to go to the movies with your friends. Which of these motives will win? What will your first course of action be in this situation? Will you eat, study, go to the movies, or fall asleep? We often find ourselves pulled in different directions by our motives. Are some types of motives inherently stronger than others? Perhaps.

Abraham Maslow, a prominent figure in humanistic psychology (Chapter 1), recognized that in certain circumstances, some motives have greater influence over our behavior than others do. Maslow conceptualized both our physiological and psychological motives as different classes of *needs* to which we assign different levels of priority. These different classes form a **hierarchy of needs**, in which the lower-level needs have the first priority (Maslow, 1970). Maslow's hierarchy of needs is usually presented as a pyramid, as shown in • FIGURE 5.3.

The lowest level of Maslow's hierarchy—the base of the pyramid—is our *physiological needs.* Maslow theorized that we seek to satisfy such basic needs as hunger and need for warmth before we are motivated to satisfy any of our other needs. If our physiological needs are met, then our next level of concern is satisfying *safety needs,* such as having a safe place to live. At the next level, Maslow identified *belongingness* and *love needs,* the motivation to be with others, to be loved, and to be appreciated by

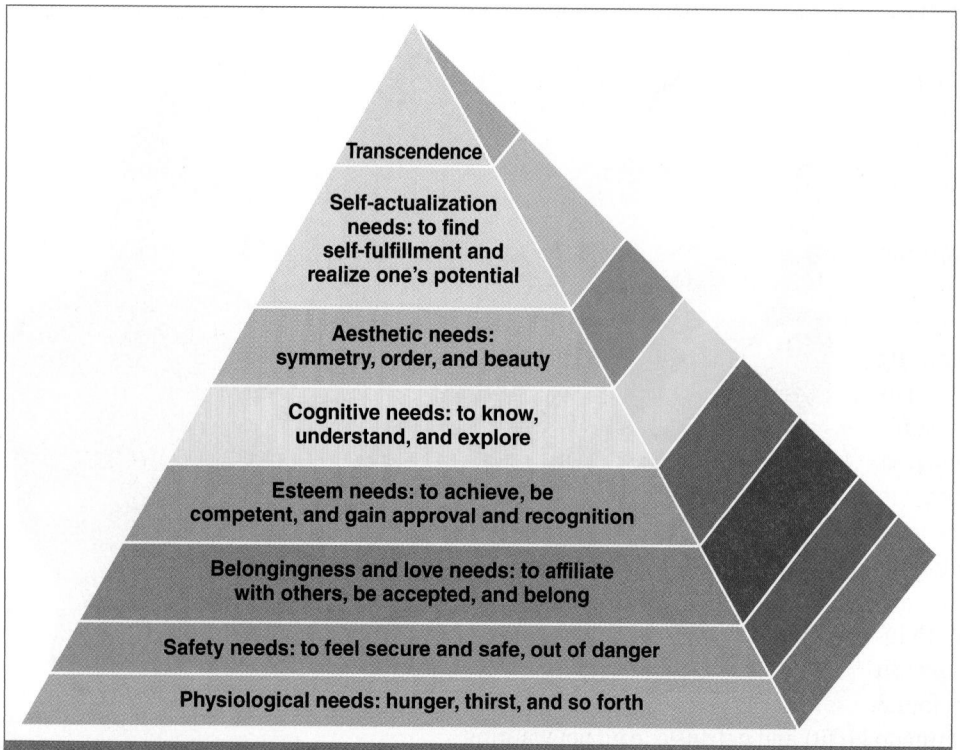

Source: Maslow, Abraham H.; Frager, Robert D. (Editor); Fadiman, James (Editor), *Motivation and Personality,* 3rd, © 1987. Electronically reproduced by permission of Pearson Education, Inc., Upper Saddle River, New Jersey.

FIGURE 5.3
Maslow's Hierarchy of Needs

Tim Graham/Hulton Archive/Getty Images

Andrew Gombert/Landov

According to Abraham Maslow, few of us will ever fulfill enough of our lower-level needs to actually reach the level of self-actualization. During her lifetime, Mother Teresa appeared to have reached the levels of self-actualization and need for transcendence. Similarly, singer Bono of the group U2 appears to be striving for self-actualization, spending much of his time engaged in humanitarian causes.

others. At the next levels we would seek to successively satisfy our *esteem needs, cognitive needs,* and *aesthetic needs* (see Figure 5.3 for descriptions).

If we meet our aesthetic needs, we may seek to move to even higher levels, toward self-fulfillment. At these levels, motives include *self-actualization needs,* or the motivation to reach our full potential, and the *need for transcendence,* the motivation to achieve spiritual fulfillment. Maslow had little hope that the average person would actually reach the self-fulfillment level. He believed that most people are unable to fulfill enough of the needs at the lower and middle levels of the pyramid, but that some of us do satisfy enough of our lower-level needs to at least try for self-actualization and transcendence. For example, Mahatma Gandhi, Martin Luther King Jr., and Mother Teresa all appeared to be motivated by these higher levels of Maslow's hierarchy.

At first glance, Maslow's hierarchy seems to make sense. If you are starving, you will probably be less concerned with whether people love you and more concerned with finding food. Indeed, a recent study conducted in China found that the degree to which a need was satisfied correlated positively with the degree to which the need at the next higher level of the hierarchy was satisfied as well (Taormina & Gao, 2013). This finding is consistent with Maslow's predictions that lower needs must be fulfilled before moving on to higher-level needs.

However, much of the work on Maslow's hierarchy of needs has failed to generate strong support for his theory (Soper, Milford, & Rosenthal, 1995). In fact, we often seem to behave in ways that contradict Maslow's notion that we must fulfill lower needs before we can be concerned with higher-order needs. For instance, have you ever gone without lunch to pursue some other activity, such as studying for an exam? In that case, you were motivated by esteem needs even though your physiological needs had not been met. Likewise, research also indicates that when we have satisfied our needs at a certain level of the hierarchy, we do not always move up to the next level and attempt to satisfy those needs (Hall & Nougaim, 1968).

We have seen that there are many different ways to look at motivation. However, whether we view motivation as an instinct, a drive, a need, or an incentive, one thing is certain: motivation is what catalyzes our behavior and moves us into action.

Quiz Yourself

5.1

1. Which of the following approaches to motivation is most closely aligned with Darwin's theory of evolution?
   a. Drive theory
   b. Instinct theory
   c. Self-determination theory
   d. Maslow's hierarchy of needs
2. Which of the following approaches to motivation assumes that motivation can come from outside the person?
   a. Instinct theory
   b. Drive theory
   c. Self-determination theory
   d. None of the above
3. Which of the following is the best example of intrinsic motivation?
   a. Studying hard to keep your scholarship
   b. Staying late at work to earn overtime
   c. Cleaning your house because you enjoy a tidy home
   d. Dressing up for a job interview because you want to make a good impression

Answers 1. b; 2. c; 3. c

5.2 Hunger and Eating

Lying in his hospital bed, being fed through a feeding tube, Jean-Dominique Bauby still fantasized about eating delectable gourmet meals. This shouldn't surprise us, given the importance of food in our daily lives. Food is part of one's culture. Eating is one of our most fundamental activities, basic to survival. To protect us from starvation, the motivation to eat remains strong even when we have competing or conflicting motivations. But what is it that initiates the hunger that motivates us to eat?

5.2.1 • The Origins of Hunger

The hunger motive is one of the primary drives that helps us maintain homeostasis in the body. The goal of hunger is to motivate us to eat when our bodies need fuel. Thus, we should feel hungry when we are lacking fuel and nutrients, but we should *not* feel the motivation to eat when we have enough fuel and nutrients in our bodies. Like a thermostat, hunger works on a *negative feedback loop* in the body that allows us to maintain homeostasis in our bodies.

set point a particular weight that our body seeks to maintain

Homeostatic regulation of hunger explains why we seem to have an individual **set point**, or a weight that our body naturally attempts to maintain. Having a set point may be one reason that the vast majority of people who lose weight tend to regain it. When the body loses weight, the person's hunger increases, the person eats more, and the weight is regained. Although having a set point makes dieting very difficult, experiencing increased hunger when we fall below our set point also protects us from starvation. In environments where people struggle to find enough to eat, this extra motivation may make them work harder to obtain enough food to survive.

To motivate us to eat enough food to maintain homeostasis and thereby our set point, our brain must receive accurate and reliable feedback from the rest of our body. Where in the body does this feedback about the current status of our body's fuel supply originate?

HUNGER FEEDBACK FROM THE BODY

One of the first places psychologists looked for clues to hunger was the stomach, and some evidence suggests that one part of the feedback that initiates hunger is an empty stomach. When our stomachs become empty, the walls of the stomach contract, and these contractions appear to stimulate hunger. Additionally, the stomach appears to release a hormone called **ghrelin** that sends strong hunger signals to the brain (Suzuki et al., 2010).

Just as the stomach signals hunger, it may also play a role in telling the brain when it is time to stop eating. When we eat, our stomach's walls must distend to increase the volume of the stomach and allow room for the food we eat. This distention of the stomach has been suggested as one source of feedback that signals to the brain that it is time to stop eating (Deutsch, 1990; Xu et al., 2008). However, the role it plays maybe complex. One study found that distending the stomach by means of an inflatable balloon placed in the stomach had no effect on subsequent food intake, but it did reduce feelings of hunger while the balloon was in place (Oesch et al., 2006). Failure of an inedible balloon to reduce subsequent eating may be explained by the fact that receptors in the walls of the stomach may actually be able to measure the nutritive value of the food we eat. Researchers have shown that the degree to which we feel hungry is directly correlated with the number of calories we have in our stomach (deCastro & Elmore, 1988) and the balance of proteins, carbohydrates, and fats we have consumed (El Khoury et al., 2010; Lomenick et al., 2009). When the stomach senses that we have eaten enough, it subsequently releases less ghrelin. This reduction in ghrelin curbs the hunger signals being sent to the brain, resulting in satiety. In a recent study of obese women, participants who exhibited a normal reduction in ghrelin after eating also exhibited less anxiety and stress compared to participants who had abnormally high postmeal ghrelin levels. This suggests that ghrelin may also play a role in anxiety-related eating (Sarker, Franks, & Caffrey, 2013).

Although the stomach is an important source of feedback in the hunger process, it is not the only source. Surprisingly, even people who have had their stomachs completely removed because of cancer usually still feel hunger (Janowitz & Grossman, 1950). The liver is another source of feedback for hunger. Our liver has the capacity to help regulate hunger by monitoring the levels of *glucose* and *glycogen* in our body (see • TABLE 5.1). **Glucose** is the form of sugar that our bodies burn for energy, and **glycogen** is the form of starch that we store along with fatty acids. When we have excess glucose in our body, we convert it into glycogen and then store it for future use. The liver determines what our energy

ghrelin [GRELL-in] a hunger-stimulating hormone produced by the stomach

glucose the form of sugar that the body burns as fuel

glycogen [GLIE-co-jen] a starchy molecule that is produced from excess glucose in the body; it can be thought of as the body's stored energy reserves

TABLE 5.1

The Liver's Role in Hunger

	THE LIVER DETECTS THAT GLUCOSE IS CONVERTING TO GLYCOGEN	THE LIVER DETECTS THAT GLYCOGEN IS CONVERTING TO GLUCOSE
Hungry		X
Not Hungry	X	

requirements are by monitoring our levels of glucose and glycogen. On the one hand, if the liver detects that we are converting glucose into glycogen, indicating that we have too much fuel in our bodies, it will send signals to the brain to shut off hunger. On the other hand, if the liver notices that glycogen is being turned back into glucose, indicating that we are dipping into our energy reserves, it will send signals to the brain to initiate hunger.

The endocrine system (Chapter 2) also plays a role in regulating hunger. The hormone **insulin** can increase feelings of hunger (see Grossman & Stein, 1948). Made in the pancreas, insulin facilitates the movement of glucose from the blood into our cells, where it is metabolized. When glucose moves into the cells, blood levels of glucose drop, so we begin to dip into our glycogen reserves, and hunger is initiated. In this indirect way, insulin can produce feelings of hunger.

insulin [IN-suh-lin] a hormone produced by the pancreas that facilitates the movement of glucose from the blood into the cells of the body

cholecystokinin [coe-lih-cyst-oh-KYE-nin] (CCK) a hormone released by the small intestines that plays a role in hunger regulation

leptin a hormone released by fat cells in the body that plays a role in hunger regulation

Foods that cause a rapid increase in blood sugar, called *high glycemic foods,* do not keep our hunger satisfied for very long. This is because the body pumps out a large amount of insulin to counteract the rapid increase in blood sugar, resulting in a subsequent drop in blood glucose levels that sets off hunger (Bornet et al., 2007). So, if you are looking for a snack and want to feel full longer, choose a low glycemic food (for example, an apple) over a high glycemic food (for example, sweetened apple sauce).

Other hormones affect hunger even more directly. When we eat, the small intestines release the hormone **cholecystokinin (CCK)** into the bloodstream. CCK appears to shut off the urge to eat (Canova & Geary, 1991; Lassman et al., 2010). However, the level of hunger that we experience is due to more than just the amount of CCK in our bloodstream. How much food we have recently eaten also seems to influence hunger. If we have not taken in enough food, CCK by itself may not be enough to stop our hunger and our eating (Muurahainen et al., 1991). Interestingly, researchers have found that certain chemicals found in green vegetables, called *thylakoids,* have the power to increase the amount of CCK released after eating a high carbohydrate meal. This increase in CCK is associated with lower postmeal hunger, which may lead to eating less later on in the day (Stenblom et al., 2013).

Fat cells may provide yet another source of feedback for hunger regulation. Fat cells make and secrete a chemical called **leptin**. When fat cells release leptin into the bloodstream, it travels to the brain, where it is picked up by receptors near the brain's *ventricles* (the fluid-filled cavities in the brain) and in the hypothalamus (the part of the brain that maintains homeostasis) (McGregor et al., 1996). Leptin is thought to inform the brain about the level of fat reserves available. When the brain senses high leptin levels, this may indicate that a large number of fat cells are full of fat reserves. Therefore, we do not need to take in more fuel, and our hunger may be reduced. In support of this hypothesis, researchers have found that mice that are bred to be genetically fat will lose weight if they are given injections of leptin (Pelleymounter et al., 1995).

Unfortunately, we are a long way from understanding the exact role of leptin in motivating human eating. For example, researchers are currently investigating the role that the neurotransmitter *dopamine* (Chapter 2) plays in mediating leptin action in the brain (Benoit et al., 2003; Burdakov, Karnani, & Gonzalez, 2013). Another issue being researched is how leptin, CCK, and other digestive tract chemicals interact to regulate hunger (Blevins & Baskin, 2010; Woods, 2013). At the moment, we have no body of evidence to support the notion that losing weight is as simple as taking a few tablets of leptin!

HUNGER REGULATION IN THE BRAIN

The brain, of course, plays a significant role in our eating behavior. It receives and processes signals from the stomach about contractions and distention, from the liver about the glucose–glycogen balance, and from leptin. The brain may also directly monitor our energy supplies. Evidence suggests that the brain, like the liver, monitors the level of glucose in the blood (Chaput & Tremblay, 2009). There appear to be specialized *glucoreceptors* in the hypothalamus that measure glucose levels in the bloodstream (Burdakov, Luckman, & Verkhratsky, 2005). If an animal is given a substance that makes its hypothalamus unresponsive to glucose, the animal goes on an eating binge (Miselis & Epstein, 1970). Disabling the hypothalamus's glucoreceptors tricks the brain into thinking that the body is critically low on fuel. The brain then signals extreme hunger to quickly replenish the body's glucose.

Further clues about the role of the hypothalamus in hunger regulation come from animal studies in which surgical lesions are made in the brain. By destroying part of the hypothalamus and observing the effect that this destruction has on behavior, psychologists have uncovered some clues about the role that the different parts of the hypothalamus play in both initiating and stopping eating.

One part of the hypothalamus, the **lateral hypothalamus**, or **LH**, seems to function as an "on switch" for hunger. When the LH is destroyed in a rat, the rat stops eating. As a result, the rat loses weight and eventually dies. Without the LH, the rat simply starves to death (Teitelbaum & Stellar, 1954), which seems to indicate that the LH turns on hunger. However, further investigation has shown that the LH is not the only "on switch" for hunger. Curiously, if a rat is force-fed for long enough after having had its LH destroyed, the rat will eventually get some of its appetite back. Its appetite will not be as great as it was prior to losing its LH, but the rat will eat, particularly very tasty foods (Teitelbaum & Epstein, 1962).

Another bit of evidence that suggests an "on switch" for hunger outside the LH comes from studies using **neuropeptide Y**, a powerful hunger stimulant (Gibbs, 1996). When an animal is injected with neuropeptide Y, its strongest effect occurs outside the LH (Leibowitz, 1991). It stands to reason that if the LH were the primary "on switch" for hunger, then this powerful stimulant would have its strongest effect in the LH. That this does not appear to be the case suggests that there is an even more important "on switch" for hunger elsewhere in the brain. To date, the research suggests that the LH plays an important role in hunger, but it is not the only brain structure involved in motivating us to eat (see Petrovich, 2013).

The hypothalamus is also thought to play a role in shutting off hunger. Some evidence suggests that a part of the hypothalamus, the **ventromedial hypothalamus**, or **VMH**, plays a role in creating a feeling of *satiety*. When we are sated, we feel full and do not wish to eat more. Rats who have had their VMH destroyed will begin to eat ravenously and will gain enormous amounts of weight (● FIGURE 5.4). If the VMH were the rat's only satiety center, or hunger "off switch," then destroying its VMH should make the rat eat

lateral hypothalamus (LH) a region of the hypothalamus once thought to be the hunger center in the brain

neuropeptide Y the most powerful hunger stimulant known

ventromedial [ven-tro-MEE-dee-al] hypothalamus (VMH) a region of the hypothalamus that plays an indirect role in creating a feeling of satiety

© Richard Howard

FIGURE 5.4

A Mouse with a Lesion in the Ventromedial Hypothalamus (VMH)

This mouse had its ventromedial hypothalamus damaged. As a result, the mouse has eaten more than normal and gained a great deal of weight. But this mouse will not eat itself to death. Rather, it will now eat just enough to maintain this new, higher set point weight.

continuously until it dies. But this doesn't happen. A rat without a VMH will eat a great deal of food and gain a great deal of weight, but after a certain amount of weight gain, its appetite will level off and the rat will then eat only enough food to maintain its new, higher weight. It's as if losing the VMH changes the rat's set point. In other words, the weight that the rat's body tries to maintain through homeostatic regulation has been shifted upward to a new, higher weight.

So, although the VMH may not be the only "off switch" for hunger, it does appear to play a role in obesity (see King, 2006; Levin & Routh, 1996). When the VMH is damaged surgically in a rat, the endocrine system's control over insulin release is disturbed. The result is an increased release of insulin into the bloodstream, which produces greater hunger and subsequent increases in eating (Valensi et al., 2003). Loss of the VMH doesn't remove the satiety center, but rather causes disturbances in the endocrine system that result in increased eating. Most of us, however, have not had our VMH surgically

You Review **Mechanisms of Hunger**

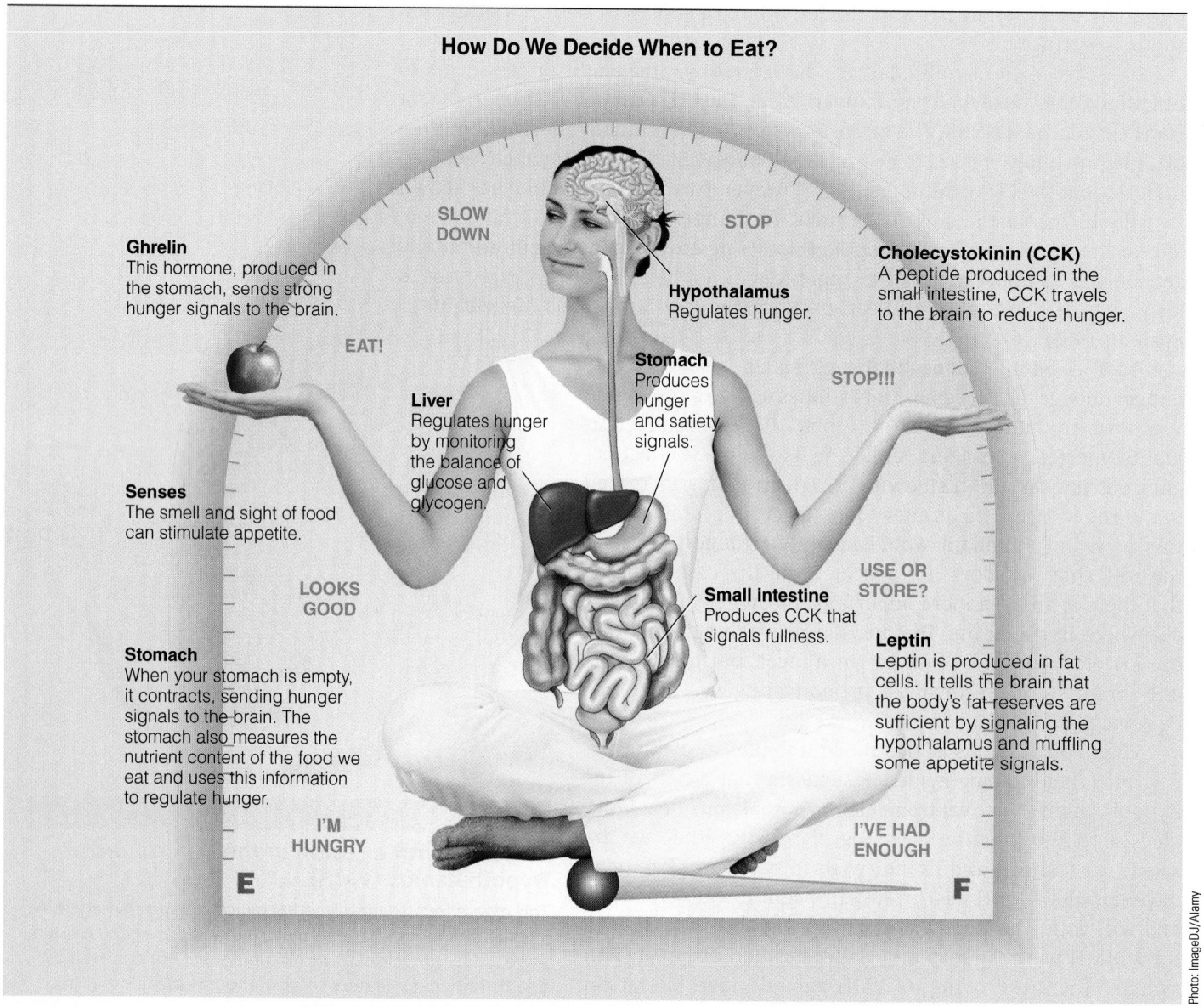

Photo: ImageDJ/Alamy

removed or damaged. Why might the system fail us under conditions seen in everyday life?

Recent research suggests that chronic challenges to the hunger-regulating centers of the brain can disrupt its ability to sense and respond to insulin, thereby damaging its ability to regulate hunger and metabolic functioning. One of these challenges seems to be eating a high-fat diet. Mice fed a high-fat diet were shown to develop less activity in certain neural pathways of the VMH as a result of increased insulin activity in the brain. This reduction in neural activity was also related to weight gain in the mice and lessened ability to control blood sugar in their bodies (Klöckener et al., 2011). This study further underscores the role of insulin in regulating hunger and body weight, and the importance of controlling insulin levels via a healthy diet.

What we have learned from studies of the hunger centers in the brain is that many mechanisms turn on and shut off feelings of hunger. There does not appear to be a single "on" or "off" switch for hunger (King, 2006). Rather, hunger seems to be regulated by a complex network of feedback to the brain from various sources in the body, as well as direct signaling in the brain (Suzuki et al., 2010) (see You Review: Mechanisms of Hunger).

OTHER CUES THAT INFLUENCE EATING: CULTURE AND CONSUMERISM

Have you ever eaten a big bag of popcorn at the movies just minutes after you finished a large meal? Have you ever consumed a fast-food meal that contained far more calories, fat, and salt than you really needed? If so, your behavior has shown that eating is often more than just satisfying biological needs and maintaining homeostasis in the body. Recently, psychologists have begun to discriminate between *intuitive eating,* or eating that is motivated by physiological hunger and satiety feedback, and eating that is motivated by emotional and situational cues that have little connection to energy requirements (Augustus-Horvath & Tylka, 2011; Avalos & Tylka, 2006). For example, the smell of popping popcorn at a theater can make you want to eat popcorn, even if you've just had a full meal. Or you may be tempted to indulge in a big bowl of ice cream after a stressful day.

Nonintuitive eating occurs for reasons other than supplying fuel for our bodies. In many cultures, food and feasting are an integral part of cultural customs. This is especially true in the United States, where our holiday celebrations—including Christmas, Thanksgiving, Halloween, Hanukkah, Passover, Kwanzaa, and New Year's—are all associated with special foods in large quantities. The same holds true for more personal celebrations—birthdays, weddings, reunions, and even funerals. Americans and many other peoples around the world use food and eating to celebrate. This connection between joy and food can lead to eating when we do not really need to.

Our obsession with weight and dieting may also contribute to nonintuitive eating. In a recent study of adolescents, researchers found that being on a restrictive diet for weight loss was associated with less intuitive eating and increased *emotional eating,* or eating to cope with emotional distress (Moy et al., 2013). Whatever its cause, nonintuitive eating can lead to unwanted weight gain. In contrast, intuitive eating is associated with lower body mass index (BMI; Herbert et al., 2013). Finding ways to enhance intuitive eating and discourage eating that is motivated by emotion and situational cues may be one key to avoiding a major health concern—*obesity* (see Psychology Applies to Your World).

Psychology Applies to Your World:

The Obesity Epidemic

One way to define overweight and obesity is to look at the *body mass index* (*BMI*; ● FIGURE 5.5). A BMI of 25–29.9 indicates **overweight**, and a BMI of 30 or more indicates **obesity** (National Institutes of Health, 2000). BMIs over 30 are correlated with higher incidences of many diseases, including type 2 diabetes, heart disease, and some cancers (Kopelman, 2000). Clearly, we have reason to be concerned about weight.

Americans are clearly obsessed with weight. Collectively we spend millions of dollars each year on diets, exercise equipment, diet pills, and gym memberships, yet roughly two-thirds of all Americans are considered to be *overweight,* and almost a third are *obese* (● FIGURE 5.6). Sadly, among children ages 9–19, 16% are considered overweight (Kaplan, 2007). Similar figures are now seen in other cultures as well. In England, the national health authority (*Public Health England*) now reports that 64% of English adults are considered overweight or obese (PHE, 2014). In France, obesity rates are also climbing, with 14% of French adults now considered to be obese (Beardsley, 2011). In Poland, over 50% of adults are overweight or obese (Dziurowicz-Kozłowska, 2010). Numbers like these suggest that the obesity epidemic is going global.

In light of these problems, the U.S. government-funded Medicare program began considering obesity a disease in the mid-2000s ("Medicare to Fund Obesity Treatment," 2004), and in 2011 it announced that it would begin funding obesity prevention services (Kennedy & Hellmich, 2011). Despite our great concern over the issues of weight and health, why did obesity take such a hold in the United States and other countries?

Poor diet is one reason that some people gain weight. One culprit is the high-fat diet common in many Western cultures. A typical fast-food lunch can contain a whole day's worth of fat and calories. Coupled with a lack of exercise, this diet leads to weight gain in many people. Another factor comes from the way our society views food. As we mentioned earlier, we tend to eat for reasons that have little to do with maintaining homeostasis. Many of us engage in emotional eating when we are lonely, sad, or nervous (Edelman, 1981). This emotional eating may be one of the factors involved in weight gain for some people, but emotional distress has not been shown to be a general cause of obesity. In general, overweight people are not more likely to experience

Body mass index (BMI) = (weight in pounds × 703) + (height in inches)^2	
Multiply your weight in pounds by 703	Example
_____ × 703 = _____	155 lbs × 703 = 108,965
Multiply your height in inches by itself (squared)	
_____^{2} = _____	68 × 68 [inches] = 4,624
Divide the first number by the second:	
_____ ÷ _____ = _____ Weight × 703 Height squared BMI	$\frac{108{,}965}{4{,}624}$ = 23.6 BMI

BMI	Weight status
below 18.5	Underweight
18.5–24.9	Normal
25.0–29.9	Overweight
30.0 and above	Obese

FIGURE 5.5

Calculating your BMI

This chart shows how to calculate your Body Mass Index (BMI). To do so, you will need a calculator, your weight in pounds, and your height in inches.

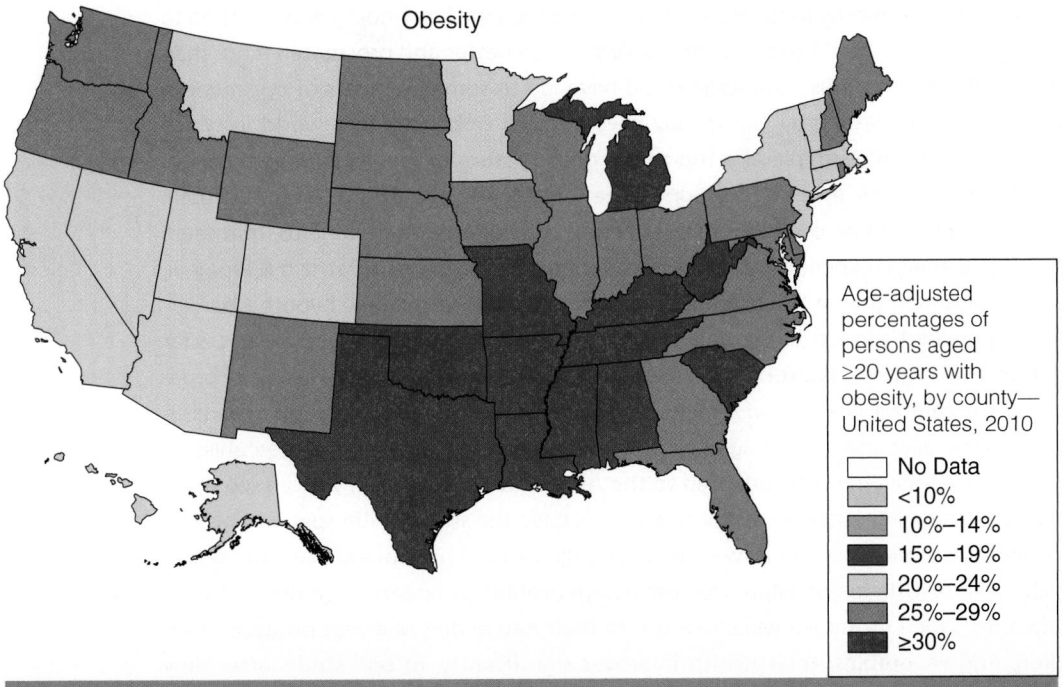

Source: Centers for Disease Control and Prevention, www.cdc.gov.

FIGURE 5.6

The Obesity Epidemic in the United States

In the United States, almost one-third of all adults are obese. This map shows the percentage of obese people across the United States. The highest concentrations of obese people (shown in dark red) seem to be in the southern states. The reasons for this epidemic are the subject of much debate, but it is likely that several causes are at work—including genetic, lifestyle, and diet factors.

anxiety or depression (Wadden & Stunkard, 1987). However, abdominal obesity (fat stored around the midsection) has been linked to some aspects of depression—namely, the somatic or body-centered symptoms of depression (e.g., fatigue, sleep disturbances, dizziness; Wiltink et al., 2013).

Biological factors may also play a role in some people's problems with weight. For example, our biological clocks or *circadian rhythms* (Chapter 4) may be tied to how our body uses the energy we take in during eating. In one recent study, participants who were assigned to eat a high-calorie breakfast lost more weight than participants who were assigned to eat a high-calorie dinner even though the daily caloric intake was similar for both groups (Garaulet & Gomez-Abellán, in press). Furthermore, our preference for the time of day in which we are most active may also affect our eating and our weight. Some of us prefer to be active in the evenings (evening types). Some of us prefer to be active in the morning (morning types). Being an evening type (as opposed to a morning type) is associated with having a harder time losing weight (Garaulet et al., 2012). Evening types are also more likely to eat later in the day and to skip breakfast (Garaulet et al., 2013). Studies such as these suggest that the biological rhythms of our bodies may influence our eating and our weight.

Another biological factor that contributes to obesity is having a low *basal metabolic rate*—the rate at which we burn energy in our bodies when resting. People differ with respect to how much energy is required to run their bodies. Some people have high metabolic rates and require large amounts of fuel; others have low metabolic rates and require relatively little energy to survive. A person with a very low metabolic rate who eats the same number of calories and exercises just as much as a person with a normal metabolic rate will still gain more weight than the normal person will. Over time, this weight gain could lead to obesity (Friedman, 1990).

Ironically, having a low metabolic rate isn't always a disadvantage. In fact, across our evolutionary history, a low metabolic rate was probably a decided advantage. Our ancestors had to hunt and forage for enough food to

Continued

eat. Those early humans who required less energy to survive probably had an easier time finding enough food to meet their needs. Therefore, those with low metabolic rates probably survived better and procreated more than their counterparts with high metabolic rates. This advantage could have led to some members of our modern society having "thrifty genes" that conserve energy, but it may have also led to obesity in a world in which hunting and gathering high-calorie foods is as simple as a trip to the grocery store or fast-food drive-through. So far, scientists have not found direct genetic evidence to support the thrifty gene hypothesis (Prentice, 2009). However, researchers are currently honing in on chemicals in the nervous system, *endocannabinoids,* that seem be able to alter our food intake and energy expenditures to conserve energy in the body (DiPatrizio & Piomelli, 2012). The presence of such mechanisms in the body would be consistent with the thrifty gene hypothesis.

Cross-cultural studies also lend indirect support to the notion of thrifty genes. The typical American diet is far different from that of our ancestors. Americans today consume large amounts of red meat, fat, eggs, and dairy products, but few fruits and vegetables. In contrast, the diets of some cultures, such as the Japanese and certain Mediterranean cultures, are much lower in red meat and contain significantly larger proportions of fruits and vegetables.

By examining cultural groups that have recently adapted to the American high-fat diet, we can see more clearly the impact of that diet on health. For example, ethnic Hawaiians have the shortest life span of any ethnic group on the Hawaiian Islands. As a group, ethnic Hawaiians show high rates of high blood pressure, type 2 diabetes, obesity, and high cholesterol. One major culprit in these health problems appears to be the fat-heavy American diet they have taken on. When ethnic Hawaiians return to their native diet of sweet potatoes, taro root, breadfruit, fish, chicken, and vegetables, their health improves significantly. In one study, after only 21 days of eating their native diet instead of the typical American diet, Hawaiians showed significant drops in blood pressure, weight, and cholesterol (Shintani et al., 1991). Perhaps many native Hawaiians are biologically unsuited to eat the American diet. The same may be true of many other obese Americans.

overweight having a body mass index of 25–29.9

obesity having a body mass index of 30 or over

basal metabolic rate the rate at which we burn energy in our bodies when resting

5.2.2 • The Battle of the Bulge: Why Is Losing Weight So Hard?

Many people spend a good deal of their time dieting. In an attempt to bring about weight loss, diets restrict the dieter's eating to varying degrees. Unfortunately, depriving yourself of food is also one reason that most diets fail. When we reduce our caloric intake to the point that we begin to lose weight, our bodies try to counteract the diet. Recall that our motivation to eat is designed to keep us from starving. When we begin to draw on our fat reserves while dieting, our body takes steps to avoid "starvation." At first, we may feel increased hunger as our body tries to avoid burning up fat reserves by urging us to eat. Later, our **basal metabolic rate** may drop as the body tries to conserve energy, again in order to avoid burning up its fat reserves. The drop in metabolic rate may offset the reduction in calories on the diet, with the end result being little or no weight loss. Even more discouraging is that our basal metabolic rate may drop even lower with each successive diet we go on (Brownell, 1988). This means that the more you diet, the harder it may become to lose weight. Our bodies appear inclined to fight against weight loss and to maintain our typical weight, or set point.

There are psychological factors in dieting, too. Depriving yourself of food often leads to bingeing. It appears that when dieters stray from their diet program, they feel as if they might as well *really* go off the diet. In one study that illustrated this reaction, dieters and nondieters were given a liquid drink. Half of each group was told that the drink was very high in calories; the other half was told that the drink was very low in calories. In reality, all the drinks had the same caloric and nutritional content. After the drink, all participants were allowed to eat as much ice cream as they wanted. The nondieters ate the same amount of ice cream regardless of whether they thought they had just consumed a high- or low-calorie drink. This was not true, however, for the dieters. The dieters who thought they had had a high-calorie drink were more likely to eat more ice cream than the dieters who thought their drink had been low-calorie. It appears that the dieters felt that having already "ruined" their diet with the high-calorie drink, there was little point in restraining themselves when it came to the ice cream (Spencer & Fremouw, 1979).

Recall that intuitive eating is less likely when one is on a restrictive diet and eating to ease emotional distress is more likely (Moy et al., 2013). Therefore, people who restrain their eating are most at risk for this bingeing when they are emotionally aroused. Emotional distress can make dieters more likely to cheat on their diet (Ruderman, 1985), but so can positive emotions (Cools, Schotte, & McNally, 1992). Whether one is happy or sad, it seems that dieting makes eating binges more likely.

The recipe for dieting success involves two factors. First, you have to make permanent changes in your eating behavior. "Dieting" is forever, and it is probably a mistake to think of losing weight as dieting. Perhaps becoming more of an intuitive eater is a better strategy. And, if you must "diet," it is generally better to focus on eating healthy, balanced meals that are lower in calories than on how many pounds you can lose in a week. The best way to lose weight is to do it slowly. People don't typically gain 15 pounds in a week, so why should we expect to lose weight that fast?

The second aspect of successful weight loss is exercise. Cultural changes that reduce physical activity, such as driving to work or school, sedentary jobs, television, and computer games, are major contributing factors to the growing obesity epidemic. Any weight loss plan that does not include exercise is likely to fail in the long run. Exercise not only burns extra calories and causes weight loss, it also increases your metabolism. Recall that when we diet, our body adjusts its metabolic rate downward to prevent starvation. You can help keep your metabolism higher by exercising, which will lead to a more permanent weight loss as your set point moves to a lower weight. Exercise, especially strength training, can also ensure that you don't lose too much muscle mass while dieting. If you diet by caloric reduction alone, you run the risk of losing beneficial muscle along with the fat (Parr, Coffey, & Hawley, 2013).

So, next time you see an advertisement for some miracle diet that allows you to eat all you want without exercising and still promises to safely take off 10 pounds a week, save your money and possibly your health. There are no quick fixes when it comes to shedding pounds. Even people who undergo *gastric bypass surgery* to drastically reduce the size of their stomach must adhere to a strict diet regimen and make lifestyle changes to achieve and sustain long-term weight loss (Powell, Calvin, & Calvin, 2007).

Envision/Encyclopedia/Corbis

foodfolio/Alamy

Which of these meals would you rather eat? Unhealthy eating habits contribute to obesity and health problems in many people.

5.2.3 • Culture and Weight-Based Prejudice

People who are overweight do not just face health threats. Being overweight also exacts an emotional toll. Americans abhor fat. People who are overweight are often ridiculed, socially isolated, and even discriminated against in the workplace. Parents have even been shown to exhibit weight bias against their own children. Parents are less likely to help their overweight children finance a car (Kraha & Boals, 2011) or their college tuition (Crandall, 1991). Even health care professionals who specialize in the treatment of obesity sometimes demonstrate negative attitudes toward the overweight. In one study, health care professionals, including psychologists, were found to have used words such as lazy and stupid to refer to overweight persons (M. Schwartz et al., 2003). Similarly, researcher Kristen Davis-Coelho and her colleagues found that some members of the American Psychological Association displayed a negative bias in their perceptions of overweight versus normal-weight women. This tendency to perceive overweight people less favorably was most evident in younger and less experienced mental health care professionals (Davis-Coelho, Waltz, & Davis-Coelho, 2000).

Prejudice against the obese seems to also extend to children. In fact, studies have shown that children's prejudice against other overweight children has grown significantly since the 1960s. This is very unfortunate because children who are teased by their peers for being overweight are at higher risk for having a negative self-image, fewer friends, and an increased likelihood of suicide (see DeAngelis, 2004).

This negative attitude about obesity is not worldwide, however. For example, one of the authors once had an overweight friend from Iceland. After living in the United States for a few years, she observed that although there were fewer obese people in her native country, she was treated more normally there than she was in the United States, where so many people are overweight. In yet other cultures, such as the African country of Mauritania, overweight women are valued for their beauty—so much so that young girls are often force-fed to make them obese. Because of health concerns, we do not advocate intentionally creating obesity in anyone. However, such cultural differences suggest that just as our perceptions of beauty and weight vary cross-culturally, so do our levels of prejudice against the overweight.

Just as cultures vary with respect to their average levels weight-based prejudice, within a given culture, there are individual differences in people's levels of prejudice. Recent research has begun to examine the individual characteristics of people who hold anti-fat prejudices. One factor that seems to be important is *fear of negative appearance evaluations* (Bissell & Hays, 2011). Likewise, having a *tendency to compare one's appearance to that of others', having a poorer body image* and *placing greater important on physical appearance* were correlated with having greater prejudice against the overweight (O'Brien et al., 2007).

Exposure to stigmatizing media depictions of overweight people may also work to exacerbate weight-based prejudice. Participants who viewed stigmatizing depictions of obese people were subsequently more likely to endorse a policy that discriminated against the obese. But, subjects who viewed nonstigmatizing depictions of obese people were less likely to endorse prejudicial policies aimed at the overweight (Brochu et al., 2014). These data suggest that eliminating stigmatizing media depictions of obesity may help reduce the weight-based prejudice. Our cultural fear of fat exacts a heavy toll on the many people who experience weight-based prejudice (Danielsdottir, O'Brien, & Ciao, 2010). Our attitudes about weight may also play a role in the development of certain eating disorders—our next topic.

5.2.4 • Eating Disorders: Bulimia Nervosa, Anorexia Nervosa, and Binge Eating Disorder

Obesity is not the only problem that involves eating. Some people also experience the devastating toll that eating disorders, or mental health disorders that are associated with eating, can take on a person's health and life. Why would food be such an issue for some of us?

BULIMIA NERVOSA

Bulimia nervosa is an eating disorder that is characterized by alternating bouts of *bingeing* and inappropriate compensatory behaviors such as *purging*, fasting, or excessive exercise. People who are bulimic gorge on large quantities of food, sometimes as much as 20,000 calories at a time; then they either go on a very rigid starvation diet or purge the food from their system (Schlesier-Stropp, 1984). Purging is achieved by self-induced vomiting or the abuse of laxatives (in the mistaken belief that laxatives prevent weight gain after overeating).

bulimia nervosa an eating disorder in which a person alternately binges on large quantities of food and then engages in some inappropriate compensatory behavior to avoid weight gain

anorexia [an-or-EX-ee-uh] nervosa an eating disorder in which a person has an intense fear of gaining weight, even though he or she is actually underweight; this irrational fear motivates the person to lose unhealthy amounts of weight through self-starvation

One of the authors once met a girl with bulimia who spent an entire semester's tuition on a 2-week cycle of bingeing and purging. She would go out at night and travel from one drive-through restaurant to another buying large quantities of tacos, hamburgers, and other fast food. She would take the food back to her dorm room, where she would quickly eat all of it and then purge it by vomiting. Luckily, this 2-week binge probably saved her life. When she was unable to explain the missing tuition money, her parents insisted she enter a treatment program. After intense treatment, she regained some measure of normalcy in her eating behavior.

Like this woman, the typical victim of bulimia is a young female who is of average to slightly above average weight. Within a given 12-month period, approximately 1% to 1.5% of young females will have bulimia nervosa (American Psychiatric Association, 2013), and an American woman has roughly a 1% chance of developing the disorder across her lifetime (Williams, Goodie, & Motsinger, 2008). Bulimia is much less likely among males; at any point in time, approximately 10 times more females than males have the disorder (American Psychiatric Association, 2013).

Bulimia is especially likely among college-age females, almost 4% of whom are estimated to have the disorder (ANRED, 2008). Not surprisingly, bulimic behavior is particularly common among female college students (Cain et al., 2010). Bulimia can be a socially isolating disorder. A college student who spends her evenings gathering up large quantities of food and bingeing and purging usually does so alone. Aside from its social toll, bulimia can sometimes be fatal. The frequent purging of food can lead to dehydration and electrolyte imbalances, which can lead to serious cardiac problems as well as other problems such as holes and erosions in the esophagus.

Given the devastating toll that bulimia can take on one's life, what would motivate anyone to engage in bulimic behavior? At this time, no one can say for sure why people become bulimic. However, many bulimic people are troubled by low self-esteem and depression (Perez, Joiner, & Lewisohn, 2004). Bulimics tend to be perfectionists who have negative views of their bodies. They tend to have grown up in families that were troubled somehow (Bardone et al., 2000; Spanou & Morogiannis, 2010). For some bulimics, bingeing and purging become a means of coping with negative emotions such as anxiety and a sense that one has no control over the events of one's own life.

ANOREXIA NERVOSA

Anorexia nervosa is an eating disorder that is characterized by self-starvation, intense fear of gaining weight, and a distorted body image. Unlike people who have bulimia, anorexics can be easily spotted because of their very low body weight. Anorexics can get down to astonishingly low weights (as low as 50 pounds), and 5% to 10% of anorexics die as a result of the disorder (Wilson, Grilo, & Vitousek, 2007). The most bizarre aspect of anorexia is that even at a life-threateningly low weight, an anorexic can look in the mirror and see herself as fat (Grant & Phillips, 2004).

Estimates of the percentage of the female population in the United States with anorexia range from 0.12% to 2.0% (Wade, 2007). But, within a given

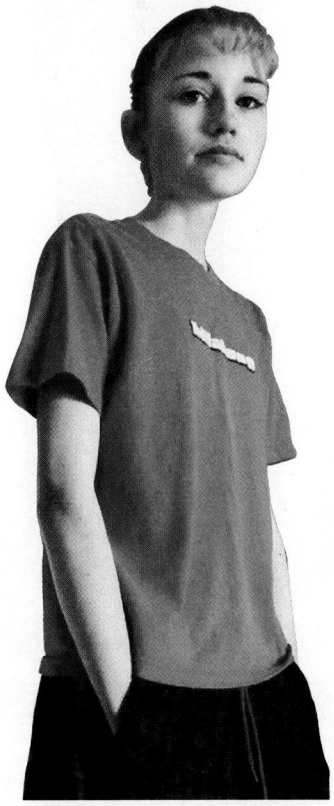

AP Images/The Grand Island Independent/Barrett Stinson

Anorexia nervosa is a devastating disorder in which people are motivated to drastically restrict their eating. Some people with anorexia also increase their level of exercise. The result is extreme weight loss, but this weight loss is never enough to please the anorectic. Anorexics like this woman still look in the mirror and feel that they need to lose more weight.

JAB Promotions/WireImage/ Getty Images

FIGURE 5.7

Too Thin?

Many models and actresses are very thin. The steady parade of these women in the media may have contributed to the increase in eating disorders seen in the 1980s and 1990s.

12-month period of time, approximately 0.4% of females have anorexia nervosa (American Psychiatric Association, 2013). Worldwide, most anorexics are females from middle- and upper-class families in industrialized countries. Anorexia is rarely found in men. For every male with anorexia, there are approximately 10 females with the disorder (American Psychiatric Association, 2013). However, there is some concern that eating disorders may be a bigger problem in the gay community, where body image concerns appear to be heightened (Russell & Keel, 2002) and among males with gender-identity confusion (Crosscope-Happel, 2000). Furthermore, as cultural pressures result in males becoming increasingly concerned with having lean and muscular body types, the incidence of male anorexia and other body image related disorders may increase (Murray & Touyz, 2012).

Anorexia is also less common in cultures that hold a fuller-figured woman up as the standard of beauty. It appears that one of the contributing factors in the development of anorexia is societal pressure on young women to be very thin—unrealistically thin. If you pick up just about any American fashion magazine or watch just about any American television show, you will find that most of the females depicted are extremely thin. Sometimes they actually look anorexic (• FIGURE 5.7). Many television stars and models wear size 0 or 2 clothes, whereas many American women wear size 10 or 12 (or larger)! If you do the math, you'll see that many American women fall short of the standard of beauty depicted in the media. What do you do if you are a young girl who aspires to look like the actors you see on TV, and a healthy diet and exercise do not allow you to meet your goals? Some girls take drastic steps to reach their "ideal" body image, and anorexia may be the result.

Researchers have found wide cultural variations in women's perceptions of their ideal body image. For example, in one study that compared U.S., Israeli, Spanish, and Brazilian women, the American women were found to be the least satisfied with their bodies. The American women also reported that they felt the most pressure to be thin (Joliot, 2001). A recent study of Mexican American college women also found that the degree to which these women had internalized American standards of female beauty was related to their levels of dissatisfaction with their own bodies (Poloskov, 2013). This is significant because in cultures that portray beautiful women as being somewhat plumper—for example, in Jamaica (Smith & Cogswell, 1994) or even in American culture prior to the 1970s—anorexia is uncommon. Pre-1970, women who were considered beautiful were considerably heavier than those who are considered beautiful today. For example, Marilyn Monroe was considered to be the standard of beauty in the 1950s and early 1960s, and before her, Mae West—these two women were not the ultrathin models of today (• FIGURE 5.8). Still, despite being bombarded with images of very thin women, most American girls do not become anorexic. Why is it that some do?

At one time, anorexia was thought to be correlated with ethnicity. Because the thin standard of female beauty is most frequently portrayed as a White woman in American culture, many predicted that White women would experience greater pressure to be unrealistically thin and therefore have higher rates of anorexia. Indeed, studies conducted in the 1980s seemed to confirm this hypothesis. However, this situation seems to have changed. A later study conducted in the United States did not find White women to have more symptoms and predictors of eating disorders than Black, Hispanic, or Asian women. The authors concluded that minority women have caught up to White women in this domain and are now equally susceptible to risk factors for eating disorders such as dissatisfaction with one's body (Shaw et al., 2004; see also Wade, 2007).

binge eating disorder an eating disorder characterized by recurrent episodes of binge eating, as in bulimia nervosa, but without regular use of compensatory measures to avoid weight gain

Characteristics that seem to be correlated with anorexia include perfectionism (Davies et al., 2009; Egan et al., 2013) and faulty thinking about food (for example, thinking one should never eat carbohydrates; Steinhausen & Vollrath, 1993), as well as biochemical abnormalities (Ferguson & Pigott, 2000; Young, 2010). Many people with eating disorders also have *personality disorders*—characteristic, maladaptive ways of dealing with the world (see Chapter 13; Marañon, Echeburúa, & Grijalvo, 2004; Sansone & Sansone, 2011). We do not yet know if these are *causal* factors or merely factors that *correlate* with eating disorders.

Another piece of the puzzle may be genetics (Keel & Klump, 2003). Some scholars have argued that genes for anorexia evolved to allow our ancestors to survive famine by helping them ignore food while migrating to better environments (Guisinger, 2003). Indeed, evidence supports the idea of a genetic basis for anorexia. If one identical twin is anorexic, the other twin's chances of becoming anorexic are drastically increased. However, having a fraternal twin who is anorexic only modestly increases one's chances of becoming anorexic (Holland, Sicotte, & Treasure, 1988). This pattern of results supports the existence of a genetic predisposition to anorexia. It is also common to see family members, particularly mothers and daughters, who both have eating disorders. However, this doesn't necessarily indicate a genetic basis for the disorders as family members also tend to have shared environmental influences. At present, it appears that both bulimia and anorexia may result from a complex mix of cultural factors, personality characteristics, environmental issues, and biological factors.

Omar Reyes/Landov

L. J. Willinger/Keystone Features/Hulton Archive/Getty Images

Hulton Archive/Getty Images

FIGURE 5.8

Standards of Female Beauty

Standards of beauty in the United States have changed over time, and they also differ across cultures. In the 1930s, Mae West was considered an icon of feminine beauty. In the 1950s and early 1960s, it was Marilyn Monroe. Today, women like Angelina Jolie are the standard of beauty.

© jackhollingsworth.com/Alamy

Greer & Associates, Inc./Alamy

Buddy Mays/Documentary Value/Corbis

In cultures like Jamaica, Fiji, and Mexico, the standard of beauty leans toward heavier women. Cultures such as these have far lower rates of eating disorders than the United States.

BINGE EATING DISORDER

Binge eating disorder is an eating disorder characterized by recurrent episodes of binge eating, such as those seen in bulimia nervosa, but without regular use of the inappropriate compensatory measures that bulimics employ to avoid weight gain. Because binge eaters do not compensate for their overeating, they may be overweight. As we've already seen, obesity and being overweight are at epidemic levels in the United States. Current estimates suggest that within a 12-month period, 1.6% of adult females and 0.8% of adult males have binge eating disorder (American Psychiatric Association, 2013). However, it is thought that the rate of binge eating disorder among people seeking weight loss treatment may be higher. Just how many obese and overweight people have binge eating disorder is uncertain at this time. However, one estimate suggests that up to 30% of people who seek professional treatment for weight control may meet the criteria for this disorder (Brody, Walsh, & Devlin, 1994; see You Review: *DSM-5* Criteria for Eating Disorders).

You Review *DSM-5* Criteria for Eating Disorders

Bulimia Nervosa

A. Recurrent episodes of binge eating. An episode of binge eating is characterized by both of the following:
   1. Eating, in a discrete period of time (e.g., within any 2-hour period), an amount of food that is definitely larger than what most individuals would eat in a similar period of time under similar circumstances.
   2. A sense of lack of control over eating during the episode (e.g., a feeling that one cannot stop eating or control what or how much one is eating).

B. Recurrent inappropriate compensatory behaviors in order to prevent weight gain, such as self-induced vomiting; misuse of laxatives, diuretics, or other medications; fasting; or excessive exercise.

C. The binge eating and inappropriate compensatory behaviors both occur, on average, at least once a week for 3 months.

D. Self-evaluation is unduly influenced by body shape and weight.

E. The disturbance does not occur exclusively during episodes of anorexia nervosa.

Anorexia Nervosa

A. Restriction of energy intake relative to requirements, leading to a significantly low body weight in the context of age, sex, developmental trajectory, and physical health. Significantly low body weight is defined as a weight that is less than minimally normal or, for children and adolescents, less than minimally expected.

B. Intense fear of gaining weight or of becoming fat, or persistent behavior that interferes with weight gain, even though at a significantly low weight.

C. Disturbance in the way in which one's body weight or shape is experienced, undue influence of body weight or shape on self-evaluation, or persistent lack of recognition of the seriousness of the current low body weight.

Binge Eating Disorder

A. Recurrent episodes of binge eating. An episode of binge eating is characterized by both of the following:
   1. Eating, in a discrete period of time (e.g., within any 2-hour period), an amount of food that is definitely larger than what most individuals would eat in a similar period of time under similar circumstances.
   2. A sense of lack of control over eating during the episode (e.g., a feeling that one cannot stop eating or control what or how much one is eating).

B. The binge eating episodes are associated with three (or more) of the following:
   1. Eating much more rapidly than normal.
   2. Eating until feeling uncomfortably full.
   3. Eating large amounts of food when not feeling physically hungry.
   4. Eating alone because of feeling embarrassed by how much one is eating.
   5. Feeling disgusted with oneself, depressed, or very guilty afterward.

C. Marked distress regarding binge eating is present.

D. The binge eating occurs, on average, at least once a week for 3 months.

E. The binge eating is not associated with the recurrent use of inappropriate compensatory behavior as in bulimia nervosa and does not occur exclusively during the course of bulimia nervosa or anorexia nervosa.

5.2

Quiz Yourself

1. A friend of yours was recently in a car accident and experienced damage to his ventromedial hypothalamus. What effect would you expect this damage to have on your friend's behavior?
   a. He will likely stop eating.
   b. He will likely die.
   c. He will likely gain a great deal of weight.
   d. He will likely gain a great deal of weight, but then he will lose the pounds and return to his normal weight.
2. A drug that acts in the intestines to help people lose weight would most likely affect which of the following chemicals in the body?
   a. Insulin
   b. CCK
   c. Leptin
   d. Serotonin
3. Gabby's liver is converting glycogen into glucose. As a result, Gabby will likely feel which of the following?
   a. Not hungry
   b. Hungry
   c. Nauseous
   d. We cannot predict from the information given.

Answers 1. c; 2. b; 3. b

5.3 Sexual Motivation

Another fundamental motive is the motivation to engage in sexual activity. Even locked inside his own body, Jean-Dominique Bauby no doubt felt sexual desire as he remembered intimacies from his past and lamented the loss of future ones. For most of us, sexuality is a healthy and important part of our lives. And, although sexual motivation is not necessary for life in the same manner that hunger is, sexual motivation does help ensure survival of the species through procreation.

5.3.1 • Sexual Desire: A Mixture of Chemicals, Thoughts, and Culture

Sexual desire is our motivation and interest in engaging in sexual activity. It is the first step in experiencing **sexual arousal**, a heightened state of sexual interest and excitement. Like many other behaviors that we have discussed, sexual desire is influenced by our biology as well as our learning experiences and cultural expectations.

Biological and psychological processes influence sexual desire. The physical desire to have sex, or **libido**, is affected by both the hypothalamus and certain hormones of the endocrine system. As discussed in Chapter 2, the brain's hypothalamus works with the master gland of the body, the pituitary gland, to release hormones into the bloodstream. In this way, the hypothalamus plays a key role in regulating sexual behavior. The hypothalamus continually monitors the level of sex hormones in the bloodstream and directs the endocrine system to either increase or decrease the release of these hormones as required.

In mammals, **estrogens** are female hormones that regulate the female animal's desire to mate. Female animals' estrogen levels increase dramatically during a period called **estrus** ("being in heat"), in which the female is receptive to males' attempts to mate with her. Estrus coincides with ovulation in the female. During ovulation, the female's egg (or eggs) matures, so that it can be fertilized by the male sperm during mating. If fertilization does not occur, the female will pass out of estrus, and she will

sexual desire one's motivation and interest in engaging in sexual activity

sexual arousal a heightened state of sexual interest and excitement

libido [leh-BEE-doe] one's physical desire, or drive, to have sex

estrogens a class of female hormones that regulate many aspects of sexuality

estrus [ess-TRUSS] in some species, a period of "being in heat" in which the female is receptive to males' attempts to mate with her

Martin Harvey/Gallo Images/Corbis

Some female mammals show visible signs when they are receptive to mating.

shed the egg along with the lining of her uterus during menstruation. If a pregnancy is going to occur, estrus is when it will happen. Therefore, it is in both the male and female animals' best interest to mate during estrus. To ensure that mating will occur, estrus is usually marked by some physical change in the female that signals to males of the species that she is in estrus and ready to mate. For example, many female chimpanzees have sexual swelling, or engorgement, of the external female genitals that indicates to male chimpanzees that it is time to mate.

Humans are a bit different from other mammals in that a human female has no defined period of estrus. Human females can mate at any time in the menstrual cycle, and although female estrogen levels do fluctuate during the menstrual cycle, estrogen is not closely related to human female libido. Evidence for the limited role of estrogen in sexual desire comes from cases of women who have had hysterectomies that involved removal of their ovaries. **Ovaries** are organs that produce eggs and estrogen in a woman's body. Without ovaries, a woman's estrogen levels plummet. Despite the drastic loss of estrogen, some women do not experience a loss of sexual desire after a hysterectomy (Sherwin & Gelfand, 1987). And for those women who do experience loss of desire, taking estrogen alone does not always increase desire or improve sexual response (El-Matary, Kemball, & Feteha, 2006).

ovaries the organs in a female's body that produce eggs, or ova

testosterone a male hormone that plays a role in many aspects of sexuality, including sexual desire

testes the organs in a male's body that produce both sperm and testosterone

In humans, the hormone that seems to govern libido is **testosterone**. Testosterone is part of a class of male hormones called *androgens*. Although testosterone is a male hormone, it is also found in females (likewise, males have estrogen). In males, the **testes** produce testosterone (in addition to sperm). In women, it is produced by the *adrenal glands* that sit above the kidneys. Adequate testosterone levels seem to be important in maintaining sexual desire. If testosterone levels fall too low, both males and females experience disinterest in sex.

Testosterone may not be the only hormone that drives our desire, however. Another hormone called *oxytocin* plays a role in adult social bonding or attachment. Oxytocin is released during sexual activity and may contribute to the feeling of closeness we feel toward our partner during sexual activity (Fisher, 2004). *Dopamine,* a neurotransmitter associated with pleasure and reward (Chapter 2), also influences sexual desire (Pfaus, 2009).

Are chemicals the sole cause of sexual desire? No. Although hormones and neurotransmitters play a significant role in our libido, sexual desire is not merely a function of chemicals in our bodies (Baumeister, 2004; Brotto et al., 2011). Our senses, our thoughts, and our culture also influence human sexual desire. Visual cues can increase or decrease sexual desire. For example, just fixating one's gaze on the chest or pelvic region of another can increase physiological arousal (Nummenmaa et al., 2012). Erotic photographs or movies may be a sexual turn-on to some people, but not to others. Seeing a lover nude or in sexy lingerie may be stimulating for some. Such visual stimulation seems to have a greater effect on men than on women (Reinisch, 1991). Sounds, such as a lover's voice or romantic music, may be appealing to some. Research also suggests that our sense of smell may play a role in sexual arousal (Stern & McClintock, 1998). For some it may be the scent of a particular cologne or perfume, whereas for others it may be natural body scents such as sweat. When fertile or at midcycle, women prefer the scent of males who have more masculine-looking faces. Similarly, men find the scent of women who are ovulating especially attractive (Gangestad, Thornhill, & Garver-Apgar, 2005), and they release more testosterone when exposed to the scent of ovulating women (Miller & Maner, 2010).

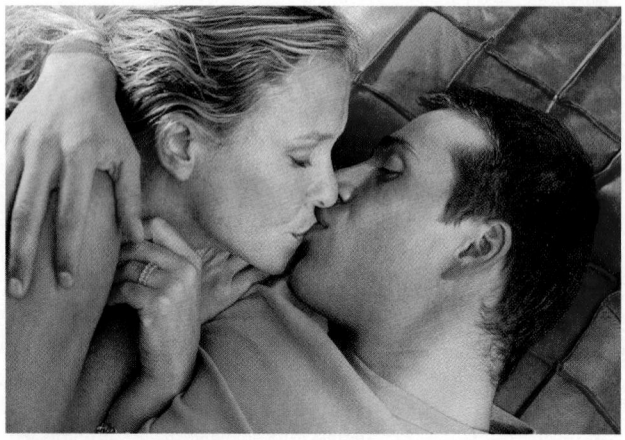

© Image Source/Alamy

Human sexual desire is more than just a matter of hormones.

Such findings suggest an evolutionary role of our sense of smell in sexual desire. However, people vary greatly in the types of smells they find arousing. For example, one study found that the aromas of pumpkin pie and lavender evoked the greatest sexual response in males, whereas the smell of candy-coated licorice, cucumbers, and baby powder elicited the greatest sexual response in females (Hirsch et al., 1998).

Our sense of touch plays a more direct role in sexual desire. Because nerve endings are unevenly distributed throughout the body, some areas of the skin are more sensitive to touch than others. These areas, called **erogenous zones**, include the genitals, buttocks, breasts, armpits, ears, navel, mouth, and the inner surfaces of the thighs. However, areas that may be highly stimulating to one person may produce a negative reaction in another; hence, our preferences in reaction to touch differ.

Many of the differences in our reactions to sensory cues exist because we all think differently about what should be or should not be sexually stimulating. Such expectations may be learned or reflect the larger influence of gender roles and culture on our behavior. For instance, in the United States, we emphasize cleanliness and the masking of natural body odors with perfumes and deodorants. As a result, Americans may learn to consider perfumes and deodorants more sexually appealing than body sweat. In a culture where perfume and deodorant are not commonly used, people may find natural body odors more appealing.

Personal experiences and cultural influences can influence our sexual desire, but once we are willing to engage in sexual activity, a predictable cycle of physical responses occurs, as described in the next section.

erogenous [eh-ROJ-en-ous] zones areas of the skin that are sensitive to touch

excitement phase the first stage of the sexual response cycle, in which males get erections and females produce vaginal lubrication

plateau phase the second stage of the sexual response cycle, in which excitement peaks

orgasm phase the third stage of the sexual response cycle, in which the pelvic and anal muscles contract

5.3.2 • The Sexual Response Cycle

In the 1960s, William Masters, a gynecologist, and Virginia Johnson, a nurse, were the first researchers to directly observe and measure the sexual responses of men and women engaged in a variety of activities. Electronic sensors were placed on the bodies of the participants to directly measure physical responses. The participants were also interviewed in detail about their experiences. The information gathered in this study, subsequently published in Masters and Johnson's *Human Sexual Response* (1966), described the common physical changes that we experience in our sexual encounters. The model includes four successive phases: *excitement, plateau, orgasm,* and *resolution* (• FIGURE 5.9). Men and women were remarkably similar in their physical responses.

During the **excitement phase**, men and women experience an increase in heart rate and blood pressure. The nipples may become erect and blood flow is increased to the genital area. Males experience penile erection, and the scrotal sac thickens. Females produce vaginal lubrication, and the inner two-thirds of the vagina expands. The clitoris, the female sex organ that is extremely sensitive to sensation, swells. During the **plateau phase**, excitement peaks and remains somewhat constant. Breathing becomes rapid, and blood pressure and heart rate continue to rise. Men experience a full penile erection and fully elevated testes. A few droplets of fluid that can contain sperm may appear at the tip of the penis. In women, the inner part of the vagina expands fully and the uterus becomes elevated. The clitoris shortens and withdraws.

During the **orgasm phase**, breathing, blood pressure, and heart rate peak. Brain imaging studies suggest that in women, at least 80 different brain structures play a role in orgasm (Komisaruk & Whipple, 2011; Komisaruk et al., 2011). In the body, contractions of the pelvic muscles and the anal sphincter produce the sensation of orgasm. And, other muscles throughout the body may also spasm during orgasm. In the male, the internal bodily contractions propel seminal fluid through the penis, causing ejaculation. Hence, in the male, the orgasm phase consists of

Art Phillips/Bettmann/Corbis

Masters and Johnson pioneered field research on the sexual response of males and females.

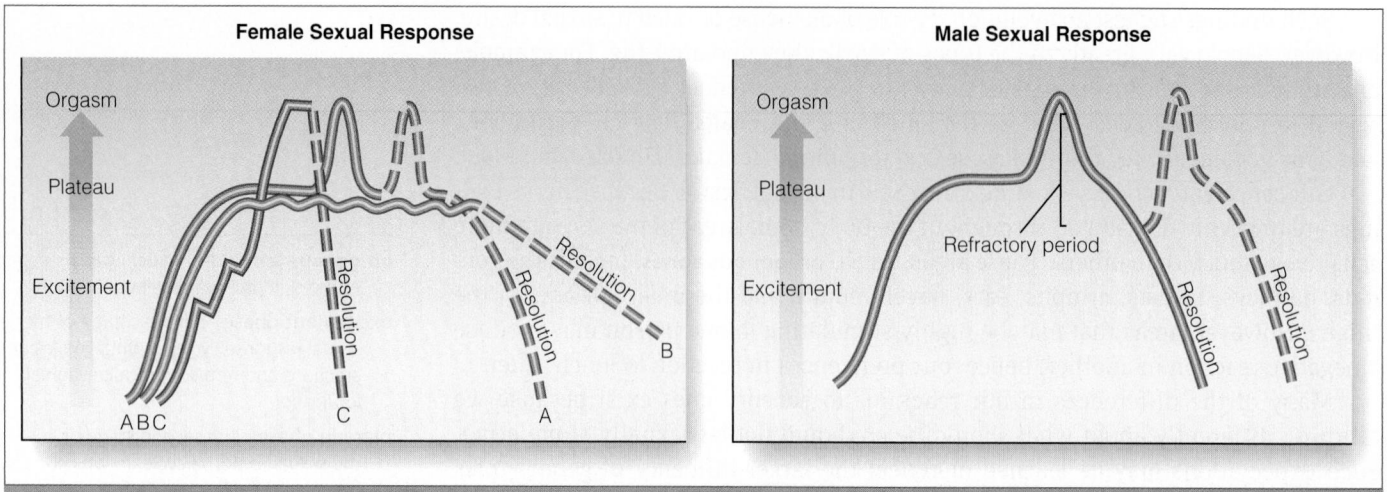

FIGURE 5.9

The Sexual Response Cycle

Masters and Johnson identified three basic patterns of response in females. A female may experience one or more orgasms (A), an extended plateau with no orgasm (B), or a rapid rise to orgasm with a quick resolution (C). Males show less variability in their sexual responses because of the refractory period.

Source: From *Human Sexual Response* by W. H. Masters and V. E. Johnson. Copyright © 1966 Little, Brown & Co. Reprinted by permission of Lippincott, Williams & Wilkins.

two processes: orgasm and ejaculation. However, males' and females' subjective experiences of orgasm are actually quite similar (Mah & Binik, 2002; Vance & Wagner, 1976). Men and women describe the experience in much the same way.

The sexual response cycle concludes with the **resolution phase**, in which the body returns to its prearoused state. Breathing, heart rate, and blood pressure return to normal. The male loses his erection, and in the female the vagina, clitoris, and uterus return to their normal size and position. Yet a distinct gender difference occurs in sexual response during the resolution phase. Unlike women, men experience a **refractory period**, or a time during which they are physically incapable of experiencing another orgasm or ejaculation. This measure of time increases as men age. For an adolescent male, the refractory period may last only a few minutes, whereas for men over age 50, it may last from several minutes to a day. Because women do not undergo a refractory period, they can more easily be rearoused after orgasm, leading some women to experience repeated or multiple orgasms. Hence, compared to males, who experience refractory periods of varying lengths, there is greater variability in the female sexual response pattern (Figure 5.9; Masters, Johnson, & Kolodny, 1993).

ENGAGE YOURSELF! Sex is a fundamental part of life, but sex (especially unprotected sex) can expose us to sexually transmitted infections. Did you know that when you have sex with someone, you may be exposing yourself to infections that this person might have picked up from previous sexual partners? In a sense, when you have sex with someone, it is as if you are sleeping with everyone that your partner has had sex with and everyone those people had sex with, and so on. London's Lloyds Pharmacy has created an online tool called the Sex Degrees of Separation Calculator that will calculate how many people you *could* have had direct and indirect sexual contact with to date (based on what is known about trends in sexuality at different ages). Check it out online. The number might surprise you.

resolution phase the final stage of the sexual response cycle, in which the body returns to homeostasis

refractory period a time during the resolution phase in which males are incapable of experiencing another orgasm or ejaculation

5.3.3 • Variations in Sexuality: Generational, Age, Gender and Sexual Orientation Differences

Although the experience of sex is similar for males and females, how we express our sexuality and the attitudes we hold about sex tend to vary more across generations and genders. Yet, despite the central role that sex plays in our lives, large-scale studies of these sexual trends in society are not as common as you might think. In fact, only a handful of good studies have ever been conducted.

In one of these studies, researchers asked 27,500 men and women aged 40–80 years from 29 different countries questions about their sexual behavior. The results indicated that across the world sexuality is an important part of people's lives. Over 80% of the males and 65% of the females surveyed indicated that they had engaged in sexual intercourse in the past year (Nicolosi et al., 2004). These data suggest that contrary to popular myths about sexuality, middle-aged and older adults are very much interested in sex! But, how do middle and older adults stack up against younger people when it comes to sex?

Additional studies have illustrated some interesting age and generational differences in sexuality. In 2010, London's Lloyds Pharmacy commissioned a survey of 3,000 British women. They found generational differences in the number of sexual partners women had had by age 24. Women who came of age between 2000 and 2009 reported having 5.65 partners by age 24. In contrast, young women of the 1970s reported having 3.72 by the same age, and women of the 1960s reported an average of 1.67 partners (Pinedo, 2010). These data suggest that women are taking more partners at a younger age than in the past—an especially important finding in light of the threat posed by HIV/AIDS and other sexually transmitted infections (see also Chapter 12).

An ABC News survey of American sexuality also revealed some generational differences in attitudes about sex ("American Sex Survey," 2004). This survey examined participants ranging from 18 to over 65 years of age, ensuring that participants came from several different generations: the *Millennial Generation* (those born after 1980), *Generation X* (those born between 1965 and 1980), *Baby Boomers* (those born between 1946 and 1964), and the *Silent Generation* (those born before 1946). ●TABLE 5.2 summarizes some of the sexual differences seen across these generations.

As you can see from Table 5.2, the more recent generations tend to have more open and accepting attitudes about sexuality. It also appears that the attitudes of the Silent Generation (those born before 1946) differ the most from those of the other generations. However, a bit of caution in interpreting these data is in order. Remember that these data were collected in 2004, when the participants were at very different stages of life. It is possible that some of the differences seen are due more to the participants' stage of life than to the generation from which they come. This difficulty in interpreting data is very common when people of different ages or cohorts are tested at a single point in time.

Likewise, the National Survey of Sexual Health and Behavior (NSSHB; Herbenick et al., 2010) revealed age-related differences in sexuality. However, it is hard to say whether these differences are due to age-related changes, generational influences, or a combination of the two. The NSSHB was conducted on 5,865 American men and women between the ages of 14 and 94. Among the more interesting findings was that 80.4% of the men 70 and older and 58.3% of women 70 and older reported having ever engaged in masturbation. Higher percentages of participants from the Millennial, Gen X, and Baby Boomer generations reported having engaged in masturbation at some point. Perhaps surprisingly, among male

TABLE 5.2

Generational Differences in Attitudes About Sexuality

AGE (IN 2004)	18–29 (MILLENNIALS & GEN X)	30–39 (GEN X)	40–49 (BABY BOOMERS)	50–64 (BABY BOOMERS & SILENT GENERATION)	65+ (SILENT GENERATION)
Discusses sexual fantasies with their partner	71%	55%	49%	37%	22%
Describes self as being sexually adventurous	55%	46%	41%	29%	19%
Feels that premarital sex is acceptable	71%	66%	69%	60%	30%
Feels that homosexuality is acceptable	65%	55%	55%	56%	40%

Source: "American Sex Survey," ABC News, 2004.

I love images/seniors/Alamy

For many people, sexuality remains an important part of life well into late adulthood.

and female participants aged 18–69, the lowest levels of reported experience with masturbation came from Millennials aged 18–19 years (86.1% of males; 66% of females). However, Millennials aged 25–29 years reported the highest levels of experience with masturbation (94.3% of males; 84.6% of females; Herbenick et al., 2010). The fact that Millennials report both the lowest and highest levels of experience with masturbation may reflect both the sexual growth that occurs in late adolescence and the openness of the Millennial generation's attitudes about sex.

NSSHB participants were also asked to report whether they had had vaginal intercourse in the last month. As you might expect, the rates increased across early adulthood (up to age 29) and then began to decrease across young, middle, and late adulthood. This trend was seen for both males and females. However, don't take this to mean that sex is just for the young. Consistent with what was seen in the global study of adults (Nicolosi et al., 2004), American men and women also expressed interest in sex later in life. In fact, a full 42.9% of the men aged 70+ and 21.6% of the women aged 70+ reported having had vaginal intercourse within the last year.

Although large-scale studies of sexuality across the life span and across generations are infrequently conducted, they do provide interesting information on our sexuality. One fact is clear: Despite the age and generation differences seen, sexuality is a vital and important aspect of our lives. For many people, sexuality remains an important part of life well into late adulthood.

5.3.4 • Whom Do We Desire? Sexual Orientation

As we have seen, sexual desire and sexual arousal are states that most of us experience. Yet there are individual differences in sexuality. Some people experience higher levels of sexual desire than others, and there is great variability in whom we desire to have sex with. **Sexual orientation**—one's sexual attraction for members of the same and/or other sex—is one of the factors that influences our choice of sexual partners.

sexual orientation one's sexual attraction for members of the same and/or other sex

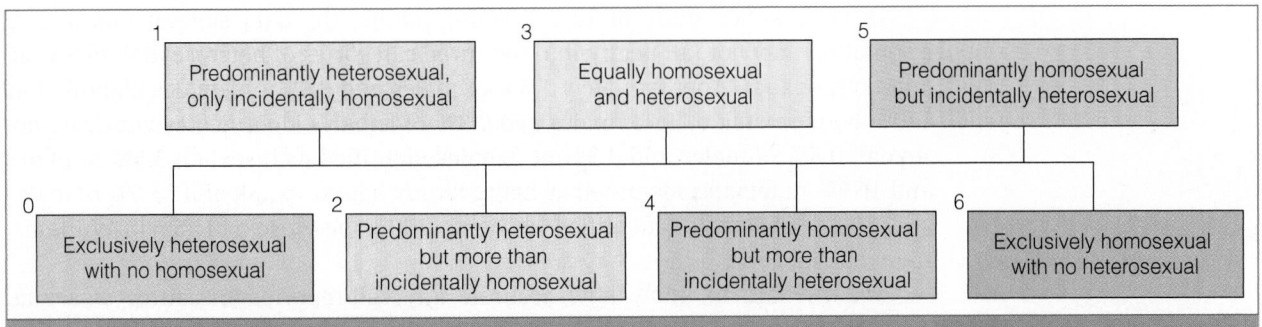

FIGURE 5.10

Kinsey's Continuum of Sexual Orientation

Sexual orientation may be expressed along a continuum of behaviors.

Source: Adapted from Kinsey et al., 1948, p. 638.

Many people never question their sexual orientation, whereas others may be in doubt as they grapple with the developmental task of establishing their identity in adolescence (Chapter 9). There are three types of sexual orientation. **Heterosexuals** are attracted to members of the other sex, **homosexuals** are attracted to members of the same sex, and **bisexuals** are attracted to members of both sexes. However, sexual orientation is not as fixed as these three terms suggest. Heterosexuality and homosexuality more often represent end points on a broad spectrum of behaviors that Kinsey and his colleagues (Kinsey, Pomeroy, & Martin, 1948) identified as a continuum of sexual orientation (● FIGURE 5.10). Moreover, sexual orientation may change over time, with women reporting greater change in orientation than men (Dickson et al., 2013; Kinnish, Strassberg, & Turner, 2005). Let's take a look at some aspects of sexual orientation, possible causes of it, and current attitudes toward gay males and lesbians.

heterosexual one who is sexually attracted only to members of the other sex

homosexual one who is sexually attracted only to members of the same sex

bisexual one who is sexually attracted to members of both sexes

SEXUAL ORIENTATION AND SEXUAL BEHAVIOR

When speaking of sexual orientation, one must be careful to distinguish between attraction and behavior. Sexual orientation is not simply a matter of whether you have sex with men or women. A man could be married to a woman, never have had sex with a man, but still be gay because he is truly attracted only to men. A woman could have sex with other women but still consider herself to be heterosexual.

In the late 1940s, Alfred Kinsey (Kinsey et al., 1948, 1953) began a series of studies on sexual behavior in which he surveyed people on many aspects of their sexuality. Kinsey found that 37% of men and 13% of women had had at least one same-sex sexual encounter, but not all of these people identified themselves as gay or lesbian. If this sounds confusing, it is. When trying to determine just how many people are homosexual, bisexual, or heterosexual, researchers have had some problems (Savin-Williams, 2006). Kinsey and his colleagues (1948) estimated that roughly 3% of the general population are exclusively homosexual. More recent figures indicate that the rate of homosexuality could be more like 4% to 6% for males and 2% to 4% for females (LeVay, 1996). In a recent survey of 5,865 Americans aged 14–94, 4.2% of adult males and 0.9% of adult females reported being homosexual. Among adolescent participants, 1.8% of males and 0.2% of females reported a homosexual orientation. Rates of bisexual orientation were 2.6% of adult males, 3.6% of adult females, 1.5% of adolescent males, and 8.4% of adolescent females (Reece et al., 2010).

In yet another study of 12,287 young adults, the data suggest that sexual orientation may not fall neatly into the three categories of heterosexual, bisexual, and homosexual. Approximately 1.7% of males and 0.9% of females identified as 100% homosexual; 0.7% of males and 0.8% of females identified as *mostly* homosexual; 0.5% of males and 2.3% of females identified as bisexual; 3.5% of males and 15.8% of females identified as being *mostly* heterosexual; and 93.6% of males and 80.2% of females identified as being 100% heterosexual (Savin-Williams, Joyner, & Rieger, 2012).

Yet it's hard to know how accurate any self-reported measures of sexual orientation are. The negative attitudes that some people hold about homosexuality make it difficult to get accurate data. It could well be that some people are reluctant to admit their true sexual feelings because they fear reprisals or feel personally stigmatized by their sexuality.

VARIATIONS: ATTITUDES TOWARD GAYS AND LESBIANS ACROSS THE WORLD

American attitudes toward gays and lesbians have become somewhat less negative over the last few decades. Television shows such as *Modern Family, Glee, Game of Thrones,* and *The L Word* suggest that the public is becoming more comfortable with homosexuality. Some corporations, as well as some governmental and nonprofit organizations, extend employee benefits to same-sex couples. In 1973, the American Psychological Association (APA) eliminated homosexuality from its list of mental illnesses and in 1980 dropped it from its *Diagnostic and Statistical Manual* (*DSM;* discussed in Chapter 13). Moreover, based on evidence that gay and lesbian relationships are influenced by the same set of variables that influence heterosexual marriages, the APA passed a resolution declaring it unfair and discriminatory to deny same-sex couples legal access to civil marriage (APA, 2004).

As attitudes become more accepting of homosexuality, societal change is clearly occurring. In 2014, Scotland became only the 17th country to legalize same-sex marriages. The Netherlands, Belgium, Spain, Canada, South Africa, Norway, Sweden, Portugal, Iceland, Argentina, England, Wales, Brazil, Uruguay, New Zealand, France, and portions of Mexico and the United States also allow same-sex marriages ("10 Countries," 2011; Goldsmith, 2014). In the United States, Massachusetts became the first state to legalize same-sex marriage in 2004. And, 10 years later, the federal government has announced that in federal matters, it will afford the same rights to same-sex marriages as it does to opposite-sex marriages (CNN, 2014). Yet, despite the federal government's stance on same-sex marriage, individual states still differ with respect to their acknowledgment of same-sex marriage rights. As of January 2014, 17 states and the District of Columbia have voted to allow same sex-marriages, but same-sex marriage is not allowed in the remaining 33 states of the union (ProCon.org, 2014).

© Kayte M. Deioma/PhotoEdit

Thinkstock/Getty Images

Gays, lesbians, and bisexuals face many prejudices in today's society. Yet their relationships are influenced by the same variables that influence heterosexual relationships.

Although societal change is taking place, **homophobia**, or prejudice against homosexuals, has not disappeared. Gays and lesbians do not have the same legal protection against discrimination as other minority groups in the United States, and gays and lesbians continue to be the victims of hate crimes. In 2012, there were 1,318 hate crime offenses that were based on sexual orientation (FBI, 2012). Approximately 80% of gay, lesbian, and bisexual youth report having experienced verbal abuse (D'Augelli, Grossman, & Starks, 2006; Meyer, 1999). Gay, lesbian, and bisexual adults also report higher levels of domestic abuse, sexual assault, and childhood abuse than heterosexuals (Balsam, Rothblum, & Beauchaine, 2005; Sweet & Welles, 2012).

homophobia prejudicial attitudes against homosexuals and homosexuality

As of 2013, 31 states and the District of Columbia had enacted laws against hate crimes motivated by sexual orientation (National Gay and Lesbian Task Force, 2013). In 2009, President Obama signed into law federal hate crime legislation called the Matthew Shepard and James Byrd Jr. Hate Crimes Prevention Act in honor of Shepard (who was killed because of his sexual orientation) and Byrd (who was killed because of his race).

Many religions condemn homosexual behavior as immoral. It is quite possible to turn on the television to see a preacher warning of the dangers of homosexual sin. Others see homosexuality as a mental illness that should be cured. Some studies do suggest that lesbian, gay, and bisexual persons are more likely to report having mental health problems (Kuyper & Fokkema, 2011; Oswalt & Wyatt, 2011). However, closer analyses reveal that these higher rates of mental health problems are likely related to what is called *minority stress* (Chapter 12), or being forced as a minority member to live an environment where majority members hold negative stereotypes and prejudices against one's group (Kuyper & Fokkema, 2011).

Furthermore, homosexual and heterosexual relationships tend to be similar in some important ways. Homosexuals are just as committed and satisfied in their romantic relationships as heterosexuals (Roisman et al., 2008). And, decades of research show that children of gay and lesbian parents do not differ in adjustment or development when compared to children raised by heterosexual couples (Patterson, 2006).

The negative attitudes that many Americans hold toward gays and lesbians are not shared by all cultures. In fact, many cultures openly accept homosexuality as a natural part of life. One study of 190 societies across the world found that approximately two-thirds of them accepted homosexuality (Ford & Beach, 1951). A historical study of 225 Native American tribes found that more than half of them accepted male homosexuality and 17% accepted female homosexuality (Pomeroy, 1965). Why do some people abhor homosexuality or see it as a mental illness, whereas others see it as a normal variation of human sexuality? Perhaps these differing points of view stem from beliefs about what causes sexual orientation.

WHAT CAUSES ONE'S SEXUAL ORIENTATION?

One common mistake that people make when trying to answer this question is to confuse sexual orientation with gender. *Gender* is the collection of personality traits that your society typically associates with either males or females. Gender is not the same thing as sexual orientation. For instance, a gay male may be very masculine or very feminine. Likewise, a heterosexual woman may be either masculine or feminine. In other words, not all feminine men are gay, and not all masculine women are lesbians.

Having said that, there is some indication in the research that early gender-related behavior may be a predictor of later sexual orientation *for some*. Some studies have shown that gender-nonconforming behavior (masculine behavior in girls, feminine behavior in boys) during childhood is correlated with later homosexuality in both men and women (Rieger, Gygax, & Bailey, 2008). Be careful about how you interpret these findings, though. Not all boys who prefer feminine activities become gay, nor do all girls who prefer masculine activities become lesbian. In fact, in one study, approximately half of the adult gay male participants had a preference for traditionally masculine activities in childhood (Bell, Weinberg, & Hammersmith, 1981). Also, even if some gays and lesbians showed a preference for gender-nonconforming activities in childhood, this does not indicate that the activities made them homosexual. It is just as likely that their homosexuality stemmed from other causes. In fact, in less stereotyped cultures in which children are not pressured to be masculine or feminine, there is less tendency for gay males to have exhibited feminine behavior in childhood (Ross, 1980).

Another reasonable question is to ask whether homosexuality could be encoded in our genes. A genetic link for homosexuality has been investigated in the traditional way—by examining pairs of identical and fraternal twins who are gay. Such studies find a higher *concordance rate* (percentage of pairs in which both twins are homosexual) among identical twins than fraternal twins (Bailey, Dunne, & Martin, 2000; Bailey & Pillard, 1991). A similar pattern has been found for females (Bailey et al., 1993, 2000). Such findings suggest a hereditary component in sexual orientation in some people.

Other investigations have found that gay men have a greater number of older brothers than heterosexual men—a phenomenon called the *fraternal birth order effect* (Blanchard, 2008; G. Schwartz et al., 2010). Discovery of this phenomenon led to development of the *maternal immune hypothesis,* which suggests that some mothers may become increasingly immune to prenatal male hormones as they bear sons. In other words, their bodies may produce more antibodies to male hormones, creating a different prenatal hormonal environment that may affect subsequent male fetuses. Similarly, research has found that homosexuals have a greater chance of being left-handed than heterosexuals, an attribute that is believed to be established prior to birth (Lippa, 2003). Such findings suggest that prenatal factors are related to sexual orientation (Rahman, 2005).

In conclusion, data indicate a strong biological role in sexual orientation. However, as of this moment, no one can say for sure just what causes our sexual orientation. The continuum of sexual orientation is in all likelihood related to the interaction among biological, psychological, and environmental forces that results in different pathways for every person. In any case, the causes of sexual orientation are likely to remain a controversial and emotional issue for some time to come.

Quiz Yourself

5.3

1. **Which is true of animals, but not of humans?**
   a. Testosterone regulates sex drive.
   b. Menstruation follows ovulation.
   c. Mating occurs only during estrus.
   d. Hormones influence sexual behavior.

2. **While dancing with his girlfriend, Malik notices that he has an erection. He is in which stage of the sexual response cycle?**
   a. Excitement
   b. Plateau
   c. Orgasm
   d. Resolution

3. **Paul has been married for 5 years to Lisa. However, he is primarily sexually attracted to men and not to women. What is Paul's sexual orientation?**
   a. Heterosexual
   b. Homosexual
   c. Bisexual
   d. Both a and b

Answers 1. c; 2. a; 3. b

5.4 Theories and Expression of Emotion

If you ask people to define emotion, you will get a variety of answers. Most people will probably say that emotions are *feelings*. Some people will give examples, such as *happiness, sadness,* or *anger,* but few will be able to produce a good definition of what an emotion actually is. Even psychologists have had trouble defining what is meant by an emotion.

One definition is that an **emotion** is a complex reaction to some internal or external event that involves physiological reactions, behavioral reactions, facial expressions, cognition, and affective responses (see Lazarus, 1991). For example, let's imagine that you are walking through the woods and you hear some rustling up ahead. You look up and see a large bear in your path. This event would likely cause an emotional reaction of *fear.* Your experience of fear would have several aspects to it:

- *Physiological reactions*: Your heart rate would increase, your respiration would increase, your pupils would dilate, and your muscles would tense.
- *Behavioral reactions*: You might freeze in your tracks. You might run (an unwise choice in this situation). You might yell at the bear.
- *Facial expressions*: Fear would show on your face. If someone were to observe you at this moment, they would likely recognize that you were afraid.
- *Cognition*: You might think about the TV show you saw on bears last week and what the experts said that you should do in this situation. You might wonder if this is a female bear with cubs just out of sight in the brush. You might think about what you will do if the bear charges.
- *Affective responses*: You would have some subjective reaction to this situation. For example, "I am scared," "I am terrified," or—if you are an animal lover—"I'm thrilled!"

As you can see, emotions are complex. Perhaps that is why psychologists have had a difficult time defining exactly what an emotion is. Another confusing aspect of emotion is that emotion is very similar to motivation. In fact, emotions can produce motivation (e.g., Mega, Ronconi, & De Beni, 2014; Zaalberg, Manstead, & Fischer, 2004). In our previous example, your fear of the bear might motivate you to run or to yell at the bear. So what separates emotions from motivation? What makes fear different from hunger? One unique element is the **affective component of emotion**, the subjective experience of what you are *feeling* that fills your consciousness during the emotion. When you are scared, you *know* that you are scared because you *feel* the affective state of fear. This affective quality of emotion allows us to clearly know when we are feeling an emotion.

Emotions can also be distinguished from motivation in that they are usually (but not always) sparked by things outside our bodies. For instance, when we see a depressing movie, we may feel sad. Or when we see a baby, we may feel happy. Motivation, in contrast, often comes from some internal source—hunger may be initiated by low blood sugar or an empty stomach. Motives tend to be sparked by a specific need or goal, but emotions can be elicited by many stimuli. For instance, many things can make us happy, but only a few conditions will lead to hunger.

Although psychologists have struggled with the concept of emotion, several notable theories of emotion have been set out over the years. Let's take a look at some of them now.

emotion a complex reaction to some internal or external event that involves physiological reactions, behavioral reactions, facial expressions, cognition, and affective responses

affective component of emotion the subjective experience of what you are feeling during the emotion

5.4.1 • The James-Lange Theory of Emotion

James-Lange theory a theory of emotion that defines an emotion as a unique pattern of physiological arousal

American psychologist William James and Danish physiologist Carl Lange each proposed one of the earliest theories of emotion at approximately the same point in history (James, 1884). Their theory, now called the **James-Lange theory** of emotion, states that emotion is *equal* to the pattern of physiological arousal that the person experiences during an emotion. In short, emotion is a physiological response to some stimulus. In our example of meeting the bear in the woods, from the James-Lange point of view, the emotion you feel is the pattern of physical and physiological reactions you have as you see the bear. Your physiological reactions—the increased heart rate, the increased respiration, the running—are the emotion of fear that you would experience in this situation. In the James-Lange view, emotion is a purely physiological event.

Renee Lynn/DLILLC/Corbis

How would you feel if you came across a bear while hiking in the woods?

WALTER CANNON'S CRITICISMS OF THE JAMES-LANGE THEORY

The James-Lange view of emotion has had many critics. One important critic was Walter Cannon, who noted that for the James-Lange theory to adequately explain emotion, there would have to be a *different* bodily response for each emotion we experience. If emotion is simply a physiological and bodily response, the only way to discriminate among emotions would be if there were different physical reactions for each emotion. Cannon doubted that this was true and, in fact, offered three good reasons to doubt the James-Lange view (Cannon, 1927). His first criticism, which we just mentioned, is that the physiological experience of emotion does not appear to vary from emotion to emotion to the degree that would be necessary to distinguish one emotion from another based purely on our physiological reaction. For example, the physiological experience of anger is not very different from that of terror—both involve increased heart rate, muscle tension, and so forth.

Second, Cannon argued that the physiological, bodily aspect of emotion sometimes follows our subjective experience of the emotion. For example, we may know that we are afraid *before* we feel our heart pounding and our muscles tensing. In the James-Lange view, there can be no emotion before there is a physiological response.

Cannon's third criticism was that artificially created physiological responses do not give rise to emotions. For example, drinking a lot of coffee may increase your physiological arousal, but it does not cause you to experience fear, excitement, love, or any other emotion. If emotion were nothing more than a physiological response, it would stand to reason that artificially caused physiological responses would also cause emotional responses.

In light of these criticisms, Cannon proposed that emotion does not originate in the body; rather, it originates in the brain. According to Cannon, when you see a bear in the woods, your fear is not due to the increased heart rate and rapid breathing you experience. Instead, when you see the bear, your brain causes you to feel fear. You may even be aware that you are afraid before you become aware of your rapidly beating heart and your panting breath. Cannon's explanation of emotion was later extended by a man named Philip Bard, and today this theory is called the **Cannon-Bard theory** of emotion.

© Blend Images/Masterfile

According to the James-Lange theory of emotion, this woman is experiencing joy because her body has reacted with a characteristic pattern of physiological changes in response to this event.

NEW SUPPORT FOR THE JAMES-LANGE THEORY

Of Cannon's three criticisms, by far the most problematic was the first one—that physiological responses are too similar to allow us to adequately discriminate among the many emotions we feel. For many years this criticism was seen as a fatal blow to the James-Lange theory. Things change, however, and in the 1990s, some new evidence gave the James-Lange theory new life. By the 1990s, psychologists had new tools for studying bodily reactions. In addition to precisely measuring heart rate, researchers could now measure minute changes in skin temperature and in the electrical conductivity of the skin that indicates small changes in the moisture of the skin. With these measurement techniques, it is now possible to examine the physiological response that accompanies emotions in greater detail than was possible in Cannon's time.

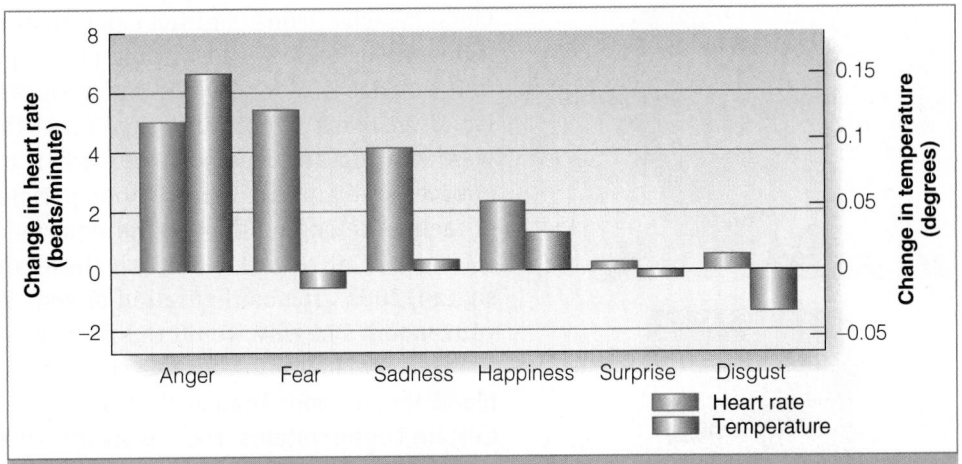

FIGURE 5.11

Physiological Changes for Six Different Emotions

Note the varying degrees of change for these different emotions.

Source: Levenson et al., 1990.

Using measures such as these, researchers have been able to show that some emotions do indeed involve different bodily reactions (for a review, see Kreibig, 2010). In one particularly clever study (Levenson, Ekman, & Friesen, 1990), participants were asked to make facial expressions for the emotions of fear, anger, happiness, disgust, sadness, and surprise and to hold these expressions for 10 seconds. While the participants held these expressions, their physiological reactions were measured very precisely. Just as the James-Lange theory predicts, there were slight but noticeable differences in heart rate, skin temperature, and other physiological reactions for the different emotions. Although all of the emotions caused changes in heart rate and skin temperature, it was the degree of change that separated the emotions from one another (● FIGURE 5.11).

These results indicate that there may be some merit to the James-Lange approach, but they do not necessarily support the entire theory. They do not address Cannon's other two criticisms—that physiological reactions sometimes follow our awareness of emotions and that artificially created arousal does not seem to directly cause the experience of emotion. Even if patterns of physiological arousal do help us discriminate among emotions, other factors may still be involved in the experience of emotion. One of these factors could be feedback from our faces.

5.4.2 • The Facial Feedback Hypothesis

You may have noticed that in the experiment we just described, the researchers induced the different emotions in an unusual way (Levensen et al., 1990): having the participants make and hold facial expressions of the desired emotion for 10 seconds. In other words, they induced the emotional state through the facial expression of the emotion. How does this work? Doesn't the emotion come *before* the facial expression? Well, maybe not entirely, according to the **facial feedback hypothesis** (McIntosh, 1996). This theory proposes that our experience of an emotion is affected by the feedback our brain gets from our

Cannon-Bard theory a theory of emotion that states that emotions originate in the brain, not the body

facial feedback hypothesis a theory that states that our emotional state is affected by the feedback our brain gets from facial muscles

© GoGo Images Corporation/Alamy

Stockbroker/MBI/Alamy

The facial feedback hypothesis maintains that feedback from facial muscles sent to the brain can affect our emotional state. Therefore, these men are experiencing different emotions, in part, because their brains are receiving very different messages from their faces.

facial muscles. Thus, smiling can influence us to feel happy, and frowning can influence us to feel bad. In one study, participants were asked to smell and rate a series of odors while either smiling or frowning. Consistent with the facial feedback hypothesis, they rated the smells more positively when they were smiling and less positively when they were frowning (Kraut, 1982). In another study, participants who experienced involuntary frowning as a result of facing the sun while walking reported increased feelings of aggressiveness (Marzoli et al., 2013). Based on these and other studies (for instance, Soussignan, 2002), the configuration of your facial muscles does seem to influence your mood. But why would this be true?

One possibility is that the configuration of your facial muscles affects the blood flow to your brain, which in turn affects the temperature of your brain. Certain configurations, such as frowns, may change blood flow to the brain in a way that increases the temperature of the brain. Other facial configurations, such as smiles, may result in blood flow changes that decrease the brain's temperature. Brain temperature, in turn, may affect the release of certain neurotransmitters that affect mood. As wild as this sounds, some evidence suggests that it might be true. In one study, one group of participants was asked to read a story that contained words that forced them to repeatedly hold their mouths in a position that was similar to smiling (Zajonc, Murphy, & Inglehart, 1989). The other group of participants was asked to read a story that did not contain such words. Both stories were of similar emotional tone. As the participants read the stories, the temperature of their forehead was measured, providing a crude measure of their brain's internal temperature.

After they had read the stories, the participants were asked to rate the stories for pleasantness. As the facial feedback hypothesis would predict, those who read the story that forced them to use their facial muscles in a manner consistent with a smile rated their story more positively than the other participants rated theirs. Furthermore, when researchers looked at the participants' forehead temperatures, those who read the story that forced them to approximate a smile had lower forehead temperatures. It appears that when we smile, we hold our facial muscles in such a way as to promote blood flow that reduces brain temperature, which somehow improves mood. There may, after all, be something to being a "hothead" or keeping a "cool head"!

5.4.3 • The Schachter-Singer Two-Factor Theory of Emotion

All the theories of emotion we have looked at so far see emotion in primarily physiological terms. Certainly physiological responses and facial expressions are part of an emotional experience—but what about cognition? Do our thoughts play a role in our emotions? Some theorists, including psychologists Stanley Schachter and Jerome Singer, believe that they do. Their **two-factor theory of emotion** states that emotions are a product of both physiological arousal and cognitive interpretations of this arousal. Schachter and Singer agreed with Walter Cannon that we do not have a separate pattern of physiological arousal for each emotion we experience; rather, when we experience an emotion, we experience a nondistinct, general physiological arousal. We then use the situational context to help us cognitively interpret the meaning of this arousal. This cognitive interpretation leads to the experience of an emotion. Going back to our example of the bear in the woods, when we see the bear, we become aroused and our heart begins to beat faster. Next, we interpret why we are reacting this way, given the context of the situation. Because we are faced

two-factor theory of emotion a theory that states that emotions result when we cognitively interpret our physiological reactions in light of the situation with a potentially dangerous wild animal, our arousal is likely to be interpreted as stemming from fear. Therefore, we label our emotional experience as fear.

In one of their studies, Schachter and Singer (1962) gave participants an injection of epinephrine, a stimulant that causes increased heart rate, respiration, and nervousness. Some of the participants were accurately informed about what to expect from the injection. Others were told that the injection was a harmless shot that would produce no symptoms. After receiving the injection, all of the participants were asked to sit in a waiting room with another participant. But the "participants" they were sent to wait with were *confederates*, or actors playing a part in the experiment. In one condition, the confederate acted angry. He complained, stomped his feet, and eventually left the waiting room in a huff. In the other condition, the confederate acted happy. He appeared joyful, tossed paper airplanes, and generally acted a bit silly.

The dependent variable in the experiment was the mood of the participants after their time in the waiting room with the confederate. Schachter and Singer reasoned that the mood of the informed participants would not be influenced by the mood of the confederate. Because the informed participants would interpret their arousal as being due to the drug and not due to some emotional state, there was no reason for their mood to be influenced by the confederate. At the same time, Schachter and Singer predicted that the mood of the uninformed participants would indeed be influenced by the mood of the confederate. Because they did not have a ready (cognitive) explanation for their arousal, the uninformed participants would look to the situation to help them interpret their reactions. If the confederate were happy, the participants would interpret their arousal as part of a positive emotional state. If the confederate were angry, then the participants would interpret their arousal as part of a negative emotional state.

The results confirmed Schachter and Singer's predictions. The mood of the informed participants was not influenced by the confederate's mood, but the confederate did influence the mood of the uninformed participants. The uninformed participants who waited with the angry confederate reported feeling angrier than did the informed participants. The uninformed participants who waited with the happy confederate reported feeling happier than did the informed participants. It appears that the uninformed participants used the situation to help them figure out their own emotions.

Although Schachter and Singer and others (for example, Brown & Curhan, 2013) have produced experimental evidence to support the notion that arousal can affect our emotional states, the two-factor theory has not stood the test of time well. Decades of research on the two-factor theory show that there is little reason to believe that emotions *require* physiological arousal or that emotions necessarily come from labeling unexplained physiological arousal. For example, people who've been given beta-blocking drugs that prevent autonomic nervous system arousal still report experiencing emotions that are relevant to their current environment (Reisenzein, 1983). Despite doubts about the two-factor theory, Schachter and Singer's contribution to the study of emotion is significant. They introduced the idea that cognition plays an important role in emotion, and many theorists recognize that thoughts are part of the emotional experience.

5.4.4 • Lazarus's Cognitive-Mediational Theory of Emotion

According to Richard Lazarus (1995), cognition is the most important part of emotion. Unlike Schachter and Singer, who thought that emotion results from the cognitive interpretation of preexisting physiological arousal, Lazarus's

cognitive-mediational theory a theory of emotion that states that our cognitive appraisal of a situation determines what emotion we will feel in the situation

cognitive-mediational theory of emotion states that our initial *cognitive appraisal* of a situation determines what emotion we will feel in the situation. Going back to the bear example, if you see a bear in the woods one day after having seen a show on TV about some hikers who were killed by a bear, you would likely feel a lot of fear! On the other hand, you might feel less fear on encountering the bear if your only knowledge of bears came from a TV show about a boy and his pet bear. According to cognitive-mediational theory, your appraisal of the situation determines your specific emotion.

Differing appraisals are one reason different people react with different emotions in the same situation (see also, Chapter 12). Cognitive-mediational theory also suggests that the best way to control our emotions is by controlling how we perceive situations in life. For instance, a student who perceives that she received a poor grade because the teacher doesn't like her will likely get angry. A calmer student may simply see the grade as a challenge to work harder and not get mad. Teaching yourself to appraise events like this as opportunities and not as threats may help you become a happier, more successful student.

VARIATIONS: GENDER DIFFERENCES IN EMOTIONAL REGULATION

Even if your initial appraisal of a situation is such that it leads to negative emotions, research shows that we can still regulate our emotions by reappraising the situation in a more positive light. For example, a woman might initially assume that a man bumped into her on purpose, leading her to feel angry. She then quickly reappraises the situation, realizing that he probably bumped into her by accident. This reappraisal is likely to lessen or even eliminate her anger.

Recently, Kateri McRae and colleagues (2008) found that although males and females did not differ with respect to how they reacted emotionally to an event, they did show different patterns of brain activity during reappraisal of these events. As the participants attempted to reduce their negative emotional reactions to upsetting pictures through reappraisal (e.g., by reminding themselves that disturbing scenes were just pictures and not real), activity levels in their prefrontal cortex, amygdala, and ventral striatal (a reward center in the brain) were monitored. Relative to the male participants, the females seemed to engage these parts of the brain more during the reappraisal process (• FIGURE 5.12).

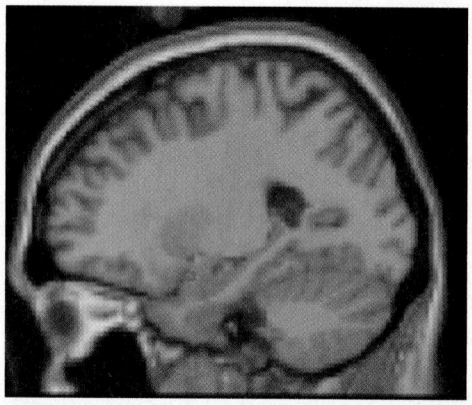

FIGURE 5.12

Gender Differences in Brain Functioning During Cognitive Reappraisal

In this fMRI scan, you can see the left amygdala in red. Relative to male participants, female participants used the amygdala, prefrontal cortex, and ventral striatal more as they attempted to reappraise an emotional situation in order to reduce their negative emotions.

Source: McRae, K., Ochsner, K. N., Mauss, I. B., Gabrieli, J. J. D., & Gross, J. J. (2008). Gender differences in emotion regulation: An fMRI study of cognitive reappraisal. *Group Processes & Intergroup Relations, 11,* 143–162. Reprinted with permission.

The meaning of these brain differences is not yet clear, but McRae and colleagues speculate that relative to women, men may not need to expend as much cognitive effort to control their negative emotions (i.e., less prefrontal and amygdala activity for men). It is also possible that during reappraisal, women must work to initiate positive emotions to help counteract their own negative emotions (i.e., more ventral striatal activity for females). Nonetheless, it is important to note that although male and female participants initiated different brain processes to control their emotion, they were equally able to do so. The stereotype that women are more emotional and less able to control their emotions was not supported in this study (McRae et al., 2008).

IS COGNITION ESSENTIAL TO EMOTION?

Although it is clear that cognitive appraisals do influence our emotional states (see, for instance, vanReekum et al., 2004), not everyone agrees that cognition is an essential part of emotion. Robert Zajonc has argued that we can have an emotional reaction to something that is completely independent of our thoughts. In one study, Zajonc (1980) showed English-speaking participants Japanese ideographs (the symbols of the Japanese language). Each ideograph was presented either frequently or infrequently. Later, the participants were asked to rate their preference for ideographs. Despite having no knowledge about the meaning of the ideographs, the participants showed a clear preference for some of them. They preferred the ideographs that they had seen more frequently to the ones they had seen infrequently. Zajonc called this phenomenon of preferring things to which we have had the most exposure the **mere exposure effect**. He reasoned that because the participants did not know the meaning of the ideographs, their emotional reactions to them could not have been influenced by cognition. Rather, their emotions were purely physiological. We will examine the mere exposure effect again in Chapter 10 when we look at its implications for romantic attraction.

mere exposure effect the idea that the more one is exposed to something, the more one grows to like it

basic emotions a proposed set of innate emotions that are common to all humans and from which other higher-order emotions may derive

5.4.5 • Communicating Emotions: Culture, Gender, and Facial Expressions

Imagine that you have traveled to a place where you do not understand the local language. You do not recognize any of the words being spoken all around you. In fact, you can't even tell how many words there are in each sentence, because they all seem to run together. You are all alone in this place, and you have to survive somehow. How will you communicate with these people? Perhaps you will try to use gestures to communicate with someone, but how will you choose which person? How will you tell if a particular person is likely to react kindly to your attempts at communication? One way would be to read the emotional expression on the person's face. Does she look happy? Does he look angry? This could be a crucial source of information for you. But what about the cultural differences in this situation? Can we read the emotional expressions of someone from an unfamiliar culture? This is another question psychologists have tried to answer.

ENGAGE YOURSELF Before you read any further, look at the pictures in • FIGURE 5.13. Can you identify the emotions that these people are feeling? These pictures represent the facial expressions of what psychologists call basic emotions. **Basic emotions** are defined as emotions that all humans are thought to have, regardless of cultural background. The idea behind basic emotions is that the capacity for these emotions is genetically programmed in us as a result of evolution. Many psychologists believe that *anger*, *happiness*, *fear*, and *sadness* are basic emotions, but there is disagreement about what other emotions might be basic. Some add disgust, shame, interest, surprise, and anxiety to the list (Turner & Ortony, 1992). But others do not. Furthermore, some believe that basic emotions

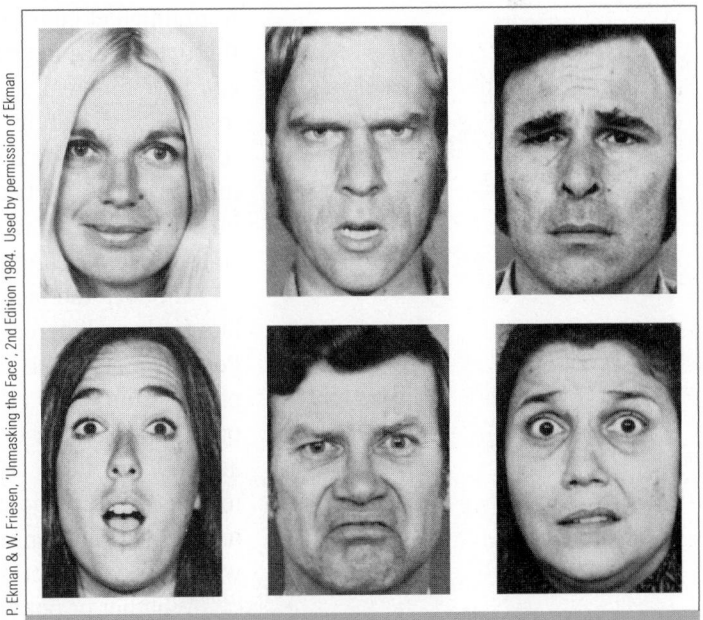

P. Ekman & W. Friesen, 'Unmasking the Face', 2nd Edition 1984. Used by permission of Ekman

FIGURE 5.13

Can You Identify These Emotions?

Source: Ekman and Friesen, 1984.

can blend together to give us more complex emotions like guilt, pride, and disappointment (Plutchik, 1984). So, were you able to accurately identify the facial expressions? From left to right, top to bottom, they are *happiness, anger, sadness, surprise, disgust,* and *fear.*

Paul Ekman (1973) showed pictures like those in Figure 5.13 to people from Argentina, Brazil, Chile, Japan, and the United States and asked participants to identify the emotions being expressed. He found that people were generally able to identify the emotions regardless of their culture, although some emotions appeared to be more universal than others. Happiness appeared to be the easiest emotion to identify (Recio, Schacht, & Sommer, 2013). People from the different cultures disagreed the most when identifying fear and anger. Other studies have shown that fear and surprise are easily confused, but that women are better than men at discriminating between these emotions. Women have also been shown to be better than men at recognizing facial expressions of arrogance, guilt, and jealousy (Simão, Justo, & Martins, 2008). This may be due to women's greater concern for relating to others and a greater tendency for women to look at other people's faces (McAndrew, 1986).

In addition to facial expression, we also seem to be able to discern the basic emotions from the sounds that people make. Recently, Ekman and colleagues found that Western and Namibian participants were both good at detecting basic emotions in each other's nonverbal vocalizations, such as laughs and screams that transcend language barriers (Sauter et al., 2010). Further support for the notion of basic emotions comes from research using neuroimaging technologies to show that specific and distinct patterns of neural activity in the brain are linked to the basic emotions (Duan et al., 2010; Vytal & Hamann, 2010).

display rules cultural rules governing when it is and isn't appropriate to display certain emotions

However, researchers have found that people from different cultures have different **display rules** governing when it is and isn't appropriate to display certain emotions. For example, in the United States, it would be considered inappropriate for a man to display fear or sadness during a business meeting. And if an Arab man is insulted, he must respond with a display of extreme anger to avoid dishonor (see Heine, 2008). People from different cultures may also have slightly different ways of displaying emotions through facial expressions—somewhat similar to how speakers of the same language can have different accents or dialects (Elfenbein et al., 2007). It is also possible that in addition to cultural display rules, we may learn to regulate our emotional reactions themselves so as to avoid the possibility of violating the rules for displaying emotion in our culture (De Leersnyder, Boiger, & Mesquita, 2013). For example, an American businessman may adjust his cognitive appraisal of the events in a business meeting so as to avoid feeling sadness because he feels it is inappropriate.

So, does the fact that at least some emotions (for example, happiness) translate fairly well across cultures guarantee that these emotions are basic emotions? Perhaps not. Some cultures list "basic" emotions that may be recognizable to people from other cultures but would not be considered basic emotions in those other cultures. For example, Hindus list *peace, wonder, amusement,* and *heroism* as basic emotions (Hejmadi, Davidson, & Rozin, 2000). Americans may be able to feel these emotions and recognize them in others, but may not consider them to be basic emotions. For reasons like these, some people have begun to question whether basic emotions truly exist (Ortony & Turner, 1990).

Whether or not we humans have basic emotions is an open question. An even more open question is: If we do have basic emotions, what are they? Regardless of whether basic emotions exist, emotions are powerful tools of communication. A smile can signal friendliness to many people—regardless of background or culture.

5.4

Quiz Yourself

1. Which of the following is not typically thought of as a basic emotion?
   a. Fear
   b. Sadness
   c. Pride
   d. Happiness
2. Derrick and Monique each went out on blind dates. Derrick took his date to dinner. Monique took her date to a football game. According to the two-factor theory of emotion, who is more likely to go out on a second date with his or her partner?
   a. Derrick
   b. Monique
   c. Monique and Derrick are equally likely to go out on a second date.
   d. Two-factor theory makes no predictions about this situation.
3. Mohammed and Betty are each stuck in a traffic jam. Mohammed remains calm, but Betty begins to get very angry. Which theory of emotion best explains Mohammed's and Betty's different emotions in this situation?
   a. Cognitive-mediational theory
   b. Two-factor theory
   c. Facial feedback theory
   d. James-Lange theory

Answers 1. c; 2. b; 3. a

5.5 Integrating Psychology: The Big Picture

When Jean-Dominque Bauby had his stroke, the loss of portions of his brainstem left him in a permanent state of locked-in syndrome. For the remainder of his life, he was unable to voluntarily move most of his body. The only part of his body that was still under his conscious control was his left eyelid, which he could blink at will. A relatively small disruption in Bauby's biological functioning had profound effects on his ability to function, changing the course of his development for the remainder of his life.

But not all of Bauby's abilities were devastated by the stroke. His ability to sense and perceive the world was left primarily intact. His conscious mind was untouched, leaving him able to process information in a normal fashion. Through blinking, he could still use language to maintain social relationships with those around him. As for many of us, social interaction was important to Bauby for he still felt emotions and he still had needs. Like most of us, Bauby felt normal emotions, including fear, sadness, love, and happiness. He also experienced normal human motivations, including hunger, sexual desire, and the need to achieve. The desire to express himself and connect with others provided Bauby with the intrinsic motivation to blink the some 250,000 times needed to write *The Diving Bell and the Butterfly.* Writing a bestselling book is a rare achievement—even for a healthy person—but then again, Bauby was a remarkable man. Where many of us would give up, Bauby was still motivated to live life to its fullest.

Bauby's story shows the crucial role that our biology plays in our ability to function in everyday life. The biological functioning of the nervous and endocrine systems underlies our ability to sense and perceive our conscious awareness, and our motivational and emotional processes. All aspects of our mental processes and behavior are affected by our biology.

In our next section, we will turn our attention to the *cognitive* dimension of psychology—the mental processes that guide our behavior and allow us to function in the world. Like our biology, our cognitive processes can have profound effects on our ability to function. In Chapter 6, we will examine how we learn. In Chapter 7, we will examine how we process information in the memory systems of our minds. And in Chapter 8, we will examine the cognitive processes that underlie our daily functioning, including the language we use to communicate with one another and the intelligence that allows us to solve the problems we face in life. As you read these chapters, keep in mind the story of Jean-Dominique Bauby and recall how your own biological processes make everything you do possible.

Studying the Chapter

Key Terms

affective component of emotion (205)
anorexia nervosa (191)
basal metabolic rate (188)
basic emotion (211)
binge eating disorder (193)
bisexual (201)
bulimia nervosa (191)
Cannon-Bard theory (206)
cholecystokinin (CCK) (182)
cognitive-mediational theory (210)
display rules (212)
drive (174)
drive reduction theory (174)
emotion (205)
erogenous zones (197)
estrogens (195)
estrus (195)
excitement phase (197)
extrinsic motivation (177)
facial feedback hypothesis (207)
ghrelin (181)
glucose (181)
glycogen (181)
heterosexual (201)
hierarchy of needs (178)
homeostasis (175)
homophobia (203)
homosexual (201)
incentive (177)
instinct (174)
insulin (182)
intrinsic motivation (177)
James-Lange theory (206)
lateral hypothalamus (LH) (183)
leptin (182)
libido (195)
mere exposure effect (211)
motive (174)
negative feedback loop (175)
neuropeptide Y (183)
obesity (186)
orgasm phase (197)
ovaries (196)
overweight (186)
plateau phase (197)
primary drive (175)
refractory period (198)
resolution phase (198)
secondary drive (176)
self-determination theory (177)
set point (180)
sexual arousal (195)
sexual desire (195)
sexual orientation (200)
testes (196)
testosterone (196)
two-factor theory of emotion (208)
ventromedial hypothalamus (VMH) (183)

What Do You Know? Assess Your Understanding

Test your retention and understanding of the material by answering the following questions.

1. According to William James, motives are best characterized as _____.

a. drives
b. instincts
c. desires
d. needs

2. Which of the following is most likely to be a primary drive?

a. Feeling sleepy and wanting to go to bed
b. Longing to be loved by others
c. Wanting a good job
d. Need for achievement

3. Most of us perform best at a _____ level of arousal.

a. low
b. moderate
c. high
d. very high

4. Which of the following is an example of a negative feedback loop?

a. Scratching a mosquito bite, making it itch more
b. Sexual arousal, leading one to desire more stimulation
c. Eating when your blood sugar is low
d. All of the above

5. Which of the following is an example of intrinsic motivation?

   a. Studying hard because you want to feel proud of your test performance
   b. Going to work to earn a paycheck
   c. Wanting to look good to impress your significant other
   d. Being nice to your grandmother in hopes that she will loan you some money

6. According to Abraham Maslow, which of the following is the highest level of motivation we experience?

   a. Belongingness
   b. Safety needs
   c. Aesthetic needs
   d. Physiological needs

7. A person with a high level of CCK in his or her bloodstream would likely _____.

   a. feel intense hunger
   b. have just finished a large meal
   c. also have a large amount of ghrelin in his/her bloodstream
   d. be on the brink of starvation

8. If you injected a hungry rat with ghrelin, what would likely happen?

   a. The rat would become even hungrier.
   b. The rat would stop eating immediately.
   c. The rat would stop eating only if it had already ingested sufficient food.
   d. The rat would slow down its eating, but it would continue to eat.

9. Damage to which area of the brain would most likely result in anorexic behavior in a rat?

   a. The ventromedial hypothalamus (VMH)
   b. The lateral hypothalamus (LH)
   c. The thalamus
   d. The hippocampus

10. Being obese is defined as _____.

   a. being at least 20 pounds overweight
   b. having a BMI of at least 30
   c. being at least 100 pounds overweight
   d. having a BMI of at least 50

11. Belinda often binges by eating large quantities of food. After these binges, she feels bad about herself but does little to change her eating behavior. As a result of these binges, Belinda is overweight. Belinda most closely meets the criteria for which eating disorder?

   a. Anorexia nervosa
   b. Bulimia nervosa
   c. Binge eating disorder
   d. Obesity

12. For men, which of the following is not correlated with having a homosexual orientation?

   a. Being Native American
   b. Being the youngest of four brothers
   c. Being left handed
   d. All of the above are correlated with homosexuality in men.

13. When a female mammal is receptive to sexual intercourse, she is said to be in _____.

   a. estrus
   b. resolution
   c. the refractory period
   d. the plateau phase

14. In humans, sexual desire is *not* influenced by which of the following chemicals?

   a. Testosterone
   b. Oxytocin
   c. Dopamine
   d. Acetylcholine

15. Male and female sexual response cycles differ most significantly in which stage?

   a. Excitement phase
   b. Orgasm phase
   c. Plateau phase
   d. Resolution phase

16. Sabrina is married with two kids. What do we know about Sabrina's sexual orientation?

   a. She's homosexual.
   b. She's bisexual.
   c. She's heterosexual.
   d. We cannot tell from this information.

17. Which theory of emotion best explains why one student panics before an exam and another remains calm?

   a. James-Lange theory of emotion
   b. Cannon-Bard theory of emotion
   c. Cognitive-mediational theory
   d. Two-factor theory

18. Which theory of emotion best explains why someone would feel more sexual attraction to his or her partner while at a concert than with the same partner in a library?
    a. James-Lange theory of emotion
    b. Cannon-Bard theory of emotion
    c. Cognitive-mediational theory
    d. Two-factor theory

19. Which of the following theories of emotion defines emotion as a pattern of physiological response in the body?
    a. James-Lange theory of emotion
    b. Cannon-Bard theory of emotion
    c. Cognitive-mediational theory
    d. Two-factor theory

20. Which of the following is a basic emotion?
    a. Guilt
    b. Pride
    c. Disappointment
    d. Sadness

Answers: 1. b; 2. a; 3. b; 4. c; 5. a; 6. c; 7. b; 8. a; 9. b; 10. b; 11. c; 12. a; 13. a; 14. d; 15. d; 16. d; 17. c; 18. d; 19. a; 20. d.

Use It or Lose It: Applying Psychology

1. Assume that you are a scientist who is trying to develop a new appetite suppressant pill for weight loss. Given your understanding of hunger, what kind of an effect would you want your pill to have on a person's body?
2. What would life be like if humans did not have the capacity for emotion?
3. Sabina was cut off in traffic on the way home from work, nearly causing her to have a serious accident. Immediately on arriving home, Sabina finds that her husband has left a dirty towel on the bathroom floor, something Sabina dislikes. What predictions would Schachter and Singer make about Sabina's emotional reaction to finding the dirty towel? Explain.
4. Pretend that you are in charge of developing a campaign to prevent eating disorders in teenage girls. What type of campaign would you develop?

Critical Thinking for Integration

1. How can the theory of natural selection (Chapter 8) explain destructive behaviors such as eating disorders and drug abuse?
2. Given your understanding of physiology (Chapter 2), what impact do you think emotion has on our health?
3. How might learning theories (Chapter 6) be used to design a therapy aimed at helping people overcome obesity?
4. How might theories of motivation and emotion help explain romantic attraction (Chapter 10)?

© Kzenon/Shutterstock.com

Are You Getting the Big Picture? Motivation and Emotion

A motive is the tendency to desire and seek out positive incentives and rewards and to avoid negative outcomes.

5.1 Theories of Motivation

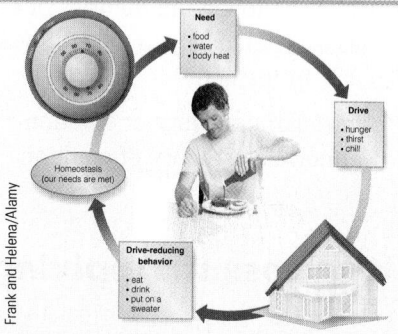

Frank and Helena/Alamy

- William James believed that motives tend to be inborn **instincts**.
- According to the **drive reduction theory**, **primary drives** maintain **homeostasis**.
- **Arousal theories** of motivation suggest that each of us has an optimal level of arousal.
- According to **self-determination theory**, as we pursue the fulfillment of basic needs, we are motivated by both **intrinsic** and **extrinsic motives**.
- Abraham Maslow proposed a **hierarchy of needs** in which some needs take priority over others.

5.2 Hunger and Eating

- Receptors in the stomach monitor the intake of food and contractions of the stomach, and signal the brain when to make us hungry or to shut off hunger.
- Liver cells, hormones, fat cells, and glucoreceptors in the hypothalamus all play a role in signaling hunger or shutting it off.
- External cues such as advertisements and the sight or smell of food can also trigger hunger.
- **Obesity** can be caused by biological factors, such as a slow metabolism and a number of behavioral factors, including a poor diet, excessive food intake, and emotional eating.
- **Bulimia nervosa** involves bingeing on food followed by purging or drastic reduction in caloric intake to rid the body of the extra calories.
- **Anorexia nervosa** is a serious eating disorder that involves extreme concern about gaining weight and reduction in caloric intake that leads to drastic weight loss.
- **Binge eating disorder** involves bingeing on food without compensatory measures to rid the body of extra calories.

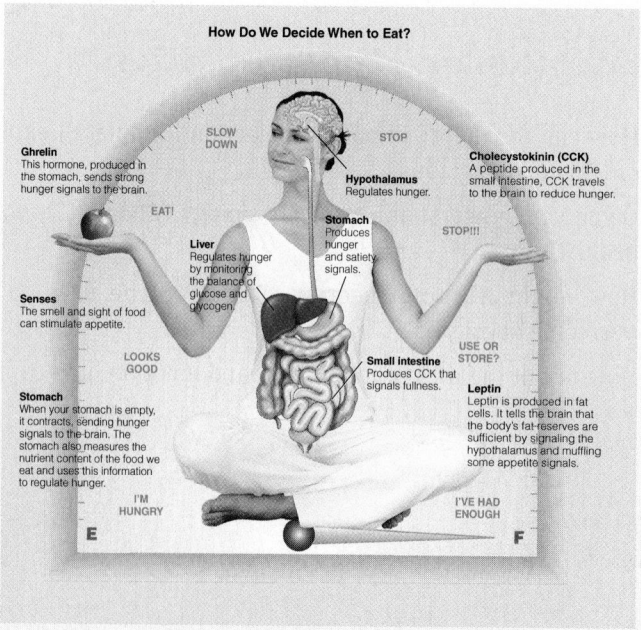

Photo: ImageDJ/Alamy

5.3 Sexual Motivation

I love images/seniors/Alamy

- **Sexual desire** is influenced by neurotransmitters, hormones, sensory cues, and cultural attitudes about what is sexually appealing.
- Masters and Johnson's research examined the physiological changes that men and women undergo during sexual activity. Their results indicate that the sexual response cycle involves **excitement**, **plateau**, **orgasm**, and **resolution phases**.
- **Sexual orientation** is not just a matter of whether you have sex with men or women. Surveys show that some people may have some same-sex encounters but not consider themselves gay or lesbian.
- Sexual orientation falls along a continuum from **heterosexual** (attracted to the other sex) to **bisexual** (attracted to both sexes) to **homosexual** (attracted to the same sex).
- **Homophobia**, prejudice against homosexuals and bisexuals, is still a big problem in some cultures, including the United States.

5.4 Theories and Expression of Emotion

© GoGo Images Corporation/Alamy

- Components of **emotion** include physiological reactions, behavioral reactions, facial expressions, cognition, and **affective** response.
- The **James-Lange theory** of emotion proposes that emotion can be understood as a physiological response to some stimulus.
- The **Cannon-Bard theory** of emotion holds that emotion is the brain responding to some stimulus or situation, then prompting an emotional reaction.
- In the **facial feedback hypothesis**, the experience of an emotion is affected by the feedback the brain receives from muscles in the face. Thus, smiling can influence us to feel happy, and frowning can influence us to feel bad.
- The Schachter-Singer **two-factor theory of emotion** states that emotions are a product of both physiological arousal and cognitive interpretations of this arousal.
- **Cognitive-meditational theory** states that our cognitive appraisal of a situation determines what emotion we will feel in the situation; thus, different people react with different emotions in the same situation.
- **Basic emotions**, including happiness, sadness, anger, and fear, have been found to be present across cultures.
- **Display rules** determine the appropriate expression of emotion in a culture.

Part 2
Foundations in Cognitive Psychology

THE BIG PICTURE **The Power of the Mind**

In previous sections, we covered the scientific foundation of psychology and the biological systems that influence our mental processes and behavior. By now, we hope that you have developed an appreciation for the complexity and importance of our biological systems, especially our remarkable brains. Many psychologists compare the brain and the mental processes of the mind to a computer (the brain) running a software program (the mind).

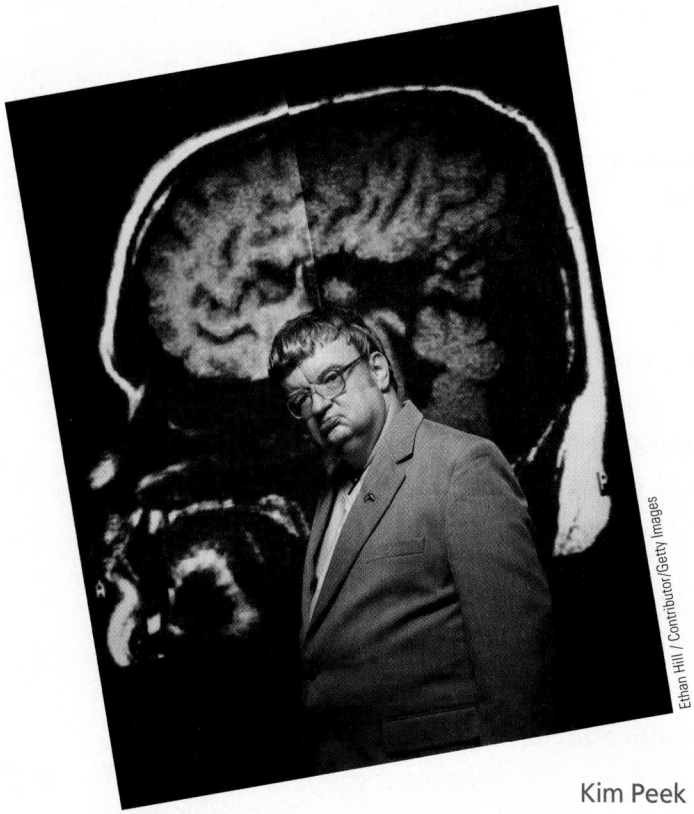

Ethan Hill / Contributor/Getty Images

Kim Peek

Like a computer, we process, store, and retrieve countless bits of information as we go about our days learning, thinking, speaking, solving problems, and so on. Collectively, these mental processes of the mind are referred to as **cognition** or the ways in which we store and use information. We engage in some form of cognition virtually every moment of our day. We store new information as we learn new concepts and behaviors. We use information that we have previously stored when solving problems in our lives. We use stored knowledge in the form of language to communicate with others. Cognition underlies much of our behavior, making an understanding of cognition an essential second foundation of the field of psychology.

As we explore cognitive psychology in this section, we will examine what decades of scientific research have taught us about cognition and its influence on our behavior. Chapter 6 describes how our experiences lead to **learning** that then affects our behavior. In Chapter 7, we will look at **memory**, the storage, processing, and retrieval of information in the mind. And, in Chapter 8, we examine the role cognition, **language**, and **intelligence** play in our daily lives. Cognitive abilities such as these play a critical role in our ability to function in life. Well-developed cognitive abilities may pave the way for success in life, whereas cognitive inabilities may make it difficult to meet some of life's challenges. Both of these situations are illustrated in our case study for this section.

Our case study for Part II tells the story of a remarkable man, Kim Peek, the real-life "Rain Man" portrayed by Dustin Hoffman in the Oscar-winning movie of that name. As you read Kim's story, think about your own cognitive processes. How do your cognitive abilities (and inabilities) measure up to his? Would you like to have Kim's cognitive abilities? Why or why not?

Kim, who passed away in December 2009 from a heart attack, was different from the moment of his birth. His head was 30% larger than normal. He did not respond normally to stimulation. His eyes moved independently of one another, and he had a large blister-like growth across the back of his head that doctors could not identify.

At age 3, the growth on Kim's head suddenly began to relocate, growing into the back of his skull, and exploding the right half of his cerebellum into many separate pieces. Later it was discovered that Kim had no corpus callosum and that the two hemispheres of his brain were fused into one large mass (see Chapter 2).

In This Part:

CHAPTER 6 **Learning**

CHAPTER 7 **Memory**

CHAPTER 8 **Cognition, Language, and Intelligence**

Despite these brain abnormalities, Kim excelled at certain aspects of memory. At age 6, Kim was memorizing parts of encyclopedias, and his ability to memorize information continued to become more impressive as he aged. By adulthood, he exhibited extraordinary mental abilities in more than a dozen topic areas. Kim spent most of his time voraciously reading—phone books, maps, history books, album covers—all with near total recall. In fact, he could simultaneously read two passages at the same time—one with his left eye and one with his right eye! If you told Kim your date of birth, he could *immediately* tell you the day of the week you were born on and the year and date when you could retire at age 65. If you told him your hometown, he could tell you your ZIP code, telephone prefix, and most likely the history of your town. He could also hum almost any piece of music on demand and do mental mathematics at an astounding level. These mathematical skills allowed Kim to do the payroll for a nonprofit organization without the use of a calculator or computer. He did all the calculations in his head! It appeared that Kim's mind was able to store and process factual information with the same efficiency as a personal computer. In fact, in tribute to his son's amazing talents, Kim's father affectionately nicknamed Kim the *Kimputer.*

Yet, Kim's genius did not extend to all types of cognitive functioning. He had extreme difficulty with certain types of learning. In particular, Kim found it impossible to learn many motor skills, most likely because of his damaged cerebellum. Despite the fact that his father showed him how to do many personal tasks on a daily basis, Kim never learned to brush his teeth or dress without assistance. By age 14, Kim completed his high school requirements at home, but he couldn't attend public school because of his extreme hyperactivity. Kim's mind constantly jumped from idea to idea, and he could not concentrate on one task at a time. He was quite poor at cognitive tasks that involve analytical reasoning or conceptual thought. For example, he could memorize a history book, but had difficulty discussing the meaning of "democracy." Kim's score on traditional intelligence tests was approximately 74, in the range that indicates intellectual disability. On tests that only measure knowledge, he scored around 175—*way* above average.

For unknown reasons, Kim's damaged brain seemed to give him the amazing ability to process massive amounts of factual information. The price for this ability seemed to be that Kim's mind was constantly besieged by its own mental connections. His mind wandered along a meandering sequence of related facts, exhausting Kim's cognitive resources and leaving him with little capacity for higher-order cognitive processes (e.g., reasoning and problem solving).

So, think about it once again. Which would you value more—the ability to memorize every word of this textbook, or the ability to understand and apply the knowledge it contains? We would certainly choose the latter. While it's true that most of us have to put much more effort into our memory than Kim did, most of us are self-sufficient in our daily tasks, and most of us are able to use reason to tackle life's challenges.

Kim's story is one of remarkable contrasts in cognition. On the one hand, he excelled at learning some tasks; on the other hand, he was also unable to learn how to execute some important skills involved in daily living. His ability to memorize information was phenomenal, yet he could not use the information he stored in memory in novel ways. In short, Kim's unusual cognitive abilities could be viewed as both a sign of genius-level intelligence or a sign of cognitive disability.

Whereas Kim was a study in the extremes of human behavior, most of us exhibit cognitive abilities that fall squarely between these extremes. In the next section, we will examine what psychologists have discovered about the cognitive abilities of the average person. As you read the chapters in this section, you will gain a deeper understanding of how you learn; how you process information in memory; and how you use stored knowledge to reason, solve problems, communicate, and, in general, exhibit intelligence in daily life. As you are on this journey, think about Kim and think about your own abilities. How might gaining insight into how your own mind works help you to better achieve your goals in life? We hope that as you learn about cognition in the coming chapters, you'll come to better appreciate the power of your mind and find ways to apply what you are learning to the improvement of your own cognitive abilities.

Kim Peek was the remarkable man who inspired the character of the Rain Man in the Oscar-winning movie of the same name.

Learning

Learning Objectives

6.1 Define learning. (APA 1.1, 1.2)

6.1 Define and give examples of orienting reflexes, habituation, and dishabituation. (APA 1.1, 1.2, 1.3)

6.2 Describe Pavlov's studies of classical conditioning. (APA 1.1, 1.2, 2.1)

6.2 Define classical conditioning and describe the factors that affect it. (APA 1.1, 1.2)

6.2 Explain how classical conditioning occurs in humans. (APA 1.1, 1.2, 1.3)

6.2 Describe the process through which classically conditioned responses are removed. (APA 1.1, 1.2, 1.3)

6.2 Describe how classical conditioning can be used to help people (APA 1.3, 3.1)

6.3 Explain Thorndike's law of effect and the experiments that led to its discovery. (APA 1.1, 1.2, 1.3, 2.1)

6.3 Describe the contributions that B. F. Skinner made to the study of operant conditioning. (APA 1.1, 1.2, 2.1)

6.3 Describe the phases of operant conditioning, including acquisition and extinction. (APA 1.1, 1.2)

6.3 Describe the factors that affect the process of operant conditioning, including schedules of reinforcement. (APA 1.1, 1.2)

6.3 Describe discrimination, generalization, and shaping as they relate to operant conditioning. (APA 1.1, 1.2)

6.3 Describe the decisions that must be made when applying operant conditioning in the real world. (APA 1.1, 1.2, 1.3, 3.1)

6.3 Describe the evidence supporting the idea that cognition plays an important role in learning. (APA 1.1, 1.2, 2.1)

6.4 Describe Albert Bandura's Bobo doll experiments and their implications for real-world behavior. (APA 1.1, 1.2, 1.3, 2.1, 3.1)

6.4 Describe the process of observational learning and the role that cognition plays in observational learning. (APA 1.1, 1.2)

Kim Peek's story at the beginning of Part II illustrates the extremes of human learning abilities. On the one hand, Kim could learn factual information with a genius-like ease. On the other hand, he found learning simple tasks such as brushing his teeth to be impossibly difficult. Most of us find that our ability to learn falls somewhere in between these extremes of genius and disability. In this chapter, we will explore the learning processes that mold and shape our behavior. Then in Chapter 7, we will examine the ways in which we learn through the processing of information in memory.

6

Ariel Skelley/Blend Images/Getty Images

Chapter Outline

6.1 Learning from the First Days of Life: Habituation / 226

6.2 Classical Conditioning: Learning Through the Association of Stimuli / 229

PSYCHOLOGY APPLIES TO YOUR WORLD: Using Taste Aversion to Help People / 239

6.3 Operant Conditioning: Learning from the Consequences of Our Actions / 241

6.4 Observational Learning or Modeling: Learning by Watching Others / 258

6.5 Integrating Psychology: The Big Picture / 262

6.1 Learning from the First Days of Life: Habituation

learning a relatively permanent change in behavior, or behavior potential, as a result of experience

orienting reflex the tendency of an organism to orient its senses toward unexpected stimuli

Let's begin by taking a formal look at what learning is. **Learning** can be defined as a relatively permanent change in behavior, or the potential for behavior, that results from experience. Learning results from many experiences in life. We learn concepts and skills in school. We learn from watching others. And we learn certain skills, like riding a bike, by doing them. Learning may show up in our behavior (as when we ride a bike), or it may not (as when we get a speeding ticket even though we've learned that speeding is wrong). Learning may stay with us for years (as with riding a bike), or it may only linger for a while (as when we observe the speed limit for only a few weeks after getting a ticket). Either way, learning is one of life's most important activities. In this chapter, we will look at four common types of learning, beginning with what is widely thought to be the simplest form of learning—*habituation*.

6.1.1 • Paying Attention and Learning to Ignore: Orienting Reflexes and Habituation

Suppose you are sitting in class, listening to your psychology professor and taking notes. All of a sudden there is a loud banging noise directly outside your classroom. What would your very first reaction to the unexpected noise be? If you are like most people, you would immediately stop listening to the lecture and turn your head in the direction of the noise. This very normal response is called an **orienting reflex** (Pavlov, 1927/1960). Orienting reflexes occur when we stop what we are doing to orient our sense organs in the direction of unexpected stimuli.

In our example, the stimulus was auditory, but this doesn't have to be the case. If you were standing in line to buy coffee and someone poked you in the back, you would most likely turn to see what the person wanted. If you were having dinner in a restaurant and someone started taking pictures using a flash camera, you would likely look in the direction of the flashes of light. In short, we exhibit the orienting reflex to any type of novel stimulus.

ENGAGE YOURSELF! Your course syllabus probably contains some admonishment about coming to class on time. Here's one reason why: Notice what happens to you and your classmates the next time a student comes in late to class. Does everyone automatically look toward the door as the student comes through it? This is also an orienting reflex—one that distracts from your ability to learn the course material. Orienting reflexes are part of everyday life. To see how common they are, tomorrow as you go about your daily routine, record as many examples of orienting reflexes in yourself (or others) as you can. Keep in mind that orienting reflexes can occur in response to any unexpected sight, sound, touch, smell, or even taste.

© Bill Aron/PhotoEdit

Why do you think we exhibit orienting reflexes? What is the benefit of automatically paying attention to novel stimuli? If you said "self-protection," you are correct. Orienting reflexes allow us to quickly gather information about stimuli that could potentially be threatening. For instance, that banging noise in the hallway could be a student dropping her books, or it could be a fight. In the case of a fight, you may want to take steps to ensure that the fight doesn't affect you in a negative way. Recall from Chapter 2 that the sympathetic branch of our nervous system is behind the *fight or flight response* that helps us survive in dangerous situations. If we perceive danger, our sympathetic system will be engaged. By orienting your senses toward the event, you can quickly assess what, if any, action is needed to protect yourself.

© Arclight/Alamy

After people live in these houses for a while, habituation will ensure that they barely even notice the sounds of jets like this one as they take off and land.

The benefit of having orienting reflexes is limited, though. Suppose that after looking up at the sound of the banging, you see that it is only a worker hammering as he installs a new bulletin board in the hallway. You would likely return your attention to the psychology lecture. If the banging noise continues, your tendency to look up at the noise in the hall would steadily decrease. In other words, your orienting reflex would diminish over time. This decrease in responding to a stimulus as it is repeated over and over is called **habituation**.

habituation [huh-bit-chew-AYE-shun]
the tendency of an organism to ignore repeated stimuli

Despite its name, habituation does not refer to forming a habit. Instead, habituation ensures that we do not waste our energy and mental resources by responding to irrelevant stimuli. In our previous example, after you have established that the noise in the hallway is not threatening, there is no reason to keep looking. If you did keep exhibiting the orienting reflex, you would needlessly miss part of your psychology lecture and waste energy that could be spent more usefully.

Almost all creatures, including those with very simple nervous systems, seem to have the capacity for habituation (Harris, 1943). This universality implies that habituation is the simplest type of learning seen in living things (Davis & Egger, 1992). Habituation can be seen in newborn infants (Lavoie & Desrochers, 2002; Rose, 1980) and even in fetuses (Van Heteren et al., 2000). Recent studies have suggested that the cerebellum, which is part of the more primitive hindbrain (see Chapter 2), plays a role in certain instances of habituation (Frings et al., 2006). These findings seem to indicate the primitive nature of habituation.

6.1.2 • Possible Benefits of Habituation: Protecting the Brain

To get a better feel for the value of habituation, imagine what life would be like if you could not habituate. Without habituation, you would reflexively respond to every sight, sound, touch, taste, and smell you encountered every time you encountered it. You would not be able to ignore these stimuli. Think of how this would limit your ability to function. Every time the worker hammered the bulletin board in the hall, your attention would move away from the lecture and toward the hall. You certainly would not learn much psychology under these circumstances! With habituation, you get the best of both worlds. You can respond to novel stimuli that may pose a danger, and you can also ignore stimuli that have been checked out and deemed to be harmless. Habituation gives you flexibility in that you don't have to continue to respond to a stimulus.

Itani/Alamy

Some researchers have suggested that migraines may result from the inability to sufficiently habituate to environmental stimuli, leading to overstimulation of the brain and migraine symptoms.

Habituation may also serve to protect our brains from overstimulation. Many people experience intense headaches called *migraines*. These debilitating headaches are frequently characterized by severe pain on one side of the head and can be associated with sensitivity to light, nausea, or vomiting. Some migraine sufferers also experience visual disturbances, called auras, which signal the impending onset of a migraine. In searching for the causes of migraines, researchers have uncovered some interesting information. First, having a specific genetic marker called the MTHFR C677T is correlated with a higher likelihood of having migraines, especially migraines with auras. This genetic marker is also associated with having higher levels of a chemical called homocysteine in the body (see de Tommaso et al., 2007). Second, researchers have discovered that migraine sufferers often appear to have a lessened ability to habituate to stimuli, perhaps at a neuronal level (Restuccia et al., 2013; Reyngoudt et al., 2011). For example, migraine sufferers showed less ability than non–migraine sufferers to habituate to a stressful sound (Huber, Henrich, & Gündel, 2005). This suggests that migraine suffers may have less ability to tune out stressful stimuli, which may lead to hyperactivity in the brain that results in migraine pain. In fact, when migraine sufferers are taught to increase their levels of habituation to environmental stimuli, they tend to experience fewer migraine attacks (see Kropp, Siniatchkin, & Gerber, 2002). Studies like these suggest that one function of habituation may be to protect our nervous system from sensory overload.

6.1.3 • Dishabituation

dishabituation [DIS-huh-bit-chew-AYE-shun] re-responding to a stimulus to which one has been habituated

Habituation may protect us from unwanted stimulation, but a permanent state of habituation would not likely be in our best interest. Imagine never again being able to attend to the sounds around you after having habituated so that you could study. Thankfully, you don't have to worry. We have the flexibility to stop habituating when the circumstances warrant it. **Dishabituation** occurs when an organism begins to respond more intensely to a stimulus to which it has previously habituated. Let's return to our example of the worker in the hallway. Although you find the hammering distracting at first, you soon habituate to the sound. Then, after several minutes of ignoring the steady hammering, you hear a new sound. The worker has turned on a radio at a rather high volume. Will you ignore this sound, too? No, you likely will not. Because the quality of the stimulus has changed dramatically, you will dishabituate. You will again find yourself orienting toward the hallway. This new sound is too dissimilar to the hammering, and you have to check it out. Once you recognize that it is the worker's radio (and that it poses no threat), you will likely habituate to this new sound as well as to the hammering.

A change in the quality of the stimulus is not the only thing that can cause dishabituation. So can the passage of time. For instance, if the worker took an hour-long lunch break and then went back to hammering, you might briefly dishabituate to the hammering. This would not last long, however—after just a few bangs of the hammer, you would reenter habituation and return your attention to the lecture. As you can see, adaptive functioning is a balance of responding—habituating and dishabituating at the appropriate time.

6.1.4 • Practical Applications of Habituation

One practical application of habituation is the use of habituation training for people who experience chronic motion sickness, or vertigo. For some vertigo sufferers, simple tasks like working at a computer may be impossible. Physical therapists often use habituation techniques to help people overcome chronic motion sickness. By repeatedly exposing clients to the stimulation that produces motion sickness, the therapist can gradually train these clients to habituate, or stop responding, to some of the visual and vestibular signals that would normally cause them to feel sick (Childs, 2011; Walak, et al., 2013; Yardley & Kirby, 2006). Similar techniques have been used to train figure skaters (Tanguy et al., 2008), pilots, and astronauts to do their jobs without experiencing motion sickness (Bagshaw, 1985).

Habituation is quite important to everyday life, but it is still a very simple type of learning. Habituation does not explain the bulk of the learning that we engage in during our lifetime, such as learning to play tennis or ride a bike. Nor does habituation explain how we come to associate certain emotions and physiological reactions with certain stimuli, such as learning to fear snakes or feeling happy when we smell Grandma's perfume. For explanations of these more complex events, we will have to turn our attention to more sophisticated and complex types of learning, discussed in the next section.

Quiz Yourself 6.1

1. **Which of the following is an example of habituation?**
   a. Juan was teasing the family dog when it bit him. Because of the pain of the bite, Juan learned not to tease the dog again.
   b. Teresa was trying to learn to knit. At first, she had to consciously think about what she was doing, but after practicing for 3 hours, Teresa could knit without thinking about it.
   c. Janel just bought a new puppy. At first, the dog's barking was distracting to Janel as she tried to watch TV, but after a while Janel did not notice the puppy's barking.
   d. Kerry loved her boyfriend very much. Now that they have broken up, every time she hears his favorite song on the radio, Kerry starts to cry.

2. **Fido the puppy tilts his head up and sniffs the air as he smells his owner cooking dinner in the kitchen. Fido is exhibiting _____.**
   a. habituation
   b. dishabituation
   c. an orienting reflex
   d. a & c

3. **Which of the following would likely have the capacity for habituation?**
   a. A 3-month-old human baby
   b. An adult monkey
   c. An adult dog
   d. All of the above

Answers 1. c; 2. c; 3. d

6.2 Classical Conditioning: Learning Through the Association of Stimuli

The discovery of classical conditioning was something of an accident. Around the turn of the 20th century, a Russian physiologist named Ivan Pavlov (1849–1936) was doing research on the digestive processes of dogs (for which he would eventually win a Nobel Prize). Pavlov was investigating the role that salivation plays in digestion. He had surgically implanted devices in the cheeks of dogs so that he could measure how much saliva they produced. His experimental method was to place the dog in a harness, present the dog with some food, and then measure the amount of saliva the dog produced (see ● FIGURE 6.1).

While conducting these studies, Pavlov noticed that sometimes the dogs began to salivate *before* the food was presented to them. Sometimes the mere sight of the food dish or the sound of the approaching experimenter was enough to produce salivation. So what was going on? Why would a dog start to salivate when it heard footsteps

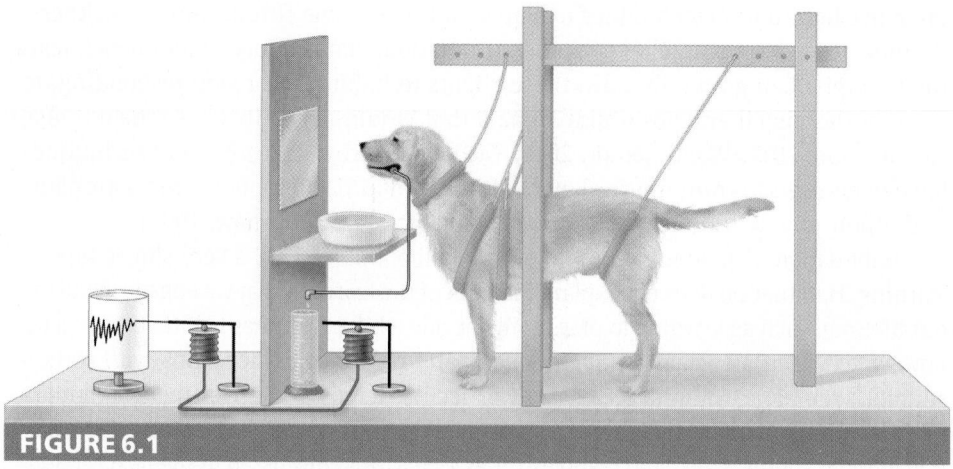

FIGURE 6.1

Pavlov's Original Experiment

The dog was held in the harness and food was placed before it. The presence of the food (unconditioned stimulus, or US) caused the dog to salivate (unconditioned response, or UR). After a while, cues in the laboratory situation (lights, sounds, or sights) became conditioned stimuli (CS) that also caused the dog to salivate (conditioned response, or CR).

or saw an empty food bowl? Pavlov reasoned that the dog had learned to associate certain cues or stimuli with the presentation of food. To the dog, the approach of footsteps had come to mean that food was soon going to appear. Consequently, the dog had become conditioned, or taught, to respond to the footsteps the same way that it responded to the food—by salivating. Unwittingly, Pavlov had discovered a learning process, one that would become extremely influential in psychology.

Pavlov began to investigate the learning process itself. He systematically paired different stimuli with food to see which could be conditioned to produce the reflexive response of salivation. In one of these investigations, Pavlov sounded a buzzer just before he gave the dog some food. He repeated these trials several times while measuring the amount of saliva the dog produced. After repeated pairing of the buzzer and the food, the dog soon began to salivate on hearing the buzzer—even on trials in which the food was not presented after the buzzer sounded. The dog had become conditioned to associate the buzzer with the presentation of food. As a result, the buzzer had taken on the same power as food to cause the dog to salivate.

6.2.1 • The Elements of Classical Conditioning

The process of learning that Pavlov discovered is commonly referred to as *classical conditioning*, or Pavlovian conditioning. We will formally define it in a minute, but first let's look at the process that produces a conditioned response:

1. *The unconditioned stimulus and response.* In order to classically condition a person or animal, you must begin with a stimulus that naturally and reliably causes some response in the organism. Because this stimulus naturally causes the reflexive response, it is referred to as an **unconditioned stimulus (US)**, and the response it evokes is called an **unconditioned response (UR)**. The term *unconditioned* refers to the fact that the association between the stimulus and the response is not learned. In Pavlov's case, the food was the unconditioned stimulus, and salivation was the unconditioned response. You do not need to teach a dog to salivate when food is presented. Instead, salivation occurs naturally when a dog sees food. • TABLE 6.1 gives some more examples of US–UR pairs that could be used in classical conditioning.

unconditioned stimulus (US) a stimulus that naturally elicits a response in an organism

unconditioned response (UR) the response that is elicited by an unconditioned stimulus

TABLE 6.1

Some Examples of US–UR Pairs

UNCONDITIONED STIMULUS (US)	UNCONDITIONED RESPONSE (UR)	
A puff of air to the eye	Eye blink	Michael L. Abramson/Time & Life Pictures/Getty Images
Ingestion of a toxin	Nausea	© Alexander Raths/Shutterstock.com
Being stuck with a pin	Flinching away from pin	Jose Luis Pelaez/Iconica/Getty Images
Sour food placed on the tongue	Salivation	© Medioimages/Photodisc/Getty Images
A light shone in the eye	Pupil constricts	© Altrendo Images/Getty Images
A firm tap to the knee	Knee-jerk reflex	Michael Donne/Science Source

neutral stimulus (NS) a stimulus that does not naturally elicit an unconditioned response in an organism

conditioned stimulus (CS) a stimulus that elicits a conditioned response in an organism

conditioned response (CR) the response that is elicited by a conditioned stimulus

2. *The neutral stimulus.* The next step is the selection of a **neutral stimulus (NS)** that does not naturally elicit the unconditioned response. In Pavlov's case, the neutral stimulus used was a buzzer. Prior to training or conditioning, a dog would not be likely to salivate when it heard a buzzer. Therefore, the buzzer is said to be neutral. It has no power to naturally cause the UR.
3. *Pairing the neutral stimulus and the unconditioned stimulus.* The third step is to systematically pair the neutral stimulus with the unconditioned stimulus. Pavlov accomplished this by repeatedly sounding the buzzer (NS) just prior to presenting the dog with the food (US). Through this repeated association of the US and the NS, the NS eventually loses its neutrality. In Pavlov's case, the dog began to salivate when the buzzer was presented without the food. At this point, classical conditioning had occurred because the buzzer was no longer neutral. The buzzer had become a **conditioned stimulus (CS)** that had the power to produce the **conditioned response (CR)** of salivation (• FIGURE 6.2).

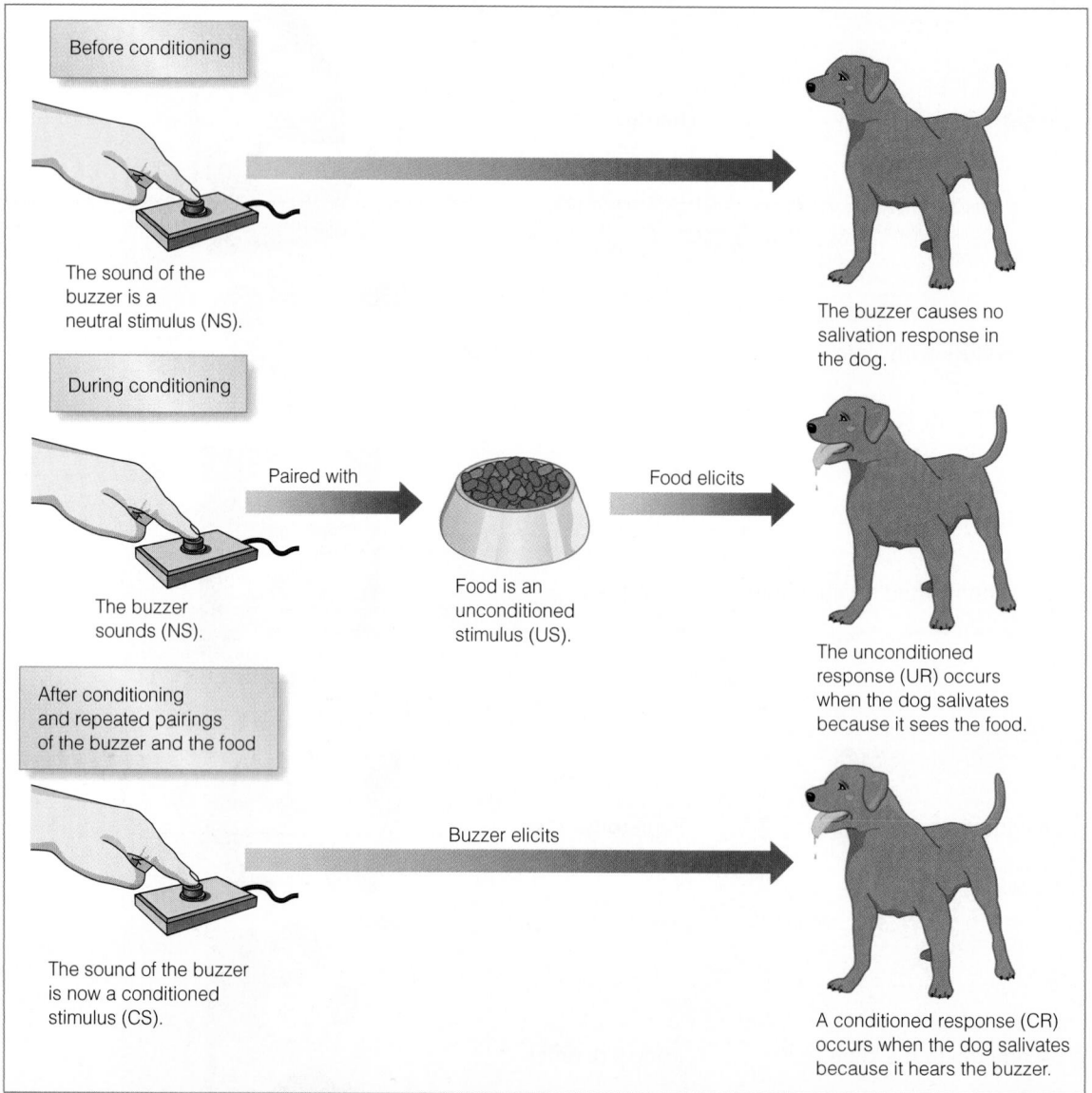

FIGURE 6.2

Pavlov's Classical Conditioning Procedure

Before conditioning, the neutral stimulus has no power to cause the response. After repeated pairings of the neutral stimulus with an unconditioned stimulus, which naturally elicits an unconditioned response, the neutral stimulus becomes a conditioned stimulus with the power to elicit the response—now called the conditioned response.

Summing up classical conditioning in a nice, neat definition is a bit awkward but nonetheless extremely important. Once, when one of us asked a student to define classical conditioning, she replied, "What Pavlov did with his dogs." This isn't, of course, a definition of classical conditioning. It does reflect the student's difficulty in trying to understand the concept of classical conditioning apart from Pavlov's particular demonstration of it, however. Keep in mind that to truly understand a concept, you must be able to define it in abstract terms as well as give an example of it. So here goes.

We would define **classical conditioning** as *learning that occurs when a neutral stimulus is paired with an unconditioned stimulus that reliably causes an unconditioned response; and because of this association, the neutral stimulus loses its neutrality and takes on the same power as the unconditioned stimulus to cause the response.* This definition may seem a bit complex, but classical conditioning is actually a fairly simple process. It merely involves learning to associate two stimuli, the unconditioned stimulus and the neutral stimulus. Through this association, the neutral stimulus becomes a conditioned stimulus (You Review: Classical Conditioning). In the next section, we will examine some of the factors that affect the strength of the association.

classical conditioning learning that occurs when a neutral stimulus is repeatedly paired with an unconditioned stimulus; because of this pairing, the neutral stimulus becomes a conditioned stimulus with the same power as the unconditioned stimulus to elicit the response in the organism

You Review **Classical Conditioning**

Abbreviation	Term	Definition
US	Unconditioned stimulus	A stimulus that naturally and reliably evokes a response in the person or animal
UR	Unconditioned response	The response that is naturally and reliably elicited by the unconditioned stimulus
NS	Neutral stimulus	A stimulus that does not initially elicit the unconditioned response in the person or animal
CS	Conditioned stimulus	A stimulus that was once neutral but, through association with the unconditioned stimulus, now has the power to elicit the response in the animal or person
CR	Conditioned response	After conditioning has occurred, the response that is elicited in the person or animal by the conditioned stimulus

6.2.2 • Factors Affecting Classical Conditioning

Exactly what is being learned in classical conditioning? We said that the organism learns to associate the NS/CS with the US. This is true, but what is the nature of this association? Why do these two particular stimuli become associated? Why did Pavlov's dog associate the buzzer with the food instead of associating other stimuli from the situation with the food? After training, why did the dog no longer begin to salivate when it heard the laboratory door open, or when the laboratory lights turned on? Why did it wait for the buzzer? To answer these questions, psychological researchers have experimentally examined different facets of the relationship between the NS/CS and the US.

contiguity [con-teh-GYU-eh-tee] the degree to which two stimuli occur close together in time

contingency [con-TINGE-en-see] the degree to which the presentation of one stimulus reliably predicts the presentation of the other stimulus

RELATIONSHIP IN TIME: CONTIGUITY

Contiguity refers to the degree to which the NS/CS and US occur close together in time. Generally speaking, for classical conditioning to occur, the NS/CS and the US must be separated by only a short period of time (Bangasser et al., 2006; Wasserman & Miller, 1997). If the interval between the presentation of the NS/CS and the US is too long, the two stimuli will not be associated, and conditioning will not occur. If Pavlov had sounded the buzzer and then 3 hours later given the dog some food, it is very unlikely that the dog would have been conditioned to salivate when it heard the buzzer.

Studies have shown that in most cases, if the US lags behind the NS/CS by more than a few seconds, conditioning will not be as strong as it could have been (Church & Black, 1958; Noble & Harding, 1963; M. C. Smith, Coleman, & Gormezano, 1969). The exact length of the optimal time interval varies depending on what response is being conditioned, but in general the longer the interval, the weaker the learning (Kryukov, 2012).

Another aspect of contiguity is the relative placement of the NS/CS and the US in time—in other words, whether the NS/CS precedes the US or follows it. Imagine if Pavlov had first given the dog the food and then sounded the buzzer. In that case the dog would not have been as likely to associate the food with the buzzer. • FIGURE 6.3 shows the five major ways to place the NS/CS and the US in classical conditioning. Of these placements, forward (delayed) conditioning produces the strongest conditioning, and backward conditioning produces the weakest conditioning (Klein, 1987).

CONSISTENCY AND RELIABILITY: CONTINGENCY

Although contiguity is necessary for conditioning, it alone does not guarantee that conditioning will occur. Conditioning also requires **contingency**, which refers to the degree to which the NS/CS reliably signals that the US is going to be presented, resulting in the NS/CS becoming associated with the CS (Díaz-Mataix, Tallot, & Doyère, 2014). If the NS/CS does not reliably predict the onset of the US, then conditioning will not occur (Bolles, 1972; Rescorla, 1967; for a review, see Wheeler & Miller, 2008). For example, if Pavlov had sometimes fed the dog after sounding the buzzer and other times did not feed the dog after sounding the buzzer, conditioning would have been weakened. This inconsistency would not send the dog a clear message that the buzzer meant food was coming. Therefore, the dog would be less likely to salivate on hearing the buzzer because he would not have made a strong association between the buzzer with the food. Given that both contiguity and contingency are necessary for strong classical conditioning, the best way to ensure strong conditioning is to consistently present only one NS/CS immediately before presenting the US.

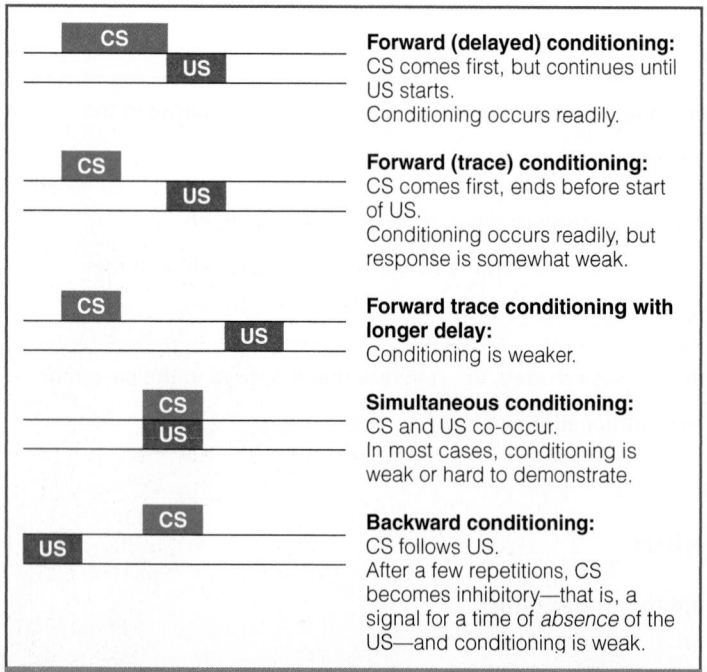

FIGURE 6.3

Possible Placements of the CS and the US in Classical Conditioning

Relative positions of the CS and US are shown for five different versions of classical conditioning: forward delayed, forward trace, forward trace with longer delay, simultaneous, and backward conditioning.

6.2.3 • Real-World Applications of Classical Conditioning

The process of classical conditioning seems a bit complex, doesn't it? It also seems as if it could occur only in a laboratory (where stimuli could be systematically paired)—but this is not true. Classical conditioning occurs frequently in everyday life. In fact, each of us has probably felt the effects of classical conditioning many times. For example, we have been classically conditioned to have certain emotional reactions in our lives. You may feel happy when you smell a perfume that reminds you of your mother. You may feel fear when you see a snake.

As you will recall, the starting point for classical conditioning is a preexisting US–UR relationship. Table 6.1 lists some unconditioned stimuli that naturally and reliably evoke unconditioned responses without prior training. These US–UR pairs can be used to produce an initial or *first-order* level of classical conditioning in a person. However, in the real world, sometimes classical conditioning occurs on top of preexisting classical conditioning. This is called *higher-order* classical conditioning. For example, if a snake bites you, the bite (US) may cause a fear (UR/CR) of snakes (CS). This is first-order conditioning. Later, if you see a snake (now a US) in the woods (NS), you may then fear (UR/CR) going into the woods (the new CS). This higher-order conditioning results in a conditioned fear of the woods.

Because of the nature of most unconditioned stimulus–unconditioned response relationships, the types of responses that can be classically conditioned usually fall into two categories: *emotional responses* and *physiological responses*.

CLASSICAL CONDITIONING OF EMOTIONAL RESPONSES

The classical conditioning of emotional responses was clearly demonstrated in a famous—now infamous—set of experiments conducted by John B. Watson and his student Rosalie Rayner in the early 1900s (Watson & Rayner, 1920). Watson set out to show that classical conditioning could be used to condition fear responses in a child. Because Watson used an 11-month-old boy named Albert, the experiments are now commonly referred to as the "Little Albert" experiments.

In the Little Albert experiments, Watson classically conditioned Albert to fear a white rat. To do this, Watson first gave Albert a white lab rat and allowed him to play with it. In the beginning, the rat was an NS for Albert because it did not cause him to be afraid. A few minutes after giving Albert the rat, Watson made a very loud noise by striking a piece of metal with a hammer. As with most 11-month-olds, a loud noise such as this was a US for Albert that reliably produced the UR of frightening Albert and making him cry. Over and over, Watson repeated this sequence of presenting the rat (NS), then making the noise (US), with the result that Albert would become afraid and cry (UR).

Can you see the parallels here between what Watson and Rayner were doing to Albert and what Pavlov did with his dogs? In the same way that Pavlov conditioned his dogs to salivate at the sound of the buzzer, Watson conditioned Albert to fear a white rat by associating the rat with a frightening noise. After several trials of pairing the noise and the rat, all Watson had to do to get Albert to cry was to show him the rat. Because the rat had been paired with the noise, the rat lost its neutrality and became a CS that was able to evoke the CR of fear.

Emotional reactions such as fear are also classically conditioned outside of the laboratory. For example, one of us once

In the Little Albert experiments, John B. Watson and his assistant, Rosalie Rayner, classically conditioned Albert to fear a white lab rat.

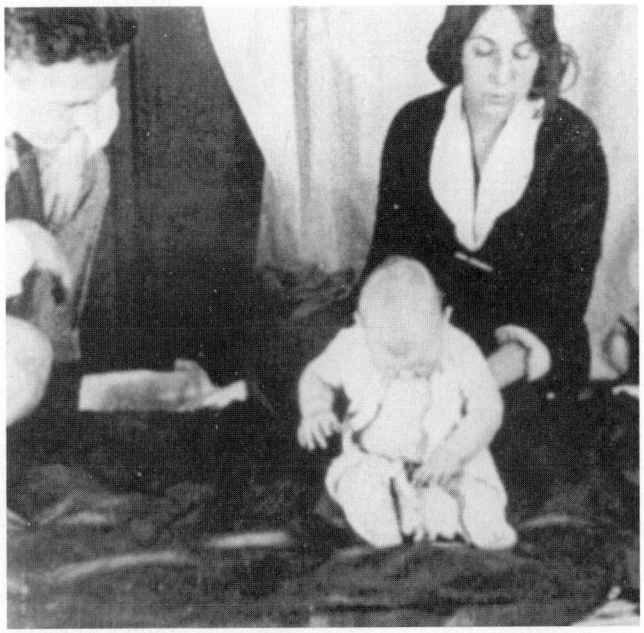

© Archives of the History of American Psychology, University of Akron, Akron, Ohio

Tony Freeman/PhotoEdit

Phobias are classically conditioned responses. A fear-producing encounter with a dog can result in the stimulus—the dog—becoming a conditioned stimulus that elicits fear.

had a professor who had an intense fear of bees because earlier in his life, several bees had stung him after he accidentally disturbed a beehive. In this case of classical conditioning, the multiple bee stings were a US that elicited the UR of fear. The bees were initially an NS, but because they were paired with the bee stings, they became a CS that could produce the CR of fear. From that day onward, all the professor had to do was to see a bee to feel intense fear.

In fact, the professor's fear of bees was so great that it spread to other insects as well. Not only was he afraid of bees, he was also afraid of wasps, yellow jackets, and any other flying insect that could sting. In psychological terms, his fear had undergone **stimulus generalization**, which occurs when stimuli that are similar to the CS have the same power to elicit the CR even though they have never been paired with the US. The professor had never been stung by a wasp, yet he feared them because they are similar to bees.

Stimulus generalization also occurred in the Little Albert experiments. After being conditioned to fear the rat, Albert also exhibited fear when presented with a dog, a rabbit, a fur coat, and a fake white Santa Claus beard. His fear of white rats had generalized to several furry things (Watson & Rayner, 1920). This may leave you wondering what happened to Little Albert. Did he suffer through life as a result of his conditioned phobias? Unfortunately, not much is known about Albert's fate. His mother withdrew him from the program and moved away before Watson and Rayner could remove the fear they had conditioned in Albert—leaving future psychologists to debate the ethics of Watson and Rayner's research.

Unlike what happened to Little Albert, all classically conditioned responses do not necessarily generalize. The opposite process, **stimulus discrimination**, often occurs. In stimulus discrimination, the conditioned response occurs in response to a particular conditioned stimulus, but it does not occur in response to other stimuli that are similar to the conditioned stimulus. For instance, a woman who works in the reptile house at the zoo is probably not afraid of most snakes, but if she found herself face to face with a poisonous king cobra, she would likely feel afraid. Sometimes, knowing when to discriminate and when to generalize is important to survival!

CLASSICAL CONDITIONING OF PHYSIOLOGICAL RESPONSES: TASTE AVERSION

Emotions are not the only responses that can be classically conditioned. Pavlov's original demonstrations of classical conditioning show a physiological response, salivation. But what other kinds of physiological responses can be classically conditioned? Table 6.1 (p. 231) lists some of the US–UR relationships that could form the basis of classical conditioning. Of these, one of the most important and common is the classical conditioning of nausea.

Have you ever eaten a food that you liked and soon after become sick to your stomach with the flu, food poisoning, motion sickness, or some other ailment? Then, after recovering from your sickness, did you find the sight, smell, or even the idea of that food nauseating? If you answered "yes" to both of these questions, you have experienced what psychologists call classically conditioned **taste aversion** (Garcia, Kimeldorf, & Koelling, 1955; Li, Hsiao, & Li, 2013).

One of the authors can vividly remember going through this type of conditioning as a child. After she ate a big dessert of peppermint ice cream, she came down with a severe case of tonsillitis that was accompanied by nausea and vomiting. After she recovered from the tonsillitis, it was years before she could even think about peppermint ice cream without feeling queasy. The same author regularly holds an informal

stimulus generalization responding in a like fashion to similar stimuli

stimulus discrimination responding only to a particular stimulus

taste aversion classical conditioning that occurs when an organism pairs the experience of nausea with a certain food and becomes conditioned to feel ill at the sight, smell, or idea of the food contest in her classes to see who has had the longest-running taste aversion. The current record stands at more than 20 years!

It seems that taste aversion is something that we learn with particular ease (Garcia & Koelling, 1966). Taste aversion is unique in two ways. First, it often occurs with only one pairing of the NS/CS and the US. Unlike most cases of classical conditioning, in taste aversion, a single pairing of the food (NS/CS) and the agent that initially causes the nausea, in this case a virus (US), is usually sufficient to cause strong conditioning. The second difference is that in taste aversion, the interval between the NS/CS and the US can be very long. Intervals as long as 24 hours can result in conditioning (Garcia, Ervin, & Koelling, 1966; Logue, 1979). Because taste aversion is an exception to some of the rules of conditioning, some psychologists believe that our genes give us a **biological preparedness** to learn taste aversion easily (Seligman, 1970).

© Cusp/Flirt/Masterfile

Eating a food and then becoming ill can result in a conditioned taste aversion. The food becomes a conditioned stimulus that results in the conditioned response of nausea.

biological preparedness a genetic tendency to learn certain responses very easily

By being biologically prepared to learn taste aversion, we are better able to avoid certain poisonous plants and substances. Once something has made us sick, we want no part of it in the future. No doubt the ability to learn taste aversion quickly, and consequently to avoid poisonous substances, has survival value. Therefore, through natural selection, genes that enabled our ancestors to learn taste aversion quickly would have been retained because animals with those genes—human and nonhuman—would have lived, whereas those with a sluggish response to taste aversion would likely die. Taste aversion is widely seen in many species of animals (Garcia, 1992).

In fact, because many other species are also susceptible to taste aversion, it can be used to help control the pesky nature of some animals. In the western United States, coyotes like to sneak into sheep pastures and kill sheep rather than hunt for food in the wild. In the past, frustrated sheep ranchers would be very tempted to either shoot the coyotes on sight or lethally poison them. But thanks to psychologists, ranchers now have a more humane and ecologically sound alternative—using taste aversion to condition the coyotes to dislike sheep as a food source. They slaughter a few sheep and treat their carcasses with a chemical that causes nausea in coyotes. These tainted carcasses are then left out for the coyotes to eat. Because the coyotes can't pass up a free meal, they eat the sheep and get very sick to their stomachs. After they recover, they want nothing to do with sheep because of conditioned taste aversion (Gustavson & Garcia, 1974). The ranchers' problem is solved. Similarly, taste aversion can be used to control problem behaviors in humans—a topic we discuss in the Psychology Applies to Your World box (p. 239).

As you continue to read and study this chapter, keep in mind the general definition of classical conditioning and try to generate your own examples of real-world classical conditioning (perhaps even some of taste aversion). By doing this, you will increase your understanding and retention of this material—both of which will help you on exam day!

ENGAGE YOURSELF! Psychologists have classically conditioned children to like healthful vegetables by pairing new vegetable flavors with the flavor of sugar to produce liking. After repeated pairings of the vegetables (NS/CS) with pleasant-tasting sugar (US), the children were conditioned to also like the vegetables (UR/CR). After conditioning, the children exhibited liking for the vegetables even when sugar was not present (Havermans & Jansen, 2007).

Similar approaches have also been shown to work in children with autism spectrum disorder getting them to accept foods that they had refused to eat in the past (Meier, Fryling, & Wallace, 2012). So, if you ever find yourself struggling with a child who doesn't want to eat healthy foods, try pairing them with a food that they do like— perhaps even a little sugar!

You can also use taste aversion to help yourself eat more healthily. Think of a food that you frequently overindulge in but wish you wouldn't (such as pizza or candy). Several times a day, imagine a delicious serving of this food. While thinking of this food, also think of something disgusting such as a bunch of worms squirming on your chosen food. If you repeat this procedure for several weeks, you may find yourself less motivated to indulge in this food!

6.2.4 • Extinction of Classically Conditioned Responses

extinction the removal of a conditioned response

acquisition the process of learning a conditioned response or behavior

aversion therapy a type of therapy that uses classical conditioning to condition people to avoid certain stimuli

Let's assume that you had the misfortune of developing a classically conditioned taste aversion to your favorite food because you ate this food just before you became ill with the flu. Furthermore, let's assume that you wanted to be able to eat your favorite food again without feeling sick to your stomach. How would you go about ridding yourself of your acquired taste aversion?

In classical conditioning, **extinction**, or removal of the conditioned response, can be brought about by presenting the conditioned stimulus to the participant without also presenting the unconditioned stimulus. In our example, extinction would begin when you ate your favorite food (CS) and you did not have the flu (US). When the CS is presented alone, it no longer predicts the onset of the US, and the CR decreases. Years later, your author finally got over her taste aversion to peppermint ice cream after she took a job in a restaurant that sold a great deal of it. After scooping many scoops of peppermint ice cream, she found that the sight and smell of it no longer made her feel sick. It wasn't long before she was even able to eat peppermint ice cream without a problem.

Pavlov's experiments with dogs also included extinction trials with the dogs. • FIGURE 6.4 shows the **acquisition**, or learning curve, for the CR and the extinction curve for the CR in Pavlov's experiment. As you can see from this figure, the CR of salivation to the buzzer was acquired over several trials in which the CS and the US were paired. In the extinction trials, the buzzer was sounded but no food was presented, and there was a fairly steady decrease in the CR. In other words, the dog became less and less likely to salivate when it heard the buzzer.

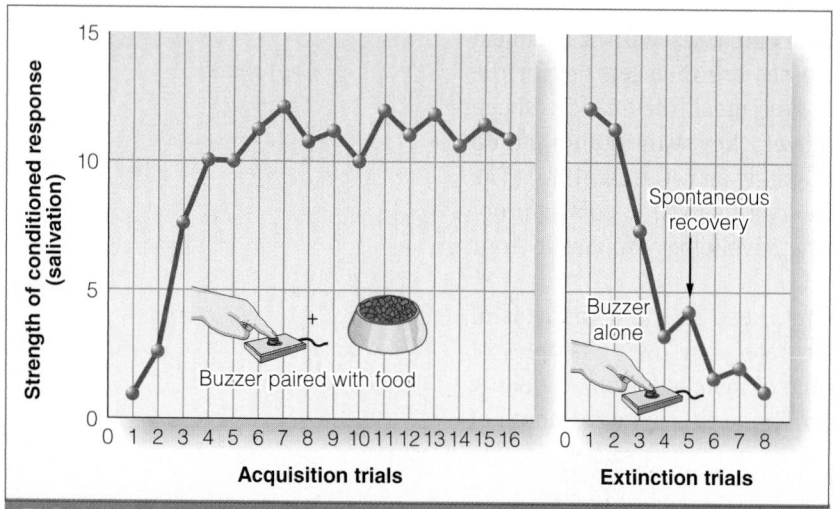

FIGURE 6.4

The Phases of Classical Conditioning

These plots show the number of conditioning trials on the *x*-axis and the strength of the conditioned response on the *y*-axis. During acquisition, the response increases in strength as a function of the number of times the CS and US have been paired together. During extinction, the CS is presented without the US, which leads to a decrease in the strength of the CR. Note that during extinction, sometimes there is a temporary increase in the strength of the CR even though the CS has not been recently presented with the US. This is called *spontaneous recovery*.

Psychology Applies to Your World:

Using Taste Aversion to Help People

Taste aversion is applicable in several therapeutic settings. One such application is in the treatment of alcoholism. The idea behind this **aversion therapy** is to condition a taste aversion to alcohol. The client takes the drug Antabuse. If he or she then drinks alcohol, the result is intense nausea and headache, which often leads to conditioned taste aversion. One of the authors' (Doyle-Portillo's) father underwent such a treatment for his alcoholism. As a result of the treatment, the smell of any alcohol made him nauseous. Family members even had to stop wearing alcohol-based cologne in his presence for fear of making him sick!

Aversion therapy has been shown to be modestly helpful in motivating people with alcoholism to remain abstinent (J. W. Smith, Frawley, & Polissar, 1997) or significantly reduce their alcohol intake (Higuchi & Saito, 2013). However, it does not represent a "cure" for alcoholism. In one study, only 20% of the people with alcoholism remained abstinent for 1 year after being treated with aversion therapy alone (Landabaso et al., 1999). Even with strong motivation (see Chapter 5) to stop drinking, clients often relapse and often must stay on Antabuse to remain sober (Kristenson, 1992). So, although aversion therapy with Antabuse may be a useful part of a comprehensive treatment program, it should not be the only treatment used for alcoholism (Finn, 2003; Hunt, 2002). Recently, researchers have found a promising new use for Antabuse. Antabuse appears to intensify the negative effects of cocaine (for example, anxiety), therefore motivating users to avoid it (Gaval-Cruz & Weinshenker, 2009; Kosten et al., 2013).

© Blue Images/Masterfile

Therapists can use classically conditioned taste aversion to help people with alcoholism overcome their desire to drink.

Another application of taste aversion is in helping people undergoing chemotherapy for cancer and other diseases. Chemotherapy drugs often cause intense nausea. If a patient receiving chemotherapy experiences nausea after eating foods that he would normally eat, there is a strong possibility that he will develop a conditioned taste aversion to those foods. This could severely affect the quality of the patient's life both during and after undergoing chemotherapy as he may develop multiple taste aversions over the course of treatment. One solution to this problem is to give the patient a novel food prior to undergoing chemotherapy. Because novel flavors are more easily associated with feelings of illness than familiar flavors are (Batsell, 2000), novel foods can act as scapegoats for the patients' regularly eaten foods. For example, patients given halva (a Middle Eastern sweet; Andresen, Birch, & Johnson, 1990) or strongly flavored candy (Broberg & Bernstein, 1987) prior to undergoing chemotherapy later experienced less taste aversion for the foods of their regular diet. Because the novel foods eaten just prior to chemotherapy were more strongly associated with their nausea, the patients' conditioned taste aversion for the novel foods was stronger than that for the familiar foods. Because novel foods can be easily avoided, the patients should be better able to resume their normal eating patterns after chemotherapy.

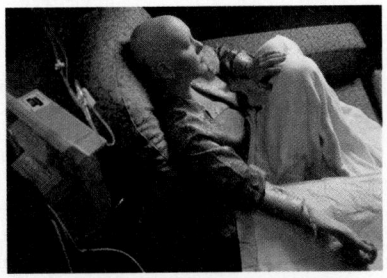
© Kevin Laubacher/Getty Images

By having chemotherapy patients consume a scapegoat food prior to undergoing chemotherapy, doctors can help ensure that the taste aversion patients experience after chemotherapy is for the scapegoat food and not for their normal diet.

Does this mean that once a response has been extinguished, it is gone forever? Note that the extinction curve in Figure 6.4 does not show a completely continuous pattern of decrease in the CR. Sometimes, after a response has been extinguished, there will be a temporary increase in the CR. This phenomenon, called **spontaneous recovery**, can occur at any point during extinction (Troisi, 2003) and may be especially likely if a response is extinguished immediately after it is originally learned (Huff et al., 2009). Let's go back to our example of taste aversion for peppermint ice cream. Today, although your author does not have an active, ongoing taste aversion for peppermint ice cream, every now and again when she thinks of peppermint ice cream, she will feel a bit sick. Thankfully, her spontaneous recovery doesn't last long. She soon reenters extinction, and she can think of peppermint ice cream and even eat it without a trace of nausea.

spontaneous recovery during extinction, the tendency for a conditioned response to reappear and strengthen over a brief period of time before re-extinguishing

What do you suppose would happen if she happened to eat some peppermint ice cream on a hot day and suffered from a small amount of heat-induced nausea? Do you think her taste aversion to peppermint ice cream would return? It is likely that it would. In fact, responses that are extinguished are usually reacquired more easily than they were acquired in the first place. Extinction does not mean that we forget that there once was a connection between the CS and the US; it simply means that the CR is less likely to occur when the CS is presented.

So far, we have seen that learning can occur through habituation and classical conditioning—learning processes that both result in rather simplistic behaviors. In the next section, we'll examine how we learn more complex behaviors through reward and punishment.

Quiz Yourself

6.2

1. Which of the following is an example of classical conditioning?
   a. Damon learns to ride a bike by watching his older brother.
   b. Sally likes the smell of rose perfume because her beloved third-grade teacher used to wear rose perfume.
   c. After 20 minutes in the day-care center, Ralph barely notices the squealing of the children at play.
   d. Ted never speeds after receiving a $500 fine for speeding.

2. Which of the following is the best example of a US–UR pair?
   a. Receiving money–happiness
   b. An electric shock to the finger–jerking one's finger away
   c. Receiving a promotion–working overtime
   d. Seeing a snake–fear

3. Janna, a real estate agent, desperately wants to sell a home. She tells the owner to place a pan of vanilla extract in the oven and heat it just before the prospective buyers arrive to look at the house. Janna knows that the smell of vanilla in the house will increase the chance that the buyers will like the house because they have been classically conditioned to respond favorably to the smell of vanilla. In this example, what is the CR?
   a. The pleasant emotions evoked by the smell of vanilla
   b. The smell of vanilla
   c. The memory of Grandma baking cookies
   d. The house

4. Jamal was eating a hotdog *on* a Ferris wheel, and *while on* the ride he became ill from motion sickness. Afterward, Jamal found himself with a conditioned taste aversion to hotdogs. Jamal's story best illustrates the fact that classically conditioned taste aversions can be learned even when there is a lack of _____.
   a. contingency
   b. contiguity
   c. both a and b
   d. None of the above

5. Wanda developed a conditioned taste aversion to pickles when she was a child. Today at age 30, she can once again eat pickles without experiencing nausea. Wanda's ability to now eat pickles is likely due to_____.
   a. dishabituation
   b. classical conditioning of a new taste aversion
   c. extinction
   d. an orienting reflex to pickles

Answers 1. b; 2. b; 3. a; 4. a; 5. c

6.3 Operant Conditioning: Learning from the Consequences of Our Actions

Suppose you are sitting in your psychology class, listening to a lecture, when your professor asks the class a question. For some reason, you raise your hand to answer the question even though you have never made a comment in this class before. The professor calls on you, and you give the correct answer. In response to your answer, the professor smiles broadly and praises you for giving such an accurate and insightful answer.

How do you think this scenario would affect you? As a result of the professor's reaction, would you be more or less likely to raise your hand in the future when she asked a question? If you are like most people, this type of praise would encourage you to raise your hand in the future. But what would happen if, instead of praising you, she frowned and said that your answer was one of the stupidest she had ever heard. How would this reaction affect your behavior? Obviously, after such a cruel response, many of us would be very unlikely to answer any more questions in that professor's class!

Both of these examples illustrate another type of learning, called **operant conditioning**. In operant conditioning, we learn from the consequences of our behavior. In our example, being praised for answering a question makes one more likely to answer questions in the future; being called "stupid" makes one less likely to answer future questions. We will see that operant conditioning is a powerful means of learning that explains how we learn many of the important lessons in our lives. But first, we will begin by looking at how operant conditioning was discovered.

operant conditioning a type of learning in which the organism learns through the consequences of its behavior

6.3.1 • E. L. Thorndike's Law of Effect

At about the same time that Ivan Pavlov was developing his theories about learning in Russia, American psychologist E. L. Thorndike (1874–1949) was busy conducting experiments on operant conditioning in New York. Thorndike was working with cats in specially constructed puzzle boxes. A puzzle box is a box with a lid or door that locks into place so that an animal can be placed inside. Once inside the box, the animal must activate some type of unlatching device to win its release. The device that unlatches the lid may be a rope pull, a pedal that needs to be pushed, or a switch that needs to be flipped. •FIGURE 6.5 shows a typical puzzle box with a foot-pedal release.

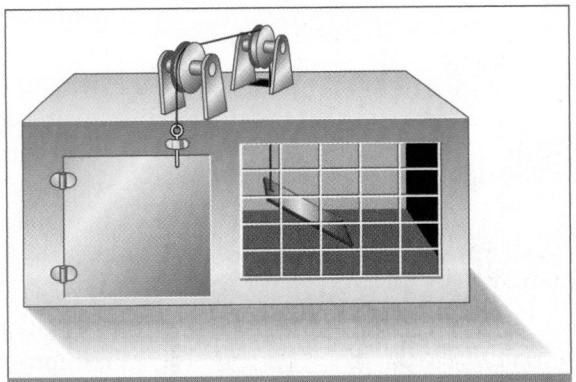

FIGURE 6.5

Puzzle Box

This is an example of a puzzle box like those used by Thorndike. To get out of the box, the cat would have to pull the string or step on the pedal.

UNLOCKING THE PUZZLE OF LEARNING

In his research, Thorndike (1898) locked a hungry cat in one of these puzzle boxes and placed some food outside the box. Then he recorded how long it took the cat to figure out how to get out of the box. Once the cat activated the device and got out of the box, Thorndike would take the cat and place it back in the puzzle box. Over and over, Thorndike repeated this procedure of imprisoning the cat and measuring the time it took the cat to win its release.

Thorndike observed in these studies that when the cat was first placed in the puzzle box, it thrashed around randomly until, by accident, it tripped the mechanism and got out of the box. After several more trials, however, the cat's behavior became less random, and the time it took to get out of the box declined. This decrease in the amount of time it took the cat to get out of the box indicated to Thorndike that learning was taking place: The cat was learning to associate its behavior with the consequences that its behavior brought about.

Based on what he observed in his puzzle box studies, Thorndike developed a principle of learning that he called the **law of effect**. The law of effect states that in a given situation, behaviors that lead to positive, satisfying consequences will be strengthened, such that the next time the situation occurs, the behavior is more likely to be repeated. In addition, the law of effect also states that in a given situation, behaviors that lead to negative, discomforting consequences will be weakened, such that the next time the situation occurs, the behavior will be less likely to be repeated (Thorndike, 1905).

law of effect a principle discovered by E. L. Thorndike, which states that behaviors that lead to positive consequences will be strengthened and behaviors that lead to negative consequences will be weakened

reinforcement the strengthening of a response that occurs when the response is rewarded

positive reinforcement strengthening a behavior by adding something pleasant to the environment of the organism

negative reinforcement strengthening a behavior by removing something unpleasant from the environment of the organism

punishment the weakening of a response that occurs when a behavior leads to an unpleasant consequence

RANDOM ACTIONS AND REINFORCEMENT

Let's examine the law of effect in terms of a hungry cat in a puzzle box. When the cat is first trapped in the box, it will likely perform many random behaviors. For instance, it may claw, hiss, bite at the bars, or meow. But none of these behaviors will open the box. The cat's early responses to being stuck in the box are random or "trial-and-error." After some time, let's say that the cat happens to step on the foot pedal that opens the puzzle box and is able to get out to where the food is waiting. This particular random behavior has led to a consequence that is far more rewarding than any of the other random behaviors the cat has tried. The law of effect states that this particular response is strengthened, or reinforced, because it results in a reward. This process of **reinforcement** means that the rewarded behavior will become more likely in the future. The next time the cat is locked in the box, it will be more likely to step on the pedal than to try the other behaviors that did not lead to release on prior trials. Over many trials, the law of effect results in the cat's becoming more and more likely to step on the pedal and less and less likely to use other behaviors that were not reinforced in the past. The behaviors that were not rewarded—and therefore not reinforced—are likely to die out.

POSITIVE AND NEGATIVE REINFORCEMENT

The two types of reinforcement are *positive reinforcement* and *negative reinforcement* (see You Review: The Four Consequences of Behavior). In **positive reinforcement**, the behavior leads to the addition of something pleasant to the organism's environment. For instance, Thorndike positively reinforced the cat for stepping on the pedal by giving the cat food when it got out of the puzzle box.

In **negative reinforcement**, the behavior is rewarded by the removal of something unpleasant from the organism's environment. In Thorndike's case, the cat was negatively reinforced for stepping on the pedal because this behavior led to the removal of its imprisonment in the puzzle box. (We are, of course, assuming that the hungry cat did not enjoy being trapped in the box.)

The difference between punishment and negative reinforcement is a point that gives many students great trouble because they tend to think that negative reinforcement is a type of punishment. This is not true! The "negative" in negative reinforcement refers to the fact that negative reinforcement removes something from the organism's environment; it does not refer to a negative or unpleasant consequence of the behavior. When you see the term *reinforcement*, keep in mind that reinforcement leads to an increase in behavior. **Punishment**, in contrast, is an unpleasant consequence that leads to a decrease in behavior.

You Review **The Four Consequences of Behavior**

Reinforcement increases the likelihood of a behavior; punishment decreases it.

	Positive	Negative
Reinforcement The consequence increases the behavior	**Positive Reinforcement** Something pleasant is added to the environment  Paul Bricknell/Dorling Kindersley/Getty Images Example: Your cat learns to use the cat door, so you give him a kitty treat.	**Negative Reinforcement** Something unpleasant is removed from the environment  Jane Burton/Dorling Kindersley/Getty Images Example: Your cat, who hates to be wet, uses his new cat door to come in out of the rain.
Punishment The consequence decreases the behavior	**Positive Punishment** Something unpleasant is added to the environment  Steve Lyne/Dorling Kindersley/Getty Images Example: Every time your cat starts to scratch your furniture, you squirt him with a water bottle	**Negative Punishment** Something pleasant is removed from the environment  blickwinkel/McPHOTO/MGO/Alamy Example: Your cat misbehaves, so you put him outside away from his toys.

POSITIVE AND NEGATIVE PUNISHMENT

As you can see from You Review: The Four Consequences of Behavior, punishment also comes in two varieties. **Positive punishment** occurs when a behavior results in the addition of something unpleasant to the organism's environment. For example, a puzzle box could be rigged to electrify the floor of the cage every time the cat stepped on the pedal. The cat would then be positively punished every time it stepped on the pedal because the resulting shock would add pain to the cat's environment.

In **negative punishment**, the behavior leads to the removal of something pleasant from the organism's environment. A puzzle box could be rigged so that when the cat presses the pedal, a drape falls over the cage, and the cat can no longer see outside the cage. If the cat enjoys seeing outside the cage, then stepping on the pedal would lead to negative punishment because it leads to the loss of a pleasant privilege for the cat. The effect of punishment is to decrease a behavior, regardless of whether the punishment is positive or negative.

positive punishment weakening a behavior by adding something unpleasant to the organism's environment

negative punishment weakening a behavior by removing something pleasant from the organism's environment

6.3.2 • B. F. Skinner and the Experimental Study of Operant Conditioning

Although E. L. Thorndike is generally credited with discovering the law of effect, American psychologist B. F. Skinner (1904–1990) is more commonly associated with the scientific study of operant conditioning. Skinner began to formally study operant conditioning in the late 1920s when he was a graduate student at Harvard University. During his long career—from the 1920s through the 1980s—Skinner made many significant contributions to our understanding of operant conditioning (Schultz & Schultz, 2012). One of his most obvious contributions was to introduce new terminology and technology to the study of this type of learning.

Skinner box device created by B. F. Skinner to study operant behavior in a compressed time frame; in a Skinner box, an organism is automatically rewarded or punished for engaging in certain behaviors

It was Skinner who introduced the term *operant conditioning* to the study of the law of effect. Skinner felt that using the term *operant* was a good way to distinguish this type of learning from classical conditioning. Skinner wanted to emphasize the fact that in classical conditioning, the organism does not actively choose to operate on the environment to produce some consequence; rather, the response is forced from the animal. Thus, Skinner referred to classically conditioned behavior as respondent behavior. In contrast, Skinner wanted to emphasize that in operant conditioning, the animal makes a choice to respond to its environment in a certain way. In this type of learning, behavior operates on the environment to produce some consequence (Skinner, 1938).

Another of Skinner's contributions to the study of operant conditioning was the development of a new device that allows researchers to condition animals in less time than is required to condition an animal in a puzzle box. This device, now called a **Skinner box**, is a chamber large enough to house a small animal, typically a rat or a pigeon. When rats are used, the chamber contains a lever or bar that the rat can press. When the rat depresses the lever or bar, it receives reinforcement in the form of a pellet of food from an automatic feeding device attached to the chamber. When pigeons are used, the pigeon receives a reward by pecking at a disk on the side of the box.

Science Source

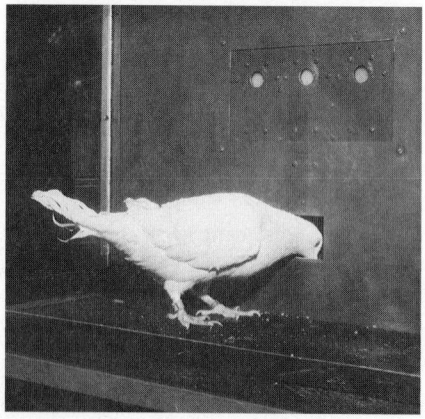

Science Source

In these operant chambers, the animals can be reinforced with food for pressing the bar or pecking the disk. Skinner boxes such as these allow researchers to efficiently gather data on operant conditioning.

To study operant behavior, Skinner would place a hungry rat in the Skinner box and wait for the rat to accidentally press the bar (which tends to happen rather quickly given the Skinner box's small size and simplicity). Once the rat pressed the bar, a pellet would drop into the chamber to reinforce this operant behavior. The rat was free to press the bar as often as it wanted and whenever it wanted. By recording the number of bar presses and when they occurred, Skinner could get a good picture of the acquisition of the operant behavior. Using the Skinner box, researchers have been able to learn a great deal about the different aspects of operant conditioning. This advance in the methodology and apparatus for studying animal learning is one of B. F. Skinner's major contributions to psychology.

APPLYING SKINNER BOX TECHNOLOGY IN THE REAL WORLD

In 1958, B. F. Skinner wrote an article entitled "Teaching Machines" in which he argued that psychologists and educators should apply their understanding of operant conditioning to develop devices that would allow children to learn at their own pace (Skinner, 1958). In Skinner's view, these teaching machines would present the learner with a question or task to answer or complete. If the learner's answer was correct, the machine would allow her to advance to the next question, thereby reinforcing the learner for getting the correct answer. If the learner's answer was incorrect, she would not be allowed to advance until she provided the right answer, thus withholding reinforcement for the incorrect response. In essence, the devices functioned as Skinner boxes for humans.

Before advanced computer technology became part of everyday life, such teaching machines were elaborate and cumbersome to construct. The personal computer changed all this. Today, we have abundant examples of these "teaching machines," although we rarely refer to them as such. They are now known as Leap Pads, Nintendo DS, Xbox, Wii, PlayStation, and so on. Some of these products were developed with the specific goal of being educational, teaching machines. Others were not.

In playing electronic games, players are rewarded for their behavior in various ways. A child selecting a correct answer on a Leap Pad hears a reward tone and is congratulated. A gamer scores points for shooting the bad guy, gets to see the next level after successful play, receives feedback on his exercise form from a Wii console, and so on. Players can also be punished. If you make a bad decision, your character might be killed or you may lose points or resources. You may hear a disappointed failure tone if you spell a word incorrectly, and so on.

Research has indicated that these devices can have both positive and negative impact on behavior. For example, college students who played video games in which women are portrayed as sex objects exhibited increased tendencies to treat women inappropriately (Yao, Mahood, & Linz, 2010). And, young men randomly assigned to play the video game Grand Theft Auto III were found to exhibit more uncooperative behavior and more permissive attitudes about alcohol and drugs than did a control group that played a low-violence game (S. S. Brady & Matthews, 2006).

But, these modern-day "Skinner boxes" may also have the power to condition us in positive ways. In a preliminary study, kindergarteners who used a Leap Pad experienced an increase in reading enjoyment, reading proficiency, and reading engagement (Munson, 2006). Another study showed that older people using Nintendo DS to play "brain training" games that exercise cognitive function were more engaged in the games and enjoyed them more than doing the same sorts of exercises in a paper and pencil format (Nacke, Nacke, & Lindley, 2009). Given that numerous studies suggest that exercising cognitive function in adulthood may help us keep our cognitive abilities longer (Valenzuela & Sachdev, 2009), having engaging devices like the Nintendo DS to encourage such exercise is a good thing. Even more exciting are consoles, such as the Wii Fit, that combine the cognitive aspects of gaming with physical exercise. Use of these so-called *exergames* has been shown to improve both the cognitive *and* physical functioning of older adults (Maillot, Perrot, & Hartley, 2012). The well-documented link between physical fitness and cognitive decline (see, Brown, Peiffer, & Martins, 2013) makes use of these newer technologies especially promising for warding off age-related cognitive decline and improving overall health.

Like many technologies, these modern-day "Skinner boxes" can have both good and bad effects on their users. We wonder what B.F. Skinner would think about the manner in which his ideas are being put to use in society today.

Bruce Laurance/The Image Bank/Getty Images

Computer and video games are examples of modern technologies that are similar to Skinner boxes, in that they are programmed to reward players for certain behaviors, while punishing them for others.

6.3.3 • Acquisition and Extinction

Although Skinner was ahead of his time in recognizing the real-world potential of the Skinner box, his main purpose for developing the device was to use it to better research the process of operant conditioning. Two areas that Skinner explored with the Skinner box were the *acquisition* and *extinction* of behavior. You may recall from our discussion of classical conditioning that acquisition refers to the conditioning of a response and extinction refers to the loss of a conditioned response. As in classical conditioning, it is possible to plot acquisition and extinction curves for operantly conditioned behaviors. The rat learns that pressing the bar leads to obtaining food, and its tendency to press the bar increases. The intensity with which the rat presses the bar continues to increase until it reaches some maximum strength. For example, the rat can eat the pellets only so fast. Therefore, the number of times the rat will press the bar in a given time frame is limited by the speed at which it eats (● FIGURE 6.6).

Extinction also occurs in operant conditioning, but it is caused by circumstances that differ from those that cause extinction in classical conditioning (see Lattal & Lattal, 2012). In classical conditioning, extinction occurs when the CS is presented without the US. In operant conditioning, extinction occurs because the behavior is no longer reinforced (see Figure 6.6). Many of us hold jobs, and going to work is an example of an operantly conditioned response. We go to work because we expect to be reinforced for this behavior on payday. What would it take to extinguish your going-to-work behavior? The answer is simple, isn't it? All it would take is the removal of your reinforcement. If your boss stopped paying you, you would likely stop going to work! In operant conditioning, withholding the reinforcement that maintains the behavior causes the extinction of that behavior.

extinction burst a temporary increase in a behavioral response that occurs immediately after extinction has begun

Like acquisition, extinction does not typically happen in one trial. Even if your boss failed to pay you on payday, you might very well return to work for a few days. In fact, you might even experience a temporary **extinction burst**, during which you worked harder in an attempt to obtain reward immediately after your boss withholds your pay (Galensky et al., 2001). At the very least, you probably would not entirely abandon work until it became very clear that reinforcement would no longer be forthcoming. Extinction tends to occur over a number of trials. Each time the organism emits the operant response without being reinforced, its tendency to repeat the response diminishes (see Figure 6.6).

Because extinction removes responses, it has many practical applications. One way to stop someone from engaging in an annoying behavior is to extinguish it by removing the reinforcement for that behavior. Take the example of a parent and child shopping together in a department store. The child sees a toy that he wants, but his parent refuses to buy it. At this refusal, the child begins to whine and cry, but instead of punishing the child for this

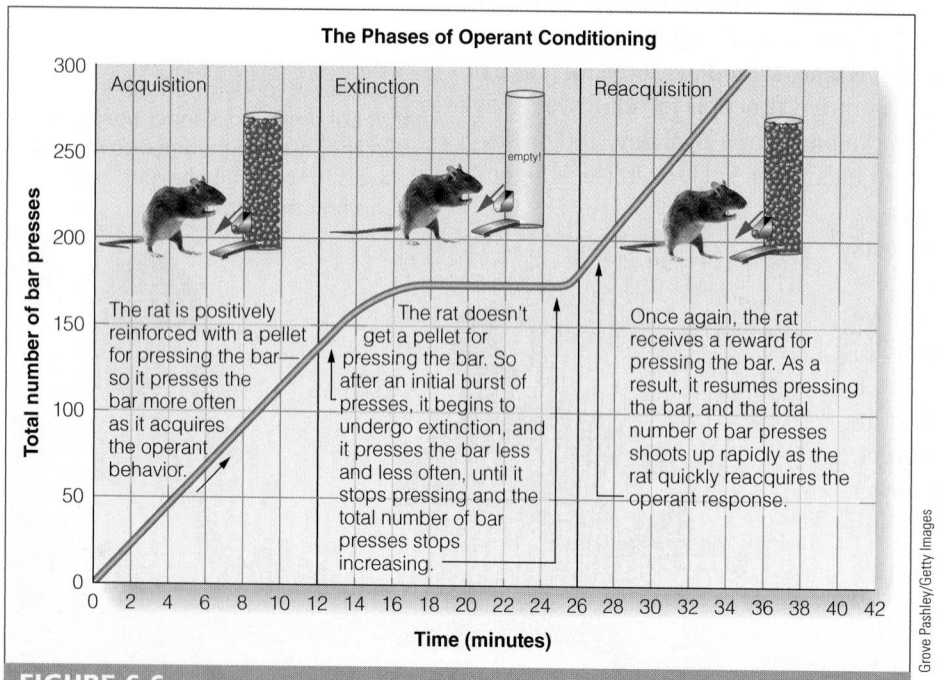

Grove Pashley/Getty Images

FIGURE 6.6

Acquisition and Extinction in Operant Conditioning

Just as we saw in classical conditioning, operant responses can also undergo acquisition, extinction, and reacquisition.

behavior, the parent ignores the child. By not reinforcing the whining and crying, the parent begins to extinguish this annoying behavior. Once the child learns that crying and whining do not lead to reward, the child will stop using this behavioral strategy to get what he wants.

The trick to using extinction to reduce unwanted behaviors is figuring out what is actually reinforcing the behavior, removing that reinforcement, and then making sure that no other reinforcement of the unwanted behavior is occurring (Martin & Pear, 2007). If Dad ignores the child's tantrums when he takes the child shopping but Mom gives in and buys the child toys, then the behavior will not be completely extinguished.

Randy Faris/Corbis/Glow Images

By ignoring this child's tantrum, the parent is placing the child on an extinction schedule. If the parent does not reward the child for this behavior, the behavior should be less likely to occur in the future, at least for this parent.

6.3.4 • Schedules of Reinforcement

Acquisition and extinction of operant behavior seem simple enough, but numerous Skinner box studies have taught us that many factors can affect the rate at which responses are acquired or extinguished. One extremely important factor is the **schedule of reinforcement**—the timing and the consistency of the reinforcement.

CONTINUOUS REINFORCEMENT

Conceptually, the simplest type of reinforcement schedule is **continuous reinforcement**, in which each and every instance of the desired behavior is rewarded. In a Skinner box study, every time the rat presses the bar, a pellet of food is delivered to the rat. In real life, many simple behaviors are reinforced on a continuous schedule. One example is when we reach for objects. The act of reaching is reinforced when we actually grasp the object we were trying to get. Except in unusual circumstances, such as reaching for an object on a shelf that is too high, reaching is rewarded every time we reach (Skinner, 1953). Unfortunately, continuous schedules of reinforcement are often not very helpful when using operant conditioning to modify behavior.

schedule of reinforcement the frequency and timing of the reinforcements that an organism receives

continuous reinforcement a schedule of reinforcement in which the organism is rewarded for every instance of the desired response

Continuous reinforcement is often not very helpful for two main reasons. The first drawback is a practical one. Let's say that you were going to use continuous reinforcement to change a child's behavior. You want your child to be polite when speaking to others, so you decide to use a continuous schedule and reinforce your child with praise every time she is polite. Would this be feasible? We doubt it. A continuous schedule of reinforcement would mean that you would have to be around your child every time she was polite, and you would have to praise or otherwise reward her for this politeness. This just isn't practical or possible.

The second problem is that continuously reinforced behaviors are vulnerable to extinction. What happens when your children are not in your presence, and you are not there to continually reinforce their good behavior? As we have already seen, when reinforcement is withheld, behavior often starts to extinguish. The problem with using continuous schedules of reinforcement is that they lead to behaviors that extinguish very quickly once the reinforcement ceases (Nevin, 2012; Nevin & Grace, 2005).

Why would this be true? When a behavior has been continuously reinforced, there is a very clear contingency between the behavior and the reward. The organism learns that the behavior should always lead to a reward. When the reinforcement stops, a clear signal is sent that the contingency no longer holds true, and extinction occurs relatively rapidly.

PARTIAL REINFORCEMENT

However, let's say the behavior is reinforced only some of the time. What is likely to happen then? The child or animal is less likely to see the lack of reinforcement as a sign that the contingency is no longer operating. Schedules of reinforcement

partial reinforcement a schedule of reinforcement in which the organism is rewarded for only some instances of the desired response

fixed ratio schedule a schedule of reinforcement in which the organism is rewarded for every *x*th instance of the desired response

variable ratio schedule a schedule of reinforcement in which the organism is rewarded on average for every *x*th instance of the desired response

that reinforce a behavior only some of the time are called **partial reinforcement** schedules. *Ratio schedules* of partial reinforcement are based on the number of responses, whereas *interval schedules* are based on the timing of the responses.

Ratio Schedules of Reinforcement In a **fixed ratio schedule**, a set number of responses must be emitted before a reward is given. For example, suppose every third response is rewarded. A rat in a Skinner box would have to press the bar three times to get a food pellet. In the real world, some people are paid on fixed ratio schedules. A person who works in a manufacturing plant and is paid a bonus for every 100 parts assembled is being reinforced on a fixed ratio, as are agricultural workers who are paid per bushel of fruit picked, garment workers who are paid per piece sewn, and so on.

Besides producing slower extinction than continuous reinforcement, fixed ratio schedules also lead to fairly high response rates (• FIGURE 6.7a). High rates of responding are especially likely if it takes many responses to get a reward (Collier, Hirsch, & Hamlin, 1972; Stephens et al., 1975). If your goal is to produce many instances of the behavior, such as many filled boxes of raspberries, in a short time frame, a fixed ratio schedule may just do the trick.

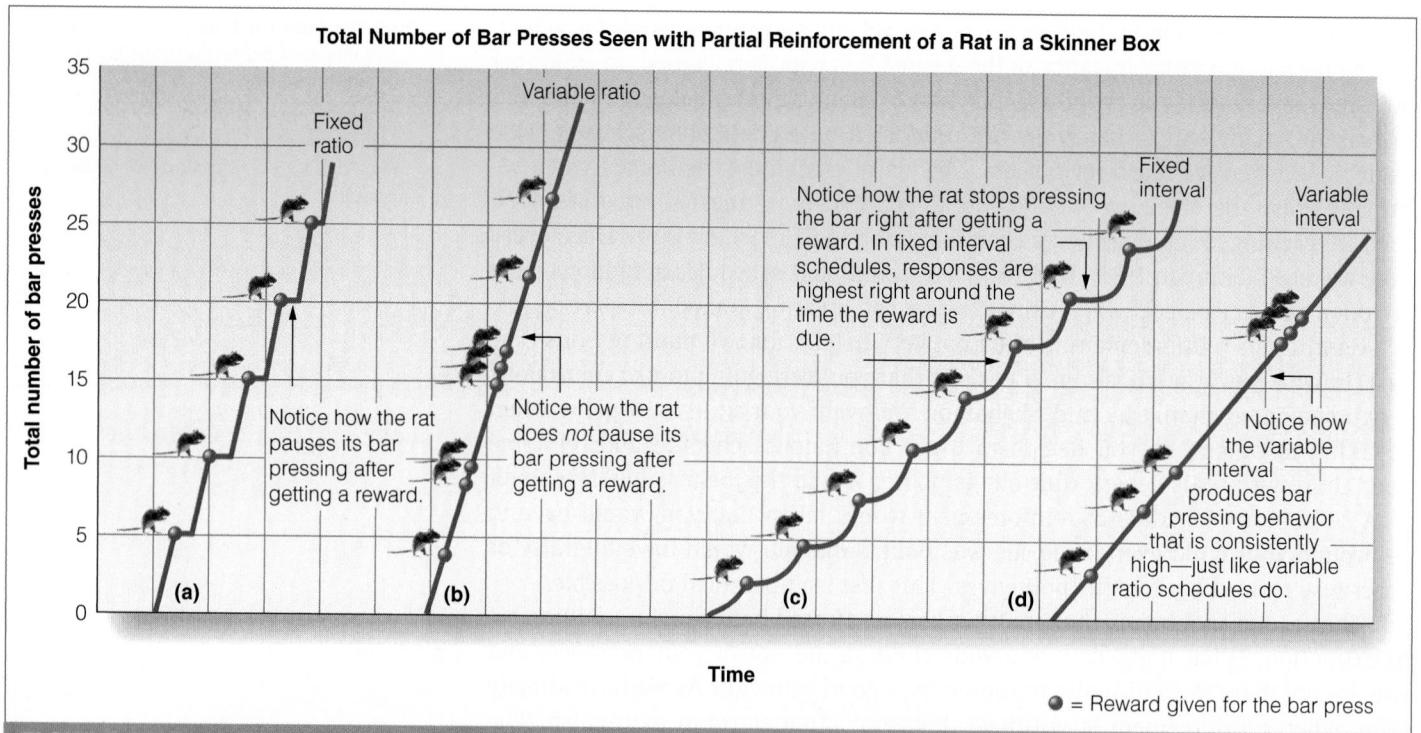

Grove Pashley/Getty Images

FIGURE 6.7

Partial Reinforcement of a Rat in a Skinner Box

This graph plots the rates of response for different schedules of reinforcement and the points at which the rat is reinforced. Notice how the rat's bar-pressing behavior changes before and after it receives a pellet on the different schedules of reinforcement. Which schedule would you use if you were going to use positive reinforcement to train your dog?

The second type of ratio schedule is the **variable ratio schedule**, in which the exact number of responses that are required to receive a reward varies around some average. For example, the rat may have to press the bar two times to receive the first reward, one time to receive the second reward, and then six times to receive the third reward.

Variable ratio schedules of reinforcement yield higher rates of response (Figure 6.7b) and even slower rates of extinction than fixed ratio schedules. A good example of this resistance to extinction comes from a real-world example of variable ratio reinforcement. Slot machines pay off on a variable ratio schedule of reinforcement. You never know how many pulls of the handle it will take to lead to the reward of a payoff. Consequently, people will play slot machines for long periods of time, even when they haven't hit the jackpot (Schreiber & Dixon, 2001). One of us once knew a person who claimed to have lost $2,000 in slot machines during a weekend in Las Vegas. That type of resistance to extinction keeps many a casino owner very happy!

© Bonnie Kamin/Photo Edit

Slot machines pay off on a variable ratio schedule of reinforcement. Because it is hard to predict when the next reward is due, people playing the machine are likely to show high rates of responding and very slow rates of extinction. This translates into big profits for the casinos!

Interval Schedules of Reinforcement Ratio schedules of reinforcement are based on the number of responses emitted by the organism. In interval schedules of reinforcement, the organism is rewarded only once per some interval of time. In a **fixed interval schedule**, the organism is rewarded for the first instance of the desired response, after which a set interval of time must pass before any other instances of the response will be rewarded. For example, if a rat in a Skinner box is reinforced on a fixed interval of 10 minutes, it will be rewarded for its first bar press, but not again until after 10 minutes has passed—no matter how many more times it presses the bar. Then the first bar press after the 10-minute mark has passed will be rewarded (● FIGURE 6.8).

fixed interval schedule a schedule of reinforcement in which the organism is rewarded for the first desired response in an *x*th interval of time

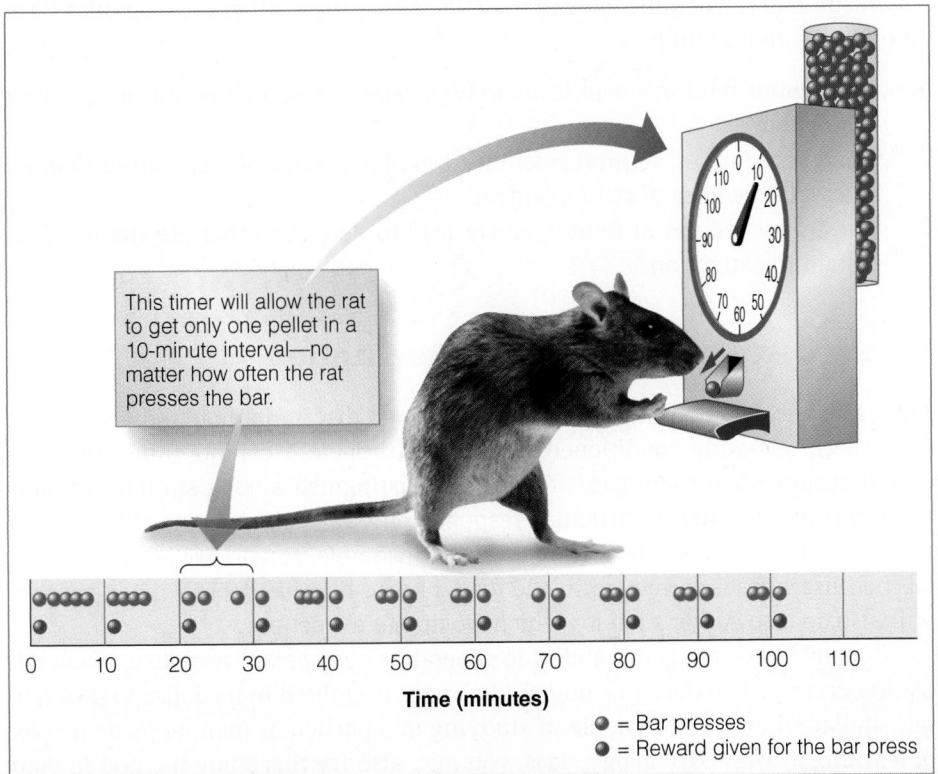

Grove Pashley/Photolibrary/Getty Images

FIGURE 6.8

Fixed Interval Schedule of Reinforcement

This is an example of an FI 10-minute schedule of reinforcement for a rat in a Skinner box. The blue dots indicate when the rat pressed the bar, and the red dots indicate when the rat was rewarded for its bar-pressing behavior. On an FI of 10 minutes, the rat will receive a maximum of one reinforcement during any 10-minute interval—no matter how often the rat presses the bar. The rat learns to press the bar only when a reward is due—right around the 10-minute interval mark. Yes, rats do have some sense of time!

Once the organism has received its reward for an interval, it usually stops responding for most of the remainder of the interval. One example of a fixed interval schedule is a yearly performance review at work. If an employee knows that she is going to be evaluated every January, she might be tempted to work her hardest in December. Immediately after being reviewed, the employee may be tempted to reduce her performance because she knows that she will not be reviewed again for another year. Then, as the end of the interval approaches and the next performance evaluation looms near, we can expect to see another increase in the employee's performance. This characteristic pause after reinforcement on a fixed interval schedule has been seen in rats (Innis, 1979) and pigeons (Berry, Kangas, & Branch, 2012), as well as humans (see Figure 6.7c; Shimoff, Cantania, & Matthews, 1981).

variable interval schedule a schedule of reinforcement in which the organism is rewarded for the first desired response in an average *x*th interval of time

One way to avoid this pause in the behavior immediately after reinforcement is to make the interval variable. Similar to what we saw in the variable ratio schedule, in a **variable interval schedule**, the length of the interval varies. What if our employee from the previous example did not know when to expect her next evaluation? What if she could be evaluated during any month of the year? Under these circumstances, her only choice would be to always perform well—assuming, of course, that she wanted to do well on her evaluation. Pop quizzes also reward students on a variable interval schedule for keeping up with their reading and studying. As you can see from Figure 6.7d, variable interval schedules produce steady rates of responding in rats. Another benefit of variable interval schedules is that they produce behaviors that are more resistant to extinction than those produced with fixed interval schedules.

In summary, when it comes to the effects that these different schedules have on operant conditioning:

1. Continuous reinforcement leads to high rates of responding but the quickest extinction.
2. Ratio schedules of reinforcement lead to higher rates of responding than do interval schedules of reinforcement.
3. Variable schedules of reinforcement lead to behaviors that are the most resistant to extinction.

6.3.5 • Discrimination and Generalization

Just as classically conditioned responses undergo discrimination and generalization, so do operantly conditioned responses. In operant conditioning, discrimination occurs when the organism learns to distinguish among similar stimulus situations and to offer a particular response only in those specific situations in which reinforcement will be forthcoming. For example, at work we learn to do our job because it leads to reward in the form of pay, but this doesn't mean that we will also do a coworker's job for which we do not expect pay.

Equally important is our ability to generalize our operant responses. Generalization occurs when the same operant behavior is emitted in response to different but similar stimuli. For example, if studying in a particular manner leads to a lot of learning in your psychology class, you may also try this study method in your history class where it may also pay off.

In the previous examples, discrimination and generalization led to positive outcomes. Unfortunately, this is not always the case. One example of the negative aspects of discrimination and generalization is found in prejudice and discrimination against certain groups of people (see Chapter 10). In prejudice, one's negative feelings about a few members of a group generalize to most or all members of that group. Similarly, one may discriminate by treating members of some groups in a kind manner and treating all or most members of a disliked group in an unkind manner. Here what we commonly refer to as discrimination in the social sense is also an example of what psychologists refer to as discrimination in learning.

6.3.6 • Shaping New Behaviors

Before a behavior can be operantly conditioned, the organism must first engage in the behavior spontaneously. Before Thorndike's cat learned to quickly receive its reward by stepping on the foot release in the puzzle box, it first had to accidentally or spontaneously step on the pedal and open the box. Learning occurs only after the behavior has been emitted and the organism has been either punished or reinforced. Given this, how can operant conditioning explain the development of novel behaviors? For example, how could an animal trainer use operant conditioning to teach a dog to do a trick that involves walking on its hind legs? If you wait for a dog to spontaneously stand up on its hind legs and begin to walk so that you can reinforce this behavior with a treat, you are going to be waiting for a long time!

shaping using operant conditioning to build a new behavior in an organism by rewarding successive approximations of the desired response

Animal trainers use an operant conditioning technique called **shaping**, in which a novel behavior is slowly conditioned by reinforcing successive *approximations* of the final desired behavior. In the case of training the dog, the trainer will reinforce any spontaneous behavior that is in the direction of the final desired behavior. The trainer may start by rewarding the dog for looking at him. Once the dog learns to pay attention, it may expand on this behavior by sitting up. This will also lead to a treat. Then the dog must sit up to get the treat. Once the dog learns to sit up, it may go a bit further and rear up a bit on its hind legs. This will also earn the dog a treat. Now that the dog can rear up, it must do so to get a treat. After rearing up for a time, the dog may spontaneously go up all the way onto its hind legs. The trainer responds with more treats. Soon the dog will progress to standing on its hind legs, and the trainer will reciprocate with more treats every time the dog stands up on its hind legs. The final step comes when the dog spontaneously takes its first steps after being conditioned to stand on its hind legs. At this point, all the trainer has to do is reward the dog for walking on its hind legs.

Shaping has many useful purposes in the real world. A parent could use shaping to help a child become more successful in school. At first the parent could reward the child for any study-related behavior, such as doing reading assignments or homework. Then the parent could progress to rewarding the child for earning good grades on individual assignments, followed by a reward only for good grades on individual exams. Then the parent could reward the child for making good grades in individual courses. Finally, the parent could reward the child only for making good grades in all courses. By slowly rewarding closer and closer approximations of the final desired behavior, the parent can shape a behavior in the child that would, perhaps, have never occurred on its own.

These last examples point to the usefulness of operant conditioning in the real world. If used correctly, operant conditioning can be very effective in modifying a child's behavior. This is not to say that operant conditioning can be used only with children. Operant conditioning can be used with any person or animal. However, the use of operant conditioning as a parental tool provides a nice backdrop for discussing some of the choices one must make before implementing an operant conditioning program of behavior modification with any person or animal.

Animal trainers such as the "Dog Whisperer" Cesar Milan, sometimes use shaping to get animals to perform new behaviors.

Neilson Barnard/Getty Images Entertainment/Getty Images

6.3.7 • Decisions That Must Be Made When Using Operant Conditioning

One of the first decisions that has to be made when using operant conditioning to change behavior is which type of consequence to use. Recall that there are two basic types of consequences that follow behavior—reinforcement and punishment. When designing an operant conditioning program of behavior modification, one must first decide whether to punish or reinforce the behavior. Sometimes this choice will be a very clear one, but often it will not be.

PUNISHMENT OR REINFORCEMENT?

At times, a parent will have a choice either to reinforce a child's good behavior or to punish the child's bad behavior. For example, suppose your child is not studying. You can punish the child for not studying, or you can reward the child for studying. Which of these methods do you think will be more successful and cause fewer problems? If you guessed that reinforcement is the safer, more effective route, you guessed correctly. In fact, one of the most effective ways of controlling children's behavior is to show them how you want them to respond and then reward them for behaving that way (Kochanska, 1995; Zahn-Waxler & Robinson, 1995). So, what makes punishment riskier and less effective?

- *Punishment doesn't teach the correct behavior in a given situation.* Think about it for a moment. Let's say you hear your daughter getting frustrated with the family dog and swearing at the dog. As a result, you immediately yell at her. What have you taught her? You have taught her not to use whatever swear word she uttered at the dog. What you have not taught her, however, is how she should have responded in this situation. The next time she is frustrated with the dog, she will not know how to express her frustration appropriately. Because punishment does not teach the correct response, any use of punishment should include a discussion of appropriate behavior and reinforcement of that behavior (Martin & Pear, 2007).
- *Harsh punishment, especially physical punishment, teaches aggressive behavior.* Harsh punishment provides an aggressive model for the child. When a parent spanks a child, the parent is teaching the child two things: first, that the child's behavior has had aversive consequences; and second, that being aggressive is a powerful means of controlling other people's behavior. In later sections of this chapter, we will see that children often imitate the behavior of others (Bandura, 1977; McGuigan, 2013). Therefore, while harsh punishment may stop an unwanted behavior, it may also teach the child to be aggressive. The next time the child feels frustrated or upset with another person, he or she may try using aggression to express those feelings. This is rarely the goal most parents have in mind!
- *Harsh punishment is often ineffective at producing behavior change* (see, Romano, Bell, & Norian, 2013; Strassberg et al., 1994). When punished, children often stop engaging in the undesired behavior, but only for as long as their parents are around. When the parents are out of sight—and the threat of immediate punishment is gone—the undesired behavior returns. Because the goal is usually to ensure that the child behaves even when the parents are not around, punishment is not always effective.
- *Harsh punishment often leads to negative emotional reactions* (Skinner, 1953). These negative reactions include anger, fear, and anxiety. If a child experiences fear and anxiety when a parent punishes him, he may come to fear the parent. Just as Little Albert came to associate the white rat with

loud, frightening noises, a child can come to associate a parent with pain and humiliation. Through classical conditioning, the parent can become a conditioned stimulus that evokes negative emotions in the child. This conditioned fear can lead to a psychologically unhealthy, fear-based parent–child relationship in which the child seeks to avoid the parent and the parent becomes resentful toward the child.

Harsh punishment, in particular, is riskier and less effective than reinforcement. Especially problematic is the use of physical punishment or spanking, which should be avoided. Years of research have shown us that children who experience physical punishment are more likely to be aggressive and experience lower levels of mental health than children who are not hit (Gershoff, 2002, 2010). Harsh physical punishment in childhood is also linked to poorer physical health in adulthood (Afifi et al., 2013). Furthermore, having experienced physical punishment as a child is correlated with relationship problems in college students (Leary et al., 2008). And, parents who use physical punishment have been shown to be more hostile and to have higher levels of conflict in their marriages (Kanoy et al., 2003).

Peter Dazeley/Photographer's Choice/Getty Images

Even though a parent may only intend to use operant conditioning when spanking a child, it is possible that the child may also experience classical conditioning. Because the parent is delivering the punishment, the parent can become a conditioned stimulus that elicits fear or other negative emotions in the child.

The Cultural Debate over the Ethics of Physical Punishment The potential risks associated with the use of physical punishment led the American Psychological Association (APA) to issue a policy statement discouraging the use of physical punishment on children decades ago (APA, 1975). However, societal change is often slow to occur. As recently as the 1990s, more than 90% of U.S. parents sampled reported using physical punishment on their children, and 100% reported using it on toddlers (Straus, 1991). Indeed, in a 2006 study, 91% of a sample of U.S. college students reported having been hit by their parents during childhood; even more troubling, 62% reported being hit with an object (Chang, Pettit, & Katsurada, 2006).

Some declines in parental use of physical punishment in the United States have also been seen. In her 2010 review of the research on physical punishment, Elizabeth Gershoff reports that only about 50% of U.S. parents still regularly use physical punishment on toddlers, while 65% to 68% use it on preschoolers. Although these numbers represent a decline, they are still high. Gershoff attributes the persistence of physical punishment in the United States in part to cultural values that are passed from generation to generation. Because we learn much of what we know about parenting from our own parents, viewing physical punishment as a successful parenting tool has been passed from parent to child for generations.

Yet change is taking place. The debate over the dangers of physical punishment has gone global, leading the Council of Europe to launch a campaign to end physical punishment of children in Europe. As of 2013, Austria, Bulgaria, Croatia, Cyprus, Denmark, Finland, Germany, Greece, Hungary, Latvia, Luxembourg, Netherlands, Poland, Portugal, Romania, Spain, and Sweden have all banned physical punishment of children. Furthermore, according to the multinational *Global Initiative to End All Corporal Punishment of Children* (2013), whose aims have been endorsed by UNICEF and UNESCO, many other countries have also banned physical punishment of children. To date, Albania, Costa Rica, Honduras, Iceland, Israel, Kenya, Liechtenstein, New Zealand, Norway, Republic of Moldova, Republic of Congo, South Sudan, Togo, Tunisia, Ukraine, Uruguay, and Venezuela have all enacted bans. Perhaps someday, future generations will also commit to eliminating the use of physical punishment on children in the United States.

Practical Alternatives to Physical Punishment The strong case we have made against physical punishment does not mean that children should not be disciplined at all. Effective parenting means teaching children to behave in socially acceptable ways, and discipline is sometimes needed to teach children appropriate self-control. Sometimes situations call for some form of punishment. Luckily, a number of alternatives to physical punishment are possible, many of which are listed in ●TABLE 6.2. If used properly, these techniques will most likely prove effective. Here are a few tips for making punishments like the ones in Table 6.2 more effective in general:

1. Tell the child what the appropriate behavior is, and then reinforce that behavior.
2. Minimize situations that tempt the child to engage in bad behavior.

TABLE 6.2

Alternatives to Physical Punishment

METHOD	EXAMPLE
Nonphysical Punishment Methods	
Timeout: The child is sent to sit in a quiet place.	Devon, 5 years old, is sent to sit in the laundry room for 5 minutes after hitting his sister. There are no toys, friends, or other reinforcements present.
Restitution: The child has to give up something.	Sabina broke her sister's toy on purpose. Now Sabina has to give one of her own toys to her sister.
Fines: The child has to pay a fine.	Every time a family member uses inappropriate language, he or she has to put 50 cents in the "swear jar."
Loss of privileges: The child loses a privilege.	Giorgio is grounded for 2 weeks for breaking curfew and talking back to his parents.
Nonpunishment Methods	
Empathy training: Teach the child to empathize with others. If the child hurts another, she is encouraged to imagine what that person might have felt as a result of being hurt. The ability to empathize reduces the motivation to hurt others.	Suzy intentionally breaks Jimmy's toy. To teach her empathy, Suzy's mother asks her to think about how she felt when Bobby broke her toy last week. Then Suzy is asked to think about whether Jimmy might be feeling the same way now that Suzy broke his toy. This should make Suzy feel bad about having hurt Jimmy's feelings.
Differential reinforcement of incompatible responses (DRI): The child is rewarded for engaging in a desirable behavior that cannot be emitted at the same time as the undesirable behavior.	Marya's parents reward her for being quiet in church as opposed to punishing her for being loud in church.

3. Use a punishment that really is punishing. If the child does not find the punishment aversive, it will fail to control the behavior.
4. Punishment must occur immediately after the bad behavior occurs.
5. Punishment must occur each and every time the bad behavior occurs. Otherwise, the bad behavior is partially reinforced when the child escapes the punishment.
6. Remain calm while you are punishing a child. This will help ensure that you do not abuse the child.

Although nonphysical punishment may be necessary at times to reduce undesirable behavior, when you have a choice, it is much safer and often more effective to use reinforcement of good behavior to control behavior. However, there are things to consider if you want to be sure your program of reinforcement has the desired effect on the behavior you are trying to change.

CHOOSING A REINFORCER THAT IS REINFORCING

It may seem like a trivial issue, but the first consideration in developing a program of reinforcement is to choose a reinforcer that is actually reinforcing for the person you are trying to condition. If the reinforcer is not something the person likes or values, it will not work. For example, if your significant other cleans the whole house, and you reward him by cooking a meal that he does not like, then he will not be more likely to clean the house again. Your attempt at operant conditioning will have failed. When in doubt, it's a good idea to discuss with the person the consequences that he or she would find reinforcing before conditioning begins.

PRIMARY AND SECONDARY REINFORCERS

Reinforcers can be categorized as either *primary* or *secondary*. A **primary reinforcer** is one that is directly reinforcing. Examples of primary reinforcers are food, water, a warm bed, and sexual pleasure. These reinforcers are primary because they are pleasurable in and of themselves. If you are hungry, then food will reinforce you by removing your hunger.

In contrast, **secondary reinforcers** are rewarding only because they lead to primary reinforcers. A wonderful example of a secondary reinforcer in Western society is money. By itself, a dollar bill is not reinforcing. What makes a dollar reinforcing is what you can buy with it—food, water, shelter, and other primary reinforcers. When you get right down to it, you don't go to work for money per se. You go to work to ensure that you will be able to purchase an adequate supply of primary reinforcers.

One method of secondary reinforcement is to use a *token economy*. A **token economy** reinforces desired behavior with a token of some sort (for example, a poker chip or a gold star) that can later be cashed in for primary reinforcers (see Martin et al., 1968). Token economies are often used to control the behavior of groups of people such as schoolchildren (Salend, 2001), children receiving treatment for intellectual disabilities (Matson & Boisjoli, 2009), or inmates (Holmqvist, Hill, & Lang, 2009). Token economies can also be used in the context of a family (Kazdin, 1977) or in the workplace (Schumacher et al., 2013).

To set up a token economy, the first step is to draw up a list of desired and undesired behaviors that you will try to control. The next step is to decide how many tokens to give (or take away) for each of the behaviors, and to develop some sort of recordkeeping system to keep track of each participant's tokens. One recordkeeping approach is to draw a chart like the one shown in ● FIGURE 6.9 and hang it on the wall in a prominent place.

primary reinforcer a reinforcer that is reinforcing in and of itself

secondary reinforcer a reinforcer that is reinforcing only because it leads to a primary reinforcer

token economy a system of operant conditioning in which participants are reinforced with tokens that can later be cashed in for primary reinforcers

Mrs. Alvarez's Class

Students	Paying attention in class, +5 tokens	On time for class, +3 tokens	Homework completely done, +7 tokens	B or better on daily quiz, +10 tokens	Talking in class, −5 tokens	Fighting, −10 tokens	Calling people names −10 tokens
Franco							
Mary							
Louisa							
Billy							
George							
Eddie							
Latesha							

Token values
25 tokens = 1 sticker, eraser, or pencil
50 tokens = 1 small toy
75 tokens = 1 medium-size toy
100 tokens = 1 coupon for free pizza
125 tokens = 1 DVD

FIGURE 6.9
A Sample Point System from a Token Economy

Using token economies has two main advantages. One is that a token economy is effective when trying to simultaneously modify a number of behaviors in a group of people. For example, a token economy can be used with an entire class, which is easier than trying to develop an individual operant conditioning program for each student.

The second major advantage is that token economies allow for immediate reinforcement with a token, even when it is not practical to immediately present the primary reinforcer. For example, it's disruptive for a teacher to stop the class to give a child a toy as a reinforcer. However, the teacher can immediately hand the child a token that can be used at week's end to purchase a toy. The use of tokens helps to bridge the gap between the behavior and the eventual primary reinforcement of the behavior.

A potential problem with token economies is that they often place the behavior on a continuous schedule of reinforcement. As we saw in previous sections, continuous reinforcement can lead to behavior that is vulnerable to extinction. It is possible that a token economy may lessen a person's desire to engage in a behavior when the behavior is not likely to lead to a token or some other reward. This potential problem may be outweighed, however, by the usefulness of the token economy in controlling the immediate behavior of the people in the program. For instance, in a prison you may be more worried about controlling the immediate, day-to-day behavior of the prison population. Facilitating the future motivation of the inmates to behave in a particular way once they are out of the token economy is likely to be less of a concern.

6.3.8 • The Role of Cognition in Learning

So far in this chapter, we have discussed three major types of learning—habituation, classical conditioning, and operant conditioning—that have some important things in common. One common feature is that all of these types of learning require that the person or animal *do something* before learning can occur. In habituation, the organism must emit an orienting reflex. In classical conditioning, the organism must have an unconditioned response. In operant conditioning, the organism must first engage in some random behavior that is either reinforced or punished.

Another common feature of these learning theories is that they do not emphasize the role that mental or cognitive processes play in learning. Researchers such as Ivan Pavlov, John B. Watson, E. L. Thorndike, and B. F. Skinner did not discuss thoughts and feelings and how these may affect the learning process. Skinner, in particular, argued that psychology should not seek to study the cognitive aspects of behavior because he believed that these things could not be studied scientifically and objectively. Skinner did not deny that humans and animals had thoughts and feelings; he simply held that they could not be studied adequately. Skinner subscribed to the psychological perspective of **behaviorism** (see Chapter 1), which states that the only aspect of living things that can and should be studied scientifically is behavior. Therefore, Skinner tried to explain behavior without discussing cognitive or mental processes (Skinner, 1953).

behaviorism a school of thought in psychology that emphasizes the study of observable behavior over the study of the mind

insight a sudden realization about how to solve a problem that occurs after an organism has studied the problem for a period of time

latent learning learning that cannot be directly observed in an organism's behavior

Because strict behaviorism totally ignores the influence of cognitive processes, it does not explain some of the learning we see in the real world, or in the lab. In the early 1900s, some researchers, including Wolfgang Köhler (1887–1967), became aware that cognitive processes must play a role in learning. Köhler observed that chimpanzees did not always attempt to solve problems in a trial-and-error fashion as predicted by the law of effect. Rather, they often seemed to study a problem for a long time as if formulating a mental plan—before attempting to solve it. In one experiment, Köhler placed a banana just out of reach outside a chimpanzee's cage, and he placed a stick inside the cage. The law of effect would predict that the chimpanzee would try many random behaviors—like shaking the bars and jumping up and down—before picking up the stick and using it to reach the banana. But this is not what Köhler observed. Instead, the chimpanzee studied the situation and then appeared to suddenly come up with the solution. After this flash of **insight** into how to solve its dilemma, the chimpanzee picked up the stick and used it to scoot the banana to a point where it could be reached (Köhler, 1925).

Köhler's work shows that learning can be a purely cognitive task. The chimpanzee did not have to wait for the consequences of its behavior to rule out behavioral strategies that would not accomplish the goal of obtaining the banana. Rather, the chimpanzee appeared to reason its way to a solution before acting.

In the 1930s, Edward Tolman (1886–1959) found additional support for the idea that cognition plays a role in learning. He discovered that rats would learn to run through a maze even when they were not rewarded for doing so (Tolman & Honzik, 1930). In Tolman's experiment, one group of rats was allowed to wander through the maze, and they were rewarded with food if they found their way to the end of the maze. Another group of rats was also allowed to explore the maze, but they were not rewarded even if they found their way to the end. As you might expect, after 10 days of training in the maze, the group that was rewarded could run through the maze more quickly than the unrewarded group could. On the 11th day, Tolman began to give rats in both groups a reward at the end of the maze. After just a few rewarded trials, the previously unrewarded rats could run through the maze just as fast as the rats that had been rewarded all along. This rapid learning in the previously unrewarded rats indicates that these rats had been learning even when they were not being rewarded.

© Penny Tweedie/Alamy

Wolfgang Köhler found that chimpanzees, like this one, can acquire insight into how to solve problems by watching and studying situations before acting. This type of problem solving suggests that cognitive processes can play an important role in learning.

Tolman's findings cannot be explained by operant conditioning alone because learning occurred *without* reinforcement. Tolman interpreted his results as being evidence that the rats had engaged in **latent learning**, or learning that cannot

cognitive map a mental representation of the environment that is formed through observation of one's environment

be directly observed through behavior. He proposed that while the unrewarded rats were wandering through the maze, they were developing a **cognitive map**, or mental representation, of the maze in their heads. Once the reward was presented, they used this map to help them get to the reward more quickly.

Although Tolman's experiments pointed to cognitive processes at work during learning, many psychologists ignored the impact of cognition on learning because of behaviorism's dominance in psychology at the time. It was not until the 1960s that learning researchers really began to look at the role of cognition in learning and behavior.

Quiz Yourself 6.3

1. **Denzel wants to increase his son, Mario's, tendency to mow the yard on Saturday mornings without having to repeatedly ask him. To do this, Denzel tells Mario that he will pay him $5 when he mows the yard without first having been told to do so. Denzel is using which schedule of reinforcement?**
   a. Fixed ratio
   b. Variable interval
   c. Variable ratio
   d. Continuous
2. **Which of the following is an example of operant conditioning?**
   a. Byron doesn't go to the dentist because the last time he did, it was very painful.
   b. Byron is afraid of dentists because the last time he went to the dentist, it was very painful.
   c. Byron wants to go to the dentist because when his friend Gina went to the dentist, the dentist gave Gina a toy.
   d. All of the above are examples of operant conditioning.
3. **Which of the following is a primary reinforcer?**
   a. Receiving good grades
   b. Food, when you're hungry
   c. Receiving a large sum of money
   d. Winning a free plane ticket in a radio contest
4. **When Kim Peek performed his feats of memory for people, they usually reacted with surprise and laughter. These reactions served as _____ that encouraged Kim to continue performing his displays of memory for others.**
   a. positive reinforcement
   b. negative reinforcement
   c. token reinforcers
   d. b and c
5. **Credit card points, earned by using the card to make purchases, are an example of _____.**
   a. conditioned stimuli
   b. primary reinforcers
   c. tokens
   d. operants

Answers 1. d; 2. a; 3. b; 4. a; 5. c

6.4 Observational Learning or Modeling: Learning by Watching Others

observational learning learning through observation and imitation of others' behavior

As we saw in the previous discussion, learning can occur without reinforcement, but even Tolman's unrewarded rats had at least engaged in the behavior of moving through the maze. Does all learning require that we actually engage in the behavior? As it turns out, we can learn by simply observing the behaviors of others. In this type of learning, called **observational learning**, we *observe* others and imitate, or *model*, their behavior. For that reason, observational learning is sometimes referred to as *social learning* or *modeling*.

As you read the following sections, keep in mind that observational learning departs from the behaviorism that Skinner so forcefully advocated on two major points. First, it acknowledges that learning can occur without an overt change in behavior; second, it takes into account the role of cognition in the learning process.

6.4.1 • Albert Bandura and the Bobo Doll Experiments

In the 1960s, psychologist Albert Bandura (b. 1925) conducted several experiments on observational learning, now considered classic psychological experiments, that contributed to his development of *social learning theory.* Collectively, these experiments are referred to as the *Bobo doll experiments* because the experimental procedure used an inflated plastic "Bobo" doll, a popular children's toy.

© Albert Bandura

FIGURE 6.10

Bandura's Bobo Doll Experiments

These photos, taken from the Bobo doll experiments, clearly show the children (panels B and C) modeling what they saw the model (panel A) doing to Bobo.

In the Bobo doll experiments, children watched films in which a woman beat up the Bobo doll. She hit him with a mallet, sat on him, threw him in the air, and so on (Bandura, Ross, & Ross, 1961). After the children viewed the films, Bandura and his colleagues placed them in a room alone with the Bobo doll and observed their behavior without their knowledge. If the children imitated the characteristic behaviors of the model, then Bandura knew that learning had occurred (• FIGURE 6.10).

In one of the Bobo doll experiments (Bandura, 1965), three groups of children watched three different films. In the *reward* film condition, the model was rewarded after beating up on Bobo. In the *punishment* film condition, she was punished after beating up on Bobo. In the *no consequences* film condition, nothing happened to the model after she beat up Bobo.

After viewing one of these films, the children were observed with Bobo, and their aggressive behaviors were recorded. As you might expect, the children who had seen the model rewarded for beating up Bobo were most likely to beat up on him themselves. However, an unexpected finding of the study was that the children who had seen the no consequences film were equally likely to beat up on Bobo. This means that seeing someone merely get away with aggressive behavior is just as likely to lead to modeling as seeing aggression rewarded. The only thing that deterred the children's aggression toward Bobo was having seen the film in which the model was punished for treating Bobo badly. Only these children were more hesitant to beat up on Bobo when they were left alone with him in the observation room.

By leaving the children alone with Bobo and recording their aggressive behavior, Bandura was able to assess how willing the children were to beat up on Bobo as a function of the consequences they expected would follow such aggression. But what had they actually learned about how to be aggressive toward Bobo? Is it possible that some of the children who did not beat up Bobo had still learned *how* to beat up Bobo? To test the children's level of *learning*, Bandura (1965) asked the children to show him exactly what they had seen in the films. Here, the children were free to model the behavior without fear of any type of punishment. Under these conditions, Bandura found that there were no significant differences across the three groups. All of the groups exhibited equal levels of learning when it came to knowing how the model had beat up Bobo.

The Bobo doll experiments show us two things. First, you don't have to engage in a behavior or experience reinforcement for learning to occur. Second, just as

Tolman discovered with his rats in the mazes, learning can be latent. The children who viewed the punishment film had learned how to beat up Bobo, but they were reluctant to beat him up because they feared there would be negative consequences for them if they did. We hope that the Bobo doll experiments make you think about the potential impact that violent movies, video games, and television may have on the children who view them because some very recent research seems to underscore the notion that kids do not merely watch TV—rather, they can learn from TV (Pinto da Mota Matos, Alves Ferreira, & Haase, 2012; Zack et al., 2009).

Researchers Donna Mumme and Anne Fernald (2003) have found that children as young as 12 months old pay attention to how a televised model reacts to certain stimuli, and they model their own reaction to the stimulus after the model's reaction. In this study, 12-month-old infants watched a televised actress interacting with certain toys. The actress responded positively, neutrally, or negatively to certain toys. Later, the infants were allowed to play with the same toys. The results showed that the infants were most likely to react favorably to the toys that the actress had either been neutral about or liked. Conversely, the infants were less likely to want to play with the toys to which the actress had reacted negatively. It seems that the infants disliked these toys simply because they had seen the actress reacting negatively toward them. Thus, the observational learning that occurs when watching TV may have the power to influence the attitudes that even very young children hold about the objects in their world. Subsequent research has suggested that infants are even more likely to pay attention to televised information when their parents also pay attention to it (Demers et al., 2013). In essence, if they are in the room, our children are likely to be watching what we are watching on TV.

Think about the impact that this process may have on learning stereotypes and prejudices. If a child is subjected to models (in real life or on TV) who react negatively to specific groups of people, could this lead to modeling in which the child comes to react negatively to certain types of people simply because they have seen this reaction in others? It seems likely that it could, and perhaps at a very young age! We will explore the causes of aggression and prejudice in our discussions of social psychology in Chapter 10. But for now, let's take a closer look at this process of observational learning and the variables that affect it.

6.4.2 • Observational Learning and Cognition

The role of cognition in observational learning can be clearly seen when you examine the conditions that are necessary for modeling to occur. According to Bandura (1986), modeling is a four-step process:

What do we learn from watching TV and playing video games?

© Jonathan Novrak/PhotoEdit

1. *Attention*. The observer must first pay attention to the model's behavior before he or she can model it. Research shows that children tend to model their behavior after people who are warm, nurturant, or powerful (Bandura, 1977). For example, a child may pay attention to the behavior of loving parents, a nurturant teacher, or a popular and seemingly powerful classmate. As we have already seen, another type of model that is particularly good at grabbing attention is a televised model (Bandura, Grusec, & Menlove, 1966). It is quite common to see children on the playground modeling the behavior of their favorite TV cartoon character. As we age and mature, however, we tend to seek out models that seem similar to us in some way (Bandura, 1986). For example, we may model our behavior after people of the same sex, ethnicity, or occupation.

2. *Retention in memory.* The observer must retain a cognitive representation or memory of the model's behavior. For children on the playground to model the behavior of TV characters, they must have memories of what they have previously seen on TV.
3. *Reproduction of the behavior.* The observer must have a mental representation of the behavior stored in memory that can be retrieved and used to reproduce the behavior. Of course, the person must have the physical abilities to actually reproduce the behavior if modeling is to occur. For instance, a child may remember seeing a cartoon superhero flying. Although the child may be able to model an approximation of this behavior, he will not be able to model the behavior precisely.
4. *Motivation.* After retrieving the memory of the behavior and figuring out how to produce the behavior, the observer must be motivated to actually execute the behavior. As we saw in the Bobo doll experiments, the observer may sometimes not want to execute the behavior. This is especially true if the observer believes that execution of the behavior may lead to punishment.

Bandura's observational learning theory brings an additional element to the study of learning, in that it addresses the role of cognition in the learning process. In the next two chapters, we will look more carefully at cognitive processes, examining how memory works in Chapter 7 and the cognitive processes involved in solving problems and making decisions and judgments in Chapter 8.

Quiz Yourself

6.4

1. **When Kim Peek's father attempted to teach Kim how to brush his teeth by modeling for him the process of brushing teeth, he was attempting to teach Kim through _____.**
   a. operant conditioning
   b. classical conditioning
   c. observational learning
   d. All of the above
2. **How do observational learning and operant conditioning differ?**
   a. In observational learning, the person is less aware that learning is taking place.
   b. In operant conditioning, the person is less aware that learning is taking place.
   c. In observational learning, the person does not have to engage in the response.
   d. In operant conditioning, the person does not have to engage in the response.
3. **Which of the following is an example of observational learning?**
   a. Henri can cook because as a child he spent a lot of time playing in the kitchen while his mother cooked dinner.
   b. Shalitha slaps another child for taking her toy away.
   c. Javier likes toy trains because they remind him of his childhood days.
   d. Billy is able to study with the neighbor's TV playing at full volume.
4. **Tyrone watches a violent TV show, but he has never imitated any of the behaviors he has seen on the show. Which of the following statements is true regarding Tyrone's learning?**
   a. Tyrone has not learned anything from watching the show.
   b. Tyrone has definitely learned something from watching the show.
   c. Tyrone may have learned something from watching the show.
   d. At some point in time, Tyrone's behavior will definitely change as a result of watching the show.

Answers 1. c; 2. c; 3. a; 4. c

6.5 Integrating Psychology: The Big Picture

In this chapter, we explored the process of *learning,* a relatively permanent change in behavior, or potential for behavior, as a result of experience. We learn to ignore repetitive stimuli when we *habituate. Classical conditioning* explains how we come to have particular physiological and emotional responses to certain stimuli. And, *operant conditioning* occurs when our behavior is shaped by the consequences it elicits from the environment. We also have the ability to engage in *observational learning* by observing the actions of others and later modeling these actions in our own behavior.

All of us have some capacity for learning. Learning is an important process through which we adapt our behavior to meet the demands of our environment. Recall the case of Kim Peek. Kim illustrated the extremes of human behavior, having both an extraordinary capacity for learning and serious learning difficulties. On the one hand, he learned to keep the payroll at his job without the use of a computer or calculator. On the other hand, no matter how many times his father demonstrated how to brush his teeth and button a shirt, Kim had great difficulty modeling these tasks. In fact, he had difficulty learning many motor-skill tasks. Most of us will fall somewhere between the extremes of Kim's learning abilities.

In our next chapter, we will continue to explore the cognitive aspect of psychology as we delve deeper into the learning process by taking a look at how we process information in memory. As you read Chapter 7, recall both the extraordinary cognitive abilities of the "Kimputer" and the difficulties Kim had with conceptual thought. Then think about your own learning and your own memory. Which types of learning come easily to you? Which types of learning are more difficult for you? And, how can you apply what you are learning about psychology to improve your learning?

Studying the Chapter

Key Terms

acquisition (238)
aversion therapy (239)
behaviorism (257)
biological preparedness (237)
classical conditioning (233)
cognitive map (258)
conditioned response (CR) (232)
conditioned stimulus (CS) (232)
contiguity (234)
contingency (234)
continuous reinforcement (247)
dishabituation (228)
extinction (238)
extinction burst (246)
fixed interval schedule (249)
fixed ratio schedule (248)
habituation (227)
insight (257)
latent learning (257)
law of effect (242)
learning (226)
negative punishment (243)
negative reinforcement (242)
neutral stimulus (NS) (232)
observational learning (258)
operant conditioning (241)
orienting reflex (226)
partial reinforcement (248)
positive punishment (243)
positive reinforcement (242)
primary reinforcer (255)
punishment (242)
reinforcement (242)
schedule of reinforcement (247)
secondary reinforcer (255)
shaping (251)
Skinner box (244)
spontaneous recovery (240)
stimulus discrimination (236)
stimulus generalization (236)
taste aversion (236)
token economy (255)
unconditioned response (UR) (230)
unconditioned stimulus (US) (230)
variable interval schedule (250)
variable ratio schedule (248)

What Do You Know? Assess Your Understanding

Test your retention and understanding of the material by answering the following questions.

1. Sasha is sitting in class, trying to listen to her professor's lecture, but she finds herself very distracted by the student next to her who is talking to another student. Sasha is exhibiting a(n) _____.

a. orienting reflex
b. habituation
c. dishabituation
d. conditioned response

2. After 2 days working at a day-care center, Roman no longer snaps to attention every time a child screams. The change in Roman's behavior is most likely due to _____.

a. orienting reflexes
b. habituation
c. dishabituation
d. classical conditioning

3. _____ is responding to a stimulus to which you have previously learned to ignore.

a. Habituation
b. Classical conditioning
c. Dishabituation
d. Operant conditioning

4. Getting an injection causes Marla to flinch. In classical conditioning terms, the needle stick is a(n) _____.

a. conditioned stimulus
b. conditioned response
c. unconditioned response
d. unconditioned stimulus

5. Which of the following types of learning does not require that the person or animal do anything in order for learning to occur?

a. habituation
b. classical conditioning
c. operant conditioning
d. social learning

6. In Pavlov's original studies, the unconditioned stimulus was _____.

a. the buzzer
b. salivation
c. food
d. the tube inserted into the dog's salivary gland

7. Every time Tyra smells apple pie baking, she feels very happy because she associates the smell of apple pie with her mother. Tyra's reaction to the smell of apple pie is most likely the result of _____.

a. habituation
b. classical conditioning
c. operant conditioning
d. observational learning

8. Amelia was in a car accident recently. Just prior to the crash, a certain song was playing on the radio. Now, whenever Amelia hears this song, she feels uneasy. This example shows that classical conditioning can sometimes occur even with low levels of _____.

a. contiguity and contingency
b. contiguity
c. contingency
d. similarity

9. Classical conditioning best explains the conditioning of what type of responses?

a. Behavioral
b. Emotional
c. Physiological
d. b & c

10. The law of effect was developed by _____.

a. Ivan Pavlov
b. E. L. Thorndike
c. B. F. Skinner
d. Albert Bandura

11. Which of the following processes best explains why a child may pretend to spank her teddy bear?

a. habituation
b. classical conditioning
c. operant conditioning
d. observational learning

12. Thelma rewards her son for making his bed by telling him that he doesn't need to mow the grass. Thelma is using _____ with _____ to condition her son's behavior.

a. classical conditioning; positive reinforcement
b. operant conditioning; positive reinforcement
c. classical conditioning; negative reinforcement
d. operant conditioning; negative reinforcement

13. _____ is responding to only a particular stimulus.

a. Stimulus generalization
b. Stimulus discrimination
c. Extinction
d. Shaping

14. _____ involves reinforcing successive approximations of the final desired behavior.

a. Extinction
b. Shaping
c. Secondary reinforcement
d. Primary reinforcement

15. Points earned for shopping at a particular store are an example of _____.

a. primary reinforcers
b. secondary reinforcers
c. fixed interval reinforcers
d. continuous reinforcers

16. Oscar is working in a manufacturing plant where he is paid $50 for every 1,000 units he produces. Oscar is being reinforced on a _____ schedule of reinforcement.

a. continuous
b. fixed interval of $50
c. fixed ratio of 1,000 units
d. variable ratio of 50 to 1,000 units

17. A token economy is an example of _____.

a. secondary reinforcement
b. operant conditioning
c. positive reinforcement
d. all of the above

18. Which of the following is *not* a true statement about using physical punishment on children?

a. Physical punishment may teach children to be aggressive.
b. Physical punishment may teach children correct behaviors.
c. Physical punishment is often less effective than positive reinforcement.
d. Physical punishment may result in classical conditioning of negative emotions in children.

19. Learning to make pizza by watching the cooking channel on TV is an example of what type of learning?

a. Habituation
b. Classical conditioning
c. Operant conditioning
d. Observational learning

20. Which of the following learning theorists would be most likely to acknowledge the role that memory plays in learning?

a. John B. Watson
b. B. F. Skinner
c. Albert Bandura
d. Ivan Pavlov

Answers: 1. a; 2. b; 3. c; 4. d; 5. d; 6. c; 7. b; 8. c; 9. d; 10. b; 11. d; 12. d; 13. b; 14. b; 15. b; 16. c; 17. d; 18. b; 19. d; 20. c.

Use It or Lose It: Applying Psychology

1. Identify a situation in which you were classically conditioned. Then identify the NS/CS, US, and UR/CR.
2. Think about two different environments that you frequently experience (for example, school, work, hanging with your friends). What behaviors are likely to be rewarded in these environments? What behaviors are likely to be punished? Are some behaviors rewarded in one environment but punished in the other? How will these rewards and punishments affect your future behavior? Explain.
3. Describe how parents use classical conditioning, operant conditioning, and social learning in their roles as parents.
4. If you were an employer who wanted to maximize employee productivity, which schedule of reinforcement would you use when creating a timetable for performance reviews of your employees? Defend your choice.

Critical Thinking for Integration

1. Design an experiment (Chapter 1) to test the hypothesis that continuous reinforcement leads to behaviors that are more easily extinguished than behaviors that are built with partial reinforcement. Describe your design in detail.
2. What role might the four types of learning play in drug addiction (Chapter 4)?
3. What role might the four types of learning play in a program designed to help people lose weight (Chapter 5)?
4. What role do the four types of learning play in your culture (Chapter 10)?

© NativeStock/PhotoEdit Inc.

Are You Getting the Big Picture? Learning

Learning is a relatively permanent change in behavior or the potential for behavior that results from experience.

6.1 Learning from the First Days of Life: Habituation

- **Orienting reflexes** allow us to respond to unexpected stimuli.
- **Habituation** allows us to stop responding to stimuli that are repeated over and over.
- **Dishabituation** allows us to re-respond to a stimulus to which we were previously habituated.

© Arclight/Alamy

6.2 Classical Conditioning: Learning Through the Association of Stimuli

- Ivan Pavlov discovered classical conditioning while studying salivation in dogs.
- **Classical conditioning** occurs when a **neutral stimulus** is paired with an **unconditioned stimulus** that reliably causes an **unconditioned response**, and because of this association, the neutral stimulus loses its neutrality and becomes a conditioned stimulus that elicits the **conditioned response**.
- Classical conditioning is most effective when the NS/CS and US are separated by only a brief period of time (**contiguity**), and the pairing must reliably predict the response (**contingency**).
- In the Little Albert experiments, John B. Watson and Rosalie Rayner studied how emotional responses could be classically conditioned in humans.
- **Stimulus generalization** occurs when we respond to similar stimuli with the same conditioned response.
- **Stimulus discrimination** occurs when the conditioned response is only elicited by a particular CS.
- **Taste aversion** occurs when a particular food is associated with some other ailment or condition that causes nausea and the food becomes a conditioned stimulus for nausea.
- The elimination of a conditioned response is known as **extinction**.

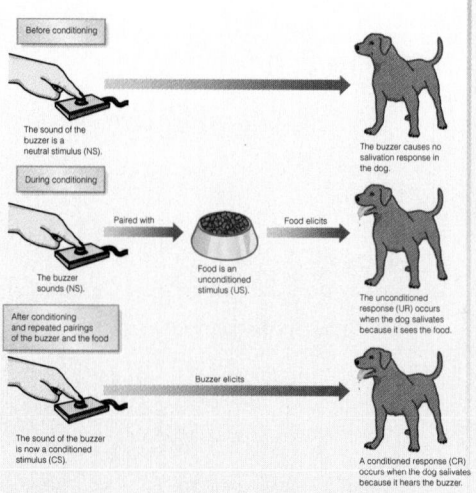

6.3 Operant Conditioning: Learning from the Consequences of Our Actions

- In **operant conditioning**, we learn from the consequences of our actions.
- E. L. Thorndike developed the **law of effect**, which emphasized the negative and positive consequences of behavior.

	Add to Environment	Remove from Environment
Increase Behavior	+ Reinforcement	– Reinforcement
Decrease Behavior	+ Punishment	– Punishment

- B. F. Skinner, a strong proponent of **behaviorism**, coined the term operant conditioning to refer to how a certain behavior operates on the environment to produce some consequence. The **Skinner box** is a chamber used to study animal learning.
- Five schedules of **reinforcement**—**continuous**, **fixed ratio**, **variable ratio**, **fixed interval**, and **variable interval**—describe the timing and number of responses required to receive reinforcement.
- In **shaping**, a novel behavior is slowly conditioned by reinforcing successive approximations of the final desired behavior.
- **Primary reinforcers** are reinforcing in themselves. **Secondary reinforcers** are rewarding because they lead to primary reinforcers.
- A **token economy** reinforces desired behavior with a token of some sort that can later be cashed in for primary reinforcers.

Steve Lyne/Getty Images

6.4 Observational Learning or Modeling: Learning by Watching Others

- **Observational learning** is learning that occurs by observing others and modeling their behavior.
- Albert Bandura's Bobo doll experiments showed that you do not have to engage in a behavior or experience for learning to occur, and that learning can be **latent**.
- In contrast to behaviorists such as Skinner, social learning theorists emphasize the role that cognitive processes (attention and retention in memory), reproduction of the behavior, and motivation play in learning

© Jonathan Novrak/PhotoEdit

Memory

Learning Objectives

7.1 Explain the functions of memory. (APA 1.1)

7.1 Explain the difference between implicit and explicit use of memory, and give examples of each. (APA 1.1, 1.3)

7.2 Describe the three-stages model of memory, including the function and characteristics of sensory, short-term, and long-term memory. (APA 1.1, 2.1)

7.2 Describe the newer conception of working memory and how it relates to the three-stages model's concept of short-term memory. (APA 1.1)

7.3 Explain how information is organized in long-term memory. (APA 1.1)

7.3 Describe the different types of long-term memory and their characteristics. (APA 1.1)

7.3 Describe the different types of amnesia and what cases of amnesia have taught us about memory. (APA 1.1, 1.2, 1.3, 2.1)

7.3 Describe age- and gender-related differences in memory. (APA 1.1, 1.2, 1.3, 2.1, 3.3)

7.4 Explain retrieval processes in memory, and give real-world examples of them. (APA 1.1, 1.3)

7.4 Describe and give examples of the various theories of forgetting in long-term memory. (APA 1.1, 1.3)

7.4 Describe some of the practical measures you can take to improve your memory. (APA 1.3, 5.2)

7.5 Describe the accuracy of memory and its implications for eyewitness memory. (APA 1.1, 1.3, 3.3)

7.6 Describe what is known about the biology of memory. (APA 1.1, 1.2)

Kim Peek's father affectionately referred to Kim as the "Kimputer." Kim's amazing ability to process and store large quantities of factual information, such as phone numbers, ZIP codes, and encyclopedia entries certainly brings to mind the workings of a computer. This notion that our minds function as computers is not unusual in psychology, either. Many psychologists use a computer analogy to help them understand the mind. The information-processing approach in cognitive psychology assumes that the mind functions like a very sophisticated computer. A computer accepts input—the information you type into it—stores and processes the information, and allows you to go back and retrieve the same information. In essence, this is also what your mind does with information.

7

© Robert Kneschke/Shutterstock.com

Chapter Outline

7.1 The Functions of Memory: Encoding, Storing, and Retrieving / 270

7.2 The Development of New Memories / 271

7.3 Long-Term Memory: Permanent Storage / 283

7.4 Retrieval and Forgetting in Long-Term Memory / 289

PSYCHOLOGY APPLIES TO YOUR WORLD: Tips for Improving Your Memory / 290

7.5 The Accuracy of Memory / 295

7.6 The Biology of Memory / 297

7.7 Integrating Psychology: The Big Picture / 300

7.1 The Functions of Memory: Encoding, Storing, and Retrieving

encoding the act of inputting information into memory

memory traces the stored code that represents a piece of information that has been encoded into memory

storage the place where information is retained in memory

retrieval the process of accessing information in memory and pulling it into consciousness

consciousness an organism's awareness of its own mental processes and/or its environment

attention an organism's ability to focus its consciousness on some aspect of its own mental processes and/or its environment

explicit memory the conscious use of memory

implicit memory the unconscious use of memory

As you read this chapter, you are inputting, or **encoding**, information into your memory in the form of **memory traces**, which are stored bits of information in memory. Your mind will process this information and put it into memory **storage**. Then, on test day or some other day when the information is needed, you will use **retrieval** processes to recall and output the information from memory. Without memory, we would not be able to learn.

However, there are important differences between computers and the human mind. One difference is the human capacity for **consciousness**, the awareness of our own thoughts and the external world. When we focus our **attention** on something, we bring the stimulus into our consciousness—we become consciously aware of it. If we turn our attention inward, we become conscious of our own thoughts. If we focus our attention outward, we become conscious of the outside world. A computer does not have such awareness.

7.1.1 • Explicit and Implicit Memory

Psychologists define **explicit memory** as the conscious use of memory (Bush & Geer, 2001; Graf & Schacter, 1985). We use explicit memory when we consciously search our memory for a previously stored bit of information. For example, try to answer the following question: "What part of the brain's cortex processes visual information?" To answer, you must consciously search your memory for the information you learned in Chapter 2. We hope your search led you to the correct answer, the occipital lobe! While you were trying to answer this question, you were fully aware that you were searching your memory for the answer. In this respect, you were utilizing your memory explicitly (see Ward, Berry, & Shanks, 2013). But do we always know what's going on inside our own memory?

Not always. Sometimes we access and retrieve memories without having consciously tried to do so. For example, have you ever pulled into your driveway, only to realize that you don't recall the last few miles of your trip home? How did you find your way home without being consciously aware of driving the car? This example illustrates the phenomenon of **implicit memory**, or the unconscious use of memory (Graf & Schacter, 1985; Reder, Park, & Kieffaber, 2009). During the trip home, you were using stored knowledge of how to drive your car, how to find your house, how to read street signs, and so on. The trick is that you did all of these things without conscious awareness. Every day, we execute many behaviors at the implicit level of memory. If we had to execute everything explicitly, we would literally not be able to think and walk at the same time! As we'll see in the coming sections, our cognitive resources for memory are limited. We simply can't do everything explicitly.

© Rick Gomez/Masterfile

Is the mind just like a computer?

7.1

Quiz Yourself

1. Which of the following abilities does a smartphone *not* possess?
   a. Encoding
   b. Storage
   c. Retrieval
   d. Attention
2. Which of the following *best* illustrates the use of explicit memory?
   a. Forgetting to get eggs at the grocery store
   b. Trying to remember the name of a woman you once met at a party
   c. Automatically thinking of a cat when you see a dog on TV
   d. Guessing the correct answer on a multiple-choice test
3. Which of the following *best* illustrates the use of implicit memory?
   a. Knowing the correct answer on a multiple-choice test
   b. Trying to remember where you left your car keys
   c. Forgetting where you left your car keys
   d. Tying your shoe while talking on your cell phone

Answers 1. d; 2. b; 3. d

7.2 The Development of New Memories

As you may recall from Chapter 1, the study of cognition grew in psychology from the 1960s to the 1980s. As it did, the information-processing approach to understanding memory also became more prominent as psychologists began to develop theories of memory that described memory using a computer analogy for the mind. In this section, we'll look at two of these models—the three-stages and working memory models of memory.

sensory memory a system of memory that very briefly stores sensory impressions so that we can extract relevant information from them for further processing

short-term memory (STM) a system of memory that is limited in both capacity and duration; in the three-stages model of memory, short-term memory is seen as the intermediate stage between sensory memory and long-term memory

long-term memory (LTM) a system of memory that works to store memories for a long time, perhaps even permanently

7.2.1 • The Traditional Three-Stages Model of Memory

Traditionally, memory has been explained as having three distinct stages of storage (Atkinson & Shiffrin, 1968). When information enters memory, its first stop is **sensory memory**. In sensory memory, information that comes in from our eyes, ears, and other senses is briefly stored in a sensory form, such as a sound or a visual image. If we pay attention to the information in our sensory memory, the information is sent on to the second stage, **short-term memory (STM)**, for further processing. Short-term memory functions as a temporary holding tank for a limited amount of information. We can hold information in short-term memory for only a few seconds before we must act either to send it further on in the memory system or to keep it in short-term memory by refreshing it. If we decide to further process the information, we can move it from temporary storage in short-term memory to the permanent storage system of **long-term memory (LTM)** (● FIGURE 7.1). Let's look at each of these stages of memory in a bit more detail.

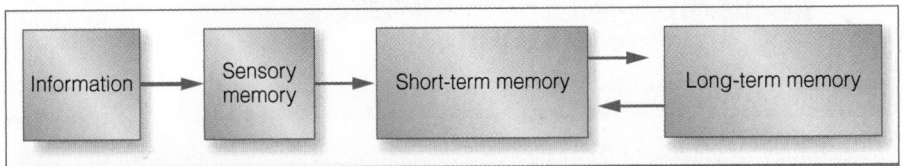

FIGURE 7.1

The Traditional Three-Stages Model of Memory

The traditional three-stages model of memory proposes that in forming new memories, information passes sequentially from sensory memory to short-term memory to long-term memory.

SENSORY MEMORY: ICONIC AND ECHOIC MEMORY

All of the information that enters our memory from the outside world must first pass through our senses. The information we receive from our sense organs lasts for a very brief time after the sensory stimulation has ended. As noted earlier, this holding of sensory information after the sensory stimulus ends is sensory memory. Perhaps you have noticed your sensory memory at work. Have you ever heard a fire engine's siren and then found that you could still hear the sound of the siren in your head for a short time after you could no longer actually hear the siren? If so, you caught your sensory memory at work.

Of all our senses, sight (*iconic memory*) and hearing (*echoic memory*), the two most studied by psychologists, are also the primary means through which we acquire information. But they are not the only useful senses. We also learn through our senses of taste, smell, and touch (*haptic memory*). Psychologists assume that we have sensory memories for each of the senses.

Asia Images/Getty Images

Michael Caulfield/Getty Images

FIGURE 7.2

Sensory Memory

As this man watches a concert video, he stores brief sensory images of what he is seeing in his iconic memory. At the same time, he stores a brief sensory image of the sound he is hearing in his echoic memory. The resulting sensory memories may last for only a fraction of a second, but in that time he will extract the information he wants to keep and send it on into short-term memory for further processing.

The function of sensory memory is to hold sensory information just long enough for us to process it and send it on to short-term memory for further processing. The amount of information that we can process in sensory memory at one time tends to be rather large. However, at least with respect to iconic memory, this capacity seems to vary, being affected by things such as our emotional state (Kuhbandner, Lichtenfeld, & Pekrun, 2011). Although the capacity of sensory memory is large, its duration is short. In the case of iconic memory, the information stays in sensory memory for merely a fraction of a second (Massaro & Loftus, 1996). Although still very brief, the exact duration of echoic (hearing) memories seems to vary across situations (Demany & Semal, 2005). In the end, if we do not send sensory information on to short-term memory within seconds (or less), it will be lost forever as our sensory memories decay (see • FIGURE 7.2).

So, how do we transfer information from sensory memory to short-term memory? It's simple, actually. To transfer information from sensory memory to short-term memory, all we have to do is pay attention to the sensory information. In paying attention to a sensory stimulus, we focus our consciousness on that stimulus. For example, as you read a phone number in a phone book, you pay attention to the number and bring it into your consciousness. As you do this, you ensure that the image of the phone number will be transferred from iconic memory into short-term memory (see • FIGURE 7.3a and b). If you are distracted or unmotivated, you may gaze at the page without paying attention to the number. In that case, the image will be lost as it decays from iconic memory. As you can see, if you don't pay attention to what you are reading, you are wasting your time!

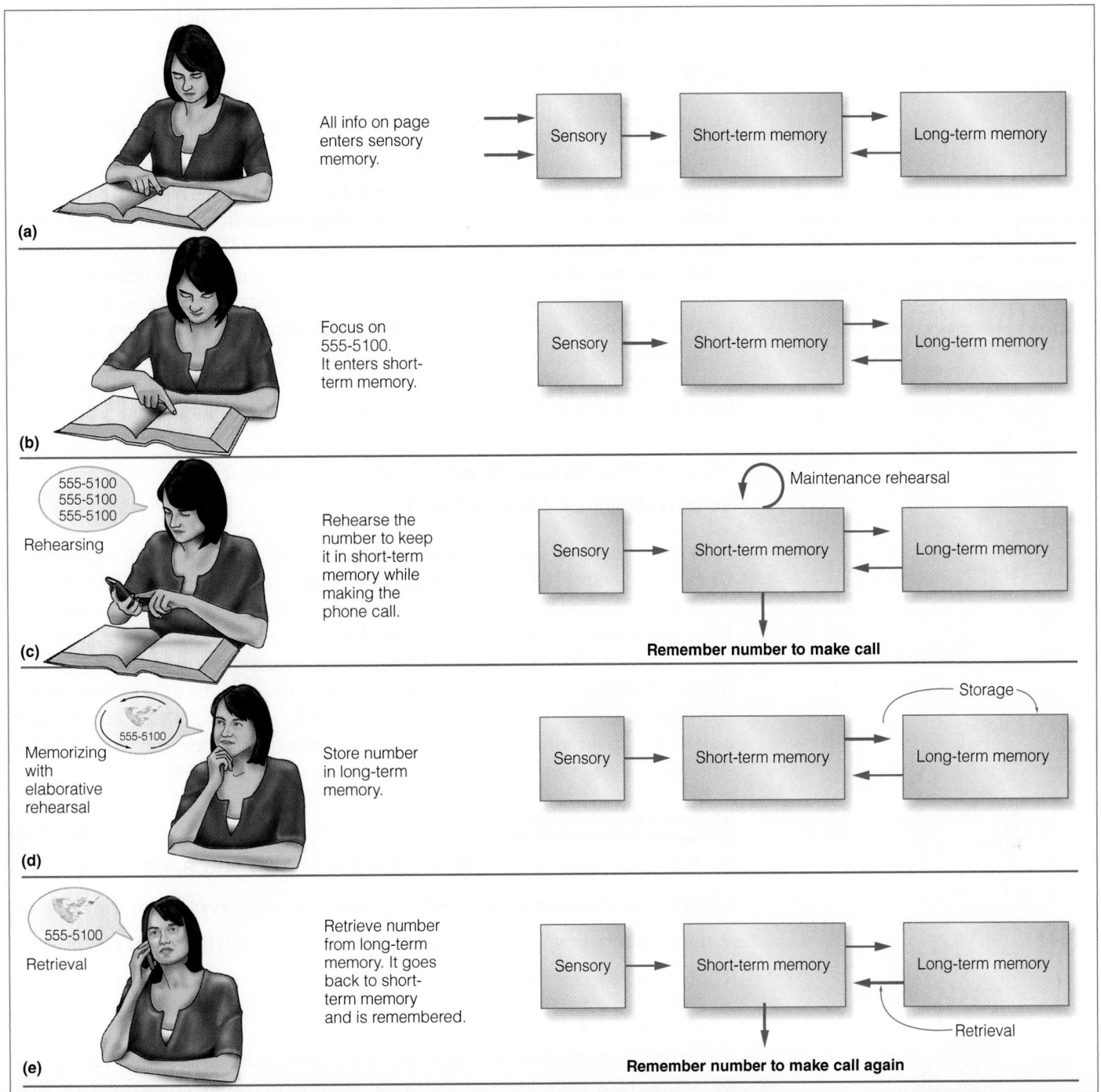

FIGURE 7.3

The Three Stages Model of Memory

As Juanita looks up the phone number of a pizza shop, the information enters her visual sensory memory. (b) As she focuses her attention on the phone number, the information now moves to her short-term memory. (c) To keep the number in mind while she dials it, Juanita uses maintenance rehearsal, repeating the number over and over to herself. (d) As Juanita continues to think about the number, she engages in elaborative rehearsal by associating the number with the idea of pizza in her mind; as a result, the number is now stored in her long-term memory. (e) Later, when Juanita wants to order pizza again, she retrieves the number from long-term memory.

Attention is a necessary step in encoding memories, but there is more to it than that. Once information makes it to your short-term memory, you have to take active steps to keep this information in memory.

SHORT-TERM MEMORY: WHERE MEMORIES ARE MADE (AND LOST)

dual coding system a system of memory that encodes information in more than one type of code or format

chunking a means of using one's limited short-term memory resources more efficiently by combining small bits of information to form larger bits of information, or chunks

The three-stages view of memory conceptualizes short-term memory as a temporary holding tank for information that has been transferred in from sensory memory. Short-term memory uses a **dual coding system** in which memories can be stored either visually or acoustically (with sound) (see Henry et al., 2012; Paivio, 1982). Although short-term memory serves us well, it is another point in the system where information can be lost. Because short-term memory is designed for temporary storage, both its capacity and its duration are limited. It can hold only a small amount of information, and only for a short time. If you've ever tried to hold a phone number in your head while you make it to the phone, you know just how limited short-term memory is and how susceptible it is to forgetting!

7.2.2 • The Capacity of Short-Term Memory: Seven (Plus or Minus Two)

In 1956, psychologist George Miller published a landmark paper on the capacity of short-term memory. In this research, Miller had participants try to remember as many items from a list as they could. He found that the average person could hold about seven, plus or minus two, items in short-term memory. Ever since, psychologists have referred to the "magic number seven" when speaking of the capacity of short-term memory. This 7 ± 2 capacity applies to such items as numbers, words, and other small bits of information. The limited capacity of short-term memory may be due to the way that neurons in the hippocampus code and store information (Migliore, Novara, & Tegolo, 2008; von Allmen et al., 2013).

ENGAGE YOURSELF! To illustrate the capacity of short-term memory, read the following list of numbers {1, 7, 3, 0, 6, 2, 4, 1, 8, 6, 7, 4, 0, 8, 1, 3, 5, 2, 8, 9, 1} to a friend and then immediately ask the person to recall as many of the numbers as possible in the same order you read them. We bet you'll find that your friend is able to remember only around 7 ± 2 of them.

Given this 7 ± 2 capacity, we can easily hold a phone number, a short grocery list, or the name of a person we just met in our short-term memory. But, if we need to, can we hold more information in our short-term memory? Maybe. One technique for extending the amount of information we can hold in short-term memory is called **chunking** (Bor & Seth, 2012; Simon, 1974). Chunking involves grouping information together into meaningful units, or chunks. For example, many of the important numbers in our culture—Social Security numbers, phone numbers, license plates, credit card numbers, and so on—are usually presented in a prechunked form so as to facilitate our remembering them. It would be harder to recall your Social Security number as nine separate digits rather than three chunks.

However, there is a limit to how much information can be chunked. The number of chunks we can store in short-term memory decreases as the chunks gets larger. In other words, you can hold more three-digit numbers in short-term memory than you can eight-digit numbers (Simon, 1974). In a sense, short-term memory is like a short bookshelf. It may hold seven skinny books of poetry, but only three thick dictionaries.

7.2.3 • The Duration of Short-Term Memory: It's Yours for 30 Seconds

Duration is the second major limitation on short-term memory. Once information passes into short-term memory, it can only be kept there for around 30 seconds without some type of rehearsal or refreshing of the material (J. A. Brown, 1958; Peterson & Peterson, 1959).

What if you have to keep some information in short-term memory for more than 30 seconds? Suppose you look up a phone number and have to remember it while you search for your cell phone. If you can't write the phone number down, you need to find a way to keep it in your short-term memory for longer than 30 seconds. What do you think you would you do in this situation? One simple solution would be to repeat the phone number over and over out loud as you look for your phone (Figure 7.3c). This repetition of the material in short-term memory, called **maintenance rehearsal**, is useful for extending the duration of short-term memory (Nairne, 2002). When you repeat the information over and over again, you resupply it to short-term memory before it can decay, extending its retention for another 30 seconds or so before you must repeat the number to yourself again. You can keep this up all day, as long as no one interrupts or distracts you!

maintenance rehearsal repeating information over and over again to keep it in short-term memory for an extended period of time

TECHNOLOGY, DISTRACTION, AND MEMORY IN THE CLASSROOM

As we have seen, attention plays a key role in memory processing (see, for example, Carlisle & Woodman, 2013). Achieving our learning goals depends in part on our ability to focus our attention on relevant information. Unfortunately, it seems as if modern life is full of potential distractions that may challenge our ability to pay attention and learn—even in the classroom. Today, students have unprecedented access to technology in the classroom and beyond. For some of us, our cell phone is vital to everyday life. We use these technologies to remain connected, store important information, find our way from here to there, and so on. But, do these technologies help us learn? Or, do they present distractions that impede our use of memory?

How many times have you been in class when another student's cell phone began to ring? Has this ever happened during an exam? Aside from being annoying, research suggests that a ringing cell phone can impair memory. In a classroom setting, Christian End and colleagues randomly assigned some students to watch a video during which the researchers called a classmate's phone twice, letting it ring for 5 seconds each time. In the control condition, students watched the video uninterrupted. Later, all students were given a multiple-choice test on the content of the video. The results showed that relative to the control group, students in the cell phone condition performed more poorly on the exam. They were also more likely to have incomplete class notes on the video content (End et al., 2010). These results indicate that ringing cell phones affect students' attention and later memory for course content. It appears that muting your cell phone is more than just a matter of politeness. Your academic success may depend on it.

TRANSFERRING INFORMATION FROM SHORT-TERM TO LONG-TERM MEMORY

Assuming that we can pay attention well enough to get information into our short-term memory, we still need to move this information into long-term memory if we wish to keep it for an extended period of time. Maintenance rehearsal may be useful for keeping information in short-term memory; however, you will likely

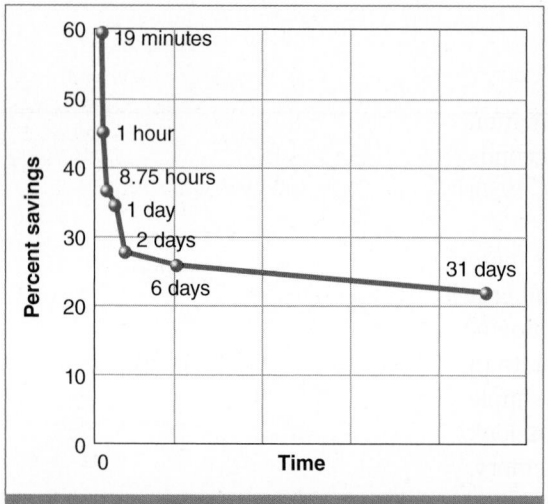

FIGURE 7.4

Retention After Maintenance Rehearsal

Psychologist Hermann Ebbinghaus learned lists of nonsense syllables (such as NID) using maintenance rehearsal and then calculated how much of this learning was retained over various periods of time—a factor he called savings in learning. A savings score of 100% would mean that no learning was lost with time. As you can see, memory for the syllables dropped off very quickly over time. After only 2 days, nearly 75% of the learning was lost. These data clearly indicate that maintenance rehearsal is a relatively poor means of storing information in long-term memory. If you want to really retain what you have learned, you should use elaborative rehearsal. (Based on data from Ebbinghaus, 1885/1913.)

have to do more than merely repeat the information if you want to store it permanently in long-term memory. Maintenance rehearsal accomplishes only a weak transfer of information into long-term memory (Glenberg, Smith, & Green, 1977; Lockhart & Craik, 1990). Memories encoded using maintenance rehearsal are easily forgotten with time.

• FIGURE 7.4 illustrates what psychologists refer to as a **forgetting curve**, or the amount of information forgotten as time passes. As you can see from Figure 7.4, when maintenance rehearsal is used to learn material, 75% of the information will be lost in only 2 days. You may have learned this lesson the hard way if repetition is your primary means of studying material for exams. If you simply repeat information over and over in your head, or repeatedly read over the information in your text and notes, your studying will not accomplish strong transfer of information into long-term memory, and you may find yourself in trouble on test day. To really learn new material, you'll have to use a more effective rehearsal strategy.

7.2.4 • Elaborative Rehearsal: Making Memories Stick

As we just saw, the main function of maintenance rehearsal is to keep information in short-term memory—and information in short-term memory is only temporary. To really get information into your long-term memory, you have to use another technique, called **elaborative rehearsal** (Craik & Lockhart, 1972). Elaborative rehearsal (Figure 7.3d) involves forming associations, or mental connections, between the information in short-term memory that you want to store and information you already have stored in your permanent long-term memory. To get customers to recall a business's phone number, for example, advertisers often use jingles. Associating the phone number with the melody serves to elaborate it in memory.

Another powerful type of elaboration is to generate personally relevant examples of the material you are learning. Every time you generate an example from your own life that demonstrates a psychological principle, you are engaging in elaborative rehearsal and increasing the chances of retrieving the material later (Figure 7.3e). For example, thinking about how you used repetition to memorize your multiplication tables in grade school as an example of maintenance rehearsal will help you retain this concept in long-term memory.

forgetting curve a graph of the amount of learned information that is forgotten over time

elaborative rehearsal forming associations or links between information one is trying to learn and information already stored in long-term memory so as to facilitate the transfer of this new information into long-term memory

ENGAGE YOURSELF! To illustrate the power that elaborative rehearsal has on memory, try this quick demonstration. Get a blank sheet of paper and try to write the lyrics to a song you have in your music collection without playing or singing the song. How well do you do? If you're like most of us, you probably found this task challenging. Now, play the song and try to sing along. Is it easier to recall the lyrics while singing? For most of us it would be. We have elaborated the lyrics by associating them with the tune in our long-term memory. Recalling the tune helps us recall the words. Elaborative rehearsal leads to better memory.

7.2.5 • Levels of Processing

This notion that the more thoroughly or deeply you process information, the more strongly you transfer it to long-term memory is referred to as the **levels-of-processing model** of memory (Craik & Lockhart, 1972). When Fergus Craik and Robert Lockhart (1972) first proposed the levels-of-processing approach, it was assumed that the only way to get information into long-term memory was to use elaborative rehearsal. Subsequent research has shown that this isn't necessarily the case. Although maintenance rehearsal is a shallow form of processing that doesn't involve much elaboration of the material, it does allow for some transfer of information into long-term memory (Lockhart & Craik, 1990).

levels-of-processing model a model that predicts that information that is processed deeply and elaboratively will be best retained in and recalled from long-term memory

For example, you may eventually remember your checking account number if you have to write it, and thus repeat it, frequently enough. However, the type of transfer to long-term memory that occurs with maintenance rehearsal doesn't really help students pass an exam in which they actually have to understand what they are talking or writing about. One study found that if you increase the amount of maintenance rehearsal by 9 times (900%), you increase your recall of the information by only 1.5% (Glenberg et al., 1977). Elaborative rehearsal, in contrast, involves a very deep level of processing. To elaborate material, you must access information stored in long-term memory and associate it with the new information you are trying to learn (see Rudner et al., 2013). This requires much more effort and thought than merely repeating the information over and over. The good news is that this effort pays off in terms of better memory for the information. Elaborative rehearsal is clearly your best bet if you want to successfully master material, whether in a course or in life.

As an example, let's say that you attend a multicultural fair at your school in which students bring foods from their native cultures for everyone to try (one of the author's schools regularly holds such an event). You sample a West African dish called a puff-puff, a type of slightly sweet fried bread that is often eaten with kidney bean stew. Finding the puff-puff delicious, you decide to commit it to memory so that you can later find some means of obtaining more—trust us, they're that good!

If you want to commit information about the puff-puff to long-term memory, you must associate it with what you already know. You might think about how a puff-puff looks very much like an American donut hole. You may note that the puff-puff contains nutmeg, which reminds you of drinking eggnog with nutmeg during the winter. You might associate the puff-puff with similar fried breads in other cultures, such as Native American fry bread or beignets from New Orleans. Or you might associate puff-puffs with your friend Denis from West Africa. Do you see what we're doing here? We are finding ways to associate and link the puff-puff to concepts that you already have stored in long-term memory, such as donuts, nutmeg, and a friend. This is what elaborative rehearsal is all about. You go beyond simply repeating information to actually thinking about the information, and in doing so, you process the information deeply enough to efficiently transfer it to long-term memory.

Susann Doyle-Portillo

If you want to commit information about the puff-puff to long-term memory, you must use elaborative rehearsal. In other words, you must associate the puff-puff with what you already know.

When you use elaborative rehearsal as you learn, you will retain the information in the permanent storage system of long-term memory in a way that maximizes the chances of being able to retrieve it when you need it—whether on test day or when searching online for West African recipes.

DOES SHORT-TERM MEMORY REALLY EXIST?

Recall that the three-stages model proposes short-term memory as a separate, intermediate stage of memory that is limited in capacity and duration (see Figure 7.1, p. 271). As you learned in Chapter 1, any scientific theory must be supported by the results of scientific experiments before we place much stock in it. As you will shortly see, not all of the available research supports the three-stages model, particularly in its conception of short-term memory. Let's take a look at the evidence that supports and that calls into doubt this model.

7.2.6 • The Serial-Position Curve and Age-related Changes in Memory

Some support for the three-stages model comes from *serial-position experiments*. In a typical experiment, participants listen to a list of around 20 words slowly read aloud by the experimenter, after which they immediately try to recall the words in any order they can. The experimenter then plots the *serial-position curve*, or the tendency for participants to recall each word correctly plotted as a function of the position of the word in the original list. • FIGURE 7.5 shows a typical serial-position curve. You will notice in Figure 7.5 that not all of the words in the list have an equal chance of being recalled. Rather, words at the beginning and the end of the list are recalled better than words in the middle of the list.

primacy effect the tendency for people to recall words from the beginning of a list better than words that appeared in the middle of the list

recency effect the tendency for people to recall words from the end of a list better than words that appeared in the middle of the list

The overall shape of the serial-position curve fits well with the three-stages view of memory. In fact, the model predicts that you will obtain a curve like that shown in Figure 7.5. The tendency for words at the beginning of the list to be better recalled, called the **primacy effect**, can be explained in terms of long-term memory. As participants listen to the list of words, they spend considerable time rehearsing the words at the beginning of the list in their short-term memory. While they are doing this, they have no short-term memory capacity left to rehearse the words in the middle of the list. Therefore, words in the middle of the list are lost from short-term memory, but the words at the beginning of the list are moved to long-term memory and thus are remembered well at recall. Interestingly, diminished primacy effects for adults have been shown to be related to having Alzheimer's disease and mild cognitive impairments that are likely to progress on to become Alzheimer's disease (Cunha et al., 2012). This diminished primacy effect presumably suggests that people with Alzheimer's disease and progressive cognitive impairments have difficulty transferring information from short-term memory to long-term memory.

The words at the end of the list are also well remembered, in what is called the **recency effect**. The recency effect is thought to occur because participants still have these words in short-term memory at the time they are asked to recall the list. Therefore, all the participants have to do is dump these words from their short-term

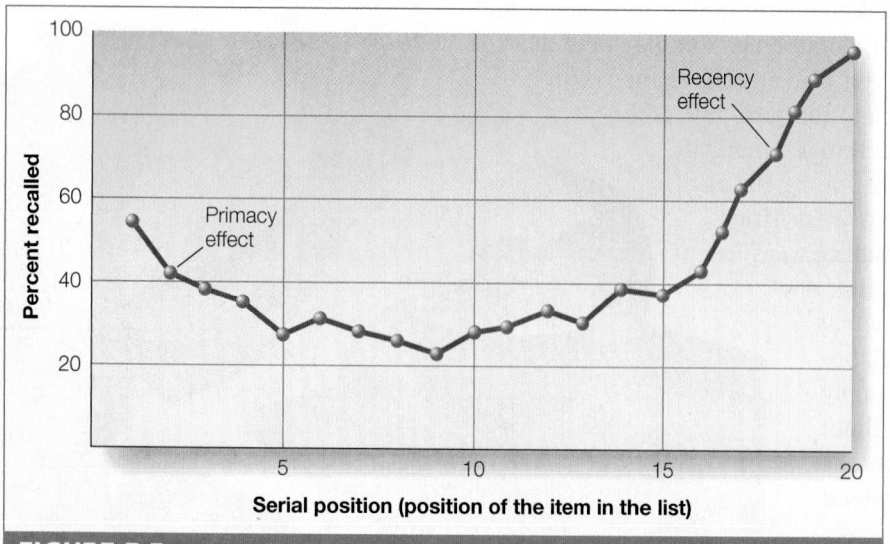

FIGURE 7.5

Serial-Position Curve

In a serial-position experiment (Murdoch, 1962), participants are asked to remember a list of words that are read aloud to them. In such experiments, words at the beginning of the list (primacy effect) and words at the end of the list (recency effect) are remembered best.

memory before going on to retrieve the other words (from the beginning of the list) from long-term memory. In the serial-position experiment, participants should be able to recall the last two or three words they heard (Glanzer & Cunitz, 1966). The recency effect does not extend to the full 7 ± 2 capacity of short-term memory because some of the capacity of short-term memory is taken up in rehearsing the words from the start of the list and in continuing to hear new words.

Interestingly, recency memory is one of the aspects of memory that is most affected by normal aging (Wingfield & Kahana, 2002). As we get older, our short-term memory tends to suffer more than our distant long-term memories. One of your authors, who is only 52, often stops by the grocery store without a list and many times leaves the store without buying everything she needs. This type of forgetting almost never occurred in her 20s. However, not all short-term memory suffers as we age. In one study, participants of different ages were shown a series of three pictures in rapid succession. Seconds later, they were shown a test picture and asked to determine whether the test picture was one of the pictures they had just seen. In this case, younger and older participants showed serial-position curves that were strikingly similar. The older participants did not have poorer recency memory than the younger participants (Sekuler et al., 2006). It appears that aging negatively affects recency memory for verbal information much more than for visual information.

Another positive finding is that older adults appear to compensate for poorer recency memory by becoming more strategic in their memory processing. Older adults tend to focus their memory processing more on the most important information, and they have been shown to re-study information strategically just before it needs to be recalled (Castel et al., 2013). Strategies such as these may help ensure that older adults remain as functional as younger people despite the normal age-related changes in memory they face.

Although numerous serial-position experiments support the three-stages model of memory, some scientists still express doubts about the model, especially its conception of short-term memory. One potential problem with the three-stages model has to do with how we process information in memory. This model proposes that the only route by which information can reach long-term memory is through short-term memory. There is some doubt as to whether this is true (Logie, 1999).

If information must pass from sensory memory into short-term memory without having made contact with long-term memory, then long-term memory is activated only *after* information is processed in short-term memory. The problem is that this is not always the case. If you are given a list of seven words to remember, you will likely use maintenance rehearsal (repeating the words over and over to yourself) to keep these words in short-term memory. To do so, however, you will have to know how to pronounce the words, which you can only know by accessing your knowledge (from long-term memory) of how to pronounce the words. You must access and retrieve information in long-term memory *before* you have processed the information into long-term memory (Logie, 1999). One criticism of the three-stages model is that it cannot account for this type of common behavior. Failure of the model to fully account for our everyday use of memory has led researchers to develop alternative views of memory. One of the most influential alternatives to the three-stages model is the *working memory view* of memory (Baddeley, 1986, 2012; Baddeley & Hitch, 1974).

working memory a multifaceted component of long-term memory that contains short-term memory, a central executive, a phonological loop, and a visuospatial sketch pad; the function of working memory is to access, move, and process information that we are currently using

7.2.7 • The Working Memory Model: Parallel Memory

Today, many researchers reject the notion that information passes sequentially through the three stages of memory and instead propose a new type of memory called **working memory** (see Baddeley, 2002, 2012). The working memory model views the memory stages in more of a parallel fashion as opposed to a serial fashion. In other words, the working memory model assumes that we process different aspects of memory at the same time, rather than in a series of stages as predicted by the three-stages model.

In this view, working memory and short-term memory are parts contained within long-term memory (• FIGURE 7.6). Working memory moves information into and out of long-term memory, whereas short-term memory operates as the part of working memory that briefly stores the information we are using at any particular time.

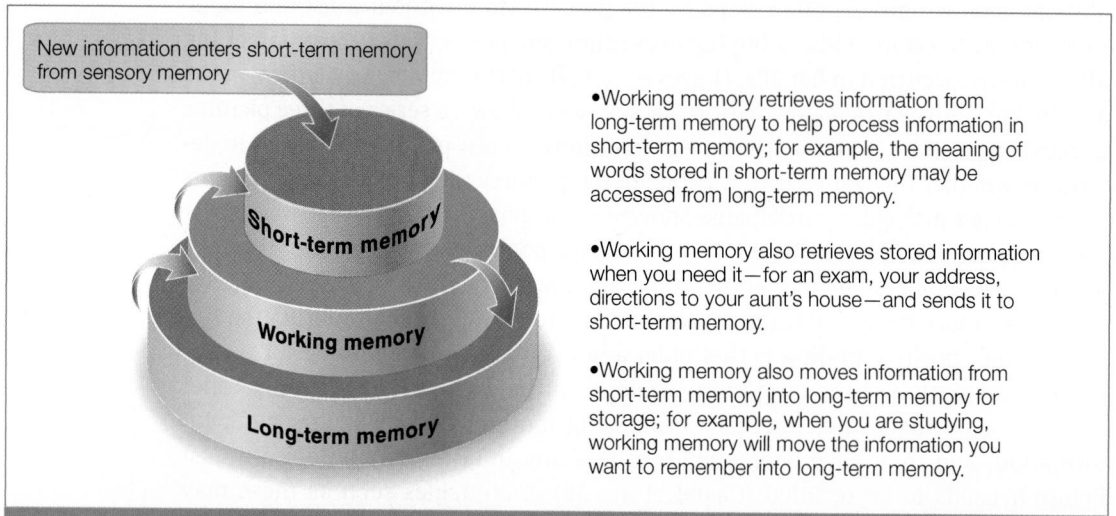

FIGURE 7.6

The Working Memory View of Memory

In the working memory view of memory, the stages of memory work in more of a parallel fashion than a sequential fashion. In this view, short-term memory and working memory are both contained within long-term memory. Working memory moves information into and out of both short-term and long-term memory as necessary.

Suppose a bee stings you. Your haptic (touch) sensory memory registers the pain of the sting, and your visual sensory memory captures the sight of the bee. These sensory impressions are then sent to working memory, where they are combined into an integrated memory representation of being stung by the bee (see Kessler & Meiran, 2006). At the same time, your working memory may activate a long-term memory of what you learned in first-aid class about allergic reactions to bee stings. Working memory pulls this information on allergic reactions into short-term memory, and you now consciously think about the signs of an allergic reaction as you check to see whether you are having one. You conclude that you are not having an allergic reaction, so you cease to think about it, and working memory transfers the new knowledge that you are not allergic to bee stings to long-term memory.

As you can see, in this view of memory, information does not flow sequentially from sensory to short-term to long-term memory. Rather, working memory plays several roles. The short-term memory part of working memory acts as a storage system for information that is currently being used. At the same time, other parts of working memory act to retrieve information, process new information, and send new and revised information on to long-term memory. The order in which the different memory stages are activated can vary depending on the circumstances.

One advantage of the working memory model is that it can explain why we sometimes seem to access long-term memory before we process information in short-term memory. For instance, as you read this page, you must access information that you have stored in long-term memory about the English language in order to pronounce and understand the words. As the words on the page enter your short-term memory, you already know what they mean and how they sound. The working memory view of memory can explain this, but the three-stages model cannot. In the working memory model, you can go to your long-term memories to help you process perceptual information in a top-down fashion, meaning that your perception is guided by your knowledge of the world (see Chapter 3; Logie, 1999).

THE CENTRAL EXECUTIVE AND DEFICITS IN MEMORY FUNCTIONING

One of the more prominent theories of a multicomponent working memory proposes that working memory contains a **central executive** component and two subordinate systems: the *phonological loop,* which processes auditory information (such as the buzzing of a bee), and the *visuospatial sketch pad,* which processes visual and spatial information (the sight of a bumblebee) (Baddeley, 1992, 2012; Baddeley & Hitch, 1974). These systems are called subordinate systems because they fall under the control of the central executive (● FIGURE 7.7).

central executive the attention-controlling component of working memory

The central executive functions as an attention-controlling mechanism within working memory. The central executive must coordinate the actions of the subordinate systems and integrate information that comes in from these systems (for example, directing you to pay attention to how close a bee gets to your arm). This makes the central executive component especially important when we are engaged in tasks that require attention and the coordination of visual and auditory information, such as when playing a video game (Baddeley, 1992). Furthermore, it appears that some aspects of central executive functioning are affected by our motivation for processing information in a given situation (Sanada et al., 2013). Being motivated to win the video game may facilitate your working memory function and help you achieve your goals. However, despite their best efforts, some people still have difficulties with memory processing.

Recently, some researchers have proposed that faulty executive functioning—an inability to direct one's attention while using working memory—may be one of the underlying mechanisms in attention deficit hyperactivity disorder (ADHD) in children (Dovis et al., 2013; Rinsky & Henshaw, 2011). Central executive impairment has also been seen in patients who have had strokes and those with Alzheimer's disease (Yang et al., 2013). The characteristic and progressive memory loss seen in Alzheimer's disease is thought by some to reflect a loss of central executive functioning (Gibbons et al., 2012; Saunders & Summers, 2011). This loss of central executive functioning can be seen when Alzheimer's patients are asked to do visual and auditory tasks at the same time. Because their central executive is not functioning properly, Alzheimer's patients have trouble coordinating and integrating information from visual and auditory sources, and they experience more problems than a healthy person does on the simultaneous tasks. However, when Alzheimer's patients are tested on a single task that is scaled to their ability, such as recalling

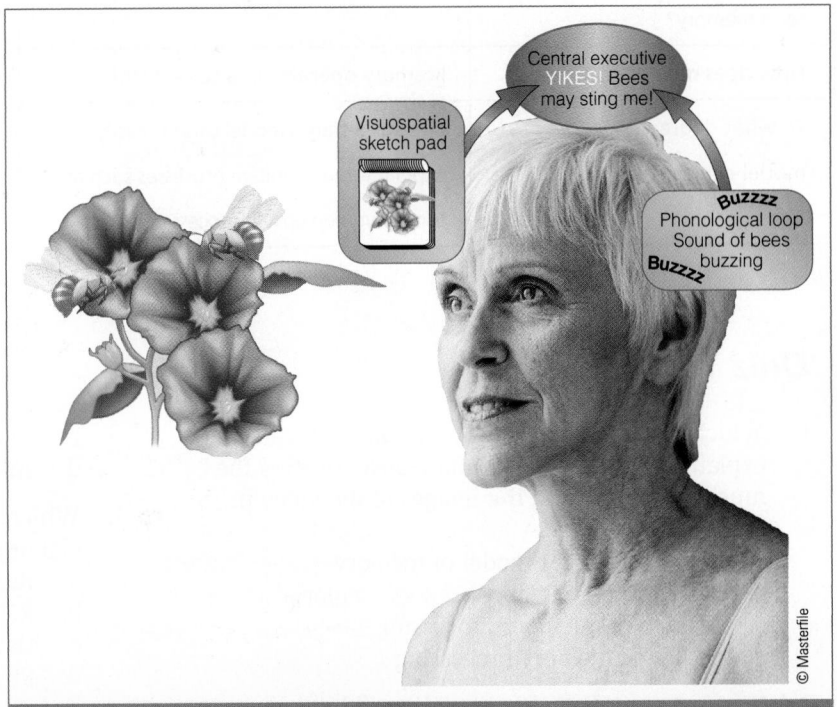

FIGURE 7.7

Baddeley's Central Executive Model of Working Memory

In Baddeley's model of working memory, the central executive integrates visual information from the visuospatial sketch pad and auditory information from the phonological loop. The integration of information that the central executive provides is crucial when we are engaged in activities that require us to use both visual and auditory information—as in deciding how to react when you both see and hear nearby bumblebees.

a list of numbers, they perform as well as control participants (Logie et al., 2000). This pattern of results supports the notion that the structure of working memory has multiple components, with at least one component that integrates information.

The working memory view offers a more complex model than the traditional three-stages model, one that explains more of what researchers observe about memory. This does not mean, however, that psychologists have a complete understanding of how memory works. Even working memory theorists disagree as to exactly what role working memory plays in the memory system (Buehner et al., 2005). Theorists also disagree as to whether working memory is separate from long-term memory. Not all researchers are convinced that working memory is composed of multiple components, and those who are convinced of its multiplicity do not agree on the number of components. Clearly, our understanding of working memory is still developing (Hurlstone, Hitch, & Baddeley, 2013; Repovs & Baddeley, 2006). Still, relative to the three-stages model, the working memory model represents a better explanation of memory (see You Review: The Three-Stages and Working Memory Models of Memory).

You Review **The Three-Stages and Working Memory Models of Memory**

Comparison	Three-Stages Model	Working Memory Model
What are the components of the memory system?	Memory consists of three separate stages: sensory memory, STM, and LTM.	Memory consists of several interacting components: sensory memory, working memory, and LTM.
What is the relationship between short-term memory and long-term memory?	STM is a single component of memory that is separate from LTM.	Working memory is a multicomponent part of LTM that includes STM, the central executive, the phonological loop, and the visuospatial sketchpad.
How does memory operate?	Memory operates in a serial fashion.	Memory operates in a parallel fashion.
To what degree does the model explain real-world behavior?	The three-stages model cannot easily explain some cognitive processes such as top-down perceptual processing.	Because the working memory model is a parallel model of memory, it can better account for processes such as top-down perceptual processing.

Quiz Yourself 7.2

1. **Which of the following views of memory can best explain our ability to simultaneously process the music of a video and the images of the video in short-term memory?**
   a. The three-stages model of memory
   b. The working memory view of memory
   c. Procedural memory processing
   d. Semantic memory processing

2. **When you are listening to and watching a music video on your computer, which component(s) of memory are you likely to be using?**
   a. The phonological loop
   b. The central executive
   c. The visuospatial sketch pad
   d. All of the above

3. **Which of the following is the *best* example of elaborative rehearsal?**
   a. Reading a chapter in your text three times
   b. Relating the material to your personal experiences
   c. Using flashcards of key concepts in the chapter
   d. Rewriting your lecture notes

Answers 1. b; 2. d; 3. b

7.3 Long-Term Memory: Permanent Storage

According to the memory models we've explored—the three-stages model and the working memory model—long-term memory is our largest and most permanent memory storage system (Figures 7.3 and 7.6, pp. 273 and 280). Long-term memory is where we store information that we wish to keep for a long period of time. It is in long-term memory that we store all of our knowledge of our self and of the world. Information stored in long-term memory is not conscious until we activate it and call it into working memory or short-term memory. Let's begin our quest to understand how we store memory for the long haul by getting a better understanding of the capacity, encoding, and organization of long-term memory.

7.3.1 • The Capacity of Long-Term Memory

For all practical purposes, long-term memory seems to have a limitless capacity. To date, psychologists have not found any reason to believe that long-term memory has a limited capacity, as short-term memory and working memory do. It is safe to say that you are unlikely to ever run out of room in your long-term memory. It may sometimes feel as though your brain is full, but you still have the capacity to store more information in long-term memory. What you are feeling is more likely to be a problem in focusing your attention or a lack of available capacity in short-term or working memory. If you can pay enough attention to move the information through sensory memory to short-term/working memory, and then rehearse the material enough to get it to long-term memory, you will find that you have ample storage space for the information.

semantic encoding encoding memory traces in terms of the meaning of the information being stored

7.3.2 • Encoding in Long-Term Memory

Information is encoded in long-term memory in several forms. As in the other parts of memory storage, information in long-term memory can be stored in both acoustic (sound) and visual forms (Paivio, 1986). However, we more often encode long-term memories semantically, in terms of the meaning of the information. **Semantic encoding** stores the gist, or general meaning, of the stimulus rather than storing all of the sensory details (Anderson, 1974; Gernsbacher, 1985; Wanner, 1968).

Semantic encoding offers some distinct advantages over acoustic and visual encoding in long-term memory (see Cherry et al., 2012), even though it sacrifices a lot of the details because all of the features of the original stimulus are not stored in memory. For example, if you read a description of a West African puff-puff in a cookbook, you could store information about the sound of the word *puff-puff* or the visual image of a puff-puff in your long-term memory, but this wouldn't really help you make a puff-puff. In fact, you could memorize an exact picture of a puff-puff and still not know what it is. On the other hand, if you stored semantic information about the puff-puff—that it is a West African food consisting of a fried ball of dough made of flour, eggs, sugar, nutmeg, shortening, milk, and baking powder—you would potentially have enough understanding of a puff-puff to actually make one. A picture couldn't give you that.

© moodboard/SuperStock

Although you may sometimes feel as if your long-term memory is "full," you always have the capacity to store information—provided that you are not too tired, distracted, or unmotivated to rehearse and elaborate the material you wish to learn.

7.3.3 • Organization in Long-Term Memory

One aspect of encoding information in long-term memory is how we organize it. Over the years, psychologists have proposed various means by which we organize our knowledge categorically (that is, by category; for a review, see Anderson, 2000). One of these strategies involves the use of a generalized knowledge structure called a **schema** (Bartlett, 1932; Rumelhart, 1980). We have schemas for people, places, concepts, events, groups of people, and just about everything else we know.

Schemas can be thought of as filing systems we use for knowledge about particular concepts. Schemas contain general information on the characteristics of the concept's category, its function, and so on. For each of these general characteristics, the schema has slots for information specific to the concept. For example, let's look at a portion of a hypothetical schema for a puff-puff. On the left are the names of the slots in the schema found for breads. On the right are the specific bits of information that would be placed in these slots for the puff-puff.

Puff-Puff

Is a:	bread
Contains:	flour, sugar, shortening, nutmeg, eggs, etc.
Method of preparation:	fried
Uses:	energy source; eaten with kidney bean stew
Appearance:	small, donut-hole sized
Origin:	West Africa

These slots can also have default values that are used when information is missing from our perception. For instance, if you did not read that the puff-puff is fried, you might assume that because a puff-puff is bread, it must be baked. One of the default values for the slot "method of preparation" may be "baked." We probably rely on these default values in schemas when we engage in *top-down perceptual processing* (see Chapter 3).

Obviously, breads are not the only objects for which we have schemas. In fact, we have schemas for many different types of information. In addition to schemas for objects, we have schemas for abstract *concepts* such as love, hate, and psychology. We also have schemas to categorize our social world. We use *person schemas* for specific people, such as best friend, mother, or brother; *stereotypes* for groups of people, such as Asians, Catholics, football fans, or artists; and *scripts* for events, such as going to the doctor, eating at a fancy restaurant, or going on a date. In Chapter 10, we will take a closer look at how schemas affect our behavior in social situations.

schema [SKEE-ma] an organized, generalized knowledge structure in long-term memory

declarative memory a type of long-term memory encompassing memories that are easily verbalized, including episodic and semantic memories

semantic memory long-term, declarative memory for conceptual information

episodic [epp-uh-SOD-ick] memory memory for the recent events in our lives

7.3.4 • Declarative and Procedural Long-Term Memories

Most research on memory has concerned itself with a type of explicit memory called **declarative memory**. Declarative memory is memory for knowledge that can be easily verbalized: names, dates, events, concepts, and so on. This is the type of memory that Kim Peek excelled so well at, memorizing phonebooks, textbooks, and so on. Declarative memory can be divided into two subtypes: **semantic memory**, which is memory for concepts, and **episodic memory**, which is memory for the recent events in one's life.

Right now, as you read this chapter, you are adding to your semantic memory by increasing your knowledge of psychology and memory processes. In doing this, you will add to the schemas you have stored in long-term memory for these (and other) concepts in the chapter. For example, you may think of semantic and episodic memories from your own life and tie your growing knowledge of psychology to the well-formed schemas you have for the world. By building and strengthening these schemas, you are helping to build a knowledge base for psychology that will later enable you to apply this information to problems that require some understanding of psychology, including the exam on test day.

As you attend school and go about the business of your everyday life, you are also adding to your episodic memory (Pause et al., 2013; Tulving, 1972; Wheeler, Stuss, & Tulving, 1997). Episodic memory contains fairly detailed memories of the recent events in your life (Conway, 2009). You store memories of your conversations with others, events you have attended, and your activities in your episodic memory. Episodic memories are associated with a unique sense of personal awareness (Wheeler et al., 1997). Later, when you remember reading this chapter, you'll think, "I was there; I remember reading that chapter." This self-awareness makes episodic memory a very personal part of our long-term memory.

Michael Dunning/Getty Images

Autobiographical memory gives us our past—such as these childhood memories.

Our lives are a series of events. Once encoded, our episodic memories are quickly integrated into **autobiographical memory**, our more general memory of our unique personal history (Burt, Kemp, & Conway, 2008). As episodic memories are integrated into autobiographical memory, some of the details are lost (Conway, 2009). So, although you can probably recall a great deal about what you did an hour ago, you probably cannot recall many of the details of what you did last week. Our cherished memories of the past are, to some degree, abstractions of the original events. Nonetheless, these memories are extremely important to us. Without autobiographical memory, we would lose an important part of our selves (Rathbone et al., 2012).

autobiographical memory memory for our past that gives us a sense of personal history

GENDER AND AUTOBIOGRAPHICAL MEMORY

Take a moment now to recall some of your own episodic memories. What comes to mind when you think of your past? Is it easy to recall the events of your life, or is it a struggle? Interestingly, researchers have found that how easily you recall episodic memories may be a function of your gender (Colley et al., 2002; Grysman & Hudson, 2013; Niedzwienska, 2003; Pillemer et al., 2003). Penelope Davis (1999) found that compared to men, women are better at recalling emotional childhood memories, such as a happy birthday party or an angry conflict with a childhood friend. Davis hypothesized that gender differences are evident only for emotional memories because females' greater tendency to elaborate is particular to emotional event memories.

To test this notion, Davis first had all participants retrieve emotion-laden childhood memories. Then they were asked to sort their memories into categories of memories that seemed to go together—for example, happy memories, memories associated with school, memories associated with family, and so on. The participants were free to use as many or as few categories as they chose. As predicted, the females sorted their memories into significantly more categories than the males did. From these data, Davis concluded that females' enhanced autobiographical memory for emotional events is due to their tendency to organize these memories into more diverse categories. In other words, women have been socialized to do more elaborative processing of emotion-laden autobiographical memories, and this processing pays off in terms of better recall.

Realistic Reflections/Getty Images

Research suggests that relative to males, females are better at recalling emotionally charged episodic memories. Later in life, this girl may recall this happy graduation day better than her male classmates do.

ARE SEMANTIC AND EPISODIC MEMORY SEPARATE SYSTEMS?

Given that semantic and episodic memory are both enhanced by elaborative rehearsal, does this mean that they are stored in the same fashion in the brain? Currently, there is some debate on this issue. Although the findings are controversial, a number of studies suggest that episodic and semantic memory may indeed be separate memory systems (Graham et al., 2000; Wheeler et al., 1997). Some of the most persuasive research on this issue comes from studies using the PET and fMRI scan technologies that you learned about in Chapter 2. These scans allow researchers to see which parts of the brain are most active while the participant is engaged in certain activities. By scanning participants' brains while they perform semantic and episodic memory tasks, researchers can get an idea of which parts of the brain are involved in these two types of memory.

These studies suggest that processing semantic and episodic memory tasks produces activation in some common areas of the brain, such as the prefrontal cortex, but also some unique patterns of activation (Levine et al., 2004; Nyberg et al., 2003). If episodic memory and semantic memory tasks involve activity in different parts of the brain, it is not a far leap to conclude that they must be separate memory systems. Additionally, researchers have found that people with certain brain disorders experience more impairment in storing long-term episodic/autobiographical memories than they do in storing semantic memories (Tramoni et al., 2011).

Recently, some researchers have proposed the existence of a memory system that lies somewhere between semantic and episodic memory, a system called *personal semantics* (Renoult et al., 2012). Personal semantic memory is thought to encompass *knowledge* about oneself, whereas episodic memory is memory for events or episodes from one's life. Both episodic and personal semantic memory are hypothesized to be part of autobiographical memory (Leyhe et al., 2009). Clearly, more research is needed to determine the exact number and configuration of the memory systems that underlie our knowledge of ourselves and the world.

PROCEDURAL MEMORY: MEMORY FOR SKILLS

procedural memory long-term memory for skills and behaviors

Regardless of whether semantic and episodic memory are part of the same memory system, they share the characteristic of being *declarative* or easily verbalized. This is not true of all of our knowledge. **Procedural memory**, our memory for skills, is not as readily put into words as our declarative (semantic and episodic) memories are. To illustrate this difference between declarative and procedural memories, take a moment to try the following demonstration.

ENGAGE YOURSELF! Use your procedural memory to think of a skill that you know how to execute very well, such as walking, riding a bike, or driving a car; then attempt to tell someone else how to execute that skill without showing him or her how to do it. You can only use words to describe the skill. Now choose something about which you have declarative memory—the directions to your favorite music store or the plot of your favorite movie—and try to communicate that using only words.

Which task did you find to be more difficult? We bet that you found the first task to be much harder than the second. The first task asked you to verbalize a procedural memory, whereas the second asked you to verbalize a semantic memory. As we said before, procedural memories are not easily verbalized, and we've demonstrated just how hard it can be to find words to describe even everyday skills.

Another defining characteristic of procedural memory is that it is often *implicit* memory (Cohen, 1984; Reber, 2013; Squire, Knowlton, & Musen, 1993). Recall that implicit memory is memory that is used unconsciously. We remember without being aware that we are remembering. For the most part, the skills we execute every day are done in an unconscious, implicit fashion. As you walk to your classes, are you consciously aware of what you need to do to get your body to walk? When you take notes in class, are you aware of what you need to do to get your hand to write? Of course not! We walk, write, drive a car, and perform many other skills without thinking about them. The fact that procedural memories are implicit may also help explain why we have a difficult time verbalizing them. How can you verbalize your execution of a behavior when you are not aware of how you do it? You can't.

A final aspect of procedural memory that separates it from declarative memory is its longevity. Procedural memories tend to last for a long time in long-term memory. You've probably heard the saying "It's like riding a bike. You never forget how to do it." There is a great deal of truth in this folk wisdom—once we have mastered a skill, it does stay with us for a long time. For example, one of your authors recently purchased a bike. She hadn't ridden one in almost 10 years, but when she tried it, it was as if she had ridden just yesterday. Declarative memory, on the other hand, does not enjoy the same longevity as procedural memory. If you put aside your study of psychology and never thought about it, how much psychology do you think you would be able to recall 10 years from now? Probably not much.

As you can see, procedural memory seems to differ substantially from declarative memory. The degree of disparity between these two types of memory brings up the question of whether they are separate memory systems. Strong evidence to support the notion that procedural memory is a separate memory system comes from studies done on people with *amnesia*.

retrograde amnesia a type of amnesia in which one is unable to retrieve previously stored memories from long-term memory

anterograde [an-TARE-oh-grade] amnesia a type of amnesia in which one is unable to store new memories in long-term memory

7.3.5 • Amnesia: What Forgetting Can Teach Us About Memory

Amnesia is a condition in which a person cannot recall certain declarative memories. Amnesia can be classified as *retrograde* or *anterograde* (● FIGURE 7.8). **Retrograde amnesia** is an inability to recall previously stored declarative memories; **anterograde amnesia** is an inability to encode new declarative memories in long-term memory. In short, retrograde amnesia is amnesia for one's past, and anterograde amnesia is amnesia for one's present and future.

Amnesia has several causes, but of most interest to us here is amnesia that is caused by brain injury or illness. In particular, studies of brain-injured people with anterograde amnesia have taught us much about the distinction between declarative and procedural memory. One of the most famous cases of anterograde amnesia involved H.M. (Corkin, 1968), who suffered from severe epilepsy that was centered in the vicinity of his hippocampal regions in the temporal lobe (Chapter 2) and did not respond to medication. In an effort to curb H.M.'s seizures, doctors removed the hippocampal regions in both hemispheres of his brain (Squire, 1992).

© Chris Hendrickson/Masterfile

FIGURE 7.8
Amnesia Affects a Person's Memory in Dramatic Ways

The surgery was successful in that H.M.'s seizures were drastically reduced. However, in another sense, the operation was a serious failure. After H.M. recovered from the surgery, it became apparent that he could no longer store new declarative memories. He could not remember seeing his doctor seconds after the doctor left the room. He was also unable to read an entire magazine article. By the time he got to the end of a long paragraph, he would have forgotten what he'd just read. It was clear that H.M. had severe anterograde amnesia, a condition he lived with for the next 55 years until his death in 2008 at age 82 (Carey, 2008).

Interestingly, however, H.M. did not completely lose his ability to store new long-term memories. After the surgery, he could still store procedural memories. For instance, H.M. could learn to do certain perceptual-motor tasks, such as tracing a stimulus while looking at its image in a mirror. Furthermore, he was seen to improve on these tasks with time (Milner, 1962). Results similar to those found in H.M. have also been found in other people with amnesia (see, for example, Cermak et al., 1973; Mulligan & Besken, 2013). The fact that H.M. and other people with amnesia can still learn new skills indicates that procedural memory is not stored in long-term memory in the same way as declarative memory.

For people with amnesia, the ability to learn new skills is very fortunate. They can still use their procedural memory to learn new skills that may allow them to perform certain jobs, such as making furniture or knitting sweaters, although they will not remember where they acquired these new skills. If they also lost their ability to encode procedural memories, they would be even more impaired. They would not be able to add anything to their long-term memory.

© Daniel Teetor/Alamy

The Washington Post/Getty Images

Recent studies suggest that concussions among high school athletes are cause for concern. When female athletes compete in sports with the same rules and protective equipment as male players, they may be at equal or higher risk than their male counterparts. For high school athletes, football, soccer, and lacrosse pose some of the highest risks.

AMNESIA IN EVERYDAY LIFE: CONCUSSIONS IN SPORTS AND RECREATION

Most of us will never face amnesia to the degree that H.M. did. However, amnesia may be more common than you think. Each year, in the United States, over 200,000 people are treated for nonfatal sport and recreation-related brain injuries, many of which are concussions (CDC, 2011). Studies of injured athletes show that many will suffer at least mild, temporary amnesia (Chrisman et al., 2013; Collins et al., 2003). If you add to these numbers the people who suffer from other forms of brain injury—from car accidents, illnesses, drug overdoses, and falls—you can see how amnesia may be more common than you might think. This is why it is important to always follow safety procedures, such as wearing a helmet while biking.

Recently, researchers have studied high school athletes to determine the frequency with which they experience concussions (Lincoln et al., 2011). The study examined data from 25 different high schools over an 11-year period; it considered boys' football, lacrosse, soccer, wrestling, basketball, and baseball and girls' soccer, lacrosse, basketball, softball, field hockey, and cheerleading. Overall, the researchers found a rate of 0.24 concussions per 1,000 practices or games, with a total of 2,651 concussions reported. Disturbingly, they also found that the rate of concussions increased 15.5% per year during the study, although it is unclear if this increase was due to increased injuries or increasing proficiency in diagnosing concussions during the study. Boys' football had the highest rate of concussions, followed by girls' soccer, boys' lacrosse, and girls' lacrosse. Boys' baseball and girls' cheerleading were tied for the safest sports of those studied.

Although girls had a lower rate of concussion overall, in specific sports (that is, soccer, basketball, and baseball/softball), girls had a higher rate of concussion than boys. Only in lacrosse, where girls play with different protective equipment and different rules, was the concussion rate lower for girls. These data suggest that under similar conditions of play, girls may be more at risk for concussions.

The effects of concussions in high school athletes were examined in another study (Schatz et al., 2011). These researchers found that athletes with a history of two or more concussions had significantly more cognitive, physical, and sleep difficulties compared to athletes with histories of one or fewer concussions. Given the overall rates of concussions and the effects of repeated concussions on young athletes, it appears that we should focus on finding ways to better protect young athletes.

Even without brain injury or amnesia, you may still encounter mild problems with your memory from time to time. Normal, everyday forgetting can be an annoyance. In the next sections, we will discuss how we retrieve information from long-term memory and theories of why we sometimes forget the information we have encoded in our memory.

Quiz Yourself

7.3

1. **Remembering the definition of elaborative rehearsal is an example of a(n) _____ memory.**
   a. semantic c. procedural
   b. episodic d. sensory
2. **You know how to behave when you go to a fast-food restaurant because you have a(n) _____ stored in long-term memory for this event.**
   a. episode c. schema
   b. icon d. proposition
3. **Which of the following is the best example of semantic encoding in long-term memory?**
   a. Remembering how to play the tune to your favorite song on a guitar
   b. Remembering the name of the artist who sings your favorite song
   c. Hearing the tune to your favorite song in your head
   d. Seeing the face of the artist who sings your favorite song in your head

Answers 1. a; 2. c; 3. b

7.4 Retrieval and Forgetting in Long-Term Memory

We store memories so that we can later retrieve them. Retrieval is the act of moving information from long-term memory back into working memory or consciousness. Retrieval occurs when we send a *probe* or *cue* into long-term memory in search of memory traces, or encoded memories that we have stored there. A probe or cue can be many things—a test question, the sight of a playground, the sound of a roller coaster, or even a particular smell. For example, the smell of a pumpkin pie in the oven may remind you of a particularly joyous holiday event with loved ones. Or, the sight of a calculator may remind you of a test you took in a high school math class. Memories such as these can be recalled into consciousness many times throughout a given day. The ability to retrieve information from long-term memory also serves important practical applications as well. For example, the ability to retrieve instructions on how to execute a mathematical problem comes in very handy on a math exam. Recalling how to cook your favorite dish allows you to have a nice dinner. And, retrieving information that you have stored about your friends facilitates your social interactions with them by giving you things to talk about. These are just some of the many examples of how we use retrieval in everyday life. Now let's take a closer look at how retrieval occurs in memory and explore ways to improve our use of memory. See Psychology Applies to Your World: Tips for Improving Memory.

Eric Audras/PhotoLibrary

Many things can function as memory probes—test questions, sights, sounds, smells, and so on. These probes have the power to retrieve memories and bring them to consciousness. For example, smelling your mother's perfume may bring a host of pleasant memories to mind.

Psychology Applies to Your World:

Tips for Improving Your Memory

Although some people, such as Kim Peek, have remarkable memories, most of us find that storing large amounts of new information requires hard work. As students, much of your academic performance relies on your ability to store and remember information. Now that you have learned a bit about how your memory works, you can apply this knowledge to your own life. Yes, you, too, can have a better memory! To be a successful student, you have to study in a way that works with these processes, not against them. We'll outline some strategies that will help maximize your memory.

© Bill Aron/PhotoEdit

You can't learn well if you don't pay attention!

Single-Task—Don't Multitask

Attention is the first step in getting information into memory. If you are distracted by other tasks (for example, watching television or participating in social media) while studying, you won't be able to devote your full attention to the information you are trying to learn, and your ability to recall the information later may be affected (Iidaka et al., 2000; Zeamer & Fox, 2013). Therefore, you should study when and where you can focus your full attention on the single task of studying the material you are trying to learn. Try studying in a quiet, distraction-free environment.

Do Not Cram for Exams

Cramming is one of the worst ways to study for an exam. Unfortunately, many students procrastinate and then try to make up for it by pulling an all-nighter right before the exam. If this is the way you approach your studies, you are asking for failure. Even if you manage to pass the exam, the information you stored in long-term memory is likely to become inaccessible shortly after the exam. In short, you waste your time when you cram.

Studies have shown that *massed practice*—when you try to learn a great deal of information in one study session—results in poor recall of the information. Recall suffers because massed practice results in fatigue, which leads to a lack of attention, and the shortened time frame does not give you time to adequately rehearse information. Without adequate attention and elaborative rehearsal, information will not be efficiently stored in long-term memory. A better way to study is to use *distributed practice,* distributing your study time across several days rather than bunching it up on one day (or night). The beauty of distributed practice is that you don't necessarily have to study longer; you just need to space out the time you spend studying.

7.4.1 • Recognition and Recall

Think for a moment about the types of exams you have had in the past—for example, multiple-choice, essay, fill-in-the-blank, and true/false. An essay question is an example of a **recall** task. In a recall task, the probe is relatively weak; it does not contain a great deal of information to go on as you search your memory for the answer. You can't guess your way through an essay test. You must really know the information to answer the question. If you have not elaborated the material in long-term memory, you will likely find it difficult to recall.

recall a type of retrieval process in which the probe or cue does not contain much information

Use Elaborative Rehearsal

To study efficiently, you must process the information at a deeper level, finding ways to elaborate on the meaning of the material in your memory. This means you must form connections or associations among the bits of information you are trying to learn and the information you already know. Outlining is one way to do this. Take all of the material you are trying to learn, and organize it into an outline. When you create an outline, you must elaborate the material because you have to think about the relationships among concepts. It also helps to come up with your own original examples of the concepts you are learning—a technique we've encouraged you to use throughout this text. By generating examples, you once again elaborate the material. If the examples are from your own life, this is even better because it ties the material to your self, and we remember information that relates to the self better than information that does not (Symons & Johnson, 1997).

Use Overlearning

Overlearning is a technique in which you learn the material until you feel that you have mastered it, and then you continue to study it some more. By doing this, you help ensure that you will be able to retrieve it at a later date, because every time you activate information in long-term memory, you help to make it more available for retrieval. Overlearning can also make you feel more confident as you sit down to take an exam. Knowing that you really know the material, as opposed to "sort of" knowing it, can lessen the anxiety that you feel during an exam, which in turn can improve your performance.

Use the SQ3R Method

SQ3R is an acronym for Survey, Question, Read, Recite, and Review. Using this method when studying a chapter, you first survey the whole chapter, noting the section headings. As you survey them, you formulate questions based on these headings. Then, as you read the chapter, you search for answers to your questions. After you read the chapter, you reread the material and recite, or summarize, the meaning of each section. Finally, you review what you have learned from reading and reciting the material. The SQ3R seems to foster memory because it encourages elaboration and integration of the material. Give it a try when you read the next chapter.

Mnemonics Make Your Memory Mighty

If you find it difficult to elaborate the material, you might try using *mnemonic devices,* memory tricks that help you recall information. A few that you might try include acronyms, taking the first letter of each word you want to remember and use these first letters to form a word; and acrostics, creating a rhyme or saying in which each word starts with the first letter of each of the to-be-remembered words. For example, ESR could be an acronym for the three memory processes of encoding, storage, and retrieval. And "Ellen steals rabbits" could be an acrostic to help you remember the three memory processes of encoding, storage, and retrieval.

A multiple-choice question, on the other hand, is an example of a **recognition** task. In recognition, the probe is stronger and contains much more information than does a recall cue. Several researchers have proposed theories to explain why recognition is typically easier than recall (for example, Gillund & Shiffrin, 1984; Tulving, 1983). One theory proposes that recognition is easier because of the overlap between the content of the probe and the content of the memory trace (Tulving, 1983). Think about it for a minute: In a multiple-choice question, the answer is actually part of the probe. Because recall is the harsher test of memory, you should always study as if you are going to take an essay exam. This way, you'll be sure to be prepared for your professor's questions.

recognition a type of retrieval process in which the probe or cue contains a great deal of information, including the item being sought

7.4.2 • Forgetting: Why Can't I Remember That?

Unfortunately, despite your best efforts at studying, there will always be instances when retrieval is difficult. We've all known times when the probes and cues we sent into long-term memory were not successful in retrieving the desired information. For a memory to actually be retrieved from long-term memory, two conditions must be met: the memory must be both *available* and *accessible*. A memory is available when it has been encoded in long-term memory and the memory trace is still present in long-term memory. Obviously, if you never encoded the memory in long-term memory, you won't be able to retrieve it later.

However, availability by itself is not enough to ensure retrieval. Accessibility of the memory trace is also important. If the probe cannot reach the memory trace in long-term memory, the memory will not be retrieved, even if it is available. As we will see in the next section, there are a variety of circumstances in which the probe fails to retrieve an available, but inaccessible, memory.

decay theory a theory of forgetting that proposes that memory traces that are not routinely activated in long-term memory will degrade

tip of the tongue phenomenon knowing that you know a piece of information, even though you cannot recall it at the moment

proactive interference a type of forgetting that occurs when older memory traces inhibit the retrieval of newer memory traces

DECAY THEORY: IF YOU DON'T USE IT, YOU LOSE IT

What student hasn't asked him- or herself this question: "I studied that material, so why did I forget it on the test?" Forgetting occurs when we cannot, for some reason, retrieve information from long-term memory. One theory of forgetting, **decay theory**, maintains that once a memory trace is stored in long-term memory, it must be routinely activated to keep it there (Ebbinghaus, 1885/1913). If we store a memory and then fail to recall it periodically, the memory trace weakens and decays. If the decay is not stopped by recalling the memory, the memory trace will be lost forever.

Although decay theory seems to make sense, there are some good reasons to doubt that memory traces decay from disuse. One is that memories seem to last a very long time, even when we do not routinely access them. For example, in one study, participants' recognition of English–Spanish vocabulary words was tested anywhere from 1 to 50 years after they had studied Spanish. The results showed that recognition memory for these vocabulary words had declined little over the years (Bahrick, 1984).

© Masterfile

On exam day, you really hope that your retrieval methods work!

INTERFERENCE: TEMPORARY FORGETTING

Have you ever found yourself unable to answer a test question, only to remember the answer later, after the test is over? Sometimes we know that we know information, even though we cannot recall it at the moment, something psychologists refer to as the **tip of the tongue phenomenon**. This frustrating experience is often due to *interference,* a condition in which the memory trace is still available, but has become temporarily inaccessible. **Proactive interference** occurs when older information inhibits our ability to retrieve other, newer information from memory. For example, one of your authors spells her first name in an unusual way that often causes proactive interference in others. Her name is pronounced "Suzanne," but it is spelled *Susann*. Because of its spelling, people often pronounce her name as "Susan" when they first see it in print. Then, no matter how many times she corrects them, they seem to always want to call her Susan. This example is one of proactive interference because the *older* (people's original) pronunciation of her name inhibits the *newer* (correct) pronunciation in people's memory. (It's also the reason she started going by Sue early in childhood!)

We can also experience **retroactive interference**, in which *newer* information inhibits the retrieval of *older* information in memory. Suppose you move to a new home and work very hard to memorize your new address and phone number. Chances are, you will soon find it hard to recall your old address and phone number. This is an example of retroactive interference, because the new phone number and address interfere with your ability to retrieve the old phone number and address from long-term memory.

Unfortunately, our susceptibility to both proactive (Jacoby, Debner, & Hay, 2001) and retroactive (Hedden & Park, 2003) interference tends to increase as we age. One explanation for why interference increases with age is that our central executive function tends to decline with advancing age. As the central executive becomes less efficient, it is also less able to suppress interfering memory traces (Biss, Campbell, & Hasher, 2013; Hedden & Yoon, 2006).

CONTEXT AND FORGETTING

Interference theory does seem to describe one way in which we forget information, but there is reason to suspect that interference may not occur as often in the real world as it does in laboratory experiments (Slameka, 1966). **Cue-dependent forgetting** may be a better explanation of forgetting in the real world. The theory of cue-dependent forgetting (Tulving, 1974) is that the amount of information we can retrieve from long-term memory is a function of the type of cue or probe we use. If the memory cues we use are not the right ones, we may experience forgetting.

Nicole Duplaix/National Geographic

Studies show that we remember information best when we retrieve it in the same context in which it was learned. Godden and Baddeley (1975) found that divers who learned a list of words while under water recalled more of the words while submerged than they did on the dock. Studies like these suggest that a change in context may be one of the reasons we sometimes forget.

The cue-dependent forgetting theory is part of the *encoding specificity principle* developed by Endel Tulving (Wiseman & Tulving, 1976). According to this principle, we encode aspects of the context in which we learn information, later using these contextual aspects as cues to help us retrieve the information from long-term memory. If the encoding specificity principle is correct, then we should have better memory when we retrieve information in the same setting that we learned it.

In one distinctive study, researchers asked divers to learn a list of words while they were either on shore or 20 feet under water (Godden & Baddeley, 1975). Later, researchers tested the divers' recall for the words in either the context in which they had studied the words or the context in which they had not studied the words. Consistent with the encoding specificity principle, the researchers found that when the divers recalled the words in the same context in which they had learned the words, their recall was better.

Encoding specificity has also been shown to hold true for mood states and states of consciousness. People can recall information they learned while drinking alcohol better when they have been drinking (Eich et al., 1975). Information learned while smoking marijuana is better recalled while smoking marijuana (Eich, 1980). And information learned while in a bad mood is better recalled in a negative mood state than when one is happy (Teasdale & Russell, 1983). These findings do not mean that it is better to learn while in these states, however. For example, alcohol can reduce one's ability to encode information in the first place (Parker, Birnbaum, & Noble, 1976).

retroactive interference a type of forgetting that occurs when newer memory traces inhibit the retrieval of older memory traces

cue-dependent forgetting a type of forgetting that occurs when one cannot recall information in a context other than the context in which it was encoded

REPRESSION: MOTIVATED FORGETTING

The final theory of forgetting we will discuss is Sigmund Freud's (1915, 1943) proposal that the emotional aspects of a memory can affect our ability to retrieve it. According to Freud, when we experience emotionally threatening events, we push or repress these memories into an inaccessible part of our mind called the unconscious (Chapter 11). This **repression** results in amnesia for this information.

repression a type of forgetting proposed by Sigmund Freud in which memories for events, desires, or impulses that we find threatening are pushed into an inaccessible part of the mind called the unconscious

Repression of memories has become a very controversial subject because of its relationship to cases of childhood sexual abuse. Some people have claimed that they suddenly "remembered" abuse that had occurred many years before. After many years have passed, there is often no corroborating evidence to support such claims. Furthermore, the content of recalled memories for events can be affected by, among other things, the stress the child was under during the event (Klemfuss et al., 2013); and some experiments indicate that the details of children's memories for past events can often be incorrect (Brainerd & Reyna, 2002; Howe, 2000). In one study, researchers found that preschool children could not distinguish memories for fictitious events from memories for real events after 10 weeks of thinking about the events. Even more alarming, the children were able to give detailed accounts of the fictitious events, and they seemed to really believe that the fictitious events had happened (Ceci, 1995).

The frequent lack of corroborating evidence for recovered memories, along with experimental evidence that questions the accuracy of memory, has led some to charge that these are in fact *false memories* (Loftus & Davis, 2006). The debate is further fueled by the lack of experimental data to support the notion that repression can occur. To test the theory of repression, researchers would have to traumatize participants and then see whether they repressed their memories of the trauma. Obviously, this type of study cannot be done for ethical reasons. So, for now, psychologists cannot say for sure whether repression is one of the reasons we forget (see You Review: Theories of Forgetting).

You Review **Theories of Forgetting**

Theory	Definition	Example
Decay	Memory traces that are not routinely activated erode and disappear over time.	You haven't thought of your best friend from kindergarten in 15 years. When you meet him/her, you cannot recall his/her name.
Proactive interference	Older memory traces inhibit the retrieval of newer memory traces.	You can't seem to remember your friend's new, married name, but you can recall her maiden name.
Retroactive interference	Newer memory traces inhibit the retrieval of older memory traces.	You can't recall your old phone number, but you can recall your new phone number.
Cue-dependent forgetting	Memories are not as easily retrieved when the retrieval cues do not match the cues that were present during encoding.	You run into a classmate at the grocery store, and you can't recall her name. But you do recall her name when you see her at school.
Repression	Threatening memories are pushed into the inaccessible unconscious part of the mind.	You are in a horrible car accident in which other people are seriously injured. Although you are uninjured, you later cannot recall details of the accident.

7.4

Quiz Yourself

1. You meet an old friend on the street and search your memory for his name. This is an example of which type of retrieval task?
   a. Recall
   b. Recognition
   c. Implicit retrieval
   d. Encoding specificity
2. Decay theory states that forgetting is due to a lack of _____, whereas interference theory states that forgetting is due to a lack of _____.
   a. availability; accessibility
   b. accessibility; availability
   c. encoding; accessibility
   d. encoding; availability
3. Mary was married 6 months ago. Much to her dismay, her friends continue to call her by her maiden name even though she has legally taken her partner's name. Mary's friends are experiencing which memory phenomenon?
   a. Encoding specificity
   b. Repression
   c. Proactive interference
   d. Retroactive interference
4. Which of the following is the most controversial theory of forgetting?
   a. Proactive interference
   b. Retroactive interference
   c. Repression
   d. The encoding specificity principle

Answers 1. a; 2. a; 3. c; 4. c

7.5 The Accuracy of Memory

Even when we are successful in retrieving memories, a lingering question is just how accurate they are. Many people report experiencing **flashbulb memories**, or unusually detailed memory for emotionally charged events (R. Brown & Kulik, 1977). Perhaps you have as well. For example, can you remember what you were doing when you heard that terrorists had attacked the World Trade Center on September 11, 2001? Do you recall watching the live TV coverage as the tragedy was taking place? If so, answer this question: How long after the plane hit the first tower did it take for both towers to fall?

flashbulb memory an unusually detailed and seemingly accurate memory for an emotionally charged event

Researchers interviewed 690 people 7 weeks after the attack and asked them this question. On average, the participants reported that it took 62 minutes for the towers to collapse—when in reality it took almost 2 hours. On the day of the attack, do you remember watching news coverage of the first plane hitting the towers? If so, you are not alone—despite the fact that this video footage did not air until the next day (Perina, 2002). So how did you do on this task? How accurate (or inaccurate) is your memory of that day?

Interestingly, some researchers now suspect that stress hormones that act on the amygdala (Chapter 2) may be responsible for certain aspects of flashbulb memories. A current theory is that when you experience an emotional event, such as watching a horrific terrorist attack, your body releases stress hormones that direct your brain's amygdala to initiate storage of a long-term memory of that event. However, these stress hormones also seem to block the formation of accurate memories for what was happening immediately before the emotional event. Therefore, you may end up with a memory for the emotional event that is not entirely accurate because you have something of a "gap" in your memory (Bower, 2003; Hirst et al., 2009).

7.5.1 • Memory Is Not Like a Video Camera

Does it surprise you to know that memory is often inaccurate? But think about it: Even when we store memories of the everyday events in our lives, we do not store memory traces for every detail. Memory does not work like a video

© Steve McCurry/Magnum Photos

Do you remember what you were doing when you heard about the September 11th attacks?

recorder. It's more like a construction project. We store the gist of the information in long-term memory with the help of schemas, but we do not store all of the details. This means that when we retrieve a memory, we do not recall all of the details and then use them to *reconstruct* the event. Memory is more than just **reconstructive**, or based on actual events; it is also *constructive*.

Memory is **constructive** in that we use the knowledge and expectations that we have stored in our schemas to help us fill in the missing details in our stored memories (Schacter & Addis, 2007). It is very possible that you filled in the gaps in your memory of September 11, 2001—such as what you were wearing that day, the setting in which you first heard the news, or specific details of the news coverage that you watched that day. Most of the time, it makes little difference whether we recall such details accurately. But sometimes the details of our recollections can be extremely important, even a matter of life and death.

7.5.2 • Eyewitness Memory

Psychologist Elizabeth Loftus (1944–) has spent a good part of her career showing that eyewitness memory can be manipulated by the expectations we hold about the world. For example, in one experiment (Loftus & Palmer, 1974), Loftus showed participants a film of a car accident. After viewing the film, the participants were randomly divided into several groups and questioned about their memory of the film. In one group, the participants were asked, "About how fast were the cars going when they *smashed* into each other?" In another group, the participants were asked, "About how fast were the cars going when they *hit* each other?" In the control group, the participants were not asked to estimate the speed of the cars. The results showed that the verb used in the question affected participants' estimates of the speed of the cars. Participants in the "smashed into" group estimated the speed of the cars, on average, at 41 mph; the average estimate for participants in the "hit" group was 34 mph.

reconstructive memory memory that is based on the retrieval of memory traces that contain the actual details of events we have experienced

constructive memory memory that utilizes knowledge and expectations to fill in the missing details in retrieved memory traces

misinformation effect the distortion of memory that occurs when people are exposed to misinformation

The participants exhibited the **misinformation effect**, or the distortion of memory that occurs when people are exposed to misinformation. In this case, the words *smashed* and *hit* activated different expectations that were used to fill in the missing details in the participants' memories of the film, and the result was that they remembered the film differently. Imagine how a lawyer's choice of words might influence a witness's memory on the witness stand.

Even more dramatic is the fact that our memories can be permanently altered by things that happen *after* we encode the memories. In another study (Loftus & Zanni, 1975), Loftus showed participants a film of a car crash and then asked them a series of questions about the accident. The participants in one group were asked, "Did you see *a* broken headlight?" In a second group, the participants were asked, "Did you see *the* broken headlight?" Although there had been no broken headlight in the film, of those who were asked about *a* broken headlight, 7% reported that they had seen a broken headlight in the film. Of the participants who were asked about *the* broken headlight, 17% said they had seen it. By subtly suggesting to these participants that there *had* been a broken headlight, Loftus caused more of them to remember seeing something that they had not seen. She created a false memory in her participants.

These false memories do not seem to be motivated by a participant's desire to please the researcher. In another study, Loftus offered participants $25 if they could recall an event accurately. Even with this motivation to be accurate, the participants could not prevent their memories from being distorted by the misleading information they heard after viewing the incident (Loftus, 1979).

Although it is clear that eyewitness memory is susceptible to errors, there is some disagreement as to why these errors occur. According to Loftus (2000), we accept subsequent misinformation as being correct, and this information becomes part of our memory for the original event. Others propose that eyewitness memory becomes faulty when we make errors in identifying the source of information we have stored in long-term memory (Johnson, Hashtroudi, & Lindsay, 1993). According to this view, when we retrieve a memory for a particular event from long-term memory, we also retrieve information from other sources relevant to the event. For instance, we might retrieve information from times when we discussed the event with others, from comments others made about the event, from things we read about the event in the newspaper, and so on. Because there is considerable overlap between our memory for the original event and our memories of information related to the event, it is easy for us to get confused about the source of these bits of information. We might misattribute the source of a particular detail to our memory of the original event, when we actually encoded it in another situation.

Regardless of which interpretation is correct, after we witness the original event, the more information we are faced with, the more likely it is that our memory will become faulty.

7.5

Quiz Yourself

1. **In recalling his date from last Saturday night, Juan assumes that she was wearing shoes, even though he did not encode the details of what her shoes looked like. Juan's memory is an example of _____.**
   a. constructive memory
   b. reconstructive memory
   c. procedural memory
   d. encoding specificity
2. **In question number 1, Juan's recollection of his date is most likely to be the result of _____.**
   a. reconstructive memory
   b. constructive memory
   c. constructive and reconstructive memory
   d. memory that is like a videotape—an exact copy of what he experienced on the date
3. **Which of the following events is most likely to produce a flashbulb memory?**
   a. Taking a difficult math test
   b. Being in a serious car accident
   c. Having a heated discussion with your best friend
   d. Going to a very scary movie on a date

Answers 1. a; 2. c; 3. b

7.6 The Biology of Memory

Much of what we know about the role that the brain plays in memory comes from studies of people with amnesia. People with amnesia often experience severe memory problems that can be traced to damage or disease in particular parts of the brain. Recall the case of H.M., discussed earlier in this chapter. H.M.'s hippocampal regions were removed in an attempt to control his epilepsy; as a result of the surgery, he could no longer achieve **memory consolidation** (the stabilization and long-term storage of memory traces in the brain). In short, he lost the ability to move new declarative memories from short-term to long-term memory (● FIGURE 7.9). Other amnesic cases, too, have supported the notion that the hippocampus plays a significant role in the storage of declarative memories (Parkin & Leng, 1993).

memory consolidation the stabilization and long-term storage of memory traces in the brain

Scientists also use brain-imaging technology, discussed in Chapter 2, to study the function of the brain during memory tasks (for example, see Finn, 2004). These

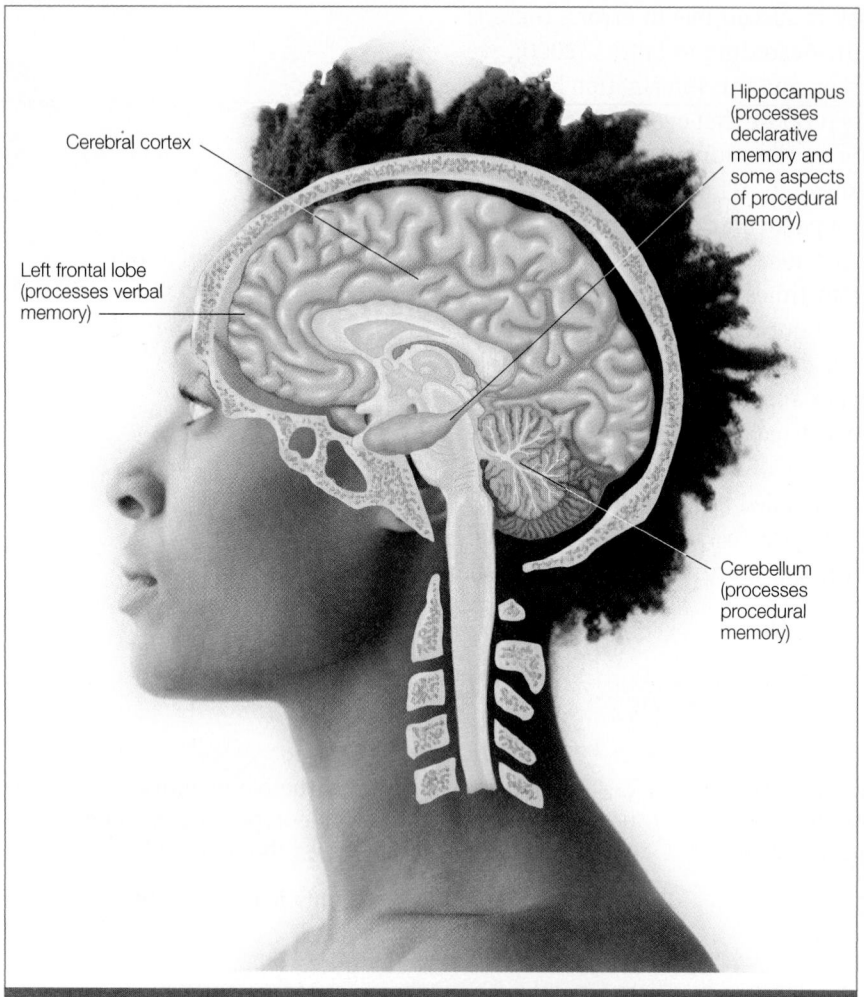

© JLP/Jose Luis Pelaez/zefa/Corbis

FIGURE 7.9

Brain Structures That Are Important to Memory

The hippocampus plays a significant role in the processing of declarative memories, but it may also process some aspects of procedural memories. The left frontal lobe processes verbal memories, and the cerebellum processes procedural memories.

studies indicate that the hippocampus plays an important role in the declarative memory function of people without amnesia. For instance, PET scans show that blood flow in the normal brain is higher in the right hippocampal region during declarative memory tasks, but not during procedural memory tasks (Schacter et al., 1996; Squire et al., 1992). Likewise, numerous studies have documented memory problems in animals that have had lesions (areas of damage) made in their hippocampal regions (see Winocur, Moscovitch, & Sekeres, 2013).

Research on both animals (Iso, Simoda, & Matsuyama, 2006) and humans (Woollett, Glensman, & Maguire, 2008) suggests that the degree to which we use our memory may have implications for the structure of our brain, particularly in the area of the hippocampus. Do you recall the study of London taxi drivers from Chapter 2? That study used MRI technology to show that London cab drivers have specific hippocampal regions that are larger than those found in London bus drivers. London's street system is old and complicated, and taxi drivers must memorize the entire city, not just a single bus route, in order to be licensed. Is it possible that these drivers experienced greater hippocampal development because they relied on their memory so much in doing their job? No one can say for sure at this time, but consistent with this notion, the researchers did find that the taxi drivers who had been driving the longest tended to have the biggest hippocampal regions (Maguire et al., 2006).

Because the hippocampus appears to play an important role in the formation of new memories, researchers are currently investigating whether drugs that stimulate neural growth and function in the hippocampus may also provide useful treatments for people suffering from memory-robbing diseases such as Alzheimer's disease (see, for example, Frielingsdorf et al., 2007).

Like the hippocampus, the frontal lobe also seems to play a significant role in the processing of declarative memory. Evoked response potential (ERP) recordings have revealed that the left frontal lobe is very active during the processing of verbal information. This makes sense because one of the language centers of the brain, Broca's area (Chapter 2), is in the left frontal lobe (Anderson, 2000). Similarly, PET scans of the brain in action have revealed that the amount of left frontal lobe activation seems to be related to the degree to which the participant is processing the material. Left frontal lobe activity is especially likely to occur when participants are deeply processing the material. In fact, the more activation there is in the participants' left frontal lobe, the better they tend to recall the information (Kapur et al., 1994). Findings like these seem to suggest that the levels-of-processing approach to memory may have some biological correlate.

© Ron Chapple Stock/Alamy

This PET scan shows that regions of the left frontal lobe, shown in red, are very active during thinking (lower right). When listening, the brain shows high activity in the temporal lobe (upper left). When a person is speaking, high activity is seen in the left frontal lobe along the motor cortex and in Broca's area (lower left).

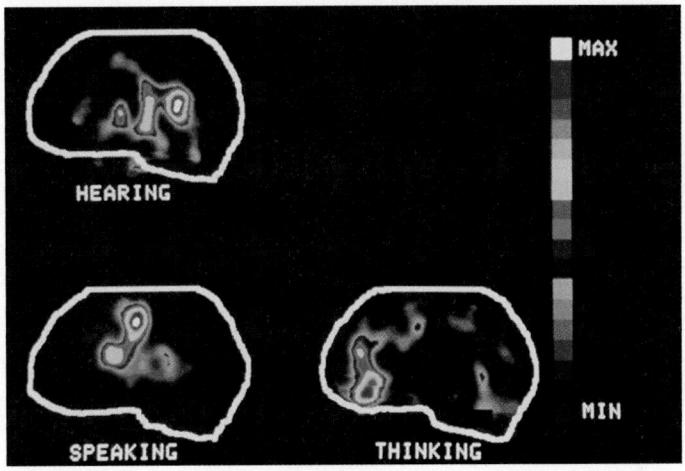

Yves Forestier/Sygma/Corbis

It appears that the hippocampus and the frontal lobes play a crucial role in the processing of declarative memory, but what about procedural memory? How is it that a person with severe hippocampal damage, like H.M., can still learn new skills? Declarative memory is usually explicit, but procedural memory is typically executed in an implicit, unconscious manner. Therefore, we may gain some insight into how the brain processes procedural memory by examining the brain function that underlies implicit memory.

To examine brain function during implicit memory processing, researchers took PET scans of participants while they completed implicit and explicit memory tasks. As expected, the explicit memory task was associated with increased blood flow in the hippocampal regions of the brain. However, when the participants used their implicit memory, all of the blood flow changes that occurred were outside the hippocampal regions of the brain (Schacter et al., 1996).

Other brain-imaging studies have shown that procedural memory is linked to brain structures outside the hippocampus. For instance, motor skill memory seems to rely, in part, on the cerebellum (Sanes, Dimitrov, & Hallett, 1990; Figure 7.9) and the *striatum* (Censor, Dayan, & Cohen, 2013). This explains why someone like Kim Peek, who had cerebellar damage, would have problems learning new motor skills, but another person like H.M., who had hippocampal damage, would still be able to acquire new procedural memory skills.

Although the role of the hippocampus in processing declarative memories has been well established and damage to the hippocampus does not eliminate the ability to store new procedural memories, exactly how procedural memories are stored is still under investigation. Some recent studies suggest that the hippocampus may play some role in processing procedural memories after all (see, for example, Gheysen et al., 2010). For example, activity in the hippocampus has been shown to coincide with the overnight memory consolidation of newly learned motor skills (Albouy et al., 2008, 2013), and that other brain regions may play a role in maintaining the procedural memories over time (Albouy et al., 2013). Studies like these suggest that we still have more to learn about the role that the hippocampus and other brain structures play in memory.

Quiz Yourself

7.6

1. Which of the following tasks would be most difficult for an adult with anterograde amnesia?
   a. Learning to jump rope
   b. Learning to play a new video game
   c. Recalling his fifth birthday party
   d. Learning psychology
2. Sarah is learning a list of new words. If you took a PET scan of Sarah's brain as she completed this task, where would you expect to see the greatest brain activity?
   a. The cerebellum
   b. The hypothalamus
   c. The hippocampus
   d. The right frontal lobe
3. José was in a car accident and he damaged his cerebellum. Which of the following tasks would be most difficult for José after his accident?
   a. Learning to play the piano
   b. Learning psychology
   c. Recalling his childhood
   d. Remembering what he had for breakfast

Answers 1. d; 2. c; 3. a

7.7 Integrating Psychology: The Big Picture

In Chapter 6, we discussed processes of learning (*habituation, classical* and *operant conditioning,* and *observational learning*) that occur throughout daily life and how this learning affects our behavior. In the current chapter, we further explored the cognitive aspect of psychology by examining the memory processes of encoding, storage, and retrieval that underlie much of our learning in life.

The case of Kim Peek, the real-life *Rainman,* illustrates the extremes of human abilities for learning and memory. On the one hand, Kim had a computer-like ability for learning. On the other hand, Kim exhibited great deficiencies in learning. Both Kim's abilities and inabilities for learning likely reside in the manner in which he processed information in memory. Kim's unique brain seemed to foster an amazing ability to encode, store, and retrieve vast quantities of factual information in his declarative memory. But it was also because of his unique brain that Kim was unable to efficiently encode, store, and retrieve procedural memories, such as how to brush his teeth each day.

Unlike Kim, you most likely cannot memorize a book chapter simply by reading it. For you (and for most of us) committing information to long-term memory requires careful encoding and elaboration of the material in working memory. As you read this chapter, your central executive directed your working memory to process the visual, auditory, and meaning aspects of what you were reading. You then elaborated the material by thinking about how this information fits with what you already know about psychology and the world. As you elaborated the material, the information became encoded in your long-term semantic memory, where you will continue to elaborate it as you study in preparation for retrieval at some point in the future—such as on exam day! So, although it takes effort, your memory most likely serves you well when you use it properly.

In our next and final chapter in this section, "Cognition, Language, and Intelligence," we will further explore our cognitive abilities and the implications they have for our ability to survive and thrive in a challenging world. As we prepare to complete our discussion of cognition in the next chapter, think again about Kim Peek. Did Kim's unique abilities help him solve problems in his daily life? Or, did they hinder his ability to function? Would you consider someone like Kim to be intelligent? Was he a genius? Or, did he have a disability? How do your own memory abilities stack up against Kim's? Are your abilities more or less advantageous than Kim's when it comes to living everyday life?

Studying the Chapter

Key Terms

anterograde amnesia (287)
attention (270)
autobiographical memory (285)
central executive (281)
chunking (274)
consciousness (270)
constructive memory (296)
cue-dependent forgetting (293)
decay theory (292)
declarative memory (284)
dual coding system (274)
elaborative rehearsal (276)
encoding (270)
episodic memory (284)
explicit memory (270)
flashbulb memory (295)
forgetting curve (276)
implicit memory (270)
levels-of-processing model (277)
long-term memory (LTM) (271)
maintenance rehearsal (275)
memory consolidation (297)
memory traces (270)
misinformation effect (296)
primacy effect (278)
proactive interference (292)
procedural memory (286)
recall (290)
recency effect (278)
recognition (290)
reconstructive memory (296)
repression (294)
retrieval (270)
retroactive interference (293)
retrograde amnesia (287)
schema (284)
semantic encoding (283)
semantic memory (284)
sensory memory (271)
short-term memory (STM) (271)
storage (270)
tip of the tongue phenomenon (292)
working memory (279)

What Do You Know? Assess Your Understanding

Test your retention and understanding of the material by answering the following questions.

1. Bits of information that are encoded into memory are known as _____.

a. memory probes
b. memory cues
c. memory traces
d. attentional foci

2. Brushing your teeth, combing your hair, and tying your shoes are all most likely to involve use of which type of memory?

a. Explicit
b. Implicit
c. Autobiographical
d. Semantic

3. As you read a book, which is the first stage of memory into which the information that you are reading is processed?

a. Short-term
b. Working memory
c. Iconic memory
d. Semantic memory

4. Which of the following types of memory has the shortest duration?

a. Long-term memory
b. Short-term memory
c. Sensory memory
d. Working memory

5. At most, the average person should be able to hold _____ single-digit numbers in her short-term memory.

a. 3
b. 5
c. 7
d. 13

6. The available research evidence suggests that the _____ may play a role in the processing of both declarative and procedural memories.

a. cerebellum
b. hippocampus
c. striatum
d. b and c

7. Which of the following would be the *best* example of maintenance rehearsal?

a. Reading your notes over and over as you study for an exam
b. Thinking about how the material you are studying relates to chapters that you have previously studied
c. Developing mnemonics to help you remember the material
d. Thinking about how the material relates to your own life

8. According to the working memory model, which of the following is not a component of working memory?

a. Short-term memory
b. The phonological loop
c. The central executive
d. Iconic memory

9. The working memory model is to _____ as the three-stages model is to _____.

a. serial processing; explicit memory
b. parallel processing; explicit memory
c. serial processing; parallel processing
d. parallel processing; serial processing

10. As you read the words on this page, which component of working memory is likely controlling the manner in which you process this information?

a. Short-term memory
b. The phonological loop
c. The central executive
d. The visuospatial sketch pad

11. Your knowledge of animals is most likely stored in _____.

a. short-term memory as acoustic memory traces
b. short-term memory as semantic memory traces
c. long-term memory as acoustic memory traces
d. long-term memory as semantic memory traces

12. Glenn suffered a concussion in a terrible car accident, after which he could no longer store new episodic or semantic memories. Glenn seems to be suffering from _____.

a. retrograde amnesia
b. anterograde amnesia
c. repression
d. cue-dependent forgetting

13. Your knowledge of psychology is an example of _____ memory.

a. long-term
b. semantic
c. declarative
d. All of the above

14. Compared to procedural memory, declarative memory is often _____.

a. less likely to be processed in working memory
b. more explicit
c. less verbal
d. more implicit

15. In _____, the memory probes and cues are stronger and contain more information.

a. recall
b. recognition
c. short-term working memory
d. long-term memory

16. When you first met your classmate, he was introduced to you as Calvin. However, Calvin never uses his first name and goes by just his initials (C.D.). Now, after a few years, you find that you cannot recall C.D.'s first name. This is most likely an example of _____.

a. retroactive interference
b. proactive interference
c. memory trace decay
d. repression

17. According to the available research, which of the following is *not* a true statement about flashbulb memories?

a. They are emotionally charged memories.
b. They are in part a function of the stress hormones that are released at the time the memory trace is encoded.
c. They are very accurate in their detail.
d. Many people experience flashbulb memories at some point in their lives.

18. Recalling the actual details of your first day in college in an accurate manner would be an example of _____ memory.

a. reconstructive
b. constructive
c. semantic
d. procedural

19. The phrase "Please excuse my dear aunt Sally," used as a tool to help people recall the order of mathematical operations, is an example of _____.

a. an acronym
b. a mnemonic
c. massed practice
d. All of the above

20. Research on concussions in high school athletes suggests that _____.

a. when playing comparable sports, boys have a higher rate of concussions than girls
b. when playing comparable sports, girls have a higher rate of concussions than boys
c. when playing comparable sports, boys and girls have an equal rate of concussions
d. surprisingly, high school cheerleading has the second highest rate of concussions

Answers: 1. c; 2. b; 3. c; 4. c; 5. c; 6. b; 7. a; 8. d; 9. d; 10.c; 11. d; 12. b; 13. d; 14. b; 15. b; 16. a; 17. c; 18. a; 19. b; 20. b

Use It or Lose It: Applying Psychology

1. If you were going to design a computer that "thinks" like a human does, what would you have your computer do?
2. Your best friend tells you about a very detailed memory she has for her first day of kindergarten 16 years ago. She claims to recall all of the details of that special day—everything from what she had for breakfast to the color and design of the dress she wore. After telling you of her memory, your friend asks you how it is possible that she can remember that day in such detail. Given what you know about memory, what would you say to your friend about her childhood memory?
3. Assume that you are a psychologist who is called to testify in court. The defense attorney asks you to describe for the jury how humans store memories for everyday events. What would your testimony be about the accuracy of memory?
4. Your grandmother thinks she is having some problems with her memory. However, her doctor has assured her that her forgetting is normal and that she does *not* have Alzheimer's disease. How would you explain to her why she sometimes forgets things that she meant to buy at the store and the names of old friends that she hasn't seen in years?

Critical Thinking for Integration

1. Explain the evolutionary value (Chapter 1) of implicit memory.
2. How does getting a good night's sleep (Chapter 4) relate to memory?
3. What types of questions would a developmental psychologist (Chapter 1) ask about memory?
4. Use what you have learned about learning in Chapter 6 *and* what you have learned about memory in this chapter to design a plan to make yourself a more motivated, successful student.

© Robert Kneschke/Shutterstock.com

Are You Getting the Big Picture? Memory

7.1 The Functions of Memory: Encoding, Storing, and Retrieving

- The human brain **encodes**, stores, and processes information. We can use memory both **explicitly** (consciously) and **implicitly** (unconsciously).

7.2 The Development of New Memories

- The **three-stages model of memory:**

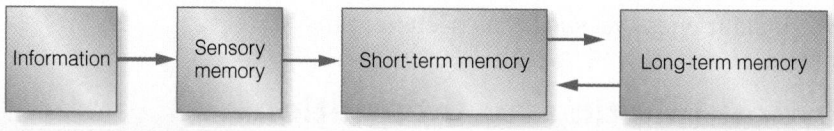

- Many researchers today reject the rigid three-stages model of memory and suggest a different type of memory, called **working memory**, that is important in moving information in and out of **long-term memory**.

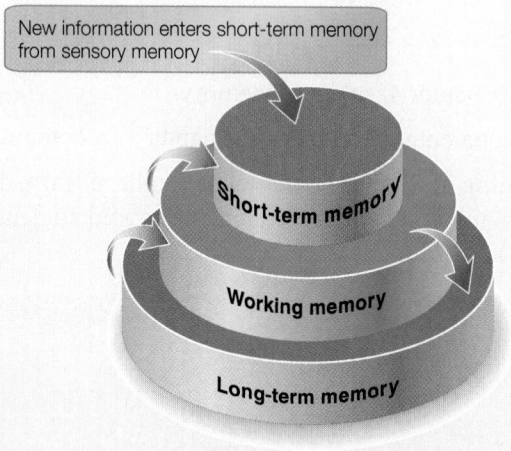

- Working memory retrieves information from long-term memory to help process information in short-term memory; for example, the meaning of words stored in short-term memory may be accessed from long-term memory.
- Working memory also retrieves stored information when you need it—for an exam, your address, directions to your aunt's house—and sends it to short-term memory.
- Working memory also moves information from short-term memory into long-term memory for storage; for example, when you are studying, working memory will move the information you want to remember into long-term memory.

7.3 Long-Term Memory: Permanent Storage

- Long-term memory is organized into **schemas**, which allow us to quickly and efficiently use our memory. In a sense, schemas are like a filing system for the library of knowledge we have stored in our long-term memory.

Susann Doyle-Portillo

ORGANIZATION OF INFORMATION IN LONG-TERM MEMORY

Declarative memory
Semantic memory
+
Personal Semantics
Episodic/autobiographical memory

Procedural memory

7.4 Retrieval and Forgetting in Long-Term Memory

© Masterfile

Despite our best efforts to retain information, sometimes forgetting occurs. Forgetting may be due to **decay** of memory traces, **interference, cue-dependent forgetting,** or perhaps even **repression.**

To improve your memory:

- Pay **attention** to what you are trying to remember; avoid distractions.
- Do not cram for exams.
- Use **elaborative rehearsal** to reinforce retention of information.
- Use overlearning.
- Use **mnemonics** to make your memory mighty.
- Use the SQ3R method: Survey, Question, Read, Recite, Review.

7.5 The Accuracy of Memory

© Steve McCurry/Magnum Photos

- **Flashbulb memories** are unusually detailed memories for emotionally charged events—memories that are quite powerful but not always accurate.
- In general, we are prone to many memory errors, including the **misinformation effect**. In cases of eyewitness testimony, these errors can have serious consequences.

7.6 The Biology of Memory

- **Memory consolidation** is the stabilization and long-term storage of memory traces in the brain.
- Brain-imaging research shows that people who use their memory a great deal may have structural differences in their hippocampal regions. The hippocampus and frontal lobe seem to play significant roles in processing declarative memory.
- The hippocampus may also play some role in the memory consolidation of procedural memories.
- Studies suggest that procedural memory is linked to the cerebellum and the striatum.

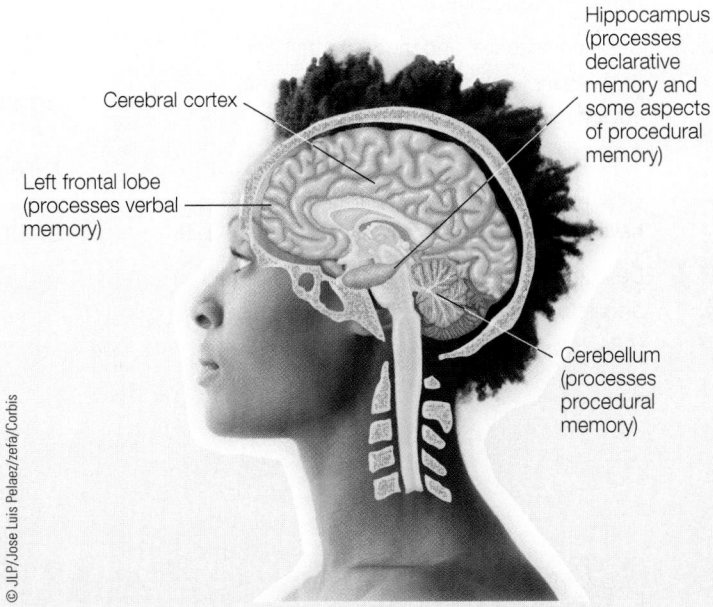

© JLP/Jose Luis Pelaez/zefa/Corbis

Cognition, Language, and Intelligence

Learning Objectives

8.1 Describe how we represent knowledge in our memory. (APA 1.1, 1.2, 1.3)

8.1 Describe how we organize knowledge in our memory. (APA 1.1, 1.2, 1.3)

8.2 Describe the different types of problems we face in life and the ways in which we may try to solve them. (APA 1.1, 1.2, 1.3)

8.2 Describe common obstacles to problem solving. (APA 1.1, 1.2, 1.3)

8.3 Describe the processes of deductive and inductive reasoning. (APA 1.1, 1.2, 1.3, 2.1)

8.3 Describe the factors that affect decision making. (APA 1.1, 1.2, 1.3)

8.3 Describe the process of judgment and heuristics that bias our judgments. (APA 1.1, 1.2, 1.3, 3.3)

8.4 Describe how children acquire language. (APA 1.1, 1.2, 1.3, 2.1)

8.4 Describe the concept of linguistic relativity. (APA 1.1, 1.2, 1.3, 2.1, 3.3)

8.4 Describe current research on the issue of nonhuman language. (APA 1.1, 1.2)

8.5 Describe historical and modern attempts to measure intelligence, and some of the advantages and disadvantages of these methods. (APA 1.1, 1.2)

8.5 Describe the various ways that psychologists have conceptualized intelligence. (APA 1.1, 1.2)

8.5 Describe the diversity seen in intelligence and discuss potential reasons for this diversity. (APA 1.1, 1.2, 1.3, 3.3)

In the last two chapters, we covered the cognitive aspect of psychology in terms of how we learn from our experiences, and how we encode, store, and retrieve information about these experiences in memory. In this final chapter of the cognitive section, we will examine how we put the results of our learning and memory to good use in everyday life by engaging in *cognition* (for example, thinking, reasoning, and so on), using *language,* and exhibiting *intelligence*. After all, what good would learning and memory be to us, if we weren't able to use the products of these processes to help us survive in the world? Recall again, the case of Kim Peek. Would you consider Kim to be a genius because he could memorize entire phonebooks? Or, would you consider him to have a disability because he could not use his memory in practically important ways, such as to live independently? Think about your own cognitive abilities. Would you be willing to trade places with Kim, or would you prefer to remain as you are? Although you may not be able to memorize entire books, we are betting that you can still use your cognitive abilities to do some pretty remarkable things, such as choosing a major; balancing the demands of school, work, and/or family; managing your budget; and many more great feats of daily life. In this chapter, we will examine how we use cognitive processes, such as thinking, problem solving, language, and intelligence, to help us cope with the challenges of everyday life.

8

©Tyler Olson/Shutterstock.com

Chapter Outline

8.1 Thinking: How We Use What We Know / 308

8.2 Problem Solving: Putting Our Thinking to Good Use / 314

8.3 Reasoning, Decision Making, and Judgment / 318

8.4 Language: Communication, Thought, and Culture / 322

PSYCHOLOGY APPLIES TO YOUR WORLD: Are Humans the Only Animals to Use Language? / 326

8.5 Defining and Measuring Intelligence / 328

8.6 Integrating Psychology: The Big Picture / 344

8.1 Thinking: How We Use What We Know

cognition the way in which we use and store information in memory

thinking the use of knowledge to accomplish some sort of goal

knowledge information stored in our long-term memory about the world and how it works

mental representation memory traces that represent objects, events, people, and so on that are not present at the time

We engage in some sort of **cognition** during every waking moment. Each day, we do a lot of thinking, but most of us would have difficulty defining what it is that we actually *do* when we think. Psychologists define **thinking** as the use of **knowledge**, the information we have stored in long-term memory, to accomplish some sort of goal. Thinking includes the ability to perceive and understand our world, to communicate with others, and to solve the problems we encounter in our lives (R. E. Mayer, 1983).

Thinking involves the use of all types of knowledge. We store our knowledge in long-term memory as **mental representations**—bits of memory that represent objects, events, people, and so on that are not actually present now. For instance, most of us can close our eyes and think about what our best friend looks like, the smell of her perfume, and her likes and dislikes. To do this, we call on the many mental representations of our friend that we have stored in long-term memory.

In general, thinking involves the use of two broad classes of mental representations: those based on *sensory* aspects of the object, such as its visual appearance, smell, taste, and so forth; and those based on the *meaning* of the object, such as its name, definition, and properties. We will now turn our attention to a discussion of the best-studied forms of these mental representations: *visual images* and *concepts*.

8.1.1 • Visual Images: How Good Is the Mental Picture?

The ability to "see" a friend's face in our mind or to visualize a map of our hometown in our head can be very useful in everyday life, but do we really store "pictures" in our memory? Over the years, psychologists have studied this question by examining how people perform on certain tasks in which they must mentally manipulate visual images (Denis & Cocude, 1999; Kosslyn, Ball, & Reiser, 1978/2004).

In a typical image-scanning experiment, like the one done by Stephen Kosslyn and colleagues (Borst & Kosslyn, 2008; Kosslyn et al., 2004), participants are asked to memorize a map of a fictitious island with several objects depicted on it (• see FIGURE 8.1). After the participants have memorized the map, they are asked to mentally scan the path that a black dot would take as it travels from one point on the map to another. Because the points are at various distances from one another, researchers can correlate the time it takes participants to mentally scan the image with the distance between the points on the actual map. If the participants' visual images of the map are copies of the actual map, the time it takes to scan longer distances should be longer than the time it takes to scan shorter distances on the map. This is exactly what Kosslyn found: the time it took to scan distances increased proportionately with the increase in the actual distances on the map. The results of this and numerous other experiments (see Jolicoeur & Kosslyn, 1985; Pylyshyn, 2006; Shepard, 1978, for a review) suggest that visual images may have all of the spatial properties of the real stimulus. In other words, the visual image we store is essentially a copy of the stimulus we see in the world.

As convincing as image-scanning experiments are in supporting the argument that visual images have spatial properties that mimic those of the actual stimulus,

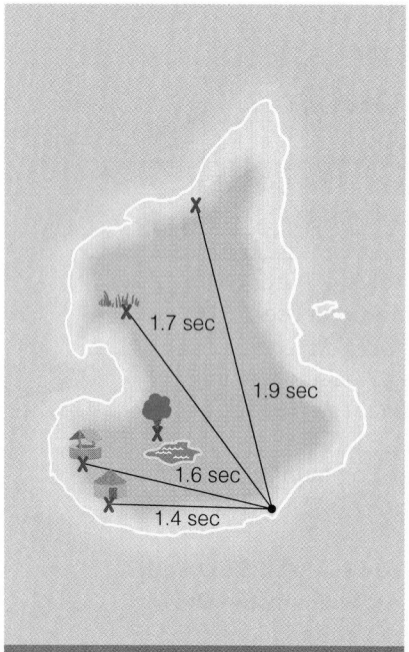

FIGURE 8.1

An Image-Scanning Task

In this task, participants were asked to imagine a black dot moving across the map to the points indicated by the *X*s. The average amount of time to do this was proportionate to the distance between the starting point and the ending point on the map.

Source: © Stephen Kosslyn 1978.

the question still remains: do we actually store photographic images of the things that we see? As it turns out, there are reasons to suspect that we generally do not. For example, try the following demonstration.

ENGAGE YOURSELF! Let's look at your ability to answer questions about a visual stimulus that you have seen many times, a map of North America.

Which is farther east: Reno, Nevada, or San Diego, California?

Which is farther north: Montreal, Canada, or Seattle, Washington?

Which is farther west: the Atlantic or the Pacific entrance to the Panama Canal?

The answers seem obvious, but researchers have found that most people answer them incorrectly (Stevens & Coupe, 1978). The correct answers are San Diego, Seattle, and the Atlantic entrance. Are you surprised? Take a look at • FIGURE 8.2, which shows that these are the correct answers.

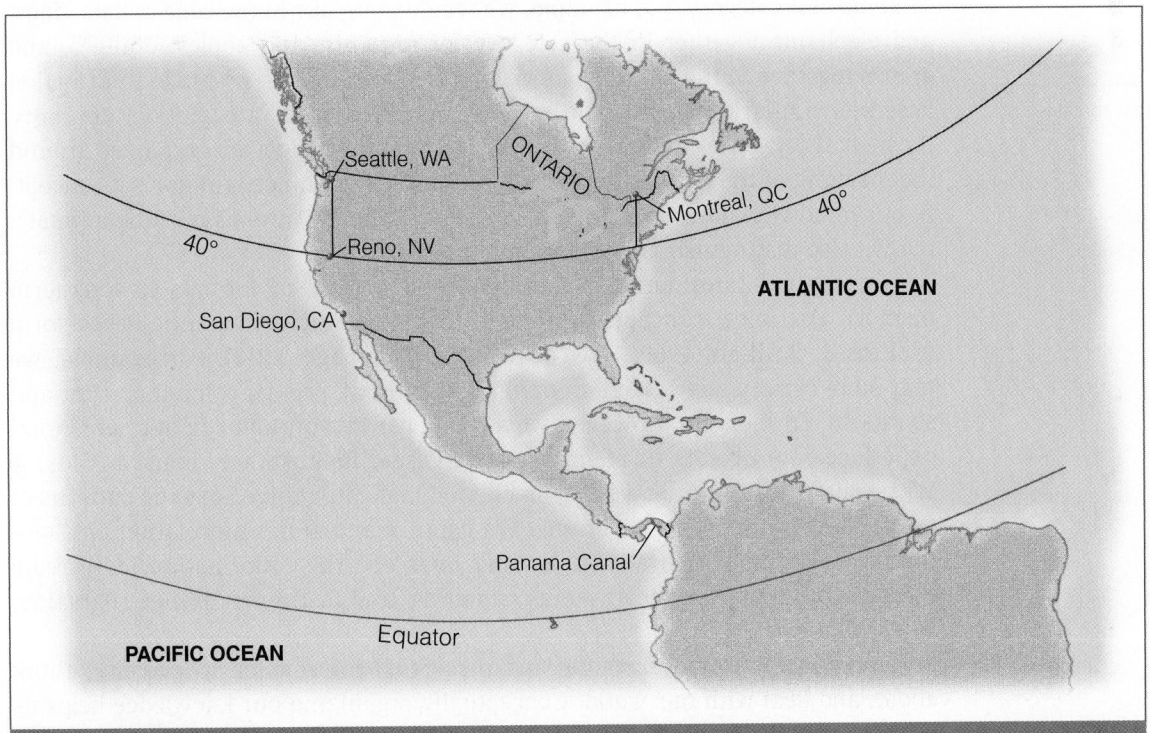

© Cengage Learning®

FIGURE 8.2

A Map of North and South America

Most people answer questions about this map incorrectly even though they have seen it many times before. It is highly unlikely that we have an exact visual image of this map stored in our long-term memory.

So, where does all of this research leave us with respect to visual images? Isn't it a bit contradictory? Some studies suggest that visual images are precise mental copies of the actual stimuli (see, for example, Shepard, 1978), but other studies show that visual images may deviate significantly from the actual stimuli (Boden, 1988; Chambers & Reisberg, 1992; Pylyshyn, 2003, 2006).

According to Stephen Kosslyn (1994), our mental representation of visual stimuli relies on both visual images *and* verbal knowledge. In other words, we use both types of mental representations—sensory (pictures) and meaning (words)—to fully represent visual stimuli. The pictures represent parts of the stimulus, and the words describe the stimulus and tell us how the pieces of the picture fit together. For example, when you look at a flower, you might store, among other things, a visual image of the shape of a petal, the stem, and the center, along with words describing the fact that the petals are placed around the center and the stem descends from the bottom of the flower. In Kosslyn's view, we do not store a carbon copy of the flower. Instead, we use this mixture of verbal and pictorial pieces to construct our visual image of the flower. Recall from Chapter 7 that memory is, after all, constructive. Unfortunately, the constructive nature of memory does sometimes lead to inaccuracies. Don't feel bad if you thought Reno was east of San Diego!

8.1.2 • Concepts: How We Organize What We Know

As we saw in Chapter 7, we have a tendency to organize our knowledge in long-term memory. We store mental representations for related objects together in the same mental category. For example, we would store our knowledge of cats, dogs, and elephants together in the category for *animals,* and apples, oranges, and grapes together in the category for *fruits*. This tendency to organize information based on similarity shows the *conceptual* nature of human cognition. **Concepts**, the mental categories that contain related bits of knowledge, are organized around the meaning of the information they represent. For instance, animal is a concept. In our mind we know what it means to be an animal. Animals must be animate, but we also distinguish animals from humans.

concept mental category that contains related bits of knowledge

Conceptual information is encoded in a variety of formats in long-term memory. At times, concepts are stored in a semantic or meaning-based form (Collins & Quillian, 1969; Hawco, Armony, & Lepage, 2013). For example, we may store certain facts about an orange—it's round, orange-colored, a fruit, and so on—in our memory. However, we also appear to store some of our perceptual experiences of objects in memory as well (see, for instance, Lanska, Olds, & Westerman, 2013). When we see, smell, and taste an orange, specific patterns of neural activity arise in our brains. We capture and store information on these unique patterns of neural activity and later use this information to recreate the perceptual experience of seeing, smelling, and tasting an orange (Barsalou, 2008; Marques, 2010).

We use this stored semantic and perceptual information to perceive, think about, and deal with our world. Conceptually organizing our knowledge helps us use that knowledge more efficiently. Concepts can be viewed as a type of mental shorthand that both organizes and saves space in our cognitive system. For example, close your eyes and picture an orange in your mind's eye. Can you see it clearly? Can you describe it in detail? Most of us can do this easily for something as familiar as an orange. Now look carefully at your mental orange. Is this concept that you have stored in your mind an actual orange that you have seen? In other words, is this orange number 123,675 that you saw one Sunday morning at the local market? Not likely! Instead, your concept of an orange is an abstraction, or a general idea, of what an orange is. You don't have to store mental representations for each and every orange you have seen. Rather, you only need to store a generalized concept of what an orange is and what it looks like. This is a great cognitive space-saver when you think about all of the oranges you'll see in your lifetime.

ORGANIZING CONCEPTS INTO CATEGORIES

Another benefit of mental concepts is that we can organize them into hierarchical categories (Markman & Ross, 2003). Psychologists have found that we tend to organize our knowledge into three levels of categorization (Rosch et al., 2004). The highest, most general level is called the **superordinate category**. The superordinate level contains concepts that are broad and general in their description. For example, fruit would be considered to be a superordinate category. The intermediate level of categorization is the **basic level category**. The basic level seems to be the level that we use most often to think about our world. For example, when we write out a shopping list, we probably list basic level concepts, such as oranges rather than fruit. Accordingly, people tend to be faster in naming and categorizing objects at the basic level, a phenomenon called the *basic level effect*. For example, determining that an animal is a *dog* should take less time than determining that an animal is a *schnauzer* (Wu & Mo, 2011).

The third level in the hierarchy is the **subordinate category**. Concepts at the subordinate level are less general and more specific than those at the basic level. When speaking of oranges, the subordinate category would contain items like Valencia oranges, navel oranges, and blood oranges. Although the subordinate level is the most specific, it is not the first level that springs to mind when we think about our world. You would be much more likely to place the basic level concept—oranges—on your shopping list than you would be to place Valencia oranges. Interestingly, the basic level is also the first level of knowledge young children acquire (Quinn & Tanaka, 2007; Rosch et al., 2004).

superordinate category the highest, most general level of a concept

basic level category the intermediate level of categorization that seems to be the level that we use most to think about our world

subordinate category the lowest level of categorization, which contains concepts that are less general and more specific than those at the basic level

formal concept a concept that is based on learned, rigid rules that define certain categories of things

natural concept a concept that develops naturally as we live our lives and experience the world

FORMAL AND NATURAL CATEGORIES

How do we acquire concepts in the first place? Simply put, we acquire concepts from an early age as we observe and learn from our world. We acquire **formal concepts** as we learn the rigid rules that define certain categories of things. For example, for an animal to be considered a member of the formal category, *female*, it must possess certain attributes or characteristics. All females are genetically designed to produce either offspring or eggs. If an animal does not have this attribute, it cannot be a female. The lines that define formal categories are very clear-cut.

Unfortunately, life is not always so neat and tidy as to provide us with formal rules for everything, and much of our knowledge of the world does not fit cleanly into only one category. For example, do you consider a tomato to be a fruit or a vegetable? How do you categorize cucumbers? Many people consider tomatoes and cucumbers to be vegetables, whereas others—including botanists—categorize them as fruits. Why the confusion? Perhaps because we associate fruits with sweetness, we tend not to classify cucumbers and tomatoes as fruit even though they do contain seeds, which is a defining attribute of fruit. Most of us are aware of the rules for membership as a female but are not aware of the botanical definition of a fruit. We have organized our fruit and vegetable concepts in a less distinct and orderly fashion based on our own experiences with them.

Concepts that develop naturally as we live our lives and experience the world are referred to as **natural concepts**. We do not learn formal rules for these concepts; rather, we intuit and create the rules as we learn about our world. As a result, the boundaries defining natural concept categories are often blurry, or "fuzzy" (Rosch, 1973; Rosch et al., 2004). Our example of the tomato is a good illustration of this. You can classify the tomato as a vegetable, a fruit, or both, depending on your experience. Because many of us see tomatoes in the vegetable section of the supermarket, we include them in the vegetable category. However, botanists scientifically classify tomatoes as fruits. How do you see them?

RTimages/Alamy

Envision/Corbis

Charles Mistral/Alamy

The basic level category *pear* falls under the superordinate category *fruit*. The label *Bosc pear* is a subordinate category of the basic level category *pear*.

Because natural concepts are a by-product of our day-to-day experience, they develop in a relatively effortless and natural manner as we live our lives. Curiously, when researchers try to force people to develop new natural concepts in the laboratory, people have a lot of trouble doing so (Makino & Jitsumori, 2007). In such situations, we may overthink and try to develop clear-cut rules for concepts that are inherently fuzzy. Even when we try to define the boundaries of preexisting natural concepts, we can have trouble. For example, if you were asked to define the criteria for identifying real-world examples of "love," you would likely find this to be a very difficult task.

ENGAGE YOURSELF! Natural categories are learned as a natural part of everyday life. No one sits us down and formally educates us about the rules that define membership in natural categories. For example, it is unlikely that anyone ever taught you the formal definition of an *animal*. Yet, you probably feel that you know what an animal is. Perhaps because of this we tend to do better with the fuzzy boundaries of natural concepts in the real world than we do in the laboratory. However, we are not perfect. The difficulty involved in deciding which items to include and which to exclude from a category varies considerably across situations. Sometimes it's an easy task, and other times it's not. For example, take a look at • FIGURE 8.3, and answer the questions as quickly as you can. Which of the questions were you able to answer quickly? Which ones took longer? Why do you think some of them were easier than others?

Most people find it easier to decide that a robin is a bird than that a penguin is a bird. Why? One possibility is that a robin is a more typical example of the category bird than a penguin is. According to some researchers, we form what are called **prototypes** for natural concept categories, much like the mental image of the orange we discussed earlier. A prototype is our concept of the most typical member of the category—in essence, a summary of all the members of the category. When we judge whether something belongs in a natural concept category, we compare it to the prototype of the category (Minda & Smith, 2002). The more similar the object is to the prototype, the faster we judge it to be a member of the concept category.

Other researchers argue that rather than using an abstracted prototype (a composite representation of the most typical category member), we judge category membership by comparing an item to the memories we have stored for actual specific examples, or preexisting **exemplars**, of that concept category

prototype our concept of the most typical member of the category

exemplar [ig-ZEM-plar] a mental representation of an actual instance of a member of a category

Frank Greenaway/ Dorling Kindersley/ Getty Images	Is a bat a mammal?	Yes ❑ No ❑
© ArchMan/ Shutterstock.com	Is a dolphin a mammal?	Yes ❑ No ❑
Digital Zoo/Getty Images	Is a penguin a bird?	Yes ❑ No ❑
Patricia Doyle/Getty Images	Is a cat a mammal?	Yes ❑ No ❑
image 100/Jupiter images	Is a robin a bird?	Yes ❑ No ❑
blickwinkel/Alamy	Is a whale a mammal?	Yes ❑ No ❑
Adam Jones/Getty Images	Is an eagle a bird?	Yes ❑ No ❑

All answers are "Yes."

FIGURE 8.3

Natural Concept Categories

Answer these questions as fast as you can.

(Nosofsky & Zaki, 2002; Rehder & Hoffman, 2005; Vanpaemel & Storms, 2008). In this view, you would determine that the robin in your backyard is a bird by comparing this robin to the memories or exemplars of the *actual* birds you have seen in your lifetime. Unless you live where penguins are common, you are likely to have many more songbird exemplars than penguin exemplars available in your memory. Because robins resemble the songbird exemplars that quickly come to mind more closely than penguins do, you are quicker to decide that a robin belongs in the category of birds.

The debate over whether we use prototypes or exemplars to judge category membership is ongoing. Some argue that we may even use both (Ashby & Maddox, 2005; Storms, DeBoeck, & Ruts, 2001) or that our categories may be based on idealized representations of concepts rather than what is most prototypical or most real (Voorspoels, Vanpaemel, & Storms, 2011). Regardless of how we go about making category judgments, these judgments are crucial to our ability to think about our world. In the next section, we will see just what we can accomplish with all of our thinking. But first, take a moment to test your knowledge of this last section.

Quiz Yourself

8.1

1. Which of the following is evidence indicating that our visual images contain all the properties of the actual stimulus?
   a. Memory for images is near perfect in children.
   b. The time it takes to mentally scan an image of an object is related to the actual size of the object.
   c. Most people can visualize familiar objects in great detail.
   d. Our mental maps of the world are perfect in their detail.
2. Which of the following would be a superordinate concept for the category car?
   a. Prius
   b. Truck
   c. Vehicle
   d. Red sports car
3. In an experiment, Dr. Kelly asks participants to name the first example of an "animal" that comes to mind. Based on what you know about concepts, which of the following would the average participant be most likely to name?
   a. Dog
   b. Lassie
   c. German shepherd
   d. Bat

Answers 1. b; 2. c; 3. a

8.2 Problem Solving: Putting Our Thinking to Good Use

Imagine that you get into your car one morning only to find that it won't start. It's 7:30 and you have an 8:00 class. Today of all days, you don't need this because you have a final exam in your psychology class. You have a problem! As you can see from this example, we never know when a problem will arise. What would you do in this situation? Call a friend for a ride? Walk to school? Call your professor and arrange to take a makeup final? Or fix your own car? In general, when we solve problems, we go through a series of six stages (Hayes, 1989), outlined in • TABLE 8.1.

TABLE 8.1

The Steps to Problem Solving

PROBLEM-SOLVING STEP	EXAMPLE
Identify the problem.	The car won't start, and I have a final exam.
Represent the problem.	If I miss this exam without permission, I'll fail the course.
Plan a solution.	I will call a taxi.
Execute the plan.	Call the taxi.
Evaluate the plan.	The taxi will get me to school, but I will be late. Maybe I should also have called my professor?
Evaluate the solution.	I did make it to school, and I took the exam. My professor was a bit angry that I didn't call to say I'd be late, but I did pass the exam. I handled this situation adequately, but next time I'll call my professor.

Source: Hayes, 1989.

Although the prospect of missing a final exam is frightening, there are a number of obvious solutions to this problem. This is not the case for all problems, however. If it were, we would have ended hunger, war, and pollution long ago. Why do some problems seem to have obvious possible solutions whereas others do not? The answer lies in the type of problem we are facing.

Image Source/Getty Images

Deciding how much paint to buy for a home improvement project is an example of a task that can be most accurately solved using an algorithm.

8.2.1 • Well-Structured and Ill-Structured Problems

Well-structured problems are problems for which there is a clear pathway to the solution. We face well-structured problems every day. Learning to use your new cell phone, balancing your bank account, and finding the cheapest hotel at your vacation destination are all examples of well-structured problems. When we solve well-structured problems, we tend to go about it in one of two ways. We use either an *algorithm* or a *heuristic* to achieve a solution.

An **algorithm** is a method of solving a particular problem that always leads to the correct solution; a **heuristic** is a shortcut or rule of thumb that may or may not lead to a correct solution. Imagine that you're going to paint your bedroom, but you don't know how much paint to buy. The algorithmic solution to this problem is to measure the height and width of all your walls, calculate the area, and look up how many gallons of paint are required to cover the area. This algorithm will lead to the correct answer, and as a result, you will buy just the right amount of paint. However, this strategy also takes considerable time. You must measure the walls, find the formula for paint coverage, and calculate the required figures. If you are in a hurry (or impatient), this strategy may not be your first choice. Instead, you might use a heuristic, such as simply guessing how much paint you will need to do the job. Guessing is quick, but you do run the risk of not buying the right amount of paint. You might have to go back to the store for more paint, or you might have a lot of paint left over. *Guessing* and repeated guessing, or *trial and error,* are two very common heuristics.

As you consider this example, you may think that it seems foolish to guess at the amount of paint to buy when a clear algorithm exists for this problem. Why would anyone approach a problem in this seemingly haphazard fashion? One might choose a heuristic over an algorithm for at least two reasons. First, as noted earlier, heuristics can save time. You might guess correctly that you need 2 gallons of paint to cover your room. Second, we do not always know the correct algorithm for the problem we are facing. What if you lack the mathematical knowledge to calculate the surface area of your bedroom walls? Even though a formula for calculating the surface area and paint coverage exists, if you don't know what it is, you cannot implement the algorithm, and you would have to use a heuristic.

In contrast, when attempting to solve an *ill-structured problem*, we have no choice but to use a heuristic. **Ill-structured problems** are problems for which there is no known algorithm, such as trying to end global warming or effect world peace. **Intuition**, simply believing that something is true independent of any reasoning process, is a common strategy for solving ill-structured problems. Often we go with a hunch or feeling that a particular strategy will lead us to solve

well-structured problem a problem for which there is a clear pathway to the solution

algorithm [AL-go-rih-thum] a method of solving a particular problem that always leads to the correct solution

heuristic [hyur-RISS-tick] a shortcut or rule of thumb that may or may not lead to a correct solution to the problem

ill-structured problem a problem for which an algorithm is not known

intuition believing that something is true independent of any reasoning process a problem without having a logical reason for believing this. For example, you might have a hunch that taking a particular side road that you've never been on will get you around a traffic jam and to school on time. The problem with intuition is that it is frequently wrong. One of your authors recently found this out when the road she chose took her miles out of her way and made her even later than the traffic jam would have.

Although intuition can fail us, it and other heuristics do sometimes lead to viable solutions to problems. For example, a man lost at sea might randomly plug a hole in his boat by shoving a shoe in the hole. Of course, to implement this problem-solving strategy, he would first have to think about trying the shoe. The danger is that we may not even think of certain possible solutions to our problems.

This is often the case with ill-structured problems. Often we get stuck in particular ways of trying to solve problems, and we lack the *insight* required to find a true solution. **Insight** occurs when we find a new way of looking at the problem that leads to a sudden understanding of how to solve it (Dominowski & Dallob, 1995; Qiu et al., 2010). Because of its perceived suddenness, insight is often referred to as the "Aha!" experience. Insight often feels as if a lightbulb has turned on, illuminating the answer for us. But current research indicates that insight isn't such a sudden process. Insight often occurs only after we have thought about the problem for a while (C. A. Kaplan & Simon, 1990). Truly understanding a problem and how to solve it often occurs only as the result of much thought and gradual acquisition of knowledge about the problem (Hamel & Elshout, 2000). Furthermore, recent studies have suggested that insight is affected by a person's level of motivation and emotion in a given situation (for example, Li et al., 2013).

insight a new way of looking at a problem that leads to a sudden understanding of how to solve it

creativity the ability to combine mental elements in new and useful ways

8.2.2 • Creativity: Overcoming Obstacles to Problem Solving

We do not need to tell you that some problems in life are more difficult to face than others. At times, all of us may encounter problems that challenge even our best problem-solving skills. Solving difficult problems often requires *creativity*.

For more than 50 years, psychologists have been trying to define exactly what creativity is and what abilities or traits creative people possess (Mumford, 2003). To date, the major agreement among researchers has been that **creativity** involves the ability to combine mental elements in new and useful ways (Sternberg, 1999; Vartanian, Martindale, & Kwiatkowski, 2003). Creativity may mean finding a novel solution to a problem or coming up with a unique approach to creating some new product—a piece of music, a painting, or a scientific theory that is widely recognized as being creative (Gelade, 2002).

Certainly all of us can think of people we believe are creative. But what makes one person more creative than another? Are there special traits or abilities that creative people possess? Over the years, psychologists have proposed several variables that may be related to creativity, including certain aspects of intelligence and executive functioning (Nusbaum & Silvia, 2011) and specific personality traits, such as how open one is to new experiences (Hughes, Furnham, & Batey, 2013).

The good news is that recently researchers have found evidence that supports the idea that we may be able to develop specific competencies that are related to being creative. Robert Epstein and Victoria Phan conducted a large-scale study of people, measuring their levels of trainable competencies and their self-reported degree of creativity. They found that *capturing* new ideas so they are not forgotten, *challenging* oneself with difficult tasks, *broadening* one's skills and knowledge through continued learning, and *surrounding* oneself with a stimulating environment were all predictors of how creative the person reported themselves to be (Epstein & Phan, 2012). These data suggest that learning to stimulate and challenge oneself are characteristics that coincide with creativity. However, is thirsting for knowledge and stimulating experience enough to guarantee creativity? Probably not. Obviously, not everyone who visits an art museum is a creative artist. What individual cognitive skills might explain why some of us turn knowledge and inspiration into feats of creativity and some of us do not?

One cognitive trait that has received a great deal of research attention is a skill called *divergent thinking* (Vartanian et al., 2003). Divergent thinking is the ability to generate many ideas quickly in response to a single prompt (Eysenck, 1995). For example, a divergent thinker can quickly come up with many different ways to tie a scarf or many different uses for an ink pen.

Divergent thinking aids creativity because it allows you to come up with many different ideas about how to solve a problem. As we will see, when you can think quickly to generate many different ideas, you are less likely to be blocked by some of the common obstacles to problem solving, including *functional fixedness* and *mental sets*.

When we attempt to solve problems, we often rely on well-used strategies. We look at the tools that we have at our disposal, and we evaluate them in terms of their common, everyday uses. We think of a hammer as a tool for pounding and a box as an object for holding other objects. We often cannot conceive of using these tools in new, novel ways. This limitation of being able to see objects only in their familiar roles is called **functional fixedness**. Functional fixedness can prevent us from solving problems that otherwise could be solved. For example, if your author could only think of her MP3 player as a device for listening to music, she might not have realized that she could use its illuminated video display to light up a darkened room during a recent power outage, allowing her to find some matches and candles!

Visions of America/Contributor/Getty Images

Creativity requires us to think divergently. In creating this piece of art, the artist has found a new use for these common items.

Another obstacle to problem solving is a *mental set*. A **mental set** is a tendency to habitually use the methods of problem solving that have worked for you in the past. Mental sets become an obstacle when we persist in trying solutions that may have worked in the past but are not working in the current situation. If you find yourself having little success in solving a problem, stop working on the problem for a while and let it *incubate*.

Incubation, or a period of not thinking about the problem, sometimes helps us solve a problem (Hélie & Sun, 2010; Sio & Ormerod, 2009). When we incubate, unproductive strategies recede from memory, and we are better able to attack the problem from a fresh, more productive perspective when we return to it (see Penaloza & Calvillo, 2012). If we are locked in a mental set, incubation may be just what is needed to solve the problem.

As we've seen in this section, problem solving is a matter of generating possible solutions and then selecting the one that will ultimately solve the problem. If your car broke down tomorrow, how would you decide which course of action to take? Would you call in absent to school? Call a mechanic? Call a taxi? Walk to school? Go back to bed and forget it? Many times, choosing the best solution from among all the possibilities is the real task. In the next section, we take a closer look at the cognitive processes that we engage in when we reason, make decisions, and make judgments.

functional fixedness being able to see objects only in their familiar roles

mental set the tendency to habitually use methods of problem solving that have worked for you in the past

incubation [in-cue-BAY-shun] a period of not thinking about a problem that helps one solve the problem

Quiz Yourself

8.2

1. Which of the following is the best example of an ill-structured problem?
   a. Balancing your monthly checking account statement
   b. Losing weight
   c. Reducing crime in your neighborhood
   d. Solving a crossword puzzle
2. Incubation sometimes aids problem solving because it _____.
   a. reduces fatigue
   b. improves deductive reasoning
   c. allows us to forget unproductive strategies
   d. improves inductive reasoning
3. Sue used a chair with wheels to carry a big load of books to her car. She piled the books in the seat of the chair and pushed it to her car. Trina made several trips carrying books by hand, even though she also had a chair with wheels in her office. Trina was most likely experiencing the effects of _____.
   a. functional fixedness
   b. an ill-structured problem
   c. heuristic thinking
   d. divergent thinking
4. Based on what you know about Kim Peek, which of the following cognitive tasks would likely be easiest for him to accomplish?
   a. Using creativity to solve a problem
   b. Solving a well-structured problem
   c. Breaking out of a mental set
   d. Using divergent thinking

Answers 1. c; 2. c; 3. a; 4. b

8.3 Reasoning, Decision Making, and Judgment

Reasoning, decision making, and judgments are cognitive processes that use some of the same strategies as problem solving. We engage in *reasoning* when we draw conclusions based on certain assumptions about the world. For example, you might reason that your friend Jamal is a nice person because he has many friends. *Decision making* is choosing among several options, as in our example of what you might do if your car breaks down. *Judgments* are also related to solving problems, often using two particular heuristics that we'll discuss.

reasoning drawing conclusions about the world based on certain assumptions

deductive reasoning reasoning from the general to the specific

inductive reasoning reasoning from the specific to the general

8.3.1 • Deductive and Inductive Reasoning

We engage in **reasoning** when we draw conclusions that are based on certain assumptions about the world. In contrast to relying on our *intuition* to draw conclusions, reasoning tends to be a slower, more deliberative and logical process. For example, you might reason that your friend Elva has money because she wears nice clothes. Or, based on your experiences, you might reason that studying leads to better grades. You may recall that reasoning was one skill that Kim Peek had trouble with. Although Kim could memorize well, he was unable to use this information to draw new conclusions about the world.

Psychologists who study reasoning have traditionally looked at two types of reasoning processes: *deductive reasoning* and *inductive reasoning*. **Deductive reasoning** involves reasoning from the *general* to the *specific*. In other words, you start with a general rule (studying leads to good grades), and apply it to particular cases (my friend Melissa makes good grades, so she must study hard).

Inductive reasoning is the opposite approach. When using inductive reasoning, we reason from the *specific* to the *general*. Here the object is to begin with specific instances (several friends who get good grades, including Melissa, are often busy studying), and then discover what general rule fits all of these instances (studying hard seems to be the factor that leads to good grades). When we use specific instances to arrive at a general rule, we are employing inductive reasoning.

We hope you see the parallels between reasoning and the scientific method that psychologists use to conduct research (see Chapter 1). When conducting studies to test theories, psychologists try to induce the general rules that explain mental processes and behavior. Once these rules have been induced, they can then be applied to individual situations to help deduce, or predict, how people and animals are likely to behave. This, of course, does not mean that reasoning is just for scientists. Deductive and inductive reasoning are equally important in everyday life. Effective reasoning can be a very important aspect of making good decisions in our lives.

8.3.2 • Decision Making: Outcomes and Probabilities

decision making making a choice from among a series of alternatives

judgment the act of estimating the probability of an event

Decision making involves choosing from among several alternatives. We must first choose a course of action before we can implement a solution to a problem. Two factors that influence our decisions are the perceived *outcomes* of our decisions and the *probability* of achieving these outcomes. For example, when you consider a major, you weigh the expected outcomes of choosing that major. How interesting is the subject area to you? What kind of job will it lead to? How difficult will the course work be? What is the pay like in this field? You also temper these judgments with your perception of how likely it is that these outcomes will actually occur. There may be high-salaried jobs in your major area, but if you see little chance of actually getting one of them, then you will be less likely to choose that major.

Logically, we would seek to make decisions that we believe have a good chance of leading to favorable outcomes. However, our decision-making processes are a bit more complex than this. Another factor that affects our decisions is how the possible courses of action are presented, or *framed* (Kahneman & Tversky, 1984; Tversky & Kahneman, 2004). For example, which of the following options would you choose? Would you choose to take a class in which you had a 60% chance of passing? Or one in which you had a 40% chance of failing? Many people would choose the first option because it is framed positively, even though the chance of succeeding in the course is the same in both cases. Whether you prefer a positively framed option or a negatively framed one depends on your orientation. Sometimes we exhibit *loss aversion*, or a tendency to focus on what a certain decision could cost us in terms of potential gain—for example, worrying that your choice of major may limit your future employment opportunities. Other times, we exhibit *risk aversion*, or concern over losing what we already have—for example, worrying that the time you need to devote to your chosen major may force you to give up your current job.

8.3.3 • Judgments: Estimating the Likelihood of Events

Judgment can be seen as a type of problem solving in which we estimate the probability of an event. If you don't know what the probability of a certain event is, and you need to have this probability to make a decision, what do you do? As with all problems, you can solve this one using either an algorithm or a heuristic. An algorithm would involve somehow looking up or calculating the exact probability that a given event will occur. This is often neither possible nor practical, as in the case of trying to figure out what the stock market will do in the coming months. So, as we saw before, we tend to rely on heuristics when we make judgments.

THE AVAILABILITY HEURISTIC

Many people are afraid to fly, even though commercial air travel is statistically safer than traveling by car (National Safety Council, 2011). In fact, commercial air travel is getting safer. According to the National Transportation Safety Board, the accident rate for commercial air carriers decreased by 80% in the 10 years leading up to 2012 (Weener, 2012). So why would people be afraid to choose a safer form of travel? The answer lies in the manner in which we make judgments about the frequency of events. When we estimate the frequency of events, we heuristically base our judgments on the ease with which we can recall instances of the event in memory. The more easily we can recall a memory for an event, the more frequent we estimate the event to be. This memory shortcut is called the **availability heuristic** (Tversky & Kahneman, 1974).

availability heuristic a heuristic in which we use the ease with which we can recall instances of an event to help us estimate the frequency of the event

representativeness heuristic a heuristic in which we rely on the degree to which something is representative of a category, rather than the base rate, to help us judge whether or not it belongs in the category

The availability heuristic explains the previous example of fearing air travel more than driving. Although fatal car accidents occur every day, they are not as widely covered by the media as plane crashes are. A fatal car crash may result in one or a few deaths, but a plane crash usually involves a larger number of fatalities. Therefore, when a plane goes down, the news coverage is graphic, horrifying, and prolonged. This leaves us with a strong, easily accessible memory for the plane crash. The result is that when we think of ways to travel, we more readily recall memories of plane crashes, and we may mistakenly overestimate the risk associated with air travel (Bahk, 2006). The result is that many people fear flying, when they really ought to be more afraid of traveling by car (see • FIGURE 8.4).

According to the availability heuristic, the ease with which we can retrieve memories of events from long-term memory biases our judgments of how frequently the event occurs in real life. Seeing news coverage of air disasters leaves us with vivid memories of plane crashes that cause us to overestimate the probability of a plane crash occurring in the future. As a result, air traffic often falls off immediately following a crash, although in general flying is still safer than driving to your destination.

©Pavel L Photo and Video/Shutterstock.com

THE REPRESENTATIVENESS AND AFFECTIVE HEURISTICS

We also make heuristic judgments when deciding whether an object, event, or person belongs in a particular category by relying on the degree to which the person or thing in question is representative of the category. This tendency, called the **representativeness heuristic**, explains some of the mistakes we make in judgment (Tversky & Kahneman, 1974).

For instance, we often ignore the true probability, or base rate, of events in favor of our heuristic judgments. In one experiment on the representativeness heuristic, participants were told that a group of 100 people contained 70 engineers and 30 lawyers. They were also given a description of one of the group members—a man—that included the following traits: conservative, ambitious, nonpolitical, likes carpentry, and enjoys solving mathematical puzzles. Then they were asked to judge the probability that he was an engineer or a lawyer. If we were to approach this question logically, we would base our judgment on the base rate and say that there is a 70% chance that the man is an engineer and a 30% chance that he is a lawyer. The participants, however, did not approach this task logically. Instead, they based their judgments on the representativeness of the description that they were given and ignored the base rate information. As a result, the participants judged that there was a 90% chance that the man was an engineer (Kahneman & Tversky, 1973). Clearly, we often place more confidence in irrational judgments based on heuristics than in rational ones based on more factual probabilities (Tversky & Kahneman, 1980).

Heuristics like representativeness can contribute to serious problems like prejudice. For example, one of your authors once met a man who had little personal contact with African Americans. His exposure to African Americans was mostly limited to watching episodes of the TV show *Cops,* in which he saw many African Americans being arrested for crimes. This left the man with the false impression that most African Americans are representative of the category criminal. As a result, the man grew uneasy when he encountered any African American—a clear and unfortunate expression of racial prejudice. Media depictions of people can interact with our tendency to use heuristics like representativeness, making them powerful influences on our judgments of others.

Another way that such media depictions can affect us is through the use of another heuristic called the *affective heuristic* (Slovic et al., 2002). The **affective heuristic** suggests that we will make quick judgments about people and things based on whether or not we have an immediate positive or negative emotional reaction to them. For example, if one has an immediate negative emotional reaction when meeting a minority member because she has learned to associate minorities with crime, this immediate emotional reaction is likely to influence the judgments she makes about this person. As you might imagine, use of the affective heuristic frequently leads to making incorrect judgments about others because the judgment is not based on the person's actual traits and behaviors.

If all of this sounds as though humans are incapable of making good judgments, don't despair. This is not the case. Often heuristics do lead to correct judgments. In addition, we do not always behave in a heuristic way. Sometimes we do pay attention to probabilities (Cosmides & Tooby, 1996). Whether we make judgments algorithmically or heuristically is a product of both the situation (Cosmides & Tooby, 1996) and the characteristic way that we as individuals tend to think (Stanovich & West, 1998). When the conditions are right, we do make good and logical judgments. This is especially true when we are making judgments in everyday, real-life situations (Anderson, 2000). Take a moment to test your knowledge of this section before moving on to learn about language and its relationship to thought.

A Comparison of Accidental Death Risk*
United States — 1999–2003

Type	Deaths Per Year (5-Yr Average)	General Population Risk Per Year**	Risk Based on Exposure
Motor Vehicles	36,676	1 out of 7,700	1.3 deaths per 100 million veh. miles
Motorcycles	3,112	1 out of 91,500	31.3 deaths per 100 million veh. miles
Railroads	931	1 out of 306,000	1.3 deaths per million veh. miles
Bicycles	695	1 out of 410,000	n/a
Air Carriers	138***	1 out of 2,067,000	1.9 deaths per 100 million aircraft miles

*These data are drawn from a more detailed table prepared by the U.S. Department of Transportation.

**The DOT used an average U.S. population figure of approximately 285,000,000 over the five-year period in computations.

***Other than those aboard the aircraft who were killed, fatalities resulting from the 9/11 terrorist acts are excluded.

FIGURE 8.4

Although Many People Fear Flying, Other Modes of Transportation are Actually Much Riskier

affective heuristic a heuristic in which we make quick judgments about people and things based on whether or not we have an immediate positive or negative emotional reaction to them

Quiz Yourself

8.3

1. It has been unseasonably hot and dry for the last month. Today, you are asked to predict the probability that prolonged heat and drought will occur in the next century. You are likely to _____ this probability because of the _____.
   a. underestimate; affective heuristic
   b. overestimate; availability heuristic
   c. underestimate; algorithm
   d. overestimate; representativeness heuristic
2. Jonas is hesitant to invest in real estate because he believes that he can make more money in the stock market than he can in the housing market. Jonas is exhibiting _____.
   a. loss aversion
   b. risk aversion
   c. the representativeness heuristic
   d. the affective heuristic
3. Of the 100 people in Harry's psychology class, 60 are education majors and 40 are psychology majors. Yet when Harry first met a classmate named Sally, he guessed that there was a 90% chance that she was a psychology major because she had a poster of Sigmund Freud on her dorm room wall. Harry likely based his judgment on _____.
   a. affective heuristic
   b. an algorithm
   c. representativeness heuristic
   d. availability heuristic
4. Which of the following is an example of *deductive* reasoning?
   a. Because Jared received a traffic ticket, he must have broken a traffic law.
   b. Because your psychology professor is friendly, professors tend to be friendly.
   c. Because it was cold this winter, winters are growing colder.
   d. b and c

Answers 1. b; 2. a; 3. c; 4. a

8.4 Language: Communication, Thought, and Culture

language a well-developed, syntactical verbal system for representing the world

Our capacity for **language** is one of the most spectacular human abilities. No other species has such a well-developed, syntactical verbal system for representing its world. As you learned in Chapter 2, Broca's and Wernicke's areas are specialized structures in the left hemisphere of the human brain that help us produce and comprehend speech. We put these brain areas to good use in that we use words in just about every aspect of our lives. As we have seen, much of our knowledge is represented in memory using words. Without words, our ability to mentally represent our world, solve problems, and make decisions would be drastically altered.

8.4.1 • How Humans Acquire Language

Some researchers have proposed that humans are born with an innate tendency to acquire language (N. R. Cattell, 2006; Chomsky, 1957). According to this view, we are born with a *language acquisition device (LAD),* or a biological makeup that gives us an innate knowledge of the syntax of a language (Chomsky, 1965). Supporters of the LAD argue that children across the world are not uniformly exposed to enough language and language coaching to account for the speed and consistency with which they learn language. This argument for the innateness of language is called the *poverty of stimulus (POS)* argument (see, for example, Berwick et al., 2011). However, other researchers argue that POS supporters significantly underestimate children's true exposure to language in early life (Behme & Deacon, 2008), and reject the notion that language is innate (see Helmuth, 2001).

Deciding which perspective is correct has challenged psychologists for decades. A complicating factor in settling this debate is that it is practically impossible to isolate the effects that our biology and our environment have on language development. How can we determine whether children are born with innate knowledge of language, when nearly all children in the world are exposed to language immediately after birth? When children begin speaking (at about 1 year), it could be due to some innate, biological mechanism, or it could be that they learned to speak from interacting with others who use language. In normal children, it is impossible to tell exactly why language develops, but what if we could find children who were never exposed to spoken language? What could these children teach us about the development of human language?

Masterfile

The speed and uniformity with which infants learn language across the world suggests to some that humans have a language acquisition device or innate knowledge of the syntax of language.

During the 1970s, researchers documented such a case of deaf children in Nicaragua who had never been exposed to sign language and were unable to hear spoken Spanish. The children's teachers did not know sign language, so they tried to teach the children to read and write in Spanish. However, when left to their own devices, such as on the playground, the children began to develop their own spontaneous form of sign language. Their language, Nicaraguan Sign Language, is today recognized as a true language complete with gestural vocabulary and its own syntactical and grammatical rules (Senghas & Coppola, 2001). Cases like this one are consistent with the notion that the drive to develop some form of language is innate.

But what about spoken language? Is there any evidence that hearing children also have an innate capacity for language? Yes, there is. Evidence for the innate nature of language also comes from cross-cultural studies on language development in hearing children. These studies show that regardless of the culture, language seems to develop in children at about the same age and in the same sequence of stages. This similarity in the developmental process, which occurs despite cultural differences, argues for some biological mechanism that underlies language.

COOING AND BABBLING: BABY STEPS TO LEARNING ONE OR MORE LANGUAGES

Most of us acquire our first language beginning in the first couple of years of life. Research indicates that newborns from birth to 1 month are capable of perceiving vowel sounds in an adult-like manner (Aldridge, Stillman, & Bower, 2001), and by about 2 months, infants begin **cooing**. Cooing involves making vowel sounds, such as "ooo" and "ah." By 4 months, infants begin to engage in **babbling**, which adds consonant sounds to the vowel sounds they emitted during cooing. For example, an infant might repeat the sound "ka, ka, ka" over and over. Infants' first babbles are very similar across cultures, but this soon changes (Stoel-Gammon & Otomo, 1986). By 7 months, infants begin to emit babbles that contain sounds that are part of the language they have been exposed to in their environment. In this fashion, the infant's language system apparently tunes itself to the language or languages that the infant hears on a regular basis (see Feldman et al., 2013). By 1 year, children's babbling contains the sounds and intonations of their native language (Levitt & Utmann, 1992).

cooing the vowel sounds made by infants beginning at 2 months

babbling the combinations of vowel and consonant sounds uttered by infants beginning around 4 months

Perhaps because the infant's language system appears to tune itself to the sounds of the language the child hears, children who grow up in bilingual households, where adults speak two languages to the children, tend to acquire both languages at high levels of proficiency (Petitto, 2009). But this does not mean that a child cannot learn a second language later in life. A child who is not exposed to a second language until elementary school can still develop near-native proficiency in the language (Hakuta, 1999). However, from childhood to adulthood, it seems to become steadily more difficult for us to become bilingual. For example, an adolescent who is just beginning to learn Spanish may never speak Spanish as fluently as a child who began learning Spanish in elementary school (Hakuta, Bailystok, & Wiley, 2003). Therefore, if true bilingualism is desired, it is best to begin learning the second language as early as possible.

phoneme [FOE-neem] the smallest unit of sound in a language

morpheme [MORE-feem] the smallest unit of sound in a language that has meaning

overextension when a child uses one word to symbolize all manner of similar instances (e.g., calling all birds "parakeet")

underextension when a child inappropriately restricts the use of a word to a particular case (e.g., using the word *cat* to describe only the family pet)

telegraphic speech two-word sentences that children begin to utter at 20–26 months

grammar the rules that govern the sentence structure in a particular language

pragmatics the rules of conversation in a particular culture

Once a child achieves the stage of babbling the basic sounds, or **phonemes**, of her native tongue, the next step in language development is learning to communicate. At around 12 months, children begin trying to communicate in earnest with others. This communication is often based on gestures before it is based on words. For example, a child may point at a toy that he wants. When parents learn to interpret these *preverbal gestures*, communication is achieved. As they catch on to their child's preverbal gestures, parents often verbalize the meaning of the gesture for the child. Parents say things like, "Oh, do you want this toy?" This verbalization of the child's intention allows the child to begin to learn **morphemes**, or the smallest sounds in a language that have meaning. As a result, by the end of the first year or so, children begin to speak their first words.

FROM "MAMA" AND "DADA" TO FULL CONVERSATIONS

A child's first words are usually the names of familiar objects, people, actions, or situations, ones with which they have had a great deal of contact. Typically, these words are *Dada, Mama, hi, hot,* and the like. Between 12 and 18 months of age, children usually utter only one word at a time, and often they convey tremendous meaning with these one-word sentences. For example, the utterance "Milk!" may stand for "I want some milk, please!"

As young children begin to speak, they may exhibit **overextension** in their language, using one word to symbolize all manner of similar instances. For instance, the word dog may be used to symbolize any animal. During this period, the opposite problem may also occur when children exhibit **underextension** of language. In this situation, children inappropriately restrict their use of a word to a particular case, such as when a child uses the word dog to refer only to the family pet.

By the time children reach 20–26 months, they begin to combine words into two-word sentences in what is called **telegraphic speech**. Telegraphic speech is often ungrammatical, but it does convey meaning, such as "Doggie bad," meaning "The dog was bad." From here, children rapidly acquire both vocabulary and **grammar**, or the rules that govern sentence structure in their language, such as word order and verb tenses. From the simple subject–verb combinations of telegraphic speech, English-speaking children progress to more complex subject–verb–object sentences between ages 2 and 3. Children who speak other languages adopt the relevant grammatical patterns of their native language. As children develop throughout the preschool years, their knowledge and use of grammar becomes increasingly complex. By age 6, the average child has an impressive vocabulary of around 10,000 words and a fairly competent mastery of grammar (Tager-Flusberg, 2005).

As children develop better vocabularies and acquire the grammatical rules of language, they exercise these abilities during social interactions with others. It's during these social interactions with peers and adults that children begin to learn **pragmatics**, or the rules of conversation operating in their culture. Pragmatics may include rules about turn taking, eye contact, tone of voice, and other aspects of conversation.

These hard-earned linguistic abilities will be very valuable to the child, as they are to us all. Let's take a closer look at what, exactly, language does for us.

8.4.2 • The Function of Language in Culture and Perception

It is not difficult to see that language affects us in many ways. Obviously, one of language's main functions is to facilitate communication. We use language to describe our world, our thoughts, and our experiences to others. Without language, we would lead lives of social isolation.

LANGUAGE AND THE DEVELOPMENT OF CULTURE

Because language brings us together and allows us to share ideas and experiences, language also plays a role in the development of culture. Russian psychologist Lev Vygotsky (1896–1934) noted the influence of language in the development of culture in his *sociocultural theory* (Vygotsky, 1934/1987) (see Chapter 9). According to sociocultural theory, older and more knowledgeable members of a society pass on the values, beliefs, and customs of their culture to children by telling the children stories and by engaging in conversations with them. The children store these dialogues in their memory and later use this knowledge to guide their behavior. Just as you learned from the stories of your elders, someday you too will pass down elements of your culture as you converse with younger people.

Language may facilitate the transmission of culture from generation to generation, but does the language we speak also affect the way we view the world? In the next section, we'll take a look at this interesting issue.

Whorfian [WORE-fee-un] hypothesis, or linguistic relativity hypothesis the theory that one's language can directly determine or influence one's thoughts

LINGUISTIC RELATIVITY: THE INFLUENCE OF LANGUAGE ON THOUGHT

One of the most intriguing theories about language came from an unlikely source. Benjamin Whorf was a Connecticut fire insurance inspector whose unusual hobby was linguistics, or the study of language. After intensive studies of the languages of Native Americans, Whorf became convinced that one's language could directly determine or influence one's thoughts (Whorf, 1956). This notion has since come to be called the **Whorfian hypothesis** or the **linguistic relativity hypothesis** (for a review, see Tohidian, 2009).

In its strongest form, the linguistic relativity hypothesis states that one's language actually determines one's thoughts and one's perception of the world. According to this view, people who have different native languages think differently and perceive the world in a different light. For example, Whorf argued that Eskimos would understand "snow" differently than Europeans because the Eskimos' native language has more words for snow than English has. Whorf claimed that differences among languages make it impossible to express all thoughts equally in all languages. Therefore, you can think and see the world only in terms of the language that you know. According to Whorf, your language *determines* what you think and how you perceive the world.

To date, the bulk of the evidence does not support the strong form of Whorf's linguistic relativity hypothesis (• see TABLE 8.2). However, there is reason to think that a modified, or weaker, interpretation of

TABLE 8.2

Different Words for Snow

Contrary to Whorf's hypothesis, like the Eskimo, English speakers do have several words for snow.

ESKIMO	ENGLISH
qanuk: "snowflake"	snowflake
qanir: "to snow"	snow
kanevvluk: "fine snow/rain particles"	snowfall
muruaneq: "soft deep snow"	powder
pirta: "blizzard, snowstorm"	blizzard, snowstorm
nutaryuk: "fresh snow"	powder
qengaruk: "snow bank"	snowbank

Psychology Applies to Your World:

Are Humans the Only Animals to Use Language?

For centuries, humans believed that they alone had the ability to use language. It was assumed that only the advanced human mind was capable of dealing with the complexities of a language. Remarkably, this assumption has been called into question. Although it is very controversial, today some researchers believe that some other animals may possess linguistic abilities (for example, Shanker, Savage-Rumbaugh, & Taylor, 1999).

In looking at the linguistic abilities of other species, we first have to make a distinction between *language* and *communication*. Language is a system of communication that has a set vocabulary and a set structure, or grammar. For instance, English sentences generally follow a subject–verb–object pattern. Though many languages reverse the order of the verb and the object, most of the world's languages place the subject at the beginning of the sentence—for example, *Mike ran home* (Ultan, 1969). Languages also differ with respect to the placement of adjectives and adverbs. English places the adjective before the noun, *blue dress*; Spanish places it after, *vestido azul*. As you can see, each language has its own set of rules.

In contrast to the structure and order of language, communication can be very unstructured. All that is required in a communication system is that your meaning be conveyed to others. There is little argument that animals can communicate. For example, a rooster will emit an alarm cry to warn other chickens of danger (Marler, Duffy, & Pickert, 1986) and domestic dogs respond to specific play signals of their owners (Rooney, Bradshaw, & Robinson, 2001). But does this ability of some animals to communicate mean they have the capacity for language?

Some of the best evidence for animal language comes from studies done on Bonobo chimpanzees. Bonobos, also known as pygmy chimpanzees, are perhaps our closest genetic relatives, even more closely related to us than the common chimpanzee. During the 1980s, researcher Sue Savage-Rumbaugh and others attempted to teach English to a Bonobo named Matata. Because Bonobos do not have vocal cords that produce humanlike speech, they cannot actually speak. To get around this problem, the researchers used a special computer keyboard during the language training. On the surface of the keyboard were pictures, and when a picture was pressed, a computer-generated voice spoke the name of the object in the picture. Using this keyboard, Savage-Rumbaugh tried to teach Matata the meaning of certain words, but Matata did not catch on well (Wise, 2000, p. 223). However, Matata's infant stepson, Kanzi, had been observing his mother's lessons. Although Savage-Rumbaugh and her colleagues never attempted to teach Kanzi to use the keyboard, he picked up this skill on his own (Savage-Rumbaugh et al., 1986). By age 2½, Kanzi had begun to use some of the symbols his mother was trying to learn on the keyboard. When experimenters gave up trying to teach Matata to use the keyboard, they separated her from Kanzi. The day Matata left, Kanzi approached the keyboard and began to use it to make requests and express himself. In fact, he used it a total of 120 times on that first day (Wise, 2000).

Michael Nichols/National Geographic creative

As an infant, Kanzi learned to use a language keyboard like this one to communicate with humans just by watching researchers who were working with his mother, Matata.

Much like a young child, Kanzi appeared to have learned some vocabulary just by observing language being used around him. Kanzi's acquisition of language seemed to occur quite naturally (Shanker et al., 1999). For example, a patch of wild strawberries grew outside Kanzi's laboratory, and when he discovered them, Kanzi began to eat them. He overheard researchers referring to them by the word *strawberries* and soon appeared to understand what the word *strawberries* meant. After apparently learning the meaning of the word *strawberries,* Kanzi would head for the berry patch whenever he heard someone speak the word (Savage-Rumbaugh, 1987).

Overall, Kanzi's use of language is quite impressive. He uses the keyboard to make requests, such as to visit another chimpanzee named Austin. If he is told that he cannot visit because it's too cold to go outside, Kanzi modifies his request to ask to see a picture of Austin on TV (Savage-Rumbaugh, 1987). Furthermore, Kanzi seems to be able to respond to very unusual and novel requests, such as "Put the pine needles in the refrigerator" or "Put the soap on the ball."

Language abilities have been shown in species other than the Bonobos as well. Researcher Irene Pepperberg (1993, 1999) had some success in training an African grey parrot named Alex to speak some English. Unlike the Bonobo, a parrot has the physical ability to produce speech as well as comprehend it. Before his death in 2007, Alex was able to speak some words in English, and identify the shape, color, and material of many objects (Pepperberg, 1991). Attempts to train other African grey parrots to use words to refer to objects in laboratory settings have yielded mixed results (Giret et al., 2010). However, one recent study conducted in an animal's home environment found that a pet African grey parrot (Cosmo) tended to utter phrases such as "Cosmo wanna talk" when her owner was in the same room and "Where are you" when her owner was out of sight. These results suggest that the parrot's speech, which she learned from her owner, was influenced by specific social contexts (Colbert-White, Covington, & Fragaszy, 2011).

Dolphins have also shown some linguistic promise. Researcher Louis Herman and his colleagues have had some success in training dolphins to understand a language that the researchers created. This created language is based on gestures, but it has a set vocabulary in which certain gestures stand for certain words, and a specific set of grammatical rules that dictate how gestures can be combined into phrases. One of the dolphins, named Phoenix, was able to follow a complex sequence of instructions delivered in this gestured language (Herman & Uyeyama, 1999). Another dolphin, Ake, seemed to notice when the grammatical laws of the language had been violated (Herman, Kuczaj, & Holder, 1993).

As impressive as the linguistic abilities of Kanzi, Alex, Cosmo, Ake, and Phoenix are, not everyone is convinced that animals truly have the capacity for language. Some argue that these animals are merely highly trained (Pinker, 1994). Skeptics propose that rather than actually using language, the animals are engaging in trained behaviors that they hope will lead to some reward. Certainly, Alex, Cosmo, Ake, and Phoenix were trained to use language, but what about Kanzi, who was never trained to use language? He learned it on his own during his early years, just as children do (Shanker et al., 1999).

Another criticism of animal language research directly questions the linguistic abilities of animals. Some argue that animal language researchers have not adequately demonstrated that animals can follow all of the grammatical and syntactical rules of human language (Kako, 1999). Animal language researchers counter that their critics have unfairly focused on the linguistic abilities that animals lack and have largely ignored the linguistic abilities that animals do have (Shanker et al., 1999).

You can see that this is a very passionate debate—as well it should be, for there is a great deal at stake here. If we ultimately determine that animals do have linguistic capacities, then we may have to reconsider what separates humans from the rest of the animal kingdom. This possibility brings up a whole host of ethical questions concerning animals and the manner in which we treat them in human society (Wise, 2000).

Rick Friedman/Corbis

Although controversial, studies of animals like Alex, the African grey parrot, challenge the presumption that language is a solely human attribute.

the Whorfian hypothesis may hold true. The weaker version states that instead of language determining thought processes, language merely *influences* them. For example, a study that compared Spanish speakers to Mayan speakers found differences in their ability to remember colors. These memory differences were related to how easy it is to verbally label colors in Spanish and Mayan (Stefflre, Castillo-Vales, & Morley, 1966). It appears that how easily you can label a color in your language does affect your memory for that color. Similarly, within English-speaking children, researchers found that the ability to correctly verbalize the plural of a word (say, *shoes*) was related to a child's ability to later recall whether she had seen a single shoe versus multiple shoes in a stimulus picture (Ettlinger, Lanter, & VanPay, 2013).

It is also likely that language can influence our perception of the world. In one study involving the sorting of color samples, participants who spoke Setswana were more likely to group blues and greens together than were those who spoke English or Russian. This finding was attributed to the fact that in Setswana, one word describes both blue and green colors (Davies, 1998). The idea that humans do not all categorize color the same way is an important premise of the linguistic relativity hypothesis.

Quiz Yourself 8.4

1. Babies begin _____ when they begin to make _____ sounds.
   a. cooing; consonant
   b. babbling; vowel
   c. cooing; vowel and consonant
   d. babbling; vowel and consonant
2. Which of the following people would be the most likely to agree with the statement "Language facilitates the development of culture"?
   a. Lev Vygotsky
   b. Benjamin Whorf
   c. Sue Savage-Rumbaugh
   d. Eleanor Rosch
3. One's language can influence one's _____.
   a. speech
   b. memory
   c. perception
   d. All of the above

Answers 1. d; 2. a; 3. d

8.5 Defining and Measuring Intelligence

intelligence abilities that enable you to adapt to your environment and behave in a goal-directed way

What makes a person intelligent? Is it being able to memorize large amounts of information like Kim Peek could? Knowing how to survive in the wilderness? Having good social skills? Today, many psychologists view **intelligence** broadly as having abilities that allow you to adapt to your environment and behave in a goal-directed way. But over the years, psychologists have found that developing a precise definition of intelligence is not as easy as it may seem, and our conception of intelligence has undergone several revisions. Equally challenging has been finding ways of measuring intelligence.

8.5.1 • Measuring Intelligence by Abilities and IQs

One of the first people to study the measurement of intelligence was British psychologist Sir Francis Galton (1822–1911). Galton claimed that intelligence is an inherited trait that is correlated with having superior physical abilities. As such, he believed that intelligence could be measured by measuring traits like reaction time, eyesight, and so on. However, early studies failed to find much support for Galton's ideas (Schultz & Schultz, 2012), and they soon fell out of favor.

ALFRED BINET: MEASURING INTELLIGENCE BY MEASURING COGNITIVE ABILITIES

The modern intelligence test is credited to Alfred Binet (1857–1911). In 1904, the French government appointed Alfred Binet and psychiatrist Théodore Simon to a commission charged with developing a means of measuring the intelligence of French schoolchildren so that the government could identify children who would not likely profit from traditional education.

Binet saw intelligence as the capacity to *find and maintain a purpose, adopt a strategy to reach that purpose, and evaluate the strategy so it can be adjusted as necessary* (Terman, 1916). In essence, Binet suggested that having intelligence makes one a good problem solver. As such, he developed an intelligence test that assessed general cognitive abilities such as the individual's attention, judgment, and reasoning skills (Binet & Simon, 1905).

Binet prepared a set of 30 tasks that measured these skills and arranged them in order of difficulty, with the easiest questions first and the hardest questions last. Not surprisingly, the brighter students could answer more of the questions than the not-so-bright students could. Also, not surprisingly, the older children tended to answer more questions correctly than the younger children. In fact, Binet noticed that the brighter younger children could sometimes answer correctly as many questions as the average child of an older age. For example, a very smart 6-year-old might be able to answer as many questions as the average 10-year-old child could. So Binet began to quantify children's intelligence in terms of **mental age**, or the age that reflects a child's mental abilities in comparison to the "average" child. In Binet's scheme, a mental age that exceeds one's chronological age indicates above-average intelligence, and a mental age that is below a child's actual age indicates a below-average level of intelligence. Binet's concept of mental age became the foundation for the IQ score, and his test became the basis for modern intelligence tests.

mental age the age that reflects the child's mental abilities in comparison to the average child of the same age

standardized test a test that uses a standard set of questions, procedures, and scoring methods for all test takers

intelligence quotient (IQ) one's mental age divided by one's chronological age times 100

LEWIS TERMAN: THE INTELLIGENCE QUOTIENT AND THE STANFORD-BINET

In 1916, Stanford psychologist Lewis Terman completed an American revision of the intelligence test that Binet and Simon had developed. He named his version of the test the Stanford Revision of the Binet-Simon Scale, which became known as the *Stanford-Binet*. The Stanford-Binet is an example of a **standardized test**—a test that uses a standard set of questions, procedures, and scoring methods for all test takers. In standardizing the Stanford-Binet, Terman gave the test to a large number of people and calculated the average test scores that people of different ages made on the test. These norms allowed Terman to establish mental age scores for people taking the Stanford-Binet.

Perhaps Terman's most significant contribution to the test was to popularize the use of an **intelligence quotient**, or **IQ**, as the measure of an individual's intelligence. An IQ score is calculated as follows:

$$IQ = (MA/CA) \times 100$$

where

$$MA = \text{mental age}$$

and

$$CA = \text{chronological, or actual, age}$$

Using the concept of an IQ, a person of average abilities has, by definition, an IQ of 100 or, in other words, a mental age equal to her or his actual age. IQs over 100 indicate above-average intelligence, and IQs below 100 indicate below-average intelligence.

The Stanford-Binet has undergone four major revisions since 1916 and is still in wide use today. The most recent edition, the Stanford-Binet Intelligence Scales, Fifth Edition (SB5), was released in 2003. However, a modern IQ test developed by psychologist David Wechsler (1896–1981) and first released in 1939 has greatly challenged the popularity of the Stanford-Binet.

DAVID WECHSLER'S INTELLIGENCE SCALES

Wechsler (1939) developed his intelligence test in response to shortcomings he saw in the Stanford-Binet. Wechsler objected to the fact that the Stanford-Binet test tried to sum up intelligence in a single score. He believed that one number could not adequately express something as complex as intelligence. Furthermore, Wechsler objected to the use of the mental age concept for adults (R. M. Kaplan & Saccuzzo, 1989). After all, would you necessarily expect a 40-year-old to correctly answer more questions than a 35-year-old? The concept of mental age doesn't apply as well to adults as it does to children because adults do not change as much from year to year as children do. Therefore, mental age has little significance in adulthood.

To correct these problems, Wechsler developed an intelligence test that yields scores on individual subscales that measure different mental abilities. Furthermore, instead of using mental age to determine IQ, Wechsler's tests compare a participant's performance to the average person's performance to determine IQ. The Wechsler tests are standardized tests that are devised so that an average person's performance on the test results in an IQ of 100. Using this number as a benchmark, people who score above average on the test are given IQ scores above 100, and people who perform below average are given IQ scores below 100. Most people can expect to score near this average IQ, somewhere in the range of 85–115 (• FIGURE 8.5).

Today there are three separate Wechsler intelligence tests. The Wechsler Preschool and Primary Scale of Intelligence, Fourth Edition (WPPSI-IV), is administered to children ages 2½ to 7. The Wechsler Intelligence Scale for Children, Fourth Edition (WISC-IV), is used for children ages 6–16. And the Wechsler Adult Intelligence Scale, Fourth Edition (WAIS-IV), is used for people ages 16–90.

The WAIS-IV consists of 11 subtests that measure various verbal and performance abilities (• TABLE 8.3). Performance on these subtests is used to calculate an overall IQ score as well as separate index scores for *verbal comprehension, perceptual reasoning, working memory,* and *processing speed.* The design of the WAIS-IV makes it flexible. Testers can administer any of the indexes alone (for example, measuring only perceptual reasoning) or all of them together to obtain an overall IQ score.

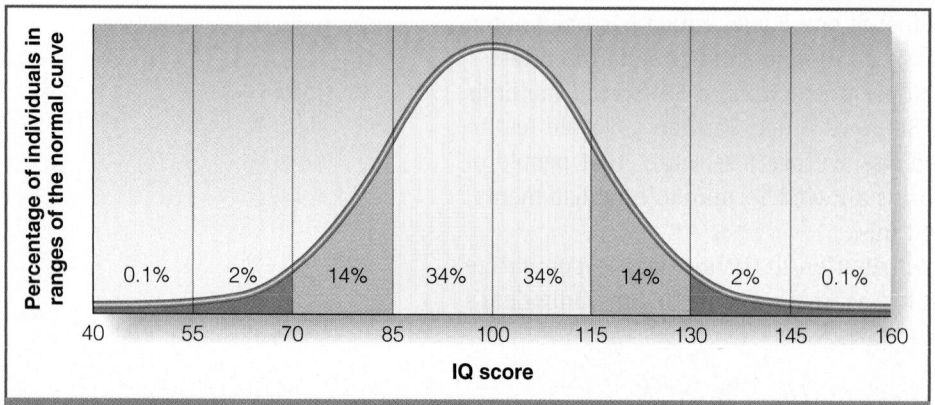

FIGURE 8.5

The Normal Distribution of IQ Scores

IQs tend to be normally distributed across the population. This means that when a frequency distribution of IQ scores is plotted, it forms a bell-shaped curve, with most people scoring near the average of 100 on the IQ test and very few scoring extremely high or low.

TABLE 8.3

The Wechsler Adult Intelligence Scale (WAIS-IV) and Its Subscales

NOTE: The test items shown are examples—they do not appear in the actual test.

CONTENT AREA	EXPLANATION OF TASKS/QUESTIONS	EXAMPLES OF POSSIBLE TASKS/QUESTIONS
		Verbal Comprehension
Vocabulary	Define the meaning of the word.	What does persistent mean? What does archaeology mean?
Information	Supply generally known information.	Who is Hillary Clinton? What are six New England states?
Similarities	Explain how two things or concepts are similar.	In what ways are an ostrich and a penguin alike? In what ways are a lamp and a heater alike?
		Perceptual Reasoning
Block design	Use patterned blocks to form a design that looks identical to a design shown by the examiner.	Assemble the blocks on the left to make the design on the right.
Matrix reasoning	Fill in the missing cell in a matrix with a picture that would logically complete the matrix.	Which of these figures would complete the logical sequence in this matrix?
Visual puzzles	Construct a figure from a series of puzzle pieces.	Which three of these pieces go together to make this puzzle?
		Working Memory
Digit span	Listen to a series of digits (numbers), then repeat the numbers either forward, backward, or both.	Repeat these numbers backward: 9, 1, 8, 3, 6.
Arithmetic	Mentally manipulate arithmetical concepts.	How many 52-cent candy bars can you buy with a 5-dollar bill?
		Processing Speed
Symbol search	When given an array of symbols, find the specified symbol and circle it.	Circle the ♣ in the following array: ♣ ψ Δ λ ♦ ⊗ ℑ ♣ θ ♣ θ Δ λ ♥ ⊕ ∑ ℑ • Δ ♣ λ ♦ ♥ ℑ ≅ ψ ♦
Digit symbol	When given a key matching particular symbols to particular numerals, copy a sequence of symbols, transcribing from symbols to numerals, using the key.	Look carefully at the key. In the blanks, write the correct numeral for the symbol below each symbol. ○ □ ⊗ ◇ ⊖ 1 2 3 4 5 □ ◇ ⊖ □ ○ ⊗ ◇ ⊖ _ _ _ _ _ _ _ _

Ray Stott/The Image Works

The WISC and WAIS use different types of tasks to assess IQ.

reliability the degree to which a test yields consistent measurements of a trait

validity the degree to which a test measures the trait that it was designed to measure

cultural bias the degree to which a test puts people from other cultures at an unfair disadvantage because of the culturally specific nature of the test items

TESTING THE TEST: WHAT MAKES A GOOD INTELLIGENCE TEST?

So far, we have looked at two widely accepted tests that psychologists and educators use to measure intelligence. These are but two of a great many tests that have been devised to measure intelligence and other psychological traits. When choosing which test to administer or when interpreting the scores yielded by these tests, we have to ask, "Is this a good test?" If psychologists never worried about the quality of their measurements, they could well find themselves making many faulty judgments about the people they measure. Think about it: How would you feel if someone gave you an IQ test and then told you that your score would determine whether you got a job? Wouldn't you want some assurance that the test actually reflected your true intellectual ability? Most of us would.

Before a test is used to make decisions about anyone's life, the test itself must be tested and evaluated. Psychologists must be assured that the test is both *reliable* and *valid* before it can be put into widespread use. The **reliability** of a test refers to the degree to which the test yields consistent measurements over time. Although intelligence can change over time, it usually does so very slowly. In general, if you are intelligent today, you will be intelligent 6 months from now. So, if we use a test to measure your IQ today and then again in 6 months, the scores should be comparable. This doesn't mean that the test has to yield exactly the same score, but the scores should be close.

Establishing the reliability of an intelligence test is very important, but the **validity** of the test is an equally important characteristic. Validity is the degree to which the test measures what it was designed to measure. In the case of an intelligence test, one must show that the test actually measures intelligence!

One way to establish a test's validity is to show that scores on the test reliably predict future behavior. For example, if we expect that intelligence is related to doing well in school, then scores on a valid IQ test should predict who does well in school and who does not. If the test is valid, IQ and GPA should correlate. Students with higher IQ scores should tend to also have higher GPAs and students with lower IQ scores should tend to have lower GPAs. If they do not, the IQ test is not a valid predictor of academic success, and it should not be used as such.

ENGAGE YOURSELF! You might be thinking that validity seems like a trivial issue. After all, if you create an IQ test that asks people questions that seem to require intelligence to answer, won't the test tell you who is smart and who is not? As it turns out, it is quite easy to devise tests that are invalid. For example, questions that require specific cultural knowledge may not assess the intelligence of people unfamiliar with that culture—even though they may be very intelligent. This validity problem is referred to as **cultural bias.** Some people have argued that intelligence tests are often biased and invalid for cultural minority members (Reynolds & Brown, 1984). To illustrate this point, try to answer the following sample IQ test question.

Choose the term that best completes this analogy:

Chayote is to soup as scissors are to _____.

a. a drawer

b. paper

c. eggs

d. a bird

Was the answer immediately apparent to you? If you are from a culture that is not familiar with the word *chayote,* which is a type of squash eaten in some Latin American cultures, you might not realize that you put scissors into a drawer the way you put chayote into soup. Does this mean you are unintelligent? Of course not—but an incorrect answer would count against you if it were on an IQ test. Some people contend that IQ tests can't help reflecting the cultural values, language, and knowledge of the people who develop them, and therefore all IQ tests carry some form of cultural bias (Greenfield, 1997). We should always keep in mind that IQ tests do not measure all human intellectual abilities, and our cultural environment can affect our performance on these tests (Sternberg, 1997a).

8.5.2 • The Nature of Intelligence: The Search Continues

Back in the early 1900s, psychological historian E. G. Boring noted that "intelligence is what the tests test" (quoted in Gardner, 1999, p. 13). By this, Boring meant that psychologists had placed a great deal of emphasis on developing tests to measure intelligence, but they had not spent adequate time exploring what intelligence actually is.

INTELLIGENCE AS A SINGLE FACTOR

A century ago, British statistician Charles Spearman argued that because test scores of separate mental abilities (such as verbal skills, mathematical ability, deductive reasoning skills) tend to correlate, there must be one general level of intelligence that underlies these separate mental abilities (Spearman, 1904). Spearman referred to this **general intelligence** as *g*. In Spearman's view, one's level of *g* would determine how well he or she functioned on any number of cognitive tasks. The idea that intelligence is a single, unitary factor helped lead to the rapid expansion of intelligence testing in schools, the workplace, and the military. But the notion of *g* would soon be challenged.

general intelligence (*g*) Charles Spearman's notion that there is a general level of intelligence that underlies our separate abilities

crystallized intelligence our accumulation of knowledge

fluid intelligence the speed and efficiency with which we learn new information and solve problems

INTELLIGENCE AS A COLLECTION OF ABILITIES

Is intelligence really a single factor? Can't a person be smart in some areas, but not in others? By the 1930s, some theorists were beginning to challenge the idea of a single intelligence. The notion of *g* fell from favor as psychologists proposed theories that described intelligence as a set of abilities rather than a single trait. In 1938, psychologist L. L. Thurstone (1938) argued that intelligence was made up of seven distinct mental abilities: reasoning, associative memory, spatial visualization, numerical fluency, verbal comprehension, perceptual speed, and word fluency. Others would eventually propose as many as 120 different factors underlying intelligence (Guilford, 1967).

However, not everyone was convinced that intelligence was made up of many different factors. In the 1960s, Raymond Cattell (1963) revived the idea of *g*. Cattell proposed that *g* does exist, but in two different forms, which he called *crystallized intelligence* and *fluid intelligence*. **Crystallized intelligence** refers to our accumulation of knowledge. For example, your knowledge of psychology is part of your crystallized intelligence. **Fluid intelligence** refers to the speed and efficiency with which we learn new information and solve problems. For instance, the higher your fluid intelligence, the more quickly you will learn the material in this chapter. As a result, both fluid and crystallized intelligence are related to educational attainment across the lifespan (Kaufman et al., 2009).

There is both good and bad news when it comes to our levels of fluid and crystallized intelligence over a lifetime. The evidence shows that crystallized intelligence can continue to grow well into late adulthood (Horn, Donaldson, & Engstrom, 1981), but fluid intelligence tends to decrease across adulthood (Schaie, 1994). The degree to which we retain these abilities throughout life is affected by our environment and our physical well-being, although environment is much more important in the case of crystallized intelligence (Horn, 1982).

As you can see, there has been much disagreement as to exactly what intelligence is. Today, many psychologists still favor the idea of a general intelligence, especially those psychologists who focus on its measurement (Gardner, 1999, p. 14). However, other psychologists have gone on to develop newer theories that conceptualize intelligence as a multifaceted set of abilities or intelligences.

HOWARD GARDNER'S MULTIPLE INTELLIGENCES

In the early 1980s, Harvard psychologist Howard Gardner proposed a theory of intelligence that views humans as possessing many different intelligences (Gardner, 1983). According to Gardner, an intelligence is "a biopsychological potential to process information that can be activated in a cultural setting to solve problems or create products that are of value in a culture" (Gardner, 1999, pp. 33–34). This definition emphasizes the fact that intelligence allows us to function efficiently in our own environment, and it also highlights the fact that different cultures and environments place different demands on our intelligence.

For example, in the United States today, we might consider the ability to understand and predict fluctuations in the stock market as a sign of intelligence. In an unindustrialized, nomadic culture, however, the ability to seek out a source of water may be a more highly valued intelligence. After carefully considering the different human abilities that allow us to function in our environment, Gardner developed a strict set of criteria for identifying an intelligence (Gardner, 1999). Using these criteria, Gardner has identified nine different intelligences and allowed for the possibility that more may someday be identified (Gardner, 2004). Gardner's theory of **multiple intelligences** is summarized in • TABLE 8.4.

multiple intelligences the idea that we possess different types of intelligence rather than a single, overall level of intelligence

As you look at Table 8.4, can you see that you have more of some types of intelligence and less of others? Most of us do not possess equal levels of all types of intelligence. Rather, we each have our own strengths and weaknesses. Therefore, Gardner doesn't have much use for tests that seek to measure general intelligence. For Gardner, it is far more important to look at a person's intelligence profile—his or her level of ability across the different types of intelligence.

ROBERT STERNBERG'S TRIARCHIC THEORY OF INTELLIGENCE

Psychologist Robert Sternberg has taken an approach somewhat similar to Howard Gardner's. Like Gardner, Sternberg rejects the usefulness of trying to measure a single, general intelligence. However, Sternberg doesn't subscribe to the idea that we possess many separate intelligences. Sternberg considers some of Gardner's intelligences as talents that some people possess. For example, it's hard to see why musical intelligence would be important in many cultures. Even if you have little or no musical ability, you could still function very well in many cultures, including American society. However, in the United States and many

TABLE 8.4

Gardner's Multiple Intelligences

INTELLIGENCE	DESCRIPTION	EXAMPLES
Linguistic	The ability to learn and use languages	An author has a good command of language and can express ideas well in written form.
Spatial	The ability to recognize and manipulate patterns of space	A surveyor is very good at judging distances. A seamstress designs a pattern for a jacket.
Logical-mathematical	The ability to attack problems in a logical manner, solve mathematical problems, and in general exhibit scientific thought	A psychologist can develop and test theories in a scientific manner. A physician examines a patient and makes a diagnosis.
Musical	The ability to perform, compose, and appreciate music	A songwriter can create unique melodies and perform them.
Bodily-kinesthetic	The ability to use one's body to solve problems and create products	A gymnast can perform intricate maneuvers on the balance beam.
Interpersonal	The ability to understand the intentions, motivations, and desires of others	A manager is good at working with others and can inspire others to perform at their optimal level of performance.
Intrapersonal	The ability to understand oneself	A student knows what she wants in terms of her career and future life, and she uses this information to choose an appropriate major.
Naturalistic	Paying attention to nature and understanding environmental issues	A homemaker recycles her trash and avoids using household cleaners that are harmful to the environment.
Existential	Being concerned with "ultimate" issues; seeking higher truths	A philosophy student ponders the meaning of life.

Source: *Intelligence Reframed: Multiple Intelligences for the 21st Century* by Howard Gardner (New York: Basic Books/Perseus). Reprinted by permission of BASIC BOOKS, a member of Perseus Books Group.

other cultures, the ability to think logically would be very important to your survival and well-being.

Sternberg suggests that *successful intelligence,* or intelligence that helps us function in our world, is composed of three types of cognitive abilities. Accordingly, Sternberg calls his theory the **triarchic theory of intelligence** (Sternberg, 1985, 1997b). According to the triarchic theory, intelligence is composed of analytical, practical, and creative abilities that help us adapt successfully to our environment.

triarchic [tri-ARK-ic] theory of intelligence Robert Sternberg's theory that proposes that intelligence is composed of analytical, practical, and creative abilities that help us adapt to our environment

Analytical intelligence is seen in our ability to use logic to reason our way through problems—for example, finding a way to fix your car when it breaks down. Analytical intelligence is also important as we implement and evaluate problem-solving strategies, allowing us to evaluate whether a particular problem-solving strategy is working well.

Practical intelligence is our ability to adapt to our environment. This is the type of intelligence that we see in people who have a great deal of common sense. People who are high in practical intelligence exhibit savvy. They know how to function efficiently within their environment. For example, a Central American farmer may be able to predict the weather by noticing changes in the environment. Or someone who lives in New York City may be very good at finding the

© mast3r/Shutterstock.com

Having good emotional intelligence allows one to remain calm and effective during life's challenging moments.

quickest way across town during rush hour. Both of these people, although they possess very different skills, exhibit practical intelligence. Keep in mind that behaviors and skills may be intelligent in some environments, but not in others.

Creative intelligence is our ability to use our knowledge of the world in novel situations. For example, suppose you found yourself in a foreign culture where you did not know the language or the customs. Would you be able to function? People who are high in creative intelligence can adapt what they know about the world to meet the unique demands of new situations. In this case, you might use pantomime skills learned while playing charades to help you communicate without words.

DANIEL GOLEMAN'S THEORY OF EMOTIONAL INTELLIGENCE

Yet another way of conceptualizing intelligence comes from psychologist Daniel Goleman. In his best-selling book *Emotional Intelligence,* Goleman (1995) argues that a concept of intelligence that is based solely on cognitive abilities is too limiting. He notes that even people with relatively high IQs can fail to succeed in life and sometimes do things that appear to be downright unintelligent. For example, a gifted student with a perfect score on the SAT may turn out to be a poor college student who fails most of his classes (Goleman, 1995). According to Goleman, the reason for this is that many times our actions are guided not by our intellectual abilities but by our emotions. Goleman contends that just as some of us are intellectually gifted, some of us are endowed with emotional prowess—an ability he calls *emotional intelligence.*

In Goleman's view, emotional intelligence includes awareness of your own emotional states, accurate assessment of your own abilities, self-confidence, self-control, trustworthiness, conscientiousness, the ability to adapt to changes, innovation or creativity, achievement motivation, commitment to completing goals, initiative or self-motivation, and a sense of optimism (Goleman, 1998; Petrides, Furnham, & Martin, 2004). In other words, an emotionally intelligent person is a confident self-starter who is ethical and adaptable—the kind of person who sets a goal and works toward it without letting minor obstacles derail his or her progress. With this sort of determination, confidence, and ability to adapt, a person with only an average IQ might be able to go far. Likewise, a bright person with low emotional intelligence might become overwhelmed with self-doubt or lack of motivation and, as a result, fail to perform well in life.

Since its introduction, the concept of emotional intelligence has sparked interest among researchers and in the workplace (Yunker & Yunker, 2002). For instance, Goleman and his colleagues have suggested that one way to increase effective leadership in the corporate world is to teach personnel to achieve higher levels of emotional intelligence (Goleman, Boyatzis, & McKee, 2002).

With an eye toward such practical applications, researchers John Mayer, Peter Salovey, and David Caruso have developed a test of emotional intelligence, the *Mayer-Salovey-Caruso Emotional Intelligence Test,* or *MSCEIT.* The MSCEIT measures four different aspects of emotional intelligence: perceiving emotions accurately, using emotions to facilitate thought, understanding emotions, and managing emotions in oneself and others (Mayer et al., 2003). In one study, MSCEIT scores were found to be positively correlated with measures of social competence in relationships with friends—but only for men. Men who scored low in emotional intelligence were found to engage in more behaviors that were harmful to their friendships than men who scored high in emotional intelligence. No such correlation was found for women (Brackett et al., 2006). At this time, the meaning of this finding is unclear, and there are doubts about the validity of the MSCEIT as a measure of emotional intelligence (R. D. Roberts et al., 2006). Researchers still have much work to do before we fully understand the nature of emotional intelligence and its importance to the everyday lives of men and women.

8.5.3 • Nature, Nurture, and IQ: Are We Born Intelligent, or Do We Learn to Be?

The issue of what intelligence is has certainly stimulated a great deal of debate among researchers (see You Review: The Nature of Intelligence), but another issue has captured the attention of the public even more. Where does intelligence come from? Are we born with a predestined level of intelligence, or do we acquire intelligence as we develop (Gardner, 1999)?

You Review The Nature of Intelligence

Theorist	View of Intelligence
Charles Spearman	Intelligence → is → Generalized Intelligence (*g*)
L. L. Thurstone	Intelligence → is → Reasoning Associative Memory Spatial Visualization Numerical Fluency Verbal Comprehension Perceptual Speed Word Fluency
Raymond Cattell	Generalized Intelligence (*g*) → has two forms → Crystallized Intelligence Fluid Intelligence
Howard Gardner	Multiple Intelligences → are → Linguistic Spatial Logical-mathematical Musical Bodily-kinesthetic Interpersonal Intrapersonal Naturalistic Existential Intelligence
Robert Sternberg	Intelligence → comprises → Cognitive Abilities: Analytical Intelligence Practical Intelligence Creative Intelligence.
Daniel Goleman	Emotional Intelligence → coexists with → Traditional Intelligence

NATURE VERSUS NURTURE AND INTERACTIONISM

nature–nurture debate the age-old debate over whether we are mostly a product of our genes or of environmental influences

genes strands of DNA found in the nuclei of all living cells

natural selection the cornerstone of Darwin's theory of evolution, which states that genes for traits that allow an organism to be reproductively successful will be selected or retained in a species and genes for traits that hinder reproductive success will not be selected and therefore will die out in a species

genotype [JEAN-oh-type] inherited genetic pattern for a given trait

phenotype [FEEN-oh-type] an actual characteristic that results from interaction of the genotype and environmental influences

interactionism the perspective that our genes and environmental influences work together to determine our characteristics

Explaining how and why we develop as we do is the central issue in the age-old **nature–nurture debate**. On the nature side of this debate is the claim that individual characteristics (such as intelligence) are largely determined by one's genes and are not learned. On the nurture side, individual characteristics are thought to be molded by environmental influences such as parents, the educational opportunities you have, and the TV shows you watch. From the nurture point of view, our traits and characteristics are acquired totally by experience.

There is little doubt that genes exert a powerful influence on the development of an organism. All living organisms develop according to a "blueprint" or plan contained in the genes that an organism inherits from its parents. **Genes** are strands of deoxyribonucleic acid (DNA) that are found in the nuclei of all living cells and direct the development of the organs and systems of the body. In 2003, scientists working on the *Human Genome Project,* a large-scale scientific project aimed at identifying the entire set of genes that are found in the DNA of the human body, completed this mapping. One of the most surprising findings of the project was that the total number of genes in the human genome is about 30,000. Originally, scientists had predicted that they would find approximately 100,000 genes. The fact that a mere 30,000 genes direct the development of something as complex as humans was a surprise (U.S. Department of Energy, 2007). So, why do humans possess these specific 30,000 genes and the characteristics that they govern? To answer this question, think back to a concept we discussed in Chapter 1—natural selection.

In 1859, Charles Darwin published *On the Origin of Species by Means of Natural Selection* (Darwin, 1859/1936), in which he outlined the process of natural selection. **Natural selection** is a simple but powerful process that can change, kill, or create a species over time. The central principle of natural selection is that for characteristics to be retained in a species, genes for these traits must be passed on to offspring. If an organism does not reproduce, its genes die with it. If a specific trait is maladaptive and tends to prevent an organism from surviving and procreating, then the genes for this trait are not as likely to be passed on to offspring. Over time, these maladaptive genes should die out in the species. In contrast, adaptive genes, which give rise to traits that help an organism reproduce, will be passed on to future generations. Through natural selection, these adaptive genes will become more widespread in the species over time. From this perspective, the genes of the human genome are present in us today because they aided our ancestors' ability to thrive and reproduce.

Even though our human genes direct our bodies to develop as human bodies, we are not all the same. As individuals, we have unique characteristics because we inherited a particular mix of genes for specific traits from our parents. At conception, we get half of our genes from each of our parents. From this combination of genes, we develop our characteristics. The genetic code that we inherit for a particular trait is called the **genotype**. But the genotypes we inherit, such as genes for dark hair, only partly determine the traits we actually acquire. The environment plays a role as well. The actual trait or characteristic we develop is referred to as the **phenotype**. The phenotype is a product of the genotype an organism inherits and the environment in which it lives. For example, the exact shade of your hair, the level of your intelligence, the speed with which you run—all are phenotypes, which are the expression of inherited genotypes and environmental influences.

Today, the dominant perspective on the nature–nurture debate is **interactionism**. Most psychologists now believe that genetic influences interact with environmental influences to produce our traits and behavior. For example, a child can inherit very "smart" genes, but if education is not provided, the child will not be as "smart" as he or she could have been. Interactionism does not end the nature–nurture debate, however. Today, many psychologists are attempting to understand the relative contributions of nature and nurture to specific traits, asking whether a trait such as intelligence is mostly genetic or mostly environmental.

GENETIC STUDIES

The same technology that made the Human Genome Project possible has also opened new doors to researchers studying the origins of intelligence and other traits. Today, researchers are able to collect blood samples from people and then using DNA analyses, correlate the presence of particular genes in the person's genome (genotype) with his or her particular levels of traits, such as intelligence (phenotype). In one of the first studies to use this approach, researchers in Scotland were able to show that intelligence is *polygenetic* or based on many genes and that an identified collection of genetic markers accounted for 40% of the variation seen in the participants' crystallized intelligence scores and 51% of the variation seen in participants' fluid intelligence scores (Davies et al., 2011). This study strongly suggests that genetics do influence intelligence. However, notice that the genetic markers they tested did not account for 100% of the variability in intelligence. Therefore, the researchers' data do *not* rule out environmental influences on intelligence.

TWIN STUDIES

Twin studies are another way to answer questions about the relative contributions of nature and nurture to intelligence. Twin studies compare specific traits between pairs of *identical twins* (twins who share 100% of their genetic code) and pairs of nonidentical or *fraternal twins* (twins no more genetically related than other siblings). If identical twins share a similar trait more often than fraternal twins do, then a genetic basis for the trait is implied. If, on the other hand, identical twins are no more similar on a trait than fraternal twins, there is less support for a genetic influence (if the trait were genetic, we would expect the genetically identical twins to be more alike). Other studies compare identical twins raised in different environments to identical twins raised in the same household. Dissimilarities between identical twins reared together and identical twins raised apart would be a powerful argument for environmental influence on the trait being measured. Through such comparisons, psychologists can isolate the influence of nature and nurture on the development of specific traits.

Across a wide variety of such studies, *heritability* estimates (the proportion of variability in a trait accounted for by genetics) have been shown to range from about 0.4 to 0.8 for intelligence (Nisbett et al., 2012). Findings such as these leave little doubt that intelligence is influenced by genetics. But once again, such findings do not negate the importance of environmental factors. For example, one interesting wrinkle is that heritability estimates for intelligence seem to vary from population to population. In particular, intelligence seems to be more heritable in upper socioeconomic status (SES) children and less heritable in lower SES children (for a review, see Nisbett et al., 2012). This suggests that environments associated with lower SES may exert more influence on intelligence, perhaps preventing some children from reaching their full genetic potential.

8.5.4 • Diversity in Intelligence: Race, Gender, and Age

In 1994, the publication of a book, *The Bell Curve,* brought the debate over the origins of intelligence into the public eye (Herrnstein & Murray, 1994). The title of this book refers to the fact that IQ scores tend to follow a normal distribution, which is shaped like a bell (see Figure 8.5, p. 330). In *The Bell Curve*, the authors argued that intelligence is primarily encoded in our genes and that environmental influences do little to change it. This extreme position was largely denounced by scholars (Gardner, 1999), but the public became engaged in heated discussions about the merits of this position, as well as the implications of the authors' claims. Of particular concern was the implication that some minority groups may be genetically inferior with respect to intelligence. Though the authors never stated that minorities were genetically inferior, this conclusion appeared to follow from their arguments and the data that have been collected on IQ differences across racial groups.

INTELLIGENCE AND RACE

Generally speaking, studies have shown that average IQ scores tend to vary across racial groups in America. As a group, African Americans tend to score about 10–15 points lower on IQ tests than European Americans, who are in turn outscored, on average, by Asian Americans (Nisbett, 1995; Rushton, 2012). Although it has traditionally received less research attention, Hispanic Americans also tend to score below non-Hispanic European Americans on IQ tests (Dickens & Flynn, 2006; Nisbett et al., 2012). If we are to believe the message of *The Bell Curve*, the inference would be that these differences exist mostly because of genetic inheritance. Furthermore, some may be tempted to conclude that if these differences are genetically based, then any attempt to raise children's IQ scores by improving their environment would be a waste of time and money. It is this sort of offensive assertion that has kept the debate on race, genetics, and intelligence ignited for decades (see Rushton & Jensen, 2005, and Sternberg, Grigorenko, & Kidd, 2005, for thorough reviews of the research from opposing points of view).

Overall, the results of twin studies (and other studies) on the inheritance of traits in families have not supported the strong nature claims made in *The Bell Curve*. Rather, these studies support an *interactionist* perspective that intelligence seems to stem from both our genes and our environment (Chipuer, Rovine, & Polmin, 1990; Nisbett et al., 2012; Polmin, 1994). In fact, there is evidence that directly challenges the notion that improving one's environment does little to change one's intelligence.

Compared to European Americans, a disproportionate number of minority group members live in poverty. An impoverished environment may contribute to lesser performance on IQ tests for a number of reasons. Poorer parents cannot afford educational toys, good schools, computers, and so on for their children. Poorer parents may themselves not be highly educated and therefore may be less able to stimulate their children in the ways that highly educated parents can. Indeed, a recent study found that many of the differences seen in IQ scores could be attributed to differences in literacy levels among the people tested (Marks, 2010). Given that literacy is a learned skill, providing an enriching environment is likely to increase IQ for all children.

One study (Moore, 1986) showed that African American middle-schoolers who had been placed in affluent European American families as infants had average IQs that were not only above average for African American children but also above average for European American children. Nisbett and colleagues (2012) review several studies showing that being adopted into a higher SES family is associated with a 12- to 18-point increase in IQ score. These studies suggest that the environment in which one grows up contributes significantly to one's IQ.

Furthermore, there is reason to suspect that certain aspects of the environment may be improving for minority members. Since the 1970's, the IQ gap between Black and White students has reduced by more than 5.5 points. This suggests that Blacks are catching up to Whites in terms of educational and intellectual attainment (Nisbett et al., 2012). Such a change in just a few decades would be hard to explain in terms of genetic differences, leaving the explanation that the narrowing of the IQ gap may be due to environmental factors such as increased access to better educational environments. However, some researchers (for example, Rushton, 2012) dispute the notion that the IQ gap is really narrowing between Blacks and Whites at all. So, the debate continues.

Whether or not the IQ gap is decreasing and whether or not IQ is mostly a product of genes or the environment, it is important to keep the practical relevance of this research in mind. It is very important to note that there is more variability in intelligence *within* racial groups than there is *between* racial groups. In other words, the range of IQ scores among European Americans or among African Americans is wider than the average difference between these groups. Furthermore, keep in mind that group characteristics do not predict individual characteristics. We cannot assume to know an individual's level of IQ (or any other characteristic) based solely on knowing his/her group membership. For example, knowing that the class average on your last psychology exam was 73 does not mean that you made a 73. You may have scored above or below average.

GENDER DIFFERENCES IN INTELLECTUAL ABILTIES

Just as we saw in our discussion on race and IQ, data are at times open to different interpretations. Another area in which the interpretation of data has been varied and sometimes contentious is in the study of how gender relates to intellectual abilities. Beliefs or stereotypes about male and female intellectual abilities abound. For example, in the United States (and many other cultures), people tend to believe that men are better at math and women are better at verbal tasks. Another common stereotype is that men are more intelligent than women and women are more emotional than men. But are there truly gender differences in intelligence?

The answer to this question has proved to be somewhat complicated. Over the last several decades, many researchers have investigated the issue of gender differences in intelligence, and often their results have been difficult to interpret (Galliano, 2003). In part, the confusion has to do with how individual researchers have defined specific abilities. For example, to evaluate mathematical ability, you could look at a person's ability to solve equations, the speed with which he or she can solve word problems, whether the person has succeeded in math classes, or any number of other measures. Another problem is that studies that fail to find predicted gender differences are often not published. Therefore, if we look only at published studies that do show gender differences in intelligence, we may falsely conclude that gender differences are more prevalent than they actually are (Galliano, 2003).

After examining the available research, many psychologists have concluded that men and women do not differ in general intelligence, or *g* (Halpern & LeMay, 2000; Nisbett et al., 2012). On the other hand, some gender differences have been indicated with respect to specific multiple intelligences. We have summarized some of these suspected differences in ● TABLE 8.5.

Keep a few things in mind as you read Table 8.5. First, many gender differences are small (see, for example, Galliano, 2003; Hyde, Fennema, & Lamon, 1990). Second, finding such differences often depends on how they were measured. For example, females tend to earn better grades in math classes, but males tend to do better on standardized tests of mathematical ability (Hyde & McKinley, 1997). Third, gender differences can vary by culture, age, and race. For instance, in Thailand, girls outperform boys in math, but in France, boys do better than girls (Galliano, 2003). And in the United States, male superiority on math SAT scores occurs only among European Americans (Robinson et al., 1996). Finally, gender differences are at times a product of bias in the tests used

TABLE 8.5

Gender Differences on Some Cognitive Tasks

TASKS ON WHICH WOMEN OFTEN HAVE HIGHER AVERAGE SCORES	TASKS ON WHICH MEN OFTEN HAVE HIGHER AVERAGE SCORES
Verbal Tasks	Visual Memory Tasks
Verbal fluency Synonym generation Spelling Anagrams Reading comprehension Writing Foreign languages Tongue twisters Knowledge about literature	Mental rotation tasks
Perceptual Tasks	Spatial Tasks
Searching for letters within lines of text Detecting touch, taste, odor, and sound at low levels of intensity	Making judgments about moving objects—for example, judging how far away a moving object is
Motor Skill Tasks	Motor Skill Tasks
Fine motor skill tasks like tracing the mirror image of a stimulus on a piece of paper	Motor skills that involve aiming, such as throwing a baseball or darts
Academic Performance	Knowledge Areas
Most subject areas at school	General knowledge Knowledge about math, geography, and science
	Fluid Reasoning Tasks
	Mechanical reasoning Quantitative reasoning Verbal analogies Scientific reasoning Proportional reasoning

Source: Adapted from Halpern, 1996.

to measure different abilities. For example, David Share and Phil Silva (2003) found that in a sample of New Zealand students, boys were more likely to be labeled as having reading disabilities because of a statistical bias in the way that reading disability scores were calculated.

Given these types of complexities in the data, it is difficult to conclude that there are broad-based, global differences between men and women when it comes to intelligence. Despite the lack of clarity concerning the differences, it is fairly clear that we tend to believe the stereotypes we have about men's and women's abilities. Belief in these stereotypes has been well documented in studies that ask men and women to assess their own intellectual abilities. For example, in one study, Adrian Furnham and colleagues found that parents tended to estimate their sons' IQs as being higher than their daughters', indicating that they had more confidence in their sons' overall intelligence, or g. When asked to rate their children on specific multiple intelligences, the parents tended to rate their sons higher on mathematical and spatial intelligence and their daughters higher on verbal and musical intelligences (Furnham, Reeves, & Budhani, 2002).

These biases also seem to extend to how we view our own levels of intelligence. In cultures as diverse as the United States, Poland, Argentina, China, Iran, New Zealand, and Slovakia, men's self-ratings of intelligence are higher than women's (see Furnham, Wytykowska, & Petrides, 2005, for a review). Men also rate themselves as having lower levels of emotional intelligence (Petrides et al., 2004), better general knowledge, and more skill on tasks of visual perception (Pallier, 2003). Studies like these seem to suggest that both men and women have (perhaps misguidedly) bought into the commonly held stereotypes about their respective abilities. This can be problematic. If a woman believes that she is less intelligent, this may actually work to lower her performance (Chamorro-Premuzic & Furnham, 2004). Furthermore, even if she performs well, stereotypes like these can be the basis for prejudice and discrimination—topics that we will discuss more in Chapter 10.

INTELLIGENCE AND AGING

Race and gender are not the only sources of stereotypes about intelligence. Older people often face stereotypes about their intelligence as well. Many people equate growing older with the certainty of dementia and other intellectual challenges. However, studies indicate that the majority of people aged 90–94 years do not require assistance with daily tasks, such as bathing (Berlau, Corrada, & Kawas, 2009). Declines in intellectual functioning that are severe enough to prevent people from functioning independently are likely due to disease and not due to normal aging.

As we age, we tend to experience some declines in the efficiency of our information processing or *fluid intelligence,* but how much decline we experience is in part related to our overall health. In one study, researchers compared middle-aged and older adults who were healthy (healthy group) with middle-aged and older adults who had high blood pressure and/or vascular disease (vascular risk group) over a 5-year period (Raz et al., 2007). They found that relative to the healthy group, the vascular risk group experienced more negative brain changes. For example, the vascular risk group experienced more brain lesions and increased shrinkage in the prefrontal cortex and hippocampus of the brain relative to the healthy participants. Recall from Chapters 2 and 7 that the hippocampus and prefrontal cortex play important roles in the processing of memories. The vascular risk group also experienced more decline in their working memory, an important aspect of fluid intelligence. These findings suggest that cardiovascular disease and cardiovascular risk factors (such as high blood pressure and diabetes) may increase your risk of experiencing declines in fluid intelligence as you age. Therefore, doing what you can to limit your cardiovascular risk—such as exercising, maintaining a healthy weight, eating well, and avoiding smoking—may also reduce your chances of experiencing cognitive declines in older age.

Losing the ability to function due to cognitive problems in older age is not a normal part of the aging process. The good news is that maintaining a healthy lifestyle may reduce your chances of facing debilitating changes in your cognitive functioning later in life.

Enigma/Alamy

Quiz Yourself 8.5

1. Which psychologist would be most likely to agree with the following statements: "Intelligence is not a single ability. We do not possess intelligence. We possess many intelligences."
   a. Robert Sternberg
   b. Francis Galton
   c. Howard Gardner
   d. Daniel Goleman

2. Gilbert recently developed a new intelligence test that he plans to administer to second-grade children, but when he wrote the questions, he used an adult-level vocabulary. Based on your understanding of intelligence tests, what would you predict the test to be?
   a. Valid and reliable
   b. Unreliable
   c. Invalid
   d. Valid, but not reliable

3. One day, Sabrina's front door started squeaking at the hinges. She was out of the spray lubricant that she would normally use for this purpose, so she went to her kitchen and got a bottle of cooking oil. She dabbed a bit of the corn oil on the hinge, and the squeak went away. Sabrina best exhibits a high level of _____ intelligence.
   a. analytical
   b. existential
   c. practical
   d. creative
4. On which of Sternberg's types of intelligence would Kim Peek likely have scored highly?
   a. analytical
   b. practical
   c. creative
   d. none of the above
5. Janelle is a14 year-old African American female. Jonah is a 14 year-old White male. Based on this information, we can assume that_____.
   a. Janelle will have a lower IQ than Jonah
   b. Janelle will be better at verbal tasks than Jonah will be.
   c. Jonah will be better at visuospatial tasks than Janelle will be.
   d. None of the above.

Answers 1. c; 2. c; 3. d; 4. d; 5. d

8.6 Integrating Psychology: The Big Picture

In this final chapter on the cognitive aspects of psychology, we explored the cognitive processes commonly referred to as *thinking.* Thinking involves the use of *knowledge* to attain our goals. Some of the goals that we strive to attain include solving the *well-structured* and *ill-structured problems* that we face in life, *reasoning, decision making,* making *judgments,* and using *language* to communicate with others. Most of us are able to engage in these cognitive processes, but some of us accomplish them better than others do. For example, although Kim Peek was easily able to memorize large amounts of information, he was not particularly good at reasoning, decision making, or solving ill-structured problems. On the other hand, you might be very skilled at such tasks, perhaps demonstrating high levels of *creativity* or *deductive reasoning* skills. Or, perhaps you might be very skilled at expressing your thoughts through language. How well we engage in such cognitive tasks determines to some degree how well we function in life. Possessing well-developed cognitive skills is conducive to exhibiting *intelligence* or adapting to your environment and behaving in a goal-directed manner. Because life challenges us in many different ways, some psychologists have argued that rather than being a single trait, intelligence is best conceptualized as a series of *multiple intelligences* or collections of domain-specific abilities. So while Kim Peek may have demonstrated very high levels of knowledge, he did not score highly on traditional tests of *generalized intelligence* (*g*). Think about your own intelligence. What are your intellectual strengths? What are your weaknesses? Whatever they may be it is likely that your own unique levels of intelligence are due to an *interaction* between the genes you inherited from your parents and the environments in which you have lived. It is this interplay of *nature* and *nurture* influences that makes each of us the unique individual we are. In our next section, we will explore the sociocultural and individual variations in our traits and behaviors that form the third section of psychology. In Chapter 9, we will examine how we develop across our lifetimes as a result of nature and nurture influences. In Chapter 10, we will explore how we understand and interact with other people in our environment and how these interactions vary across cultures. And, in Chapter 11, we will look at variations in our personality traits and how they relate to our behavior. As you read these coming chapters, think about your own unique cognitive abilities, the influences that helped these abilities develop in you, and how these abilities affect your interactions with others and the world.

Studying the Chapter

Key Terms

affective heuristic (321)
algorithm (315)
availability heuristic (320)
babbling (323)
basic level category (311)
cognition (308)
concept (310)
cooing (323)
creativity (316)
crystallized intelligence (333)
cultural bias (332)
decision making (319)
deductive reasoning (318)
exemplar (312)
fluid intelligence (333)
formal concept (311)
functional fixedness (317)
general intelligence (*g*) (333)
genes (338)
genotype (338)
grammar (324)
heuristic (315)
ill-structured problem (315)
incubation (317)
inductive reasoning (318)
insight (316)
intelligence (328)
intelligence quotient (IQ score) (329)
interactionism (338)
intuition (315)
judgment (319)
knowledge (308)
language (322)
mental age (329)
mental representation (308)
mental set (317)
morpheme (324)
multiple intelligences (334)
natural concept (311)
natural selection (338)
nature–nurture debate (338)
overextension (324)
phenotype (338)
phoneme (324)
pragmatics (324)
prototype (312)
reasoning (318)
reliability (332)
representativeness heuristic (320)
standardized test (329)
subordinate category (311)
superordinate category (311)
telegraphic speech (324)
thinking (308)
triarchic theory of intelligence (335)
underextension (324)
validity (332)
well-structured problem (315)
Whorfian hypothesis/linguistic relativity hypothesis (325)

What Do You Know? Assess Your Understanding

Test your retention and understanding of the material by answering the following questions.

1. _____ is the information we have stored in our long-term memory about the world.

a. Thinking
b. Memory
c. Cognition
d. Knowledge

2. The idea of what a giraffe is, is an example of a(n) _____.

a. mental representation
b. judgment
c. image
d. heuristic

3. The available evidence most strongly suggests that we store mental representations of stimuli that are _____ of what we see.

a. exact visual copies
b. only verbal descriptions
c. both verbal descriptions and visual images
d. only prototypes

4. Given the concepts crab, seafood, King crab, and Opilio crab, which one represents the basic level category?

a. Crab
b. Seafood
c. Opilio crab
d. King crab

5. Which of the following is most likely an example of a natural concept?

a. Furniture
b. Sofa
c. Wing-back chair
d. Housewares

6. Using a formula to calculate the gas mileage on your car is an example of a(n) _____.

a. algorithm
b. heuristic
c. exemplar
d. judgment

7. Determining the best location for the family vacation is most likely an example of a(n) _____.

a. well-structured problem
b. ill-structured problem
c. judgment
d. insight

8. Which of the following is *not* an aid to problem solving?

a. A mental set
b. Incubation
c. Creativity
d. Insight

9. Reasoning that because many larger cars and trucks get poorer gas mileage, a Hummer must get very poor mileage is an example of _____.

a. inductive reasoning
b. deductive reasoning
c. decision making
d. problem solving

10. After watching a show on global warming, Mitch overestimates the average yearly temperature for his hometown. Mitch's error is most likely due to _____.

a. the availability heuristic
b. the representativeness heuristic
c. framing
d. poor decision making

11. The English prefix *pro-* is an example of a(n) _____.

a. phoneme
b. morpheme
c. pragmatic
d. overextension

12. Lamond is 5 months old. At which stage of language development would you most expect him to be?

a. Cooing
b. Babbling
c. One-word speech
d. Telegraphic speech

13. Who would most agree with the statement "A Spanish-speaking person and an English-speaking person will necessarily have different perceptions of the world"?

a. Lewis Terman
b. Noam Chomsky
c. Benjamin Whorf
d. Alfred Binet

14. According to the text, which of the following species have not been shown to possibly possess linguistic skills?

a. Parrots
b. Chimpanzees
c. Horses
d. Dolphins

15. _____ is credited with being the father of the modern intelligence test.

a. Francis Galton
b. Alfred Binet
c. Robert Sternberg
d. Lewis Terman

16. Six-year-old Tasha scores as well as the average 10-year-old on an intelligence test. Tasha's IQ score is approximately _____.

a. 100
b. 134
c. 167
d. 182

17. David Wechsler did which of the following?

a. He developed the first intelligence test.
b. He moved psychologists away from using the concept of mental age to calculate IQ scores.
c. He introduced the idea that humans possess multiple intelligences as opposed to a general level of intelligence, or *g*.
d. All of the above.

18. An intelligence test must be _____ to be of use to psychologists.

a. reliable
b. valid
c. culturally biased
d. a and b

19. As we age, _____ intelligence tends to decline, but _____ intelligence tends to increase.

a. fluid; crystallized
b. crystallized; fluid
c. practical; analytical
d. analytical; practical

20. Your specific level of intelligence is due to your _____.

a. genotype
b. genotype and nurture influences
c. genotype and nature influences
d. nature influences

Answers: 1. d; 2. a; 3. c; 4. a; 5. b; 6. a; 7. b; 8. a; 9. b; 10. a; 11. b; 12. b; 13. c; 14. c; 15. b; 16. c; 17. b; 18. d; 19. a; 20. b.

Use It Or Lose It: Applying Psychology

1. What abilities define our concept of an intelligent person in the United States? What abilities do you think would define the concept of an intelligent person in rural Africa?
2. Make a case for why one would want to use heuristics for solving problems and making decisions and judgments.
3. Give an original example of an ill-structured and a well-structured problem.
4. Describe the stages that children go through as they develop language and give an example of each. If you wanted to raise a bilingual child, how do you think you could best accomplish this?
5. Examine the theories of multiple intelligences that you read about in this chapter. Are there any types of intelligence that you feel were overlooked in these theories? Why or why not?

Critical Thinking for Integration

1. How could Lev Vygotsky's idea (see Chapter 9) of the zone of proximal development be useful to child caregivers who wish to improve a child's language development?
2. Presume that someday we finally do provide conclusive evidence that animals have linguistic abilities. How do you think this would change research in psychology and other sciences?
3. Given what you have learned about language, intelligence, and psychology in general, what advice would you give a first-time parent who is concerned about raising the best child he or she can?
4. Damage to which areas of the brain (Chapter 2) would be most likely to impair a person's ability to use language? Would this damage also affect the person's problem-solving skills? Explain.
5. How could cultural bias in intelligence testing facilitate the development or maintenance of racial prejudices (Chapter 10)?

© Tyler Olson/Shutterstock.com

Are You Getting the Big Picture? Cognition, Language, and Intelligence

8.1 Thinking: How We Use What We Know

- **Cognition** is the way in which we store and use information.
- Our knowledge comprises the mental representations of the world that we have stored in long-term memory.
- **Thinking** is the use of **knowledge** to accomplish a goal.
- Visual images are powerful **mental representations** that allow us to remember a person's face or a map.
- **Concepts** are mental categories that contain related bits of knowledge and are organized around the meaning of the information they represent.
- We tend to organize our knowledge into three levels of categorization: the general, broad **superordinate category**; the **basic level category**; and the **subordinate category**, which is the most specific.

RTimages/Alamy

Envision/Corbis

Charles Mistral/Alamy

- We acquire **formal concepts** as we learn the rigid rules that define certain categories of things, but **natural concepts** develop naturally as we live our lives and experience the world.
- A **prototype** is our concept of the most typical member of a category—in essence, a summary of all members of that category.
- **Exemplars** are stored representations of actual category members we have experienced.

8.2 Problem Solving: Where Does Our Thinking Get Us?

- An **algorithm** is a method of solving a **well-structured problem** that always leads to the correct solution. A **heuristic** is a shortcut, or rule of thumb, that may or may not lead to the solution of a problem. **Ill-structured problems** must be solved with heuristics.
- **Insight**, **creativity**, and **incubation** help us overcome common obstacles to problem solving like **functional fixedness** and **mental sets**.

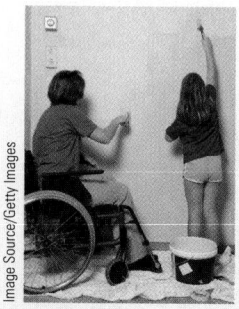

Image Source/Getty Images

8.3 Reasoning, Decision Making, and Judgment

- We engage in **reasoning** when we draw conclusions that are based on certain assumptions about the world. **Deductive reasoning** involves reasoning from the general to the specific, whereas **inductive reasoning** involves reasoning from the specific to the general.
- **Decision making** involves choosing among several alternatives and is often part of the problem-solving process.
- Framing, or how possible courses of action are presented, can affect our decisions.
- Two mental shortcuts that can be useful but that can also lead to mistakes are the **availability** and **representativeness heuristics**.

8.4 Language: Communication, Thought, and Culture

Masterfile

- Human **language** is a well-developed, syntactical, verbal system for representing the world.
- Scientists debate the idea that humans are born with an innate language acquisition device (LAD)—a programmed capacity for language.
- Research indicates that infants generally proceed from **cooing** to **babbling** to **morphemes** on their road to language skills. By age 2, most children exhibit **telegraphic speech**. Soon after, children learn the rules of **grammar** and **pragmatics** for their language.
- One theory, known as the **Whorfian hypothesis** or the **linguistic relativity hypothesis**, suggests that one's language actually determines one's thoughts and perceptions of the world. A more widely held view is that language influences, rather than determines, our thoughts.
- Although animals communicate, it is hotly debated whether they have the capacity for language.

8.5 Defining and Measuring Intelligence

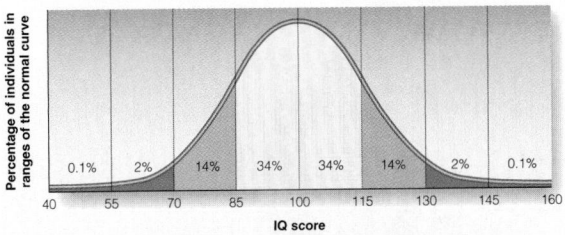

- Many modern psychologists broadly view **intelligence** as those abilities that allow you to adapt to your environment and behave in a goal-oriented way.
- Alfred Binet established the measurement of **mental age** that reflected a child's mental abilities compared to those of the "average" child at a specific age.
- Stanford psychologist Lewis Terman revised Binet's testing procedures and introduced the **intelligence quotient**, or **IQ**, which is a score obtained by dividing one's mental age by one's chronological age.
- The adult version of David Wechsler's test (WAIS-IV) yields several separate index scores and an overall score.
- Intelligence tests are frequently criticized for having a **cultural bias**.
- The idea of mental ability as a single unitary factor is known as **general intelligence**, or ***g***.
- **Crystallized intelligence** refers to our accumulation of knowledge, whereas **fluid intelligence** refers to the speed and efficiency with which we learn new information and solve problems.
- Some theorists argue that we have **multiple intelligences**. Examples are Robert Sternberg's **triarchic theory of intelligence** and Howard Gardner's theory of multiple intelligences.
- Daniel Goleman's theory of emotional intelligence argues that emotions are also an important component of successful living.
- Although a heated debate continues over whether intelligence is inherited, most research suggests that an interaction of heredity (**nature**) and environment (**nurture**) contributes to our intellectual capabilities.

Part 3
Foundations in Developmental and Social Psychology

THE BIG PICTURE **The Changes and Challenges of Life**

The two previous sections included chapters that focused on specific psychological processes such as neuroscience, consciousness, learning, and memory. The third section or foundation expands on these topics by illustrating how a person's behavior is better understood by evaluating individual variability and the sociocultural environment. This section includes three chapters: human development, social psychology, and personality. **Development** consists of changes in our behavior and abilities over our lifetime. **Social psychology** examines how we think and behave in the company of others. **Personality** is our unique collection of attitudes, emotions, thoughts, habits, impulses, and behaviors that define how we behave across situations. The Part III case study powerfully illustrates these mutually influential forces. It is the life story of Hongyong Baek, as told by her granddaughter Helie Lee in *Still Life with Rice* (1996). As you read about the challenges she faced, think about how her development, personality, and social environment may have influenced her behavior, as sometimes it is easier to see these patterns and influences in others than it is in ourselves. Then examine how these same areas may be influencing your own behavior. At the same time, consider and imagine what challenges may still be ahead of you.

Hongyong Baek was born in Korea in 1912, the second of four children and the first daughter of wealthy parents. She was strong and willful and curious to conquer life, behaviors that were not in

Helie Lee recounts the eventful life of her Korean grandmother, Hongyong Baek, in her memoir, *Still Life with Rice.*

line with acceptable gender roles for Korean females at that time. So, as was the custom for Korean girls, at the age of 9, Hongyong began daily lessons in virtue, womanhood, and managing a household. She preferred the household lessons as they were "something I could touch, see, and use freely," but her headstrong temperament often incurred her mother's wrath and discipline. She understood obedience, but the idea of chastity was difficult to grasp. For example, when her mother told her to protect her "private parts," she thought her mother meant her knees, because she was constantly being told to keep her knees covered. At age 12 when she started to menstruate, her mother told her it was a woman's curse. Ashamed, she hid in her room fearing that everyone would know.

Unwed at 22, Hongyong feared she was too plain and clumsy to marry. She prayed to Buddha for a husband; without one she was considered a burden on her family. A marriage was arranged, to 19-year-old Dukpil Lee. Hongyong now belonged to another man's family. To her surprise, Hongyong's husband encouraged her to share her ideas and opinions, and her affection for him grew. She gave birth to a boy, Yongwoon, fulfilling her most important wifely duty by giving her husband a son. Over the next 15 years, Hongyong bore four more children, two daughters and two sons.

In This Part:

CHAPTER 9 **Human Development**

CHAPTER 10 **Social Psychology**

CHAPTER 11 **Personality**

In 1939, as Hongyong gloried in the role of wife and mother, civil unrest in her country, long occupied by the Japanese, grew. Not wanting to lose their Korean heritage, the Lee family went to China, leaving behind all that was familiar. At Hongyong's suggestion, they started a sesame oil business. The business prospered, but Hongyong grew bored. Against her husband's wishes (which at that time and place was considered uncommon for a wife), she began to smuggle opium. Soon they had more money than they could spend. However, her husband spent more time away from her and had affairs with other women. Hongyong's insecurities about her appearance resurfaced. To keep her husband's attention, they opened a restaurant to entertain the most prominent and powerful people in China.

In her 30s, Hongyong was plagued with health problems. She discovered the ancient art of *ch'iryo,* a healing technique in which the flesh is pinched and slapped in order to improve blood circulation. Hongyong used ch'iryo to improve her health and treated herself and her children daily.

In 1945, Americans dropped the atomic bomb on Japan, and the Japanese surrendered Korea. Thousands of Koreans boarded trains for their homeland, the Lee family among them. The Lee family returned to North Korea, which was quickly occupied by Korean communists. Most of the family's land and money were confiscated. As her husband turned to alcohol, Hongyong converted to Christianity and developed a thirst for religious knowledge. She questioned her reason for living, learned how to read and write, and gave away what little riches they had left.

In 1950, the Korean War erupted at the 38th parallel. Because of her religion, Hongyong was imprisoned for "treasonous" activities. She spent 30 days in an overcrowded prison cell. Her daughter Dukwah dodged bombs and gunfire to bring her baby sister Dukhae to be breastfed by Hongyong every day. Once she was released, Hongyong knew her family would not be safe unless they went to South Korea.

Hongyong watched her husband leave for South Korea and then bid farewell to her eldest son. Unable to bear the waiting, Hongyong packed up her children to cross the Taedong River. Thousands of other refugees had the same idea. During the crossing, Hongyong and her baby were trampled. Once across, Hongyong prepared to bury her baby. Miraculously, Dukhae was still breathing, although barely. With frozen feet, empty bellies, and little energy, the family continued to walk, hoping to find shelter and peace. At one point, Hongyong was so exhausted that she wanted to leave Dukhae under a tree to die. Because the baby was practically dead, Hongyong thought to sacrifice her in hopes that the rest of the family would survive. But Dukwah refused to leave her sister, and the two women took turns carrying her.

Amid exploding bombs, throngs of people, and piles of wreckage, the Lee family made it to Seoul, 2 weeks before the South Korean borders closed. Hongyong found her husband in a refugee camp, but her eldest son, Yongwoon, never appeared. The agony was too much for Hongyong. For 8 months, she was a living ghost, ignoring her husband and children, forgetting to pray. She sat on a crate all day, staring into space, barely eating or sleeping. Her husband took care of the children and made ends meet by selling gum and cigarettes. Finally, Hongyong's two sisters found her and took in the entire family.

Just as their lives were returning to some sort of normalcy, Hongyong's husband contracted diphtheria and quickly died. Hongyong vowed to find her way back to God. Just shy of 40 years old, she was now a widow. For the first time in her life she would have to make decisions on her own without anyone's approval. She again questioned her purpose in life and turned back to her ch'iryo. As her patients' health improved, more clients came looking for her services. Her hands could not keep up with the demand, so she developed an internship program to train other women in the art of ch'iryo.

As Hongyong's practice expanded, her children grew, went to college, married, and had children. She enjoyed being a grandmother and doted on her grandchildren with affection. As her 60th birthday approached, Hongyong waved good-bye to her daughter and granddaughters, as they emigrated to the United States. Eight years later, Hongyong bid farewell to Korea and emigrated to America herself, but she never stopped searching for her eldest son. After 40 years, she finally received news. He was alive! He had been caught behind the lines in North Korea. At 80 years of age, Hongyong finally achieved peace of mind.

Hongyong's story illustrates the sometimes dramatic turning points that shape our behavior. A multitude of forces help or hinder our development: the love or ridicule of others, our ability to deal with death, our quest to find personal meaning in our lives, to name just a few. Every person is also influenced by a multitude of social environments: family, school, friends, neighborhoods, religion, and culture. Hongyong followed the prescribed social roles for her time and for her culture. Her parents arranged her marriage. As a female, her role was to be a good wife and mother. Yet, Hongyong's natural curiosity and strong personality violated cultural expectations of how a female should behave. Fortunately, her husband accepted her despite her willfulness, allowing Hongyong to explore her talents as an entrepreneur through the sesame oil business, as an opium madam, and as a restaurant owner.

Consider how learning about development, social psychology, and personality will help you appreciate the sociocultural forces and individual experiences that make each person unique—just as Hongyong's journey makes her tale one of a kind. We hope this understanding will lead to a deeper appreciation of why you behave the way you do and to more productive and enjoyable interactions with the people around you.

Cover used by permission of Simon & Schuster Adult Publishing Group.

Human Development

Learning Objectives

9.1 Explain the nature–nurture issue and how it leads to diversity in behavior. (APA 1.2, 2.1)

9.1 Identify and describe the three stages of prenatal development, and explain the importance of a positive prenatal environment. (APA 1.1, 1.3, 2.2, 5.1)

9.2 9.5 Describe major physical changes across the lifespan and how they impact cognitive and psychosocial development. (APA 1.1, 1.3, 5.1)

9.3 Describe the development of perceptual abilities of infants, and explain how it relates to cognitive development. (APA 1.1, 1.3)

9.3 Compare and contrast Piaget's and Vygotsky's theories of cognitive development, and apply these theories to children's behavior. (APA 1.1, 1.2, 2.1, 2.5, 5.1)

9.3 Compare and contrast Kohlberg's and Gilligan's theories of moral reasoning, and apply these theories to moral decisions. (APA 1.1, 1.2, 2.1, 2.5)

9.4 Define temperament, and distinguish among the three temperamental styles of infants. (APA 1.1)

9.4 Describe behaviors that indicate that an attachment has been formed, and distinguish among different attachment patterns. (APA 1.1, 1.3, 2.1, 2.4, 2.5, 5.1)

9.4 9.7 Describe and apply the parenting styles that Baumrind documented, and explain the new roles and responsibilities of being a parent. (APA 1.1, 1.3, 2.1, 2.2, 4.1)

9.4 9.7 Detail Erikson's theory of psychosocial development, and indicate the possible positive and negative outcomes at each stage. (APA 1.1. 1.2)

9.4 Explain gender-schema theory, and describe how nature and nurture influence gender-role behavior and gender identity. (APA 1.1, 1.2, 1.3, 5.1)

9.6 Compare and contrast formal operations and postformal thought in adolescence and adulthood, and apply them to behavior. (APA 1.1, 1.2)

9.6 Describe changes in mental abilities in adulthood. (APA 1.1, 1.3, 2.2, 4.1)

9.7 Define and describe the transitional phase of development referred to as emerging adulthood. (APA 1.1, 2.5)

9.7 Describe the varieties of social relations in adolescence and adulthood. (APA 1.1, 1.3, 2.2, 2.5, 4.1)

9.7 Explain the predictable changes people experience in career development. (APA 1.1, 1.3)

9.8 Describe and apply the emotional reactions that characterize dying people, according to Kübler-Ross. (APA 1.1, 1.2, 1.3, 5.1)

9.8 Describe and apply the three phases of grief. (APA 1.1, 1.3)

This chapter outlines the processes of development. **Development** consists of changes in behavior and abilities. As we saw in the opening story in Part III about Hongyong Baek, and may understand from our own experiences, human development is complicated. Physical changes are occurring along with emotional, social, and mental (or cognitive) development. At the same time, social forces (such as people around us) and our environment also affect these processes. We hope that by understanding the physical, cognitive, and social aspects of development, you will be able to appreciate the many forces that make each child, teenager, and adult unique.

9

Masterfile

Chapter Outline

9.1 Human Development: How Does It All Begin? / 356

9.2 Physical Development in Infancy and Childhood / 360

9.3 Cognitive Development in Infancy and Childhood / 363

9.4 Psychosocial Development in Infancy and Childhood / 374

9.5 Physical Changes in Adolescence and Adulthood / 383

9.6 Cognitive Changes in Adolescence and Adulthood / 389

9.7 Psychosocial Changes in Adolescence and Adulthood / 393

PSYCHOLOGY APPLIES TO YOUR WORLD: Career Development / 400

9.8 Death and Dying / 402

9.9 Integrating Psychology: The Big Picture / 404

9.1 Human Development: How Does It All Begin?

Psychologists study development in order to understand the changes that humans experience from conception to the end of life. Because development covers such a large time span, developmental psychologists typically specialize by limiting their investigations to a particular period of life, such as infancy, childhood, adolescence, or adulthood. Within any one of these age stages, psychologists may focus on different aspects of development: physical, mental, social, or personality development. One developmental psychologist may study how language develops in infants while another may research how peer pressure affects drug use in adolescents.

Recall from Chapter 1 that psychology seeks to *describe, predict, control,* and *explain* behavior. If psychologists can accomplish these goals, then we can promote healthy development and prevent or alter maladaptive patterns of development. For example, if we understand how children think, we can then create appropriate educational environments, thus maximizing each child's potential. Understanding the dynamics of peer pressure during adolescence may suggest strategies to reduce drug use, delinquency, and teenage pregnancy. Stories like Hongyong's illustrate the importance of understanding more fully how experiences such as war, miscarriage, or alcoholism affect people's development. Knowing about developmental processes, therefore, has numerous real-world applications. However, as we'll read about next, explaining developmental changes is not easy. Part of the difficulty is that some but not all of human development is predictable, and it is the combinations of these life events that add to the complexity and uniqueness of each person's story.

9.1.1 • Nature–Nurture Revisited: How Biology and Culture Lead to Diversity

Think about all the variables that can potentially influence how a person grows and changes. In addition to a unique biological foundation (genetics), every person is also influenced by a multitude of environments: family, school, friends, neighborhoods, religion, and culture. The potential contribution of these biological and environmental factors to development has become a central issue for developmental psychologists. Recall from Chapter 8 that this is referred to as the **nature–nurture issue** or debate. Psychologists are interested in how much one's biology, or *nature,* contributes to a person's development versus how much one's environment and culture, or *nurture,* influence this process.

development changes in behavior or abilities or both

nature–nurture issue the degree to which biology (nature) or the environment (nurture) contributes to a person's development

Genes—or *nature*—influence almost every aspect of development, from personality and physical development to cognitive processes such as language development and intelligence (Bouchard, 2004; Davis, Haworth, & Plomin, 2009; Gottlieb, Wahlsten, & Lickliter, 1998). *Nurture* is the total effect of all the external environmental events and circumstances that influence your development. It includes your family, friends, how others perceive and behave toward you, events that happen to you, television programs that you watch, music that you listen to, the customs and rituals of your ethnic background, your gender, your culture, your schooling, and so on.

Recall that it is not really a case of nature *or* nurture. Rather, it is the *interaction* of these two forces that influences behavior. Genes may moderate the influence of environmental forces; likewise, gene expressions may be altered by the environment (Champagne, 2010; Champagne & Mashoodh, 2009; Eagly & Wood, 2013; Tucker-Drob, Briley, & Harden, 2013). As you read about the various types of development that we experience, keep this nature–nurture issue in mind, as the influences of nature and nurture seem to interact in a complex fashion.

9.1.2 • Prenatal Development

From the outside, all we see is a woman with a swollen belly who walks with a waddle. We may even have the opportunity to see or feel movement occurring inside her belly. Any woman who has been pregnant has experienced having some people want to touch her stomach or to treat her more delicately because of her "condition." Both tendencies speak to our fascination with the developments going on inside.

All the genetic material for development is inherited from your biological parents at the time of conception. The male sperm cell, containing 23 single chromosomes, fertilizes the female ovum, also containing 23 single chromosomes, to create a fertilized egg, called a **zygote**, that has 23 pairs of chromosomes. Over the next 38–40 weeks, the average gestation period for a human, the zygote will experience dramatic changes as it evolves into a baby. So many changes occur during this time that scientists divide the prenatal period into three stages: the *germinal* or *zygotic stage,* the *embryonic stage,* and the *fetal stage.*

The first 14 days after conception are the **germinal stage** of development. The major characteristic of this stage is cell division. Following conception, the zygote starts to replicate itself and divide. This process ensures that all the cells of the organism contain the same genetic material. The zygote divides into 2 cells, which then replicate and divide again, creating a 4-cell organism. The cells continue replicating and dividing, and around the 5th day after conception the zygote has become a 100-cell organism, called a *blastocyst*. During this process of cell division, the mass of cells also travels down the fallopian tube to the uterus. On approximately the 9th day after conception, the blastocyst implants itself in the lining of the uterine wall. Cell division continues through the 2nd week.

The **embryonic stage** covers development of the organism, now called an *embryo,* from the 3rd through the 8th week. After the blastocyst attaches to the uterine wall, its outside cells develop into the support structures: the *placenta, umbilical cord,* and *amniotic sac*. The inner cells become the embryo.

The major characteristic of the embryonic period is the formation and development of the major organs and systems. Cells start to specialize into bone, muscle, and body organs. All the major biological systems—the cardiovascular system, the digestive system, the skeletal system, the excretory system, the respiratory system, and the nervous system—are forming. Given the importance of these systems for survival and well-being, the embryonic stage is perhaps the most precarious stage of prenatal development. Most miscarriages occur and genetic defects surface during this stage. The embryo's development may also be harmed by outside environmental factors, producing devastating effects. We will return to these topics in a moment.

By the end of the embryonic stage, all basic bodily structures and systems have formed. About 4 weeks after conception, the heart is beating, the spinal cord is forming, the liver is producing red blood cells, and ovaries or testes have formed (but the embryo's sex is not apparent by ultrasound until between 12 and 18 weeks). Although only an inch long, the embryo already looks human. Facial features, such as the eyes, lips, nose, and jaw, have taken shape. Short stubs represent arms and legs, and the beginnings of fingers and toes are apparent.

The third prenatal development period, the **fetal stage**, begins the 9th week after conception. From now until birth, the organism is referred to as a *fetus*. The major characteristic of the fetal stage is continued growth and maturation. The fetus grows larger and starts to move. By 14 weeks, the fetus can kick, open its

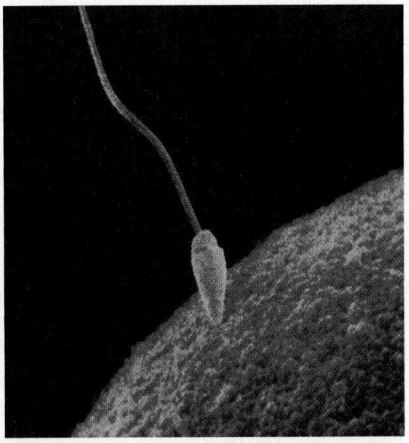

Don W. Fawcett/Science Source

Human sperm and egg at the moment of penetration. The sperm cell fertilizes the female ovum to create a zygote.

zygote [ZIE-goat] a fertilized egg

germinal stage the first stage of prenatal development, from conception to 14 days

embryonic [em-bree-AH-nik] stage the second stage of prenatal development, lasting from the 3rd through the 8th week

fetal stage the third stage of prenatal development from the 9th week through the 9th month

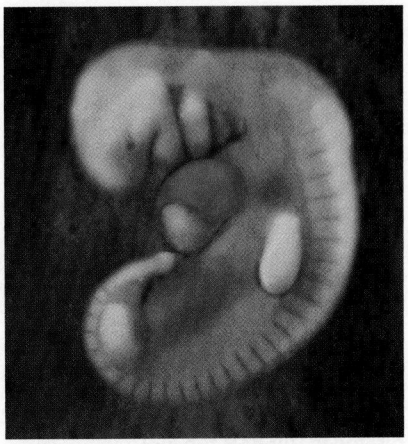

Anatomical Travelogue/Science Source

Micro-MRI, reconstructed with 3-D imagery, actual size of embryo 4.0 mm. The image depicts a human embryo during its 4th week of development. Age is calculated from the day of fertilization. In this image, the fusing tubes of the heart are highlighted in red. Early growth of the cardiovascular system begins during the 3rd week, when blood vessels form, and continues into the following weeks of development. Image from the book *From Conception to Birth: A Life Unfolds.*

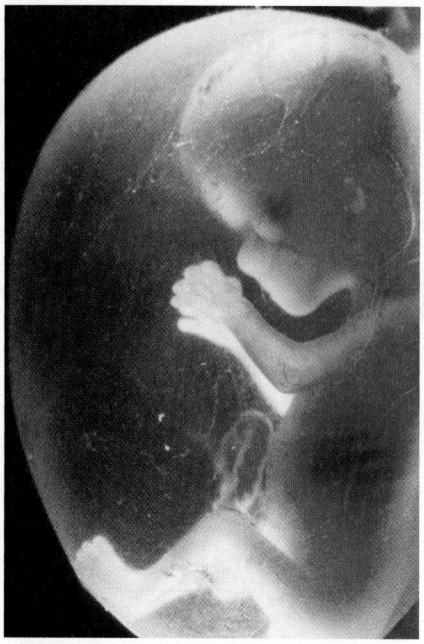

Claude Edelmann/Science Source

At 14 weeks, the fetus's lungs and external sex organs have developed.

mouth, swallow, and turn its head. Its lungs and external sex organs have developed. By the end of the 6th month (24 weeks), the organs are sufficiently formed that the fetus has reached *viability*—the possibility of surviving outside the womb (but only in a neonatal intensive care unit). During the last 3 months, the fetus is responsive to sound, light, and touch.

From the union of a single sperm cell and egg, the fetus has undergone significant and complex changes over the course of 40 weeks. However, not all zygotes experience these changes. About half of all fertilized eggs die and are miscarried, usually before the woman knows she is pregnant. Of pregnancies that the mother knows about (because of a missed menstrual cycle), approximately 15% to 20% end in miscarriage (American College of Obstetricians and Gynecologists, 2002).

9.1.3 • Application: The Importance of a Positive Prenatal Environment

The support structures of the intrauterine environment are designed to protect the developing organism. However, internal and external forces can still interfere with this natural defense system and cause birth defects.

When internal chromosomal abnormalities are present at conception, their effects typically arise during the embryonic stage. For example, **Down syndrome** results from an extra 21st chromosome. Babies with Down syndrome are characterized by distinct facial features (such as almond-shaped eyes or a flat nose) and are more likely to experience heart defects and varying degrees of intellectual disability. Medical tests can identify the presence of Down syndrome and hundreds of other inherited genetic disorders so that parents can prepare themselves or terminate the pregnancy (Rappaport, 2008). This possibility highlights the importance of regular prenatal consultations with a physician.

Birth defects may also be caused by outside environmental forces. Any environmental agent that has the potential to harm the embryo is referred to as a **teratogen**. It may be a drug that the mother takes, such as cocaine or alcohol; a disease, such as German measles (rubella); or chemicals that the mother inhales, such as certain cleaning fluids. All these substances have the potential to cause birth defects. The critical factor seems to be *when* the mother is exposed to these agents. These **sensitive periods** emphasize the complex interplay of nature and nurture on development. Certain organs and systems are more vulnerable to the effects of teratogens during particular stages of prenatal development (● FIGURE 9.1). Notice that the most severe effects are most likely to occur during the embryonic stage of development. Because a woman usually does not discover that she is pregnant until the embryo is already formed and developing, she may unknowingly expose her developing baby to harm.

Women who use any type of drug during pregnancy can potentially affect their babies. Women who smoke during pregnancy reduce the flow of oxygen to the fetus; their babies tend to be irritable, have respiratory problems, and have lower birth weight (Lester, Andreozzi, & Appiah, 2004; Shea & Steiner, 2008). Women who drink alcohol heavily during pregnancy put their unborn children at risk for **fetal alcohol syndrome (FAS)**. Children with FAS tend to have low birth weight, brain abnormalities, and lowered intellectual functioning, and tend to exhibit limb, head, and facial deformities (Dalen et al., 2009; Ikonomidou et al., 2000; Ornoy & Ergaz, 2010). Even moderate drinking can affect the embryo's brain development, resulting in later intellectual impairments (Kraft, 1996; Rasmussen, Soleimani, & Pei, 2011). Prenatal alcohol exposure has also been linked to an increased risk of low birth weight and poorer visual acuity in infancy (R. C. Carter et al., 2005; Mariscal et al., 2006).

Down syndrome a genetic birth disorder resulting from an extra 21st chromosome, characterized by distinct facial features and a greater likelihood of heart defects and intellectual disability

teratogen [tur-RAH-tuh-jun] an environmental substance that has the potential to harm the developing organism

sensitive period in prenatal development, a time when genetic and environmental agents are most likely to cause birth defects

fetal alcohol syndrome (FAS) a birth condition resulting from the mother's chronic use of alcohol during pregnancy that is characterized by facial and limb deformities and intellectual disability

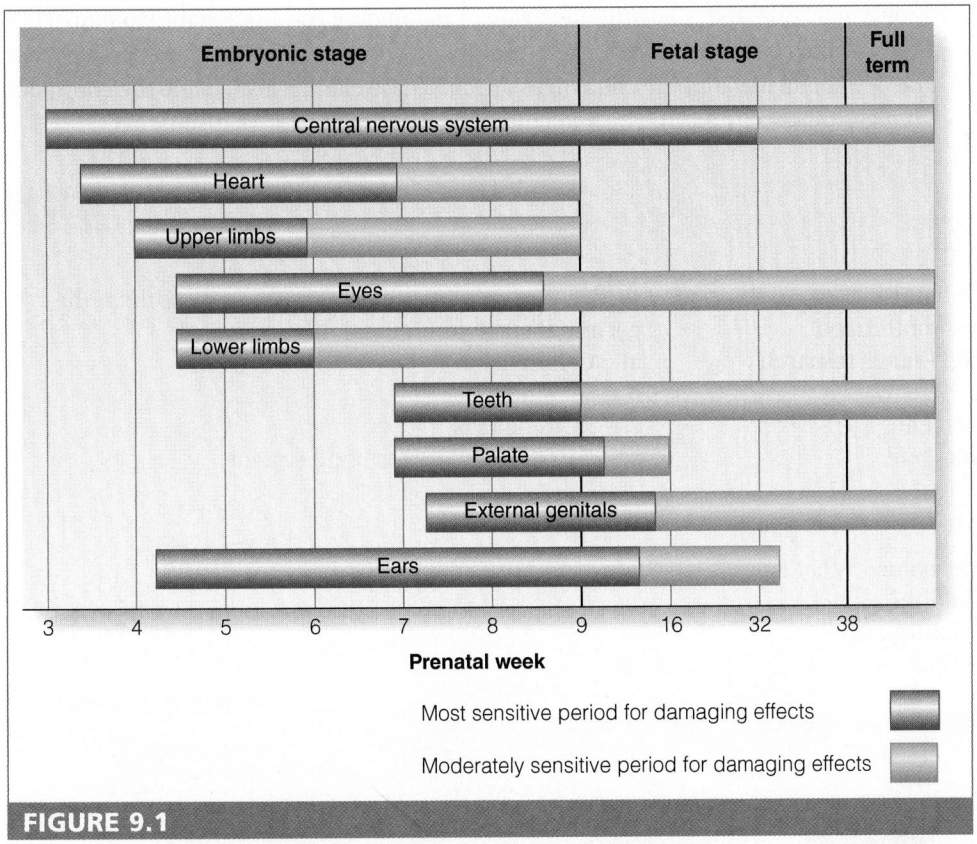

FIGURE 9.1

Sensitive Periods and Effect on Prenatal Development

The darker bars indicate the most sensitive period for certain organs and structures; the lighter bars indicate lessened vulnerability. Sensitivity is greatest during the embryonic period, although some structures remain vulnerable throughout the prenatal period.

Source: Adapted from K. L. Moore and T. V. N. Persaud, *Before We Are Born: Essentials of Embryology and Birth Defects.* Philadelphia: Saunders. Copyright © 1998 Elsevier Science (USA). All rights reserved. Reprinted by permission.

Illegal drugs also produce damaging effects. If the mother is a heroin addict, the baby will be born addicted and have to undergo withdrawal. Crack or cocaine babies are often born premature, underweight, and irritable, and tend to have poor feeding habits (Frank et al., 2002; Gouin et al., 2011).

Prenatal exposure to teratogens may also have long-term effects. Children exposed to drugs during pregnancy tend to be more impulsive, less adaptable, and evidence more behavioral problems later in life than children not exposed to drugs during pregnancy (Espy, Riese, & Francis, 1997; Richardson et al., 2011). In southern Japan, adults whose mothers took in high levels of methylmercury (found in fish) during pregnancy have shown accelerated rates of aging (Newland & Rasmussen, 2003). There is also increasing evidence that maternal stress and anxiety during pregnancy may influence the offspring's development. High levels of maternal stress hormones during pregnancy increase the risk of preterm birth and are associated in childhood with higher blood pressure, behavioral and emotional problems, as well as a higher risk of obesity (Coussons-Read, 2012; Harris & Secjkl, 2011; Reynolds, 2013; Rinaudo & Wang, 2012).

Prescription and over-the-counter medicines may also influence fetal development. Read the warning labels on any over-the-counter medication, and you will see that pregnant women are cautioned to seek a doctor's advice before using any medicine. Whatever the mother takes in during pregnancy or breastfeeding, so does the baby.

Proper nutrition and a healthy lifestyle are paramount for a pregnant woman. They increase the chances of producing a healthy newborn who is better prepared to face the developmental and life challenges ahead. These challenges include the enormous changes that occur in infancy and childhood—our next topic of discussion.

Quiz Yourself

9.1

1. Dr. Newhart is investigating if mental stimulation in infancy can impact childhood intelligence and behavior. Dr. Newhart's research emphasizes _____.
   a. nature's influence on development
   b. nurture's influence on development
   c. the influence of teratogens
   d. viability and development
2. Loretta is in her 5th month of pregnancy. What stage of development is her unborn child in?
   a. Germinal
   b. Zygote
   c. Embryonic
   d. Fetal
3. Which of the following is *most* characteristic of the germinal stage of prenatal development?
   a. Cell division
   b. Viability
   c. Birth defects
   d. Formation of major body systems

Answers 1. b; 2. d; 3. a

9.2 Physical Development in Infancy and Childhood

neonate a newborn during the first 28 days of life

The average **neonate**, or newborn up to 28 days old, enters the world 20 inches long, weighing 7 pounds. One year later, the average infant is 29 inches long and will have tripled in weight, emphasizing how rapidly babies grow during infancy. Physical growth and developmental changes result from the complex interaction of the forces of nature and nurture. Our genes lay the foundation for how tall we grow and how our body fat is distributed. The environmental factors of nutrition, health care, and lifestyle also influence our height and build. A similar interplay of nature and nurture is seen in brain and motor development.

9.2.1 • Brain Development

What is your very first childhood memory? How old were you then? Most people do not recall events in infancy or before 3 years old. This lack of memory may be related to the development of the nervous system. At birth, an infant's brain has billions of neurons, but the connections between the neurons are very limited, and myelin (see Chapter 2) is incomplete. Experience and learning mix with heredity to shape brain development. Neural pathways grow rapidly, and by the time a child is 3 years old, 1,000 trillion synapses have formed (Garlick, 2003). A 2-month-old has very few neural connections compared to the billions a 2-year-old has. More experience plus increased activity equals more neural connections.

During childhood and early adolescence, the brain prunes and discards unnecessary connections, reducing the total number of synapses (Cook & Cook, 2005; Thompson et al., 2000). Those connections that are used repeatedly become permanent, whereas those that are used infrequently or not at all are unlikely to survive (National Scientific Council on the Developing Child [NSCDC], 2007).

This discovery has altered researchers' thinking on infant care and early education. Providing stimulating age-appropriate activities fosters and strengthens brain development. Impoverished environments weaken neural connections—fewer connections are made, and unexercised connections are likely to be discarded.

A young child's brain is highly *plastic,* or changeable, and very dense with neurons when compared to adults' brains. If a certain area of the brain is damaged in infancy, other areas of the brain can compensate by reorganizing neural connections (Xiong, Mahmmod, & Chopp, 2010). However, there are individual inherited differences in this process; some brains may be better able to adapt than others (Garlick, 2002). As children age, the brain is less able to change and adapt because neural connections have already been formed, and in some cases discarded, although some plasticity remains throughout adulthood (Huttenlocher, 2002; Kelsch, Sim, & Lois, 2010). The plasticity and density of the brain ensure a child's best chance of adapting to his or her environment. This adaptation is also evident in the development of children's motor skills.

9.2.2 • Reflexes and Motor Development

Infants are born relatively helpless creatures. They cannot feed themselves and are unable to walk. Infants do have certain sensory abilities, a good set of lungs that enable them to cry, and a set of *reflexes,* all of which biologically prepare them to get the help they need to survive.

reflex an automatic response to a specific environmental stimulus

A **reflex** is an *automatic* response to a particular stimulus. Reflexes enable infants to learn about their environment, thus establishing important neural connections for *voluntary* motor behaviors. Hence, reflexes serve as the foundation for behaviors such as walking, eating, crying, smiling, and grasping. For example, infants are born with a sucking reflex. They will automatically suck on any object that touches their lips. Infants also have a *rooting reflex*. When you touch the side of infants' cheeks, they will turn in that direction and open their mouth. These two reflexes teach infants how to use their mouths to get food. Infants are also born with a grasping reflex. When an object is placed on their palm, they will automatically grasp it. The grasping reflex is the foundation of *prehension,* when infants learn to handle items with their hands. Their brains and bodies learn, through grasping, the necessary skills that will later be used to write with a pen, play a musical instrument, tie their shoes, or give a parent a hug.

Infants are also biologically prepared to communicate, despite lacking formal language skills. A crying reflex—automatically crying when distressed—alerts the caretaker to the infant's needs. In a matter of weeks, the baby learns to use crying to get the caretaker's attention. Luckily, infants are also born with a smiling reflex to use when they are pleased (which also serves as positive reinforcement for their caregivers). This reflex evolves into a *social smile* during the second month of life, when the infant smiles at everybody. Infants' smiles then become more discriminating; by 6 months of age, they reserve their smiles for familiar voices and faces.

Reflexes also initiate *locomotive* ability, or the ability to move around. Crawling and stepping reflexes prepare the brain and body for motions involved in pulling oneself up, crawling, and walking. These abilities develop in much the same sequence for all infants around the world, evidence of our genetic heritage. However, cross-cultural research suggests that child-rearing practices and variations in the environment may speed up or slow down this process. For example, despite living in poverty and poor sanitary conditions, Ugandan infants sit independently on average at 4 months compared to 6 months for U.S. infants. This advantage is lost when Ugandan infants are raised in Western culture—evidence of a nurture influence (Adolph, Karasik, & Tamis-Lemonda, 2009).

gross motor skills motor behaviors involving the large muscles of the body

fine motor skills motor behaviors involving the small muscles of the body

By age 2, most infants are walking, running, and getting into everything. However, motor development, the changes in a child's body activities, does not end there. As children age, *gross motor skills* become more proficient. **Gross motor skills** refer to behaviors that involve large muscle groups such as the biceps or quadriceps. These include running, walking, jumping, and hopping. This proficiency is apparent when you watch a toddler, a preschooler, and an 8-year-old run. The toddler waddles and is unsteady on her feet. The preschooler is more coordinated compared to the toddler, but less fluid and not as fast as the 8-year-old.

Similar changes occur in **fine motor skills**, which involve small muscle groups. Fine motor skills include such activities as writing, using utensils, and playing a musical instrument. Toddlers and preschoolers are less adept at tasks involving fine motor skills, but as the school years approach, children become much more proficient. • TABLE 9.1 shows average age ranges for specific gross and fine motor skills achieved in infancy and early childhood in the United States. Notice that the achievement of a particular task lays the foundation for attaining the subsequent,

TABLE 9.1

Motor Milestones in Infancy and Early Childhood

3 MOS.	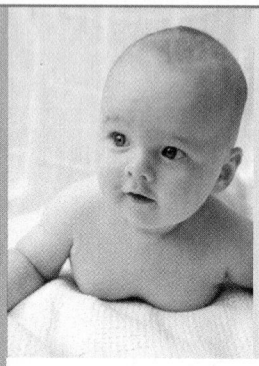 Leila Cutler/Alamy • Lifts head and chest when lying on stomach • Grasps rattle • Waves arms • Kicks legs	2 YRS.	 Clayton Sharrard/PhotoEdit • Drinks from a straw • Tosses a ball • Feeds self with a spoon • Bends over without falling
6 MOS.	• Reaches for and grasps objects • Helps hold a bottle • Shakes a rattle • Sits with little support • Rolls over	3 YRS.	• Puts on shoes • Dresses self with help • Kicks a ball • Hops on one foot • Pedals • Climbs
1 YR.	 © Monkey Business Images/Shutterstock.com • Sits alone • Crawls and pulls self up • Uses finger to point • Grasps object with thumb and index finger	4 YRS.	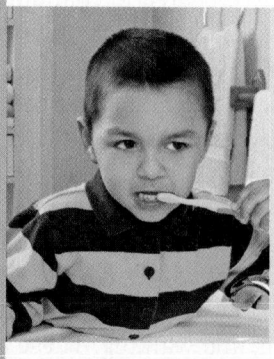 © 3445128471/Shutterstock.com • Runs, jumps, hops, and skips • Brushes teeth • Jumps over objects • Catches, bounces, and throws a ball
18 MOS.	• Pulls and pushes objects • Turns pages in a book • Scribbles • Stacks a few blocks • Walks and runs stiffly	5 YRS.	• Rides a bicycle with training wheels • Balances on one foot • Cuts with scissors • Jumps rope • Copies simple designs • Capable of swimming and skating

more difficult, task. In other words, babies must be able to sit up before they can crawl. Children must walk before they learn to jump rope.

Enormous changes occur in physical development through the infancy and childhood years. The same magnitude of change characterizes cognitive development, or how children think, which we'll turn to next.

9.2

Quiz Yourself

1. Which of the following infants is *most* likely to have the fewest neural connections?
   a. A 1-month-old
   b. A 4-month-old
   c. A 1-year-old
   d. A 2-year-old
2. The rooting reflex is to eating as the grasping reflex is to _____.
   a. locomotion
   b. crawling
   c. gross motor skills
   d. prehension
3. Children in preschool learn how to use scissors in order to help develop their _____ skills.
   a. gross motor
   b. fine motor
   c. reflex
   d. locomotive

Answers 1. a; 2. d; 3. b

9.3 Cognitive Development in Infancy and Childhood

Television shows, movies, and comic strips capitalize on the unique way in which children develop mentally (their *cognitive development*). What is it about children's thinking that makes adults laugh? This section reviews psychological research into how infants first learn to conceptualize the world and how this thinking changes as they proceed through childhood. We will start with perceptual development.

9.3.1 • Perceptual Development: Gathering Information from the Environment

Infants are hard to study. They sleep most of the time, and they can't talk much. We can't remember what it's like to be an infant. Researchers must therefore study infants when they are awake and active, and devise clever ways to measure what infants know. The best way to gather information about what infants can and cannot perceive seems to be to measure certain behaviors and see how those behaviors change under particular conditions. For example, researchers may measure how long an infant spends looking at a stimulus or how long an infant sucks when exposed to different sounds. As researchers create more precise ways of measuring infant behavior, we are discovering that infants know a lot more than we once believed.

VISION

Babies are very nearsighted at birth. Objects need to be close in order for babies to see them, and even then, the objects look blurry. In addition, a baby's eyes lack *convergence,* or the ability to focus both eyes on an object. This may be why newborns typically look cross-eyed in photographs. However, as the structure of the eyes and the neural connections in the brain mature, babies attain visual convergence.

Newborns show a preference for looking at complex, high-contrast stimuli. If given a choice among various complex visual stimuli, infants will spend most of their time looking at faces (Frank, Amso, & Johnson, 2014; Pascalis & Kelly, 2009; Turati, 2004; Turati & Simion, 2002). This preference is adaptive, as it helps foster a social bond with the primary caretaker. By 3 months old, a baby can tell the difference between its primary caretaker's face and that of a stranger and more easily recognizes faces from its own race (Bar-Haim et al., 2006; Kelly et al., 2007; Sangrigoli & de Schonen, 2004). Infants also have more difficulty processing male faces than female faces (Ramsey-Rennels & Langlois, 2006).

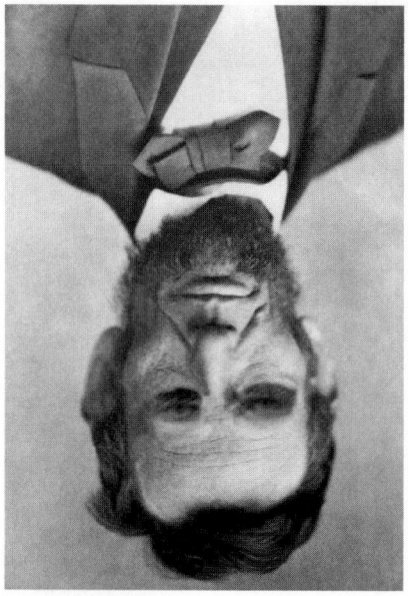

©Historical/Corbis

ENGAGE YOURSELF! Our brains are predisposed to recognize a face, and this predisposition is present in babies. Look closely at the upside-down image of Lincoln on this page before looking at it right side up. Notice anything? Even when presented with an inverted portrait, we ignore the distortions and recognize that it is a face. When you look at Lincoln's portrait right side up, you notice all the distortions.

We also have the tendency to see faces in random patterns that strongly resemble the configuration of a face, a psychological phenomenon referred to as *pareidolia* (Hadjikhani et al., 2009; Voss, Federmeier, & Paller, 2012). Have you ever seen the "man in the moon" or faces in arrangements of food or clouds even though there is not a literal face visible? Face perception develops quite early and may even be "hard-wired" at birth, bestowing an evolutionary advantage in quickly detecting friend or foe that enhances human survival (Leopold & Rhodes, 2010).

DEPTH PERCEPTION

During their first year, infants develop *depth perception*. In a classic experiment conducted in 1960, researchers Eleanor Gibson and Richard Walk created an apparatus called a "visual cliff" (see photo). They then observed at what age infants would or would not cross over the surface where it appeared to drop off. Infants as young as 6 months of age hesitated when approaching this perceived cliff. Again, we see that biology prepares us for developmental challenges. Babies acquire depth perception at about the same time they become mobile. Because depth perception and body coordination may not yet be developed in some infants, it is extremely important to never leave a baby unattended on a bed, a changing table, or any other elevated surface. Immature depth perception, as well as inadequate body control, makes it more likely that infants will fall and hurt themselves.

Eleanor Gibson and Richard Walk's visual cliff apparatus tests depth perception in infants.

Mark Richards/PhotoEdit

HEARING

Unborn babies react to sounds in the intrauterine environment at around the 20th week. A mother's voice is one of those sounds, which may explain why babies are likely to recognize their mothers' voices soon after birth (L. S. Black et al., 2004; DeCasper & Fifer, 1980).

Infants can locate the direction of sounds. They readily learn the difference between similar consonant sounds, such as /d/ and /p/, and appear to remember simple speech sounds a day after hearing them (Gerken, 2002). Research suggests that these abilities to discriminate sounds and familiar voices from unfamiliar ones may also be present in fetuses (Draganova et al., 2007; Kisilevsky et al., 2003; Lecanuet, Manera, & Jacquet, 2002).

Babies prefer soft and rhythmic sounds, which explains why they enjoy lullabies so much. They prefer most to listen to voices, specifically *motherese* or baby talk, the drawn-out vowels, exaggerated syllables, and rhythmic, up-and-down inflection used by women across the world (Pool, 2005). Infants do not like loud noises, which may explain why some children become classically conditioned to fear thunderstorms (see Chapter 6).

THE OTHER SENSES

Taste, touch, and smell are other ways that infants gather meaning from their environment. Infants' taste buds are functional at birth, and infants prefer sweet tastes. Infants are also born with an acute sense of smell. As soon as 3 days after birth, breastfed infants can discriminate the smell of their own mother from that of an unfamiliar female (Cernoch & Porter, 1985; R. H. Porter, 1999).

Infants are also very responsive to touch. Touching and caressing infants stimulates their growth and can improve brain development and cognitive development (Diamond & Amso, 2008). In one study, two groups of premature infants were given the same neonatal care with one exception—half the infants were routinely massaged, and the other half were not. Those receiving the massages gained weight faster, developed faster neurologically, and were therefore able to leave the hospital sooner than those in the control group (Field et al., 1986). Today, it is standard practice to encourage parents of preterm babies to hold them often. Holding and touching infants also fosters their social development.

Infants' perceptual abilities allow them to gather much needed information from the environment—how their caretakers look, sound, and smell, where the food is, and what sounds contribute to language. From these beginnings, infants develop the abilities to know, think, and remember, a process called *cognition*. Perhaps no one has advanced our understanding of children's thinking more than Jean Piaget, whose ideas and research are presented next.

schema [SKEE-ma] a mental idea, concept, or thought

9.3.2 • Piaget's Theory of Cognitive Development

Swiss psychologist Jean Piaget (1896–1980) interviewed and observed infants and children, including his own, to discover and describe the changes in thinking that occur in childhood. Piaget gave children certain tasks to perform, observed their problem-solving strategies, and then asked them how they came to their conclusions.

From these observations and interviews, Piaget (1929, 1952) developed a theory about how children acquire their mental abilities. His theory traces the shifts in thinking from infants' reflexes to a teenager's reasoning abilities. He believed that cognition advances in a series of distinct stages, and that how a preschooler thinks differs dramatically from how an elementary school student thinks. Three concepts central to his theory are *schemas*, *assimilation*, and *accommodation*.

Bill Anderson/Science Source

Piaget observed children's problem-solving strategies to discover and describe the changes in thinking that they experience.

SCHEMAS, ASSIMILATION, AND ACCOMMODATION

To Piaget, any mental idea, concept, or thought is a **schema**. We form these schemas based on our experiences of the world. For example, a baby may have a sucking schema, "Is this object suckable?" or a mother schema, "Does this person fit with my cognitive framework of mother?" A preschooler may have the schema "The sun follows me wherever I go." Adults' schemas may be very simple—"A key will start a car"—or more complex, such as individual ideas of justice, morality, or love.

Piaget believed that our brains are biologically programmed to seek understanding of our world. So, we form schemas to fit with our perceptions of the world. When we achieve this fit, so that our cognitions correspond with the environment, we have *mental equilibrium*. For example, an infant may grab her pacifier, put it in her mouth, and suck it—an experience that confirms her schema that a pacifier is suckable. When there is not a fit between our schemas and the world, we experience *mental disequilibrium*, an uncomfortable state that we are motivated to get rid of so our mental harmony can be restored. For example, an infant may grab a fistful of sand at the beach, put it in his mouth, and determine it is not suckable; therefore, he will not suck on sand in the future. The processes of assimilation and accommodation explain how we use existing schema and create new ones to fit our experiences and, therefore, maintain mental equilibrium.

assimilation [uh-sim-uh-LAY-shun] the process by which an existing schema is used to understand something new in the environment

accommodation [uh-com-muh-DAY-shun] the process by which a schema is changed, modified, or created anew in order to understand something new in the environment

Assimilation is the process by which we apply an existing schema to our understanding of the environment. For example, a young child is traveling in a car with her parents. As they pass an open field, the child sees some cows. The only schema the child has for a four-legged animal is dog. So the child points and says, "Doggies!" The parents may correct the child—"No, those are called cows"—but she may persist in calling them "doggies" because that is her framework for understanding four-legged animals. The child has *assimilated* her experience of "cow" into her existing schema of "dog." However, many times our existing schema will not fit our new experiences. At times like these, the process of accommodation takes center stage.

Accommodation is the process we use to change or modify our existing schema—or even create new ones—to adapt to some change in the environment. For example, suppose the child in the previous example sees a dog and a cow side by side. The differences in the animals cannot be ignored and will create disequilibrium in the child's mental state. In this situation, she may come to call the new animal "cow." Her existing schema for four-legged animals has now been modified. The child will go through the same process when she sees a horse, a cat, or a hippopotamus.

PIAGET'S STAGES OF COGNITIVE DEVELOPMENT

According to Piaget, assimilation and accommodation create shifts in mental processing that allow the child to progress through four stages of cognition: *sensorimotor, preoperational, concrete operations,* and *formal operations* (1952; summarized in You Review: Piaget's Stages of Cognitive Development). Each stage has characteristics that permit the child to conceptualize the world in a unique fashion.

You Review **Piaget's Stages of Cognitive Development**

Sensorimotor (birth–2 yrs.)	Preoperational (2–6/7 yrs.)	Concrete Operations (6/7–11/12 yrs.)	Formal Operations (12 yrs.–adult)
Reflexes	Symbolic thinking	Conservation	Abstract reasoning
Object permanence	Illogical thinking	Logical thinking	
	Centration	Decentration	
	Egocentrism		

Bill Anderson/Science Source

Sensorimotor Stage During the first cognitive stage, the **sensorimotor stage**, from birth to 2 years, Piaget suggested that infants acquire knowledge through their senses and through their motor abilities—hence the name *sensorimotor.* For example, infants quickly recognize and prefer to look at their mothers' faces. Similarly, infants use their hearing to form schemas of what certain utterances mean, establishing the foundation for language. Taste, touch, and smell are also used to gather information and to form schemas as infants explore objects with their hands, mouths, and feet. We also saw that infant reflexes help establish schemas for later voluntary behaviors such as grasping, sitting, crawling, and walking.

Piaget believed that during this stage, infants can only form schemas of objects and actions that are in their immediate perception—in other words, what they currently see, hear, or touch. They learn by doing and by acting on objects. They lack the ability to represent an object when it is not present. For infants, it is truly "out of sight, out of mind," according to Piaget. The baby thinks of his pacifier when it is present by manipulating it with his mouth or hands. An infant can think about her "blankie" only when it is present. If these objects are not present, they no longer exist for the infant. However, as the infant grows and the brain matures, babies begin to have mental representations. One sign of this milestone is *object permanence.*

Object permanence is the understanding that an object continues to exist even when it is not present. We can see this in infants' behavior when they start to search for hidden objects. For example, Piaget would show a baby an interesting toy and then cover it. Before the age of 6 months, infants would not search for the toy, lacking the understanding that the toy still existed. It seemed as if the infant could not keep a mental representation of the object and its location in mind. However, by 8 months, infants will begin to search for the toy, suggesting the beginnings of object permanence. This ability steadily improves through 24 months, when infants will search long and hard for hidden objects, indicating that they have fully achieved object permanence.

Although Piaget accurately described the process of object permanence in infancy, he may have underestimated infants' abilities. Current research suggests that infants as young as 3–6 months old have a rudimentary understanding of object permanence and that they gradually develop stronger mental representations of objects through experience (Bremner, Bryant, & Mareschal, 2006; Kibbe & Leslie, 2011; Ruffman, Slade, & Redman, 2005; Shinskey & Munakata, 2005; Wang, Baillargeon, & Brueckner, 2004).

Once infants acquire object permanence, they are on their way to **symbolic thinking**. This is the understanding that an object can be represented with symbols such as gestures or language (Ganea et al., 2007). For example, a toddler may imitate the sound or walk of a monkey even when there is no monkey in sight. This ability to use symbols propels the child to the second stage of cognitive development: the preoperational stage.

Preoperational Stage During the **preoperational stage**, from about age 2 to age 6 or 7, preschoolers and young schoolchildren are actively acquiring and using symbols (DeLoache, 2001). Being able to use symbols opens up a new world to the preschooler. It is the foundation of a child's language development. A word symbolizes

sensorimotor stage Piaget's first stage of cognitive development, in which infants learn schemas through their senses and motor abilities

object permanence the understanding that an object continues to exist even when it is not present

symbolic thinking the understanding that objects can be represented with symbols such as bodily gestures or language

preoperational stage Piaget's second stage of cognitive development, characterized by the use of symbols and illogical thought

Pretend play indicates advancement in cognition as children acquire the ability to use symbols.

©istockphoto.com/Pamela Moore

Marmaduke St. John/Alamy

Marmaduke St. John/Alamy

Lacking the ability of conservation, young children are likely to believe that the amount of liquid has changed when it is poured into the taller, thinner glass. Centering on the height of the liquid, they believe the taller, thinner glass has more.

or stands for an object that may or may not be present. A child's vocabulary and understanding of language dramatically increase during these years. Recall from Chapter 8 that children progress from one-word utterances at 12–18 months to two-word sentences at 20–26 months, and that by age 6, the average child has a vocabulary of around 10,000 words. So, when a parent asks, "Do you want some juice?" the preoperational child knows what juice is and may even go to the refrigerator to get it. Young children's pretend play also demonstrates their use of symbols, such as using a stick to represent a sword or taking on family roles when they play "house." However, the child's new ability to symbolize objects is still illogical and does not always make sense to adults. For example, a child may believe that a switch turns on ocean waves, or that there are monsters hiding under the bed.

The illogical thinking of preschoolers is due to cognitive limitations that include *centration* and *egocentrism*. **Centration** occurs when the child focuses on only one feature or aspect of an object. For instance, a child who sees a man with long hair or an earring may conclude that the man is a woman. She focuses on one feature, the man's hair length, and this man's hair length fits with her schema for females. For preschoolers, if it looks like a duck, it is a duck; they have difficulty distinguishing between appearance and reality. Centration so dominates children's thinking at this stage that they do not realize that something can remain the same if its appearance changes, an ability called **conservation**.

In classic experiments, Piaget tested preschoolers and school-age children's conservation abilities (see photos). Children were shown two identical glasses containing the same amount of liquid. In front of the child, Piaget poured the liquid from one of these glasses into a taller, thinner glass. Children were then asked whether the glasses had equal amounts of liquid or whether one glass had more liquid than the other. Children in the preoperational stage were most likely to reply that the tall, thin glass had more because they were focused on the height of the liquid in the narrower glass. It looked as though it had more, so it must have more. For preschoolers at a party, then, adults should be aware that it must *look* as though the children all have the same amount of cake or punch. Otherwise the preschoolers will think they are receiving different amounts—which can create havoc!

An additional limitation to the preschooler's thinking is **egocentrism**, or the belief that everyone else thinks as you do. For example, when one of your authors was playing hide-and-seek with her then 3-year-old son, he hid in his room in the corner. His face was turned into the wall, much like a child who is sent to stand in a corner for misbehaving. On entering the room, your author said, "I see you." Her son replied, "No, you don't." From her son's perspective, he could not see his mother; therefore she could not see him. Preschoolers believe that others see things as they do, and therefore think as they do, a finding that has been repeatedly replicated using a range of different methods (Wellman, Cross, & Watson, 2001).

centration the act of focusing on only one aspect or feature of an object

conservation the understanding that an object retains its original properties even though it may look different

egocentrism [ee-go-SEN-trih-zum] the belief that everyone thinks as you do

Rose is Rose © reprinted by permission of United Feature Syndicate, Inc.

Although adults may find it frustrating, the illogical thinking of a preschooler lends an almost magical quality to their thought processes. For example, they believe in monsters, bad-dream catchers over their beds to prevent nightmares, the tooth fairy, imaginary friends, and fantasy. However, current research suggests that here, too, Piaget's ideas probably underestimate children's thinking abilities. Egocentrism, centration, and the inability to tell the difference between appearance and reality do not *always* characterize preschoolers' thoughts and may to some degree be a result of the testing method used (Deak 2006; Jenkins & Astington, 1996). Rather, these limitations are *sometimes* present in children's thinking and gradually fade as the child matures and develops more logical thought processes.

Concrete Operations Stage During Piaget's third cognitive stage, **concrete operations**, from about age 6 or 7 through age 11 or 12, schoolchildren become logical thinkers. They no longer center on one feature or facet of an object as the preschooler did, and their conservation abilities improve (●TABLE 9.2). By age 11 or 12,

concrete operations Piaget's third stage of cognitive development, characterized by logical thought

TABLE 9.2

Piaget's Conservation Experiments

Mastery of conservation tasks begins gradually during the concrete operations stage. Children typically master conservation of number by age 6 or 7. Conservation of area may not be grasped until age 8 or 9.

Typical tasks used to measure conservation		Typical age of mastery
	Conservation of number Two equivalent rows of objects are shown to the child, who agrees that they have the same number of objects.	6–7
	One row is lengthened, and the child is asked whether one row has more objects.	
	Conservation of mass The child acknowledges that two clay balls have equal amounts of clay.	7–8
	The experimenter changes the shape of one of the balls and asks the child whether they still contain equal amounts of clay.	
	Conservation of length The child agrees that two sticks aligned with each other are the same length.	7–8
	After moving one of the sticks to the left or right, the experimenter asks the child whether the sticks are of equal length.	
	Conservation of area Two identical sheets of cardboard have wooden blocks placed on them in identical positions; the child confirms that the same amount of space is left on each piece of cardboard.	8–9
	The experimenter scatters the blocks on one piece of cardboard and again asks the child whether the two pieces of cardboard have the same amount of unoccupied space.	

children realize that although the tall, thin glass looks as though it has more liquid, in reality the glasses have equivalent volume. Changes in these abilities force the child to recognize that previous beliefs may be mistaken, so accommodation occurs. It also brings about a reduction in egocentrism as the child can now consider the perspectives of others. This enables empathy, persuasion, and a sense of humor to grow.

Although the concrete operational child thinks more logically, these schemas are limited to actual experience or concrete objects and situations. School-age children have difficulty reasoning abstractly about what may be or what could be without being able to test their ideas in an observable way. This is why hands-on activities and class demonstrations of abstract ideas for school subjects such as math and science are necessary in elementary and middle school. Notice that Hongyong preferred the household lessons as they were "something I could touch, see, and use freely." When told to protect her "private parts," Hongyong thought her mother meant her knees because she was constantly being told to keep her knees covered. Being able to think about situations that are not present occurs in the final stage of Piaget's theory, *formal operations*.

formal operations Piaget's final stage of cognitive development, characterized by the ability to engage in abstract thought

private speech Vygotsky's term describing the behavior of young children who talk to themselves to guide their own actions

Formal Operations Stage According to Piaget, as children approach their teenage years, they may achieve the final cognitive stage, **formal operations**. They are no longer limited to concrete objects and situations; they can now engage in abstract reasoning. Teenagers can imagine and hypothesize what *could* be. This ability expands their horizons. They are able to understand more abstract, scientific, and mathematical concepts. They can imagine potential careers and envision future consequences for current behavior.

PIAGET'S INFLUENCE ON COGNITIVE DEVELOPMENT RESEARCH

Piaget's theory revolutionized our understanding of children's thinking abilities and stimulated much research in cognition. The changes in thinking that Piaget proposed do not always proceed according to the precise stages and timetable he originally suggested (Haith & Benson, 1998). Children's mental abilities develop at different ages. Nurture, culture, or experience can facilitate growth and change in these abilities. However, Piaget very accurately described the *sequence* in which these changes occur, even in diverse societies (Dasen, 1994; Lourenco & Machado, 1996). One final criticism of Piaget's theory is that it overlooks the important effects of culture on cognitive development. The ideas of Lev Vygotsky explore this connection between culture and cognition.

9.3.3 • Vygotsky's Theory of Cognitive Development: Culture and Thinking

Lev Vygotsky (1896–1934) was a Russian psychologist whose ideas have influenced how psychologists and educators think about children's cognitive development, and have provided an alternative to Piaget's theory (John-Steiner & Mahn, 1996). In contrast to Piaget's emphasis on the internal origin of schemas, Vygotsky (1978, 1986) emphasized that mental processes begin externally with our social interactions with others. For example, babies smile at caretakers or toddlers raise their arms to signal that they want to be picked up. A child internalizes these mental processes to create a cognitive framework for understanding the world.

Young children often talk to themselves as they play, a behavior Vygotsky called **private speech**. For Vygotsky, private speech represents an internal monitor that guides the child's actions. Private speech, or self-talk, as it is sometimes called, is common among preschoolers and peaks around 5–7 years of age. Around 9 years of age, these spoken words are internalized as silent lip movements. Eventually, children just think the thoughts rather than saying them. However, private speech can return at any age when we are confused or having difficulties in problem solving or learning new skills. Such inner speech guides our thinking and can help regulate our behavior. *Self-talk* strategies that support Vygotsky's ideas on private speech have been developed to help deaf children use sign language, help students with emotional and behavioral disorders, and to enhance sports performance (Berk & Spuhl, 1995; Hatzigeorgiadis et al., 2011; Kelman, 2001). It makes sense, therefore, to allow and even encourage children and adults to use self-talk when problem solving or learning new skills.

According to Vygotsky, because cognition is so intimately tied to our social interactions, culture has a profound influence on our mental processing. The language, measurement systems, rituals, beliefs, and technology of a culture both limit and support certain ways of thinking (Tomasello, 2000). For instance, if your language does not have a word to capture an idea or expression, it is difficult to imagine or understand that concept. Similarly, children who have the opportunity to read books, use the Internet, travel, and attend cultural events will be more capable of conceptualizing ideas than will children without such tools. According to Vygotsky, cognitive development does not occur in fixed stages as Piaget theorized. Rather, cognitive development may proceed in any number of directions, depending on our culture, social interactions with others, and the environment we live in.

Representing concepts is not achieved simply by having these tools. Conceptual thinking is taught to children by parents, teachers, siblings, coaches, and other important people in their lives. This instruction is most helpful when it is within a child's **zone of proximal development (ZPD)**—the gap between what a child can already do and what he or she is not yet capable of doing without help. Through collaborative interaction, the adult initially guides and supports the child's efforts to master a task. The less able a child is to do a task, the more direction and guidance an adult must give. The adult then gradually minimizes the guidance and support until the child can do the task alone, in a process called **scaffolding**. For example, when teaching a child how to dress, an adult first supports the child by holding the shirt out as the child puts her arms into the sleeves and then buttons the shirt for the child. When the child seems ready, less support is given until the child is putting the shirt on by herself and buttoning it on her own. It is through these interactions with others that children internalize strategies, reasoning skills, and problem-solving abilities. For this reason, Vygotsky believed that a child's cognitive development benefits most from interactions with people who are more capable or advanced in their thinking than the child.

zone of proximal development (ZPD) according to Vygotsky, the gap between what a child is already able to do and what he or she is not yet capable of doing without help

scaffolding [SKAH-fol-ding] a process in which adults initially offer guidance and support in helping a child to reason, solve a problem, or master a task; as the child becomes more proficient and capable, the adult helps less and less until the child can master the task on his or her own

Mike Theiss/National Geographic Image Collection/Alamy

Vygotsky emphasized the importance of culture and social interactions in his theory of cognitive development.

9.3.4 • Moral Reasoning: How We Think About Right and Wrong

Consider the following situation: An automatic teller machine (ATM) dispenses $10,000 to you, and there is no way that this error would ever be discovered. You keep the money, but you donate half of it to the soup kitchen in your town. Should you have kept the money? How did you decide what to do? Your answer to this situation would provide clues to psychologists about your level of **moral reasoning**, or how you distinguish right from wrong. Two well-known theories on moral development are Lawrence Kohlberg's *stages of moral reasoning* and Carol Gilligan's *ethic of care*.

moral reasoning how you decide what is right and what is wrong

KOHLBERG'S THEORY OF MORAL DEVELOPMENT

Lawrence Kohlberg (1927–1987) developed moral dilemmas or situations like the one we posed to you, and then asked participants to describe what the main character should do and why. After analyzing data from thousands of participants, Kohlberg created a theory of how people morally reason and the changes in this reasoning that occur as they develop (Kohlberg, 1969; Kohlberg, Levine, & Hewer, 1983). He proposed that our moral reasoning develops in six stages, which he arranged in three levels: preconventional, conventional, and postconventional (● TABLE 9.3).

TABLE 9.3

Kohlberg's Stages of Moral Reasoning

PRECONVENTIONAL LEVEL (MOST CHILDREN)
Stage 1: Obedience and Punishment Orientation. Children obey rules to avoid punishment. "Taking a cookie without asking is wrong because you get a timeout."
Stage 2: Naively Egoistic Orientation. Children view morally right action as that which increases their personal rewards and meets their needs. "You scratch my back, and I'll scratch yours."
CONVENTIONAL LEVEL (MOST ADOLESCENTS AND ADULTS)
Stage 3: Good Boy/Good Girl Orientation. Moral rightness is based on maintaining the approval and/or avoiding the disapproval of others such as family and friends. "I will return the rest of the money so my parents won't be disappointed in me."
Stage 4: Law and Order Orientation. Moral rightness is based on following the rules or laws of the society. Exceptions to the rules are not allowed. "Stealing is wrong because it is against the law."
POSTCONVENTIONAL LEVEL (SOME BUT NOT ALL ADULTS)
Stage 5: Contractual/Legalistic Orientation. Exceptions to rules can now be considered, as the protection of individual rights is emphasized over societal laws. "I confessed to the crime, but I was not told I had a right to remain silent, so the confession is not valid."
Stage 6: Universal Principles Orientation. Individuals develop their own set of universal principles that guide their judgments of right and wrong across all situations and all societies. "All people, regardless of skin color, should have access to education."

At the *preconventional level* of reasoning, children make decisions about right or wrong based on their ability to avoid punishment or to gain rewards. For example, it is wrong to take the money because you may get caught and then punished. It is right to take the money because you can use it and no one will find out about it. Recall that at this age, children are egocentric and have difficulty understanding the nature of rules. Consequently, children are centered on the immediate consequences of their actions.

With the ability to think logically and to understand another person's perspective, children at the *conventional level* of reasoning can now understand rules and expectations that others may have for them. Therefore, their moral reasoning is based on the standards of the group or society. They believe behaviors are right or wrong because they gain the approval or avoid the disapproval of parents, teachers, or peers. You may not take the money because you are afraid your parents would find out and be disappointed in you, or you may take the money to gain acceptance from your friends. At this level, children can appreciate society's rules or laws for moral behavior. However, because they lack the ability to reason abstractly, children apply these laws to every situation and every person very rigidly. Exceptions based on circumstances are not considered.

At the *postconventional level* of moral reasoning, people base their judgments of right or wrong on contractual or universal principles of morality. The person can appreciate extenuating circumstances and realizes that external standards handed down from society cannot always be applied to all the situations in the same manner. The person develops internal standards of right and wrong to guide moral behavior. These abstract principles may include the "Golden Rule" (Do unto others as you would have them do unto you) or values such as respecting the dignity of all persons regardless of race, creed, or culture. You may not take the money because you did not earn it and you may be financially hurting someone else.

Kohlberg's theory has stimulated much research—as well as much criticism and controversy (Narvaez, 2010). Kohlberg-like studies in 27 cultures support his stage sequence of moral reasoning. People typically move through these stages in the way that Kohlberg proposed (Damon, 1999; Helwig, 1997; Walker & Taylor, 1991). By adulthood, most people have progressed to conventional moral reasoning, but few people move on to postconventional reasoning, especially the highest stage. Postconventional reasoning emphasizes the individual rights that each person in a society should be afforded. Such reasoning may apply more to people from Western cultures. In other parts of the world, moral systems tend to emphasize the well-being of the group in regulating values (Haidt, 2008; Snarey, 1995). Research on infants also posits that humans have a built-in or innate moral sense that evolved to facilitate cooperative living (Hamlin, 2013). Another perspective from which Kohlberg's theory has been criticized is that of gender, a controversy initiated by one of his students, Carol Gilligan.

Carol Gilligan's classic work *In a Different Voice* challenged Kohlberg's theory of moral reasoning.

Paul Hawthorne/Getty Images Entertainment/Getty Images

GILLIGAN'S THEORY: GENDER AND MORAL REASONING

Carol Gilligan (b. 1936) hypothesized that males and females do not judge right and wrong in the same manner. She believed that Kohlberg's model emphasized the male perspective on moral reasoning more than the female view. In her book *A Different Voice* (1982), Gilligan speculated that males and females focus on different principles for deciding what is right and wrong. Males tend to be more focused on concepts of fairness and justice. Females are more likely to emphasize concern, care, and relations with others in making judgments about right and wrong. Gilligan asserts that women's focus on caring is a different, but not a less valid, basis for moral reasoning.

Research evaluating gender differences in moral reasoning has not strongly supported Gilligan's claims. On hypothetical dilemmas, *both* males and females emphasize themes of justice and caring in their responses (Jadack et al., 1995; Jaffee & Hyde, 2000; Walker, 1995). Thus, moral reasoning may be based on justice or caring independent of gender (Jorgensen, 2006).

Quiz Yourself 9.3

1. Which of the following statements about infants' sensory abilities is *false*?
   a. Infants prefer looking at complex, high-contrast stimuli.
   b. Infants have functioning taste buds at birth.
   c. Infants prefer to listen to voices.
   d. Infants perceive depth at birth.
2. Simone sees a military tank on the highway and calls it a "truck." According to Piaget, which process is Simone engaged in?
   a. disequilibrium
   b. private speech
   c. assimilation
   d. accommodation
3. Pedro has four nickels in his pocket. His sister has a dollar. Pedro thinks he has more than his sister because it looks like and feels like more. Pedro is *most* likely in Piaget's _____ stage of development.
   a. sensorimotor
   b. preoperational
   c. concrete operations
   d. formal operations
4. Zahara can pull her pants on but has not yet mastered how to button them. Zahara's behavior best exemplifies which developmental concept?
   a. Private speech
   b. Zone of proximal development
   c. Egocentrism
   d. Scaffolding
5. Kayla, a 4-year-old, shares her toys with June so that June will also share her toys. At what level of Kohlberg's theory is she operating?
   a. Preconventional
   b. Preoperational
   c. Conventional
   d. Postconventional

Answers 1. d; 2. c; 3. b; 4. b; 5. a

9.4 Psychosocial Development in Infancy and Childhood

A close connection between nature and nurture also influences a child's social and personality development. Children come into the world with a biological tendency to behave in a certain way. How parents and others respond to these behaviors can influence the child's personality as well as the relationships the child develops with others. We explore these issues as we look at the topics of *temperament, attachment, parenting styles,* Erik Erikson's theory of *psychosocial development,* and *gender-role development.*

9.4.1 • Temperament: The Influence of Biology

Babies come into the world showing a general disposition to behave in certain ways in response to their surroundings. These differences are believed to be due more to the child's biological makeup than to his or her environment, especially because the child has not yet been exposed to any environment other than the womb. These differences at birth in behavioral style are referred to as **temperament**. In pioneering research, Stella Chess and Alexander Thomas (Chess & Thomas, 1984; Thomas & Chess, 1977, 1986) gathered information on numerous infant behaviors such as these:

- General activity level
- General mood
- Ability to establish a regular pattern of eating and sleeping
- Likelihood of approaching or withdrawing from new people and new situations
- Ability to adapt to changes from their normal routine

From observing babies' behaviors on these variables, these researchers described three temperamental styles: easy infants, difficult infants, and slow-to-warm-up infants.

As the label implies, *easy infants* are generally in a good mood, establish a regular pattern of eating and sleeping, readily approach new objects and people, and adapt readily to changes in their routines. *Difficult infants,* in contrast, show more intense negative emotions such as crying. They have a more irregular pattern of eating and sleeping and are not as likely to approach new people and situations. Parents may even call such babies "colicky." *Slow-to-warm-up infants* are in between these two extremes. They are not as negative in response as difficult infants, but it takes them some time to adapt to new situations.

A child's temperament and the parents' responses to this temperament influence the parent–child bond called *attachment.*

temperament a person's general pattern of attention, arousal, and mood that is evident at birth

attachment the emotional bond between caretaker and infant that is established by 8 or 9 months

9.4.2 • Attachment: Learning About Relationships

Attachment, the emotional tie between the infant and the primary caretaker, is usually firmly established by 8–9 months. Initially, psychologists believed that feeding provided the basis for building the attachment relationship: the baby feels connected to the primary caretaker because the parent satisfies the infant's hunger. However, animal research by Harry Harlow (1905–1981) in the 1950s changed the way we view the attachment process today.

THE ORIGINS OF ATTACHMENT

In a classic study, Harlow and Zimmerman (1959) wanted to investigate the nature of attachment. They used infant rhesus monkeys as subjects because ethical principles would prohibit such a study with human infants. They designed two artificial monkeys to act as surrogate mothers for the babies. One of the "surrogate mothers" was covered with a soft terry cloth fabric. The other "surrogate mother" was made of wire and had a feeding tube attached. The researchers wanted to see which "surrogate mother" the infants preferred. The data showed that while the infant monkeys went to the wire "surrogate mother" for food, they clung to and spent most of their time with the cloth-covered "surrogate mother." This showed that feeding was not the reason the monkeys attached; rather, it was the close, warm contact that facilitated this bond. Establishing close, warm contact through holding and caressing facilitates attachment. Human infants can thus easily attach to multiple people and objects, including fathers, grandparents, siblings, and teddy bears.

Courtesy of Harlow Primate Lab, University of Wisconsin-Madison

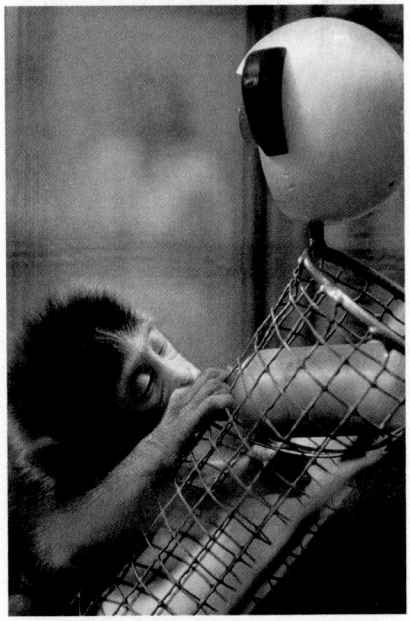

Courtesy of Harlow Primate Lab, University of Wisconsin-Madison

Harlow's studies showed that while the infant monkeys went to the wire "surrogate mother" for food, they clung to and spent most of their time with the cloth-covered "surrogate mother."

The attachment bond is readily seen in specific infant behaviors by the end of the first year. For example, most babies reserve certain behaviors for their parents. Infants smile when a parent approaches them, raise their hands toward the parent to be picked up, and nestle closer when the parent holds them. Two additional signs of attachment include *separation anxiety* and *stranger anxiety*. **Separation anxiety** is a fear the infant expresses when separated from the primary caretaker. This distress normally appears at about 6 or 7 months of age, and peaks at about 14–18 months. Separation anxiety gradually becomes less frequent and less intense throughout the toddler and preschool years. However, it is not uncommon for even older children to become anxious or homesick when separated from their parents for a long period (Thurber, 1995).

separation anxiety the fear an infant expresses when separated from the primary caretaker

stranger anxiety the distress an infant expresses when faced with unfamiliar people

In **stranger anxiety**, the infant becomes distressed when approached by unfamiliar people. Stranger anxiety typically appears between 8 and 10 months of age. It may intensify through the end of the first year, but usually subsides over the second year. Therefore, it is not unusual for a 1- or 2-year-old to cry or cling to a parent when approached by a doctor, an unfamiliar relative, or a new babysitter.

VARIATIONS IN ATTACHMENT PATTERNS

Although most infants establish an attachment with a caregiver by the end of the first year, the quality of these attachments is not necessarily the same from infant to infant. Mary Ainsworth (1913–1999) and her colleagues (Ainsworth et al., 1978) designed a research technique called the *strange situation* procedure to try to measure qualitative differences in infant attachments. In the strange situation, infants and their parents are placed in an unfamiliar playroom. The infant's behavior is observed and measured as certain events occur. For example, does the infant explore the new situation and the toys when left in the playroom with the parent? How does the infant behave when a stranger enters the room? What is the baby's response when the parent leaves the room? What is the infant's reaction when the parent returns?

Observations of infants under these circumstances uncovered several patterns, or styles of attachment. Ainsworth and others (Ainsworth et al., 1978; Hesse & Main, 2006; Main & Solomon, 1990) described four patterns of attachment: secure, avoidant, resistant, and disorganized/disoriented.

- *Secure attachment.* Infants who are securely attached use the parent as a supportive base from which to operate and explore. They explore the toys while in the new situation, paying attention to any new strangers who may enter the room. They may or may not cry when the parent leaves, but this emotional upset quickly subsides once the parent returns.
- *Avoidant attachment.* Infants who show avoidant attachment appear to ignore the parent. They pay the parent little attention. They do not appear to be distressed when the parent leaves, and they show little emotional response when the parent reappears.
- *Resistant attachment.* Infants who display resistant attachment resemble a "clinging" baby. They remain close to the parent and do not actively explore the new situation. They show extreme distress when the parent leaves and appear to be angry when the parent returns. They may hit and push at the parent and are less easily consoled.
- *Disorganized/disoriented attachment.* Infants showing disorganized attachment seem confused or disoriented. They look away from the

parent while being comforted and have a blank facial expression after being calmed by her.

Although most children worldwide appear to have secure attachments to their caretakers, we must be cautious in interpreting the "insecure" patterns of attachment. Different child-rearing practices and cultural attitudes influence how we interact with our children, and these interactions as well as the larger social context appear to influence attachment. In some countries, children's independence is encouraged; in other countries, a closeness with the caretaker is emphasized. However, these same styles of attachment have generally emerged across cultures, suggesting that these styles of attachment are common worldwide (van Ijzendoom & Sagi-Schwartz, 2008).

Many psychologists endorse the notion that the quality of this first attachment relationship lays the foundation for the quality of all other relationships with friends and romantic partners. Research supports this reasoning to a certain degree. Securely attached infants are more likely to become curious, resilient, and self-controlled preschoolers. Such children are more likely to persist in problem-solving tasks, do well in school, interact more skillfully with their peers during the school years, and recover from conflict better in romantic relationships in young adulthood (Kerns et al., 2007; Orina et al., 2011; Salvatore et al., 2011; Simpson, Collins, & Salvatore, 2011; Simpson et al., 2007).

However, being securely attached at an early age does not guarantee an absence of problems later. Moreover, research has not been able to consistently document a negative or unfavorable picture of development for the other attachment patterns. Some studies suggest that insecurely attached infants are more prone to behavioral and adjustment problems in their social relations with others, whereas other studies do not (C. E. Hamilton, 2000; Hill-Soderlund & Braungart-Rieker, 2008; Rothbaum et al., 1995). Bonds with individuals other than the caretaker can compensate for insecure attachments at home. Moreover, given the number of variables that can influence attachment, an early pattern of insecure attachment does not guarantee a lifelong pattern of insecure relationships. As family circumstances improve, so too may the quality of the attachment. Similarly, social relationships *after* infancy must also be considered when we evaluate children's psychological adjustment.

9.4.3 • Variations in Parenting Styles

Parents' responses to their infants and children also influence the parent–child relationship. Diana Baumrind (b. 1927) (1967, 1971) investigated these responses by observing parents' interactions with their children. From her observations, three styles of parenting emerged.

Authoritarian parents tend to exhibit a high level of control and a low level of affection toward their children. They set high expectations for their children but without communicating the reasons behind their expectations. "It's my way or the highway" would be a characteristic attitude of authoritarian parents. The children are not included in discussions of family issues, rules, or roles. They are to do what they are told. If they do not obey, force and physical punishment are used to ensure compliance. Baumrind found that children from authoritarian households tended to be more withdrawn, anxious, and conforming than other children.

Authoritative parents tend to exhibit moderate control and are warm toward their children. Authoritative parents are least likely to spank or hit their children. Rules—and the consequences for violating them—are established in a democratic

authoritarian [ah-thor-uh-TARE-ee-an] parent a parenting style characterized by high levels of control and low levels of affection

authoritative [ah-thor-uh-TAY-tive] parent a parenting style characterized by moderate levels of control and affection

Simon Marcus/Corbis

Parents who are warm and moderate in discipline are more likely to have competent and happy children.

manner, and children are included in family discussions. Reasonable expectations and demands are made of the children, and the children respond accordingly. Baumrind found that parents who use this style of parenting tended to have competent, happy, and self-confident children. It appears to be the most effective approach to parenting. Although Baumrind's sample was predominantly restricted to European Americans, these benefits of authoritative parenting have also been found to apply to several U.S. ethnic groups, including African Americans, Korean Americans, Chinese Americans, and Hispanic Americans (Abar, Carter, & Winsler, 2009; Cheah et al., 2009; H. Kim & Chung, 2003; Querido, Warner, & Eyberg, 2002; Steinberg et al., 1992).

Permissive parents have very little control over their children. Discipline is lax. Children make their own decisions even when they may not be capable of doing so. Very few demands are made of the children in terms of rules or chores. Permissive parenting includes two distinct types: indulgent and neglectful. *Permissive-indulgent* parents are very warm, affectionate, and involved with their children but still make few demands on their children, hence the name "indulgent". *Permissive-neglectful* parents make few demands and show little affection or warmth toward their children; they are uninvolved with parenting and neglect the emotional needs of their children. Children of permissive-indulgent parents tend to be impulsive, disobedient, yet emotionally secure, whereas children of permissive-neglectful parents tend to have the poorest outcomes in terms of social skills, self-esteem, and academic achievement.

permissive parent a parenting style characterized by low levels of control or discipline

Do parents always *cause* children to act a certain way? Perhaps not. Recall that these are correlations, and causal connections cannot be made from correlational data. A parent–child relationship is not a one-way street. Children's temperaments influence the way parents treat them just as much as a parent's responsiveness influences the development of a child (Raby et al., 2012). Moreover, other variables such as the quality of the parents' relationship or the level of family functioning can influence how parents and children interact (Caldera & Lindsey, 2006; Schoppe-Sullivan et al., 2007). How a child develops socially and emotionally will depend in part on the *goodness of fit* between the child's temperament and his or her surrounding social relationships, including those with parents (Bradley & Corwyn, 2008; Chess & Thomas, 1984; Reiss, 2005; Roisman & Fraley, 2006; Stright, Gallagher, & Kelley, 2008).

Ted Streshinsky/Historical/Corbis

For Erikson, the child-rearing practices of a culture fulfill basic psychological and emotional needs to influence healthy personality development.

9.4.4 • Erikson's Stages of Psychosocial Development: The Influence of Culture

After studying child-rearing practices in several cultures, Erik Erikson (1902–1994) believed that children and adults progress through eight stages, or *developmental crises* (Erikson, 1963, 1968, 1980). At each stage, the environment and the person's responses to the environment influence the development of either a healthy or an unhealthy personality characteristic. At each stage, the person incorporates a new quality into his or her personality. Resolving earlier stages with healthy outcomes makes it easier to resolve later stages with positive outcomes. An unhealthy resolution of a stage can have potential negative effects throughout life, although damage can sometimes be repaired at later stages. Four of Erikson's eight stages pertain to the childhood years and are discussed here. The other four stages focus on the adolescent and adult years and are discussed later in the chapter. You Review: Erikson's Stages of Psychosocial Development summarizes all eight stages.

You Review **Erikson's Stages of Psychosocial Development**

Age	Stage	Developmental Challenge
Birth–1 year	Trust versus mistrust	Sense of security
1–3 years	Autonomy versus shame and doubt	Independence
3–6 years	Initiative versus guilt	Trying new things
6–12 years	Industry versus inferiority	Sense of mastery and competence
Adolescence	Identity versus role confusion	Sense of self, personal values, and beliefs
Young adulthood	Intimacy versus isolation	Committing to a mutually loving relationship
Middle adulthood	Generativity versus stagnation	Contributing to society through one's work, family, or community services
Late adulthood	Ego integrity versus despair	Viewing one's life as satisfactory and worthwhile

Ted Streshinsky/Historical Pics

1. *Trust versus mistrust.* This stage occurs during the first year of life, when infants are totally dependent on others in their environment to meet their needs. An infant whose needs are met is more likely to develop trust in others than one whose needs are not met. Developing a sense of trust also fosters the development of a secure attachment.
2. *Autonomy versus shame and doubt.* From 1 to 3 years of age, toddlers struggle with separating from their primary caretaker. They must negotiate an appropriate balance between autonomy, or independence, and dependence. If people in the toddler's environment belittle the child's efforts at independence or encourage dependence by being overly protective, then Erikson believed the child will be more likely to develop shame and doubt.
3. *Initiative versus guilt.* Erikson believed that during the preschool years (ages 3–6), children's environments encourage the development of either initiative or guilt. When children develop initiative, they are motivated to take the first step, to start something on their own, and to be ambitious. Preschoolers are actively exploring their environments through trial and error. At the same time, they start to understand that others have expectations for their behavior, and they learn to read people's reactions to their explorations. From these explorations and observations, they begin to develop schemas of what they "ought to do." If these schemas conflict with what others in their environment expect from them, guilt may develop. Hongyong's curious nature encouraged a sense of initiative. Yet this initiative at a later age was discouraged because it violated cultural expectations of how a female should behave.
4. *Industry versus inferiority.* During the elementary school years (ages 6–12), children receive a great deal of feedback on their performance. They are in school usually 6 hours a day, where they receive a steady stream of information on their abilities. Their papers may have stars, red marks, or numbers on them. Children may be grouped according to ability. Because children this

age can think logically, they can compare their performance on a task with that of their peers. In this way, they form opinions about which activities make them feel industrious, masterful, or competent, as well as ideas about activities or tasks that make them feel inferior or less capable of performing.

According to Erikson, by the time children approach adolescence, their personality has been shaped by the resolution of each of these developmental challenges. How the child resolves these issues has encouraged the development of either a healthy or a not so healthy personality.

Young children lack gender permanence, the knowledge that our assigned gender does not change. Playing dress-up allows them to explore the gender roles of the other sex.

9.4.5 • Gender-Role Development

By 2 or 3 years old, children know whether they are a boy or a girl and can label the gender of others. These labels then provide a framework for understanding what clothes, toys, colors, jobs, and behaviors are "appropriate" for each sex. Thus, children at a very early age are processing and developing schemas about **gender roles**, or society's expectations for how a female and a male should behave (Leaper & Friedman, 2007).

Gender permanence or *gender constancy* is the knowledge that our assigned gender will not change. Typically, children under the age of 6 years do not yet understand that their gender is permanent (De Lisi & Gallagher, 1991; Szkrybalo & Ruble, 1999). Although young children lack gender permanence, they are especially rigid in gender stereotyping even across ethnic groups (Bussey & Bandura, 1999; Halim et al., 2013). Recall that at this age children focus on only one aspect of a situation or an object. If one of your features or behaviors looks like that of a male, then you are a male. If the feature fits with the child's concept of a female, then you are a female. Consequently, if a little boy puts on his mother's dress, he may believe that he is now a girl.

BEM'S GENDER-SCHEMA THEORY: INTEGRATING LEARNING AND COGNITION

The process by which a child develops gender roles and comes to label specific behaviors and activities as either masculine or feminine is not completely understood. Psychologists currently endorse Sandra Bem's (1944–2014) **gender-schema theory**, a perspective that combines elements of social learning theory and cognitive development. Gender-schema theory suggests that the learning processes of modeling and reinforcement work together with a child's developing mental abilities to facilitate the child's understanding of gender (Bem, 1981; Crane & Markus, 1982; Markus et al., 1982; Martin & Halverson, 1981, 1987).

From a very early age, children are keen observers of their environment. They see which behaviors men and women engage in, and which of those behaviors are reinforced or punished. With these observations, children actively construct schemas on gender behaviors. These schemas then guide children's decisions about how they and others should behave (Martin & Ruble, 2004).

The schemas for gender-role behavior are culturally defined and vary from society to society. In many cultures, traditional gender roles are emphasized for children (Shiraev & Levy, 2010). Males are seen as aggressive,

gender roles society's expectations for how males and females should behave

gender permanence the understanding that one's gender will not change

gender-schema theory the idea that gender roles are acquired through modeling and reinforcement processes that work together with a child's mental abilities unemotional, and dominant, whereas females are seen as passive and emotional. These traditional gender roles were evident in Hongyong's culture. Yet within U.S. society, one's ethnic background may convey different gender stereotypes (Markus, 2013). For example, traditional Hispanic American gender roles stress the faithful, self-giving female who is subordinate to her husband and is seen as the preserver of family and tradition. The male is strong, dominant, and the head of the household who is responsible for the safety and honor of the family (McNeill et al., 2001; Reid & Bing, 2000). Among African Americans, females often assume the dominant role in the family. Females are independent, emotionally strong, and obliged to help others (Woods-Giscombé, 2010). Strong extended family bonds and high levels of adaptability in gender roles are emphasized (Reid & Bing, 2000). Asian Americans tend to value group solidarity. Often, for females, family obligations are expected to be of higher priority than individual achievement, and males are seen as dominant (Pyke & Johnson, 2003).

NATURE AND NURTURE INFLUENCES ON GENDER-ROLE BEHAVIOR

Psychologists have explored the extent to which gender-role behavior is due to nature and nurture. For example, research suggests that many gender differences appear across cultures and in other species, such as the preference to develop same-sex friendships, the higher level of activity and physical aggression in males, and gender-specific toy preferences (Beatty, 1992; Hassett, Siebert, & Wallen, 2008; Martin & Ruble, 2010). For example, Hassett et al. (2008) found that male rhesus monkeys showed consistent preference for wheeled toys, whereas female rhesus monkeys tended to show a broader range of toy preferences. These findings suggest that gender differences may in part be influenced by genetic or hormonal differences, particularly during prenatal development. Females prenatally exposed to high levels of male hormones show increased male-typical play and aggression (Auyeung et al., 2009; Drea, 2009). At the same time, a child's environment is filled with messages about gender. These messages come from parents, teachers, peers, and the larger society and suggest the powerful impact of nurture on gender behavior (Bussey & Bandura, 1999).

Parents are the first source of information for babies on gender. In many ways, sons and daughters are treated similarly. Mothers and fathers encourage both sons and daughters to be independent. Parents are equally warm to their children regardless of gender. Both mothers and fathers have high educational aspirations for their children and value achievement in both their sons and daughters (Paulson & Sputa, 1996; Spera, Wentzel, & Matto, 2009). Yet daughters experience more parental involvement with their education than do sons, and girls perceive their parents as more encouraging of higher education than do boys (Carter & Wojtkiewicz, 2000; Reynolds & Burge, 2008). However, in the area of science achievement (a traditionally male-stereotyped activity), parents were more likely to believe that science was less interesting and more difficult for their daughters, even when there were no differences in the children's interest or science grades (Tenenbaum & Leaper, 2003).

In addition, most parents expect their children to play with gender-appropriate toys. Boys play with guns, cars, blocks, and balls. Girls are expected to play with dolls and tea sets and to enjoy activities such as playing dress-up, house, and school. Parents often assign different household chores to their

Paul Bradbury/Getty Images

Fuse/Getty Images

Parents' interactions with their children influence their developing schemas of gender roles.

sons and daughters. Girls wash the dishes and do chores inside the house such as vacuuming and dusting. Boys take out the trash and do outdoor chores such as mowing the lawn, washing cars, and cleaning out the garage. Fathers are much more likely to hold to these gender stereotypes and tend to be less accepting of cross-gender behaviors, especially in their sons (Lytton & Romney, 1991; O'Bryan, Fishbein, & Ritchey, 2004).

Parents who are less likely to hold these gender expectations tend to have children who are less gender-typed (Warner & Steel, 1999; Witt, 1997). Moreover, children who *see* their parents behave in a less stereotypical fashion—moms taking out the trash or dads performing household tasks—also tend to be less gender-typed (Hupp et al., 2010; Turner & Gervai, 1995). Parents, however, are not the only ones who influence children's gender roles. Once children begin school, teachers and peers influence gender schemas as well.

Research suggests that *gender bias* exists in many classrooms (Stromquist, 2007). Gender bias is the favoring of one gender over the other because of different views of male and female roles. Boys tend to receive both more positive and more negative attention from teachers, and are called on more often (Einarsson & Granstrom, 2004; Jones & Dindia, 2004; Swinson & Harrop, 2009). Teachers are also more likely to accept wrong answers from girls, encourage boys to try harder when they make errors, and see boys as more clever (Horgan, 1995; Skelton, 2006). Teachers also tend to stereotype mathematics as a male domain even when boys and girls performed similarly (Keller, 2001; Tiedemann, 2002). When it comes to career counseling, boys are more likely to be encouraged to pursue careers in math and science, such as engineering, whereas girls are encouraged to pursue education, nursing, and social work (Halpern et al., 2007; Sadker, 2000).

Children's notions about gender are also reinforced within their peer groups, starting as early as age 3. Same-sex peers praise the child for engaging in gender-appropriate behaviors. Children who engage in gender-inappropriate behavior may be teased, laughed at, and even isolated from the group. Boys are particularly critical of same-sex peers who engage in "girlish" behavior, resulting in harsher punishment for their activities (G. D. Levy, Taylor, & Gelman, 1995; A. J. Rose & Smith, 2009).

Society in general also contributes to children's gender stereotypes. Fast-food chains offer boy and girl toys with their children's meals. Some toy stores still have aisles marked "Boys" and "Girls." Many television shows still hold to traditional gender stereotypes (Aucoin, 2000). Males appear more frequently and tend to be the dominant characters. Male characters are more likely than female characters to engage in active tasks such as climbing or riding a bike. Females are more often depicted as passive, dependent, and emotional. Many of the female characters on television are not employed. When they do have jobs, they are often stereotypical ones such as teachers, nurses, and secretaries (Huston & Wright, 1998; Signorielli & Bacue, 1999).

Gender portrayals in film paint a similar picture. In 100 of the top-grossing G-rated children films released between 1990 and 2005, only 28% of the speaking characters were female. Yet, in a positive trend, the female characters were less likely to be portrayed as a damsel in distress and were sometimes depicted acting heroically or altruistically. Among the 400 U.S. top-grossing released films in the four main rating categories (G, PG, PG-13, and R) between 1990 and 2006, 73% of the characters were male. Females were more likely than males to be depicted as parents or as hypersexualized (overemphasizing their sexuality and attractiveness) (Smith & Cook, 2008).

Analyses of television advertisements in more than 20 countries echo these findings. Women are more likely to be the user of the product, whereas men are more often portrayed as the wise, knowledgeable expert. Women appear more often in domestic roles selling body care and household cleaning products and appear less often in occupational settings. Men are rarely shown in private residences or with children in the background (Furnham & Paltzer, 2010; Nassif & Gunter, 2008). Children who watch television frequently may adopt these gender-role stereotypes.

Anna Stowe/Alamy

Society encourages stereotypical gender schema by prescribing what are appropriate "girl" and "boy" toys, as indicated by this obviously girl-oriented display.

9.4

Quiz Yourself

1. As a child Hongyong was described as willful and strong. If as a baby she had difficulty adapting to new situations and showed intense negative emotions, her temperament would best be described as _____.
   a. easy
   b. difficult
   c. slow-to-warm-up
   d. sensitive
2. In the strange situation procedure, a baby who clings to the mother while she is present and who shows extreme distress when the mother leaves would be exhibiting which style of attachment?
   a. Secure
   b. Avoidant
   c. Disorganized
   d. Resistant
3. Of the different styles of parenting, _____ parenting seems to result in the best developmental outcomes for most children.
   a. authoritative
   b. authoritarian
   c. permissive-indulgent
   d. permissive-neglectful
4. Jose is a very active toddler who prefers to do things by himself. According to Erikson, Jose appears to be successfully resolving which developmental crisis?
   a. Trust versus mistrust
   b. Autonomy versus shame and doubt
   c. Initiative versus guilt
   d. Industry versus inferiority
5. Which of the following statements about gender-role development is *false*?
   a. At 3 years old, toddlers can label their gender.
   b. At 4 years old, preschoolers have gender permanence.
   c. At 6 years old, children have gender roles.
   d. At 8 years old, children have gender constancy.

Answers 1. b; 2. d; 3. a; 4. b; 5. b

9.5 Physical Changes in Adolescence and Adulthood

Development is not limited to the childhood years; changes continue during the adult years, too. In adulthood, however, these changes are much more variable than in childhood. In this section, we describe the physical changes that characterize adolescence and adulthood. As in childhood, both nature and nurture influence our development.

During adolescence and adulthood, we both peak and decline in terms of our physical development. How much and how rapidly we decline are very much influenced by both nature and nurture. Genes affect how we age, but so do the degree to which we exercise mind and body and the experiences we have as we age. What we think of as aging is an incremental and gradual process, but growing into our sexual maturation can be abrupt and actually quite dramatic. We are referring, of course, to the onset of *puberty*.

9.5.1 • Puberty: Big Changes, Rapid Growth, and Impact on Behavior

puberty [PEW-bur-tee] the process of sexual maturation

menarche [MEN-ar-kee] a girl's first menstruation

Puberty is the process of sexual maturation. These developmental changes involve overall body growth and maturation of sex characteristics that enable people to sexually reproduce. Puberty generally occurs 2 years earlier in girls than in boys, with an average onset at age 10 in females and age 12 for males, but the timing of puberty varies greatly from one person to another and from one culture to another (Parent et al., 2003). Over the past 100 years, the age at which puberty begins has dropped in the United States, Western Europe, and Japan. Even within the United States, ethnic variations exist with African American and Hispanic girls entering puberty a year earlier, on average, than European American girls (Butts & Seifer, 2010; Kaplowitz et al., 1999).

A growth spurt shortly after age 10 for girls and after age 12 for boys adds almost 10 inches in height and about 40 pounds in weight to the average body through adolescence. Girls' hips broaden relative to their shoulders, and boys' shoulders widen relative to their hips. Both sexes gain muscle and fat during puberty; however, girls gain more fat and boys gain more muscle. Because these changes are abrupt and uneven at times, early adolescence is regarded as an especially awkward phase of development (Malina, 1990).

In addition to overall growth, puberty includes internal and external signs of sexual maturity, caused by the release of sex hormones. In girls, sex hormones cause the breasts, ovaries, uterus, and vagina to mature, and initiate the start of their first menstrual cycle, or **menarche**. Pubic hair and underarm hair also develop. In boys, sex hormones cause the penis, scrotum, and testes to mature. These changes are accompanied by the growth of body hair and a deepening of the voice as the larynx enlarges. On average, males and females complete the process of puberty within 4–5 years (Rogol, Roemmich, & Clark, 2002). • FIGURE 9.2 summarizes the physical changes that boys and girls experience during puberty.

Puberty has a definite emotional and psychological impact, particularly on the adolescent's self-image and mood. Typically, adolescents' reactions to these physical changes are mixed, but if they are prepared for the upcoming changes and have a supportive family, psychological adjustment to puberty is better (Mrug et al., 2008; Omar, McElderry, & Zakharia, 2003). As we saw in the section case study, Hongyong's lack of knowledge and understanding of these changes made puberty confusing for her. Many adults attribute teenagers' moodiness to "raging hormones." Although higher hormone levels may influence teenagers' moods, it is also likely that teenagers' emotions influence hormone levels (Adam, 2006; Nottelmann et al., 1990). Teenagers often juggle multiple activities such as school, sports, clubs, band, or part-time work while interacting with varying groups of people—teachers, peers, family, coworkers, or coaches. Regulating their emotions and expectations within these different interactions and activities can be stressful and result in moodiness.

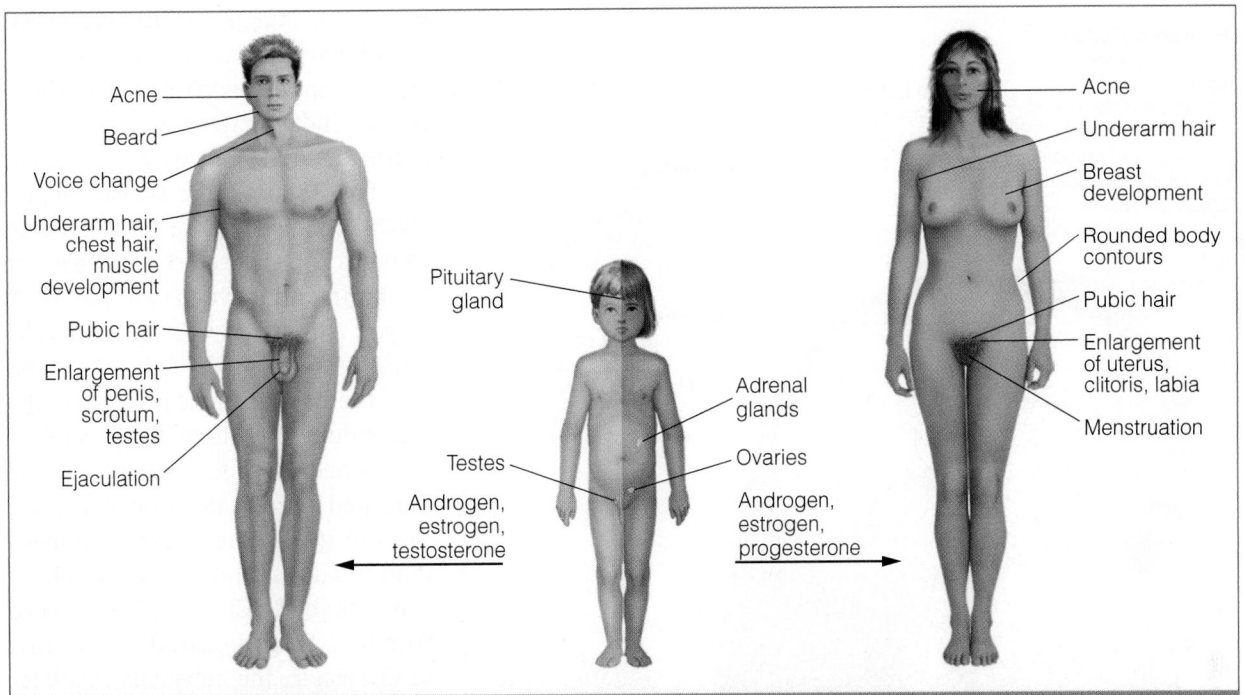

FIGURE 9.2

Physical Changes in Adolescent Males and Females During Puberty

Hormonal changes during puberty cause the development of sexual characteristics. These include physical changes to the organs directly involved in reproduction.

The timing of puberty also has a psychological impact on the self-image of an adolescent, one that differs for boys and girls. For boys who mature early, the growth in stature and muscle brings with it a better self-image and body image than for boys who mature later. However, early-maturing boys report somewhat more stress than late-maturing boys (Huddleston & Ge, 2003). Early-maturing females experience more adjustment difficulties and are more likely to smoke and drink alcohol during adolescence and to do less well in school than are those who mature later (Bratberg et al., 2005; Ge et al., 2006; Graber, Brooks-Gunn, & Warren, 2006; Tanner-Smith, 2010). Girls whose breasts develop early may find the attention they receive hard to cope with and fraught with pressures to become sexually active when they may not be ready cognitively and emotionally to do so. Girls who develop later are better adjusted to these changes because the pressure to become sexually active occurs at an older age, when their cognitive abilities are better able to handle such pressures. Long-term studies suggest that the effects of early versus late maturation in puberty may be short-lived, except for early-maturing girls. At age 24, early-maturing girls report poorer family and peer relationships, lower life satisfaction, and higher rates of depression compared to other females (Graber et al., 2004).

The physical changes of puberty and the cognitive ability to think abstractly often make teenagers self-conscious about their appearance.

Jerzyworks/MasterFile

9.5.2 • Brain Changes in Adolescence and Adulthood

In addition to pubertal changes, a tremendous amount of brain development takes place during adolescence and into early adulthood. Medical technology such as magnetic

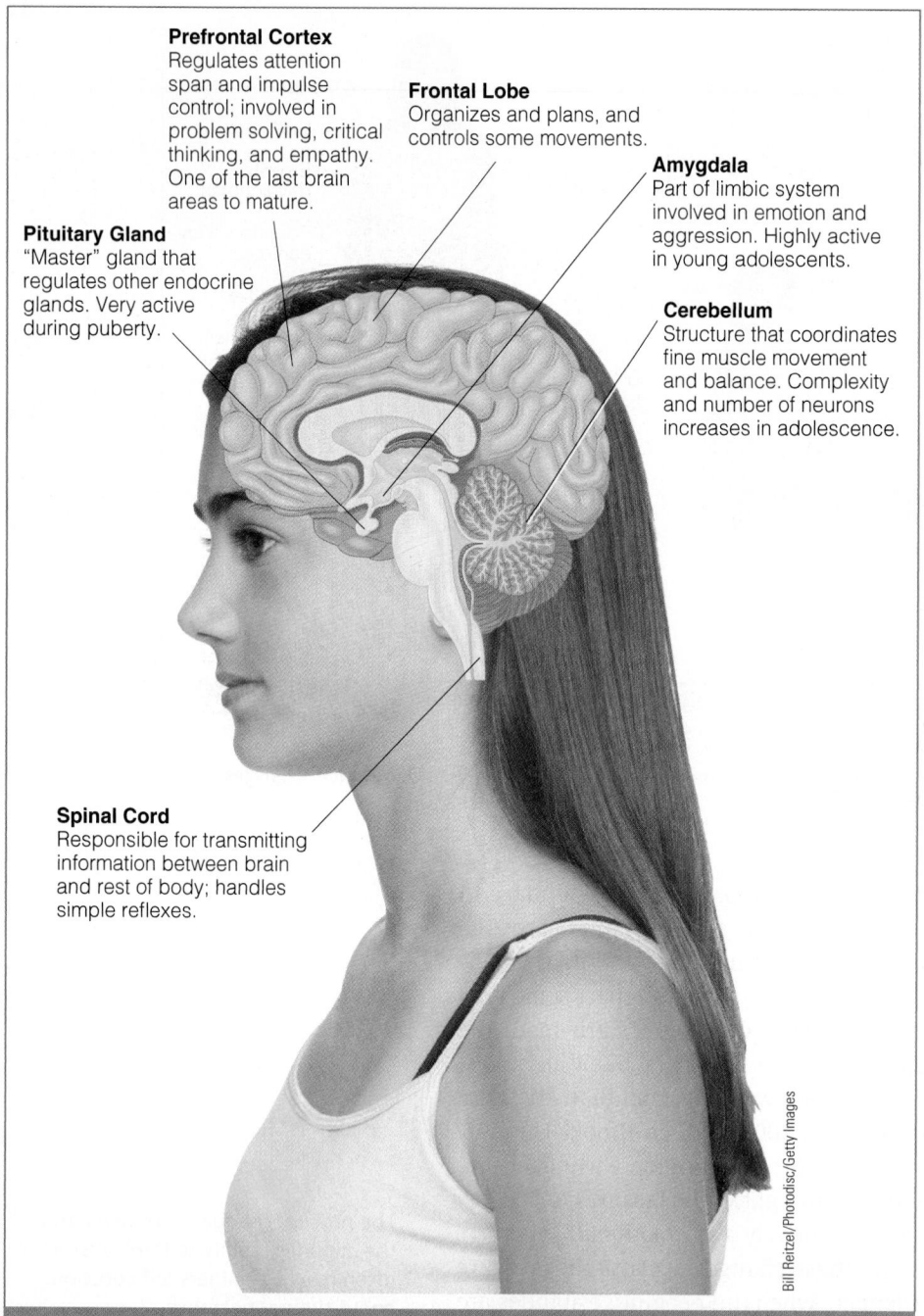

FIGURE 9.3

Changes in the Adolescent Brain

Changes in the adolescent brain generally start at the back of the brain and move toward the front. Hence the areas of the brain that are most involved in problem solving, planning, and critical thinking are the last areas to mature.

resonance imaging (MRI and fMRI; see Chapter 2) has allowed researchers to examine people's brains. These studies indicate dynamic changes in brain anatomy into early adulthood (Ashtari et al., 2007; Galvan et al., 2007; J. N. Porter et al., 2011). These changes appear to start at the back of the brain and move toward the front, as you can see in • FIGURE 9.3. The number of neurons and the complexity of their connections increase in the cerebellum. Recall that the cerebellum is necessary for balance, muscle tone, and performance of motor skills. The amygdala is more active in teens than in adults, and is larger in males (Koolschijn & Crone, 2013; Scherf, Smyth, & Delgado, 2013). As we saw in Chapter 2, the amygdala regulates our emotional reactions. Nerve fibers in the corpus callosum—the band of nerves that connects the two cerebral hemispheres—also thicken before and during puberty (J. N. Porter et al., 2011; Thompson et al., 2000).

Just prior to puberty there appears to be a second wave of overproduction of cortical gray matter—the tissue that covers the outside of the cerebral hemispheres that appears gray because of the absence of myelin on the axons (Durston et al., 2001; Sowell et al., 2001). The brain then prunes these connections as it did earlier in life—keeping the connections that are used while those that are not used wither away (see • FIGURE 9.4). This gray matter growth spurt predominates in the prefrontal cortex—the area that plays a major role in cognitive processes such as problem solving, judgment, reasoning, impulse control, and the planning and execution of behavior. This is among the latest brain areas to mature, not reaching adult dimensions until the early 20s (Casey, Giedd, & Thomas, 2000; Giedd, 2004).

Do these brain changes *cause* teenagers' behavior? Changes in the cerebellum *may* explain why young teens tend to be more physically uncoordinated and awkward than older teens and adults. The immaturity of the prefrontal cortex *may* explain why teenagers' judgment and reasoning may not always be sound. However, although structural changes in the brain *correlate* with teenage behavior, that does not mean they *cause* the behavior. Adolescent brain research does not take into account other aspects of development, such as cognitive abilities and the psychosocial challenge of forming an identity. Moreover, adolescent behavior is also influenced by environmental and cultural factors, such as parenting, peer pressure, the influence of school and the media, and other factors that contribute to brain processing. Adolescents all over the world experience roughly the same process of brain development, yet teenagers in different cultures and environments do not all behave the same way. Attributing a specific teenager's behavior solely to brain changes ignores variations among individuals and across development. Yet, we do know that teenagers have continued opportunities to develop their brains through activities in which they participate (Brant et al., 2013). Exercising their minds by reading, doing mathematics, and playing sports or music can strengthen neural connections.

Nerve Proliferation...
By age 11 for girls and 12 for boys, the neurons in the front of the brain have formed thousands of new connections. Over the next few years many of these links will be pruned.

...and Pruning
Those that are used and reinforced—the pathways involved in language, for example—will be strengthened, while the ones that aren't used will die out.

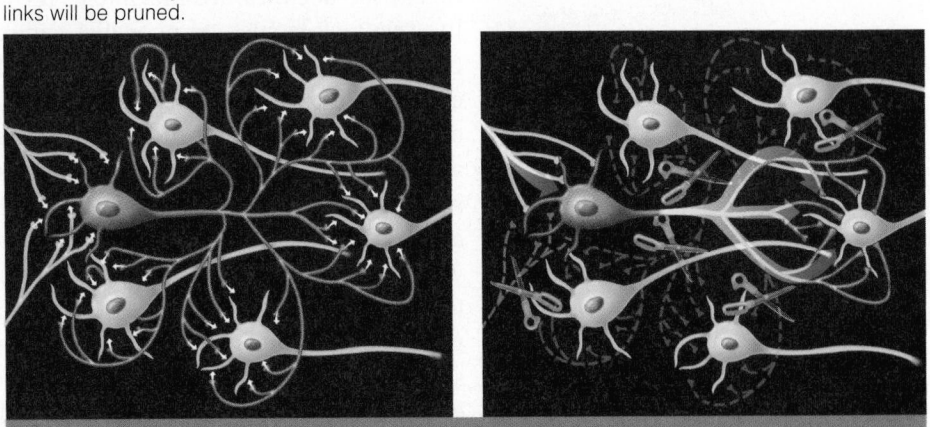

FIGURE 9.4

Neural Growth and Pruning

During early adolescence, new neural connections are formed. In a process called pruning, those that are used are strengthened, whereas those that are not wither away. Hence, engaging in stimulating and interesting activities during adolescence is good for our brains.

Source: *Time,* May 10, 2004. Reprinted with permission.

Is the brain completely developed at adolescence? No. Under normal conditions, stem cells in some regions of the brain continuously generate neurons throughout life and neural networks reorganize (Park & McDonough, 2013; Schmidt-Hieber, Jonas, & Bischofberger, 2004). The brain remains *plastic*—able to adapt in response to new experiences such as new jobs, marriage, divorce, children, new friends, and financial responsibilities.

9.5.3 • Physical Changes from Early to Later Adulthood

We hit our biological prime during early adulthood, when all major biological systems reach full maturation. Both women and men peak during their late 20s and early 30s in terms of physical strength, stamina, coordination, dexterity, and endurance (Whitbourne, 1996). These abilities gradually decline in middle and late adulthood.

A similar process occurs in our sensory abilities. Visual acuity, or the ability to focus vision, peaks in our early 20s and remains fairly high until middle adulthood. As we age, we lose the ability to focus on close objects (*presbyopia*), so that reading glasses or bifocals may become necessary in middle or late adulthood. Age-related hearing loss is also common among older adults, especially for high-pitched tones such as a distant telephone or a doorbell. However, people's senses of taste, smell, and touch remain fairly stable until late adulthood.

We see additional signs of the aging process in people's physical appearance as they approach their 40s and 50s. The skin starts to show wrinkles, and the hair may thin and turn gray. Weight gain is likely as metabolism slows, causing noticeable "love handles" or a "pot belly." Then, as people approach their 60s, they typically begin to lose weight and muscle, which may result in a sagging of the skin (Haber, 1994). The compression of vertebrae combined with a loss of bone tissue results in a loss of height as people age.

Although many physical abilities decline over the adult years, it is not clear that these declines are inevitable. As we discuss in more detail in Chapter 12, lifestyle factors such as poor diet, smoking, drinking alcohol, and lack of exercise contribute to the decline in physical functioning for some people. Moreover, culture markedly influences the way we think about aging and our expectations of our physical abilities in middle and later adulthood. In Western cultures such as the United States, becoming old is associated with being frail, useless, and ill, so that many people attempt to push back the aging process. Yet in countries such as Brazil, China, Japan, and Russia, where older people are more valued, aging is viewed more positively and is perceived as a time to look forward to rather than to dread (Gardiner, Mutter, & Kosmitzki, 1998; Lockenhoff et al., 2009). People with positive perceptions of aging engage in more preventive health behaviors, such as exercising, and tend to live longer (B. R. Levy & Myers, 2004; B. R. Levy et al., 2002). Across the world, many older people, despite changes in physical functioning, still lead active lifestyles (Baltes, 1997). As people age, they can usually continue their daily activities by making some adjustments and allowing themselves more time.

9.5.4 • Gender and Reproductive Capacity

Our reproductive capacity also changes during the adulthood years. Women's fertility steadily decreases from age 15 to age 50 (McFalls, 1990; Rowe, 2006). Sometime around age 50, on average, women undergo changes associated with the process of **menopause**. Menopause signals the end of a woman's childbearing years. Her body produces less and less estrogen, affecting the number of eggs that are released from the ovaries. Eventually, as she ages, ovulation and menstruation stop altogether. Decreasing levels of estrogen also cause the breasts and the uterus to shrink. The vaginal walls produce less lubrication, which may make sexual intercourse somewhat painful.

menopause the period when a female stops menstruating and is no longer fertile

Although men do not experience a "male menopause," they, too, undergo hormonal changes after age 60, termed *andropause* (Finch, 2001; Mohr et al., 2005; Whitbourne, 2001). They gradually produce fewer male hormones as they age, which lowers the concentration of sperm in the semen and results in hair loss on the legs and face. However, men are still capable of producing offspring into their 70s, 80s, and 90s.

Despite these reproductive changes, older adults continue to have active and satisfying sex lives. For example, in one national survey of U.S. adults between the ages of 57 and 85, 73% of 57- to 64-year olds reported regular sexual activity, more than half of the 65- to 74-year-olds reported regular sexual activity, and 26% of the 75- to 85-year olds reported regular sexual activity (Lindau et al., 2007).

Because many cultures equate "looking old" with being unattractive, especially for women, middle age and later life may not seem very appealing. However, despite the effects of aging, 40% of noninstitutionalized people over 65 report being in very good to excellent health compared to 65% for persons 18–64 years old (Administration on Aging [AOA], 2011). Although older adults may not be pleased with certain aspects of physical aging, they are no less content with their lives. Several studies show that older adults often report higher levels of well-being than do younger adults (Cacioppo et al., 2008; Stawski et al., 2008). Happiness and contentment perhaps have more to do with people's ability to adjust to these changes rather than with the changes themselves.

9.5

Quiz Yourself

1. **Which of the following people tend to have the most difficult time adjusting during adolescence?**
   a. Early-maturing males
   b. Late-maturing males
   c. Early-maturing females
   d. Late-maturing females
2. **Andre, a 65-year-old man, is likely to experience all of the following as the result of aging except _____.**
   a. weight loss
   b. andropause
   c. loss in visual acuity
   d. hearing loss for low-pitched tones
3. **Which of the following lists the brain structures in the correct order in which they change (from earliest to latest) in adolescence?**
   a. Cerebellum, prefrontal cortex, amygdala
   b. Cerebellum, amygdala, prefrontal cortex
   c. Prefrontal cortex, cerebellum, amygdala
   d. Amygdala, prefrontal cortex, cerebellum

Answers 1. c; 2. d; 3. b

9.6 Cognitive Changes in Adolescence and Adulthood

Adolescence and adulthood are also marked by changes in the way that we think. Consider how Hongyong's thoughts and focus changed over time. Initially, as a young adolescent, her concerns and thoughts predominantly centered on herself. With her marriage, her focus expanded to include her husband and her family's views on herself. Then, as she grew older, she became more accepting of others. This section examines these changes in cognition.

9.6.1 • Formal Operations Revisited: Applying Cognition to Adolescent Behavior

As we saw earlier in this chapter, children think and reason in ways that are qualitatively different from the thinking of adolescents and adults. Similarly, teenagers do not necessarily think like adults, but they are beginning to practice the reasoning skills and the ability to think outside themselves that characterize later cognitive development.

Recall that Piaget (1952) proposed that teenagers begin to think abstractly during the formal operations stage. This ability to reason abstractly allows them to imagine what could be and to hypothesize about future events and future outcomes. As a result, adolescents experience what they believe are—and sometimes are—tremendous insights into how things could be rather than how they are. This phenomenon is often labeled the *idealism of youth* (Elkind, 1998). Adolescents believe that they have the answers to problems such as world hunger or conflicts. This mental ability also helps adolescents in discovering who they are as individuals—a topic that will be discussed later in this chapter.

Formal operational thinking also allows teenagers to tackle more challenging academic subjects (science, geometry, calculus) that rely on abstract visualization and reasoning powers. It also

The ability to reason abstractly allows teenagers to successfully tackle complex academic topics.

Michael J. Doolittle/The Image Works

enables adolescents to argue more effectively, a power that may not be seen positively by their parents! They are more capable of suggesting hypothetical scenarios ("What if...") to justify their position, making them more effective debaters (Elkind, 1998). However, along with this ability to think abstractly comes the return of *egocentrism*.

Egocentrism in adolescence involves teenagers' imagining what others must be thinking. However, teens believe that other people are concerned with the same things they are. Because adolescents' ideas focus mainly on themselves, they believe that others are equally concerned about them (Elkind & Bowen, 1979). For example, a teen with a pimple on his face may imagine that his peers and teachers are thinking only about the pimple on his face. Recall how Hongyong hid in her room ashamed that everyone would know that she was menstruating. Teenagers may not ask or answer questions in class because they are so sure that everyone is talking about them and thinking about them. They are newly and acutely aware of their own being, and self-consciousness peaks. Because teens believe that others are focused on them, they behave as if they are on stage—playing to an audience—a phenomenon referred to as the **imaginary audience** (Elkind, 1998). They may laugh especially loudly or behave dramatically because of their belief that they are being constantly watched. Neuroimaging research and adolescent self-reports support this heightened sensitivity to others' evaluation in adolescence (Somerville, 2013; Somerville et al., 2013). Although the imaginary audience and egocentrism are most associated with the teenage years, they may still be somewhat present later in life as young adults choose clothing, jobs, or interests to impress an audience that is largely imaginary (Frankenberger, 2000; Schwartz, Maynard, & Uzelac, 2008).

imaginary audience the belief held by adolescents that everyone is watching what they do

personal fable the belief held by adolescents that they are unique and special

Another feature of adolescents' thought that relates to egocentrism is the **personal fable** (Elkind, 1998). Teenagers develop the "personal fable" that they are special and unique, that their thoughts and feelings cannot be adequately understood by others (Elkind, 1994). Reflect back on your first love. When that relationship ended, you may have felt as if no one in the world could identify with what you were feeling. The story you tell yourself is that this person, who is the only person in the world for you, has now gone away, and your life will never be happy again. This is one personal fable of adolescence.

Personal fables may contribute to adolescent risk taking. Because teenagers feel that they are special and unique, they often feel that their own risks are less than those of their peers. For example, they may engage in unprotected sexual intercourse, believing that they won't be the ones to contract a sexually transmitted disease or conceive a child. They may experiment with drugs, believing that they will not become addicted. In their minds, addiction happens to other people. However, some research suggests that this *optimistic bias* is no more prevalent in adolescents than it is in adults (Reyna & Farley, 2006). Moreover, adolescent risk-taking behavior is much more likely in emotionally charged situations than in cool, less emotional ones (Casey & Caudle, 2013; Figner & Weber, 2011).

Although formal operational thinking is often perceived as the hallmark of adolescent thinking, this does not mean that *all* adolescents think abstractly in this way. Cross-cultural research (Hollos & Richards, 1993; Rogoff & Chavajay, 1995) suggests that the development of formal operational thinking is very much influenced by experience and culture. If abstract thought is necessary to "get by" in one's society or for a particular task, then humans may learn it. This thinking is more likely to be found in youths who are formally educated and in societies with more specialized and technical occupations (Flieller, 1999; Kuhn & Crowell, 2011).

In addition to Piaget's stage of formal operations, research has documented that adolescents think in other ways that are qualitatively different from adults. One such discovery is from research studies on *postformal thought*.

9.6.2 • Postformal Thought: Developing Adult Reasoning

Suppose you were in the same situation as Hongyong. You are traveling in the middle of a war with a baby strapped to your back and three young children. Your baby's survival is questionable because she has been crushed by the crowds, and all of you are tired, hungry, and cold. Her added weight makes it difficult for you to walk, especially because you have been traveling for days with little food or water. What do you do? Would you, like Hongyong, consider leaving the baby under a tree in the hope of ensuring the survival of the rest of your family? Or would you, like Dukwah, insist that the baby continue to be carried? Is there a right or a wrong answer?

When situations like this are presented to adolescents and adults, differences emerge in their thinking. Adolescents often reason in terms of black or white, right or wrong, good or bad—what is called **dualistic thinking** (Perry, 1981). They tend to believe that there is only one solution. However, as people enter adulthood, they are more capable of **relativistic thinking**, the idea that in many situations there is not necessarily one right or wrong answer. As adults we become aware that sometimes solutions and answers are relative to the situation or to the people in the situation. In Hongyong's dilemma, for example, adults typically would consider additional situational aspects such as how much farther the family has to travel, whether the younger children can help carry the baby, and the likelihood of the mother's surviving if she continues to carry the baby. The adolescent, thinking dualistically, may still believe the adult can do everything—carry the baby, lead the family, and reach safety.

Numerous research investigations support the notion that relativistic thinking represents a qualitative change beyond formal operations (Sinnott, 1998; Yang, Wan, & Chiou, 2010). In this context, it has been termed as a type of **postformal thought**. It is characterized by the appreciation that a correct solution or answer may vary from situation to situation and that there may be multiple solutions, all equally viable, to a given problem. As adults age, their experiences truly do help them reason, resolve conflicts, and make decisions in a more pragmatic way (Grossmann et al., 2012; Worthy et al., 2011).

dualistic [do-uhl-LIS-tik] thinking reasoning that divides situations and issues into right and wrong categories

relativistic [rell-uh-tah-VIS-tik] thinking the idea that in many situations there is not necessarily one right or wrong answer

postformal thought the idea that a correct solution (or solutions) may vary, depending on the circumstances

fluid intelligence abilities that rely on information-processing skills such as reaction time, attention, and working memory

9.6.3 • Changes in Mental Abilities

The most comprehensive research to date, undertaken by Schaie (1983, 1994, 1996; Schaie & Willis, 2000), reveals that patterns of aging differ for different mental abilities. Recall from Chapter 8 that there are two broad categories of skills called *fluid intelligence* and *crystallized intelligence*.

Fluid intelligence, which develops during early childhood, relies heavily on processing skills such as reaction time, attention, and working memory. It is presumed to be based primarily on nature or biology, peaking when brain maturity has been reached (Li et al., 2004). Within the category of fluid intelligence, some mental abilities remain stronger than others. For example, perceptual speed and numeric ability tend to decline in one's late 20s and early 30s. Other fluid skills such as spatial orientation and inductive reasoning remain strong and steady through one's 50s, declining after that (Bucur & Madden, 2010; Salthouse, 2012; Schmiedek, Lovden, & Lindenberger, 2013).

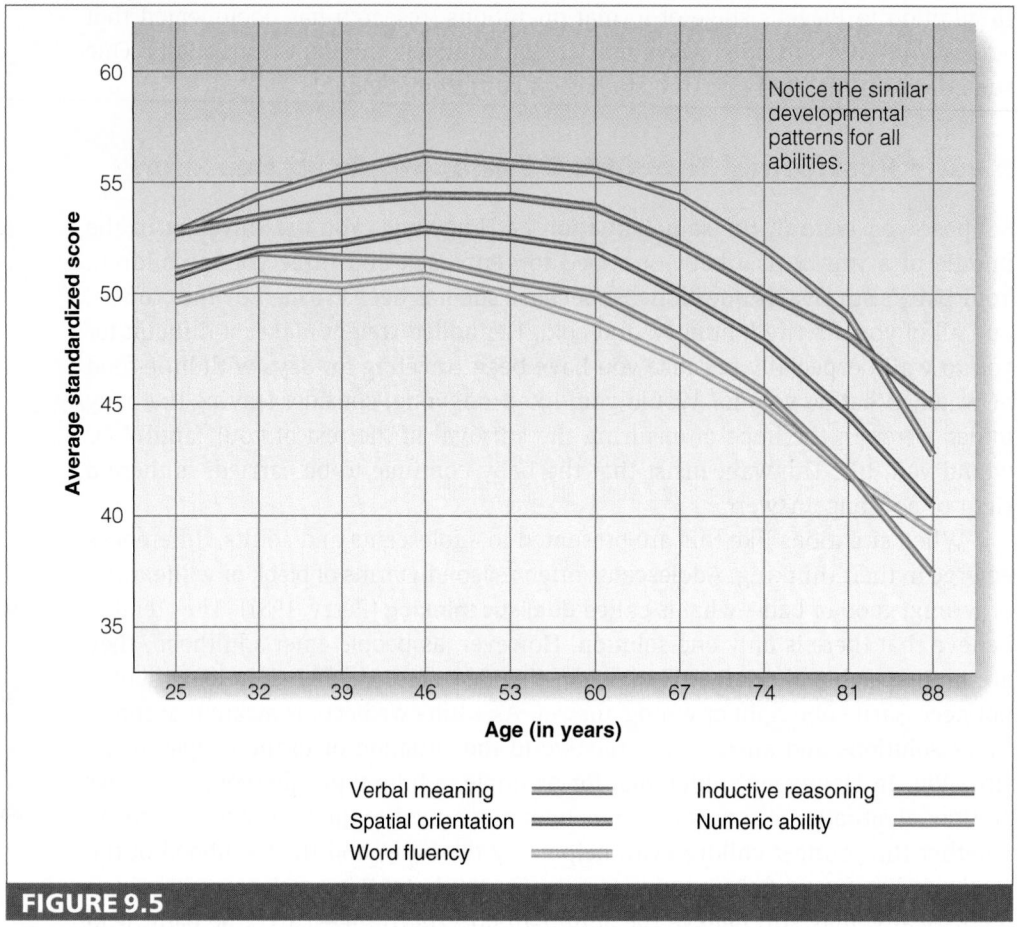

FIGURE 9.5

Age Trends in Mental Abilities

In his ongoing study of mental abilities, Schaie (1983, 1994, 1996) has documented that most mental abilities remain strong through early and middle adulthood. Eighty percent of his participants showed no declines by age 60, and almost two-thirds were still stable through age 80.

Source: "The Course of Adult Intellectual Development," by K. W. Schaie, 1994, *American Psychologist, 49,* 304–313. Copyright © by the American Psychological Association. Reprinted by permission of the author.

crystallized intelligence abilities that rely on knowledge, expertise, and judgment

Crystallized intelligence, in contrast, involves the use of knowledge, expertise, and good judgment. Crystallized intelligence depends more on nurture or experience, such as educational background and occupational expertise. These abilities increase into adulthood and then decline somewhat after one's mid-60s (Li et al., 2004; Salthouse, 2012; van Hooren et al., 2007). Crystallized skills include vocabulary, verbal memory, and responses to social situations. These age-related trends in mental abilities are summarized in • FIGURE 9.5.

Many factors other than age shape how well we function mentally. Poor health, diseases, and prescription medications contribute to a rapid decline in mental abilities. Older adults can benefit cognitively from regular physical exercise (Colcombe & Kramer, 2003; Emery, Finkel, & Pedersen, 2012). A mentally inactive lifestyle is also a potential factor in cognitive decline and Alzheimer's disease (Schaie, 1996; Wilson & Bennett, 2003). The motto "Use it or lose it!" seems most appropriate in this context. Doing crossword puzzles, watching *Jeopardy,* and continuing to read, travel, or participate in educational pursuits are all activities that help sustain cognitive functioning (Hertzog et al., 2008; Stine-Morrow et al., 2007).

9.6

Quiz Yourself

1. The idea that a correct solution (or solutions) may vary depending on the circumstances is called _____.
   a. dualistic thinking
   b. egocentrism
   c. postformal thought
   d. formal operations
2. When at the mall with her friends, Maria acts as if everyone is watching her. Maria's behavior is an example of _____.
   a. egocentrism
   b. an imaginary audience
   c. idealism
   d. a personal fable
3. Which one of the following mental abilities shows the *least* amount of decline after age 25?
   a. Inductive reasoning
   b. Numeric ability
   c. Perceptual speed
   d. Reaction time

Answers 1. c; 2. b; 3. a

9.7 Psychosocial Changes in Adolescence and Adulthood

How people's individuality and character develop and change in adolescence and adulthood, and how people navigate their social environments are challenging research areas in contemporary psychology. Erik Erikson sees adolescence and adulthood as a process of building, modifying, and sustaining a personal identity. This identity is influenced by our social relationships as well as the world of work.

9.7.1 • Erikson's Psychosocial Stages of Adolescence and Adulthood

Recall Erikson's psychosocial stages of development (You Review, p. 379) in which children, adolescents, and adults face developmental crises that establish their individuality. Successfully mastering each stage strengthens the person's capacity to confront and negotiate the next stages. Here we examine the four stages Erikson attributed to the adolescent and adult years.

IDENTITY VERSUS ROLE CONFUSION: KNOW WHO YOU ARE

For Erikson (1956, 1958, 1959), adolescence represents the integration and summation of the previous crises of childhood into an appropriate *identity*. Teenagers must figure out who they are and what they believe in, what their values are, and how they may be similar to or different from peers and parents. This search for personal identity is thought to be very much influenced by both the biological changes of puberty and the newly acquired cognitive ability of abstract reasoning (Grysman & Hudson, 2010). Teenagers begin to imagine what they want to be and experiment with new roles and responsibilities as they figure out their personal identity. For example, teenagers may try out different styles of clothing or listen to many types of music. They may join different peer groups or try out different college courses to explore various career options. Sometimes adolescents and young adults become so involved in constantly trying out new roles that they fail to form a stable identity. Erikson referred to this condition as *role confusion*.

Even when a teen fully attains an identity, this identity is not permanently etched in stone. Rather, adolescence represents a time when the core of our identity is established. We continue to refine and modify our identity as we transition to adult roles and responsibilities (Marcia, 2002). Think back to Hongyong's identity. Although headstrong, she adopted the values specified for her as a Korean female. Yet, given a husband who valued her opinions, she was able to explore her potential as a businessperson.

INTIMACY VERSUS ISOLATION: CONNECT WITH OTHERS

In Erikson's theory, successful resolution of the identity crisis prepares the young adult for the next developmental crisis: *intimacy versus isolation*. Having formed a stable identity, the person is now prepared to make a long-term commitment to a partner. Intimacy requires that people refine and modify their identity to accommodate the values and interests of another. In successfully meeting this challenge, neither partner's identity would be sacrificed. For Erikson, *intimacy* is characterized by cooperation, tolerance, and an acceptance of others' different views and values. This secure sense of intimacy may be expressed through marriage or long-term romantic partnerships, through close friendships, or through work relationships. Some people may lose their sense of identity—or fear losing it—and therefore be reluctant to connect with others. Erikson referred to this state as *isolation*. Isolated individuals are easily threatened by close relations with others and hesitate to establish close ties. They are more defensive in the relationships they do form, and they have less tolerance for the varying views and opinions of others.

Consider Hongyong and her husband Dukpil's relationship. They met for the first time when they were joined in marriage, but were fortunate to build an intimate relationship. They confided in one another and valued each other's opinions. They each deferred to the other when the other had more interest or expertise on the subject. Hongyong forgave Dukpil and accepted him despite his infidelities and drinking. He accepted her despite her willfulness and conversion to Christianity. They were tolerant of one another.

GENERATIVITY VERSUS STAGNATION: MAKE THE WORLD A BETTER PLACE

According to Erikson, resolving the intimacy versus isolation stage prepares adults for the developmental crisis of the middle adulthood years: *generativity versus stagnation*. This stage of development has to do with our feeling that we have made significant and meaningful contributions to our society. Middle adulthood is often the time when people become aware of their mortality. They recognize that their time here on Earth is limited. As a result, they begin to think about their accomplishments and effect on society. Erikson believed that if a middle-aged adult feels that he or she has contributed something worthwhile to society, then a sense of *generativity* has been achieved. Marriage, long-term relationships, child rearing, career accomplishments, and service to the community may all contribute to this sense of having lived a productive life (Westermeyer, 2004). On the one hand, generativity is associated with positive personality characteristics and life satisfaction (Peterson & Duncan, 2007). On the other hand, middle-aged adults who conclude that they have contributed very little to society will experience *stagnation*, a sense of failure, and an absence of meaningful purpose in life.

People cope with feelings of stagnation in a variety of ways. Some remain disenchanted and bitter. Others attempt to change their lives to regain a sense of generativity and identity. Society often perceives such attempts as a *midlife crisis*. However, the number of people who actually experience such dramatic shifts in their life structure is actually quite small (Wrightsman, 1994). For example, in a 12-year study of people over age 40, Sadler (2000) found that a significant number of middle-aged adults are productive, enjoy their close relationships, and have begun to take risks. They experience what Sadler calls a "second growth" in midlife, characterized by enjoyment of life as Hongyong did with her ch'iryo practice.

INTEGRITY VERSUS DESPAIR: NO REGRETS

At the end of the life span, adults begin to review their lives and judge their satisfaction with the choices they have made and the direction that their lives have taken. Erikson believed that the issue facing people in their 60s and beyond was one of *integrity versus despair.* When this evaluation is generally positive and satisfying, individuals have achieved a sense of *integrity,* which allows them to face their eventual death without fear or regret. However, if this life review results in dissatisfaction and a sense of regret over roads not taken, the person is more likely to experience *despair* or hopelessness stemming from the knowledge that one cannot relive one's life. In such a case, the person may become fearful of death.

John Henley/Cusp/Corbis

For older adults, reminiscing about their experiences provides a sense of integrity and life satisfaction.

9.7.2 • Emerging Adulthood

In industrialized nations such as the United States, the time between the teenage years and when one assumes adult responsibilities is not as short as it used to be. This added length has resulted in a new transitional phase of development from one's late teens to one's mid-20s referred to as **emerging adulthood** (Arnett, 2007).

emerging adulthood the transitional period between late adolescence and the mid-20s when young people have left adolescence but have not yet assumed adult roles and responsibilities

More young people are attending college, especially women. The median age of marriage has risen and parenthood is often delayed such that emerging adulthood prolongs identity development as young people pursue education, travel, explore various career paths, and experiment with varying love relationships (Arnett, 2010). Even at a subjective level, young people don't feel like they have assumed adult responsibilities. For example, in one large diverse sample of college and noncollege young adults between the ages of 18 and 35, 56% reported feeling "somewhat like an adult" (Lowe et al., 2013).

However, emerging adulthood does not occur for all young people. In many non-Western cultures, there is no delay between the teen years and adult roles; young people work, get married, and raise families in adolescence or soon after (UNICEF, 2009). Even in Western nations like the United States that have postponed adult roles, a transitional period of emerging adulthood is not possible for young people with limited economic resources or little education or for those who experience early parenthood (P. Cohen et al., 2003).

Emerging adults may participate in career fairs to further explore their identity options.

Kim Kulish/Corbis News/Corbis

9.7.3 • Variations in Social Relations in Adolescence and Adulthood

Hongyong followed the prescribed social roles for her time and for her culture. She did not socialize with boys or date, and her parents arranged her marriage. Despite her husband's infidelities, she never considered divorce. She and her husband expected to have children. If they did not, they would have been viewed as abnormal. Although in many cultures such prescribed social roles may still be the norm, in Western cultures, today's adolescents and adults express intimacy in relationships in a wide range of lifestyles, including dating, marriage, cohabitation, divorce, and parenthood.

Maria Teijeiro/Photodisc/Getty Images

Dating gives teenagers a chance to learn how to cooperate and compromise with people in a variety of situations.

DATING AND SINGLEHOOD

Most teens date at some point in adolescence, but regular dating has declined in recent years. In 2011, 66% of high school seniors reported dating, compared to 82% in 2000 (Bachman, Johnston, & O'Malley, 2001; Johnston, Bachman, & O'Malley, 2013). However, this difference could reflect a change in teens' language. Nowadays, young people more often talk of "hanging out" or "going together" rather than dating. In these initial romantic relationships, young people look for social support, affection, and someone who has similar interests (B. B. Brown, 2004; Collins & van Dulmen, 2006). Males rate the attractiveness of a potential partner as especially important, whereas females rate the attractiveness and social status of a potential partner as important factors in whom to date (Ha, Overbeek, & Engels, 2010).

Dating serves several functions for teenagers. Besides being an outlet for fun and recreation, dating gives teenagers a chance to learn how to cooperate and compromise with people in a variety of situations (Lambeth & Hallett, 2002). For example, choosing a movie or a restaurant entails listening to the other person's wishes and then resolving any differences. Teens can discover more about themselves and how others' needs may differ from their own. Sexual experimentation may also be involved (Sanderson & Cantor, 1995; Smetana, Campione-Barr, & Metzger, 2006). Dating and romantic relationships during adolescence pave the way for establishing adult intimate relationships.

It is typical to start one's adulthood as unmarried—and the number of young adults who are single is growing. In 2011, 62% of U.S. residents 18 and older had never married (U.S. Census Bureau, 2012b). Among African American women, 43% remain unmarried into their late 30s, compared to 18% of Hispanic, 12% of Asian, and 14% of European American women (U.S. Census Bureau, 2012b). Worldwide, young adults are delaying marriage (● FIGURE 9.6). In the United States, the average age for first marriages is 28.3 for men and 25.8 for women (Copen et al., 2012). Being single allows young adults a chance to explore different types of friendships and relationships as well as to continue refining and defining their identities. Young single adults also may be moving or traveling as part of building careers, which can make it harder to start or maintain a relationship.

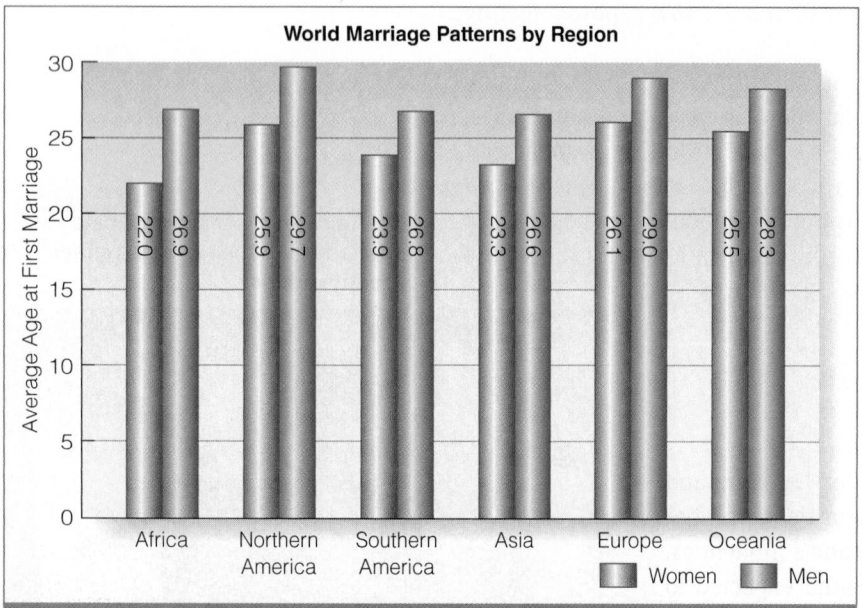

FIGURE 9.6

World Trends in Age at First Marriage for Men and Women

Worldwide, the average age when men and women first marry is rising, resulting in a larger number of singles in young adulthood.

Source: United Nations, 2003.

COHABITATION

Some adults choose to live together, or *cohabit,* with an intimate partner, one with whom they enjoy a sexual relationship. Cohabitation rates have been increasing steadily over the past 20 years in the United States. Currently, 6.7 million unmarried opposite-sex couples live together (U.S. Census Bureau, 2010). These unions tend to be short-lived; about half of cohabiting couples either get married or break up within a year (Bumpass & Lu, 2000; Lichter, Qian, & Mellott, 2006). The increased rate of cohabiting couples is not unique to the United States—an even higher level exists in many other countries, such as Sweden, Finland, and Denmark (Loveless & Holman, 2007). However, cohabitation is rarer in more traditional societies. It is frowned on in Asian societies and discouraged in Islamic societies.

Couples cohabit for various reasons. Many gay and lesbian couples cohabit because their states' laws do not recognize civil unions or marriages. Heterosexual couples may feel that cohabiting before marriage will give them the opportunity to see whether they are truly compatible before undertaking the serious commitment of marriage. Some couples cohabit after divorce as an alternative to remarriage (S. L. Brown, Lee, & Bulanda, 2006).

MARRIAGE: ADAPTATION, SATISFACTION, AND GENDER DIFFERENCES

More than 95% of Americans choose to get married at some point in their lives (U.S. Census Bureau, 2010). Survey research indicates that married couples in the United States are as happy today as they were 20 years ago (Amato et al., 2003). In some cultures, marriages are still arranged with up to 90% of marriages arranged in India and less than 10% of marriages arranged in Japan (Ferrante, 2011; Toledo, 2009)). Parents, relatives, and friends choose marriage partners based on their finances, family values, social status, and perceived compatibility with the potential bride or groom (Batabyal, 2001).

Marriage, like any other lifestyle choice, involves adaptation. A new role as spouse has been added, and people must adjust to living as a couple rather than as an individual. Researchers have found that many aspects of the marital relationship change after the first year. The "I love you's" become less frequent, sexual activity becomes less frequent, and couples spend more time performing daily chores and tasks together rather than talking and having fun. Despite these changes, many couples continue to report satisfaction in their marital relationships.

Research has discovered many factors that are related to marital satisfaction. For example, when both people are similar in family background, social class, education, and religion, couples report more satisfying relationships (Gaunt, 2006). Couples who wait to marry until after age 20 are more likely to report happier marriages than those who marry before age 20. Warm and positive family relationships (before and during marriage), supportive spouse behavior, a willingness to sacrifice, seeing one's partner as an ideal mate, and secure financial circumstances also increase the chances of a satisfying marital or romantic relationship (Ackerman et al., 2013; Clark et al., 2010; Karney & Bradbury, 2005; Kogan et al., 2010; Murray, Griffin et al., 2011; Stanley et al., 2006). Perhaps the biggest detriments to a satisfying long-term relationship are boredom, negative comments, contempt, defensiveness, and criticism (Gottman, 1999a, 1999b; Lavner & Bradbury, 2010; Robles & Kiecolt-Glaser, 2003; Tsapelas, Aron, & Orbuch, 2009).

Research also shows some interesting gender differences in marital satisfaction. Although married people report greater life satisfaction than single people (Holt-Lunstad, Birmingham, & Jones, 2008; Myers, 2000), husbands typically report higher marital satisfaction than wives (Schumm, Webb, & Bollman, 1998). For example, Corra and colleagues (2009) investigated trends in marital happiness from 1973 to 2006 and found that Whites and husbands reported greater marital happiness than Blacks and wives. Marriage is associated with better physical and mental health for men (Kaslow, Hansson, & Lundblad, 1994; Read & Grundy, 2011). Health advantages for married women are more likely when the marriage is characterized as highly satisfying (Gallo, Troxel,

More than 95% of people in the United States choose to get married at some point in their lives.

Michael Doolittle/Alamy

Kuller, et al., 2003; Gallo, Troxel, Matthews, et al., 2003). Today, more married women are employed, but they still perform the majority of household tasks and have more responsibility for child rearing than married men. In dual-earner couples, wives average almost 10 hours more per week on childcare and household tasks than their husbands (Coltrane, 2001; Offer & Schneider, 2011; University of Michigan, 2008). Given these circumstances, it is not surprising that when divorce does occur, it is more likely to be initiated by the female (Amato & Rogers, 1997).

DIVORCE

About 1 in 5 adults will at some time in their lives experience divorce. First marriages that end in divorce last, on average, about 8 years (Kreider, 2005). Divorce rates are higher among couples who do not have children, who marry at a young age, or whose parents divorced (Amato & DeBoer, 2001; Goodwin, Mosher, & Chandra, 2010; Shulman et al., 2001). Divorce rates are also higher among African Americans (10.6%) and European Americans (9.8%) than among Hispanic Americans (7.5%) and Asian Americans (4.2%), and higher among lower-income couples than higher-income couples (Rank, 2000; U.S. Census Bureau, 2010).

Like other lifestyle changes, divorce brings with it stresses and adaptations that the couple and the family must negotiate. Typically, divorce is preceded by a period of conflict and dissatisfaction (Lucas, 2005). Emotional, economic, legal, and practical difficulties follow. What was once one household must now be divided into two. If there are children involved, custody arrangements must be made. Identities are reshaped and redefined as the couple mentally shifts from thinking in terms of "us" to "me." Friendships with other couples may fade. Simultaneously, each member of the couple is resolving feelings of anger, rejection, disappointment, or loneliness (Amato, 2000). Given these changes, it is not surprising that at least initially divorced people are more likely to report higher levels of psychological distress or experience physical health problems (Hughes & Waite, 2009; Lorenz et al., 2006). Over time, many adjust to their new lives (Amato, 2010; Mancini, Bonanno, & Clark, 2011). Many divorced adults, especially young people, choose to marry again. However, it is more common for men to remarry than for women (Kreider, 2005).

Divorce also affects the family. Previous styles of parenting may change, as the custodial parent must assume more responsibility for disciplining the children. The noncustodial parent may become more permissive because he or she spends less time with the children. Children experience many of the same emotions as their parents, such as loss, grieving for the family that was, and anger that their parents were not able to make the marriage work. As a result, they are more likely to misbehave. Children of divorce may be more aggressive, disrespectful, disobedient, withdrawn, or moody, and school performance may deteriorate, at least over the short term (Lansford, 2009). Their misbehavior makes it even more difficult for parents to be effective. Studies suggest that it is this breakdown in parenting and children's exposure to marital conflict both prior to and following a divorce that are most detrimental to a child's development (Amato, 1993; Amato & Booth, 1996). Hence, a two-parent household filled with strife and discord is as difficult for a child as the experience of divorce (Booth & Amato, 2001; Lansford, 2009).

9.7.4 • Parenting

At one time, marriage was synonymous with becoming a parent, but that is not necessarily the case today. With increasing numbers of birth control options available, parenthood is more of a choice today than it used to be. About 15% of U.S.

adults ages 40–44 in 2009 had never had a child (U.S. Census Bureau, 2010). At the same time, more single women and cohabitating couples are having or adopting children (Manning, 2001; Teachman et al., 2000; U.S. Census Bureau, 2010). For those who do have children, parenthood becomes another life transition that includes adaptation to new roles and responsibilities.

Although most prospective parents look forward to the birth of their child, children radically change people's lives. With the joy and elation of a newborn baby comes less sleep, leisure time, and time spent together as a couple. Life satisfaction typically decreases (Luhmann et al., 2012). Financial planning is a must; it will cost about $300,000 to raise one child born in 2012 over the next 17 years—and that's not including college expenses (USDA, 2013). Life becomes a juggling act as the couple tries to keep an eye on all the responsibilities of work and family at the same time. Although fathers today are more involved in child care and housework than ever before (Coley, 2001), most heterosexual couples become more traditional in their gender roles following the birth of a child (Katz-Wise, Priess, & Hyde, 2010). Mothers, even working mothers, are more likely to become the primary caregiver of the child as the man intensifies his role as provider (Cowan & Cowan, 2000; Deutsch, 2001).

Barbara Peacock/ The Image Bank/Getty Images

Parenting may bring changes in gender roles and the division of labor in the home. Such changes may increase or decrease marital satisfaction.

Other variables also influence life satisfaction following the birth of a baby. For example, the baby's temperament (see p. 375) may create more or less stress on new parents (Schoppe-Sullivan et al., 2007). Difficult babies who cry all the time are more of a challenge than babies who are quiet or who are generally cheerful. The parent makes a difference too. Generally, older parents who have waited longer after marrying to have children are better able to adjust to parenthood (Belsky & Rovine, 1990; Umberson et al., 2005). Younger couples who have children right away are adjusting to marriage at the same time that they are coping with being new parents. The levels of income, spousal support, and support from extended family and friends also increase or decrease the amount of stress that comes with parenting (Levy-Shiff, 1994).

As the child grows older, the demands of parenting do not ease up. Parents adjust their styles of discipline to meet the new challenges their children pose as they grow older and become established (O'Brien, 1996). As the child enters middle school, parenthood may become even more stressful, and marital satisfaction tends to decrease (● FIGURE 9.7; Cui & Donnellan, 2009; Kurdek, 1999; Waldron-Hennessey & Sabatelli, 1997). Parent–child conflicts increase

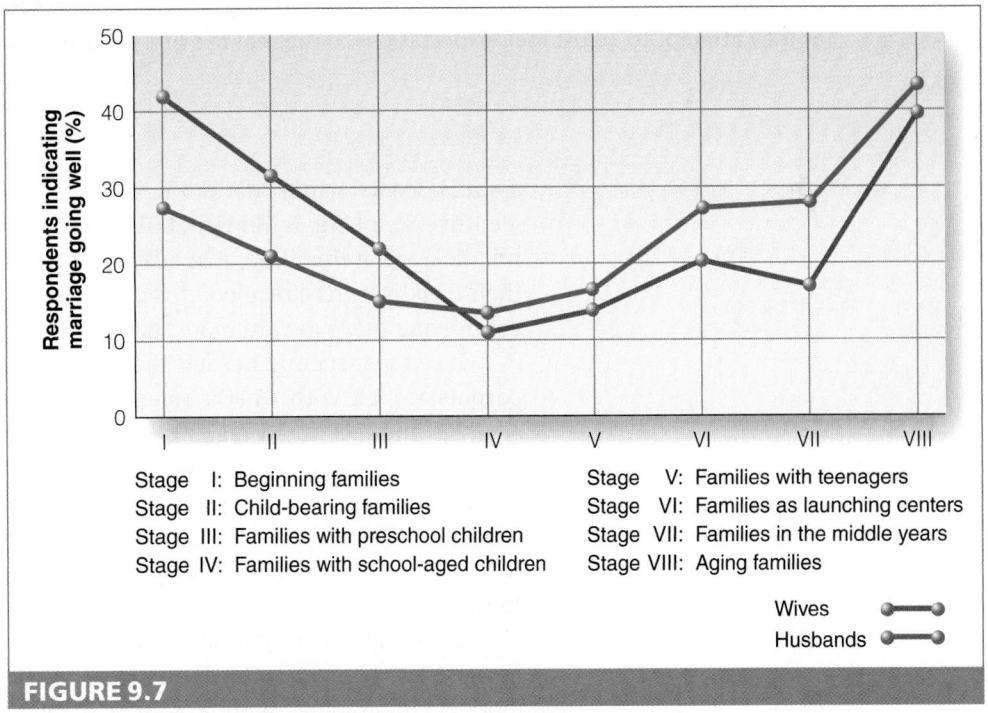

FIGURE 9.7

Marital Satisfaction and Stages of Parenting

First documented by Rollins and Feldman (1975) and later replicated in many studies, the graph shows the percentage of husbands and wives who said their marriage was going well "all the time" at various stages while raising children.

Source: Adapted from Boyd C. Rollins and Harold Feldman, "Marital Satisfaction over the Family Life Cycle," *Journal of Marriage and the Family, 32* (February), 25. Copyrighted 1975 by the National Council on Family Relations, 3989 Central Ave., N.E., Suite 550, Minneapolis, MN 55421. Reprinted by permission.

Psychology Applies to Your World:

Career Development

What do you want to be when you grow up? As a child, you have been asked this question thousands of times, with the expectation that you will answer it with some type of career choice. What we do for a living, or what we hope to do for a living, becomes an integral part of our identity. It may also determine who we socialize with and where we live. For four decades, Donald Super (1957, 1976, 1980, 1991) addressed such issues, outlining a progression of career development.

In early adolescence, as teenagers form their identities, they experiment with how various career options fit with their ideas of who they are and what they want to be. During this *crystallization phase,* potential career options are reduced to a few choices. For example, a teenager who views himself as outgoing, quick thinking, and motivated may imagine himself in a marketing or law career. Teenagers and young adults further explore career options by testing out prospective career choices in the *specification phase*. For example, a young woman who is considering becoming a doctor may volunteer at a hospital or take a part-time job in a physician's office to determine whether medicine fits her interests and abilities. Although somewhat older, Hongyong explored her talents as an entrepreneur through the sesame oil business, as an opium madam, and as a restaurant owner.

Young people enter the workforce and begin to learn about jobs firsthand in the *implementation phase*. The young adult learns both the actual tasks of the job and job-related skills such as getting along with coworkers, getting to work on time, and responding to authority figures. The reality of the work may not meet the person's initial expectations. For example, a teacher's aide may discover that working with children 6 hours a day is not what he expected it to be. Everyone experiences this sort of *reality shock* in some form. However, it is the degree of reality shock that typically determines our willingness to stay on a particular career path. For this reason, the implementation phase can be quite unsettling and unstable. Young adults may find themselves changing positions frequently as they attempt to adjust their expectations to the realities of a particular career.

as adolescents achieve formal operational abilities and begin defining their own identity (Steinberg & Morris, 2001). At the same time, parents, who are typically middle-aged at this time, may also be evaluating and questioning the direction of their own lives. As a result of this conflict and tension, parents may relinquish some control and move toward more shared decision making with their teenagers.

Once the last child has left the family home for college or an independent life, parents are left with what is referred to as the *empty nest*. Parents may be lonely at times and feel that a major chapter in their family life is over. The parents are also aware of their own aging. Yet this stage presents lots of opportunity, too. Most parents, especially women, enjoy the changes brought about by the empty nest. Marital satisfaction tends to increase, and women generally feel better about themselves as the stress and responsibilities of parenthood decrease (Gorchoff, John, & Helson, 2008; White & Edwards, 1990).

What happens to parents if their children don't leave—or if they come back because of divorce, limited finances, or extended schooling? This situation is more common today, with 36% of U.S. young adults aged 18–31 living with their parents (Fry, 2013). This phenomenon is referred to as the *full nest* or the *boomerang generation*. It is more common among Hispanic Americans, African Americans, and Asian Americans, perhaps because of the greater emphasis on family closeness in these ethnic groups (Arnett, 2004). Some parents gladly support their emerging adults (Igarashi et al., 2013). If these young adults act responsibly, going to school or working, parents appear to adjust well. However, some parents do find living with their young adult children stressful (Gitelson & McDermott, 2006).

When a young adult decides on a specific occupation, he or she enters the *establishment phase*. Career expectations continue to be adjusted as the person settles into an occupation and advances in his or her career. Today, however, it is unlikely that this establishment will be with one company or on one career path. The establishment phase may also be more characteristic of men's career pathways. Women's careers may be interrupted during these years for childbearing and child rearing (Preston, 2005). For Hongyong, the establishment phase came with her ch'iryo practice. She knew this was what she wanted to do.

During middle adulthood, career development is characterized by a *maintenance phase*. Although some people may question their career choices and opt for a career change, most middle-aged adults strengthen their commitment to their careers and are more likely to find personal meaning in their work.

Workers enter the *deceleration phase* when they begin planning for their upcoming retirement. Older adults consider such things as finances, where they want to live, and how they want to spend their retirement years. When people stop working full-time, the *retirement phase* begins. Most Americans choose to retire sometime in their 60s and look forward to retirement living. As with other developmental processes that we have discussed, retirement is a process of adjustment that is influenced by many factors such as health, finances, one's control over the decision to retire, and the ability to maintain social ties with others (Lowis, Edwards, & Burton, 2009; Price & Balaswamy, 2009; Reitzes & Mutran, 2004; van Solinge & Henkens, 2005).

Peter Beck/Bridge/Corbis

During the establishment phase, young adults settle into an occupation or a career.

We see, then, that children complicate the lives of adults. Parenthood tends to correlate with lower rates of marital satisfaction and higher levels of stress. Despite these negative effects, most parents don't regret the experience and report higher levels of happiness, positive emotion, and meaning in life than do nonparents (Nelson et al., 2013). Children bring many joys and experiences that enrich their parents' lives. However, the association between parenthood and well-being varies by age and gender. Compared with nonparents, male and middle-aged parents evidence greater well-being, while young and single parents evidence lower well-being (Nelson et al., 2014).

Quiz Yourself

9.7

1. **According to Erikson, feeling that you have made important contributions to society will lead to a sense of _____.**
   a. integrity
   b. generativity
   c. industry
   d. identity

2. **Which of the following statements is *false*?**
   a. Emerging adulthood occurs for all young people.
   b. Emerging adulthood prolongs identity development.
   c. Emerging adulthood typically occurs in one's late teens to one's mid-20s.
   d. Emerging adulthood is when young people have not yet assumed adult roles and responsibilities.

3. **Which of the following is *false* in regard to social relations in adulthood?**
   a. Cohabitation rates have increased over the past decade.
   b. More males than females report being happily married.
   c. Singlehood is associated with better mental and physical health for males.
   d. Divorced people are more likely to experience physical health problems.

4. Parents' marital satisfaction tends to _____ when their children enter middle school.
   a. increase
   b. decrease
   c. marginally get better
   d. stay the same

5. "Reality shock" is most likely to happen during which phase of career development?
   a. Specification phase
   b. Establishment phase
   c. Implementation phase
   d. Deceleration phase

Answers 1. b; 2. a; 3. c; 4. b; 5. c

9.8 Death and Dying

Hongyong Baek witnessed many people's deaths due to war, disease, and starvation. She also personally grieved for her husband. What do people experience psychologically at times like these? Psychologists are also interested in these issues of the last life stage.

Death is a process rather than a point in time. Decades ago it was a process that took place at home, with family members present. Today, it is more likely to occur in a hospital or medical facility, surrounded by doctors, nurses, and machines. In our society, death is more removed from our everyday experiences. As a result, when we face death, we and our families are often unprepared for it. Nevertheless, loss is an inevitable part of our development. Knowing what happens when a loved one is dying and how people respond to the death of a loved one may better prepare us for this final journey.

9.8.1 • Emotional Reactions to Death: Kübler-Ross's Stages

If you were told today that you only had 6 months to live, how would you react? Elisabeth Kübler-Ross (1926–2004) (1969, 1974), a pioneer researcher on death and dying, interviewed more than 200 terminally ill people to address this question. She wanted to investigate any predictable emotional and psychological changes that people might experience as they confront their own death. From her research, she identified five reactions that may characterize dying people: denial, anger, bargaining, depression, and acceptance.

When people first learn that they have a terminal illness, a typical reaction is *denial*. They behave as if they have not just been told that they are going to die. For example, they may insist on a second or third medical opinion. Others may continue in their normal activities, behaving as if they had never received this news. Denial is an effective coping strategy that allows the person time to come to terms with impending death.

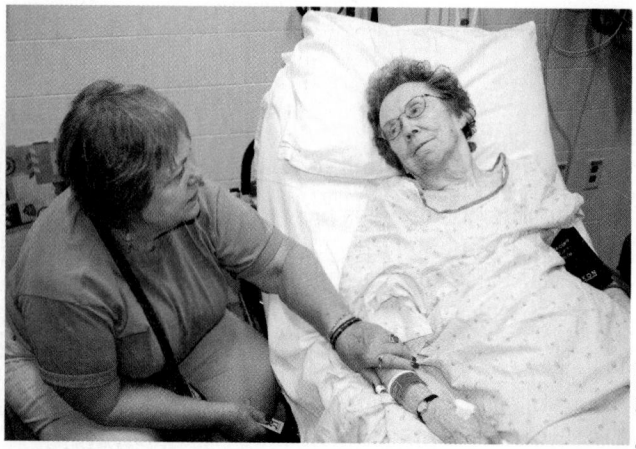

Steve Skjold/Alamy

Terminally ill patients experience a variety of emotional reactions to their deaths, according to Elisabeth Kübler-Ross's research on death and dying.

As denial dwindles, it is replaced by the emotional reaction of *anger*. People lash out at loved ones and medical personnel over the unfairness of death. "Why me?" may be a common response during this stage. Looking for others to blame may also be an expression of this anger.

Following denial and anger, some dying people may also express emotions indicative of *bargaining*. They attempt to strike a deal for more time with the doctors, a supreme being, or the universe. For example, a man may want to live just long enough to see his daughter graduate from college. Another person may bargain to make it through a particular holiday. These bargains may be unrealistic and impossible to fulfill.

People who are dying may become *depressed* or extremely sad when denial, anger, and bargaining fail to delay the progress of their illness. They may lose interest in their usual activities or refuse to participate. This depression may be one way for those who are near the end of life to mourn their own death.

The final emotional state described by Kübler-Ross is *acceptance*. A peace and calm characterize the dying as they face the end of life. They may separate themselves from all but a few of their loved ones as they prepare for life's ending.

Research confirms the legitimacy of Kübler-Ross's reaction stages (Kalish, 1985; Samarel, 1995). However, not every dying person experiences all these reactions. Moreover, not all dying persons go through these reactions in the same order. Death, like many other developmental processes, is influenced by a variety of factors, including one's personality and coping style, the type of support received from family members and health professionals, and the nature of the terminal illness. Yet Kübler-Ross's model is useful for understanding the emotions of dying people and for supporting anyone suffering from loss. People may also experience similar reactions when they face a divorce, unemployment, or the impending death of a loved one.

Hongyong experienced many of these emotions as she wondered over the fate of her son and watched her husband die. At first, she denied the possibility that her son was dead or that her husband's illness was fatal. She turned away in anger from her religion when her son did not appear at the refugee camp. Her depression was so intense that she ignored her living children. But as time went by, she slowly accepted her husband's death as well as not knowing the fate of her son.

9.8.2 • Bereavement and Grief: How We Respond to Death

When a loved one dies, *bereavement* and *grief* follow. **Bereavement** is the experience of losing a loved one; **grief** is our emotional reaction to that loss. Just as death is a highly personal experience, so too is grief. However, research on bereaved people has identified common themes and emotional reactions within three phases: impact/shock, confrontation, and accommodation/acceptance (Bowlby, 1980; Parkes, 1986, 1991; Rando, 1995).

bereavement [bee-REEVE-munt] the experience of losing a loved one

grief one's emotional reaction to the death of a loved one

Most people's first reaction to the loss of a loved one is shock. This *impact phase* may include disbelief on hearing that a loved one has died. It may feel as if a numbness has settled within one's body or mind. This numbness is adaptive, dulling the painful emotions of loss. People in this stage may perform such actions as picking out a casket, making arrangements for a funeral or a burial, and even calling friends and relatives to inform them of the death, as if in a dream. This shock is particularly intense if the person's death was sudden. Think about the emotional numbness and body aches that Hongyong experienced when she thought that her son was dead. She operated as if she were in a fog, a living ghost.

Shock, disbelief, and numbness are common emotional reactions to the loss of a loved one.

Mark Richards/PhotoEdit

Deep despair and agony may soon follow the numbness and shock in the *confrontation phase*. Uncontrollable weeping, anxiety, and feelings of guilt and anger are not uncommon as the grieving person yearns for the loved one to return. The survivor must confront the reality of the loss, and this can be especially painful. The person may have difficulty concentrating, sleeping, and eating. By confronting each wave of despair, the person moves closer to realizing that the loved one is gone.

As the pain of the confrontation phase subsides, the survivors begin to accept the death of the loved one in the *accommodation phase*. The survivors reengage with life, and the memories of the deceased are internalized. People are now able to refocus their emotional energies on normal daily events and relationships with the living.

How long does this grieving process take? A definitive answer is not possible. The course and intensity of these phases differ from person to person. Personality traits, cultural background, and the circumstances surrounding the death of the loved one are all factors that influence one's grief responses. Some people function considerably better after a year or two; others may take several years. Some may never recover, especially from the death of a child (Murphy, 2008). This may explain Hongyong's 40-year search for her son. Research also suggests that men and women may cope differently with grief, as women are more likely than men to seek social support and express their feelings more openly (Rando, 1995; Stroebe, 2001). There also are different cultural norms when it comes to grieving and bereavement. Views on death, dying, and grief are influenced by our cultural upbringing and influence how one expects to grieve and the customs and rituals of the death process (Rosenblatt, 2008).

Quiz Yourself

9.8

1. Caryn has just started chemotherapy to treat breast cancer. Each day she prays that she will be a better person if she is given a second chance and recovers from her illness. Which Kübler-Ross stage is Caryn most likely in?
   a. Acceptance
   b. Bargaining
   c. Anger
   d. Denial
2. Our emotional reaction to the loss of a loved one is called _____.
   a. bereavement
   b. grief
   c. bargaining
   d. reality shock
3. The most intense emotional reactions to the loss of a loved one typically occur during which grief phase?
   a. Impact
   b. Shock
   c. Confrontation
   d. Accommodation

Answers 1. b; 2. b; 3. c

9.9 Integrating Psychology: The Big Picture

In this chapter, we examined the many different ways in which people develop. We hope that as you read this chapter, you were able to see how Hongyong Baek's development contributed to the unique person she became. Although the chapter separately outlined physical, cognitive, and social aspects of development, it is only by integrating these forces, that we can truly appreciate and understand Hongyong's life story.

For example, Hongyong's difficult temperament (biology) did not help her conform to the prescribed social roles for her gender and culture. This may have been a factor in why she married at a later age than other Korean females and in why she was imprisoned. Her culture and gender roles, in turn, influenced her cognitions and psychosocial development. She thought she was ugly and that her value was in being a good wife and mother. Her internal conflict between what she thought she should be and what she wanted to do resulted in role confusion as she searched for meaning in her life through a variety of careers. Her relationships with her husband and children at times complicated and at times nurtured this quest for meaning. Her morality and beliefs were tested not only by these relationships but also by the political environment of her time. As you can see, development is quite complex and requires an understanding of physical, cognitive, and social variables to fully comprehend how it leads to variations in human behavior. Keep these concepts in mind, as many of them will be reinforced in the next two chapters as we explore how social psychology and personality also contribute to variations in behavior.

Studying the Chapter

Key Terms

accommodation (366)
assimilation (366)
attachment (375)
authoritarian parent (377)
authoritative parent (377)
bereavement (403)
centration (368)
concrete operations (369)
conservation (368)
crystallized intelligence (392)
development (354)
Down syndrome (358)
dualistic thinking (391)
egocentrism (368)
embryonic stage (357)
emerging adulthood (395)
fetal alcohol syndrome (FAS) (358)
fetal stage (357)
fine motor skills (362)
fluid intelligence (391)
formal operations (370)
gender permanence (380)
gender roles (380)
gender-schema theory (380)
germinal stage (357)
grief (403)
gross motor skills (362)
imaginary audience (390)
menarche (384)
menopause (388)
moral reasoning (372)
nature–nurture issue (356)
neonate (360)
object permanence (367)
permissive parent (378)
personal fable (390)
postformal thought (391)
preoperational stage (367)
private speech (370)
puberty (384)
reflex (361)
relativistic thinking (391)
scaffolding (371)
schema (365)
sensitive period (358)
sensorimotor stage (367)
separation anxiety (376)
stranger anxiety (376)
symbolic thinking (367)
temperament (375)
teratogen (358)
zone of proximal development (ZPD) (371)
zygote (357)

What Do You Know? Assess Your Understanding

Test your retention and understanding of the material by answering the following questions.

1. Enrique believes that genes are primarily responsible for development. He is emphasizing the _____.

a. nurture side of the nature–nurture issue
b. nature side of the nature–nurture issue
c. influence of the environment
d. influence of unconscious desires

2. Organs and systems form during the _____ stage of prenatal development.

a. zygote
b. germinal
c. embryonic
d. fetal

3. _____ are environmental factors, such as alcohol or cleaning fluids, that may cause birth defects.

a. Chromosomes
b. Teratogens
c. Sensitive periods
d. Myelins

4. _____ serve as the foundation for behaviors such as walking, eating, crying, smiling, and grasping.

a. Temperaments
b. Attachments
c. Formal operations
d. Reflexes

5. Learning how to skip, jump on a trampoline, or ride a bike are examples of _____ motor skills.

a. gross
b. fine
c. big
d. scaffolding

6. Which of the following stimuli do infants prefer to look at?

a. Circles
b. Colors
c. Faces
d. Machines

7. Pablo sees a porpoise for the first time and exclaims, "Fishy, Daddy!" Pablo is engaging in the cognitive process of _____.

a. assimilation
b. accommodation
c. scaffolding
d. formal operations

8. Ms. Lucy, the kindergarten teacher, tries her best to coach her students by making each task somewhat more difficult than the last and modeling how best to approach each task. Ms. Lucy's practice is consistent with _____.

a. assimilation
b. accommodation
c. scaffolding
d. sensorimotor thought

9. Some students think it is wrong to cheat because they could get caught and punished. Such students are operating at the _____ level of moral reasoning.

a. preconventional
b. conventional
c. postconventional
d. preoperational

10. Jamal sees two differently shaped glasses filled with liquid. He recognizes that even though they look different, the glasses hold the same amount of liquid. Piaget would say that Jamal is operating at the _____ stage of cognitive development.

a. sensorimotor
b. preoperational
c. concrete operations
d. preconventional

11. As a baby, Reece did not cry a lot, regularly approached new people and situations, and had a regular pattern of eating and sleeping. Reece's temperament is best described as _____.

a. easy
b. slow-to-warm-up
c. difficult
d. avoidant

12. While at the state fair, Cicily remains close to her dad and does not explore the games or rides. She shows extreme distress if her dad leaves her side. Cicily most likely has a(n) _____ attachment style.

a. avoidant
b. resistant
c. secure
d. disorganized

13. Which part of the brain is among the last to fully develop during adolescence and young adulthood?

a. Cerebellum
b. Amygdala
c. Pituitary gland
d. Prefrontal cortex

14. Older adults evaluate how satisfying their lives have been in Erikson's psychosocial crisis of _____.

a. identity versus role confusion
b. intimacy versus isolation
c. generativity versus stagnation
d. integrity versus despair

15. Consuelo dresses and acts like a girl. She feels that she is a female. This describes Consuelo's _____.

a. gender role
b. gender identity
c. gender typing
d. gender bias

16. Tomas believes that there is only one right answer or single solution to a situation. Tomas is engaging in _____.

a. dualistic thinking
b. relativistic thinking
c. postformal thought
d. All of the above

17. The development of one's personal values and character is referred to as _____.

a. industry
b. integrity
c. generativity
d. identity

18. How are teenagers and preschoolers similar in their thinking?

a. Both cannot think abstractly.
b. Both have developed conservation abilities.
c. Both are egocentric in their thinking.
d. Teenagers and preschoolers are not similar in their thinking.

19. Marital satisfaction is associated with _____.

a. similar educational background
b. warm and positive extended family relationships
c. secure financial circumstances
d. All of the above

20. Pilar's partner died a week ago and she is in the impact stage of grief. What emotions is Pilar most likely feeling?

a. Numbness and shock
b. Deep despair and agony
c. Anxiety and feelings of guilt
d. Acceptance and reengagement with her daily living

Answers: 1. b; 2. c; 3. b; 4. d; 5. a; 6. c; 7. a; 8. c; 9. a; 10. c; 11. a; 12. b; 13. d; 14. d; 15. b; 16. a; 17. d; 18. c; 19. d; 20. a

Use It or Lose It: Applying Psychology

1. At what age would you introduce your child to the following games and toys? Defend your reasoning by considering physical, cognitive, and psychosocial aspects of development.
   a. A board game
   b. Building blocks
   c. Constructing a model spaceship
   d. Hide-and-seek
   e. A chemistry set
2. Analyze your parent(s)' style of discipline during your childhood. How would Baumrind classify their parenting style? How well did their style complement your temperament? What impact do you think your parent(s)' style of discipline had on your cognitive, psychosocial, and emotional development? Be specific, and cite examples to support your answer.
3. For each of Erikson's psychosocial stages, detail what specific behaviors may suggest that an individual is having difficulty resolving that particular stage.
4. Imagine that you have just been told that you are going to have a baby. Use your knowledge about infant physical, cognitive, and psychosocial development to design a nursery for your baby. Create a list of items you'd like to include, such as furniture, toys, and bedding, and describe how you would decorate the walls. Explain your choices in terms of developmental processes.
5. Describe what you feel are benefits to aging and give examples to support your arguments.
6. Spend an hour watching television shows aimed at children, playing children's video games, or using computer programs developed for children. What messages, schemas, or concepts will children acquire from these sources? How might these messages influence their ideas about gender? In your opinion, are these messages appropriate for children? Explain.

Critical Thinking for Integration

1. Review the information on memory processing (Chapter 7) and problem solving (Chapter 8). What strategies and activities would Piaget and Vygotsky suggest are best for improving children's memory and problem-solving skills? Would they suggest the same techniques or different ones?
2. How might operant conditioning (Chapter 6) influence children's understanding of gender? In your opinion, are males and females reinforced for the same behaviors? Do they receive the same reinforcers? Similarly, are males and females punished for the same behaviors? How do their punishments differ? How might differences in reinforcers and punishers influence gender behavior in males and females?
3. Use each of the different psychological perspectives introduced in Chapter 1 to explain career choice in adulthood.
4. Explain how the aging trends described in this chapter relate to the information on sensation and perception discussed in Chapter 3? Consider the physical structure of the sense organs as well as how aging may influence our ability to sense and perceive the world.

Masterfile

Are You Getting the Big Picture? Human Development

9.1 Human Development: How Does It All Begin?

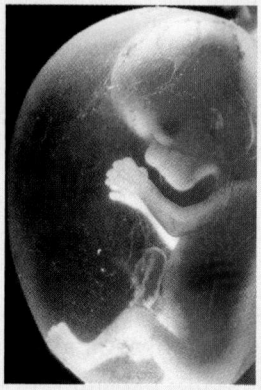

Claude Edelmann/Science Source

Development includes changes in physical, emotional, social, and cognitive behavior and abilities over time through an interaction of **nature** (one's biology) and **nurture** (one's environment and culture).

- **Germinal stage** (0–14 days): The **zygote** undergoes rapid cell division and duplication.
- **Embryonic stage** (2–8 weeks): Major organs and organ systems form.
- **Fetal stage** (week 9–birth): Body organs and systems more fully develop

9.2 How Do Infants and Children Develop Physically?

© Monkey Business Images/Shutterstock.com

- Infants' and children's brains are highly *plastic*, or changeable.
- **Reflexes** such as sucking, rooting, and grasping help the infant survive.
- **Gross motor skills** (behaviors that involve large muscle groups) allow the child to run, walk, jump, and hop. **Fine motor skills** (involving small muscle groups) aid in activities such as writing, using utensils, and playing a musical instrument.

9.3 How Do Infants and Children Develop Cognitively?

Marmaduke St. John/Alamy

- According to Jean Piaget, infants and children apply **schemas** (**assimilation**) to understand their environment and adapt to change through **accommodation** when existing schema are changed or modified in four stages of cognitive development: **sensorimotor**, **preoperational**, **concrete operations**, and **formal operations**.
- Lev Vygotsky stressed the importance of culture and social interactions in cognitive development.
- Lawrence Kohlberg's research on **moral reasoning** suggests that children's understanding of right and wrong develops progressively from a focus on the self to the external world.

9.4 How Do Infants and Children Develop Psychosocially?

Paul Bradbury/Getty Images

- An infant's **temperament** can influence the **attachment** or emotional tie between the infant and the primary caregiver.
- Diana Baumrind identified three styles of parenting: **authoritarian**, **authoritative**, and **permissive**. Permissive parenting may be indulgent or neglectful.
- Psychologist Erik Erikson proposed that the environment and the child's responses to the environment influence the development of either a healthy or an unhealthy personality.
- At a very early age, children process and develop schema about **gender roles**, or society's expectations for how a female and a male should behave.

9.5 Physical Changes in Adolescence and Adulthood

© Jerzyworks/Masterfile

- **Puberty** involves maturation of sex characteristics that enable us to reproduce. At around age 50, women experience **menopause** and hormonal changes that eventually bring an end to reproductive capacity.
- During adolescence and throughout life, the brain remains highly plastic, allowing us to adapt to changing conditions.

9.6 Cognitive Changes in Adolescence and Adulthood

- Teenagers tend to be **egocentric**, believing that others are concerned with the same things that they are.
- **Postformal thought** is characterized by **relativistic thinking**, an appreciation that the correct solution or answer may vary from situation to situation. Remaining cognitively active helps adults avoid steep declines in mental abilities.

9.7 Psychosocial Changes in Adolescence and Adulthood

Michael Doolittle/Alamy

- Erik Erikson considered adolescence the key stage for developing *identity*, but he believed adults continue to develop when they establish *intimacy*, *generativity*, and *integrity*.
- Adolescent and adult relationships are expressed in a wide range of lifestyles, including dating, cohabitation, marriage, divorce, and parenthood.
- Finding satisfying work and holding a job are part of adult development.

9.8 How Do People Cope with Death and Dying?

Mark Richards/Photo Edit

- Death is a process rather than a point in time and is an inevitable part of our development.
- Researcher, Elizabeth Kübler-Ross, identified five reactions that may characterize people who know they are dying: denial, anger, bargaining, depression, and acceptance.

Social Psychology

Learning Objectives

10.1 Describe attitudes, how they develop, and how they affect behavior. (APA 1.1, 1.3)

10.1 Describe dissonance theory, and explain the role of dissonance in attitude change. (APA 1.1, 1.2, 1.3)

10.1 Describe the major theories of persuasion and how the communicator, the message, and the audience affect persuasion. (APA 1.1, 1.2, 1.3, 2.1)

10.2 Describe how we form impressions about ourselves and others by making attributions. (APA 1.1, 1.3, 3.2)

10.2 Describe the common heuristics and biases that affect the attribution process. (APA 1.1, 1.3)

10.3 Define and distinguish among prejudice, stereotypes, discrimination, and stereotype threat. (APA 1.1, 1.3, 3.2, 3.3)

10.3 Describe how prejudice develops. (APA 1.1, 1.2, 1.3, 3.2, 3.3)

10.3 Describe ways to reduce prejudice. (APA 1.1, 1.2, 1.3, 3.2, 3.3)

10.4 Describe the factors affecting attraction: proximity, exposure, similarity, and physical attractiveness. (APA 1.1, 1.3, 3.2)

10.5 Describe how cohesiveness and norms function within groups. (APA 1.1, 1.2, 1.3, 3.2)

10.5 Describe the factors that affect our tendency to conform to the norms of a group. (APA 1.1, 1.2, 1.3, 3.2)

10.5 Describe how working in a group can affect both performance and decision making within the group. (APA 1.1, 1.3, 3.2)

10.6 Describe the process of compliance and commonly used compliance techniques. (APA 1.1, 1.3)

10.6 Describe obedience, destructive obedience, and the factors that affect our tendency to obey. (APA 1.1, 1.2, 1.3, 3.3)

10.7 Define aggression and its different types. (APA 1.1, 1.3)

10.7 Describe how biology, learning, and situational factors affect aggression. (APA 1.1, 1.3, 3.2, 3.3)

10.8 Describe the steps involved in deciding whether to help another. (APA 1.1, 1.3, 3.2, 3.3)

10.8 Describe the factors that influence helping. (APA 1.1, 1.3, 3.2, 3.3)

The story of Hongyong Baek illustrates how those around us affect our thoughts and behaviors. Hongyong's feelings about her body were influenced by both her mother's teachings and the cultural values placed on women in Korea at the time. As a result, she felt ashamed and inadequate. In the presence of her mother, she tried to behave as her mother expected her to behave—as a chaste and obedient woman—but often failed. Then when Hongyong's parents arranged for her marriage to Dukpil Lee, it was through his encouragement that she learned to become more assertive and independent. If Hongyong had married a more domineering man, who never let her speak her mind, it is possible that she might not have developed the independence that ultimately allowed her to survive the challenges she faced during the Korean War.

Similarly, Hongyong's own behavior likely had influence on the thoughts and behaviors of those around her. Her decision to smuggle opium resulted in her husband's decision to spend more time away from home. Hongyong's change of career influenced her husband to spend more time with her. As you can see, in the social world each of us is capable of being both influenced by others *and* being an influence that changes others. The **social influence** goes both ways. Take a moment to reflect: In what ways have others influenced your thoughts and behaviors? In what ways have you influenced the thought and behavior of others? These are the questions that we will explore in this chapter on *social psychology.*

10

© Tyler Olson/Shutterstock.com

Chapter Outline

10.1 Evaluating the World: Attitudes / 412

10.2 Forming Impressions of Others / 417

10.3 Prejudice: Why Can't We All Just Get Along? / 421

10.4 Being Drawn to Others: The Nature of Attraction / 429

10.5 Group Influence / 433

10.6 Requests and Demands: Compliance and Obedience / 439

10.7 Aggression: Hurting Others / 447

PSYCHOLOGY APPLIES TO YOUR WORLD: Does Television Portray Violence Accurately? / 450

10.8 Choosing to Help Others: Prosocial Behavior / 451

10.9 Integrating Psychology: The Big Picture / 455

10.1 Evaluating the World: Attitudes

social influence social pressures that serve to modify our thoughts and/or behavior

social psychology the branch of psychology that studies how we think and behave in social situations

social cognition the area of social psychology that deals with the ways in which we think about other people and ourselves

attitude an evaluative belief that we hold about something

Social psychology is the study of how we think and behave in the vast array of social situations that we experience. One area of social psychology, **social cognition**, investigates the ways in which we think (cognition) about ourselves and others—for example, studying how we develop **attitudes**, our liking or disliking for the people, places, and things in our world. We all have attitudes about a multitude of things that represent the evaluative beliefs we hold about the contents of our world (e.g., liking country music or disliking lazy people). But how do we acquire these attitudes?

10.1.1 • Acquiring Attitudes Through Learning

As with many of our beliefs, we learn to have many of the attitudes we hold. One learning process that affects our attitudes about the world is *classical conditioning* (Chapter 6). Recall that classical conditioning is often responsible for the development of certain learned *emotional* and *physiological* responses in humans (• FIGURE 10.1). Because classical conditioning has the power to change the way we feel about certain stimuli, it also has the power to influence our attitude toward these stimuli. For example, if a man is robbed by a gang member, he may be classically conditioned to fear (CR) people who wear gang colors and clothes (CS). In short, classical conditioning can often explain the gut-level emotional and physiological aspects of our attitudes (Grossman & Till, 1998). Similarly, if a celebrity (US) makes us feel positive emotion (UR), then seeing this celebrity marketing a product (NS/CS) may condition us to have a positive emotional reaction (CR) when we encounter the product (Till, Stanley, & Priluck, 2008).

Operant conditioning, or learning through the consequences of our behavior (Chapter 6), also affects our attitudes. If you are rewarded for having certain attitudes, the attitude will be strengthened. But if you are punished for having certain attitudes, the attitude will be weakened. For example, if your friends applaud your

FIGURE 10.1

Classically Conditioning a Negative Attitude Toward Dogs

For a young child, a fear response in her mother (US) will naturally cause fear in the child (UR). On the other hand, the sight of a dog will not reliably elicit fear in a small child. Therefore, the dog is initially a neutral stimulus (NS). When the sight of the dog (NS) is repeatedly paired with a fear response in the mother (US), the child can easily acquire a conditioned fear of dogs (CR) that is elicited by the mere sight of a dog (CS).

efforts to "go green" and recycle your trash, then your pro-green attitude is likely to strengthen.

Operant conditioning can also influence our attitudes through the consequences of our direct interaction with the objects of our attitude. For example, if you try a Jamaican dish with lots of very hot peppers that burns your mouth so badly your eyes water, you might develop a negative attitude about eating hot Jamaican food. As a result, the next time you visit a Jamaican restaurant, your behavior will likely change—you'll order one of the blander dishes!

At times, we also model the attitudes of others. Recall that in *observational learning* we learn by watching the actions of others and storing mental representations of their behavior in memory (Chapter 6). For example, Hongyong Baek's early attitudes about the role of women in society were very similar to the attitudes espoused by her mother. Because Hongyong spent a lot of time with her mother, she may have simply modeled the attitudes that she saw her mother express. Take a minute to think about your attitudes and the attitudes of those closest to you. Are your views on the roles of men and women in society similar to those of your closest loved ones? If so, the similarity may be due to observational learning. If you are like most people, you will find that overall, your attitudes are quite similar to those of your parents (Rohan & Zanna, 1996) and those around you (Kowalski, 2003). There will, of course, be some notable differences, but overall we tend to be more like those we love when it comes to attitudes.

As you can see, we learn attitudes the way that we learn everything in life—through experience. Once we form our attitudes about the world, they then have the power to affect what we know, how we feel, and how we behave toward just about everything we encounter in our lives. But is this always the case—do our attitudes always predict our behavior?

© Jim West/Alamy

We often take on the attitudes of our parents through observational learning. This little girl is likely to adopt the pro–public education attitudes of her mother.

10.1.2 • Attitude–Behavior Consistency

Do you ever find yourself behaving in a manner that contradicts your attitudes? For example, have you ever laughed at a joke you didn't find very funny? Do you sometimes engage in behavior that you know is harmful to you? If so, your behavior is not unusual. We often behave in ways that go against our attitudes. This lack of *attitude–behavior consistency* has intrigued researchers because it seems so counterintuitive and illogical.

If social pressures can make it difficult for us to behave consistently with our attitudes, what factors make it more likely that we will behave in ways that are consistent with our attitudes? Answers to this question have great practical value in society. For instance, under what circumstances might people's positive attitudes toward safer sex actually lead them to engage in protected sex? When might political attitudes accurately predict voting behavior? And in which situations can a company assume that consumer attitudes toward their products will actually translate into sales? Researchers have been diligently trying to answer such questions. ● TABLE 10.1 describes some of the variables that have been shown to influence attitude–behavior consistency.

Given that our attitudes develop through experience and that once in place they influence our behavior at least part of the time, many psychologists are interested in how attitudes can be changed. This information also has great practical value. If we knew how to change attitudes, we might be able to reverse social problems such as prejudice and alcoholism. These and other pragmatic concerns have fueled a great deal of research on attitude change.

TABLE 10.1

Factors That Affect Attitude–Behavior Consistency

FACTOR	EXAMPLE
If your attitude about the object is low in ambivalence, the attitude will be a better predictor of behavior (Cooke & Sheeran, 2004).	Feeling completely positive about spinach (rather than having mixed feelings about spinach) increases your chance of eating it.
If the cognitive and affective aspects of the attitude are both positive (or both negative), the attitude will be a better predictor of behavior (Cooke & Sheeran, 2004).	Both enjoying spinach and knowing that it is good for you increases the chances that you will eat it.
Attitudes that are quickly and automatically retrieved from long-term memory are better predictors of behavior (Cooke & Sheeran, 2004).	If the first thing you think of when ordering dinner is your love of spinach, you are more likely to order it.
Attitudes that have been stable over time are likely to be better predictors of behavior (Cooke & Sheeran, 2004).	If you have loved spinach since early childhood, you are more likely to continue eating it than you would be if you only recently developed a liking for spinach.
Attitudes that are certain are better predictors of behavior (Cooke & Sheeran, 2004).	If you are very sure about your love of spinach, you are more likely to eat it than you would be if you were not very certain about liking spinach.
Attitudes that are learned through direct experience with the attitude object are likely to be better predictors of behavior (Cooke & Sheeran, 2004).	If you first learned to love spinach by actually eating it, you are more likely to eat it again.
Being in a negative mood has been shown to enhance attitude–behavior consistency (Elen et al., 2013).	You have loved spinach since childhood. Today, you had a bad day and are in a bad mood. When your friend offers you corn at the picnic today, instead you eat the spinach.
Attitudes best predict behavior when the attitude and behavior have the same level of attitude-relevant action activity (Paulson et al., 2012).	You love spinach and believe in promoting spinach as a healthy food (active attitude). When planting your garden, you choose to grow spinach (active behavior).

10.1.3 • Cognitive Consistency and Attitude Change

Throughout our lifetime, our attitudes will change as we acquire new knowledge and have different experiences. For example, a favorable attitude toward a particular restaurant may change if you read in the paper that the restaurant failed its last health inspection. In light of this new information, the old attitude may be discarded in favor of a less favorable one. In this example, the attitude change was motivated from within the attitude holder. The change was not the result of a concerted effort on the part of others. It was motivated more by your desire to maintain what psychologists refer to as **cognitive consistency**, or the desire to avoid contradictions in our attitudes and behaviors (Festinger, 1957). Cognitive consistency theories (Festinger, 1957; Heider, 1946) propose that humans find it uncomfortable when there is inconsistency among their attitudes or between their

cognitive consistency the idea that we strive to have attitudes and behaviors that do not contradict one another attitudes and their behavior. Most of us believe that we are intelligent, logical beings. This attitude about being intelligent and logical would be inconsistent with the attitude that an unhealthy restaurant is a good place to eat. So we adjust one of our attitudes (the one concerning the restaurant) to avoid such an inconsistency. But why does inconsistency make us uncomfortable and therefore motivate attitude change?

One explanation of how cognitive inconsistency motivates attitude change is **dissonance theory** (Festinger, 1957). According to dissonance theory, inconsistencies among attitudes or between attitudes and behavior cause an unpleasant physical state called *dissonance*. Think of dissonance as a state of unease much like being hungry or being anxious. It stems from the realization that we have behaved in a way that is contrary to our self-concept (Aronson, 1998). Because dissonance makes us feel bad, we are motivated to stop this unpleasant feeling, which can lead to attitude and/or behavior change (Joule & Azdia, 2003; Martinie, Milland, & Olive, 2013; Powers & Jack, 2013). For example, a health-conscious person who smokes is likely to experience dissonance because smoking is inconsistent with being health conscious. Once the person experiences dissonance, she will be motivated to stop the dissonance by removing the inconsistency.

Colin Young-Wolff/Photo Edit

Because smoking is inconsistent with being health conscious, this person is likely to experience dissonance that may lead to attitude or behavior change.

In general, there are three ways to remove the inconsistencies that cause dissonance. First, she can change her behavior (stop smoking). Second, she can change her attitudes (decide that she is not health conscious after all). Or third, she can remove the inconsistency by bringing new beliefs and attitudes to bear on the situation (convince herself that smoking has never really been proven to cause health problems). Any of these three methods will reduce the dissonance felt by the person and restore a state of *consonance,* in which there is no inconsistency among attitudes and behavior.

10.1.4 • Persuasion and Attitude Change

Dissonance theory can explain certain aspects of how we change and grow as human beings, but dissonance is not the only means through which our attitudes change. We also encounter frequent **persuasion** situations in which others directly attempt to change our attitudes. Every day we face persuasive attempts from friends, family members, politicians, the media, and advertisers. A widely quoted figure estimates that the average American encounters a whopping 3,000 advertisements per day (Stanton, 2004). However, some dispute this figure. The American Association of Advertising Agencies (2014) suggests that the actual number may be more in line with 600–625 potential exposures per day from various sources. They specify *potential* exposures, because it is quite possible that some of these go unnoticed by us. Whether the actual number is 600 or 3,000, most agree that persuasive attempts are a common daily occurrence. With all of these persuasive attempts being hurled at us on a daily basis, an understanding of how persuasion occurs becomes almost a necessity.

Obviously, not all of the persuasive attempts we are subjected to actually produce attitude change. We do not become loyal to every product we see advertised on TV. We do not vote for every political candidate we hear speak. So just what makes persuasion successful—or what makes it fail?

One very important factor in the effectiveness of persuasion is the type of *cognitive processes* that we engage in during the persuasive attempt. The degree to which we analyze persuasive arguments can influence whether those arguments are effective in changing our attitudes (Petty & Cacioppo, 1986; Wegener & Carlston, 2005). When we process on the **central route to persuasion**, we carefully

dissonance theory a theory that predicts that we will be motivated to change our attitudes and/or our behaviors to the extent that they cause us to feel dissonance, an uncomfortable physical state

persuasion a type of social influence in which someone tries to change our attitudes

central route to persuasion a style of thinking in which the person carefully and critically evaluates persuasive arguments and generates counterarguments; the central route requires motivation and available cognitive resources

peripheral route to persuasion a style of thinking in which the person does not carefully and critically evaluate persuasive arguments or generate counterarguments; the peripheral route ensues when one lacks motivation and/or available cognitive resources

and critically evaluate the logic of the persuasive arguments we encounter. When we process on the **peripheral route to persuasion**, we do not attempt to critically evaluate the arguments and are instead persuaded by superficial aspects of the arguments such as the likability of the person making them or the attractiveness of the ad. For example, when viewing job ads online, participants who were motivated to carefully evaluate the ad's content (central route processing) developed attitudes toward the company that were less affected by the aesthetics of the website. In contrast, if the participants were motivated to focus on superficial aspects of the ads rather than carefully evaluating their content (peripheral route processing), they developed attitudes toward the company that were more affected by the aesthetics of the website (Gregory, Meade, & Thompson, 2013).

Whether or not persuasion is successful depends in large measure on the cognitive processing we employ. However, other variables can also affect our chances of being persuaded. These variables fall into three categories: variables associated with the *communicator* of the message, variables associated with the persuasive *message* itself, and variables associated with the *audience* that receives the persuasive message.

COMMUNICATOR VARIABLES

We tend to be most persuaded when the person communicating the message to us is attractive (Eagly & Chaiken, 1975; Evans & Clark, 2012), appears to be credible (Hovland & Weiss, 1951; Tormala, Briñol, & Petty, 2007), or appears to be an expert (Evans & Clark, 2012; Petty, Cacioppo, & Goldman, 1981). We are also most persuaded when the communicator does not appear to be trying to persuade us—unless he or she is attractive, in which case persuasion is not reduced by the awareness that the communicator is trying to persuade us (Messner, Reinhard, & Sporer, 2008). This is one reason that advertisers hire well-respected, attractive actors and actresses to sell their products. They know that we will be more likely to be persuaded because we place our trust in such people—especially if we are processing on the peripheral route (Petty et al., 1981; Shavitt et al., 1994).

MESSAGE VARIABLES

The logic of the persuasive argument has its greatest impact when we are processing on the central route, for it is here that we can truly appreciate the goodness of the argument (see Petty & Briñol, 2008). We are more likely to be persuaded if the communicator effectively presents both the pros (why we should accept the arguments) and cons (why we might not accept the arguments) of the proposal. This is especially true when the communicator can effectively argue against objections to accepting the proposal (Crowley & Hoyer, 1994). Two-sided arguments generally work best because we tend to trust a communicator who is willing to openly discuss the drawbacks of a proposal.

Attractiveness of a communicator can be one factor that makes you more likely to accept an argument. This is especially true when you are processing on the peripheral route to persuasion.

Bloomberg via Getty Images

AUDIENCE VARIABLES

Effective persuasion is heavily dependent on who is being

persuaded. In general, all of us are easier to persuade on the peripheral rather than the central route to persuasion. However, individual differences among us can also influence whether we are persuaded. Variables such as intelligence (Rhodes & Wood, 1992), self-esteem (Petty, Fabrigar, & Wegener, 2003), self-monitoring (our tendency to change our behavior to meet other's expectations; Evans & Clark, 2012), and mood (Sanaktekin & Sunar, 2008) can all affect our tendency to be persuaded. Yet, after decades of research, it is impossible to make blanket statements about the effect these variables have on persuasion because our individual differences interact in a complex fashion with other variables, such as the route we are processing on (Petty & Briñol, 2008). Under the right circumstances, either high or low levels of intelligence, self-esteem, or positive emotion can all lead to high or low persuasion.

Quiz Yourself 10.1

1. **If Mike wishes to make the best possible decision about how to vote in the upcoming presidential election, he should watch the presidential debates while processing on the _____.**
   a. central route
   b. algorithmic route
   c. peripheral route
   d. shortest route
2. **A politician is attempting to persuade people to vote for her in an upcoming election. With which of the following types of arguments would you expect her to have the most success in winning over a skeptical audience?**
   a. A short argument that lacks great detail
   b. A very long and detailed argument
   c. A one-sided argument explaining why voters should vote for her
   d. A two-sided argument explaining why voters should vote for her, as well as some concerns they may have about voting for her
3. **Thelma recently discovered that her favorite actress supports a radical political group that Thelma despises. According to dissonance theory, what is most likely to happen in this situation?**
   a. She will begin to like the actress more.
   b. She will begin to like the actress less.
   c. She will begin to dislike the political group more.
   d. Her attitudes toward the actress and the group will not change.

Answers 1. a; 2. d; 3. b

10.2 Forming Impressions of Others

One of the most important aspects of social cognition is **impression formation**, or how we understand and make judgments about others. When we meet someone for the first time, we usually attempt to determine what type of person he is. Is this person kind, smart, aggressive, or untrustworthy? We want to know. Why do we want to know what other people are like? In short, if we have a good understanding of other people's traits and abilities, we can predict how they will behave in certain situations. This allows us to guide our own behavior in social situations. Without some understanding of others, social interactions would be much more awkward and uncertain.

impression formation the way that we understand and make judgments about others

10.2.1 • The Attribution Process

One of our basic social cognitive tendencies is to try to explain the behavior of ourselves and others, but how do you determine the traits and characteristics of

attribution the act of assigning cause to behavior

trait attribution an attribution that assigns the cause of a behavior to the traits and characteristics of the person being judged

situational attribution an attribution that assigns the cause of a behavior to some characteristic of the situation or environment in which the behavior occurs

someone you've just met? If you're thinking that we pay attention to what the person says and does, you're correct. When we judge a person, we observe his behavior, and then we attempt to determine the cause of this behavior (Heider, 1958). This process of assigning cause to behavior is called **attribution**. For example, imagine that you enter a local café and see a woman yelling at a man in the corner booth. Witnessing her outburst, you would likely try to determine why the woman is yelling. Is it because she is an aggressive person? Or did the man somehow provoke this type of outburst in an otherwise kind woman? Questions like these may pass through your mind as you watch the scene unfold.

In this example, we can attribute the woman's behavior to one of two types of causes. We can attribute the behavior to her traits, abilities, or characteristics, in which case we are making a **trait attribution**. Or we may attribute the behavior to something in the environment, in which case we are making a **situational attribution**. If we make a trait attribution about the yelling woman, we assume that she is yelling because she is an aggressive person. If we make a situational attribution, we assume that something happened in the environment that caused the woman to yell—perhaps her companion accidently spilled hot coffee in her lap. Note that when we make a situational attribution, we do not attribute the woman's behavior to her personality.

Denise Hager/Catchlight Visual Services/Alamy

If you witnessed this scene, what attributions would you make about this woman's behavior? Would you assume that her behavior reflects her personality traits? Or would you assume that the situation must have elicited her behavior?

10.2.2 • Heuristics and Biases in Attribution

Ideally, we would weigh all the available evidence before making either a trait attribution or a situational attribution. Unfortunately, the realities of the world do not always allow us to make careful, analytic attributions. Humans are *cognitive misers*, meaning that we try to conserve our cognitive resources whenever we can (Fiske & Taylor, 2013). We have seen evidence of our miserliness in earlier discussions. As we saw in Chapter 8, when we have to quickly solve a problem, we often use shortcuts, or heuristics, in hopes of finding a solution. Heuristics may lead to quick answers, but they do not always lead to accurate answers. People have been shown to employ several timesaving heuristics while making attributions, and these shortcuts often lead to errors and biases in the attribution process.

ENGAGE YOURSELF! Try the following demonstration. Look at the photos in • FIGURE 10.2 and follow the instructions. What type of personality traits did you list for these people? How confident were you in these judgments? Now ask yourself this question: What evidence do I have that these people actually possess these personality traits? If you're like most people, your perceptions of these celebrities are based on the roles they play on TV or in the movies. Most of us assume that their behavior on TV is indicative of their personality traits in real life. Did you? If so, what situational explanations for these people's TV behavior did you fail to take into account? Did you take into account that on TV, these celebrities are acting? Did you think about the fact that even reality shows and talk shows involve someone directing the actors' behavior and the actors are aware that they are being watched by millions of people? Probably not. The bottom line is that unless you've spent time with

Jim Parsons of *The Big Bang Theory*	Shakira of *The Voice*	Oprah Winfrey of *Oprah's Next Chapter*	Jimmy Fallon of *The Tonight Show Starring Jimmy Fallon*
Trait:	Trait:	Trait:	Trait:
Trait:	Trait:	Trait:	Trait:
Trait:	Trait:	Trait:	Trait:
Confidence rating:	Confidence rating:	Confidence rating:	Confidence rating:

FIGURE 10.2

What Do You Think About These Celebrities?

Take a look at these celebrities. Would you like to be friends with these people? What kind of people do you think they are? In the spaces below each photo, write down some of the traits you think this person possesses. Then rate your confidence in the accuracy of your judgments on a scale from 1 to 10, where 1 = not at all confident that your judgment is correct and 10 = very confident that your judgment is correct.

these celebrities in real life, you've never really seen their natural behavior; therefore, it's somewhat illogical to draw firm conclusions about their personality traits. If you did just that, don't feel bad. This tendency to rely on trait attributions and to discount situational explanations of behavior is so common that it is called the **fundamental attribution error**.

fundamental attribution error our tendency to overuse trait information when making attributions about others

individualistic culture a culture, like many Western cultures, in which individual accomplishments are valued over group accomplishments

collectivistic culture a culture, like many Asian cultures, in which group accomplishments are valued over individual accomplishments

FUNDAMENTAL ATTRIBUTION ERROR

Why we tend to engage in the fundamental attribution error is not entirely clear. Perhaps it reflects our preference to know more about a person's traits than about a person's environment. After all, the goal of forming attributions is to understand the person, not the environment (Jones, 1979). For example, in one study participants were found to make negative *trait* attributions about the author of an email that contained spelling and grammatical errors. However, when they were given *situational* information that indicated that the author was from a different culture, the participants formed less negative impressions of the author (Vignovic & Thompson, 2010).

Another explanation for the fundamental attribution error is that when we view someone in a social setting, we tend to focus our attention on the person and her behavior, paying less attention to the situation. If we don't pay much attention to the situation, we are unlikely to give situational factors much weight when making our attributions.

Engaging in the fundamental attribution error varies with the degree to which our culture emphasizes individual behavior over group behavior. Some cultures, such as those in North America and Western Europe, are **individualistic cultures**, emphasizing the behavior and success of individuals rather than groups. Some other cultures, such as those in India and Japan, are **collectivistic**

cultures, emphasizing the behavior and success of groups more than individuals (Triandis, 1994). Research has shown that people from individualistic cultures are more likely to engage in the fundamental attribution error (Choi & Nesbitt, 1998), but people from collectivistic cultures are less likely to engage in this bias (Morris & Peng, 1994). Presumably, the Western focus on the individual accounts for this difference in attribution, but more research needs to be done to pinpoint the exact causes of the fundamental attribution error and its connection to culture (see, e.g., Lien et al., 2006).

One piece of good news is that education in social psychology, such as you are getting right now, can reduce our tendency to engage in the fundamental attribution error (Stalder, 2012). It seems that being aware of our own potential biases can help us behave in a less biased fashion when making attributions and forming impressions of others.

ACTOR/OBSERVER BIAS

What kind of attributions do we make when we are examining our own behavior? What if you found yourself yelling at a companion in a café? Would you be as likely to label yourself as a mean person as you would the woman in the previous example? Probably not. When we observe our own behavior, we tend to take situational factors more into account than we do for others. This tendency has been called the **actor/observer bias** because we make different attributions as *actors* than we make as *observers* of others (Choi & Nesbitt, 1998; Jones & Nesbitt, 1971). The actor/observer bias predicts that you are likely to attribute your own yelling to some situational factor. Perhaps your significant other angered you, or you had a bad day. The explanation you would likely use for others, being a mean person, would be low on your list of attributions for your own behavior.

actor/observer bias our tendency to make the fundamental attribution error when judging others, while being less likely to do so when making attributions about ourselves

self-serving bias our tendency to make attributions that preserve our own self-esteem—for example, making trait attributions for our successes and situational attributions for our failures

The actor/observer bias may seem self-serving, but this is not always the case. You would also be more likely to attribute a classmate's unexpected A on an exam to his traits than you would your own unexpected A. In this case, the actor/observer bias predicts that you would consider situational causes, such as an easy exam, more for yourself than for others. So why do we treat ourselves differently from others when it comes to attribution?

One potential reason for the actor/observer bias is that when we are the actor, we cannot literally see our own behavior, and our attention is generally focused outward on the environment. But when we are the observer, our attention is generally focused on the other person's behavior. Therefore, because we are relatively unaware of our own behavior and very aware of the environment, we are more likely to consider situational factors in making attributions for ourselves (Hennessy & Jakubowski, 2007; Storms, 1973).

The actor/observer bias may also stem from the different knowledge we have about ourselves and other people (Eisen, 1979). When we are making attributions about our own behavior, we are usually very aware of the way in which the environment influences it. Because we do not typically know other people's thoughts, we usually do not know how other people perceive the situation and whether it indeed influences their behavior.

SELF-SERVING BIAS

Although the actor/observer bias does not stem from a desire to enhance one's self-esteem, this does not mean that we never seek to make ourselves look better. Often we do make self-esteem-boosting attributions. The **self-serving bias** refers to our tendency to make trait attributions for our successes and situational attributions for our failures (Miller & Ross, 1975). If you were to earn an A on your next psychology exam, you would likely attribute this grade to your ability or your study habits. However, if you were to fail your next psychology exam (and we hope that you do not!), you would be more likely to attribute your grade to some situational factor, such as your professor's teaching or the fact that your roommate interfered with your studying.

Most people, regardless of age, gender, or culture, engage in the self-serving bias (Mezulis et al., 2004). The major reason for the self-serving bias appears to be our desire to feel good about ourselves (Brown & Rogers, 1991; Trafimow, Armendariz, & Madsen, 2004). For example, in a recent study, Indian parents attributed their own children's negative behavior to situational factors not related to parenting. However, they attributed the negative behaviors of other people's children to personality factors and parenting factors (Montemayor & Ranganathan, 2012). Attributions such as these presumably allowed the parents to still think of themselves as good parents, despite negative behavior in their own children. The self-serving bias may help us protect our self-esteem, but it can also cause problems if we become too self-serving. For instance, not taking responsibility for our failures can lead others to like us less (Carlston & Shovar, 1983).

As we have seen in this section, we often take shortcuts, or heuristics, when making attributions about others. Heuristics may save time, but often they lead to incorrect attributions and judgments. As we will see in the next section, our tendency to use mental shortcuts can also lead to bigger problems, including prejudice and discrimination.

Quiz Yourself 10.2

1. **Our tendency to overuse trait attributions and to ignore the situational influences on behavior is known as the _____.**
   a. fundamental attribution error
   b. self-serving bias
   c. social desirability bias
   d. actor/observer bias

2. **Which of the following people would be *least* likely to exhibit the fundamental attribution error?**
   a. Henri from Canada
   b. Hongyong from Korea
   c. Lamont from the United States
   d. Greta from Germany

3. **Jasper was quick to assume that Susan was intelligent when he saw that she earned an A on her last psychology exam. However, when Jasper earned an A on his history test, he was not so quick to assume that he was intelligent. Which of the following biases in social cognition *best* explains Jasper's behavior?**
   a. The fundamental attribution error
   b. The self-serving bias
   c. The social desirability bias
   d. The actor/observer bias

Answers 1. a; 2. b; 3. d

10.3 Prejudice: Why Can't We All Just Get Along?

Prejudices based on race, gender, sexual orientation, age, religion, country of origin, and other perceived differences still hamper many people's ability to live a productive and happy life. People have been harassed and belittled, lost jobs, and even been killed because of prejudice. In 2012, the Federal Bureau of

Investigation (FBI) reported a total of 5,790 incidents of hate crimes. Most of these incidents were motivated by racial prejudice (48.3%), with prejudice based on sexual orientation (19.6%) and prejudice based on religion (19.0%) being the next most frequent motives for hate crimes (FBI, 2012a).

Besides violent crimes and crimes against property, discrimination can also manifest in subtler forms. For example, Hispanics are often quoted higher rents than Whites for the same property and given less help in securing mortgages for home purchases (Department of Housing and Urban Development [HUD], 2005). Real estate agents often direct African Americans to poorer, segregated minority neighborhoods (HUD, 2005). And despite gains in equal rights over the last several decades, women have still not achieved equal status in the workforce, academia, or the government (Blackwell, Snyder, & Mavriplis, 2009; Cheung & Halpern, 2010; Sanchez-Hucles & Davis, 2010; Stephens & Levine, 2011). Prejudice remains a serious social problem. Because prejudice poses a threat to all of us, understanding where prejudice comes from is essential.

We can view prejudice as an extension of normal cognitive processes in that prejudices are attitudes that develop like all other attitudes. At the same time, prejudices are unique because they are especially problematic and divisive attitudes that can cause great harm to countless individuals and to society at large. As we look at the development of prejudice, we will examine the similarities between normal cognition and prejudiced thought.

10.3.1 • Stereotypes, Prejudice, and Discrimination

You will recall from Chapter 7 that as we acquire knowledge about the world, we store that information in generalized knowledge structures called schemas. Schemas reside in our long-term memory and allow us to more efficiently encode, store, and retrieve information (Fiske & Taylor, 2013). When we form a schema for a particular group of people, that schema is referred to as a **stereotype**. All of us have stereotypes for the various groups of people—such as professors, children, or females—we encounter in life. Our stereotypes allow us to make assumptions about others and to have certain expectations about how others will behave.

stereotype a schema for a particular group of people

prejudice a largely negative stereotype that is unfairly applied to all members of a group regardless of their individual characteristics

Although stereotypes are generally helpful to us, they are related to the prejudices that cause untold difficulties for humankind. One way to conceptualize a **prejudice** is as a stereotype gone awry. A stereotype can be thought of as the *cognitive* component of an attitude (Aronson, Wilson, & Akert, 2005) or the knowledge you have stored in memory about some group of people. Stereotypes become problematic when we generically apply them to all members of a group without regard to those individuals' unique characteristics. Furthermore, when a stereotype contains biased and negative information about a particular group of people, the stereotype begins to look like a prejudice (see, for example, Chory-Assad & Tamborini, 2003). For example, in a study of stereotypes held in the United States, United Kingdom, and Australia, researchers found similarities between the stereotypes participants held for people with low-socioeconomic standing and the stereotypes they held for apes. These results suggest that many people in these cultures hold stereotypes about the poor that are dehumanizing (Loughnan et al., 2014). Finally, when a biased, negative stereotype becomes coupled with a negative *affective* or emotional reaction toward all (or most) people belonging to that group, a prejudice results.

In the mind of the prejudiced person, members of a particular group are disliked and labeled as having negative characteristics, regardless of their individual qualities. Additionally, prejudice can affect how the prejudiced person behaves toward others. All too often, prejudice motivates people to treat others poorly. **Discrimination** is the behavioral expression of a prejudice. For example, not considering a woman for a job as a forklift operator simply because she is female would be an act of discrimination.

Discrimination doesn't always take such a blatant form. It can be much more subtle. Psychologists Samuel Gaertner and John Dovidio (1986, 2005) have argued that modern-day racial prejudice in the United States takes the form of **aversive racism**. According to this theory, European Americans who outwardly support equality and fairness may still feel negative emotions in the presence of African Americans (Hodson, Dovidio, & Gaertner, 2010). These negative or *aversive* emotions may motivate the person to discriminate against or avoid interaction with minority members. Aversive racism may be more likely when stressful situations heighten such aversive feelings. For example, European Americans were found to be slower to help African Americans than they were to help other European Americans during a severe emergency, but equally likely to help members of either group during a minor emergency (Kunstman & Plant, 2008). These results suggest that under stress, hidden prejudices can surface and give rise to discrimination.

discrimination the behavioral expression of a prejudice

aversive racism a proposed form of subtle racism in which European Americans feel aversive emotions around African Americans, which may lead them to discriminate against African Americans

stereotype threat a phenomenon in which fears of being discriminated against elicit stereotype-confirming behaviors

Jack Hollingsworth/Photodisc/Getty Images

Studies suggest that Hispanic people are more likely to be quoted higher rental rates than their White counterparts. These findings suggest that prejudice and discrimination are still part of our world.

10.3.2 • Stereotype Threat: Prejudice Can Be a Self-Fulfilling Prophecy

Like a woman seeking employment in a male-dominated field, many people live with the fear that others may harbor prejudices about them. Psychologist Claude Steele proposes that some victims of prejudice actually end up reinforcing certain aspects of the prejudices held against them because of a phenomenon called **stereotype threat**. Stereotype threat exists when a person fears that others will judge her not on her own qualities but rather on prejudicial stereotypes held about the group(s) to which she belongs (Steele, 1997). Understandably, this fear can lead to considerable anxiety in minorities because of the negative nature of the prejudices they face. For example, women often experience stereotype threat when performing mathematical and scientific tasks (Good, Woodzicka, & Wingfield, 2010). Widespread negative stereotyping of women in the workplace also leads women to expect that coworkers will give them less credit for successes and more blame for failures (see, e.g., Heilman & Kram, 1983).

Studies have shown that stereotype threat can actually inhibit performance on a task. For example, normally high-achieving females tend to score less well on mathematics problems but not on verbal tasks when they are asked to perform these tasks in an environment where they are outnumbered by men (Inzlicht & Ben-Zeev, 2000). In this situation, females presumably become aware of the prejudicial stereotypes that many people hold—that men are better at math—and the fear of being perceived to be mathematically inept (stereotype threat) then impairs their math performance. Females are not stereotyped as being poor at verbal tasks, so there is no stereotype threat for verbal tasks, and females exhibit no impairment in performance even when they are outnumbered by males. Stereotype threat can thus become a *self-fulfilling prophecy* in which a woman behaves in a manner that actually reinforces negative stereotypes about females (Keller & Dauenheimer, 2003).

The effect of stereotype threat may be due to increased physiological arousal that results when we perceive that others expect us to perform poorly. As such, the effects of stereotype threat appear to be especially strong when the task being performed is a difficult one (Hively & El-Alayli, 2014). Recall from Chapter 5 that high or low levels of arousal can degrade performance on tasks (Yerkes & Dodson, 1908). When a task is difficult, the amount of arousal needed to impair performance is lower than the level needed to impair performance on easy tasks (Martinie, Olive, & Milland, 2010). As a result, when stereotype threat is experienced while performing a difficult task, performance is more likely to suffer (Keller, 2007). Unfortunately, stereotype threat may discourage some people from attempting certain challenges in life.

For example, stereotype threat has been shown to impair African Americans' academic performance (see, e.g., Steele & Aronson, 1995), and it may contribute to some African Americans' experiencing *disidentification* with certain aspects of European American culture. If young African Americans experience stereotype threat in school (they perceive that others expect them to fail), one way they may protect themselves emotionally is by devaluing education. If one does not feel that academic achievement is important, then if one fails at academics, it is not damaging to his or her self-esteem (Steele, 1997). Unfortunately, this not only prevents some African Americans from achieving academically, it may also place pressure on those African Americans who do wish to pursue academic success. If your friends devalue your dreams, you must either abandon your plans or distance yourself from your friends—both of which can be painful. One thing is certain: as long as negative stereotypes persist, it's a safe bet that many people will suffer as a result.

10.3.3 • Social Transmission of Prejudice

Like other attitudes, prejudices can develop through the processes of classical conditioning, operant conditioning, and observational learning (Duckitt, 1992). As you can see in You Review: The Learning of a Prejudice Against Men, these types of learning allow prejudices to develop and also be passed from person to person within a culture. The experiences we have with other groups of people, the models we are exposed to (Kowalski, 2003), and the rewards and punishments we receive in life all have the power to mold our stereotypes and prejudices.

You Review **The Learning of a Prejudice Against Men**

Type of Learning	Situation	Outcome
Classical conditioning	Marlita is robbed at knifepoint (US) by a man (CS). During the attack, she feels terror and anger (UR/CR).	After the attack, Marlita feels anger and terror when she sees men. She has been classically conditioned to feel negative emotions in response to men.
Operant conditioning	Bobbi makes fun of some boys at her school. She calls them "stupid crybabies" (behavior). All of Bobbi's friends laugh when they see her behaving this way (reward).	Bobbi is more likely to make fun of boys in the future because she has been rewarded for doing so. Her friends have operantly conditioned her prejudiced, discriminatory behavior.
Observational learning	From a young age, Jackie hears her mother frequently say that men are sloppy, stubborn, insensitive creatures.	Jackie is likely to model her mother's prejudices and adopt her mother's belief that men are sloppy, stubborn, and insensitive.

How easily prejudices can be learned was dramatically demonstrated in one of the most famous classroom exercises ever done on prejudice. In the late 1960s, grade school teacher Jane Elliot decided to teach her third-grade class an important lesson about prejudice. She believed that her students, who were all rural White children, could benefit from learning about prejudice from both sides of the fence.

One day in class, Elliot told her students that she had recently heard that scientists had determined that brown-eyed people were inferior to blue-eyed people. She told the class that brown-eyed people were less intelligent, trustworthy, and nice than the "superior" blue-eyed people. To make the group differences very salient, Elliot had all the brown-eyed children wear brown cloth collars over their clothing so they could be immediately identified as members of the "inferior" group of students.

Within hours of her announcement concerning eye color, Elliot had created a strong prejudice in her classroom. The blue-eyed children made fun of the brown-eyed children. The blue-eyes called the brown-eyes names, ostracized them, and in general treated them cruelly. A fight even occurred on the playground as a result of the prejudice. In less than a day, Elliot turned a peaceful, egalitarian classroom into a hotbed of prejudice and discrimination (Monteith & Winters, 2002). Elliot's study showed the world how easily prejudice can be learned from others—especially when we learn it from those we look up to.

Admittedly, the environment Elliot created in her classroom was deliberately designed to create prejudice. What other types of environments may contribute to the development of prejudices? Can prejudice be developed within a family, for instance? Some evidence suggests that we do adopt the prejudices of our parents (Degner & Dalege, 2013; Dhont, Roets, & Van Hiel, 2013). However, having prejudiced parents does not guarantee that we will become prejudiced. In one study that examined the match between parental values and those held by their children, it was found that children are most likely to have attitudes similar to those of their parents when the parents hold egalitarian beliefs. When parents hold prejudicial attitudes, the match between their values and their children's values is less strong (Rohan & Zanna, 1996).

It appears that when parents hold strong prejudices, the children may pick up these prejudices but later find that their peers do not reinforce them for holding such negative views. Because they are not reinforced and may even be punished by their peers for holding prejudices, they experience a decline in prejudice that distances them from their parents' values. But when parents hold egalitarian values, their children may pick up these values and be reinforced by their peers for having them. Their values then remain more like those of their parents (Aronson et al., 2005). This line of research makes a powerful argument for teaching tolerance in schools and in society because if tolerance becomes prevalent in a culture, it may have the power to override what happens in the home.

Mark Peterson/Corbis News/Corbis

Is this child likely to adopt the prejudices of her parents through modeling?

10.3.4 • Intergroup Dynamics and Prejudice

We all belong to certain groups: families, schools, clubs, states, countries, religions, and races. These groups and the roles we play in them help define who we are as individuals and our connection to others (Gergen & Gergen, 1988; Halsam et al., 2014). Because we tend to identify with the groups to which we belong, we also tend to prefer the groups of which we are members (Roth & Steffens, 2014).

IN-GROUP BIAS: US VERSUS THEM

We tend to like the people in our group a little more than we like the people who are not members. In other words, we exhibit an **in-group bias** (Hewstone, Rubin, & Willis, 2002). We tend to like our family members more than strangers. We like those who attend our school more than those who do not. We have a bias toward liking our country's citizens a little more than foreigners.

Think of the groups of spectators at a sporting event. Each group sits on its team's side, and at times the rivalry between the two sides erupts into name-calling and even violence. If these same people met under other conditions in which their team affiliations were not obvious, such as at the grocery store or library, do you think they would be as likely to call each other names and fight? Probably not. Why do we sometimes allow our group affiliations to bias how we feel about and treat others? It appears to boil down to self-esteem.

We apparently derive some of our self-esteem from the groups of which we are members. One way to enhance self-esteem is by belonging to a group we perceive as good and desirable. For example, if you perceive your religion as being the best religion, then belonging to this religious group increases your self-esteem. Unfortunately, one way to perceive your particular group as being good is to believe that other groups are not as good (Tajfel, 1982). When our group succeeds at something, we tend to be especially proud (Cialdini et al., 1976). In the absence of meaningful victory, we still tend to view our in-group members as superior to out-group members (Brewer, 1979; Molero et al., 2003; Tajfel, 1982).

The in-group bias tends to make us prejudiced against those who are not part of our social groups. Furthermore, the in-group bias tends to affect the way we perceive out-group members, causing us to see members of an out-group as being pretty much all alike. Researchers call this tendency the **out-group homogeneity bias** (Linville, Fischer, & Salovey, 1989; Rubin & Badea, 2012). Individual characteristics are perceived not to differ much from the stereotype that defines the group. So once we have knowledge about one member of an out-group, we tend to apply it to all people in that group (Quattrone & Jones, 1980).

in-group bias our tendency to favor people who belong to the same groups that we do

out-group homogeneity [home-uh-juh-NEE-it-tee] bias our tendency to see out-group members as being pretty much all alike

realistic-conflict theory the theory that prejudice stems from competition for scarce resources

scapegoat an out-group that is blamed for many of society's problems

CONFLICT AND PREJUDICE: IT'S THEIR FAULT

Realistic-conflict theory (Levine & Campbell, 1972) proposes that conflict among groups for resources motivates the development of prejudice. In the United States, immigrants are often the targets of prejudice because they are perceived as coming here "to steal jobs away from hard-working Americans" (Esses et al., 2001). Minority out-group members often play the role of **scapegoat**, the out-group members we blame for our problems, when times are hard (Allport, 1954/1979). In modern America, as you might expect, racial prejudice most often exists when groups are in direct competition for the same jobs (Simpson & Yinger, 1985).

Possibly the most famous study ever conducted on conflict and prejudice is Muzafer Sherif's Robber's Cave experiment (Sherif et al., 1961). Sherif and his colleagues conducted this experiment in a naturalistic setting, a summer boys' camp at Robber's Cave State Park in Oklahoma (hence the experiment's nickname). The participants were normal, healthy, middle-class, White, Protestant, 11- to 12-year-old boys who attended Boy Scout camp at the park. Prior to participation in the camp, the boys were all strangers to one another.

As they arrived at the camp, the boys were randomly assigned to one of two cabins, the Eagles' cabin or the Rattlers' cabin. The cabins were situated fairly far apart to ensure that the two groups would not have much contact with each other. The boys in each group lived together, ate together, and spent much of their time together. Under these conditions of isolation from each other, the Eagles and the Rattlers became separate, tight-knit in-groups. Once each group bonded, the experimenters placed the Eagles and Rattlers together under conditions of conflict.

In this next phase, the experimenters had the Eagles and Rattlers compete with each other in sporting events. The winning group would get prizes that 12-year-old boys find attractive, such as pocketknives. The losers got nothing for their efforts except defeat. As a result of this competition, the Eagles and the Rattlers began to call each other names, sabotage each other's cabins and belongings, and even engage in physical violence against one another. In short, the Eagles hated the Rattlers, and the Rattlers hated the Eagles. A prejudice based on the relatively meaningless distinctions of being Eagles or Rattlers was fully developed in the boys. When the prejudice between the Eagles and Rattlers reached the point of physical violence, the experimenters stopped the competition between the boys and sought ways to reduce the prejudice that had developed.

10.3.5 • Reducing Prejudice in the Real World

One of Sherif's strategies to reduce prejudice was to increase noncompetitive contact between the Eagles and the Rattlers (e.g., watching movies together). In fact, the idea that contact between groups is enough to reduce prejudice, the so-called **contact hypothesis**, has been around for quite some time (Lee & Humphrey, 1943, cited in Allport, 1954/1979). If people from different in-groups see a lot of each other, won't they realize that the prejudices they hold about one another are unfounded and abandon them?

contact hypothesis the theory that contact between groups is an effective means of reducing prejudice between them

superordinate goal a goal that is shared by different groups

As Sherif found out, mere contact often does little to reduce prejudice (e.g., Poore et al., 2002). One reason contact doesn't work is that when people from different groups are thrown together, they tend to self-segregate (Binder et al., 2009). A drive through any big city illustrates this point. Neighborhoods are often well defined on the basis of ethnicity and race—even though people are legally free to live where they choose. Such segregation can prevent meaningful contact between groups from happening, precluding much chance of reducing prejudice.

To bring groups together in meaningful contact, they have to be motivated to really spend time together—not just occupy the same space. Not surprisingly, *cooperative contact,* in which the groups work together on a common task, has been shown to be more effective in reducing prejudice than merely forcing groups together (Pettigrew & Tropp, 2006).

After experimenting with increased contact between the Eagles and the Rattlers, Sherif and his colleagues (1961) tried facilitating cooperation between the two groups of boys. Sherif and his colleagues created *superordinate goals* for the Eagles and the Rattlers. A **superordinate goal** is a goal that both groups want to accomplish but cannot without the help of the other group. For instance, the researchers disrupted the water supply that both groups used by tampering with the water pipes. To reestablish water to the camp, the Eagles and Rattlers had to work together to find the source of the trouble. While they were trying to solve their mutual problem, the Eagles and Rattlers did not seem to have much time to hate one another. In another instance, a food supply truck broke down, and the two groups had to work together to push-start the truck. Without their combined efforts, both groups would have gone hungry.

After a series of such contacts, the prejudice between the groups began to dissolve, perhaps because the Eagles and Rattlers now saw themselves as part of the same group—the group that was trying to find food and water. Without clear lines between the boys, there was no basis for in-group or out-group bias or prejudice.

Stock Connection Blue/Alamy

Superordinate goals are an effective means of reducing prejudice. These people are likely to see themselves as members of the same in-group as they work together to accomplish their goals. As a result, they are likely to experience less prejudice toward one another.

The researchers noted that friendships began to form between individual Eagles and Rattlers, and as a whole, the Rattlers and Eagles began to cooperate, spend time together, and even share their money. The prejudice that was once so strong was dramatically reduced (Sherif, 1966).

Based in part on the results of the Robber's Cave study, researchers have attempted to outline the characteristics of the type of contact between groups that reduces prejudice. The most effective strategies are ones with these factors:

- The different groups need each other.
- The different groups have a common, superordinate goal that requires everyone's effort to achieve.
- The different groups work shoulder to shoulder on an equal playing field to accomplish the goal.
- The contact is hospitable, informal, and free from negative emotional interaction.
- Contact with out-group members lasts for a significant period of time.
- The norms governing the contact situation promote harmony and mutual respect.

One practical application of these conditions is called a *jigsaw classroom* (Aronson, 2000). A jigsaw classroom is one in which students from diverse ethnic groups are asked to work together on a project in a cooperative way. Each child is responsible for a different piece of the project, which forces the children to be interdependent. Because they must rely on each other, the children begin to focus more on the tasks at hand and less on their differences. According to psychologist Elliot Aronson (2000; 2011), 25 years of research on the outcomes of jigsaw classrooms consistently indicates that as participants begin to identify as members of the same in-group, prejudice and hostility among the children are reduced, and self-esteem and academic performance are increased. These findings further underscore the message of the Robber's Cave experiment—that cooperation rather than competition can work to lower prejudice in the world.

We have seen that prejudices can affect the judgments we make about other people. When we attribute negative characteristics to people simply because they belong to a certain social group, we are behaving prejudicially. Our prejudices can, in turn, affect the way we treat other people.

Regardless of whether we base our impressions on a prejudice or on actual behavior, we tend to want to spend more time with people we like. We may decide to enter into a friendship or a romantic relationship with someone about whom we have formed a positive impression. The relationship may turn out to be wonderful, or it may fail. In the aftermath of the breakup of a relationship, we often ask ourselves, "What did I ever see in this person?" This is the question that we will tackle next as we look at what attracts us to others.

10.3

Quiz Yourself

1. **Kelly is a manager at a firm that has been troubled by considerable prejudice between its male and female employees. Kelly wants to institute a program that will reduce the level of prejudice between the sexes. Which of the following plans has the *best* chance of working?**
   a. Appoint opposite-sex managers to supervise workers.
   b. Have a "battle of the sexes" to see which sex can outperform the other on the job.
   c. Form work teams to solve company problems, and make sure that the teams contain both male and female members.
   d. Threaten to fire anyone who says or does anything prejudicial, and post this message around the workplace to ensure that everyone knows about the policy.

2. **Relative to in-group members, we tend to view out-group members as being _____.**
   a. less like us
   b. less favorable
   c. more homogeneous
   d. All of the above

3. **Which of the following is the *best* example of cooperative contact?**
   a. Teachers supervising students taking a math test
   b. A manager meeting with employees to discuss sales figures
   c. A police officer speaking to an elementary school class about the dangers of drugs
   d. A citizens' group meeting to find ways to reduce crime in their neighborhood

Answers 1. c; 2. d; 3. d

10.4 Being Drawn to Others: The Nature of Attraction

The attitudes that we form about a person determine whether we will be attracted to this person as a friend or as a romantic partner. The affective component of the attitudes we hold about someone is particularly important. If a person produces positive emotional reactions in us, we are much more likely to find him or her attractive. Think about the people closest to you. How do you feel about your best friend and your significant other? We are betting that most of you generally feel positive emotions about those you love. Most of us do. When it comes to attraction, the most important question is: What makes us feel good about another person?

10.4.1 • Proximity and Exposure: Attraction to Those That Are Nearby

One of the most intriguing findings in the area of attraction concerns how much exposure we have to certain people and how the exposure affects our feelings of attraction for them. Recall from Chapter 5 that the more often we see a person or an object, the more we tend to like it. This trend, called the *mere exposure effect* (A. Y. Lee, 2001; Zajonc, 1968), appears to be true for a variety of stimuli, including people (Moreland & Topolinski, 2010; Zebrowitz, White, & Wieneke, 2008).

proximity physical closeness

Many studies have shown that we tend to be friends and lovers with those who live and work close to us (Clarke, 1952; Festinger, 1951; Festinger, Schachter, & Back, 1950; Ineichen, 1979; Segal, 1974). The more **proximity**, or geographic closeness, we have to someone in our daily lives, the more exposure we have to them, and the more we tend to like them. For example, within an apartment building, the closer a person's apartment is to yours, the higher the probability that you will be friends with that person (Festinger, 1951). This is true even when apartments are assigned on a random basis, as you might find in university housing (Festinger et al., 1950). Attraction to those who live and work nearby seems to hold across cultures as well. Studies have found evidence supporting a relationship between proximity and liking in both Africa (Brewer & Campbell, 1976) and France (Maisonneuve, Palmade, & Fourment, 1952).

10.4.2 • Similarity: Having Things in Common

Two old adages describe the people we tend to choose as friends or romantic partners. One says, "Birds of a feather flock together," and the other says, "Opposites attract." You probably know some couples who demonstrate both views of attraction. But what does the average person look for? Do we want someone who is similar to us, or are we looking for someone who is different to complement our personality?

People who work in close proximity to each other are more likely to become friends and lovers.

Phil Boorman/Photodisc/Getty Images

Research on this issue indicates that, indeed, "birds of a feather flock together." When choosing a romantic partner, we tend to gravitate to people who are of similar age, socioeconomic status, education, intelligence, race, religion, attitudes, power, and physical attractiveness (Brehm, 1992; Browning et al., 1999; Hendrick & Hendrick, 1983). For example, it was after Hongyong discovered that she and Dukpil shared some similar attitudes that she began to feel real affection for him. Having things in common seems to be important in romantic relationships. Accordingly, similarity seems to predict attraction across a variety of cultures, including Mexico, India, and Japan (Byrne et al., 1971). Similarity also seems to be a factor in the friends we choose (Kandel, 1978; Newcomb, 1961; Rubin et al., 1994).

Self-esteem may play a role in our preference for similar others. Being attracted to similar others may be motivated in part by a desire to maintain high self-esteem. After all, valuing similar others is, in a way, valuing one's self (Heine, Foster, & Spina, 2009).

It is also possible that we are attracted to similar others because finding ourselves attracted to dissimilar others might produce dissonance (Heider, 1958). For example, if you were attracted to someone who did not share your spiritual views, the conflict between your attitudes about the person and your attitudes about spirituality might produce dissonance. In the face of this dissonance, it might be easier to change your attitudes about the person (as opposed to your spirituality), lessening your attraction to him or her and reducing the dissonance. Overall, it is more comfortable to be attracted to those who share our attitudes.

10.4.3 • The Importance of Physical Attractiveness

One of the first things we notice about a potential romantic partner is his or her physical attractiveness. Although standards of physical attractiveness vary across cultures (see • FIGURE 10.3), it is an important factor in determining our attraction to others. In a classic study that examined physical attractiveness and attraction in a blind-date scenario, physical attractiveness was the only factor found to predict whether a person wanted to go out on a second date (Walster et al., 1966).

When it comes to choosing potential partners, physical attractiveness seems to be important to both men and women (Luo, 2009), but men seem to place particular emphasis on how attractive their potential romantic partners are (Jonason, 2009). This special emphasis that men place on physical attractiveness seems to hold for both homosexual and heterosexual men. Heterosexual and homosexual women, in contrast, place more importance on the psychological traits of their potential partners. For example, heterosexual women place more emphasis on a man's social status when choosing a mate (Alterovitz & Mendelsohn, 2009). So it seems that although physical attractiveness is important to women, it is not the most important aspect of a partner (Deaux & Hanna, 1984).

Yuri Arcurs/Alamy

FIGURE 10.3

Cultural Differences in Physical Attractiveness

Standards of physical attractiveness can vary across cultures. All of these people would be considered attractive in their respective cultures. Which of these people do you find attractive?

Cusp/SuperStock

Remi Benali/Terra/Corbis

ImageDB103/Alamy

matching hypothesis the theory that we are attracted to people whose level of physical attractiveness is similar to our own

Although we may be attracted to good-looking people, we tend to be romantically involved with people whose level of physical attractiveness is comparable to our own. This tendency, called the **matching hypothesis**, seems to be true of both dating and married couples (Zajonc et al., 1987). Matching is so pervasive that we actually expect to date people at our same level of attractiveness (Montoya, 2008).

Interestingly, the influence of physical attractiveness on romantic relationships seems to be mirrored in our same-sex friendships. The matching hypothesis predicts that our same-sex friends will be, on average, about as attractive as we are (McKillip & Reidel, 1983). And although both men and women seem to choose their friends on the basis of their physical attractiveness, again men place more emphasis on this characteristic than do women (Berscheid et al., 1971; Feingold, 1988; Perlini, Bertolissi, & Lind, 1999). The importance of physical attractiveness in social relationships isn't surprising in light of findings that we tend to perceive attractive people more positively than unattractive people (Lemay, Clark, & Greenberg, 2010). For example, attractive people are perceived to be more interesting, sociable, kind, sensitive, and nurturing than unattractive people (Dion, Berscheid, & Walster, 1972). With all these perceived qualities, no wonder we want to be friends and lovers with attractive people!

However, another reason may also explain why we prefer attractive people. Perhaps being attracted to others is in part biological and instinctive. In an interesting study, researchers found that babies as young as 2 months old looked longer at attractive faces than they did at unattractive ones (Langlois et al., 1987), indicating that they preferred the attractive faces. Because it is hard to imagine that 2-month-old babies have had time to learn to be biased toward attractive people, these findings suggest that we are born with an instinctive preference for good-looking people. Indeed, research has suggested that we find faces to be attractive if they tend to be *symmetric, average* (nondistinctive), and have a *level of masculinity/femininity that is appropriate* to the sex of the face (Griffey & Little, 2013). Perhaps we evolved to be drawn to certain facial traits (e.g., symmetrical facial features) because they indicate good health (Bronstad, Langlois, & Russell, 2008). In terms of natural selection and evolution, it makes sense for us to be sexually attracted to people who are healthy and therefore able to facilitate our ability to produce offspring.

10.4.4 • The "Chemistry" of Lust, Love, and Romance

When it comes to love and romance, is there anything to the notion of "chemistry" between people? Perhaps. Neuroimaging studies suggest that many brain areas are involved in our complex feelings for our romantic partners (Acevedo et al., 2011). Furthermore, psychologists have identified three separate emotional systems involved in romantic relationships. *Lust* is our sex drive or desire for sexual gratification. *Romantic attraction* is our physical and emotional desire for a specific person. Attachment is *companionate love*, or our desire to be close with our partner. Interestingly, psychologists have discovered that each of these emotional systems seems to be related to the action of different chemicals in the body. Lust is governed by hormones—in particular, estrogens and androgens (Chapter 2). Experiencing romantic attraction is related to increased dopamine and norepinephrine, but lowered serotonin, in the brain. Experiencing attachment or love is associated with the action of other neurotransmitters and hormones, including neuropeptides, oxytocin, and vasopressin (Fisher, 2000).

R1/Alamy

When it comes to romance, several chemicals in our bodies influence the lust, romantic attraction, and attachment we feel for others.

In one fascinating study, single men and men in monogamous relationships were given an intranasal dose of oxytocin. Afterward, they were allowed to interact with an attractive woman. The dose of oxytocin did not affect how close or proximal the single men got to the female target, but for men in monogamous relationships, having been exposed to oxytocin made them keep a greater distance from the female. Oxytocin did not affect how close either type of man got to a male experimenter. It appears that oxytocin may also work to maintain monogamous relationships by motivating men to avoid signaling romantic interest (via physical proximity) in other women (Scheele et al., 2012).

If love and romance are related to chemical action in the brain, does this mean that altering the chemical environment of the brain can affect our romantic feelings for our partner? Some researchers believe so. Psychologist Dixie Meyer suggests that antidepressant drugs such as selective serotonin reuptake inhibitors that increase serotonin action in the brain may also interfere with the brain chemicals that support romantic attraction, resulting in the person's experiencing reduced satisfaction with his or her romantic relationship (Meyer, 2007). Based on her preliminary work, Meyer suggests that therapists should be aware that satisfaction with one's romantic life is affected by many things, including perhaps one's biochemistry and medications.

Although the idea of "chemistry" in romance may have some merit, we are drawn to others for many reasons. Sexual attraction is just one of these reasons. Sometimes our desire to be with others serves a purpose other than romance, sex, and reproduction. In the next section, we will further explore our social nature by examining some of the reasons we are driven to be with others in the form of social groups.

Quiz Yourself

10.4

1. **Based on the available psychological research, you are *most* likely to end up in a romantic relationship with _____.**
   a. a neighbor who shares your values
   b. a person from another state who shares your values
   c. a fellow student who does not share your values
   d. a coworker who has opposite views

2. **Attractive people are assumed to be all of the following things, except _____.**
   a. interesting
   b. sociable
   c. proud
   d. nurturant

3. **Which of the following statements is true?**
   a. Women are unconcerned with physical attractiveness when choosing a romantic partner.
   b. Women and men are equally interested in physical attractiveness when choosing a romantic partner.
   c. Neither men nor women pay that much attention to physical attractiveness when choosing a romantic partner.
   d. Men pay more attention to physical attractiveness when choosing a romantic partner.

Answers 1. a; 2. d; 3. d

10.5 Group Influence

Throughout our lifetime, we will belong to a multitude of groups—some of which we join and some of which we belong to by circumstance—families, communities, clubs, teams, professional organizations, and so on. For many of us, belonging to such groups is something that we value, but why? Psychologists suggest several potential explanations for why we join groups (Baumeister & Leary, 1995; Paulus, 1989). Groups may give us companionship, make us feel safe, make us feel proud, provide us with information, or help us achieve our goals in life. Regardless of why we join a group, once we do join, the group and its collective members then have the power to influence our behavior.

10.5.1 • Social Forces Within Groups: Norms and Cohesiveness

norm unwritten rule or expectation for how group members should behave

Groups are characterized by the expectations and attitudes of their members. Group **norms** are the rules that guide the behavior of group members. Norms can be explicitly stated rules or unwritten expectations that members have for behavior within the group. Norms tell us how to dress, how to behave, how to interact with each other, and so on. Virtually every group has its own unique set of norms—each family, culture, workplace, and group of friends may have different expectations for how its members should behave. For an example of how norms can vary across ethnic groups in the United States, take a look at • TABLE 10.2.

TABLE 10.2

Some Cross-Cultural Differences in Norms Governing Conversation within the United States

CULTURE → NORM ↓	NATIVE AMERICAN CULTURE	EUROPEAN AMERICAN CULTURE	ASIAN AMERICAN CULTURE	AFRICAN AMERICAN CULTURE	HISPANIC AMERICAN CULTURE
Level of eye contact  © Andy Dean Photography/Alamy	Direct eye contact is seen as invasive and disrespectful.	Direct eye contact is generally expected—especially when being spoken to.	Direct eye contact that lasts more than a second or two is considered disrespectful—especially with one's superiors.	Direct eye contact is expected and prolonged during speaking, but less when listening.	Direct eye contact is often viewed as disrespectful—especially when one is being spoken to.
Level of emotion displayed  J Lange/PYMCA/Alamy	Conversations are often unemotional and dispassionate.	Highly emotional, animated conversation is not preferred in public settings.	Controlling one's display of emotion is very important.	Conversations are often passionate and animated.	Conversations that take place among Hispanics may be very emotional and animated. Conversations that occur in ethnically mixed settings tend to be more low-key.
Level of gesture use  Masterfile	In daily conversation, gesture use tends to be restrained.	Moderate gesture use is typical.	Gesture use is restrained. Asian Americans tend to use fewer gestures than European Americans.	Frequent and large gestures are the norm.	Moderate to high use of gestures is typical.

Source: Adapted from Elliott, C. E. (1999). *Cross-cultural communication styles.* Available online at http://www.awesomelibrary.org/multiculturaltoolkit-patterns.html.

In general, we do not like to break the norms of the groups to which we belong. When we do, we may face several unpleasant consequences. Group members may ridicule us or try to persuade us to change our behavior, or—perhaps most threatening—we might be thrown out or ostracized from the group. Recall that groups often fulfill social needs and give us a sense of security and identity. Because of these benefits, we often value our group memberships and wish to protect them. The degree to which members wish to maintain membership in the group is referred to as **cohesiveness**. In groups whose members have very positive attitudes about their membership in the group, cohesiveness is high, and the group tends to be close-knit. When cohesiveness is high, the pressure we feel to meet group norms is also high. This means that as our attraction for certain groups increases, so does the influence these groups have over us. The more we value our membership in a group, the less willing we are to risk losing that membership. Therefore, group cohesiveness helps ensure **conformity** within a group as group members modify their behavior to avoid breaking the group's norms (Crandall, 1988; Latané & L'Herrou, 1996; Schachter, 1951).

Joseph Reid/Alamy

We are likely to conform to the norms of groups because we do not want to be ostracized or ridiculed.

cohesiveness [coe-HEE-siv-ness] the degree to which members of a group value their group membership; cohesive groups are tight-knit groups

conformity behaving in accordance with group norms

10.5.2 • Conformity Within a Group

One of the most influential psychologists to formally study the process of conformity was Solomon Asch (1907–1996). During the 1950s, Asch conducted a series of classic experiments on conformity and the factors that make us more or less likely to conform in a given situation. Asch (1951) had male participants engage in a perceptual task with eight other men. The participants were unaware that the eight other men in the experiment were *confederates*, or actors posing as participants. Each participant, along with the eight confederates, was shown a series of lines and asked to match the length of a test line to one of three other comparison lines (• FIGURE 10.4). The experiment was set up so that the confederates made their judgments first. The participant heard all of the confederates in turn choose—aloud—the wrong line. By the time the true participant's turn came, he had heard all the others choose what was clearly the wrong line. A norm had formed in the group, the norm of choosing the wrong line. The dependent variable in Asch's study was whether the participant would conform to the norm or whether he would go with his own perception and choose the correct comparison line.

What do you think Asch found? What would you have done in this situation? In fact, Asch found that 74% of his participants conformed at least once during the experiment. Apparently, many people can be easily made to conform. Only 26% of the participants consistently stood by their convictions and refused to conform.

Asch also found that as the *majority group* (the number of confederates who choose the wrong line) increased, so did the participants' tendency to conform. However, Asch found that maximum conformity was reached in the participants when only three confederates were present.

Since Asch's original experiments, others have studied the factors that affect conformity in groups. Overall, the picture that emerges from the research on conformity is that we are most likely to conform if one or more these factors is present:

- We do not feel confident of our abilities.
- Cohesiveness is high in the group.

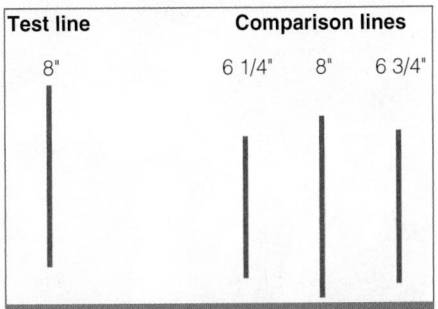

FIGURE 10.4

The Asch Procedure for Testing Conformity

In Asch's study, 74% of the subjects conformed and chose the 6¼-inch line as the match for the comparison line after hearing the confederates make this obviously incorrect choice.

Source: Based on Asch, 1951.

- Our responses are made public (we are not anonymous).
- The group has at least three members who are unanimous in their dedication to the norm.
- The idea that one should conform is itself a norm in our culture and/or we do not feel a personal need to be individuated.

EXPLAINING CONFORMITY: THE EFFECTS OF CULTURE AND CONFIDENCE

Asch showed us that conformity is rather easy to obtain, but why are we so willing to adhere to group norms? As part of his *debriefing* at the end of his experiments, Asch asked participants why they had chosen the wrong line. Their answers were interesting.

Some participants indicated that they chose the wrong line even though they knew it was wrong. This type of conformity, involving a change of behavior to fit a norm but no real attitude change or persuasion, is called **normative conformity**. The primary motive for normative conformity seems to be a desire to fit in with the group and be liked by others. This is one reason that cohesiveness tends to increase conformity. When we like being in the group, we want others to like us as well (Sakari, 1975). Research has shown that people in cultures that value individualism (such as the United States) are less likely to conform than are people from cultures that place more value on being part of a group (such as Japan; Bond & Smith, 1996; Killen, Crystal, & Watanabe, 2002; Takano & Sogon, 2008). In cultures in which nonconformists are admired, you can expect to see less conformity.

normative conformity conformity that occurs when group members change their behavior to meet group norms but are not persuaded to change their beliefs and attitudes

informational conformity conformity that occurs when conformity pressures actually persuade group members to adopt new beliefs and/or attitudes

Interestingly, these differences in conformity that exist between collectivistic and individualistic cultures may not hold up in all situations. For example, researchers found increased conformity in people from collectivistic cultures in face-to-face interactions, but when examining interactions online, the cultural differences in conformity were not seen. It appears that conformity pressures in the cyberworld differ from those felt in face-to-face social interactions (Cinnirella & Green, 2007).

Although many of Asch's participants suggested that they conformed to be liked, some had other reasons for conforming. Some reported that they chose the wrong line because they became convinced that it was the correct choice. These participants were actually persuaded by the majority group. Recall that persuasion leads to attitude change. The way these participants perceived the lines and what they believed to be true about the lines changed as a function of the majority opinion. The majority opinion informed these participants of what the correct choice was. For this reason, conformity that results in actual attitude change is referred to as **informational conformity**. Informational conformity is heightened when people are unsure of their opinions and insecure about their abilities (Cacioppo & Petty, 1980).

Nonconformists seem to enjoy violating the norms of the majority group.

Anthony Redpath/Flirt/Corbis

THE DARK SIDE OF CONFORMITY: THE STANFORD PRISON EXPERIMENT

In 1971, Stanford University psychologist Phillip Zimbardo set out to conduct an experiment on the effects of a prison setting on the behavior of prisoners and guards. Twenty-four healthy male participants were randomly assigned to play the role of either a prisoner or a guard in a mock prison set up in the basement of a campus building. All participants wore uniforms appropriate to their roles as guards or prisoners. The prisoners wore prison uniforms and were referred to by serial numbers rather than their names. The guards had dark sunglasses, wore khaki uniforms, and carried clubs.

The experiment was slated to last 2 weeks, with the prisoners remaining in the "prison" for the entire experiment. Within days, some very disturbing behavior began to emerge. The men assigned to play the guards became abusive toward the mock prisoners. The men assigned to play the prisoners became docile and depressed, allowing the so-called guards to abuse and manipulate them. The mock guards hooded the prisoners, called them names, and subjected them to a host of demeaning, humiliating activities. Their behavior got so out of hand that Zimbardo had to cancel the experiment before the end of the first week (Zimbardo, 1972).

Why would 24 healthy young men begin to behave so abnormally in such a short time? A great deal of their behavior stemmed from the fact that they were isolated from the outside world and the norms of society. Within the prison-like setting, a new set of norms sprang up—ones that called for the guards to be abusive and the prisoners to be submissive. Another factor at work was **deindividuation**. In deindividuation, a person's behavior becomes controlled more by external norms than by the person's own internal values and morals. In short, the roles that the men were playing became stronger determinants of their behavior than their own attitudes and beliefs. Several factors aided the deindividuation process:

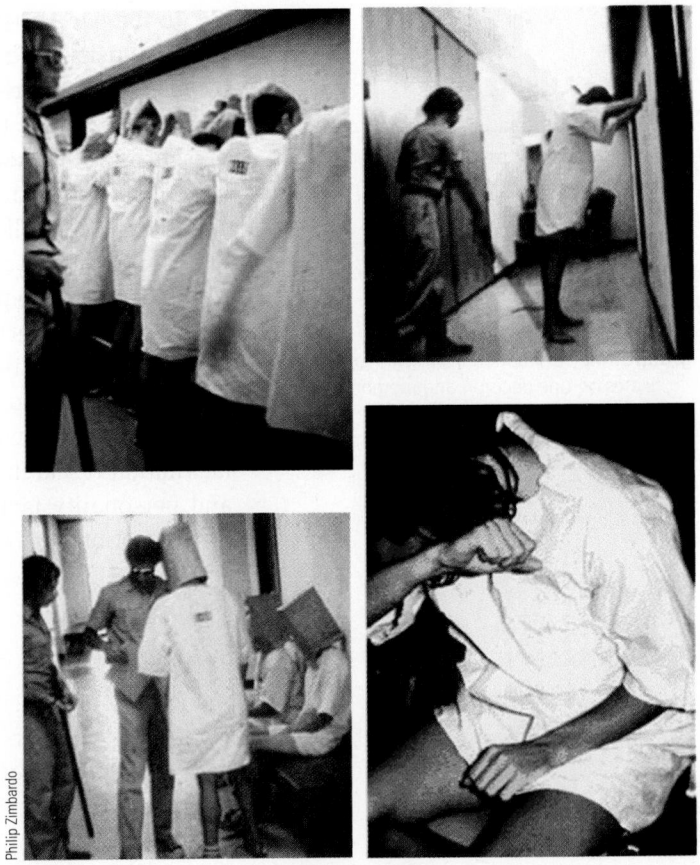

Phillip Zimbardo

Phillip Zimbardo's Stanford prison experiment shows that when we become deindividuated, we lose track of our own internal values and beliefs, and our behavior comes under the control of the group's norms. When deindividuated, we may find ourselves doing things we never thought we would do

- All participants wore uniforms, which heightened their anonymity.
- All participants were "playing" an assigned social role. As "actors," the participants' behavior was more controlled by their roles and their ideas about how prison guards and prisoners typically behave than it was by their own internal values and beliefs.
- The guards hid behind dark glasses, which heightened their anonymity.
- The prisoners were referred to by numbers, not names, which made them seem less human.
- The experiment was conducted in a basement, away from the outside world and its norms.
- There was no strong leader who argued for fair treatment of the prisoners.

When deindividuation occurs, dangerous things can happen. All it takes is one person to begin behaving badly, and even good people may blindly conform to this new norm of behavior.

Sometimes being part of the group can be problematic, but working in a group can also enhance our performance. We'll explore both possibilities further in the next section.

10.5.3 • Is Working in a Group Better Than Working Alone?

Have you ever heard that "many hands make light work"? Or "two heads are better than one"? Such sayings extol the virtues of working in groups. Do we really accomplish more when we are part of a group?

deindividuation [DEE-in-dih-vid-you-AYE-shun] a state in which a person's behavior becomes controlled more by external norms than by the person's own internal values and morals

social facilitation performing better on a task in the presence of others than you would if you were alone

social loafing when group members exert less effort on a group task than they would if they were performing the task alone

groupthink a situation in which a group fixates on one decision and members blindly assume that it is the correct decision

In the late 1800s, psychologist Norman Triplett observed that people seem to perform tasks faster when they perform in the presence of others. For example, bicyclers seem to ride faster when riding along with other cyclists than they do when riding alone (Triplett, 1898). This enhanced performance when others are present is called **social facilitation**. Over the last century, social facilitation has been demonstrated in humans and many other species across a wide variety of situations (see Aiello & Douthitt, 2001).

But do we always perform better when others are around? Not always. For example, when we perform unfamiliar or complex tasks, having others around is likely to impede performance (Zajonc, 1965). For many of us, giving a speech is an example of an unfamiliar task that becomes more daunting when others are present. And many of us can think of times when we "choked" in front of others despite the fact that we could recite our speech perfectly when alone. Today, social facilitation researchers seek to explain the complex interplay of situational, task, and personality factors that result in either enhanced or impaired performance in front of others (Aiello & Douthitt, 2001; see also Snyder, Anderson-Henley, & Arciero, 2012).

SOCIAL LOAFING

Having an audience can affect performance, but what happens when we are working with others? How does working toward a common goal affect individual performance? Sometimes **social loafing** occurs when group members fail to work as hard as they would if they were working alone (Harkins, 1987). Social loafing occurs in part because group members perceive that others will not hold them accountable for their individual performance (Pearsall, Christian, & Ellis, 2010). For example, if everyone receives the same grade for a group project, some members may be tempted to slack off in hopes that other members will pick up the slack. One way to reduce social loafing is to encourage individual effort as well as teamwork by rewarding group members for both the quality of the group's output and their individual performance (Pearsall et al., 2010).

So many hands only *sometimes* make light work. What about cognitive processes? Are two heads better than one? We often seek out others when we have important decisions to make. We form committees to set policy for organizations. We choose juries to try court cases. The assumption is that important decisions are best placed in the hands of many. Ironically, psychological research indicates that in some instances, our faith in the wisdom of groups may be misplaced. Group decisions are not necessarily better, more effective, or more logical than decisions made by individuals.

GROUPTHINK

One factor that can contribute to poor group decisions is known as **groupthink**. Groupthink occurs when a group fixates on one decision and members assume that it must be the correct one without carefully examining other alternatives (Janis, 1982). When groupthink occurs, the group does not weigh all of the options, often resulting in disastrous decisions. For example, in 1986, NASA decided to launch the space shuttle *Challenger* despite troubling data from engineers indicating that O-rings on the rocket booster could fail. The resulting explosion claimed the lives of all aboard and brought intense public and governmental scrutiny of NASA.

Group isolation, group cohesiveness, strong dictatorial leadership, and *stress within the group* have all been implicated as factors that promote groupthink (Janis, 1985, 2007). Sometimes groups must work in isolation because the issues they are dealing with are secret or confidential. An isolated group cannot get information from or call on outside sources; they can only consider solutions that are generated within the group. Because the group cannot consider all possible solutions, some potentially good solutions may be overlooked, and groupthink is more likely.

Group cohesiveness also contributes to groupthink. As we have seen, when a group is very cohesive, members highly value their membership in the group. When this is the case, the group's norms become powerful influences on the members' behavior. In a cohesive group, members may be hesitant to voice their objections to the prevailing group attitude because they do not want to "rock the boat." When members hesitate to voice objections, groupthink becomes more likely and potentially poor decisions are not adequately critiqued and rejected (Packer, 2009).

For the same reason, a dictatorial group leader would also facilitate groupthink. When members are afraid to disagree with a leader, they tend to go along with the leader's position, and groupthink is more likely (Janis, 2007; Shafer & Crichlow, 1996). If a group wants to make good decisions, thoughtful critique of all ideas should be encouraged rather than discouraged in the group.

A final reason for groupthink is stress. When a group is making decisions under some form of duress, they may not behave in as logical a manner as they would if they were not stressed. Time pressure is one such stressor that can contribute to groupthink. When a group has a very short time in which to generate a solution to some problem, they are less likely to be able to examine all possible options, and groupthink becomes more likely.

10.5

Quiz Yourself

1. **When Hongyong behaved submissively, even though she wanted to speak her mind, because she didn't want to violate the norms of her culture, her behavior was an example of _____.**
   a. deindividuation
   b. consistency
   c. dissonance
   d. conformity

2. **Bill is working on a group project for his psychology class. To Bill's dismay, some of his fellow group members haven't contributed very much to the project, leaving Bill to do most of the work. Which of the following *best* explains Bill's situation?**
   a. deindividuation
   b. social facilitation
   c. social loafing
   d. fundamental attribution error

3. **What do groupthink and deindividuation have in common?**
   a. They both involve persuasion.
   b. They both are more common in individualistic cultures.
   c. They both involve dissonance.
   d. They both involve conformity.

Answers 1. d; 2. c; 3. d

10.6 Requests and Demands: Compliance and Obedience

Imagine that you answer the phone one evening and hear a telemarketer on the other end. After she identifies herself as a telemarketer, she asks you to contribute to the local police organization. Would you agree to contribute, or would you refuse? Now compare this situation with a similar one. This time, you answer the phone and hear a police officer on the other end. After identifying herself as a local officer, she asks you to contribute to the police organization. Would you be more inclined to agree to the officer's request? Many people would, but why? What makes these two situations different?

One difference is the source of the request. A police officer represents an authority figure to many people. Many of us would perceive a request coming from an authority figure to be more of a *demand* for **obedience**. On the other hand, we are less likely to be intimidated by a telemarketer, and therefore we would likely perceive her request as just that, a simple *request* for **compliance**. Although the differences between compliance and obedience situations may appear to be subtle, they have great implications for how we respond.

obedience yielding to a demand

compliance yielding to a simple request

foot-in-the-door compliance increasing compliance by first asking people to give in to a small request, which then paves the way for compliance with a second, larger request

10.6.1 • Compliance Techniques: Getting People to Say "Yes"

Compliance situations are very common in life. For instance, salespeople try to get us to agree to buy their products. Doctors ask us to follow their instructions. Spouses ask their partners to do household chores. Given that pressures to comply are inescapable, psychologists are interested in identifying successful compliance techniques and the reasons that make them work well. Marketers and other professionals also want to understand compliance so that they can create more effective campaigns for changing public behavior—for example, to increase sales (Weyant, 1996), to adhere to weight-loss programs (Nyer & Dellande, 2010), or to follow a doctor's orders for the taking of prescribed medications (Holt et al., 2014). It's a good idea for us to become familiar with compliance techniques because others will be using them on us.

FOOT-IN-THE-DOOR COMPLIANCE

Suppose a friend asks to borrow a dollar, and you comply. Later, if that same friend asks to borrow $5, would it be harder to refuse the request because you had previously lent him or her the dollar? Research on compliance suggests that it would. Once a person gets a foot in the door, so to speak, by getting us to comply with a small request, it seems to open the way to getting us to comply with another, larger request. In a classic experiment on **foot-in-the-door compliance**, researchers approached some homes and asked the person answering the door to sign a petition to promote safe driving. The researchers also selected other homes in the neighborhood to participate in the study but did not approach them at this time. Two weeks later, the researchers returned to the neighborhood and approached the homes they had previously visited as well as the homes that were not visited on the first day. This time, the researchers asked if they could put up a huge billboard that said "Drive Carefully" in the front yard. The data showed that those people who had complied with the first request to sign the petition were more

James Shaffer/PhotoEdit

Compliance techniques such as foot-in-the-door can be used to influence our behavior. Agreeing to these signs may pave the way for future campaign contributions.

likely to comply with the request for the billboard (Freedman & Fraser, 1966). Similarly, researchers in Israel found that people who had previously signed a petition for a specific charity were more likely to agree to donate money to the charity at a later date (Schwarzwald, Bizman, & Raz, 1983). It appears that giving in to a small request paves the way for us to give in to a larger request.

One explanation for foot-in-the-door's effectiveness is that our general desire to behave in a consistent fashion makes it hard for us to refuse subsequent requests. When you give in to the initial small request, your self-image changes ever so slightly. Having already complied, you are now the type of person who complies with requests made by this person or group. Because your self-image has changed, you now feel compelled to behave consistently with this new self-image. Recall that to not act in accordance with one's attitudes would likely produce dissonance. So when the person or group makes a subsequent request, to deny it would mean going against one's self-image and perhaps feeling dissonance. Therefore, compliance is more likely. When a clever manipulator gets a person to give in on a small matter, it does indeed seem to lead to a greater chance of future compliance (Cialdini, 2001; Girandola, 2002; Pascual et al., 2013).

DOOR-IN-THE-FACE COMPLIANCE

In **door-in-the-face compliance**, a very large request is followed by a smaller target request. For example, researchers asked college students whether they would agree to commit to volunteering 2 hours a week for the next 2 years in a program to help juvenile delinquents. As you might guess, all the students declined. Then the researchers asked if the students would be willing to volunteer to take the juveniles to the zoo for a couple of hours. A full 50% of the students agreed to take the trip to the zoo after they had refused to volunteer weekly. This number was significantly higher than the 17% of students in a control group who agreed after being asked only whether they would take the trip to the zoo (Cialdini et al., 1975). It appears that if we figuratively "slam the door" in the face of a person's request, we are more likely to comply if she makes a more reasonable request later (for review, see Feeley, Anker, & Aloe, 2012).

door-in-the-face compliance increasing compliance by first asking people to give in to a very large request and then, after they refuse, asking them to give in to a smaller request

reciprocity [reh-cih-PRAH-cih-tee] a strong norm that states that we should treat others as they treat us

One explanation for door-in-the-face compliance centers on the *perceptual contrast* between the two requests. After the extremity of the first request, the second, smaller request may seem more reasonable to you than if it had been the only request you received (Cialdini et al., 1975).

Another explanation for door-in-the-face compliance centers on **reciprocity**, a very strong norm in many cultures that requires that we reciprocate others' behavior (Lecat, Hilton, & Crano, 2009; Mowen & Cialdini, 1980). For example, if we are nice, others should be nice to us. If we are mean, others may be mean in return. Reciprocity explains in part why we feel more obligated to comply in a door-in-the-face situation than with a single request. In a door-in-the-face situation, after you refuse the initial request, the requester then concedes the initial position and makes a more reasonable request. Because the requester has made a concession, we feel as though we must reciprocate and also make a concession. The easiest way to do this is to comply with the second request. If we don't make this concession, then we may feel as if we are breaking an important social norm.

Finally, some researchers (e.g., O'Keefe & Figge, 1997) propose that emotion plays a role in compliance. When we turn down the initial large request, we feel negative emotions, such as guilt. Because we do not enjoy feeling bad, we look for a way to reduce these negative emotions. With the opportunity to comply when a second, more reasonable, request is presented, we are more likely to comply to relieve our guilt and make ourselves feel better (Millar, 2002).

LOW-BALLING AND THAT'S-NOT-ALL

low-balling increasing compliance by first getting the person to agree to a deal and then changing the terms of the deal to be more favorable to yourself

that's-not-all increasing compliance by sweetening the deal with additional incentives

destructive obedience obedience to immoral, unethical demands that cause harm to others

Salespeople often use compliance techniques to increase sales. If you think about it, salespeople are in fact asking us to do something. They are asking us to buy their products. One technique that is a favorite among salespeople is **low-balling**, or increasing compliance by first getting the person to agree to a deal and then changing the terms of the deal to be more favorable to the salesperson (Cialdini et al., 1978). For example, a salesperson might offer you a car for $16,750, which you agree to pay. Then, when you go to sign the contract, you find that several charges have been added on, bringing the price up to $17,435. Because you agreed to the original price ($16,750), you are more likely to agree to the $17,435.

This technique works, in part, because we have given our word that we will purchase the car, and we don't like to break promises. We are also likely to be happy to be buying the car, and $17,435 doesn't seem like that much more than $16,750 (perceptual contrast). So, we comply.

If we do quibble about the additional money, the salesperson might also try the **that's-not-all** technique by sweetening the deal with additional incentives (Burger, 1986, 2011). He might throw in some new floor mats or some free car washes to get us to sign. These incentives will not be worth $685, but they might still get us to comply. That's-not-all works, in part, on the norm of reciprocity. The salesperson does something nice for you, and you are supposed to reciprocate by saying "yes."

Many salespeople are professional compliance experts. Even if you know about compliance techniques, they can still work on you. If you feel pressured, it might be best to leave the situation before doing something that you will regret.

10.6.2 • Obedience: Doing What We Are Told to Do

The research on compliance shows that we are fairly likely to give in to simple requests from others. Given this, how do we respond when others *demand* our obedience?

In many instances, obedience is a good thing. For instance, we want people to obey the laws of our society; otherwise, chaos would ensue. However, sometimes we are asked to do things that we know are wrong—things that may even cause harm to others. In these instances, if we give in to the demands, we would be engaging in what psychologists call **destructive obedience**. Recall from Chapter 1 the controversial work of Yale psychologist Stanley Milgram (1933–1984). In the 1960s, Milgram set out to discover just how likely the average person is to engage in destructive obedience. Milgram ran an ad in a New Haven, Connecticut, newspaper that solicited participants for an experiment that would investigate the role of punishment in learning. In actuality, the experiment would measure the participants' willingness to obey an order to administer a very painful electric shock to another person. The participants weren't told this until *after* the experiment was over. As far as the participants knew, they were participating in a study on learning, not obedience.

In all, 40 men participated in Milgram's first study (Milgram, 1963). These men ranged from 20 to 50 years of age, and they represented a variety of professions, including teachers, engineers, and postal clerks. All of the men were paid $4.50 (approximately $30 in today's money) for their participation *before* the experiment began.

When they arrived at the lab, the participants were told that they would be playing the role of a teacher in the experiment. As the teacher, their job would be to administer electric shocks, using an apparatus that delivered shocks ranging from 15 volts to 450 volts, to a participant playing the role of the learner (• FIGURE 10.5).

The learner was supposed to learn a list of words, and the teachers were told that the purpose of the experiment was to see whether the shocks would improve the learner's rate of learning. In actuality, the learner was a confederate, an actor who only pretended to be shocked, but the participants did not know this until after the experiment ended.

During the procedure, the experimenter, a 31-year-old high school biology teacher dressed in a lab coat, stood slightly behind the seated teacher. Throughout the experiment, the teacher and learner communicated via an intercom system, but they did not have visual contact. The teacher was instructed to read a list of words to the learner over the intercom, and then to listen as the learner recalled the words from memory. Every time the learner made a mistake, the teacher was told to deliver a shock to the learner by flipping one of the switches on the apparatus. The procedure began with the 15-volt switch, and the teacher was instructed to move progressively up the scale toward the 450-volt switch as the learner made more and more mistakes.

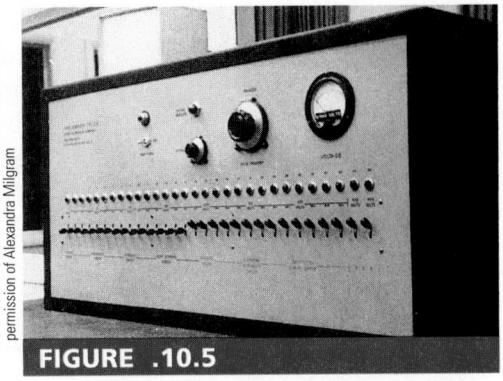

From the film Obedience ©1965 by Stanley Milgram and distributed by Penn State Media Sales. Reprinted by permission of Alexandra Milgram

FIGURE .10.5

The Apparatus Used by Milgram in His Famous Obedience Studies

How far would you go before you refused to obey?

Milgram was primarily interested in seeing how far up the scale the teachers would go before they refused to obey orders to shock the learner further. At the 300-volt mark, the learner began to pound on the wall as if in great pain, protesting the continued shocking. At this point, most participants began to question the experimenter as to whether they should continue to shock the learner, who was obviously in pain. The teachers began to show clear signs of distress, including shaking, stuttering, sweating, nervous laughter, and biting their lips and fingernails. The teachers often protested verbally and indicated that they didn't feel good about continuing to shock the learner.

In response to such displays and protests, the experimenter calmly prodded the participants to continue with the procedure. The experimenter never yelled. He never made verbal or physical threats. He never threatened to take away their $4.50. The experimenter merely requested that the participants continue following orders. The strongest statement by the experimenter was "You have no other choice, you must go on" (Milgram, 1963, p. 374).

After the 315-volt mark, the learner fell completely silent and unresponsive, as if he had lost consciousness or was injured. Because the learner missed all the words on the trial by not responding, the experimenter instructed the teacher to continue delivering the shocks. At this point, it is likely that the teacher believed that he was being asked to shock an injured—or even unconscious—man! What would you do in this situation? What do you think the teachers did?

The results of Milgram's study were nothing short of shocking. A full 65% of the teachers continued to shock the learner all the way up to the 450-volt mark. Despite believing the learner to be ill or worse, most of the teachers continued to follow the experimenter's orders. Even Stanley Milgram was surprised by his findings. Prior to the experiment, Milgram had surveyed psychology students and behavioral science professionals to get a feel for how many participants they thought would go all the way to 450 volts (Milgram, 1963, 1974). Most people believed that only 1% to 3% would. The results showed, of course, a very different picture. Approximately 65% of the participants did go all the way to 450 volts, and no participant refused to obey before the 300-volt mark had been reached!

As you might imagine, Milgram's findings generated a great deal of skepticism. Some people questioned whether the participants in Milgram's (1963) study were abnormal in some way. To answer such skepticism and to further investigate the variables that affect the rate of obedience, Milgram repeated his procedure with different participants. He replicated the study in another town (Bridgeport, CT) and found similar results (Milgram, 1965). Milgram also conducted the study using female participants and again found high rates of obedience (Milgram, 1974).

Other researchers have since replicated Milgram's findings. High school students were found to be even more willing to obey orders (Rosenhan, 1969). Cross-cultural research in other Western cultures has also yielded high rates of obedience using Milgram's procedure (Triandis, 1994). However, a recent partial replication of Milgram's study (Burger, 2009) has sparked a debate over whether societal changes since the 1960s have made people less obedient. Could it be that relative to their grandparents, the young people of today would be less likely to follow orders to hurt others?

VARIATIONS: OBEDIENCE 45 YEARS AFTER MILGRAM

Today, most institutions will not allow researchers to use Milgram's experimental procedure because of concerns over the amount of distress it would cause participants and the possibility that it might violate the ethical rule of doing no harm to research participants (see Chapter 1). Reluctance to replicate Milgram's study has largely left open the question of how people today would react when asked to obey destructive commands. Given that Millennials (people born after 1980) are thought to be more self-focused and assertive than the relatively conformist Baby Boomers (people born between 1945 and 1964), would they be more likely to assert themselves by disobeying destructive orders (Twenge, 2009)?

Recently, psychologist Jerry Burger (2009) found a way to address this question. Burger modified Milgram's procedure to reduce the amount of stress it causes participants and therefore make the procedure more ethical. In his so-called *150-volt solution,* participants are first carefully screened to eliminate those who are likely to experience psychological harm during the study; second, the participants are asked to go only to 150 volts—not the 450 volts used in Milgram's studies (Miller, 2009). Using this less stressful, more ethical procedure, Burger found that his participants were just as likely as Milgram's participants to obey at the 150-volt level (Burger, 2009).

However, Burger's sample of participants was very different from the sample Milgram used. For example, Milgram used only males in his original study. Burger had both male and female participants (Twenge, 2009). When the data were reanalyzed using only the male participants, the results showed that nearly twice as many males disobeyed in 2009 (33.3%) as did in Milgram's original study (17.5%). Although this difference did not reach statistical significance, some researchers argue that it at least suggests that obedience may be decreasing (Twenge, 2009). Clearly, more research is needed to determine whether this is true. Perhaps Burger's 150-volt solution will prove to be a valuable tool in these investigations (Miller, 2009).

Have things changed since the 1960s when Milgram conducted his original studies? Are young people today as willing to engage in destructive obedience as their grandparents were? Today, would research participants go all the way to 450 volts?

© Rido/Shutterstock.com

FACTORS THAT AFFECT OBEDIENCE

Regardless of whether destructive obedience has decreased somewhat over the generations or not, it appears that Milgram's results were not flukes. Unfortunately, even today, many people seem willing to follow orders to hurt others (Burger, 2009). What accounts for this tendency?

One factor that contributed to the high rate of obedience in the Milgram studies was the presence of a *perceived authority figure*. During the procedure, the experimenter, dressed in a lab coat and looking official, stood close by the participant and issued orders to deliver the shocks. Authority figures work in two ways to ensure obedience. First, the fact that the authority figure is ultimately in charge may seem to relieve the person following orders from responsibility for his actions. A person can always tell himself that he was only following orders. Second, the presence of official-looking authority figures tends to intimidate us, and we are therefore more likely to obey their orders (Bushman, 1988). Sometimes it makes sense to be intimidated by authority figures because some authority figures have true power (for example, police officers). If you perceive that authority figures can observe your behavior and that you may suffer negative consequences for disobeying, you might obey out of fear alone.

In later experiments, Milgram found that he could reduce obedience in his participants by increasing the physical distance between the experimenter and the teacher. If the experimenter was not physically present to watch the teacher's behavior, the teachers were much less likely to obey the orders to shock the participant. • TABLE 10.3 summarizes some of the later experimental manipulations

TABLE 10.3

Some Experimental Conditions in Milgram's Experiments and Their Resultant Rates of Obedience

EXPERIMENTAL MANIPULATION	PERCENTAGE OF PARTICIPANTS WHO OBEYED ALL THE WAY TO THE 450-VOLT LEVEL
The learner was seated in the same room with the teacher.	40%
The teacher had to hold the learner's hand down on the shock plate.	30%
The experimenter delivered his orders by telephone instead of in person.	27.5%
The teacher was tested with two confederates who pretended to be participants also playing the role of teacher. Halfway through the experiment, the two confederates refused to shock the learner any further.	10% of participants continued to obey after the confederates refused to further shock the learner.
The teacher was tested with two confederates who pretended to be participants also playing the role of teacher. One of the confederates was the one who actually flipped the switch to shock the learner. The real participant only played an auxiliary role in shocking the learner.	92.5%
Female participants played the role of teacher.	65%

Source: Milgram, 1965.

that Milgram (1965) used to test variables that affect rates of obedience. From Table 10.3, you can see that when the experimenter telephoned his orders to the teachers, obedience dropped to 27.5%.

Another reason for the high rates of obedience in Milgram's studies is the *timing of the requests* made by the experimenter. When the participants arrived at the lab, they very quickly found themselves faced with orders from an authority figure to shock another human being. Because the orders began almost immediately after the participants arrived, they did not have much time to think about their actions. As we saw earlier, when we do not have time to think things through, we are more susceptible to persuasive attempts.

Another factor that contributed to high rates of obedience was the fact that the shock levels were increased incrementally. In essence, Milgram's procedure was a textbook example of foot-in-the-door compliance in action. The first orders were for the teachers to deliver a 15-volt shock, a mere tingle compared to the final shock level of 450 volts. Few people would have qualms about following an order to deliver an almost painless shock, so why not obey? What the participants did not know was by obeying the order to deliver the 15-volt shock, they were paving the way for their own obedience to further orders to shock the learner. Every time the participants obeyed an order to shock, it became harder for them to refuse to continue. Some have likened this type of incremental obedience to standing on a **slippery slope**. Once you begin to obey, it's like beginning to slide down the slope. The farther you go, the more momentum you gain, and the harder it is to stop obeying. If Milgram's procedure had begun with an order to deliver the potentially dangerous shock of 450 volts, it is unlikely that he would have obtained such high rates of obedience.

slippery slope the use of foot-in-the-door compliance in an obedience situation to get people to obey increasing demands

psychological distance the degree to which one can disassociate oneself from the consequences of his/her actions

Another factor that affects obedience is the **psychological distance** we feel between our actions and the results of those actions. In Milgram's first experiment (Milgram, 1963), the teacher could not see the learner during the procedure. In this type of condition, psychological distance is large, meaning that it was relatively easy for the teachers to not think about the consequences of their actions. If you don't think about the consequences of your actions, then you don't have to consciously come to terms with and take responsibility for those actions. This allows you to obey even in situations in which your actions may harm others.

In one dramatic experiment, Milgram had the teacher and learner sit side by side during the procedure. In this variation of the experiment, the teacher had to reach over and hold the learner's hand down on the shock plate. As you might guess, this procedure dramatically reduced the psychological distance for the teacher. It's hard to dissociate yourself from the consequences of your actions when you're actually touching your victim. Under these conditions, only 30% of the participants delivered the maximum 450-volt shock. Note, however, that although obedience was cut in half by reducing the psychological distance, obedience was *not* eliminated. Almost one-third of participants still continued to obey the experimenter, even under these conditions.

A final reason that people may exhibit destructive obedience may reside in the people themselves. In his replication of Milgram's work, Jerry Burger recorded the comments of the participants for later analysis. Burger found some interesting trends. For example, he found that participants who refused to obey were more likely to have expressed a sense of *personal responsibility* than the participants who obeyed to the end of the experiment. Those participants who expressed concern for the learner were also more reluctant to continue to obey, but their reluctance was *not* great enough for them to ultimately disobey (Burger, Girgis, & Manning, 2011). These data suggest that a sense of *personal responsibility* and *concern for others* may be traits that serve to reduce our tendency to engage in destructive obedience. Further research will be needed to fully investigate the effects of these traits.

Despite the controversy generated by Milgram's studies, his work remains one of the most powerful statements ever made about human behavior. Aside from demonstrating our obedience to authority, Milgram's work also brings up some important and perhaps frightening questions about basic human nature. For instance, how can psychologists explain the tendency of some people to behave aggressively? We will look at this issue next.

Quiz Yourself

10.6

1. **You want your friend to lend you $50. If you want to use the door-in-the-face compliance technique to ensure that your friend will comply with your request, what should you do?**
   a. First ask for $1,000 before asking for the $50.
   b. First ask for $10 before asking for the $50.
   c. Wash your friend's car before you ask for the $50.
   d. Tell your friend that you will pay the money back in one week.
2. **In Milgram's original experiment, what percentage of participants went all the way to 450 volts when "shocking" the learner?**
   a. 5%
   b. 35%
   c. 65%
   d. 75%
3. **Which of the following compliance techniques *best* explains Milgram's findings in his study on obedience?**
   a. Foot-in-the-door
   b. Door-in-the-face
   c. Reciprocity
   d. Low-balling

Answers 1. a; 2. c; 3. a

10.7 Aggression: Hurting Others

Psychologists define aggression as an action that is intended to cause harm to another person who does not want to be harmed (Baron & Richardson, 1992; Brehm, Kassin, & Fein, 2002; Huesmann, 1994). Aggressive acts can be classified as *instrumental* or *hostile*. **Instrumental aggression** is aimed at achieving some goal. For example, a child may hit a playmate to distract her so the child can grab her toy. **Hostile aggression** is motivated solely by a desire to hurt others. For example, a bully may punch another child on the playground just to see the child cry.

instrumental aggression aggression that is used to facilitate the attainment of a goal

hostile aggression aggression that is meant to cause harm to others

Although both types of aggression are widespread in many cultures, the overall prevalence of aggression varies across cultures. Among developed countries, the United States is considered to be an aggressive society (see Osterman et al., 1994). Pick up a major American metropolitan newspaper any day of the week, and you will see abundant evidence of this in the daily crime reports. In 2012, a total of 1,214,462 violent crimes were reported in the United States. This represents approximately 386.9 violent crimes for every 100,000 people in the United States (FBI, 2012b).

Besides the almost daily reports of violent crime in the United States, it appears that even noncriminals have aggression on their minds. Researchers

Barbara Stitzer/PhotoEdit

Instrumental aggression is aimed at achieving some goal. The older child is being aggressive to obtain a toy.

surveyed 312 college students at a U.S. university about whether they had ever thought about killing someone. Fully 73% of male students and 66% of female students reported that they had (Kenrick & Sheets, 1993)! What could account for such numbers? Could aggressive feelings be more natural than we like to think?

10.7.1 • Biological Theories of Aggression

It has been widely documented that among many species, including humans, males tend to be more aggressive than females (see e.g., Sysoeva et al., 2010). In 2012, males accounted for 80.1% of those arrested for violent crimes (FBI, 2012b). Because males have more of the hormone testosterone in their bodies, researchers have long suspected that testosterone and aggressive behavior are related. But the research on the relationship between aggression and testosterone has yielded a somewhat confusing picture. Sometimes higher levels of testosterone are associated with higher levels of aggression in animals (Müller, Moe, & Groothuis, 2013; Wagner, Beuving, & Hutchinson, 1980), but sometimes they are not (Eaton & Resko, 1974). Likewise, human studies sometimes show a correlation between high testosterone levels and aggression (Dabbs & Morris, 1990; Sánchez-Martín et al., 2011; Van Goozen, Frijda, & de Poll, 1994), but sometimes they fail to find a clear relationship (Coccaro et al., 2007).

Even if the correlation between testosterone and aggressive behavior were more consistent in the literature, it would still be difficult to determine the actual cause(s) of aggressive behavior. Recall that *correlation* does not imply *causation*. Higher levels of testosterone are associated with muscularity and strength, which may simply give one the physical ability to be a bully. Some researchers have found that in adolescent boys, aggression is correlated with physical size but not correlated with levels of testosterone (Tremblay et al., 1998).

A POSSIBLE ROLE FOR SEROTONIN

Research has suggested that another chemical, serotonin (see Chapter 2), may also play a role in regulation of aggressive behavior (for a review, see Duke et al., 2013; Libersat & Pflueger, 2004). Researchers measured levels of the neurotransmitter serotonin in the bloodstream of three groups of people: survivors of suicide attempts, people institutionalized since childhood for aggressive behavior, and a normal control group (Marazzitti et al., 1993). They found that the suicide survivors and the aggressive patients had lower levels of serotonin than those in the normal control group.

Recently, researchers found that giving healthy participants an antidepressant that increases serotonin made them less likely to take action that would financially harm other players in a monetary game. This change in behavior seemed to stem from the participants becoming more empathetic and therefore more averse to harming others (Crockett et al., 2010).

Low levels of serotonin are associated with conditions such as obsessive-compulsive disorders, in which the person has difficulty controlling his or her behavior and feels compelled to repeat certain actions (see Chapter 13). If we extend this thinking to the relationship between serotonin and aggression, we can speculate that people with lower levels of serotonin may have difficulty in controlling their aggressive impulses toward themselves (as in suicide) and toward others (as in the institutionalized patients). However, more research is needed before any firm conclusions can be drawn about the role of serotonin in aggression.

CHILDHOOD ABUSE AND AGGRESSION

Another connection between biology and aggression comes from research into the backgrounds of incarcerated criminals. During the 1980s and 1990s, psychiatrist Dorothy Otnow Lewis interviewed more than 100 murderers in an attempt to discover whether they had experienced abuse as children (Lewis, 1992). During these interviews, Lewis discovered that an overwhelming majority of these murderers had suffered extreme abuse during childhood. In particular, many had suffered severe head injuries as a result of the abuse, which led Lewis and her colleagues to hypothesize that the murderers' aggressive tendencies may have resulted from brain damage (Lewis et al., 2004).

More recent research seems to reinforce Lewis's notions. It is now thought that childhood abuse and neglect are related to the development of several brain abnormalities. Using some of the techniques for studying the brain that we discussed in Chapter 2 (such as EEG, MRI, and fMRI), researchers have found that childhood abuse and neglect correlate with having structural abnormalities in the amygdala, hippocampus, corpus callosum, left frontal lobe, left temporal lobe, and cerebellum (Teicher, 2002). Research has also shown a correlation between damage in the area of the frontal lobe adjoining the limbic system and agitated/aggressive behavior in people with mild cognitive impairment and Alzheimer's disease (Trzepacz et al., 2013).

Virtually no one would disagree that an end to child abuse would be good for society. Aside from a possible link between the physical damage caused by child abuse and later aggression, psychologists have other reasons to fear the destructive influence of child abuse. An aggressive model, such as an aggressive, punitive parent or a violent TV character, can teach a child to be aggressive.

10.7.2 • Learning Theories of Aggression

In Chapter 6, we described Albert Bandura's *Bobo doll* experiments, in which children who watched an adult model beat up a plastic Bobo doll were likely to mimic the model's aggression when later left alone with the doll (Bandura, Ross, & Ross, 1963). After being exposed to an aggressive model, the children acquired new and aggressive behaviors. Many psychologists believe that aggression is often learned through this type of *observational learning*.

However, exposure to violence and aggression may promote more than just modeling of aggressive behavior. Such exposure may actually influence the cognitive, emotional, and behavioral responses we have to events in our daily lives. One model of aggression, the **cognitive neoassociation theory**, proposes that cues present during an aggressive event can become associated in memory with the thoughts and emotions experienced during that event (Anderson & Bushman, 2002; Berkowitz, 1990). For example, if you see many instances (real or televised) in which people use guns to shoot and hurt those who have humiliated them, you may begin to associate concepts from these events in your memory. You may begin to associate guns with anger, hurt, fear, and

cognitive neoassociation theory proposes that cues present during an aggressive event can become associated in memory with the thoughts and emotions experienced during that event

Psychology Applies to Your World:

Does Television Portray Violence Accurately?

TV and movies have been shown to portray many aspects of life unrealistically, including mental health therapy (Sharma & Malik, 2013), marriage (Segrin & Nabi, 2002), the medical profession (Chory-Assad & Tamborini, 2001), and violence. One study reported a total of 2,126 antisocial acts in 65.5 hours of so-called reality television programming, or shows that are supposed to document real life, such as *Cops*. The problem is that these "reality shows" do not give an accurate picture of real life. They portray acts of aggression at rates that are far above the actual rates at which they occur in U.S. society (Potter et al., 1997). Furthermore, violence on television is not just confined to a few "reality" shows. In fact, a review of studies conducted over the last 40 years indicates that nearly 70% of prime-time shows contain violence (Weaver, Zelenkauskaite, & Samson, 2012).

And the children are watching. According to the Nielsen Company, children ages 2–5 watch 32 hours of television a week and children ages 6–11 watch 28 hours a week (Associated Press, 2009). By the time a child reaches age 18, she will have witnessed some 200,000 acts of televised violence, of which 16,000 will have been murders (APA cited in Muscari, 2002). Saturday morning children's programming exposes children to 20–25 acts of violence per hour (Kaiser Family Foundation, 2006). Even more disturbing is that many televised acts of aggression are ones in which the aggressor experiences no negative repercussions for his or her actions. In 1996, a report sponsored by the National Cable Television Association indicated that perpetrators go unpunished in 73% of all violent scenes on TV and that only 16% of all violent acts on TV portrayed long-term negative consequences of violence for the victim. These false impressions may increase the likelihood that children will actually model the behavior they see on TV (Bandura, 1965; Hogben, 1998).

foto-begsteiger/vario Images RM/Age Fotostock

Are these children learning to be aggressive as they watch television?

humiliation; or you may begin to associate conflict with shooting. Because these concepts become tightly linked in memory, activation of one of them can prime other related concepts and cause them to become active. In other words, merely seeing a gun may cause you to have aggressive thoughts. Being humiliated may activate feelings of anger and the desire to use a gun to retaliate against those who hurt you. Indeed, research participants have been shown to have aggressive thoughts after simply being shown pictures of weapons (Anderson, Benjamin, & Bartholow, 1998).

If our behavior is heavily influenced by the cues we perceive to be associated with aggression and violence, then the nature of such perceptions is very important. Given that many of our ideas about the world are influenced by the media, it is worthwhile to ask the question, does television portray violence and its consequences accurately? For a look at this issue, see the Psychology Applies to Your World box.

10.7.3 • Situations That Promote Aggressive Behavior

When are you most likely to behave aggressively? Are there circumstances in which you might behave in a physically aggressive manner toward another? What would it take?

One key factor in aggression appears to be frustration. According to the **frustration-aggression hypothesis** (Dollard et al., 1939), when we become frustrated, we activate a motive to harm other people or objects. These motives are likely to be directed at those people or objects that we perceive to be the source of our frustration. Most physically abusive parents never intend to threaten or harm their children. But in the heat of the moment, some parents take out their frustration on their children. A recent study of fathers with 3-year-old children found that the more parenting stress a father was under, the more likely he was to use corporal punishment on his child (S. J. Lee et al., 2011). Likewise, parents in high-stress situations—such as extreme poverty—who do not have good coping skills are most at risk for becoming abusive (Garbarino, 1997; see also Guterman et al., 2013). Recall from Chapter 5 that motives drive and catalyze behavior. Consequently, when we are frustrated, our chances of behaving aggressively increase. Therefore, during stressful, frustrating situations, we have to be on guard for possible aggressive behavior in ourselves and in others.

frustration-aggression hypothesis the idea that frustration causes aggressive behavior

Quiz Yourself

10.7

1. Which neurotransmitter has been implicated as possibly playing a role in aggressive behavior?
   a. Testosterone
   b. Serotonin
   c. Dopamine
   d. Estrogen
2. Road rage incidents are more likely to occur in heavy traffic. This fact can *best* be explained as due to the increase in _____ that occurs among drivers in heavy traffic.
   a. frustration
   b. fatigue
   c. fear
   d. anxiety
3. Little Sabina wants to play with her sister's doll, but her sister will not let Sabina have the doll. So Sabina hits her sister and takes the doll away while her sister cries. Sabina's behavior is *best* characterized as an example of _____.
   a. hostile aggression
   b. instrumental aggression
   c. biological aggression
   d. learned aggression

Answers 1. b; 2. a; 3. b

10.8 Choosing to Help Others: Prosocial Behavior

By now you might be thinking that humans are pretty rotten creatures. We seem to be easily biased against others, easily influenced by others, aggressive, and even easily convinced to do real harm to others. But it is also true that humans

prosocial behavior behavior that helps others

altruism helping another without being motivated by self-gain

helping behavior another term for altruism

often engage in **prosocial behavior**, or behavior that helps others. Recall how Hongyong engaged in prosocial behavior when she used *ch'iryo* to heal others of their ailments. In doing so, Hongyong not only helped others, she also helped herself. But, helping need not involve some sort of benefit. Sometimes we demonstrate **altruism**, or a willingness to help others without considering any possible benefit for ourselves. Just as we have the capacity for violence, we also have the capacity for kindness and compassion.

10.8.1 • The Murder of Kitty Genovese

As is sometimes the case, the psychological study of altruism, or **helping behavior**, was prompted by a tragedy, the murder of Kitty Genovese in New York City on March 13, 1964. Kitty Genovese, age 28, was returning to her apartment in Queens at 3:20 A.M. when she was approached and stabbed by a man in a prolonged assault that lasted 30 minutes. During the attack, Kitty's screams were heard by 38 of her neighbors. Yet Kitty did not get the help she needed, and she died from her injuries. A *New York Times* article that reported the murder claimed that although 38 people witnessed Kitty's murder, none of them called the police until after she was dead (Gansberg, 1964). As you might imagine, people reacted with shock and outrage to this news. Further reports of interviews with some of the witnesses only fanned the flames. Some of the witnesses explained their inaction by saying, "I didn't want to get involved." Even a man who finally did call the police first called a friend for advice because he was so afraid of getting involved (Mohr, 1964).

Today, some people allege that these early reports misrepresented some of the facts of the case and overstated the witnesses' apathy. For example, many of the witnesses may not have been in a position to actually see the attack; they may have only heard some commotion on the street. It is also possible that some witnesses may have tried to call the police immediately after Kitty was attacked but for unknown reasons the calls were ineffective (De May, 2006). Perhaps we will never know exactly how the witnesses, many of whom have since passed away, actually responded that night. However, what is certain is how the public perceived the situation back in 1964—they perceived that the witnesses were apathetic and callous. What is also certain is that examples of apparent bystander apathy have periodically reappeared in the decades since Kitty's murder. When they do, people once again express outrage that such a thing can happen in a civilized society (for example, see Livingston, 2010).

Soon after Kitty's murder and the uproar that followed, researchers Bibb Latané and John Darley (1969) set out to determine which factors influence whether we help others in need. They found that apathy or lack of concern is not the reason that people fail to help in situations like the Genovese murder. They also discovered that deciding whether to help someone is not necessarily a single decision, nor is it a simple decision to make. You must first notice that something out of the ordinary is occurring. Second, you must correctly interpret the situation as one that requires your aid. It is very possible that some of those who heard Kitty Genovese's cries did not realize that they were anything other than the normal sounds of a New York City street at night. Third, you must feel that you have a responsibility to intervene in the situation. Some of the 38 witnesses may have believed that someone else was coming to Kitty's aid. Fourth, you must decide how to help the person in distress. If you don't know what to do, you cannot offer help to someone in need. Finally, you must implement your helping strategy, and actually help the person in need.

10.8.2 • The Bystander Effect

Because deciding to help is a multistep process, failure can occur at any of the five steps. Early studies of helping behavior focused on responsibility and the thought processes that might contribute to one person's feeling responsible to help another in need. Latané and Darley hypothesized what they called the **bystander effect**. As the number of bystanders increases in an emergency situation, the probability that any one of the bystanders will actually intervene *decreases*.

bystander effect the idea that the more witnesses there are to an emergency, the less likely any one of them is to offer help

diffusion of responsibility the idea that responsibility for taking action is diffused across all the people witnessing an event

pluralistic ignorance the idea that we use the behavior of others to help us determine whether a situation is an emergency requiring our help; if no one else is helping, we may conclude that help isn't needed

To test their theory, Latané and Darley conducted a number of experiments (Latané & Darley, 1969). In one study, participants worked on a questionnaire either alone or in the presence of two other people. Halfway through the questionnaire, smoke began to filter into the room through a wall vent, as if there were a fire nearby. The dependent variable in the study was whether the participant got up to investigate the source of the smoke and how quickly he or she did so. The results of this experiment supported the idea of the bystander effect. When participants were in the room alone, 75% of them got up to investigate the source of the smoke. When there were two other people in the room, only 10% of the participants got up to investigate. It appears that even when you may be helping yourself, the presence of other bystanders can reduce your tendency to help. Why would this be the case?

One explanation for the bystander effect is **diffusion of responsibility**, or the idea that all bystanders share equally in the responsibility for helping in an emergency. Each of the 38 witnesses would thus have borne only a small fraction of the responsibility for helping Kitty Genovese. As the number of bystanders decreases, the amount of responsibility any one bystander bears increases. When you are the only witness, you bear all of the responsibility for helping. So, what can you do if you need help and there are several bystanders present? You can reduce the bystander effect by clearly identifying one bystander and requesting his or her help. By singling out one person, you eliminate the diffusion of responsibility, placing all of the responsibility on that one person. Remembering this could save your life someday!

Diffusion of responsibility is not the only factor that prevents people from helping others. Another possible explanation for a bystander's failure to help is **pluralistic ignorance**, or the failure of a group of witnesses to perceive there is a problem that requires their help (Latané & Darley, 1969). When the witnesses saw the others doing nothing to help Kitty, this lack of action and excitement on the part of others may have caused each individual to inaccurately perceive that Kitty did not need help (Sexton, 1995). In other words, when we see that others are not interpreting a situation as an emergency, we are less likely to interpret the situation as an emergency, and therefore we are less likely to help.

Researchers now believe that the number of witnesses to an emergency is only one factor that influences helping. Several other variables that have been shown to influence helping behavior are summarized in ● TABLE 10.4. As you read through Table 10.4, you'll notice that, unfortunately, not all people are equally likely to receive help.

10.8.3 • When People Choose to Help

Although Kitty did not receive the help she needed, there are many examples of people who have helped others both in heroic ways and through simple,

TABLE 10.4

Variables That Affect Helping Behavior

VARIABLE	DESCRIPTION
Level of bystander's hurry (Darley & Batson, 1973)	Bystanders who are in a hurry are less likely to stop and help someone in distress.
Bystander's relationship to other bystanders (Gottlieb & Carver, 1980)	When bystanders expect to interact with each other in the future, they are more likely to help a stranger in need.
Relationship between victim and bystander (Kogut & Ritov, 2011)	A bystander who knows something about the victim is more likely to help.
Bystander's perceived ambiguity (Solomon, Solomon, & Maiorca, 1982)	If the situation is ambiguous, bystanders will tend to see it as a nonemergency and therefore be less likely to help.
Bystander's fear for own safety (Tobin, Davey, & Latkin, 2005)	If bystanders are afraid they will be harmed in some way (e.g., arrested), they are less likely to help.
Bystander's prejudice against the victim or belief that the victim is an out-group member (Saucier, McManus, & Smith, 2010)	Bystanders who are prejudiced against the victim or see the victim as an out-group member are less likely to help.
Victim's level of dependency (Bornstein, 1994)	Bystanders are more likely to help a victim they perceive to be dependent—for example, a child.
Victim's responsibility for own plight (DePalma et al., 1999)	Bystanders are less likely to help if they perceive the emergency to be the victim's own fault.

Tom Stewart/Bridge/Corbis

Humans often do come to the aid of others.

everyday acts of kindness. In 2012, when Superstorm Sandy devastated portions of the east coast of the United States, people from many walks of life came to the aid of their neighbors and many more contributed financial support to relief efforts. In the spring of 2011, when deadly tornadoes destroyed large portions of towns like Tuscaloosa, Alabama, and Joplin, Missouri, many bystanders rushed to help pull people from the trapped vehicles and debris. In the aftermath of the earthquakes and tsunami that devastated Japan in 2011, many ordinary citizens rushed to help the thousands of victims. From around the world, many more rushed to send money and supplies to aid the Japanese. As these examples indicate, we do not always think of ourselves first, and we frequently are motivated to help others in need.

When we fail to help, it is usually not out of a sense of apathy or cruelty, but rather out of misunderstanding, confusion, or fear (Latané & Darley, 1969). Perhaps by becoming aware of the factors that affect our tendency to help others, we can find ways to make the world a more altruistic place.

10.8

Quiz Yourself

1. **What did Darley and Latané conclude about the witnesses in the Kitty Genovese murder case?**
   a. Many of the witnesses were uncaring people, and that is why they failed to help.
   b. The witnesses were too busy doing other things to stop and help Kitty.
   c. Many of the witnesses did not help because they assumed that someone else would help.
   d. Fear was the best explanation for why the witnesses did not help.

2. **Recently, one of the authors was sitting in her office when the fire alarms in her building went off. To her amazement, everyone seemed to ignore the alarms, and no one evacuated the building until security forced them to leave. Which of the following best explains their reluctance to leave the building?**
   a. Diffusion of responsibility
   b. Apathy
   c. Pluralistic ignorance
   d. A lack of conformity

3. **If you are ever the victim of an accident and there are many witnesses, what should you do to help ensure that one of the witnesses helps you?**
   a. Scream for help.
   b. Remain quiet so as not to scare the witnesses.
   c. Single out one of the witnesses, and request that he or she help you.
   d. Yell "Fire!"

Answers 1. c; 2. c; 3. c

10.9 Integrating Psychology: The Big Picture

The life of Hongyong Baek illustrates many of the processes that social psychologists study. The *attitudes* she held about herself as a woman were influenced in large part by the *stereotypes* and *prejudices* that many in her culture held about women at the time—for example, that women should be obedient to men and that a woman's opinion was not worth as much as a man's opinion. As she developed during childhood, many of these cultural ideas became imprinted in her mind. Yet, as she continued to develop throughout adulthood, her attitudes also changed over time; showing us that as we are exposed to new experiences, processes such as *persuasion* and *cognitive dissonance* can change the attitudes we hold about the world and ourselves.

Despite an arranged marriage to a man she barely knew, the *similarity* of attitudes she shared with her husband led Hongyong to fall in love with him. For a period of time, she reveled in her role as wife and mother, and when her husband began to wander, she *attributed* his infidelity to her lack of *attractiveness* as a woman.

Throughout her life, Hongyong felt pressure to *conform* to the norms of her culture. In her traditional Korean culture, these norms often called for *compliance* and *obedience*. However, at times, Hongyong failed to conform, comply, and obey. She went against her husband's wishes. She smuggled opium. She spoke her mind. She considered abandoning her child under desperate circumstances. All these behaviors violated the norms and sometimes the laws of her society.

Yet, she also met society's expectations in many ways. She cared for her husband and children. She worked at several honest professions. She educated herself. She tried to help others with her practice of ch'iryo. She searched for decades until she found the son she had lost in the chaos of the war. In many ways, Hongyong engaged in *prosocial behavior.*

Like Hongyong, you too are affected by others. All of us feel social pressures toward persuasion, conformity, compliance, obedience, and so on. Many of us have dealt with prejudice, aggression, love, and the need to help others. We can't escape these forces, for we are social beings. Yet, despite the social influences we all feel, we are still individuals. For Hongyong, her determined and independent personality may have helped drive her to overcome some of the pressures and challenges that she faced in life. In our next chapter, we will examine personality and individual traits that affect our behavior in the social world. As you read Chapter 11, think about Hongyong and all that she experienced. Also, think of the ways that you have been influenced by others and how your own unique personality has guided your behavior in the social world.

Studying the Chapter

Key Terms

actor/observer bias (420)
altruism (452)
attitudes (412)
attribution (418)
aversive racism (423)
bystander effect (453)
central route to persuasion (415)
cognitive consistency (414)
cognitive neoassociation theory (449)
cohesiveness (435)
collectivistic cultures (419)
compliance (440)
conformity (435)
contact hypothesis (427)
deindividuation (437)
destructive obedience (442)
diffusion of responsibility (453)
discrimination (423)
dissonance theory (415)
door-in-the-face compliance (441)
foot-in-the-door compliance (440)
frustration-aggression hypothesis (451)
fundamental attribution error (419)
groupthink (438)
helping behavior (452)
hostile aggression (447)
impression formation (417)
individualistic cultures (419)
informational conformity (436)
in-group bias (426)
Instrumental aggression (447)
low-balling (442)
matching hypothesis (432)
normative conformity (436)
norms (434)
obedience (440)
out-group homogeneity bias (426)
peripheral route to persuasion (416)
persuasion (415)
pluralistic ignorance (453)
prejudice (422)
prosocial behavior (452)
proximity (430)
psychological distance (446)
realistic-conflict theory (426)
reciprocity (441)
scapegoat (426)
self-serving bias (420)
situational attribution (418)
slippery slope (446)
social cognition (412)
social facilitation (438)
social influence (441)
social loafing (438)
social psychology (412)
stereotype (422)
stereotype threat (423)
superordinate goal (427)
that's-not-all (442)
trait attribution (418)

What Do You Know? Assess Your Understanding

Test your retention and understanding of the material by answering the following questions.

1. Which of the following is *not* an attitude?

a. Liking rap music
b. Believing that honesty is the best policy
c. Believing that Atlanta is the capital of Georgia
d. All of the above are attitudes.

2. When Hongyong tried to convince her husband that smuggling opium was a good idea, she was attempting to employ which technique of social influence?

a. Dissonance
b. Persuasion
c. Conformity
d. Compliance

3. If you are in the market for a new car, you should process television ads from car dealers on the _____ route to persuasion.

a. central
b. peripheral
c. cognitive
d. emotional

4. Which of the following is *least* likely to affect persuasion?

a. How distracted the audience members are
b. How intelligent the audience members are
c. How attractive the audience members are
d. The mood of the audience members

5. Assuming that your professor is a happy person because she was smiling today in class is most likely an example of _____.

a. dissonance
b. the fundamental attribution error
c. the actor/observer bias
d. the in-group/out-group bias

6. Believing that your roommate is to blame for your poor performance on your history exam is most likely an example of _____.

a. a trait attribution
b. the fundamental attribution error
c. the actor/observer bias
d. the self-serving bias

7. Believing that because Joe is over 70 years old, he would not be a very good waiter is an example of a _____.

a. stereotype
b. prejudice
c. situational attribution
d. All of the above

8. Jane Elliott's study of prejudice in brown-eyed and blue-eyed grade school students showed us that _____.

a. prejudices are already present in us
b. prejudices develop easily in us
c. prejudices develop slowly over time
d. children do not form prejudices as easily as adults do

9. When Mary says, "All men hate to ask for directions," she is most likely exhibiting the _____.

a. out-group homogeneity bias
b. in-group/out-group bias
c. actor-observer bias
d. fundamental attribution error

10. Muzafer Sherif's study of the Eagles and Rattlers indicated that _____ is the most useful way to reduce prejudice.

a. punishment
b. mere contact with out-group members
c. cooperative contact between groups
d. competition between groups

11. Living and working in close proximity to someone is likely to increase our liking for that person because of _____.

a. in-group/out-group bias
b. the mere exposure effect
c. similarity
d. the out-group homogeneity effect

12. Being in love with someone is associated with increased _____ in the brain.

a. dopamine
b. serotonin
c. GABA
d. acetylcholine

13. Immediately after a famous actor wears Cooldog brand jeans in a movie, the Cooldog company sees sales of its jeans increase by 500%. This sales increase is most likely the result of _____.

a. compliance
b. conformity
c. persuasion
d. obedience

14. Sasha loves to knit. She notices that when she knits with her knitting group, she seems to get more done than she would in the same amount of time knitting alone at home. Sasha's experience is most likely an example of _____.

a. informational conformity
b. social loafing
c. social facilitation
d. the self-serving bias

15. Which of the following would be *least* likely to reduce the risk of groupthink in a group?

a. Having a strong group leader
b. Allowing ample time for discussion of ideas
c. Allowing visitors to attend group meetings
d. Having low cohesiveness

16. The destructive obedience that Stanley Milgram demonstrated in his experiments is *most* closely related to which of the following social psychological phenomena?

a. Realistic conflict
b. Attribution
c. Foot-in-the-door compliance
d. The frustration-aggression hypothesis

17. Which of the following has *not* been linked to aggressive behavior?

a. Low serotonin levels
b. High testosterone
c. Frustration
d. High norepinephrine levels

18. The bystander effect predicts that you are *most* likely to receive help from an individual when he or she _____.

a. is the only witness to your plight
b. is one of many witnesses to your plight
c. is knowledgeable about helping
d. is a compassionate person

19. Altruism is helping someone _____.

a. without concern for your own gain
b. because you expect a reward
c. because you are afraid you'll be sued if you fail to help
d. because other people are watching

20. Pluralistic ignorance prevents helping because _____.

a. everyone decides that someone else is responsible for helping
b. no one knows how to help
c. no one recognizes that help is needed
d. no one cares enough to help

Answers: 1. c; 2. b; 3. a; 4. c; 5. b; 6. d; 7. b; 8. b; 9. a; 10. c; 11. b; 12. a; 13. b; 14. c; 15. a; 16. c; 17. d; 18. a; 19. a; 20. c.

Use It or Lose It: Applying Psychology

1. Given what you have learned about obedience and compliance, what precautions would you urge people to take if they wanted to make themselves less vulnerable to requests and demands from others?

2. Pretend you have just been appointed to a committee at your place of work. Your mission is to develop a strategic plan that will take your company into the future. What precautions would you take to ensure that your group does not develop groupthink?

3. Pretend you are an advertising account executive working for a new client. Using your knowledge of persuasion, design a television ad campaign to sell a new type of dishwashing detergent called Squeeky Clean Suds. Then justify to your client why your plan should be successful.

4. Pretend you are a community leader in a racially divided community. Design a program to reduce racial tensions among your community's citizens. Then explain why your plan should work.

5. Watch two television shows that feature male and female characters, one modern show and one older show from prior to the 1990s. What gender stereotypes are portrayed in these two shows? How do the shows differ in their depiction of male and female roles? How do these differences reflect changes in our culture over the past 50 years?

6. Keep a log of the attributions you make in a single day. How often did you use the heuristics discussed in this chapter? How often did you engage in careful attributions?

7. Find an article from a major metropolitan newspaper that discusses an instance in which someone committed an act of altruism. Then find an article that describes an emergency in which no one came to the aid of the victim. Compare and contrast the two situations in terms of the variables that affect helping behavior. Do these situations fit with what you have learned about helping behavior? If not, how do they differ?

Critical Thinking for Integration

1. Give examples, not cited in the text, of how the learning theories from Chapter 6 (that is, classical conditioning, operant conditioning, and observational learning) can contribute to the development of a prejudice.

2. Given what you have learned about developmental psychology in Chapter 9, when would you expect to see prejudice develop in children? Explain your answer.

3. Use what you learned in Chapter 1 to design an experiment to test the matching hypothesis.

4. Use what you learned in Chapter 1 to design an experiment to test the hypothesis that bystanders will be less likely to help a victim who they perceive to be responsible for his own plight.

© Tyler Olson/Shutterstock.com

Are You Getting the Big Picture? Social Psychology

Social psychology is the study of how we think and behave in social situations. **Social cognition** refers to the ways in which we think about ourselves and others.

10.1 Evaluating the World: Attitudes

Hulton Archive/Getty Images

- **Attitudes** are evaluative beliefs that contain affective, behavioral, and cognitive components.
- Attitudes develop through learning processes, including classical conditioning, operant conditioning, and observational learning or modeling.
- Attitudes sometimes predict how we will behave in certain situations.
- **Dissonance** results from a lack of **cognitive consistency**; it motivates us to change either our attitudes or our behavior.
- **Persuasion** occurs when someone makes a direct attempt to change our attitudes.
- We tend to be most persuaded by people who appear to be attractive, credible, and expert.
- Typically, people are easier to persuade when they are processing on the **peripheral route** rather than the **central route.**

10.2 Forming Impressions of Others

- In forming impressions of others, we make **trait** or **situational attributions** when we assign cause to their behavior.
- The **fundamental attribution error** is the tendency to overuse trait explanations during attribution.
- The **actor/observer bias** and the **self-serving bias** are two other sources of mistaken or biased attributions.

10.3 Prejudice: Why Can't We All Just Get Along?

Mark Peterson/Corbis News/Corbis

- **Prejudices** are negatively biased **stereotypes** that are applied to all members of a social group regardless of the members' individual characteristics.
- Like most attitudes, prejudices are learned.
- Intergroup dynamics such as **in-group bias** and **out-group homogeneity bias** often play a role in prejudice.
- The **contact hypothesis** states that mere contact between in-group and out-group members can reduce prejudice. Cooperative contact and **superordinate goals** have been shown to be more effective in reducing prejudice.

10.4 Being Drawn to Others: The Nature of Attraction

- Some of the factors that affect our attraction to others include **proximity**, similarity of their attitudes and characteristics to ours, physical attractiveness, and the biochemical processes in our bodies.

10.5 Group Influence

Joseph Reid/Alamy

- **Conformity** is the tendency to behave in ways that are consistent with the **norms** or expectations of a group.
- In **normative conformity**, we conform just to avoid breaking norms. In **informational conformity**, we conform because we are persuaded by conformity pressure to believe the group's stance is correct.
- Conformity is influenced by such factors as majority group size, unanimity of the majority group, anonymity, group cohesion, and self-esteem.
- **Social facilitation** occurs when we perform better in the presence of others, but sometimes working with others can lead to **social loafing** as group members decrease their effort.
- **Groupthink** occurs when groups working under conditions of isolation, high **cohesiveness**, stress, and dictatorial leadership make poor decisions after failing to examine all possible solutions to a problem.

10.6 Requests and Demands: Compliance and Obedience

From the film Obedience ©1965 by Stanley Milgram and distributed by Penn State Media Sales. Reprinted by permission of Alexandra Milgram

- **Compliance** is giving in to a simple request.
- In **foot-in-the-door compliance**, one is more likely to yield to a second larger request after having already complied with a first, smaller request.
- In **door-in-the-face compliance**, one is more likely to yield to a second, smaller request after having refused an earlier large request.
- **Reciprocity**, or feeling obligated to return others' favors, is a major reason why we comply.
- **Obedience** is giving in to a demand. Factors that make us more likely to obey orders, even when they direct us to behave destructively, include: the presence of an authority figure; the foot-in-the door compliance of the **slippery slope;** and increased **psychological distance.**

10.7 Aggression: Hurting Others

- Aggression is causing harm or injury to someone who does not wish to be harmed.
- **Instrumental aggression** is goal-directed aggression; **hostile aggression** is aimed solely at hurting others.
- Potential causes of aggression include high levels of testosterone, a lack of serotonin, brain damage caused by child abuse, observational learning or modeling the aggression of others, **cognitive neoassociation theory**, and the **frustration-aggression hypothesis.**

10.8 Choosing to Help Others: Prosocial Behavior

Tom Stewart/Bridge/Corbis

- **Helping behavior**, or **altruism**, is the tendency to help others in need with little concern for our own gain.
- One of the factors affecting helping behavior is the **bystander effect**, in which **diffusion of responsibility** reduces the likelihood of obtaining help when there are many witnesses. **Pluralistic ignorance** may also prevent witnesses from perceiving the situation as an emergency.

Personality

Learning Objectives

11.1 Discuss Freud's perspective on personality, describing how his levels of awareness, psychosexual stages, and personality structures interact to generate behavior. (APA 1.1, 1.2)

11.1 Discuss neo-Freudian perspectives on personality, indicating their differences from and similarities to Freud's theory. (APA 1.1, 1.2)

11.1 Indicate the strengths and weaknesses of the psychoanalytic approach in explaining personality. (APA 1.2, 2.1)

11.2 Define traits, and apply the various trait approaches to understanding personality (Allport, Cattell, Eysenck, and the five factor theory). (APA 1.1, 1.2, 1.3)

11.2 Discuss genetic contributions to personality, and address whether personality is consistent and stable over time. (APA 1.2, 1.3, 2.1)

11.2 Indicate the strengths and weaknesses of the trait approach in explaining personality. (APA 1.2, 2.1)

11.3 Describe social cognitive approaches to personality, such as Bandura's reciprocal determinism and Rotter's locus of control. (APA 1.1, 1.2)

11.3 Indicate the strengths and weaknesses of the social cognitive approach in explaining personality. (APA 1.2, 2.1)

11.4 Define self-actualization, and describe how the humanistic views of Maslow and Rogers propose that it can be achieved. (APA 1.1, 1.2)

11.4 Indicate the strengths and weaknesses of the humanistic approach in explaining personality. (APA 1.2, 2.1)

11.5 Compare and contrast the advantages and disadvantages of using personality inventories, projective tests, and rating scales to measure personality. (APA 1.3, 2.1, 2.4, 5.5)

11.5 Describe the purpose of direct observation and the clinical interview. (APA 1.1, 1.3, 5.5)

In the previous two chapters, we outlined how social and developmental processes contribute to variations in behavior across people. This chapter extends that discussion by examining personality. **Personality** is the unique collection of attitudes, emotions, thoughts, habits, impulses, and behaviors that define how a person typically behaves across situations. Hongyong Baek story at the opening of this section illustrated a complex and rich array of personalities within one family. Hongyong Baek was willful, curious, and insecure about her appearance. Her husband, Dukpil was compromising, resourceful, and sociable. Some of the children were more outgoing and independent, whereas others were more quiet and unassuming. Perhaps your family is similarly varied, seeming like a cast of actors put together for an off-Broadway play! How can we understand these similarities and differences in personality? That is the focus of this chapter as we explore this critical question: how do we develop our personalities, and how stable—or changeable—are they?

11

Psychologists do not agree on a single, specific answer to this question—personality is difficult to define, difficult to measure, and influenced by many factors (Schultz & Schultz, 2005). As such, four dominant scientific perspectives have emerged to explain our personalities: the *psychoanalytic approach,* the *trait approach,* the *social cognitive approach,* and the *humanistic approach*. No single approach can explain all facets of personality in all people, and each perspective has advantages and disadvantages. As we describe each approach, consider your own ideas about personality. Do you think you inherit your personality, or is it formed through experiences? Examining such ideas speaks to whether you think personality is stable and consistent over time or whether it can change. It also will help you connect the material to your experiences and current way of thinking.

Fancy/Alamy

Chapter Outline

11.1 The Psychoanalytic Approach: Sigmund Freud and the Neo-Freudians / 464

11.2 The Trait Approach: Consistency and Stability in Personality / 472

PSYCHOLOGY APPLIES TO YOUR WORLD: Are You a Sensation Seeker? / 474

11.3 The Social Cognitive Approach: The Environment and Patterns of Thought / 482

11.4 The Humanistic Approach: Free Will and Self-Actualization / 485

11.5 Scientifically Measuring Personality / 488

11.6 Integrating Psychology: The Big Picture / 492

Hulton Archive/Stringer/Archive Photos/Getty Images

The psychoanalytic perspective on personality originated with Sigmund Freud. Freud saw personality as the product of driving forces within a person that were often conflicting and sometimes unconscious.

11.1 The Psychoanalytic Approach: Sigmund Freud and the Neo-Freudians

The **psychoanalytic perspective** on personality originated with Sigmund Freud (1856–1939). We introduced his approach to understanding behavior in Chapter 1. Freud practiced medicine, specializing in "nervous diseases." However, soon after beginning private practice, Freud moved away from physical explanations of nervous disorders and focused more on investigating psychological causes of these disorders. His ideas about personality were based on case studies of his patients, his reading of literature, and his own self-analysis. Freud saw personality as the product of driving forces within a person that were often conflicting and sometimes unconscious. As we saw in Chapter 4, Freud believed that dreams were one of the ways these unconscious forces expressed themselves. Freud's theory is unique in that it strongly emphasizes unconscious aspects of personality.

11.1.1 • Freud's Levels of Awareness

Freud (1940/1964) proposed that human personality operates at three different levels of awareness or consciousness and that each level of awareness influences behavior. Freud viewed consciousness as being like an iceberg (• FIGURE 11.1). When we look at behavior, all we usually see is the tip of the iceberg, or the **conscious level**: the thoughts, perceptions, and explanations of behavior of which the person is aware. The major portion of the iceberg, according to Freud, is below the surface. These impulses, memories, and thoughts are unseen but have a huge impact on personality. Because so large a portion of one's personality lies below the surface of consciousness, or awareness, Freud believed, any explanation of personality and behavior must focus on these unconscious forces.

Your conscious level, as previously stated, includes any memories, thoughts, or urges of which you are currently aware. You know you want to download the new Wiz Khalifa song, or you know that it is important to read this chapter and study for the test next week. But the things you could potentially be aware of at any one time are infinite, and you cannot hold more than a couple of thoughts, urges, and memories in consciousness at any one time. So, according to Freud, it is necessary to have a holding place for easily accessible memories, thoughts, or impulses of which you could become aware. This is the role of the **preconscious level**.

The **unconscious level** contains all those thoughts, impulses, memories, and behaviors of which you are unaware. However, although you are unaware of them, they always influence your behavior. Consider the 4-year-old boy who stops his parents from hugging or inserts himself between them to prevent them from kissing. According to Freud, he is not aware that this behavior stems from a need or wish to bond with his mother, yet it is still influencing his behavior.

11.1.2 • Freud's Structure of Personality

To Freud (1940/1964), human personality is an energy system comprised of three major personality structures: the *id*, the *ego*, and the *superego*. At birth, all of the

personality the unique collection of attitudes, emotions, thoughts, habits, impulses, and behaviors that define how a person typically behaves across situations

psychoanalytic perspective [psi-co-an-uh-LIH-tic] a personality approach developed by Sigmund Freud that sees personality as the product of driving forces within a person that are often conflicting and sometimes unconscious

conscious [CON-shus] level the level of consciousness that holds all the thoughts, perceptions, and impulses of which we are aware

preconscious [pre-CON-shus] level the level of consciousness that holds thoughts, perceptions, and impulses of which we could potentially be aware

unconscious [un-CON-shus] level the level of awareness that contains all the thoughts, perceptions, and impulses of which we are unaware energy of the personality is contained within a structure called the **id**. The id is an unconscious energy force that seeks pleasure and gratification. Hungry infants cry for food or because they are wet or tired. The id operates according to the **pleasure principle**; it drives people to feel good and to maximize pleasure and gratification. Freud saw the impulses driving the id as *sexual* and *aggressive* in nature. In this way, he viewed humans as very similar to animals—unconsciously and selfishly motivated by basic sexual and aggressive instincts. Such basic instincts ensure and promote the survival of the individual, and therefore the survival of the species as a whole.

When we grow and begin to interact with our environment, we realize that our demands cannot always be immediately fulfilled. For example, when a baby's cry for food is not met every time, the baby has encountered reality. As a result, part of the energy of the id becomes directed to a second personality structure, the **ego**. The ego acts as a negotiator between the instinctual needs of the id and the demands of membership in human society. Children learn that their id demands can be fulfilled only when they behave appropriately. The ego operates according to the **reality principle**. It realizes that the desires of the id can be met only by successfully dealing with the environment, by finding appropriate or attainable means by which to fulfill id impulses. Suppose a 4-year-old wants something to eat. Does he immediately cry like a baby? Not typically. The 4-year-old with a functioning ego knows that there are more appropriate and acceptable ways of getting food. He will probably ask for something to eat and be willing to wait (at least for a little while) for his caregiver to prepare it for him. We see the ego functioning in the

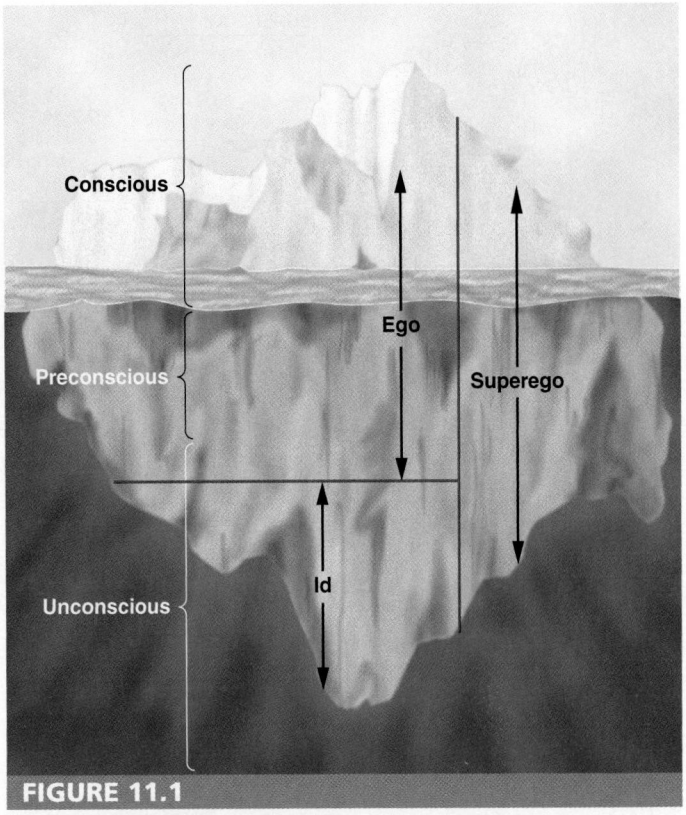

FIGURE 11.1

Iceberg Analogy of Freud's Levels of Awareness

In Freud's "iceberg" analogy of the mind, the id and parts of the ego and superego are submerged below the water in the unconscious. Parts of the ego and superego also operate in the conscious and preconscious.

id the unconscious part of the personality that seeks pleasure and gratification

pleasure principle the basis on which the id operates; the urge to feel good and maximize gratification

ego the conscious part of the personality that attempts to meet the demands of the id in a socially appropriate way

reality principle the basis on which the ego operates; finding socially appropriate means to fulfill id demands

Mel Yates/The Image Bank/Getty Images

According to Freud, it is a child's superego that drives feelings of guilt after wrongdoing.

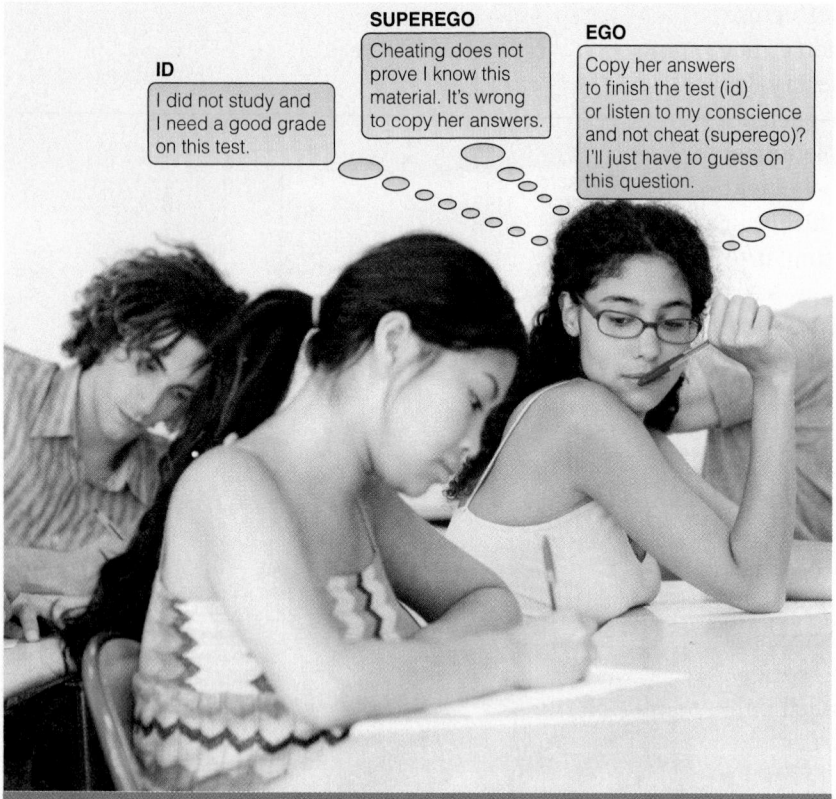

PhotoAlto/SuperStock

FIGURE 11.2

Freud's Personality Structures

According to Freud, adult behavior results from the interaction among the three personality structures of the id, ego, and superego.

child's ability to delay his desire for food. But the ego's job is still to fulfill the instinctual demands of the id—the unseen force beneath the tip of the iceberg (see Figure 11.1).

As the child continues to grow, parents and other important people impart their values and standards of behavior to the child. Parents convey the right and wrong ways to feel, think, and behave. The child incorporates these standards as the energy of the personality further divides into a third personality structure. The **superego** typically emerges during the resolution of the *phallic stage* (discussed shortly) and represents our moral conscience. Our superego judges the rightness or wrongness of our actions. When we have the sense that we did something wrong, our superego is talking. The moral directives of the superego must also be taken into account by the ego. Just like id demands, superego demands must be met realistically by the ego in order to function in society.

The energy that these three personality components use cannot be cut apart. For Freud, personality is a dynamic, or active, process. The id, ego, and superego are not fixed entities but rather parts of our personality that serve different functions. A healthy personality will have developed a strong ego that appropriately releases and controls instinctual energy. However, problems may arise in personality functioning if id energy or superego energy overwhelms the functioning of the ego.

To Freud, all adult behaviors are a reflection of the interplay among these three structures (• FIGURE 11.2). When examining behavior, we see only the functioning of the ego, but this ego is simultaneously being influenced by the unconscious demands of the id and the superego. *Freudian slips* illustrate this interaction. A Freudian slip is the expression of an unconscious impulse from the id before the ego controls the impulse. The ego may then state that it did not mean to say something and corrects the slip to conform to socially approved behavior. For example, one might say to a rival businessperson at a meeting, "Would you like to hit in this chair?" instead of "Would you like to sit in this chair?" and then quickly correct the error. Freud would state that what "slipped out" was meant. It just hadn't yet been socially screened by the ego.

You can see that the demands of the id and the superego are often in direct opposition to one another. This internal conflict sometimes overwhelms the ego, creating *anxiety*. According to Freud, the ego handles this anxiety by using **defense mechanisms** (A. Freud, 1936). Defense mechanisms, discussed more thoroughly in Chapter 12, protect the ego by reducing the anxiety it feels when faced with the conflicting demands of the id and the superego. We all make use of these *emotional coping mechanisms*, as they are now familiarly called. We tend to use those defense mechanisms that have been previously reinforced or that successfully reduce anxiety. For example, if you *rationalized*

superego the part of the personality that represents your moral conscience

defense mechanism a process used to protect the ego by reducing the anxiety it feels when faced with the conflicting demands of the id and the superego behavior as a child, you would probably continue to use this defense mechanism as an adult.

Consider the section case story. From a psychoanalytic perspective, Hongyong's business endeavors would be related to her efforts to cope with her husband's unfaithfulness. Emotionally, Hongyong would feel anger at this betrayal. It is normal to feel anger when a loved one cheats, to be mad at him or her for betraying trust. We cannot direct our anger toward its true source if our culture sees this behavior as not okay. We may also feel it is wrong to be angry with someone we love. So Hongyong's superego would attempt to squelch her anger, but the energy of those feelings would still need an outlet. Hongyong's ego satisfied both the id and the superego by directing her anger into something more productive—a successful restaurant that perhaps would also serve to keep her husband busy and away from other women, using the defense mechanism of *sublimation* (see p. 521).

Differences in personality, then, arise from internal energy conflicts among the id, ego, and superego (called *intrapsychic conflicts*). Freud further believed that personality is shaped by differences in how we resolve psychosexual stages of development.

11.1.3 • Freud's Psychosexual Stages of Development

According to Freud (1940/1964), personality develops through a series of five *psychosexual stages*. These stages represent a complex interaction between natural shifts of pleasure from one part of the body to another and the environmental factors that influence how we handle these sexual desires. From birth through adolescence, children must resolve numerous unconscious conflicts that arise from sexual pleasure associated with stimulation of certain body parts, or what Freud called *erogenous zones*. For example, the infant nursing (from the mother's breast or from a bottle) derives a great deal of sensual pleasure from the feel of the nipple on his or her lips, and the satisfaction in reducing the sensation of hunger that the milk brings. However, the pleasure received from any erogenous zone must be balanced with parental restrictions or permissiveness placed on one's behavior. This creates an internal struggle, or "conflict," that significantly influences the resulting personality. Freud uses the term *psychosexual* to refer to the psychological significance of these sexual drives in the formation of a healthy personality. Because environmental circumstances vary in terms of how we are parented or how we respond to these socialization experiences, the result is individual differences in personality. Let's take a brief look at each of Freud's psychosexual stages.

Ryan McVay/Photodisc/Getty Images

Parents' toilet-training practices influence a toddler's attempt to resolve the anal psychosexual stage, according to Freud.

ORAL STAGE

The **oral stage** lasts from birth until approximately 18 months of age. The mouth, tongue, and lips are the erogenous zones, or focus of pleasure. Babies receive pleasure from sucking, licking, biting, and chewing.

oral stage Freud's first psychosexual stage of development, which occurs during the first year of life, in which the handling of the child's feeding experiences affects personality development

ANAL STAGE

The **anal stage** lasts from approximately 18 months to 3 years. The anus and rectum are the erogenous zones. Freud viewed production of feces as a creative act. The toddler typically feels quite proud of them, either holding their feces in or spreading them around. How the parent then responds to this or how the parent

anal stage Freud's second psychosexual stage, which occurs from approximately 18 months to 3 years of age, in which the parents' regulation of the child's biological urge to expel or retain feces affects personality development

phallic [FAH-lick] stage Freud's third psychosexual stage of development, which occurs between 3 and 6 years of age, in which little boys experience the Oedipus complex and little girls the Electra complex

Oedipus [ED-uh-puss] complex in the male, an unconscious sexual urge for the mother that develops during the phallic psychosexual stage

Electra complex in the female, an unconscious sexual urge for the father that develops during the phallic psychosexual stage

latency [LATE-an-see] stage Freud's fourth psychosexual stage of development, which occurs from around age 6 to puberty, in which the child's sexuality is suppressed due to widening social contacts with school, peers, and family

genital stage Freud's final psychosexual stage of development, which begins at puberty, in which sexual energy is transferred toward peers of the other sex (heterosexual orientation) or same sex (homosexual orientation)

attempts to control this production through toilet-training practices is the key to adequately resolving this stage.

PHALLIC STAGE

During the **phallic stage**, from 3 to 6 years of age, the genitals are the primary erogenous zone, and children receive pleasure from self-stimulation. This stage is particularly important for personality development as it represents the time when the **Oedipus complex** and the **Electra complex** occur. Freud believed that at this age, young children develop unconscious sexual urges for the parent of the other sex. The child wants to bond with the parent of the other sex as the child sees the parents bonding. Using the terms *Oedipus* and *Electra* from two ancient Greek tragedies, Freud believed that at this psychosexual stage, little boys unconsciously fall in love with their mothers and experience hostile feelings toward their fathers much as Oedipus (unknowingly) married his mother and killed his father. Like Electra, little girls unconsciously fall in love with their fathers and feel jealousy toward their mothers. Children at this age may prevent their parents from hugging or be jealous of the parents' spending time alone together. Children then resolve these complexes by identifying with and behaving more like the same-sex parent. A young boy may start to imitate the way his father eats, or a young girl may mimic the way her mother brushes her hair. The child incorporates the values and standards of the same-sex parent, thus ending the rivalry. The child's psychic energy is then redirected to the growth of the superego.

LATENCY STAGE

The **latency stage** occurs from age 6 until puberty. During the latency stage, sexual impulses are pushed into the background. The child's energy focuses on other demands of the environment, most noticeably school and peer relations. Sexuality reappears at puberty as reflected in the final psychosexual stage, the genital stage.

According to Freud, the genital stage of psychosexual development unconsciously motivates teens to interact with potential sexual partners.

Adrian Sherratt / Alamy

GENITAL STAGE

The **genital stage** begins with puberty. The genitals again become the source of pleasure, as the adolescent must revisit the sexual urges that first appeared during the phallic stage. Recall that during the phallic stage, children developed unconscious attractions to the other-sex parent. Recognizing now that the sexual love for the parent cannot be fulfilled, the adolescent seeks resolution of the genital stage by transferring this love to an other-sex mate. Consequently, for Freud, adult heterosexual intimate relations reflect the unconscious desire to choose a mate in the image of one's other-sex parent. If during the phallic stage the child develops unconscious attractions to the same-sex parent, then during the genital stage, homosexual intimate relations arise from transferring love to a same-sex partner.

VARIATIONS IN PERSONALITY AND FIXATIONS

As Freud saw it, all children develop through these predictable stages, which are primarily sexual but are psychologically significant in forming a healthy personality. Successfully resolving these stages entails receiving an optimal amount of gratification at each stage—not too much and not too little. A child who receives too much satisfaction at one stage may be reluctant to move on to the next stage. Too little satisfaction may result in frustration for the child, who may continue to seek gratification instead of moving on. These examples of inadequate resolution of a stage result in what Freud called a *fixation*. Those who fixate at one stage remain stuck, and their personalities remain immature or underdeveloped. Part of the personality remains focused on the concerns of this stage.

For Freud, problems in adult personality reflect these unresolved issues or fixations from childhood. For example, a person whose oral urges were not adequately satisfied in infancy would develop an *oral fixation*. An oral fixation might be expressed in the adult behaviors of overeating, nail biting, constantly chewing on pens or pencils, or boasting. More serious behaviors reflecting oral fixations include smoking, alcoholism, and binge eating. Fixation at the anal stage may express itself in the adult personality as *anal-retentiveness* or *anal-expulsiveness*. Being overly neat, stingy, or orderly (anal-retentive) or being excessively sloppy, generous, or carefree (anal-expulsive) both result from inadequate resolution of the anal stage. These are just two examples of how fixations might manifest themselves in an adult personality.

11.1.4 • Neo-Freudian Theories Explaining Variations in Personality: Carl Jung, Alfred Adler, and Karen Horney

Freud's work created much controversy among professionals in the developing field of psychology. Many physicians and psychologists were initially intrigued by Freud's ideas but had their differences with aspects of his theory and eventually separated from Freud. These *neo-Freudians* agreed with Freud that unconscious conflicts were important to understanding personality, but they placed less emphasis on the role of the instinctual impulses of sex and aggression in motivating behavior. We have already introduced one neo-Freudian, Erik Erikson, whose theory of *psychosocial development* we discussed in Chapter 9. His eight stages described the influence of the environment on the developing ego over the life span. Three other examples of neo-Freudian theories are presented here, in the ideas of Carl Jung, Alfred Adler, and Karen Horney.

Hulton Archive/Stringer/Archive Photos/Getty Images

Carl Jung divided the unconscious into the personal unconscious (forgotten memories and repressed experiences) and the collective unconscious (the collected images and ideas from the earliest development of the human psyche).

CARL JUNG AND THE COLLECTIVE UNCONSCIOUS

Carl Jung (1875–1961) was a student of Freud's who came to reject his ideas about personality, particularly the sexual aspects of his theory. Like Freud, Jung maintained that personality was a function of the interplay between conscious and unconscious processes. However, Jung (1917/1967) divided the

Indeed/Getty Images

Children's small stature and dependence on parents create inferiority feelings that motivate them toward achievement, according to Adler.

unconscious into the *personal unconscious* and the *collective unconscious*. The **personal unconscious**, much like Freud's unconscious, consisted of forgotten memories and repressed experiences. The **collective unconscious** is universal to all people of all time periods and cultures. The collective unconscious represents the collected images and ideas from the earliest development of the human psyche.

In particular, the collective unconscious includes **archetypes**, mental representations or symbols of themes and predispositions to respond to the world in a certain way. According to Jung, two of the major archetypes of the personality are the *anima* and the *animus*, the female and male aspects of each person. Among the other archetypes Jung identified are the *persona* and the *shadow*. The persona is the appearance we present to the world, the role or character we assume when relating to others, such as the martyr, the rebel, or the teacher. The shadow includes those negative tendencies or qualities of the self that a person tries to deny or hide from the world. Jung's emphasis on the collective unconscious, and his belief that spiritual and religious drives are just as important as sexual ones, continues to draw attention. He also stressed the importance of enduring personality traits such as *introversion* and *extraversion* (discussed shortly).

ALFRED ADLER AND THE INFERIORITY COMPLEX

Alfred Adler (1870–1937) also began as a student of Freud's but disagreed with his emphasis on aggressive and sexual urges as the major force in personality development. Adler (1928) believed that it is the child's desire to overcome feelings of helplessness and to master the environment that directs behavior. In the world of adults, children are small and helpless and feel inadequate and weak. Children have to be bathed by a parent and hold a parent's hand when crossing the street. These feelings of inferiority motivate the child—and later the adult—toward achievement. For Adler, personality develops from our attempts to compensate for inferiority feelings. Moderate feelings of inferiority will result in constructive achievement and creative growth, but deep feelings of inferiority will impede positive growth and development and result in an *inferiority complex*.

Adler also emphasized the importance of birth order as a factor in personality development. He argued that firstborns, middle-borns, and youngest children grow up in differing family environments and are not necessarily treated the same by parents. These different experiences are likely to affect personality development. Adler's ideas have resulted in hundreds of studies on the effects of birth order. These studies have generally not found any reliable relationships between birth order and personality (Abdel-Khalek & Lester, 2005; Harris, 2000). Yet people generally believe that birth order affects personality, which may then actually encourage those in various birth ranks to differ in their personalities (Herrera et al., 2003).

KAREN HORNEY, BASIC ANXIETY, AND CULTURE

Although Karen Horney (1885–1952) agreed with Freud on the significance of early childhood in personality development, she rejected his belief that this development arose from instinctual conflicts. Instead, Horney (1937, 1939) suggested that family environments and disturbances in early relationships lead to **basic anxiety**, or a feeling of helplessness in children. Children cope with this basic anxiety by pursuing love, power, prestige, or detachment. Horney further argued, in contrast

personal unconscious according to Jung, the part of the unconscious that consists of forgotten memories and repressed experiences from one's past

collective unconscious according to Jung, the part of the unconscious that contains images and material universal to people of all time periods and cultures

archetypes [ARE-kuh-types] according to Jung, mental representations or symbols of themes and predispositions to respond to the world in a certain way that are contained in the collective unconscious

basic anxiety according to Horney, the feeling of helplessness that develops in children from early relationships to Freud, that culture plays a larger role in personality development than biology and instinct. For Horney, personality is not merely the result of psychosexual conflicts, as Freud would argue, but rather is influenced by all the events and people in the culture that make a child feel unsafe and unloved, giving rise to basic anxiety.

Bettmann/Corbis

Karen Horney argued that culture plays a larger role in personality development than does biology and suggested that family environments and disturbances in early relationships lead to basic anxiety in children. Children cope with this basic anxiety by pursuing love, power, prestige, or detachment.

11.1.5 • Contributions and Criticisms of the Psychoanalytic Approach

Freud's contributions to psychology have been immense (Erwin, 2002). He is regarded as one of the most influential thinkers of the 20th century (Gedo, 2002). His presence is still felt among the general public through literature, arts, and the movies. His theory on dreams stimulated much research on the nature of sleep. His notion of defense mechanisms was extensively elaborated on by his daughter, Anna Freud, and his focus on coping and well-being sparked interest and research in health psychology. His ideas are evident in tests designed to measure personality (discussed later in this chapter) and in therapy approaches to help people with mental health problems (Chapter 14). Freud's basic notion of the unconscious influencing our behavior also has merit. Research in the area of cognitive neuroscience does support *unconscious cognition*—thought processes that occur outside conscious awareness that potentially influence judgments and behavior (Atas et al., 2014; Bargh & Morsella, 2008; Gedo, 2002; Greenwald & Draine, 1997; Kihlstrom, 1993; Westen, 1999).

Furthermore, Freud was one of the first to see the importance of early development in later adult behavior (Gedo, 2002). In the early 1900s, children were seen as mini-adults. People did not believe as strongly as we do now that how infants and children are treated influences their adult behavior. Although we know that infancy and childhood experiences do not *determine* adult behavior, as Freud asserted, his emphasis on the importance of these early years was a critical departure from accepted beliefs at that time. Through his psychosexual stages, Freud placed much emphasis on explaining the developmental nature of personality, probably more so than any other theorist. His views on sexuality and the impact of culture on sexuality continue to influence research (Hartmann, 2009; Person, 2005).

Freud's perspective has been criticized on several counts, however. First, many believe that Freud placed too much emphasis on sexual and aggressive instincts. His perspective shines very little light on environmental and social conditions that may affect personality functioning. We have just noted how many neo-Freudians diverged from Freud on this point, creating alternate views of the ego and personality that take our interactions with others into account (Horgan, 1996). His ideas and themes have also been attacked for their focus on male development and their perpetuation of the idea of male superiority (Person, 1990).

Much more problematic are Freud's methods of data collection and the fact that his theories cannot be readily tested experimentally (Crews, 1996). His theories are based almost entirely on case study research and his own self-analysis. His observations may not have been objective, and his case studies involved patients who were diagnosed with nervous disorders. What his patients told him may not have been accurate, and their statements were not corroborated by other sources. These issues make it difficult to generalize Freud's observations. Scientifically testing Freud's theoretical concepts is also quite challenging. Measuring the unconscious is difficult if participants are unaware of these impulses. It is equally difficult to measure psychosexual stages of development. For this reason, we cannot prove that Freud's theory is true, but we also cannot disprove it. Thus, it remains a possible explanation of personality functioning, though not as popular as it was in the past. Freud's ideas have not been supported by data from other cultures, possibly because his theories reflect the Western cultural value of individualism. They may not apply in collectivist cultures that emphasize the importance of the group (Matsumoto, 1994).

Quiz Yourself 11.1

1. The psychoanalytic perspective emphasizes the influence of _____ on personality.
   a. unconscious desires
   b. traits
   c. self-actualization
   d. environmental factors
2. Your memories of your high school graduation or first date reside at the _____ level of consciousness.
   a. conscious
   b. preconscious
   c. unconscious
   d. subconscious
3. Maria often feels guilty when she engages in even the slightest offensive behavior. Freud would say that Maria has a strong _____.
   a. id
   b. ego
   c. superego
   d. collective unconscious
4. Neo-Freudian Alfred Adler emphasized _____ as motivators of personality development.
   a. fears
   b. basic anxiety
   c. archetypes
   d. feelings of inferiority
5. One of the major criticisms of Freud's theory concerns its _____.
   a. overemphasis on environmental and cognitive factors in explaining behavior
   b. difficulty in being experimentally tested and validated
   c. emphasis on the conscious
   d. assumption that all people are good

Answers 1. a; 2. b; 3. c; 4. d; 5. b

11.2 The Trait Approach: Consistency and Stability in Personality

trait approach a personality perspective that attempts to describe personality by emphasizing internal, biological aspects of personality called traits

trait tendency to behave in a certain way across most situations

A second major perspective on personality is called the **trait approach**. The trait approach, like the psychoanalytic approach, focuses on internal aspects of personality. Whereas the psychoanalytic approach attempts to explain personality by focusing on unconscious forces, the trait perspective describes personality and emphasizes its biological aspects. Trait theory assumes that we all have internal **traits**, or tendencies to behave in a certain way across most situations. These traits remain relatively stable as we age and explain why individuals generally behave the same way across a variety of situations. Yet because people differ in the degree to which they possess various traits, we develop unique personalities. We will describe four major approaches to understanding these personality traits in the theories of Gordon Allport, Raymond Cattell, Hans Eysenck, and in the *five factor theory.*

11.2.1 • Gordon Allport's Trait Theory

Psychologist Gordon Allport (1897–1967) believed that three types of traits help us understand a person's uniqueness: *central traits, secondary traits,* and *cardinal traits* (Allport, 1961). **Central traits** are those tendencies we have across most situations; they are the core qualities your friends would state if they were asked to describe you. For example, if you are friendly in most situations, then friendly would be considered a central trait. We all have central traits, but the specific qualities that are considered a central trait may differ from person to person. Hongyong was generally driven and industrious, two examples of her central traits.

Secondary traits describe how we behave in certain situations; they are tendencies that are less consistent and more situation-specific. Many of us behave aggressively in certain situations, such as when we are frustrated or when we see others behave aggressively. Again, we all have secondary traits, but whether a specific quality is considered a secondary trait may differ from person to person.

Cardinal traits describe how we behave across all situations. Allport considered these a very basic and permanent element of our personalities—but he had difficulty finding cardinal traits in all people that he studied. Consequently, the validity of cardinal traits became suspect. Recall from Chapter 6 on learning and Chapter 10 on social psychology the powerful effect the environment can have on our behavior. This effect often makes us behave differently across situations.

Allport's goal in describing traits was to understand the behavior of a specific individual. Other research focused on identifying and understanding core or universal traits that direct the behavior of people in general, relying heavily on the use of statistics. This set the stage for Raymond Cattell's statistical analysis of personality traits.

central traits according to Allport, the tendencies we have to behave in a certain way across most situations

secondary traits according to Allport, the tendencies we have that are less consistent and describe how we behave in certain situations

cardinal traits according to Allport, those dominant elements of our personalities that drive all of our behaviors

surface traits basic traits that describe people's personalities, according to Cattell

source traits universal tendencies that underlie and are at the core of surface traits, according to Cattell

introversion [in-tro-VER-shun] personality traits that involve energy directed inward, such as being calm or peaceful

extraversion [ex-tra-VER-shun] personality traits that involve energy directed outward, such as being easygoing, lively, or excitable

11.2.2 • Raymond Cattell's Factor Analytic Trait Theory

Raymond Cattell (1905–1998) attempted to document relationships among traits using a sophisticated statistical technique called *factor analysis* (Cattell, 1943). In contemporary factor analysis, the possible traits that could be used to describe people are entered into a computer program; then the program groups related traits into factors. In this way, Cattell reduced the number of personality traits that could be used to describe all people.

Cattell's research (1965) originally yielded 36 **surface traits** that could describe personality. He then hypothesized that there must be common underlying factors that account for the 36 surface traits. Cattell referred to these qualities or dimensions as **source traits**. Source traits are basic, broad, and relatively universal tendencies at the core of our personalities. We may differ in the amount or quality of these traits, but they are present in everyone's personality to some degree. Through subsequent analysis and research, Cattell identified 16 source traits (● TABLE 11.2, p. 476). However, Cattell's 16 source traits did not easily lend themselves to research. Research led by British psychologist Hans Eysenck would further reduce the number.

© Courtesy of Cattell Family

Using factor analysis, Raymond Cattell reduced the number of core personality traits to 16 basic traits, referred to as source traits.

11.2.3 • Hans Eysenck Narrows the Traits: The PEN Model

Building on Cattell's factor analytic studies, Eysenck and Rachman (1965) found two factors that they believed measured people's key characteristics: *introversion/extraversion* and *emotional stability/neuroticism*. Introversion and extraversion define where a person's energy is directed. **Introversion** means that the person's energy is directed inward. This tendency could include being rigid, reliable, sober, or controlled. **Extraversion** means that the person's energy is directed outward. This tendency could include being easygoing, lively, or excitable.

Emotional stability and neuroticism refer to control over one's emotions. Being even-tempered and calm are traits that include more control over emotions and

Psychology Applies to Your World:

Are You a Sensation Seeker?

One trait of particular interest to psychologists is that of sensation seeking. Some people seem to crave arousal, seeking out higher levels of arousal than the rest of us. In fact, sometimes they seek out levels of arousal that the rest of us would find aversive or unpleasant. These people are what psychologists call **sensation seekers**; they habitually tend to seek out high levels of physiological arousal by engaging in intensely stimulating experiences (Zuckerman, 1978, 1994). Some sensation seekers pursue daring activities such as mountain climbing, skydiving, bungee jumping, and fast driving, whereas others may be stimulated by engaging in problem behaviors such as drug use, aggression, or delinquency (Lynne-Landsman et al., 2011).

One theory that seeks to explain the causes of sensation seeking looks at biological differences in the brains of sensation seekers. Psychologist Marvin Zuckerman found that sensation seekers tend to have low levels of a substance called *monoamine oxidase*, or MAO (Zuckerman & Kuhlman, 2000). MAO is an enzyme that breaks down neurotransmitters like serotonin, dopamine, and norepinephrine (Chapter 2). One of these neurotransmitters, dopamine, seems to be responsible for motivating us to obtain rewards. The low level of MAO in the brains of sensation seekers may mean that they experience more dopamine activity than other people. Without MAO to break it down, the dopamine would remain in the synapse longer, continuing to stimulate the neuron. This increased dopamine action may be related to sensation seekers' motivation to experience reward from intense arousal.

Research examining brain region responses to high arousal stimuli between individuals high and low in sensation seeking supports this view. Individuals high in sensation seeking tend to show more activation in brain regions associated with reward and show less inhibition or the ability to regulate this activation compared to those low in sensation seeking (Joseph et al., 2009). What causes these brain differences? Current research suggests that multiple dopamine genes that we inherit may be at the heart of sensation-seeking behavior (Derringer et al., 2010).

According to psychologist Marvin Zuckerman, some people are high in the trait of sensation seeking. They engage in highly energizing and stimulating activities such as skydiving and extreme sports.

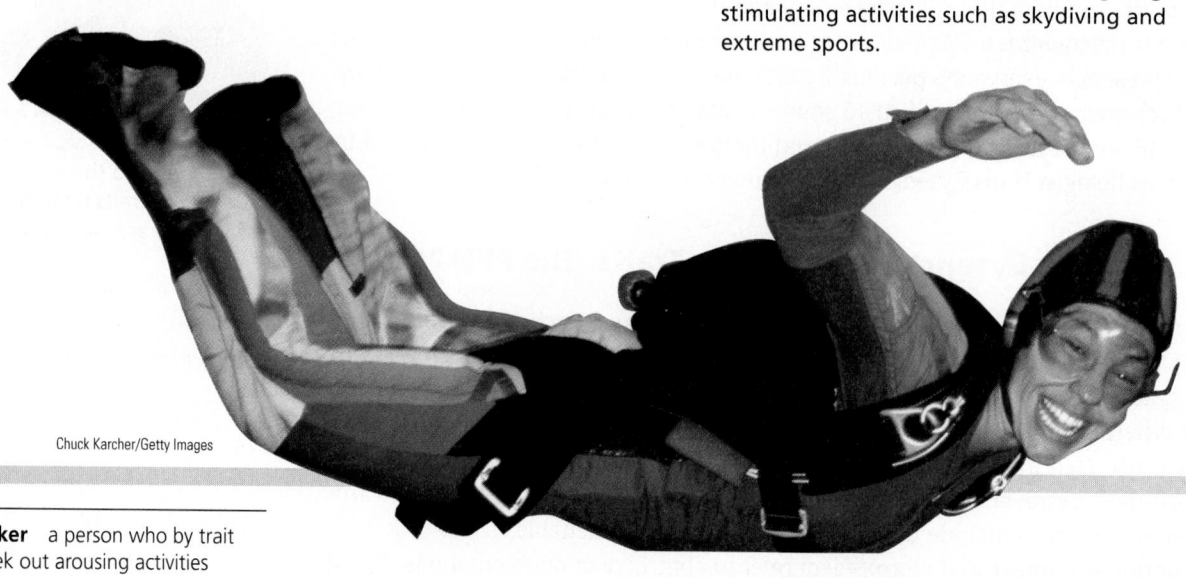

Chuck Karcher/Getty Images

sensation seeker a person who by trait tends to seek out arousing activities

TABLE 11.1

Brief Sensation-Seeking Questionnaire

Answer "true" or "false" to each item listed below by circling *T* or *F*. A "true" means that the item expresses your preference most of the time. A "false" means that you do not agree that the item is generally true for you. After completing the test, score your responses according to the instructions that follow the test items.

T F 1. I would really enjoy skydiving.

T F 2. I can imagine myself driving a sports car in a race and loving it.

T F 3. My life is very secure and comfortable—the way I like it.

T F 4. I usually like emotionally expressive or artistic people, even if they are sort of wild.

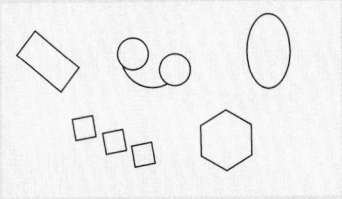

A

T F 5. I like the idea of seeing many of the same warm, supportive faces in everyday life.

T F 6. I like doing adventurous things and would have enjoyed being a pioneer in the early days of this country.

T F 7. A good photograph should express peacefulness creatively.

T F 8. The most important thing in living is fully experiencing all emotions.

T F 9. I like creature comforts when I go on a trip or vacation.

T F 10. Doing the same things each day really gets to me.

B

T F 11. I love snuggling in front of a fire on a wintry day.

T F 12. I would like to try several types of drugs as long as they didn't harm me permanently.

T F 13. Drinking and being rowdy really appeals to me on weekends.

T F 14. Rational people try to avoid dangerous situations.

T F 15. I prefer figure A to figure B.

Give yourself 1 point for answering "true" to the following items: 1, 2, 4, 6, 8, 10, 12, and 13. Also give yourself 1 point for answering "false" to the following items: 3, 5, 7, 9, 11, 14, and 15. Add up your points, and compare your total to the following norms: 11–15, high sensation seeker; 6–10, moderate sensation seeker; 1–5, low sensation seeker. Bear in mind that this is a shortened version of the Sensation Seeking Scale and that it provides only a rough approximation of your status on this personality trait.

Source: A. F. Grasha & D. S. Kirschenbaum (1986). *Adjustment and competence: Concepts and applications.* St. Paul, MN: West Publishing. Reprinted by permission of Anthony F. Grasha.

Are you a sensation seeker? To get a feel for your level of sensation seeking, take the questionnaire in ● TABLE 11.1. This questionnaire is only a brief version of the full Zuckerman Sensation Seeking Scale (Zuckerman, 1994). Therefore, your true level of sensation seeking may differ from that indicated by your test results. The questionnaire will give you some insight into your sensation-seeking tendencies, but please recognize that this test gives you only a rough idea of where you fall on this dimension.

TABLE 11.2

Cattell's 16 Personality Factors

FACTOR	DESCRIPTION (Extremes of Each Factor From Low to High Levels)
Warmth	Reserved - Warm
Reasoning	Less intelligent - More intelligent
Emotional stability	Easily upset - Emotionally stable
Dominance	Submissive - Dominant
Liveliness	Serious - Expressive
Rule consciousness	Nonconforming - Conforming
Social boldness	Shy - Venturesome
Sensitivity	Tough-minded - Sensitive
Vigilance	Trusting - Suspicious
Abstractedness	Practical - Imaginative
Privateness	Open - Shrewd
Apprehension	Unworried - Worried
Openness to change	Conservative - Experimenting
Self-reliance	Dependent - Self-sufficient
Perfectionism	Undisciplined - Precise
Tension	Relaxed - Tense

emotional stability having control over one's emotions

neuroticism [nur-RAH-tuh-siz-um] the degree to which one is emotionally unstable

psychoticism [psi-COT-uh-siz-um] the degree to which one is hostile, nonconforming, impulsive, and aggressive

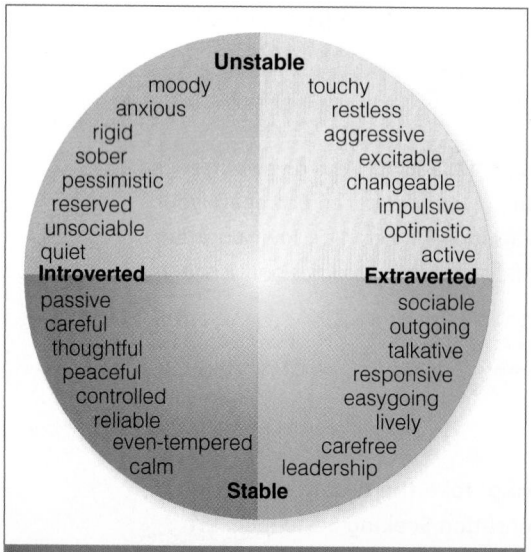

FIGURE 11.3

Eysenck's Trait Theory

British psychologist Hans Eysenck arrived at two universal traits using factor analysis. The stable–unstable axis defines one's emotionality; the introverted–extraverted axis defines the degree to which a person's energy is directed inward or outward. The traits in each quadrant indicate where they are placed with respect to these two factors.

represent **emotional stability**, whereas moody and touchy describe traits that represent **neuroticism**. We all are somewhere on the introversion/extraversion scale and somewhere on the emotional stability/neuroticism continuum; however, we all differ in the degree to which we express the two factors (• FIGURE 11.3).

In the 1970s, Hans Eysenck (1916–1997), in collaboration with his wife, Sybil Eysenck, added a third dimension called *psychoticism* to the model (Eysenck & Eysenck, 1969, 1976). **Psychoticism** includes tendencies toward recklessness, disregard for common sense and cultural norms, inconsideration, hostility, anger, and impulsivity. Eysenck originally characterized impulsivity as a dimension of extraversion. However, once the dimension of psychoticism was added, he moved this trait from extraversion to psychoticism. Eysenck's three-factor model of personality is referred to as the PEN (psychoticism, extraversion, neuroticism) model (• TABLE 11.3).

THE NEUROBIOLOGY OF EXTRAVERSION AND INTROVERSION

Eysenck (1967, 1982, 1991) proposed that introverts inherit the tendency toward higher levels of physical arousal than extraverts. Introverts are more likely to avoid social situations because such experiences will elevate their arousal and lead to overstimulation and discomfort. Hence, they are more likely than extraverts to turn inward and become introverted. Extraverts, by contrast, seek out stimulating environments to increase

TABLE 11.3

Eysenck's PEN Model

PSYCHOTICISM	EXTRAVERSION	NEUROTICISM
Aggressive	Sociable	Anxious
Assertive	Optimistic	Depressed
Impulsive	Expressive	Guilt feelings
Manipulative	Active	Moody
Tough-minded	Dominant	Obsessive
Hostile	Lack of reflection	Tense

their naturally lower arousal levels. Research has generally supported Eysenck's *arousal theory;* several studies confirm that introverts tend to show higher levels of physical arousal than extraverts (Beauducel, Brocke, & Leue, 2006; Bullock & Gilliland, 1993; Kumari et al., 2004; LeBlanc, Ducharme, & Thompson, 2004). Another prominent explanation of introversion and extraversion is the *reward-processing theory.* It suggests that extraverts' brains are more sensitive to both rewards and dopamine functioning, which leads them to gravitate to more stimulating social activities (Cohen et al., 2005; Depue & Collins, 1999; Depue & Fu, 2013; Smillie, 2013). Future research on the neuroscience of personality traits will further expand our knowledge in this area.

11.2.4 • The Five Factor Trait Theory

Currently, the most widely accepted trait theory derived from factor analysis is Paul Costa and Robert McCrae's (1992) **five factor theory**. This theory proposes five core dimensions that can be measured along a continuum in all people.

five factor theory Costa and McCrae's trait theory that proposes five core dimensions to personality: openness, conscientiousness, extraversion, agreeableness, and neuroticism

- *Openness*: the degree to which one is thoughtful and rational in considering new ideas. People who score high in openness tend to be imaginative, creative, and curious and to prefer variety; those who score low in openness prefer routine and are more narrow-minded in their ideas and experiences.
- *Conscientiousness*: the degree to which one is aware of and attentive to other people, to the details of a task, or to both. People who are high in conscientiousness tend to be hardworking, ambitious, reliable, and self-controlled, whereas individuals low on this dimension are more often described as unreliable, lazy, and spontaneous.
- *Extraversion*: the degree to which one's energy is directed inward or outward. People high in extraversion are talkative and sociable and prefer to be around others. At the other end of the continuum are people low in extraversion (introverts), who are quiet, reserved, and more comfortable on their own.
- *Agreeableness*: the degree to which one gets along well with others. Being easygoing and trusting are traits characteristic of one high in agreeableness. At the other end of the spectrum are people who are unfriendly, antagonistic, and suspicious (low agreeableness).
- *Neuroticism*: the degree to which one is emotionally stable or unstable. People high in neuroticism are temperamental, worrisome, and pessimistic. People who score low on this factor tend to be more even-tempered and calm.

You Review **Summary of Trait Theories**

Theorist/Theory	Method of Collection	Results
Allport	Subjectively collected traits	Three trait levels: central, secondary, and cardinal
Cattell	Factor analysis	36 surface traits; 16 source traits
Eysenck's PEN model	Factor analysis	Three basic traits labeled PEN: psychoticism, extraversion, and neuroticism
Costa & McCrae's five factor theory	Factor analysis	Five basic traits that form the acronym OCEAN: openness, conscientiousness, extraversion, agreeableness, and neuroticism

These five dimensions appear in all cultures, suggesting that these five factors may represent universal personality components (Katigbak et al., 2002; McCrae & Costa, 1998; Yamagata et al., 2006). An easy way to remember the five factors is with the acronym OCEAN. Each letter in OCEAN stands for one of the five factors: O = openness, C = conscientiousness; E = extraversion; A = agreeableness; and N = neuroticism.

You Review: Summary of Trait Theories compares the four trait theories. Notice that the main difference in these theories is the number of source traits that are proposed. Allport's theory proposes 3 types, Eysenck's theory proposes 3, Cattell's theory proposes 16, and Costa and McCrae's model proposes 5.

11.2.5 • Genetic Contributions to Personality

The trait perspective assumes that people have internal dispositions to behave consistently across situations. Thus, some researchers have speculated that we inherit some aspects of our personalities. Recall that newborn infants do show differences in behavior that we refer to as *temperament* (see Chapter 9), that these temperamental differences appear strongly related to genes (Braungart et al., 1992; Plomin et al., 2008), and that they are quite stable over time (Jaffari-Bimmel et al., 2006; Majdandzic & van den Boom, 2007; McCrae et al., 2000; Rothbart, Ahadi, & Evans, 2000). As we saw in the section case study, Hongyong had a difficult temperament that was relatively stable at least through childhood. It seems possible that other characteristics or personality dispositions are also inherited.

behavioral genetics field of study that examines the influence of genetics and hereditary factors on personality traits

Researchers in the field of **behavioral genetics** study the degree to which personality traits are influenced by genetics and hereditary factors. One way to study genetic contributions—the nature side of personality—is to look at children who are adopted. On the one hand, because adopted children have no genes in common with their adoptive family members, any similarities in personality characteristics between these children and their adoptive parents are likely due to learning or modeling. On the other hand, because these children have genes in common with their biological parents but do not share a family environment, any similarities to them are likely due to genetics. These research studies have found more personality similarities between adoptive children and their biological parents (Carey & DiLalla, 1994). These findings suggest a strong genetic component to personality.

Another method for investigating the contribution of genes—or nature—is to study identical twins (W. Johnson et al., 2009). Research on identical twins provides even more compelling evidence that at least *some* personality tendencies may be inherited (Bouchard, 2004; Weiss, Bates, & Luciano, 2008). Identical twins reared in separate environments appeared to show remarkable similarities in behavior years later when they were reunited (Bouchard et al., 1990; Holden, 1980; Lykken et al., 1992). One of the more famous separated pairs is James Springer and James Lewis, known as the "Jim twins." Both drove Chevrolets and chain-smoked Salem cigarettes. They both worked as sheriff's deputies and listed stock car racing, carpentry, and mechanical drawing as interests and hobbies (Holden, 1980). Studies have indeed found more similarities between the personalities of identical twins than of nonidentical (fraternal) twins (Buss, 1995; Laceulle et al., 2013; Plomin et al., 2008; Saudino et al., 1995). Such evidence indicates a significant genetic role in the personalities we exhibit.

Ashley Cooper/Alamy

Studies have found more similarities between identical twins' personalities than between nonidentical twins' personalities, indicating a significant genetic role in the personalities that we exhibit.

Other research on the heritability of personality traits in a domain called *personality neuroscience* has focused on genes that direct neurotransmitter functioning, specifically serotonin and dopamine. For example, several studies have found an association between the *serotonin transporter gene* and anxiety-related personality traits (Hayden et al., 2007; Sen, Burmeister, & Ghosh, 2004; Sen, Villafuerte et al., 2004). This gene influences the levels of serotonin in the brain and may account for differences in anxiety levels from person to person. Other studies have investigated the relationship between a *dopamine receptor gene* and the personality trait of novelty seeking (Jonsson et al., 2003; Munafo et al., 2008; Schinka, Letsch, & Crawford, 2002). Such results suggest a complex interaction between biology, environment, and personality. Human behavior is the product of many genes working simultaneously, together with multiple environmental and developmental events (Ebstein et al., 2002; Hamer, 2002). Unraveling these connections and influences will keep scientists very busy in the years ahead.

11.2.6 • Stability and Change in Personality

The trait approach not only assumes that traits are inherited; it also assumes that these internal tendencies are consistent and stable over time. What does the research indicate? Research does support the stability of *some* personality traits over the course of adulthood. However, age, culture, and gender are important when considering stability and change in personality.

DIVERSITY: THE INFLUENCE OF AGE, CULTURE, AND GENDER ON PERSONALITY

After the age of 30, changes in personality traits are smaller than in childhood and young adulthood (Costa & McCrae, 1997; McCrae, 2009; Roberts, Walton, & Viechtbauer, 2006; Spengler, Gottschling, & Spinath, 2012; Terracciano, Costa, & McCrae, 2006). As a part of the developmental process, children, adolescents, and young adults experiment with new identities and ways of behaving. They may adopt new values and attitudes or revise existing ones (McAdams & Olson, 2010). Changes in personality, therefore, are more frequent during these periods.

Some studies suggest that at least for some traits, there is a consistency from childhood to adulthood (Edmonds et al., 2013; Roberts, Caspi, & Moffitt, 2001). For example, McCrae and colleagues (2002) found stability in the traits of extraversion, agreeableness, and conscientiousness from age 12 to age 18. Hampson and Goldberg (2006) found stability for the traits of extraversion and conscientiousness from elementary school to midlife. Shiner, Masten, and Roberts (2003) found modest continuity in academic conscientiousness and agreeableness from childhood to adulthood. Another study (Robins et al., 2001) found consistency in the five factor personality traits when following the same people from the beginning to the end of their college years.

However, research on U.S. and cross-cultural samples also suggests substantial *changes* in personality even during the course of adulthood. People generally become more conscientious, agreeable, and emotionally stable, slightly less open to experience, and less extraverted across adulthood (Bleidorn et al., 2013; Carducci, 2009; Jackson et al., 2012; Laceulle et al., 2013; Ludtke, Trautwein, & Husemann, 2009; Roberts & Mroczek, 2008; Roberts, Walton, & Viechtbauer, 2006; Scollon & Diener, 2006). Many people also become more *androgynous,* exhibiting both male and female traits, as they age (Fiske, 1980). Even McCrae and colleagues' (1999, 2000) cross-cultural research did not find consistency across all of the five factor traits. For example, despite being headstrong as a child, Hongyong learned to temper her willfulness and became more accommodating in her marriage and her businesses as she got older.

Age differences in personality have also been investigated in other cultures, and a similar picture has emerged. Data from 62 nations over 5 continents (America, Australia, Africa, Asia, and Europe) are consistent with findings on the five factor model of personality in U.S. samples (Bleidorn et al., 2013; McCrae et al., 1999, 2000, 2009). Older men and women in these cultures also tended to be lower in extraversion and openness to experience and higher in agreeableness and conscientiousness. Such findings appear to support the universality of *some* personality traits. These societies differ dramatically in language, culture, and historical experiences from one another and from the experiences of most people in the United States. Yet the cultural differences seemed to have little impact on age differences in personality traits.

Gender differences in personality traits also show evidence of both stability and change. Across cultures and for both college-age and older adult samples, women report themselves to be higher in neuroticism, extraversion, agreeableness, and openness to feelings, whereas men report themselves higher in assertiveness and openness to ideas (Costa, Terracciano, & McCrae, 2001; McCrae, 2009; Schmitt et al., 2008; Weisberg, DeYoung, & Hirsh, 2011). Yet these personality traits varied more *within* each gender than they did between genders. Gender differences in neuroticism and extraversion also become smaller over time as men and women age (Carducci, 2009; Srivastava et al., 2003). Moreover, the research demonstrates that not all people change at the same rate over their lives. Some people's traits may be stable, whereas other people's traits may change (Mroczek & Spiro, 2003; Roberts & Mroczek, 2008; Small et al., 2003). Why personality change occurs for some people and not others is a question that continues to be researched.

THE INFLUENCE OF THE ENVIRONMENT ON TRAITS

Situational factors also influence the stability and consistency of traits. Many of us display the same trait (behave the same way) when faced with similar circumstances—that is, when the environmental cues are the same. However, when the situation is different, our behavior may change. This relationship among traits, situations, and behavior is referred to as the **person–situation interaction** (Mischel & Shoda, 1995). For example, the students of one of the authors of this textbook are always surprised to hear that she has a fear of public speaking. They see her speak every week in class with little anxiety. They know that she has been teaching

person–situation interaction the influence of the situation on the stability of traits; when in the same situation, we display similar behavior, but when the situation is different, behavior may change for more than 25 years. From such knowledge, they predict that she would not fear public speaking in other situations, such as at a research conference or at a community function. But in these different situations, she is extremely anxious, panicked, and nauseated at the thought of speaking in front of a group. The cues of the two different situations evoke different behaviors and reactions. Thus, our traits do not always predict how we will behave across different situations. Discovering how loved ones will behave in specific situations is just as important as knowing their traits (Friesen & Kammrath, 2011).

How do psychologists reconcile these seemingly contradictory findings? Psychologists recognize that personality is both stable *and* changeable. Some traits are probably more consistent across the life span and from culture to culture, whereas others are more easily influenced by one's society, gender, environment, and daily situations (Fleeson, 2004). Such flexibility enables individuals to face developmental changes and challenges throughout their lives.

11.2.7 • Contributions and Criticisms of the Trait Approach

The trait perspective has contributed to our understanding of personality by providing psychologists with a common vocabulary to describe people's personalities. Because this common language facilitates communication within the field, the trait approach has been particularly useful in the area of personality assessment, a topic we will turn to shortly. Knowing a person's tendencies or traits also helps psychologists predict future behavior. These predictions, however, will be influenced by the nature of the situation (J. A. Johnson, 1997). The assumptions of the trait perspective—that traits are internal and stable—have also fueled research investigating the biological aspects of personality and the consistency and stability of personality traits across the life span.

However, the objective of personality research is to uncover how we differ from one another. Although the trait perspective does a good job of *describing* people's personalities, it is criticized for not *explaining* why we behave in a particular way (Digman, 1997; McCabe & Fleeson, 2012). Critics further argue that it portrays personality too simplistically and fails to reflect its complexity and depth (Block, 1995; Epstein, 1994; Gladwell, 2004). Can everyone really be reduced to 3, 5, or 16 dimensions? Can we cleanly divide personality into biological and environmental components without taking into account the complex interactions among them? We have also seen the trait perspective's shortcomings in predicting people's behavior across different situations (Wiggins, 1997). This should not be surprising, though, given the powerful influence of situational forces on behavior.

Sharie Kennedy/LWA/Comet/Corbis

Sharie Kennedy/LWA/Comet/Corbis

Often our personality interacts with our environment. A behavior we display in one context (texting on our cell phone when the teacher is not looking) may not be the same behavior we exhibit at other times (being studious and engaged when the teacher is attentive).

Quiz Yourself

11.2

1. The trait perspective attempts to describe _____.
   a. person–situation interactions
   b. a person's key characteristics
   c. cultural influences on personality
   d. factor analysis
2. Terrence is outgoing in most situations. Allport would describe this tendency in Terrence as a _____.
   a. source trait
   b. secondary trait
   c. cardinal trait
   d. central trait
3. Which of the following is *not* considered one of the five factor traits of personality?
   a. Achievement
   b. Extraversion
   c. Conscientiousness
   d. Agreeableness
4. Research on the stability of personality traits over the lifespan shows that in general after age _____ changes in one's personality traits are small.
   a. 12
   b. 20
   c. 30
   d. 50
5. Malcolm is hostile, aggressive, and impulsive. According to Eysenck, Malcolm is high in _____.
   a. conscientiousness
   b. neuroticism
   c. psychoticism
   d. introversion

Answers 1. b; 2. d; 3. a; 4. c; 5. c

social cognitive approach a personality perspective that emphasizes the influence of one's thoughts and social experiences in formulating personality

reciprocal determinism [ree-SIP-pra-cull dee-TER-min-iz-um] according to Bandura, the constant interaction among one's behavior, thoughts, and environment determines personality

11.3 The Social Cognitive Approach: The Environment and Patterns of Thought

The **social cognitive approach** sees personality as influenced by both the environment and one's thoughts. Whereas Freud focused on how unconscious forces influence behavior, and the trait perspective investigates internal dispositions, the social cognitive approach looks at the characteristic ways a person perceives and interprets events in the environment. For example, the person who assumes that others are unlikely to treat her fairly is more likely to have a quarrelsome personality than a person who tends to assume that things generally happen for the best. These patterns of thoughts are established through our interactions with and observations of other people. Two examples of this approach are Albert Bandura's *reciprocal determinism* and Julian Rotter's *locus of control theory.*

Albert Bandura speculates that personality is the product of reciprocal determinism, or the mutual interaction among one's environment, behavior, and thoughts.

Jon Brenneis/Life Magazine/Time & Life Pictures/Getty Images

11.3.1 • Reciprocal Determinism: Albert Bandura's Interacting Forces

Albert Bandura (b. 1925) speculates that personality is the product of three interacting forces: *environment, behavior,* and *thoughts* (Bandura, 1986). Bandura called the constant interaction among these three factors **reciprocal determinism** (• FIGURE 11.4). We choose to place ourselves in certain environments, and these environments then influence our behavior and the way we think. However, the way we think—our attributions, goals, values, and perceptions—may guide which environments we choose to be in as well as the behavior we exhibit (Dweck, 2008). Our behavior, in turn, may change the environment as well as the way we think. All three variables influence each other in a *reciprocal* manner.

For example, when we were children, we were placed in a family environment that modeled specific child-rearing techniques. We tend to think that everything we experienced in our home was normal, and that these same experiences occurred everywhere else, too. We tend to think that everyone else grew up with the parental discipline style we had. When we ourselves have children, if we have not learned anything different, we tend to behave in the same way toward our children. The family environment and our understanding of the way we were raised have now influenced our own parenting behavior.

A critical cognitive element in this interplay is what Bandura (1997) termed **self-efficacy**, or one's expectation of success in a given situation. Self-efficacy can differ among different domains in one's life. People with high self-efficacy in a certain domain believe that they will be successful in that domain. Approaching a situation with this belief is more likely to result in actual success. In contrast, people with low self-efficacy in a particular domain are more likely to approach a task believing that they won't succeed at it. This mindset then decreases their chance of succeeding by causing them to give up too easily or to not even really try in the first place.

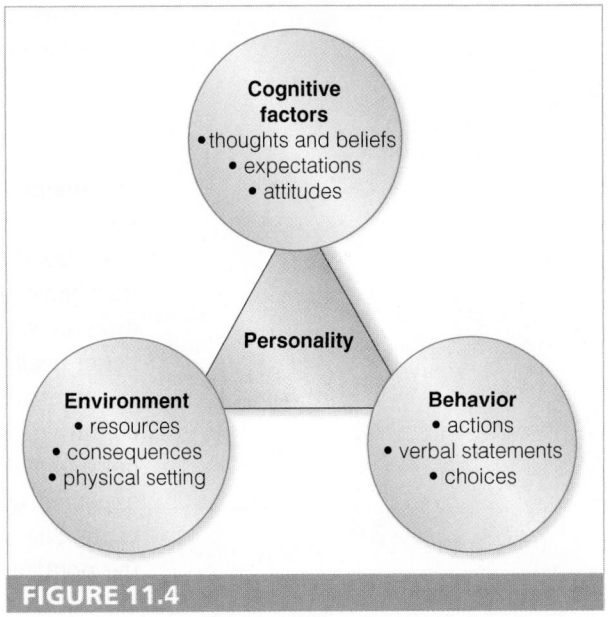

FIGURE 11.4

Bandura's Reciprocal Determinism

Albert Bandura speculates that the constant interaction among our behavior, thoughts (cognitive factors), and environment determines our personalities.

Let's return to our previous example. If you believe that you will be a successful parent by using the same discipline techniques that your parents used with you, you will be more likely to use such measures. If such practices are successful—in other words, your children behave as you would like—you feel even better as a parent. However, if you do not believe that you will be a successful parent, you may constantly change the methods you use to discipline your children. Such inconsistency will make it even less likely that your children will behave the way you want, which only reinforces your lack of confidence in your parenting ability.

self-efficacy [self-EF-fuh-kah-see] the expectation that one has for success in a given situation

locus [LOW-cus] of control the expectation of control we have over the outcome of an event; an internal locus means we expect some degree of personal control, whereas an external locus means we expect little personal control

11.3.2 • Julian Rotter's Locus of Control: Internal and External Expectations

Julian Rotter (1916–2014) provides another example of a social cognitive approach to personality. His theory (Rotter, 1982) is referred to as **locus of control**, or *location of control*. Rotter believes that we all have expectations regarding how much control we have over the outcome of an event. These expectations fall on a continuum from internal to external. For example, you probably enter the testing room on exam day already expecting to do well, average, or poorly on the exam. This is your expectation of the event. Some people attribute the outcome of an event to internal forces, such as hard work. If you expect to do well on an exam because you studied hard, you are exhibiting an *internal locus of control*. As an "internal," you are attributing the outcome of the event to factors within your control. However, other people attribute the outcome of an event to external forces, such as good luck, fate, or environmental factors. If you believe you will do well on the exam because the course or test is easy or because the professor likes you, these expectations demonstrate an *external locus of control*. As an "external," you attribute the outcome to factors outside your control. Not

People who exercise may be more likely to believe that they can control their health—an example of an internal locus of control.

IE134/Image Source Plus/Alamy

surprisingly, internals demonstrate higher academic achievement than externals. Externals tend to believe that only fate or the luck of a sympathetic teacher will get them a good grade, and so they do not study as much as internals (Schultz & Schultz, 2005).

Rotter suggests that these varying expectations of control lead to differences in personality. Think about your health. Who would be more likely to exercise regularly and maintain a healthy lifestyle? Externals are more likely to attribute their weight, health, or medical condition to fate. "What will be, will be" could be their motto. They feel that when their time is up, their time is up. Internals, however, believe that they can control their health and are therefore more likely to exercise, follow doctors' directions, get regular checkups, and eat wisely, behaviors that actually contribute to better health (Phares, 1991; Ryon & Gleason, 2014; Strickland, 1989).

In examining the section case study, how would Bandura's and Rotter's social cognitive perspectives explain Hongyong's personality? They would probably see her as having an internal locus of control and a strong sense of self-efficacy. She expected to succeed in business, in her marriage, and in learning to read and write. She was determined to get her family to freedom and to find her son despite the political and cultural upheaval around her.

11.3.3 • Contributions and Criticisms of the Social Cognitive Approach

The social cognitive approach has made major contributions to the field of psychology. By focusing on the cognitive processes such as thinking, expectations, and other mental events that influence our behavior, it has expanded our conceptualization and understanding of personality. This knowledge in turn has stimulated an enormous amount of research, as we saw in the second section of this text that examined how cognition influences behavior. Our knowledge of memory, attributions, and problem solving stem directly from this perspective, which easily lends itself to research, specifically experimental testing. Objectively measuring social and cognitive processes is easier than measuring unconscious forces or biological tendencies. Despite these contributions, the social cognitive approach has been criticized for not addressing biological, unconscious, and emotional factors that influence personality (Liebert & Spiegler, 1998). It also has been criticized for not specifying the exact nature of personality development.

Quiz Yourself

11.3

1. **The social cognitive perspective emphasizes the influence of _____ on personality**
   a. unconscious impulses
   b. internal control
   c. self-actualization and self-esteem
   d. the environment and patterns of thoughts

2. **Dylan is sure he will do poorly on his next psychology exam. Dylan often thinks this way in regard to his academic studies. Bandura would say that Dylan has _____.**
   a. low self-actualization
   b. low self-efficacy
   c. an external locus of control
   d. reciprocal determinism

3. **Juanita believes that finding a job is a matter of being in the right place at the right time. Rotter would classify Juanita as having _____.**
   a. low self-efficacy
   b. low determinism
   c. an internal locus of control
   d. an external locus of control

Answers 1. d; 2. b; 3. d

11.4 The Humanistic Approach: Free Will and Self-Actualization

The fourth and final personality perspective we will discuss is the **humanistic approach**. Humanistic psychology viewed itself as a "third force" in American psychology, following psychoanalytic and behavioral views. The humanistic approach emphasizes the individual, personal choice, and free will in shaping personality. The individual is seen as an active participant in his or her growth as a person. The humanistic view further assumes that humans have a built-in drive toward fulfilling their own natural potential. The attainment of this potential is referred to as **self-actualization**. Two well-known humanistic theorists have charted somewhat different paths to achieving self-actualization. One is Abraham Maslow, whose *hierarchy of needs theory* was introduced in Chapter 5. The other is Carl Rogers and his *self theory*.

humanistic approach a personality perspective that emphasizes the individual, personal choice, and free will in shaping personality; assumes that humans have a built-in drive toward fulfilling their own natural potential

self-actualization [self-ack-shu-lih-ZAY-shun] the fulfillment of one's natural potential

actualizing [ACK-shu-lies-ing] tendency according to Rogers, the natural drive in humans to strive for fulfillment and enhancement

11.4.1 • Abraham Maslow and the Hierarchy of Needs Theory

Recall from Chapter 5 that Maslow (1908–1970) believed that the pathway to achieving self-actualization was in the form of a hierarchy, with physical or biological needs at the bottom and more psychological or social needs at the top (Maslow, 1968, 1970, 1971). According to Maslow, a person must satisfy lower-level needs before higher-level needs can be attained. At the bottom of the hierarchy are basic physiological needs, such as the need for food and water. Without food and water, we cannot proceed to the next rung of the ladder. At this next level, safety becomes the concern: the need to be free from harm and to feel secure. Once this safety need is met, the person focuses on psychological needs, such as feeling a sense of belongingness (the need to fit in), feeling esteem or respect from others, and meeting cognitive and aesthetic needs. Once these needs have been satisfied, self-actualization can be attained. Maslow estimated that only 1 person in 10 operates from self-actualization needs. While in Chapter 5 we discussed how Maslow's theory relates to motivation, here we are revisiting Maslow's theory as it applies to personality and explaining why people may consistently behave the way they do.

Unfortunately, Maslow's hierarchy does not explain why some people would deprive themselves of lower food and safety needs in favor of higher needs, such as esteem or self-actualization. For example, Nelson Mandela preferred to remain imprisoned in South Africa for many years than to lose his right to criticize the apartheid government. Maslow's hierarchy has also been criticized for not capturing the power of culture in influencing and shaping human needs (Kesebir, Graham, & Oishi, 2010). Some critics contend that Maslow's hierarchy is just too simple a view of motives and personality (Kenrick et al., 2010; Neher, 1991). Another view of self-actualization is Carl Rogers's self theory.

Shaun Best/Reuters/Corbis

People who meet the criteria for self-actualization, such as the late Nelson Mandela, might actually deprive themselves of lower-level needs (remaining imprisoned) in favor of higher needs (the right to criticize one's government).

11.4.2 • Carl Rogers and Self Theory

Carl Rogers (1902–1987) believed that understanding human personality required an understanding of how people view themselves and how they interpret events around them (Rogers, 1942, 1951, 1961, 1970, 1980). He believed that human beings naturally strive for fulfillment and enhancement, a basic motive that he referred to as the **actualizing tendency**.

Michael Rougier/Time & Life Pictures/Contributor/Getty Images

Carl Rogers believed that understanding human personality requires an understanding of how people view themselves and how they interpret events around them.

THE DEVELOPMENT OF SELF-CONCEPT

Rogers's proposed actualizing tendency is set at birth and moves the infant to recognize that she is separate from the mother and an independent being. The infant begins to experience the self as "I" or "me." This self gradually evolves into the person's self-concept. **Self-concept** is our perception or image of our abilities and our uniqueness. At first one's self-concept is very general and changeable, as in the 4-year-old who describes herself as a girl with brown hair or the 3-year-old who states in one moment that he is happy but 5 minutes later that he is sad. As we grow older, these self-perceptions become much more organized, detailed, and specific. For example, a 15-year-old is more likely to describe himself in terms of his academic abilities, athletic abilities, social abilities, and talents. For example, he may say, "I'm a decent second baseman, a B student, and I have a lot of friends."

Underlying Rogers's actualizing tendency is an *organismic valuing process.* Experiences that maintain or enhance the person are valued, and therefore are preferred and liked. Experiences that do not maintain or enhance the person are not valued, and therefore are rejected (Sheldon, Arndt, & Houser-Marko, 2003). An infant's valuing process is direct and simple. We know as infants what we like and what we dislike. We value food because it reduces the sensation of hunger. We value being held in a parent's arms because it makes us feel secure. However, such an internal evaluation of our values is soon influenced by our social interactions and cultural environments and by our basic need for love and acceptance (Fulmer et al., 2010; Markus & Kitayama, 2010; McAdams, 2013).

As children, we come to realize that other important people in our lives (such as parents, teachers, siblings, or other relatives) also place value on our experiences. They communicate to us the "right" and "wrong" ways to think, feel, and behave. Cultural, racial, and gender norms may become especially powerful influences on our behavior. Because we desire their love and affection, we incorporate these messages into our valuing process. Experiences that meet these imposed values tend to be incorporated into our self-concept. For example, if a parent has communicated to a child that good grades are valued and the child gets good grades, the child may describe herself as a good student. A child may come home every day from school reporting on how well she did in school. This accomplishment gives the child the opportunity to gain acceptance and love from the parent. Conversely, suppose the child does not get good grades at school. This child may hide test scores from parents for fear of being rejected and unloved. This example illustrates the enormous influence of others' standards and values on our self-concepts. We may no longer listen to our own internal valuing system but pay more attention to the views and values of loved ones and our society. Our worth and regard are now judged on the basis of the imposed opinions, judgments, and values of others in our social interactions and culture, rather than our own internal organismic valuing process. We have come to see ourselves as others see us.

THE VALUE OF UNCONDITIONAL POSITIVE REGARD

What determines the degree to which we "listen" to, or incorporate, these parental and societal norms and standards? For Rogers, it is the degree of **unconditional positive regard**, or acceptance and love with no strings attached, that we receive from others. Our good points as well as bad points are accepted. People accept us and love us for who we are. This does not mean that a person's *actions* always receive approval. For example, suppose a youngster kicks the dog because the dog chewed a cherished toy. A parent can express displeasure at the child's actions, yet still let the child know that the angry behavior is understood and that the

self-concept one's perception or image of his or her abilities and uniqueness

unconditional positive regard acceptance and love of another's thoughts and feelings without expecting anything in return child is still loved by the parent despite the behavior. However, if the parent attacks the child's self, calling the child "bad," the parent has now communicated *conditional* positive regard. The child will believe that feeling angry is wrong because feeling angry will lose his parent's love and acceptance. In other words, unconditional positive regard communicates respect for a person's thoughts and feelings.

On the one hand, if a child experiences unconditional positive regard, especially during the early years of life, he or she is less likely to lose contact with the organismic valuing process established at birth. In this way, the child grows into an adult who chooses to act, feel, or think on the basis of his or her inner evaluations, taking into consideration the effect of his or her behavior on others. For Rogers, this represented a healthy personality. On the other hand, if a child experiences primarily conditional positive regard during these years, he or she is more likely to develop a self-concept that is based on how others see him or her and disregard the inner guiding voice in his or her behavior. Such people think, act, or behave in a certain way in hope of ensuring the continued love and acceptance of others. They believe that if they don't meet certain self-imposed expectations, their parents will not love them anymore. These perceptions, whether accurate or not, impede our ability to fulfill our potential, according to Rogers. In such situations, healthy development of the personality is hindered, and psychological discomfort may occur (Assor, Roth, & Deci, 2004).

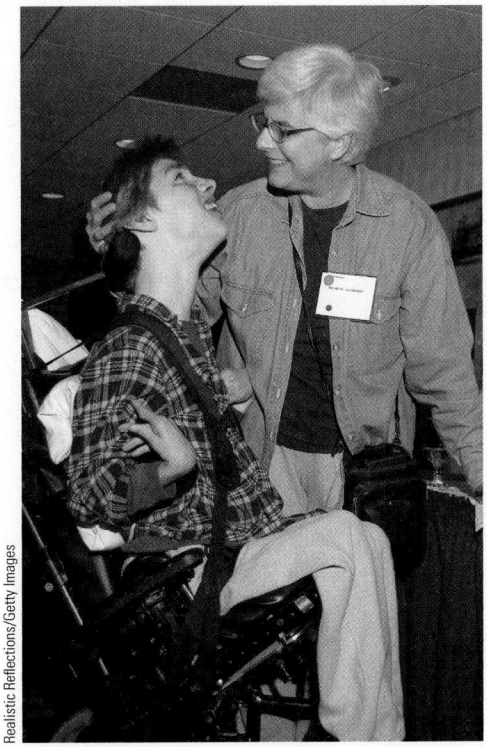

Realistic Reflections/Getty Images

The approval (or disapproval) we receive from others influences our self-concept, according to Rogers.

Let's take one more look at Hongyong Baek from a humanistic perspective. Growing up female in the Korean culture, during a time of political and cultural upheaval, potentially influenced Hongyong's perception of reality and the evaluation of her self-concept. Others' opinions and judgments (such as her husband's) affected her view of herself. Moreover, her struggle at times to fulfill basic biological, security, and belongingness needs may have influenced the attainment of higher psychological needs. Her self-concept influenced her experiences and behaviors.

11.4.3 • Contributions and Criticisms of the Humanistic Approach

Many humanistic ideas have been incorporated into individual, family, and group therapy approaches, as we will see in Chapter 14. The humanistic approach has encouraged many people to become more aware of themselves and their interactions with others. However, the humanistic perspective has been criticized for its seemingly naïve and optimistic assumption that all people are good and are motivated toward attaining self-actualization. Critics argue that all people are not necessarily good and that humanists underestimate the capacity for evil in some individuals (Coffer & Appley, 1964; Ellis, 1959). Equally problematic is the difficulty in validating through experiments many of the humanistic concepts such as actualizing tendency, organismic valuing process, and unconditional positive regard (Burger, 2004). The major source of data for Rogers's self theory has been under scrutiny as well, as it was derived from clients' self-statements. How reliable and valid are such statements? It's possible that clients did not always present their "true" selves to Rogers and that as a listener Rogers was biased. As a result, humanistic psychology has not become as major a force in psychology as Maslow once hoped—although many consider the emergence of *positive psychology* (see Chapter 12) a rebirth of humanistic goals and its enduring legacy (Diener, Oishi, & Lucas, 2003).

Quiz Yourself

11.4

1. The humanistic perspective emphasizes the influence of _____ on personality.
   a. unconscious impulses
   b. internal traits
   c. an actualizing tendency
   d. environmental and cognitive factors
2. Maslow's hierarchy of needs theory would have the most difficulty explaining which one of the following?
   a. A teenager shopping for the "right" clothes to wear to school.
   b. A starving child stealing food at the grocery store.
   c. A person who lives in a dangerous part of town tries to find a job that makes him feel important.
   d. A successful business person with a satisfying relationship searches for spiritual fulfillment.
3. Which of the following elements does Rogers believe promotes the fulfillment of one's potential?
   a. Unconditional positive regard
   b. Esteem
   c. Sympathy
   d. Adaptability

Answers 1. c; 2. c; 3. a

11.5 Scientifically Measuring Personality

We have described four different approaches to personality. Each perspective tends to employ certain tools to measure or assess personality. The results of these tests can be used in clinical settings to inform therapists about their clients' behavior, as well as in research to explore variations in personalities across individuals.

As with any tool or measuring device, it is important that the test be *reliable* and *valid*. **Reliability** refers to the consistency of a measurement tool. If we were to assess your height as an adult with a tape measure, we would want to get a consistent "reading" every time we measured your height. Personality tests also need to be reliable, or yield similar results over time. This reliability will not be perfect as we are not consistent in our behavior at all times. However, personality tests should report similar trends if they are reliable.

reliability the degree to which a test yields consistent measurements of a trait

validity the degree to which a test measures the trait that it was designed to measure

personality inventory an objective paper-and-pencil or computerized self-report form that measures personality on several dimensions

Measurement tools like personality tests also need to be valid. **Validity** refers to the ability of a test to measure what it says it is measuring. If a test states that it is measuring your intelligence and it does so by measuring your foot size, this test would not be valid. There is no relationship between foot size and intelligence. Notice that this test would be reliable (that is, yield a consistent measure from time to time), but it does not measure what we think of as intelligence. Therefore, personality tests should measure what we believe personality to be.

Each of the four major perspectives has developed its own way of measuring personality. These measures include *personality inventories, projective tests, rating scales,* and *clinical interviews.*

11.5.1 • Personality Inventories: Mark Which One Best Describes You

Personality inventories are objective paper-and-pencil or computerized self-report forms. You are typically asked to indicate how well a statement describes you

TABLE 11.4

Sample MMPI-2 Items

I have trouble with my bowel movements.	T	F
I do not sleep well.	T	F
At parties, I sit by myself or with one other person.	T	F
A lot of people have it in for me.	T	F
In school, I was frequently in trouble for acting up.	T	F
I am anxious most of the time.	T	F
I hear strange things that others do not hear.	T	F
I am a very important person.	T	F

or to answer true or false to a specific statement. Perhaps you have completed a personality questionnaire for a potential job or on an online dating site? In college settings, many students have completed the *Myers-Briggs Personality Inventory*. This test assesses an individual's personality on four different dimensions. In clinical settings, the most frequently used personality inventory is the **Minnesota Multiphasic Personality Inventory (MMPI-2)**.

Minnesota Multiphasic [mul-tee-FAZE-ick] Personality Inventory (MMPI-2) a personality inventory that is designed to identify problem areas of functioning in an individual's personality

The MMPI-2 is a 567-item true/false questionnaire that takes about 1 hour to complete. The questions describe a wide range of behaviors (●TABLE 11.4). The purpose of the MMPI-2 is to identify problem areas of functioning in an individual's personality. It is organized into 10 groups of items, called *clinical scales*. These scales measure patterns of responses or traits associated with specific mental health disorders such as depression, paranoia, and schizophrenia. A person's response patterns are reviewed to see whether they resemble the pattern of responses from groups of people who have these disorders. Interpreting the MMPI-2 involves comparing the test taker's responses to those of the "norming" population.

As part of its construction, the MMPI-2 was given to thousands of people, called a *norming group*. Individuals in the norming group included people who had no mental health disorders and people who had particular disorders. In this way the test constructors could see how frequently someone without the disorder would respond "true" to these items and how frequently someone with the mental health disorder would respond "true." The first group established the average, or "normal," number of items for each of these clinical scales, whereas the second group gave an indication of what would be considered problematic functioning. A psychologist is interested in examining any areas of your personality that fall outside the normal range. These areas would be considered problem areas of your personality and might suggest issues for therapy.

Another widely used personality inventory is the *California Psychological Inventory (CPI)*. The CPI contains 434 true/false items, including 194 from the original MMPI. Unlike the MMPI, the CPI was developed to measure positive traits such as sociability, independence, and responsibility in healthy individuals. The CPI norming groups did not contain people who had been diagnosed with mental health problems.

One of the main problems with self-report measures such as the MMPI-2 and CPI is the test taker's honesty or truthfulness. For this reason, both the

projective test a less structured and subjective personality test in which an individual is shown an ambiguous stimulus and is asked to describe what he or she sees

Rorschach [ROAR-shock] Inkblot Test a projective personality test consisting of 10 ambiguous inkblots in which a person is asked to describe what he or she sees; the person's responses are then coded for consistent themes and issues

Thematic Apperception [thee-MAT-ick ap-per-SEP-shun] Test (TAT) a projective personality test consisting of a series of pictures in which the respondent is asked to tell a story about each scene; the responses are then coded for consistent themes and issues

FIGURE 11.5

Sample Rorschach Inkblot

After being shown an inkblot like this one, the person indicates what he or she sees on the card.

FIGURE 11.6

Sample Thematic Apperception (TAT) Card

In taking the TAT, a person is asked to tell a story about a scene such as this one.

MMPI-2 and CPI contain *validity scales* to assess the truthfulness of the individual's responses.

11.5.2 • Projective Tests: Tell Me What You See

Another type of tool used to measure personality, the **projective test**, is less structured than the personality inventory. When taking this test, you are shown an ambiguous image and then asked to describe what you see or to tell a story about the picture. Such tests rely on the idea that whatever stories, motives, or explanations you offer reflect your own issues and concerns, projected onto the image.

One of the most famous projective tests is the **Rorschach Inkblot Test**. The Rorschach test consists of 10 inkblots on cards. As each card is presented, you indicate what images you see. Your responses are then coded according to specific guidelines to decrease subjectivity and enhance the validity of the results. A sample card is shown in • FIGURE 11.5.

Another widely used projective test is the **Thematic Apperception Test (TAT)**. In the TAT, you are shown images that are not as ambiguous as inkblots yet still allow for a variety of interpretations. You are asked to tell a story about the image, and your responses are then coded for any consistent themes, emotions, or issues. A sample TAT image is depicted in • FIGURE 11.6. After being shown this image, a client might relate the following story: "It's a picture of a young man who has been waiting several hours at a park for his partner to arrive. He is tired, anxious, and angry. He is hoping that nothing bad has happened to his partner. He is also hoping that he wasn't stood up."

The purpose of projective tests is similar to that of personality inventories. Psychologists want to pinpoint healthy and unhealthy areas of functioning in the individual being tested. However, unlike personality inventories, projective tests are derived from the psychoanalytic perspective; the images and stories described are thought to reflect underlying unconscious urges and desires. Because projective tests are more subject to the interpretation of the clinician than are personality inventories, coding systems have been devised to decrease variation in interpretation and increase their reliability in measuring personality. Projective tests are most useful for identifying themes in a person's life or for delineating an individual's problem-solving style.

11.5.3 • Rating Scales and Direct Observation

A third type of tool used by psychologists to measure personality is the *rating scale*. Rating scales are formatted similarly to checklists. You check off the statements or behaviors that most apply to you. Because the person being evaluated may not answer the statements truthfully, teachers, parents, partners, and clinicians can also complete rating scales on the person being evaluated. These alternate perspectives minimize the self-distortions that are associated with self-report instruments.

Psychologists may also rely on directly observing a client's behavior and interactions with others to assess personality. Closely watching how you behave in particular situations can be helpful in determining what happens before and after your responses. Such information is particularly important to clinicians who favor a social cognitive approach and who want to understand the social or environmental factors that may be influencing problem behavior.

TABLE 11.5

Rosenberg Self-Esteem Scale

Below is a list of statements dealing with your general feelings about yourself. If you Strongly Agree, circle *SA*. If you Agree with the statement, circle *A*. If you Disagree, circle *D*. If you Strongly Disagree, circle *SD*.

		STRONGLY AGREE	AGREE	DISAGREE	STRONGLY DISAGREE
1.	I feel that I'm a person of worth, at least on an equal plane with others.	SA	A	D	SD
2.	I feel that I have a number of good qualities.	SA	A	D	SD
3.	All in all, I am inclined to feel that I am a failure.	SA	A	D	SD
4.	I am able to do things as well as most other people.	SA	A	D	SD
5.	I feel I do not have much to be proud of.	SA	A	D	SD
6.	I take a positive attitude toward myself.	SA	A	D	SD
7.	On the whole, I am satisfied with myself.	SA	A	D	SD
8.	I wish I could have more respect for myself.	SA	A	D	SD
9.	I certainly feel useless at times.	SA	A	D	SD
10.	At times I think I am no good at all.	SA	A	D	SD

Scoring:
For items 1, 2, 4, 6, 7 Strongly Agree = 3; Agree = 2; Disagree = 1; Strongly Disagree = 0
For items 3, 5, 8, 9, 10 Strongly Agree = 0; Agree = 1; Disagree = 2; Strongly Disagree = 3
The scale ranges from 0 to 30, with 30 indicating the highest score possible. There are no discrete cutoff points for high and low self-esteem.
Higher scores indicate more positive feelings toward the self while lower scores indicate more negative feelings toward the self.

Source: Rosenberg, M. (1989). *Society and the adolescent self-image*. Middletown, CT: Wesleyan University Press.

ENGAGE YOURSELF! Psychologists may find rating scales on self-esteem and self-concept useful for understanding how a person perceives reality and feels about him or herself. Take a moment to complete the self-esteem scale provided in ●TABLE 11.5.

clinical interview the initial meeting between a client and a clinician in which the clinician asks questions to identify the difficulty in functioning that the person is experiencing

11.5.4 • Clinical Interviews

One tool used by most clinical psychologists is the **clinical interview**. This interview typically takes place during the first meeting between the client and the clinician and involves the clinician asking the client questions to identify the client's difficulty in functioning. The format and length of the interview, as well as the questions that are asked during the interview, may differ from clinician to clinician. These differences again relate to the alternate views on personality that were discussed in this chapter. For example, a clinician who favors the social cognitive approach is more likely to ask specific questions about social situations and patterns of thoughts. This clinician may want to know what you were thinking about prior to, during, and after a particular behavior occurred. A humanist is more likely to focus on the client's interpretation and perception of reality. The focus of any clinical interview, however, is to identify as clearly

Zigy Kaluzny/The Image Bank/ Getty Images

A clinical interview typically takes place during the first meeting between the client and the clinician. The focus is on identifying as clearly as possible the difficulty in functioning that the person is experiencing.

as possible the difficulty in functioning that the person is experiencing. This difficulty is often given a name, or *diagnosis*. The exact nature of these diagnoses is covered in Chapter 13.

Quiz Yourself 11.5

1. **The major disadvantage of self-report instruments, such as the MMPI-2 and the CPI, is _____.**
   a. the subjective interpretation of the results by the clinician
   b. the respondents may not tell the truth
   c. the scoring criteria are very vague and unreliable
   d. there are no norms to compare one's responses against
2. **Tamara goes to see a clinical psychologist. The psychologist asks her to look at some vague pictures and report what she sees. Most likely Tamara is taking a _____.**
   a. personality inventory
   b. projective test
   c. rating scale
   d. clinical interview
3. **When one goes to a clinical psychologist, the first session is most likely to involve _____.**
   a. personality testing
   b. a physical examination
   c. hypnosis
   d. a clinical interview

Answers 1. b; 2. b; 3. d

11.6 Integrating Psychology: The Big Picture

This chapter presented four different views of personality: the *psychoanalytic perspective*, the *trait approach*, the *social cognitive perspective*, and the *humanistic approach*. Rather than debating which of these perspectives is "right," many psychologists prefer instead to see these viewpoints as complementary. Just as a photographer may take the same picture from many different angles, psychologists, too, like to understand personality from varying viewpoints. When taken together, these theories provide a much more complex and richer view of the forces that make us unique than any single perspective could do.

These complementary perspectives also underscore the necessity in understanding and integrating the different areas of contemporary psychology. Reconsider all the potential forces that influenced Hongyong's Baek's personality. Biologically, she may have inherited traits and drives that motivated her to succeed at business and have the fortitude to move her family to freedom. Her cognitive processes helped her solve problems and learn how to read and write, despite being raised at a time when women did not learn these skills. Yet, Hongyong fulfilled the valued cultural roles as mother and wife while still finding meaning in her life with her ch'iryo practice. However, her journey was not without challenges as she battled health problems and depression when she thought she lost her son and then after her husband's death. Such challenges illustrate the importance of understanding physical and mental health processes—our next and last foundation of psychology to explore.

Studying the Chapter

Key Terms

actualizing tendency (485)
anal stage (467)
archetypes (470)
basic anxiety (470)
behavioral genetics (478)
cardinal traits (473)
central traits (473)
clinical interview (491)
collective unconscious (470)
conscious level (464)
defense mechanism (466)
ego (465)
Electra complex (468)
emotional stability (476)
extraversion (473)
five factor theory (477)
genital stage (468)
humanistic approach (485)
id (465)
introversion (473)
latency stage (468)
locus of control (483)
Minnesota Multiphasic Personality Inventory (MMPI-2) (489)
neuroticism (476)
Oedipus complex (468)
oral stage (467)
personal unconscious (470)
personality (462)
personality inventory (488)
person–situation interaction (480)
phallic stage (468)
pleasure principle (465)
preconscious level (464)
projective test (490)
psychoanalytic perspective (464)
psychoticism (476)
reality principle (465)
reciprocal determinism (482)
reliability (488)
Rorschach Inkblot Test (490)
secondary traits (473)
self-actualization (485)
self-concept (486)
self-efficacy (483)
sensation seeker (474)
social cognitive approach (482)
source traits (473)
superego (466)
surface traits (473)
Thematic Apperception Test (TAT) (490)
trait (472)
trait approach (472)
unconditional positive regard (486)
unconscious level (464)
validity (488)

What Do You Know? Assess Your Understanding

Test your retention and understanding of the material by answering the following questions.

1. Which perspective suggests that human beings have genetic dispositions to behave in a certain way across situations?

a. Psychoanalytic perspective
b. Trait perspective
c. Humanistic perspective
d. Social cognitive perspective

2. Meera's friends describe her as warm and giving across most situations. According to Allport, warm and giving are _____ of Meera's.

a. central traits
b. source traits
c. cardinal traits
d. primary traits

3. Which personality perspective emphasizes the influence of unconscious forces on personality?

a. Psychoanalytic perspective
b. Trait perspective
c. Humanistic perspective
d. Social cognitive perspective

4. Timothy feels very confident about his writing abilities. Bandura would say that Timothy has high _____ for his writing.

a. extraversion
b. self-efficacy
c. determinism
d. self-concept

5. Even though her mother told her not to, Gretchen had a second piece of chocolate cake. Which personality structure, according to Freud, motivated Gretchen's behavior?

a. Superego
b. Ego
c. Id
d. The preconscious

6. Which of the following is *not* one of the traits of the five factor theory?

a. Openness
b. Extraversion
c. Conformity
d. Agreeableness

7. Defense mechanisms are used to handle intrapsychic conflict between which two personality structures?

a. Id and ego
b. Id and superego
c. Ego and superego
d. The ego and the preconscious

8. Which theory examines the influence of one's environment, behaviors, and thoughts on personality?

a. Hierarchy of needs
b. Locus of control
c. Self theory
d. Reciprocal determinism

9. The Oedipus and Electra complexes occur during which psychosexual stage?

a. Phallic
b. Latency
c. Anal
d. Genital

10. People generally become more _____ and less _____ across adulthood.

a. neurotic; introverted
b. emotionally stable; extraverted
c. extraverted; conscientious
d. open to experience; agreeable

11. Melinda believes that her hard work and determination have led to her successful career. According to Rotter, Melinda has a(n) _____.

a. positive self-concept
b. external locus of control
c. internal locus of control
d. overactive superego

12. You take a personality test in which you are asked to indicate how well a statement describes you. Most likely you are taking which of the following personality tests?

a. MMPI-2
b. IQ test
c. Rorschach Inkblot Test
d. TAT

13. Your long-term memories most likely reside in which level of consciousness?

a. Unconscious
b. Subconscious
c. Preconscious
d. Conscious

14. Wally is described as moody, tense, and anxious. According to Eysenck, Wally is high in _____.

a. extraversion
b. neuroticism
c. fearfulness
d. psychoticism

15. Marley is in high school and very much wants to be a part of the in-crowd. According to Maslow, Marley is trying to fulfill _____ needs.

a. peer
b. safety
c. belongingness
d. esteem

16. Donny's mother is very upset when Donny's grades slip below a B level. Donny feels that he must make good grades in order to receive his mother's love and acceptance. According to Rogers, Donny perceives _____ from his mother.

a. unconditional positive regard
b. conditional positive regard
c. actualizing tendency
d. self-actualization

17. Shanique takes a personality test in which she is asked to count to 10 and identify pictures of animals. This personality test most lacks _____.

a. validity
b. reliability
c. consistency
d. norming

18. In what way did Karen Horney agree with Freud on personality development?

a. Development arises from instinctual conflicts.
b. Personality is the result of psychosexual conflicts.
c. Culture plays a large role in personality development.
d. Early childhood is a significant time for personality development.

19. The humanistic approach has been criticized for _____.
    a. not detailing personality development
    b. relying too heavily on experimental data
    c. its optimistic view that all people are good
    d. All of the above
20. Which of the following is *not* a contribution of the psychoanalytic perspective?
    a. Stimulated research on sleep and dreaming
    b. Stimulated research on coping and health
    c. Created personality tests and therapy approaches
    d. Stimulated experimentation on learning and perception

Answers: 1. b; 2. a; 3. a; 4. b; 5. c; 6. c; 7. b; 8. d; 9. a; 10. b; 11. c; 12. a; 13. c; 14. b; 15. c; 16. b; 17. a; 18. d; 19. c; 20. d.

Use It or Lose It: Applying Psychology

1. Which theory of personality do you find most compelling, and why?
2. Using one of the personality perspectives discussed in this chapter, analyze the personality of a favorite television or movie character.
3. How has your personality changed over the years? How has it remained the same? What theory or theories can best explain these changes and consistencies?
4. How would you go about constructing a personality test? How does the structure of your test relate to your perspective on personality?
5. Try to describe your personality in detail from each of the perspectives discussed in this chapter.

Critical Thinking for Integration

1. Review the theories of motivation discussed in Chapter 5. How do they correlate with the views on personality discussed in this chapter?
2. In Chapter 10, we discussed behaviors such as conformity, aggression, and helpfulness in relation to the effect that others have on our behavior. How would the psychoanalytic perspective explain such behaviors? How would they be explained from the humanistic perspective?
3. Discuss how memory (Chapter 7), problem solving (Chapter 8), and intelligence (Chapter 8) relate to personality.

Fancy/Alamy

Are You Getting the Big Picture? Personality

Personality is the unique collection of attitudes, emotions, thoughts, habits, impulses, and behaviors that defines how a person typically behaves across situations.

11.1 The Psychoanalytic Approach: Sigmund Freud and the Neo-Freudians

- Emphasizes unconscious aspects of personality. It proposes that personality operates at the **conscious**, **preconscious**, and **unconscious** levels.

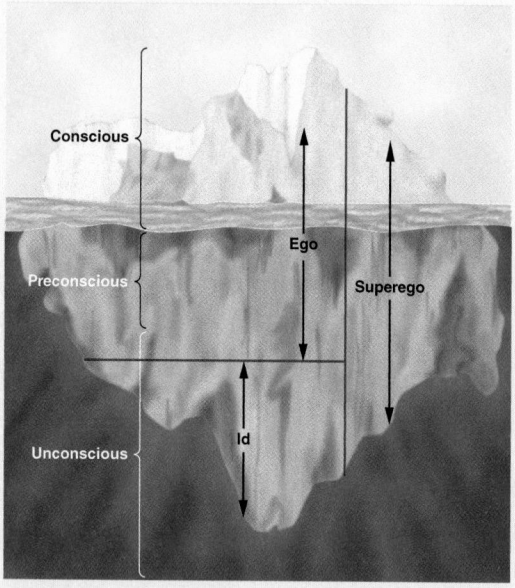

- According to Freud, personality is comprised of the unconscious **id** that operates according to the **pleasure principle**, the conscious **ego** that operates according to the **reality principle**, and the moral directives of the **superego**.
- For Freud, personality develops through a series of five psychosexual stages (**oral**, **anal**, **phallic**, **latency**, **genital**) that represent a complex interaction between natural sexual urges and our socialization experiences.
- Neo-Freudians such as Jung, Adler, and Horney placed less emphasis on the role of the instinctual impulses in motivating behavior.

Hulton Archive/Getty Images

11.2 The Trait Approach: Consistency and Stability in Personality

- Attempts to describe personality by identifying the internal **traits**, or tendencies that we have across most situations.
- Allport classified traits into three types: **central**, **cardinal**, and **secondary** traits.
- Cattell's factor analysis of traits yielded 16 **source traits** that could be measured in everyone. Eysenck proposed three universal traits in his PEN model: **psychoticism**, **extraversion**, and **neuroticism**.
- Costa and McCrae's **five factor theory** proposes five core universal traits: openness, conscientiousness, extraversion, agreeableness, and neuroticism (OCEAN).
- Research suggests a complex interaction between genes and the environment in producing personality. Some traits remain stable over the course of adulthood, but situational factors also influence the consistency of traits.

© Ashley Cooper/Alamy

11.3 The Social Cognitive Approach: The Environment and Patterns of Thought

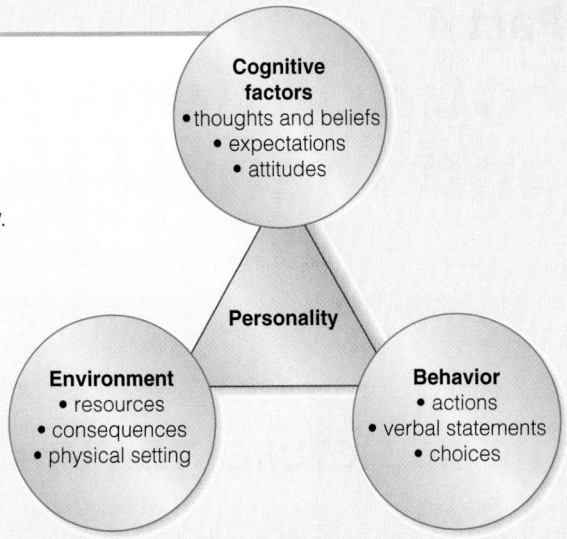

- Evaluates environmental and cognitive factors that influence personality.
- Bandura's **reciprocal determinism** suggests that personality is due to the constant interaction between one's environment, behaviors, and thoughts. A critical cognitive element is **self-efficacy**, or the expectation one has for success in a given situation.
- Rotter believes that one's **locus of control**, or one's expectations of whether the outcome of an event is due to internal or external forces, influences personality.
- The **social cognitive approach** is comprehensive, has many applications, and is easily tested experimentally.

11.4 The Humanistic Approach: Free Will and Self-Actualization

Michael Rougier/Time & Life Pictures/Contributor/Getty Images

- Emphasizes one's drive toward uniqueness and **self-actualization**.
- Maslow believed that the pathway to self-actualization lies in fulfilling a hierarchy of needs, with physical needs at the bottom and psychological needs at the top.
- Rogers's self theory emphasizes how one's **self-concept**, or perception of self, is influenced by the standards and values of others, most notably the degree to which we perceive and receive **unconditional positive regard** from others.
- The **humanistic approach** promotes self-awareness and positive interactions with others, and its ideas have been incorporated into several therapy approaches.

11.5 Scientifically Measuring Personality

- Tools that assess personality should be **reliable** and **valid**.
- **Personality inventories** such as the **MMPI-2** and CPI are objective paper-and-pencil or computerized self-report forms that can reliably describe a person's traits if answered honestly.
- **Projective tests** such as the **Rorschach Inkblot Test** and the **Thematic Apperception Test** are less structured tests in which a person is shown an ambiguous image and asked to describe it. According to the psychoanalytic perspective a person's responses are believed to reflect underlying unconscious concerns.
- Psychologists may also use rating scales and direct observation to measure behaviors and interactions with others.
- The focus of the **clinical interview** is to identify the difficulty in functioning that a person is experiencing.

Part 4
Foundations in Physical and Mental Health

THE BIG PICTURE **The Ups and Downs of Life**

The final foundation of psychology focuses on *physical* and *mental health*. It emphasizes a "biopsychosocial" approach that highlights how biological, psychological, and social factors contribute to both physical and mental health behaviors. The term *biopsychosocial* underscores how interrelated these factors are in understanding a person's physical and mental functioning. This section includes three topics: health, mental health disorders, and mental health therapies. Chapter 12 introduces **health psychology**, the study of how people's behavior influences their health for better and for worse. This chapter examines how stress, coping, personality, and lifestyles influence our behavior. Chapter 13 outlines the major **mental health disorders** such as depression, anxiety, and schizophrenia. It includes the main symptoms of these disorders as well as our current understanding of what causes such problems. Chapter 14 explores therapy. **Therapy** consists of techniques that are used to help people with mental health or interpersonal problems. Because all of us sometimes experience difficulty in functioning, these topics offer much psychological research that will be relevant to your day-to-day living. It will help you realize how some of your personal habits, thoughts, or daily actions may be problematic, and hopefully will enable you to change them and enhance your personal well-being. To illustrate, consider for a moment the following story.

Emily Fox Gordon

Emily Fox Gordon

When most adolescents enter adulthood, especially when they come from privilege, it is thought of as a carefree, exciting time in life. It is often considered a time to go to college, enter the workforce or both, and discover and nurture one's talents and ambitions. But this is often not the case for young people who struggle with mental health issues. Emily's teenage years centered around mental health institutions. Her childhood was not entirely unhappy. By outward appearances, her early childhood was enriched with music, literature, and engaging activities. But inwardly, Emily felt emotionally neglected by her parents. Emily's father, a professor of economics, was tense, intellectual, judgmental, easily angered, and focused on work and achievement. Her mother was often sad and depressed, and an alcoholic.

Emily gained her parents' attention by being disobedient and acting out. She was an underachiever at school, had difficulty learning, and spent hours in detention for misbehavior. Her father called her careless and clumsy. Her mother was embarrassed by her. Her behavior and academic performance were unacceptable to her achievement-oriented parents—children of immigrant parents who cut their religious and cultural ties to achieve the "American dream." Emily was curious about religion, but it was scorned by her parents. She felt awkward, fat, and hopeless, and spent more and more time reading or alone. Emily had difficulty fitting in and felt like a misfit. She experienced unprecedented rages and panic, developing a spastic colon and rapid heartbeat. She regarded herself as the difficult child, the family scapegoat, and a pariah at school. She felt forgotten and was hungry for spiritual and emotional connections.

In This Part:

CHAPTER 12 **Health, Stress, and Coping**

CHAPTER 13 **Mental Health Disorders**

CHAPTER 14 **Mental Health Therapies**

In the eighth grade, Emily was sent to Dr. V., a therapist, following another incident at school in which she angrily chased another student with what school administrators described as an intention to inflict physical harm. In these therapy sessions, Emily would lie down on a couch while Dr. V. remained silent in a chair. Not knowing what to do, Emily remained silent as well, listening to Dr. V. steadily scribbling on a notepad. After a year, Emily's family moved, and she continued therapy to deal with her rage and panic. She was sent to see Dr. H. There, Emily sat on a couch, and Dr. H. remained silent in a nearby chair, knitting a sweater. After a year of listening to the click-clacking of knitting needles, therapy with Dr. H. was terminated.

Emily's problems at home and school continued. She was kicked out of several private schools for misbehavior and truancy. She often snuck out of her parents' house at night to hang out with two brothers who were also social outcasts. They would stay out half the night smoking cigarettes and roaming the town. On one of these occasions, at 16, Emily's father found her at an unchaperoned party with a boy in a dark room, where they were kissing and groping one another. Her father dragged her out of the party and drove her home. Furious with her parents, Emily broke an aspirin jar and, using a piece of the glass, scratched her wrists in a half-hearted suicide attempt. Her parents sent her to see another therapist, Dr. G.

Therapy with Dr. G. was different from what Emily had experienced before. She sat facing him and was encouraged to talk freely about her dreams, stress, and problems while Dr. G. looked for themes threaded through her discussions. She saw Dr. G. on and off through her high school years. After she again attempted suicide at age 18, Dr. G. recommended an inpatient facility for Emily. She was placed in the highly regarded Austen Riggs treatment center in Massachusetts. Her intelligence was measured and she was given the Rorschach personality test. During her interview she stated she felt detached and disengaged. Emily was diagnosed as having an anxiety problem with borderline personality trends. She stayed at Riggs for 3 years, 1 year as an inpatient and another 2 years as an outpatient in residential apartments.

As an inpatient, Emily was told when to eat and sleep, and she attended group meetings. If she did not get her work jobs done or go to bed at the appropriate time, she lost privileges. Patients received medication at regular intervals. Her first therapist in the hospital was considerably different from her previous therapists. He took walks with Emily, drank wine with her and her roommate, and on one occasion put his arm around her waist. On the one hand, Emily craved his affection and attention; but on the other hand, she knew he was becoming inappropriately attached to her, and so she searched for a new therapist. She was fortunate enough to find Dr. Leslie Farber.

Dr. Farber's approach seemed radically different. He emphasized the presence of will in human behavior, and he communicated to Emily that he believed in her and her value. He shared with Emily anecdotes about his own life that were similar to her experiences and feelings. He treated her with warmth and understanding rather than aloofness or pity. He challenged her personal beliefs and highlighted her negative self-remarks. Emily felt as if she was being treated as a fellow human being. At Dr. Farber's urging, Emily studied for and passed her GED certification. She completed a few courses at the local college. Yet, she still had times of difficulty while an outpatient. She would hang out at the local bar, drink heavily, and wait to be picked up by men. She had many sexual partners. When Dr. Farber moved to New York to set up a practice, Emily followed. She found an apartment and a job and continued to meet with Dr. Farber. Through many years and many therapy sessions, Dr. Farber helped Emily "recover" her life and discover her "best self."

In her adulthood, Emily married, gave birth to a daughter, and went on to earn a bachelor's and a master's degree in English. She taught English at a local college and joined women's writing groups. She reentered therapy in her adulthood to cope with her emotional anger, neediness, and marital conflict, and at this time was diagnosed with depression. Since ending therapy, Emily has realized writing as a way to make sense of her thoughts, history and the world. She has written four books and has taught writing workshops at several U.S. universities.

As you can see, Emily experienced many stressors and did not effectively cope with them. Despite having money, she did not always receive effective help to learn coping. Her journey, detailed in one of her books, *Mockingbird Years: A Life In and Out of Therapy* (2000), highlights how biological, psychological, and social factors can influence our ability to function in a healthy or unhealthy way. As you read the chapters in this section, you will gain a deeper understanding of how stress and coping impact our health, the criteria for various mental health disorders, and the therapy techniques that can improve our functioning. As you are on this journey, think about your own behaviors. How do you cope with stress? How did you learn to do so? How might gaining insight into difficulty in functioning improve your own physical and mental health? By understanding stress and coping, mental health disorders, and therapy as an intersection of biological, psychological, and social factors, you hopefully will be able to recognize healthy and unhealthy patterns of functioning in yourself and the people around you, learn how to endure the difficult times, and be better able to weather the ups and downs of life.

Courtesy of Emily Fox Gordon

Emily Fox Gordon's novel, *Mockingbird Years*, highlights how biological, psychological, and social factors can influence our ability to function in a healthy or unhealthy way.

Health, Stress, and Coping

Learning Objectives

12.1 Define stress, and discriminate among the four types of stressors. (APA 1.1, 1.3)

12.1 Distinguish among the four types of conflict situations, and give examples of each. (APA 1.2, 1.3)

12.2 Discuss the role of cognitive appraisal in the biological stress response. (APA 1.2, 5.1)

12.2 Explain how the body responds to stress and how this physiological response may vary in males and females. (APA 1.1, 2.5, 3.2, 3.3)

12.2 Discuss how the stress response influences immunity to disease. (APA 1.2, 2.1, 5.1)

12.3 Distinguish between problem-focused and emotion-focused coping styles, providing examples of each. (APA 1.1, 1.2, 1.3)

12.3 Describe adaptive ways to manage stress, and explain how these techniques influence the stress response and one's health. (APA 1.3, 5.1)

12.4 Discriminate among Type A, Type B, and Type C personalities, and critically examine the research on the relationship between these personality types and health. (APA 1.1, 2.1, 3.2)

12.4 Define learned helplessness, and explain its influence on stress and health. (APA 1.1, 1.3, 5.1)

12.4 Explain the three factors of a hardy personality and its relationship to stress and coping. (APA 1.2, 3.2)

12.5 Identify health-defeating behaviors, and describe how alcohol use and smoking negatively influence health. (APA 1.2, 1.3, 5.1)

12.5 Discriminate among the various sexually transmitted infections, understanding their causes, modes of transmission, and treatment options. (APA 1.1, 1.2, 3.3)

12.5 Identify health-promoting behaviors, and apply how physical activity, eating habits, and sleep influence stress and health. (APA 1.3, 5.1)

12.5 Identify the five factors that contribute to happiness and well-being. (APA 1.3, 3.2, 3.3)

In this chapter, we'll explore the field of **health psychology.** Health psychologists study how a person's behavior, thoughts, personality, and attitudes influence his or her health for better and for worse. In this regard, health is seen as a result of the interaction among biological, psychological, and social forces highlighting a "biopsychosocial" approach introduced in the section opening (Brannon & Feist, 2004; S. E. Taylor, 2003). The main topics of this chapter are stress, coping, and health. We saw in this section's case study how the stress of Emily's home life and her difficulty at school, combined with her ineffective ways of coping, influenced her thoughts, behavior, and feelings of well-being. Because all of us cope with stress on a daily basis, this chapter offers much psychological research that will be relevant to your day-to-day living. We hope that you will be able to apply the information in this chapter to Emily's story as well as your own life and realize how personal habits, thoughts, and daily actions influence one's health. Hopefully, this analysis will encourage you to live a healthier, longer life!

12

Kathleen Finlay/Masterfile

Chapter Outline

12.1 What Is Stress? Stress and Stressors / 504

12.2 The Stress Response / 512

12.3 Coping with Stress / 518

12.4 Personality and Health / 525

12.5 Lifestyle, Health, and Well-Being / 529

PSYCHOLOGY APPLIES TO YOUR WORLD: Technology's Health Effects / 531

12.6 Integrating Psychology: The Big Picture / 537

12.1 What Is Stress? Stress and Stressors

health psychology the subfield of psychology that investigates the relationship between people's behaviors and their health

stress any event or environmental stimulus (stressor) that we respond to because we perceive it as challenging or threatening

life event a change in one's life, good or bad, that requires readjustment

You are running late for school and your car breaks down—today of all days, when you have a major project due in one class and a midterm in another. Or maybe you're a working parent, trying to get the kids off to school in the morning, when your youngest can't find her shoes and the dog just got into the garbage. Perhaps you have just fallen in love and have decided to make the relationship more serious. Or maybe you have grown dissatisfied with your relationship and are contemplating ending it. All of these situations have one thing in common: they all include *stress*, an inevitable and unavoidable fact of life.

Stress can be defined as any event or environmental stimulus (stressor) that we respond to because we perceive it as challenging or threatening. This definition implies three aspects to stress. First, we all encounter stressors—stimuli in our lives that we perceive as challenges or threats, such as traffic, an approaching midterm exam, or a hurricane. Second, our reactions to these stressors include bodily reactions. Third, by perceiving and then reacting, we cope with the challenges or threats (successfully or not, as we will see). This chapter explores these three aspects of stress.

Briefly reflect on an ordinary day in your life. You probably perceive many events or stimuli as provoking or annoying: a long line at the fast-food drive-through, a confrontation with your boss, or the need to do several errands in a limited amount of time. There probably have also been events in your life that you found to be particularly trying or traumatic, such as the death of a loved one, an unplanned pregnancy, or a termination from your job. Stressors come in all shapes and sizes. Emily's story illustrated several stressors: difficulty at school, conflicts with her father, frequent changes in schools and therapists. Psychological research classifies these stressors into four types:

- Major life events
- Catastrophes
- Daily hassles
- Conflict

Let's take a look at how each of these stressors is defined and explore the impact that they have on our health.

Image Source/Digital Vision/Getty Images

Life events, both good and bad, can be perceived as stressful and require us to adjust to them.

12.1.1 • Life Events: Change Is Stressful

How do we know which events in our life qualify as major, rather than minor, stressors when they all feel stressful? Believe it or not, psychologists have tried to measure this difference. Pioneering research by Thomas Holmes and Richard Rahe in 1967 set out to measure the impact of particular stressors on people's health. They asked a large sample group to rate **life events**, or changes in one's living, both good and bad, that require us to adjust to them. In other words, which life events did the respondents perceive as more or less stressful? From these ratings, Holmes and Rahe developed the Social Readjustment Rating Scale (SRRS), reprinted in • TABLE 12.1.

Holmes and Rahe assigned each major life event a numerical value, referred to as a *life change unit*. The higher the number, the more stressful this life event was rated by Holmes and Rahe's sample. Notice that the life events on the scale include positive as well as negative changes—for example, marriage, a new family member, and outstanding personal achievement. However, it is not just experiencing one of

TABLE 12.1

Holmes and Rahe's Social Readjustment Rating Scale

RANK	LIFE EVENT	LIFE CHANGE UNITS	RANK	LIFE EVENT	LIFE CHANGE UNITS
1	Death of spouse	100	23	Son or daughter leaving home	29
2	Divorce	73	24	Trouble with in-laws	29
3	Marital separation	65	25	Outstanding personal achievement	28
4	Jail term	63	26	Spouse begins or stops work	26
5	Death of a close family member	63	27	Begin or end school	26
6	Personal injury or illness	53	28	Change in living conditions	25
7	Marriage	50	29	Revision of personal habits	24
8	Fired at work	47	30	Trouble with boss	23
9	Marital reconciliation	45	31	Change in work hours or conditions	20
10	Retirement	45	32	Change in residence	20
11	Change in health of family member	44	33	Change in school	20
12	Pregnancy	40	34	Change in recreation	19
13	Sex difficulties	39	35	Change in church activities	19
14	Gain of new family member	39	36	Change in social activities	18
15	Business readjustment	39	37	Take out loan less than $20,000	17
16	Change in financial state	38	38	Change in sleeping habits	16
17	Death of a close friend	37	39	Change in number of family get-togethers	15
18	Change to different line of work	36	40	Change in eating habits	15
19	Change in number of arguments with spouse	35	41	Vacation	13
20	Take out mortgage or loan for major purchase	31	42	Christmas	12
21	Foreclosure of mortgage or loan	30	43	Minor violation of the law	11
22	Change in responsibilities at work	29			

Note: In Holmes and Rahe's Social Readjustment Rating Scale, each major life event is assigned a numerical value. The higher the number, the more stressful the life event is perceived to be. Add up the life change units for all those events you have experienced in the past year. Then compare your total to the standards indicated in the text.

Source: Reprinted with permission from T. H. Holmes & R. H. Rahe (1967), "The Social Readjustment Rating Scale," in the *Journal of Psychosomatic Research*, Vol. 11, No. 2, pp. 213–218. Copyright © 1967 Elsevier Science

these events that is at issue. Rather, it is reacting to several of these events within a year that Holmes and Rahe found may influence one's health.

ENGAGE YOURSELF! Take a moment to look at the Social Readjustment Rating Scale (Table 12.1). Add up the life change units for all those events you have experienced in the last year. Compare your total to the standards devised by Holmes and Rahe.

0–150	No significant problems
150–199	Mild life crisis
200–299	Moderate life crisis
300 or more	Major life crisis

Holmes and Rahe (1967) found that the higher people scored on the SRRS, the more prone they were to illness. Of those who scored within the mild life crisis range, 37% had experienced deteriorated health. This figure rose to 51% for those whose scores indicated they were experiencing a moderate life crisis, and 79% for those in the major life crisis range. Follow-up studies have supported Holmes and Rahe's findings (Gruen, 1993; Scully, Tosi, & Banning, 2000). If you scored high on the scale, you may want to consider adjusting your lifestyle in ways that reduce your chances of becoming ill. However, keep in mind that these are correlations and, as we discussed in Chapter 1, correlation does not mean causation. Life events do not directly cause illness, but they may make a person more vulnerable to illness and disease.

Subsequent research (Pearlin, 1993) evaluating Holmes and Rahe's scale indicates that the impact of these life changes is not simply a matter of how many of them one experiences. We need to take several other variables into account, including these:

- The voluntary or involuntary nature of the life change
- How desirable or undesirable the life change is perceived to be
- Whether the life change is scheduled or unscheduled

For example, when Emily's family moved, she had to change schools. This can be considered involuntary because she did not decide to move her family, undesirable as she would have to make new friends, and unforeseeable from a child's perspective. Consider as another example a couple about to break up. Typically, the partner who initiates the breakup feels less stress after she has informed her significant other of her decision. In this context, the breakup is seen as voluntary, desirable, and scheduled. At the same time, her partner may experience increased stress, as the dissolution of the relationship is involuntary (not of the partner's choosing), undesirable, and unscheduled. As this example illustrates, the amount of stress one experiences when faced with life changes may vary across people. We can consider Holmes and Rahe's scale as a rough index of how susceptible some people may be to illness, given the number of major stressors the person encounters.

You may have noticed that the scale has very few life events that are likely to be experienced by college students and younger people. The SRRS has been criticized for not adequately defining stress events among younger age groups. Yet research supports the notion that major changes—such as the breakup of a relationship, academic pressure, or even college itself—may influence the physical and mental health of college students (Crandall, Preisler, & Aussprung, 1992; Mohr et al., 2014). This is important because perceived stress also seems to predict how well students perform academically. High levels of perceived stress in college and medical students correlate with lower grade point averages (Maville & Huerta, 1997; Sohail, 2013). For example, in one survey of college students (ACHA, 2006), stress was the most frequent reason given for academic problems. You may find that the Undergraduate Stress Questionnaire (• TABLE 12.2) includes more of the stressors that you typically face than does Holmes and Rahe's SRRS. It was specifically designed to measure life event stress in college students. Undergraduates who have experienced more of these life events are more likely to report more physical symptoms and are less likely to report a positive mood (Crandall et al., 1992). It may therefore provide a more accurate assessment of your stress level and hence your susceptibility to illness.

TABLE 12.2

Undergraduate Stress Questionnaire

Have any of the following stressful events happened to you at any time during the past semester? If any has, check the space next to it. If an item has not occurred, leave it blank. Stressful life events are listed in descending order of severity. Students with more checkmarks are more likely to need health care than students with fewer checkmarks.

___ 1. Death (family member or friend)
___ 2. Had a lot of tests
___ 3. It's finals week
___ 4. Applying to graduate school
___ 5. Victim of a crime
___ 6. Assignments in all classes due the same day
___ 7. Breaking up with boy/girlfriend
___ 8. Found out boy/girlfriend cheated on you
___ 9. Lots of deadlines to meet
___ 10. Property stolen
___ 11. You have a hard upcoming week
___ 12. Went into a test unprepared
___ 13. Lost something (especially wallet)
___ 14. Death of a pet
___ 15. Did worse than expected on test
___ 16. Had an interview
___ 17. Had projects, research papers due
___ 18. Did badly on a test
___ 19. Parents getting a divorce
___ 20. Dependent on other people
___ 21. Having roommate conflicts
___ 22. Car/bike broke down, flat tire
___ 23. Got a traffic ticket
___ 24. Missed your menstrual period and waiting
___ 25. Thoughts about future
___ 26. Lack of money
___ 27. Dealt with incompetence at the Registrar's Office
___ 28. Thought about unfinished work
___ 29. No sleep
___ 30. Sick, injury
___ 31. Had a class presentation
___ 32. Applying for a job
___ 33. Fought with boy/girlfriend
___ 34. Working while in school
___ 35. Arguments, conflict of values with friends
___ 36. Bothered by not having family's social support
___ 37. Performed poorly at a task
___ 38. Can't finish everything you need to do
___ 39. Heard bad news
___ 40. Had confrontation with an authority figure
___ 41. Maintaining a long-distance boy/girlfriend
___ 42. Crammed for a test
___ 43. Feel unorganized
___ 44. Trying to decide on major
___ 45. Feel isolated
___ 46. Parents controlling with money
___ 47. Couldn't find a parking space
___ 48. Noise disturbed you while trying to study
___ 49. Someone borrowed something without your permission
___ 50. Had to ask for money
___ 51. Ran out of ink while printing
___ 52. Erratic schedule
___ 53. Can't understand your professor
___ 54. Trying to get into your major or college
___ 55. Registration for classes
___ 56. Stayed up late writing a paper
___ 57. Someone you expected to call did not
___ 58. Someone broke a promise
___ 59. Can't concentrate
___ 60. Someone did a "pet peeve" of yours
___ 61. Living with boy/girlfriend
___ 62. Felt need for transportation
___ 63. Bad haircut today
___ 64. Job requirements changed
___ 65. No time to eat
___ 66. Felt some peer pressure
___ 67. You have a hangover
___ 68. Problems with your computer
___ 69. Problem getting home when drunk
___ 70. Used a fake I.D.
___ 71. No sex in a while
___ 72. Someone cut ahead of you in line
___ 73. Checkbook didn't balance
___ 74. Had a visit from a relative and entertained him/her
___ 75. Decision to have sex on your mind
___ 76. Spoke with a professor
___ 77. Change of environment (new doctor, dentist, etc.)
___ 78. Exposed to upsetting TV show, book, or movie
___ 79. Got to class late
___ 80. Holiday
___ 81. Sat through a boring class
___ 82. Favorite sports team lost

Source: C. S. Crandal et al., "Measuring Life Event Stress in the Lives of College Students: The Undergraduate Stress Questionnaire (USQ)," in *Journal of Behavioral Medicine, 15*(6), pp. 627–662, © 1992. Reprinted with kind permission of Springer Science and Business Media.

12.1.2 • Catastrophes: Natural Disasters and Wars

Unexpected traumatic events or *catastrophes* that almost all people perceive as threats also qualify as stressors. Catastrophes may affect one's physical and mental health (Bonanno et al., 2010). After catastrophic events such as floods, earthquakes, hurricanes, tornadoes, or fires, people are generally more likely to experience depression or anxiety (Brende, 2000; Davidson, 2000; Dewaraja & Kawamura, 2006; Neria, Nandi, & Galea, 2008; Weems et al., 2007).

Tony Arruza/Encyclopedia/Corbis

Unexpected catastrophes or traumatic events also cause stress and can affect one's physical and mental health.

We have for a long time recognized the stress of war on soldiers, as evidenced by the various names we have given to the pattern of symptoms that some soldiers experience when they return. It was called *shell shock* in World War I, *battle fatigue* in World War II, and *posttraumatic stress disorder* (*PTSD*) following the Vietnam War and Operation Desert Storm. Soldiers often experience nightmares, flashbacks, and vivid memories as they relive their war experiences. They may evidence intense startle responses to loud noises and have difficulty concentrating and getting along with others. Rape victims report similar physical and psychological symptoms that may meet the criteria for what is referred to as *rape trauma syndrome*—more evidence that unexpected events may take their toll on one's health. Traumatic events and catastrophes are often involuntary, undesirable, and unscheduled, in that we typically don't have a lot of time to prepare for them; it is relatively easy to see how they might influence our health and well-being. We'll discuss PTSD in more detail in Chapter 13.

Do catastrophes or traumatic events always affect health negatively? Not necessarily. Some people exposed to disaster may show chronic dysfunction, yet many others show remarkable *resilience* (discussed shortly), experiencing only temporary distress (Bonanno et al., 2010). Moreover, research has documented a potential positive effect of stressful life experiences for some people, referred to as *posttraumatic growth* or *benefit-finding*. People report that these events have changed their lives in positive ways, such as building stronger relationships with others, emphasizing enjoyment in life, and initiating positive changes in health behaviors (Bower, Moskowitz, & Epel, 2009; Updegraff, Silver, & Holman, 2008). It seems that for some people, a severe life-threatening event provides an opportunity to reevaluate their lives and prompts them to initiate positive changes.

12.1.3 • Daily Hassles: Little Things Add Up!

daily hassles the everyday irritations and frustrations that individuals face

When psychologists evaluate the relationship between stress and health, they not only measure life changes and analyze the influence of catastrophes; they also evaluate the impact of everyday irritations and frustrations. These **daily hassles** also appear to play a role in our health. At times these irritants add to the stress of major life changes and catastrophic events, such as the daily planning for a wedding or getting stuck in traffic during an evacuation due to a natural disaster. But for most of us, the routine annoyances and frustrations we experience on a daily basis are stressful in themselves. Can you think of any examples of daily hassles? Waiting in lines, lack of money, losing your keys, or fights with loved ones are a few examples that may come to mind. Such daily hassles may in fact be the most significant source of stress, placing a great burden on our physical and mental health and on our relationships (Charles et al.,

2013; Lazarus, 1990; Repetti, Wang, & Saxbe, 2009). As the number of daily hassles increases, our physical and mental health tends to decrease (O'Connor et al., 2008; Sim, 2000). However, whether we perceive these frustrations as stressful is of prime importance in determining our susceptibility to illness. Some people easily shrug off these annoyances, whereas others find them particularly perturbing. Emily faced several daily hassles in school that she found upsetting and frustrating—difficulty learning, interactions with peers—which contributed to her upset stomach and rapid heartbeat.

Rubberball/Mike Kemp/Getty Images

Everyday irritations and frustrations increase our stress level and can influence our health.

VARIATIONS IN STRESS

Gender, race, age, socioeconomic status, sexual orientation, and education all seem to influence our perception of stress (Almeida, 2005; Dunkel Schetter et al., 2013; H. Taylor, 2002). Women are more likely than men to perceive stress from concerns about money, having a lot of things to do, health concerns, and trouble relaxing. In general, younger people report more daily hassles in their lives than older people. Those with more money and more education also report lower levels of perceived stress from daily hassles than do those with lower income and less education. Although people who make more money and have more education may lead full and hectic lives, they generally perceive that they have more control over their lives and report having more fun. They are less likely to experience hassles concerning their own health, illness of a family member, trouble relaxing, problems at work, and exposure to excessive noise than are people with less education and lower incomes.

Racial and ethnic differences also appear in reports on daily hassles. African Americans are more likely than Hispanic or European Americans to report economic hassles, exposure to noise, feeling lonely, and invasion of personal privacy as frequent day-to-day hassles. Hispanic Americans are more likely than European or African Americans to report problems with aging parents as a hassle of daily living. Some minorities and immigrants may experience *acculturative stress,* or the difficulties associated with adapting to a new culture (Hovey, 2000; Torres et al., 2012).

Prejudice and discrimination are unique sources of stress for members of racial and sexual minority groups termed *minority stress* and members of lower-income groups (called *social-class discrimination*) (Bernstein et al., 2011; D'Anna et al., 2010; Dunkel Schetter et al., 2013; Fuller-Rowell et al., 2012; McClure et al., 2010; Padela & Heisler, 2010). Anticipating being discriminated against or interpreting others' behaviors as discriminatory can increase stress in some people. They worry that their behavior will be interpreted in a way that confirms negative stereotypes. Such situations are potentially stressful and can influence people's physical and mental health. For example, lesbian, gay, and bisexual adults who experience high levels of minority stress report more health problems and poorer overall health than those who experience less minority stress (Hatzenbuehler, 2014; Lick, Durso, & Johnson, 2013). Such research illustrates the impact that our interactions with others can have on our physical and mental well-being.

RESILIENCE

As we have seen, considerable evidence indicates that negative life events, catastrophes, trauma, and daily stressors can have negative effects on physical and mental health. However, we also have reason to believe that under the right conditions, facing adversity can build **resilience** or adapting well to significant stressors. Resilience essentially conveys "bouncing back" from adversity.

resilience the capacity to adapt well to significant stressors

conflict a situation in which a person must choose between two or more needs, desires, or demands

approach–approach conflict a situation in which a person must choose between two likable events

Consider the situation of childhood poverty. Living in poverty is a significant source of stress. It may include housing problems, limited access to health care, fewer educational and employment opportunities, and/or limited economic resources for food, shelter, or the common necessities of life. Children raised in poor families tend to have elevated rates of medical problems later in adulthood (Cohen et al., 2010). Yet, remarkably, some of these children stay in good physical and mental health later in life and evidence high academic achievement despite their exposure to such challenges. What accounts for their resilience? The answer is quite complex.

Key factors in resilience may be related to biopsychosocial factors. For example, a child's temperament or internal locus of control may play a role. Family factors such as social support and maternal warmth and nurturance may buffer children from the harmful effects of poverty (Miller et al., 2011). Some research suggests that successfully recovering from significant stress especially early in life may strengthen health neural networks in our bodies such that we are less vulnerable or tougher to subsequent stressors later in life. In contrast, chronic, uncontrollable stress in childhood may weaken neural networks and alter immune system functioning such that one is more vulnerable to physical and mental health disorders in adulthood (Fagundes et al., 2013; Russell et al., 2014). Canadian psychologist Edith Chen (2012; Chen & Miller, 2012) proposes that some individuals from low socioeconomic conditions may develop *"shift-and-persist"* strategies that reduce their physical responses to the chronic stress they face, which then lessens their susceptibility to chronic disease. *Shifting* involves accepting stressors as uncontrollable and less threatening to reduce their emotional impact. *Persisting* involves enduring by finding meaning when times get tough and remaining optimistic about one's future.

Several investigations also indicate that experiencing moderate cumulative adversity is related to resilience. That is, people who are sheltered from experiencing adversity or experience a high amount of lifetime adversity are both more likely to report poorer physical and mental health and well-being compared to people who experience some or a moderate amount of lifetime adversity (Seery, 2011; Seery et al., 2013). Similar to the shift-and-persist model, Seery and his colleagues speculate that perhaps some adversity allows a person to generate the necessary biopsychosocial resources to prepare for subsequent stressors. Future research will hopefully shed more light on the nature and development of resilience.

12.1.4 • Conflict: Approach and Avoidance

Conflict, or having to choose between two or more needs, desires, or demands, can also place stress on us. Should you take the required science course or the required math course? Should you wear the blue or the gray suit to the job interview? Whether we perceive these options as positive or negative results in four basic forms of conflict (• FIGURE 12.1):

1. *Approach–approach conflicts.* The easiest conflict to resolve, and therefore the conflict that is accompanied by the least amount of perceived stress, is the **approach–approach conflict**, in which a person must choose between two

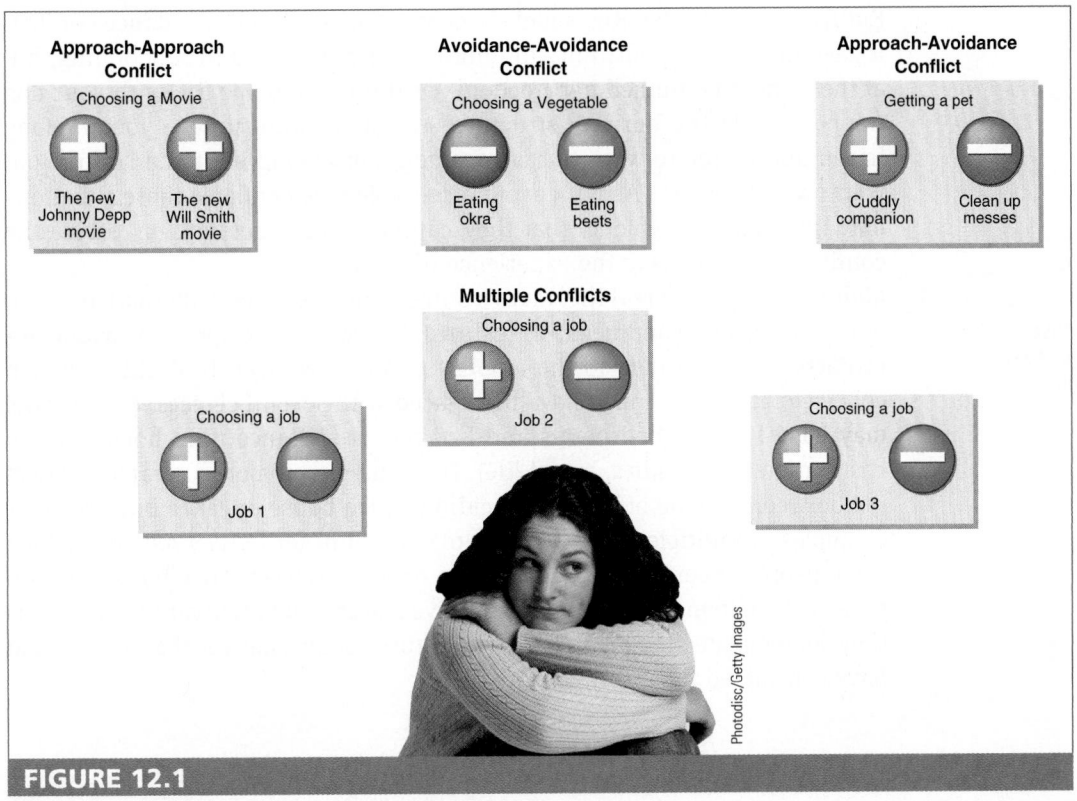

FIGURE 12.1

Four Common Conflict Situations

In an approach–approach conflict, a person must choose between two appealing choices—in this example, two movies one would like to see. In an avoidance–avoidance conflict, a person must choose between two undesirable choices—in this example, two disliked vegetables. In an approach–avoidance conflict, a person faces a decision that has both positive and negative features—in this example, owning a pet that cuddles yet also makes messes. Multiple conflicts involve several choices that have both positive and negative qualities—in this example, choosing among three jobs.

likable, or positive, events. Choosing between seeing an old friend who is passing through town or going out with someone you've been hoping would ask you out is an example of an approach–approach conflict. A more stressful approach–approach example could be liking and being challenged in your job and being offered another attractive and challenging position in the same company. In this type of conflict, you really can't lose because both options are favorable.

2. *Avoidance–avoidance conflicts.* The opposite of the approach–approach conflict is the **avoidance–avoidance conflict**, in which a person has to choose between two undesirable, or negative, events. You can think of this type of conflict as a Catch-22 situation. For example, do you spend the morning in line to register your car, or do you get your car towed because the registration has expired? Because both options in an avoidance–avoidance conflict are unappealing, many people remain undecided and inactive, or "frozen." They don't do anything. Consequently, avoidance–avoidance conflicts are accompanied by a greater degree of perceived stress than are approach–approach conflicts.
3. *Approach–avoidance conflicts.* Another stressful conflict to resolve is the **approach–avoidance conflict**, in which a person is faced with a desire or need that has both positive and negative qualities. He or she is drawn to the situation because of its positive features (approach), but is also repelled by and would rather not experience the negative aspects of the situation (avoidance).

avoidance–avoidance conflict a situation in which a person must choose between two undesirable events

approach–avoidance conflict a situation in which a person is faced with a desire or need that has both positive and negative aspects

Emily's stay at Austen Riggs had elements of an approach–avoidance conflict. It gave Emily the opportunity to improve her mental health functioning, but at the same time limited her freedom. Or think of a home fire with your dog trapped inside the burning structure. You don't want to lose your lifelong friend and therefore want to save the dog, but attempting to do so may put your own life at risk. As with avoidance–avoidance conflicts, these situations may immobilize people so that they cannot make a decision or resolve the conflict, which leads to the experience of stress.

multiple approach–avoidance conflict a situation that poses several alternatives that each have positive and negative features

4. *Multiple conflicts.* In real life, many conflicts involve several alternatives, each with both positive and negative features. These **multiple approach–avoidance conflicts** can contribute to the amount of stress we feel. In deciding which college to attend, you may have been faced with several choices. Each school may have had its good points and bad points (distance from home, tuition cost, program of studies, social life). Deciding on a major or a career, choosing between two job offers, and deciding which house or car to buy are other examples of multiple conflicts. This may account for *buyer's remorse,* which some people experience after making a major purchase. They bought, or approached, an item because of its attractive features but afterward felt regret as they contemplated the item's negative features or alternatives that they should have considered more seriously.

Quiz Yourself

12.1

1. You go to the dentist and find out that you have to get a tooth extracted. The only time the dentist can schedule your appointment is at the same time as a traffic court appointment. This situation is an example of a(n) _____.
   a. approach–approach conflict
   b. approach–avoidance conflict
   c. avoidance–avoidance conflict
   d. multiple conflict
2. Which of the following does the Social Readjustment Rating Scale consider the most stressful major life event for adults?
   a. A jail term
   b. Death of a spouse
   c. Divorce
   d. Pregnancy
3. Getting stuck in traffic on your way to a job interview is an example of a _____.
   a. daily hassle
   b. major life event
   c. catastrophe
   d. stress response
4. Which of the following are more likely to report problems with aging parents as a hassle of daily living?
   a. Asian Americans
   b. European Americans
   c. African Americans
   d. Hispanic Americans

Answers 1. c; 2. b; 3. a; 4. d

12.2 The Stress Response

Now that we have looked at the types of stressors that may influence health, we will examine the second feature of stress: the reactions that accompany stress. This analysis will further your understanding of the relationship between stress and health.

12.2.1 • Cognitive Appraisal: Assessing Stress

We all experience stressors, especially daily hassles. We all wait in lines, sit in traffic, and pay bills. Yet not all of us interpret these events as equally stressful. Some people view giving blood as less stressful than others. You may feel excited about giving a speech, whereas others cringe at the same prospect. Therefore, the first step in experiencing stress is how you think about or interpret an event or situation. Our initial interpretation of an event is called our **primary appraisal** (Lazarus, 1991, 1993). This primary appraisal can be irrelevant, positive, or stressful.

primary appraisal [uh-PRAY-zull] our initial interpretation of an event as irrelevant, positive, or stressful

If your primary appraisal of an event is *irrelevant,* you interpret the situation as unrelated to your happiness or safety. For example, the number of students in a particular course you are taking may not make a difference to you one way or another. Class size may be appraised as not relevant to your performance in the class, and therefore viewed as not stressful. Primary appraisals also can be *positive.* For example, you may take a class in which there is a small number of students and view this situation as something good. Again, we typically don't feel much stress in situations such as these. However, when we appraise a situation as *stressful,* we believe it will require a great deal of our emotional and psychological resources. For example, you may view a small class size as stressful if you fear speaking in front of a group and are expected to participate in class discussion.

Our primary appraisal of an event as stressful can lead to positive or negative emotions that either increase or decrease our perceived stress levels (Barlow, 2002; Bovin & Marx, 2011). How much stress we experience will depend on whether we see the situation as a threat, a harm, or a challenge. If we appraise a stressful event as *threatening,* we believe that the situation will cause us some harm in the future. When we interpret an event in this manner, we typically feel fear, anxiety, or anger—negative emotions that increase our stress levels and decrease our performance (Gildea, Schneider, & Shebilske, 2007). For example, having to give an oral presentation on a project later in the term may be perceived as threatening by a student. He may fear negative evaluations by the professor or other students or be anxious that his voice will crack or that he will stammer. If we appraise an event as *harmful,* we believe it will do us some damage or injury. For example, one of the authors of your textbook appraised putting holiday lights up on her house as stressful because she believed that getting on the roof of her house would lead to injury. Again, such appraisals typically lead to feelings of fear and anxiety that increase our feelings of stress. However, situations can also be appraised as *challenging,* as a means toward personal growth or personal gain. For example, taking a new job may be appraised as an opportunity for career growth, or getting married may be appraised as an opportunity to deepen and expand the nature of an intimate relationship. Challenge appraisals typically elicit positive emotions such as excitement and happiness, and are therefore perceived as less stressful.

Do you perceive an oral presentation as a threat or a challenge? A primary appraisal of threat will make you feel more stressed than viewing it as a challenge.

Tony Freeman/PhotoEdit

Not all primary appraisals break down easily into the categories of threat, harm, or challenge. A situation or event may involve a combination of appraisals. For example, starting a relationship, finding a job, and having a baby are complex situations that may involve appraisals of both threat and challenge. Also, the appraisal process is a personal one. Not everyone appraises the same situation in the same manner. For example, some students may perceive course exams as threats, whereas other students may see them as challenges.

Once you appraise a situation or event as a threat or a challenge, you must evaluate what can be done to cope with or manage the stressor,

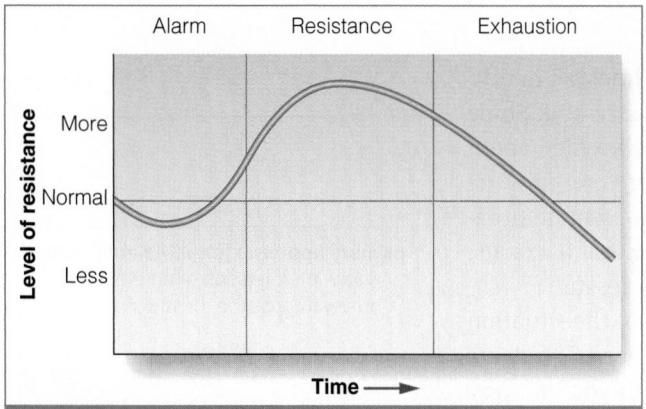

FIGURE 12.2

General Adaptation Syndrome

According to Hans Selye, the biological stress response consists of three phases. In the alarm reaction, the body releases chemicals to deal with a stressor. These chemicals lower the body's resistance. In the resistance stage, the body shores up additional resources to cope with the stressor. If the stressor persists, the body enters the exhaustion stage, in which bodily resources dwindle and we function at less than normal. Wear and tear on the body begin.

referred to as **secondary appraisal** (Lazarus & Folkman, 1984). In secondary appraisal, people take into account the resources available to cope with the stressor. It includes an assessment of how they might cope, if that strategy or behavior will be successful in managing the stressor, and the likelihood that they can actually produce the necessary coping behaviors and strategies (discussed later in the chapter). Primary appraisals of threat or challenge interact with secondary appraisals of coping options to influence one's overall feelings of stress. If these appraisals lead to feelings of stress, your body changes to deal with the stressor.

12.2.2 • Selye's General Adaptation Syndrome: The Body's Response to Stress

Many of us recognize stressful situations because of the bodily reactions that accompany them. For example, if you perceive giving a speech as a stressor, when faced with doing so, you may feel shaky, perspire more, feel your heart race, or even experience difficulty breathing. You may experience these same reactions when accepting an award or before an important job interview. These reactions are a part of a general bodily pattern termed the **general adaptation syndrome** (**GAS**; Selye, 1976). • FIGURE 12.2 shows the GAS as three phases that we all experience when we perceive a stressor in the environment: an initial *alarm reaction, resistance,* and *exhaustion.*

secondary appraisal an evaluation of resources available to cope with a stressor

general adaptation syndrome (GAS) the general physical responses we experience when faced with a stressor

alarm reaction the first phase of the general adaptation syndrome, characterized by immediate activation of the nervous and endocrine systems

ALARM REACTION

The **alarm reaction** consists of those bodily responses that are immediately triggered when we initially appraise an event as stressful. It is much like the car alarm that goes off the moment an intruder tries to open the car door. In the body, this involves activation of the nervous system and the endocrine system (• FIGURE 12.3).

Recall from Chapter 2 that your nervous system has two branches: the central nervous system, consisting of the brain and the spinal cord, and the peripheral nervous system, including the somatic and autonomic divisions. The autonomic division includes two systems: the parasympathetic branch, which operates when we are calm and relaxed; and the sympathetic nervous system, our fight-or-flight mechanism that prepares us to face a threat in the environment. This sympathetic branch of the nervous system is at the heart of the stress response.

When a person perceives a threat in the environment—or what we have now referred to as a stressor—the sympathetic nervous system is activated. In order to prepare the body to deal with the stressor, the sympathetic nervous system works in conjunction with the endocrine (or hormonal) system. It stimulates the adrenal gland to secrete two types of hormones: *adrenalin* and *corticosteroids.* These hormones travel to the major organs (liver, heart, lungs) to prepare the body for fight or flight. Our heart rate and blood pressure increase, our lungs expand, and our liver releases stored sugars that can be used for energy. At the same time, the brain stimulates the pituitary gland to release endorphins, the body's natural painkillers. The body continues to expend these resources for as long as the stressor persists. Once the stressor passes, the brain turns off the sympathetic nervous system, which in turn shuts off the release of these stress hormones, and the body returns to its parasympathetic mode of calm and relaxation. However, if the stressor continues, the body enters the resistance stage.

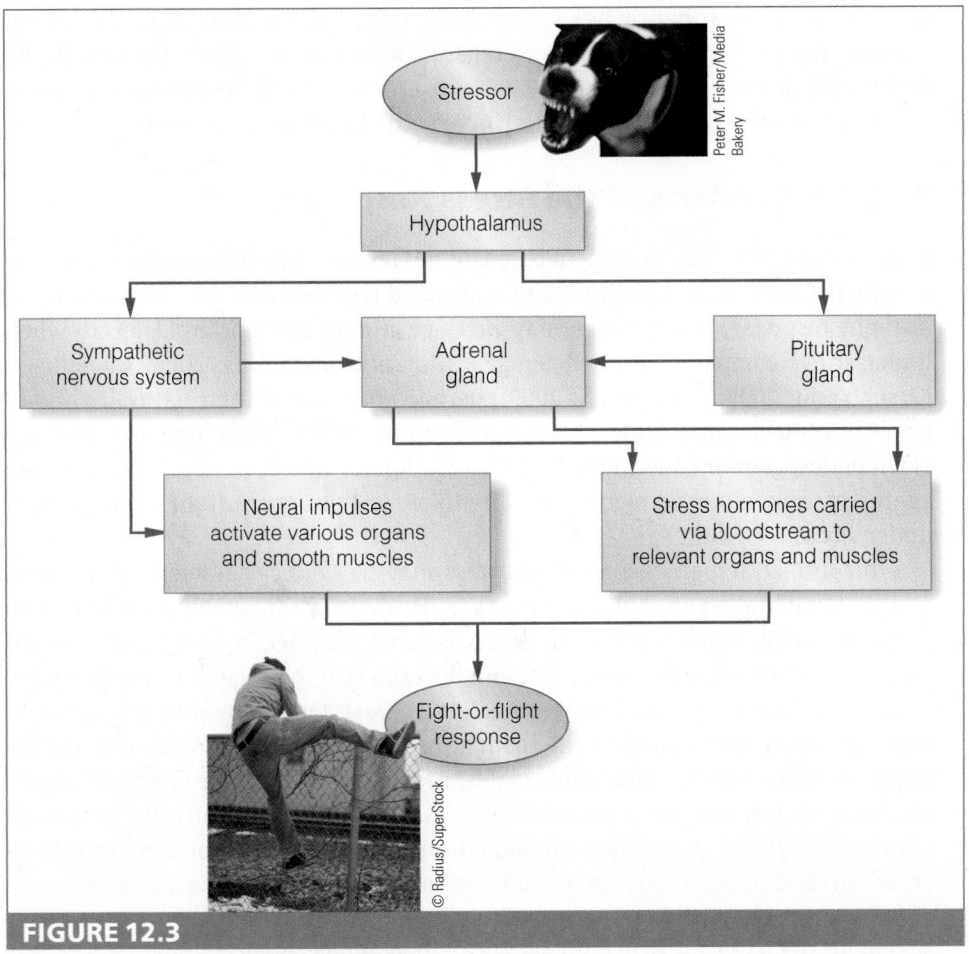

FIGURE 12.3

Biological Pathway of the Stress Response

When we perceive an event as stressful, the hypothalamus in the brain activates two systems: the sympathetic branch of the nervous system and the pituitary gland of the endocrine system. The nervous system sends neural messages to the major glands, organs, and muscles to prepare for fight or flight. At the same time, neural messages activate the adrenal gland to secrete the stress hormone adrenalin. The pituitary gland sends hormonal messages to the adrenal gland to secrete the stress hormones corticosteroids. The combined effects of these stress hormones prepare our bodies to face stressors.

RESISTANCE STAGE

During the **resistance stage**, the body continues its efforts to cope with the stressor. The sympathetic nervous system and endocrine system continue to be activated. However, the bodily reactions associated with resistance are less intense than the alarm reaction, as the body's resources begin to dwindle. When the body has drained its resources so that energy is no longer available, we enter the exhaustion stage.

resistance stage the second phase of the general adaptation syndrome, in which the nervous and endocrine systems continue to be activated

exhaustion stage the third and final phase of the general adaptation syndrome, in which bodily resources are drained and wear and tear on the body begins

EXHAUSTION STAGE

It is during the **exhaustion stage** that wear and tear on the body begins. High levels of adrenalin and corticosteroids in the body over a prolonged period of time damage the heart and lessen the effectiveness of the immune system. The result is that you become more vulnerable to heart disease, ulcers, high blood pressure, and colds and flus (Cohen, 1996; Kiecolt-Glaser et al., 2002; G. E. Miller & Blackwell, 2006; Rice, 2000). Excessive and prolonged exposure to stress hormones may also produce headaches, backaches, indigestion, constipation, diarrhea, fatigue, insomnia, mood swings, and muscle tension (Chou et al., 2007; De Benedittis, Lorenzetti, & Pieri, 1990; Nash & Thebarge, 2006). Recall Emily's spastic colon and rapid heartbeat when she had difficulty fitting in with her peers.

12.2.3 • Gender and the Stress Response

Evidence suggests that women and men do not respond physiologically to stress in exactly the same way. Although both males and females have the necessary fight-or-flight response, adult males may produce higher corticosteroid levels when under stress compared to adult females (Kajantie & Phillips, 2006; Kudielka & Kirschbaum, 2005; Wang et al., 2007), perhaps because of their naturally higher levels of testosterone (Girdler, Jamner, & Shapiro, 1997). These higher steroid levels in males, combined with the male's evolutionary role as protector, hunter, and aggressor, may motivate men to be more likely to fight or confront a threat when under stress.

In contrast, female responses to stress may be better characterized as "tend and befriend" rather than fight or flight (S. E. Taylor et al., 2000). In response to stress or threat, women are more likely to come together in groups, seek social support, and care for offspring. These behaviors may be related to the hormone *oxytocin,* which is released in response to at least some stressors and tends to have a calming effect on the fight-or-flight response. Estrogen, which is naturally higher in adult females than adult males, seems to enhance the effects of oxytocin, whereas testosterone seems to reduce its effects. Consequently, the enhanced effects of oxytocin in females, combined with the female's evolutionary role as child nurturer and gatherer, may motivate women to be more likely to seek social contact when under threat or stress (S. E. Taylor, 2006). Perhaps Emily's frequent sexual affairs were a way to connect with others when she was under stress. This is not to say that men do not or cannot tend and befriend, or that women do not or cannot fight or flee. Each gender just may be more specifically adapted to one response or the other in times of stress.

12.2.4 • Stress and the Immune System: Resistance to Disease

As we have seen, our body's reaction to stress, particularly during the exhaustion phase, can influence the effectiveness of our immune system. Researchers' interest in the connection between the immune system and stress has generated a new field of study called **psychoneuroimmunology**, which investigates the connections among psychology (behaviors, thoughts, emotions), the nervous system, and immune system functioning. The immune system is our body's best defense against illness because it fights and destroys bacteria, viruses, and other foreign substances that may invade our bodies. If this system is impaired, as in the case of prolonged stress, we are more prone to illness and disease (Fagundes, Glaser, & Kiecolt-Glaser, 2013; Kiecolt-Glaser, 2009; Webster Marketon & Glaser, 2008).

psychoneuroimmunology [sigh-ko-nur-o-im-ya-NAH-la-gee] the field of study that investigates the connections among psychology (behaviors, thoughts, emotions), the nervous system, and immune system functioning

immunosuppression [im-mew-no-suh-PREH-shun] the reduction in activity of the immune system

The corticosteroids and endorphins that are released into our body during the stress response actually reduce and dampen the activity of our immune system. This effect is referred to as **immunosuppression**. Consequently, turning on our stress response, which ensures our ability to survive immediate danger, comes at the expense of our immune system, our long-term survival mechanism.

Much research supports the notion that stress suppresses the functioning of the immune system, which then increases the chances of developing infections such as the common cold (Anderson, 2003; Kiecolt-Glaser et al., 2002; Rice, 2000). During final exam time and other periods of academic pressure, students show a weakened immune system (Chandrashekara et al., 2007; Gilbert et al., 1996). This may explain why you catch a cold or are more likely to experience allergies and sinus infections during finals week or when you have several projects or papers due at the same time. Immunosuppression also occurs in both men and women following the death of a spouse or partner (Beem et al., 1999; Schleifer et al., 1983) and in people going through separation and divorce (Kiecolt-Glaser & Glaser, 1992; Kiecolt-Glaser et al., 2003). People who are caregivers for someone with a terminal disease or dementia experience chronic stress that also results in immunosuppression (Damjanovic et al., 2007; Vitaliano, Young, & Zhang, 2004). Lower socioeconomic status and family chaos are related to higher stress hormones in children, which may increase their risk of later health problems (Bower, Crosswell, & Slavich, 2014; Chen, Cohen, & Miller, 2010).

More serious, though, is the correlation among stress, the immune system, and cancer. Most people's initial reaction to a cancer diagnosis is panic, anger, or depression—emotions that activate the stress response and momentarily retard immune system functioning (Ader, 2001). Moreover, our response and attitude toward having cancer may influence the eventual spread and fatality of the disease. For example, emotional distress in breast cancer patients is associated with a lower survival rate (Luecken & Compas, 2002; Osborne et al., 2004). Patients who express their emotions about the disease—both positive and negative—tend to have a higher chance of survival than patients who hold in their emotions (Lehto et al., 2006; Reynolds et al., 2000). Similarly, cancer patients with an optimistic attitude who are determined to beat the disease often outlive patients with a less positive attitude (Carver et al., 2000; Shen, McCreary, & Myers, 2004). Notice that this research does not say that stress *causes* cancer, but rather that stress may influence the rate at which cancer cells grow. If your immune system is functioning at reduced levels during times of stress, it is less available to fight these life-threatening cells.

We are by no means saying that surviving or not surviving cancer is totally up to the individual. The onset, course, and magnitude of cancer in patients are influenced by variables that include one's genetics, the type of cancer, when it is detected, social support, and the treatments available. Our attitude about developing cancer and receiving cancer treatment is only one factor among many to consider when examining the connection between stress and health. There is virtually no scientific evidence that our mental state *causes* cancer or that our mental state *cures* cancer.

We don't yet understand the exact relationship among stress, cancer, and immune system functioning. Current studies speculate that chronic stress leads to an imbalance in our immune system, in which some immune responses are suppressed while others are enhanced; it is this *disruption* of the normal balance in our immune system that increases our vulnerability to illness and disease (Robles, Glaser, & Kiecolt-Glaser, 2005; Segerstrom, 2007). Moreover, the

The Palm Beach/ZUMA Press, Inc./Alamy

Our attitude about developing cancer and receiving cancer treatment is only one factor among many to consider when examining the connection between stress and health.

exact nature of our physical response to stress depends on the frequency, intensity, and duration of the stressors and our cognitive appraisals or perceptions of those stressors (Costa-Pinto & Palermo-Neto, 2010; Kemeny, 2003). We look to future research to fill in the blanks and make our knowledge more complete.

Quiz Yourself 12.2

1. You are more vulnerable to illness during which stage of Selye's stress response model?
   a. Alarm reaction
   b. Resistance
   c. Rejuvenation
   d. Exhaustion
2. Immunosuppression refers to _____.
   a. the activation of the immune system when we are faced with a stressor
   b. a reduction in the activity of the immune system
   c. the immune system's ability to survive immediate danger
   d. the release of endorphins and corticosteroids to help the immune system function
3. Eniesha was shopping at the mall when she heard a person yelling angrily close by. Eniesha turned around to see who was yelling and saw that two adults were arguing. So, Eniesha went back to her shopping. In psychological terms, Eniesha just _____.
   a. made a primary appraisal
   b. made a secondary appraisal
   c. had an avoidance–avoidance conflict
   d. experienced stress
4. The stress response experienced by women may be better characterized as _____ in part due to the hormone called _____.
   a. "tend and befriend"; oxytocin
   b. "tend and befriend"; estrogen
   c. "fight or flight"; oxytocin
   d. "fight or flight"; estrogen

Answers 1. d; 2. b; 3. a; 4. a

12.3 Coping with Stress

Think of the exam or exams you will take for this course. Does your body evidence the telltale signs of the stress response when thinking about your exam? What do you do when faced with stress like this? Are you likely to react emotionally, becoming very anxious and worrying about what the test will be like? Are you likely to tackle the stressor directly, focusing all your energy on studying and preparing for the exam? Or do you simply ignore your stress, hoping for a miracle such as postponement or cancellation of the exam? Maybe you experience some or all of these reactions.

coping the behaviors that we engage in to manage stressors

Whatever you do to manage an event or stimulus that you perceive as threatening is part of **coping**. How we cope with stress influences the way stress affects us. We will discuss two broad types of strategies for coping: *problem-focused coping* and *emotion-focused coping* (Folkman & Lazarus, 1988). Some research suggests that females are somewhat more likely to use emotion-focused strategies and males are somewhat more likely to use problem-focused coping, but these gender differences are dependent on the nature of the stressor (Matud, 2004; Ptacek, Smith, & Dodge, 1994; Tamres, Janicki, & Helgeson, 2002). Anyone may use one or both types of coping when faced with a stressor. Each has its benefits and costs (Lazarus & Folkman, 1984; Roth & Cohen, 1986).

12.3.1 • Problem-Focused Coping: Change the Situation

problem-focused coping behaviors that aim to control or alter the environment that is causing stress

emotion-focused coping behaviors aimed at controlling the internal emotional reactions to a stressor

Problem-focused coping is aimed at controlling or altering the environment that is causing the stress. Let's say, for example, that you are working while going to school and your boss just increased your work hours. You now feel that you don't have enough time for school or your social life. A problem-focused approach to coping with this increased workload might be finding another job without as many required hours or reducing the number of credit hours you are taking in school. Both of these strategies are aimed at changing the situation to reduce the amount of perceived stress. One benefit of either of these problem-focused coping strategies would be elimination of the perceived stressor. At the same time, you benefit by experiencing more control over your environment, which may also enhance your self-esteem. However, it is also possible that you have misdiagnosed the problem, which is a cost of problem-focused coping. Maybe the number of work hours isn't affecting your college work as much as your motivation or your social schedule is. You may actually increase your long-term level of stress by choosing an inappropriate course of action. For example, reducing your college hours increases the time it will take to complete your college education. Alternately, changing jobs may result in lower wages, making it more difficult to pay for your education.

Generally, problem-focused coping tends to be most useful when we feel that we can actually do something about a situation (Folkman & Moskowitz, 2000). Under these circumstances, problem-focused coping is more likely to lead to a more positive health outcome (Largo-Wight, Peterson, & Chen, 2005; Penley, Tomaka, & Wiebe, 2002; Smith & Dust, 2006). However, when we do not feel that a situation is controllable, we often rely more on emotion-focused coping strategies (Lazarus, 1993).

12.3.2 • Emotion-Focused Coping: Change Your Reaction

Emotion-focused coping is aimed at controlling your internal, subjective, emotional reactions to stress. You either express your emotions or alter the way you feel or think in order to reduce stress. Stressors activate a variety of emotions, including anxiety, worry, guilt, shame, jealousy, envy, and anger. Because these emotions are usually experienced as unpleasant, we are motivated to release, reduce, or avoid them. Recall from the section case study Emily's emotion-focused coping. Her anger, panic, and depression were typical ways in which she reacted to the stress in her life. Or suppose that a young woman is anticipating the arrival of her partner at a party where they planned to meet, and he is already an hour late. The stress of this situation not only activates the physical sensations that we have discussed previously but also triggers emotional reactions. She may be angry with him because she feels that he is purposely ignoring her. She may take her anger out on a friend, or she may turn all of her emotional energy into being the life of the party. Conversely, she may experience anxiety and worry, fearing that something harmful has happened to him. When he arrives, she may express her anger by complaining about his lateness or ignoring him altogether, or she may

Jetta Productions/Getty Images

Taking your anger out on someone to relieve stress is an example of emotion-focused coping.

be especially loving and attentive. Either way, her coping behavior is directed at regulating the emotions that she is experiencing.

We attempt to lessen the effects of these negative emotions in two ways: by engaging in *cognitive reappraisal* and by using psychological *defense mechanisms*. **Cognitive reappraisal** is an active and conscious process in which we alter our interpretation of the stressful event. In the previous example, the young woman has appraised her partner's lateness in a negative manner (he's ignoring her or something bad has happened to him). These appraisals have led to feelings of anger and anxiety. She can reappraise or reinterpret his lateness in a more realistic manner—he got caught in traffic or he had to work late. These reappraisals are less likely to lead to negative emotional states. Thus, cognitive reappraisal can be an emotionally constructive way of coping with a stressful event (Gross, Halperin, & Porat, 2013; Jamieson, Mendes, & Nock, 2013; Mauss et al., 2007; Ray, Wilhelm, & Gross, 2008; Troy et al., 2010). In one study, positive reappraisal even led to less immunosuppression during a chronic stress period (Koh et al., 2006). Cognitive reappraisal is effective for regulating negative emotions when the perceived stressor is uncontrollable—when the only thing a person can control is his or her emotions. When stressors can be controlled, problem-focused coping (changing the situation) may be better (Troy, Shallcross, & Mauss, 2013).

cognitive reappraisal [re-uh-PRAY-zull] an active and conscious process in which we alter our interpretation of a stressful event

defense mechanisms unconscious, emotional strategies that are engaged in to reduce anxiety and maintain a positive self-image

A more automatic and unconscious way in which we lessen the effects of our emotions is by using **defense mechanisms**. Sigmund Freud was one of the first theorists to identify psychological defense mechanisms. Recall Freud's ideas on personality and coping in Chapter 11. Freud suggested that we use coping strategies unconsciously to reduce our anxiety and maintain a positive self-image and self-esteem. Because of these features, we now consider these defense mechanisms emotion-focused coping strategies. We use them to avoid or reduce the emotions associated with a stressor, but they do not necessarily eliminate the source of stress. For example, you might use the defense mechanism of *displacement* to deal with your anger toward a boss, a parent, or a significant other. You take your anger out on a friend by yelling at her, or on an object by throwing it against the wall. Afterward, you may *feel* better, but it does not resolve the issue that made you angry in the first place. The stressor is still present and may resurface again in the future.

Everyone uses defense mechanisms from time to time. Some of these defense mechanisms are adaptive. Directing your anger into a more constructive activity such as washing your car is more productive than hurting someone else (see "Sublimation" in • TABLE 12.3). Other defense mechanisms, especially when we use them to excess, can prevent us from developing effective ways of coping. For example, the student who fails to study for a test may decide that his roommate who watches television is at fault. Such a defense on the part of the student does not promote an adaptive way of coping with failure. The more common defense mechanisms are displayed in Table 12.3. See if you can identify the defense mechanisms that you tend to use.

The use of defense mechanisms involves costs and benefits. The main reason we use them is to restore our self-image. We also benefit because defense mechanisms reduce anxiety. They may also give us the confidence to handle additional stressors. However, the benefits of defense mechanisms are typically outweighed by the costs. Defense mechanisms often inhibit our ability to resolve a problem. Using our emotions to cope with stressors may impede our functioning in other daily activities—Emily's rages and panic often distanced her further from her friends and family. Most important, using

TABLE 12.3

Common Defense Mechanisms

DEFENSE MECHANISM	DEFINITION	EXAMPLES
Denial	Refusing to accept or acknowledge the reality of a situation or idea	Going out partying the night before an exam denies how this behavior will affect your exam performance. Having unprotected sex denies the possibility of an unwanted pregnancy or contracting an STI.
Rationalization	Devising a plausible reason or motive to explain one's behavior	You rationalize your excessive consumption of alcohol by saying it makes you more sociable or improves your personality.
Reaction formation	Engaging in a behavior or attitude that is at the opposite extreme of one's true motive or impulse	A young boy pulls the ponytail of the girl sitting in front of him, behaving aggressively to cover up the opposite emotion—liking her. After seeing someone at the mall whom you dislike, you approach and say warmly, "Hi. How have you been? You look great!"
Regression	Returning to an earlier stage of development in one's behavior, thinking, or attitudes	Adults who throw tantrums, pout, or whine are engaging in childlike behaviors. An older child may react to the birth of a sibling by wetting the bed or sucking her thumb again.
Sublimation	Directing emotions into an activity that is more constructive and socially acceptable	Some people exercise or clean their room when they are angry or upset. Others direct their emotions into writing, sculpting, music, or painting.
Repression	Excluding wishes, impulses, ideas, or memories from consciousness	A person may forget the details of an accident, crime, or other situation associated with trauma or harm.
Projection	Attributing one's own ideas, feelings, or attitudes to other people	You accuse another student of brown-nosing the professor when in reality it is you who engages in this behavior. A person in a relationship may accuse his partner of wanting to date other people when this is his own desire.
Displacement	Directing emotions toward a less threatening source	You yell at your partner after an argument with your boss. An athlete throws objects or kicks the bench after a missed play.

defense mechanisms keeps us in a state of unawareness as to the true source of any stress-related symptoms. Given these disadvantages, why do we continue to use defense mechanisms? Basically, they are easier and produce quicker results in reducing our feelings of anxiety. Unfortunately, these advantages are often at the expense of our well-being as we may experience more distress and negative mood over the long run (Littleton et al., 2007; O'Brien, Terry, & Jimmieson, 2008).

Emotion-focused coping is not *always* maladaptive. Intentionally expressing one's emotions in reaction to a stressor can be beneficial depending on the stressor, the environment, and the person (Bonanno & Burton, 2013; Stanton & Low, 2012; Tullett, Teper, & Inzlicht, 2011). Writing in a journal or expressing feelings with friends often helps people manage their responses to stressors—our next topic of discussion.

12.3.3 • Managing Stress: Applying the Research

Because stress affects our health, considerable research has addressed what strategies may reduce our risk of illness and disease. These techniques all focus on changing one or more aspects of the stress response. Many of these methods address both problem-focused and emotion-focused coping:

- *Exercise.* Some form of regular aerobic exercise, such as swimming, walking, or dancing, can be an effective strategy for reducing physical stress reactions (Huang et al., 2013; Langreth, 2000; Stear, 2003). Exercise reduces negative emotions such as depression and anxiety that we often feel in response to stress (Brugman & Ferguson, 2002; Long & van Stavel, 1995). Exercise raises energy levels, strengthens the heart, and lowers muscle tension. We sleep more soundly after exercise and also feel better as the body increases its production of natural mood elevators like serotonin and endorphins (Chapter 2).
- *Relax.* One of the most successful nonchemical ways to manage stress is through the application of relaxation techniques. Such methods may include **progressive relaxation training**, in which you learn to alternately tense and then relax each muscle group of the body in a systematic fashion. This activity gives you an awareness of when and where you feel tension when you're under stress. You then learn to manage and control the tension that you feel by relaxing on command. Other relaxation techniques may include regular massages, meditation, yoga, deep breathing exercises, engaging in a hobby, or listening to music. Daily use of relaxation procedures are effective in lessening symptoms of asthma, insomnia, headaches, rheumatoid arthritis, high blood pressure, chronic pain conditions, intestinal problems, and chronic anxiety (Astin, 2004; Fumal & Schoenen, 2008; Hughes et al., 2013; Lebovits, 2007; McCallie, Blum, & Hood, 2006; Ostelo et al., 2007). Relaxation techniques also have been helpful in reducing anxiety and stress levels of cancer patients (Isa et al., 2013; Song et al., 2013).
- *Develop social support.* As social animals, humans are motivated to maintain social connections with others. Having friends, a shoulder to cry on, or someone to discuss an issue or trying event with are all examples of **social support**—having close and positive relationships with others. Social support buffers the effects of stress (S. Cohen et al., 2003; Diener & Seligman, 2004; Shields, 2004; Uchino, 2009). Family stability, a partner's support, or simply having friends to confide in is related to a longer life span, as well as a longer survival rate for those with cancer or heart disease (Antoni & Lutgendorf, 2007; Cohen & Janicki-Deverts, 2009; Hawkley & Cacioppo, 2007; Holt-Lunstad, Smith, & Layton, 2010). Even giving social support to others appears to buffer the effects of stress (Brown et al., 2003). Social support also may act to decrease the release of stress hormones and reduce stress-induced immune responses (Eisenberger et al., 2007; Fagundes et al., 2011; Koh et al., 2006; Pietromonaco, DeBuse, & Powers, 2013). Yet cultural norms influence the appropriateness of seeking and using social support networks. For example, Asians and Asian Americans are less likely to ask directly for emotional support in times of distress as it is more likely to be viewed negatively in their culture (Kim, Sherman, & Taylor, 2008; Sherman, Kim, & Taylor, 2009).

  The impact of social support on health can also be seen in the research on loneliness. Feeling lonely or socially rejected, as Emily did,

progressive relaxation training a stress management technique in which a person learns how to systematically tense and relax muscle groups in the body

social support having close and positive relationships with others has a major impact on health and well-being (DeWall & Bushman, 2011; Hawkley & Cacioppo, 2010; Jaremka et al., 2013). Higher levels of loneliness, smaller social networks, or experiencing social rejection have been found to be associated with higher levels of cortisol (a corticosteroid secreted during the stress response), a lower antibody response to flu shots, and poorer immune system functioning. High levels of cortisol are not good for one's health. Poor antibody response means the body's immune system produces fewer protective antibodies and puts the person at greater risk for illness (Pressman et al., 2005).

Leonora Hamill/Stone/Getty Images

Having close relationships with others helps us weather stress.

- *Be spiritual.* Spiritual faith, prayer, church or temple membership, and strong value systems may promote physical health and well-being for *some* people (Inzlicht & Tullett; 2010; McCullough et al., 2000; McIntosh et al., 2011; Miller & Thoresen, 2003; Powell, Shahabi, & Thoresen, 2003). Spirituality often means having a purpose in life, self-awareness, and connectedness with self, others, and a larger community. Religiousness is typically defined as participation in an institutionalized doctrine. For example, several studies have found that prayer and spirituality are associated with reduced symptoms of distress in cancer patients (Laubmeier, Zakowski, & Bair, 2004; Lynn, Yoo, & Levine, in press; Taylor & Outlaw, 2002). Religiousness and spirituality have also been shown to be significantly associated with reduced symptoms in people with serious mental illness (Corrigan et al., 2003). One study found a relationship between prayer and better health, but only among less educated and, to a lesser extent, lower-income people (Banthia et al., 2007). Recall Emily's desire for spiritual and emotional connections; resources that may have helped her well-being.

Religion, spirituality, and health are correlated. We cannot conclude that religiousness or spirituality *causes* better health. Which, if any, specific religious or spiritual factors enhance or undermine health and well-being remains unclear (Jordan et al., in press). One must also consider the importance of religion and spirituality within one's culture (Masters & Hooker, 2013). Many of the studies have significant methodological flaws, and they define religion and spirituality in a variety of ways (Hill & Pargament, 2003; Schreiber & Brockopp, 2012; Sloan & Bagiella, 2002). As more sound research is conducted, psychologists may be able to uncover the distinct contribution of religion and spirituality to health and well-being.

- *Imagine a calm environment.* **Guided imagery** is a technique in which you learn to use your mind to achieve a state of relaxation. You imagine that you are in a safe, pleasant, calming environment, perhaps walking along a beach or in a forest. You maintain your focus on this image as you feel the tensions associated with stress leave your body. Similar to progressive relaxation, you become trained to automatically summon up this image when you feel stressed. For some people, guided imagery is just as effective as the relaxation techniques discussed previously (Astin, 2004). Can you think of your own image, scene, or memory that would provide these benefits for you? How does your body feel as you think about it?

guided imagery a technique in which you focus on a pleasant, calming image to achieve a state of relaxation when you feel stressed

Joachen Schlenker/Masterfile

The stress management technique of guided imagery involves using your mind to achieve a state of relaxation. Whenever you feel stressed, you focus on a pleasant, calming environment like the image shown here to relieve bodily tensions and promote relaxation.

meditation mental exercises in which people consciously focus their attention to heighten awareness and bring their mental processes under more control

- *Meditate.* **Meditation** in the form of yoga, Zen, mindfulness, or transcendental meditation also may reduce tension and anxiety caused by stress (Grossman et al., 2004; Holzel et al., 2011; Hughes et al., 2013; Paul et al., 2007). These practices are mental exercises in which people consciously focus their attention on thoughts, emotions, or body sensations to heighten awareness. The person sits in a comfortable position with her eyes closed and silently focuses her attention on a specially assigned word that creates a resonant sound or on a bodily state such as her breathing. Meditation appears to decrease heart rate, respiration, and oxygen consumption (Carrington, 1993; Tang et al., 2009). Some studies have also found that meditation can improve mood, lessen tiredness, and enhance immune system response (Fan et al., 2010; Moyer et al., 2011; Rosenkranz et al., 2013; Solberg, Halvorsen, & Holen, 2000). Isolating the key element common to the different meditation practices may help us draw more solid conclusions on the specific health benefits of meditation (Xiong & Doraiswamy, 2009).
- *Be optimistic.* Simply expecting good things to happen may influence your health. For example, in a study on first-year law students, those students who endorsed optimistic beliefs, such as believing they could succeed and having confidence about their abilities, had better immune system functioning at mid-semester than did students with a more pessimistic outlook (Segerstrom & Sephton, 2010). Optimists report lower stress levels and have fewer stress-related physical complaints (Finkelstein et al., 2007; Peterson & Bossio, 2001; Pritchard, Wilson, & Yamnitz, 2007). Optimists also evidence lower levels of the stress hormone, cortisol, upon awakening than pessimists (Endrighi, Hamer, & Steptoe, 2011; Jobin, Wrosch, & Scheier, 2014). Cancer and heart disease patients with an optimistic attitude often show a better response to treatment than patients with a less positive attitude (Carver et al., 2000; Shen et al., 2004). Focusing on the half of the glass that is full is better for your health than focusing on the half that is empty.
- *Laugh.* Laughter promotes relaxation, which may explain why good-humored people perceive less stress when faced with life's challenges (Lefcourt, 2001; Lefcourt & Davidson-Katz, 1991). Laughter may buffer stress by reducing blood pressure, increasing deep breathing, boosting the immune system, increasing feelings of well-being, and raising energy levels (Bennett et al., 2003; Christie & Moore, 2005). Any one or all of these factors may be responsible for the positive health effects. Even smiling through stress has been linked to lowered levels of heart rate during stress response recovery (Kraft & Pressman, 2012), giving credence to the saying "Grin and bear it."
- *Manage your time wisely.* Many of us experience stress because we feel that there is not enough time to accomplish all the tasks, errands, and work that we have established for ourselves. Feelings of time pressure can negatively affect our health and well-being (Menzies, 2005). One way to minimize the stress resulting from such pressures is to organize your time better. Keeping a daily planner, electronic calendar, or formal time schedule to record your obligations, commitments, and deadlines for study, work, and leisure activities can ease tension. Keeping a formal time schedule also allows you to evaluate the number and importance of your commitments. One of the most common time management mistakes that college students make is not allowing enough time to study all of the

assigned material (Buehler, Griffin, & Ross, 1994; Jacobs & Hyman, 2013). The key to effective time management is to treat each responsibility—whether work, study, or play—as a serious commitment.

By using these methods, you have the opportunity to reduce the ill effects of stress on your health right now, as well as the cumulative effect of stress on your body in the future. However, if you sometimes feel that you cannot manage the stress in your life, or you aren't coping well with your stressors, then it may be time to seek professional help. Chapter 14 describes the different types of mental health professionals who can help us cope more effectively.

12.3

Quiz Yourself

1. Organizing your time better would be best classified as a(n) _____ coping skill.
   a. problem-focused
   b. emotion-focused
   c. avoidance-focused
   d. encounter-focused
2. It is common for young children to react to the birth of a sibling by regressing to earlier behaviors such as sucking their thumb again or wanting to feed from a bottle. Such behaviors exemplify _____ coping skills.
   a. problem-focused
   b. emotion-focused
   c. avoidance-focused
   d. encounter-focused
3. Which of the following is the *least* effective stress management technique?
   a. Guided imagery
   b. Physical exercise
   c. Defense mechanisms
   d. Relaxation techniques

Answers 1. a; 2. b; 3. c

12.4 Personality and Health

Health psychologists have also been interested in how personality influences our health. A number of personality dimensions have been related to health—specifically, to the functioning of our cardiovascular and immune systems (Segerstrom, 2000; T. W. Smith, 2006). We consider three such avenues of research here: the *Type A personality, learned helplessness,* and the *hardy personality.*

12.4.1 • Type A Personality: Ambition, Drive, and Competitiveness

Take a moment to look at •TABLE 12.4. Which of these descriptions most accurately reflects your personality? Would you consider yourself more of a **Type A personality**, a person who is aggressive, competitive, and driven to achieve? Do you characterize yourself as more of a **Type B personality**, a person who is more relaxed, easygoing, patient, and flexible? Or do you consider yourself more like a **Type C personality**, describing a person who is cautious, careful, overly patient and nice, and who avoids conflict and suppresses negative emotions such as anger? Emily's father probably fit the Type A description more than the Type B or Type C.

Type A personality a personality that is aggressive, ambitious, and competitive

Type B personality a personality characterized by patience, flexibility, and an easygoing manner

Type C personality a personality that is cautious, serious, sensitive to criticism, and results oriented, and that suppresses negative emotions such as anger

TABLE 12.4

The ABCs of Personality: Which Type Are You?

TYPE A	TYPE B	TYPE C
 © iStockphoto.com/repinanatoly	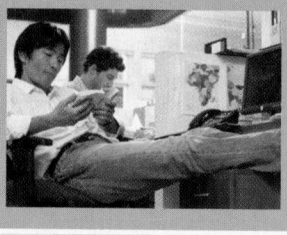 Christopher Robbins/Digital Vision/Getty Images	 Image Studios/UpperCut Images/Alamy
Competitive	Easygoing	Cautious
Verbally aggressive	Calm	Careful
Overcommitted to achieving	Relaxed	Detached
Impatient	Patient	Introspective
Hostile attitude when frustrated	Trusting	Sensitive to criticism
Sense of time urgency	Good-natured	Serious
Workaholic	Lower need for achievement	Results oriented
Easily angered	Supportive	Suppressed emotion

At one time, having a Type A personality was considered a risk factor for heart disease. Cardiologists Meyer Friedman and Ray Rosenman (1974) were the first to examine the connection between personality and heart disease. They suspected that personality or behavior patterns might play a role in the lives of men who were more likely to develop heart disease or more likely to die from a heart attack. To test their idea, the researchers gathered a sample of 3,000 men between the ages of 35 and 59 with no known health problems. Each man was interviewed, and based on his behavior during the interview, each was designated as a Type A personality, a Type B personality, or somewhere in between. A label of Type A or Type B was given to those men who very much exemplified those traits listed in Table 12.4. The majority of the sample fell somewhere in between, but in comparing the two types, Friedman and Rosenman found that over the next decade, those with Type A personalities were two to three times more likely to suffer a heart attack. Keep in mind that the majority of the sample could not easily be categorized as either Type A or Type B.

Friedman and Rosenman's landmark study stimulated additional research on how personality factors may place people at risk for disease. However, subsequent research on the connection between Type A personality and the risk of heart disease has not been able to replicate these results (Booth-Kewley & Friedman, 1987; T. Q. Miller et al., 1991).

Later research attempted to isolate which specific aspects of the Type A personality might predispose a person to heart problems. The key features include anger, mistrust, and hostility. People who are frequently angry, suspicious, bitter, antagonistic, and distrustful of others seem more likely to experience heart-related health problems and have a shorter life span (Deary, Weiss, & Batty, 2010; Mommersteeg & Pouwer, 2012; B. W. Roberts et al., 2007; T. W. Smith et al., 2004).

People with a Type A personality who do not show these specific behaviors appear to be no more at risk for heart disease than their Type B counterparts.

Research on the Type C or cancer-prone personality has proceeded in a similar fashion. That is, at one time, having a Type C personality was suggested as a major factor in the development of cancer, specifically breast cancer in women (see Scheier & Bridges, 1995, for review). However, subsequent research suggests that it is the suppression or denial of anger, one specific aspect of the Type C personality, that may put a woman more at risk for breast cancer. There is little evidence for a so-called cancer-prone personality, yet a modest to weak relationship has been found between not expressing one's negative emotions and the risk of breast cancer (Bleiker et al., 2008; Butow et al., 2000; McKenna et al., 1999).

12.4.2 • Learned Helplessness: I Can't Do It

Do you believe that you have no control over stressful life events? Do you believe that even your best efforts will result in failure? When you blame yourself for any failure you experience, are you more likely to attribute your failure to a specific factor—you're just not good at soccer—or to a more global feature—you're just too uncoordinated to do any athletic activity? These questions illustrate the key features of a personality factor called **learned helplessness**, in which people develop a passive response to stressors based on their exposure to previously uncontrolled, negative events.

learned helplessness a passive response to stressors based on exposure to previously uncontrolled, negative events

Learned helplessness was first demonstrated in dogs in a psychological laboratory (Seligman & Maier, 1967). The dogs were placed in a cage that was equipped with an electrified grid. When the dogs received a shock they could not escape from, after repeated trials, the dogs' escape responses slowly decreased. Recall from Chapter 6 that this decrease in responding is called *extinction*. Even when they were later given the opportunity to escape the shock, the dogs remained in the cage. The dogs had learned to be helpless. Experiments using human participants (not using shock) have produced similar results (Hiroto, 1974; W. R. Miller & Seligman, 1975). Consequently, when previous experiences lead you to believe that you cannot "fix" the problems facing you, you may approach new situations with this perceived lack of control and passively endure whatever comes your way (Dweck, Chiu, & Hong, 1995; Peterson, Maier, & Seligman, 1993). You are likely to view stressors as threats rather than as challenges. As a result, your levels of stress increase, and you are more likely to develop stress-related physical illnesses (Overmier, 2002; Stern, Dhanda, & Hazuda, 2009). Remember Emily's failures at school and her resulting feelings of hopelessness. It is possible that her attitude of learned helplessness contributed to her emotional distress.

Digital Vision/Getty Images

If you fail an exam, do you go and get help, or do you just assume that you'll never understand the material and withdraw from the class? Expecting to fail and believing you have no control over the outcome of events are key qualities of learned helplessness.

Research supports the notion that college students who feel helpless are less likely to persist and more likely to give up easily; as a result, they earn poor grades and report unhappiness

(Fazio & Palm, 1998; McKean, 1994). Adults and adolescents (like Emily) who react to stress by feeling at a loss to do anything about the situation are more prone to depression and other stress problems (Diener et al., 2009; Rotenberg et al., 2012; Waschbusch et al., 2003). Learned helplessness has also been documented in children with a history of reading failure (Fowler & Peterson, 1981). It can develop in elderly people in nursing homes who are not given choices about their daily activities and routines (Seligman, 1989). In all these situations, the *expectation* of failure and lack of control is what influences one's perceived level of stress, one's subsequent response to stress, and ultimately, one's mental and physical health.

12.4.3 • The Hardy Personality: Control, Commitment, and Challenge

Do you view stressors as challenges or as threats? For example, if you try out for the tennis team one year and don't make it, do you try out again the next year, or do you simply give up? Do you stay committed to the pursuit of your goals and values? If you fail an exam, do you get help, or do you just assume that you'll never understand the material and withdraw from the class? Do you believe that your actions influence the outcome of a situation? Your answers to these questions outline three factors that appear to be related to health: challenge, commitment, and control.

hardy personality a personality, high in the traits of commitment, control, and challenge, that appears to be associated with strong stress resistance

- The tendency to see life as a series of *challenges*
- A sense of personal *commitment* to self, work, family, and other values
- A perception of *control* over life and work

These "three Cs" taken together were labeled by psychologists Salvatore Maddi and Suzanne Kobasa (1984) as the **hardy personality**.

This term resulted from Kobasa's (1982) research on upper-level executives and attorneys who had experienced considerable stress over a 3-year period. Those who exemplified hardy traits were less likely to get ill during this time of stress. Even Type A people who scored high on measures of hardiness were less likely to get ill than Type A people who scored low on hardiness. This observation led Kobasa to conclude that hardiness traits may decrease stress levels, thereby decreasing one's chances of developing illness.

© s_bukley/Shutterstock.com

After surviving being kidnapped and held captive for 9 months at the age of 14, Elizabeth Smart still perceives life as a challenge. She testified against her kidnappers and is now an activist fighting human trafficking and sex crimes against children. She exemplifies the three traits of a hardy personality.

Psychological research confirms that hardy people seem to be unusually resistant to stress (Bonanno, 2004; Maddi, 2005). They endorse a positive worldview in which stressors are appraised as challenges rather than threats, so they feel less potential harm from them. Notice that these qualities are in direct contrast to learned helplessness. This positive attitude appears to promote more problem-focused coping, enabling such people to handle conflict better and be more willing to rely on the help of others when weathering stress (Maddi et al., 2006; Scheir & Carver, 1992). Hardy people also report higher levels of personal satisfaction with their work (Rush, Schoel, & Barnard, 1995) and show greater immune system responses to bacteria (Dolbier et al., 2001).

What does all this research on personality tell us? First, we can recognize that how one expresses negative emotions such as anger and hostility can influence one's health. Frequent anger and hostility as well as suppressing one's negative emotions do not promote good health. Similarly, negative cognitions such as expecting failure or a lack of control do not appear to be good for our health. In contrast, the three Cs of hardiness—a sense of control, being comfortable with challenge, and maintaining commitment—appear to be most beneficial to our ability to deal with stress and therefore most advantageous to our health.

12.4

Quiz Yourself

1. Donald is described by his friends as easygoing, calm, and patient. Donald would most likely be classified as a _____.
   a. Type A personality
   b. Type B personality
   c. Type C personality
   d. learned helpless personality
2. Which of the following personality factors has been strongly linked to depression and other stress problems?
   a. Type A traits
   b. Type B traits
   c. Hardiness
   d. Learned helplessness
3. After working on a project for more than 3 years, Zilmarie is told by her boss to redesign the project in a new way. Zilmarie considers such a task a challenge and commits herself to the new project with gusto. Zilmarie is probably high on which personality dimension?
   a. Type A personality
   b. Optimism
   c. Hardiness
   d. Type C personality

Answers 1. b; 2. d; 3. c

12.5 Lifestyle, Health, and Well-Being

Health psychologists also examine lifestyle and environmental factors that may play a role in our susceptibility to illness and disease. Considerable research has examined voluntary lifestyle behaviors that put us at higher risk for illness and disease. However, lifestyle choices can also benefit our physical and mental health. Consistent with this view, research over the past decade in the field of *positive psychology* describes those factors that contribute to happiness and well-being (Ruark, 2009; Wallis, 2005).

12.5.1 • Health-Defeating Behaviors

We already have seen that high levels of stress may increase your chances of illness. Some of these events may or may not be under your control. Health psychologists define **health-defeating behaviors** as those behaviors that increase the chance of illness, disease, or death. They include risky behaviors such as driving at excessive speeds or while texting, carrying a weapon, or being a passenger in a car with a driver who is under the influence of drugs or alcohol. Risky behaviors endanger your health because you place yourself in a situation in which you have a higher risk of physical injury.

In fact, many of the leading causes of death are related to unsafe health practices (• FIGURE 12.4). The top four leading causes of death—heart disease, cancer, lower respiratory diseases, and stroke—have been linked to personal habits that damage our health. We will examine behavior patterns, usually engaged in over a long period of time, that are controllable and that seriously put your health at risk. These behaviors include alcohol consumption, smoking, distracted driving, and unsafe sex practices that can lead to contracting a sexually transmitted infection (STI). Notice that Emily engaged in many of these health-defeating behaviors.

health-defeating behaviors behaviors that increase the chance of illness, disease, or death

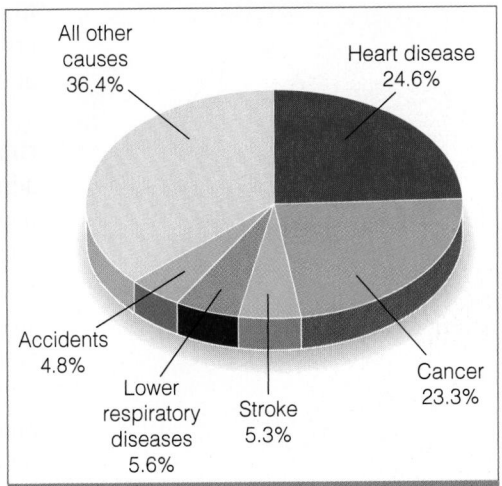

FIGURE 12.4

Leading Causes of Death in the United States

In 2009, heart disease, cancer, respiratory diseases, stroke, and accidents were the top five causes of death in the United States. The top two causes of death, heart disease and cancer, were the same for males and females and for Whites, Blacks, and American Indians; for Asian/Pacific Islanders, cancer was the leading cause of death with heart disease second. Many of these deaths could have been prevented by engaging in better health practices.

Source: *National Vital Statistics Report*, Vol. 61, No. 7, 2012.

ALCOHOL

Recall from Chapter 4 the specific effects that alcohol has on the body and brain. These effects can be seen within a larger context by examining the social and physical ramifications of alcohol abuse on people's health and well-being. Consider that the majority of manslaughter convictions, assaults, and domestic violence incidents involve alcohol. Nearly half of all U.S. highway deaths involve alcohol. Fetal alcohol syndrome (FAS), caused by a mother's excessive ingestion of alcohol during pregnancy, is the leading preventable cause of intellectual disability. In one national survey (Johnston et al., 2013), 22% of high school seniors admitted to binge drinking in the past 2 weeks, despite being underage. For college men and women, the rate is even higher.

Alcohol abuse not only leads to social problems but is also associated with major health problems, including heart disease, stroke, cancer, liver disease, memory blackouts, and erectile dysfunction in males. These statistics convey the drastic impact that alcohol abuse has on our nation's health and suggest that alcohol should be used only in moderation, if at all.

SMOKING

Another easily preventable behavior is cigarette smoking. Recall from Chapter 4 that nicotine affects several neurotransmitters in the brain that act as stimulants, increasing arousal, feelings of pleasure and reward, and metabolic rate, which is why smokers tend to be thinner than nonsmokers. However, in high doses, nicotine causes vomiting, diarrhea, sweating, and dizziness. Most first-time users report nausea and dizziness from smoking cigarettes. Yet users quickly develop nicotine dependence and cravings for cigarettes (J. E. Rose et al., 2007).

In some developing countries, smoking is the norm. In the United States, smoking has declined over the past 30 years, yet 21.5% of adult men and 17.3% of adult women still smoke; American Indian/Alaska Native and multiracial adults have the highest rates of tobacco use (Schiller et al., 2012). Rates are lower among adults aged 65 and older, perhaps because many longtime smokers die (CDC, 2009a). Level of education and income level also differentiate smokers from nonsmokers, with people living below poverty level and people with lower levels of education having higher smoking rates (Wetter et al., 2005).

Why do people smoke? Many adolescents experiment with smoking in middle and high school. In 2012, nearly 9% of 12- to 17-year-olds were current cigarette smokers (SAMHSA, 2013). Many of these young people are aware of the health hazards associated with smoking, yet they begin anyway. Smoking is related to both biological and environmental factors. On the side of biology, there is considerable evidence that specific genes and gene combinations are involved in nicotine dependence (Erblich et al., 2005; Kremer et al., 2005; Ling et al., 2004). However, social pressure also contributes to smoking. For example, peer pressure is often cited as a reason why young people start smoking (Hayes & Plowfield, 2007). Seeing their favorite celebrities or music idols smoke, or even watching movies in which many characters smoke, also glamorizes smoking (Cin et al., 2007; Distefan, Heatherton, & Sargent, 2009; Pierce, 2005). For this reason, many antismoking programs are aimed at teenagers because this seems to be the prime age when smoking begins. Health officials have determined that the cost of treating the health problems associated with smoking far outweighs the cost of prevention programs.

Psychology Applies to Your World:

Technology's Health Effects

Technology has the potential for great benefit and great harm to our health. On the plus side, social networking sites, e-mail, and text messaging can reduce loneliness and offer companionship and social support that can help combat stress and improve well-being (Barker, 2009; Shaw & Gant, 2002). The Internet provides instant access to health information and resources that can reduce stress and worry. Fitness video games offer a fun, enjoyable, and often inexpensive way to remain physically active. However, being inundated with constant communication 24/7 creates stress and can make it more difficult to relax. Feeling like you are being left out of a social loop can create social anxiety. People may disengage from loved ones and pay more attention to the person on the phone or on the computer than to the people who are actually present. The Internet may produce information overload or give contradictory or unreliable health information that creates stress and worry (Abbott, 2010).

However, there are more serious, adverse health effects of technology use. After prolonged cell phone use, people may notice aching, burning, numbness, or tingling in the forearm and hand called "cell phone elbow" (Darowish, Lawton, & Evans, 2009). It is associated with people who use their cell phones for extended periods while holding their neck crooked and elbow bent. It can aggravate a painful and disabling condition called *cubital tunnel syndrome,* or the compression of the ulnar nerve near the elbow. Similarly, irritation and compression of the median nerve in the wrist, known as *carpal tunnel syndrome,* can result from repetitive work such as uninterrupted computer typing and frequent mouse use, depending on the frequency of use and wrist position of the user (Rempel, Keir, & Bach, 2008). Excessive texting uses short little motions that do not effectively use the muscles. This action can lead to painful cramping in the thumbs, hands, or joints, popularly called "BlackBerry thumb" or "teenager tendonitis" (Gordon, 2008). Staring at computer, tablet, or cell phone screens for long periods can lead to dry eyes, eye irritation, redness, blurred vision, and eye strain, a condition referred to as *computer vision syndrome* and that can cause headaches, pain, and fatigue (Blehm et al., 2005). Perhaps one of the most dangerous behaviors that has resulted from technology is an increase in distracted driving.

In 2011, 10% of fatal car crashes involved distracted driving, and an additional 400,000 people were injured in crashes related to driver distraction (NHTSA, 2013). People do not turn off their connection to the outside world when they get into their cars, yet our brain is not capable of fully concentrating on two things simultaneously. Nearly 70% of U.S. drivers reported talking on the phone, and 31% reported sending or receiving a text while driving (CDC, 2013b). Text messaging and conversing on either a handheld or hands-free cell phone while driving slows reaction time more than being drunk or high (Drews et al., 2009; Strayer, Drews, & Crouch, 2006). Text messaging takes drivers' eyes off the road for the longest time (an average of 4.6 seconds) compared to drivers talking on a cell phone and those not using a phone. That is the equivalent of driving 55 mph with one's eyes shut the entire length of a football field (Olson et al., 2009). Drivers who are text messaging show more missed lane changes and more variability in lane position and following distances (Hosking, Young, & Regan, 2009). Driving safely is keeping your eyes and your mind on the road. Text messaging while driving compromises both.

fStop/SuperStock

Texting and driving is a health-defeating behavior as it increases one's chances of injury or death.

UNSAFE SEX AND THE RISK OF SEXUALLY TRANSMITTED INFECTIONS (STIs)

sexually transmitted infection (STI) an infection that is passed from one person to another primarily through sexual contact

Sexually transmitted infections (STIs) are infections that are passed from one person to another, usually through sexual contact. However, some STIs may be spread by nonsexual contact as well as from a mother to her unborn child. Every day we hear news accounts of the spread of AIDS and the HIV virus. Yet AIDS and the HIV virus are not the only types of STIs, many of which are more widespread, especially in the United States.

The Centers for Disease Control and Prevention (2014) estimates that nearly 20 million people in the United States become infected with an STI each year. In fact, the United States has one of the highest rates of STIs in the industrialized world.

Risk Factors for STIs

Why are STIs so widespread? One reason is that younger people today are more likely to engage in sexual intercourse. Almost half of new cases of STIs occur among teenagers and young adults, who may not use condoms or may use them infrequently, or in women "on the pill" using oral contraceptives, which do not prevent STIs (CDC, 2014; Crosby & Danner, 2008). A second reason is that many STIs often have no symptoms, so they are unknowingly passed from one person to the next. A third reason is the social stigma attached to those infected with an STI. Such negative perceptions may prevent people from openly discussing their condition with medical personnel, partners, and other loved ones.

Women, teenagers, men who have sex with men, and some ethnic groups are more likely to have an STI in the United States. Men and women between the ages of 15 and 24 are most at risk (Calvert, 2003; CDC, 2014; Crosby & Danner, 2008). Young people are at increased risk because they engage in many high-risk sexual behaviors, such as having multiple partners and engaging in unprotected sexual intercourse. Women are at higher risk for contracting an STI than men because the warm, moist environment of the vagina renders women more susceptible to infection (Bolton, van der Straten, & Cohen, 2008). Younger women are especially vulnerable as viruses and bacteria can more easily invade immature cervical cells than mature ones (Parker-Pope, 2002). According to data from the Centers for Disease Control and Prevention (2010a, 2010b, 2014), higher rates of STIs are found among gay and bisexual men, and all ethnic minority populations except Asians/Pacific Islanders when compared to European Americans.

Engaging in certain sexual behaviors also puts one at a higher risk for contracting an STI. High-risk sexual behaviors include oral–genital sex without a condom or dental dam, semen in the mouth, and vaginal or anal intercourse without a condom (Hatcher et al., 1994). Sex with multiple partners, as Emily evidenced, also increases one's chances of contracting an STI. Moreover, some STIs are contracted through nonsexual means. Certain forms of drug use increase the risk, as sharing contaminated needles can directly transmit organisms such as HIV. An infected pregnant woman also risks transmitting the infection to her unborn child and causing serious birth defects.

STIs can cause irreparable damage. Left untreated, STIs can cause pelvic inflammatory disease (PID), chronic pelvic pain, and infertility in women (CDC, 2010b). They can also result in arthritis, heart problems, brain damage, and even death. The financial cost to our health care system is enormous, while the human cost to partners, families, and infected persons is incalculable. It's a cost that does not necessarily have to be paid, as many STIs are easily treated and prevented.

Types of STIs

There are three basic categories of STIs: bacterial infections, viral infections, and parasitic infections.

Bacterial infections include *chlamydia, gonorrhea,* and *syphilis.* Bacteria are microorganisms or germs that can quickly reproduce and cause disease in the body. Chlamydia, gonorrhea, and syphilis are transmitted primarily through vaginal, anal, or oral sexual activity. If present in the vagina, these infections also can be transmitted from a mother to a newborn during delivery. An unusual discharge and sore or painful urination are common symptoms of these infections. However, many men and women show no symptoms during the early stages and therefore do not seek treatment until more serious symptoms develop. Antibiotics are typically used to treat bacterial infections (Cates, 1998).

Viral infections include *genital herpes, human papillomavirus* (*HPV*), and *HIV/AIDS.* Viruses are incapable of reproducing on their own. They invade a normal cell and direct that cell to make new viral copies. These copies then invade other healthy cells, causing infection. Many of the symptoms of these infections can be treated, but the virus remains in the body and is yours for life. Most people with genital herpes or HPV do not initially develop symptoms or health problems. When symptoms do occur in genital herpes, noticeable sores appear. About one in six people between the ages of 14 and 49 are infected with genital herpes (CDC, 2010a). Similarly, most people who become infected with any of the more than 40 strains of HPV do not know they have it. However, certain types of HPV can cause *genital warts,* small bumps, or groups of bumps, usually in the genital area. Approximately 20 million people in the United States are currently infected with HPV. It is estimated that most sexually active men and women will get infected with HPV at some point in their lives, making it the most common STI in the United States (CDC, 2013a). A controversial vaccine, consisting of three treatment doses, can be administered to young females from 11 to 26 years of age to protect them from four types of HPV that cause most cervical cancers and genital warts. The vaccine also protects young males from 11 to 21 years of age against two HPV types that cause most genital warts. The vaccine is most effective when a person completes the treatment before becoming sexually active.

Being HIV-positive means that a person has been infected with the human immunodeficiency virus (HIV). In HIV/AIDS, the HIV attacks the immune system, resulting in mild flu-like symptoms that may then disappear for years before developing into a full-blown case of AIDS. Although symptoms may not be present, a person still carries the virus and is therefore capable of transmitting it to a partner during sexual activity. HIV/AIDS can also be contracted through the exchange of contaminated blood or passed to a fetus during pregnancy or to an infant during breastfeeding.

It is estimated that more than 1.1 million people are currently living with HIV in the United States (CDC, 2013c). People with HIV tend to come from lower socioeconomic groups; are more likely to be less educated; are more likely to be gay, bisexual, and other men who have sex with men; and are more likely to be African American (CDC, 2013c). However, anyone—regardless of age, income, race, or sexual orientation—can contract this potentially deadly disease. Treatment to suppress HIV/AIDS infection typically consists of a steady regime of antiretroviral drugs. This treatment slows the disease's progression and has significantly decreased the number of HIV- and AIDS-related deaths (Crum et al., 2006; Venkatesh, Biswas, & Kumarasamy, 2008).

Parasitic infections include *pubic lice* and *scabies.* A parasite lives off another organism or host. Pubic lice, or "crabs," survive by feeding on human blood. Scabies are tiny mites that burrow under the skin and lay eggs. Both infections can be spread through sexual contact or by contact with infested towels, linens, or clothing. The most common symptom is intense itching in the genital area. Parasitic infections are typically treated with a solution that kills the lice or mites and their

Eye of Science /Science Source

Pubic lice are often called "crabs" because of the organism's resemblance to a crab.

eggs. It is important to carefully reexamine the body 4 to 7 days after treatment to ensure that all the eggs have been killed. Towels, linens, and clothing also need to be treated to prevent reinfection. You Review: Sexually Transmitted Infections (STIs) shows the main types of sexually transmitted infections, modes of transmission, symptoms, and treatment.

You Review **Sexually Transmitted Infections (STIs)**

STI	Transmission Modes	Symptoms	Treatments
BACTERIAL			
Chlamydia	Vaginal, oral, or anal sexual activity, or from an infected mother to her newborn during vaginal birth	In females: frequent and painful urination, lower abdominal pain, and vaginal discharge. In males: burning or painful urination, and slight penis discharge. However, many people show no symptoms.	Antibiotics
Gonorrhea	Vaginal, oral, or anal sexual activity, or from an infected mother to her newborn during vaginal birth	In females: increased vaginal discharge, burning urination, or irregular menstrual bleeding (many women show no early symptoms). In males: yellowish, thick penile discharge, or burning urination.	Antibiotics
Syphilis	Vaginal, oral, or anal sexual activity, or by touching an infected chancre or sore	A hard, round, painless chancre or sore appears at site of infection within 2 to 4 weeks.	Penicillin or other antibiotics for penicillin-allergic patients
VIRAL			
Genital herpes	Vaginal, oral, or anal sexual activity	Painful, reddish blisters around the genitals, thighs, or buttocks, and for females on the vagina or cervix. Other symptoms may include burning urination, flu-like symptoms, or vaginal discharge in females.	No cure, although certain drugs can provide relief and help sores heal
HPV	Vaginal, oral, or anal sexual activity	Some strains cause painless warts to appear in the genital area or anus; other strains may cause abnormal cell changes in the cervix.	Vaccine, cryotherapy (freezing), acid burning, or surgical removal of warts
HIV/AIDS	Sexual contact, infusion with contaminated blood, or from mother to child during pregnancy, childbirth, or breast feeding.	May develop flu-like symptoms that may disappear for many years before developing full-blown AIDS. AIDS symptoms include fever, weight loss, fatigue, diarrhea, and susceptibility to infection.	No cure; treatment includes a combination of antiretroviral drugs
PARASITES			
Pubic lice	Sexual contact or contact with infested linens or toilet seats	Intense itching in hairy regions of the body, especially the pubic area	Prescription shampoos or nonprescription medications
Scabies	Sexual contact or contact with infested linens or toilet seats	Intense itching, reddish lines on skin, welts, and pus-filled blisters in affected area	Prescription shampoos

12.5.2 • Health-Promoting Behaviors

health-promoting behaviors behaviors that decrease the chance of illness, disease, or death

Health psychologists define **health-promoting behaviors** as those that decrease the chance of illness, disease, or death. Throughout this chapter we have indicated behaviors that you can engage in that appear to be related to better physical and mental health. Three additional behaviors that benefit the body and mind are *physical activity, healthy eating,* and *getting enough sleep.* Regular physical activity, healthful eating habits, and a good night's sleep promote a longer and healthier life.

PHYSICAL ACTIVITY

Physical activity improves health. Such activity may include taking the stairs instead of the elevator at school or at work; parking farther away from stores when shopping; or walking or biking to campus instead of driving. However, moderate physical activity for at least 30 minutes a day is recommended by most health experts. Moderate physical activity includes walking briskly, swimming, cycling, or jogging—aerobic activities that stimulate heart and lung functioning.

Regular physical activity plays an important role in people's health. In addition to combating stress, physical activity helps us live longer, improves mental health, and positively affects memory and cognition (Collins et al., 2009; Lee et al., 2011; Williams & Kemper, 2010). Engaging in regular physical activity also protects against cardiovascular disease, some kinds of cancer, and bone density loss, and can help with weight control (Bassuk & Manson, 2010; Huang et al., 2013; Slattery et al., 2010). Regular exercise is one of the most critical elements in any weight-loss program. Another important factor is eating right.

EATING RIGHT

Being overweight or obese is associated with a higher risk of several types of health problems such as type 2 diabetes, sleep apnea, migraine headaches, heart disease, and some cancers. It also shortens one's life span (National Research Council, 2011). Healthful eating when combined with physical activity can decrease one's risk of disease and death.

Eating right means choosing foods that are nutritious and healthy. Nutritious foods such as fruits, vegetables, and grains are high in vitamins, minerals, and fiber. Processed foods and foods high in sugar, salt, oil, or fat (like fast food) increase cholesterol, which contributes to the development of heart problems (Phelan et al., 2009). One should strive to eat well-balanced meals that meet one's nutritional needs and include a variety of foods from each of the major food groups.

Eating right also means eating breakfast. Skipping breakfast is one of the biggest nutritional mistakes that people make. Breakfast is your first chance to refuel your body to prepare it for the day's activities. Regularly eating a healthy breakfast is associated with increased attention span, less risk of chronic diseases, and living a longer life (Hoyland, Dye, & Lawton, 2009; Schoenborn, 1986). Eating a healthy breakfast also makes us less likely to overeat later in the day.

GETTING ENOUGH SLEEP

As we saw in Chapter 4, adults and teenagers require at least 8 hours of sleep a night, yet few of us achieve this. Why is getting enough sleep so important? For one, doing so enhances your immune system (Lange et al., 2006; Motivala & Irwin, 2007). When you deprive your body of sleep, your natural immune responses are reduced (Murphy & Delanty, 2007; Ruiz et al., 2012). The right amount of sleep also activates chemicals that influence your emotions and enhance mood. If you are deprived of sleep, you are more likely to be irritable, cranky, and unhappy, in addition to being tired (Lemola, Ledermann, & Friedman, 2013; Short et al., 2013). Sleep offers many benefits to our functioning and ensures that we will be healthy, alert, and happy.

Soul/Iconica/Getty Images

People who are happy are healthier and live longer.

12.5.3 • Happiness and Well-Being

Healthy living promotes happiness and life satisfaction. So, it is fitting to end this chapter by investigating what makes people happy. Research typically measures happiness by asking people how satisfied they are with their lives. This is referred to as *subjective well-being*. People who score high on measures of subjective well-being live longer and healthier lives (Chida & Steptoe, 2008; Xu & Roberts, 2010). The factors that contribute to happiness nicely summarize many of the health behaviors that this chapter has explored (Diener & Biswas-Diener, 2008):

- *Social relationships*. People who are happy have close, strong, and positive relationships with others. Higher well-being is associated with social rather than solitary pursuits that involve meaningful conversations with others (Mehl et al., 2010; Mogilner, 2010). Strong ties increase subjective well-being and help moderate the ill effects of stress. Emily's loneliness and lack of connections with others often made her depressed and unhappy.
- *Cognitive patterns*. People think in ways that contribute to happiness. Happy people view stressors as opportunities rather than as threats, engage in more intentional positive activities such as expressing gratitude and thinking optimistically, and remember positive experiences rather than dwelling on negative ones (Lyubomirsky & Layous, 2013; Sin & Lyubomirsky, 2009).
- *Temperament*. Good and bad events happen to everyone and affect levels of happiness. However, individuals differ in their ability to adapt to these events. People who bounce back from negative events by using positive emotions to cope can more easily reset their point of being happy to the same or a new adjusted level. This ability may stem from inherited differences in temperament and thus be greatly influenced by genetics.
- *Wealth*. Can money buy happiness? Only to a small extent. In poor societies, people who have more money report higher levels of happiness. However, once people rise above poverty level in terms of wealth, money doesn't buy more happiness. Income level has only a modest impact on subjective well-being (Aknin, Norton, & Dunn, 2009; Anderson et al., 2012). However, income loss and economic troubles can have a negative effect on well-being (Boyce et al., 2013; Sutin et al., 2013). Moreover, valuing money above relationships, love, and personal satisfaction is negatively associated with happiness (Bauer et al., 2012). How one spends their money is equally important to consider. People who spend money on others report more happiness (Dunn, Aknin, & Norton, 2014).
- *Culture*. One's feeling of happiness is also influenced by the values that characterize one's society. Cultural norms dictate whether happiness is important and what constitutes a good life. Individualistic cultures

endorse the value of personal happiness, whereas collectivistic cultures value group identity. Not surprisingly, East Asians and Asian Americans report lower levels of happiness than Europeans and European Americans (Wirtz et al., 2009). People in war-torn nations report less happiness and well-being than do people in stable countries (Inglehart et al., 2008).

Future research will help us discover more about the nature of happiness and life satisfaction. This knowledge will enable health psychologists to continue their efforts at understanding stress, preventing illnesses, and promoting lifelong well-being.

Quiz Yourself 11.4

1. **Which of the following is *not* a health-promoting behavior?**
   a. Viewing stressors as challenges rather than as threats
   b. Perceiving events as controllable
   c. Relying exclusively on one defense mechanism for coping
   d. Engaging in problem-focused coping

2. **Pedro has experienced an intense, burning sensation during urination and a thick, yellowish penile discharge. Pedro most likely has which STI?**
   a. Gonorrhea
   b. Genital herpes
   c. Genital warts
   d. HPV

3. **Which of the following people is most likely to report being the happiest?**
   a. Haifa, who is extremely wealthy, has a few close friends, and focuses on negative experiences
   b. Sam, who is moderately wealthy, optimistic, and adapts well to negative events
   c. Agustin, who is moderately wealthy, optimistic, and lives in a war-torn nation
   d. All of these would report similar levels of happiness

4. **Which one of the following statements is *true*?**
   a. Collectivistic cultures most value personal happiness.
   b. Higher well-being is associated with solitary pursuits.
   c. Skipping breakfast helps to focus one's attention.
   d. Income level has only a modest impact on happiness.

Answers 1. c; 2. a; 3. b; 4. d

12.6 Integrating Psychology: The Big Picture

This chapter explored the topics of stress, coping, and health—topics that are bound to be relevant to you. Notice how the information in this chapter emphasizes a *biopsychosocial* approach. The physical aspect of the stress response and the functioning of our immune systems constitute biological elements that influence our health. What we perceive as stressors and how we cope with stress, as well as our personality illustrate psychological factors involved in our general health. How we deal with different social, cultural, and environmental types of stressors such as major life events, daily hassles, and catastrophes also influence our health and happiness.

Think about Emily's story from the section opener. Her emotional responses of rage and panic often resulted in a spastic colon and elevated heart rate—biological effects from how she coped with stress. Her learned helplessness and negative self-evaluations only contributed to her difficulty in functioning. Acting out, smoking, drinking excessively, and sex with multiple partners were not effective means of coping with the emotional neglect she felt from those around her. Even despite a privileged background, Emily lacked social support, optimism, and other forms of adaptive coping techniques even from some of her therapists. Once she established a trusting and respectful relationship with Dr. Farber, she was able to make some progress toward her "best self."

Think about how the information in this chapter might apply to you. Examine the ways in which you handle stress. Do you spend a significant amount of your time on social media or watching television, drinking alcohol, smoking, exercising, or using drugs? Are these methods adaptive or maladaptive? Do you experience any stress-related symptoms such as headaches, backaches, muscle tension, anxiety, or upset stomach? How might your coping style be influencing your health? What stress management techniques do you use and could you adopt the use of more adaptive ones? Are there any improvements that you could make in your personality or lifestyle that would enhance your health, and how might you begin to make these changes? Addressing issues such as these will help you master the material and hopefully will make you pause for a moment to contemplate how your health may be improved for today and for the future.

Studying the Chapter

Key Terms

alarm reaction (514)
approach–approach conflict (510)
approach–avoidance conflict (511)
avoidance–avoidance conflict (511)
cognitive reappraisal (520)
conflict (510)
coping (518)
daily hassles (508)
defense mechanisms (520)
emotion-focused coping (519)
exhaustion stage (515)
general adaptation syndrome (GAS) (514)
guided imagery (523)
hardy personality (528)
health psychology (502)
health-defeating behaviors (529)
health-promoting behaviors (534)
immunosuppression (516)
learned helplessness (527)
life event (504)
meditation (524)
multiple approach–avoidance conflict (512)
primary appraisal (513)
problem-focused coping (519)
progressive relaxation training (522)
psychoneuroimmunology (516)
resilience (510)
resistance stage (515)
secondary appraisal (514)
sexually transmitted infection (STI) (532)
social support (522)
stress (504)
Type A personality (525)
Type B personality (525)
Type C personality (525)

What Do You Know? Assess Your Understanding

Test your retention and understanding of the material by answering the following questions.

1. Which of the following events is likely to produce the most stress for the average person?

a. Losing your job after months of talk about a buyout
b. Losing your job without any warning
c. Quitting your job to look for a different line of work
d. Keeping your job after others have lost their jobs due to downsizing

2. Which of the following is *not* considered a major life event?

a. Marriage
b. Losing your job
c. Buying a home
d. Being late to work

3. The adrenal gland secretes which two hormones during the stress response?

a. Adrenalin and corticosteroids
b. Adrenalin and GABA
c. Corticosteroids and insulin
d. Insulin and GABA

4. Cecilia feels stressed from her full-time job and taking care of her two children. Cecilia finds a more flexible job that allows her to spend more time with her children. Which style of coping does Cecilia's behavior illustrate?

a. Emotion-focused
b. Problem-focused
c. Defensive
d. Both a and c

5. Which of the following behaviors promotes health and well-being?

a. Perceiving events as controllable
b. Engaging in defense mechanisms
c. Expecting failure
d. All of these help your health

6. Ryan can't decide whether to vacation in the mountains or at the beach. Ryan is experiencing a(n) _____.

a. approach–avoidance conflict
b. approach–approach conflict
c. avoidance–avoidance conflict
d. multiple approach–avoidance conflict

7. Matresha is driving when a van pulls out in front of her and almost causes an accident. Matresha's heart begins to pound, and her blood pressure shoots up. Matresha is likely in the _____ phase of the general adaptation syndrome.

a. alarm
b. resistance
c. exhaustion
d. final

8. A weakened immune system and vulnerability to disease are most likely to occur in which stage of the general adaptation syndrome?

a. Alarm
b. Resistance
c. Exhaustion
d. Resilience

9. Jariel is a workaholic. He never takes a vacation. He won't even speak to friends and family on the phone when they call him at work. He is often angry and impatient with others. What type of personality does Jariel appear to have?

a. Type A
b. Type B
c. Type C
d. A hardy personality

10. April recently lost her high-paying job. While talking to a friend about her job loss, April told her that she was looking forward to finding a job in a new field. April appears to be *most* exhibiting the hardy trait of _____.

a. challenge
b. commitment
c. control
d. resistance

11. Which of the following is *not* an effective means of managing stress?

a. Exercise
b. Relaxation techniques
c. Talking to friends
d. Be spontaneous with your time

12. Tom views his new job as a positive and challenging change. Tom's appraisal of stress in this situation is most likely to elicit the emotion of _____.

a. anger
b. fear
c. excitement
d. anxiety

13. Lucinda believes she has no control over what happens to her. She expects failure and often feels stressed out. What type of personality does Lucinda appear to have?

a. Learned helplessness
b. Type C personality
c. Type A personality
d. Type B personality

14. Which of the following is an accurate statement concerning the relationship between stress and the immune system?

a. Stress always decreases the effectiveness of our immune system.
b. Stress always increases the effectiveness of our immune system.
c. If stress disrupts normal immune system functioning, we increase our vulnerability to illness and disease.
d. If stress disrupts normal immune system functioning, we decrease our vulnerability to illness and disease.

15. The 2013 typhoon in the Philippines powerfully illustrates the stressful nature of _____.

a. daily hassles
b. major life events
c. catastrophes
d. both a and b

16. Jeffrey has been feeling like he has the flu. He also has noticed reddish bumps around his genital area. Jeffrey most likely has which STI?

a. Gonorrhea
b. Genital herpes
c. Syphilis
d. Chlamydia

17. Which of the following is *not* a factor that contributes to happiness?

a. social support
b. cultural norms
c. wealth
d. eating breakfast

18. Florangel feels really stressed. Her child was up most of the night coughing. She has a major project due for her Economics course, and she is not sure if she will have enough money to pay her monthly bills. Florangel's high stress level is most due to _____.

a. major life events
b. daily hassles
c. catastrophes
d. approach–approach conflict

19. When Alexandra gets in a fight with her partner, she stomps her feet, covers her ears, and refuses to listen. Alexandra's behavior *best* illustrates the defense mechanism called _____.

a. regression
b. repression
c. reaction formation
d. displacement

20. Health-defeating behaviors _____.

a. are not controllable
b. are engaged in over a short period of time
c. make us more susceptible to illness and disease
d. All of the above

Answers: 1. b; 2. d; 3. a; 4. b; 5. a; 6. b; 7. a; 8. c; 9. a; 10. a; 11. d; 12. c; 13. a; 14. c; 15. c; 16. b; 17. d; 18. b; 19. a; 20. c.

Use It or Lose It: Applying Psychology

1. What defense mechanisms do you think are more often employed by people who engage in health-defeating behaviors? Provide examples to illustrate and support your answer.

2. Using your own behavior, give an example of each of the following defense mechanisms: projection, denial, reaction formation, displacement, and sublimation.

3. Using your own behavior, give an example of each of the conflict situations discussed in the section on stress and stressors in this chapter. How did you respond to each of these situations? Indicate whether your response reflected a problem-focused coping strategy or an emotion-focused coping strategy.

4. Develop a formal time schedule to better manage your time. First create a chart showing all the hours in a day and all the days of the week. Block out all those times that are already committed, such as sleeping, class time, work, and daily chores. Now allocate a specific amount of time to study for your classes and to exercise. Follow this plan for a week to see whether you need to make any modifications. Provide an analysis of your time use.

Critical Thinking for Integration

1. Review the four types of learning detailed in Chapter 6. Integrate and apply the theories to explain why people smoke or engage in unsafe sex practices.

2. After reviewing the processes of memory in Chapter 7, suggest how learned helplessness can be explained as a process of memory.

3. What obstacles or aids to problem solving (Chapter 8) can be linked to maladaptive and adaptive forms of coping?

4. Integrating information from Chapters 4, 6, and 12, develop an antialcohol campaign that addresses the effects of alcohol (Chapter 4), the learning processes that accompany alcohol use (Chapter 6), and the effects that alcohol has on one's health (Chapter 12).

5. Given that pregnancy is a stressor, how might women best cope with the immediate changes associated with pregnancy and childbirth, as well as the transition to parenthood (Chapter 9)? What might be indicators of maladaptive coping patterns during pregnancy?

6. Review the cognitive changes that take place in adolescence (Chapter 9). How might adolescent cognitive development account for teenagers' willingness to engage in health-defeating behaviors?

Kathleen Finlay/Masterfile

Are You Getting the Big Picture? Health, Stress, and Coping

Health psychologists study how people's behavior influences their health for better and for worse.

12.1 What Is Stress? Stress and Stressors

- **Stress** is any event or environmental stimulus (stressor) that we respond to because we perceive it as challenging or threatening.
- *Catastrophes* and significant **life events**, such as the death of a loved one or a new job, are major stressors. Everyday frustrations—called **daily hassles**—are less serious stressors, but can have a negative effect on health.
- **Resilience** or adapting well to significant stressors may be a protective factor for some people who experience chronic stress.
- **Conflict** also produces stress.

Hulton Archive/Getty Images

12.2 The Stress Response

- If our initial interpretation or **primary appraisal** of an event is one of stress, we may view it as a threat, as harmful, or merely as a challenge.
- Our body responds to stress in a three-phase **general adaptation syndrome**:
  - The **alarm reaction** consists of those bodily responses, including the nervous system and endocrine system, that are immediately triggered when we initially appraise an event as stressful.
  - In the **resistance stage**, the body continues to cope with the stressor, but the bodily reactions are less intense than during the alarm reaction.
  - In the **exhaustion phase**, wear and tear on the body begins, causing serious damage if stress continues over an extended period of time.

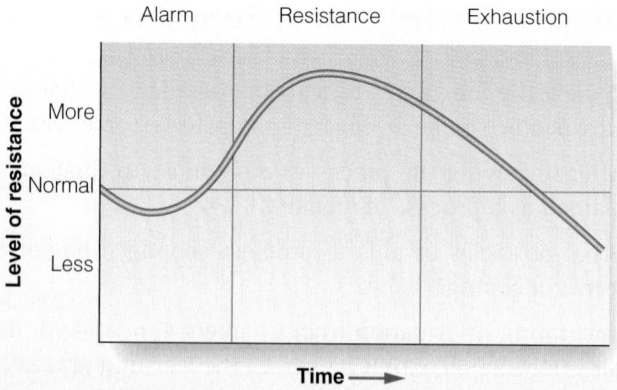

- The corticosteroids and endorphins that are released into our body during the stress response dampen the activity of our immune system (**immunosuppression**), making us more vulnerable to health problems.

12.3 Coping with Stress

Leonora Hamill/Stone/Getty Images

- **Coping** is how we manage a threatening event or stimulus.
- **Problem-focused coping** controls or alters the environment that caused the stress. It is most useful when we feel that we can do something about the stressor.
- **Emotion-focused coping** controls our internal, subjective, emotional responses to stress. We alter the way we feel or think in order to reduce stress.
- **Defense mechanisms** are unconscious coping strategies that allow us to reduce our anxiety and maintain a positive self-image and self-esteem.
- A number of strategies can be used to reduce stress in one's life, including exercise, **social support**, **guided imagery**, **meditation**, laughter, and time management.

12.4 Personality and Health

- A person with a **Type A personality** is aggressive, competitive, and driven to achieve; a person with a **Type B personality** is relaxed, easygoing, patient, and flexible; a person with a **Type C personality** is careful and patient and suppresses negative emotions such as anger. The Type A personality trait of hostility is related to a higher incidence of heart disease.
- **Learned helplessness** results from believing that you have no control over stressful life events. You view stressors as threats, your level of stress increases, and you are more likely to develop stress-related illnesses.
- The **hardy personality** is resistant to stress; it includes characteristics such as
  - A tendency to see life as a series of *challenges*;
  - A sense of personal *commitment* to self, work, family, and other values;
  - A perception of *control* over one's life and work.

12.5 What Behaviors Promote Health and Well-Being?

Soul/Iconica/Getty Images

- **Health-defeating behaviors**, such as alcohol and substance abuse, smoking, distracted driving, and unsafe sex, increase the chance of illness, disease, or death.
- **Sexually transmitted infections** are passed from one person to another primarily through sexual contact. Young people are at greater risk for contracting STIs because they are more likely to engage in high-risk sexual behaviors.
- **Health-promoting behaviors** decrease the chance of illness, disease, or death. Regular physical activity, healthful eating, and getting enough sleep promote a longer and healthier life. Happiness is related to a strong social support network, an optimistic outlook, economic resources, temperament, and cultural values.

Mental Health Disorders

Learning Objectives

13.1 Define a mental health disorder and identify and apply the criteria that psychologists use for determining abnormal behavior. (APA 1.1, 1.2, 1.3)

13.1 Indicate the lifetime and annual prevalence rates of mental health disorders, and describe variations by development, gender, and ethnicity. (APA 1.1, 1.3, 2.5)

13.1 Compare and contrast the varying perspectives on explaining mental health disorders, and apply a biopsychosocial or integrated perspective to explain a particular behavior. (APA 1.2, 2.1)

13.2 Identify the structure of the *DSM* model, and explain the research on its strengths and weaknesses. (APA 1.1, 2.1, 3.3)

13.3 Describe the components of excessive anxiety and distinguish among the symptoms of anxiety, trauma-, obsessive-compulsive and related disorders. (APA 1.1, 1.2)

13.3 Discuss research on our current understanding of the biopsychosocial factors that contribute to anxiety, trauma-, obsessive-compulsive and related disorders. (APA 2.1, 2.5)

13.4 Distinguish among the symptoms of the various dissociative disorders, and describe their link to stressful or traumatic events. (APA 1.1, 1.3)

13.4 Distinguish among the symptoms of the various somatic symptom disorders, and discuss their link to health anxiety. (APA. 1.1, 1.2)

13.5 Distinguish between the symptoms of the depressive and bipolar disorders. (APA 1.1, 1.3)

13.5 Describe common misconceptions that people hold about suicide. (APA 1.3)

13.5 Discuss research on our current understanding of the biopsychosocial factors that play a role in mood disorders. (APA 1.2, 2.1, 2.5)

13.5 Explain the role of biopsychosocial factors in women's higher vulnerability to depression. (APA 1.3, 2.1, 2.5)

13.6 Describe the typical onset and prognosis for schizophrenia and its variation by gender, social class, and ethnicity. (APA 1.1, 2.5)

13.6 Identify and discriminate among the positive and negative symptoms of schizophrenia. (APA 1.1, 1.2)

13.6 Discuss the research on our current understanding of the causes of schizophrenia. (APA 2.1, 2.5)

13.7 Describe the nature of personality disorders and give a brief description of the different types of personality disorders. (APA 1.1, 1.2)

This chapter outlines several major categories of mental health disorders and explains the symptoms used to diagnose particular disorders. For each type of disorder, we will consider the possible reasons why a person behaves this way. Although the research presented may seem overwhelming at times, keep in mind that these explanations are closely tied to topics with which you are already familiar. For example, many of the symptoms of mental health disorders are physical in nature, involving brain functioning, neurotransmitters, hormones, and genetics—biological factors that were introduced in Chapter 2. Many of the symptoms also relate to psychological concepts such as learning, cognition, and emotions—again, topics that have been addressed in previous chapters. Furthermore, we will see that certain disorders are more common among certain segments of the population. Your familiarity with previous discussions on gender, race, personality, development, and culture will assist you in understanding these sociocultural factors and individual variations that influence mental health.

13

Cusp and Flirt/Masterfile

Chapter Outline

13.1 What Is Abnormal Behavior? / 546

13.2 The *DSM* Model for Classifying Abnormal Behavior / 549

13.3 Anxiety, Trauma-, Obsessive-Compulsive and Related Disorders: It's Not Just "Nerves" / 553

13.4 Dissociative and Somatic Symptom Disorders: Other Forms of Anxiety? / 562

13.5 Mood Disorders: Beyond the Blues / 565

PSYCHOLOGY APPLIES TO YOUR WORLD: Suicide Facts and Misconceptions / 568

13.6 Schizophrenia: Disintegration / 575

13.7 Personality Disorders: Maladaptive Patterns of Behavior / 581

13.8 Integrating Psychology: The Big Picture / 584

13.1 What Is Abnormal Behavior?

mental health disorder a dysfunction in thinking (cognition), emotions, and/or social behavior that impairs functioning and is not culturally expected

Defining what is normal from abnormal behavior is not an easy task. Simply being different does not qualify as abnormal. There is no simple test that a person can take to uncover a mental health disorder. As such mental health professionals define a **mental health disorder** as a dysfunction in thinking (cognition), emotions, and/or social behavior that impairs functioning and is not culturally expected (Insel et al., 2010; Sanislow et al., 2011). Recall from the section case study that Emily's difficulty in functioning would meet these criteria. Her rage, panic, and suicide attempts were emotional responses that impaired her functioning and were not typical or normal behaviors for her circumstances. Let's look more closely at how this definition distinguishes normal from abnormal behavior:

1. *Not typical or culturally expected.* If we judge normal as what most people do, then engaging in a behavior less or more frequently than others would be atypical. For example, it is considered crucial for survival to ingest a minimum amount of food per day. People who engage in this behavior a lot less than most people—as in the case of people with anorexia—would qualify as abnormal. Persons with autism engage in social communication far less than most people. As such, their behavior may be considered abnormal. Atypical can also mean engaging in a behavior that most people do not. For example, believing that you are from another planet or galaxy is a thought that most people do not have.

   Also implied in this definition is whether the behavior violates social and cultural norms of how people are supposed to behave. However, it is extremely important to emphasize that social norms vary widely across cultures, within cultures, and across historical times. What is considered socially acceptable in San Francisco, California, may be considered unacceptable in Keokuk, Iowa. Similarly, what was deemed unacceptable in the 1950s may be considered acceptable today. For example, changing views on homosexuality in part influenced the American Psychiatric Association to remove homosexuality from its list of mental health disorders in 1973. Because social norms vary so widely, judging the abnormality of behavior on this aspect alone is especially problematic.
2. *Distress.* A mental health disorder causes great personal distress to the individual or those around him or her. Often people seek treatment when a behavior causes such emotional or physical pain. Alternatively, a person with a mental health disorder may cause distress in others through chronic lying or violence.
3. *Dysfunction.* In defining abnormality, psychologists consider whether a behavior interferes with a person's ability to function. Can the person hold a job, go to school, or form close relationships? The more difficulty a person has in functioning in everyday life, the more likely his or her behavior is considered to be abnormal.

Michael Macor/San Francisco Chronicle/Corbis

Autism is a childhood disorder that is marked by disordered communication.

13.1.1 • Prevalence of Mental Health Disorders

In 2010, there were an estimated 20% of Americans 18 and older with a mental health disorder in the past year (SAMHSA, 2012b). Lifetime prevalence estimates are quite a bit higher, with more than half of U.S. adults meeting the criteria for a mental health disorder at some time in their lives (National Comorbidity Survey Replication [NCS-R], 2007; see • FIGURE 13.1). And yet, this may be a conservative estimate as many people who have difficulty functioning may not want or have access to mental health services (Moffitt et al., 2009). Mental health disorders are the leading cause of disability in the United States and Canada for people between the ages of 15 and 44 (World Health Organization, 2004). Although there is little overall gender difference in the lifetime risk of a mental health disorder, adult females were more likely than adult males to have both any mental health disorder (23% vs. 16.8%) and a serious mental health disorder (6.5% vs. 3.4%) in the last year (SAMHSA, 2012b). Moreover, males and females do show differences in the types of mental health disorders they are more likely to experience (NCS-R, 2007; see • FIGURE 13.2).

Rates of mental illness also have risen dramatically in the last 10–15 years among high school and college students (Twenge, 2006). College mental health counseling is on the rise, and suicide is the third leading cause of death among those aged 15–24 (Heron, 2013). Self-rated emotional health for first-year college students is at its lowest level since it was first assessed 25 years ago (Pryor et al., 2010). Data from national surveys indicate that 22% of U.S. teens were likely to experience a mental health disorder with severe impairment or distress at some time in their lives (Merikangas et al., 2010).

Does this mean that our society today is more likely to be psychologically distressed? Not necessarily. Over the past several decades, much has changed in our understanding and assessment of mental health. Public awareness of mental health disorders has increased, and methods for assessing mental illness have improved dramatically (Costello, Egger, & Angold, 2005). Mental health services are more open to people, and the stigma surrounding mental illness is less today than it was in previous decades, so that people may be less reluctant to seek treatment. Consequently, it is likely that you or someone close to you will at some time experience a mental health disorder. Being familiar with psychology's current understanding of such behavior may help you manage such a situation.

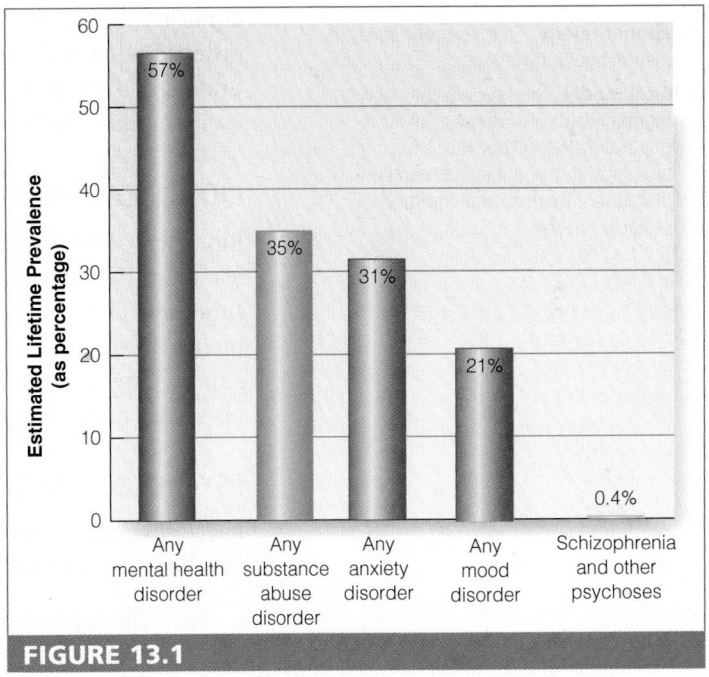

FIGURE 13.1

Lifetime Prevalence of Mental Health Disorders

More than half of U.S. adults will be diagnosed with a mental health disorder at some time in their lives.

Source: National Comorbidity Survey Replication data, Table 1. Updated 2007. http://www.hcp.med.harvard.edu/ncs

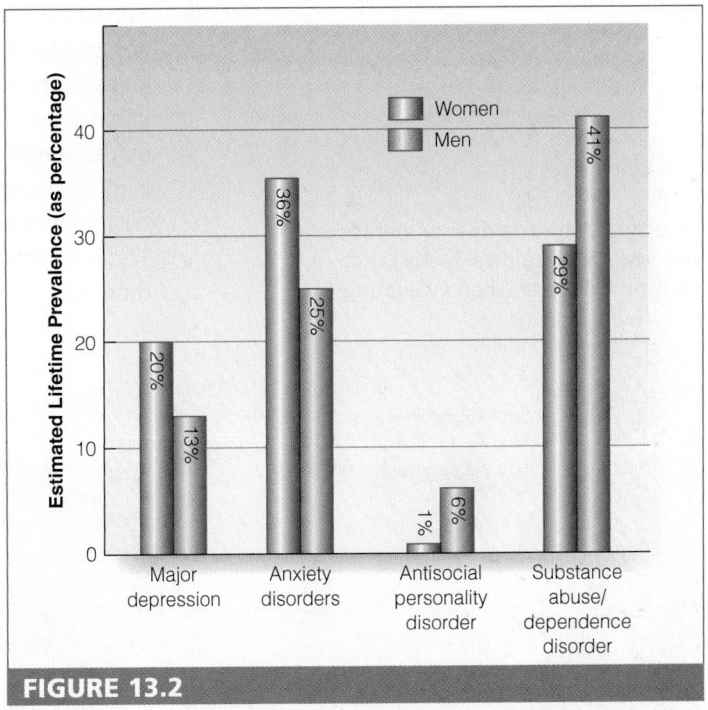

FIGURE 13.2

Prevalence of Depression, Anxiety, Substance Abuse, and Antisocial Personality Disorder in Women and Men

Males and females differ in the types of mental health disorders they are more likely to experience.

Source: National Comorbidity Survey Replication data, Table 1. Updated 2007. http://www.hcp.med.harvard.edu/ncs

13.1.2 • Explaining Abnormal Behavior: Perspectives Revisited

Since the beginning of recorded history, doctors and philosophers have tried to understand why people exhibit

psychopathology the scientific study of mental health disorders

medical model perspective that views mental health disorders as similar to physical diseases; they result from biological disturbances and can be diagnosed, treated, and cured like physical illnesses

abnormal behavior. **Psychopathology** is the scientific study of mental health disorders. Today, Western cultures lean toward three main models or approaches for understanding abnormal behavior: *biological theories, psychological theories,* and *social* or *cultural* theories.

BIOLOGICAL THEORIES: THE MEDICAL MODEL

Biological theories attribute abnormal behavior to some physical process: genetics, an imbalance in hormones or neurotransmitters, or some brain or bodily dysfunction. The biological perspective is also known as the **medical model** because mental health disorders are viewed as similar to physical diseases. As such, they can be diagnosed, treated, or cured in much the same way as other physical illnesses by prescribing medications or through surgery.

PSYCHOLOGICAL THEORIES: INTERNAL AND EXTERNAL INFLUENCES

Psychological theories attribute abnormal behavior to internal or external stressors. Recall from Chapter 11 on personality that four perspectives predominate:

- *The psychoanalytic perspective.* This perspective attributes abnormal behavior to unresolved unconscious conflicts. According to Freud, mental health disorders result from the conflict between the unconscious sexual and aggressive instinctual desires of the id and the outward demands of society. Newer theories, referred to as *psychodynamic theories* and developed by Freud's followers such as Alfred Adler and Karen Horney (Chapter 11), downplay the role of sexual and aggressive instincts and instead emphasize the role of the ego and interpersonal relationships in maintaining or restoring mental health.
- *The social learning perspective.* Learning theorists (particularly B. F. Skinner and his successors) explain abnormal behavior as a result of the same learning processes that produce normal behavior—classical conditioning, operant conditioning, and social learning. A person's responses to stimuli in the environment and the consequences of these behaviors are what lead to abnormal behavior. A person's past learning and modeling along with current experiences can explain mental health disorders.
- *The cognitive perspective.* This perspective emphasizes the role of thoughts, expectations, assumptions, and other mental processes in abnormal behavior. Think about the little voice inside you that comments on your behavior. Does it encourage you to do well, or does it criticize you for your stupidity? Is it possible that such internal messages influence your behavior? The cognitive perspective maintains that they do.
- *The humanistic perspective.* Humanists like Carl Rogers see abnormal behavior as resulting from a distorted perception of the self and reality. When people lose touch with their personal values and their sense of self, or when they fail to fulfill their basic biological and psychological needs, they cannot attain self-actualization. Instead, they experience personal distress and are more likely to engage in maladaptive behavior.

Poverty and adverse environments are important sociocultural factors that must be looked at when evaluating abnormal behavior.

Owen Franken/Encyclopedia/Corbis

SOCIOCULTURAL THEORIES: THE INDIVIDUAL VARIES IN CONTEXT

Sociocultural theories emphasize social or cultural factors that may play a role in mental health. Such a perspective argues that internal biological and psychological processes can be understood only in the context of the larger society and culture that shape and influence people's behavior. Abnormal behavior, therefore, can be fully understood only when social factors such as age, race, gender, social roles, and socioeconomic status are taken into account. In addition, social conditions such as poverty, discrimination, and environmental stressors must be looked at when evaluating abnormal behavior (see e.g., Zvolensky et al., 2010).

A BIOPSYCHOSOCIAL MODEL: INTEGRATING PERSPECTIVES

Despite decades of research, no single theory or perspective is correct. It is only by integrating all the perspectives that our explanations of abnormality become comprehensive. We often hear in the popular press and in television commercials that a mental health disorder such as depression or anxiety is caused by "a specific gene" or "a chemical imbalance." But such reports are too simplistic to explain the complexity of mental illness. Most mental health disorders result from a combination of biological, psychological, and social factors (hence the name of the *biopsychosocial model*); they do not have just one cause.

For example, as we will soon see, people diagnosed with major depressive disorder often show changes in brain chemistry—a biological factor. They also are likely to engage in a negative pattern of thinking, a psychological factor. In addition, major depression is more likely to be diagnosed in women—a sociocultural factor. Current research in psychology focuses on understanding how these forces operate together, much as the pieces of a jigsaw puzzle fit together.

Quiz Yourself 13.1

1. **Susan enjoys eating garbage when she is hungry. By which criteria can Susan's behavior be considered abnormal?**
   a. Danger to others
   b. Violates social norms
   c. Distress
   d. All of the above
2. **What is the likelihood that you or someone close to you will be diagnosed with a mental health disorder sometime in your life?**
   a. About 15%
   b. About 25%
   c. About 50%
   d. About 75%
3. **Dr. Kwan believes that Ken's abnormal behavior has resulted from a distorted sense of self and a loss of personal values. Dr. Kwan is adopting which psychological perspective?**
   a. Humanistic
   b. Psychoanalytic
   c. Social learning
   d. Cognitive

Answers 1. b; 2. c; 3. a

13.2 The *DSM* Model for Classifying Abnormal Behavior

In 1952, the American Psychiatric Association (APA) published a book listing the symptoms that must be shown in order for a person to be diagnosed with a specific mental health disorder. Emily, featured in this section's case study, was

Diagnostic and Statistical Manual of Mental Disorders (DSM) a book published by the American Psychiatric Association that lists the criteria for close to 300 mental health disorders

diagnosed as having an anxiety problem with borderline personality trends. More than 60 years later, the ***Diagnostic and Statistical Manual of Mental Disorders*** (***DSM***) is in its fifth edition, published in 2013. This most recent edition, known as the *DSM-5*, lists specific and concrete criteria for diagnosing nearly 300 disorders in children, adolescents, and adults. Here we outline the general structure of the *DSM* and describe its strengths and weaknesses.

13.2.1 • The Structure of the *DSM*

The *DSM-5* includes 20 major categories of mental health disorders. Many of these disorders are the focus of this chapter and are listed in • TABLE 13.1. It also indicates the length of time that a person must show these symptoms to

TABLE 13.1

***DSM-5* Major Categories of Disorders**

MAJOR CATEGORY	SOME INCLUDED DISORDERS
Neurodevelopmental Disorders	• Intellectual Disabilities • Communication Disorders • Autism Spectrum Disorders • Attention-Deficit/Hyperactivity Disorder • Specific Learning Disorder • Motor Disorders
Schizophrenia Spectrum and Other Psychotic Disorders	• Delusional Disorder • Brief Psychotic Disorder • Schizophrenia • Schizoaffective Disorder
Bipolar and Related Disorders	• Bipolar I Disorder • Bipolar II Disorder • Cyclothymic Disorder
Depressive Disorders	• Major Depressive Disorder • Persistent Depressive Disorder (Dysthymia) • Premenstrual Dysphoric Disorder
Anxiety Disorders (see You Review, p. 559)	• Separation Anxiety Disorder • Social Anxiety Disorder (Social Phobia) • Panic Disorder • Generalized Anxiety Disorder • Specific Phobia
Obsessive-Compulsive and Related Disorders (see You Review, p. 559)	• Obsessive-Compulsive Disorder • Body Dysmorphic Disorder • Hoarding Disorder
Trauma- and Stressor-Related Disorders (see You Review, p. 559)	• Reactive Attachment Disorder • Posttraumatic Stress Disorder • Acute Stress Disorder

(continued)

TABLE 13.1

DSM-5 Major Categories of Disorders (continued)

MAJOR CATEGORY	SOME INCLUDED DISORDERS
Dissociative Disorders (see Table 13.2, p. 563)	• Dissociative Identity Disorder • Dissociative Amnesia • Depersonalization/Derealization Disorder
Somatic Symptom and Related Disorders (see Table 13.3, p. 564)	• Somatic Symptom Disorder • Conversion Disorder • Illness Anxiety Disorder
Feeding and Eating Disorders (see Chapter 5)	• Rumination Disorder • Anorexia Nervosa • Bulimia Nervosa
Elimination Disorders	• Enuresis • Encopresis
Sleep–Wake Disorders (see Chapter 4)	• Insomnia Disorder • Central Sleep Apnea • Restless Legs Syndrome
Sexual Dysfunctions	• Erectile Disorder • Female Orgasmic Disorder • Genito-Pelvic Pain/Penetration Disorder
Gender Dysphoria	• Gender Dysphoria
Disruptive, Impulse-Control, and Conduct Disorders	• Oppositional Defiant Disorder • Conduct Disorder • Kleptomania
Substance-Related and Addictive Disorders (see Chapter 4)	• Alcohol-Related Disorders • Opioid-Related Disorders • Stimulant-Related Disorders • Gambling Disorder
Neurocognitive Disorders	• Delirium • Major and Mild Neurocognitive Disorders
Personality Disorders (see Table 13.4, p. 582)	• Paranoid Personality Disorder • Antisocial Personality Disorder • Dependent Personality Disorder • General Personality Disorder
Paraphilic Disorders	• Voyeuristic Disorder • Fetishistic Disorder • Sexual Sadism Disorder
Other Mental Disorders	• Unspecified Mental Disorder

Source: Reprinted with permission from the *Diagnostic and Statistical Manual of Mental Disorders, Fifth Edition*, Copyright 2013. American Psychiatric Association.

qualify for a diagnosis. These criteria require that the symptoms interfere with the person's ability to function, adopting the definition of abnormality that we discussed at the start of this chapter and that is accepted by many professionals today. However, the current version of the *DSM* does not speculate as to the causes of the individual's behavior—it is *atheoretical*. This atheoretical position underscores the complex biopsychosocial nature of the causes of mental illness. Moreover, because the *DSM-5* is relatively new, much of the research described herein is derived from individuals who met the diagnostic criteria from previous editions of the *DSM*.

13.2.2 • How Good Is the *DSM* Model?

How *reliable* and *valid* is the *DSM* model? Recall from Chapter 11 that *reliability* refers to the consistency of a measurement system. We would expect two different clinicians to give a similar judgment or a consistent rating when presented with the same symptoms. Similar diagnoses should also be made when different people exhibit the same symptoms.

Validity refers to how well a rating system does what it was intended to do; it refers to the accuracy of the test. We would expect that the *DSM* model should be accurate in diagnosing people who are having difficulty functioning. In addition, it should be accurate in the label it applies to a person's condition. People who are depressed should be diagnosed as depressed, and people addicted to drugs should be diagnosed as having a substance-related disorder.

The numerous revisions of the *DSM* have attempted to improve its reliability and validity based on sound scientific data. As a result, the reliability and validity for many of the diagnostic categories have improved (T. A. Brown et al., 2001; Hasin et al., 2006; Lahey et al., 2004). However, the reliability of the personality disorders is considered low, calling into question the validity of diagnosing the personality disorders (Clark, 2007; Falkum, Pedersen, & Karterud, 2009; Widiger & Trull, 2007). The reliability and validity of the changes incorporated into the *DSM-5* diagnoses have yet to be determined.

Having a standard system such as the *DSM* does not guarantee an accurate diagnosis. Making diagnostic judgments will always involve some subjectivity and personal bias on the part of the clinician, as people's symptoms often do not fit neatly into one category. Moreover, certain symptoms may be listed as a part of several disorders. As a result, sometimes people meet the criteria for more than one disorder, and can be diagnosed with both, a situation called *comorbidity*. Biases having to do with gender, race, or culture—whether conscious or unconscious—can also skew a diagnosis (Jane et al., 2007; Skodol & Bender, 2003; Widiger & Chaynes, 2003).

Critics of the *DSM* model also point out the possible negative effects of labeling someone with a mental health disorder (Baumann, 2007; Grover, 2005). A diagnostic label may serve as a *self-fulfilling prophecy*, encouraging a person to behave in a way that is consistent with the disorder. Remember how Emily's father called her careless and clumsy, which only contributed to Emily's feelings of awkwardness. Others in the person's environment may also treat the person in a way that encourages the symptoms of the disorder. We as a society tend to treat people with any diagnostic label negatively, perhaps increasing their maladaptive functioning through prejudice and discrimination. Such negative treatment may persist even after the person's behavior returns to normal (Rosenhan, 1973; Szasz, 1987).

The *DSM* model is not perfect and can provide only a general description of the problem a person is experiencing. It does not consider the uniqueness of each individual, nor can it tell us how this person will behave in the future. Yet the *DSM* provides a useful framework and common language for clinicians and researchers to diagnose and study people with mental health problems. Having a common language also allows researchers to more effectively study the possible underlying causes of mental health disorders. Keep in mind the advantages and criticisms of the *DSM* system as we review some of the more prevalent and more interesting mental health disorders.

13.2

Quiz Yourself

1. The purpose of the *DSM* is to _____.
   a. explain the causes of mental health disorders
   b. describe the symptoms of mental health disorders
   c. indicate the frequency of mental health disorders
   d. prescribe treatment methods for mental health disorders
2. The *DSM* model most emphasizes which aspect of the definition of abnormality?
   a. Atypical
   b. Violation of social norms
   c. Inability to function
   d. Mental insanity
3. Which of the following is *true* about diagnosis?
   a. A diagnostic system is valid if two different clinicians give a similar judgment or a consistent rating when presented with the same symptoms.
   b. The *DSM-5* has eliminated the problem of comorbidity.
   c. A diagnostic label may serve as a self-fulfilling prophecy.
   d. The *DSM-5* guarantees accurate diagnoses.

Answers 1. b; 2. c; 3. c

13.3 Anxiety, Trauma-, Obsessive-Compulsive and Related Disorders: It's Not Just "Nerves"

We all experience anxiety from time to time. Many students are anxious when they have to make an oral presentation. Other people are nervous when they have to meet new people or fly in an airplane. In these examples, however, the anxiety tends to decrease once the situation is over. People with excessive anxiety are different in that they experience chronic anxiety that seriously interferes with their ability to function. We saw in the section case study how Emily's panic caused distress and difficulty in coping.

13.3.1 • Components of Excessive Anxiety

Typically, excessive anxiety can be characterized by four components: *physical, cognitive, emotional,* and *behavioral.* These components interact powerfully, creating an unpleasant experience of fear or dread, although there may not be a specific fear-producing stimulus present.

The *physical* components of anxiety include dizziness, elevated heart rate and blood pressure, muscle tension, sweating palms, and dry mouth. These physical symptoms stem from the activation of the sympathetic nervous system (Chapter 2). The hormonal system is also activated as adrenalin is released into the bloodstream. Recall that this process is referred to as the fight-or-flight response. This fight-or-flight response occurs every time we perceive a threat in our environment.

People with excessive anxiety have concerns that are unrealistic and out of proportion to the amount of harm that could occur. *Cognitive* components of anxiety may include worrying, fearing loss of control, exaggerating (in one's mind) the danger of a situation, exhibiting paranoia, or being extremely wary and watchful of people and events. These thoughts may lead to *emotional* reactions such as a sense of dread, terror, panic, irritability, or restlessness. These thoughts and emotions propel the person to behave in ways meant to cope with the anxiety.

Coping with abnormal anxiety may include *behaviors* such as escaping or fleeing from the situation; behaving aggressively; "freezing," which results in being unable to move; or avoiding the situation in the future. Again, these symptoms are so intense that they disrupt the quality of the person's life and cause significant distress.

generalized anxiety disorder (GAD) an anxiety disorder characterized by chronic, constant worry in almost all situations

13.3.2 • Types of Excessive Anxiety Disorders

Approximately 19% of Americans over 18 years of age are diagnosed with an anxiety disorder in a given year (NCS-R, 2007) (see • FIGURE 13.3). Women have consistently higher rates of anxiety disorders than do men (McLean et al., 2011). African Americans have a lower lifetime risk of anxiety disorders than European Americans and Hispanic Americans (Breslau et al., 2005). Anxiety disorders typically begin in childhood or adolescence and are highly *comorbid,* meaning that the anxiety disorder occurs along with another mental health disorder (Copeland et al., 2014; Kessler et al., 2010). Recall that Emily's anxiety was evident by the early teen years, and she was diagnosed as having not just an anxiety disorder but also borderline personality disorder.

We will discuss three *DSM-5* categories of disorders characterized by excessive anxiety: anxiety disorders, trauma-related disorders, and obsessive-compulsive and related disorders. The anxiety disorders include *generalized anxiety disorder, panic disorder, agoraphobia, specific phobia,* and *social anxiety disorder.* The obsessive-compulsive and related disorders include *obsessive-compulsive disorder* and *hoarding disorder. Posttraumatic stress disorder* is a trauma-related disorder.

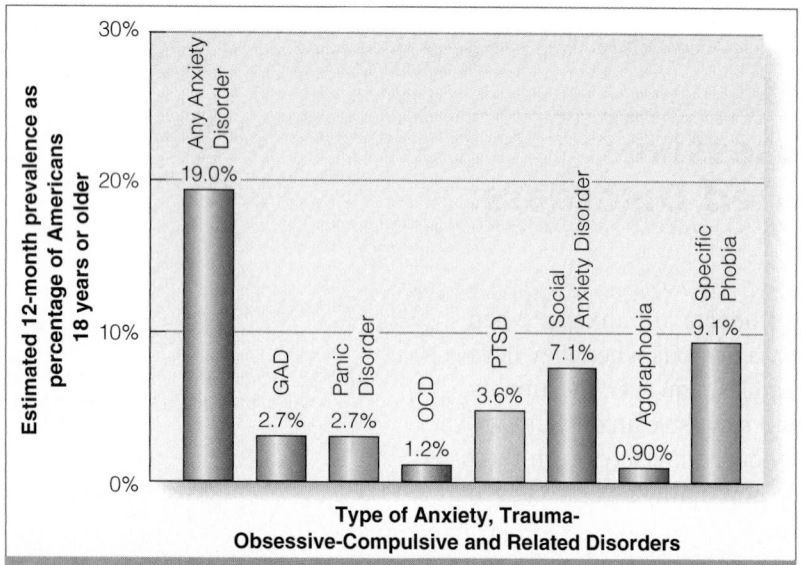

FIGURE 13.3

Prevalence of Anxiety, Trauma-, Obsessive-Compulsive and Related Disorders in a Given Year

Among adults 18 years of age or older, social anxiety disorder and specific phobia are the most commonly diagnosed disorders in any given year because the age of onset is typically earlier for these disorders than for the other excessive anxiety disorders.

Source: National Comorbidity Survey Replication data, Table 2. Updated 2007. http://www.hcp.med.harvard.edu/ncs

GENERALIZED ANXIETY DISORDER (GAD)

Some people are anxious all the time in almost all situations. These individuals may be diagnosed with **generalized anxiety disorder (GAD)**. Symptoms of GAD include excessive anxiety, worry, and difficulty in controlling such worries.

The person may be easily fatigued, restless, and irritable, and may experience difficulty concentrating or sleeping (American Psychiatric Association, 2013). People with GAD chronically worry not only about major issues, such as which car or house to buy, their children's health, or their job performance, but also about minor issues such as being late, wearing the right outfit, or what to make for dinner. It is estimated that about 3% of American adults experience GAD in any given year (Kessler, Chiu et al., 2005) with 14% meeting the criteria for the disorder some time in their lives (Moffitt et al., 2010). European Americans are at higher risk of GAD than African Americans and Hispanic Americans (Breslau et al., 2006).

PANIC DISORDER AND AGORAPHOBIA

Imagine that you are attending a party given by a good friend. When you arrive at the party, a feeling of panic suddenly overwhelms you. Your heart begins to pound, you hear ringing in your ears, your skin feels tingly and numb, and it becomes harder and harder to breathe. These are common symptoms that occur during a *panic attack,* a short but intense episode of severe anxiety. As many as 30% of adults in the United States report occasional panic attacks that do not interfere with their daily functioning (Kessler, Chiu et al., 2006). However, when panic attacks are more common, and a person begins to fear having panic attacks to the extent that it interferes with the ability to function, a diagnosis of **panic disorder** may be given (American Psychiatric Association, 2013).

panic disorder an anxiety disorder characterized by intense fear and anxiety in the absence of danger that is accompanied by strong physical symptoms

agoraphobia [agg-or-uh-FOE-bee-uh] an anxiety disorder characterized by excessive fear of being in places from which escape might be difficult or where help might not be available if one were to experience panic

It is estimated that between 1.5% and 5% of people will develop panic disorder at some time in their lives (Grant et al., 2006). It typically develops in late adolescence or early adulthood and is twice as common in women as in men (Grant et al., 2006; Kessler, Berglund et al., 2005). European Americans and Native Americans tend to have a higher prevalence rate of panic disorder than do African Americans, Asian Americans, and Hispanic Americans (Breslau et al., 2006; Grant et al., 2006).

People with panic disorder often feel so overwhelmed by the feelings of panic that they think they are having a heart attack or a seizure. They may believe that they are "going crazy" or going to die, and many seek medical attention to find out what is wrong with them. The panic attacks may occur frequently or only sporadically. Most people with panic disorder cannot identify any specific thing that might have triggered the attack. However, when a panic attack occurs, the same situation may then trigger a future attack. Emily's teenage behavior was probably most consistent with panic disorder.

Fear of having another panic attack may lead to **agoraphobia**, or fear of being in places from which escape may be difficult or where help may not be available if one were to experience panic (American Psychiatric Association, 2013). People affected with agoraphobia avoid any place—the mall, the grocery store, or the movie theater—in which they believe a panic attack may occur. Such fears can leave people housebound for years. At least 75% of those who are diagnosed with agoraphobia are women (Barlow, 2002).

For many college students, taking a test is an anxiety-producing event.

Image Source/Getty Images

SPECIFIC PHOBIA AND SOCIAL ANXIETY DISORDER

All of us have fears. Some of us get anxious when we think of or see a snake or a spider. Others may fear public speaking or eating in public. As children, we may have been afraid of the dark or the dentist. These are common fears. However, when our fears become so intense that they cause severe anxiety, possibly even panic attacks that interfere with our ability to function, then a diagnosis of *specific phobia* or *social anxiety disorder* is made (American Psychiatric Association, 2013).

specific phobia an anxiety disorder characterized by persistent fear and avoidance of a specific object or situation

social anxiety disorder an anxiety disorder characterized by an irrational, persistent fear of being negatively evaluated by others in a social situation; also called social phobia

obsession a recurrent thought or image that intrudes on a person's awareness

compulsion repetitive behavior that a person feels a strong urge to perform

obsessive-compulsive disorder (OCD) a disorder involving a pattern of unwanted intrusive thoughts and/or the urge to engage in repetitive actions that interferes with a person's functioning

Specific phobias involve a persistent fear and avoidance of a specific object or situation—animals, heights, bridges—or other specific stimuli. They are one of the most common disorders worldwide, affecting approximately 9% of American adults (NCS-R, 2007), 4% of the general population in Mexico (Medina-Mora et al., 2005), 2.7% in Japan (Kawakami et al., 2005), and 7.7% across several European countries (ESEMed/MHEDEA, 2004). Specific phobias typically begin in childhood (Kessler, Berglund et al., 2005).

Social anxiety disorder (social phobia) includes an irrational, persistent fear of being negatively evaluated by others in a social situation. A person with social anxiety disorder may have an extreme fear of rejection, embarrassment, or humiliation. This disorder may include fear of public speaking, fear of eating or undressing in front of others, or fear of meeting new people. The person endures intense anxiety or avoids these social situations such that his or her functioning is impaired (American Psychiatric Association, 2013). It is estimated that 12% of American adults will experience social anxiety disorder at some time in their lives (Ruscio et al., 2008). Social anxiety disorder tends to develop in the early preschool years and in adolescence, and it is somewhat more likely to develop in women than in men (Bogels et al., 2010; Kessler, Berglund et al., 2005; Lang & Stein, 2001). African Americans and Hispanic Americans tend to have a lower lifetime risk of social anxiety disorder than do European Americans (Breslau et al., 2006).

People with specific phobia and social anxiety disorder typically recognize that their fears are irrational, but they cannot stop the overwhelming anxiety they feel when faced with the feared object or situation.

OBSESSIVE-COMPULSIVE DISORDER (OCD) AND HOARDING DISORDER

Obsessions are recurrent thoughts or images that intrude on a person's consciousness or awareness. **Compulsions** are repetitive behaviors that a person feels a strong urge to perform. All of us experience intrusive thoughts and strong urges. For example, on your way to school or work, the thought pops into your head that you left the stove on, and you start worrying about a house fire. What do you do? Many of us feel compelled to turn the car around to check that everything is okay. However, what if this scenario occurred every time you got in the car, and you felt compelled to check each time? In such a case, you might be diagnosed with **obsessive-compulsive disorder (OCD)**.

Obsessive-compulsive disorder is a disorder in which a person experiences recurrent obsessions or compulsions or both that he or she feels cannot be controlled (American Psychiatric Association, 2013). Obsessions often center on dirt and contamination, doing harm to oneself or others, sexual thoughts, or repeated doubts (such as not having locked the house). Common compulsions include cleaning, checking, counting things, or arranging and straightening things in a particular fashion. The compulsions are often performed with the hope of preventing the obsessive thoughts or making them go away. However, performing these "rituals" provides only temporary relief. Not performing the rituals increases the person's anxiety.

Recurrent obsessions cause great personal distress, and compulsions can be time-consuming and in some cases harmful—as when a person washes his or her hands so frequently that they bleed. It is estimated that between 1% and 3% of individuals will develop OCD at some time in their lives; in the United States, the rates are higher among European Americans than among Hispanic Americans and African Americans (Calamari et al., 2012; Kessler Chiu et al., 2005; Leckman et al., 2010).

Hoarding disorder is related to OCD but is now considered a separate disorder in the *DSM-5*. People who hoard have persistent difficulty throwing away possessions, even when the item is of very little value. The person's compulsion to hoard impairs their ability to function, yet having to part with or discard their possessions causes significant distress and anxiety. As a result, the person's living environment becomes cluttered, unusable, and in some cases even hazardous (American Psychiatric Association, 2013). It is estimated that between 2% and 5% of the population engage in hoarding with nearly equal numbers of males and females (Frost, Steketee, & Tolin, 2012; Iervolino et al., 2009).

WR Publishing / Alamy

In hoarding disorder a person keeps large amounts of items that others consider excessive or worthless such that it interferes with his or her safety and/or ability to function.

POSTTRAUMATIC STRESS DISORDER (PTSD)

Excessive anxiety can also develop following a traumatic event as in the case of **posttraumatic stress disorder (PTSD)**. PTSD develops after exposure to a terrifying event or ordeal in which grave physical harm occurred or was threatened. Traumatic events may include the following:

- Violent personal assaults such as rape, physical abuse, or sexual abuse
- Natural or human-caused disasters such as an earthquake, a hurricane, a terrorist attack, or an outbreak of an infectious disease
- Military combat
- Events that anyone might experience—the sudden, unexpected death of a loved one or witnessing a violent crime or a deadly traffic accident

A diagnosis of PTSD requires that the person repeatedly reexperience the ordeal in the form of distressing memories, nightmares, frightening thoughts, or flashback episodes, especially when exposed to situations that are similar to the original trauma. For example, a car backfire might trigger a flashback to a combat trauma or being the victim of an armed robbery. Anniversaries of the event also can trigger symptoms. At the same time they persistently avoid situations, thoughts, or memories that are associated with the trauma. In addition, people diagnosed with PTSD may experience emotional numbness or withdrawal from themselves or others such that they lose interest in usual activities or are regarded as distant and emotionally unavailable. Finally, people with PTSD are always on guard and alert to any real or imagined potential threats in their environments—showing *hypervigilance,* having difficulty concentrating, or having difficulty sleeping (American Psychiatric Association, 2013). They may experience depression, anxiety, irritability, or outbursts of anger; physical symptoms such as headaches, dizziness, or chest pain; or feelings of intense guilt. For some people, such symptoms can seriously disrupt the ability to work or to meet social, professional, and family obligations.

Approximately 3.5% of U.S. adults are diagnosed with PTSD in a given year (Kessler, Chiu et al., 2005). In the United States, the rates are higher among African Americans than among Hispanic Americans, Asian Americans, and European Americans (Roberts et al., 2011). More than twice as many females as males

hoarding disorder an obsessive-compulsive-related disorder characterized by persistent difficulty in discarding possessions such that they accumulate and clutter living areas causing significant distress and impairment in functioning

posttraumatic stress disorder (PTSD) a trauma-related disorder, characterized by distressing memories, emotional numbness, and hypervigilance, that develops after exposure to a traumatic event

Mike Goldwater/Photonica World/Getty Images

Exposure to a trauma can lead to the development of PTSD.

experience PTSD following exposure to a trauma, typically sexual assault (Tolin & Foa, 2006; Zinzow et al., 2012). Women's higher PTSD risk has been attributed to a number of variables that reinforce the biopsychosocial perspective on mental health disorders. For example, sex differences in the responses of the *amygdala,* the brain structure that mediates fear, have been documented (Hamann, 2005). Moreover, women are more likely to perceive threat and loss of control than men—psychological factors that may influence the risk of PTSD (Olff et al., 2007). Women are more likely to be victims of sexual abuse and experience these traumas at younger ages than men—social factors that also play a role in PTSD (Olff et al., 2007; Tolin & Foa, 2006; Zinzow et al., 2012).

Soldiers (male or female) are also at high risk for developing PTSD, as military conflict is a source of trauma (Creamer et al., 2011). About 19% of Vietnam veterans developed PTSD at some point after the war (Dohrenwend et al., 2006). The disorder has also been reported among Persian Gulf War veterans, with estimates running as high as 8% (Wolfe et al., 1999). After two decades of conflict in Afghanistan, 42% of Afghan participants in a national population-based survey reported PTSD symptoms (Cardozo et al., 2004). Studies of U.S. military personnel in Iraq and Afghanistan also indicate problems in mental health, most notably PTSD (Felker et al., 2008; Sundin et al., 2010, 2014).

Research on the effects of the September 11th attacks on mental health revealed a remarkable degree of PTSD, at least initially (Calderoni et al., 2006; Grieger, Fullerton, & Ursano, 2004; Lating et al., 2004). A comprehensive mental health screening of more than 11,000 rescue and recovery workers and volunteers at the World Trade Center revealed that more than 20% of the participants experienced symptoms of PTSD, and 13% met the diagnostic criteria for PTSD (CDC, 2004). Even nonrescue utility workers deployed to the disaster sites had risk of PTSD (Cukor et al., 2011). Years later, many of these individuals are faring better; however, people who were directly exposed to the attacks are more likely to have persistent symptoms of PTSD (Cukor et al., 2011; Laugharne, Janca, & Widiger, 2007).

You Review: Symptoms of Some of the Anxiety, Trauma-, Obsessive-Compulsive and Related Disorders summarizes those disorders that we have discussed.

13.3.3 • Research Explaining Anxiety, Trauma-, Obsessive-Compulsive and Related Disorders

What causes the disorders characterized by excessive anxiety? Research on people with excessive anxiety suggests biological, psychological, and sociocultural factors that may contribute to such behavior, underscoring the biopsychosocial nature of mental health disorders presented at the beginning of the chapter.

BIOLOGY: NEUROTRANSMITTERS, GENETICS, AND THE BRAIN

The functioning of several neurotransmitters has been linked to excessive anxiety. For example, abnormal activity of norepinephrine, serotonin, or GABA may be involved in panic attacks (Charney et al., 2000; Goddard et al., 2010). Abnormal activity of GABA has been linked to people with GAD, and problems in serotonin regulation have been suggested as a cause for OCD and PTSD (Kuzelova, Ptacek, & Milan, 2010; Mellman et al., 2009).

You Review **Symptoms of Some of the Anxiety, Trauma-, Obsessive-Compulsive and Related Disorders**

ANXIETY DISORDERS	SYMPTOMS
Generalized Anxiety Disorder	Excessive worry for at least 6 months about a number of events accompanied by physical symptoms such as muscle tension, difficulty concentrating, and irritability that impair a person's functioning.
Panic Disorder	Recurrent abrupt experiences of unexpected intense fear accompanied by physical symptoms such as heart palpitations, shortness of breath, or dizziness (panic attacks) followed by 1 month of either persistent worry over additional panic attacks or behavior designed to avoid panic attacks that interfere with a person's functioning.
Specific Phobia	Persistent fear of a specific object or situation that is excessive and unreasonable, lasts for 6 months or more, and interferes with a person's functioning.
Social Anxiety Disorder (Social Phobia)	Persistent fear of one or more social situations in which the person is possibly judged by others that is excessive and unreasonable, lasts for 6 months or more, and interferes with a person's functioning.
Agoraphobia	Excessive and unreasonable anxiety about two or more of the following: public transportation, open spaces, enclosed spaces, being in a crowd or outside the home alone, that the person avoids because of fear of no escape or help if panic-like symptoms develop; lasts for 6 months or more, and interferes with a person's functioning.
TRAUMA-RELATED DISORDER	**SYMPTOMS**
Posttraumatic Stress Disorder	Exposure to a traumatic event during which one feels helplessness or fear followed by recurrent and intrusive memories or nightmares of the event, avoidance of stimuli associated with the event, numbing of emotions, and increased arousal that impair the person's functioning.
OBSESSIVE-COMPULSIVE AND RELATED DISORDERS	**SYMPTOMS**
Obsessive-compulsive Disorder	Presence of recurrent, persistent, intrusive thoughts or images (obsessions), and/or repetitive behaviors or mental acts that a person feels driven to perform (compulsions) to reduce distress or to prevent some event from happening. The thoughts or behaviors are time-consuming and interfere with a person's functioning.
Hoarding Disorder	Persistent difficulty discarding possessions such that they accumulate and clutter living areas causing significant distress and impairment in functioning.

A genetic predisposition to excessive anxiety also may exist. Children of parents with anxiety disorders have a greater risk for anxiety disorders than children of parents with no mental health disorders (Micco et al., 2009). Even relatives of a person (siblings, aunts, uncles) with an anxiety disorder are more likely to have one compared with relatives of someone without a disorder (Hanna, 2000). Twin and family studies have found high heritability especially for panic disorder and OCD (Mosing et al., 2009; Nicolini et al., 2009; Wittchen et al., 2010). Recall that Emily's father was described as tense and keyed-up, so it is possible that Emily inherited a tendency to be anxious herself.

Other studies have focused on specific brain areas that are involved in anxiety and fear. As stated previously, our fear response is coordinated by the amygdala, a small structure deep inside the brain that also plays a role in our emotional memories. Neuroimaging studies on people with GAD and PTSD suggest an overactive amygdala that may contribute to their heightened level of anxiety and memory-related symptoms (Etkin et al., 2010; Hettema et al., 2012; Rogers et al., 2009; Shin et al., 2011). Abnormal functioning of a part of the forebrain called the *striatum* has been investigated as a possible factor in OCD (Choi et al., 2007; Milad & Rauch, 2012). For example, in one study (Rauch et al., 1997), PET scans of individuals with OCD showed different brain activity in the striatum when performing a cognitive task than did the PET scans of people without OCD.

PSYCHOLOGICAL FACTORS: LEARNING AND COGNITIONS

Psychological factors also help in explaining excessive anxiety. For example, specific phobias can be learned in the same way that Watson and Rayner were able to condition Little Albert to fear a white rat (see Chapter 6; Field, 2006). A neutral stimulus (the phobic object) gets paired with a stimulus that naturally elicits fear. So, when a thunderstorm gets paired with a loud noise (thunder) that naturally evokes fear, we learn to be fearful of thunderstorms.

Conditioning processes also may play a role in panic disorder. Neutral stimuli that are present during an initial panic attack may then become conditioned

LWA-Dann Tardif/Lithium/AGE Fotostock

We may acquire fears by observing others' negative experiences.

stimuli that trigger panic symptoms on subsequent occasions. These conditioned stimuli are then thought to generalize to other neutral stimuli, resulting in a variety of cues that evoke panic symptoms (Lissek et al., 2010).

Direct experience is not always necessary to develop a specific phobia. We may acquire fears simply by observing or hearing about others' negative experiences (Kelly & Forsyth, 2007). How many of us have come face to face with a bear? But after hearing someone's account on the news or seeing Internet videos of people's encounters, we may also now fear bears.

Reinforcement is a learning process that helps explain compulsions. If you engage in a certain behavior following an anxiety-provoking obsession, your anxiety is often reduced. The next time the obsession occurs, you feel more compelled to engage in the behavior so that you can reduce your anxiety (Barlow, 2002). Learning and conditioning theories have also been useful in understanding PTSD. Sights, sounds, or images of the trauma all become conditioned stimuli that trigger the fear reaction.

Cognitive research suggests that our thinking processes play a role in developing excessive anxiety. In particular, people who perceive situations and objects as uncontrollable, unpredictable, dangerous, and disgusting are more vulnerable to excessive anxiety disorders (Armfield, 2006; Newman et al., 2013). People with disorders marked by excessive anxiety also may have the tendency to process more negative information rather than positive or neutral information about an event (Fox, Cahill, & Zougkou, 2010; Hertel & Brozovich, 2010; Kleim et al., 2014). For example, studies show that people with panic disorder sometimes misinterpret their bodily sensations, thinking they are beginning a panic attack. Their negative and catastrophic thinking then heightens their anxiety (Clark & Beck, 2010; Craske & Barlow, 2001). People diagnosed with GAD tend to anticipate that something bad will happen to them and that they will feel out of control. While driving in a car, they may worry that they will get lost or in an accident. These worries become constant and almost automatic in their thought processes (Beck, 1997; Riskind et al., 2000).

The shattering of common cognitive beliefs about life may bring on PTSD. An unpredictable trauma—such as a rape, an earthquake, or an automobile accident—may make us question our assumptions that the world is safe and just and that events happen for a reason. It dispels our illusion of control and invincibility, and our assumption that bad things only happen to bad people (Edmondson et al., 2011; Janoff-Bulman, 1992).

SOCIOCULTURAL VARIATIONS: STRESS, GENDER, AND CULTURE

Sociocultural factors must also be considered when explaining the development of disorders characterized by excessive anxiety. For example, in cultures experiencing rapid social change or war, people are more likely to exhibit anxiety symptoms than are people in more stable countries (Compton et al., 1991). Similarly, people who had adverse childhood experiences such as abuse or violence or who have had other previous traumatic or stressful experiences are more likely to develop excessive anxiety disorders (Berntsen et al., 2012; Green et al., 2010; McLaughlin et al., 2010; Ogle et al., 2013). Available social support from family, friends, or the community also makes a difference such that people with emotional support may function better following a traumatic event than those who are isolated or rely on more problematic coping strategies such as avoidance or drug use (Friedman, 2009; La Greca et al., 2010). In the section case study Emily's difficulty with learning at school, high expectations for success, and social rejection at home could be sociocultural factors that contributed to her feelings of anxiety. We have also seen that European Americans and women are more likely than other ethnic groups and men to be diagnosed with an anxiety disorder. More research will have to examine the role of gender and culture in the experience of excessive anxiety before we fully understand their influence.

Quiz Yourself 13.3

1. Marilu is anxious and nervous all the time. She constantly worries over her family, her job, and her schoolwork. Which disorder *best* describes Marilu's behavior?
   a. Panic disorder
   b. Generalized anxiety disorder
   c. Specific phobia
   d. Obsessive-compulsive disorder
2. Learning theories suggest that obsessive-compulsive disorder is the result of _____.
   a. reinforcement processes
   b. faulty cognitions
   c. low self-esteem
   d. unconscious impulses
3. Abdul was involved in a four-car pileup on the interstate 8 months ago. Since then, he has been having nightmares and flashback episodes of the accident. He has difficulty concentrating and has withdrawn from his family and friends. Abdul would most likely be diagnosed with which disorder?
   a. Panic disorder
   b. Posttraumatic stress disorder
   c. Social anxiety disorder
   d. Generalized anxiety disorder

Answers 1. b; 2. a; 3. b

13.4 Dissociative and Somatic Symptom Disorders: Other Forms of Anxiety?

Dissociative and *somatic symptom disorders* are quite rare in the general population but often are of much interest to students. Here we outline the general nature of these disorders and the factors that may a play a role in their development.

13.4.1 • Dissociative Disorders: Multiple Personalities

dissociative [dih-SO-shee-tive] disorder a mental health disorder marked by a loss of awareness of some part of one's self or one's surroundings that seriously interferes with the person's ability to function

To *dissociate* means to break or pull apart. Thus, the **dissociative disorders** involve a loss of awareness of some part of our self, our surroundings, or what is going on around us. Mild dissociative experiences are common (Aderibigbe, Bloch, & Walker, 2001; Hunter, Sierra, & David, 2004). For instance, have you ever driven somewhere and on arrival did not remember driving there? Have you ever missed a part of a conversation but can tell from the speaker's demeanor that you appeared to have been listening the whole time? Have you ever appeared attentive in class while you were daydreaming about your plans for the weekend? All of these are common, everyday dissociative experiences.

However, when loss of awareness becomes more extreme, a diagnosis of a dissociative disorder may apply. Such extreme dissociation is typically linked to severe stress or a series of emotionally traumatic events (Isaac & Chand, 2006; Kihlstrom, 2001). • TABLE 13.2 provides a brief description of the dissociative

TABLE 13.2

Types of Dissociative Disorders

DISORDER	MAJOR FEATURES
Depersonalization disorder	Frequent episodes in which the person feels detached from own mental state or body that causes significant distress or impairs functioning.
Dissociative amnesia	Memory loss of important personal information, not due to substance use or brain injury that causes significant distress or impairs functioning. May occur with or without dissociative fugue in which person unexpectedly travels away from home with memory loss of identity or other personal information.
Dissociative identity disorder	Two or more separate personalities in the same individual that cause significant distress or impaired functioning.

disorders listed in the *DSM-5*. Here we will confine our discussion to perhaps the most controversial and fascinating one, *dissociative identity disorder.*

dissociative identity disorder (DID) a disorder in which two or more personalities coexist within the same individual; formerly called multiple personality disorder

Dissociative identity disorder (**DID**), formerly called *multiple personality disorder,* involves the existence of two or more separate personalities in the same individual (American Psychiatric Association, 2013). The separate personalities—referred to as alters (for alternate personalities)—may or may not be known to the "core," or "host," personality—the person who asks for treatment. Each personality has its own perceptions, thoughts, mannerisms, speech characteristics, and gestures. Each alter appears to have a specific function. For example, one alter may arise to deal with romantic relationships, whereas another alter deals with academic work. The alter personalities may be of different ages, gender, or ethnicities. The majority of people diagnosed with DID are women.

Frequent blackouts or episodes of amnesia are common in people with dissociative identity disorder. They may notice money missing from their bank accounts that they don't remember spending, or find objects in their home that they do not recognize. Self-mutilating behavior is also common in people with this disorder. They may repeatedly burn or cut themselves and have a history of suicide attempts (Foote et al., 2008). Often they have been previously diagnosed with other disorders such as major depressive disorder, PTSD, a substance-related disorder, or schizophrenia, especially if they have reported hearing voices (Loewenstein & Putnam, 2004; Rodewald et al., 2011).

One striking similarity among people with DID is their backgrounds. Almost all have reported experiencing chronic, horrific childhood physical and/or sexual abuse at the hands of family members (Coons, 1994; Ellason, Ross, & Fuchs, 1996; Ross & Ness, 2010). Many clinicians believe that in an attempt to deal with such trauma, these people defensively dissociate, developing alter personalities that can protect them from experiencing such events in life or in memory. People with DID also are highly susceptible to hypnosis (Kihlstrom, 2005; Kihlstrom, Glisky, & Angiulo, 1994). Thus, the ability to dissociate may have become an effective coping mechanism early in life (Spiegel et al., 2011). In contrast, others propose that social learning, expectancies, and sleep dysfunction account for DID. That is, inadvertent suggestive cueing by therapists, hypnosis as a method of memory recovery, and media portrayals of the disorder lead individuals over time to assume the role of someone with DID

(Lynn et al., 2012). Moreover, traumatic experiences disrupt the normal sleep–wake cycle and these disruptions increase one's vulnerability to dissociative symptoms (van der Kloet et al., 2012).

As you can see, explaining the occurrence of DID is highly debated. Some psychologists even question the validity of the dissociative identity disorder (Kihlstrom, 2005; Piper & Merskey, 2004). There has been a great increase in the number of reported cases since 1980 (American Psychiatric Association, 2000a), and it is more frequently diagnosed in the United States (Boysen, 2011). Verifying the claims of amnesia and blackouts is difficult, and people with DID have often been diagnosed with other mental health disorders (Kluft, 1999; Loewenstein & Putnam, 2004; Rodewald et al., 2011). Some believe that DID may represent an extreme form of posttraumatic stress disorder (Butler et al., 1996). A subset of people with PTSD do experience dissociative symptoms, especially those who have experienced repeated sexual trauma (Wolf et al., 2012). As such, a *dissociative-PTSD subtype* has been included in the *DSM-5*. Future research may help us better understand the nature of both dissociation and its relationship to PTSD.

13.4.2 • Somatic Symptom Disorders: "Doctor, I'm Sure I'm Sick"

somatic [so-MAA-tic] symptom disorder a mental health disorder marked by physical complaints that have no apparent physical cause

illness anxiety disorder a somatic symptom disorder in which the person persistently worries over having a serious illness, without any evident physical basis; formerly called *hypochondriasis* [high-po-con-DRY-uh-sis])

Somatic means "related to the body." The **somatic symptom disorders** involve physical complaints for which there is no apparent physical cause. The physical symptoms are real to the person, but physicians can find no medical reason why the individual is experiencing such symptoms. For example, a person may complain of constant hip pain. Numerous medical tests are completed, but there is no apparent physical cause for the hip ache. Because no physical cause can be found, it is assumed that psychological distress underlies the physical problem. In Emily's case, we saw that her anxiety often caused her to have a spastic colon—a somatic symptom related to her emotional distress. ●TABLE 13.3 describes the somatic symptom disorders listed in the *DSM-5*. Our discussion in this section will focus on one of them, *illness anxiety disorder,* formerly called *hypochondriasis.*

In **illness anxiety disorder**, a person believes that he or she has a serious medical illness despite evidence to the contrary (American Psychiatric Association, 2013). Many of us know someone who frequently complains about physical ailments. However, people with illness anxiety disorder are convinced that they

TABLE 13.3

Types of Somatic Symptom Disorders

DISORDER	MAJOR FEATURES
Conversion disorder	Loss of functioning in some part of the body, but no physical cause can be found; causes significant distress or impaired functioning.
Somatic Symptom disorder	Six months of persistent physical complaints with excessive thoughts, feelings, or behaviors related to the symptoms that cause distress or disrupt one's life. The person has sought medical attention, but no physical cause can be found.
Illness Anxiety Disorder	Persistent worry over having a serious illness for at least 6 months. The person may frequently seek or rarely use medical care.

have a serious illness, not just one or two specific symptoms. People with illness anxiety disorder may undergo extensive medical testing by several doctors to confirm the existence of their illness. When a doctor suggests that they may have a mental health problem, people with illness anxiety disorder are likely to seek out another physician rather than seek mental health counseling (Kirmayer & Looper, 2007). Alternatively, others with the disorder may believe they have a serious illness but refuse to seek medical attention. People with illness anxiety disorder often have a family history of depression or anxiety, leading some researchers to speculate that this disorder is an intense form of health anxiety related to panic disorder and obsessive-compulsive disorder (Abramowitz & Moore, 2007; Gropalis et al., 2012). Illness anxiety disorder has an estimated prevalence between 1% and 5% in the general population (American Psychiatric Association, 2000a).

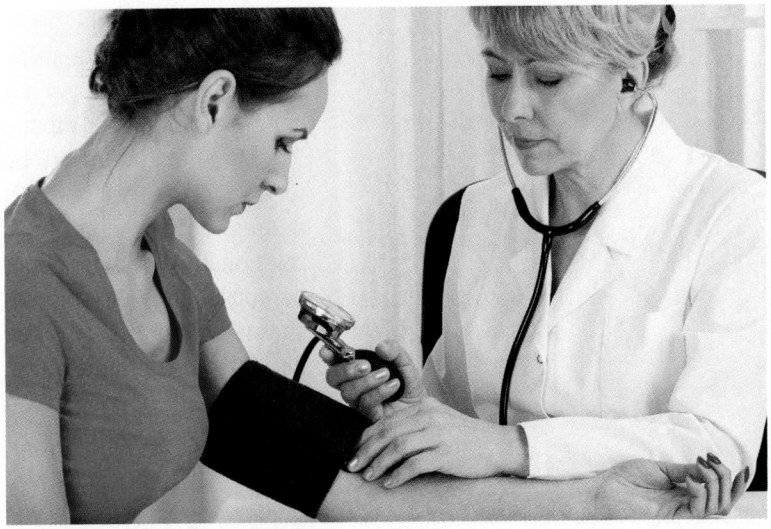

© Photographee.eu/Shutterstock.com

Somatic symptom disorders involve physical complaints with no apparent physical cause. Numerous medical tests may be completed, but no physical cause can be found for the patient's complaint.

13.4

Quiz Yourself

1. **Dissociative disorders involve _____.**
   a. the disintegration of one's personality
   b. physical symptoms without any physical cause
   c. a splitting off of one's conscious mind
   d. a numbness or paralysis in some part of the body
2. **Alphonsia has recurrent abdominal pain. Her doctors have conducted numerous medical tests and can find no physical cause for her symptom. Alphonsia appears to have a(n)_____.**
   a. anxiety disorder
   b. somatic symptom disorder
   c. dissociative disorder
   d. obsessive-compulsive disorder
3. **What do the dissociative and somatic symptom disorders have in common?**
   a. They both occur more frequently in men than in women.
   b. They both involve a preoccupation with the body.
   c. They both include a loss of identity.
   d. They both may represent alternate expressions of anxiety.

Answers 1. c; 2. b; 3. d

13.5 Mood Disorders: Beyond the Blues

A third major category of disorders described in the *DSM-5* is mood disorders. **Mood disorders** involve a significant change in a person's emotional state. This change may include feeling depressed or extremely elated for an extended time. Following anxiety disorders, mood disorders are one of the more common mental health disorders, affecting approximately 9.5% of adult Americans in a given year (Kessler, Chiu et al., 2005). Like anxiety disorders, mood disorders are also likely to have a high rate of comorbidity, or coexist with another mental health disorder.

Many of us experience sadness, but typically this period of sadness lasts only a few days. In clinical depression, the mood change is persistent and interferes significantly with a person's ability to function. Also, normal periods of sadness

mood disorder a mental health disorder marked by a significant change in one's emotional state that seriously interferes with one's ability to function are usually brought on by environmental events—the loss of a loved one, the breakup of a relationship, or a disappointment in one's life. People with clinical depression are sad over a longer period, sometimes in the absence of such external events or long after most people would have adjusted to such changes.

Mood disorders can be devastating to personal relationships and to the ability to work or go to school. Recall that later in adulthood Emily was diagnosed with depression. Her emotional neediness and anger negatively impacted her marital relationship. Many people think that the symptoms are not "real" and that the person should be able to "snap out of it." These inaccurate beliefs may cause shame, which discourages people from seeking appropriate treatment. Fortunately, Emily reentered therapy to address her mood disorder.

We will discuss two basic types of mood disorders: *depressive disorders* and *bipolar disorders*.

major depressive disorder a mood disorder involving sadness, feelings of worthlessness, loss of interest in one's usual activities, and changes in bodily activities such as sleep and appetite that persists for at least 2 weeks

persistent depressive disorder a mood disorder that is a less severe but more chronic form of major depressive disorder; also called dysthymic [dis-THIGH-mik] disorder

13.5.1 • Depressive Disorders: A Change to Sadness

The *DSM-5* indicates several different forms of depression. Here we discuss two types: *major depressive disorder* and *persistent depressive disorder* (*dysthymic disorder*).

MAJOR DEPRESSIVE DISORDER

A diagnosis of **major depressive disorder** requires that a person experience either depressed mood or loss of interest or pleasure in one's usual activities plus at least four other symptoms of depression for a period of at least 2 weeks. These symptoms must be severe enough that they interfere with the person's ability to function but not be due to a general medical condition or the effects of a substance (drug abuse or medication) (American Psychiatric Association, 2013). The other symptoms of depression may include these:

Physical and Behavioral Symptoms

- Change in sleep patterns—either sleeping too much (hypersomnia) or too little (insomnia)
- Change in appetite—either eating too much (resulting in weight gain) or too little (resulting in weight loss)
- Change in motor functioning—either moving slowly and sluggishly or appearing agitated in movement
- Fatigue, or loss of energy

Cognitive Symptoms

- Inability to concentrate or difficulty in making decisions
- Exaggerated feelings of worthlessness or guilt
- Thoughts of suicide (see Psychology Applies to Your World, pp. 568–569)

Major depressive disorder may occur as a single episode or as repeated episodes over the course of years. Some episodes may be so severe that the person requires hospitalization, especially in the presence of frequent suicide attempts or *delusions* (believing something that is not true) and *hallucinations* (perceiving things that are not there).

martin-dm/Getty Images

Major depressive disorder is marked by physical, behavioral, and cognitive symptoms, in addition to depressed mood.

PERSISTENT DEPRESSIVE DISORDER (DYSTHYMIA)

Persistent depressive disorder or *dysthymic disorder* is a less severe but more chronic form of major depressive disorder. The person seems sad and downcast over a longer time. A diagnosis of persistent depressive disorder requires the symptom of depressed mood plus at least two other symptoms of depression for a period of at least 2 years (American Psychiatric Association, 2013). Persistent depressive disorder generally begins in childhood, adolescence, or early adulthood. Typically, the symptoms of persistent depressive disorder are not severe enough to require hospitalization. However, most people with persistent depressive disorder eventually experience a major depressive episode (Klein, Lewinsohn, & Seeley, 2001; Klein, Shankman, & Rose, 2006).

INDIVIDUAL VARIATIONS IN DEPRESSION

Worldwide, depression is projected as the single most burdensome disease in terms of disability by 2030 (World Health Organization, 2008). In the United States, 17% of adults will experience an acute episode of depression at some time in their lives, and 6% will experience more chronic depression (Kessler, Chiu et al., 2005; Kessler & Wang, 2009). Depression also appears to be related to age and gender. Although major depressive disorder can develop at any age, the majority of people who experience a major depressive episode do so by early adulthood (Kessler, Berglund et al., 2005; Rohde et al., 2013). People between 15 and 24 years of age are at high risk for experiencing a major depressive episode, whereas 45- to 54-year-olds experience the lowest rates of major depressive episodes (Kessler et al., 2003; Merikangas et al., 2010). Women are twice as likely as men to experience both mild and more severe depression, a difference found in many different countries, ethnic groups, and across adolescent and adult age groups (Bradley & Hopcroft, 2007; Rohde et al., 2013; Schuch et al., 2014; D. R. Williams et al., 2007). Although African Americans and Hispanic Americans have a lower lifetime risk for a major depressive disorder, when they do experience one, it tends to be more chronic and severe (Breslau et al., 2005, 2006; D. R. Williams et al., 2007). Yet, Hispanics in the United States do show a higher prevalence of depression in the previous year than non-Hispanic people (Anderson & Mayes, 2010).

Unfortunately, many people with depression never receive treatment. In one study, only 51% of participants who met the criteria for major depressive disorder during the prior year received some type of treatment for it. African Americans and Mexican Americans were least likely to receive any care (Gonzalez et al., 2010).

13.5.2 • Bipolar-Related Disorders: The Presence of Mania

Bipolar-related disorders are a second type of mood disorder. The *DSM-5* includes several diagnoses under bipolar-related disorders. Here we will discuss two of them: *bipolar disorder* and *cyclothymic disorder.*

Bipolar disorder involves a shift in mood between two states, or *poles*. One of these shifts is to a depressed state, with symptoms similar to those of major depressive disorder. The person feels sad, lacks self-worth, and may show changes in sleeping and eating over a 2-week period. The second mood change is to the opposite extreme—to a "high" or euphoric state, called **mania**. During a manic state, people feel elated and have high self-esteem, have a decreased need for sleep, are more talkative than usual, and are highly distractible. Much energy is directed at achieving goals, although many projects may be started and few finished. People in this state have an inflated sense of self, feeling confident and able to accomplish anything. This may result in delusional thinking or hallucinations. Also, their boundless energy often results in more impulsive and risk-taking behaviors. When such symptoms of mania, or mania and depression, interfere with a

bipolar disorder a mood disorder characterized by both depression and mania

mania a period of abnormally excessive energy and elation

Psychology Applies to Your World:

Suicide Facts and Misconceptions

Suicidal thoughts are one symptom of depression. Research suggests that nearly 90% of all people who commit suicide have some diagnosable mental health disorder, commonly a depressive disorder or a substance-related disorder (Borges et al., 2010). In 2010, suicide was the 11th-leading cause of death in the United States (higher than homicide). Among 25- to 34-year-olds, it was the second-leading cause of death; among 35- to 44-year-olds, it was the fourth-leading cause of death. Among 15- to 24-year-olds, suicide was the third-leading cause of death. However, these rates are probably grossly underestimated given the negative stigma attached to suicide in the United States (Heron, 2013; Kung et al., 2008; Xu, Kochanek, & Tejada-Vera, 2009).

Women are two to three times more likely than men to *attempt* suicide, but four times as many men actually kill themselves, in part because of the means chosen (Kung et al., 2008; National Center for Health Statistics, 2013). Men tend to shoot, hang, or stab themselves. Women are more likely to choose less lethal means, such as drug overdoses. This gender difference appears in many countries across the world (Weissman et al., 1999; Welch, 2001) except China, where more women commit suicide than men (Phillips, Li, & Zhang, 2002). As seen in • FIGURE 13.4, in the United States, Whites and American Indian/Alaska Natives have higher rates of suicide than other ethnic groups (National Center for Health Statistics, 2013). As we saw in the section case study, Emily had several suicide attempts. Because many of us will encounter or already have

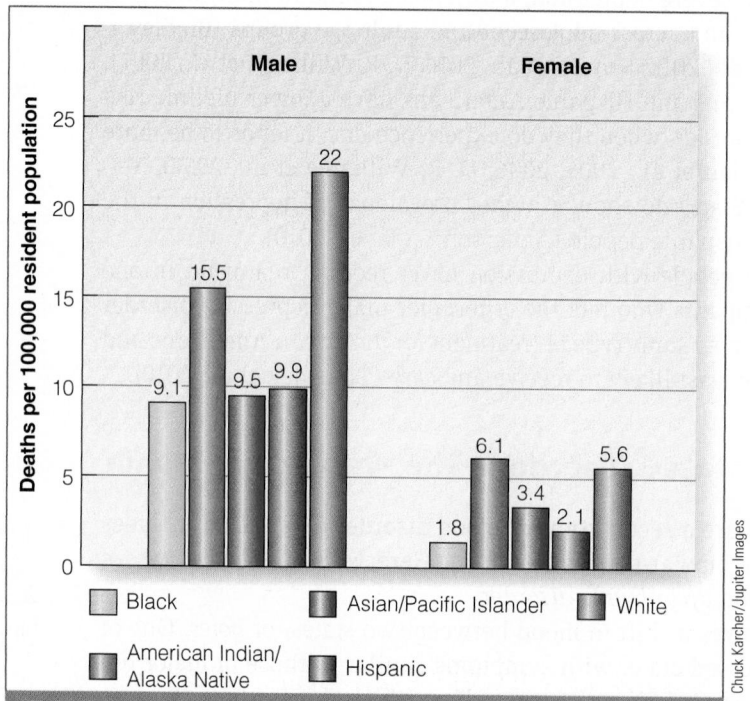

Chuck Karcher/Jupiter Images

FIGURE 13.4

U.S. Death Rates for Suicide by Gender and Ethnicity in 2010

Although women attempt suicide more often, men across all ethnic groups are more likely to commit suicide.

Source: National Center for Health Statistics. (2013). *Health, United States*, 2012. Hyattsville, MD: Author.

encountered someone who is suicidal, let's take a moment to dispel some of the more common misconceptions concerning suicide.

Misconception #1: People who talk of suicide will not kill themselves.

Although most people who talk of suicide do not go on to attempt suicide, people who commit suicide typically have expressed their intentions at some time to family members or friends before their attempt (Ortega & Karch, 2010; Shneidman, 1987). They may have talked about "going away" or be preoccupied in general with the notion of death. Therefore, any talk of suicide should be taken seriously. A person who is suicidal should not be left alone. You may need to contact a mental health professional, call 911, or call a suicide crisis hotline in your area.

Misconception #2: If you ask someone who is depressed whether he or she has thoughts of suicide, it will only plant the idea of suicide in his or her head.

Asking direct questions about a person's plan for suicide is the only way to assess the person's risk for committing suicide. Bringing up the subject can also give the person an opportunity to talk about his or her problem. People who have a concrete plan in mind for when or how they will end their life are more likely to attempt suicide than those whose plans are less specific (Nock et al., 2008; SAMHSA, 2009b).

Misconception #3: People who have unsuccessfully attempted suicide will not try again.

In the United States from 2003 to 2007, among women aged 15–44 who committed suicide, 37% had a history of suicide attempts (Ortega & Karch, 2010). Similarly, among adolescents, a previous history of suicide attempts is the single best predictor of future suicide attempts and completions (Lewinsohn, Rohde, & Seeley, 1994; Miranda et al., 2014). Therefore, a previous suicide attempt puts adolescents and young adult and middle-aged women in particular at a higher risk for future suicide attempts.

Misconception #4: A better mood means the risk of suicide is gone.

Suicide does not typically happen when a person is in the depths of a deep depression. Rather, suicide attempts are more likely to occur when people with depression have energy and can think more clearly and make decisions. This energy and clearer thinking make it appear to loved ones that the person is getting better and is therefore at a lower risk of suicide, when sometimes a better mood can indicate an increased risk of suicide.

Misconception #5: Only people who are depressed attempt suicide.

Although suicidal thoughts are a symptom of depression and depressed people are 30 times more likely to commit suicide than are healthy individuals (Joiner, 2010), people with other serious mental health disorders, including bipolar disorder, substance-related disorders, dissociative disorders, borderline personality disorder, and schizophrenia, are also at risk for suicide (Foote et al., 2008; Nock et al., 2008; Soloff & Chiapetta, 2012). According to findings from the WHO World Mental Health Surveys, the strongest predictors of suicide attempts in developed countries are mood disorders; whereas in developing countries, they are substance use, PTSD, and impulse control disorders (Nock et al., 2009).

Though overall women attempt suicide more often, males who are depressed are especially at risk, with a rate four times higher than that for women who are depressed (National Institute of Mental Health, 2007). A number of other events and situations also increase one's risk of suicide, including economic hardship, serious illness, problems with a partner or the loss of a relationship, childhood sexual or physical abuse, and the presence of a firearm in the home (Borges et al., 2010; Bruffaerts et al., 2010; Karch et al., 2009; Ortega & Karch, 2010). Suicide occurs among people who have mental health disorders as well as those who face environmental stressors. The majority of suicide attempts are expressions of extreme distress and helplessness, not just "harmless" bids for attention.

© s_bukley/Shutterstock.com

Catherine Zeta-Jones recently sought treatment after being diagnosed with bipolar disorder.

person's ability to function, a diagnosis of bipolar disorder is appropriate (American Psychiatric Association, 2013).

Cyclothymic disorder is a less severe but more chronic form of bipolar disorder. In cyclothymic disorder, a person alternates between milder periods of mania and more moderate depression for at least 2 years (American Psychiatric Association, 2013). The person functions reasonably well during the mild mania but is likely to be more impaired during the depressive phase.

Bipolar disorders are less common than depressive disorders, with 2.6% of adult Americans experiencing an episode of bipolar disorder at some time in their lives (Kessler, Chiu et al., 2005; Lewinsohn, Klein, & Seeley, 2000). Men are just as likely as women to be diagnosed with bipolar disorder. The median age of onset for bipolar disorder is late adolescence and early adulthood (Kessler, Berglund et al., 2005; Merikangas et al., 2011).

13.5.3 • Research Explaining Mood Disorders

What causes mood disorders? Not surprisingly, research has identified biological, psychological, and sociocultural factors that may contribute to mood disorders. Again, this highlights the biopsychosocial nature of mental health.

BIOLOGICAL FACTORS: GENES, NEUROTRANSMITTERS, STRESS HORMONES, AND BRAIN STRUCTURES

Several biological factors have been investigated as contributing to depressive disorders: *genes*, *neurotransmitters*, *stress hormones*, and *specific brain areas*.

cyclothymic [sigh-clo-THIGH-mik] disorder a mood disorder that is a less severe but more chronic form of bipolar disorder

Genes The evidence from family history studies and twin studies suggests that mood disorders may be genetically transmitted, especially in the case of bipolar disorder. For example, first-degree relatives (parent, child, or sibling) of persons with bipolar disorder are much more likely to develop the disorder than are relatives of people without the disorder (Perlis et al., 2006; Saunders et al., 2008). Similarly, if an identical twin is diagnosed as having bipolar disorder, the other identical twin has a higher probability of developing the disorder than if they were fraternal twins (McGuffin et al., 2003; Wallace, Schneider, & McGuffin, 2002). In one twin study, the heritability of bipolar disorder was estimated as high as 93% (Kieseppa et al., 2004).

The evidence for genetic factors in major depressive disorder is less clear. The trend toward genetic transmission is present, particularly in women and when the depression begins early in life (Abkevich et al., 2003; Ebmeier et al., 2006; Mosing et al., 2009). Emily's mother was often sad and depressed, perhaps increasing Emily's chances of inheriting a mood disorder. One specific gene that may play a role in depression is the *serotonin transporter gene* (Saveanu & Nemeroff, 2012). Specific regions of chromosomes also have been identified that may contribute to one's risk for depression and bipolar disorder (Duric et al., 2010; Hayden et al., 2010; Holmans et al., 2007; Kuzelova et al., 2010; Levinson et al., 2007).

Neurotransmitters The malfunctioning of certain neurotransmitters has also been linked to mood disorders, specifically serotonin and norepinephrine (Carver, Johnson, & Joormann, 2009; Goddard et al., 2010; Saveanu & Nemeroff, 2012). Antidepressant drugs that act on serotonin and norepinephrine to relieve the symptoms of depression seem to offer evidence for the role of these neurotransmitters in depression. Similarly, abnormalities in the neurotransmitters norepinephrine, dopamine, and glutamate have been investigated as possible factors for proneness to mania in bipolar disorder (Carlson et al., 2006; Cousins, Butts, & Young, 2009; Keck, McElroy, & Arnold, 2001). Unstable circadian rhythm functions may also affect the normal functioning of these neurotransmitters (Bullock & Murray, 2014).

Stress Hormones The connection between depression and hormones has also been studied. Hormones regulate functions such as sleep, appetite, sexual desire, and pleasure. Symptoms of depression relate to these bodily functions (McClung, 2007). Of particular interest to psychologists is the link between stress hormones and depression. When stress hormones are released, they tend to inhibit the activity of brain neurotransmitters that are related to mood. Hence, repeated activation of the hormonal stress system may lay the groundwork for depression (Gillespie & Nemeroff, 2007; Gotlib, Joormann, & Foland-Ross, 2014; Saveanu & Nemeroff, 2012). Excessive levels of stress hormones have also been linked to the shrinkage of certain brain areas that may be related to depression (Kunugi et al., 2010; Sheline, 2000).

Brain Structures Other studies have focused on brain areas that are involved in depression, specifically abnormal functioning of the prefrontal cortex and limbic system (Gotlib et al., 2014; Saveanu & Nemeroff, 2012; Thase, 2010). Recall from Chapter 2 that the prefrontal cortex is involved in planning, attention, working memory, problem solving, and goal-oriented behavior. The limbic system includes the amygdala and hippocampus, structures that regulate emotion, memory, motivation, and mood.

Research is also investigating how connections in the brain *between* the cortex and the limbic system may be associated with depressive symptoms (Gotlib & Hamilton, 2008; Gotlib et al., 2014). Studies by Helen Mayberg and her colleagues (1997, 1999, 2005) as well as others have demonstrated a consistent relationship between depression and dysfunction in an area of the brain's cortex called the *subgenual cingulate*, also known as *Brodmann's area 25* (Dobbs, 2006; Drevets, Savitz, & Trimble, 2008; Tripp et al., 2011). Overactivity in this area allows negative emotions to overwhelm the thinking part of the brain. Additional evidence for this brain region's role in depression comes from treatment studies. Effective antidepressant treatment reduces abnormal activation in this area in people who are depressed (Fu et al., 2004). Using electrodes to reduce activity in this area has also been moderately successful in alleviating symptoms in people with treatment-resistant depression (symptoms that do not respond to at least one trial of antidepressant medication) (Hamani et al., 2009; Kito, Hasegawa, & Koga, 2011; Mayberg et al., 2005).

Research on the biological factors that may contribute to mood disorders indicates a complex relationship among genes, neural activity, hormones, and brain functioning (Dannlowski et al., 2007; Gotlib et al., 2014; Kraft et al., 2007). Future technologies may assist us in sorting out the precise relationship between biology and mood disorders.

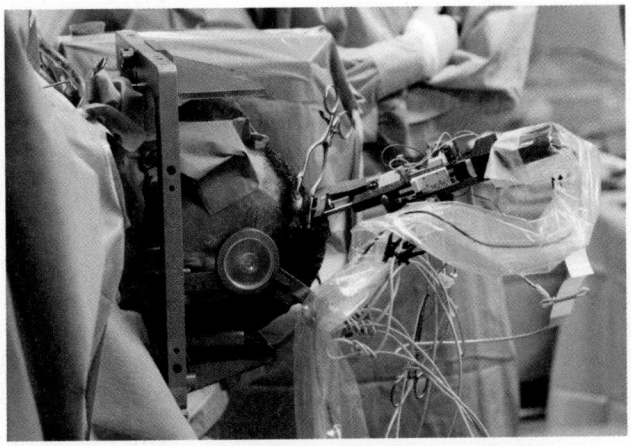

Ian HANNING/REA/Redux

Deep brain stimulation involves implanting electrodes in the part of the brain that affects mood. This surgery has been moderately successful in alleviating depression in clinical trials in participants with treatment-resistant depression.

PSYCHOLOGICAL FACTORS: EARLY ADVERSE LIFE EVENTS, LEARNED HELPLESSNESS, AND NEGATIVE THINKING

Psychological factors also help in explaining mood disorders, especially depression. Specifically, psychologists have examined how *negative life events, learned helplessness*, and *negative patterns of thinking* may put one more at risk for depression.

Early Adverse Life Events Psychoanalytic theory suggests that depression is linked to unresolved childhood issues of abandonment, rejection, and loss that result in self-blame, self-hatred, and other symptoms of depression (Freud, 1917). Some research is consistent with this view. A history of early adverse experiences such as insecure attachments, abuse, separations, and losses can make one vulnerable to depression (Green et al., 2010; Heim et al., 2008; McLaughlin et al., 2010; Nederhof, Ormel, & Oldehinkel, 2014; Vergne & Nemeroff, 2006). Emily's childhood feelings of parental neglect coincide with this viewpoint. While it is possible that early feelings of abandonment and rejection may play a role in depression, it is also possible that such early stressful life events may adversely affect brain chemistry and immune system responses that contribute to depression (Heim et al., 2008; Hennessy, Schiml-Webb, & Deak, 2009).

learned helplessness the belief that one cannot control the outcome of events

ruminative [RUE-muh-nay-tive] coping style the tendency to persistently focus on how one feels without attempting to do anything about one's feelings

cognitive distortion thought that tends to be pessimistic and negative

Learned Helplessness Another psychological explanation of depression is **learned helplessness**, which involves the belief that you cannot control the outcome of events or what is going to happen (see Chapter 12). Therefore, you do not respond even when your response could lead to success. Initial evidence for learned helplessness came from studies in which dogs were administered controllable shock, uncontrollable shock, or no shock (Overmier & Seligman, 1967; Seligman & Maier, 1967). The dogs in the controllable shock situation had to learn to jump a barrier in order to turn off the shock. They quickly learned this behavior. The dogs in the uncontrollable shock situation could not turn off the shock. Later, when the dogs that had been in the uncontrollable shock situation were given the opportunity to jump the barrier to avoid the shock, they failed to respond. They had *learned* to be helpless and just sat there taking the shock *even when they could escape it*. Such research suggests that people who are depressed may respond similarly—they do not take steps to solve or even prevent problems when such action could be helpful because they believe that life is uncontrollable (Ilgen & Hutchison, 2005).

Negative Thinking Research by Susan Nolen-Hoeksema (1959–2013) and her colleagues (Nolen-Hoeksema, 2001, 2002; Nolen-Hoeksema, Larson, & Grayson, 1999; Nolen-Hoeksema et al., 2007; Nolen-Hoeksema, Wisco, & Lyubomirsky, 2008) indicates that coping styles play a role in depression. People who are depressed are more likely to engage in what is called a **ruminative coping style**. To ruminate means to focus on your thoughts. People who are depressed spend a lot of time thinking about their depression and why they are depressed. They tend not to do anything about their depression or its causes but rather remain focused on repetitively analyzing their feelings and concerns. This focus makes it more likely that they will become more severely depressed and also stay depressed longer. Many studies support an association among rumination, negative mood and vulnerability to depression (Aldao, Nolen-Hoeksema, & Schweizer, 2010; Huffziger, Reinhard, & Kuehner, 2009; Jones et al., 2009; Joormann, 2010; Joormann, Levens, & Gotlib, 2011; Marchetti, Koster, & De Raedt, 2013; McIntosh, Gillanders, & Rodgers, 2010).

Research also highlights the role of negative thinking patterns and attributions in the development of mood disorders. If you have ever been around someone who is "down," or depressed, you realize that his or her thoughts tend to be pessimistic and negative. People who are depressed are more likely to engage in negative thinking errors, called **cognitive distortions**, according to classic research by Aaron Beck (1967, 1976). For example, people who are depressed tend to reject positive experiences and focus only on the negative aspects of a situation. Beck believes that these people engage in a negative view so automatically that they may not even realize their errors in thinking.

ENGAGE YOURSELF! To help you understand the impact of negative thinking errors on mood, try this demonstration. Before you go to bed tonight, write down how you feel generally—for example, happy, sad, or stressed. Tomorrow, carry a notepad or tablet around with you all day. Every time you have a positive thought or experience, write it down. At the end of the day, again write down how you feel generally. It is likely that noting positive feelings all day will create a more positive overall feeling. If we had asked you to note negative thoughts for an entire day, how do you think that would affect your outlook on your day?

Research on the *attributions* of people who are depressed further supports Beck's model. An attribution is assigning a cause to behavior (see Chapter 10). People who are depressed tend to feel undeserving of positive outcomes and attribute negative environmental events to factors within themselves (Alloy, Abramson, & Francis, 1999; Wood et al., 2009). For instance, failing an exam is interpreted to mean that one is stupid, will always be stupid, and will probably fail more exams. A relationship breakup is interpreted to mean that one is not lovable and will always be unlovable. These negative attributions and cognitive distortions appear related to depressed mood (Abramson et al., 2002; Gibb et al., 2004; Moore & Fresco, 2007). Beck (2008) has suggested that early adverse experiences combined with biological vulnerabilities (genetics and neurochemistry) may influence the development of these cognitive deficits in people who are depressed. The negative cognitions then influence the interpretation and processing of future stressors as well as neurochemistry and brain activation, creating a vicious cycle of biopsychosocial factors and the maintenance of depression (Foland-Ross et al., 2013).

SOCIOCULTURAL VARIATIONS: SOCIAL STATUS, STRESS, AND GENDER

Sociocultural factors must also be considered when explaining mood disorders. Depression is more likely among people of lower social status (Blazer et al., 1994), especially those from adverse neighborhoods (Cutrona, Wallace, & Wesner, 2006). A considerable body of research also documents a consistent relationship between major stressful life events and the onset of depression, especially among people who are genetically predisposed to depression (Green et al., 2010; Hammen, 2009; Monroe & Reid, 2009; Nederhof et al., 2014; Taylor et al., 2006). Explaining such differences is further complicated by the worldwide gender difference in depression. As we have noted, women are more likely to be diagnosed with depression than men.

13.5.4 • Gender and Depression

Biopsychosocial forces that are unique to women may explain their higher vulnerability to depressive disorders (see • FIGURE 13.5; Gorman, 2006; Mazure, Keita, & Blehar, 2002; Nolen-Hoeksema & Hilt, 2013). We have already seen that the genetic risk of depression appears stronger in women than in men. Research has also investigated—over many years and many studies—the relationship between the female ovarian hormones, estrogen and progesterone, and mood in an effort to understand pathways to depression. However, it is not as simple as saying ovarian hormones *cause* depression. Symptoms of depression do not appear to correspond to changes in levels of estrogen and progesterone across the menstrual cycle

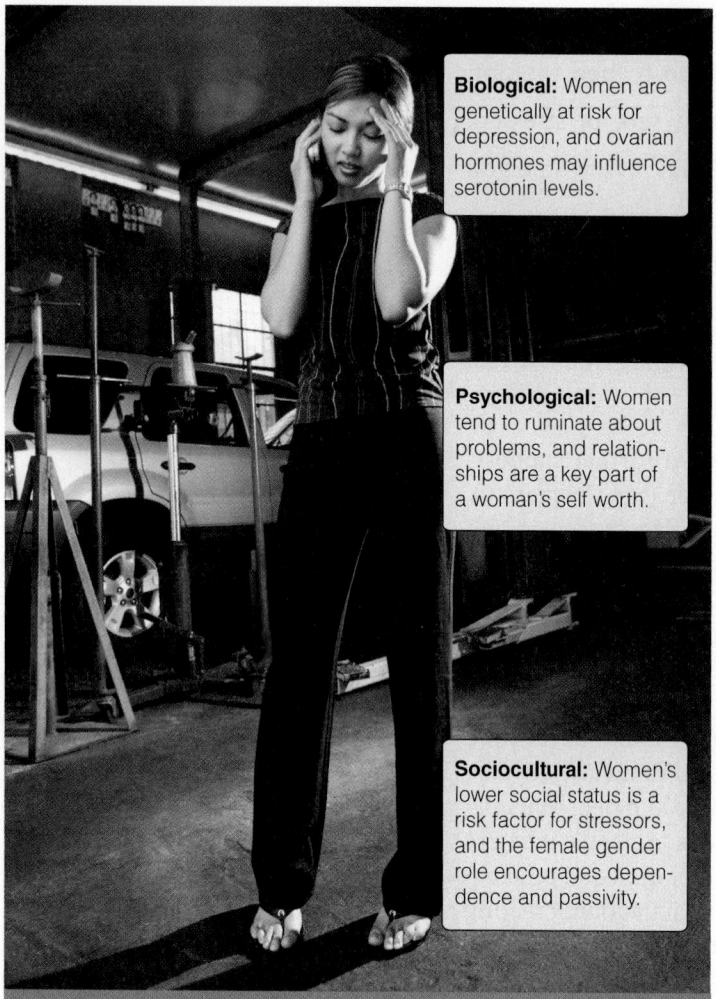

Masterfile

FIGURE 13.5

Women and Depression

Biopsychosocial forces unique to women may explain their higher vulnerability to depressive disorders.

(Steiner & Born, 2000). Rather, research suggests that women's estrogen and progesterone levels may influence the functioning of the neurotransmitter serotonin, which plays a central role in mood. However, researchers don't yet understand the precise actions by which estrogen and progesterone influence serotonin functioning (Hughes et al., 2009; Lu et al., 2003; Parker & Brotchie, 2004; Steiner, Dunn, & Born, 2003). Similarly, some argue that stress hormones differentially contribute to gender differences in depression (Parker & Brotchie, 2010; Young & Korszun, 2010).

Psychological factors unique to women must also be considered when examining gender differences in depression. For example, females are more likely than males to engage in a ruminative coping style (Li, DiGiuseppe, & Froh, 2006; Lopez, Driscoll, & Kistner, 2009; Nolen-Hoeksema, 2001; Papadakis et al., 2006). That is, women tend to focus on how they feel and to fret about their feelings. Even co-rumination, or excessively talking about problems with friends, though offering women social support, can also amplify or increase one's depressive symptoms (Byrd-Craven et al., 2008; Rose, Carlson, & Waller, 2007). In contrast, men are more likely to engage in some activity to take their minds off their feelings, to withdraw, or to abuse drugs (Nolen-Hoeksema & Hilt, 2013). As Nolen-Hoeksema and her colleagues (1999) put it, "Women think and men drink."

Women are also more likely to have an interpersonal orientation that puts them at risk for depression (Mazure et al., 2002). Relationships are more important to a woman's sense of self-worth than they are to a man's. As a result, women are more likely to silence their own demands in order to maintain a positive relationship and are more likely to place their needs secondary to those of others. This relational style may also predispose women to depression.

Tied to these biological and psychological factors are the social circumstances that women face. Women are at a disadvantage in society: They earn less and have less power than men. They report less satisfaction with work and family and are more likely to be victims of violence, discrimination, sexual abuse, and poverty (Heim et al., 2009; Klonoff, Landrine, & Campbell, 2000; Koss & Kilpatrick, 2001). Negative life events such as these foster feelings of uncontrollability and helplessness, perceptions that are intimately connected to mood disorders (Browne, 1993; Ilgen & Hutchison, 2005). Traditional gender roles also discourage women from being masterful, independent, and assertive and encourage them to be dependent and passive. These prescribed roles may increase women's feelings of uncontrollability and helplessness (Barlow, 2002).

Although rates of major depression are higher in women, approximately 13% of U.S. men will experience a major depressive disorder sometime in their lives (NCS-R, 2007). We have also seen that men are at a much higher risk for committing suicide than women. Yet some men may not express the symptoms of depression in the same manner as women. Although men may report the physical symptoms of depression—fatigue, sleep problems, and loss of interest in their usual activities—men are less likely to cry and express sadness and are more likely to hide their feelings, be irritable, lash out at others, and abuse alcohol. Male gender-role socialization encourages men to be strong and in control, which may discourage men from admitting and expressing emotional distress (Cochran & Rabinowitz, 2000; Pollack, 1998).

For both men and women, depression is a complex behavior affected by biological, psychological, and sociocultural variables. Each of us probably has some biological vulnerability to mood disorders. However, social and psychological factors may act to protect us from such vulnerability or, alternatively, make us more likely to express this vulnerability. Research continues to explore the exact role these factors play. People's lives depend on it.

Quiz Yourself 13.5

1. **Maria has been sad for 3 weeks. She can't sleep, eat, or concentrate, and is constantly crying. She has lost interest in her usual activities. Maria would most likely be diagnosed with which disorder?**
   a. Bipolar disorder
   b. Cyclothymic disorder
   c. Major depressive disorder
   d. Persistent depressive disorder
2. **People who are depressed are more likely to engage in _____ or repetitively analyze their feelings and concerns.**
   a. cognitive distortions
   b. rumination
   c. pessimism
   d. negative attributions
3. **Which of the following statements about suicide is *true?***
   a. People who talk of suicide are often just looking for attention and will not kill themselves.
   b. Among adolescents, previous suicide attempts are a predictor of future attempts.
   c. A better mood means the risk of suicide is gone.
   d. Only people who are depressed commit suicide.
4. **Which of the following statements about women's higher vulnerability to depression is *false?***
   a. Women are more likely to have higher levels of estrogen and progesterone which cause depression.
   b. Women are more likely to experience negative life events that lead to feelings of helplessness.
   c. Women are more likely to have an interpersonal orientation that puts them at risk for depression
   d. Women are more likely to focus on how they feel, which can increase feelings of depression.

Answers 1. c; 2. b; 3. b; 4. a

13.6 Schizophrenia: Disintegration

Schizophrenia is a chronic, disabling mental health disorder that affects roughly 1%–2% of the general population worldwide (Ho, Black, & Andreasen, 2003; Lieberman, Stroup, & Perkins, 2012). It involves the disintegration of one's personality.

schizophrenia [skit-suh-FREE-nee-uh] a severe mental health disorder characterized by disturbances in thought, perceptions, emotions, and behavior

Is schizophrenia the same thing as multiple personalities? No. Multiple personalities (now called *dissociative identity disorder,* as previously discussed) involve the existence of several *intact* personalities within a person. In schizophrenia, the one personality is no longer intact, or held together and connected. If we think of someone's personality as a related set of cognitive, emotional, perceptual, and motor behaviors, then in schizophrenia we see the disconnection among

Jean-Michel Girand/Science Source

Schizophrenia is a severe mental health disorder marked by disordered thoughts, perceptions, emotions, and/or motor behavior, as depicted in this drawing by someone with schizophrenia.

these personality elements. As these elements lose their connections with one another, the person loses his or her connection with reality. This results in impaired functioning.

13.6.1 • Individual Variations: Onset, Gender, Ethnicity, and Prognosis

Symptoms of schizophrenia typically appear in adolescence or young adulthood. In some cases, the symptoms come on gradually; in others, they appear more abruptly. Schizophrenia affects men and women with equal frequency, although it typically appears earlier in men than in women. Men tend to develop the disorder in their late teens or early 20s, and women are generally affected in their 20s or early 30s (American Psychiatric Association, 2000a; Robins & Regier, 1991). This gender difference may be related to hormonal and sociocultural factors. The hormone estrogen may protect women by lessening abnormal brain development associated with schizophrenia (Canuso & Pandina, 2007; Seeman, 2008). In addition, women's higher social competence and more extensive social networks may delay the onset of the disorder (Combs & Mueser, 2007; Hooley, 2010). Perhaps because of the earlier onset, men with schizophrenia tend to be more chronically impaired (Grossman et al., 2008; Ho et al., 2003).

Schizophrenia is diagnosed more often in African Americans and Asian Americans. However, this difference may be due to racial bias and cultural insensitivity (Barnes, 2004; Bresnahan et al., 2007). Lifetime prevalence rates of schizophrenia are lower among Hispanics than among European Americans (Zhang & Snowden, 1999). Schizophrenia also is more prevalent in lower socioeconomic groups (Escobar, 1993; Kirkbride et al., 2007).

Most people with schizophrenia suffer throughout their adult lives, losing opportunities for careers and relationships (Hooley, 2010; Jobe & Harrow, 2010). Several factors contribute to this suffering: the negative stigma that a schizophrenia diagnosis brings, the lack of public understanding, and inaccurate media portrayals of people with schizophrenia as criminally violent. Most people with schizophrenia are not violent toward others but are withdrawn and prefer to be left alone (Steadman et al., 1998). Although there currently is no cure, a diagnosis of schizophrenia does not necessarily mean progressive deterioration in functioning, as most people believe. Rather, for reasons not yet understood, schizophrenic symptoms and episodes tend to decrease as a person ages (Eaton et al., 1998; Harrow et al., 2005; Jablensky, 2000). However, recovery is very much related to social factors such as economic and social support. Most people with schizophrenia continue to experience difficulties throughout their lives (Jobe & Harrow, 2010).

13.6.2 • Symptoms of Schizophrenia

Schizophrenia may express itself in many forms, depending on which symptoms are present. People diagnosed with schizophrenia show two or more of the following symptoms nearly every day during a 1-month period with continued disturbance for at least 6 months; and one of the symptoms must be *delusions, hallucinations,* or *disorganized speech* (discussed shortly). These symptoms are not due to substance use or a medical condition, and they interfere with the person's ability to function (American Psychiatric Association, 2013). Symptoms of schizophrenia fall into two broad categories: positive and negative symptoms.

POSITIVE SYMPTOMS OF SCHIZOPHRENIA

Positive symptoms of schizophrenia represent an excess or distortion of normal functions and are more obvious signs of a break with reality called *psychosis*. They include *delusions, hallucinations, disorganized speech,* and *grossly disorganized* or *catatonic behavior.*

- **Delusions** are thoughts and beliefs that the person believes to be true but that have no basis in reality. For example, *persecutory delusions* involve beliefs about being followed or watched, usually by agents of authorities such as the FBI or the government. *Grandiose delusions* involve beliefs about being a famous or special person. For instance, a person with schizophrenia may believe that he is the president of France. People with schizophrenia may also hold *delusions of reference* (believing that others are talking about them) or *delusions of thought control* (believing that their thoughts are controlled by another person or force).
- People who are diagnosed with schizophrenia also may experience **hallucinations**, in which the person sees, hears, tastes, smells, or feels something that others do not perceive. In schizophrenia, hearing voices or other sounds (called *auditory hallucinations*) is the most common altered perception, followed by *visual hallucinations* (seeing things that aren't there). The hallucinations may tell the person to perform certain acts or may be frightening in nature.
- The speech of individuals with schizophrenia is often disorganized in a variety of ways that impair effective communication. **Disorganized speech** (*formal thought disorder*) involves a lack of associations between ideas and events. Because the ideas of people with schizophrenia lack connection, we refer to this disconnection as *loose associations*. Their ideas seem unrelated to one another, and their speech is often characterized as a *word salad* (words seem tossed together without any apparent syntax or organization). They may be saying a lot, but what they say is not communicating anything to the receiver.
- **Disordered behavior** may also characterize some people with schizophrenia. This may take the form of unusual, odd, or repetitive behaviors and gestures. Head banging, finger flapping, or tracing a pattern over and over again are examples. Childlike silliness, inappropriate sexual behavior (such as public masturbation), or difficulty maintaining hygiene may be present. Some people with schizophrenia may show an absence of all motor behaviors, remaining totally motionless and rigid for hours on end and resisting efforts to be moved. Such behavior is referred to as a **catatonic stupor**. Other people with schizophrenia may show **catatonic excitement**, in which they are suddenly agitated, fidgety, shouting, swearing, or moving around rapidly.

delusion a thought or belief that a person believes to be true but in reality is not

hallucination perceiving something that does not exist in reality

disorganized speech a positive symptom of schizophrenia in which one's speech lacks association between one's ideas and the events that one is experiencing

disordered behavior a positive symptom of schizophrenia that includes inappropriate or unusual behavior such as silliness, catatonic excitement, or catatonic stupor

catatonic [cat-uh-TAWN-ick] stupor a positive symptom of schizophrenia marked by disorder in motor behavior involving immobility

catatonic excitement a positive symptom of schizophrenia marked by disorder in motor behavior involving excited agitation

NEGATIVE SYMPTOMS OF SCHIZOPHRENIA

Negative symptoms of schizophrenia represent a restriction or absence of normal functions. These include *blunted affect, alogia,* and *avolition* (American Psychiatric Association, 2013). Approximately 25% of persons with schizophrenia display these symptoms (Cohen et al., 2013; Ho et al., 2003).

Grunnitus Studio/Science Source

In a catatonic stupor, the person may remain in a "posed" position for hours on end.

- *Affect,* in psychological terms, refers to expressing emotions. Some people with schizophrenia show **blunted affect**, or a lack of emotional expression. They appear passive, with immobile facial expressions. Their vocal tone does not change even when the conversation is emotional in tone. They do not respond to events in their environment with any emotion. Their speech lacks the inflection that usually communicates a speaker's mood.
- **Alogia**, also called *poverty of speech,* refers to decreased quality and/or quantity of speech. The person with schizophrenia gives brief and empty replies.
- **Avolition** is the inability to follow through on one's plans. A person with schizophrenia may seem apathetic, sitting for long periods of time, showing little interest in his or her usual activities.

Many people with schizophrenia exhibit both positive and negative symptoms. People with schizophrenia who show predominantly positive symptoms tend to have a less severe course of schizophrenia and respond better to medication (Kendler et al., 1994; Kutscher, 2008). Such findings have led researchers to believe that positive symptoms of schizophrenia may have a different cause than negative symptoms.

13.6.3 • Research Explaining Schizophrenia: Genetics, the Brain, and the Environment

To date, biological factors account for the strongest evidence in the development of schizophrenia, although environmental factors must also be considered. It is likely that environmental conditions interact with biological factors to make a person either more or less susceptible to the illness. Biological research has focused on three main areas: *genetics, brain abnormalities,* and the malfunctioning of *specific neurotransmitters* in the brain. Environmental research has focused on prenatal and development factors, as well as the role of family and the environment.

blunted affect a negative symptom of schizophrenia involving lack of emotional expression

alogia [uh-LO-jeeuh] a negative symptom of schizophrenia involving decreased quality and/or quantity of speech

avolition [AA-vuh-lish-un] a negative symptom of schizophrenia marked by the inability to follow through on one's plans

A STRONG GENETIC FACTOR

Family, twin, and adoption studies have routinely demonstrated a high heritability of schizophrenia (Allen et al., 2008; Levy et al., 2010; NIMH Genetics Workgroup, 1998). As • FIGURE 13.6 shows, although the incidence of schizophrenia in the general population is 1%–2%, the more genetically similar a person is to someone with schizophrenia, the more likely he or she will also develop the disorder (Cardno & Gottesman, 2000). In identical twin pairs, if one twin develops schizophrenia, the other twin has about a 48% chance of developing the disorder. However, in fraternal twins (who are not genetically identical), the probability is only 17%. Adoption studies show a similar pattern (Tienari et al., 2003; Tienari, Wahlberg, & Wynne, 2006). Adopted children who have biological parents with schizophrenia are 10 times more likely to develop the disorder than are adopted children whose biological parents are not diagnosed with schizophrenia.

Despite these results, it is unlikely that a single gene is responsible for the illness; if it were, the heritability rates would be higher. Research has therefore moved toward exploring several chromosomal regions that may work together to increase a person's vulnerability to schizophrenia, as well as altered gene expressions that may give rise to brain abnormalities (Nicodemus et al., 2010;

Pogue-Geile & Yokley, 2010; Shi et al., 2009; Walker & Tessner, 2008; Walker et al., 2010). The exact nature of these pathways has yet to be identified.

Another genetic explanation for schizophrenia stems from the association between advanced paternal age and an increased risk of schizophrenia. That is, some people with schizophrenia are more likely to have had older fathers (45 years or older) at birth. Such an association has led to the hypothesis that mutations in male sperm cells (which are more likely to occur as a male ages) may be in part a genetic mechanism for schizophrenia in at least some people (Byrne et al., 2003; Dalman & Allebeck, 2002; Malaspina et al., 2001; Torrey et al., 2009).

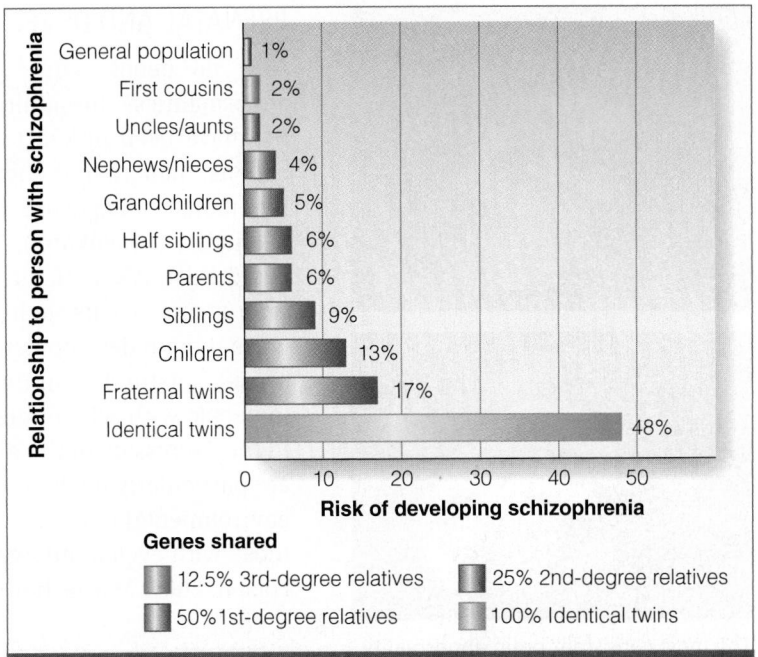

FIGURE 13.6

Risk of Schizophrenia and Genetic Relatedness

The incidence of schizophrenia in the general population is 1%–2%. However, the more closely one is genetically related to a person with schizophrenia, the higher the risk of developing the disorder.

Source: Reprinted by permission of Irving I. Gottesman.

THE BRAIN: NEUROTRANSMITTERS AND STRUCTURAL ABNORMALITIES

A second area of research on the development of schizophrenia looks at neurotransmitters and abnormalities in certain brain structures. It was originally believed that schizophrenia was caused by excess activity of the neurotransmitter dopamine in the brain. The drugs that are prescribed for schizophrenia, called *phenothiazines,* reduce dopamine activity in the brain and are typically more effective in reducing the positive symptoms of schizophrenia. However, many people with schizophrenia do not respond to treatment with phenothiazines. One of the newer drugs used to treat schizophrenia, called *clozapine,* does not block the same dopamine receptors as the phenothiazines, clearly indicating that dopamine is involved, but in a more complex way (Conklin & Iacono, 2002; Grace, 2010). Researchers continue to investigate the exact role of dopamine in the development of schizophrenia (Howes & Kapur, 2009).

Other research suggests a potential role for the neurotransmitter glutamate (Coyle, 2006; Grace, 2010). Drugs such as PCP and ketamine (see Chapter 4) that block the action of glutamate can cause normal research participants to exhibit cognitive impairments and negative symptoms similar to those found in people with schizophrenia (Deakin et al., 2008). Current research is focused on how glutamate and dopamine dysfunction may interact to contribute to the development of schizophrenia (Javitt, 2007; Stahl, 2007; Stone, Morrison, & Pilowsky, 2007). Obviously, the relationship between neurotransmitters and schizophrenia remains a complex one.

Abnormalities in certain brain structures have also been investigated for their links to schizophrenia. The most consistent abnormality found in people with schizophrenia is enlarged ventricles (see photos on next page) (Lieberman et al., 2001; Mitelman et al., 2005; Wright et al., 2000). A *ventricle* is a fluid-filled cavity in the brain. Enlarged ventricles reduce the overall size of the brain, which in turn may contribute to the development of schizophrenia. Brain dysfunction in the frontal and temporal lobes has also been implicated in the development of schizophrenia (Karlsgodt, Sun, & Cannon, 2010; Weinstein, Woodward, & Ngan, 2007; Wolf et al., 2007). The frontal lobe is responsible for language, emotions, and social behavior, and the temporal lobe plays an important role in memory. The symptoms of schizophrenia (disordered speech, blunted affect, and catatonic behavior) are associated with these brain areas.

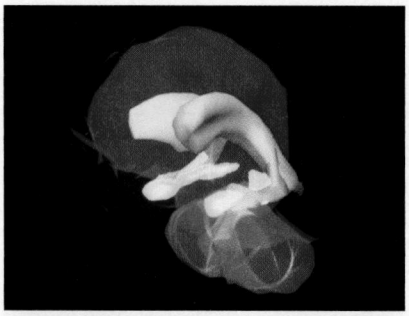

Dr. Nancy C. Andreasen/Science Source

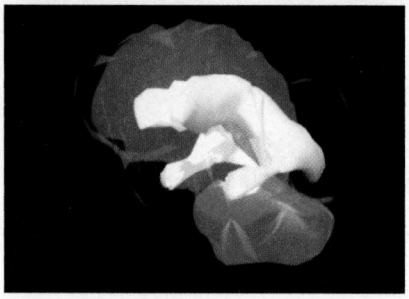

Dr. Nancy C. Andreasen/Science Source

The most consistent brain abnormality that has been found in people with schizophrenia is enlarged ventricles. Shown here are 3-D magnetic resonance images (MRI) of the brain of a person with schizophrenia (bottom) and the brain of a person without schizophrenia (top). The hippocampus (yellow, at center) is shrunken and the fluid-filled ventricles (white) enlarged in the brain of the person with schizophrenia.

PRENATAL AND DEVELOPMENTAL FACTORS

How do people with schizophrenia develop these neurochemical or brain abnormalities? In addition to possible hereditary factors, these abnormalities have been linked to factors of pregnancy and birth such as birth complications, maternal diabetes, low birth weight, prenatal maternal stress, and the mother's exposure to prenatal viruses (A. S. Brown et al., 2004; King, St-Hilaire, & Heidkamp, 2010; Walker et al., 2010), although many other causes could exist. A genetic predisposition to schizophrenia interacts with prenatal environmental agents such as a maternal virus or poor nutrition, causing changes in normal brain development. Then, as the brain reaches maturation (during adolescence), a natural trimming away of brain synapses occurs. It is hypothesized that in people with schizophrenia, the brain trims away too many synapses, resulting in the expression of the disorder in the teenage years. Symptoms of schizophrenia are particularly likely to appear if the person has a strong genetic disposition or if environmental circumstances have encouraged the expression of the disorder in those with even a mild genetic link (Barch, Cohen, & Csernansky, 2014; Fatemi & Folson, 2009; McGlashan & Hoffman, 2000; Rapoport et al., 2005).

THE ROLE OF FAMILY AND ENVIRONMENT

Two critical factors that appear to contribute to the onset and course of schizophrenia are family support and exposure to stressful living conditions. Studies on the families of people with schizophrenia have found that the quality of family communications and interactions may either encourage or discourage the onset of schizophrenia in people who are genetically at high risk (Hooley, 2010). The quality of family interactions may also influence whether future psychotic episodes are triggered. Families that are critical, harsh, hostile, and poor communicators may make a high-risk person more susceptible to the disorder (Hooley, 2007; Schlosser et al., 2010). Chronic stress from living a low-income lifestyle or within a family with poor communication also appears to influence future relapses (Ventura et al., 2000). Although it appears that family and lifestyle do not *cause* schizophrenia, they are critical factors in people's susceptibility to the disorder and must be taken into account when designing prevention or treatment programs for those with schizophrenia.

Quiz Yourself 13.6

1. **Which of the following is a negative symptom of schizophrenia?**
   a. Delusions
   b. Hallucinations
   c. Alogia
   d. Catatonic stupor
2. **The most consistent brain abnormality found among people with schizophrenia is _____.**
   a. a small frontal lobe
   b. a small temporal lobe
   c. enlarged ventricles
   d. an enlarged frontal lobe
3. **Loose associations and word salad characterize which symptom of schizophrenia?**
   a. Disorganized speech
   b. Avolition
   c. Delusions
   d. Blunted affect

Answers 1. c; 2. c; 3. a

13.7 Personality Disorders: Maladaptive Patterns of Behavior

The **personality disorders** consist of long-standing patterns of malfunctioning. All of us have personality "quirks." Some people may be excessively neat. Others may be somewhat suspicious and mistrustful of others. However, these traits do not necessarily qualify someone for a personality disorder. In personality disorders, the person's emotions, thoughts, and behavior result in persistent distress to self or others and interfere with one's ability to function. As we saw in the section case study, Emily was diagnosed as having borderline personality trends indicating that her personality was contributing to her difficulty in functioning.

People with personality disorders also can be diagnosed with any of the mental health disorders previously discussed, and they typically seek treatment for these disorders or because someone else has a problem with their behavior and encourages them to undergo therapy. Individuals with a personality disorder often don't see a problem with their behavior and, therefore, seldom seek treatment on their own. It is estimated that as many as 10%–14% of adults in the United States meet the criteria for at least one personality disorder (Grant et al., 2004; Lenzenweger et al., 2007). Worldwide, about 6% of adults may have a diagnosable personality disorder (Huang et al., 2009). The *DSM-5* lists 10 personality disorders, and space considerations prohibit a discussion of all of them, but we give a brief description of them in ●TABLE 13.4. Here we will confine our discussion to two: *antisocial personality disorder* and *borderline personality disorder.*

personality disorder a mental health disorder marked by maladaptive behavior that has been stable over a long period and across many situations

antisocial personality disorder a personality disorder marked by a pattern of disregard for and violation of the rights of others with no remorse or guilt for one's actions

13.7.1 • Antisocial Personality Disorder: Impulsive and Dangerous

People who are impulsive and disregard the rights of others without showing any remorse or guilt are diagnosed with **antisocial personality disorder** (American Psychiatric Association, 2013). *Antisocial* in this context does not mean shy or unsociable, but rather indicates harmful acts against (anti) others (social). People who have antisocial personalities lack impulse control and often act hastily and recklessly with little concern for the consequences of their behavior. They are irresponsible, blame others for their problems, and frequently have difficulty maintaining social relationships. They repeatedly lie and may manipulate others into doing what they want. Such antisocial or harmful behavior has often been present since childhood or adolescence (Loney et al., 2007). It is one of the more common personality disorders, and men are 5 times more likely than women to be diagnosed with this disorder (Grant et al., 2004; Lenzenweger, 2008).

People with antisocial personality disorder are more often sent to prison than to treatment. However, this does not mean that all criminals have antisocial personality disorder. Although antisocial behavior is highly correlated with delinquency and criminal behavior, not all criminals are antisocial. One of the key features distinguishing the two is the lack of remorse and guilt for one's actions. A person can commit armed robbery yet afterward regret his actions. The antisocial person does not experience such regret or remorse. People with antisocial personality disorder may not be violent. They may be

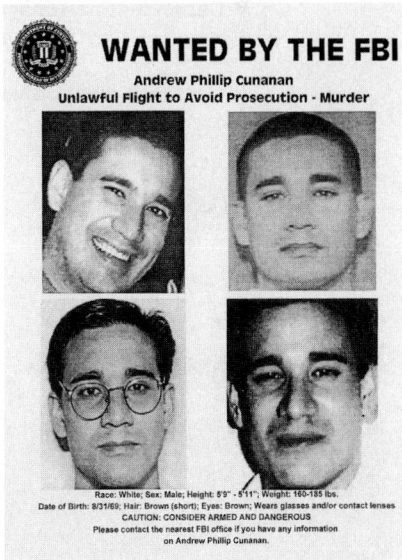

AP Photo/FBI

Andrew Cunanan murdered famous clothes designer Gianni Versace after killing several others. He was described by many as a charming and bright young man.

TABLE 13.4

Types of Personality Disorders

DISORDER	MAJOR FEATURES
CLUSTER A: ODD OR ECCENTRIC DISORDERS	
Paranoid personality disorder	Excessive suspicion and mistrust of others
Schizoid personality disorder	Lack of desire to form close relationships with others; emotional detachment and coldness toward others
Schizotypal personality disorder	Considered a mild version of schizophrenia. The person shows inappropriate social and emotional behavior, and unusual thoughts and speech.
CLUSTER B: DRAMATIC, EMOTIONAL, OR ERRATIC DISORDERS	
Antisocial personality disorder	Chronic pattern of impulsive behavior; violates rights of others and does not show remorse or guilt for actions
Borderline personality disorder	Instability in mood, self-concept, and interpersonal relationships
Histrionic personality disorder	Intense need for attention; always wants to be the center of attention; excessively dramatic behavior; rapidly changing moods
Narcissistic personality disorder	Preoccupation with own sense of importance and view of self as above others; typically ignores the needs and wants of others
CLUSTER C: ANXIOUS OR FEARFUL DISORDERS	
Avoidant personality disorder	Intense and chronic anxiety over being negatively evaluated by others, so avoids social interactions
Dependent personality disorder	Excessive need to be cared for by others; denies own thoughts and feelings and clings to others
Obsessive-compulsive personality disorder	Pattern of rigid and perfectionist behavior; preoccupied with details, rules, order, and routine; experiences upset when routine is disrupted (This is not the same as the disorder OCD.)

"con artists," and more of them may live outside prison than in it. They may function successfully in business, politics, or entertainment (Stout, 2005).

What causes antisocial personality disorder? Some research suggests biological factors. Twin studies, adoption studies, and family studies support a genetic influence (Hicks et al., 2004; Moffitt, 2005). For example, family members of people with antisocial personality disorder have higher rates of the disorder than the general population. Other research suggests low levels of the neurotransmitter serotonin (Moffitt et al., 1998); deficits in brain areas that control impulsivity, attention, and decision making (Kiehl et al., 2006; Raine, 2008; Raine et al., 2011); elevated levels of the hormone testosterone (van Honk & Schutter, 2007); and low arousal of the nervous system (Raine, 1997; Raine et al., 2000).

However, psychological and social variables cannot be ruled out. People with antisocial personality disorder often experience conflict-filled childhoods. Their parents may be neglectful, inconsistent in discipline, harsh, hostile, or less warm. As a result, they often learn to expect such treatment from others and adopt a mistrustful and aggressive stance toward others (Afifi et al., 2011; Dishion & Patterson, 1997; Feinberg et al., 2007). In all likelihood, a complex interplay between genes and the environment best explains the development of antisocial personality disorder (Arias et al., 2011; Fowles & Dindo, 2009; Raine, 2008; van Goozen, Fairchild, & Harold, 2008).

13.7.2 • Borderline Personality Disorder: Living on Your Fault Line

Borderline personality disorder (BPD) is characterized by instability in moods, interpersonal relationships, self-image, and behavior (American Psychiatric Association, 2013). This key feature of instability often disrupts people's relationships, career, and identity. Their unstable emotions result in intense bouts of anger, depression, or anxiety that may occur for hours or for a day. Their unstable self-concepts are reflected in extreme insecurity at some times and exaggerated feelings of importance at other times. This instability may prompt frequent changes in goals, jobs, friendships, and values because people with borderline personalities lack a clear definition of themselves. They have little idea of who they are. Their interpersonal relationships are also characterized by instability. They may admire, idealize, and cling to loved ones at first; but when conflict occurs, feelings of abandonment and rejection surface, and their feelings quickly turn to anger and dislike. They then seek out new friends or loved ones, and the cycle repeats itself. People with this disorder often feel unworthy, bad, or empty inside. At times of extreme insecurity and depression, self-injury and suicide attempts are common (D. W. Black et al., 2004; Soloff & Chiapetta, 2012). Notice how much of Emily's problems in her teenage years match these symptoms. Her emotions often vacillated between rage and panic. Her feelings of inadequacy often made her feel insecure and unlovable, and she had several suicide attempts.

borderline personality disorder (BPD) a personality disorder marked by a pattern of instability in mood, relationships, self-image, and behavior

Like Emily, people with BPD are often diagnosed with other mental health disorders such as major depression, substance-related disorder, or anxiety (Eaton et al., 2011). It is estimated that approximately 2%–6% of the population could be diagnosed with BPD at some point in their lives, and it is diagnosed slightly more often in young women than in men (Torgersen, 2012; Zanarini et al., 2012). Extensive mental health services are often needed to treat people with BPD.

Research on the causes of BPD has focused on biopsychosocial factors. Low levels of serotonin are related to impulsive behaviors (Ni et al., 2007; Siever & Koenigsberg, 2000). Difficulty in regulating emotions may be related to abnormal brain functioning (Leichsenring et al., 2011; L. M. Williams et al., 2006). However, many people with BPD report a history of adverse life events such as abuse or neglect, making environment a probable factor (Bornovalova et al., 2006; Leichsenring et al., 2011). For example, in one study (Zanarini, 2000), a large percentage of patients with BPD had reported being sexually abused. Such social stressors may impede normal attachment patterns, identity development, and the ability to express appropriate emotions.

Quiz Yourself

13.7

1. Which of the following is *not* a feature of antisocial personality disorder?
   a. Lack of remorse
   b. Shyness and unsociability
   c. Poor impulse control
   d. Disregard for the rights of others

2. Felicia is extremely insecure and lacks a clear sense of identity. She often clings to new friends and then hates them a month later. She has an intense fear of abandonment and rejection. Felicia's behavior *best* fits which personality disorder?
   a. Narcissistic
   b. Antisocial
   c. Borderline
   d. Paranoid

3. Personality disorders _____.
   a. do not coexist with other mental health disorders such as depression or anxiety
   b. generally appear in early or middle adulthood
   c. are stable patterns of malfunctioning
   d. do not pose any threat to others

Answers 1. b; 2. c; 3. c

13.8 Integrating Psychology: The Big Picture

In this chapter, we have provided examples of disorders from nine of the major categories of mental health disorders listed in the *DSM-5*. Each disorder meets the criterion of abnormality endorsed at the beginning of the chapter—inability to function. Although research continues into the exact origins of each disorder, we have seen that in many cases, a person's biological vulnerability appears to combine with psychological and sociocultural factors—learning experiences, thinking patterns, development, family interactions, cultural attitudes, gender roles—to trigger the onset of the disorder.

Such an interaction of variables is helpful in understanding Emily's difficulty in functioning. Biologically, Emily may have been genetically predisposed to anxiety and depression as her father was a tense and driven man while her mother was often sad and depressed. Yet, psychological variables such as learning, cognitions, and emotions also need to be considered. Emily could have been modeling her parents coping mechanisms. We also saw that Emily's delinquent and disruptive behavior was often a way for her to get parental attention. In addition, her negative cognitions and feelings of parental and peer rejection could have also contributed to her psychological distress. Such stress could have further affected her biological functioning. Traditional female gender roles that perhaps went against a family culture of high expectations for achievement are sociocultural variables that could have further compounded Emily's problems, especially as she evidenced difficulty in learning. Only by integrating and examining all these variables can we achieve a comprehensive picture of Emily's behavior.

Like Emily, many people with mental health disorders seek help in the form of therapy. So, keep the symptoms of these disorders in mind. It will assist you in mastering the material of the next chapter, where we explore the different therapies psychologists and psychiatrists use to treat mental health disorders.

Studying the Chapter

Key Terms

agoraphobia (555)

alogia (578)

antisocial personality disorder (581)

avolition (578)

bipolar disorder (567)

blunted affect (578)

borderline personality disorder (BPD) (583)

catatonic excitement (577)

catatonic stupor (577)

cognitive distortion (572)

compulsion (556)

cyclothymic disorder (570)

delusion (577)

***Diagnostic and Statistical Manual of Mental Disorders* (DSM)** (550)

disordered behavior (577)

disorganized speech (577)

dissociative disorder (562)

dissociative identity disorder (DID) (563)

generalized anxiety disorder (GAD) (554)

hallucination (577)

hoarding disorder (557)

illness anxiety disorder (564)

learned helplessness (572)

major depressive disorder (566)

mania (567)

medical model (548)

mental health disorder (546)

mood disorder (565)

obsession (556)

obsessive-compulsive disorder (OCD) (556)

panic disorder (555)

persistent depressive disorder (dysthymic disorder) (566)

personality disorder (581)

posttraumatic stress disorder (PTSD) (557)

psychopathology (548)

ruminative coping style (572)

schizophrenia (575)

social anxiety disorder (556)

somatic symptom disorder (564)

specific phobia (556)

What Do You Know? Assess Your Understanding

Test your retention and understanding of the material by answering the following questions.

1. Allison can't help feeling sad most of the time. It upsets her that she can't be happy and seem "normal." Allison's behavior *best* fits which criterion of abnormality?

a. Violation of social norms
b. Personal distress
c. Danger to others
d. All of the above

2. If a person had "stage fright" or fear of public speaking to the degree that it interfered with his or her ability to function, these would be examples of which mental health disorder?

a. Specific phobia
b. Social anxiety disorder
c. Major depressive disorder
d. Agoraphobia

3. Dr. Sanchez believes that abnormal behavior is the result of irrational assumptions and negative thinking patterns. Dr. Sanchez views mental illness from a _____ perspective.

a. social learning
b. biological
c. psychoanalytic
d. cognitive

4. Julissa repeatedly complains about stomach pains and nausea. Numerous medical tests and procedures cannot find a physical cause for Julissa's symptoms. Julissa may be diagnosed with what type of mental health disorder?

a. A mood disorder
b. An anxiety disorder
c. A somatic symptom disorder
d. A dissociative disorder

5. Alogia and avolition represent _____ symptoms of schizophrenia.

a. positive
b. negative
c. neutral
d. undifferentiated

6. Some clinicians question the validity of dissociative identity disorder, suggesting that it represents an extreme form of which mental health disorder?

a. bipolar disorder
b. panic disorder
c. generalized anxiety disorder
d. posttraumatic stress disorder

7. Men are more likely than women to be diagnosed with _____.

a. anxiety disorders
b. substance-related disorders
c. mood disorders
d. schizophrenia

8. A young woman reports frequent blackouts, consistently receives phone calls and mail addressed to a person with a different name, and often finds items in her closet that she cannot remember buying. This woman is most likely to be diagnosed with which type of mental health disorder?

a. Dissociative disorder
b. Somatic symptom disorder
c. Mood disorder
d. Borderline personality disorder

9. Which mental health disorder is characterized by delusions, hallucinations, incoherent thought and speech, and inappropriate emotions?

a. Dissociative identity disorder
b. Schizophrenia
c. Panic disorder
d. Generalized anxiety disorder

10. For the last month, Dimitri has been sad, has felt worthless, has been losing weight, can't concentrate, and constantly feels tired. Dimitri is most likely to be diagnosed with which mental health disorder?

a. Bipolar disorder
b. Major depressive disorder
c. Cyclothymic disorder
d. Persistent depressive disorder

11. Jayne was shopping at the local mall when all of a sudden her chest felt tight, she couldn't catch her breath, her heart began to pound, and she felt shaky and dizzy. Since that day, Jayne has had several more episodes like this. They always strike without warning and in different types of situations. It is most likely that Jayne has _____.

a. generalized anxiety disorder
b. bipolar disorder
c. panic disorder
d. agoraphobia

12. Which of the following symptoms distinguishes bipolar disorder from major depressive disorder?

a. Mania
b. Alogia
c. Apathy
d. Delusions

13. Betta is always worried. She worries that her kids will get sick. She worries that she will lose her job. She worries that her husband will get cancer. Sometimes she is worried without even knowing why she is worried. Betta is most likely to be diagnosed with _____.

a. posttraumatic stress disorder
b. obsessive-compulsive disorder
c. generalized anxiety disorder
d. agoraphobia

14. Which personality disorder is characterized by instability in moods, interpersonal relationships, self-image, and behavior?

a. Histrionic
b. Narcissistic
c. Antisocial
d. Borderline

15. The *DSM* is an abbreviation for _____.

a. *Disorders and Statistics for Mental Health*
b. *Diagnostic and Statistical Manual of Mental Disorders*
c. *Dimensions and Symptoms of Mental Disorders*
d. *Disorders and Symptoms of Mental Health Disorders*

16. Which brain structure is *most* involved in anxiety and fear?

a. Frontal lobe
b. Temporal lobe
c. Hippocampus
d. Amygdala

17. When depressed, Katelyn constantly thinks about her depression and why she is depressed. This often results in Katelyn being even more depressed. Katelyn's behavior is most consistent with _____.

a. learned helplessness
b. negative attributions
c. a ruminative coping style
d. compulsions

18. The most consistent brain abnormality found in people with schizophrenia is _____.

a. a damaged frontal lobe
b. enlarged ventricles
c. less white matter
d. larger brain size

19. Ozzie always wants to be the center of attention and is excessively dramatic. His moods rapidly change. Which personality disorder *best* fits Ozzie's behavior?

a. Histrionic personality disorder
b. Antisocial personality disorder
c. Schizoid personality disorder
d. Borderline personality disorder

20. Sociocultural theories emphasize the role of _____ in explaining abnormal behavior.

a. negative thoughts
b. unconscious conflicts
c. unrealistic self-images
d. environmental stressors

Answers: 1. b; 2. b; 3. d; 4. c; 5. b; 6. d; 7. b; 8. a; 9. b; 10. b; 11. c; 12. a; 13. c; 14. d; 15. b; 16. d; 17. c; 18. b; 19. a; 20. d

Use It or Lose It: Applying Psychology

1. What behaviors do you believe would be considered abnormal in every culture and society (present and past) and in all situations? Are these behaviors symptoms of any of the disorders discussed in this chapter? How does this list help or hinder psychologists' understanding of abnormality?

2. Which disorders would people be most likely AND least likely to seek treatment for, and why? How might this search differ by gender, age, or ethnicity?

3. Create a program that would best address the treatment and care of people with schizophrenia.

4. After reading this chapter, what factors appear to be most linked to mental health and illness? What can our society do to improve mental health?

5. Which mental health disorders do you think you are most at risk for, and why? Be sure to consider biopsychosocial factors in formulating your response.

Critical Thinking for Integration

1. How might memory processes (Chapter 7) be linked to the development of anxiety, trauma-, or obsessive-compulsive-related disorders?

2. How might gender role development (Chapter 9) explain the gender differences in the prevalence of anxiety and depressive disorders? Describe what might be the attributions (Chapter 10) for individual success and failure of a person with an anxiety or depressive disorder. How might these individuals judge the behavior of others? Provide examples to support your ideas.

3. Refer to the section on research methods in Chapter 1. In a study on the causes of schizophrenia, how might the presence of various symptoms of schizophrenia in your sample complicate a study's conclusions? How could more valid research on the origin of schizophrenia be conducted? What might make your solution difficult to implement?

Cusp and Flirt/Masterfile

Are You Getting the Big Picture? Mental Health Disorders

13.1 What Is Abnormal Behavior?

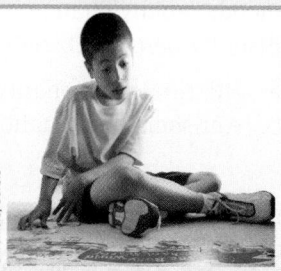

Michael Macor/San Francisco Chronicle/Corbis

- A **mental health disorder** is a dysfunction in thinking (cognition), emotions, and/or social behavior that impairs functioning and is not culturally expected.
- Mental health disorders result from a combination of biological, psychological, and social factors (*biopsychosocial* perspective). They do not have just one cause.

13.2 The *DSM* Model for Classifying Abnormal Behavior

- The ***Diagnostic and Statistical Manual of Mental Disorders (DSM)***, currently in its fifth edition, is an atheoretical system that describes specific criteria for a diagnosis of a mental health disorder.
- Labeling someone with a mental health disorder can have negative effects because it may encourage the person to behave in a way that is consistent with the disorder.

13.3 Anxiety, Trauma-, Obsessive-Compulsive and Related Disorders

WR Publishing/Alamy

- **Generalized anxiety disorder** is characterized by excessive anxiety, worry, and difficulty in controlling such worries. **Panic disorder** is characterized by recurrent panic attacks or the persistent fear of having a panic attack. **Specific phobia** is a persistent fear of an object and **social anxiety disorder** is a persistent fear of being negatively evaluated by others in a social situation.
- In **obsessive-compulsive disorder**, a person experiences recurrent **obsessions, compulsions** or both that cannot be controlled. **Hoarding disorder** involves persistent difficulty in throwing away possessions, even when the items are of very little value.
- **Posttraumatic stress disorder** develops after exposure to a terrifying event. The person experiences distressing memories, nightmares, thoughts, or flashback episodes of the event that interfere with functioning.
- Potential biopsychosocial factors for anxiety, trauma-, obsessive-compulsive and related disorders include:
  - Biological factors (genetics, neurotransmitter imbalances, and abnormal brain functioning)
  - Psychological factors such as conditioning and maladaptive cognitions
  - Social factors such as rapid social change, stress, low social status, and gender

13.4 Dissociative and Somatic Symptom Disorders: Other Forms of Anxiety?

- **Dissociative disorders** are characterized by a loss of awareness of some part of the self. In **dissociative identity disorder**, separate multiple personalities exist in the same person. It is believed to be related to severe stress or a series of emotionally traumatic events.
- **Somatic symptom disorders** are characterized by physical complaints or symptoms with no apparent physical cause, as in **illness anxiety disorder**. Psychological distress appears to underlie the physical complaints of these disorders.

13.5 Mood Disorders: Beyond the Blues

martin-dm/Getty Images

- **Mood disorders** are characterized by a significant change in one's emotional state over an extended period.
- In **major depressive disorder**, the person experiences extreme or chronic sadness or loss of pleasure.
- **Bipolar disorder** involves a shift in mood between two states: sadness and **mania**.
- Potential biopsychosocial factors explaining mood disorders include:
  - Biological factors such as genetics, neurotransmitter imbalances, stress hormones, and abnormal brain functioning
  - Psychological factors such as unresolved issues of loss and rejection, **learned helplessness**, **ruminative coping style**, **cognitive distortions**, and pessimistic attributions
  - Social factors such as lower social status, stressful life events, and gender

13.6 Schizophrenia: Disintegration

Grumitus Studio/Science Source

- **Schizophrenia** is a chronic mental health disorder characterized by positive symptoms (**delusions**, **hallucinations**, **disorganized speech**, **catatonic stupor**, or **catatonic excitement**), and/or negative symptoms (**blunted affect**, **alogia**, **avolition**).
- Potential causes of schizophrenia are primarily biological, including genetics, dopamine and glutamate activity, and abnormal brain functioning. However, family support and stressful living conditions may influence the course of the disorder.

13.7 What Are Personality Disorders?

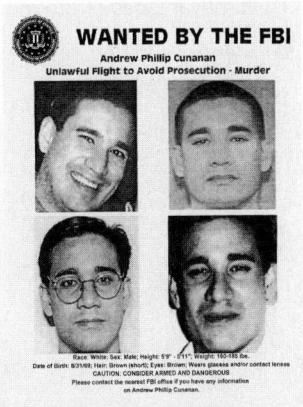

AP Photo/FBI

- The **personality disorders** consist of long-standing patterns of malfunctioning typically evident in childhood or adolescence.
- People who disregard the rights of others without showing any remorse or guilt are diagnosed with **antisocial personality disorder**.
- **Borderline personality disorder** is characterized by instability in moods, interpersonal relationships, self-image, and behavior.
- Personality disorders are related to biological factors (genetics, neurotransmitters, abnormal brain functioning) and psychosocial factors (inconsistent parenting practices, gender, conflict-filled childhood).

Mental Health Therapies

Learning Objectives

14.1 Distinguish between psychotherapy and biomedical therapy, and describe the trained professionals who are qualified to give each. (APA 1.1, 5.5)

14.1 Describe the four essential ethical principles that psychotherapists must follow when conducting treatment. (APA 3.1)

14.1 Identify when a person should consider seeking therapy. (APA 1.3)

14.2 Describe the aim of psychoanalytic therapies, and distinguish between traditional and modern psychoanalysis. (APA 1.1, 1.2)

14.3 Describe the aim of humanistic therapy, and distinguish among the three key characteristics of client-centered therapy. (APA 1.1, 1.2)

14.4 Explain systematic desensitization, flooding, and aversion therapy, and describe how they change behavior through classical conditioning processes. (APA 1.1, 1.2, 1.3)

14.4 Discuss how operant conditioning techniques are used in therapy to modify or change problem behavior. (APA 1.1, 1.3)

14.5 Describe the aim of cognitive therapy approaches. (APA 1.1)

14.5 Compare and contrast Ellis's rational-emotive therapy and Beck's cognitive therapy. (APA 1.1, 1.2)

14.6 Understand the advantages and disadvantages of group therapy. (APA 1.3)

14.6 Identify and describe the types of group therapy. (APA 1.1, 1.2)

14.7 Examine the complexity of conducting research on the effectiveness of psychotherapy. (APA 1.2, 2.1, 2.5)

14.7 Identify and describe the factors that contribute to effective psychotherapy. (APA 1.2, 1.3, 3.2)

14.7 Describe how technology has influenced the delivery of psychotherapy, and examine the effectiveness and ethical concerns of technology-assisted interventions. (APA 1.3, 2.1, 3.1)

14.8 Distinguish the treatment effects and side effects of antianxiety drugs, antipsychotic drugs, antidepressants, and antimanic drugs. (APA 1.2, 1.3)

14.8 Understand the symptoms treated and the side effects of noninvasive brain stimulation procedures (TMS and ECT) and psychosurgery. (APA 1.2)

Therapy consists of techniques that are used to help people with mental health or interpersonal problems. All therapies attempt to change a person's behavior. However, the techniques that are used differ because each therapy approach stems from one of the main theoretical perspectives introduced in Chapter 1 and

14

Laurence Mouton/Â·s/Canopy/Corbis

explained in more detail in subsequent chapters. This chapter explores the principal approaches to therapy that are common today. We will begin by defining therapy, examining who is qualified to give it, and addressing when it is appropriate for a person to seek therapy.

Chapter Outline

14.1 Providing Psychological Assistance / 592

PSYCHOLOGY APPLIES TO YOUR WORLD: When Does One Need to Consider Psychotherapy? / 595

14.2 Psychoanalytic Therapies: Uncovering Unconscious Conflicts / 596

14.3 Humanistic Therapy: Facilitating Self-Actualization / 599

14.4 Behavior Therapies: Learning Healthier Behaviors / 601

14.5 Cognitive Therapies: Changing Thoughts / 607

14.6 Group Therapy Approaches: Strength in Numbers / 611

14.7 Effective Psychotherapy: Do Treatments Work? / 614

14.8 Biomedical Therapies: Applying Neuroscience / 618

14.9 Integrating Psychology: The Big Picture / 626

14.1 Providing Psychological Assistance

Mental health professionals today use two broad forms of therapy to help people who are having difficulty functioning: *psychotherapy* and *biomedical therapy*. Many people, like Emily in the section case study, receive therapy that combines both approaches.

14.1.1 • Psychotherapy Versus Biomedical Therapy

therapy techniques that are used to help people with mental health or interpersonal problems

psychotherapy the use of psychological principles and techniques to treat mental health disorders

biomedical therapy the use of medications or other medical interventions to treat mental health disorders

Psychotherapy is the use of psychological principles and techniques to treat the symptoms of mental health disorders, such as depression, or to treat interpersonal problems, such as troubled relationships. *Psychotherapy* is a general term that encompasses many different forms of therapy. However, all psychotherapies are based on the central assumption that underlying psychological factors such as emotions, cognitions, behavior, or relationships are at the root of interpersonal problems and mental illness. In contrast, **biomedical therapy** uses medications or other medical interventions to treat the symptoms of mental health problems. Biomedical therapy assumes that biological factors, such as abnormal brain functioning or chemistry, are at the root of mental illness.

As we saw in Chapter 13 on mental health disorders, both assumptions are supported by substantial research. Indeed, American attitudes toward both psychotherapy and biomedical therapy have become more favorable over the years. For example, Ramin Mojtabai (2007) compared data on adults' attitudes toward seeking mental health services from two large representative surveys of the U.S. population, one from 1990–1992 and one from 2001–2003. Compared to the earlier survey, participants from the more recent survey reported being more willing to seek professional help for a mental health problem, more comfortable talking with a professional about their problems, and less likely to report feeling embarrassed if others discovered they were seeking help for mental health issues. Attitudes of younger participants improved more than attitudes of middle-aged participants. Another study found that African Americans and Hispanics or Latinos may have more positive attitudes toward seeking mental health treatment than non-Hispanic whites (Shim et al., 2009).

Mojtabai (2009) also assessed attitudes toward psychiatric medications by comparing data from adult participants in the U.S. General Social Survey of 1998 and of 2006. Participants in 2006 were more likely to say that medications help people deal with day-to-day stress, make it easier to deal with family and friends, and help people feel better about themselves. Participants in 2006 were also more likely to report a willingness to take medications for personal problems, depression, panic attacks, and to cope with life stresses.

Negative attitudes toward mental health services can influence a person to deny symptoms or delay treatment. Fortunately, as these studies have shown, attitudes toward psychotherapy and medications appear to be improving at least in the United States.

14.1.2 • Who Is Qualified to Give Therapy?

Trained professionals administer psychotherapy and biomedical therapy. A variety of educational and experiential backgrounds characterize psychotherapists (• TABLE 14.1). These include clinical psychologists, psychoanalysts, licensed counselors or social workers, and marital or family therapists. A master's degree

TABLE 14.1

Types of Mental Health Professionals

PROFESSION	EDUCATION	TRAINING
Clinical Psychologist	• College degree • Graduate school in clinical psychology to earn a doctorate (PhD or PsyD; requires 5–8 years after college degree)	Supervised research and/or training in psychotherapy techniques, psychological testing, and the diagnosis of mental health disorders
Counseling Psychologist	• College degree • Graduate school in counseling psychology or education to earn a doctorate (PhD or EdD; requires 4–6 years after college degree)	Supervised training in assessment, counseling, and therapy techniques
Licensed Professional Counselor	• College degree • Graduate school to earn a master's degree in counseling (requires 3–5 years after college degree)	Supervised training in assessment, counseling, and therapy techniques
Licensed Social Worker	• College degree • Graduate school in social work to receive a master's degree (MSW; requires 3–5 years after college degree)	Supervised training in a social service agency or a mental health center; may or may not include training in psychotherapy
Couple or Family Therapist	• College degree • Graduate school to receive a master's degree in counseling, psychology, or social work (requires 3–5 years after college degree)	Supervised training in family and couple therapy; may also include training in individual psychotherapy methods
Psychiatrist	• College degree • Medical school to receive a medical degree (MD or DO) and then specialize in psychiatry (requires 5–10 years after college degree)	Training in the diagnosis and prevention of mental health disorders with a focus on pharmaceutical treatment approaches; may include training in psychotherapy methods

is the minimum educational requirement for any of these professions, and some require doctorate-level degrees. Many therapists receive training in specialty areas or in specific forms of psychotherapy. For example, a *psychoanalyst* is trained in Freud's methods of treatment. Therapists' backgrounds often include internships in which they have been supervised in administering treatment. In addition, most states require licensing and/or certification of mental health professionals.

Only licensed psychiatrists or other medical doctors can legally administer biomedical therapies. Certification as a psychiatrist requires completion of medical school before specializing in psychiatry. In general, a psychiatrist is the only mental health professional who can prescribe medication. However, the right of clinical psychologists to prescribe medications has long been a topic of hot debate. Only three states, Louisiana, Illinois, and New Mexico, currently grant prescription privileges to clinical psychologists who have completed additional training.

14.1.3 • Ethical Standards for Psychotherapists

In addition to being adequately trained and educated, mental health professionals are required to behave ethically and according to certain professional standards

Jacky Chapman/Janine Wiedel Photolibrary/Alamy

Psychotherapists are ethically bound to provide culturally sensitive, competent treatment.

when conducting treatment. These are not legal statutes but rather standards established by the American Psychological Association (APA, 2002) indicating how psychotherapists should behave toward their clients. Violations of these standards should be reported to professional review boards that oversee the licensing of psychotherapists. Four essential ethical principles are *competent treatment, informed consent, confidentiality,* and *appropriate interactions.*

CULTURALLY SENSITIVE, COMPETENT TREATMENT AND INFORMED CONSENT

The primary responsibility of the clinician toward a client is to provide *appropriate and adequate treatment.* Such a guideline prevents clinicians from merely warehousing clients in a treatment center, a practice that was common in previous decades and centuries. When providing treatment, psychotherapists must get *informed consent* from their clients. This guideline involves fully informing clients of the nature of treatment and the details of their participation, including any potential side effects or consequences of treatment. These requirements are especially critical if any experimental types of treatment will be used. Additionally, clinicians must possess the necessary training to provide *culturally sensitive* and competent care to clients from diverse backgrounds including age, gender, race, ethnicity, religion, sexual orientation, disability, language, or socioeconomic status.

CONFIDENTIALITY

Psychotherapists must respect the *confidentiality* of their communications with clients. They do not repeat to family members or friends any client discussions that occur within the context of therapy. Consultations with other professionals are permitted only when the client has agreed. Using client stories or experiences in a published work is not permitted without the express permission of the client. This ensures trust within the therapist–client relationship.

However, there are exceptions to this guideline. One exception occurs when the therapist believes that the client should be committed to a treatment facility. In this circumstance, the therapist will have to break confidentiality to convince a court that the client is a danger to him- or herself. Another exception to maintaining confidentiality occurs when others might be in danger. For example, if during therapy a client expresses violent intent toward another person, therapists are legally required to inform the potential victim of this potential harm. In addition, if a therapist suspects child abuse, partner abuse, or elder abuse, he or she is legally required to report such cases to the appropriate authorities.

APPROPRIATE INTERACTIONS

Therapists must *interact appropriately* with clients for successful therapy to occur. For example, psychotherapists are forbidden from becoming sexually or romantically involved with any client, and are not to socialize with their clients. Psychotherapists do not drink alcohol with their clients or engage in intimate demonstrations of affection such as an arm around the waist. The behavior of Emily's first therapist in the hospital was inappropriate and therefore unethical. Psychotherapists are not to go into business with clients or establish any other form of social relationship that would impede the course of therapy.

Psychology Applies to Your World:

When Does One Need to Consider Psychotherapy?

People seek psychotherapy for a variety of reasons. Many come to therapy because they are in distress from one of the many mental health disorders discussed in Chapter 13. Their behavior is maladaptive, or they are experiencing difficulty functioning in everyday life. They may be dealing with depression, extreme anxiety, or schizophrenia. Others who seek treatment have a history of mental illness and exhibit significant symptoms of a disorder. Some people are legally mandated to receive therapy by the court system. Unfortunately, for many people with mental illness, seeking and receiving treatment often depend on one's ability to pay, either through their own resources and/or by private or public insurance (SAMHSA, 2011; Wang et al., 2005). For example, in 2010, approximately 60% of the 45.9 million adults with mental health problems had not received mental health services in the past year. The most frequently cited reason for not receiving or continuing treatment was an inability to afford care (SAMHSA, 2012b).

You do not have to be diagnosed with a mental health disorder in order to benefit from psychotherapy. Millions of people seek professional help to cope with other life problems. For example, couples and families in conflict may consider counseling to deal with their troubled relationships. People who have experienced major life transitions such as divorce, unemployment, retirement, or the death of a loved one may seek therapy to help them adjust to these changes. People are more likely to receive therapy if they have some type of insurance and are educated. Females are more likely than males, and multiracial and white groups are more likely than other ethnic groups to use mental health services (SAMHSA, 2012b; see ● FIGURE 14.1).

You may want to consider therapy if you feel helpless, sad, blue, or anxious for a prolonged period or if such feelings do not improve despite several efforts to change them. You also may want to consider therapy if you are having difficulty carrying out your everyday activities. Therapy may also be useful if you want to make decisions differently, improve the functioning of important relationships, or change your life to feel more satisfied.

FIGURE 14.1

Who Uses Therapy?

People are more likely to use mental health services if they have some type of health insurance. Therapy is also more likely to be used by females, and white and multiracial groups.

Source: Substance Abuse and Mental Health Services Administration (SAMHSA). (2012). *Results from the 2010 National Survey on Drug Use and Health: Mental health findings.* NSDUH Series H-42, HHS Publication No. (SMA) 11-4667. Rockville, MD: Author.

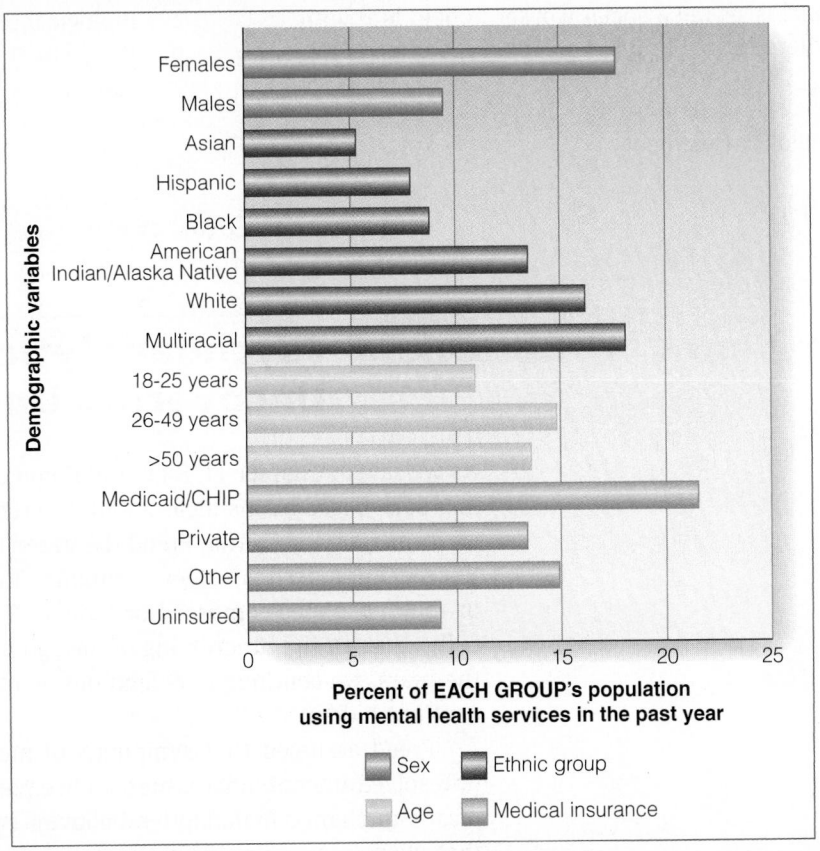

Unfortunately, when therapists are depicted in movies and on television, they often do not maintain these ethical standards. Such media portrayals confuse the public as to the appropriate behavior of therapists.

14.1.4 • Seeking Therapy

How do you find a therapist? Talk to family and friends for recommendations, use directories on the Internet, consult your local or state psychological association, or inquire at your community mental health center. Your place of worship, physician, or local college may also be a useful resource for finding a therapist.

Given the many psychotherapy approaches, which one should you choose? The next five sections of this chapter describe the main psychotherapy approaches. After reading about them, you may find that you are more comfortable with the philosophy, goals, and techniques of some over others. This information will assist you in understanding the nature of therapy, and in choosing a therapist if the need ever arises.

Quiz Yourself

14.1

1. **Psychotherapy should be considered when _____.**
   a. you get in trouble with your boss
   b. you are having difficulty functioning in some aspect of your life
   c. you have physical problems
   d. All of the above
2. **Michael is seeing a social worker to help him with his interpersonal problems. Michael is undergoing _____.**
   a. psychiatric counseling
   b. medical treatment
   c. psychotherapy
   d. biomedical therapy
3. **Which of the following professionals is most likely to prescribe medication as a form of therapy?**
   a. Clinical psychologist
   b. Social worker
   c. Biological psychologist
   d. Psychiatrist

Answers 1. b; 2. c; 3. d

14.2 Psychoanalytic Therapies: Uncovering Unconscious Conflicts

As we saw in Chapter 11, Sigmund Freud originally developed the psychoanalytic approach based on his ideas about different levels of consciousness and personality formation. Recall that Freud theorized that each of us has an unconscious level that contains desires, urges, thoughts, and memories of which we are unaware or that have been repressed or hidden. These unconscious conflicts psychologically threaten the functioning of the ego by causing us distress and anxiety. Over the years, we continue to defend our ego by erecting more barriers to keep these conflicts hidden.

Freud assumed that symptoms of mental health disorders stem from these unresolved unconscious issues. Consequently, the goal of psychoanalytic therapies is to change maladaptive behavior by uncovering unconscious conflicts so that clients can gain *insight* into the real source of their problems (Wolitzky,

1995). Freud named this approach **psychoanalysis**. Professionals who administer this type of therapy are called *psychoanalysts*. Here we will describe two forms of psychoanalysis: *traditional psychoanalysis* and the more modern *psychodynamic approach*.

Jose Luis Pelaez, Inc./Cusp/Corbis

In psychoanalysis, the client lies down on a couch away from the therapist so that the client may freely associate and express whatever comes to mind.

14.2.1 • Traditional Psychoanalysis

In traditional psychoanalysis as developed by Freud, the client lies down on a couch and talks about his or her concerns. It is the psychoanalyst's job to listen carefully and attentively to the client and discover what unconscious conflicts, themes, or concerns may be affecting the person. The first two therapists that Emily went to adopted this approach. Uncovering unconscious conflicts is not an easy task. Therefore, the psychoanalyst uses several methods to help clients gain insight and uncover critical issues from their pasts (Freud, 1949). These methods include *free association, dream analysis,* and *interpretation*. The psychoanalyst also observes the client's behaviors for clues as to unconscious conflicts. Two examples of client behaviors that give such clues are *resistance* and *transference*.

Free association involves talking freely about a subject without censoring any thoughts. The client is fully awake and is asked to talk about a specific topic. The client says whatever comes to mind. The psychoanalyst makes very few comments during free association, instead focusing on important themes or issues that may be revealed.

Dream analysis is a tool that some psychoanalysts use to reveal unconscious conflicts (Pesant & Zadra, 2004). Dreams do not directly represent unconscious conflicts but rather are comprised of symbols that reflect these underlying unconscious impulses (see Chapter 4). It is the psychoanalyst's job to decipher the true meaning, or *latent content*, of these dreams and thereby reveal important unconscious issues. Recall from the section case study that one of Emily's therapists was very interested in the content of her dreams and would attempt to find the themes embedded within them.

Free association and dream analysis provide the psychoanalyst with information on the unconscious workings of the client's mind. The psychoanalyst can then make interpretations to the client. **Interpretations** are the psychoanalyst's views on the themes and issues that may be influencing the client's behavior. These interpretations may help the client gain insight into his or her problems.

However, if the client is not psychologically ready to deal with these issues, he or she may resist these interpretations. **Resistance** occurs when a client behaves in such a way as to deny or avoid certain topics or issues. A client may resist a psychoanalyst's interpretation because it is too close to the truth and therefore creates anxiety. Clients may miss appointments or arrive late as a way of resisting the revealing nature of the therapy session. Clients may laugh or joke about topics that are actually quite painful for them. These resistant behaviors provide the psychoanalyst an additional clue to the unconscious conflicts affecting the client.

The process of **transference** also provides a clue to a client's unconscious conflicts. Freud (1949) believed that at some point during therapy, clients would unconsciously react to the therapist as if the therapist were his or her parent, friend, sibling, or romantic partner. Freud termed this unconscious reaction *transference* because the client was unknowingly transferring feelings and emotions toward a loved one onto the therapist. The psychoanalyst can explore such instances of

psychoanalysis [sigh-co-uh-NAL-uh-sis] a method of therapy formulated by Freud that focuses on uncovering unconscious conflicts that drive maladaptive behavior

free association a technique in psychoanalysis in which the client says whatever comes to mind

dream analysis a technique in psychoanalysis in which the therapist examines the hidden symbols in a client's dreams

interpretation the psychoanalyst's view on the themes and issues that may be influencing the client's behavior

resistance a process in psychoanalysis whereby the client behaves in such a way as to deny or avoid sensitive issues

transference a process in psychoanalysis in which the client unconsciously reacts to the therapist as if the therapist were a parent, friend, sibling, or romantic partner transference to reveal how the dynamics of clients' relationships may be influencing their behavior.

Traditional psychoanalysis was a dominant treatment approach through the 1950s. However, uncovering unconscious conflicts often took years and called for as many as five sessions per week. The long-term nature of traditional psychoanalysis made it increasingly impractical and expensive for the average person and for the growing involvement of the health insurance industry. The development of other psychotherapies as well as the advent of drug therapy (discussed later) also led to a decrease in the popularity of traditional psychoanalysis (Henry et al., 1994). Hence, psychoanalysis was forced to move in a new direction.

14.2.2 • Modern Psychoanalysis

psychodynamic therapy modern psychoanalysis delivered in a shorter time that focuses less on the client's past and more on current problems and the nature of interpersonal relationships

Modern psychoanalysis, often referred to as **psychodynamic therapy**, or *short-term dynamic therapy,* is evident in many different forms. Such therapies are consistent with the views of Freud and the psychoanalytic approach. They continue to rely on the therapist's interpretations of the client's feelings and behavior, and on identifying instances of transference and resistance. However, modern psychoanalysis tends to focus less on the client's past. Current problems and the nature of interpersonal relationships are seen as more important in improving the client's behavior. The therapist also plays a more direct role, rapidly interviewing and questioning the client to uncover unconscious issues and themes in a shorter time. Then the therapist and client agree to focus on a limited set of problems that are seen as causing the client the most trouble. For example, in *interpersonal therapy,* extensive attention is given to the client's relationships and interpersonal behaviors that seem to be the most important in the onset and/or maintenance of depression. Modern psychoanalysis tends to be more short term, lasting no more than a few months, and appears to be effective in improving clients' symptoms (Abbass, Town, & Driessen, 2011; Cortina, 2010; Jakobsen et al., 2012; Schottenbauer et al., 2008; Shedler, 2010; Slavin-Mulford et al., 2011).

Quiz Yourself 14.2

1. The goal of psychoanalysis is to change behavior by _____.
   a. uncovering unconscious conflicts so that the client can gain insight into the source of his or her problems
   b. uncovering negative cognitive patterns that impede the client's ability to function
   c. examining environmental conditions and how they influence the client's responses
   d. providing the client with unconditional support and love so that he or she makes adaptive and healthy behavioral choices

2. Song often arrives late for her psychoanalysis appointment and sometimes forgets her appointments altogether. Her psychoanalyst might interpret Song's behavior as a sign of _____.
   a. transference
   b. challenge interpretation
   c. resistance
   d. free association

3. Modern psychoanalysis differs from traditional psychoanalysis in that _____.
   a. it is shorter in duration
   b. it is focused less on the client's past and more on present relationships and issues
   c. the therapist is more direct
   d. All of the above

Answers 1. a; 2. c; 3. d

14.3 Humanistic Therapy: Facilitating Self-Actualization

As we have just seen, problems with psychoanalysis forced it to move in a new direction that resulted in briefer psychodynamic therapies that were still connected to the ideas of Freud. However, some psychoanalysts departed radically from these views and developed different forms of therapy. One example is *humanistic therapy.*

14.3.1 • The Aim of Humanistic Therapy Approaches

The *humanistic approach* focuses less on unconscious forces and more on the conscious actions we take in controlling our behavior. Even though Dr. Farber was a trained psychoanalyst, his belief in Emily's value and his emphasis on her free will exemplify this humanistic perspective. In Emily's words:

> Dr. Farber was both far humbler than his more conventional colleagues and far bolder. He was humbler because he approached his patients as a whole human being. . . . He was bolder because . . . he committed himself to a risky, open-ended friendship and to all the claims of responsibility that friendship entails. (Gordon, 2000, p. 125)

Humanists believe that behavior is driven not by unconscious impulses, but by how we interpret the world and our awareness of our feelings. The only way to understand a person's behavior, therefore, is to connect with and understand the person's worldview. Humanism further assumes that people will naturally strive toward personal growth and achievement of their full potential when raised in a positive and accepting environment. When a person holds distorted perceptions or lacks self-awareness, mental health problems arise, preventing the person from becoming *self-actualized.* Yet people are capable of healing themselves, if only the right environment is provided. The therapist's role is to create this safe environment for self-exploration and facilitate the journey toward self-fulfillment (Greenberg & Rice, 1997). One of the most influential and best known of the humanistic therapies is *client-centered therapy.*

client-centered therapy a humanistic psychotherapy approach formulated by Carl Rogers that emphasizes the use of empathy, genuineness, and unconditional positive regard to help the client reach his or her potential

14.3.2 • Client-Centered Therapy: Three Key Ingredients

Disillusioned with the goals, methods, and assumptions of psychoanalysis, Carl Rogers (1902–1987) developed a different therapy approach that exemplifies the humanistic perspective. Whereas Freud saw the analyst as all-knowing and responsible for client change, Rogers believed that the therapist should serve more as a facilitator or coach to help move the client in the direction of change. Such a viewpoint resulted in **client-centered therapy**, or *person-centered therapy.* As the names imply, in client-centered therapy, the focus and direction of therapy comes from the person, or client. The client decides what to talk about, without interpretation or judgment from the therapist. The therapist, according to Rogers (1951, 1980, 1986), creates a positive and accepting environment to facilitate self-awareness and personal growth by providing three key characteristics: *empathy, genuineness,* and *unconditional positive regard.*

In humanistic therapy, therapist and client sit face-to-face as they work together in solving the client's problems.

AP Images/FBI

empathy the ability of a therapist to understand a client's feelings and thoughts without being judgmental

genuineness the ability of a therapist to openly share his or her thoughts and feelings with a client

unconditional positive regard the ability of a therapist to accept and value a person for who he or she is, regardless of his or her faults or problems

EMPATHY: UNDERSTANDING THE CLIENT

Are you a good listener? Do friends and family frequently confide in you? If so, then you may possess empathy. According to Rogers, **empathy** is the ability to understand a client's feelings and thoughts without being judgmental. The therapist does not express disapproval toward the client but rather indicates understanding of the client's feelings. Conveying empathy involves actively listening to the client—making eye contact, nodding as the client speaks, and assuming an interested and attentive pose. Empathy also involves *reflection*. The therapist restates, repeats, or summarizes the thoughts and feelings that he or she hears the client express. Reflected statements communicate to the client the active attention of the therapist and mirror the client's perceptions and views of reality. Consider this example of empathy and reflection from Irvin Yalom's work, *Love's Executioner and Other Tales of Psychotherapy* (1989, p. 29).

> **Client:** I believe he is intentionally trying to drive me to suicide. Does that sound like a crazy thought?
>
> **Therapist:** I don't know if it's crazy, but it sounds like a desperate and terribly painful thought.

Notice in this example that the therapist does not judge the client's thoughts as crazy and reflects the emotions underlying the statement of suicide. Ideally, empathy and reflection will help clients see themselves and their problems more clearly, promoting a realistic self-image and greater self-acceptance.

GENUINENESS: SHARING THOUGHTS, FEELINGS, AND EXPERIENCES

A second key therapist quality in client-centered therapy is genuineness. **Genuineness** is the ability to openly share one's thoughts and feelings with others. The therapist expresses his or her true feelings and thoughts to the client and does not hide behind the mask of being the "professional," "doctor," or authority figure. The therapist self-discloses a fair amount to the client, which allows the client to see the therapist as a real, living person. Such disclosure also creates an open environment that promotes trust and an honest expression of thoughts and feelings. Rogers believed that such an environment would model to the client how relationships can be built on a foundation of trust and honesty. Emily learned such a lesson from Dr. Farber. His genuineness made her believe he truly cared about her well-being.

UNCONDITIONAL POSITIVE REGARD: VALUING THE CLIENT

The third key quality in client-centered therapy, unconditional positive regard, was introduced in the chapter on personality (Chapter 11). Recall that Rogers defined **unconditional positive regard** as the ability to accept and value a person for who he or she is, regardless of his or her faults or problems. Rogers believed that receiving unconditional positive regard in one's childhood is a key factor in healthy personality adjustment. A therapist who offers unconditional positive regard to a client does not indicate shock, dismay, or disapproval to any client statements. Instead, the therapist communicates caring and respect toward the client regardless of what the client says.

This does not mean that the therapist has to personally *agree* with everything the client states. Rather, the therapist's job is to reflect the client's feelings and thoughts in order to further the client's self-knowledge and enable the client to solve problems in his or her own way. Unconditional positive regard enables the client to believe that he or she has value and is competent at making decisions. Such attitudes foster self-confidence and self-acceptance that lead to healthier growth choices.

For Rogers, a therapist who demonstrates all three qualities—empathy, genuineness, and unconditional positive regard—establishes a positive and nurturing environment. A person feels accepted, understood, and valued. These feelings help the client self-explore a more realistic self-image and perception of the world. This in turn removes the obstacles to personal growth so that self-actualization can be realized.

Does client-centered therapy work? Compared to no-treatment control groups, people in client-centered therapy do change their behavior (Greenberg & Rice, 1997; Hill & Nakayama, 2000). Compared to more structured therapy approaches, client-centered therapy is equally effective (Stiles et al., 2006, 2008).

Quiz Yourself

14.3

1. **The goal of humanistic therapy is to change behavior by _____.**
   a. confronting unconscious conflicts through therapist interpretations
   b. uncovering negative thoughts that cause the client anxiety and distress
   c. examining stimuli in the environment and how they influence the client's responses
   d. providing the client with a safe environment for self-exploration and facilitating the journey toward self-fulfillment
2. **Which of the following is *not* one of the elements used in client-centered therapy to help the client achieve self-fulfillment?**
   a. Genuineness
   b. Free association
   c. Unconditional positive regard
   d. Empathy
3. **Marcos is receiving client-centered therapy. His therapist openly shares his thoughts and feelings with Marcos, relating his own experiences that are similar to those of Marcos's. Marcos's therapist is exhibiting which quality of client-centered therapy?**
   a. Genuineness
   b. Reflection
   c. Unconditional positive regard
   d. Empathy

Answers 1. d; 2. b; 3. a

14.4 Behavior Therapies: Learning Healthier Behaviors

Psychoanalytic and humanistic therapies focus on internal reflection by the client. In contrast, **behavior therapy** focuses directly on changing current problem behaviors rather than delving into the client's past. Behavior therapies, also called *behavior modification*, consist of techniques and methods that use learning principles to change problem behavior. Chapter 6 described the learning processes of classical conditioning and operant conditioning. The behavioral perspective relies on these principles to modify behavior. Recall that the *behavioral perspective* assumes that behavior is a result of environmental variables such as stimuli and consequences in the environment. It further assumes that people learn maladaptive behavior in the same way that they learn adaptive behavior. So, changing behavior involves changing the environmental circumstances that seem to elicit negative behavior. Learning principles that focus on *extinction* are used to stop disruptive behaviors.

behavior therapy therapy that applies the principles of classical and operant conditioning to help people change maladaptive behaviors

Similarly, learning principles that focus on *shaping* or acquiring behaviors are used to replace undesirable behaviors with more adaptive ones.

Behavior therapy can take many forms. Here we discuss two broad categories of behavior therapy: *classical conditioning techniques* and *operant conditioning techniques*.

14.4.1 • Applying Classical Conditioning Techniques in Therapy

Some behavior therapies rely on the principles of classical conditioning outlined in Chapter 6. Briefly, classical conditioning occurs when stimuli in the environment become associated so that both produce the same response. For example, as a child, one of the authors was bitten by a dog twice within a 2-year period. In both instances, the dog was a German shepherd. Following those incidents, she developed an intense fear of large dogs. Her dog-biting experiences became associated with pain, so that now she feared pain from all large dogs and routinely avoided them. Her fear was a learned behavior. Behavior therapy would focus on having her unlearn her response to large dogs. Three behavior therapy techniques that rely on classical conditioning principles are *systematic desensitization*, *flooding*, and *aversion therapy*.

SYSTEMATIC DESENSITIZATION: RELAX AND HAVE NO FEAR

systematic desensitization [sis-tuh-MAT-ick dee-sen-sih-tuh-ZAY-shun] a behavior therapy technique that uses a gradual, step-by-step process to replace fear or anxiety with an incompatible response of relaxation and positive emotion

One effective tool for treating phobias and anxiety is systematic desensitization (Wolpe, 1958). **Systematic desensitization** involves replacing a fear or anxiety response with an incompatible response of relaxation and positive emotion. Anxiety and relaxation are *competing responses*. You cannot feel both at the same time; you can only feel one or the other. So the aim of systematic desensitization is to have a client learn how to relax and then slowly and systematically introduce the feared object, situation, or thought while the client maintains a positive state of pleasure or relaxation. An early example of systematic desensitization was an experiment by Mary Cover Jones (1924) in which she treated a 3-year-old's fear of rabbits. The child, Peter, sat at a distance from a caged rabbit while eating one of his favorite foods. The cage was gradually moved closer to Peter until he was able to play with the rabbit and not experience any fear. Jones had countered Peter's negative emotional reaction of fear with a positive one of pleasure from the food.

Systematic desensitization is accomplished in three basic steps. First, the client is trained in *progressive muscle relaxation*. As discussed in Chapter 12, this method involves alternately tensing and relaxing different muscle groups, beginning with the head and working down to the toes, so that the client learns to distinguish when muscles are tense and when they are relaxed.

ENGAGE YOURSELF! Try progressive muscle relaxation training on your own. Close your eyes and take deep breaths for a minute. Then tighten your jaw muscles and clench your teeth. Hold the tension for a few moments and then relax and take several deep breaths. Do the same for your eyes, forehead, neck, and shoulders, alternating between tensing your muscles and then relaxing them. You will be pleasantly surprised by how a few minutes of this procedure can reduce tension and promote relaxation.

An Anxiety Hierarchy for Systematic Desensitization

Degree of fear	
5	I'm standing on the balcony of the top floor of an apartment tower.
10	I'm standing on a stepladder in the kitchen to change a light bulb.
15	I'm walking on a ridge. The edge is hidden by shrubs and treetops.
20	I'm sitting on the slope of a mountain, looking out over the horizon.
25	I'm crossing a bridge 6 feet above a creek. The bridge consists of an 18-inch-wide board with a handrail on one side.
30	I'm riding a ski lift 8 feet above the ground.
35	I'm crossing a shallow, wide creek on an 18-inch-wide board, 3 feet above water level.
40	I'm climbing a ladder outside the house to reach a second-story window.
45	I'm pulling myself up a 30-degree wet, slippery slope on a steel cable.
50	I'm scrambling up a rock, 8 feet high.
55	I'm walking 10 feet on a resilient, 18-inch-wide board which spans an 8-foot-deep gulch.
60	I'm walking on a wide plateau, 2 feet from the edge of a cliff.
65	I'm skiing an intermediate hill. The snow is packed.
70	I'm walking over a railway trestle.
75	I'm walking on the side of an embankment. The path slopes to the outside.
80	I'm riding a chair lift 15 feet above the ground.
85	I'm walking up a long, steep slope.
90	I'm walking up (or down) a 15-degree slope on a 3-foot-wide trail. On one side of the trail the terrain drops down sharply; on the other side is a steep upward slope.
95	I'm walking on a 3-foot-wide ridge. The slopes on both sides are long and more than 25 degrees steep.
100	I'm walking on a 3-foot-wide ridge. The trail slopes on one side. The drop on either side of the trail is more than 25 degrees.

FIGURE 14.2

Sample Anxiety Hierarchy

An anxiety hierarchy like the one shown here is used during systematic desensitization. This hierarchy was developed for a woman who had a fear of heights.

From K. E. Rudestam, *Methods of Self Change: An ABC Primer,* © 1980 Wadsworth. Reprinted with permission of the author.

Once the client has learned progressive relaxation, the client and therapist develop an anxiety hierarchy. An **anxiety hierarchy** (● FIGURE 14.2) is a list of situations or items that trigger a client's anxiety or fear. The items on the hierarchy start with the least anxiety-provoking situations or items and progress to the most distressing.

anxiety hierarchy a list that orders, according to the degree of fear, the situations or items that trigger anxiety; the list starts with the least frightening images and progresses to the most distressing

In the third step, progressive relaxation and the anxiety hierarchy are combined. Relaxation is paired with each item in the hierarchy. As the client becomes able to imagine a feared situation and remain relaxed, the next item in the hierarchy is addressed. Over several therapy sessions, this systematic process continues until the client has become desensitized to all items in the hierarchy.

You may be skeptical at this point, unconvinced that thinking about a feared stimulus is similar to actually encountering the object or situation. This skepticism is somewhat warranted, so once the client has mastered the mental images, behavior therapists can extend systematic desensitization to a simulated or actual environment. For many fears, this is when systematic desensitization is most effective (Antony & Barlow, 2002). For example, flight simulators can be used to help desensitize people to a fear of flying. Combining systematic desensitization with the actual situation, called *in vivo exposure,* is also a very effective tool in treating a variety of anxiety disorders (Choy, Fyer, & Lipsitz, 2007; Foa et al., 2013; Meyerbroeker et al., 2013; Tolin, 2010).

Virtual reality computer technology also can be used to simulate a feared situation. Virtual reality bridges the gap between imagining feared stimuli in a therapist's office and in vivo exposure in the field by simulating a feared situation. The client wears a head-mounted display with small video monitors

AP Images/Bebeto Matthews

Virtual reality exposure therapy allows clients to experience their fears in a simulated, nonthreatening environment.

and stereo earphones that integrate visual and auditory cues to immerse the client in a computer-generated virtual environment. For example, a person with a fear of flying may be exposed to stimuli that simulate sitting in a plane and hearing the plane's engines revving for takeoff. A person with a fear of public speaking may experience simulation of standing at a podium. The therapist can control the images the client receives while monitoring heart rate, respiration, and skin temperature to assess the client's fear responses during the session (Bender, 2004).

Virtual reality exposure therapy has become an increasingly common, effective treatment for people with excessive anxiety disorders such as specific phobias, social anxiety disorders, panic disorders, and posttraumatic stress disorder (P. L. Anderson et al., 2005; J. G. Beck et al., 2007; de Carvalho, Freire, & Nardi, 2010; Gerardi et al., 2010; Klinger et al., 2005; McLay et al., 2010; Motraghi et al., 2014; Parsons & Rizzo, 2008; Rothbaum, Rizzo, & Difede, 2010).

FLOODING: FACING OUR FEARS

flooding a behavior therapy technique in which a client is exposed to a feared object or situation for a prolonged period until his or her anxiety extinguishes

Another exposure behavior therapy that relies on classical conditioning processes is flooding. In **flooding**, the client remains exposed to the feared object, situation, or image for a prolonged period (1–2 hours) until his or her anxiety decreases. Recall from Chapter 6 that this is a process called *extinction* in which the conditioned stimulus (CS) (the feared item) is presented by itself until it no longer produces the conditioned response (CR) of anxiety and fear. In contrast to systematic desensitization, flooding starts with the *most* feared item or situation rather than the least distressing item. In addition, instead of relaxing, the client is told to experience the fear fully and is prevented from escaping the situation or engaging in any other anxiety-avoiding behaviors. Whatever terrible consequences the client imagined would happen do not occur, and his or her anxiety decreases.

Flooding can be an effective and efficient way to reduce anxiety and fear (McNeil & Kyle, 2009; Tryon, 2005). A client's anxiety subsides rather quickly; however, relapses (return of the fear) are common (Escobar, 2008). This should not be surprising if you recall the concept of *spontaneous recovery* in which the conditioned response (anxiety) can reappear after it has been extinguished. For this reason, flooding is often used in combination with other therapy techniques (Corey, 2009). Because of the discomfort associated with flooding, it is ethically imperative that clients be fully informed and prepared for flooding treatment.

AVERSION THERAPY: WE WON'T DO SOMETHING IF WE DISLIKE IT

Do you bite your nails? As a child, did you suck your thumb? Did loved ones try to get you to stop such behaviors? Many parents put a foul-tasting or spicy liquid such as Tabasco sauce on their child's nails or thumb to stop nail biting or thumb sucking. These parents may not know that they are performing aversion therapy, another example of a behavior therapy that relies on classical conditioning principles. **Aversion therapy** involves pairing an unpleasant stimulus (foul or spicy taste) with a specific undesirable behavior such as biting one's fingernails. Ideally, the aversive stimulus becomes associated with the undesirable response so that the person is less likely to engage in the response again.

aversion [uh-VER-shun] therapy a behavior therapy technique in which a specific behavior is paired with an unpleasant stimulus in order to reduce its occurrence

covert sensitization [co-VERT sen-sih-tuh-ZAY-shun] therapy a milder form of aversion therapy in which graphic imagery is used to create unpleasant associations with specific stimuli

Aversive conditioning occurs frequently in everyday life. Food poisoning is a prime example. If a particular food has ever made you sick, normally it will be months or even years before you touch that food again. The food (stimulus) becomes associated with being sick (response) so that you avoid it at all costs. Therapists use this knowledge to treat a variety of undesirable habits and behaviors. For example, an aversion therapy method for treating alcoholism involves taking a drug called Antabuse (Cannon & Baker, 1981). Antabuse interacts with alcohol, causing nausea and vomiting. If a person with alcohol use disorder drinks while using Antabuse, it makes him or her ill. The unwanted stimulus (alcohol) becomes associated with the response of feeling ill and nauseated. The person with alcoholism learns to avoid alcohol in order to avoid the associated unpleasant response. Unfortunately, the person with alcohol use disorder can also simply avoid taking the medication, thereby nullifying the effectiveness of the procedure.

In clinical trials, Antabuse has demonstrated mixed results in helping people abstain from alcohol use. When Antabuse is given under supervision and in conjunction with a drug that specifically reduces alcohol cravings, its effectiveness on short-term abstinence and days until relapse is improved (Barth & Malcolm, 2010; Johnson, 2008; Jorgensen, Pedersen, & Tonnesen, 2011; Krampe & Ehrenreich, 2010; Skinner et al., 2014).

An alternative form of aversion therapy is called **covert sensitization therapy**. In this procedure, graphic imagery is used to create unpleasant associations with specific stimuli. For example, a person who smokes cigarettes may have to repeatedly imagine black and diseased lungs when faced with the stimulus of a cigarette. At this point, you may be disturbed by the knowledge that therapists use such unpleasant procedures in treatment. Keep in mind, though, that therapists are ethically bound to get informed consent from clients. Clients are informed of the procedure and must agree before such a method can be used.

14.4.2 • Applying Operant Conditioning Techniques in Therapy

Whereas systematic desensitization, flooding, and aversion therapy rely on classical conditioning principles, some behavior therapies rely on the principles of operant conditioning outlined in Chapter 6. Briefly, operant conditioning focuses on the consequences of a behavior. It assumes that reinforced behavior will be maintained and punished behavior will be extinguished. For instance, in the previous example in which your author developed a fear of large dogs, recall that following the dog-biting episodes she responded by avoiding large dogs. The consequence of this response was reinforcing—it reduced her fear. She learned that the next time she encountered a large dog, avoiding it would quickly rid her of any anxiety.

Changing undesirable behavior, therefore, involves changing the consequences of a behavior. These changes can be accomplished in a variety of ways (Kazdin, 2013).

© Ilike/Shutterstock.com

Children's tantrums can be eliminated if their inappropriate behavior is not reinforced. However, keep in mind that the child's tantrums will initially get worse as the child attempts to get a reaction from loved ones.

- *Positive reinforcement*. Positive reinforcement is used to encourage or maintain a behavior. For example, every time a child complies with a parental request, verbal praise follows. After the child's compliance increases, verbal praise need not occur every single time.
- *Nonreinforcement and Extinction*. To discourage unwanted behavior, any reinforcers of the behavior are removed. For instance, to discourage a child from throwing tantrums at home, the child's parent ignores the behavior so that no attention (even negative attention, such as a reprimand) reinforces the behavior. If a reinforcer does not follow a behavior, the behavior will occur less frequently. Eventually the behavior will be eliminated or extinguished. However, keep in mind that often the unwanted behavior will increase before it goes away because a person is expecting the reinforcer. The child's tantrums will initially be longer or more frequent in an attempt to get a reaction from the parent. Misbehavior may also continue because all subtle forms of reinforcers have not been eliminated. For example, consider what happens when the same child acts up in school. Although the teacher may scold or reprimand the child, the child still receives a form of attention, and therefore the behavior may not subside. Even if the teacher ignores the child's misbehavior, classmates may reinforce the behavior by laughing and paying attention to him or her.
- *Punishment*. Sometimes punishment is used to decrease undesirable behaviors. Recall that punishment occurs when an undesired behavior is immediately followed by a negative or unpleasant consequence such as loss of a privilege. But also remember the side effects of punishment. It can produce negative emotions such as anger or fear, or negative behaviors, such as avoidance. For these reasons, punishment is used sparingly.
- *Shaping*. Recall from Chapter 6 that shaping involves positively reinforcing each successive attempt at a behavior. It is used to teach a person new, desired behaviors. For example, shaping may be used to teach children with autism how to speak. If the child makes a "t" sound to say toy, this attempt is rewarded. Shaping has also been successfully used to teach people with intellectual disabilities self-help skills, such as washing their face or brushing their teeth.
- *Token economy*. A **token economy** involves rewarding people with tokens, or symbolic rewards, for desired behavior. Because not everyone is influenced by the same reward, tokens—such as chips, points, or stars—are given each time a person engages in a desired behavior. These tokens can then be exchanged for a variety of reinforcers such as food, privileges, goods, phone time, and so on.

token economy a behavior therapy technique in which people are rewarded with tokens for desired behavior; the tokens can then be exchanged for what is reinforcing to the individuals

You may recall having had a treasure chest or goody box in elementary school. Students who had acquired a certain number of points or tokens could visit the prize box at the end of the week. Today, your consumer behavior may be unknowingly reinforced by a token economy. Many credit card companies, restaurants, and retail stores offer points for purchases. These points can then be exchanged for merchandise, food, or future discounts. Airlines do the same thing with frequent flyer points. Their aim is to increase your consumption of their services.

The same principle can be used in hospitals, halfway houses, prisons, substance abuse treatment centers, and other institutional settings. People earn tokens for desired behavior and constructive activities, and then exchange them for passes, free time, snacks, access to television, or private rooms. Recall that Emily's behavior in the Riggs treatment center was monitored in this fashion. To receive privileges, she had to get her work jobs done and go to bed at the appropriate time. In some institutions, patients may lose or be charged tokens for undesired behavior such as fighting, noncompliance, or not completing their chores. A token economy can be a very effective tool for treating children with intellectual disabilities and autism, and for managing behavior in a group setting (Matson & Boisjoli, 2009; Mottram & Berger-Gross, 2004; Park & Lee, 2012; Petry et al., 2004).

Although behavior therapies have been very successful in treating a variety of psychological and behavioral problems, particularly in children, they do not address the thoughts and perceptions that often accompany behavior. For this reason, behavioral strategies have been increasingly used in conjunction with cognitive therapy, our next topic of discussion.

Quiz Yourself

14.4

1. **Behavior therapies change behavior by _____.**
   a. examining unconscious conflicts and replacing them with subconscious memories
   b. focusing on negative cognitive patterns that impede the client's ability to function
   c. examining and then changing the environmental circumstances that seem to elicit negative behavior
   d. identifying the client's worldview to facilitate the journey toward self-fulfillment
2. **Celia goes to a therapist to try to reduce her fear of driving. The therapist teaches Celia how to relax and then has her imagine those aspects of driving that make her fearful while maintaining her relaxed mode. Celia is most likely undergoing _____.**
   a. aversion therapy
   b. a token economy
   c. systematic desensitization
   d. client-centered therapy
3. **Which of the following is a therapy approach based on the principles of classical conditioning?**
   a. A token economy
   b. Shaping
   c. Positive reinforcement
   d. Aversion therapy

Answers 1. c; 2. c; 3. d

14.5 Cognitive Therapies: Changing Thoughts

Many mental health disorders such as anxiety and depression may stem from negative and distorted thought patterns. *Cognitive therapies* focus on changing these maladaptive patterns of thinking and perceiving, and replacing them with more adaptive ways of interpreting events. Two of the most widely used cognitive therapies are Albert Ellis's *rational-emotive therapy* and Aaron Beck's *cognitive therapy.*

14.5.1 • Ellis's Rational-Emotive Therapy: Reinterpret One's Viewpoint

Developed by Albert Ellis (1913–2007) (1973, 1995), **rational-emotive therapy** is based on the premise that many mental health problems stem from how people think about and interpret events in their lives. It is not the actual event that causes

rational-emotive therapy a cognitive therapy approach created by Albert Ellis that focuses on changing the irrational beliefs that are believed to impede mental health

Courtesy of Ellis Institute

Albert Ellis developed rational-emotive therapy to deal with clients' faulty or irrational beliefs that lead to self-defeating behaviors such as anxiety, depression, or anger.

the emotional upset, but rather the person's *interpretation* of the event that results in emotional distress. Specifically, rational-emotive therapy identifies the client's faulty or irrational beliefs that lead to self-defeating behaviors, anxiety, depression, anger, or other mental health problems. Research supports Ellis's notion that people who think more irrationally experience more psychological distress (Hyland et al., 2014; Nieuwenhuijsen et al., 2010; Taghavi et al., 2006; Ziegler & Smith, 2004).

Ellis identified common irrational beliefs (1991) that often impede people's functioning (see • TABLE 14.2). Identifying such irrational beliefs is the first step in rational-emotive therapy. For example, one client may have an excessive need for approval because she believes that she "must be loved by everyone." Another client may irrationally believe that there is a "right" solution for every problem and become frustrated or depressed because a problem recurs. Once these beliefs have been identified, the therapist challenges their validity. The therapist confronts and disputes these fallacies in a logical and persuasive manner, pushing the client to recognize that such beliefs are irrational and unhealthy. The therapist might make statements such as "What evidence do you have to support this belief?" or "In what other ways could this evidence be interpreted?" Additionally, the client may be asked "What is the worst thing that could happen?" and "If that happened, what could you do?" Asking such questions forces clients to consider alternative viewpoints, face their fears and anxieties, and explore possible problem-solving methods.

After a client's irrational beliefs have been recognized and refuted, they can then be replaced with more realistic and rational beliefs. These beliefs may be reflected in such statements as "Not everyone will like me, but that is okay and not a measure of my worth" or "There are several ways to solve a problem, and if one approach fails I can try another."

Rational-emotive therapy is a very direct and confrontational approach. Admitting that our way of thinking is irrational and unhealthy and radically changing our interpretation of events in our lives is not an easy task. Yet despite these obstacles, rational-emotive therapy has generally been effective in treating mood and excessive anxiety disorders (David et al., 2008; Lewinsohn et al., 1990; Sava et al., 2009).

cognitive therapy a therapy created by Aaron Beck that focuses on uncovering negative automatic thought patterns that impede mental health

cognitive distortions distorted thinking patterns, such as overgeneralization or all-or-none thinking, that, according to Aaron Beck, lead to depression, anxiety, and low self-esteem

TABLE 14.2

Examples of Irrational Assumptions

1. I must be loved by or approved of by everyone.
2. I must be competent and achieving in all things I do; otherwise I am worthless.
3. Some people are bad and should be severely blamed and punished for it. I should be extremely upset over the wrongdoings of others.
4. It is awful and upsetting when things are not the way I would like them to be.
5. Unhappiness is caused by external events, and I cannot control my bad feelings and emotional reactions.
6. If something unpleasant happens, I should dwell on it.
7. Avoiding difficulties, rather than facing them, will make you happy.
8. Always rely on someone who is stronger than you.
9. Your past will always affect your present life.
10. There is a perfect solution for every problem, and it is awful and upsetting if this solution is not found.

14.5.2 • Beck's Cognitive Therapy: Replace Negative Thoughts

A second illustration of focusing on thought patterns in therapy is Aaron Beck's (b. 1921) **cognitive therapy**. Noticing that many of his clients who were depressed expressed a negative view of themselves and the world almost habitually, Beck turned his attention to the role cognitions play in emotional distress. He developed a cognitive therapy based on the principle that distorted thinking, in the form of **cognitive distortions** and negative, automatic thought patterns, leads to depression, anxiety, and low self-esteem (Beck et al., 1979). For example, do you ever make critical remarks to yourself such as "Oh, I am so stupid" or "I am such an idiot"? Recall Emily's declarations that she was fat, awkward, and a misfit. Such personal negative statements depress mood and lower self-esteem. Beck believed that such maladaptive patterns could be identified and changed, resulting in more adaptive behavior. ● TABLE 14.3 illustrates some of the more common cognitive distortions that Beck identified in people who are depressed.

Beck's cognitive therapy is not as confrontational in its approach as rational-emotive therapy. Rather, Beck (1991) saw the client and therapist as a collaborative team, working together to identify and evaluate the accuracy and biases of the client's thought patterns. At first, the therapist teaches the client how to recognize and keep track of negative automatic thoughts, such as "I never do anything right" or "I always fail at whatever I do." The therapist and client then test the validity or accuracy of these thoughts. For example, a client may be asked to list

Courtesy of Beck Institute for Cognitive Therapy and Research

Aaron Beck developed cognitive therapy based on the principle that distorted thinking and negative, automatic thought patterns lead to depression, anxiety, and low self-esteem.

TABLE 14.3

Examples of Cognitive Distortions

COGNITIVE ERROR	DESCRIPTION	EXAMPLE
All-or-nothing thinking	Seeing each event as completely good or bad, right or wrong, a success or a failure	"If I don't get this job, I am a failure."
Arbitrary inference	Concluding that something negative will happen or is happening even though there is no evidence to support it	"My neighbor did not say hello to me. She must be mad at me."
Disqualifying the positive	Rejecting positive experiences	"Anyone can paint. It's no big deal."
Emotional reasoning	Assuming that negative emotions are accurate without questioning them	"I feel fat, so I must be fat."
Labeling	Placing a negative, global label on a person or situation	"I can't do anything right, so why should I try?"
Magnification and minimization	Overestimating the importance of negative events and underestimating the impact of positive events	"In my job evaluation, my boss said I need to work on my time management skills. She only said I was a productive worker and good team manager to be nice."
Overgeneralization	Applying a negative conclusion of one event to other unrelated events and areas of one's life	"I messed up on my math test, so I won't do well in history or Spanish. I should drop out of school."
Personalization	Attributing negative events to oneself without reason	"My parents are in a bad mood because they have an idiot for a son."
Selective abstraction	Focusing on a single, irrelevant, negative aspect of a situation while ignoring more relevant and important aspects of the situation	"It doesn't matter that I got a raise and a promotion. I now have to go to work an hour earlier."

all the tasks assigned to him or her in a week and then indicate whether each task was completed. The therapist hopes that such an exercise will not only point out the inaccuracy of the client's beliefs, but also teach the client how to evaluate negative automatic thoughts in the future. We saw that as a part of therapy, Dr. Farber would often highlight Emily's negative thought patterns as a way of improving her self-image.

Cognitive therapy, like rational-emotive therapy, has been very effective in treating depression and excessive anxiety disorders (David et al., 2008; Gibbons et al., 2010). In some studies, it has been just as effective as drugs (Sava et al., 2009). More important, clients who have adopted new and more adaptive patterns of thinking are less likely to become depressed in the future—a benefit that drugs cannot provide (Jarrett et al., 2001; Teasdale et al., 2001).

cognitive-behavior therapy (CBT)
a range of treatment approaches to alter faulty cognitions and maladaptive behaviors

Currently, the elements of cognitive therapy are often combined with the techniques of behavioral therapy (discussed previously) and called **cognitive-behavior therapy** (**CBT**). CBT is considered as the best established psychological treatment for people with obsessive-compulsive and related disorders and chronic pain (Ehde, Dillworth, & Turner, 2014; Lack, 2012; Olatunji et al., 2013) and has been shown to be highly effective in treating other anxiety disorders and depression (Baker, McFall, & Shoham, 2008; Hofmann & Smits, 2008; Lang et al., 2011; McEvoy & Nathan, 2007; Miskovic et al., 2011; Norton & Price, 2007). It is also effective in treating eating disorders and substance-related disorders (Baker et al., 2008; Ricca et al., 2010; Schmidt et al., 2007). CBT has more recently been adapted to target the positive symptoms of schizophrenia such as delusional thought processes and disorganized speech (Addington, Piskulic, & Marshall, 2010).

You Review: Psychotherapy Approaches contrasts the goals and therapeutic techniques of the psychotherapy approaches we have discussed in this chapter.

You Review **Psychotherapy Approaches**

Psychological Perspective	Therapy Approaches	Therapy Goals	Therapy Techniques
Psychoanalytic	Traditional psychoanalysis and modern psychodynamic therapy	Insights and resolution regarding unconscious conflicts	Free association, dream analysis, interpretation
Humanistic	Client-centered therapy	Acceptance of genuine self and personal growth	Genuineness, empathy, and unconditional positive regard
Behavioral/Learning	Behavior modification	Eliminate maladaptive behaviors and acquire adaptive behaviors	Systematic desensitization, flooding, aversion therapy, shaping, reinforcement, extinction, token economy
Cognitive	Rational-emotive therapy, cognitive therapy	Reduce negative thinking and irrational beliefs; develop more realistic thinking	Challenge irrational beliefs, record negative automatic thoughts

Quiz Yourself

14.5

1. **Svetlana goes to a therapist who focuses on her negative automatic statements. Svetlana is most likely undergoing what type of therapy?**
   a. Rational-emotive therapy
   b. Cognitive therapy
   c. Systematic desensitization
   d. Client-centered therapy
2. **The goal of cognitive therapy approaches is to change behavior by _____.**
   a. uncovering unconscious conflicts so that the client can gain insight into the source of his or her problems
   b. uncovering negative cognitive patterns that impede the client's ability to function
   c. changing reinforcers in the environment that seem to elicit negative behavior
   d. examining the client's self-awareness to increase self-exploration and facilitate self-actualization
3. **The cognitive therapies have been most effective in treating which type of disorders?**
   a. Schizophrenia
   b. Personality disorders
   c. Depression
   d. Autism

Answers 1. b; 2. b; 3. c

14.6 Group Therapy Approaches: Strength in Numbers

The psychotherapies we have described so far focus on a one-to-one relationship between a client and a therapist. This is known as *individual psychotherapy*. However, therapy can be administered to many people at one time with one or more therapists, in a process called **group therapy**. Group therapy approaches are often used in psychiatric facilities, group homes, the military, addiction centers, and mental institutions. They are also frequently offered by community mental health centers and outpatient treatment programs. Emily attended many group meetings, not only at the hospital as an inpatient but also as an outpatient at the community center. Group therapy often centers on one type of problem (such as substance use or depression) or is offered for a specific type of client (such as women who have been battered, teenagers, or sex offenders). Group therapy may be administered by any of the different types of professionals discussed at the beginning of this chapter.

group therapy therapy that is administered to more than one person at a time

14.6.1 • The Benefits of Group Therapy

Group therapy has several distinct advantages over individual therapy (Dies, 1993; Yalom & Leszcz, 2005). First, group therapy tends to be less expensive than individual therapy. The cost of one or more therapists is shared by several people. However, clients do receive less one-on-one or individualized treatment in a group therapy setting. Second, group therapy offers therapists a view into the client's social interactions with others. Because many people receive therapy to address interpersonal problems, group therapy offers a safe mini-environment in which to explore new social behaviors or to understand how our interactions with others may be impeding our mental health.

Group therapy can be a less expensive alternative to individual psychotherapy.

Jon Bradley/Stone/Getty Images

Group therapy also enables clients to recognize that they are not the only ones struggling with difficulties. Group members can offer acceptance, trust, and support for someone who is having problems. They can offer ideas or suggestions for solving problems and can learn from one another. Studies on group therapy have found it to be generally comparable in outcomes to individual psychotherapy for some mental health disorders (Barrera et al., 2013; Mulcahy et al., 2010; Nevonen & Broberg, 2006).

14.6.2 • The Nature and Types of Group Therapy

Group therapy, like individual psychotherapy, can take many forms. Any one of the four approaches previously described can be used for treating groups of people. For example, group cognitive-behavior therapy can be used to reduce people's fear of flying. Group interpersonal psychotherapy can be used to improve people's interpersonal relations. Three unique forms of group therapy are *family therapy*, *couple therapy*, and *self-help groups*.

FAMILY THERAPY: THE WHOLE SYSTEM

family therapy therapy that focuses on creating balance and restoring harmony to improve the functioning of the family as a whole system

In **family therapy**, the family unit is the group. Often families come to therapy with an "identified patient," such as a misbehaving or rebellious teenager. Yet the focus of family therapy is not on the functioning of the individual but, rather, on the functioning of the family as a whole system. The goal of family therapy is to create balance and restore harmony within the family system to improve its functioning. If one person in the family is having problems, these problems are seen as a symptom of disharmony within the family unit (Lebow & Gurman, 1995).

Think of your own family for a moment. All members of a family have roles, expectations, or labels placed on them, usually at a very young age. One member of the family may be considered "the brain." Another family member may be viewed as "the peacemaker." These roles are not spoken but rather are communicated through our interactions with our family members. If a family member does not conform to his or her assigned role, the rest of the family system will be disrupted. Many times we try to make family members behave in a way that is consistent with our expectations of their perceived roles. Do you ever feel that your family does not know the "real" you? Have you ever tried to step out of your assigned role, only to find family members so concerned or shaken by your new behavior that it is easier to just go back to your old pattern of behaving? If so, you have experienced the power of the family system.

The goal of family therapy is to improve the functioning of the family system.

Nancy Sheehan/PhotoEdit

Family therapists view the "identified patient" as merely the focus for problems in the family system. Rather than simply treating the individual, they explore and analyze the interactions and communications between family members. They address sources of conflict and note how unspoken rules or expected roles may be interfering with healthy family functioning. Although Emily never underwent family therapy, in her book she acknowledges how a family therapist might have viewed her situation: "A family therapist would have identified me as the family scapegoat, the child designated to 'act out' the conflicts between my tense, driven father and my incipiently alcoholic mother" (Gordon, 2000, p. 63).

COUPLE THERAPY: IMPROVING COMMUNICATION AND SECURING ATTACHMENT

Couple therapy focuses on improving communication and intimacy between two people in a committed relationship. The unspoken rules that couples use to communicate, and the ways in which they miscommunicate, are identified and addressed. The couple therapist then replaces ineffective or unhealthy patterns of communicating with more adaptive ones (Gurman & Jacobson, 2002). For example, each partner is encouraged to paraphrase what the other has said to confirm that the correct message has been heard. Criticism and derogatory labels or names are discouraged. These are just two examples of the "new rules" therapists suggest to improve communication and intimacy within couples.

couple therapy therapy that focuses on improving communication and intimacy between two people in a committed relationship

self-help group a group comprised of people who share the same problem and meet to help one another

Another form of couple therapy is *emotionally focused therapy* (*EFT*). EFT, developed by Sue Johnson and Les Greenberg (1988), helps couples identify, manage, and ultimately transform negative, reactive emotions that arise when a couple is in conflict and a person's attachment to his or her loved one is uncertain or threatened. Research on EFT shows positive impact on alleviating couple distress (Greenberg, Warwar, & Malcolm, 2010; Johnson & Williams-Keeler, 1998; Lebow et al., 2012; MacIntosh & Johnson, 2008; Makinen & Johnson, 2006).

SELF-HELP GROUPS: HELPING EACH OTHER COPE

Self-help groups are comprised of people who share the same problem and meet to help one another. Self-help groups differ from other forms of group therapy in that they are organized and led by nonprofessionals. Self-help organizations are becoming increasingly popular, and you, a family member, or a friend may have attended one of their meetings. It is estimated that 1.1% of the U.S. population received support from a mental health self-help group in the past year (SAMHSA, 2009c). In one study of Michigan and Massachusetts psychiatrists, 75% reported referring clients with depression to a self-help group (Powell, Silk, & Albeck, 2000). Self-help groups can be found for anything from grief and eating disorders to people who have a loved one dealing with a substance-related disorder. The main purpose of these groups is to offer social support and help one another cope, but they often provide useful information and advice as well.

The format and purpose of self-help groups vary widely. For example, group meetings may be highly structured or conducted more loosely. Many self-help groups adopt a 12-step program format originated by the well-known Alcoholics Anonymous (AA). Such a format includes admitting that you have a problem and that you are powerless over the problem. It encourages people to seek strength from a "greater power," to admit one's shortcomings, and to make amends to people they have harmed. Although such 12-step programs are not therapy, mental health professionals often encourage clients to participate in such groups to receive additional emotional support and encouragement. Such groups can increase a client's adherence to treatment, encourage drug abstinence, and reduce the severity of mental health symptoms (Donovan et al., 2013; Kaskutas, 2009; Sussman, 2010). However, research has been unable to specify what elements of self-help groups make them effective or what types of people they benefit most. For many people, mental health self-help groups complement professional mental health treatment (SAMHSA, 2009c).

14.6

Quiz Yourself

1. Which of the following is *not* an advantage of group therapy approaches?
   a. Less expensive
   b. More individual attention
   c. Focus on interpersonal interactions
   d. None of the above
2. The goal of family therapy is to _____.
   a. fix the person with the most problems
   b. improve communication between the parents
   c. create harmony and balance within the family unit
   d. understand the past problems of the family
3. Many self-help groups, such as Alcoholics Anonymous and Narcotics Anonymous, assume that a critical factor in improving one's mental health is _____.
   a. social support
   b. physical health
   c. financial status
   d. medication

Answers 1. b; 2. c; 3. a

14.7 Effective Psychotherapy: Do Treatments Work?

After reading about all these different forms of psychotherapy, you may be asking yourself, "Does psychotherapy work? And if it does work, which approach is the best?" Researchers analyzing the effectiveness of therapy have asked themselves similar questions. As we shall soon see, the answers to these questions are neither simple nor straightforward. Many factors influence and contribute to the effectiveness of therapy.

14.7.1 • Conducting Research on Therapy's Effectiveness

To answer the question "Does psychotherapy work?" research typically compares clients who are receiving therapy with clients who are receiving a placebo treatment or no treatment at all. Such studies have generally shown that psychotherapy has positive effects and is better than a placebo treatment or no treatment at all. They also suggest that the different approaches—*psychodynamic*, *humanistic*, *behavioral*, and *cognitive*—produce relatively equivalent results in terms of client improvement (Baker et al., 2008; Chambless & Ollendick, 2001; Nathan, Stuart, & Dolan, 2000; Westen & Bradley, 2005). This finding has been termed the *Dodo Bird verdict* after the Dodo Bird in *Alice in Wonderland* who, following the race, stated, "Everyone has won, and all must have prizes." The Dodo Bird verdict implies that it doesn't matter which therapy approach a therapist selects because all are equivalent in effectiveness.

Other research suggests that certain forms of therapy work better for certain types of mental health disorders (Chambless & Ollendick, 2001; Crits-Christoph, 1997; Lambert & Bergen, 1994). For example, panic disorder and obsessive-compulsive-related disorders may respond best to cognitive-behavior therapy, whereas phobias may respond best to behavioral methods (Allen et al., 2010; Ponniah, Magiati, & Hollon, 2013; Roshanaei-Moghaddam et al., 2011).

Some evidence shows that psychotherapy can even alter the functioning of the brain. For example, A. L. Brody and colleagues (1998) took PET scans of persons with obsessive-compulsive disorder before and after receiving 2 months of behavioral therapy. Metabolic activity of the brain decreased in the clients following treatment. Excessive activity in certain areas of the brain may in part explain the intrusive and uncontrollable obsessions that inundate people with this disorder. It appears that psychotherapy, like medication, can reduce these faulty signals. Neuroimaging studies on people with other mental health disorders (panic disorder, major depressive disorder, specific phobias, PTSD) have also documented changes in brain metabolism following psychotherapy treatment (Beauregard, 2007; Dichter, Felder, & Smoski, 2010; Felmingham et al., 2007; Frewen, Dozois, & Lanius, 2008; Kennedy et al., 2007).

Conducting research on therapy's effectiveness is quite complex. First, think about the selection of participants for such a study. It is hard to find people who all have the same disorder to the same degree, and many people like Emily in the section case study may be diagnosed with symptoms of more than one disorder (*comorbidity*). Such differences in symptoms introduce potential sampling problems into the research. Next, think about the administration of the *independent variable*. In an experiment, therapists would be trained to deliver a very specific type of therapy. To ensure consistency among therapists, deviations from these methods would not be allowed. As you might imagine, this is much different from the way treatment is administered in the real world (Chambless & Hollon, 1998). In addition, it is difficult to design a "no treatment" control group. Add to these issues the problem of defining what a good outcome is and how it will be measured (the *dependent variable*; Westen & Bradley, 2005). Do we rely on the therapist's judgment of improvement, the client's self-report of well-being, or some other measure? How long should the client be free of symptoms for treatment to be considered effective? Although you may not feel that such research questions are important to you, the results of such studies are important to health insurance companies. They use this research to determine the most cost-effective and efficient means of treatment. Consequently, outcome research may indirectly affect you or a loved one in the future.

eclectic [ee-KLECK-tick] therapy approach therapy that incorporates an integrated and diverse use of therapeutic methods

eye movement desensitization and reprocessing (EMDR) therapy an eclectic therapy approach to treat trauma in which the client attends to emotionally disturbing images while simultaneously focusing on an external stimulus

Perhaps a more appropriate question to ask about therapy is "Which treatment is most effective for this person, with this problem, under these circumstances?" Such a personalized approach to treatment is becoming more common as many therapists are adopting an *eclectic approach* to treatment (Kopta et al., 1999). An **eclectic therapy approach** involves an integrated and diverse use of therapeutic methods.

For example, **eye movement desensitization and reprocessing (EMDR) therapy** (Shapiro, 1991) is an eclectic therapy approach recommended by the American Psychiatric Association as an effective treatment for trauma (American Psychiatric Association, 2004). The client's distressing memories are identified, along with positive beliefs the client will need to cope with future stressful situations. The client then focuses on the most vivid image of the trauma while simultaneously attending to another stimulus for 20–30 seconds, such as moving one's eyes back and forth or tapping one's fingers. The client

GARO/PHANIE/Age Fotostock

EMDR therapy is an eclectic therapy approach designed to reduce distress in people who have experienced trauma.

is directed to notice whatever thoughts, feelings, or images come to mind. This process is repeated until the client's distress is reduced. The client then focuses on the positive belief while engaging in the dual attention task (Shapiro, 2001). EDMR therapy appears to be effective in reducing symptoms of PTSD (Kemp, Drummond, & McDermott, 2010; Nijdam et al., 2012; Ponniah & Hollon, 2009; Rodenburg et al., 2009; Watts et al., 2013). EMDR therapy also has shown promise as a treatment option for people with chronic pain or obsessive-compulsive disorder (Nazari et al., 2011; Tesarz et al., 2014). However, the sample sizes of these studies are small. Further replication of EMDR therapy's effectiveness for these disorders is warranted.

14.7.2 • Factors That Contribute to Effective Psychotherapy

Although research has provided mixed results on the question "Which psychotherapy is most effective?" evidence suggests that all successful psychotherapies share certain common elements, even when the specific methods used differ greatly. The term **therapeutic alliance** describes the interactive and collaborative relationship between the client and the therapist. The nature and development of this relationship can influence the effectiveness of therapy (Kozart, 2002; Lorenzo-Luaces, Derubeis, & Webb, 2014; Norcross & Wampold, 2011; Watson, Schein, & McMullen, 2010).

therapeutic alliance [thair-uh-PEW-tick uh-LIE-unce] the interactive and collaborative relationship between the client and the therapist

Therapists contribute to a successful alliance in many ways. First, the therapist establishes a positive relationship with the client. This involves creating an atmosphere of mutual respect and trust. Clients who trust their therapist are more likely to believe that they will benefit from therapy. The clients, therefore, are more likely to engage in the therapy process by revealing important information about themselves and by trying the new skills, behaviors, or techniques that the therapist suggests. Second, effective therapists are empathetic and warm, evidencing a caring attitude toward the client and the ability to listen (Norcross & Wampold, 2011; Teyber & McClure, 2000). Third, successful therapists offer an explanation or interpretation of why the client is having a problem and encourage clients to confront painful emotions (Ingram, Hayes, & Scott, 2000; Snyder et al., 2000).

Finally, effective therapists provide *culturally sensitive* treatment by adapting psychotherapy to the client's cultural background (Smith, Rodriguez, & Bernal, 2011; Thomas, Solorzano, & Cobb, 2007). Given that most providers of mental health services come from the majority culture and clients may be members of minority cultures, it is important to the success of therapy that therapists acknowledge and understand the experiences and values of diverse ethnocultural populations in the United States (Pedersen, 2002; White, Gibbons, & Schamberger, 2006). Otherwise, therapists may unintentionally introduce bias (based on race, gender, sexual orientation, or social class) into therapist–client interactions, making empathy and trust more difficult to achieve (Draguns, 2002; Vasquez, 2007).

Therapist characteristics are not the only determinant of a successful alliance. Client attitudes and behaviors also make a difference (Kwan, Dimidjian, & Rizvi, 2010; Leon et al., 1999; Lorenzo-Luaces et al., 2014). Clients who are motivated and committed to therapy tend to experience more positive results. Those who are actively involved in the therapy process and optimistic about the benefits of therapy also fare better. Moreover, clients who can express their feelings and thoughts and who are more psychologically mature experience more gains from therapy. Clients who have no previous history of mental health disorders also tend to benefit more. The social environment of the client is also important. Clients who have supportive loved ones and stable, rather than chaotic, living conditions tend to benefit more from therapy.

Notice that none of these characteristics is specific to any one of the therapy approaches we have described. So if you or a loved one is in need of a therapist, it is important to find a therapist and an approach that make you comfortable. Believing in the therapist and his or her approaches will establish a positive therapeutic alliance, thereby enhancing the effectiveness of your therapy.

14.7.3 • The Effectiveness and Ethics of Technology in the Delivery of Psychotherapy

The rapid development of computer technology, smartphones, and the Internet has started to influence psychotherapy in the form of *behavioral intervention technologies* (*BITs*) (Kazdin & Blase, 2011; Schueller, Munoz, & Mohr, 2013; C. B. Taylor & Luce, 2003). Computer-based programs can now be used to administer personality assessments such as the MMPI-2. Smartphones can be used to collect data from clients on their thoughts, behaviors, and mood, allowing clinicians and people in general to become more aware of their behavior across many situations. Videoconferencing and Skype can provide a link to therapists for clients who live too far away for face-to-face meetings. These are just some of the technological tools that can enhance the delivery of psychotherapy.

Are there online psychological services? You bet! The Internet has produced mental health treatment called *cybertherapy* and *e-health interventions* through e-mail, real-time online counseling, professionally assisted chat rooms, self-help groups, and mental health information and education sites. However, technology-assisted treatments present a number of professional and ethical issues (Hilgart et al., 2012; Hsiung, 2001; Spriggs, 2009). Online psychological services lack the close, personal contact of face-to-face interactions. Establishing a therapeutic alliance is more difficult when you cannot hear the tone of someone's voice or read his or her body language and facial expressions. "Cybershrinks" may or may not have adequate training or be appropriately licensed (Bloom, 1998). Client confidentiality is of great concern because information on the Internet can be easily accessed. Despite these concerns, the effectiveness of these programs shows promise. For example, the U.S. Department of Veteran Affairs (VA) mental health care facilities have launched multiple technology-assisted programs to help treat close to 2 million veterans with encouraging results (Brief et al., 2013; Morland et al., 2010; Tuerk et al., 2010). Effective technology-assisted interventions have shown to reduce symptoms in people with anxiety, depressive, and substance-related disorders (Carlbring et al., 2011; Carroll et al., 2008; Cavanagh et al., 2009; Klein et al., 2010; Mohr et al., 2010; Munoz et al., 2012). Studies on cybertherapy treatments for grief, anxiety, and anger management suggest improved client functioning (Hirai & Clum, 2005; Morland et al., 2011; Wagner, Knaevelsrud, & Maercker, 2006). However, more research is needed to better understand for which people technology-assisted treatments work best (Griffiths, Calear, & Banfield, 2009; Shoham & Insel, 2011). At this time, technology and the Internet appear to be promising and impactful resources that may help people struggling with mental illness (Castelnuovo et al., 2003; Teachman, 2014).

Videoconferencing can provide mental health services to people who live a long distance away such as in large rural areas.

Artiga Photo/Cusp/Corbis

Quiz Yourself

14.7

1. **Which of the following statements about the effectiveness of psychotherapy is *true*?**
   a. Cognitive therapy is considerably more effective than other forms of therapy.
   b. Psychoanalysis is considerably more effective than other forms of therapy.
   c. The main types of therapy appear to be equally effective.
   d. Receiving therapy appears to be no more effective than no therapy.
2. **Which of the following is an element associated with successful therapy?**
   a. Free association
   b. Chaotic living conditions of the client
   c. Being forced to receive therapy
   d. A positive therapist–client relationship
3. **An eclectic approach to therapy refers to _____.**
   a. an integrated and diverse use of therapeutic methods
   b. a reliance on free association and interpretation
   c. a mutual bond of respect and warmth between the therapist and client
   d. deepening the client's knowledge of psychology

Answers 1. c; 2. d; 3. a

14.8 Biomedical Therapies: Applying Neuroscience

psychopharmacology [sigh-co-farm-uh-KAH-lo-gee] the use of medications to treat mental health problems

antianxiety medications minor tranquilizers such as Valium that are prescribed to reduce tension and anxiety

Now that we have described psychological treatments for mental health disorders, it is time to turn our attention to biomedical approaches. The two dominant biomedical approaches are *drug therapy* and *brain stimulation procedures*. Far less used, but still a dramatic last resort, is *psychosurgery*.

14.8.1 • Drug Therapies: Chemically Altering the Brain

Today, the most common biomedical therapy used to treat mental health problems is medication. Recall that medications are generally prescribed by physicians or psychiatrists who have extensive training in **psychopharmacology**, or the use of drugs to treat mental health problems. Medications are generally not prescribed by psychologists. As with any prescribed medication, side effects can occur and must be considered in any treatment plan.

The most common form of biomedical therapy is psychopharmacology, or prescribing medication for mental health disorders.

Brian Pieters/Masterfile

Medication cannot cure a mental health disorder. Rather, it reduces the symptoms of the disorder while the person is taking the medication. Often, therefore, medications are prescribed jointly with psychotherapy. The medication stabilizes the person sufficiently so that psychological issues can be addressed. Here we present the major types of medications that are prescribed for specific mental health disorders.

ANTIANXIETY DRUGS: REDUCE TENSION

As the name implies, **antianxiety medications** are sedatives prescribed to reduce tension and anxiety. The best-known antianxiety drugs are the *benzodiazepines* such as *Valium, Ativan,* and *Xanax*. These medications reduce tension, relax the muscles, and promote sleep by depressing the central nervous system. They influence the functioning of three neurotransmitters: GABA, serotonin, and norepinephrine (Chapter 2). They are fast-acting drugs, calming feelings of anxiety within an hour or so. These medications are useful in treating people who are diagnosed with generalized anxiety disorder, social anxiety disorder, panic disorder, posttraumatic stress disorder, agoraphobia, and insomnia (Barlow, 2002; Nardi et al., 2010; Offidani et al., 2013).

The benzodiazepines are highly addictive if taken over a long period. People quickly build up a tolerance to these medications, requiring higher and higher dosages to achieve a reduction in anxiety. If dependence does occur, the person must be gradually weaned from the drug because abrupt withdrawal can be life threatening. Withdrawal symptoms can include tremors, irritability, insomnia, tingling sensations, a return of intense anxiety, and in rare cases even seizures and paranoia.

A second drawback of taking benzodiazepines is the effect on cognitive and motor functioning. As a depressant drug, the benzodiazepines reduce coordination, alertness, and reaction time (van Laar, Volkerts, & Verbaten, 2001). These impairments can affect a person's ability to drive a car or perform tasks at work or school. These effects are even more severe when alcohol is used with these medications.

Finally, *relapse rates* for patients taking benzodiazepines are high. This means that many people taking these drugs experience the anxiety symptoms again when they discontinue treatment or are taken off the drugs. The drugs appear to provide only short-term relief from anxiety symptoms. Long-term benefits are more likely when benzodiazepine treatment is combined with cognitive-behavioral therapies or antidepressant medication (Roy-Byrne, 2014).

Because of the disadvantages of benzodiazepine treatment, a nonbenzodiazepine drug, called *buspirone* (trade name BuSpar), is sometimes prescribed to treat anxiety, particularly generalized anxiety disorder and social anxiety disorder (Asnis et al., 2004; Chessick et al., 2006; Halaby, Haddad, & Naja, in press; Loane & Politis, 2012; Mokhber et al., 2010; Varley & Smith, 2003). A modest success, buspirone has a lower risk of dependence, but it takes considerably longer for the drug to reduce anxiety. The person must take this medication for several days or weeks before a noticeable reduction in anxiety symptoms is achieved.

ANTIPSYCHOTIC DRUGS: REDUCE SYMPTOMS OF PSYCHOSIS

Over the centuries, many medical treatments had been unsuccessful in treating psychotic symptoms, especially in people diagnosed with schizophrenia. Such treatments included brain surgery (lobotomy), insulin injections, and shock treatment. Because these treatments were ineffective, most people with schizophrenia were merely warehoused in mental hospitals. Then, in the 1950s, *chlorpromazine* (trade name Thorazine) was discovered as an effective drug in treating psychosis, or a loss of touch with reality. As Thorazine and the numerous drugs that followed, such as *Mellaril* and *Haldol*, were the first drugs to effectively reduce psychosis for some people, they are referred to as *conventional* or first-generation *antipsychotic medications*.

antipsychotic medications major tranquilizers such as Haldol that are prescribed to relieve psychotic symptoms such as delusions and hallucinations

Antipsychotic medications are major tranquilizers prescribed to relieve psychotic symptoms such as agitation, delusions, disordered thinking, and hallucinations. They may be prescribed for people with schizophrenia, bipolar disorder, or major depressive disorder when such individuals have lost touch with reality. These drugs appear to work by reducing the action of the neurotransmitter dopamine in the brain (Sanyal & vanTol, 1997). Recall that dopamine has long been suspected as a major link in understanding psychotic behavior (Chapter 13).

Although conventional antipsychotic drugs dramatically decreased the number of patients in mental hospitals for several decades, they are effective for only 60% of persons who try them (American Psychiatric Association, 2000b). They are more effective in treating the positive symptoms of schizophrenia, such as delusions (false beliefs) and hallucinations (hearing voices), than the negative symptoms, such as blunted affect (lack of emotional reactions), alogia (poverty of speech), and avolition (lack of motivation) (see Chapter 13). The conventional antipsychotic medications also have significant side effects, including sleepiness, dry mouth, blurred vision, weight change, drooling, constipation, sexual dysfunction, and depression. Motor side effects also occur, including tremors, spasms, frozen facial expressions, and motor agitation, causing people with schizophrenia to pace. These motor side effects often look like Parkinson's disease. This should not be surprising given that Parkinson's disease has been related to a reduced functioning of dopamine in the brain, precisely the effect of conventional antipsychotic medications.

tardive dyskinesia [TAR-div dis-kuh-NEE-juh] a possible long-term side effect of conventional antipsychotic medications involving involuntary motor movements of the mouth, tongue, and face

antidepressants medications prescribed to alleviate the symptoms of depression, eating disorders, and some anxiety disorders

Long-term use of such drugs can lead to an irreversible motor disorder called **tardive dyskinesia** that involves involuntary motor movements of the mouth, tongue, and face. People experiencing this side effect may repeatedly smack their lips, stick out their tongues, puff out their cheeks, or make other odd facial movements. It is estimated that this serious side effect occurs in 10–20% of people with long-term use of conventional antipsychotic drugs (Chakos et al., 1996; Oosthuizen et al., 2003).

Newer drugs, called *atypical antipsychotics* or second-generation antipsychotics, have renewed hope of successfully treating schizophrenia. These drugs influence the action of serotonin and dopamine in the brain and cause less serious side effects and a lower incidence of tardive dyskinesia (Correll, Leucht, & Kane, 2004; Jeste, 2004). They are effective in reducing both the positive and negative symptoms of schizophrenia (Lieberman et al., 2003; Lindenmayer et al., 2007; Macfadden et al., 2010; Stahl, 2001a, 2001b). Side effects include sedation, nausea, headaches, seizures, dizziness, and an increased risk of sleep apnea (Rishi et al., 2010), but for people who do not respond to conventional antipsychotic medications, these newer drugs can be a lifesaver. As a result, they have become the most commonly used antipsychotic drugs in clinical practice. Examples of such drugs include *risperidone*, and *aripiprazole*. Atypical antipsychotic medications are approved by the FDA for treatment of schizophrenia and bipolar disorder (to treat manic episodes) and as augmentation for major depressive disorder and autism spectrum disorders (Cipriani et al., 2011; Maher & Theodore, 2012).

ANTIDEPRESSANT DRUGS: MOOD, COMPULSIONS, AND CRAVINGS

Antidepressants are prescribed to alter mood and alleviate the symptoms of major depressive disorder. Antidepressants have also been effective in treating people with obsessive-compulsive disorders, panic disorders, eating disorders, and drug cravings (Barlow, 2002). As shown in ● TABLE 14.4, there are three main classes of antidepressants: *tricyclics, MAO inhibitors,* and *selective serotonin reuptake inhibitors* (*SSRIs*).

Tricyclics

Tricyclic antidepressants, such as *Tofranil* and *Elavil,* elevate mood and reduce the symptoms of depression by influencing the action of norepinephrine and serotonin in the brain (Stahl, 1998). However, it takes from 4 to 8 weeks on such medication before noticeable relief from depression occurs. Tricyclics are effective in relieving depressive symptoms in 60–85% of people who are depressed (Arroll et al., 2005; Fawcett, 1994; Guze & Gitlin, 1994). As with any drug, tricyclics have a number of side effects, including dry mouth, weight gain, dizziness, blurred vision, constipation, and sexual dysfunction. The tricyclics can also be fatal in overdose amounts, which is why they are seldom prescribed to patients who are suicidal.

MAO Inhibitors

The monoamine oxidase (MAO) inhibitors are a class of antidepressants that elevate mood by increasing the monoamine neurotransmitters in

TABLE 14.4

Antidepressant Drugs

GENERIC NAME	TRADE NAME	COMMON SIDE EFFECTS
TRICYCLIC ANTIDEPRESSANTS		
Amitriptyline	Elavil	Dizziness, drowsiness, constipation, dry mouth, water retention, low blood pressure, hair loss, blurred vision
Desipramine	Norpramin Pertofrane	Dizziness, drowsiness, dry mouth, low blood pressure, headache, increased appetite/weight, nausea, tiredness, unpleasant taste
Doxepin	Adepin Sinequan	Dizziness, drowsiness, diarrhea, dry mouth, water retention, low blood pressure, blurred vision
Imipramine	Tofranil	Dizziness, drowsiness, diarrhea, dry mouth, water retention, low blood pressure
Nortriptyline	Aventyl Pamelor	Dizziness, drowsiness, constipation, dry mouth, water retention, low blood pressure, blurred vision
MAO INHIBITORS		
Phenelzine	Nardil	Dizziness, drowsiness, change in appetite, low blood pressure, constipation, dry mouth, headache, liver problems, sexual problems, sleep disturbances, stomach and intestinal problems, water retention, weight gain
Tranylcypromine	Parnate	Dizziness, drowsiness, dry mouth, diarrhea, change in appetite, insomnia, nausea, rapid or irregular heartbeat, water retention, weakness, weight loss
SELECTIVE SEROTONIN REUPTAKE INHIBITORS (SSRIs)		
Fluoxetine	Prozac	Headache, insomnia, drowsiness, tremor, dizziness, fatigue, poor concentration, abnormal dreams, agitation, nausea, diarrhea, dry mouth, change in appetite, constipation, cramps, vomiting, flatulence, sweating, rash, nasal congestion, cough, heart palpitations, muscle pain, decreased sexual desire, urinary frequency
Paroxetine	Paxil	Nausea, prolonged sleepiness, headache, dry mouth, constipation, dizziness, insomnia, diarrhea, sweating
	Zoloft	Insomnia or prolonged drowsiness, dizziness, headache, tremor, fatigue, male sexual dysfunction, diarrhea, nausea, constipation, change in appetite, dry mouth, vomiting, flatulence
OTHER ANTIDEPRESSANTS		
Bupropion	Wellbutrin, Zyban	Headache, agitation, dizziness, confusion, insomnia, tremors, hypertension, nausea, vomiting, dry mouth, constipation, menstrual irregularities, rash, sweating, blurred vision, weight loss or gain

the brain (Stahl, 1998). They are just as effective as the tricyclic antidepressants but are less frequently prescribed because of their more serious side effects (M. Fava & Rosenbaum, 1995). These include lowered blood pressure, liver damage, and weight gain. These drugs also interact with substances high in an amino acid called *tyramine*. Tyramine is present in common foods such as cheese, smoked meats, and chocolate, liquids such as beer and wine, and even over-the-counter medications. This interaction can produce a sudden rise in blood pressure that is potentially fatal. You may have noticed the caution statements on the back of any over-the-counter cold medication stating that it is not to be used by a person who is taking an MAO inhibitor. Yet MAO inhibitors may be more effective in the treatment of severe depression than the newer antidepressants (Parker et al., 2001).

selective serotonin reuptake inhibitor (SSRI) a type of antidepressant drug that inhibits the reuptake of the neurotransmitter serotonin, thereby improving mood

antimanic medications drugs that are prescribed to alleviate manic symptoms of bipolar disorder

lithium a naturally occurring mineral salt prescribed to control manic symptoms in people with bipolar disorder; it influences several neurotransmitters in the brain, including glutamate, serotonin, and dopamine

Selective Serotonin Reuptake Inhibitors (SSRIs) Currently, the most frequently prescribed antidepressant medications are the **selective serotonin reuptake inhibitors (SSRIs)** such as *Prozac*, *Lexapro* and *Zoloft*. Recall from Chapter 2 that reuptake is the process whereby the neurotransmitters that are left over in the synapse are recycled back into the presynaptic neuron. SSRIs elevate mood by leaving the neurotransmitter serotonin in the synapse longer. They have several advantages over the other two categories of antidepressants.

The side effects of SSRIs are less severe and are not fatal in overdose. These include increased nervousness, headaches, insomnia, nausea, stomach cramps, decreased sexual drive, and sexual dysfunction (Fisher, Kent, & Bryant, 1995; Michelson et al., 2000). Some of these side effects may diminish after a few weeks of treatment. Other antidepressants, such as *Zyban* and *Wellbutrin*, are similar to SSRIs but influence the norepinephrine and dopamine systems. These antidepressants do not decrease one's sexual drive and are therefore sometimes used in combination with SSRI drugs to elevate mood while lessening the sexual side effects (Leuchter et al., 2008; Zisook et al., 2006). Zyban is also prescribed as a tobacco cessation treatment. SSRIs are also useful in treating anxiety disorders, eating disorders, and substance-related disorders, especially alcohol use disorder (Barlow & Durand, 2005; Lenze et al., 2009; Romanelli et al., 2014; van Apeldoorn et al., 2010). For all of these reasons, the SSRIs are quite popular.

However, there is considerable debate over the SSRIs effectiveness in treating mild to moderate depression. Some research suggests that they are just as effective as the other classes of antidepressants (Arroll et al., 2005; Garnock-Jones & McCormack, 2010; Gartlehner et al., 2005; Stewart et al., 2012). Other research suggests that they have modest to insignificant effects and are most beneficial in the treatment of severe depression (Fournier et al., 2010; Kirsch et al., 2008).

Antidepressant medication has been associated with an increased risk of suicidal thoughts and behaviors in children and adolescents, especially in the first few months of treatment (FDA Public Health Advisory, 2004). In 2004, the Food and Drug Administration directed that manufacturers of antidepressants include a "black box" warning—the FDA's strongest—on all antidepressant medication for children and adolescents.

ANTIMANIC DRUGS: MOOD STABILIZERS

The **antimanic medications** are prescribed to alleviate manic symptoms of bipolar disorder. The first mood-stabilizing drug approved by the FDA was **lithium**, a naturally occurring mineral salt. Lithium has the advantage of controlling both manic and depressive symptoms in people with bipolar disorder, although it is far more effective in treating mania (Amsterdam & Shults, 2010; Nivoli, Murru, & Vieta, 2010; Young et al., 2010). For this reason, people with bipolar disorder may be prescribed antidepressant drugs in addition to lithium to stabilize their moods. Lithium achieves its effect by influencing several neurotransmitters in the brain: glutamate, serotonin, and dopamine (Dixon & Hokin, 1998). It is taken even when people have no symptoms of mania to prevent future manic episodes.

Research on the effectiveness of lithium treatment is challenging as there is extreme variability in people's absorption of lithium. Some people absorb lithium rather quickly and can therefore tolerate only small dosages, whereas others absorb the chemical more slowly. Lithium dosage amounts, therefore, vary considerably from one person to the next. Too little lithium can lead to manic episodes, whereas too much can lead to lithium poisoning, causing vomiting, nausea, slurred speech, and impaired muscle coordination. For any one person, the difference between the correct, or "therapeutic," amount of lithium and a toxic amount is a very fine line. For this reason, lithium levels must be carefully monitored in people with bipolar disorder.

Lithium, like all the drugs discussed so far, also has side effects, including nausea, vomiting, diarrhea, blurred vision, reduced concentration, weight gain, and increased risk of diabetes and kidney problems (Maj et al., 1997). It can also lead to birth defects if taken by pregnant women during their first trimester.

For those people with bipolar disorder who do not respond to lithium or who cannot tolerate its side effects, other drug options are available. For example, *anticonvulsant drugs* such as carbamazepine (*Tegretol*) and valproate (*Depakote*) are effective in treating severe mania and produce fewer side effects than lithium. *Valproate,* approved by the FDA to treat mania in 1995, has recently overtaken lithium as the most frequently prescribed mood-stabilizing drug. However, the anticonvulsant drugs are less effective than lithium in preventing suicide (Goodwin & Goldstein, 2003; Tondo & Baldessarini, 2009). The anticonvulsant drugs can also cause birth defects when taken by pregnant women. However, when compared to placebo, both lithium and the anticonvulsant drugs have been shown to be effective treatments for bipolar disorder (Bowden et al., 2010; Calabrese et al., 2005; Cipriani et al., 2013; Goldberg, 2007; Woo et al., 2014).

The effectiveness of medications for treating bipolar disorder is further complicated by patient compliance (Sachs & Rush, 2003). Some people with bipolar disorder miss the euphoric feelings of the manic state and, against the advice of their physicians, go off their medications when they are feeling better. They often believe that they can control their symptoms without medication. For example, in one large study of patients with bipolar disorder receiving treatment in VA settings, almost 50% did not take their medications as prescribed (Sajatovic et al., 2007). Unfortunately, manic symptoms often return, thus requiring a recalibration of appropriate medication levels.

You Review: Drug Therapy and Mental Health Disorders summarizes which medications are typically prescribed for specific mental health disorders.

You Review **Drug Therapy and Mental Health Disorders**

Medication Type	Type of Drug	Examples	Symptoms Treated
Antianxiety drugs	Benzodiazepines Nonbenzodiazepines	Valium, Xanax BuSpar	Anxiety and tension; insomnia
Antipsychotic drugs	Conventional antipsychotics	Thorazine, Mellaril, Haldol	Psychotic symptoms such as agitation, delusions, disordered thinking, and hallucinations
	Atypical antipsychotics	Clozaril, Risperdal, Zyprexa	Psychotic symptoms such as agitation, delusions, disordered thinking, and hallucinations; negative symptoms of schizophrenia
Antidepressant drugs	Tricyclics MAO inhibitors Selective serotonin reuptake inhibitors (SSRIs)	Elavil, Tofranil Nardil, Parnate Prozac, Paxil, Zoloft	Depressed mood; excessive anxiety disorders; eating disorders; substance-related disorders
Antimanic drugs	Lithium Anticonvulsants	Lithium carbonate Tegretol, Depakote	Relieves manic symptoms; prevents future manic episodes

14.8.2 • Noninvasive Brain Stimulation Procedures: TMS and ECT

Some people with mental health disorders evidence *treatment resistance*. That is, despite psychotherapy and/or drug therapy, their symptoms do not improve. In cases such as these, directly stimulating the brain has produced promising and unexpected results. Two such procedures include *transcranial magnetic stimulation* and *electroconvulsive therapy*.

TRANSCRANIAL MAGNETIC STIMULATION (TMS): STIMULATING NEURONS

transcranial magnetic stimulation (TMS) a biomedical treatment approach in which electromagnetic impulses stimulate brain neurons; used for treatment resistant depression

electroconvulsive therapy (ECT) a series of treatments in which electrical current is passed through the brain, causing a seizure; used to alleviate severe depression

First developed in 1985, **transcranial magnetic stimulation** (**TMS**) uses brief magnetic impulses to stimulate brain neurons to ease symptoms of depression. In TMS, an electromagnetic device is placed against the forehead, near an area of the brain involved in regulating mood. Short electromagnetic pulses are administered which pass through the skull to stimulate neurons in the brain. As the pulses are administered, the person will feel a slight tapping on the head. The strength of the pulse is equivalent to that of an MRI scan. A typical session lasts 30–60 minutes. Common side effects include headaches, lightheadedness, and scalp discomfort. In 2008, the FDA approved TMS as a treatment for major depressive disorder for people who have not responded to at least one antidepressant medication.

Research on the effectiveness of TMS in treating depression has produced mixed results. Some studies have found insignificant results (Loo et al., 2003), others have found an effect (Fitzgerald et al., 2003; Gaynes et al., 2011; Slotema et al., 2010); some have found an effect only for distinct subtypes of depression (Downar et al., 2014; Ren et al., 2014), and others suggest that TMS's effectiveness is tied to other variables such as the location of stimulation, frequency and duration of pulses, length of treatment period, and its use alone or in conjunction with medication (Aleman, 2013; Xie, Chen, & Wei, 2013). More research is needed to understand the most effective use of TMS.

ELECTROCONVULSIVE THERAPY (ECT): INDUCING A BRIEF SEIZURE

Before the birth of drug therapy in the 1950s, the most common form of biomedical therapy consisted of administering electrical shocks to the brains of patients to induce seizures. This procedure, called **electroconvulsive therapy** (**ECT**), was a routine therapy approach used on people with schizophrenia. It was believed that producing a seizure would calm the hallucinations, agitation, and delusions that people with schizophrenia experience. In fact, ECT was *not* effective in treating people with these symptoms of schizophrenia. However, for reasons that aren't clear, it can be effective in treating people with severe depression.

Although still highly controversial, ECT today consists of a series of treatments, usually performed in a hospital, in which electrical current is passed through the brain, causing a seizure. After administration of anesthesia and a muscle relaxant, metal electrodes are placed on the head of the now unconscious patient. A current of 70–130 volts is passed through one side of the brain for roughly one-half second. A seizure occurs, causing the patient to have muscle tremors for about 1 minute. Violent convulsions do not occur because of the administration of the muscle relaxant prior to the procedure. The patient undergoes this procedure about every other day for 6–12 sessions. It is a quick and painless medical procedure.

Many students are appalled and even frightened by ECT. It seems so archaic and primitive. These are natural and common reactions. However, keep in mind that ECT is not the first treatment for depression, but rather a last resort. It is administered to patients who are depressed and are not responding to psychotherapy or drug therapy and remain in a severely depressed state. These patients may be suicidal or even psychotic. For these patients, ECT may be the only form of treatment that is effective (Nemeroff, 2007).

ECT is effective for people who are severely depressed, and it is very effective in treating psychotic depression (Damm et al., 2010; Gaynes et al., 2011; Kellner et al., 2010; Merkl, Heuser, & Bajbouj, 2009; Ren et al., 2014). It also relieves depression faster than drug therapy. Most patients improve within a few days. It is not currently understood how ECT lifts depression. It is speculated that the seizure may alter the functioning of specific brain structures, of neurotransmitters in the brain, or both (Abbott et al., 2014; S. M. Taylor, 2008; Yatham et al., 2010). Identifying the precise effect of shock on all brain functions is rather like finding a needle in a haystack, but research continues to investigate the effect of ECT on depression.

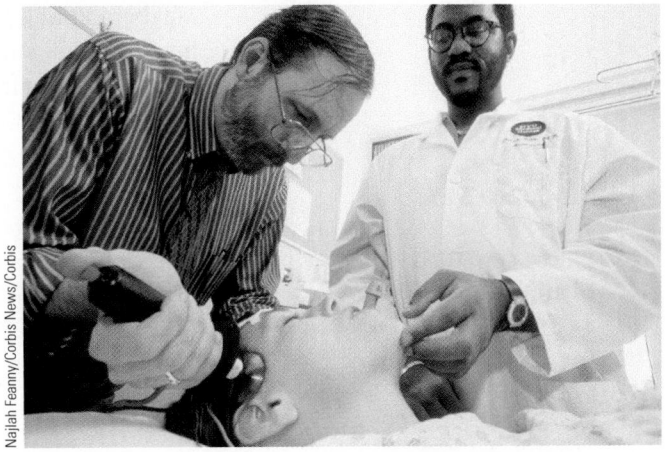
Najlah Feanny/Corbis News/Corbis

Electroconvulsive therapy (ECT) is a last-resort treatment option administered to patients who are depressed and are not responding to psychotherapy or drug therapy and remain in a severely depressed state.

ECT does have its drawbacks. It can lead to cognitive impairments, such as memory loss, learning difficulties, or disturbances in verbal abilities. A second concern in using ECT is the high relapse rate. Many ECT patients relapse into depression. Such relapses may occur as soon as 4 months after treatment. Thus, the effects of ECT seem to be short-lived (Swartz, 1995). Despite ECT's short-term effectiveness, these concerns—as well as people's fears about administering electrical shock to the brain—continue to make ECT a very controversial treatment approach.

14.8.3 • Psychosurgery: Deep Brain Stimulators and Targeted Brain Lesions

Another dramatic last resort for the treatment of mental health disorders is **psychosurgery**. Psychosurgery involves surgically altering the brain to alleviate symptoms in someone with a mental health disorder. First introduced in the 1940s and 1950s, probably the best-known psychosurgery is the *prefrontal lobotomy*, in which the neurons connecting the frontal lobe to the rest of the brain were surgically disconnected. However, with the rise and success of drug therapies, psychosurgery declined considerably, as lobotomies were generally ineffective and produced seizures and a loss in intellectual functioning.

psychosurgery a biomedical treatment approach involving neurosurgery to alleviate symptoms in someone with a mental health disorder

Is psychosurgery still used today? Yes. Many neurosurgeons continue to use psychosurgery for treating people with mental illness who do not respond to conventional biomedical or psychotherapy treatments. Today, psychosurgery methods are more precise, thanks to recent improvements in surgical techniques. For example, a neurosurgeon may lesion (destroy) a small target area of the brain to reduce symptoms of obsessive-compulsive disorder. Research suggests that approximately 25–30% of patients who have undergone this procedure improve significantly (Patel et al., 2013; Read & Greenberg, 2009; Shah et al., 2008).

Since 1993, neurosurgeons have been implanting deep brain stimulators in people who have Parkinson's disease (Benabid et al., 2001). It is the most commonly practiced surgical treatment for this disease, improving motor function by at least 60%, leading to a significant improvement in the quality of life for people with Parkinson's (Ashcan et al., 2004). Deep brain stimulation for the treatment of resistant depression and severe cases of obsessive-compulsive disorder also shows promising results (Blomstedt et al., 2013; Hamani et al., 2009; Huff et al., 2010;

Mayberg et al., 2005; Read & Greenberg, 2009; Shah et al., 2008). Keep in mind, however, that such operations are performed very infrequently and only as a last resort. Psychosurgery continues to be a controversial biomedical technique.

Quiz Yourself

14.8

1. **Electroconvulsive therapy is most effective for the treatment of _____.**
   a. schizophrenia
   b. panic attacks
   c. severe depression
   d. bipolar disorder
2. **Which of the following is the most serious side effect of taking conventional antipsychotic medication?**
   a. Rebound anxiety
   b. Physical dependence
   c. Hallucinations
   d. Tardive dyskinesia
3. **Prozac is what type of antidepressant drug?**
   a. SSRI
   b. MAO inhibitor
   c. Tricyclic
   d. Benzodiazepine

Answers 1. c; 2. d; 3. a

14.9 Integrating Psychology: The Big Picture

This chapter has outlined the major types of psychotherapies and biomedical therapies. We have seen that each therapeutic approach stems from one of the main theoretical perspectives introduced in the beginning of this textbook: *biological*, *psychoanalytic*, *cognitive*, *behavioral*, and *humanistic*. The aim of all therapies is to improve a person's ability to function, yet some focus on altering biology (drug therapy), while others focus on psychological factors (cognitions, emotions, learning) or one's social relationships and interpersonal functioning. We have also seen that therapy is generally effective, regardless of the specific techniques endorsed and that in many cases using an eclectic approach that combines *biopsychosocial* methods can be very effective. Of course, the effectiveness of therapy also will be related to the characteristics of the therapist and the client as was illustrated by Emily and Dr. Farber's therapeutic alliance.

We hope that you have enjoyed your journey through psychology. We have provided you with a *foundation* of psychological concepts and research that we encourage you to *apply* to your life. Remember that behavior and mental processes are never due to just one cause and that there is a complicated interaction among biological, psychological, and social variables that best explains behavior, and this explanation may vary from individual to individual. Acknowledging this *integration* and complexity will further your understanding of not only your behavior but also the behavior of those around you. Good luck!

Studying the Chapter

Key Terms

antianxiety medications (618)
antidepressants (620)
antimanic medications (622)
antipsychotic medications (619)
anxiety hierarchy (603)
aversion therapy (605)
behavior therapy (601)
biomedical therapy (592)
client-centered therapy (599)
cognitive-behavior therapy (CBT) (610)
cognitive distortions (608)
cognitive therapy (608)
couple therapy (613)
covert sensitization therapy (605)
dream analysis (597)
eclectic therapy approach (615)
electroconvulsive therapy (ECT) (624)
empathy (600)
eye movement desensitization and reprocessing (EMDR) therapy (615)
family therapy (612)
flooding (604)
free association (597)
genuineness (600)
group therapy (611)
interpretation (597)
lithium (622)
psychoanalysis (597)
psychodynamic therapy (598)
psychopharmacology (618)
psychosurgery (625)
psychotherapy (592)
rational-emotive therapy (607)
resistance (597)
selective serotonin reuptake inhibitor (SSRI) (622)
self-help group (613)
systematic desensitization (602)
tardive dyskinesia (620)
therapeutic alliance (616)
therapy (590)
token economy (606)
transcranial magnetic stimulation (TMS) (624)
transference (597)
unconditional positive regard (600)

What Do You Know? Assess Your Understanding

Test your retention and understanding of the material by answering the following questions.

1. Most psychotherapists hold at least a _____ degree and in most states hold an appropriate license or certificate.

a. bachelor's
b. associate's
c. master's
d. doctorate

2. Which of the following is *not* an ethical guideline of psychotherapists?

a. Inform the client of the nature of the treatment
b. Never break the confidentiality of communications with client
c. Interact appropriately with clients
d. Provide adequate treatment

3. _____ uses techniques such as free association and dream analysis to uncover hidden conflicts.

a. Psychoanalysis
b. Cognitive therapy
c. Behavior therapy
d. Client-centered therapy

4. Which psychotherapy would use systematic desensitization to treat a person with a specific phobia?

a. Psychoanalysis
b. Cognitive therapy
c. Behavior therapy
d. Client-centered therapy

5. In which psychotherapy does the therapist challenge the illogical beliefs of the client?

a. Behavior therapy
b. Rational-emotive therapy
c. Client-centered therapy
d. Psychodynamic therapy

6. Dr. Ramon expresses genuineness and empathy to her client. Dr. Ramon is most likely engaging in _____.

a. psychoanalysis
b. cognitive therapy
c. behavior therapy
d. client-centered therapy

7. Dr. Andrews reinforces appropriate client behavior and ignores inappropriate behavior. Dr. Andrews is engaging in _____.
   a. psychoanalysis
   b. cognitive therapy
   c. behavior therapy
   d. client-centered therapy

8. Dr. Shu reflects her client's thoughts and feelings so that she can better understand the client's problems. Dr. Shu is engaging in _____.
   a. behavior modification
   b. client-centered therapy
   c. rational-emotive therapy
   d. free association

9. Which type of therapy pairs an unpleasant stimulus with the problem behavior in the hopes of reducing its occurrence?
   a. Aversion therapy
   b. Systematic desensitization
   c. Token economy
   d. Client-centered therapy

10. Dr. Tyler teaches his client how to recognize negative automatic thought patterns. Dr. Tyler is engaging in _____.
   a. rational-emotive therapy
   b. systematic desensitization
   c. cognitive therapy
   d. psychodynamic therapy

11. Which of the following is *not* a benefit of group therapy?
   a. It is less expensive than individual psychotherapy.
   b. Therapists can view clients' social interactions.
   c. It offers more one-on-one treatment.
   d. It provides social support from others experiencing the same problem.

12. Dr. Mendel encourages Maurice to paraphrase what his partner says to confirm that he has understood the comment. It is most likely that Maurice is engaged in _____.
   a. psychoanalysis
   b. family therapy
   c. couple therapy
   d. drug therapy

13. The "Dodo Bird" verdict refers to _____.
   a. the effect of psychotherapy on the brain
   b. how the main psychotherapy approaches are equivalent in effectiveness
   c. the high relapse rates among people with mental health disorders
   d. the higher effectiveness of group therapy over individual therapy

14. Dr. Garfield and his client have an interactive and collaborative relationship, commonly referred to as a(n) _____.
   a. eclectic approach
   b. therapeutic alliance
   c. psychotherapeutic effect
   d. transference

15. Which of the following is a disadvantage of cybertherapy?
   a. The increased client confidentiality
   b. Provides clients who live far away from therapists access to mental health services
   c. Lacks the close personal contact of face-to-face interactions
   d. It costs more than face-to-face therapy.

16. Juanita has been diagnosed with generalized anxiety disorder. A psychiatrist is most likely to prescribe _____ to treat Juanita's symptoms.
   a. lithium
   b. Xanax
   c. Prozac
   d. clozapine

17. Antipsychotic medications affect which neurotransmitter?
   a. Endorphins
   b. Glutamate
   c. GABA
   d. Dopamine

18. Craig has been diagnosed with schizophrenia. His psychiatrist has prescribed Thorazine to reduce Craig's delusions and hallucinations. Which of the following side effects might Craig experience from taking this medication?
   a. Loss of sense of smell
   b. Tardive dyskinesia
   c. Fluid retention and rash
   d. Kidney problems

19. Electroconvulsive therapy has been shown to be particularly effective for the treatment of _____.
   a. schizophrenia
   b. severe depression
   c. panic disorder
   d. obsessive-compulsive disorder

20. Which of the following medications has been associated with an increased risk of suicidal thoughts and behaviors in children and adolescents?

a. Antianxiety drugs
b. Lithium
c. SSRI drugs
d. Antipsychotic drugs

Answers: 1. c; 2. b; 3. a; 4. c; 5. b; 6. d; 7. c; 8. b; 9. a; 10. c; 11. c; 12. c; 13. b; 14. b; 15. c; 16. b; 17. d; 18. b; 19. b; 20. c

Use It or Lose It: Applying Psychology

1. Compare and contrast psychoanalysis and client-centered therapy. What qualities do they have in common? What are their major differences?
2. Which psychotherapy approach do you find the most appealing, and why? Which psychotherapy approach do you find the least appealing, and why?
3. What can the critical components of therapy effectiveness teach us about resolving our own problems? How might these components be useful in group therapy approaches?
4. What are the advantages and disadvantages of using medication to treat mental health problems?
5. Think about a behavior or problem that you have had or are having. Apply a behavior therapy method to change this behavior. What would the behavior and the method be, and how would you go about changing the behavior?

Critical Thinking for Integration

1. Design an experiment (Chapter 1) that would test the effectiveness of a drug therapy versus a psychotherapy. Be sure to carefully define your dependent measure of effectiveness.
2. Refer to the conditioning of Little Albert's fear of a white rat in Chapter 6, and apply a therapy approach to reduce Albert's fear.
3. How might some of the psychotherapy techniques described in this chapter promote problem-focused coping styles in response to stress (Chapter 12)?

Laurence Mouton/Ã¯s/Canopy/Corbis

Are You Getting the Big Picture? Mental Health Therapies

Therapy consists of techniques that are used to help people with mental health or interpersonal problems.

14.1 What Is the Nature of Psychotherapy?

Nancy Sheehan / PhotoEdit

- **Psychotherapy** is administered by clinical psychologists, licensed counselors, social workers, and therapists.
- Psychotherapists abide by ethical standards of *confidentiality, competent treatment* that is culturally sensitive, *informed consent,* and *appropriate interactions.*
- You should consider therapy if you feel helpless, sad, or nervous for a prolonged period of time or if such feelings do not improve despite several efforts to change them.

14.2 Psychoanalytic Therapies

Jose Luis Pelaez, Inc./Cusp/Corbis

- Traditional **psychoanalysis** has clients gain insight into the underlying source of their problems. Modern **psychodynamic therapy** also relies on the therapist's **interpretations** of the client's feelings and behaviors but places more emphasis on current problems and interpersonal relations and less on the client's past.

14.3 Humanistic Therapy

© Photofusion Picture Library/Alamy

- Humanistic therapy such as **client-centered therapy** connects with and understands the client's worldview. The therapist offers **genuineness**, **empathy**, and **unconditional positive regard** to encourage self-exploration and self-fulfillment.

14.4 Behavior Therapies

AP Images/Bebeto Matthews

- **Behavior therapies** use learning principles to change maladaptive behavior.
  - Classical conditioning therapies use techniques such as **systematic desensitization**, virtual reality technology, **flooding**, and **aversion therapy** to change the client's responses to stimuli.
  - Operant conditioning therapies use techniques such as shaping, extinction, positive reinforcement, and **token economies** to change behavior.

14.5 Cognitive Therapies

Courtesy of Beck Institute for Cognitive Therapy and Research

- In cognitive therapies, maladaptive patterns of thinking and perceiving are replaced with more adaptive ways of interpreting events.
  - In **rational-emotive therapy**, the therapist confronts, questions, and challenges the validity of client's irrational beliefs.
  - In **cognitive therapy**, the therapist identifies and tracks negative automatic thoughts and has the client test the accuracy of these **cognitive distortions**.

14.6 What Happens in Group Therapy?

Jon Bradley/Stone/Getty Images

- The goal of **group therapy** is to improve the functioning and interactions among individuals, couples, families, or other groups.
- Group therapy tends to be less expensive than individual therapy and offers a safe mini-environment in which to explore new social behaviors or to understand how our interactions with others may be impeding our mental health.

14.7 Effective Psychotherapy: Do Treatments Work?

GARO/PHANIE/Age Fotostock

- Generally, the different psychotherapy approaches produce relatively equivalent results in terms of client improvement.
- A personalized approach to treatment is becoming more common as many therapists adopt an **eclectic therapy approach** that involves an integrated and diverse use of therapeutic methods.
- Behavioral intervention and e-health technologies as well as cybertherapy are tools that can enhance the delivery of psychotherapy, yet present ethical considerations.

14.8 Biomedical Therapies

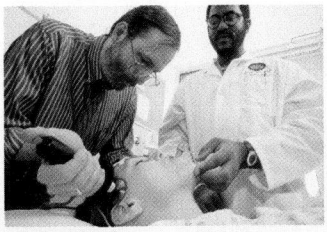
Najlah Feanny/Corbis News/Corbis

- **Biomedical therapies** are administered by psychiatrists and other medical professionals.
- The most common biomedical therapy is **psychopharmacology**, or the use of medications to treat mental health problems. Drug therapies influence brain neurotransmitters to alter behavior.
  - **Antianxiety medications** are prescribed to reduce tension and anxiety.
  - **Antipsychotic medications** are prescribed to relieve psychotic symptoms such as agitation, delusions, disordered thinking, and hallucinations.
  - **Antidepressants** are prescribed for mood and anxiety disorders, eating disorders, and substance-related disorders.
  - **Antimanic medications** are used primarily to treat mania.
- More controversial biomedical therapies include noninvasive brain stimulation procedures such as **transcranial magnetic stimulation** (**TMS**) and **electroconvulsive therapy** (**ECT**), and **psychosurgery**.

Statistics in Psychology

Learning Objectives

A.1 Define the terms data and statistics, and explain how they are used in science. (APA 2.4)

A.1 Describe the different types of graphs and distributions used in statistical analyses, including frequency distributions, frequency polygons, histograms, and scatter plots. (APA 2.4)

A.1 Calculate and interpret the different measures of central tendency used in statistics: the mean, median, and mode. (APA 2.4)

A.1 Calculate and interpret the different measures of variability used in statistics: the range, variance, and standard deviation. (APA 2.4)

A.1 Explain what a normal and standard normal distribution are. (APA 2.4)

A.1 Calculate and interpret a *z* score and a correlation coefficient. (APA 2.4)

A.2 Explain the logic behind inferential statistics, hypothesis testing, and statistical significance. (APA 2.4)

A

Appendix Outline

A.1 Using Statistics to Describe Data / 633

A.2 Using Statistics to Draw Conclusions / 643

A.3 Summary / 644

A.1 Using Statistics to Describe Data

As you learned in Chapter 1, psychology is the scientific study of behavior and mental processes. Psychologists develop hypotheses about behavior and mental processes and then test these hypotheses using experiments, case studies, surveys, naturalistic observations, or other research methods. In the course of their research, psychologists collect a variety of information, or **data**, from their research participants.

data information gathered in scientific studies

Imagine that you are a health psychologist interested in whether the legal drinking age in a country affects the rate of underage drinking in that society. More specifically, you might ask questions like these: "Does having a lower legal drinking age encourage drinking among 15-year-olds? And if so, does the legal drinking age equally affect both male and female 15-year-olds?" To see whether such relationships exist, you must first collect data on the number of 15-year-olds who drink in particular countries along with each country's legal drinking age (see • TABLE A.1).

Take a moment to look at the data in Table A.1. By just looking at the table, can you tell whether a relationship exists between the percentage of 15-year-old students who drink and a country's minimum legal drinking age? If you cannot,

TABLE A.1

Percent of Students Who Report Drinking Alcohol Weekly at Age 15, Selected Countries

COUNTRY	MINIMUM LEGAL DRINKING AGE	MALES	FEMALES
Austria	16	39%	23%
Belgium	16	38	22
Canada	18	22	17
Czech Republic	18	32	19
Denmark	15	46	38
England	18	47	36
Estonia	18*	21	10
Finland	18	11	8
France	16	31	15
Germany	16	29	22
Greece	16*	52	31
Greenland	18	13	10
Hungary	16	29	11
Ireland	18	27	12
Israel	18	26	10
Latvia	18	28	12
Lithuania	21	16	9
Northern Ireland	18	33	20
Norway	18	16	12
Poland	18	20	8
Portugal	16	29	9
Russia	18	28	24
Scotland	18	37	33
Slovakia	18	32	16
Sweden	18	17	11
Switzerland	16	19	9
United States	21	23	15
Wales	18	53	36

Source: Except where noted, data taken from Kaul, C. (2002). *Statistical Handbook on the World's Children* (p. 447). Westport, CT: Oryx Press.

*These data taken from http://www2.potsdam.edu/alcohol-info/LegalDrinkingAge.html#worlddrinkingages.

you are in good company—it's impossible to tell from just a table whether the data support one's hypothesis. Instead, psychologists must use a type of applied mathematics, called **statistics**, to describe and analyze their data. Only then can a researcher determine what the data say about his or her hypothesis.

statistics a type of applied mathematics used to describe data and test hypotheses

graph a visual depiction of data

A.1.1 • Graphs: Depicting Data Visually

Take another look at the data in Table A.1. Where would you start if you wanted to see whether the legal drinking age is related to drinking rates among 15-year-olds? Well, have you ever heard that *a picture is worth a thousand words*? One way to start would be to create a **graph**, or pictorial representation, of the data.

Psychologists use many different types of graphs to help analyze their data. One of the more common graphs is a **frequency distribution**. A graph of a frequency distribution is a two-dimensional illustration that plots how frequently certain events occur. For example, it might be useful to see the frequency, or rate, at which countries have set certain minimum drinking ages. This information could be depicted using several types of graphs to illustrate the frequency distribution; two of the more common ones are **frequency polygons** (a line graph) and **histograms** (a bar graph). ● FIGURE A.1 shows the frequency distribution of legal drinking age depicted in a frequency polygon; ● FIGURE A.2 shows the same frequency distribution using a histogram. By looking at either one of these graphs, we can see that most of these selected governments have set their minimum drinking age below 21 and that the most commonly set drinking age is 18.

An even more useful type of graph for this investigation would be a **scatter plot**. In a scatter plot, two variables are plotted as a function of each other. For example, we could plot the percentage of 15-year-old drinkers as a function of the country's minimum drinking age. ● FIGURE A.3 shows such plots separately

frequency distribution a graph of data that plots the frequency of data points on the *y*-axis and the data points themselves on the *x*-axis

frequency polygon a line graph that is used to illustrate a frequency distribution

histogram a bar graph that is used to illustrate a frequency distribution

scatter plot a graph of data that plots pairs of data points, with one data point on the *x*-axis and the other on the *y*-axis

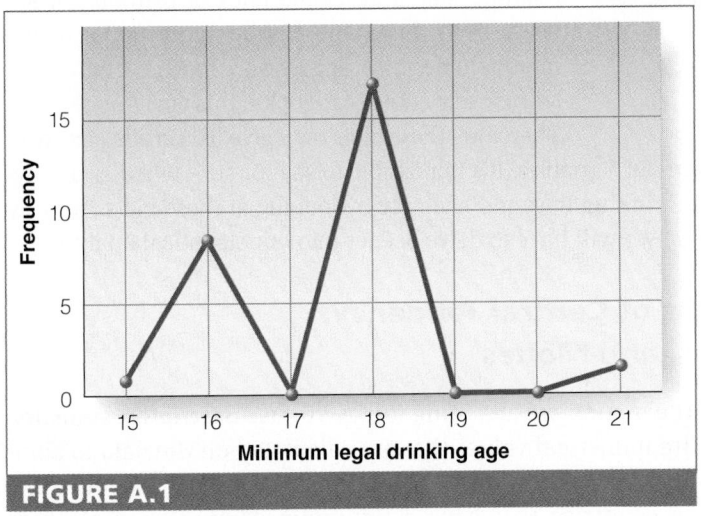

FIGURE A.1

Frequency Polygon

Frequency polygon showing the frequency distribution for minimum drinking age in 28 countries (data from Table A.1).

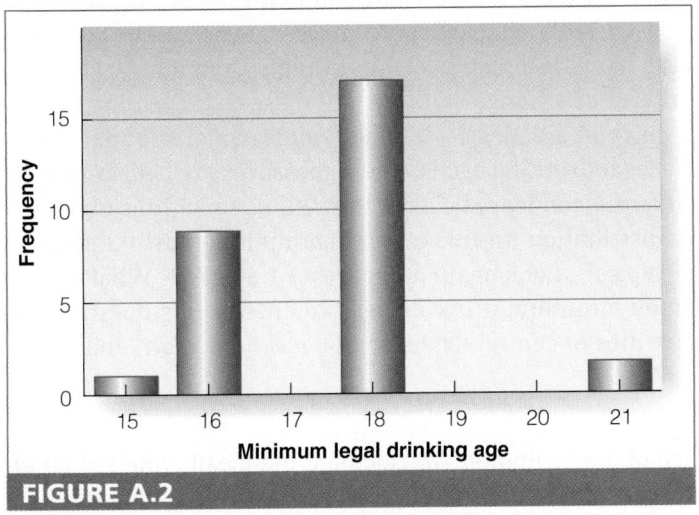

FIGURE A.2

Histogram

Histogram showing the frequency distribution for minimum drinking age in 28 countries (data from Table A.1).

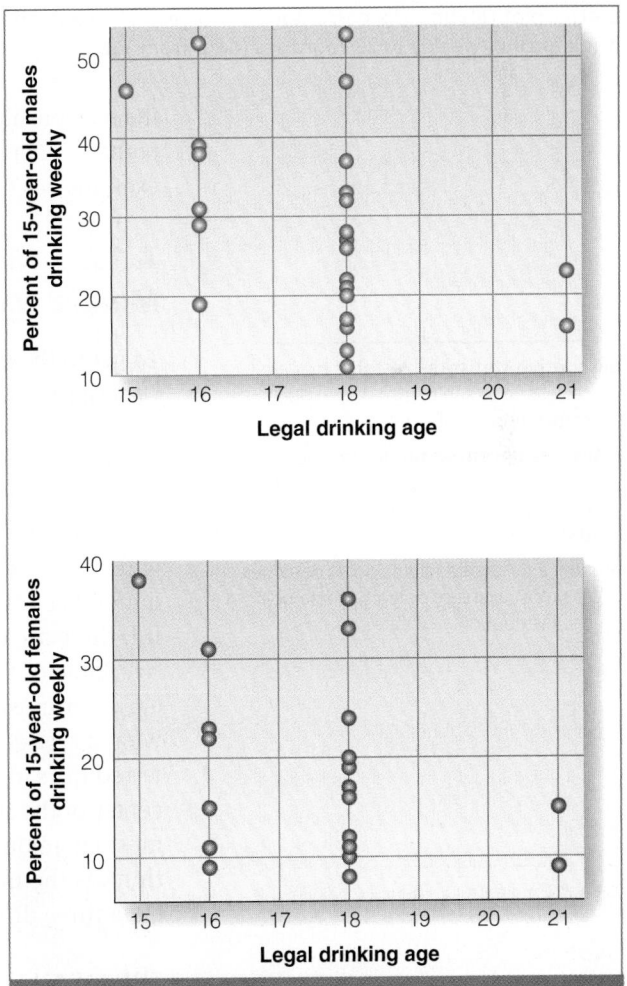

FIGURE A.3

Drinking at Age 15 as a Function of Minimum Legal Drinking Age

Scatter plots of the percentage of 15-year-olds who drink weekly as a function of minimum legal drinking age in 28 countries (data from Table A.1).

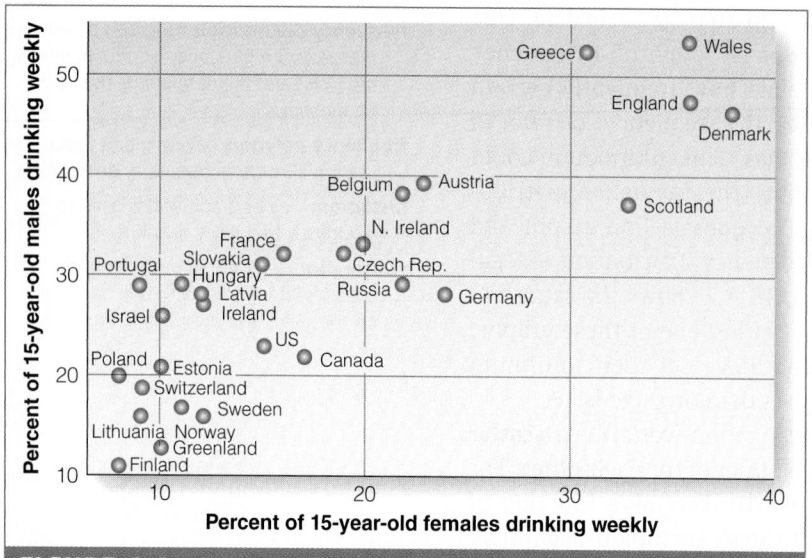

FIGURE A.4

Drinking at Age 15 of Males Versus Females

Scatter plot relating the percentage of 15-year-old males and females who drink alcohol weekly in 28 countries (data from Table A.1).

for males and females. By looking at the scatter plots in Figure A.3, you can get a *very crude* picture of the relationship between drinking age and the rate of underage drinking at age 15. Looking at Figure A.3, as the minimum drinking age decreases, does the rate of underage drinking increase? Do these data confirm or discount our hypothesis that lowering the drinking age encourages underage drinking? Although it is true that countries with a minimum drinking age of 16 or younger have relatively high levels of underage drinking, there are also a number of countries with a minimum drinking age of 18 that have high levels of underage drinking by 15-year-olds.

• FIGURE A.4 is another scatter plot, this time relating male and female rates of drinking. It appears from this graph that as more males drink, more females also engage in drinking—but if you look closely at the scatter plot, this isn't *always* true. Therefore, these plots only give us a crude picture of the relationship between our variables. It's impossible to say for sure whether our hypotheses about teenage drinking have merit simply by looking at these plots. To truly examine our hypotheses, we will have to delve deeper into our statistical analysis.

A.1.2 • Measures of Central Tendency: Means, Medians, and Modes

descriptive statistics statistics that are calculated to summarize or describe certain aspects of a data set

measures of central tendency descriptive statistics that describe the most central, or typical, data points in the frequency distribution

mean a descriptive statistic that describes the most average, or typical, data point in the distribution

To get to the heart of the matter, we are going to have to use **descriptive statistics**. Descriptive statistics are numerical values that are calculated on the data to summarize and describe the data as a whole. For example, you could calculate the percentage of these 28 countries that have a minimum drinking age of 18 or higher. This percentage would be 19 of the 28 countries, or 67.9%. Or you could calculate the percentage of countries with a minimum drinking age under 18 in which more than 25% of their male sample indicated that they drank weekly (8 out of 9 countries, or 88.9%). Although such percentages can sometimes be helpful, there are other, better statistical methods to use in this situation.

Some of the most useful descriptive statistics are those that describe the average, or most typical, entry in a data set—in other words, a statistic that shows what a *typical* country's legal drinking age is. These measures are collectively referred to as **measures of central tendency** because they tell us something about the center of the frequency distribution (in this case, what minimum drinking age is most common, or most typical). Look again at Figures A.1 and A.2. What do you think is the most common minimum drinking age? To answer this question, we have three different measures of central tendency: the *mean*, *median*, and *mode*.

THE MEAN

The **mean** is the average of a distribution. To calculate the mean, you add up all of the data points and then divide the total by the number of data points. This formula can be expressed with this equation:

$$\overline{X} = \frac{\Sigma X}{N}$$

where

$\overline{X}$ = the symbol for the mean;

Σ = a mathematical symbol that means to sum up the items that follow it;

X = the individual data points in the distribution;

N = the total number of data points or scores in the distribution.

The calculations for the average minimum drinking age and the average percentages of males and females who drink weekly at age 15 are shown in ● TABLE A.2.

median a descriptive statistic that identifies the center of the frequency distribution; 50% of the scores are above and 50% are below this point in the distribution

outliers unusual data points that are at the extremes of the frequency distribution and either far above or below the mean

THE MEDIAN

Another measure of central tendency is the **median**, or the score that is at the center of a frequency distribution. To find the median, you must first list all of the scores in ascending order. Once this is done, simply find the score that is at the center of this ordered list of scores. The calculation of the median legal drinking age is shown in ● FIGURE A.5. As you can see by comparing Figure A.5 and Table A.2, the median and the mean are not the same number. This shows one advantage of the median over the mean.

The mean is highly affected by unusual scores, or **outliers**, in the distribution. In this case, one country, Denmark, has an unusually low drinking age of 15. Although Denmark's minimum drinking age of 15 does not differ very much from the more common limit of 16, Denmark is the only country to set the age this low, and this outlying score works to lower the mean somewhat. However, because the median is simply the center score of the distribution, it is unaffected by unusual scores. So, whereas the mean drinking age is 17.5, the median drinking age is somewhat higher at 18.

When a distribution contains outliers, the median is the better choice for measuring central tendency. This is especially true for situations in which the outliers are more extreme than in our drinking-age example. For instance, assume that in a class of 10 students, 9 students score a 75 on an exam, and 1 student scores a 15. The mean for the class would be 69, but the median would be 75. That's a difference of more than half a letter grade between these two measures of central tendency, with the median more accurately reflecting how most students scored on the exam.

TABLE A.2

Average Minimum Drinking Age and Average Percentage of Students Who Report Drinking Alcohol Weekly at Age 15, Selected Countries

COUNTRY	MINIMUM LEGAL DRINKING AGE	% MALES	% FEMALES
Austria	16	39	23
Belgium	16	38	22
Canada	18	22	17
Czech Republic	18	32	19
Denmark	15	46	38
England	18	47	36
Estonia	18*	21	10
Finland	18	11	8
France	16	31	15
Germany	16	29	22
Greece	16*	52	31
Greenland	18	13	10
Hungary	16	29	11
Ireland	18	27	12
Israel	18	26	10
Latvia	18	28	12
Lithuania	21	16	9
Northern Ireland	18	33	20
Norway	18	16	12
Poland	18	20	8
Portugal	16	29	9
Russia	18	28	24
Scotland	18	37	33
Slovakia	18	32	16
Sweden	18	17	11
Switzerland	16	19	9
United States	21	23	15
Wales	18	53	36
ΣX	491	814	498
$\overline{X} = \frac{\Sigma X}{N}$	491/28 = 17.5	814/28 = 29.1	498/28 = 17.8

Source: Except where noted, data taken from Kaul, C. (2002). *Statistical Handbook on the World's Children* (p. 447). Westport, CT: Oryx Press.
*These data taken from http://www2.potsdam.edu/alcohol-info/LegalDrinkingAge.html#worlddrinkingages.

First take all of the minimum legal drinking ages for the countries and list them in ascending order:

15, 16, 16, 16, 16, 16, 16, 16, 16, 18, 18, 18, 18, 18, 18, 18, 18, 18, 18, 18, 18, 18, 18, 18, 18, 21, 21

Now find the score at the center of this distribution. In this case, because there is an even number of scores ($N = 28$) the center of this distribution would be between the 14th and 15th score in the list. Therefore, to find the median or X_{50}, we would average the 14th and 15th score:

$$(18 + 18)/2 = 18$$

$$X_{50} = 18$$

FIGURE A.5

Calculation of the Median Legal Drinking Age

THE MODE

The final measure of central tendency is the **mode,** or the most frequent score in the distribution. If you look again at Figure A.1 (or Figure A.2), you will see that the most frequent, or most common, drinking age is 18. Therefore, like the median, the mode is also 18. The mode is an especially useful measure of central tendency when the data being examined are not numerical (for example, the most typical car color in the student parking lot).

Measures of central tendency tell us something about the most representative scores at the center of the frequency distribution, but they do not tell us anything about the range, or breadth, of the scores in the distribution. To determine this characteristic of the distribution, we will have to look at *measures of variability.*

A.1.3 • Measures of Variability: Analyzing the Distribution of Data

Variability refers to the degree to which the individual scores of the distribution tend to *differ* from the central tendency of the distribution. In other words, variability measures how spread out the frequency distribution is. Look back at Figure A.1. As we just saw, the mean drinking age is 17.5. As you would expect, most of the scores in the frequency distribution are clustered around 18, but that does not mean that *all* of the scores are close in value to 18. Some scores are as low as 15, and some are as high as 21. Measures of variability tell us about the degree to which these more extreme scores differ from the mean. The simplest measure of variability is the **range** of the distribution, or the difference between the highest and lowest values in the distribution. In this case, the range of drinking ages would be 21−15 = 6 years.

Although the range is a measure of variability, it is fairly crude in that it doesn't really tell us how much most scores differ from the mean. Another measure of variability, called the **variance**, takes into account the difference between the individual scores of the distribution and the mean of the distribution. The first step to calculating the variance is to calculate the mean of the distribution. The next step is to calculate the **sum of squares** of the distribution. Here, *squares* refers to the difference between each score in the distribution and the mean of the distribution, with this difference being taken to the second power (that is, squared, or multiplied by itself). So, the sum of squares (*SS*) can be calculated using the following equation:

$$SS = \Sigma(X - \overline{X})^2$$

Once you have calculated *SS*, to calculate the variance (S^2), simply divide by the total number of scores (N)[1]:

$$S^2 = \frac{\Sigma(X - \overline{X})^2}{N}$$

Another measure of variability is the **standard deviation** (S), or the square root of the variance:

$$S = \sqrt{\frac{\Sigma(X - \overline{X})^2}{N}}$$

mode a measure of central tendency that identifies the most common, or frequent, score in the distribution

range a measure of variability that is the difference between the high score and the low score of the distribution

variance a measure of variability that shows on average how much the scores vary from the mean

sum of squares the sum of the squared errors, or deviations, from the mean for the scores in the distribution; the numerator of the variance equation

standard deviation a measure of variability equal to the square root of the variance; often used to gauge the degree to which an individual score deviates from the mean of a distribution

[1]When using a sample variance to estimate a population's variance, a better estimate is obtained using the formula $S^2 = \frac{\Sigma(X - \overline{X})^2}{N-1}$.

All three measures of variability indicate the degree to which the scores in the distribution are dispersed. The higher these measures are, the more dispersion, or spread, there is among the scores. Although it may be difficult to see why you would want to know the variability of a distribution, one reason is that you can use the standard deviation as a ruler, or guideline, for judging how atypical or typical a score in the distribution is.

To see how this works, take a look at • FIGURE A.6. Figure A.6 shows the calculation of the standard deviation for the male drinking percentages across the 28 countries. As you can see, the standard deviation for the distribution of male drinking scores is 11.03. We can use this figure to gauge how unusual a specific score in the distribution is. Using the standard deviation and the mean of the distribution, we can calculate a ***z* score**. A z score expresses the degree to which an individual score differs from the mean of the distribution in terms of the standard deviation of the distribution.

$$Z_x = \frac{X - \overline{X}}{S}$$

For example, in Germany, 29% of 15-year-old males drink weekly. This means that Germany's score would be

$$Z_x = (29 - 29.1)/11.03 = -.009.$$

Germany's z score indicates that the percentage of German 15-year-old boys who drink is far less than one standard deviation below the mean of 29.1 for all of the 28 countries. This is illustrated graphically in • FIGURE A.7.

Now look at the figure reported for Wales. In Wales, 53% of the 15-year-old males surveyed were drinking. Wales's z score of 2.17 indicates that their score of 53% is more than 2 standard deviations above the mean. This indicates that Wales's experience is not very typical of the average country's experience with male underage drinking at age 15. Wales *seems* to have a bigger problem with this issue than the average country does, but is this deviation from the mean enough of a problem to worry about? To answer this, we have to assess the probability that a given country would have a particular percentage of its young men drinking alcohol on a weekly basis. Luckily, we might be able to do this.

Country $N = 28$	X = Percent of 15-Year-Old Males Drinking	$X - \overline{X} = X - 29.1$	$(X - \overline{X})^2 = (X - 29.1)^2$
Austria	39	9.9	98.01
Belgium	38	8.9	79.21
Canada	22	– 7.1	50.41
Czech Republic	32	2.9	8.41
Denmark	46	16.9	285.61
England	47	17.9	320.41
Estonia	21	– 8.1	65.61
Finland	11	–18.1	327.61
France	31	1.9	3.61
Germany	29	– .1	.01
Greece	52	22.9	524.41
Greenland	13	–16.1	259.21
Hungary	29	– .1	.01
Ireland	27	– 2.1	4.41
Israel	26	– 3.1	9.61
Latvia	28	– 1.1	1.21
Lithuania	16	–13.1	171.61
Northern Ireland	33	3.9	15.21
Norway	16	–13.1	171.61
Poland	20	– 9.1	82.81
Portugal	29	– .1	.01
Russia	28	– 1.1	1.21
Scotland	37	7.9	62.41
Slovakia	32	2.9	8.41
Sweden	17	–12.1	146.41
Switzerland	19	–10.1	102.01
United States	23	– 6.1	37.21
Wales	53	23.9	571.21
	$\sum X = 814$		$\sum(X - \overline{X})^2 = 3407.88$
	$\overline{X} = \sum X/N = 814/28 = 29.1$		$S^2 = \sum (X - \overline{X})^2 / N = 3407.88/28 = 121.71$
			$S = \sqrt{\sum (X - \overline{X})^2 / N} = \sqrt{121.71} = 11.03$

Legend: $\overline{X}$ = the mean; S^2 = the sample variance; S = the standard deviation; $\sum$ = a symbol that means sum up the items that follow; N = the total number of scores or data points

FIGURE A.6

Calculation of the Standard Deviation for the Percentage of Males Drinking Weekly at Age 15

A.1.4 • Normal and Standard Normal Distributions

Many variables, such as height, weight, IQ, and so on, have a **normal distribution**. In other words, if you measured these characteristics for a very large number of people and plotted them in a frequency distribution, the resulting graph would be bell-shaped and symmetrical, like the one in Figure A.7. If we assume that drinking

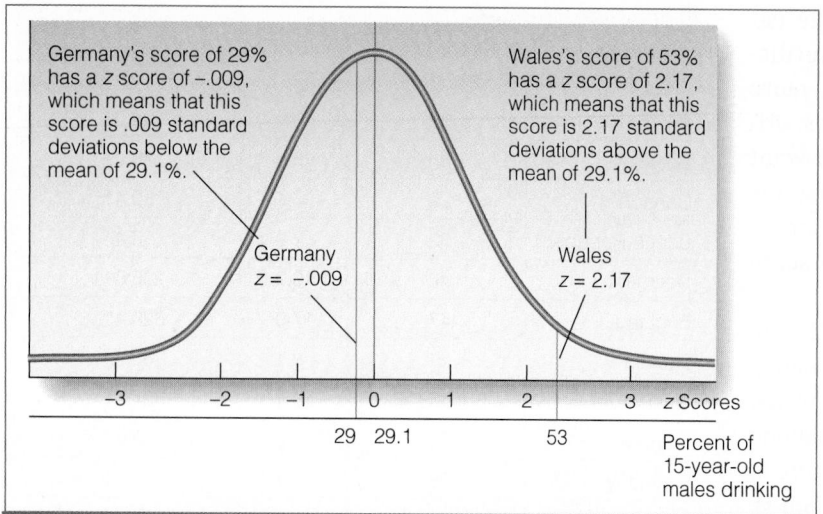

FIGURE A.7

z Scores for Germany and Wales

The mean, or average, percentage of 15-year-old males who drank was 29.1% and the standard deviation was 11.03 across the 28 countries. This figure shows the individual *z* scores for the percentage of 15-year-old males drinking in Germany and Wales. *Z* scores indicate how many standard deviations away from the mean a particular score falls. As you can see, Germany has a slightly below average percentage of 15-year-old male drinkers, with a raw score of 29% and a *z* score of –.009. Wales is quite a bit above average in its male underage drinking, with a raw score of 53% and a *z* score of 2.17.

behavior is normally distributed, then we can also assume that if we calculated the *z* scores for all of the different countries and plotted them in a frequency distribution, that distribution of *z* scores would also be a normal distribution, with $\bar{Z} = 0$, $S = 1$.

When a distribution of *z* scores is normal in shape, it is referred to as the **standard normal distribution**. The great thing about the standard normal distribution is that we know exactly what percentage of the distribution falls between any two scores, as shown in • FIGURE A.8. As you can see, 68.26% of the *z* scores should fall within the range of *z* scores from −1 to +1, whereas only 0.26% of the scores will be above a *z* score of +3 or below a *z* score of −3. The probability that a country would have a *z* score of +2.13 or higher is on the order of a mere 1.5%. So, indeed, Wales seems to have some possible cause for concern here because the number of 15-year-old boys consuming alcohol on a weekly basis is unusual compared to other countries.

A.1.5 • The Correlation Coefficient: Measuring Relationships

Take a look again at Figure A.4, the scatter plot for underage drinking in males versus females in the 28 countries. Do you notice anything interesting about this scatter plot? Don't the data points of the scatter plot tend to fall along a line that slopes up to the right of the graph? Doesn't this seem to indicate that there might be a linear relationship between the percentage of 15-year-old males and females drinking alcohol

z score a measure of relative standing that measures the distance of a score from the mean of the distribution in standard deviation units

normal distribution a bell-shaped, symmetric frequency distribution

standard normal distribution The standard normal distribution is a symmetric, bell-shaped distribution of *z* scores with ($\bar{z} = 0$, $S = 1$) for which we know the exact area under the curve

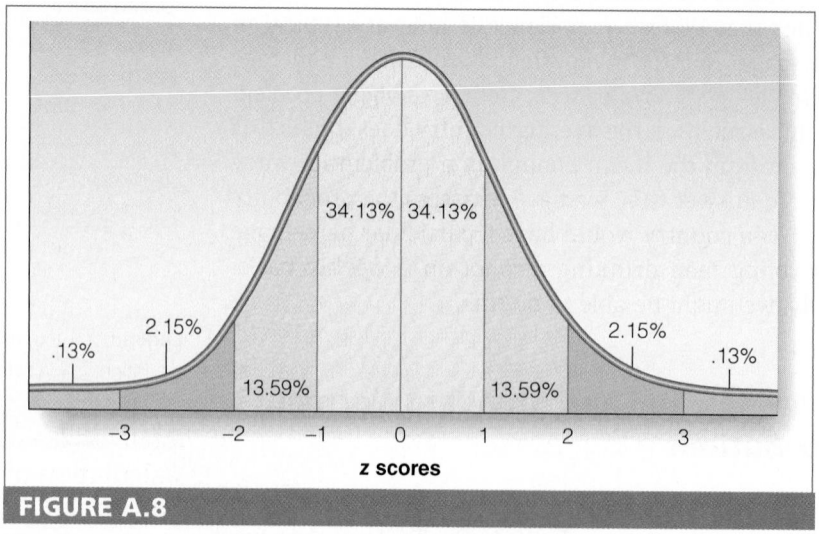

FIGURE A.8

The Standard Normal Distribution of *z* Scores

The standard normal distribution is a symmetric, bell-shaped distribution of *z* scores with $\bar{z} = 0$, $S = 1$. The *z* score is the number of standard deviations from the mean that the score is.

in a country? As one sex drinks more, doesn't the other seem to generally follow suit? To examine the degree to which such a relationship might exist, psychologists would use yet another statistic to describe these data—the **correlation coefficient**. Simply put, the correlation coefficient measures the degree to which pairs of data points fall along a straight line on a scatter plot. The formula for the correlation coefficient is

correlation coefficient the average product of *z* scores calculated on pairs of scores; describes the degree to which the scores in the pairs are linearly related

$$r = \frac{\Sigma z_x z_y}{N}$$

where

r = the correlation coefficient;

z_x = the z score for one of the variables in a pair;

z_y = the z score for the other variable of the pair;

N = the total number of pairs of scores.

The correlation coefficients that can be calculated with this formula have a possible range of $-1 \leq r \leq +1$. See ● FIGURE A.9 for an interpretation of these values. As you can see, an r value of 0 (Figure A.9a) indicates no linear relationship between the two variables. As r approaches either −1 (Figure A.9b) or +1 (Figure A.9c), the linear relationship between the two variables becomes stronger. Positive r values indicate a *direct* relationship between the variables—as one variable increases, so does the other. Negative r values indicate an *indirect* relationship between the variables—as one variable increases, the other decreases.

Now let's return to our question of a relationship between the percentage of males and females in a country who at age 15 drink weekly. ● FIGURE A.10 shows the calculation of the correlation coefficient for these data. As you can see, there is a strong positive correlation (r = .8715) between the percentage of males and females who drink alcohol weekly at age 15. This makes sense, because one might expect many of the factors that influence male underage drinking in a country to influence females similarly. One might think that one of these factors would be the legal drinking age in the country—that countries with a younger drinking age would have a higher percentage of 15-year-olds drinking alcohol illegally.

The data, however, do not fully support this hypothesis. In our sample, the correlation between legal drinking age and the percentage of males drinking at 15 is $r = -.412$. This moderately negative correlation indicates that countries with a lower legal drinking age tend to have higher rates of males drinking illegally at age 15. However, such a clear relationship was not found for females. Therefore,

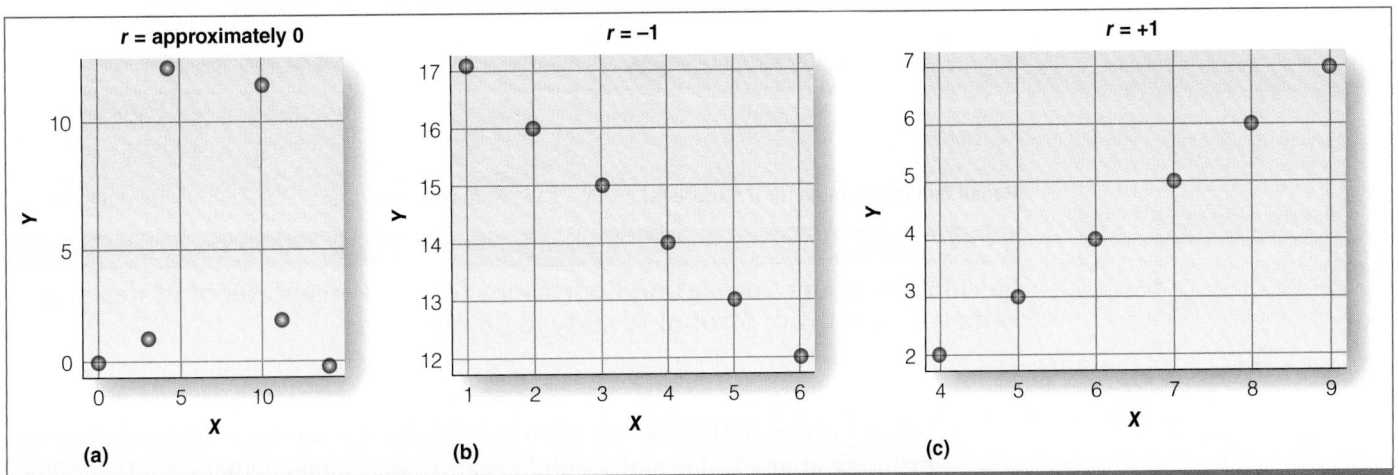

FIGURE A.9

The Correlation Coefficient (*r*)

Graphic depictions of different values of the correlation coefficient: (a) r = approximately 0; (b) $r = -1$; (c) $r = +1$.

Country	Percent of 15-yr-old Males Drinking	z Score for Percent of Males Drinking	Percent of 15-yr-old Females Drinking	z Score for Percent of Females Drinking	$z_{male}z_{female}$
Austria	39	.90027	23	.56263	.50652
Belgium	38	.80961	22	.45464	.36808
Canada	22	–.64098	17	–.08531	.05468
Czech Republic	32	.26564	19	.13067	.03471
Denmark	46	1.53490	38	2.18251	3.34994
England	47	1.62557	36	1.96652	3.19671
Estonia	21	–.73164	10	–.084125	.61549
Finland	11	–1.63826	8	–1.05724	1.73203
France	31	.17498	15	–.30130	–.05272
Germany	29	–.00635	22	.45464	–.00289
Greece	52	2.07888	31	1.42657	2.96565
Greenland	13	–1.45694	10	–.84125	1.22565
Hungary	29	–.00635	11	–.73326	.00465
Ireland	27	–.18767	12	–.62527	.11734
Israel	26	–.27833	10	–.84125	.23415
Latvia	28	–.09701	12	–.62527	.06066
Lithuania	16	–1.18495	9	–.94924	1.12481
Northern Ireland	33	.35630	20	.23866	.08504
Norway	16	–1.18495	12	–.62527	.74091
Poland	20	–.82230	8	–1.05724	.86937
Portugal	29	–.00635	9	–.94924	.00602
Russia	28	–.09701	24	.67063	–.06506
Scotland	37	.71895	33	1.64255	1.18091
Slovakia	32	.26564	16	–.19330	–.05135
Sweden	17	–1.09429	11	–.73326	.80240
Switzerland	19	–.91296	9	–.94924	.86663
United States	23	–.55032	15	–.30130	.16581
Wales	53	2.16954	36	1.96652	4.26644
					$\sum z_{male}z_{female}$ = 24.403
					$r = \sum z_{male}z_{female} / N$ = 24.403/28 = .8715

Recall that the formula for a z score is: $z = (X - \bar{X})/S$, where $\bar{X}$ = the mean and S = the standard deviation.

FIGURE A.10

Calculation of the Correlation Coefficient for the Percentage of Males and Females Who Drink Alcohol Weekly in 28 Countries

we can conclude that having a lower drinking age is *related* to higher rates of drinking at age 15 for males only. Recall from Chapter 1 that correlation does not imply causation here. We cannot say that a lower drinking age *causes* males to drink at 15. We can only say that the two variables are related in a linear fashion.

A.2 Using Statistics to Draw Conclusions

Inferential statistics are statistics that psychologists use to test hypotheses about their data. In short, inferential statistics help psychologists judge whether observed differences in their data are large enough to be **significant** or meaningful. To illustrate this issue, let's look at the difference in the average rate of drinking for males and females across the 28 countries (see Table A.2). The mean percentage of males drinking at 15 is 29.1%, but the mean percentage of females who report drinking at 15 is only 17.8%. Thus, it appears that males and females are not equally likely to drink at age 15. But is this difference (29.1 − 17.8 = 11.3) large enough to convince us that males really differ from females in their underage drinking? Is it possible that these data are merely a fluke or coincidence? How big a difference must we see between the sexes before we can say that our results are *significant*? These are the questions that inferential statistics tackle.

inferential statistics statistics that psychologists use in hypothesis testing to tell them when they should reject or accept their hypotheses about the population

significant results are considered significant when there is a very small chance (usually less than 5%) of finding those results given the assumption that the null hypothesis is true

null hypothesis (H_0) the hypothesis that contains a statement of what we do *not* believe is true about our variables in the population

alternative hypothesis (H_1) the hypothesis that contains a statement of what we do believe is true about our variables in the population

The first step to understanding inferential statistics is to understand the nature of hypotheses. In all studies that use inferential statistics, the researcher sets forth two hypotheses. The first one, called the **null hypothesis** (H_0), is a statement of what the researcher does not believe to be true about the variables. The second one, called the **alternative hypothesis** (H_1), is a statement of what the researcher *does* believe to be true about the variables. In our example, these would be

$$H_0: \mu_{males} = \mu_{females}$$

$$H_1: \mu_{males} \neq \mu_{females}$$

where

μ_{males} = the mean percent of males drinking in the entire population of all 15-year-old males;

$\mu_{females}$ = the mean percent of females drinking in the entire population of all 15-year-old females.

In other words, we do *not* believe that the rate of drinking is the same for males and females across the world at age 15. Rather, we believe that 15-year-old males drink at a different rate than 15-year-old females. Although it may seem odd, the way that scientists proceed from this point is to try to show that the null hypothesis is correct. Rather than directly testing the notion set forth in the alternative hypothesis, we instead test the hypothesis that contains the statement of what we do *not* believe to be true about our variables. So for the moment, we will assume that there is no difference between the rates of drinking for males and females at age 15. We will analyze our data to see whether they support this notion or whether we must reject this null hypothesis in favor of the alternative hypothesis that at age 15, males and females do indeed differ in their rates of drinking alcohol.

To test the null hypothesis, we must determine the probability of finding our results (that 29.1% of males and 17.8% of females were drinking), given the *assumption* that there is no real difference between the males and females when it comes to drinking at age 15. This is where a standard distribution comes in handy. If we can calculate a statistic on our data for which we know the distribution and the probabilities of obtaining certain values of the statistic, then we can determine how likely or unlikely it would be to get our results simply by accident or fluke. In a sense, we did this earlier when we looked at the probability of finding that Wales had a rate of drinking for males that was 2.17 standard deviations above the mean. When we found that the probability of Wales having a z score of 2.17 was only 1.5%, we were then fairly confident that the rate of male drinking in Wales was significantly different from most of the other countries. So, how low a probability is low enough for us to say that our results are significant? Generally speaking, psychologists are comfortable dealing with results that have probabilities less than 5%, although in some cases the significance level might be placed at a lower percentage.

Going back to our current example, the question now is this: "Is there a 5% or less probability of finding that 29.1% of the males and 17.8% of the females in our sample drink, if there is indeed *no* difference between 15-year-old males and females in the population at large?" If we find that the probability of obtaining our results is less than 5%, then we can safely conclude that our null hypothesis is likely incorrect, and we should *reject* it in favor of the alternative hypothesis. If we find that the probability of obtaining our results is greater than 5%, then we must accept our null hypothesis and admit that we were likely wrong in formulating our alternative hypothesis.

So how do we go about finding the probability of our results? Unfortunately, a detailed explanation of how we would determine this probability is beyond the scope of this text. If you ever take a statistics class, you will learn how this number is determined. However, so as not to leave you in suspense, we will tell you how the story ends. If the null hypothesis is true and there is no difference between male and female drinking in the population, the probability of finding our results (that 29.1% of males and 17.8% of females drink at age 15) is close to 0. This means that it is highly unlikely that males and females drink equally at age 15, and we can safely reject our null hypothesis in favor of the alternative hypothesis.

A.3 Summary

We hope that this appendix has helped you get a very basic understanding of how psychologists use statistics. Statistics are the major tool through which we as scientists judge the validity of our research results. Without statistics, we would have no way to separate the flukes and coincidences of life from the true, meaningful differences that exist in the world. We use statistics to describe our data, and in doing so, we use graphs or plots to visually depict data. We use measures of central tendency, such as the mean, median, and mode, to describe the center, or most typical, score in a frequency distribution. We use measures of variability, such as the range, variance, or standard deviation, to describe the dispersion, or spread, of the scores within the frequency distribution.

Another descriptive statistic that is commonly used is the correlation coefficient. The correlation coefficient describes the degree to which two variables are linearly related. A linear relationship between variables indicates that as one variable changes in magnitude, the other variable also experiences some change. The range of the correlation coefficient is $-1 \leq r \leq +1$. Positive correlations indicate a direct relationship between the variables: as one variable increases, so does the other. Negative correlations indicate an indirect relationship between the variables: as one variable increases, the other tends to decrease. As the correlation coefficient approaches -1 and $+1$, the described relationship between the variables is stronger or more linear.

Statistics are also used to test hypotheses about variables in the population being studied using a representative sample. When statistics are used to test hypotheses and thus to draw inferences about the population, they are referred to as inferential statistics. In testing hypotheses, researchers always set up two competing hypotheses. The null hypothesis contains a statement of what the researcher does not believe about the variables. The alternative hypothesis contains a statement of what the researcher believes to be true about the variables. The researcher then uses inferential statistics to test the null hypothesis.

To do this, the researcher must calculate some statistic on the data in the sample, and this statistic must be one for which we know what its distribution looks like. For instance, if the variable being studied is normally distributed in the population, then one could calculate z scores on the data and know that the distribution of these z scores in the population would be the standard normal distribution. The standard normal distribution is a bell-shaped, symmetric curve that has a mean of 0 and a standard deviation of 1. Because we know the shape, mean, and variance of the standard normal distribution, we also know exactly how much of the distribution falls between any two z scores. This allows us to determine the exact probability of obtaining any particular z score in our data.

In practice, z scores are not used very often to test hypotheses because psychologists frequently study more than one variable, and z scores can help us determine only the probability of obtaining a single data point in a sample. Therefore, psychologists often use other inferential statistics. The principle is still the same, however. You calculate an inferential statistic with a known distribution on your sample data. Next, you use the distribution to determine the probability of obtaining this particular value of the statistic, given the assumption that the null hypothesis is true. If the probability of obtaining this value of the inferential statistic when the null hypothesis is true is less than 5%, then you can safely say that within an acceptable margin of error, it appears that the null hypothesis is not true and it should be rejected in favor of the alternative hypothesis. In other words, your results are significant, and your data support your hypothesis.

In conclusion, please realize that this appendix has just skimmed the surface of what statistics is all about. All psychologists must undergo fairly extensive training in statistics before completing their degrees so that they have all the tools they need to discover the true nature of mental processes and behavior.

Studying the Appendix

Key Terms

alternative hypothesis (H_1) (643)
correlation coefficient (641)
data (633)
descriptive statistics (636)
frequency distribution (635)
frequency polygon (635)
graph (634)
histogram (635)
inferential statistics (643)
mean (636)
measures of central tendency (636)
median (637)
mode (638)
normal distribution (639)
null hypothesis (H_0) (643)
outliers (637)
range (638)
scatter plot (635)
significant (643)
standard deviation (638)
standard normal distribution (640)
statistics (634)
sum of squares (638)
variance (638)
***z* score** (639)

What Do You Know? Assess Your Understanding

Test your retention and understanding of the material by answering the following questions.

1. _____ are bits of knowledge gathered in scientific studies.

a. Statistics
b. Data
c. Hypotheses
d. Correlations

2. If we want to know if a person's height is a good predictor of his shoe size, which statistic(s) would be the most useful?

a. The mean
b. The mode
c. The correlation coefficient
d. A *z* score

3. If you want to describe the most common pet in America, after surveying 20,000 people to determine the type(s) of pet(s) they own, you should calculate the _____ of your data.

a. mean
b. median
c. mode
d. variance

4. A small company employs 10 people. At this company, three employees earn $20,000 a year, four employees earn $17,000, two employees earn $21,000, and the president earns $210,000 a year. Which of the following measures of central tendency is the most appropriate measure for accurately depicting the typical salary at this company?

a. Mean
b. Median
c. Mode
d. Variance

5. The mean of the standard normal distribution is equal to _____.

a. 0
b. 2
c. 3
d. –1

6. Which of the following statistics would be most useful for describing how the grades in a psychology course differ across the students in the class?

a. Mean
b. Variance
c. Correlation coefficient
d. *z* score

7. A *z* score of 2.66 means that the raw score in question is _____ the mean of the distribution.

a. 1.33 standard deviations below
b. 1.33 standard deviations above
c. 2.66 standard deviations below
d. 2.66 standard deviations above

8. Assuming that IQ scores are normally distributed, what percentage of the population can be expected to score 2 or more standard deviations above the mean on an IQ test?

a. 2.28%
b. 5.36%
c. 8.77%
d. 52.35%

9. The hypothesis that psychologists actually test is called the _____ hypothesis.

a. true
b. null
c. alternative
d. testable

10. A(n) _____ distribution is a bell-shaped, symmetric frequency distribution.

a. normal
b. histogram
c. scatter plot
d. frequency polygon

Answers: 1. b; 2. c; 3. c; 4. b; 5. a; 6. b; 7. d; 8. a; 9. b; 10. a

Applying Psychology in the Workplace

KATHY A. HANISCH, Iowa State University

Learning Objectives

B.1 Define industrial and organizational psychology and discuss the value of work in people's lives. (APA 1.1, 1.2, 5.1, 5.5)

B.1 Describe the different types of jobs available. (APA 1.1, 1.3)

B.2 Detail how employers decide which job applicants to hire. (APA 1.2, 1.3, 5.1)

B.3 Describe how new employees become socialized to their work and organization through culture, groups, leadership, and performance appraisal. (APA 1.2, 1.3, 3.2, 5.1, 5.5)

B.4 Detail how employee satisfaction is influenced by employees' attitudes and behaviors at work. (APA 1.2, 1.3, 5.1)

B

Appendix Outline

B.1 Industrial and Organizational Psychology / 649

B.2 Selecting Employees: The Hiring Process / 652

B.3 Socializing Employees: Culture, Groups, Leadership, and Performance Appraisal / 657

B.4 Employee Satisfaction: Attitudes and Behaviors at Work / 661

B.5 Summary / 665

Psychologists who study people's behavior at work using psychological principles are called *industrial* and *organizational psychologists*, and their field of study is **industrial and organizational (I/O) psychology**. I/O psychologists study employee selection, performance appraisal, training, job design, communication, work stress, motivation, leadership, groups and teams, organizational culture/climate, human factors, job attitudes, well-being, and work behavior. This appendix will introduce you to the field of I/O psychology. You will experience many of the topics discussed here when you seek, obtain, and keep a job.

B.1 Industrial and Organizational Psychology

You have applied for a job, submitted your résumé, and taken a series of tests. You have been interviewed by your potential supervisor and been given a tour of the company. You now find yourself sitting across from the co-owners, who have just

industrial and organizational (I/O) psychology the study of people's behavior at work using psychological principles

offered you a position. They tell you that their organization is a great place to work. As evidence, they tell you that no one has quit in the last 5 years and that employees are rarely absent. They also tell you that they have flexible policies. You can work whatever hours you like and take vacation whenever you want. And if you decide to work for them, you'll have access to spending cash as well as keys to the company.

You try to maintain your composure. You'd heard interesting things about this company but didn't really believe them. Finally, the co-owners ask you what you are worth, indicating they will pay you whatever you wish. Now you're really dumbfounded and wonder what the catch is, but sit quietly while they talk about other issues. Does this sound too good to be true? Wouldn't this be ideal?

Almost this exact scenario played out in an organization owned and managed by an Oakland appliance dealer in the 1970s. His name was Arthur Friedman, and he had decided to change how he ran his business. Art, as reported in the *Washington Post* (Koughan, 1975), announced at one of his staff meetings that employees could work the hours they wanted, be paid what they thought they were worth, take vacation time when they wanted, and help themselves to petty cash if they were in need of spending money. New employees would be allowed to set their own wages, too. As you might imagine, the employees weren't sure how to take this news. It was reported that no one said anything during the meeting when Art first described his plan (Koughan, 1975).

When asked why he was changing his business practices, Art replied, "I always said that if you give people what they want, you get what you want. You have to be willing to lose, to stick your neck out. I finally decided that the time had come to practice what I preached" (Koughan, 1975). In the final analysis, Art's experiment worked. The organization was profitable. Friedman signed union contracts without reading them (the employees didn't need a union with Art in charge). Employees didn't quit, they didn't steal from the company, and they were rarely absent. Net profits increased, and the company was a success. The employees realized that to make the organization work and remain in business, they had to be reasonable in their requests and behavior (Koughan, 1975).

A present-day company with some enticing work perks is SAS, the largest privately held software company. In 2010, *Fortune* magazine rated it the number one company to work for. Included among its many perks are 90% coverage of the health care premium, unlimited sick days, free health care with an on-site medical center that has a $4.5 million budget (it still saves the company $5 million a year; Kaplan, 2010), subsidized child care and cafeteria, free fitness center, swimming pool, and summer camps for employees' children. In addition, SAS has an on-site billiards hall, sauna, manicurist, and hair salon, and offers massages. The company also has picnics and other family events (which employees and their families want to attend) as well as snacks (fruit, donuts, and M&Ms) on different days. In addition to these benefits, SAS rewards innovation and risk taking while supporting the growth of its employees both personally and professionally (www.sas.com).

Jim Goodnight has been the CEO of SAS since incorporation in 1976. His organization was rated as the #1 company to work for by *Forbes* in 2010.

Adam Berry/Bloomberg via Getty Images

Organizations like SAS and Art Friedman's company are interesting because of how they deal with their employees and how that treatment affects the employees' behaviors. This interest is what is at the heart of industrial and organizational psychology. I/O psychology studies human behavior in work settings.

B.1.1 • Work in Our Lives

You have learned about work since you were a small child. You may have asked where your parent was going when you went to day care or why your parent left the house before 8 a.m. and did not return until after 5 p.m. You likely "played" at different jobs by dressing up as an astronaut, a firefighter, a teacher, a chef, or a construction worker. As you got older, other information about work may have come from your friends, other family members, school, and the media. In high school, more education and a part-time job may have given you additional details about the meaning of work. As you pursue a college degree, you may receive information about the work and jobs available in your chosen field through classes, service learning, internships, or other job or research experiences.

Courtsey of k.Hanisch

Children learn about work through play and dress-up.

Work is an important part of life for many people. We often ask people we meet what they "do," which translates into "What is your job and whom do you work for?" Many people identify with their work because they spend so much of their waking lives at work. Work is important because it provides many of the things people need and value. Income from work provides us with the money necessary to satisfy our basic needs for food, shelter, and security (for example, health care or retirement income), while the "leftover" money provides us with discretionary funds to use as we see fit. These funds may be used to buy a round of golf, an iPad, or a fancy place to live; to support charities or attend athletic or fine art performances; or to save for college. Essentially, money, typically from work, provides us with a standard of living that varies from person to person depending on our income and how we choose to spend it. In addition, work provides much more. It provides a source of social interactions and friendships, independence, a sense of accomplishment, satisfaction, a reason to get up in the morning, happiness, a sense of identity, recognition, and prestige (see • TABLE B.1).

Although most researchers and practitioners agree that money and recognition are nearly universal motivators (R. E. Clark, 2003), many of the things we value or seek from work vary from person to person. For example, the prestige of a job may not be important to you, but it might be important to your best friend. Perhaps you will want your work to provide you with a sense of accomplishment or be a source of social interactions, while those attributes may not be valued by another person. It is important to understand what you want from your work as well as what a job can provide.

From an employer's perspective, it is useful to determine what employees want because satisfied employees will be more likely than

TABLE B.1

Jobs with the Highest and Lowest Prestige (2009)*

JOB DESCRIPTION	PERCENTAGE RATING JOB AS HIGH PRESTIGE
Highest Prestige	
Firefighter	61%
Scientist	54%
Teacher	53%
Doctor	52%
Military officer	51%
Lowest Prestige	
Real Estate Agent/Broker	4%
Actor	9%
Banker	10%
Accountant	11%
Stockbroker	13%

*It is interesting to note that some of the professions with the highest prestige (firefighter, teacher) are not considered high-paying jobs, while some of those with the least prestige (actor, stockbroker, real estate agent) are associated with fame or high earning potential or both. It appears that the polled individuals do not equate money and fame with high prestige; they appear to be unique concepts.

Sources: www.harrisinteractive.com and U.S. Department of Labor.

dissatisfied employees to work to meet organizational goals. Part of a supervisor's job is to ascertain what employees value because those values can be used to motivate employees to perform well in their jobs.

B.1.2 • Types of Jobs

There are many types of work, in many types of jobs, in many different organizational settings. These settings include multinational conglomerates; public and private companies; nonprofits; federal, state, and local government organizations; and home businesses.

People in the United States work a variety of schedules, from extended workweeks (45 to 99 hours) to standard workweeks (35 to 44 hours) to part-time workweeks (fewer than 35 hours). Some people, such as police officers, medical personnel, and factory workers, because of the nature of their jobs, work shifts other than the typical 8 a.m. to 5 p.m. workday. Others are offered flexible working schedules that best fit their lives as long as they work the required number of hours and accomplish the work. Telecommuting is becoming more and more popular with the increase in appropriate technology. Some people work for virtual organizations that use communication technologies to outsource the majority of their functions.

Regardless of the type of job or your work schedule, you will likely spend most of your waking hours in some type of employment for many years. Many people spend their weekends working, too. Because work is critical to who we are and what we do, studying the psychological principles and some of the topics examined by I/O psychologists will provide you with information that may be useful to you in your future careers.

Quiz Yourself

B.1

1. Nearly all people value _____ and _____ from their work.
   a. money; prestige
   b. prestige; social interactions
   c. money; recognition
   d. satisfaction; prestige
2. Which of the following would an I/O psychologist be *least* likely to study?
   a. leadership
   b. life satisfaction
   c. employee selection
   d. performance appraisal
3. SAS offers many enticing work perks. CEO Jim Goodnight chooses to do this primarily because _____ .
   a. it makes inconveniences easy to deal with so employees can focus on their work
   b. most other companies offer these same perks
   c. he wanted SAS to be rated the number one company to work for in 2010
   d. there is a powerful employee union at SAS

Answers 1. c; 2. b; 3. a

B.2 Selecting Employees: The Hiring Process

Industrial and organizational psychologists first became involved in the process of selecting employees when the U.S. government needed help selecting and placing officers and soldiers in World War I (Aamodt, 2010). Psychologists used mental ability tests to determine who would become officers and who would be in the infantry. The process many employers now use to hire employees is very detailed, typically consisting of five components: *job analysis, testing, legal issues, recruitment,* and the *selection decision.*

B.2.1 • Job Analysis

Job analysis is the identification of the critical elements of a job. I/O psychologists have helped devise effective strategies for determining three basic aspects of any job: (1) What tasks and behaviors are essential to the job? (2) What knowledge, skills, and abilities are needed to perform the job? (3) What are the conditions (such as stress, safety, and temperature) under which the job is performed? A job analysis can be conducted in many ways. An analyst (an I/O psychologist, human resources employee, manager, or outside consultant) may interview current employees, have them complete questionnaires, observe people in the job, or talk to people knowledgeable about the job (Gael, 1988).

The information from a job analysis is used in many types of personnel functions. These include employee selection, performance appraisal, training, and human resources planning. Within the hiring process, job analysis is used to write job descriptions; to determine what tests might be used to assess the relevant knowledge, skills, and abilities of job applicants; and to assist in meeting legal requirements that affect the selection process.

job analysis the identification of the critical elements of a job, including tasks, skills required, and working conditions

test the measurement of a carefully chosen sample of behavior

unstructured interview an informal, unplanned interview conducted by an untrained interviewer using random questions and no scoring key

structured interview an interview conducted by a trained interviewer using standardized questions, a specific question order, and a predetermined scoring or answer key

B.2.2 • Testing

You are familiar with tests and taking tests. **Tests** are defined here as the measurement of carefully chosen samples of behavior. These include the standard paper-and-pencil or computerized tests used to measure specific skills or abilities in a class, or more general abilities as in the SAT or ACT. They also include personality assessments (see Chapter 11) such as conscientiousness and honesty tests. In addition, work samples, in which applicants do a replica of the work they will be asked to do on the job, are useful tests. Tests are vital to the success of organizations. They are used to ascertain differences between people. The goal of these tests is to help employers choose the person best suited for the job and the organization. Regardless of the type of test or how it is administered, the reliability and validity of a test are very important (see Chapter 8).

Another type of test is the *employee interview.* Nearly all organizations use some type of interview in their selection of employees (Salgado, Viswesvaran, & Ones, 2003). Even though interviews are often viewed as subjective, more than 85 years of research has provided evidence regarding when interviews are useful and when they are not.

Selection interviews can be broadly classified as *unstructured* and *structured*. **Unstructured interviews** are informal and unplanned. They are conducted by an untrained interviewer, with random questions and no scoring key. Some typical questions asked during an unstructured interview are listed in • TABLE B.2. **Structured interviews** are conducted by a trained interviewer. They have standardized questions, a specific question order, and a predetermined scoring or answer key. Examples of structured interview questions are listed in • TABLE B.3. Structured interviews, based on a job analysis, have greater reliability and validity than unstructured interviews (Huffcutt & Arthur, 1994; Macan, 2009).

TABLE B.2

Typical Unstructured Interview Questions

1. What are your weaknesses?
2. Why should we hire you?
3. Why do you want to work here?
4. What are your goals?
5. Why did you leave (or why are you leaving) your job?
6. When were you most satisfied in your job?
7. What can you do for us that other candidates can't?
8. What are three positive things your last boss would say about you?
9. What salary are you seeking?
10. If you were an animal, which one would you want to be?

Source: C. Martin, 2006, Monster.com.

TABLE B.3

Structured Behavior-Based Interview Questions

1. Tell me in specific details about a time when you had to deal with a difficult customer.
2. Give me an example of a time when you had to make a decision without a supervisor present.
3. Give me a specific example of when you demonstrated your initiative in an employment setting.
4. Give me an example of a time when you had to work with a team.
5. Describe a time when you had to be creative at solving a problem.

Source: Adapted from The Job Centre, Niagara College Canada, 2005, http://jobs.niagarac.on.ca/.

B.2.3 • Legal Issues

Title VII of the Civil Rights Act of 1964 the law that prohibits discrimination based on race, color, religion, sex, and national origin

One of the most important pieces of legislation regarding employment, and specifically the hiring of employees, is **Title VII of the Civil Rights Act of 1964** (Equal Employment Opportunity Commission, 2002). Title VII "prohibits discrimination based on race, color, religion, sex, and national origin," known as the "Big 5." Providing protection for people comprising the Big 5 helps to ensure that they have equal employment opportunities. Exceptions to this provision include national security, seniority systems, and *bona fide occupational qualifications (BFOQs)*. BFOQs permit organizations to discriminate in hiring persons in a protected class if the qualification is determined to be reasonably necessary to the operation of the business. For example, women can be discriminated against when hiring someone to model men's swimwear, and vice versa. It is reasonably necessary to the marketing and selling of swimwear that organizations hire men to model male swimwear and women to model female swimwear; sex is a BFOQ. It is not reasonably necessary, however, that a secretary in a church who does secretarial work and not church or religious work believe in the same religion as the church that employs him; religion in this case could not be used as a BFOQ.

Mike Flanagan/www.cartoonstock.com

It is important for employers to abide by laws that protect people against discrimination because the costs of litigation can be very high, both monetarily and in terms of an organization's reputation. This protection applies to discrimination based not only on the Big 5, covered under the Civil Rights Act, but on other characteristics such as age (Age Discrimination in Employment Act, 1967) and disability (Americans with Disabilities Act, 1990). Employment law in the United States is meant to protect and provide equal opportunities for all individuals.

Bookkeeper - Johannesburg East

Expiry Date: 2010-07-02

Location: Johannesburg East
Category: Banking and Financial Services
Job Type: Permanent
Salary: R8000.00 to R10000.00 MONTHLY COST TO COMPANY

Apply Now!

Job Details:

We are urgently looking for a 40 year or older lady to perform full bookkeeping duties.

We will consider the candidate with an accounting degree or diploma in bookkeeping. She must have a Pastel Partner, Pastel Evolution experience and also be able to work on books to trial balance.

Duties:
Invoicing
Full
Creditors
Cashbook
Pettycash
Management
Reports

Software Proficiency:
Microsoft Excel: Intermediate
Microsoft Word: Intermediate
Pastel Partner: Intermediate
Pastel Evolution: Basic

Minimum Education: National Diploma (NQF5)

Required Experience: 3 Years

FIGURE B.1

Legal issues in employment vary in different countries, however. The advertisement shown in • FIGURE B.1 for a bookkeeper in Johannesburg, South Africa would not be legal in the United States. It specifies that the applicant must be female, which would be illegal under Title VII of the Civil Rights Act. It also specifies age 40 or older, which would be illegal in some states that protect younger individuals against age discrimination. U.S. federal law prohibits discrimination based on age once a person reaches the age of 40 (Age Discrimination in Employment Act). The employer is seeking an older woman, which is likely not related to expected job performance; people younger than 40 could perform just as well in the job of a bookkeeper.

Employment legislation offers fair treatment for people looking for a job. In the United States, organizations with several employees are required to abide by the employment laws. These laws make the U.S. job market fairer than in many other countries.

B.2.4 • Recruitment

The process organizational managers use to identify potential employees for a job is called **recruitment**. Depending on the job, a manager or owner may recruit from inside the company or seek someone outside the organization. The owner or manager may advertise on the company website or on a website such as Indeed.com or Simply.hired.com for specific types of jobs. In addition, websites like Monster.com and CareerBuilder.com link potential employees and employers in a variety of jobs and locations. Other recruitment sources include college career centers, newspapers, radio and television advertisements, trade magazines, professional publications, and employee referrals.

recruitment the process organizations use to identify potential employees for a job

Research indicates that employees recruited through inside sources such as employee referrals or rehires work for the organization longer and have better job performance than those recruited through outside sources including advertisements, employment agencies, or recruiters (Zottoli & Wanous, 2000). Studies have supported the idea that those recruited using inside sources receive more accurate information about the job than those recruited through external sources (Conrad & Ashworth, 1986; McManus & Baratta, 1992). In effect, the new employees receive realistic job previews.

A survey of the 50 best small and medium organizations to work for in the United States found that 92% use employee referrals, and that nearly 30% of all hires were referred by a current employee (NAS, 2012; Pomeroy, 2005). Because of their effectiveness, some companies provide rewards to employees who recommend an applicant who is hired. These rewards include cash, vacations, and prizes such as televisions and free house cleaning services for a year (R. Stewart et al., 1990). Typically, the new employee must work for the organization a set period of time before the referring employee can receive the award (R. Stewart et al., 1990). SAS Canada offers a bonus up to $8,000 for a successful employee referral (http://www.eluta.ca/top-employer-sas-canada).

After applicants have submitted either a résumé or an application, someone from the organization such as the human resources manager or supervisor, or a "bot" (a software application that screens résumés for the right qualifications and skills before a human sees them), will determine which applicants should be considered further. In that process, he or she may make telephone inquiries of previous employers or other references and conduct criminal background checks.

A growing phenomenon is employers' use of social networking sites such as Facebook, LinkedIn, and Twitter to learn about and even seek job candidates. In a 2012 CareerBuilder survey, 37% of employers reported that they use social networking sites in their selection process, and 11% plan to start using them. On these sites employers have found promising candidates reporting on their own drug use, sexual exploits, and drinking, as well as posting inappropriate photographs and bad-mouthing their previous employer (Haefner, 2009). In addition to identifying risky behavior patterns, managers are using social networking sites to determine whether applicants would fit in well with the company culture and to evaluate their professionalism (Hargis, 2008). It would be wise to closely look at any publicly accessible information before a job search and to establish privacy settings for any material that you do not want a potential employer to see. Legislation in many states prohibits employers from requiring passwords to access social media sites.

"can-do" factors factors that determine the maximum performance an employee can exhibit

"will-do" factors factors that determine the normal or typical performance by an employee

B.2.5 • Making the Decision

When selecting employees, employers are looking for a good match between the employee and the organization. They would like to match the requirements for excellent performance in the job with the person's knowledge, skills, abilities, personality, and motivation for the job. They attempt to accomplish this by using the different types of tests discussed earlier.

Based on this photo, would you hire this job candidate?

© Louis Quail/Corbis

Researchers have posited two groups of factors that determine an employee's performance in a job. They are the *"can-do"* and the *"will-do" factors* (Schmitt et al., 2003). **"Can-do" factors** suggest what an employee is capable of doing on the job if he is working to the best of his ability. Personality factors such as conscientiousness and need for achievement as well as integrity have been classified as important **"will-do" factors** in performance (Schmitt et al., 2003). "Will-do" factors suggest the time and effort an employee is willing to exert for the organization. A person's "can-do" and "will-do" factors may change as she moves from organization to organization. Once a person is selected, the important process of being accepted and socialized into the organization at all levels, including a work group or team, begins.

B.2

Quiz Yourself

1. Asking employees to describe their job is one way of conducting a _____.
   a. job evaluation
   b. job analysis
   c. performance appraisal
   d. job review
2. Zachary is usually a conscientious and hardworking employee, but the company has hired a new boss who is really lazy and doesn't motivate his employees. It is likely that Zachary's _____ will be compromised in this situation.
   a. try-to factors
   b. will-do factors
   c. can-do factors
   d. must-do factors
3. Alexander, a television reporter, wants access to the women's locker room right after the basketball game to conduct interviews with the team members. The women's team lets female reporters in to interview them but wants Alexander to wait until after they have showered and changed. Alexander argues he needs to be treated the same as the female reporters. What would be the likely outcome if this issue goes before a court?
   a. The women's team would win because sex is a BFOQ in this case.
   b. The women's team would win because they can discriminate against Alexander because they don't like his reporting style.
   c. Alexander would win because the women's team members can't discriminate against him because they don't like his reporting style.
   d. Alexander would win because sex is not a BFOQ in this case.

Answers 1.b; 2. b; 3. d

B.3 Socializing Employees: Culture, Groups, Leadership, and Performance Appraisal

When you report for your first day of work in an organization, you will need to learn many things to be successful in your job. The process of learning these things is called **organizational socialization**, which has been defined as "the process by which organizational members become a part of, or are absorbed into, the culture of the organization" (Jablin, 1982, p. 255). Organizational socialization consists of people learning how the organization operates by using information provided by management, coworkers, observation, and company handbooks or memos.

organizational socialization the process by which members of an organization become a part of, or are absorbed into, the culture of the organization

Nowadays, electronic communication is an important part of how employees are socialized (Flanagin & Waldeck, 2004). Employees communicate through e-mail, texting, company websites, chat groups, and blogs. Job applicants also use these resources to learn about the organization before submitting their applications, and employers often screen job applicants through some of these same mediums.

Often, one of the first things an employee encounters on the job is new employee orientation training that focuses on the goals and expectations of the organization. These clearly help to set the expectations and culture of the organization. Other common types of training in organizations are diversity and harassment training. These training programs are usually required company-wide to ensure that all employees are aware of the policies of the organization; they also are used by organizations to try to prevent and correct harassment problems in an attempt to limit liability in harassment complaints (Equal Employment Opportunity Commission, 2010).

mentoring the pairing of a current and often long-term employee (the mentor) with a new employee

organizational culture the shared cognitive assumptions and beliefs of an organization

organizational climate the behavioral norms of an organization

work teams/groups two or more employees who together perform organizationally relevant tasks, share one or more common goals, interact socially, and exhibit task interdependencies

Supervisors and coworkers are also important sources of socialization information. **Mentoring** is a form of training in which a current and often long-term employee (the mentor) is paired with a new employee. The mentor's role is to help the new employee adapt to the job by assisting with advice or resources. The mentor may provide information about how the organization works, career advancement opportunities, and how performance is evaluated. Good mentoring helps new employees become successful on the job and learn the formal and informal rules of the organization (Aamodt, 2010).

Research indicates that both mentors and those they mentor often benefit from the relationship. For example, in one study of health care employees, it was found that those who were mentored reported higher salaries, greater promotion rates, and more positive career success than those who did not receive mentoring (Allen, Lentz, & Day, 2006). Employees who have been mentored experience more effective socialization and better compensation, advancement, career satisfaction, job satisfaction, job involvement, and organizational commitment than those with no mentoring (Eby et al., 2013; Greenhaus, 2003).

B.3.1 • Organizational Culture and Climate

Organizational culture includes the shared assumptions and beliefs of the organization. These cognitions then influence the **organizational climate**, or actions and behaviors of the people in the group or organization (Schein, 1985). These behaviors are considered the norm for the organization; they represent the "normal behaviors" expected from its members. Because culture and climate generally operate in unison, our discussion will refer to these elements collectively as culture (Ostroff, Kinicki, & Tamkins, 2003). Organizational culture is important because it lets employees know what is expected of them and affects how they think and behave. Culture is often determined by the founders of the organization and may be modified over time by the successes and failures of an organization. See • FIGURE B.2 for factors that affect organizational culture.

Some organizations like SAS have cultures that appear to have been successful from the start, as suggested by low turnover and organizational profitability. Several case studies have described organizations that have successfully changed their culture from poor to better or great. Remember Art Friedman from the beginning of this appendix? He allowed his employees to set their own wages and decide the hours they worked; he also required employees to belong to the union. After Friedman made these changes, employee grumbling stopped (Koughan, 1975). The organizational culture changed, resulting in better morale, increased productivity, and employee longevity. No one wanted to quit working in a culture where the employees got to make their own decisions that affected the organization's bottom line. Finding an organizational culture that fits your working style will have consequences for your attitudes, performance, and tenure in an organization. *Work teams* and the *leadership* of an organization have a large influence on the culture of an organization.

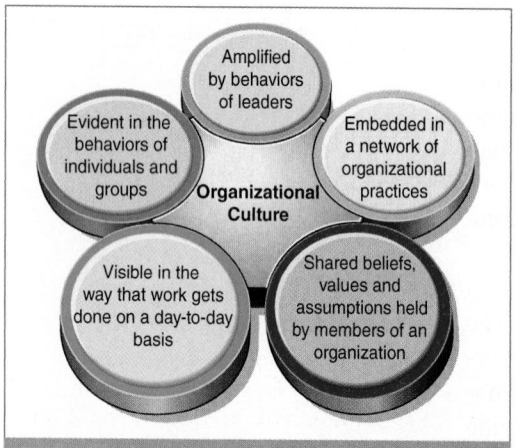

FIGURE B.2

Several factors affect the organizational culture of an organization.

B.3.2 • Groups and Teams

Work teams and **groups** can be defined as two or more employees who have common goals, have tasks that are interdependent, interact socially, and work on relevant organizational tasks within specific requirements and rules (Kozlowski & Bell, 2003). Just as there can be a culture in an organization, groups or teams also exhibit cultures that may encourage or discourage certain types of work-related behaviors and attitudes. These cultures then form the basis for the socialization of new group or team members.

Although most organizations provide formal means of socializing new employees (for example, new employee orientation training), the group or team dynamics have immediate and direct effects on employees' socialization (Anderson & Thomas, 1996). The outcomes of organization socialization and work group socialization may be different. Teams may have leaders or may be self-managing. Self-managing teams tend to show better productivity, an increase in work quality, improved quality of life for employees, decreased absenteeism, and decreased turnover than teams with leaders (Cohen & Ledford, 1994). When teams fail, often the failure is linked to the team leader, who may be too autocratic, wielding too much power or influence, or too lax and providing too little monitoring. As a result, the team does not realize the autonomy and control levels it needs to be successful (Langfred, 2004; G. L. Stewart & Manz, 1995).

B.3.3 • Leadership

Leadership is the art of getting someone else to do something you want done because he wants to do it.
—Dwight D. Eisenhower

leadership a social influence process in which a person steers others toward a goal

transformational leadership characterized by high ethical standards, inspirational motivation, intellectual stimulation, and individual consideration

Leadership has many definitions, including one person influencing another person or a team toward a goal (Bryman, 1996). Leadership has received a lot of research attention in industrial/organizational psychology. Yet it is still difficult to describe how to make or select the ideal or best leader. Many theories exist, and most have been useful in helping us understand what makes a good leader and how to improve leadership style.

Personality plays a role in many leadership theories. Certainly, it is an important aspect of successful or unsuccessful leaders. Kirkpatrick and Locke's (1991) review suggests that drive, honesty and integrity, self-confidence, cognitive abilities, and knowledge are associated with successful leaders. Leaders with poor cognitive abilities and social skills and those who are indecisive, low in self-confidence and self-esteem, dishonest, and lacking in ambition tend to be less successful (Kaplan, Drath, & Kofodimos, 1991).

Art Friedman's integrity likely made him a successful leader. He decided to give employees what he would want, providing them with the capabilities to make major decisions that could either make or break the organization. In his case, he created a self-managing group that had no need for external assistance from unions or other entities. As a result, Friedman demonstrated the *transformational leadership* approach (Bass, 1990). **Transformational leadership** is characterized by high ethical standards, inspirational motivation, intellectual stimulation, and individual consideration—all clearly evident in Friedman's leadership style.

Jim Goodnight, the CEO of SAS, has the philosophy that you should "treat employees like they make a difference and they will" (www.sas.com/jobs/corporate/index.html). Undoubtedly, his philosophy is working because SAS, even with the economic turbulence of the past several years, has continued to grow and has remained profitable. Other indicators include the company's number one ranking in 2010 by *Forbes* magazine, employee turnover of 2% in 2009 compared to the software industry average of 22%, and an employee average of only 2 sick days per year (there is no limit). Goodnight wants a balanced work and personal life for his employees so they work 35-hour workweeks with many of them setting

Amy Sussman/Getty Images for Discovery Communications

Oprah Winfrey is a modern-day charismatic leader. She is probably best known as host for 25 years of *Oprah*. In addition, she has started a television network (OWN), established *O* magazine, and created multiple charity groups, donating millions of dollars across the globe.

their own hours. He wants his employees to work well during their 7-hour days so his company tries to take care of inconveniences by having many services on-site (e.g., fitness center, day care, cafeteria, medical center). Employees rave about how great it is to work at SAS (Kaplan, 2010).

Leaders today must contend with information-based team environments requiring the capacity for sifting large amounts of information coming from computer networks (Avolio, Kahai, & Dodge, 2000). The widely varying working environments that result from global competition require leaders to be adaptable (Mann, 1959), capable of handling stress (Goleman, 1998), knowledgeable about competitors and products (Kirkpatrick & Locke, 1991), and able to solve complex problems quickly (Zaccaro et al., 2000). Leaders in organizations today also need to be concerned with human resources planning (the hiring and maintenance of an employee workforce) and the appropriate evaluation of employee performance to ensure their organizations will be competitive and profitable in the ensuing years.

B.3.4 • Performance Appraisal

performance appraisals the evaluations or reviews of employees' job performance

Performance appraisals are the evaluations or reviews of employees' performance. Employees should continually be told about their job performance, both the good and the bad, by their employers. Formal employee performance appraisals are times for management to systematically evaluate employee performance and productivity on the job, set performance goals, and directly convey information about the culture of the organization (see Fletcher & Perry, 2001, for a review of research and future trends in performance appraisal). Performance appraisals are important for many reasons, including (1) determining areas of employees' work needing improvement and areas to be complimented, (2) effectively managing employee raises and promotions, (3) dealing with unproductive employees in a fair and appropriate manner that may include termination, and (4) assisting in workforce planning that may be particularly important in difficult economic times but should be done routinely to have the best employees in the organization.

Performance appraisals vary in frequency, with some organizations evaluating new employees 30 or 60 days after hire while others evaluate new employees' performance 3 or 6 months after hire. Once an employee has been working for an organization for one year, most organizations formally evaluate performance annually or semiannually (Aamodt, 2010). A typical performance review consists of some type of form that is filled out by the employee's supervisor; some organizations have both the employee and the employer fill out the same form to allow them to compare their views of the employee's performance. This is followed by a meeting between the manager and the employee to discuss the employee's performance. This meeting should be held in a neutral, distraction-free location with an appropriate amount of time for discussion.

Performance review meetings should be conducted in a distraction-free, neutral location with a prepared and trained employer.

PM Images/Getty Images

Because the performance appraisal will often clearly define the most important components of employees' jobs and help shape the culture of the organization, it is recommended that employers provide performance appraisal forms to new employees when they are hired or on their first day of work. This will send a clear message to the employees about the work that is valued by the organization and about whether they will be evaluated according to criteria set by management (this may suggest a more collaborative or cooperative culture) or will be appraised relative to their coworkers (this may suggest a more competitive culture). It is in the best interest of both the employer (for performance management) and the employee (as a road map to success) that the job performance requirements be known at the time of hire. Once employees are hired who can complete the work tasks and be effective in the organization (that is, they have the ability to do the job), then their attitudes become important because their attitudes will directly influence their work behaviors.

B.3

Quiz Yourself

1. Spencer, a new employee of the company, has learned most of the behaviors required to do his job effectively. This would illustrate that Spencer has learned the _____ of the organization.
   a. organizational climate
   b. organizational culture
   c. transformational culture
   d. transformational climate
2. Performance appraisals are important because they _____.
   a. help define the culture of the organization
   b. provide employees needed information on their job performance
   c. aid employers in determining the type of training needed by their employees
   d. all of the above
3. Carol is part of a successful self-managing team in an organization that produces handcrafted furniture. Compared to her coworkers in traditional-leader teams, Carol and her work team should have _____.
   a. better productivity, lower work quality, and a decrease in absenteeism
   b. an increase in work quality, decrease in work quantity, and better quality of life
   c. an increase in absenteeism, lower work quality, and higher work quantity
   d. better productivity, better work quality, and a better quality of life

Answers 1. b; 2. d; 3. d

B.4 Employee Satisfaction: Attitudes and Behaviors at Work

One of the most important factors influencing whether you will be motivated to do a good job hinges on your *attitudes* and *behaviors* at work. The causes and consequences of work attitudes have been extensively researched. Some of the outcomes of attitudes include work behaviors such as volunteering for a project, helping out a coworker, quitting, absenteeism, tardiness, early retirement, and performance.

B.4.1 • Attitudes at Work

Attitudes at work are many and varied. In general, you can be satisfied or dissatisfied with the tasks and conditions at work, the people in your work environment, and the rewards you get from work. Employee satisfaction is important because it has been shown to be related to employee behaviors at work (Hanisch, 1995; Judge et al., 2001). Two of the most commonly studied work attitudes are *job satisfaction* and *organizational commitment*.

attitudes at work satisfaction with the work itself, pay and benefits, supervision, coworkers, promotion opportunities, working conditions, and job security

job satisfaction the positive or negative affect associated with a job

JOB SATISFACTION

The positive or negative feelings associated with a job define **job satisfaction** (Thurstone, 1931). Some of the ways organizations can create satisfied employees include flexible working hours, professional growth opportunities, interesting work (Hackman & Oldham, 1976), autonomy, job security, a good supervisor, good benefits, competitive pay, opportunities for promotion (Cranny, Smith, & Stone, 1992), respect, recognition, and being part of something or being included. It is important to note that what makes one worker satisfied may not make another worker satisfied. For some people, interesting work is paramount. Others place higher emphasis on having coworkers they like. Still others feel that the pay and benefits they receive are most important. Virtually all employees value recognition (some acknowledgment of their work), respect, and being part of the organization. These rewards are all inexpensive and typically require very little time to implement. Just as in selection, a match between what you want and what the organization can provide will result in a successful outcome for both parties.

ENGAGE YOURSELF! One measure often used to assess employee work attitudes, and specifically different facets of job satisfaction, is the *Job Descriptive Index* (JDI; P. C. Smith, Kendall, & Hulin, 1969). This index has been improved based on years of research (for example, Balzer et al., 1997; Hanisch, 1992). The JDI measures five facets of satisfaction: Work on Present Job, Supervisor, Coworkers, Present Pay, and Opportunities for Promotion. Try filling out the JDI Work on Present Job scale in • TABLE B.4.

A recent survey found that listening to music at work leads to higher levels of reported employee satisfaction. About one-third of those participating in a Spherion Workplace Snapshot survey conducted by Harris Interactive in 2006

TABLE B.4

Work on Present Job

Think of the work you do at present. How well does each of the following words or phrases describe your job? In the blank beside each word or phrase below, write:
Y for "Yes" if it describes your work
N for "No" if it does not describe your work
? if you cannot decide

____1. Fascinating	____6. Creative	___ 11. Tiring	___ 16. Simple
____2. Routine	____7. Respected	____12. Healthful	____17. Repetitive
____3. Satisfying	____8. Uncomfortable	____13. Challenging	____18. Gives sense of accomplishment
____4. Boring	____9. Pleasant	____14. Too much to do	
____5. Good	____10. Useful	____15. Frustrating	
Scoring Key:			
1. Y=3, N=0, ?=1;	6. Y=3, N=0, ?=1;	11. Y=0, N=3, ?=1;	16. Y=0, N=3, ?=1;
2. Y=0, N=3, ?=1;	7. Y=3, N=0, ?=1;	12. Y=3, N=0, ?=1;	17. Y=0, N=3, ?=1;
3. Y=3, N=0, ?=1;	8. Y=0, N=3, ?=1;	13. Y=3, N=0, ?=1;	18. Y=3, N=0, ?=1
4. Y=0, N=3, ?=1;	9. Y=3, N=0, ?=1;	14. Y=0, N=3, ?=1;	
5. Y=3, N=0, ?=1;	10. Y=3, N=0, ?=1;	15. Y=0, N=3, ?=1;	

To interpret your score on the work scale, 27 is considered the neutral value (Balzer et al., 1997). Values considerably higher would be evaluated as very satisfied; values considerably lower would be evaluated as very dissatisfied with the work on your present job.

reported they listened to an iPod or other personal music device while working (www.spherion.com). Seventy-nine percent of the participants reported that listening to music improved their job satisfaction or productivity or both at work. Allowing workers to listen to music may become more and more popular in jobs where music does not interfere with coworkers, safety, or job performance. Having happy workers contributes to an organization's success.

Digital Vision/Photolibrary

Employees report their job satisfaction and productivity increase if they are allowed privileges such as listening to music while they work.

ORGANIZATIONAL COMMITMENT

Employee commitment to an organization is related to employee retention within the organization. There are three types of organizational commitment: *affective, normative,* and *continuance* (Meyer & Allen, 1991). Meyer and Allen define **affective commitment** as an employee's emotional attachment to the organization that makes the employee want to stay in the organization. **Normative commitment** is based on feelings of obligation. **Continuance commitment** results when an employee remains with a company because of the high cost of losing organizational membership, including monetary (for example, pension benefits) and social (such as friendships) costs. Meyer and Herscovitch (2001) argue that employees have an organizational commitment profile at any given time in their job, with high or low values on each of the three types of commitment. In other words, an employee may have high scores on normative and continuance commitment, but be lower on affective commitment. Depending on the profile, the employee may engage in different behaviors such as quitting or helping out the organization.

Students may experience these different types of commitment to their college. Affective commitment occurs when a student feels an emotional attachment to her college because she really likes the school, including classes, the football team, and the town. Normative commitment might be evidenced by a student whose parent attended that college and who feels obligated to do the same regardless of whether it is the best school for him. Staying at a college because your friends are there and you have already paid for 2 years would typify acting under continuance commitment. The three levels of commitment could be represented as a commitment profile for a student.

Organizational commitment is related to job satisfaction. Employees who are satisfied with their job are more committed to their organization than are those who are less satisfied (Mosedeghrad, Ferlie, & Rosenberg, 2008; Mueller et al., 1994). Other correlates of organizational commitment include trust in one's supervisor and human resources practices that are supportive of employees (Arthur, 1994). The organizational commitment of Friedman's employees was very high, as evidenced by no turnover in 5 years; the low turnover at SAS also supports strong organizational commitment by its employees.

affective commitment an employee's emotional attachment to the organization

normative commitment commitment to the organization based on feelings of obligation

continuance commitment remaining with an organization because of the high cost (monetary or social or both) of losing organizational membership

B.4.2 • Behaviors at Work

Employers want their employees to engage in behaviors that will make them successful in the job because their success helps the organization meet its goals, including earning profits and fulfilling its mission. Employees have control over two aspects of their work: their time and their effort (Naylor, Pritchard, & Ilgen, 1980). Having employees at work instead of late or absent as well as exerting effort while at work are important to performance and productivity. Positive behaviors such as *organizational citizenship behaviors* generally help an organization meet its goals while negative behaviors such as *organizational withdrawal* and *counterproductive behaviors* detract from goal attainment.

organizational citizenship behaviors (OCBs) employee behaviors that go beyond what is expected by the organization

organizational withdrawal work withdrawal or job withdrawal

work withdrawal behaviors employees use to avoid their work (e.g., lateness, absenteeism)

job withdrawal behaviors employees use to avoid their job (e.g., quitting, retiring)

counterproductive behaviors intentional behaviors on the part of an organizational member viewed by the organization as contrary to its legitimate interests

ORGANIZATIONAL CITIZENSHIP BEHAVIORS

Organizational citizenship behaviors (OCBs), or prosocial behaviors, are often described as extra-role behaviors because they are behaviors not specifically required by the job and not usually evaluated during performance reviews. These behaviors go beyond what is expected by the organization (C. A. Smith, Organ, & Near, 1983). Examples include staying late to finish a project, mentoring a new employee, volunteering for work, and helping a coworker. Some reasons why people engage in organizational citizenship behaviors are job satisfaction, high job autonomy, a positive organizational culture, high agreeableness (as a personality dimension; Witt et al., 2002), and high conscientiousness (Borman et al., 2001). OCBs have positive consequences for the organization and for employees in their day-to-day interactions with others in the organization.

ORGANIZATIONAL WITHDRAWAL AND COUNTERPRODUCTIVE BEHAVIORS

Unhappy employees cause problems for organizations because they sometimes engage in behaviors that researchers refer to as *organizational withdrawal* and *counterproductive* behaviors. **Organizational withdrawal** has been defined as behaviors employees use to avoid their work (**work withdrawal**) or their job (**job withdrawal**) (Hanisch, 1995; Hanisch & Hulin, 1990, 1991). Examples of work withdrawal are being absent from work, leaving work early, arriving to work late, missing meetings, and using work equipment for personal use without permission. Examples of job withdrawal are quitting one's job, transferring to another department within an organization, and retiring.

College students are familiar with withdrawal behaviors when it comes to certain college courses. Some classes may fail to keep your attention, and you may find yourself taking a nap in class or texting with a friend during lecture. You may even look for legitimate reasons not to attend class, such as offering to fill in for another employee at work or deciding to attend an optional session for another class.

Counterproductive behaviors, although similar in some ways to withdrawal behaviors, are defined as "any intentional behavior on the part of an organizational member viewed by the organization as contrary to its legitimate interests" (Sackett & DeVore, 2001). An example of a counterproductive behavior would be an intentional violation of safety procedures that puts the employee and the organization at risk. Other examples of counterproductive behavior are theft, destruction of property, unsafe behavior, poor attendance, drug use, and inappropriate physical actions such as attacking a coworker.

B.4.3 • Relation Between Attitude and Behavior

Organizational citizenship behaviors are positively related to job satisfaction and organizational commitment. In other words, employees with good attitudes and who feel committed to their organization are more likely to do positive things to assist the organization (LePine, Erez, & Johnson, 2002; Riketta, 2008). Research indicates that those employees who demonstrate organizational citizenship behaviors are less likely to engage in counterproductive behaviors (Dalal, 2005). Some research indicates a negative association between job satisfaction and specific withdrawal or counterproductive behaviors such as absenteeism, and job withdrawal (Falkenburg & Schyns, 2007; Hackett, 1989; Hanisch & Hulin, 1990).

Employers need to evaluate their work environment and benefit packages and make modifications where necessary to ensure that they have employees who are satisfied and committed. Art Friedman made modifications in the work environment of his organization that resulted in high satisfaction and commitment among his employees. To help with the inconvenience of going to the doctor, SAS built an on-site medical center for employees and their families; there is no charge unless you fail to show up for an appointment (Kaplan, 2010). Employees need to learn how to seek out satisfying work and perks that will result in their commitment to the organization. Satisfaction and commitment facilitate OCBs and decrease withdrawal and counterproductive behaviors. Together the right employee attitudes and behaviors will lead to successful organizational functioning.

B.4

Quiz Yourself

1. **Quitting one's job would be an example of _____.**
   a. normative commitment
   b. job withdrawal
   c. organizational citizenship behavior
   d. work withdrawal
2. **_____ would be an example of an organizational citizenship behavior while _____ would be an example of a counterproductive behavior.**
   a. Mentoring a new employee; engaging in safe work practices
   b. Being late; staying late to help a coworker
   c. Missing a meeting; being late for work
   d. Volunteering to serve on a committee; physically attacking your supervisor
3. **Gordon's organizational commitment has been decreasing in the last year. Which of the following is Gordon *most* likely to do if his organizational commitment doesn't improve soon?**
   a. quit
   b. be absent
   c. ask for a raise
   d. steal from the organization

Answers 1. b; 2. d; 3. a

B.5 Summary

This appendix has described the role of I/O psychologists in the workplace, including job analysis, employee recruitment and selection, organizational culture, performance appraisal, and the effect of employees' work attitudes on their work behaviors.

Now that you have an understanding of the process organizations use to hire successful employees, you have some of the tools necessary to help you in your search for a job. You have also learned about the appropriate matches you might strive for in seeking employment that will make your work with an organization fulfilling for both you and the company.

If you enjoyed learning about I/O psychology and think it might be a possible career for you, education and employment opportunities may interest you. Most I/O psychologists earn a master's or doctoral degree from a graduate school. This may take an additional 2 to 5 years beyond a bachelor's degree. Job opportunities are varied and often lucrative. For example, people with master's degrees in I/O psychology may work for an organization in its human resources office or conduct research on the best ways to train its employees. They may also work for the government, be employed in a consulting firm, or start their own consulting firm after obtaining some experience in the workplace. Those who earn a doctoral degree may secure the same types of jobs as those with master's degrees, but will typically be paid more for their expertise. In addition, they may work for a university or college teaching courses or conducting research on topics of their choosing, or both. I/O psychology is an excellent career choice for many students interested in business who wish to have an impact on the work lives of employees.

Studying the Appendix

Key Terms

affective commitment (663)
attitudes at work (661)
"can-do" factors (656)
continuance commitment (663)
counterproductive behaviors (664)
industrial and organizational (I/O) psychology (649)
job analysis (653)
job satisfaction (661)
job withdrawal (664)
leadership (659)
mentoring (658)
normative commitment (663)
organizational citizenship behaviors (OCBs) (664)
organizational climate (658)
organizational culture (658)
organizational socialization (657)
organizational withdrawal (664)
performance appraisals (660)
recruitment (655)
structured interview (653)
test (653)
Title VII of the Civil Rights Act of 1964 (654)
transformational leadership (659)
unstructured interview (653)
"will-do" factors (656)
work teams/groups (658)
work withdrawal (664)

What Do You Know? Assess Your Understanding

Test your retention and understanding of the material by answering the following questions.

1. Industrial and organizational psychologists may be employed in _____.

a. organizations
b. universities
c. government agencies
d. all of the above

2. On Sharon's first day working for the Campbell Company, she will most likely be required to attend _____.

a. diversity training
b. safety training
c. employee orientation training
d. job rotation training

3. Mentoring of new employees, in general, has been found to have positive outcomes or consequences for _____.

a. both the mentor and the employee
b. the mentor
c. the employee
d. organizations with autocratic leaders

4. Structured interviews are better than unstructured interviews because they are _____.

a. easier to conduct
b. more valid and reliable
c. liked better by job applicants
d. less time-consuming

5. Giving new employees a copy of their performance appraisal forms would be important in helping to _____.

a. determine employees' organizational citizenship behaviors
b. shape the culture and climate of the organization
c. determine employees' organizational withdrawal behaviors
d. increase affective commitment

6. SAS has company picnics and provides tickets to rodeos and the circus to help employees with the process of _____.

a. organizational withdrawal
b. organizational socialization
c. organizational transformation
d. organizational productivity

7. Todd stays late to help a coworker who has gotten behind in his work. Todd is exhibiting which type of behavior?

a. work withdrawal
b. productive behavior
c. organizational citizenship behavior
d. job withdrawal

8. The employees of SAS believe they have a great place to work with a fair employer and a trusting environment. In I/O psychology terms, they have a positive _____.

a. organizational culture
b. organizational climate
c. work-group climate
d. transformational leader

9. Don has been offered a position in another company that pays better and has a more liberal leave policy than his current company. He is having a hard time deciding whether to accept the position because his current company has given him a lot of time off to care for his mother. Don's decision-making problem is likely due to his _____.

a. normative commitment
b. occupational commitment
c. affective commitment
d. continuance commitment

10. Howard refers Lucille for a position in his organization. Based on research on employee referral programs, Lucille should _____.

a. be more satisfied with her job
b. be a poor performer
c. file fewer grievances with the company
d. stay longer with the organization

Answers: 1. d; 2. c; 3. a; 4. b; 5. b; 6. b; 7. c; 8. a; 9. a; 10. d

Glossary

absolute threshold the minimum intensity of a stimulus at which participants can identify its presence 50% of the time

accommodation [uh-com-muh-DAY-shun] Chap. 3: the process through which the lens is stretched or squeezed to focus light on the retina; Chap. 9: the process by which a schema is changed, modified, or created anew in order to understand something new in the environment

acetylcholine [uh-see-til-COE-leen] (ACh) a neurotransmitter related to muscle movement and perhaps consciousness, learning, and memory

acquisition the process of learning a conditioned response or behavior

action potential a neural impulse fired by a neuron when it reaches −55 mv

activation-synthesis theory suggests that dreams do not have symbolic meaning, but are the by-product of the brain's random firing of neural impulses during REM sleep

actor/observer bias our tendency to make the fundamental attribution error when judging others, while being less likely to do so when making attributions about ourselves

actualizing [ACK-shu-lies-ing] tendency according to Rogers, the natural drive in humans to strive for fulfillment and enhancement

adrenal [uh-DREEN-ull] cortex the outside part of the adrenal gland that plays a role in the manufacture and release of androgens, and therefore influences sexual characteristics

adrenal [uh-DREEN-ull] medulla the center part of the adrenal gland that plays a crucial role in the functioning of the sympathetic nervous system

affective commitment an employee's emotional attachment to the organization

affective component of emotion the subjective experience of what you are feeling during the emotion

agoraphobia [agg-or-uh-FOE-bee-uh] an excessive fear of being in places from which escape might be difficult or where help might not be available if one were to experience panic

alarm reaction the first phase of the general adaptation syndrome, characterized by immediate activation of the nervous and endocrine systems

algorithm [AL-go-rih-thum] a method of solving a particular problem that always leads to the correct solution

all-or-none fashion all action potentials are equal in strength; once a neuron begins to fire an action potential, it fires all the way down the axon

alogia [uh-LO-jeeuh] a negative symptom of schizophrenia involving decreased quality and/or quantity of speech

alternative hypothesis (H_1) the hypothesis that contains a statement of what we do believe is true about our variables in the population

altruism helping another without being motivated by self-gain

amplitude a physical property of some energies that corresponds to the height of wave peaks

amygdala [uh-MIG-duh-luh] part of the limbic system that plays a role in the emotions of fear and aggression

anal stage Freud's second psychosexual stage, which occurs from approximately 18 months to 3 years of age, in which the parents' regulation of the child's biological urge to expel or retain feces affects personality development

androgens [ANN-dro-jens] a class of male hormones that regulate many aspects of sexuality and are found in both males and females

anorexia [an-or-EX-ee-uh] nervosa an eating disorder in which a person has an intense fear of gaining weight, even though he or she is actually underweight; this irrational fear motivates the person to lose unhealthy amounts of weight through self-starvation

anterograde [an-TARE-oh-grade] amnesia a type of amnesia in which one is unable to store new memories in long-term memory

antianxiety medications minor tranquilizers such as Valium that are prescribed to reduce tension and anxiety

antidepressants medications prescribed to alleviate the symptoms of depression, eating disorders, and some anxiety disorders

antimanic medications drugs that are prescribed to alleviate manic symptoms of bipolar disorder

antipsychotic medications major tranquilizers such as Haldol that are prescribed to relieve psychotic symptoms such as delusions and hallucinations

antisocial personality disorder a personality disorder marked by a pattern of disregard for and violation of the rights of others with no remorse or guilt for one's actions

anxiety hierarchy a list that orders, according to the degree of fear, the situations or items that trigger anxiety; the list starts with the least frightening images and progresses to the most distressing

approach–approach conflict a situation in which a person must choose between two likable events

approach–avoidance conflict a situation in which a person is faced with a desire or need that has both positive and negative aspects

archetypes [ARE-kuh-types] according to Jung, mental representations or symbols of themes and predispositions to respond to the world in a certain way that are contained in the collective unconscious

assimilation [uh-sim-uh-LAY-shun] the process by which an existing schema is used to understand something new in the environment

association cortex areas of the cortex involved in the association or integration of information from the motor-sensory areas of the cortex

attachment the emotional bond between caretaker and infant that is established by 8 or 9 months

attention conscious awareness; can be focused on events that are taking place in the environment or inside our minds

attitude an evaluative belief that we hold about something

attitudes at work satisfaction with the work itself, pay and benefits, supervision, coworkers, promotion opportunities, working conditions, and job security

attribution the act of assigning cause to behavior

auditory cortex a region of cortex found in the temporal lobe that governs the processing of auditory information in the brain

auditory nerve the nerve that carries information from the inner ear to the brain

authoritarian [ah-thor-uh-TARE-ee-an] parent a parenting style characterized by high levels of control and low levels of affection

authoritative [ah-thor-uh-TAY-tive] parent a parenting style characterized by moderate levels of control and affection

autobiographical memory memory for our past that gives us a sense of personal history

autonomic nervous system the branch of the peripheral nervous system that primarily governs involuntary organ functioning and actions in the body

availability heuristic a heuristic in which we use the ease with which we can recall instances of an event to help us estimate the frequency of the event

aversion [uh-VER-shun] therapy a type of therapy that uses classical conditioning to condition people to avoid certain stimuli

aversive racism a proposed form of subtle racism in which European Americans feel aversive emotions around African Americans, which may lead them to discriminate against African Americans

avoidance–avoidance conflict a situation in which a person must choose between two undesirable events

avolition [AA-vuh-lish-un] a negative symptom of schizophrenia marked by the inability to follow through on one's plans

axon [AXE-on] a long tail-like structure growing out of the cell body of a neuron that carries action potentials that convey information from the cell body to the synapse

babbling the combinations of vowel and consonant sounds uttered by infants beginning around 4 months

basal metabolic rate the rate at which we burn energy in our bodies when resting

basic anxiety according to Horney, the feeling of helplessness that develops in children from early relationships

basic emotions a proposed set of innate emotions that are common to all humans and from which other higher-order emotions may derive

basic level category the intermediate level of categorization that seems to be the level that we use most to think about our world

basilar membrane the structure in the cochlear duct that contains the hair cells, which convert sound waves into action potentials

behavior therapy therapy that applies the principles of classical and operant conditioning to help people change maladaptive behaviors

behavioral genetics field of study that examines the influence of genetics and hereditary factors on personality traits

behavioral perspective an approach that focuses on external, environmental influences on behavior

behaviorism a psychological perspective that emphasizes the study of observable responses and behavior
bereavement [bee-REEVE-munt] the experience of losing a loved one
binge eating disorder an eating disorder characterized by recurrent episodes of binge eating, as in bulimia nervosa, but without regular use of compensatory measures to avoid weight gain
binocular [bye-NOCK-you-lar] depth cues depth cues that utilize information from both eyes
biological perspective an approach that focuses on physical causes of behavior
biological preparedness a genetic tendency to learn certain responses very easily
biomedical therapy the use of medications or other medical interventions to treat mental health disorders
bipolar disorder a mood disorder characterized by both depression and mania
bisexual one who is sexually attracted to members of both sexes
blindspot the point where the optic nerve leaves the retina, the optic disk, where there are no rods or cones
blunted affect a negative symptom of schizophrenia involving lack of emotional expression
borderline personality disorder (BPD) a personality disorder marked by a pattern of instability in mood, relationships, self-image, and behavior
bottom-up perceptual processing perception that is not guided by prior knowledge or expectations
brightness the intensity of light; it corresponds to the amplitude of the light waves
Broca's [BRO-kuz] aphasia [ah-FAYZ-yah] a condition resulting from damage to Broca's area of the brain that leaves the person unable to produce speech.
Broca's [BRO-kuz] area a region in the left frontal lobe that plays a role in the production of speech
bulimia nervosa an eating disorder in which a person alternately binges on large quantities of food and then engages in some inappropriate compensatory behavior to avoid weight gain
bystander effect the idea that the more witnesses there are to an emergency, the less likely any one of them is to offer help
"can-do" factors factors that determine the maximum performance an employee can exhibit
Cannon-Bard theory a theory of emotion that states that emotions originate in the brain, not the body
cardinal traits according to Allport, those dominant elements of our personalities that drive all of our behaviors
case study an in-depth observation of one participant
catatonic [cat-uh-TAWN-ick] excitement a positive symptom of schizophrenia marked by disorder in motor behavior involving excited agitation
catatonic [cat-uh-TAWN-ick] stupor a positive symptom of schizophrenia marked by disorder in motor behavior involving immobility
causal hypothesis an educated guess about how one variable will influence another variable
cell body the part of the neuron that contains the nucleus and DNA
central executive the attention-controlling component of working memory
central nervous system (CNS) the brain and the spinal cord
central route to persuasion a style of thinking in which the person carefully and critically evaluates persuasive arguments and generates counterarguments; the central route requires motivation and available cognitive resources
central traits according to Allport, the tendencies we have to behave in a certain way across most situations
centration the act of focusing on only one aspect or feature of an object
cerebellum the hindbrain structure that plays a role in balance, muscle tone, and coordination of motor movements
cerebral cortex the thin, wrinkled outer covering of the brain in which high-level processes such as thinking, planning, language, interpretation of sensory data, and coordination of sensory and motor information take place
cerebral hemispheres the right and left sides of the brain that to some degree govern different functions in the body
cholecystokinin [coe-lih-cyst-oh-KYE-nin] (CCK) a hormone released by the small intestines that plays a role in hunger regulation
chunking a means of using one's limited short-term memory resources more efficiently by combining small bits of information to form larger bits of information, or chunks
circadian rhythm [sir-KAY-dee-un RI-thum] changes in bodily processes that occur repeatedly on approximately a 24- to 25-hour cycle
classical conditioning learning that occurs when a neutral stimulus is repeatedly paired with an unconditioned stimulus; because of this pairing, the neutral stimulus becomes a conditioned stimulus with the same power as the unconditioned stimulus to elicit the response in the organism
client-centered therapy a humanistic psychotherapy approach formulated by Carl Rogers that emphasizes the use of empathy, genuineness, and unconditional positive regard to help the client reach his or her potential
clinical interview the initial meeting between a client and a clinician in which the clinician asks questions to identify the difficulty in functioning that the person is experiencing
closure a Gestalt principle of perception that states that when we look at a stimulus, we tend to see it as a closed shape rather than lines
cochlea [COCK-lee-uh] the curled, fluid-filled tube in the inner ear that contains the basilar membrane
cognition the way in which we use and store information in memory
cognitive-behavior therapy (CBT) a range of treatment approaches to alter faulty cognitions and maladaptive behaviors
cognitive consistency the idea that we strive to have attitudes and behaviors that do not contradict one another
cognitive distortion Chap. 13: thought that tends to be pessimistic and negative; Chap. 14: distorted thinking patterns, such as overgeneralization or all-or-none thinking, that, according to Aaron Beck, lead to depression, anxiety, and low self-esteem
cognitive map a mental representation of the environment that is formed through observation of one's environment
cognitive-mediational theory a theory of emotion that states that our cognitive appraisal of a situation determines what emotion we will feel in the situation
cognitive neoassociation theory proposes that cues present during an aggressive event can become associated in memory with the thoughts and emotions experienced during that event
cognitive perspective an approach that focuses on how mental processes influence behavior
cognitive psychology the study of mental processes such as reasoning and problem solving
cognitive reappraisal [re-uh-PRAY-zull] an active and conscious process in which we alter our interpretation of a stressful event
cognitive therapy a therapy created by Aaron Beck that focuses on uncovering negative automatic thought patterns that impede mental health
cohesiveness [coe-HEE-siv-ness] the degree to which members of a group value their group membership; cohesive groups are tight-knit groups
collective unconscious according to Jung, the part of the unconscious that contains images and material universal to people of all time periods and cultures
collectivistic culture a culture, like many Asian cultures, in which group accomplishments are valued over individual accomplishments
color blindness a condition in which a person cannot perceive one or more colors because of altered cone activity in the retina
compliance yielding to a simple request
compulsion repetitive behavior that a person feels a strong urge to perform
concept a mental category that contains related bits of knowledge
concrete operations Piaget's third stage of cognitive development, characterized by logical thought
conditioned response (CR) the response that is elicited by a conditioned stimulus
conditioned stimulus (CS) a stimulus that elicits a conditioned response in an organism
cones the cells of the retina that are sensitive to specific colors of light and send information to the brain concerning the colors we are seeing
confidentiality ethical principle that researchers do not reveal which data were collected from which participant
conflict a situation in which a person must choose between two or more needs, desires, or demands
conformity behaving in accordance with group norms
confounding variable any factor other than the independent variable that affects the dependent measure
conscious [CON-shus] level the level of consciousness that holds all the thoughts, perceptions, and impulses of which we are aware
consciousness [CON-shis-nus] feelings, thoughts, and aroused states of which we are aware
conservation the understanding that an object retains its original properties even though it may look different
constructive memory memory that utilizes knowledge and expectations to fill in the missing details in retrieved memory traces
contact hypothesis the theory that contact between groups is an effective means of reducing prejudice between them
contiguity [con-teh-GYU-eh-tee] the degree to which two stimuli occur close together in time
contingency [con-TINGE-en-see] the degree to which the presentation of one stimulus reliably predicts the presentation of the other stimulus
continuance commitment remaining with an organization because of the high cost (monetary or social or both) of losing organizational membership
continuous reinforcement a schedule of reinforcement in which the organism is rewarded for every instance of the desired response

control group the group of participants who do not receive the manipulation that is being tested
cooing the vowel sounds made by infants beginning at 2 months
coping the behaviors that we engage in to manage stressors
cornea [COR-nee-ah] the clear, slightly bulging outer surface of the eye that both protects the eye and begins the focusing process
corpus callosum [COR-puss cal-OH-sum] a thick band of neurons that connects the right and left hemispheres of the brain
correlation [cor-ruh-LAY-shun] the relationship between two or more variables
correlation coefficient the average product of z scores calculated on pairs of scores; describes the degree to which the scores in the pairs are linearly related
counterproductive behaviors intentional behaviors on the part of an organizational member viewed by the organization as contrary to its legitimate interests
couple therapy therapy that focuses on improving communication and intimacy between two people in a committed relationship
covert sensitization [co-VERT sen-sih-tuh-ZAY-shun] therapy a milder form of aversion therapy in which graphic imagery is used to create unpleasant associations with specific stimuli
creativity the ability to combine mental elements in new and useful ways
critical thinking thought processes used to evaluate and analyze information and apply it to other situations
crystallized intelligence abilities that rely on knowledge, expertise, and judgment
cue-dependent forgetting a type of forgetting that occurs when one cannot recall information in a context other than the context in which it was encoded
cultural bias the degree to which a test puts people from other cultures at an unfair disadvantage because of the culturally specific nature of the test items
cycle a physical characteristic of energy defined as a wave peak and the valley that immediately follows it
cyclothymic [sigh-clo-THIGH-mik] disorder a mood disorder that is a less severe but more chronic form of bipolar disorder
daily hassles the everyday irritations and frustrations that individuals face
dark adaptation the process through which our eyes adjust to dark conditions after having been exposed to bright light
data information gathered in scientific studies
debriefing the ethical principle that after participating in an experiment involving deception participants be fully informed of the nature of the study
decay theory a theory of forgetting that proposes that memory traces that are not routinely activated in long-term memory will degrade
decibels [DESS-uh-bells] (dB) the unit of measurement used to determine the loudness of a sound
decision making making a choice from among a series of alternatives
declarative memory a type of long-term memory encompassing memories that are easily verbalized, including episodic and semantic memories
deductive reasoning reasoning from the general to the specific
defense mechanisms Chap. 11: a process used to protect the ego by reducing the anxiety it feels when faced with the conflicting demands of the id and the superego; Chap. 12: unconscious, emotional strategies that are engaged in to reduce anxiety and maintain a positive self-image
deindividuation [DEE-in-dih-vid-you-AYE-shun] a state in which a person's behavior becomes controlled more by external norms than by the person's own internal values and morals
delusion a thought or belief that a person believes to be true but in reality is not
dendrites [DEN-drights] branchlike structures on the head of the neuron that receive incoming signals from other neurons in the nervous system
dependent variable the variable in an experiment that measures any effect of the manipulation
depressants drugs that inhibit or slow down normal neural functioning
dermis the inner layer of the skin
descriptive statistics statistics that are calculated to summarize or describe certain aspects of a data set
destructive obedience obedience to immoral, unethical demands that cause harm to others
development changes in behavior or abilities or both
Diagnostic and Statistical Manual of Mental Disorders (DSM) a book published by the American Psychiatric Association that lists the criteria for close to 300 mental health disorders
diffusion of responsibility the idea that responsibility for taking action is diffused across all the people witnessing an event
discrimination the behavioral expression of a prejudice
dishabituation [DIS-huh-bit-chew-AYE-shun] re-responding to a stimulus to which one has been habituated
disordered behavior a positive symptom of schizophrenia that includes inappropriate or unusual behavior such as silliness, catatonic excitement, or catatonic stupor
disorganized speech a positive symptom of schizophrenia in which one's speech lacks association between one's ideas and the events that one is experiencing
display rules cultural rules governing when it is and isn't appropriate to display certain emotions
dissociation [dis-so-see-AYE-shun] theory Hilgard's proposal that hypnosis involves two simultaneous states: a hypnotic state and a hidden observer
dissociative [dih-SO-shee-tive] disorder a mental health disorder marked by a loss of awareness of some part of one's self or one's surroundings that seriously interferes with the person's ability to function
dissociative identity disorder (DID) a disorder in which two or more personalities coexist within the same individual; formerly called multiple personality disorder
dissonance theory a theory that predicts that we will be motivated to change our attitudes and/or our behaviors to the extent that they cause us to feel dissonance, an uncomfortable physical state
DNA the chemical found in the nuclei of cells that contains the genetic blueprint that guides development in the organism
door-in-the-face compliance increasing compliance by first asking people to give in to a very large request and then, after they refuse, asking them to give in to a smaller request
dopamine [DOPE-uh-mean] a neurotransmitter that plays a role in movement, motivation, learning, and attention
double-blind study an experiment in which neither the experimenters nor the participants know to which group (experimental or control) participants have been assigned
Down syndrome a genetic birth disorder resulting from an extra 21st chromosome, characterized by distinct facial features and a greater likelihood of heart defects and intellectual disability
dream analysis a technique in psychoanalysis in which the therapist examines the hidden symbols in a client's dreams
drive an uncomfortable internal state that motivates us to reduce this discomfort through our behavior
drive reduction theory a theory of motivation that proposes that people seek to reduce internal levels of drive
dual coding system a system of memory that encodes information in more than one type of code or format
dualistic [do-uhl-LIS-tik] thinking reasoning that divides situations and issues into right and wrong categories
duplicity theory a theory that proposes that a combination of volley and place theory explains how our brain decodes pitch
eclectic [ee-KLECK-tic] approach an approach that integrates and combines several perspectives when explaining behavior
eclectic [ee-KLECK-tick] therapy approach therapy that incorporates an integrated and diverse use of therapeutic methods
ego the conscious part of the personality that attempts to meet the demands of the id in a socially appropriate way
egocentrism [ee-go-SEN-trih-zum] the belief that everyone thinks as you do
elaborative rehearsal forming associations or links between information one is trying to learn and information already stored in long-term memory so as to facilitate the transfer of this new information into long-term memory
Electra complex in the female, an unconscious sexual urge for the father that develops during the phallic psychosexual stage
electroconvulsive therapy (ECT) a series of treatments in which electrical current is passed through the brain, causing a seizure; used to alleviate severe depression
embryonic [em-bree-AH-nik] stage the second stage of prenatal development, lasting from the 3rd through the 8th week
emerging adulthood the transitional period between late adolescence and the mid-20s when young people have left adolescence but have not yet assumed adult roles and responsibilities
emotion a complex reaction to some internal or external event that involves physiological reactions, behavioral reactions, facial expressions, cognition, and affective responses
emotion-focused coping behaviors aimed at controlling the internal emotional reactions to a stressor
emotional stability having control over one's emotions
empathy the ability of a therapist to understand a client's feelings and thoughts without being judgmental
encoding the act of inputting information into memory
endocrine [EN-doe-crin] glands organs of the endocrine system that produce and release hormones into the blood
endocrine [EN-doe-crin] system a chemical system of communication in the body that uses chemical messengers, called hormones, to affect organ function and behavior
endorphins [in-DOOR-fins] neurotransmitters that act as a natural painkiller
enuresis [en-your-REE-sus] a condition in which a person over the age of 5 shows an inability to control urination during sleep
epidermis the outer layer of the skin
episodic [epp-uh-SOD-ick] memory memory for the recent events in our lives

erogenous [eh-ROJ-en-ous] zones areas of the skin that are sensitive to touch
estrogens [ESS-tro-jens] a class of female sex hormones that regulate many aspects of sexuality and are found in both males and females
evolutionary perspective an approach that focuses on how evolution and natural selection influence behavior
excitation when a neurotransmitter makes the postsynaptic cell more positive inside, it becomes more likely to fire an action potential
excitement phase the first stage of the sexual response cycle, in which males get erections and females produce vaginal lubrication
exemplar [ig-ZEM-plar] a mental representation of an actual instance of a member of a category
exhaustion stage the third and final phase of the general adaptation syndrome, in which bodily resources are drained and wear and tear on the body begins
experiment a research method that is used to test causal hypotheses
experimental group the group of participants who receive the manipulation that is being tested
explicit memory the conscious use of memory
extinction the removal of a conditioned response
extinction burst a temporary increase in a behavioral response that occurs immediately after extinction has begun
extrasensory perception (ESP) also known as *psi*, the purported ability to acquire information about the world without using the known senses
extraversion [ex-tra-VER-shun] personality traits that involve energy directed outward, such as being easygoing, lively, or excitable
extrinsic motivation motivation that comes from outside the person
eye movement desensitization and reprocessing (EMDR) therapy an eclectic therapy approach to treat trauma in which the client attends to emotionally disturbing images while simultaneously focusing on an external stimulus
facial feedback hypothesis a theory that states that our emotional state is affected by the feedback our brain gets from facial muscles
family therapy therapy that focuses on creating balance and restoring harmony to improve the functioning of the family as a whole system
feature detection theory a theory of perception that proposes that we have specialized cells in the visual cortex, feature detectors, that fire only when they receive input that indicates we are looking at a particular shape, color, angle, or other visual feature
fetal alcohol syndrome (FAS) a birth condition resulting from the mother's chronic use of alcohol during pregnancy that is characterized by facial and limb deformities and intellectual disability
fetal stage the third stage of prenatal development from the 9th week through the 9th month
figure–ground a Gestalt principle of perception that states that when we perceive a stimulus, we visually pull the figure part of the stimulus forward while visually pushing backward the background, or ground, part of the stimulus
fine motor skills motor behaviors involving the small muscles of the body
five-factor theory Costa and McCrae's trait theory that proposes five core dimensions to personality: openness, conscientiousness, extraversion, agreeableness, and neuroticism
fixed interval schedule a schedule of reinforcement in which the organism is rewarded for the first desired response in an *x*th interval of time
fixed ratio schedule a schedule of reinforcement in which the organism is rewarded for every *x*th instance of the desired response
flashbulb memory an unusually detailed and seemingly accurate memory for an emotionally charged event
flooding a behavior therapy technique in which a client is exposed to a feared object or situation for a prolonged period until his or her anxiety extinguishes
fluid intelligence abilities that rely on information-processing skills such as reaction time, attention, and working memory
foot-in-the-door compliance increasing compliance by first asking people to give in to a small request, which then paves the way for compliance with a second, larger request
forebrain brain structures, including the limbic system, thalamus, hypothalamus, and cortex, that govern higher-order mental processes
forgetting curve a graph of the amount of learned information that is forgotten over time
formal concept a concept that is based on learned, rigid rules that define certain categories of things
formal operations Piaget's final stage of cognitive development, characterized by the ability to engage in abstract thought
free association a technique in psychoanalysis in which the client says whatever comes to mind
frequency a physical characteristic of energy defined as the number of cycles that occur in a given unit of time
frequency distribution a graph of data that plots the frequency of data points on the *y*-axis and the data points themselves on the *x*-axis
frequency polygon a line graph that is used to illustrate a frequency distribution
frequency theory a theory that proposes that our brain decodes pitch directly from the frequency at which the hair cells of the basilar membrane are firing
frontal lobe cortical area directly behind the forehead that plays a role in thinking, planning, decision making, language, and motor movement
frustration-aggression hypothesis the idea that frustration causes aggressive behavior
functional fixedness being able to see objects only in their familiar roles
functionalism an early psychological perspective concerned with how behavior helps people adapt to their environment
fundamental attribution error our tendency to overuse trait information when making attributions about others
gamma amino butyric [GAM-ma uh-MEAN-oh bee-you-TREE-ick] acid (GABA) the body's chief inhibitory neurotransmitter, which plays a role in regulating arousal
gender permanence the understanding that one's gender will not change
gender roles society's expectations for how males and females should behave
gender-schema theory the idea that gender roles are acquired through modeling and reinforcement processes that work together with a child's mental abilities
general adaptation syndrome (GAS) the general physical responses we experience when faced with a stressor
general intelligence (*g*) Charles Spearman's notion that there is a general level of intelligence that underlies our separate abilities
generalizability [jen-er-uh-lies-uh-BILL-uh-tee] how well a researcher's findings apply to other individuals and situations
generalized anxiety disorder (GAD) an anxiety disorder characterized by chronic, constant worry in almost all situations
genes strands of DNA found in the nuclei of all living cells
genital stage Freud's final psychosexual stage of development, which begins at puberty, in which sexual energy is transferred toward peers of the other sex (heterosexual orientation) or same sex (homosexual orientation)
genotype [JEAN-oh-type] inherited genetic pattern for a given trait
genuineness the ability of a therapist to openly share his or her thoughts and feelings with a client
germinal stage the first stage of prenatal development, from conception to 14 days
Gestalt [gush-TALLT] approach a psychological school of thought originating in Germany that proposed that the whole of a perception must be understood rather than trying to deconstruct perception into its parts
ghrelin [GRELL-in] a hunger-stimulating hormone produced by the stomach
glia [GLEE-uh] cells brain cells that provide important support functions for the neurons and are involved in the formation of myelin
glucose the form of sugar that the body burns as fuel
glutamate [GLUE-tuh-mate] the chief excitatory neurotransmitter in the brain, found at more than 50% of the synapses in the brain
glycogen [GLIE-co-jen] a starchy molecule that is produced from excess glucose in the body; it can be thought of as the body's stored energy reserves
gonads [go-NADS] endocrine glands that directly affect sexual reproduction by producing sperm (testes) or eggs (ovaries)
good continuation a Gestalt principle of perception that states that we have a preference for perceiving stimuli that seem to follow one another as part of a continuing pattern
grammar the rules that govern the sentence structure in a particular language
graph a visual depiction of data
grief one's emotional reaction to the death of a loved one
gross motor skills motor behaviors involving the large muscles of the body
group therapy therapy that is administered to more than one person at a time
groupthink a situation in which a group fixates on one decision and members blindly assume that it is the correct decision
guided imagery a technique in which you focus on a pleasant, calming image to achieve a state of relaxation when you feel stressed
gustation [gus-TAY-shun] the sense of taste
habituation [huh-bit-chew-AYE-shun] the tendency of an organism to ignore repeated stimuli
hair cells neurons that grow out of the basilar membrane and convert sound waves into action potentials
hallucination perceiving something that does not exist in reality
hallucinogens [huh-LOO-sin-no-gens] drugs that simultaneously excite and inhibit normal neural activity, thereby causing distortions in perception
hardy personality a personality, high in the traits of commitment, control, and challenge, that appears to be associated with strong stress resistance
health psychology the subfield of psychology that investigates the relationship between people's behaviors and their health
health-defeating behaviors behaviors that increase the chance of illness, disease, or death
health-promoting behaviors behaviors that decrease the chance of illness, disease, or death
helping behavior another term for *altruism*

heterosexual one who is sexually attracted only to members of the other sex
heuristic [hyur-RISS-tick] a shortcut or rule of thumb that may or may not lead to a correct solution to the problem
hierarchy of needs Maslow's theory that humans are motivated by different needs, some of which take precedence over others
hindbrain the primitive part of the brain that comprises the medulla, pons, and cerebellum
hippocampus [HIP-po-CAM-puss] the part of the brain that plays a role in the transfer of information from short- to long-term memory
histogram a bar graph that is used to illustrate a frequency distribution
hoarding disorder an obsessive-compulsive related disorder characterized by persistent difficulty in discarding possessions such that they accumulate and clutter living areas causing significant distress and impairment in functioning
homeostasis [hoe-mee-oh-STAY-suss] an internal state of equilibrium in the body
homophobia prejudicial attitudes against homosexuals and homosexuality
homosexual one who is sexually attracted only to members of the same sex
hormones chemical messengers of the endocrine system
hostile aggression aggression that is meant to cause harm to others
hue the color of light; it corresponds to the light's wavelength
humanism a psychological perspective that emphasizes the personal growth and potential of humans
humanistic approach a personality perspective that emphasizes the individual, personal choice, and free will in shaping personality; assumes that humans have a built-in drive toward fulfilling their own natural potential
humanistic perspective an approach that focuses on how an individual's view of him- or herself and the world influences behavior
hypnosis a state of heightened suggestibility
hypothalamus [high-poe-THAL-uh-muss] the part of the forebrain that plays a role in maintaining homeostasis in the body, involving sleep, body temperature, sexual behavior, thirst, and hunger; also the point where the nervous system intersects with the endocrine system
hypothesis an educated guess
id the unconscious part of the personality that seeks pleasure and gratification
illness anxiety disorder a somatic symptom disorder in which the person persistently worries over having a serious illness, without any evident physical basis; formerly called *hypochondriasis* [high-po-con-DRY-uh-sis])
ill-structured problem a problem for which an algorithm is not known
imaginary audience the belief held by adolescents that everyone is watching what they do
immunosuppression [im-mew-no-suh-PREH-shun] the reduction in activity of the immune system
implicit memory the unconscious use of memory
impression formation the way that we understand and make judgments about others
in-group bias our tendency to favor people who belong to the same groups that we do
incentive a goal or desire that we are motivated to fulfill
incubation [in-cue-BAY-shun] a period of not thinking about a problem that helps one solve the problem
independent variable the variable in an experiment that is manipulated
individualistic culture a culture, like many Western cultures, in which individual accomplishments are valued over group accomplishments
inductive reasoning reasoning from the specific to the general
industrial and organizational (I/O) psychology the study of people's behavior at work using psychological principles
inferential statistics statistics that psychologists use in hypothesis testing to tell them when they should reject or accept their hypotheses about the population
informational conformity conformity that occurs when conformity pressures actually persuade group members to adopt new beliefs and/or attitudes
informed consent ethical principle that research participants be told about various aspects of the study, including any risks, before agreeing to participate
inhibition when a neurotransmitter makes the postsynaptic cell more negative inside, it becomes less likely to fire an action potential
inner ear the innermost portion of the ear that includes the cochlea
insight a new way of looking at a problem that leads to a sudden understanding of how to solve it
insomnia a sleep disorder in which a person cannot get to sleep and/or stay asleep
instinct an innate impulse from within a person that directs or motivates behavior
Institutional Review Board (IRB) a committee that reviews research proposals to ensure that ethical standards have been met
instrumental aggression aggression that is used to facilitate the attainment of a goal
insulin [IN-suh-lin] a hormone produced by the pancreas that facilitates the movement of glucose from the blood into the cells of the body
intelligence abilities that enable you to adapt to your environment and behave in a goal-directed way
intelligence quotient (IQ) one's mental age divided by one's chronological age times 100
interactionism the perspective that our genes and environmental influences work together to determine our characteristics
interpretation the psychoanalyst's view on the themes and issues that may be influencing the client's behavior
intrinsic motivation motivation that comes from within the person
introspection observing one's own thoughts, feelings, or sensations
introversion [in-tro-VER-shun] personality traits that involve energy directed inward, such as being calm or peaceful
intuition believing that something is true independent of any reasoning process
ions [EYE-ons] charged particles that play an important role in the firing of action potentials in the nervous system
James-Lange theory a theory of emotion that defines an emotion as a unique pattern of physiological arousal
job analysis identification of the critical elements of a job, including tasks, skills required, and working conditions
job satisfaction the positive or negative affect associated with a job
job withdrawal behaviors employees use to avoid their job (e.g., quitting, retiring)
judgment the act of estimating the probability of an event
just noticeable difference (JND) the minimum change in intensity of a stimulus that participants can detect 50% of the time
kinesthesis [kin-ess-THEE-sis] the ability to sense the position of our body parts in relation to one another and in relation to space
knowledge information stored in our long-term memory about the world and how it works
language a well-developed, syntactical verbal system for representing the world
latency [LATE-an-see] stage Freud's fourth psychosexual stage of development, which occurs from around age 6 to puberty, in which the child's sexuality is suppressed due to widening social contacts with school, peers, and family
latent content according to Freud, the symbolic meaning of a dream
latent learning learning that cannot be directly observed in an organism's behavior
lateral hypothalamus (LH) a region of the hypothalamus once thought to be the hunger center in the brain
law of effect a principle discovered by E. L. Thorndike, which states that behaviors that lead to positive consequences will be strengthened and behaviors that lead to negative consequences will be weakened
leadership a social influence process in which a person steers others toward a goal
learned helplessness Chap. 12: a passive response to stressors based on exposure to previously uncontrolled, negative events; Chap. 13: the belief that one cannot control the outcome of events
learning a relatively permanent change in behavior, or behavior potential, as a result of experience
lens the part of the eye that lies behind the pupil and focuses light rays on the retina
leptin a hormone released by fat cells in the body that plays a role in hunger regulation
levels-of-processing model a model that predicts that information that is processed deeply and elaboratively will be best retained in and recalled from long-term memory
libido [leh-BEE-doe] one's physical desire, or drive, to have sex
life event a change in one's life, good or bad, that requires readjustment
light adaptation the process through which our eyes adjust to bright light after having been exposed to darkness
limbic system system of structures, including the amygdala and hippocampus, that govern certain aspects of emotion, motivation, and memory
lithium a naturally occurring mineral salt prescribed to control manic symptoms in people with bipolar disorder; it influences several neurotransmitters in the brain, including glutamate, serotonin, and dopamine
lock-and-key theory a theory that proposes that olfactory receptors are excited by odor molecules in a way that is similar to the way in which neurotransmitters excite receptor sites
locus [LOW-cus] of control the expectation of control we have over the outcome of an event; an internal locus means we expect some degree of personal control, whereas an external locus means we expect little personal control
long-term memory (LTM) a system of memory that works to store memories for a long time, perhaps even permanently
loudness the psychophysical property of sound that corresponds to the amplitude of a sound wave
low-balling increasing compliance by first getting the person to agree to a deal and then changing the terms of the deal to be more favorable to yourself

maintenance rehearsal repeating information over and over again to keep it in short-term memory for an extended period of time
major depressive disorder a mood disorder involving sadness, feelings of worthlessness, loss of interest in one's usual activities, and changes in bodily activities such as sleep and appetite that persists for at least 2 weeks
mania a period of abnormally excessive energy and elation
manifest content according to Freud, what the dreamer recalls on awakening
matching hypothesis the theory that we are attracted to people whose level of physical attractiveness is similar to our own
mean a descriptive statistic that describes the most average, or typical, data point in the distribution
measures of central tendency descriptive statistics that describe the most central, or typical, data points in the frequency distribution
median a descriptive statistic that identifies the center of the frequency distribution; 50% of the scores are above and 50% are below this point in the distribution
medical model perspective that views mental health disorders as similar to physical diseases; they result from biological disturbances and can be diagnosed, treated, and cured like physical illnesses
meditation mental exercises in which people consciously focus their attention to heighten awareness and bring their mental processes under more control
medulla [meh-DOO-luh] part of the hindbrain that controls basic, life-sustaining functions such as respiration, heart rate, and blood pressure
melatonin [mel-uh-TONE-in] the hormone in the body that facilitates sleep
memory consolidation the stabilization and long-term storage of memory traces in the brain
memory traces the stored code that represents a piece of information that has been encoded into memory
menarche [MEN-ar-kee] a girl's first menstruation
menopause the period when a female stops menstruating and is no longer fertile
mental age the age that reflects the child's mental abilities in comparison to the average child of the same age
mental health disorder a dysfunction in thinking (cognition), emotions, and/or social behavior that impairs functioning and is not culturally expected
mental representation memory traces that represent objects, events, people, and so on that are not present at the time
mental set the tendency to habitually use methods of problem solving that have worked for you in the past
mentoring the pairing of a current and often long-term employee (the mentor) with a new employee
mere exposure effect the idea that the more one is exposed to something, the more one grows to like it
microsleep brief episode of sleep that occurs in the midst of a wakeful activity
midbrain brain structure that connects the hindbrain with the forebrain
middle ear the part of the ear behind the ear drum and in front of the oval window, including the hammer, anvil, and stirrup
Minnesota Multiphasic [mul-tee-FAZE-ick] Personality Inventory (MMPI-2) a personality inventory that is designed to identify problem areas of functioning in an individual's personality
misinformation effect the distortion of memory that occurs when people are exposed to misinformation
mode a measure of central tendency that identifies the most common, or frequent, score in the distribution
monocular depth cues depth cues that require information from only one eye
mood disorder a mental health disorder marked by a significant change in one's emotional state that seriously interferes with one's ability to function
moral reasoning how you decide what is right and what is wrong
morpheme [MORE-feem] the smallest unit of sound in a language that has meaning
motive a tendency to desire and seek out positive incentives or rewards and to avoid negative outcomes
motor cortex a strip of cortex at the back of the frontal lobe that governs the execution of motor movement in the body
motor neurons neurons that transmit commands from the brain to the muscles of the body
multiple approach–avoidance conflict a situation that poses several alternatives that each have positive and negative features
multiple intelligences the idea that we possess different types of intelligence rather than a single, overall level of intelligence
myelin [MY-eh-lynn] the fatty, waxy substance that insulates portions of some neurons in the nervous system
myelin sheath [MY-eh-lynn SHEE-th] the discontinuous segments of myelin that cover the outside of some axons in the nervous system
narcolepsy [NAR-co-lep-see] a rare sleep disorder in which a person falls asleep during alert activities during the day
natural concept a concept that develops naturally as we live our lives and experience the world
natural selection a cornerstone of Darwin's theory of evolution, which states that genes for traits that allow an organism to be reproductively successful will be selected or retained in a species and genes for traits that hinder reproductive success will not be selected and therefore will die out in a species
naturalistic observation observing behavior in the environment in which the behavior typically occurs
nature–nurture debate/issue the degree to which biology (nature) or the environment (nurture) contributes to a person's development
negative correlation a relationship in which increases in one variable correspond to decreases in the other variable
negative feedback loop a system of feedback in the body that monitors and adjusts our motivation level so as to maintain homeostasis
negative punishment weakening a behavior by removing something pleasant from the organism's environment
negative reinforcement strengthening a behavior by removing something unpleasant from the environment of the organism
neonate a newborn during the first 28 days of life
nervous system an electrochemical system of communication within the body that uses cells called neurons to convey information
neurons [NUR-ons] cells in the nervous system that transmit information
neuropeptide Y a powerful hunger stimulant
neuroplasticity [NUR-o-plas-TI-city] the nervous system's ability to rewire its structures as a result of experience
neuroscience a field of science that investigates the relationships between the nervous system and behavior/mental processes
neuroticism [nur-RAH-tuh-siz-um] the degree to which one is emotionally unstable
neurotransmitters [NUR-oh-TRANS-mitt-ers] chemical messengers that carry neural signals across the synapse
neutral stimulus (NS) a stimulus that does not naturally elicit an unconditioned response in an organism
night terrors very frightening non-REM sleep episodes
nightmare a brief scary REM dream that is often remembered
non-REM sleep relaxing state of sleep in which the person's eyes do not move
norepinephrine [nor-ep-in-EF-rin] (NOR) neurotransmitter that plays a role in regulating sleep, arousal, and mood
norm an unwritten rule or expectation for how group members should behave
normal distribution a bell-shaped, symmetric frequency distribution
normative commitment commitment to the organization based on feelings of obligation
normative conformity conformity that occurs when group members change their behavior to meet group norms but are not persuaded to change their beliefs and attitudes
null hypothesis (H_0) the hypothesis that contains a statement of what we do not believe is true about our variables in the population
obedience yielding to a demand
obesity having a body mass index of 30 or over
object permanence the understanding that an object continues to exist even when it is not present
observational learning learning through observation and imitation of others' behavior
obsession a recurrent thought or image that intrudes on a person's awareness
obsessive-compulsive disorder (OCD) an anxiety disorder involving a pattern of unwanted intrusive thoughts and/or the urge to engage in repetitive actions that interferes with a person's functioning
occipital [ox-SIP-it-ull] lobe cortical area at the back of the brain that plays a role in visual processing
Oedipus [ED-uh-puss] complex in the male, an unconscious sexual urge for the mother that develops during the phallic psychosexual stage
olfaction the sense of smell
olfactory epithelium [ole-FACT-uh-ree epp-ith-THEEL-ee-um] a special piece of skin at the top of the nasal cavity that contains the olfactory receptors
operant conditioning a type of learning in which the organism learns through the consequences of its behavior
opiates [OH-pee-ates] painkilling drugs that depress some brain areas and excite others
opponent-process theory the idea that we have dual-action cells beyond the level of the retina that signal the brain when we see one of a pair of colors
optic chiasm the point in the brain where the optic nerve from the left eye crosses over the optic nerve from the right eye
optic nerve the structure that conveys visual information away from the retina to the brain
oral stage Freud's first psychosexual stage of development, which occurs during the first year of life, in which the handling of the child's feeding experiences affects personality development

organizational citizenship behaviors (OCBs) employee behaviors that go beyond what is expected by the organization
organizational climate the behavioral norms of an organization
organizational culture the shared cognitive assumptions and beliefs of an organization
organizational socialization the process by which members of an organization become a part of, or are absorbed into, the culture of the organization
organizational withdrawal work withdrawal or job withdrawal
orgasm phase the third stage of the sexual response cycle, in which the pelvic and anal muscles contract
orienting reflex the tendency of an organism to orient its senses toward unexpected stimuli
out-group a group that is distinct from one's own and so usually an object of more hostility or dislike than one's in-group
out-group homogeneity [home-uh-juh-NEE-it-tee] bias our tendency to see out-group members as being pretty much all alike
outer ear the outermost parts of the ear, including the pinna, auditory canal, and surface of the ear drum
outliers unusual data points that are at the extremes of the frequency distribution, either far above or far below the mean
ovaries the organs in a female's body that produce eggs, or ova
overextension when a child uses one word to symbolize all manner of similar instances (e.g., calling all birds parakeet)
overweight having a body mass index of 25–29.9
panic disorder an anxiety disorder characterized by intense fear and anxiety in the absence of danger that is accompanied by strong physical symptoms
papillae [puh-PILL-ee] bumps on the tongue that many people mistake for taste buds
parasympathetic nervous system the branch of the autonomic nervous system most active during times of normal functioning
parietal [puh-RYE-it-ull] lobe cortical area on the top sides of the brain that play a role in touch and certain cognitive processes
partial reinforcement a schedule of reinforcement in which the organism is rewarded for only some instances of the desired response
perception the process through which we interpret sensory information
performance appraisals the evaluations or reviews of employees' job performance
peripheral nervous system (PNS) all of the nervous system except the brain and the spinal cord
peripheral route to persuasion a style of thinking in which the person does not carefully and critically evaluate persuasive arguments or generate counterarguments; the peripheral route ensues when one lacks motivation and/or available cognitive resources
permissive parent a parenting style characterized by low levels of control or discipline
persistent depressive disorder a mood disorder that is a less severe but more chronic form of major depressive disorder; also called *dysthymic* [dis-THIGH-mik] *disorder*
person–situation interaction the influence of the situation on the stability of traits; when in the same situation, we display similar behavior, but when the situation is different, behavior may change
personal fable the belief held by adolescents that they are unique and special
personal unconscious according to Jung, the part of the unconscious that consists of forgotten memories and repressed experiences from one's past
personality the unique collection of attitudes, emotions, thoughts, habits, impulses, and behaviors that define how a person typically behaves across situations
personality disorder a mental health disorder marked by maladaptive behavior that has been stable over a long period and across many situations
personality inventory an objective paper-and-pencil or computerized self-report form that measures personality on several dimensions
persuasion a type of social influence in which someone tries to change our attitudes
phallic [FAH-lick] stage Freud's third psychosexual stage of development, which occurs between 3 and 6 years of age, in which little boys experience the Oedipus complex and little girls the Electra complex
phenotype [FEEN-oh-type] actual characteristic that results from interaction of the genotype and environmental influences
pheromones [FAIR-uh-moans] airborne chemicals that are released from glands and detected by the vomeronasal organs in some animals and perhaps humans
phoneme [FOE-neem] the smallest unit of sound in a language
photopigments light-sensitive chemicals that create electrical changes when they come into contact with light
pitch the psychophysical property of sound that corresponds to the frequency of a sound wave
pituitary [peh-TOO-uh-tare-ee] gland the master gland of the endocrine system that controls the action of all other glands in the body
place theory a theory that proposes that our brain decodes pitch by noticing which region of the basilar membrane is most active
placebo effect a measurable change in participants' behavior due to the expectation or belief that a treatment will have certain effects
plateau phase the second stage of the sexual response cycle, in which excitement peaks
pleasure principle the basis on which the id operates; the urge to feel good and maximize gratification
pluralistic ignorance the idea that we use the behavior of others to help us determine whether a situation is an emergency requiring our help; if no one else is helping, we may conclude that help isn't needed
pons the hindbrain structure that plays a role in respiration, consciousness, sleep, dreaming, facial movement, sensory processes, and the transmission of neural signals from one part of the brain to another
population of interest the entire universe of animals or people that could be studied
positive correlation a relationship in which increases in one variable correspond to increases in the other variable
positive psychology the study of factors that contribute to happiness, positive emotions, and well-being
positive punishment weakening a behavior by adding something unpleasant to the organism's environment
positive reinforcement strengthening a behavior by adding something pleasant to the environment of the organism
postformal thought the idea that a correct solution (or solutions) may vary, depending on the circumstances
postsynaptic neuron [post-sin-AP-tic NUR-on] the neuron that is receiving the signal at a synapse in the nervous system
posttraumatic stress disorder (PTSD) a trauma-related disorder, characterized by distressing memories, emotional numbness, and hypervigilance, that develops after exposure to a traumatic event
pragmatics the rules of conversation in a particular culture
preconscious [pre-CON-shus] level the level of consciousness that holds thoughts, perceptions, and impulses of which we could potentially be aware
prediction an expected outcome of how variables will relate
predictive hypothesis an educated guess about the relationships among variables
prejudice a largely negative stereotype that is unfairly applied to all members of a group regardless of their individual characteristics
preoperational stage Piaget's second stage of cognitive development, characterized by the use of symbols and illogical thought
presynaptic neuron [pre-sin-AP-tic NUR-on] the neuron that is sending the signal at a synapse in the nervous system
primacy effect the tendency for people to recall words from the beginning of a list better than words that appeared in the middle of the list
primary appraisal [uh-PRAY-zull] our initial interpretation of an event as irrelevant, positive, or stressful
primary drive a drive that motivates us to maintain homeostasis in certain biological processes within the body
primary reinforcer a reinforcer that is reinforcing in and of itself
private speech Vygotsky's term describing the behavior of young children who talk to themselves to guide their own actions
proactive interference a type of forgetting that occurs when older memory traces inhibit the retrieval of newer memory traces
problem-focused coping behaviors that aim to control or alter the environment that is causing stress
procedural memory long-term memory for skills and behaviors
progressive relaxation training a stress management technique in which a person learns how to systematically tense and relax muscle groups in the body
projective test a less structured and subjective personality test in which an individual is shown an ambiguous stimulus and is asked to describe what he or she sees
prosocial behavior behavior that helps others
prototype our concept of the most typical member of the category
proximity Chap. 3: a Gestalt principle of perception that states that we tend to group close objects together during perception; Chap. 10: physical closeness
pseudopsychology psychological information or conclusions that sound scientific but that have not been systematically tested using the scientific method
psychoactive drugs substances that influence the brain and thereby the individual's behavior
psychoanalysis [sigh-co-uh-NAL-uh-sis] a method of therapy formulated by Freud that focuses on uncovering unconscious conflicts that drive maladaptive behavior

psychoanalytic [psi-co-an-uh-LIH-tic] perspective a personality approach developed by Sigmund Freud that sees personality as the product of driving forces within a person that are often conflicting and sometimes unconscious
psychoanalytic theory Sigmund Freud's view that emphasizes the influence of unconscious desires and conflicts on behavior
psychodynamic perspective an approach that focuses on internal unconscious mental processes, motives, and desires that may explain behavior
psychodynamic therapy modern psychoanalysis delivered in a shorter time that focuses less on the client's past and more on current problems and the nature of interpersonal relationships
psychological distance the degree to which one can disassociate oneself from the consequences of his/her actions
psychology the scientific study of behavior and mental processes
psychoneuroimmunology [sigh-ko-nur-o-im-ya-NAH-la-gee] field of study that investigates the connections among psychology (behaviors, thoughts, emotions), the nervous system, and immune system functioning
psychopathology the scientific study of mental health disorders
psychopharmacology [sigh-co-farm-uh-KAH-lo-gee] the use of medications to treat mental health problems
psychophysics the study of how the mind interprets the physical properties of stimuli
psychosurgery a biomedical treatment approach involving neurosurgery to alleviate symptoms in someone with a mental health disorder
psychotherapy the use of psychological principles and techniques to treat mental health disorders
psychoticism [psi-COT-uh-siz-um] the degree to which one is hostile, nonconforming, impulsive, and aggressive
puberty [PEW-bur-tee] the process of sexual maturation
punishment the weakening of a response that occurs when a behavior leads to an unpleasant consequence
pupil the hole in the iris through which light enters the eye
quasi-experiment a research study that is not a true experiment because participants are not randomly assigned to the different conditions
random assignment a method of assigning participants in which they have an equal chance of being placed in any group or condition of the study
range a measure of variability that is the difference between the high score and the low score of the distribution
rational-emotive therapy a cognitive therapy approach created by Albert Ellis that focuses on changing the irrational beliefs that are believed to impede mental health
realistic-conflict theory the theory that prejudice stems from competition for scarce resources
reality principle the basis on which the ego operates; finding socially appropriate means to fulfill id demands
reasoning drawing conclusions about the world based on certain assumptions
recall a type of retrieval process in which the probe or cue does not contain much information
recency effect the tendency for people to recall words from the end of a list better than words that appeared in the middle of the list
reciprocal determinism [ree-SIP-pra-cull dee-TER-min-iz-um] according to Bandura, the constant interaction among one's behavior, thoughts, and environment determines personality
reciprocity [reh-cih-PRAH-cih-tee] a strong norm that states that we should treat others as they treat us
recognition a type of retrieval process in which the probe or cue contains a great deal of information, including the item being sought
reconstructive memory memory that is based on the retrieval of memory traces that contain the actual details of events we have experienced
recruitment the process organizations use to identify potential employees for a job
reflex an automatic response to a specific environmental stimulus
refractory period Chap. 2: the brief period of time after a neuron has fired an action potential during which the neuron is inhibited and unlikely to fire another action potential; Chap. 5: the time during the resolution phase in which males are incapable of experiencing another orgasm or ejaculation
reinforcement the strengthening of a response that occurs when the response is rewarded
relativistic [rell-uh-tah-VIS-tik] thinking the idea that in many situations there is not necessarily one right or wrong answer
reliability the degree to which a test yields consistent measurements of a trait
REM behavior disorder a condition in which normal muscle paralysis does not occur, leading to violent movements during REM sleep
REM rebound the loss of REM sleep being recouped by spending more time in REM on subsequent nights
REM sleep an active state of sleep in which the person's eyes move
representativeness heuristic a heuristic in which we rely on the degree to which something is representative of a category, rather than the base rate, to help us judge whether or not it belongs in the category
repression a type of forgetting proposed by Sigmund Freud in which memories for events, desires, or impulses that we find threatening are pushed into an inaccessible part of the mind called the unconscious
resilience the capacity to adapt well to significant stressors
resistance a process in psychoanalysis whereby the client behaves in such a way as to deny or avoid sensitive issues
resistance stage the second phase of the general adaptation syndrome, in which the nervous and endocrine systems continue to be activated
resolution phase the final stage of the sexual response cycle, in which the body returns to homeostasis
response an organism's reaction to a stimulus
response set theory of hypnosis asserts that hypnosis is not an altered state of consciousness, but a cognitive set to respond appropriately to suggestions
resting potential the potential difference that exists in the neuron when it is resting (approximately –70 mv in mammals)
restless legs syndrome (RLS) a neurological movement disorder occurring primarily at night in which a person has unpleasant sensations in the legs and an irresistible urge to move them to relieve the pain
reticular formation the part of the midbrain that regulates arousal and plays an important role in attention, sleep, and consciousness
retina the structure at the back of the eye that contains cells that convert light into neural signals
retinal disparity a binocular depth cue that uses the difference in the images projected on the right and left retinas to inform the brain about the distance of a stimulus
retrieval the process of accessing information in memory and pulling it into consciousness
retroactive interference a type of forgetting that occurs when newer memory traces inhibit the retrieval of older memory traces
retrograde amnesia a type of amnesia in which one is unable to retrieve previously stored memories from long-term memory
reuptake the process through which neurotransmitters are recycled back into the presynaptic neuron
rods the light-sensitive cells of the retina that pick up any type of light energy and convert it to neural signals
Rorschach [ROAR-shock] inkblot test a projective personality test consisting of 10 ambiguous inkblots in which a person is asked to describe what he or she sees; the person's responses are then coded for consistent themes and issues
ruminative [RUE-muh-nay-tive] coping style the tendency to persistently focus on how one feels without attempting to do anything about one's feelings
sample the portion of the population of interest that is selected for a study
sample variance a measure of variability that shows on average how much the scores vary from the mean
saturation the purity of light; light that consists of a single wavelength produces the richest or most saturated color
scaffolding [SKAH-fol-ding] a process in which adults initially offer guidance and support in helping a child reason, solve a problem, or master a task; as the child becomes more proficient and capable, the adult helps less and less until the child can master the task on his or her own
scapegoat an out-group that is blamed for many of society's problems
scatter plot a graph of data that plots pairs of data points, with one data point on the *x*-axis and the other on the *y*-axis
schedule of reinforcement the frequency and timing of the reinforcements that an organism receives
schema [SKEE-ma] Chap. 7: an organized, generalized knowledge structure in long-term memory; Chap. 9: a mental idea, concept, or thought
schizophrenia [skit-suh-FREE-nee-uh] a mental health severe disorder characterized by disturbances in thought, perceptions, emotions, and behavior
scientific method a systematic process used by psychologists for testing hypotheses about behavior
secondary appraisal an evaluation of resources available to cope with a stressor
secondary drive a learned drive that is not directly related to biological needs
secondary reinforcer a reinforcer that is reinforcing only because it leads to a primary reinforcer
secondary traits according to Allport, the tendencies we have that are less consistent and describe how we behave in certain situations
selective serotonin reuptake inhibitor (SSRI) a type of antidepressant drug that inhibits the reuptake of the neurotransmitter serotonin, thereby improving mood
self-actualization [self-ack-shu-lih-ZAY-shun] the fulfillment of one's natural potential
self-concept one's perception or image of his or her abilities and uniqueness

self-determination theory a theory of motivation that proposes that as we pursue the fulfillment of basic needs, we experience different types of motivation that come from both the self and the outside world
self-efficacy [self-EF-fuh-kah-see] the expectation that one has for success in a given situation
self-help group a group comprised of people who share the same problem and meet to help one another
self-serving bias our tendency to make attributions that preserve our own self-esteem—for example, making trait attributions for our successes and situational attributions for our failures
semantic encoding encoding memory traces in terms of the meaning of the information being stored
semantic memory long-term, declarative memory for conceptual information
sensation the process through which our sense organs convert environmental energy such as light and sound into neural impulses
sensation seeker a person who by trait tends to seek out arousing activities
sensitive period in prenatal development, a time when genetic and environmental agents are most likely to cause birth defects
sensorimotor stage Piaget's first stage of cognitive development, in which infants learn schemas through their senses and motor abilities
sensory memory a system of memory that very briefly stores sensory impressions so that we can extract relevant information from them for further processing
sensory neurons neurons that transmit information from the sense organs to the central nervous system
separation anxiety the fear an infant expresses when separated from the primary caretaker
serotonin [ser-uh-TOE-nin] a neurotransmitter that plays a role in many different behaviors, including sleep, arousal, mood, eating, and pain perception
set point a particular weight that our body seeks to maintain
sexual arousal a heightened state of sexual interest and excitement
sexual desire one's motivation and interest in engaging in sexual activity
sexual orientation one's sexual attraction for members of the same and/or other sex
sexually transmitted infection (STI) an infection that is passed from one person to another primarily through sexual contact
shaping using operant conditioning to build a new behavior in an organism by rewarding successive approximations of the desired response
short-term memory (STM) a system of memory that is limited in both capacity and duration; in the three stages model of memory, short-term memory is seen as the intermediate stage between sensory memory and long-term memory
significant results are considered significant when there is a very small chance (usually less than 5%) of finding those results given the assumption that the null hypothesis is true
similarity a Gestalt principle of perception that states that we tend to group like objects together during perception
situational attribution an attribution that assigns the cause of a behavior to some characteristic of the situation or environment in which the behavior occurs
Skinner box a device created by B. F. Skinner to study operant behavior in a compressed time frame; in a Skinner box, an organism is automatically rewarded or punished for engaging in certain behaviors
sleep apnea [APP-nee-uh] a sleep disorder in which a person stops breathing during sleep
sleep disorder a disturbance in the normal pattern of sleeping
sleepwalking a sleep disorder in which a person is mobile and may perform actions during stage IV sleep
slippery slope the use of foot-in-the-door compliance in an obedience situation to get people to obey increasing demands
social anxiety disorder an anxiety disorder characterized by an irrational, persistent fear of being negatively evaluated by others in a social situation; also called social phobia
social cognition the area of social psychology that deals with the ways in which we think about other people and ourselves
social cognitive approach a personality perspective that emphasizes the influence of one's thoughts and social experiences in formulating personality
social facilitation performing better on a task in the presence of others than you would if you were alone
social loafing when group members exert less effort on a group task than they would if they were performing the task alone
social psychology the branch of psychology that studies how we think and behave in social situations
social support having close and positive relationships with others
sociocultural perspective an approach that focuses on societal and cultural factors that may influence behavior
somatic nervous system branch of the peripheral nervous system that governs sensory and voluntary motor action in the body
somatic [so-MAA-tic] symptom disorder a mental health disorder marked by physical complaints that have no apparent physical cause
somatosensory [so-MAT-oh-SEN-sor-ee] cortex a strip of cortex at the front of the parietal lobe that governs the sense of touch
source traits universal tendencies that underlie and are at the core of surface traits, according to Cattell
specific phobia a persistent fear and avoidance of a specific object or situation
split brain a brain with its corpus callosum severed; sometimes done to control the effects of epilepsy in people who do not respond to other therapies
spontaneous recovery during extinction, the tendency for a conditioned response to reappear and strengthen over a brief period of time before re-extinguishing
standard deviation a measure of variability equal to the square root of the sample variance; often used to gauge the degree to which an individual score deviates from the mean of a distribution
standard normal distribution a bell-shaped, symmetric distribution ($\bar{X} = 0, S = 1$) for which we know the exact area under the curve
standardized test a test that uses a standard set of questions, procedures, and scoring methods for all test takers
statistics a type of applied mathematics used to describe data and test hypotheses
stereotype a schema for a particular group of people
stereotype threat a phenomenon in which fears of being discriminated against elicit stereotype-confirming behaviors
stimulants drugs that speed up normal brain functioning
stimulus any object or event that is perceived by our senses
stimulus discrimination responding only to a particular stimulus
stimulus generalization responding in a like fashion to similar stimuli
storage the place where information is retained in memory
stranger anxiety the distress an infant expresses when faced with unfamiliar people
stress any event or environmental stimulus (stressor) that we respond to because we perceive it as challenging or threatening
structuralism an early psychological perspective concerned with identifying the basic elements of experience
structured interview an interview conducted by a trained interviewer using standardized questions, a specific question order, and a predetermined scoring or answer key
subliminal perception when the intensity of a stimulus is below the participant's absolute threshold and the participant is not consciously aware of the stimulus
subordinate category the lowest level of categorization, which contains concepts that are less general and more specific than those at the basic level
substance dependence a condition in which a person needs a drug in order to maintain normal functioning
sum of squares the sum of the squared errors, or deviations, from the mean for the scores in the distribution; the numerator of the sample variance equation
superego the part of the personality that represents your moral conscience
superordinate category the highest, most general level of a concept
superordinate goal a goal that is shared by different groups
suprachiasmatic [sue-pra-kigh-as-MAT-ick] nucleus (SCN) a group of brain cells located in the hypothalamus that signal other brain areas when to be aroused and when to shut down
surface traits basic traits that describe people's personalities, according to Cattell
survey a research method that asks a large group of people about their attitudes, beliefs, and/or behaviors
symbolic thinking the understanding that objects can be represented with symbols such as bodily gestures or language
sympathetic nervous system the branch of the autonomic nervous system most active during times of danger or stress
synapse [SIN-aps] the connection formed between two neurons when the axon bulb of one neuron comes into close proximity with the dendrite of another neuron
systematic desensitization [sis-tuh-MAT-ick dee-sen-sih-tuh-ZAY-shun] a behavior therapy technique that uses a gradual, step-by-step process to replace fear or anxiety with an incompatible response of relaxation and positive emotion
tardive dyskinesia [TAR-div dis-kuh-NEE-juh] a possible long-term side effect of antipsychotic medications involving involuntary motor movements of the mouth, tongue, and face
taste aversion classical conditioning that occurs when an organism pairs the experience of nausea with a certain food and becomes conditioned to feel ill at the sight, smell, or idea of the food
taste buds the sense organs for taste that are found between the papillae on the tongue
telegraphic speech two-word sentences that children begin to utter at 20–26 months

temperament a person's general pattern of attention, arousal, and mood that is evident at birth
temporal [TEM-por-ull] lobe the cortical area directly below the ears that play a role in auditory processing and language
teratogen [tur-RAH-tuh-jun] an environmental substance that has the potential to harm the developing organism
test the measurement of a carefully chosen sample of behavior
testes the organs in a male's body that produce both sperm and testosterone
testosterone a male hormone that plays a role in many aspects of sexuality, including sexual desire
thalamus [THAL-uh-muss] the part of the forebrain that functions as a sensory relay station
that's-not-all increasing compliance by sweetening the deal with additional incentives
THC (tetrahydrocannabinol) [tet-rah-high-dro-can-NAH-bin-all] the active ingredient in marijuana that affects learning, short-term memory, coordination, emotion, and appetite
Thematic Apperception [thee-MAT-ick ap-per-SEP-shun] Test (TAT) a projective personality test consisting of a series of pictures in which the respondent is asked to tell a story about each scene; the responses are then coded for consistent themes and issues
theory an explanation of why and how a behavior occurs
therapeutic alliance [thair-uh-PEW-tick uh-LIE-unce] the interactive and collaborative relationship between the client and the therapist
therapy techniques that are used to help people with mental health or interpersonal problems
thinking the use of knowledge to accomplish some sort of goal
threat simulation theory (TST) suggests that dreaming is an ancient biological defense mechanism that allows us to repeatedly simulate potentially threatening situations so that we can rehearse our responses to these events
threshold of excitation the potential difference at which a neuron will fire an action potential (–55 mv in mammals)
tip of the tongue phenomenon knowing that you know a piece of information, even though you cannot recall it at the moment
Title VII of the Civil Rights Act of 1964 the law that prohibits discrimination based on race, color, religion, sex, and national origin
token economy Chap. 6: a system of operant conditioning in which participants are reinforced with tokens that can later be cashed in for primary reinforcers; Chap. 14: a behavior therapy technique in which people are rewarded with tokens for desired behavior; the tokens can then be exchanged for what is reinforcing to the individuals
tolerance a condition in which after repeated use, more of a drug is needed to achieve the same effect
top-down perceptual processing perception that is guided by prior knowledge or expectations
trait the tendency to behave in a certain way across most situations
trait approach a personality perspective that attempts to describe personality by emphasizing internal, biological aspects of personality called traits
trait attribution an attribution that assigns the cause of a behavior to the traits and characteristics of the person being judged
transcranial magnetic stimulation (TMS) a biomedical treatment approach in which electromagnetic impulses stimulate brain neurons; used for treatment resistant depression
transference a process in psychoanalysis in which the client unconsciously reacts to the therapist as if the therapist were a parent, friend, sibling, or romantic partner
transformational leadership characterized by high ethical standards, inspirational motivation, intellectual stimulation, and individual consideration
triarchic [tri-ARK-ic] theory of intelligence Robert Sternberg's theory that proposes that intelligence is composed of analytical, practical, and creative abilities that help us adapt to our environment
trichromatic [try-crow-MAT-ick] theory of color vision the idea that color vision is made possible by the presence of three different types of cones in the retina that react, respectively, to red, green, or blue light
two-factor theory of emotion a theory that states that emotions result when we cognitively interpret our physiological reactions in light of the situation
Type A personality a personality that is aggressive, ambitious, and competitive
Type B personality a personality characterized by patience, flexibility, and an easygoing manner
Type C personality a personality that is cautious, serious, sensitive to criticism, and results oriented, and that suppresses negative emotions such as anger
unconditional positive regard Chap. 11: acceptance and love of another's thoughts and feelings without expecting anything in return; Chap. 14: the ability of a therapist to accept and value a person for who he or she is, regardless of his or her faults or problems
unconditioned response (UR) the response that is elicited by an unconditioned stimulus
unconditioned stimulus (US) a stimulus that naturally elicits a response in an organism
unconscious [un-CON-shus] level the level of awareness that contains all the thoughts, perceptions, and impulses of which we are unaware
underextension when a child inappropriately restricts the use of a word to a particular case (e.g., using the word cat to describe only the family pet)
unstructured interview an informal, unplanned interview conducted by an untrained interviewer using random questions and no scoring key
validity the degree to which a test measures the trait that it was designed to measure
variable interval schedule a schedule of reinforcement in which the organism is rewarded for the first desired response in an average *x*th interval of time
variable ratio schedule a schedule of reinforcement in which the organism is rewarded on average for every *x*th instance of the desired response
variance a measure of variability that shows on average how much the scores vary from the mean
ventromedial [ven-tro-MEE-dee-al] hypothalamus (VMH) a region of the hypothalamus that plays an indirect role in creating a feeling of satiety
vestibular [ves-STIB-you-lar] sense the sense of balance
visible spectrum the spectrum of light that humans can see
visual cortex a region of cortex found at the back of the occipital lobe that processes visual information in the brain
volley theory a theory that proposes that our brain decodes pitch by noticing the frequency at which groups of hair cells on the basilar membrane are firing
wavelength a physical property of some energies that corresponds to the distance between wave peaks
Weber's [VAY-bers] law a psychological principle that states that for each of our five senses, the amount of change in the stimulus that is necessary to produce a just noticeable difference depends on the intensity at which the stimulus is first presented
well-structured problem a problem for which there is a clear pathway to the solution
Wernicke's [WURR-neh-kees] aphasia [ah-FAYZ-yah] a condition resulting from damage to Wernicke's area of the brain that leaves a person unable to comprehend speech
Wernicke's [WURR-neh-kees] area a region of the left temporal lobe that plays a role in the comprehension of speech
Whorfian [WORE-fee-un] hypothesis, or linguistic relativity hypothesis the theory that one's language can directly determine or influence one's thoughts
"will-do" factors factors that determine the normal or typical performance by an employee
withdrawal symptoms physical or behavioral effects that occur after a person stops using a drug
work teams/groups two or more employees who together perform organizationally relevant tasks, share one or more common goals, interact socially, and exhibit task interdependencies
work withdrawal behaviors employees use to avoid their work (e.g., lateness, absenteeism)
working memory a multifaceted component of long-term memory that contains short-term memory, a central executive, a phonological loop, and a visuospatial sketch pad; the function of working memory is to access, move, and process information that we are currently using
***z* score** a measure of relative standing that measures the distance of a score from the mean of the distribution in standard deviation units
zone of proximal development (ZPD) according to Vygotsky, the gap between what a child is already able to do and what he or she is not yet capable of doing without help
zygote [ZIE-goat] a fertilized egg

References

Aamodt, M. G. (2010). *Industrial/organizational psychology: An applied approach*. Belmont, CA: Thomson Wadsworth.

Abad, V. C., & Guilleminault, C. (2004). Review of rapid eye movement behavior sleep disorders. *Current Neurology Neuroscience Reports, 4,* 157–163.

Abar, B., Carter, K. L., & Winsler, A. (2009). The effects of maternal parenting style and religious commitment on self-regulation, academic achievement, and risk behavior among African-American parochial college students. *Journal of Adolescence, 32,* 259–273.

Abbass, A., Town, J., & Driessen, E. (2011). The efficacy of short-term psychodynamic psychotherapy for depressive disorders with comorbid personality disorder. *Psychiatry, 74,* 58–71.

Abbott, C. C., Gallegos, P., Rediske, N., Lemke, N. T., & Quinn, D. K. (2014). A review of longitudinal electroconvulsive therapy: Neuroimaging investigations. *Journal of Geriatric Psychiatry and Neurology, 27,* 33–46.

Abbott, R. (2010). Delivering quality-evaluated healthcare information in the era of Web 2.0: Design implication for Intute: Health and Life Sciences. *Health Informatics Journal, 16,* 5–14.

Abdel-Khalek, A., & Lester, D. (2005). Sibship size, birth order, and personality. *Psychological Reports, 97,* 387–388.

Abkevich, V., Camp, N. J., Hensel, C. H., Neff, C. D., Russell, D. L., Hughes, D. C. et al. (2003). Predisposition locus for major depression at chromosome 12q22–12q23.2. *American Journal of Human Genetics, 73,* 1271–1281.

Abramowitz, J. S. (1997). Effectiveness of psychological and pharmacological treatments for obsessive-compulsive disorder: A quantitative review. *Journal of Consulting and Clinical Psychology, 65,* 44–52.

Abramowitz, J. S., & Moore, E. L. (2007). An experimental analysis of hypochondriasis. *Behaviour Research and Therapy, 45,* 413–424.

Abrams, D. B., & Wilson, G. T. (1983). Alcohol, sexual arousal, and self-control. *Journal of Personality and Social Psychology, 45,* 188–198.

Abramson, L. Y., Alloy, L. B., Hankin, B. L., Haeffel, G. J., MacCoon, D. G., & Gibb, B. E. (2002). Cognitive vulnerability: Stress models of depression in a self-regulatory and psychobiological content. In I. H. Gotlib & C. L. Hammen (Eds.), *Handbook of depression* (pp. 268–294). New York: Guilford Press.

Acevedo, B. P., Aron, A., Fisher, H. E., & Brown, L. L. (2012). Neural correlates of long-term intense romantic love. *Social Cognitive and Affective Neuroscience, 7,* 145–159. doi:10.1093/scan/nsq092.

Ackerman, J. P., Riggins, T., & Black, M. M. (2010). A review of the effects of prenatal cocaine exposure among school-aged children. *Pediatrics, 125,* 554–565.

Ackerman, R. A., Kashy, D. A., Donnellan, M. B., Neppi, T., Lorenz, F. O., & Conger, R. D. (2013). The interpersonal legacy of a positive family climate in adolescence. *Psychological Science, 24,* 243–250.

Adachi, T., Fujino, H., Nakae, A., Mashimo, T., & Sasaki, J. (2014). A meta-analysis of hypnosis for chronic pain problems: A comparison between hypnosis, standard care, and other psychological interventions. *International Journal of Clinical and Experimental Hypnosis, 62,* 1–28.

Adam, E. K. (2006). Transactions among adolescent trait and state emotion and diurnal and momentary cortisol activity in naturalistic settings. *Psychoneuroendocrinology, 31,* 664–679.

Adams, C. D., Girolami, P. A., Joseph, K. E., Sauvageot, S. A., & Slater, H. (2002). Use of a token reinforcement system to promote appropriate behavior at a pediatric burn summer camp. *Journal of Burn and Care Rehabilitation, 23,* 297–305.

Adams, K. F., Schatzkin, A., Harris, T. B., Kipnis, V., Mouw, T., Ballard-Barbash, R. et al. (2006). Overweight, obesity, and mortality in a large prospective cohort of persons 50 to 71 years old. *New England Journal of Medicine, 355,* 763–778.

Adams, M. (2009). *Slang: The people's poetry.* Oxford: Oxford University Press.

Adan, A., & Natale. V. (2002). Gender differences in morningness–eveningness preference. *Chronobiology International, 19,* 709–720.

Addington, J., Piskulic, D., & Marshall, C. (2010). Psychosocial treatments for schizophrenia. *Current Directions in Psychological Science, 19,* 260–263.

Ader, R. (2001). Psychoneuroimmunology. *Current Directions in Psychological Science, 10,* 94–98.

Aderibigbe, Y. A., Bloch, R. M., & Walker, W. R. (2001). Prevalence of depersonalization and derealization experiences in a rural population. *Social Psychiatry and Psychiatric Epidemiology, 36,* 63–69.

Adler, A. (1928). *Understanding human nature.* London: Allen & Unwin.

Adler, J., & Rosenberg, D. (1994, December 19). The endless binge. *Newsweek,* p. 72.

Administration on Aging (AOA). (2011). *A profile of older Americans: 2011.* U.S. Department of Health and Human Services. Retrieved from www.aoa.gov

Adolph, K. E., Karasik, L. B., & Tamis-Lemonda, C. S. (2009). Moving between cultures: Cross-cultural research on motor development. In M. Bornstein (Ed.), *Handbook of cross-cultural developmental science, Vol. 1. Domains of development across cultures* (pp. 61–88). Mahwah, NJ: Erlbaum.

Adolphs, R. (2002). Neural systems for recognizing emotion. *Current Opinion in Neurobiology, 12,* 169–177.

Adolphs, R., Tranel, D., & Damasio, A. R. (1998). The human amygdala in social judgment. *Nature, 393,* 470–474.

Afifi, T. O., Mather, A., Boman, J., Fleisher, W., Enns, M. W., MacMillan, H., & Sareen, J. (2011). Childhood adversity and personality disorders: Results from a nationally representative population-based study. *Journal of Psychiatric Research, 45,* 814–822.

Afifi, T. O., Mota, N., MacMillan, H. L., & Sareen, J. (2013). Harsh physical punishment in childhood and adult physical health. *Pediatrics, 132,* 333–340. doi: 10.1542/peds.2012-4021.

Aghajanian, G. K. (1994). Serotonin and the action of LSD in the brain. *Psychiatric Annala, 24,* 137–141.

Aiello, J. R., & Douthitt, E. A. (2001). Social facilitation from Triplett to electronic performance monitoring. *Group Dynamics: Theory, Research, and Practice, 5,* 163–180.

Aiken, L. R. (1996). *Personality assessment methods and practices* (2nd ed.). Seattle: Hogrefe & Huber.

Ainsworth, M. D., Blehar, M. C., Waters, E., & Wall, S. (1978). *Patterns of attachment.* Hillsdale, NJ: Erlbaum.

Aknin, L. B., Norton, M. I., & Dunn, E. W. (2009). From wealth to well-being? Money matters, but less than people think. *Journal of Positive Psychology, 4,* 523–527.

Albouy, G., King, B. R., Maquet, P., & Doyon, J. (2013). Hippocampus and striatum: Dynamics and interaction during acquisition and sleep-related motor sequence memory consolidation. *Hippocampus, 11,* 985–1004. doi: 10.1002/hipo.22183

Albouy, G., Sterpenich, V., Balteau, E., Vandewalle, G., Desseilles, M., Dang-Vu, T. et al. (2008). Both the hippocampus and striatum are involved in consolidation of motor sequence memory. *Neuron, 58,* 261–272.

Aldao, A., Nolen-Hoeksema, S., & Schweizer, S. (2010). Emotion-regulation strategies across psychopathology: A meta-analytic review. *Clinical Psychology Review, 30,* 217–237.

Aldridge, M. A., Stillman, R. D., & Bower, T. G. R. (2001). Newborn categorization of vowel-like sounds. *Developmental Science, 4,* 220–232.

Aleman, A. (2013). Use of repetitive transcranial magnetic stimulation for treatment in psychiatry. *Clinical Psychopharmacology and Neuroscience, 11,* 53–59.

Alexander, G. M. (2003). An evolutionary perspective on sex-typed toy preferences: Pink, blue, and the brain. *Archives of Sexual Behavior, 32,* 7–14.

Alexander, G. M., Wilcox, T., & Woods, R. (2009). Sex differences in infants' visual interest in toys. *Archives of Sexual Behavior, 38,* 427–433.

Allen, L. B., White, K. S., Barlow, D. H., Shear, M. K., Gorman, J. M., & Woods, S. W. (2010). Cognitive-behavior therapy (CBT) for panic disorder: Relationship of anxiety and depression comorbidity with treatment outcome. *Journal of Psychopathology and Behavioral Assessment, 32,* 185–192.

Allen, N. C., Bagade, S., McQueen, M. B., Ioannidis, J. P., Kavvoura, F. K., Khoury, M. J. et al. (2008). Systematic meta-analyses and field synopsis of genetic association studies in schizophrenia: The SzGene database. *Nature Genetics, 40,* 827–834.

Allen, T. D., Lentz, E., & Day, R. (2006). Career success outcomes associated with mentoring others: A comparison of mentors and nonmentors. *Journal of Career Development, 32,* 272–285.

Alloy, L. B., Abramson, L. Y., & Francis, E. L. (1999). Do negative cognitive styles confer vulnerability to depression? *Current Directions in Psychological Science, 8,* 128–132.

Allport, G. W. (1961). *Pattern and growth in personality.* New York: Holt, Rinehart, & Winston.

Allport, G. W. (1979). *The nature of prejudice.* Reading, MA: Addison-Wesley. (Original work published 1954)

Almeida, D. M. (2005). Resilience and vulnerability to daily stressors assessed via diary methods. *Current Directions in Psychological Science, 14,* 64–68.

Alonso, A., & Swiller, H. I. (1993). Introduction: The case for group therapy. In A. Alonso & H. I. Swiller (Eds.), *Group therapy in clinical practice* (pp. xxi–xxv). Washington, DC: American Psychiatric Press.

Alterovitz, S. S., & Mendelsohn, G. A. (2009). Partner preferences across the lifespan: Online dating by older adults. *Psychology and Aging, 24,* 513–517.

Aly, M., & Moscovitch, M. (2010). The effects of sleep on episodic memory in older and younger adults. *Memory, 18,* 327–334.

Amato, P. R. (1993). Children's adjustment to divorce: Theories, hypotheses, and empirical support. *Journal of Marriage and the Family, 55,* 23–38.

Amato, P. R. (2000). The consequences of divorce for adults and children. *Journal of Marriage and Family, 62,* 1269–1287.

Amato, P. R. (2010). Research on divorce: Continuing trends and new developments. *Journal of Marriage and Family, 72,* 650–666.

Amato, P. R., & Booth, A. (1996). A prospective study of divorce and parent-child relationships. *Journal of Marriage and Family, 58,* 356–365.

Amato, P. R., & DeBoer, D. D. (2001). The transmission of marital instability across generations: Relationship skills or commitment to marriage? *Journal of Marriage and Family, 63,* 1038–1051.

Amato, P. R., & Rogers, S. J. (1997). A longitudinal study of marital problems and subsequent divorce. *Journal of Marriage and Family, 59,* 612–624.

Amato, P. R., Johnson, D. R., Booth, A., & Rogers, S. J. (2003). Continuity and change in marital quality between 1980 and 2000. *Journal of Marriage and Family, 65,* 1–22.

American Association of Advertising Agencies. (2014). How many advertisements is a person exposed to in a day? Retrieved from https://ams.aaaa.org/eweb/upload/faqs/adexposures.pdf

American College Health Association (ACHA). (2006). American College Health Association National College Health Assessment (ACHA-NCHA) spring 2005 reference group data report. *Journal of American College Health, 55,* 5–16.

American College of Obstetricians and Gynecologists. (2002). ACOG practice bulletin: Management of recurrent pregnancy loss, 24. *International Journal of Gynaecology and Obstetrics: The Official Organ of the International Federation of Gynaecology and Obstetrics, 78,* 179–190.

American Psychiatric Association (APA). (2000a). *Diagnostic and statistical manual of mental disorders* (4th ed., Text Revision). Washington, DC: Author.

American Psychiatric Association (APA). (2000b). Substance use disorders: Alcohol, cocaine, opiods. In *Practice guidelines for the treatment of psychiatric disorders: Compendium 2000* (pp. 139–238). Washington, DC: Author.

American Psychiatric Association (APA). (2004). *Practice guideline for the treatment of patients with acute stress disorder and posttraumatic stress disorder.* Arlington, VA: Author.

American Psychiatric Association (APA). (2013). *Diagnostic and statistical manual of mental disorders* (5th ed.). Washington, DC: Author.

American Psychological Association (APA). (1975). *Council policy manual.* Retrieved from http://www.apa.org/about/governance/council/policy/index.aspx

American Psychological Association (APA). (1997). *Visions and transformations.* Washington, DC: APA's Commission on Ethnic Minority Recruitment, Retention and Training in Psychology.

American Psychological Association (APA). (2000). *Women in academe: Two steps forward, one step back.* Washington, DC: Author.

American Psychological Association (APA). (2002). Ethical principles of psychologists and code of conduct. *American Psychologist, 57,* 1060–1073.

American Psychological Association (APA). (2004). Resolution on sexual orientation and marriage. Retrieved from http://www.apa.org/releases/gaymarriage.html

American Psychological Association (APA). (2010). *Stress in America findings.* Washington, DC: Author.

American Psychological Association. (2013). *APA guidelines for the undergraduate psychology major: Version 2.0.* Retrieved from http://www.apa.org/ed/precollege/undergrad/index.aspx.

American Psychological Associaton. (2014). *Strengthening the Common Core of the Introductory Psychology Course.* Washington, DC: Author.

Amoore, J. E. (1970). *Molecular basis of odor.* Springfield, IL: Thomas.

Amorapanth, P. X., Widick, P., & Chatterjee, A. (2010). The neural basis for spatial relations. *Journal of Cognitive Neuroscience, 22,* 1739–1753. doi:10.1162/jocn.2009.21322

Amsterdam, J. D., & Shults, J. (2010). Efficacy and safety of long-term fluoxetine versus lithium monotherapy of bipolar II disorder: A randomized, double-blind, placebo substitution study. *American Journal of Psychiatry, 167,* 792–800.

Anderson, B. J., Greenwood, S. J., & McCloskey, D. (2010). Exercise as an intervention for the age-related decline in neural metabolic support. *Frontiers in Aging Neuroscience, 2,* 2–9. doi:10.3389/fnagi.2010.00030

Anderson, C. (2003). Social stress and support factors in susceptibility to the common cold. *APS Observer, 16,* 37.

Anderson, C. A., & Arciniegas, D. B. (2004). Neurosurgical interventions for neuropsychiatric syndromes. *Current Psychiatry Reports, 6,* 355–363.

Anderson, C. A., & Bushman, B. J. (2002). Human aggression. *Annual Review of Psychology, 53,* 27–51.

Anderson, C. A., Benjamin, A. J., & Bartholow, B. D. (1998). Does the gun pull the trigger? Automatic priming effects of weapon pictures and weapon names. *Psychological Science, 9,* 308–314.

Anderson, C., Kraus, M. W., Galinsky, A. D., & Keltner, D. (2012). The local-ladder effect: Social status and subjective well-being. *Psychological Science, 23,* 764–771.

Anderson, E. R., & Mayes, L. C. (2010). Race/ethnicity and internalizing disorders in youth: A review. *Clinical Psychology Review, 30,* 338–348.

Anderson, J. R. (1974). Verbatim and propositional representation of sentences in immediate and long-term memory. *Journal of Verbal Learning and Verbal Behavior, 13,* 149–162.

Anderson, J. R. (2000). *Cognitive psychology and its applications* (5th ed.). New York: Worth.

Anderson, N., & Thomas, H. D. C. (1996). Work group socialization. In M. A. West (Ed.), *Handbook of work group psychology* (pp. 423–450). New York: Wiley.

Anderson, P. L., Zimand, E., Hodges, L. F., & Rothbaum, B. O. (2005). Cognitive behavioral therapy for public-speaking anxiety using virtual reality for exposure. *Depression and Anxiety, 22,* 156–158.

Andresen, G. V., Birch, L. L., & Johnson, P. A. (1990). The scapegoat effect on food aversions after chemotherapy. *Cancer, 66,* 1649–1653.

Andresen, J. (2000). Meditation meets behavioural medicine: The story of experimental research on meditation. *Journal of Consciousness Studies, 7,* 17–73.

Andrews-Hanna, J. R., Snyder, A. Z., Vincent, J. L., Lustig, C., Head, D., Raichle, M. E. et al. (2007). Disruptions of large-scale brain systems in advanced aging. *Neuron, 56,* 924–935.

Angst, J., & Sellaro, R. (2000). Historical perspectives and natural history of bipolar disorder. *Biological Psychiatry, 48,* 445–457.

Anorexia and Related Eating Disorders. (ANRED). (2008). Eating disorder statistics. Retrieved from http://www.anred.com

Anshel, M. H. (1995). Effect of chronic aerobic exercise and progressive relaxation on motor performance and affect following acute stress. *Behavioral Medicine, 21,* 186–196.

Antoni, M. H., & Lutgendorf, S. (2007). Psychosocial factors and disease progression in cancer. *Current Directions in Psychological Science, 16,* 42–46.

Antony, M. M., & Barlow, D. H. (Eds.). (2002). *Handbook of assessment and treatment planning for psychological disorders.* New York: Guilford Press.

APA Center for Psychology Workforce Analysis and Research. (2007a). 2006–07 Faculty salary survey. Retrieved from http://www.apa.org/workforce/publications/07-fac-sal/index.aspx

APA Center for Psychology Workforce Analysis and Research. (2007b). 2008 Graduate study in psychology. Retrieved from http:/www.apa.org/workforce/snapshots/2007/figure-15.aspx

APA Center for Workforce Studies. (2007). 2007 Doctorate employment survey. Retrieved from http://www.apa.org/workforce/publications/07-doc-empl/table-3.pdf

APA Center for Workforce Studies. (2010a). 2009–2010 faculty salaries in graduate departments of psychology. Retrieved from http://www.apa.org/workforce/publications/10-fac-sal/index.aspx

APA Center for Workforce Studies. (2010b). Master's- and doctoral-level students in U.S. and Canadian graduate departments of psychology, 2008–2009. Retrieved from http://www.apa.org/workforce/publications/10-grad-study/students.aspx

Applbaum, K. D. (1995). Marriage with the proper stranger: Arranged marriage in metropolitan Japan. *Ethnology, 34,* 37–51.

Appleby, D. (1997). *The handbook of psychology.* New York: Longman.

Arendt, J. (2006). Melatonin and human rhythms. *Chronobiology International, 23,* 21–37.

Arendt, R. E., Short, E. J., Singer, L. T., Minnes, S., Hewitt, J., Flynn, S. et al. (2004). Children prenatally exposed to cocaine: Developmental outcomes and environmental risks at seven years of age. *Journal of Developmental and Behavioral Pediatrics, 25,* 83–90.

Arent, S. M., & Landers, D. M. (2003). Arousal, anxiety, and performance: A reexamination of the inverted-U hypothesis. *Research Quarterly for Exercise and Sport, 74,* 436–444.

Arias, J. M. C., Palacio Acosta, C. A., Valencia, J. G., Montoya, G. J., Arango Viana, J. C. et al. (2011). Exploring epistasis in candidate genes for antisocial personality disorder. *Psychiatric Genetics, 21,* 115–124.

Armfield, J. M. (2006). Cognitive vulnerability: A model of the etiology of fear. *Clinical Psychology Review, 26,* 746–768.

Armitage, R. (1995). The distribution of EEG frequencies in REM and NREM sleep stages in healthy young adults. *Sleep, 18,* 334–341.

Arnett, J. J. (2004). *Emerging adulthood: The winding road from the late teens through the twenties.* New York: Oxford University Press.

Arnett, J. J. (2007). Emerging adulthood: What is it and what is it good for? *Child Development Perspectives, 1,* 68–73.

Arnett, J. J. (2010). Oh, grow up! Generational grumbling and the new life stage of emerging adulthood—Commentary on Trzesniewski & Donnellan (2010). *Perspectives on Psychological Science, 5,* 89–92.

Aronson, E. (1998). Dissonance, hypocrisy, and the self-concept. In E. Harmon-Jones & J. S. Mills (Eds.), *Cognitive dissonance theory: Revival with revisions and controversies* (pp. 103–126). Washington, DC: American Psychological Association.

Aronson, E. (2000). The jigsaw strategy. *Psychology Review, 7,* 2.

Aronson, E. (2011). Reducing prejudice and building empathy in the classroom. In M. Gernsbacher, R. W. Pew, L. M. Hough, & J. R. Pomerantz (Eds.), *Psychology and the real world: Essays illustrating fundamental contributions to society* (pp. 230–236). New York: Worth.

Aronson, E., Wilson, T. D., & Akert, R. M. (2005). *Social psychology* (5th ed.). Englewood Cliffs, NJ: Prentice Hall.

Arroll, B., Macgillivray, S., Ogston, S., Reid, I., Sullivan, F., Williams, B., & Crombie, I. (2005). Efficacy and tolerability of tricyclic antidepressants and SSRIs compared with placebo for treatment of depression in primary care: A meta-analysis. *Annals of Family Medicine, 3,* 449–456.

Arthur, J. B. (1994). Effects of human resource systems on manufacturing performance and turnover. *Academy of Management Journal, 37,* 670–687.

Asay, T. P., & Lambert, M. J. (1999). The empirical case for the common factors in therapy: Quantitative findings. In M. A. Hubble, B. L. Duncan, & S. D. Miller (Eds.), *The heart and soul of change: What works in therapy* (pp. 33–56). Washington, DC: American Psychological Association.

Asch, S. E. (1951). Effects of group pressure upon modification and distortion of judgments. In H. Guetzkow (Ed.), *Groups, leadership, and men* (pp. 117–190). Pittsburgh: Carnegie.

Ashby, F. G., & Maddox, W. T. (2005). Human category learning. *Annual Review of Psychology, 56,* 149–178.

Ashcan, K., Wallace, B., Bell, B. A., & Benabid, A. L. (2004). Deep brain stimulation of the subthalamic nucleus in Parkinson's disease 1993–2003: Where are we ten years on? *British Journal of Neurosurgery, 18,* 19–34.

Ashtari, M., Cervellione, K. L., Hasan, K. M., Wu, J., McIlree, C., Kester, H. et al. (2007). White matter development during late adolescence in healthy males: A cross-sectional diffusion tensor imaging study. *NeuroImage, 35,* 501–510.

Ashwin, C., Baron-Cohen, S., Wheelwright, S., O'Riordan, M., & Bullmore, E. T. (2006). Differential activation of the amygdala and the "social brain" during fearful face-processing in Asperger syndrome. *Neuropsychologia, 45,* 2–14.

Asnis, G. M., Kohn, S. R., Henderson, M., & Brown, N. L. (2004). SSRIs versus non-SSRIs in post-traumatic stress disorder: An update with recommendations. *Drugs, 64,* 383–404.

Associated Press. (2009). Study reinforces that kids watch a lot of TV. Retrieved from http://news.yahoo.com/s/ap/20091026/ap_en_tv/us_preschool_tv/print

Assor, A., Roth, G., & Deci, E. L. (2004). The emotional costs of parents' conditional regard: A self-determination theory analysis. *Journal of Personality, 72,* 47–88.

Astin, J. A. (2004). Mind–body therapies for the management of pain. *Clinical Journal of Pain, 20,* 27–32.

Atas, A., Faivre, N., Timmermans, B., Cleeremans, A., & Kouider, S. (2014). Nonconscious learning from crowded sequences. *Psychological Science, 25,* 113–119.

Atkinson, J. W. (1983). Towards experimental analysis of human motivation in terms of motives, expectancies, and incentives. In J. W. Atkinson (Ed.), *Personality, motivation, and action: Selected papers* (pp. 81–97). New York: Praeger. (Original work published 1958)

Atkinson, R. C., & Shiffrin, R. W. (1968). Human memory: A proposed system and its control processes. In K. Spence & J. Spence (Eds.), *The psychology of learning and motivation* (Vol. 2, pp. 89–195). New York: Academic Press.

Aucoin, D. (2000, May 25). Feminist report says "sexist stereotypes" abound in prime time. *Oregonian,* E9.

Augustine, G. J. (2012). Neurotransmitters and their receptors. In D. Purves, G. J. Augustine, D. Fitzpatrick, W. C. Hall, A. LaManita, & L. E. White (Eds.), *Neuroscience* (5th ed., pp. 109–140). Sunderland, MA: Sinauer Associates.

Augustus-Horvath, C. L., & Tylka, T. L. (2011). The acceptance model of intuitive eating: A comparison of women in emerging adulthood, early adulthood, and middle adulthood. *Journal of Counseling Psychology, 58,* 110–125.

Auyeung, B., Baron-Cohen, S., Ashwin, E., Knickmeyer, R., Taylor, K., Hackett, G. et al. (2009). Fetal testosterone predicts sexually differentiated childhood behavior in girls and in boys. *Psychological Science, 20,* 144–148.

Avalos, L. C., & Tylka, T. L. (2006). Exploring a model of intuitive eating with college women. *Journal of Counseling Psychology, 53,* 486–497.

Avolio, B. J., Kahai, S. S., & Dodge, G. (2000). E-leading in organizations and its implications for theory, research and practice. *Leadership Quarterly, 11,* 615–670.

Azar, B. (1998). A genetic disposition for certain tastes may affect people's food preferences. *American Psychological Association Monitor,* 29. Retrieved from http://www.apa.org/monitor/jan98/food.html

Azevedo, F. A., Carvalho, L. R., Grinberg, L. T., Farfel, J. M., Ferretti, R. E., Leite, R. E. et al. (2009). Equal numbers of neuronal and nonneuronal cells make the human brain an isometrically scaled-up primate brain. *Journal of Comparative Neurology, 513,* 532–541.

Bachman, J. G., Johnston, L. D., & O'Malley, P. M. (2001). *Monitoring the future: Questionnaire responses from the nation's high school seniors, 2000.* Ann Arbor, MI: Institute for Social Research.

Bachman, J. G., Johnston, L. D., & O'Malley, P. M. (2009). *Monitoring the future: Questionnaire responses from the nation's high school seniors, 2008.* Ann Arbor, MI: Institute for Social Research.

Baddeley, A. (2012). Working memory: Theories, models, and controversies. *Annual Review of Psychology, 63,* 1–29. doi: 10.1146/annurev-psych-120710-100422

Baddeley, A. D. (1986). *Working memory.* Oxford: Clarendon Press.

Baddeley, A. D. (1992). Working memory. *Science, 255,* 556–559.

Baddeley, A. D. (2002). Is working memory still working? *European Psychologist, 7,* 85–97.

Baddeley, A. D., & Hitch, G. J. (1974). Working memory. In G. H. Bower (Ed.), *The psychology of learning and motivation* (Vol. 8, 47–89). London: Academic Press.

Baer, L., Rauch, S. L., Ballantine, T., Martuza, R., Cosgrove, R., Cassem, E. et al. (1995). Cingulotomy for intractable obsessive-compulsive disorder. *Archives of General Psychiatry, 52,* 384–392.

Bagshaw, S. M., Jr. (1985). The desensitisation of chronically motion sick aircrew in the Royal Air Force. *Aviation Space Environmental Medicine, 56,* 1144–1151.

Bahk, C. (2006). College students' perceived risk and anxiety after reading airplane crash news. *Psychological Reports, 99,* 107–110.

Bahrick, H. P. (1984). Semantic memory content in permastore: Fifty years of memory for Spanish learned in school. *Journal of Experimental Psychology: General, 113,* 1–24.

Bailey, J., & Pillard, R. C. (1991). A genetic study of male sexual orientation. *Archives of General Psychiatry, 48,* 1089–1096.

Bailey, J., Dunne, M., & Martin, N. (2000). Genetic and environmental influences on sexual orientation and its correlates in an Australian twin sample. *Journal of Personality and Social Psychology, 78,* 524–536.

Bailey, J., Pillard, R. C., Neale, M. C., & Agyei, Y. (1993). Heritable factors influence female sexual orientation in women. *Archives of General Psychiatry, 50,* 217–223.

Baird, A. A., Gruber, S. A., Fein, D. A., Maas, L. C., Steingard, R. J., Renshaw, P. F. et al. (1999). Functional magnetic resonance imaging of facial affect recognition in children and adolescents. *Journal of the American Academy of Child and Adolescent Psychiatry, 38,* 195–209.

Baker, T. B., Japuntich, S. J., Hogle, J. M., McCarthy, D. E., & Curtin, J. J. (2006). Pharmacologic and behavioral withdrawal from addictive drugs. *Current Directions in Psychological Science, 15,* 232–236.

Baker, T. B., McFall, R. M., & Shoham, V. (2008). Current status and future prospects of clinical psychology: Toward a scientifically principled approach to mental and behavioral health care. *Psychological Science in the Public Interest, 9,* 67–103.

Ball, E. M. (1997). Sleep disorders in primary care. *Comprehensive Therapy, 23,* 25–30.

Balsam, K. F., Rothblum, E. D., & Beauchaine, T. P. (2005). Victimization over the life span: A comparison of lesbian, gay, bisexual, and heterosexual siblings. *Journal of Consulting and Clinical Psychology, 73,* 477–487.

Baltes, P. B. (1997). On the incomplete architecture of human ontogeny: Selection, optimization, and compensation as foundation of developmental theory. *American Psychologist, 52,* 366–380.

Balthazart, J., & Ball, G. F. (2006). Is brain estradiol a hormone or neurotransmitter? *Trends in Neurosciences, 29,* 241–249.

Balzer, W. K., Kihm, J. A., Smith, P. C., Irwin, J. L., Bachiochi, P. D., Robie, C. et al. (1997). *Users' manual for the Job Descriptive Index (JDI, 1997 revision) and the Job in General Scales.* Bowling Green, OH: Bowling Green State University.

Bandura, A. (1965). Influence of model's reinforcement contingencies on the acquisition of imitative responses. *Journal of Personality and Social Psychology, 1,* 589–595.

Bandura, A. (1977). *Social learning theory.* Englewood Cliffs, NJ: Prentice Hall.

Bandura, A. (1986). *Social foundations of thought and action: A social cognitive theory.* Englewood Cliffs, NJ: Prentice Hall.

Bandura, A. (1997). *Self-efficacy: The exercise of control.* New York: W. H. Freeman.

Bandura, A., Grusec, J. E., & Menlove, F. L. (1966). Observational learning as a function of symbolization and incentive set. *Child Development, 37,* 499–506.

Bandura, A., Ross, D., & Ross, S. (1961). Transmission of aggression through imitation of aggressive models. *Journal of Abnormal and Social Psychology, 63,* 575–582.

Bandura, A., Ross, D., & Ross, S. (1963). Imitation of film-mediated aggressive models. *Journal of Abnormal and Social Psychology, 66,* 3–11.

Bangasser, D. A., Waxler, D. E., Santollo, J., & Shors, T. J. (2006). Trace conditioning and the hippocampus: The importance of contiguity. *Journal of Neuroscience, 26,* 8702–8706.

Banich, M. T., & Heller, W. (1998). Evolving perspectives on lateralization of function. *Current Directions in Psychological Science, 74,* 1–2.

Banthia, R., Moskowitz, J. T., Acree, M., & Folkman, S. (2007). Socioeconomic differences in the effect of prayer on physical symptoms and quality of life. *Journal of Health Psychology, 12,* 249–260.

Baraas, R. C., Foster, D. H., Amano, K., & Nascimento, S. M. (2006). Anomalous judgments of surface color in natural scenes under different daylights. *Visual Neuroscience, 23,* 629–635.

Barakat, M., Carrier, J., Debas, K., Lungu, O., Fogel, S. et al. (2013). Sleep spindles predict neural and behavioral changes in motor sequence consolidation. *Human Brain Mapping, 34,* 2918–2928.

Barbee, J. G. (1993). Memory, benzodiazepines, and anxiety: Integration of theoretical and clinical perspectives. *Journal of Clinical Psychiatry, 54*(10 supplement), 86–101.

Barber, J. P., Connolly, M. B., Crits-Christoph, P., Gladis, L., & Siqueland, L. (2000). Alliance predicts patients' outcome beyond in-treatment change in symptoms. *Journal of Consulting and Clinical Psychology, 68,* 1027–1032.

Barber, T. X. (2000). A deeper understanding of hypnosis: Its secrets, its nature, its essence. *American Journal of Clinical Hypnosis, 42,* 208–272.

Barch, D. M., Cohen, R., & Csernansky, J. G. (2014). Altered cognitive development in the siblings of individuals with schizophrenia. *Clinical Psychological Science, 2,* 138–151.

Bardone, A. M., Vohs, K. D., Abramson, L. Y., Heatherton, T. F., & Joiner, T. E., Jr. (2000). The confluence of perfectionism, body dissatisfaction, and low self-esteem predicts bulimic symptoms: Clinical implications. *Behavior Therapy, 31,* 265–280.

Barger, L. K., Lockley, S. W., Rajaratnam, S. M., & Landrigan, C. P. (2009). Neurobehavioral, health, and safety consequences associated with shift work in safety-sensitive professions. *Current Neurology and Neuroscience Reports, 9,* 155–164.

Bargh, J. A., & Morsella, E. (2008). The unconscious mind. *Perspectives on Psychological Science, 3,* 73–79.

Bar-Haim, Y., Ziv, T., Lamy, D., & Hodes, R. M. (2006). Nature and nurture in own-race face processing. *Psychological Science, 17,* 159–163.

Barker, J., Jones, M., & Greenlees, I. (2010). Assessing the immediate and maintained effects of hypnosis on self-efficacy and soccer wall-volley performance. *Journal of Sport and Exercise Psychology, 32,* 243–252.

Barker, V. (2009). Older adolescents' motivations for social network site use: The influence of gender, group identity, and collective self-esteem. *Cyberpsychology & Behavior, 12,* 209–213.

Barlow, D. H. (2000). Unraveling the mysteries of anxiety and its disorders from the perspective of emotion theory. *American Psychologist, 55,* 1247–1263.

Barlow, D. H. (2002). *Anxiety and its disorders: The nature and treatment of anxiety and panic* (2nd ed.). New York: Guilford Press.

Barlow, D. H., & Durand, V. M. (2005). *Abnormal psychology: An integrative approach* (4th ed.). Belmont, CA: Wadsworth.

Barnes, A. (2004). Race, schizophrenia, and admission to state psychiatric hospitals. *Administration and Policy in Mental Health, 31,* 241–252.

Barnes, J., Dong, C. Y., McRobbie, H., Walker, N., Mehta, M., & Stead, L. F. (2010). Hypnotherapy for smoking cessation. *Cochrane Database of Systematic Reviews (Online), 6,* CD001008.

Baron, R. A., & Richardson, D. R. (1992). *Human aggression* (2nd ed.). New York: Plenum Press.

Barrera, T. L., Mott, J. M., Hofstein, R. F., & Teng, E. J. (2013). A meta-analytic review of exposure in group cognitive behavioral therapy for posttraumatic stress disorder. *Clinical Psychology Review, 33,* 24–32.

Barsalou, L. W. (2008). Grounded cognition. *Annual Review of Psychology, 59,* 617–645.

Barth, K. S., & Malcolm, R. J. (2010). Disulfiram: An old therapeutic with new applications. *CNS and Neurological Disorders Drug Targets, 9,* 5–12.

Bartlett, F. C. (1932). *Remembering.* Cambridge: Cambridge University Press.

Bartoshuk, L. M. (2000). Comparing sensory experiences across individuals: Recent psychophysical advances illuminate genetic variation in taste perception. *Chemical Senses, 25,* 447–460.

Bartoshuk, L. M., & Beauchamp, G. K. (1994). Chemical senses. *Annual Review of Psychology, 45,* 419–449.

Bass, B. M. (1990). From transactional to transformational leadership: Learning to share the vision. *Organizational Dynamics, 18,* 19–31.

Bassuk, S. S., & Manson, J. E. (2010). Physical activity and cardiovascular disease prevention in women: A review of the epidemiological evidence. *Nutrition, Metabolism, and Cardiovascular Diseases, 20,* 467–473.

Batabyal, A. A. (2001). On the likelihood of finding the right partner in an arranged marriage. *Journal of Socio-Economics, 30,* 273–281.

Bates, B. L. (1994). Individual differences in response to hypnosis. In J. W. Rhue, S. J. Lynn, & I. Kirsch (Eds.), *Handbook of clinical hypnosis* (pp. 23–54). Washington, DC: American Psychological Association.

Batsell, W. R., Jr. (2000). Augmentation: Synergistic conditioning in taste-aversion learning. *Current Directions in Psychological Science, 9,* 164–168.

Bauby, J. D. (1997). *The diving bell and the butterfly.* New York: Vintage.

Bauer, M. A., Wilkie, J. E., Kim, J. K., & Bodenhausen, G. V . (2012). Cuing consumerism: Situational materialism undermines personal and social well-being. *Psychological Science, 23,* 517–523.

Baumann, A. E. (2007). Stigmatization, social distance and exclusion because of mental illness: The individual with mental illness as a "stranger." *International Review of Psychiatry, 19,* 131–135.

Baumeister, R. F. (2004). Gender and erotic plasticity: Sociocultural influences on the sex drive. *Sexual and Relationship Therapy, 19,* 133–139. doi: 10.1080/14681990410001691343

Baumeister, R. F., & Leary, M. R. (1995). The need to belong: The desire for interpersonal attachments as a fundamental human motivation. *Psychological Bulletin, 117,* 497–529.

Baumrind, D. (1964). Some thoughts on ethics of research: After reading Milgram's "Behavioral Study of Obedience." *American Psychologist, 19,* 421–423.

Baumrind, D. (1967). Child care practices anteceding three patterns of preschool behavior. *Genetic Psychology Monographs, 75,* 43–88.

Baumrind, D. (1971). Current patterns of parental authority. *Developmental Psychology Monograph, 4*(1, Pt. 2).

Beal, C. R. (1994). *Boys and girls: The development of gender roles.* New York: McGraw-Hill.

Beardsley, E. (2011). The French are getting fatter too. *National Public Radio, Special Series. Living Large: Obesity in America.* Retrieved from http://www.npr.org/2011/08/06/139042221/the-french-are-getting-fatter-too.

Beardsley, T. (1996, July). Waking up. *Scientific American,* pp. 14, 18.

Beatty, W. W. (1992). Gonadal hormones and sex differences in nonreproductive behaviors. In A. A. Gerall, H. Moltz, & I. L. Ward (Eds.), *Handbook of behavioral neurobiology: Vol. 11. Sexual differentiation* (pp. 85–128). New York: Plenum Press.

Beauducel, A., Brocke, B., & Leue, A. (2006). Energetical bases of extraversion: Effort, arousal, EEG, and performance. *International Journal of Psychophysiology, 62,* 212–223.

Beauregard, M. (2007). Mind does really matter: Evidence from neuroimaging studies of emotional self-regulation, psychotherapy, and placebo effect. *Progress in Neurobiology, 81,* 218–236.

Beck, A. T. (1967). *Depression: Clinical, experimental, and theoretical aspects.* New York: Harper & Row.

Beck, A. T. (1976). *Cognitive therapy and the emotional disorders.* New York: International Universities Press.

Beck, A. T. (1991). Cognitive therapy: A 30-year retrospective. *American Psychologist, 46,* 368–375.

Beck, A. T. (1997). Cognitive therapy: Reflections. In J. K. Zeig (Ed.), *The evolution of psychotherapy: The third conference* (pp. 55–67). New York: Brunner/Mazel.

Beck, A. T. (2008). The evolution of the cognitive model of depression and its neurobiological correlates. *American Journal of Psychiatry, 165,* 969–977.

Beck, A. T., Rush, A. J., Shaw, B. F., & Emery, G. (1979). *Cognitive therapy of depression.* New York: Guilford Press.

Beck, J. G., Palyo, S. A., Winer, E. H., Schwagler, B. E., & Ang, E. J. (2007). Virtual reality exposure therapy for PTSD symptoms after a road accident: An uncontrolled case series. *Behavior Therapy, 38,* 39–48.

Becker, P. M., Schwartz, J. R., Feldman, N. T., & Hughes, R. J. (2004). Effect of modafinil on fatigue, mood, and health-related quality of life in patients with narcolepsy. *Psychopharmacology, 171,* 133–139.

Beem, E. E., Hooijkaas, H., Cleiren, M. H., Schut, H. A., Garssen, B., Croon, M. A. et al. (1999). The immunological and psychological effects of bereavement: Does grief counseling really make a difference? A pilot study. *Psychiatry Research, 85,* 81–93.

Behme, C., & Deacon, S. H. (2008). Language learning in infancy: Does the empirical evidence support a domain specific language acquisition device? *Philosophical Psychology, 21,* 641–671.

Békésy, G. von. (1960). *Experiments in hearing.* New York: McGraw-Hill.

Bell, A. R., Weinberg, M. S., & Hammersmith, S. K. (1981). *Sexual preference: Its development in men and women.* Bloomington: Indiana University Press.

Belsky, J., & Rovine, M. (1990). Patterns of marital change across the transition to parenthood: Pregnancy to three years postpartum. *Journal of Marriage and Family, 52,* 5–19.

Bem, D. J. (2011). Feeling the future: Experimental evidence for anomalous retroactive influences on cognition and affect. *Journal of Personality and Social Psychology, 100,* 407–425. doi:10.1037/a0021524

Bem, S. L. (1981). Gender schema theory: A cognitive account of sex typing. *Psychological Review, 88,* 354–364.

Benabid, A. L., Koudsie, A., Benazzouz, A., Vercueil, L., Fraix, V., Chabardes, S. et al. (2001). Deep brain stimulation of the corpus luysi (subthalamic nucleus) and other targets in Parkinson's disease. Extension to new indications such as dystonia and epilepsy. *Journal of Neurology, 248*(Suppl. 3), III37–III47.

Bender, E. (2004). Virtual reality treatment combats phobias, PTSD. *Psychiatric News, 39,* 45.

Benham, G., Woody, E. Z., Wilson, K. S., & Nash, M. R. (2006). Expect the unexpected: Ability, attitude, and responsiveness to hypnosis. *Journal of Personality and Social Psychology, 91,* 342–350.

Benjamin, L. T., Jr., Henry, K. D., & McMahon, L. R. (2005). Inez Beverly Prosser and the education of African Americans. *Journal of the History of the Behavioral Sciences, 41,* 43–62.

Bennett, M. P., Zeller, J. M., Rosenberg, L., & McCann, J. (2003). The effect of mirthful laughter on stress and natural killer cell activity. *Alternative Therapies in Health and Medicine, 9,* 38–45.

Bennett, W. I. (1990, December). Boom and doom. *Harvard Health Letter, 16,* 1–3.

Benoit, S. C., McQuade, J.-A., Clegg, D. J., Xu, M., Rushing, P. A., Woods, S. C. et al. (2003). Altered feeding responses in mice with targeted disruption of the dopamine-3 receptor gene. *Behavioral Neuroscience, 117,* 46–54.

Benson, H. (1996). *Timeless healing: The power and biology of belief.* New York: Scribner.

Berger, A. M., & Hobbs, B. B. (2006). Impact of shift work on the health and safety of nurses and patients. *Clinical Journal of Oncology Nursing, 10,* 465–471.

Berk, L. E., & Spuhl, S. T. (1995). Maternal interaction, private speech, and task performance in preschool children. *Early Childhood Research Quarterly, 10,* 145–169.

Berkowitz, L. (1990). On the formation and regulation of anger and aggression: A cognitive-neoassociationistic analysis. *American Psychologist, 45,* 494–503.

Berlau, D. J., Corrada, M. M., & Kawas, C. (2009). The prevalence of disability in the oldest-old is high and continues to increase with age: Findings from The 90+ Study. *International Journal of Geriatric Psychiatry, 24,* 1217–1225. doi:10.1002/gps.2248

Bernstein, K. S., Park, S. Y., Shin, J., Cho, S., & Park, Y. (2011). Acculturation, discrimination and depressive symptoms among Korean immigrants in New York City. *Community Mental Health Journal, 47,* 24–34.

Berntsen, D., Johannessen, K. B., Thomsen, Y. D., Bertelsen, M., Hoyle, R. H., & Rubin, D. C. (2012). Peace and war: Trajectories of posttraumatic stress disorder symptoms before, during, and after military deployment in Afghanistan. *Psychological Science, 23,* 1557–1565.

Berry, A. K. (2006). Helping children with nocturnal enuresis: The wait-and-see approach may not be in anyone's best interest. *American Journal of Nursing, 106,* 56–63.

Berry, M. S., Kangas, B. D., & Branch, M. N. (2012). Development of key-pecking, pause, and ambulation during extended exposure to a fixed-interval schedule of reinforcement. *Journal of Experimental Analysis of Behavior, 97,* 333–346.

Berscheid, E., Dion, K., Walster, E., & Walster, G. W. (1971). Physical attractiveness and dating choice: A test of the matching hypothesis. *Journal of Experimental Social Psychology, 7,* 173–189.

Berwick, R. C., Pietroski, P., Yankama, B., & Chomsky, N. (2011). Poverty of the stimulus revisited. *Cognitive Science, 35,* 1207–1242. doi:10.1111/j.1551-6709.2011.01189.x

Betz, N. E. (1993). Women's career development. In F. L. Denmark & M. A. Paludi (Eds.), *Psychology of women* (pp. 627–684). Westport, CT: Greenwood Press.

Beutler, L. E., Machado, P. P., & Neufeldt, S. A. (1994). Therapist variables. In A. E. Bergin & S. L. Garfield (Eds.), *Handbook of psychotherapy and behavior change* (4th ed., pp. 229–269). New York: Wiley.

Bezchlibnyk-Butler, K. Z., & Jeffries, J. J. (Eds.). (1998). *Clinical handbook of psychotropic drugs* (8th ed.). Seattle: Hogrete & Huber.

Bhaskara, R. M., Brijesh, C. M., Ahmed, S., & Borges, R. M. (2009). Perception of ultraviolet light by crab spiders and its role in the selection of hunting sites. *Journal of Comparative Physiology. A, Neuroethology, Sensory, Neural, and Behavioral Physiology, 195,* 409–417.

Bianchi, S. M., Kilkie, M. A., Sayer, L. C., & Robinson, J. P. (2000). Is anyone doing the housework? Trends in the gender division of household labor. *Social Forces, 79,* 191–228.

Binder, J., Zagefka, H., Brown, R., Funke, F., Kessler, T., Mummendey, A. et al. (2009). Does contact reduce prejudice or does prejudice reduce contact? A longitudinal test of the contact hypothesis among majority and minority groups in three European countries. *Journal of Personality and Social Psychology, 96,* 843–856.

Binet, A., & Simon, T. (1905). Méthodes nouvelles pour le diagnotics du niveau intéllectuel des anormaux. *L'Année Psychologique, 11,* 191–244.

Biss, R. K., Campbell, K. L., & Hasher, L. (2013). Interference from previous distraction disrupts older adults' memory. *Journals of Gerontology: Series B: Psychological Sciences And Social Sciences, 68B,* 558–561.

Bissell, K., & Hays, H. (2011). Understanding anti-fat bias in children: The role of media and appearance anxiety in third to sixth graders' implicit and explicit attitudes toward obesity. *Mass Communication & Society, 14,* 113–140. doi: 10.1080/15205430903464592

Bisson, J. I., Ehlers, A., Matthews, R., Pilling, S., Richards, D., & Turner, S. (2007). Psychological treatments for chronic post-traumatic stress disorder. Systematic review and meta-analysis. *British Journal of Psychiatry, 190,* 97–104.

Black, D. W., Blum, N., Pfohl, B., & Hale, N. (2004). Suicidal behavior in borderline personality disorder: Prevalence, risk factors, prediction, and prevention. *Journal of Personality and Disorders, 18,* 226–239.

Black, L. S., deRegnier, R. A., Long, J., Georgieff, M. K., & Nelson, C. A. (2004). Electrographic imaging of recognition memory in 34–38 week gestation intrauterine growth restricted newborns. *Experimental Neurology, 190,* S72–S83.

Blackwell, L. V., Snyder, L. A., & Mavriplis, C. (2009). Diverse faculty in STEM fields: Attitudes, performance, and fair treatment. *Journal of Diversity in Higher Education, 2,* 195–205.

Blagys, M. D., & Hilsenroth, M. J. (2000). Distinctive features of short-term psychodynamic-interpersonal psychotherapy: A review of the comparative psychotherapy process literature. *Clinical Psychology: Science and Practice, 7,* 167–188.

Blanchard, B., Heurtaux, T., Garcia, C., Moll, N. M., Caillava, C., Grandbarbe, L. et al. (2013). Tocopherol derivative TFA-12 promotes myelin repair in experimental models of multiple sclerosis. *Journal of Neuroscience, 33,* 11633–11642. doi:10.1523/JNEUROSCI.0774-13.2013

Blanchard, R. (2008). Review and theory of handedness, birth order, and homosexuality in men. *Laterality, 13,* 51–70.

Blane, H. T. (1988). Prevention issues with children of alcoholics. *British Journal of Addiction, 83,* 793–798.

Blatt, S. J., & Shahar, G. (2004). Psychoanalysis—with whom, for what, and how? Comparisons with psychotherapy. *Journal of the American Psychoanalysis Association, 52,* 393–447.

Blazer, D. G., Kessler, R. C., McGonagle, K. A., & Swartz, M. S. (1994). The prevalence and distribution of major depression in a national community sample: The National Comorbidity Study. *American Journal of Psychiatry, 151,* 979–986.

Blehm, C., Vishnu, S., Khattak, A., Mitra, S., & Yee, R. W. (2005). Computer vision syndrome: A review. *Survey of Ophthalmology, 50,* 253–262.

Bleidorn, W., Klimstra, T. A., Denissen, J., Rentfrow, P. J., Potter, J., & Gosling, S. D. (2013). Personality maturation around the world: A cross-cultural examination of social-investment theory. *Psychological Science, 24,* 2530–2540.

Bleiker, E. M., Hendriks, J. H., Otten, J. D., Verbeek, A. L., & van der Ploeg, H. M. (2008). Personality factors and breast cancer risk: A thirteen-year follow-up. *Journal of the National Cancer Institute, 100,* 213–218.

Bleiker, E. M., van der Ploeg, H. M., Hendriks, J. H., & Ader, H. J. (1996). Personality factors and breast cancer development: A prospective longitudinal study. *Journal of the National Cancer Institute, 88,* 1478–1482.

Blevins, J. E., & Baskin, D. G. (2010). Hypothalamic-brainstem circuits controlling eating. *Forum of Nutrition, 63,* 133–140.

Blincoe, L., Seay, A., Zaloshnja, E., Miller, T., Romano, E., Luchter, S. et al. (2002). *The economic impact of motor vehicle crashes, 2000.*

Washington, DC: National Highway Traffic Safety Administration.

Block, J. A. (1995). A contrarian view of the five-factor approach. *Psychological Bulletin, 117,* 187–215.

Blomstedt, P., Sjöberg, R. L., Hansson, M., Bodlund, O., & Hariz, M. I. (2013). Deep brain stimulation in the treatment of obsessive-compulsive disorder. *World Neurosurgery, 80,* e245–e253.

Bloom, F., Nelson, C. A., & Lazerson, A. (2001). *Brain, mind and behavior* (3rd ed.). New York: Worth.

Bloom, J. W. (1998). The ethical practice of Web-Counseling. *British Journal of Guidance and Counselling, 26,* 53–59.

Boden, M. (1988). *Computer models of the mind.* Cambridge: Cambridge University Press.

Boeri, M. W., Sterk, C. E., & Elifson, K. W. (2004). Rolling beyond raves: Ecstasy use outside the rave setting. *Journal of Drug Issues, 34,* 831–860.

Bogels, S. M., Alden, L., Beidel, D. C., Clark, L. A., Pine, D. S., Stein, M. B., & Voncken, M. (2010). Social anxiety disorder: Questions and answers for the DSM-V. *Depression and Anxiety, 27,* 168–189.

Bohnen, N. I., Muller, M. I., Kuwabara, H., Constantine, G. M., & Studenski, S. A. (2009). Age-associated leukoarasosis and cortical cholinergic deafferentation. *Neurology, 72,* 1411–1416.

Boivin, D. B., Czeisler, C. A., Kijk, D. J., Duffy, J. F., Folkard, S., Minors, D. S. et al. (1997). Complex interaction of sleep-wake cycle and circadian phase modulates mood in healthy subjects. *Archives of General Psychiatry, 54,* 145–152.

Bolles, R. C. (1972). Reinforcement, expectancy, and learning. *Psychological Review, 79,* 394–409.

Bolton, M., van der Straten, A., & Cohen, C. (2008). Probiotics: Potential to prevent HIV and sexually transmitted infections in women. *Sexually Transmitted Diseases, 35,* 214–225.

Bonanno, G. A. (2004). Loss, trauma, and human resilience. *American Psychologist, 59,* 20–28.

Bonanno, G. A., & Burton, C. L. (2013). Regulatory flexibility: An individual differences perspective on coping and emotion regulation. *Perspectives on Psychological Science, 8,* 591–612.

Bonanno, G. A., Brewin, C. R., Kaniasty, K., & La Greca, A. M. (2010). Weighing the costs of disaster: Consequences, risks, and resilience in individuals, families, and communities. *Psychological Science in the Public Interest, 11,* 1–49.

Bonanno, G. A., Galea, S., Bucciarelli, A., & Vlahov, D. (2006). Psychological resilience after disaster: New York City in the aftermath of the September 11th terrorist attack. *Psychological Science, 17,* 181–186.

Bond, R., & Smith, P. B. (1996). Culture and conformity: A meta-analysis of studies using Asch's (1952, 1956) line judgment task. *Psychological Bulletin, 119,* 111–137.

Bonne, O., Vythilingam, M., Inagaki, M., Wood, S., Neumeister, A., Nugent, A. C. et al. (2008). Reduced posterior hippocampal volume in posttraumatic stress disorder. *Journal of Clinical Psychiatry, 69,* 1087–1091.

Bonte, M. (1962). The reaction of two African societies to the Mueller-Lyer illusion. *Journal of Social Psychology, 58,* 265–268.

Booth, A., & Amato, P. R. (2001). Parental predivorce relations and offspring post-divorce well-being. *Journal of Marriage and Family, 63,* 197–212.

Booth-Kewley, S., & Friedman, H. S. (1987). Psychological predictions of heart disease: A quantitative review. *Psychological Bulletin, 101,* 343–362.

Bootzin, R. R., & Rider, S. P. (1997). Behavioral techniques and biofeedback for insomnia. In M. R. Pressman & W. C. Orr (Eds.), *Understanding sleep: The evaluation and treatment of sleep disorders* (pp. 315–338). Washington DC: American Psychological Association.

Bor, D., & Seth, A. K. (2012). Consciousness and the prefrontal parietal network: Insights from attention, working memory, and chunking. *Frontiers in Psychology, 3, ArtID 63.* doi:10.3389/fpsyg.2012.00063

Borges, G., Nock, M. K., Haro Abad, J. M., Hwang, I., Sampson, N. A. et al. (2010). Twelve-month prevalence of and risk factors for suicide attempts in the World Health Organization World Mental Health Surveys. *Journal of Clinical Psychiatry, 71,* 1617–1628.

Borman, W. C., Penner, L. A., Allen, T. D., & Motowidlo, S. J. (2001). Personality predictors of citizenship performance. *International Journal of Selection and Assessment, 9,* 52–69.

Bornet, F. R., Jardy-Gennetier, A. E., Jacquet, N., & Stowell, J. (2007). Glycaemic response to foods: Impact on satiety and long-term weight regulation. *Appetite, 49,* 535–553.

Bornovalova, M. A., Gratz, K. L., Delany-Brumsey, A., Paulson, A., & Lejuez, C. W. (2006). Temperamental and environmental risk factors for borderline personality disorder among inner-city substance users in residential treatment. *Journal of Personality Disorders, 20,* 218–231.

Bornstein, M. H. (1985). On the development of color naming in young children: Data and theory. *Brain and Language, 26,* 72–93.

Bornstein, R. F. (1994). Dependency as a social cue: A meta-analytic review of research on the dependency-helping relationship. *Journal of Research in Personality, 28,* 182–213. doi:10.1006/jrpe.1994.1015

Borst, G., & Kosslyn, S. M. (2008). Visual mental imagery and visual perception: Structural equivalence revealed by scanning processes. *Memory & Cognition, 36,* 849–862. doi:10.3758/MC.36.4.849

Bosch, J. A., de Geus, E. J., Kelder, A., Veerman, E. C., Hoogstraten, J., & Amerongen, A. V. (2001). Differential effects of active versus passive coping on secretory immunity. *Psychophysiology, 38,* 836–846.

Botella, C., Villa, H., Garcia Palacios, A., Quero, S., Banos, R. M., & Alcaniz, M. (2004). The use of VR in the treatment of panic disorders and agoraphobia. *Student Health and Technology Information, 99,* 73–90.

Bouchard, T. J. (2004). Genetic influence on human psychological traits: A survey. *Current Directions in Psychological Science, 13,* 148–151.

Bouchard, T. J., Lykken, D. T., McGue, M., Segal, N. L., & Tellegen, A. (1990). Sources of human psychological differences: The Minnesota study of twins reared apart. *Science, 250,* 223–228.

Bovin, M. J., & Marx, B. P. (2011). The importance of the peritraumatic experience in defining traumatic stress. *Psychological Bulletin, 137,* 47–67.

Bowden, C. L., Calabrese, J. R., Sachs, G., Yatham, L. N., Asghar, S. A., Hompland, M. et al. (2003). A placebo-controlled 18-month trial of lamotrigine and lithium maintenance treatment in recently manic or hypomanic patients with bipolar I disorder. *Archives of General Psychiatry, 60,* 392–400.

Bowden, C. L., Mosolov, S., Hranov, L., Chen, E., Habil, H., Kongsakon, R. et al. (2010). Efficacy of valproate versus lithium in mania or mixed mania: A randomized, open 12-week trial. *International Clinical Psychopharmacology, 25,* 60–67.

Bower, B. (2003, November 8). Forgetting to remember: Emotion robs memory while reviving it. *Science News, 164,* 293.

Bower, J. E., Moskowitz, J. T., & Epel, E. (2009). Is benefit finding good for your health? Pathways linking positive life changes after stress and physical health outcomes. *Current Directions in Psychological Science, 18,* 337–341.

Bower, J. F., Crosswell, A. D., & Slavich, G. M. (2014). Childhood adversity and cumulative life stress: Risk factors for cancer-related fatigue. *Clinical Psychological Science, 2,* 108–115.

Bowers, K. S., & LeBaron, S. (1986). Hypnosis and hypnotizability: Implications for clinical intervention. *Hospital and Community Psychiatry, 37,* 457–467.

Bowlby, J. (1980). *Attachment and loss: Vol. 3. Loss: Sadness and depression.* New York: Basic Books.

Boyce, C. J., Wood, A. M., Banks, J., Clark, A. E., & Brown, G. D. (2013). Money, well-being, and loss aversion: Does an income loss have a greater impact on well-being than an equivalent income gain? *Psychological Science, 24,* 2557–2562.

Boysen, G. A. (2011). The scientific status of childhood dissociative identity disorder: A review of published research. *Psychotherapy and Psychosomatics, 80,* 329–334.

Bozarth, M. A., & Wise, R. A. (1984). Anatomically distinct opiate receptor fields mediate reward and physical dependence. *Science, 224,* 516–518.

Brackett, M. A., Rivers, S. E., Shiffman, S., Lerner, N., & Salovey, P. (2006). Relating emotional abilities to social functioning: A comparison of self-report and performance measures of emotional intelligence. *Journal of Personality and Social Psychology, 91,* 780–795.

Braddock, A. E., & Abramowitz, J. S. (2006). Listening to hypochondriasis and hearing health anxiety. *Expert Review of Neurotherapeutics, 6,* 1307–1312.

Bradley, D. B., & Hopcroft, R. L. (2007). The sex difference in depression across 29 countries. *Social Forces, 85,* 1483–1507.

Bradley, R. H., & Corwyn, R. F. (2008). Infant temperament, parenting, and externalizing behavior in first grade: A test of the differential susceptibility hypothesis. *Journal of Child Psychology and Psychiatry and Allied Disciplines, 49,* 124–131.

Brainerd, C. J., & Reyna, V. F. (2002). Recollection rejection: How children edit their false memories. *Developmental Psychology, 38,* 156–172.

Bramlett, M. D., & Mosher, W. D. (2002). Cohabitation, marriage, divorce, and remarriage in the United States. *Vital Health Statistics, 23*(22). Hyattsville, MD: National Center for Health Statistics.

Brannon, L., & Feist, J. (2004). *Health psychology: An introduction to behavior and health* (5th ed.). Belmont, CA: Wadsworth.

Brant, A. M., Munakata, Y., Boomsma, D. I., DeFries, J. C., Haworth, C. M. et al. (2013). The nature and nurture of high IQ: An extended sensitive period for intellectual development. *Psychological Science, 24,* 1487–1495.

Bratberg, G. H., Nilsen, T. I., Holmen, T. L., & Vatten, L. J. (2005). Sexual maturation in early adolescence and alcohol drinking and cigarette smoking in late adolescence: A prospective study of 2,129 Norwegian girls and boys. *European Journal of Pediatrics, 164,* 621–625.

Braungart, J. M., Plomin, R., DeFries, J. C., & Fulker, D. W. (1992). Genetic influence on tester-rated infant temperament as assessed by Bayley's Infant Behavior Record. *Developmental Psychology, 28,* 40–47.

Brehm, S. S. (1992). *Intimate relationships* (2nd ed.). New York: McGraw-Hill.

Brehm, S. S., Kassin, S. M., & Fein, S. (2002). *Social psychology* (5th ed.). Boston: Houghton Mifflin.

Bremner, A. J., Bryant, P. E., & Mareschal, D. (2006). Object-centered spatial reference in 4-month-old infants. *Infant Behavior and Development, 29,* 1–10.

Brende, J. O. (2000). Stress effects of floods. In G. Fink (Ed.), *Encyclopedia of stress* (Vol. 2, pp. 153–157). San Diego: Academic Press.

Breslau, J., Aguilar-Gaxiola, S., Kendler, K. S., Su, M., Williams, D., & Kessler, R. C. (2006). Specifying race-ethnic differences in risk for psychiatric disorder in a USA national sample. *Psychological Medicine, 36,* 57–68.

Breslau, J., Kendler, K. S., Su, M., Gaxiola-Aguilar, S., & Kessler, R. C. (2005). Lifetime risk and persistence of psychiatric disorders across ethnic groups in the United States. *Psychological Medicine, 35,* 317–327.

Bresnahan, M., Begg, M. D., Browm, A., Schaefer, C., Sohler, N., Insel, B. et al. (2007). Race and risk of schizophrenia in a U.S. birth cohort: Another example of health disparity? *International Journal of Epidemiology, 36,* 751–758.

Brewer, M. B. (1979). In-group bias in the minimal intergroup situation: A cognitive-motivational analysis. *Psychological Bulletin, 86,* 307–324.

Brewer, M. B., & Campbell, D. T. (1976). *Ethnocentrism and intergroup attitudes: East African evidence.* New York: Halstead.

Brief, D. J., Rubin, A., Keane, T. M., Enggasser, J. L., Roy, M. et al. (2013). Web intervention for OEF/OIF veterans with problem drinking and PTSD symptoms: A randomized clinical trial. *Journal of Consulting and Clinical Psychology, 81,* 890–900.

Britt, G. C., & McCance-Katz, E. F. (2005). A brief overview of the clinical pharmacology of "club drugs." *Substance Use & Misuse, 40,* 1189–1201.

Broberg, D. J., & Bernstein, I. L. (1987). Candy as a scapegoat in the prevention of food aversions in children receiving chemotherapy. *Cancer, 60,* 2344–2347.

Brochu, P. M., Pearl, R. L., Puhl, R. M., & Brownell, K. D. (2014). Do media portrayals of obesity influence support for weight-related medical policy? *Health Psychology, 33,* 197–200. doi: 10.1037/a0032592

Brody, A. L., Saxena, S., Schwartz, J. M., Stoessel, P. W., Maidment, K., Phelps, M. E. et al. (1998). FDG-PET predictors of response to behavioral therapy and pharmacotherapy in obsessive compulsive disorder. *Psychiatry Research: Neuroimaging, 84,* 1–6.

Brody, J. E. (2007, April 17). When a brain forgets where memory is. *New York Times.* Retrieved from http://www.nytimes.com/2007/04/17/health/psychology/17brody.html

Brody, M. J., Walsh, B. T., & Devlin, M. (1994). Binge eating disorder: Reliability and validity of a new diagnostic category. *Journal of Consulting and Clinical Psychology, 62,* 381–386.

Bronstad, P. M., Langlois, J. H., & Russell, R. (2008). Computational models of facial attractiveness judgments. *Perception, 37,* 126–142.

Brookoff, D., O'Brien, K. K., Cook, C. S., Thompson, T. D., & Williams, C. (1997). Characteristics of participants in domestic violence: Assessment at the scene of domestic assault. *JAMA, 277,* 1369–1373.

Brotto, L. A., Petkau, A., Labrie, F., & Basson, R. (2011). Predictors of sexual desire disorders in women. *Journal of Sexual Medicine, 8,* 742–753. doi: 10.1111/j.1743-6109.2010.02146.x

Brown, A. D., & Curhan, J. R. (2013). The polarizing effect of arousal on negotiation. *Psychological Science, 24,* 1928–1935.

Brown, A. S., Begg, M. D., Gravenstein, S., Schaefer, C. A., Wyatt, R. J., Brenahan, M. et al. (2004). Serological evidence of prenatal influenza in the etiology of schizophrenia. *Archives of General Psychiatry, 61,* 774–780.

Brown, B. B. (2004). Adolescents' relationship with peers. In R. Lerner & L. Steinberg (Eds.), *Handbook of adolescent psychology* (2nd ed., pp. 363–394). Hoboken, NJ: Wiley.

Brown, B. M., Peiffer, J. J., & Martins, R. N. (2013). Multiple effects of physical activity on molecular and cognitive signs of brain aging: Can exercise slow neurodegeneration and delay Alzheimer's disease? *Molecular Psychiatry, 18,* 864–874. doi:10.1038/mp.2012.162

Brown, J. A. (1958). Some tests of the decay theory of immediate memory. *Quarterly Journal of Experimental Psychology, 10,* 12–21.

Brown, J. D., & Rogers, R. J. (1991). Self-serving attributions: The role of physiological arousal. *Personality and Social Psychology Bulletin, 17,* 501–506.

Brown, R., & Kulik, J. (1977). Flashbulb memories. *Cognition, 5,* 73–99.

Brown, S. L., Lee, G. R., & Bulanda, J. R. (2006). Cohabitation among older adults: A national portrait. *Journals of Gerontology, Series B: Psychological Sciences and Social Sciences, 61,* S71–S79.

Brown, S. L., Nesse, R. M., Vinokur, A. D., & Smith, D. M. (2003). Providing social support may be more beneficial than receiving it: Results from a prospective study of mortality. *Psychological Science, 14,* 320–327.

Brown, T. A., DiNardo, P. A., Lehman, C. L., & Campbell, L. A. (2001). Reliability of DSM-IV anxiety and mood disorders: Implications for the classification of emotional disorders. *Journal of Abnormal Psychology, 110,* 49–58.

Browne, A. (1993). Violence against women by male partners: Prevalence, outcomes, and policy implications. *American Psychologist, 48,* 1077–1087.

Brownell, K. (1988, January). Yo-yo dieting. *Psychology Today, 22,* 22–23.

Browning, J. R., Kessler, D., Hatfield, E., & Choo, P. (1999). Power, gender, and sexual behavior. *Journal of Sex Research, 36,* 342–348.

Bruffaerts, R., Demyttenaere, K., Borges, G., Haro, J. M., Chiu, W. T., Hwang, I. et al. (2010). Childhood adversities as risk factors for onset and persistence of suicidal behavior. *British Journal of Psychiatry, 197,* 20–27.

Brugman, T., & Ferguson, S. (2002). Physical exercise and improvements in mental health. *Journal of Psychosocial Nursing and Mental Health Services, 40,* 24–31.

Bryant, R. A., & Guthrie, R. M. (2005). Maladaptive appraisals as a risk factor for posttraumatic stress: A study of trainee firefighters. *Psychological Science, 16,* 749–752.

Bryman, A. S. (1996). The importance of context: Qualitative research and the study of leadership. *Leadership Quarterly, 7,* 353–370.

Brzezinski, A. (1997). Melatonin in humans. *New England Journal of Medicine, 336,* 186–195.

Buchanan, R. W., Breier, A., Kirkpatrick, B., Ball, P., & Carpenter, W. T. (1998). Positive and negative symptom response to clozapine in schizophrenic patients with and without the deficit syndrome. *American Journal of Psychiatry, 155,* 751–760.

Buckingham-Howes, S., Berger, S. S., Scaletti, L. A., & Black, M. M. (2013). Systematic review of prenatal cocaine exposure and adolescent development. *Pediatrics, 131,* e1917–e1936.

Buckley, K. W. (1989). *Mechanical man: John Broadus Watson.* New York: Guilford Press.

Bucur, B., & Madden, D. J. (2010). Effects of adult age and blood pressure on executive function and speed of processing. *Experimental Aging Research, 36,* 153–168.

Buehler, R., Griffin, D., & Ross, M. (1994). Exploring the "planning fallacy": Why people underestimate their task completion times. *Journal of Personality and Social Psychology, 67,* 366–381.

Buehner, M., Mangels, M., Krumm, S., & Ziegler, M. (2005). Are working memory and attention related constructs? *Journal of Individual Differences, 26,* 121–131.

Bueno-Nava, A., Montes, S., DelaGarza-Montano, P., Alfaro-Rodriguez, A., Ortiz, A., & Gonzalez-Pina, R. (2008). Reversal of noradrenergic depletion and lipid peroxidation in the pons after brain injury correlates with motor function recovery in rats. *Neuroscience Letters, 443,* 32–36.

Bullock, B., & Murray, G. (2014). Reduced amplitude of the 24 hour activity rhythm: A biomarker of vulnerability to bipolar disorder? *Clinical Psychological Science, 2,* 86–96.

Bullock, W. A., & Gilliland, K. (1993). Eysenck's arousal theory of introversion–extraversion: A converging measures investigation. *Journal of Personality and Social Psychology, 64,* 113–123.

Bumpass, L. L., & Lu, H. H. (2000). Trends in cohabitation and implications for children's family contexts in the United States. *Population Studies, 54,* 29–41.

Burdakov, D., Karnani, M. M., & Gonzalez, A. (2013). Lateral hypothalamus as a sensor-regulator in respiratory and metabolic control. *Physiology & Behavior, 121,* 117–124. doi: 10.1016/j.physbeh.2013.03.023

Burdakov, D., Luckman, S. M., & Verkhratsky, A. (2005). Glucose-sensing neurons of the hypothalamus. *Philosophical Transactions of the Royal Society of London, Series B, Biological Sciences, 360,* 2227–2235.

Burgard, S. A. (2011). The needs of others: Gender and sleep interruptions for caregivers. *Social Forces, 89,* 1189–1215.

Burger, J. M. (1986). Increasing compliance by improving the deal: The that's-not-all technique. *Journal of Personality and Social Psychology, 51,* 277–283.

Burger, J. M. (2004). *Personality* (6th ed.). Belmont, CA: Wadsworth.

Burger, J. M. (2009). Replicating Milgram: Would people still obey today? *American Psychologist, 64,* 1–11.

Burger, J. M. (2011). Is that all there is? Reaction to the that's-not-all procedure. In R. M. Arkin (Ed.), *Most underappreciated: 50 prominent social psychologists describe their most unloved work* (pp. 213–216). New York: Oxford University Press.

Burger, J. M., Girgis, Z. M., & Manning, C. C. (2011). In their own words: Explaining obedience to authority through an examination of participants' comments. *Social Psychological and Personality Science, 2,* 460–466. doi:10.1177/1948550610397632

Burke, T. M., Markwald, R. R., Chinoy, E. D., Snider, J. A., Bessman, S. C. et al. (2013). Combination of light and melatonin time cues for phase advancing the human circadian clock. *Sleep, 36,* 1617–1624.

Burnham, D. (1993). Visual recognition of mother by young infants: Facilitation by speech. *Perception, 22,* 1133–1153.

Burt, C. D. B., Kemp, S., & Conway, M. (2008). Ordering the components of autobiographical events. *Acta Psychological, 127,* 36–45.

Bush, S. I., & Geer, J. H. (2001). Implicit and explicit memory of neutral, negative emotional, and sexual information. *Archives of Sexual Behavior, 30,* 615–631.

Bushman, B. J. (1988). The effects of apparel on compliance: A field experiment with a female authority figure. *Personality and Social Psychology Bulletin, 14,* 459–467.

Buss, D. M. (1995). Psychological sex differences. *American Psychologist, 50,* 164–168.

Buss, D. N. (2009). The great struggles of life: Darwin and the emergence of evolutionary psychology. *American Psychologist, 64,* 140–148.

Bussey, K., & Bandura, A. (1999). Social cognitive theory of gender development and differentiation. *Psychological Review, 106,* 676–713.

Butler, L. D., Duran, R. E. F., Jasiukaitis, P., Koopman, C., & Spiegel, D. (1996). Hypnotizability and traumatic experience: A diathysis stress model of dissociative symptomatology. *American Journal of Psychiatry, 153,* 42–63.

Butow P. N., Hiller, J. E., Price, M. A., Thackway, S. V., Kricker, A., & Tennant, C. C. (2000). Epidemiological evidence for a relationship between life events, coping style, and personality factors in the development of breast cancer. *Journal of Psychosomatic Research, 49,* 169–181.

Butt, M., Dwivedi, G., Khair, O., & Lip, G. Y. (2010). Obstructive sleep apnea and cardiovascular disease. *International Journal of Cardiology, 139,* 7–16.

Butts, S. F., & Seifer, D. B. (2010). Racial and ethnic differences in reproductive potential across the life cycle. *Fertility and Sterility, 93,* 681–690.

Butzlaff, R. L., & Hooley, J. M. (1998). Expressed emotion and psychiatric relapse. *Archives of General Psychiatry, 55,* 547–552.

Byrd-Craven, J., Geary, D. C., Rose, A. J., & Ponzi, D. (2008). Co-ruminating increases stress hormone levels in women. *Hormones and Behavior, 53,* 489–492.

Byrne, D., Gouaux, C., Griffitt, W., Lamberth, J., Murakawa, N., Prasad, M. B. et al. (1971). The ubiquitous relationship: Attitude similarity and attraction: A cross-cultural study. *Human Relations, 24,* 201–207.

Byrne, M., Agerbo, E., Ewald, H., Eaton, W. W., & Mortensen, P. B. (2003). Parental age and risk of schizophrenia: A case-control study. *Archives of General Psychiatry, 60,* 673–678.

Cacioppo, J. T., & Petty, R. E. (1980). Sex differences in influenceability: Toward specifying the underlying processes. *Personality and Social Psychology Bulletin, 6,* 651–656.

Cacioppo, J. T., Hawkley, L. C., Kalil, A., Hughes, M. E., Waite, L., & Thisted, R. A. (2008). Happiness and the invisible threads of social connection: The Chicago Health, Aging, and Social Relations Study. In M. Eid & R. Larsen (Eds.), *The science of well-being* (pp. 195–219). New York: Guilford Press.

Cain, A. S., Epler, A. J., Steinley, D., & Sher, K. J. (2010). Stability and change in patterns of concerns related to eating, weight, and shape in young adult women: A latent transition analysis. *Journal of Abnormal Psychology, 119,* 255–267.

Cain, W. S. (1988). Olfaction. In R. C. Atkinson, R. J. Herrnstein, G. Lindzey, & R. D. Luce (Eds.), *Steven's handbook of experimental psychology* (2nd ed., Vol. 1, pp. 409–459). New York: Wiley.

Calabrese, J. R., Shelton, M. D., Rapport, D. J., Youngstrom, E. A., Jackson, K., Bilali, S. et al. (2005). A 20-month, double-blind, maintenance trial of lithium versus divalproex in rapid-cycling bipolar disorder. *American Journal of Psychiatry, 162,* 2152–2161.

Calamari, J. E., Chik, H. M., Pontarelli, N. K., & DeJong, B. L. (2012). Phenomenology and epidemiology of obsessive compulsive disorder. In G. Steketee (Ed.), *The Oxford handbook of obsessive compulsive and spectrum disorders* (pp. 11–47). New York: Oxford University Press.

Caldera, Y. M., & Lindsey, E. W. (2006). Coparenting, mother–infant interaction, and infant–parent attachment relationships in two-parent families. *Journal of Family Psychology, 20,* 275–283.

Calderoni, M. E., Alderman, E. M., Silver, E. J., & Bauman, L. J. (2006). The mental health impact of 9/11 on inner-city high school students 20 miles north of Ground Zero. *Journal of Adolescent Health, 39,* 57–65.

Caldwell, J. A. (2012). Crew schedules, sleep deprivation, and aviation performance. *Current Directions in Psychological Science, 21,* 85–89.

Calvert, H. (2003). Sexually transmitted diseases other than human immunodeficiency virus infection in older adults. *Clinical Infectious Diseases, 36,* 609–614.

Camper, J. (1990, February 7). Drop pompom squad, U. of I. rape study says. *Chicago Tribune,* 1.

Campos, B., Graesch, A. P., Repetti, R., Bradbury, T., & Ochs, E. (2009). Opportunity for interaction? A naturalistic observation study of dual-earner families after work and school. *Journal of Family Psychology, 23,* 798–807.

Cannon, D. S., & Baker, T. B. (1981). Emetic and electric shock alcohol aversion therapy: Assessment of conditioning. *Journal of Consulting and Clinical Psychology, 49,* 20–33.

Cannon, W. B. (1927). The James-Lange theory of emotions: A critical examination and an alternative theory. *American Journal of Psychology, 39,* 106–124.

Canova, A., & Geary, N. (1991). Intraperitoneal injections of nanogram CCK-8 doses inhibits feeding in rats. *Appetite, 17,* 221–227.

Canuso, C. M., & Pandina, G. (2007). Gender and schizophrenia. *Psychopharmacology Bulletin, 40,* 178–190.

Cardno, A. G., & Gottesman, I. I. (2000). Twin studies of schizophrenia: From bow-and-arrow concordances to Star Wars Mx and functional genomics. *American Journal of Medical Genetics, 97,* 12–17.

Cardozo, B. L., Bilukha, O. O., Crawford, C. A., Shaikh, I., Wolfe, M. I., Gerber, M. et al. (2004). Mental health, social functioning, and disability in postwar Afghanistan. *Journal of the American Medical Association, 292,* 575–584.

Carducci, B. J. (2009). *The psychology of personality: Viewpoints, research, and applications.* Malden, MA: Wiley-Blackwell.

Carey, B. (2007, October 23). An active, purposeful machine that comes out at night to play. *New York Times.*

Carey, B. (2008). H.M., an unforgettable amnesiac, dies at age 82. *New York Times.* Retrieved from http://www.nytimes.com

Carey, G., & DiLalla, D. L. (1994). Personality and psychopathology: Genetic perspectives. *Journal of Abnormal Psychology, 103,* 32–43.

Carey, G., & Goldman, D. (1997). The genetics of antisocial behavior. In D. M. Stoff, J. Breiling, & J. D. Maser (Eds.), *Handbook of antisocial personality disorder* (pp. 243–254). New York: Wiley.

Carlbring, P., Martin, L., Torngren, C. Linna, E., Eriksson, T., Sparthan, E. et al. (2011). Individually-tailored, internet-based treatment for anxiety disorders: A randomized controlled trial. *Behaviour Research and Therapy, 49,* 18–24.

Carlisle, N. B., & Woodman, G. F. (2013). Reconciling conflicting electrophysiological findings on the guidance of attention by working memory. *Attention, Perception, & Psychophysics, 75,* 1330–1335. doi:10.3758/s13414-013-0529-7

Carlson, P. J., Singh, J. B., Zarate, C. A., Jr., Drevets, W. C., & Manji, H. K. (2006). Neural circuitry and neuroplasticity in mood disorders: Insights for novel therapeutic targets. *NeuroRx, 3,* 22–41.

Carlston, D. E., & Shovar, N. (1983). Effects of performance attributions on others' perceptions of the attributor. *Journal of Personality and Social Psychology, 44,* 515–525.

Carney, C. E., Edinger, J. D., Meyer, B., Lindman, L., & Istre, T. (2006). Daily activities and sleep quality in college students. *Chronobiology International, 23,* 623–637.

Carpenter, J. C. (2012). *First sight: ESP and parapsychology in everyday life.* Lanham, MD: Rowman & Littlefield.

Carrington, P. (1993). Modern forms of meditation. In P. M. Lehrer & R. L. Woolfolk (Eds.), *Principles and practice of stress management* (2nd ed., pp. 139–168). New York: Guilford Press.

Carroll, K. M., Ball, S. A., Martino, S., Nich, C., Babuscio, T. A., Nuro, K. F. et al. (2008). Computer-assisted delivery of cognitive-behavioral therapy for addiction: A randomized trial of CBT4CBT. *American Journal of Psychiatry, 165,* 793–795.

Carskadon, M. A., Acebo, C., & Jenni, O. G. (2004). Regulation of adolescent sleep: Implications for behavior. *Annals of the New York Academy of Sciences, 1021,* 276–291.

Carstensen, L. L., Turan, B., Scheibe, S., Ram, N., Ersner-Hershfield, H., Samanez-Larkin, G. R. et al. (2011). Emotional experience improves with age: Evidence based over 10 years of experience sampling. *Psychology and Aging, 26,* 21–33.

Carter, R. C., Jacobson, S. W., Molteno, C. D., Chiodo, L. M., Viljoen, D., & Jacobson, J. L. (2005). Effects of prenatal alcohol exposure on infant visual acuity. *Journal of Pediatrics, 14,* 473–479.

Carter, R. S., & Wojtkiewicz, R. A. (2000). Parental involvement with adolescents' education: Do daughters or sons get more help? *Adolescence, 35,* 29–44.

Cartwright, R. D. (1993). Who needs their dreams? The usefulness of dreams in psychotherapy. *Journal of the American Academy of Psychoanalysis, 21,* 539–547.

Carver, C. S., Harris, S. D., Lehman, J. M., Durel, L. A., Antoni, M. H., Spencer, S. M. et al. (2000). How important is the perception of personal control? Studies of early stage breast cancer patients. *Personality and Social Psychology Bulletin, 26,* 139–149.

Carver, C. S., Johnson, S. L., & Joormann, J. (2009). Two-mode models of self-regulation as a tool for conceptualizing effects of the serotonin system in normal behavior and diverse disorders. *Current Directions in Psychological Science, 18,* 195–199.

Cascio, W. F. (1995). Whither industrial and organizational psychology in a changing world of work? *American Psychologist, 50,* 928–939.

Casey, B. J., & Caudle, K. (2013). The teenage brain: Self-control. *Current Directions in Psychological Science, 22,* 82–87.

Casey, B. J., Giedd, J. N., & Thomas, K. M. (2000). Structural and functional brain development and its relation to cognitive development. *Biological Psychology, 54,* 241–257.

Caspi, A., Sugden, K., Moffitt, T. E., Taylor, A., Craig, I. W., Harrington, H. et al. (2003). Influence of life stress on depression: Moderation by a polymorphism in the 5-HTT gene. *Science, 301,* 386–389.

Castel, A. D., Murayama, K., Friedman, M. C., McGillivray, S., & Link, I. (2013). Selecting valuable information to remember: Age-related differences and similarities in self-regulated learning. *Psychology and Aging, 28,* 232–242. doi:10.1037/a0030678

Castelnuovo, G., Gaggioli, A., Mantovani, F., & Riva, G. (2003). From psychotherapy to e-therapy: The integration of traditional techniques and new communication tools in clinical settings. *Cyberpsychology and Behavior, 6,* 375–382.

Cates, W., Jr. (1998). Reproductive tract infections. In R. A. Hatcher et al. (Eds.), *Contraceptive technology* (17th rev. ed., pp. 179–210). New York: Ardent Media.

Cattell, N. R. (2006). *An introduction to mind, consciousness and language.* London: Continuum.

Cattell, R. B. (1943). The description of personality: Basic traits resolved into clusters. *Journal of Abnormal and Social Psychology, 38,* 476–506.

Cattell, R. B. (1963). Theory of fluid and crystallized intelligence: A critical experiment. *Journal of Educational Psychology, 54,* 1–22.

Cattell, R. B. (1965). *The scientific analysis of personality.* Baltimore: Penguin.

Cavanagh, K., Shapiro, D. A., Van Den Berg, S., Swain, S., Barkham, M., & Proudfoot, J. (2009). The acceptability of computer-aided cognitive behavioural therapy: A pragmatic study. *Cognitive Behaviour Therapy, 38,* 235–246.

Ceci, S. J. (1995). False beliefs: Some developmental and clinical considerations. In D. L. Schacter (Ed.), *Memory distortions* (pp. 91–125). Cambridge, MA: Harvard University Press.

Censor, N., Dayan, E., & Cohen, L. G. (2014). Cortico-subcortical neuronal circuitry associated with reconsolidation of human procedural memories. *Cortex, 58,* 281–288. doi: 10.1016/j.cortex.2013.05.013

Centers for Disease Control and Prevention (CDC). (2002). Involvement by young drivers in fatal alcohol-related motor-vehicle crashes—United States, 1982–2001. *Morbidity and Mortality Weekly Report, 51,* 1089–1091.

Centers for Disease Control and Prevention (CDC). (2004). Mental health status of World Trade Center rescue and recovery workers and volunteers—New York City, July 2002–August 2004. *Morbidity and Mortality Weekly Report, 53,* 812–815.

Centers for Disease Control and Prevention (CDC). (2006). Tobacco use among adults—United States, 2005. *Morbidity and Mortality Weekly Report, 55,* 1145–1148.

Centers for Disease Control and Prevention (CDC). (2007). Nonfatal Traumatic Brain Injuries from Sports and Recreation Activities—United States, 2001–2005. *Morbidity and Mortality Weekly Report, 56,* 733–737.

Centers for Disease Control and Prevention (CDC). (2008a). HIV prevalence estimates—2006. *Morbidity and Mortality Weekly Report, 57,* 1073–1076

Centers for Disease Control and Prevention (CDC). (2008b). *Sexually transmitted disease surveillance, 2008.* Atlanta, GA: Author.

Centers for Disease Control and Prevention (CDC). (2008c). Smoking-attributable mortality, years of potential life lost, and productivity losses—United States, 2000–2004. *Morbidity and Mortality Weekly Report, 57,* 1226–1228.

Centers for Disease Control and Prevention (CDC). (2009a). Cigarette smoking among adults and trends in smoking cessation—United States, 2008. *Morbidity and Mortality Weekly Report, 58,* 1227–1232.

Centers for Disease Control and Prevention (CDC). (2009b). Web-based Injury Statistics Query and Reporting System (WISQARS). *Fatal Injury Reports.* Atlanta, GA: National Center for Injury Prevention and Control.

Centers for Disease Control and Prevention (CDC). (2010a). Seroprevalence of herpes simplex virus type 2 among persons aged 14–49 years—United States, 2005–2008. *Morbidity and Mortality Weekly Report, 59,* 456–459.

Centers for Disease Control and Prevention (CDC). (2010b). *Sexually transmitted disease surveillance, 2009.* Atlanta, GA: Author.

Centers for Disease Control and Prevention (CDC). (2011a). Nonfatal traumatic brain injuries related to sports and recreation activities among persons aged ≤19 years—United States, 2001–2009. *Morbidity and Mortality Weekly Report, 60,* 1337–1342.

Centers for Disease Control and Prevention. (2011b). Unhealthy sleep-related behaviors—12 states, 2009. *Morbidity and Mortality Weekly Report, 60,* 233–238.

Centers for Disease Control and Prevention (CDC). (2011c). Vital signs: Current cigarette smoking among adults aged ≥18 years—United States, 2005—2010. *Morbidity and Mortality Weekly Report, 60,* 1207–1212.

Centers for Disease Control and Prevention (CDC). (2013a). *Incidence, prevalence, and cost of sexually transmitted infections in the United States.* Atlanta, GA: National Center for HIV/AIDS, Viral Hepatitis, STD, and TB Prevention.

Centers for Disease Control and Prevention (CDC). (2013b). Mobile device use while driving-United States and seven European countries. *Morbidity and Mortality Weekly Report, 62,* 1–6.

Centers for Disease Control and Prevention (CDC). (2013c). Monitoring selected national HIV prevention and care objectives by using HIV surveillance data—United States and 6 U.S. dependent areas—2011. *HIV Surveillance Supplemental Report, 18* (No. 5).

Centers for Disease Control and Prevention (CDC). (2014). *Reported STDs in the United States, 2012 National data for chlamydia, gonorrhea, and syphilis.* Atlanta, GA: National Center for HIV/AIDS, Viral Hepatitis, STD, and TB Prevention.

Cermak, L. S., Lewis, R., Butters, N., & Goodglass, H. (1973). Role of verbal mediation in performance of motor tasks by Korsakoff patients. *Perceptual and Motor Skills, 37,* 259–262.

Cernoch, J., & Porter, R. H. (1985). Recognition of maternal axillary odors by infants. *Child Development, 56,* 1593–1598.

Chakos, M. H., Alvir, J. M., Woerner, M., & Koreen, A. (1996). Incidence and correlates of tardive dyskinesia in first episode of schizophrenia. *Archives of General Psychiatry, 53,* 313–319.

Chamberlain, K., & Zika, S. (1990). The minor events approach to stress: Support for the use of daily hassles. *British Journal of Psychology, 81,* 469–481.

Chambers, D., & Reisberg, D. (1992). What an image depicts depends on what an image means. *Cognitive Psychology, 24,* 145–174.

Chambless, D. L., & Hollon, S. D. (1998). Defining empirically-supported therapies. *Journal of Consulting and Clinical Psychology, 66,* 7–18.

Chambless, D. L., & Ollendick, T. H. (2001). Empirically supported psychological interventions: Controversies and evidence. *Annual Review of Psychology, 52,* 685–716.

Chamorro-Premuzic, T., & Furnham, A. (2004). A possible model for understanding the personality–intelligence interface. *British Journal of Psychology, 95,* 249–264.

Champagne, F. A. (2010). Early adversity and development outcomes: Interaction between genetics, epigenetics, and social experiences across the life span. *Perspectives on Psychological Science, 5,* 564–574.

Champagne, F. A., & Mashoodh, R. (2009). Genes in context: Gene-environment interplay and the origins of individual differences in behavior. *Current Directions in Psychological Science, 18,* 127–131.

Chandrashekar, J., Hoon, M. A., Ryba, N. J. P., & Zuker, C. S. (2006). The receptors and cells for mammalian taste. *Nature, 444,* 288–294.

Chandrashekara, S., Jayashree, K., Veeranna, H. B., Vadiraj, H. S., Ramesh, M. N., Shobha, A. et al. (2007). Effects of anxiety on TNF-a levels during psychological stress. *Journal of Psychosomatic Research, 63,* 65–69.

Chang, I. J., Pettit, R. W., & Katsurada, E. (2006). Where and when to spank: A comparison between U.S. and Japanese college students. *Journal of Family Violence, 21,* 281–286.

Chaput, J. P., & Tremblay, A. A. (2009). The glucostatic theory of appetite control and the risk of obesity and diabetes. *International Journal of Obesity, 33,* 46–53. doi: 10.1038/ijo.2008.221

Charles, S. T., Piazza, J. R., Mogle, J. M., Sliwinski, M. J., & Almeida, D. M. (2013). The wear and tear of daily stressors on mental health. *Psychological Science, 24,* 733–741.

Charney, D. S., Nagy, L. M., Bremner, J. D., Goddard, A. W., Yehuda, R., & Southwick, S. M. (2000). Neurobiologic mechanisms of human anxiety. In B. S. Fogel (Ed.), *Synopsis of neuropsychiatry* (pp. 273–288). Philadelphia: Lippincott Williams & Wilkins.

Chaves, J. F. (1994). Recent advances in the application of hypnosis to pain management. *American Journal of Clinical Hypnosis, 37,* 117–129.

Cheah, C. S., Leung, C. Y., Tahseen, M., & Schuz, D. (2009). Authoritative parenting among immigrant Chinese mothers of preschoolers. *Journal of Family Psychology, 23,* 311–320.

Chen, E. (2012). Protective factors for health among low-socioeconomic-status individuals. *Current Directions in Psychological Science, 21,* 189–193.

Chen, E., & Miller, G. E. (2012). "Shift-and-persist" strategies: Why low socioeconomic status isn't always bad for health. *Perspectives on Psychological Science, 7,* 135–158.

Chen, E., Cohen, S., & Miller, G. E. (2010). How low socioeconomic status affects 2-year hormonal trajectories in children. *Psychological Science, 21,* 31–37.

Chen, Y. L., Su, M. C., Liu, W. H., Wang, C. C., Lin, M. C., & Chen, M. C. (2014). Influence and predicting variables of obstructive sleep apnea on cardiac function and remodeling in patients without congestive heart failure. *Journal of Clinical Sleep Medicine, 10,* 57–64.

Cherry, K. E., Brown, J., Walker, E., Smitherman, E. A., Boudreaux, E. O., Volaufova, J., & Jazwinski, S.

(2012). Semantic encoding enhances the pictorial superiority effect in the oldest-old. *Aging, Neuropsychology, and Cognition, 19,* 319–337. doi:10.1080/13825585.2011.619645

Chess, S., & Thomas, A. (1984). *Origins and evolution of behavior disorders: From infancy to early adult life.* New York: Brunner/Mazel.

Chessick, C. A., Allen, M. H., Thase, M., Batista Miralha da Cunha, A. B., Kapczinski, F. F., de Lima, M. S. et al. (2006). Azapirones for generalized anxiety disorder. *Cochrane Database of Systematic Reviews, 19,* CD006115.

Cheung, F. M., & Halpern, D. F. (2010). Women at the top: Powerful leaders define success as work + family in a culture of gender. *American Psychologist, 65,* 182–193.

Chiang, A. A. (2006). Obstructive sleep apnea and chronic intermittent hypoxia: A review. *Chinese Journal of Physiology, 49,* 234–243.

Chida, Y., & Steptoe, A. (2008). Positive psychological well-being and mortality: A quantitative review of prospective observational studies. *Psychosomatic Medicine, 70,* 741–756.

Childress, J. E., McDowell, E. J., Dalai, V. K., Bogale, S. R., Ramamurthy, C., Jawaid, A. et al. (2013). Hippocampal volumes in patients with chronic combat-related posttraumatic stress disorder: A systematic review. *Journal of Neuropsychiatry and Clinical Neurosciences, 25,* 12–25. doi:10.1176/appi.neuropsych.12010003

Childs, L. A. (2011). Assessing vestibular dysfunction. Exploring treatments of a complex condition. *Rehab Management, 23,* 24–25.

Chipuer, H. M., Rovine, M. J., & Polmin, R. (1990). LISREL modeling: Genetic and environmental influences on IQ revisited. *Intelligence, 14,* 11–29.

Cho, J. R., Joo, E. Y., Koo, D. L., & Hong, S. B. (2013). Let there be no light: The effect of bedside light on sleep quality and background electroencephalographic rhythms. *Sleep Medicine, 14,* 1422–1425.

Choi, I., & Nesbitt, R. E. (1998). Situational salience and cultural differences in the correspondence bias and actor-observer bias. *Personality and Social Psychology Bulletin, 24,* 949–960.

Choi, J. S., Kim, S. H., Yoo, S. Y., Kang, D. H., Kim, C. W., Lee, J. M. et al. (2007). Shape deformity of the corpus striatum in obsessive-compulsive disorder. *Psychiatry Research, 155,* 257–264.

Chollar, S. (1989, April). Dreamchasers. *Psychology Today,* pp. 60–61.

Chomsky, N. (1957). *Syntactic structures.* The Hague: Mouton.

Chomsky, N. (1965). *Aspects of the theory of syntax.* Cambridge, MA: MIT Press.

Chory-Assad, R. M., & Tamborini, R. (2001). Television doctors: An analysis of physicians on fictional and non-fictional television programs. *Journal of Broadcasting and Electronic Media, 45,* 499–521.

Chory-Assad, R. M., & Tamborini, R. (2003). Television exposure and the public's perceptions of physicians. *Journal of Broadcasting and Electronic Media, 47,* 197–215.

Chou, R., Qaseem, A., Snow, V., Casey, D., Cross, J. T., Jr., Shekelle, P. et al. (2007). Diagnosis and treatment of low back pain: A joint clinical practice guideline from the American College of Physicians and the American Pain Society. *Annals of Internal Medicine, 147,* 478–491, W118–W120.

Chou, S. P., Dawson, D. A., Stinson, F. S., Huang, B., Pickering, R. P., Zhou, Y. et al. (2006). The prevalence of drinking and driving in the United States, 2001–2002: Results from the national epidemiological survey on alcohol and related conditions. *Drug and Alcohol Dependence, 83,* 137–146.

Choy, Y., Fyer, A. J., & Lipsitz, J. D. (2007). Treatment of specific phobia in adults. *Clinical Psychology Review, 27,* 266–286.

Chrisman, S. P., Rivara, F. P., Schiff, M. A., Zhou, C., & Comstock, R. (2013). Risk factors for concussive symptoms 1 week or longer in high school athletes. *Brain Injury, 27,* 1–9. doi:10.3109/02699052.2012.722251

Christensen, A., & Jacobson, N. S. (1994). Who (or what) can do psychotherapy: The status and challenge of nonprofessional therapies. *Psychological Science, 5,* 8–14.

Christie, W., & Moore, C. (2005). The impact of humor on patients with cancer. *Clinical Journal of Oncology Nursing, 9,* 211–218.

Church, R. M., & Black, A. H. (1958). Latency of the conditioned heart rate as a function of the CS–US interval. *Journal of Comparative and Physiological Psychology, 51,* 478–482.

Cialdini, R. B. (2001). *Influence: Science and practice* (4th ed.). Needham Heights, MA: Allyn & Bacon.

Cialdini, R. B., Borden, R. J., Thorne, A., Walker, M. R., Freeman, S., & Sloan, L. R. (1976). Basking in the reflected glory: Three (football) field studies. *Journal of Personality and Social Psychology, 34,* 366–375.

Cialdini, R. B., Cacioppo, J. T., Bassett, R., & Miller, J. A. (1978). Low-ball procedure for producing compliance: Commitment then cost. *Journal of Personality and Social Psychology, 36,* 463–476.

Cialdini, R. B., Vincent, J. E., Catalan, J., Wheeler, D., & Darby, B. L. (1975). Reciprocal concessions procedure for inducing compliance: The door-in-the-face technique. *Journal of Personality and Social Psychology, 31,* 206–215.

Cin, S. D., Gibson, B., Zanna, M. P., Shumate, R., & Fong, G. T. (2007). Smoking in movies, implicit associations of smoking with the self, and intentions to smoke. *Psychological Science, 18,* 559–563.

Cinnirella, M., & Green, B. (2007). Does "cyber-conformity" vary cross-culturally? Exploring the effect of culture and communication medium on social conformity. *Computers in Human Behavior, 23,* 2011–2025. doi:10.1016/j.chb.2006.02.009

Cipriani, A., Barbui, C., Salanti, G., Rendell, J., Brown, R., Stockton, S. et al. (2011). Comparative efficacy and acceptability of antimanic drugs in acute mania: A multiple-treatments meta-analysis. *Lancet, 378,* 1306–1315.

Cipriani, A., Reid, K., Young, A. H., Macritchie, K., & Geddes, J. (2013). Valproic acid, valproate and divalproex in the maintenance treatment of bipolar disorder. *The Cochrane Database of Systematic Reviews, 10,* CD003196.

Citirik, M., Acaroglu, G., Batman, C., & Zilelioglu, O. (2005). Congenital color blindness in young Turkish men. *Opthalmic Epidemiology, 12,* 133–137.

Clark, D. A., & Beck, A. T. (2010). Cognitive theory and therapy of anxiety and depression: Convergence with neurobiological findings. *Trends in Cognitive Sciences, 14,* 418–424.

Clark, K. B. (1950). *Effect of prejudice and discrimination on personality development.* Paper written for the White House Mid-Century Conference on Children and Youth.

Clark, K. B., & Clark, M. P. (1950). Emotional factors in racial identification and preference in Negro children. *Journal of Negro Education, 19,* 341–350.

Clark, L. A. (2007). Assessment and diagnosis of personality disorder: Perennial issues and emerging conceptualization. *Annual Review of Psychology, 58,* 227–257.

Clark, M. S., Lemay, E. P., Jr., Graham, S. M., Pataki, S. P., & Finkel, E. J. (2010). Ways of giving benefits in marriage: Norm use, relationship satisfaction, and attachment-related variability. *Psychological Science, 21,* 944–951.

Clarke, A. C. (1952). An examination of the operation of residential propinquity as a factor in mate selection. *American Sociological Review, 17,* 17–22.

Clay, R. A. (1996, May). Modern hypnosis wins clinical respect, praise. *APA Monitor.*

Cloninger, C. R., & Gottesman, I. I. (1987). Genetic and environmental factors in antisocial behavior disorders. In S. A. Mednick, T. E. Moffitt, & S. A. Stack (Eds.), *The causes of crime: New biological approaches* (pp. 92–109). New York: Cambridge University Press.

Cloninger, C. R., Bayon, C., & Przybeck, T. (1997). Epidemiology and axis I comorbidity of antisocial personality disorder. In D. M. Stoff, J. Breiling, & J. D. Maser (Eds.), *Handbook of antisocial personality disorder* (pp. 12–21). New York: Wiley.

CNN. (2014, February 8). Attorney general to extend recognition of same-sex marriage rights. *CNN News Wire.* Retrieved from http://www.ozarksfirst.com/story/d/story/attorney-general-to-extend-same-sex-marriage-right/96446/TtsHUHtAJkuCUylOdqdEjw

Coccaro, E. F., Beresford, B., Minar, P., Kaskow, J., & Geracioti, T. (2007). CSF testosterone: Relationship to aggression, impulsivity, and venturesomeness in adult males with personality disorder. *Journal of Psychiatric Research, 41,* 488–492.

Cochran, S. V., & Rabinowitz, F. E. (2000). *Men and depression: Clinical and empirical perspectives.* San Diego: Academic Press.

Coffer, C. N., & Appley, M. (1964). *Motivation: Theory and research.* New York: Wiley.

Cohen, C. I., Natarajan, N., Araujo, M., & Solanki, D. (2013). Prevalence of negative symptoms and associated factors in older adults with schizophrenia spectrum disorder. *American Journal of Geriatric Psychiatry, 21,* 100–107.

Cohen, M. X., Young, J., Baek, J., Kessler, C., & Ranganath, C. (2005). Individual differences in extraversion and dopamine genetics predict neural reward responses. *Cognitive Brain Research, 25,* 851–861.

Cohen, N. J. (1984). Preserved learning capacity in amnesia: Evidence for multiple memory systems. In L. R. Squire & N. Butters (Eds.), *Neuropsychology of memory* (pp. 83–103). New York: Guilford Press.

Cohen, P., Kasen, S., Chen, H., Hartmark, C., & Gordon, K. (2003). Variations in patterns of developmental transitions in the emerging adulthood period. *Developmental Psychology, 39,* 657–669.

Cohen, S. (1996). Psychological stress, immunity, and upper respiratory infections. *Current Directions in Psychological Science, 5,* 86–90.

Cohen, S. G., & Ledford, G. E., Jr. (1994). The effectiveness of self-managing teams: A quasi-experiment. *Human Relations, 47,* 13–43.

Cohen, S., & Janicki-Deverts, D. (2009). Can we improve our physical health by altering our social networks? *Perspectives on Psychological Science, 4,* 375–378.

Cohen, S., Doyle, W. J., Turner, R., Alper, C. M., & Skoner, D. P. (2003). Sociability and susceptibility to the common cold. *Psychological Science, 14,* 389–395.

Cohen, S., Janicki-Deverts, D., Chen, E., & Matthews, K. A. (2010). Childhood socioeconomic status and adult health. *Annals of the New York Academy of Sciences, 1186,* 37–55.

Cohen, S., Tyrrell, D., & Smith, A. (1991). Psychological stress and susceptibility to the common cold. *New England Journal of Medicine, 325,* 606–612.

Colado, M. I., O'Shea, E., & Green, A. R. (2004). Acute and long-term effects of MDMA on cerebral dopamine biochemistry and function. *Psychopharmacology (Berlin), 173,* 249–263.

Colbert-White, E. N. , Covington, M. A., & Fragaszy, D. M. (2011). Social context influences the vocalizations of a home-raised African grey parrot (*Psittacus erithacus erithacus*). *Journal of Comparative Psychology, 125,* 175–184.

Colcombe, S., & Kramer, A. F. (2003). Fitness effects on the cognitive function of older adults: A meta-analytic study. *Psychological Science, 14,* 125–130.

Cole, S. W. (2009). Social regulation of human gene expression. *Current Directions in Psychological Science, 18,* 132–137.

Coleman, M., Ganong, L., & Fine, M. (2000). Reinvestigating marriage: Another decade of progress. *Journal of Marriage and Family, 62,* 1288–1307.

Coley, R. L. (2001). (In)visible men: Emerging research on low-income, unmarried, and minority fathers. *American Psychologist, 56,* 743–753.

Colley, A., Ball, J., Kirby, N., Harvey, R., & Vingelen, I. (2002). Gender-linked differences in everyday memory performance: Effort makes the difference. *Sex Roles: A Journal of Research, 47,* 577–582.

Collier, G., Hirsch, E., & Hamlin, P. H. (1972). The ecological determinants of reinforcement in the rat. *Physiology and Behavior, 9,* 705–716.

Collins, A. M., & Quillian, M. R. (1969). Retrieval time from semantic memory. *Journal of Verbal Learning and Verbal Behavior, 8,* 240–248.

Collins, A., Hill, L. E., Chandramohan, Y., Witcomb, D., Droste, S. K., & Reul, J. M. (2009). Exercise improves cognitive responses to stress through enhancement of epigenetic mechanisms and gene expression in the dentate gyrus. *PLoS One, 4,* e4330.

Collins, M. W., Field, M., Lovell, M. R., Iverson, G., Johnston, K. M., Maroon, J. et al. (2003). Relationship between postconcussion headache and neuropsychological test performance in high school athletes. *American Journal of Sports Medicine, 31,* 168–173.

Collins, W. A., & van Dulmen, M. (2006). Friendships and romance in emerging adulthood: Assessing distinctiveness in close relationships. In J. J. Arnett & J. L. Tanner (Eds.), *Emerging adults in America: Coming of age in the 21st century* (pp. 219–234). Washington, DC: APA.

Cologan, V., Schabus, M., Ledoux, D., Moonen, G., Maquet, P., & Laureys, S. (2010). Sleep in disorders of consciousness. *Sleep Medicine Reviews, 14,* 97–105.

Coltrane, S. (2001). Research on household labor: Modeling and measuring the social embeddedness of routine family work. In R. M. Milardo (Ed.), *Understanding families in the new millennium: A decade in review* (pp. 427–452). Minneapolis: National Council on Family Relations.

Comaty, J. E., Stasio, M., & Advokat, C. (2001). Analysis of outcome variables of a token economy in a state psychiatric hospital: A program evaluation. *Research in Developmental Disabilities, 22,* 233–253.

Combs, D. R., & Mueser, K. T. (2007). Schizophrenia. In M. Hersen, S. Turner, & D. Beidel (Eds.), *Adult psychopathology and diagnosis* (5th ed., pp. 234–285). New York: Wiley.

Compton, W. M., Helzer, J. E., Hwu, H., Yeh, E., McEvoy, L., Tipp, J. E. et al. (1991). New methods in cross-cultural psychiatry: Psychiatric illness in Taiwan and the United States. *American Journal of Psychiatry, 148,* 1697–1704.

Conklin, H. M., & Iacono, W. G. (2002). Schizophrenia: A neurodevelopmental perspective. *Current Directions in Psychological Science, 11,* 33–37.

Connelly, W. M., & Errington, A. C. (2012). Temporally selective firing of cortical and thalamic neurons during sleep and wakefulness. *Journal of Neuroscience, 32,* 7415–7417. doi:10.1523/JNEUROSCI.1164-12.2012

Conrad, M. A., & Ashworth, S. D. (1986). *Recruiting source effectiveness: A meta-analysis and re-examination of two rival hypotheses.* Paper presented at the First Annual Meeting of the Society for Industrial and Organizational Psychology, Chicago.

Conway, B. R. (2003). Colour vision: A clue to hue in V2. *Current Biology, 13,* R308–R310.

Conway, B. R. (2009). Color vision, cones, and color-coding in the cortex. *Neuroscientist, 15,* 274–290.

Conway, B. R., & Livingstone, M. S. (2005). A different point of hue. *Proceedings of the National Academy of Sciences of the United States of America, 102,* 10761–10762.

Conway, M. A. (2009). Episodic memories. *Neuropsychologia, 47,* 2305–2313.

Cook, J. L., & Cook, G. (2005). *Child development: Principles and perspectives.* Boston: Allyn & Bacon.

Cooke, R., & Sheeran, P. (2004). Moderation of cognition-intention and cognition-behaviour relations: A meta-analysis of properties of variables from the theory of planned behaviour. *British Journal of Social Psychology, 43,* 159–186.

Cookson, J. (1997). Lithium: Balancing risks and benefits. *British Journal of Psychiatry, 171,* 113–119.

Cools, J., Schotte, D. E., & McNally, R. J. (1992). Emotional arousal and overeating in restrained eaters. *Journal of Abnormal Psychology, 69,* 390–400.

Coons, P. M. (1994). Confirmation of childhood abuse in child and adolescent cases of multiple personality disorder and dissociative disorder not otherwise specified. *Journal of Nervous and Mental Disease, 182,* 461–464.

Cooper, M. L. (2002). Alcohol use and risky sexual behavior among college students and youth. *Journal of Studies on Alcohol, 14,* 101–117.

Cooper, Z. D., & Haney, M. (2008). Cannabis reinforcement and dependence: Role of the cannabinoid CB1 receptor. *Addiction Biology, 13,* 188–195.

Copeland, W. E., Angold, A., Shanahan, L., & Costello, E. J. (2014). Longitudinal patterns of anxiety from childhood to adulthood: The Great Smoky Mountains Study. *Journal of the American Academy of Child and Adolescent Psychiatry, 53,* 21–33.

Copen, C. E., Daniels, K., Vespa, J., & Mosher, W. D. (2012). First marriages in the United States: Data from the 2006–2010 National Survey of Family Growth. *National Health Statistics Report,* No. 49. Atlanta: U.S. Department of Health & Human Services.

Coren, S., Porac, C., Aks, D. J., & Morikawa, K. (1988). A method to assess the relative contribution of lateral inhibition to the magnitude of visual-geometric illusions. *Perception and Psychophysics, 43,* 551–558.

Coren, S., Ward, L. M., & Enns, J. T. (1999). *Sensation and perception* (5th ed.). Fort Worth, TX: Harcourt Brace.

Corey, G. (2009). *Theory and practice of counseling and psychotherapy* (8th ed.). Belmont, CA: Brooks/Cole.

Corkin, S. (1968). Acquisition of motor skill after bilateral medial temporal-lobe excision. *Neuropsychologia, 6,* 255–265.

Corra, M., Carter, S. K., Carter, J. S., & Knox, D. (2009). Trends in marital happiness by gender and race, 1973 to 2006. *Journal of Family Issues, 30,* 1379–1404.

Correll, C. U., Leucht, S., & Kane, J. M. (2004). Lower risk for tardive dyskinesia associated with second-generation antipsychotics: A systematic review of 1-year studies. *American Journal of Psychiatry, 161,* 414–425.

Corrigan, P., McCorkle, B., Schell, B, & Kidder, K. (2003). Religion and spirituality in the lives of people with serious mental illness. *Community Mental Health Journal, 39,* 487–499.

Cortina, L. M., & Kubiak, S. P. (2006). Gender and posttraumatic stress: Sexual violence as an explanation for women's increased risk. *Journal of Abnormal Psychology, 115,* 753–759.

Cortina, M. (2010). The future of psychodynamic psychotherapy. *Psychiatry, 73,* 43–56.

Cosmides, L., & Tooby, J. (1996). Are humans good intuitive statisticians after all? Rethinking some conclusions from the literature on judgment under uncertainty. *Cognition, 58,* 1–73.

Costa, P. T., & McCrae, R. R. (1992). Multiple uses for longitudinal personality data. *European Journal of Personality, 6,* 85–102.

Costa, P. T., & McCrae, R. R. (1997). Longitudinal stability of adult personality. In R. Hogan, J. A. Johnson, & S. R. Briggs (Eds.), *Handbook of personality psychology* (pp. 269–290). San Diego, CA: Academic Press.

Costa, P. T., Terracciano, A., & McCrae, R. R. (2001). Gender differences in personality traits across cultures: Robust and surprising findings. *Journal of Personality and Social Psychology, 81,* 322–331.

Costa-Pinto, F. A., & Palermo-Neto, J. (2010). Neuroimmune interactions in stress. *Neuroimmunomodulation, 17,* 196–199.

Costello, E. J., Egger, H., & Angold, A. (2005). 10-year research update review: The epidemiology of child and adolescent psychiatric disorders: I. Methods and public health burden. *Journal of the American Academy of Child and Adolescent Psychiatry, 44,* 972–986.

Council of Europe. (2008). Children and corporal punishment: "The right not to be hit, also a children's right." CommDH/IssuePaper(2006)1REV. Retrieved from https://www.wcd.coe.int/ViewDoc.jsp?id=1237635

Cousins, D. A., Butts, K., & Young, A. H. (2009). The role of dopamine in bipolar disorder. *Bipolar Disorders, 11,* 787–806.

Coussons-Read, M. (2012). The psychoneuroimmunology of stress in pregnancy. *Current Directions in Psychological Science, 21,* 323–328.

Coutinho-Budd, J., & Freeman, M. R. (2013). Probing the enigma: Unraveling glial cell biology in invertebrates. *Current Opinion in Neurobiology, 23,* 1073–1079. doi:10.1016/j.conb.2013.07.002

Cowan, C. P., & Cowan, P. A. (2000). *When partners become parents: The big life change for couples.* Mahwah, NJ: Erlbaum.

Cowan, R. L. (2007). Neuroimaging research in human MDMA users: A review. *Psychopharmacology (Berlin), 189,* 539–556.

Crabbe, J. C., Harris, R. A., & Koob, G. F. (2011). Preclinical studies of alcohol binge drinking. *Annals of the New York Academy of Sciences, 1216,* 24–40.

Craik, F. I. M., & Lockhart, R. S. (1972). Levels of processing: A framework for memory research. *Journal of Verbal Learning and Verbal Behavior, 11,* 671–684.

Crandall, C. S. (1988). Social contagion of binge eating. *Journal of Personality and Social Psychology, 55,* 588–598.

Crandall, C. S. (1991). Do heavy-weight students have more difficulty paying for college? *Personality and Social Psychology Bulletin, 17,* 606–611.

Crandall, C. S., Preisler, J. J., & Aussprung, J. (1992). Measuring life event stress in the lives of college students: The Undergraduate Stress Questionnaire (USQ). *Journal of Behavioral Medicine, 15,* 627–662.

Crane, M., & Markus, H. (1982). Gender identity: Benefits of a self-schema approach. *Journal of Personality and Social Psychology, 43,* 1195–1197.

Cranny, C. J., Smith, P. C., & Stone, E. F. (1992). *Job satisfaction: How people feel about their jobs and how it affects their performance.* New York: Lexington Books.

Craske, M. G., & Barlow, D. H. (2001). Panic disorder and agoraphobia. In D. H. Barlow (Ed.), *Clinical handbook of psychological disorders* (3rd ed., pp. 1–59). New York: Guilford Press.

Crawford, H. J., Brown, A. M., & Moon, C. E. (1993). Sustained attentional and disattentional abilities: Differences between low and highly hypnotizable persons. *Journal of Abnormal Psychology, 102,* 534–543.

Creamer, M., Wade, D., Fletcher, S., & Forbes, D. (2011). PTSD among military personnel. *International Review of Psychiatry, 23,* 160–165.

Crews, F. (1996). The verdict on Freud. *Psychological Science, 7,* 63–68.

Crick, F., & Mitchison, G. (1995). REM sleep and neural nets. *Behavioural Brain Research, 69,* 147–155.

Crits-Christoph, P. (1997). Limitations of the dodo bird verdict and the role of clinical trials in psychotherapy research: Comment on Wamplod et al. (1997). *Psychological Bulletin, 122,* 216–220.

Crits-Christoph, P., Baranackie, K., Kurcias, J. S., & Beck, A. T. (1991). Meta-analysis of therapist effects in psychotherapy outcome. *Psychotherapy Research, 1,* 81–91.

Crockett, M. J., Clark, L., Hauser, M. D., & Robbins, T. W. (2010). Serotonin selectively influences moral judgment and behavior through effects on harm aversion. *Proceedings of the National Academy of Sciences, 107,* 17433–17438.

Crombag, H. S., & Robinson, T. E. (2004). Drugs, environment, brain, and behavior. *Current Directions in Psychological Science, 13,* 107–111.

Crosby, R., & Danner, F. (2008). Adolescents' STD protective attitudes predict sexually transmitted disease acquisition in early adulthood. *Journal of School Health, 78,* 310–313.

Cross, E. S., Mackie, E. C., Wolford, G., & Hamilton, A. F. (2010). Contorted and ordinary body postures in the human brain. *Experimental Brain Research, 204,* 397–407. doi: 10.1007/s00221-00902093-X

Crosscope-Happel, C. L. (2000). Male anorexia nervosa: A new focus. *Journal of Mental Health Counseling, 22,* 365.

Crowley, A. E., & Hoyer, W. D. (1994). An integrative framework for understanding two-sided persuasion. *Journal of Consumer Research, 20,* 561–574.

Crowley, S. J., Acebo, C., & Carskadon, M. A. (2007). Sleep, circadian rhythms, and delayed phase in adolescence. *Sleep Medicine, 8,* 602–612.

Croxford, J. L. (2003). Therapeutic potential of cannabinoids in CNS disease. *CNS Drugs, 17,* 179–202.

Croy, I., Bojanowski, V., & Hummel, T. (2013). Men without a sense of smell exhibit a strongly reduced number of sexual relationships, women exhibit reduced partnership security—A reanalysis of previously published data. *Biological Psychology, 92,* 292–294. doi:10.1016/j.biopsycho.2012.11.008

Crum, N., Riffenburgh, R., Wegner, S., Agan, B., Tasker, S., Spooner, K. et al., and the Triservice AIDS Clinical Consortium. (2006). Comparisons of causes of death and mortality rates among HIV-infected patients: Analysis of the pre-, early, and late HAART (highly active antiretroviral therapy) eras. *Journal of Acquired Immune Deficiency Syndromes, 41,* 194–200.

Cui, M., & Donnellan, M. B. (2009). Trajectories of conflict over raising adolescent children and marital satisfaction. *Journal of Marriage and Family, 71,* 478–494.

Cukor, J., Wyka, K., Jayasinghe, N., Weathers, F., Glosan, C., Leck, P. et al. (2011). Prevalence and predictors of posttraumatic stress symptoms in utility workers deployed to the World Trade Center following the attacks of September 11, 2001. *Depression and Anxiety, 28,* 210–217.

Cunha, C., Guerreiro, M., de Mendonça, A., Oliveira, P., & Santana, I. (2012). Serial position effects in Alzheimer's disease, mild cognitive impairment, and normal aging: Predictive value for conversion to dementia. *Journal of Clinical and Experimental Neuropsychology, 34,* 841–852. doi:10.1080/13803395.2012.689814

Curry, K., & Stasio, M. J. (2009). The effects of energy drinks alone and with alcohol on neuropsychological functioning. *Human Psychopharmacology, 24,* 473–481.

Cutrona, C. E., Wallace, G., & Wesner, K. A. (2006). Neighborhood characteristics and depression: An examination of stress processes. *Current Directions in Psychological Science, 15,* 188–192.

D'Anna, L. H., Ponce, N. A., & Siegel, J. M. (2010). Racial and ethnic health disparities: Evidence of discrimination's effects across the SEP spectrum. *Ethnicity and Health, 15,* 121–143.

D'Augelli, A. R., Grossman, A. H., & Starks, M. T. (2006). Childhood gender atypicality, victimization, and PTSD among lesbian, gay, and bisexual youth. *Journal of Interpersonal Violence, 21,* 1462–1482.

Dabbs, J. M., Jr., & Morris, R. (1990). Testosterone, social class, and antisocial behavior in a sample of 4,462 men. *Psychological Science, 1,* 209–211.

Daiello, L. A. (2007). Atypical antipsychotics for the treatment of dementia-related behaviors: An update. *Medicine and Health, 90,* 191–194.

Dalal, R. S. (2005). A meta-analysis of the relationship between organizational citizenship behavior and counterproductive work behavior. *Journal of Applied Psychology, 90,* 1241–1255.

Dalen, K., Bruaroy, S., Wentzel-Larsen, T., & Laegreid, L. M. (2009). Cognitive functioning in children prenatally exposed to alcohol and psychotropic drugs. *Neuropediatrics, 40,* 162–167.

Dalman, C., & Allebeck, P. (2002). Paternal age and schizophrenia: Further support for an association. *American Journal of Psychiatry, 159,* 1591–1592.

Damak, S., Rong, M., Yasumatsu, K., Kokrashvii, Z., Varadarajan, V., Zou, S. et al. (2003). Detection of sweet and umami taste in the absence of taste receptor T1r3. *Science, 301,* 850–851.

Damasio, H., Grabowski, T., Frank, R., Galaburda, A. M., & Damasio, A. R. (1994). The return of Phineas Gage: Clues about the brain from the skull of a famous patient. *Science, 264,* 1102–1105.

Damjanovic, A. K., Yang, Y., Glaser, R., Kiecolt-Glaser, J. K., Huy, N., Laskowski, B. et al. (2007). Accelerated telomere erosion is associated with a declining immune function of caregivers of Alzheimer's disease patients. *Journal of Immunology, 179,* 4249–4254.

Damm, J., Eser, D., Schule, C., Obermeier, M., Moeller, H. J., Rupprecht, R. et al. (2010). Influence of age on effectiveness and tolerability of electroconvulsive therapy. *Journal of ECT, 26,* 282–288.

Damon, W. (1999). The moral development of children. *Scientific American, 281,* 73–78.

Danesi, M. (2010). The form and function of slang. *Semiotica: Journal of the International Association for Semiotic Studies, 182,* 507–517.

Dang-Vu, T. T., Schabus, M., Desseilles, M., Sterpenich, V., Bonjean, M., & Maquet, P. (2010). Functional neuroimaging insights into the physiology of human sleep. *Sleep, 33,* 1589–1603.

Danhauer, J. L., Johnson, C. E., Byrd, A., DeGood, L., Meuel, C., Pecile, A. et al. (2009). Survey of college students on iPod and hearing health. *Journal of the American Academy of Audiology, 20,* 5–27.

Danielsdottir, S., O'Brien, K. S., & Ciao, A. (2010). Anti-fat prejudice reduction: A review of published studies. *Obesity Facts, 3,* 47–58.

Dannlowski, U., Ohrmann, P., Bauer, J., Kugel, H., Baune, B. T., Hohoff, C. et al. (2007). Serotonergic genes modulate amygdale activity in major depression. *Genes, Brain and Behavior, 6,* 672–676.

Darley, J. M., & Batson, C. (1973). "From Jerusalem to Jericho": A study of situational and dispositional variables in helping behavior. *Journal of Personality and Social Psychology, 27,* 100–108. doi:10.1037/h0034449

Darowish, M., Lawton, J. N., & Evans, P. J. (2009). Q: What is cell phone elbow, and what should we tell our patients? *Cleveland Clinic Journal of Medicine, 76,* 306–308.

Darwin, C. (1936). *On the origin of species by means of natural selection.* New York: Random House. (Original work published 1859)

Dasen, P. R. (1994). Culture and cognitive development from a Piagetian perspective. In W. J. Lonner & R. Malpass (Eds.), *Psychology and culture* (pp. 141–150). Boston: Allyn & Bacon.

Dasgupta, A. M., Juza, D. M., White, G. M., & Maloney, J. F. (1995). Memory and hypnosis: A comparative analysis of guided memory, cognitive interviews, and hypnotic hyperamnesia. *Imagination, Cognition, and Personality, 14,* 117–130.

David, D., Szentagotai, A., Lupu, V., & Cosman, D. (2008). Rational emotive behavior therapy, cognitive therapy, and medication in the treatment of major depressive disorder: A randomized clinical trial, posttreatment outcomes, and six-month follow-up. *Journal of Clinical Psychology, 64,* 728–746.

Davidson, J. R. T. (2000). Trauma: The impact of post-traumatic stress disorder. *Journal of Psychopharmacology, 14,* S5–S12.

Davidson, R. J., Jackson, D. C., & Kalin, N. H. (2000). Emotion, plasticity, context, and regulation: Perspectives from affective neuroscience. *Psychological Bulletin, 126,* 873–889.

Davidson, R. J., Putnam, K. M., & Larson, C. L. (2000). Dysfunction in the neural circuitry of emotion regulation: A possible prelude to violence. *Science, 289,* 591–594.

Davies, H., Liao, P. C., Campbell, I. C., & Tchanturia, K. (2009). Multidimenional self reports as a measure of characteristics in people with eating disorders. *Eating and Weight Disorders, 14,* e84–e91.

Davies, I. R. L. (1998). A study of colour grouping in three languages: A test of the linguistic relativity hypothesis. *British Journal of Psychology, 89,* 433–452.

Davis, K. C., George, W. H., Norris, J., Schacht, R. L., Stoner, S. A., Hendershot, C. S. et al. (2009). Effects of alcohol and blood alcohol concentration limb on sexual risk-taking intentions. *Journal of Studies on Alcohol and Drugs, 70,* 499–507.

Davis, M., & Egger, M. D. (1992). Habituation and sensitization in vertebrates. In L. R. Squire, J. H. Byrne, L. Nadel, H. L. Roediger, D. L. Schacter, & R. F. Thompson (Eds.), *Encylcopedia of learning and memory* (pp. 237–240). New York: Macmillan.

Davis, O. S., Haworth, C. M., & Plomin, R. (2009). Dramatic increase in heritability of cognitive development from early to middle childhood: An 8-year longitudinal study of 8,700 pairs of twins. *Psychological Science, 20,* 1301–1308.

Davis, P. J. (1999). Gender differences in autobiographical memory for childhood emotional experiences. *Journal of Personality and Social Psychology, 76,* 498–510.

Davis-Coelho, K., Waltz, J., & Davis-Coelho, B. (2000). Awareness and prevention of bias against fat clients in psychotherapy. *Professional Psychology: Research and Practice, 31,* 682–684.

De Benedittis, G., Lorenzetti, A., & Pieri, A. (1990). The role of stressful life events in the onset of chronic primary headache. *Pain, 40,* 65–75.

De Carvalho, M. R., Freire, R. C., & Nardi, A. E. (2010). Virtual reality as a mechanism for exposure therapy. *World Journal of Biological Psychiatry, 11,* 220–230.

de Castro, J. M. (2002). The influence of heredity on self-reported sleep patterns in free-living humans. *Physiology and Behavior, 76,* 479–486.

de Fonseca, F., Carrera, M. R. A., Navarro, M., Koob, G. F., & Weiss, F. (1997). Activation of corticotropin-releasing factor in the limbic system during cannabinoid withdrawal. *Science, 276,* 2050–2054.

De Leersnyder, J., Boiger, M., & Mesquita, B. (2013). Cultural regulation of emotion: Individual, relational, and structural sources. *Frontiers in Psychology, 4,* 55. doi: 10.3389/fpsyg.2013.00055

De Lisi, R., & Gallagher, A. M. (1991). Understanding gender stability and constancy in Argentinean children. *Merrill-Palmer Quarterly, 37,* 483–502.

De May, J. (2006). A critical review of the March 27, 1964, New York Times article that first broke the story. Retrieved from http://www.oldkewgardens.com/ss-nytimes-3.html html

de Tommaso, M., Difruscolo, O., Sardaro, M., Losito, L., Serpino, C., Pietrapertosa, A. et al. (2007). Influence of MTHFR genotype on contingent negative variation and MRI abnormalities in migraine. *Headache, 47,* 253–265.

Deak, G. O. (2006). Do children really confuse appearance and reality? *Trends in Cognitive Science, 10,* 546–550.

Deakin, J. F., Lees, J., McKie, S., Hallak, J. E., Williams, S. R., & Dursun, S. M. (2008). Glutamate and the neural basis of the subjective effects of ketamine: A pharmaco-magnetic resonance imaging study. *Archives of General Psychiatry, 65,* 154–164.

DeAngelis, T. (2004). Size-based discrimination may be hardest on children. *American Psychological Association Monitor on Psychology, 35,* 62.

Deary, I. J., Weiss, A., & Batty, G. D. (2010). Intelligence, personality, and health outcomes. *Psychological Science in the Public Interest, 11,* 53–79.

Deaux, K., & Hanna, R. (1984). Courtship in the personals column: The influence of gender and sexual orientation. *Sex Roles, 11,* 363–375.

DeCasper, A. J., & Fifer, W. P. (1980). Of human bonding: Newborns prefer their mothers' voices. *Science, 208,* 1174–1176.

DeCastro, J. M., & Elmore, D. K. (1988). Subjective hunger relationships with meal patterns in the spontaneous feeding behavior of humans: Evidence for a causal relationship. *Physiology and Behavior, 43,* 159–165.

Deci, E. L., & Ryan, R. M. (1985). *Intrinsic motivation and self-determination in human behavior.* New York: Plenum Press.

Deci, E. L., & Ryan, R. M. (2008). Self-determination theory: A macrotheory of human motivation, development, and health. *Canadian Psychology, 49,* 182–185.

Degner, J., & Dalege, J. (2013). The apple does not fall far from the tree, or does it? A meta-analysis of parent–child similarity in intergroup attitudes. *Psychological Bulletin, 139,* 1270–1304. doi:10.1037/a0031436

Degroot, A. B. (2004). The role of the septo-hippocampal system in fear and anxiety. *Dissertation Abstracts International: Section B: The Sciences and Engineering, 65*(1-B), 475.

DeLacoste-Utamsing, C., & Holloway, R. L. (1982). Sexual dimorphism in the human corpus callosum. *Science, 216,* 1431–1432.

DeLoache, J. (2001). The symbol-mindedness of young children. In W. W. Hartup & R. A. Weinberg (Eds.), *Child psychology in retrospect and prospect* (Vol. 32, pp. 73–101). Mahwah, NJ: Erlbaum.

Demany, L., & Semal, C. (2005). The slow formation of a pitch percept beyond the ending time of a short tone burst. *Perception and Psychophysics, 67,* 1376–1383.

Dement, W. (1960). The effect of dream deprivation. *Science, 131,* 1705–1707.

Dement, W., & Kleitman, N. (1957). Cyclic variations in EEG during sleep and their relation to eye movements, body motility, and dreaming. *Electroencephalography and Clinical Neurophysiology, 9,* 673–690.

Dement, W., & Vaughan, C. (1999). *The promise of sleep: A pioneer in sleep medicine explains the vital connection between health, happiness, and a good night's sleep.* New York: Delacorte.

Demers, L. B., Hanson, K. G., Kirkorian, H. L., Pempek, T. A., & Anderson, D. R. (2013). Infant gaze following during parent–infant coviewing of baby videos. *Child Development, 84,* 591–603. doi:10.1111/j.1467-8624.2012.01868.x

Denis, M., & Cocude, M. (1999). On the metric properties of visual images generated from verbal descriptions: Evidence for the robustness of the mental scanning effect. *Journal of Cognitive Psychology, 9,* 353–379.

DePalma, M., Madey, S. F., Tillman, T. C., & Wheeler, J. (1999). Perceived patient responsibility and belief in a just world affect helping. *Basic and Applied Social Psychology, 21,* 131–137. doi:10.1207/15324839951036470

Department of Housing and Urban Development (HUD). (2005). *Discrimination in metropolitan housing markets: National results from Phase 1, Phase 2, and Phase 3 of the housing discrimination study (HDS).* Retrieved from http://www.huduser.org/publications/hsgfin/hds.html

Depression and Bipolar Support Alliance (DBSA). (2002). *National DMDA support groups: An important step on the road to wellness.* Chicago: Author.

Depue, R. A., & Collins, P. F. (1999). Neurobiology of the structure of personality: Dopamine, facilitation of incentive motivation, and extraversion. *The Behavioral and Brain Sciences, 22,* 491–517.

Depue, R. A., & Fu, Y. (2013). On the nature of extraversion: Variation in conditioned contextual activation of dopamine-facilitated affective, cognitive, and motor processes. *Frontiers in Human Neuroscience, 7,* 288. doi: 10.3389/fnhum.2013.00288

Derringer, J., Krueger, R. F., Dick, D. M., Saccone, S., Grucza, R. A., Agrawal, A. et al. (2010). Predicting sensation seeking from dopamine genes: A candidate-systems approach. *Psychological Science, 21,* 1282–1290.

Desseilles, M., Dabg-Vu, T. T., Sterpenich, V., Schwartz, S. (2011). Cognitive and emotional processes during dreaming: A neuroimaging view. *Consciousness and Cognition, 20,* 998–1008.

Deutsch, F. M. (2001). Equally shared parenting. *Current Directions in Psychological Science, 10,* 25–28.

Deutsch, J. A. (1990). Food intake. In E. M. Stricker (Ed.), *Handbook of behavioral neurobiology: Vol. 10. Neurobiology of food and fluid intake* (pp. 151–182). New York: Plenum Press.

DeValois, R. L., & DeValois, K. K. (1975). Neural coding of color. In E. C. Carterette & M. P. Friedman (Eds.), *Handbook of perception* (pp. 117–166). New York: Academic Press.

DeWall, C. N., & Bushman, B. J. (2011). Social acceptance and rejection: The sweet and the bitter. *Current Directions in Psychological Science, 20,* 256–260.

Dewaraja, R., & Kawamura, N. (2006). Trauma intensity and posttraumatic stress: Implications of the tsunami experience in Sri Lanka for the management of future disasters. *International Congress Series, 1287,* 69–73.

Dhabhar, F. S., Miller, A. H., McEwen, B. S., & Spencer, R. L. (1995). Effects of stress on immune cell distribution. Dynamics and hormonal mechanisms. *Journal of Immunology, 154,* 5511–5527.

Dhont, K., Roets, A., & Van Hiel, A. (2013). The intergenerational transmission of need for closure underlies the transmission of authoritarianism and anti-immigrant prejudice. *Personality and Individual Differences, 54,* 779–784. doi:10.1016/j.paid.2012.12.016

Di Lorio, C. R., Watkins, T. J., Dietrich, M. S., Cao, A., Blackford, J. U., Rogers, B. et al. (2012). Evidence for chronically altered serotonin function in the cerebral cortex of female 3,4-methylenedioxymethamphetamine polydrug users. *Archives of General Psychiatry, 69,* 399–409.

Diamond, A., & Amso, D. (2008). Contributions of neuroscience to our understanding of cognitive development. *Current Directions in Psychological Science, 17,* 136–141.

Diaz, R. M., & Berk, L. E. (Eds.). (1992). *Private speech: From social interaction to self-regulation.* Hillsdale, NJ: Erlbaum.

Díaz-Mataix, L., Tallot, L., & Doyère, V. (2014). The amygdala: A potential player in timing CS–US intervals. *Behavioral Processes, 101,* 112–122. doi.10.1016/j.beproc.2013.08.007

Dichter, G. S., Felder, J. N., & Smoski, M. J. (2010). The effects of brief behavioral activation therapy for depression on cognitive control in affective contexts: An fMRI investigation. *Journal of Affective Disorders, 126,* 236–244.

Dick, D. M., Meyers, J. L., Latendresse, S. J., Creemers, H. E., Lansford, J. E., Pettit, G. S. et al. (2011). CHRM2, parental monitoring, and adolescent externalizing behavior: Evidence for gene–environment interaction. *Psychological Science, 22,* 481–489.

Dickens, W. T., & Flynn, J. R. (2006). Black Americans reduce the racial IQ gap. Evidence from standardization samples. *Psychological Science, 17,* 913–920.

Dickson, N., van Roode, T., Cameron, C., & Paul, C. (2013). Stability and change in same-sex attraction, experience, and identity by sex and age in a New Zealand birth cohort. *Archives of Sexual Behavior, 42,* 753–763. doi: 10.1007/s10508-012-0063-z

Diekelmann, S., & Born, J. (2010). The memory function of sleep. *Nature Reviews: Neuroscience, 11,* 114–126.

Diener, C., Kuehner, C., Brusniak, W., Struve, M., & Flor, H. (2009). Effects of stressor controllability on psychophysiological, cognitive, and behavioral responses in patients with major depression and dysthymia. *Psychological Medicine, 39,* 77–86.

Diener, E., & Biswas-Diener, R. (2008). *Happiness: Unlocking the mysteries of psychological wealth.* Malden, MA: Blackwell.

Diener, E., & Seligman, M. E. (2004). Beyond money: Toward an economy of well-being. *Psychological Science in the Public Interest, 5,* 1–31.

Diener, E., Oishi, S., & Lucas, R. E. (2003). Personality, culture, and subjective well-being: Emotional and cognitive evaluations of life. *Annual Review of Psychology, 54,* 403–425.

Dies, R. R. (1993). Research on group psychotherapy: Overview and clinical applications. In A. Alonso & H. I. Swiller (Eds.), *Group therapy in clinical practice* (pp. 473–518). Washington, DC: American Psychiatric Press.

Difede, J., & Hoffman, H. G. (2002). Virtual reality exposure therapy for World Trade Center post-traumatic stress disorder: A case report. *Cyberpsychology and Behavior, 5,* 529–535.

Digman, J. M. (1997). Higher-order factors of the Big Five. *Journal of Personality and Social Psychology, 73,* 1246–1256.

Dillon, S. (2009, August 11). Disabled students are spanked more. *New York Times,* p. A10.

Dingfelder, S. F. (2010). How artists see. *Monitor on Psychology, 41,* p. 40.

Dion, K. K., Berscheid, E., & Walster, E. (1972). What is beautiful is good. *Journal of Personality and Social Psychology, 24,* 285–290.

DiPatrizio, N. V., & Piomelli, D. (2012). The thrifty lipids: Endocannabinoids and the neural control of energy conservation. *Trends in Neurosciences, 35,* 403–411. doi: 10.1016/j.tins.2012.04.006

Dishion, T. J., & Patterson, G. R. (1997). The timing and severity of antisocial behavior: Three hypotheses within an ecological framework. In D. M. Stoff, J. Breiling, & J. D. Maser (Eds.), *Handbook of antisocial personality disorder* (pp. 205–217). New York: Wiley

Distefan, J. M., Pierce, J. P., & Gilpin, E. A. (2004). Do favorite movie stars influence adolescent smoking initiation? *American Journal of Public Health, 94,* 1239–1244.

Dixon, J. F., & Hokin, L. E. (1998). Lithium acutely inhibits and chronically up-regulates and stabilizes glutamate uptake by presynaptic nerve endings on mouse cerebral cortex. *Neurobiology, 95,* 8363–8368.

Do, J., & Schenk, S. (2013). Self-administered MDMA produces dose- and time-dependent serotonin deficits in the rat brain. *Addiction Biology, 18,* 441–447.

Dobbs, D. (2006). Turning off depression. *Scientific American, 17,* 26–31.

Dobson, K. S., Backs-Dermott, B. J., & Dozois, D. J. A. (2000). Cognitive and cognitive-behavioral therapies. In C. R. Snyder & R. E. Ingram (Eds.), *Handbook of psychological change: Psychotherapy processes and practices for the 21st century* (pp. 409–428). New York: Wiley.

Doctor, R. M., & Doctor, J. N. (1994). Stress. In *Encyclopedia of human behavior* (Vol. 4). San Diego, CA: Academic Press.

Dohrenwend, B. P., Turner, J. B., Turse, N. A., Adams, B. G., Koen, K. C., & Marshall, R. (2006). The psychological risk of Vietnam for U.S. veterans: A revisit with new data and methods. *Science, 313,* 979–982.

Dolbier, C. L., Cocke, R. R., Leiferman, J. A., Steinhardt, M. A., Schapiro, S. J., Nehete, P. N. et al. (2001). Differences in functional immune responses of high vs. low hardy healthy individuals. *Journal of Behavioral Medicine, 24,* 219–229.

Dollard, J., Doob, L., Miller, N., Mowrer, O. H., & Sears, R. R. (1939). *Frustration and aggression.* New Haven, CT: Yale University Press.

Dominowski, R. L., & Dallob, P. (1995). Insight and problem solving. In R. J. Sternberg & J. E. Davidson (Eds.), *The nature of insight* (pp. 33–62). Cambridge, MA: MIT Press.

Domjan, M., & Purdy, J. E. (1995). Animal research in psychology: More than meets the eye of the general psychology student. *American Psychologist, 50,* 496–503.

Donovan, D. M., Daley, D. C., Brigham, G. S., Hodgkins, C. C., Perl, H. I., Garrett, S. B. et al. (2013). Stimulant abuser groups to engage in 12-step: A multisite trial in the National Institute on Drug Abuse Clinical Trials Network. *Journal of Substance Abuse Treatment, 44,* 103–114.

Doty, R. L. (2001). Olfaction. *Annual Review of Psychology,* 52, 423–452.

Dougherty, D. D., Baer, L., Cosgrove, G. R., Cassem, E. H., Price, B. H., Nirenberg, A. A. et al. (2002). Prospective long-term follow-up of 44 patients who received cingulotomy for treatment of refractory obsessive-compulsive disorder. *American Journal of Psychiatry, 159,* 269–275.

Dovis, S., Van der Oord, S., Wiers, R. W., & Prins, P. M. (2013). What part of working memory is not working in ADHD? Short-term memory, the central executive and effects of reinforcement. *Journal of Abnormal Child Psychology, 41,* 901–917. doi:10.1007/s10802-013-9729-9

Downar, J., Geraci, J., Salomons, T. V., Dunlop, K., Wheeler, S., McAndrews, M. P. et al. (2014). Anhedonia and reward-circuit connectivity distinguish nonresponders from responders to dorsomedial prefrontal repetitive transcranial magnetic stimulation in major depression. *Biological Psychiatry, 76,* 176–185.

Draganova, R., Eswaran, H., Murphy, P., Lowery, C., & Preissi, H. (2007). Serial magnetoencephalographic study of fetal and newborn auditory discriminative evoked responses. *Early Human Development, 83,* 199–207.

Draguns, J. G. (2002). Universal and cultural aspects of counseling and psychotherapy. In P. B. Pedersen, J. G. Draguns, W. J. Lonner, & J. E. Trimble (Eds.), *Counseling across cultures* (5th ed., pp. 29–50). Thousand Oaks, CA: Sage.

Drea, C. M. (2009). Endocrine mediators of masculinization in female mammals. *Current Directions in Psychological Science, 18,* 221–226.

Drevets, W. C., Savitz, J., & Trimble, M. (2008). The subgenual anterior cingulated cortex in mood disorders. *CNS Spectrums, 13,* 663–681.

Drews, F. A., Yazdani, H., Godfrey, C. N., Cooper, J. M., & Strayer, D. L. (2009). Text messaging during simulated driving. *Human Factors, 51,* 762–770.

Driver, H. S., & Taylor, S. R. (2000). Exercise and sleep. *Sleep Medicine Reviews, 4,* 387–402.

Druckman, D., & Bjork, R. A. (1994). *Learning, remembering, believing: Enhancing human performance.* Washington, DC: National Academy Press.

Duan, X., Dai, Q., Gong, Q., & Chen, H. (2010). Neural mechanism of unconscious perception of surprised facial expression. *Neuroimage, 52,* 401–407. doi:10.1016/j.neuroimage.2010.04.021

Duckitt, J. (1992). Psychology and prejudice: A historical analysis and integrative framework. *American Psychologist, 47,* 1182–1193.

Duckworth, T. S., Kreiner, D. S., Stark-Wroblewski, K., & Marsh, P. A. (2011). Effects of experiencing the eyewitness identification procedure on juror decisions. *Journal of Police and Criminal Psychology, 26,* 11–19. doi:10.1007/s11896-010-9071-X

Duke, A. A., Bègue, L., Bell, R., & Eisenlohr-Moul, T. (2013). Revisiting the serotonin–aggression relation in humans: A meta-analysis. *Psychological Bulletin, 139,* 1148–1172. doi:10.1037/a0031544

Dunkel Schetter, C., Schafer, P., Gaines Lanzi, R., Clark-Kauffman, E., Raju, T. N. K., & Hillemeier, M. M. (2013). Shedding light on the mechanisms underlying health disparities through community participatory methods: The stress pathway. *Perspectives on Psychological Science, 8,* 613–633.

Dunn, E. W., Aknin, L. B., & Norton, M. I. (2014). Prosocial spending and happiness: Using money to benefit others pays off. *Current Directions in Psychological Science, 23,* 41–47.

Duric, V., Banasr, M., Licznerski, P., Schmidt, H. D., Stockmeier, C. A., Simen, A. A. et al. (2010). A negative regulator of MAP kinase causes depressive behavior. *Nature Medicine, 16,* 1328–1332.

Durmer, J. S., & Dinges, D. F. (2005). Neurocognitive consequences of sleep deprivation. *Seminars in Neurology, 25,* 117–129.

Durrence, H. H., & Lichstein, K. L. (2006). The sleep of African Americans: A comparative review. *Behavioral Sleep Medicine, 4,* 29–44.

Durston, S., Hulshoff Pol, H. E., Casey, B. J., Giedd, J. N., Buitelaar, J. K., & van Engeland, H. (2001). Anatomical MRI of the developing human brain: What have we learned? *Journal of the American Academy of Child and Adolescent Psychiatry, 40,* 1012–1020.

Dweck, C. (2008). Can personality be changed? The role of beliefs in personality and change. *Current Directions in Psychological Science, 17,* 391–394.

Dweck, C. S., Chiu, C., & Hong, Y. (1995). Implicit theories and their role in judgments and reactions: A world from two perspectives. *Psychological Inquiry, 6,* 267–285.

Dziurowicz-Kozłowska, A. H. (2010). Health-related quality of life in obesity. *Acta Neuropsychologica, 8,* 284–296.

Eagly, A. H., & Chaiken, S. (1975). An attribution analysis of communicator characteristics on opinion change: The case of communicator attractiveness. *Journal of Personality and Social Psychology, 32,* 136–144.

Eagly, A. H., & Wood, W. (2013). The nature–nurture debates: 25 years of challenges in understanding the psychology of gender. *Perspectives on Psychological Science, 8,* 340–357.

Eaton, A. H., & Resko, J. A. (1974). Plasma testosterone and male dominance in a Japanese macaque (Macca fuscata) troop compared with repeated measures of testosterone in laboratory males. *Hormones and Behavior, 5,* 251–259.

Eaton, D. K., Kann, L., Kinchen, S., Shanklin, S., Ross, J., Hawkins, J. et al. (2010). Youth risk behavior surveillance—United States, 2009. *Morbidity & Mortality Weekly, 59,* 1–148.

Eaton, N. R., Krueger, R. F., Keyes, K. M., Skodol, A. E., Markon, K. E., Grant, B .F., & Hasin, D. S. (2011). Borderline personality disorder co-morbidity: Relationship to the internalizing-externalizing structure of common mental disorders. *Psychological Medicine, 41,* 1041–1050.

Ebbinghaus, H. (1910). *Abriss der psychologie.* Leipzig: Veit & Comp.

Ebbinghaus, H. (1913). *Memory: A contribution to experimental psychology* (H. Ruyer & C. E. Bussenius, Trans.). New York: Teachers College, Columbia University. (Original work published 1885)

Ebmeier, K. P., Donaghey, C., & Steele, J. D. (2006). Recent developments and current controversies in depression. *Lancet, 367,* 153–167.

Ebstein, R. P., Zohar, A. H., Benjamin, J., & Belmaker, R. H. (2002). An update on molecular genetic studies of human personality traits. *Applied Bioinformatics, 1,* 57–68.

Eby, L. T., Allen, T. D., Hoffman, B. J., Baranik, L. E., Sauer, J. B., Baldwin, S. et al. (2013). An interdisciplinary meta-analysis of the potential antecedents, correlates, and consequences of protégé perceptions of mentoring. *Psychological Bulletin, 139,* 441–476.

Edelman, B. (1981). Binge eating in normal and overweight individuals. *Psychological Reports, 49,* 739–746.

Edenberg, H. J., & Foroud, T. (2006). The genetics of alcoholism: Identifying specific genes through family studies. *Addiction Biology, 11,* 386–396.

Edmonds, G. W., Goldberg, L. R., Hampson, S. E., & Barckley, M. (2013). Personality stability from childhood to midlife: Relating teachers' assessments in elementary school to observer- and self-ratings 40 years later. *Journal of Research in Personality, 47,* 505–513.

Edmondson, D., Chaidoir, S. R., Mills, M. A., Park, C. L., Holub, J., & Bartkowiak, J. M. (2011). From shattered assumptions to weakened worldviews: Trauma symptoms signal anxiety buffer disruption. *Journal of Loss & Trauma, 16,* 358–385.

Egan, S. J., Watson, H. J., Kane, R. T., McEvoy, P., Fursland, A., & Nathan, P. R. (2013). Anxiety as a mediator between perfectionism and eating disorders. *Cognitive Therapy and Research, 37,* 905–913. doi: 10.1007/s10608-012-9516-X

Egner, T., Jamieson, G., & Gruzelier, J. (2005). Hypnosis decouples cognitive control from conflict monitoring processes of the frontal lobe. *Neuroimaging, 27,* 969–978.

Egner, T., Monti, J. M., & Summerfield, C. (2010). Expectation and surprise determine neural population responses in the ventral visual stream. *Journal of Neuroscicence, 49,* 16601–16608.

Ehde, D. M., Dillworth, T. M., & Turner, J. A. (2014). Cognitive-behavioral therapy for individuals with chronic pain: Efficacy, innovations, and directions for research. *American Psychologist, 69,* 153–166.

Ehlers, A. (1995). A 1-year prospective study of panic attacks: Clinical course and factors associated with maintenance. *Journal of Abnormal Psychology, 104,* 164–172.

Eich, J. E. (1980). The cue-dependent nature of state-dependent retrieval. *Memory and Cognition, 8,* 157–173.

Eich, J. E., Weingartner, H., Stillman, R. C., & Gillin, J. C. (1975). State-dependent accessibility of retrieval cues in the retention of a categorized list. *Journal of Verbal Learning and Verbal Behavior, 14,* 408–417.

Einarsson, C., & Granstrom, K. (2004). Gender-biased interaction in the classroom: The influence of gender and age in the relationship between teacher and pupil. *Scandinavian Journal of Educational Research, 46,* 117–127.

Eisen, S. V. (1979). Actor-observer differences in information inference and causal attribution. *Journal of Personality and Social Psychology, 37,* 261–272.

Eisenberger, N. I., Taylor, S. E., Gable, S. L., Hilmert, C. J., & Liberman, M. D. (2007). Neural pathways link social support to attenuated neuroendocrine stress responses. *NeuroImage, 35,* 1601–1612.

Eiser, A. S. (2005). Physiology and psychology of dreams. *Seminars in Neurology, 25,* 97–105.

Ekman, P. (1973). Cross-cultural studies of facial expression. In P. Ekman (Ed.), *Darwin and facial expression* (pp. 169–222). New York: Academic Press.

Ekman, P., & Friesen, W. V. (1984). *Unmasking the face* (2nd ed.). Palo Alto, CA: Consulting Psychologists Press.

El Khoury, D., El-Rassi, R., Azar, S., & Hwalla, N. (2010). Postprandial ghrelin and PYY responses of male subjects on low carbohydrate meals to varied balancing proportions of proteins and fats. *European Journal of Nutrition, 49,* 493–500. doi:10.1007/s00394-010-0108-9

Elen, M., D'Heer, E., Geuens, M., & Vermeir, I. (2013). The influence of mood on attitude–behavior consistency. *Journal of Business Research, 66,* 917–923. doi:10.1016/j.jbusres.2011.12.011

Elfenbein, H. A., Beaupre, M., Levesque, M., & Hess, U. (2007). Toward a dialect theory: Cultural differences in the expression and recognition of posed facial expressions. *Emotion, 7,* 131–146.

Elicker, J., Englund, M., & Sroufe, L. A. (1992). Predicting peer competence and peer relationships in childhood from early parent–child relationships. In R. D. Parke & G. W. Ladd (Eds.), *Family–peer relationships: Modes of linkage* (pp. 77–107). Hillsdale, NJ: Erlbaum.

Elkind, D. (1994). *A sympathetic understanding of the child: Birth to sixteen* (3rd ed.). Boston: Allyn & Bacon.

Elkind, D. (1998). *All grown up and no place to go* (Rev. ed.). Reading, MA: Perseus Books.

Elkind, D., & Bowen, R. (1979). Imaginary audience behavior in children and adolescents. *Developmental Psychology, 15,* 38–44.

Ellason, J. W., & Ross, C. A. (1997). Two-year follow up of inpatients with dissociative identity disorder. *American Journal of Psychiatry, 154,* 832–839.

Ellason, J. W., Ross, C. A., & Fuchs, D. L. (1996). Lifetime Axis I and II comorbidity and childhood trauma history in dissociative identity disorder. *Psychiatry, 59,* 255–266.

Ellenbogen, J. M., Hu, P. T., Payne, J. D., Titone, D., & Walker, M. P. (2007). Human relational memory requires time and sleep. *Proceedings of the National Academy of Science,* U.S.A., *104,* 7723–7728.

Ellis, A. (1959). Requisite conditions for basic personality change. *Journal of Consulting Psychology, 23,* 538–540.

Ellis, A. (1973, February). The no cop-out therapy. *Psychology Today, 7,* 56–60, 62.

Ellis, A. (1991). *Reason and emotion in psychotherapy.* New York: Carol Publishing.

Ellis, A. (1995). Changing rational-emotive therapy (RET) to rational emotive behavior therapy (REBT). *Journal of Rational-Emotive and Cognitive Behavior Therapy, 13,* 85–89.

El-Matary, A., Kemball, G., & Feteha, H. (2006). Loss of libido in postmenopausal women. *Journal of Obstetrics and Gynaecology, 26,* 495–500.

Emery, C. F., Finkel, D., & Pedersen, N. L. (2012). Pulmonary function as a cause of cognitive aging. *Psychological Science, 23,* 1024–1032.

Emmelkamp, P. M. (1994). Behavior therapy with adults. In A. E. Bergin & S. L. Garfield (Eds.), *Handbook of psychotherapy and behavior change* (4th ed., pp. 379–427). New York: Wiley.

Endrighi, R., Hamer, M., & Steptoe, A. (2011). Associations of trait optimism and diurnal neuroendocrine activity, cortisol responses to mental stress, and subjective stress measures in healthy men and women. *Psychosomatic Medicine, 73,* 672–678.

Eng, T. R., & Butler, W. T. (1997). *The hidden epidemic: Confronting sexually transmitted diseases.* Washington, DC: National Academy Press.

Engels, G. I., Garnefski, N., & Diekstra, R. F. W. (1993). Efficacy of rational-emotive therapy: A quantitative analysis. *Journal of Consulting and Clinical Psychology, 61,* 1083–1090.

Enns, M. W., Cox, B. J., Afifi, T. O., De Graaf, R., Ten Have, M., & Sareen, J. (2006). Childhood adversities and risk for suicidal ideation and attempts: A longitudinal population-based study. *Psychological Medicine, 36,* 1769–1778.

Epley, N., Savitsy, K., & Kachelski, R. A. (1999). What every skeptic should know about subliminal persuasion. *Skeptical Inquirer, 23,* 40–45.

Epping-Jordan, M. P., Watkins, S. S., Koob, G. F., & Markou, A. (1998). Dramatic decreases in brain reward function during nicotine withdrawal. *Nature, 393,* 76.

Epstein, R., & Phan, V. (2012). Which competencies are most important for creative expression? *Creativity Research Journal, 24,* 278–282. doi:10.1080/10400419.2012.726579

Epstein, S. (1994). Trait theory as personality theory: Can a part be as great as the whole? *Psychological Inquiry, 5,* 120–122.

Equal Employment Opportunity Commission. (2002, May 24). *Federal laws prohibiting job discrimination questions and answers.*

Equal Employment Opportunity Commission. (2010). *Sexual harassment charges EEOC and FEPAs combined: FY 1997–FY 2009.* Washington, DC: Author.

Erblich, J., Lerman, C., Self, D. W., Diaz, G. A., & Bovbjerg, D. H. (2005). Effects of dopamine D2 receptor (DRD2) and transporter (SLC6A3) polymorphisms on smoking cue-induced cigarette craving among African-American smokers. *Molecular Psychiatry, 10,* 407–414.

Erdur-Baker, O., Aberson, C. L., Barrow, J. C., & Draper, M. R. (2006). Nature and severity of college students' psychological concerns: A comparison of clinical and nonclinical national samples. *Professional Psychology: Research and Practice, 37,* 317–323.

Erikson, E. H. (1956). The problem of ego identity. *Journal of American Psychoanalysis Association, 4,* 56–121.

Erikson, E. H. (1958). *Young man Luther.* New York: Norton.

Erikson, E. H. (1959). Identity and life cycle: Selected papers. *Psychological Issues, 1,* 1–171.

Erikson, E. H. (1963). *Childhood and society* (2nd ed.). New York: Norton.

Erikson, E. H. (1968). *Identity, youth and crisis.* New York: Norton.

Erikson, E. H. (1980). *Identity and the life cycle* (2nd ed.). New York: Norton.

Eroglu, C., & Barres, B. A. (2010). Regulation of synaptic connectivity by glia. *Nature, 468,* 223–231.

Erwin, E. (Ed.). (2002). *The Freud encyclopedia: Theory, therapy, and culture.* London: Routledge.

Escobar, J. I. (1993). Psychiatric epidemiology. In A. C. Gaw (Ed.), *Culture, ethnicity, and mental illness* (pp. 43–73). Washington, DC: American Psychiatric Press.

Escobar, J. I., Gara, M., Waitzkin, H., Cohen Silver, R., Holman, A., & Compton, W. (1998). DSM-IV hypochondriasis in primary care. *General Hospital Psychiatry, 20,* 155–159.

Escobar, M. (2008). Classical conditioning. In S. F. Davis & W. Buskist (Eds.), *21st century psychology: A reference handbook* (pp. 300–309). Thousand Oaks, CA: Sage.

ESEMed/MHEDEA 2000 Investigators. (2004). Prevalence of mental disorders in Europe: Results from the European Study of the Epidemiology of Mental Disorders (ESEMed). *Acta Psychiatrica Scandivavia, 109,* 21–27.

Espy, K. A., Riese, M. L., & Francis, D. J. (1997). Neurobehavior in preterm neonates exposed to cocaine, alcohol, and tobacco. *Infant Behavior and Development, 20,* 297–309.

Essed, N. H., van Staveren, W. A., Kok, F. J., & de Graaf, C. (2007). No effect of 16 weeks flavor enhancement on dietary intake and nutritional status of nursing home elderly. *Appetite, 48,* 29–36.

Esses, V. M., Dovidio, J. F., Jackson, L. M., & Armstrong, T. L. (2001). The immigration dilemma: The role of perceived group competition, ethnic prejudice, and national identity. *Journal of Social Issues, 57,* 389–412.

Etkin, A., Prater, K. E., Hoeft, F., Menon, V., & Schatzberg, A. F. (2010). Failure of anterior cingulated activation and connectivity with the amygdala during implicit regulation of emotional processing in generalized anxiety disorder. *American Journal of Psychiatry, 167,* 545–554.

Ettlinger, M., Lanter, J., & Van Pay, C. K. (2014). Learning to remember by learning to speak. *Developmental Psychology, 50,* 431–438. doi:10.1037/a0033317

Evans, A. T., & Clark, J. K. (2012). Source characteristics and persuasion: The role of self-monitoring in self-validation. *Journal of Experimental Social Psychology, 48,* 383–386. doi:10.1016/j.jesp.2011.07.002

Eynon, R., Schroeder, M., & Fry J. (2009). New techniques in online research: Challenges for research ethics. *21st Century Society, 4,* 187–199.

Eysenck, H. J. (1967). *The biological basis of personality.* Springfield, IL: Charles C. Thomas.

Eysenck, H. J. (1982). *Personality, genetics, and behavior: Selected papers.* New York: Praeger.

Eysenck, H. J. (1991). Dimensions of personality: 16, 5 or 3? Criteria for a taxonomic paradigm. *Personality and Individual Differences, 12,* 773–790.

Eysenck, H. J. (1995). *Genius: The natural history of creativity.* Cambridge: Cambridge University Press.

Eysenck, H. J., & Eysenck, S. B. G. (1969). *Personality structure and measurement.* London: Routledge.

Eysenck, H. J., & Eysenck, S. B. G. (1976). *Psychoticism as a dimension of personality.* London: Hodder and Stoughton.

Eysenck, H. J., & Rachman, S. (1965). *The causes and cures of neurosis: An introduction to modern behavior therapy based on learning theory and the principle of conditioning.* San Diego: Knapp.

Fagot, B. I., & Kavanaugh, K. (1990). The prediction of antisocial behavior from avoidant attachment classifications. *Child Development, 61,* 864–873.

Fagundes, C. P., Bennett, J. M., Derry, H. M., & Kiecolt-Glaser, J. K. (2011). Relationships and inflammation across the lifespan: Social developmental pathways to disease. *Social and Personality Psychology Compass, 5,* 891–903.

Fagundes, C. P., Glaser, R., & Kiecolt-Glaser, J. K. (2013). Stressful early life experiences and immune dysregulation across the lifespan. *Brain, Behavior, and Immunity, 27,* 8–12.

Falkenburg, K., & Schyns, B. (2007). Work satisfaction, organizational commitment and withdrawal behaviors. *Management Research News, 30,* 708–723.

Falkum, E., Pedersen, G., & Karterud, S. (2009). Diagnostic and Statistical Manual of Mental Disorders, Fourth Edition, paranoid personality disorder diagnosis: A unitary or a two-dimensional construct? *Comprehensive Psychiatry, 50,* 533–541.

Fan, W., & Yan, Z. (2010). Factors affecting response rates of the web survey: A systematic review. *Computers in Human Behaviour, 26,* 132–139.

Fan, Y., Tang, Y. Y., Ma, Y., & Posner, M. I. (2010). Mucosal immunity modulated by integrative meditation in a dose-dependent fashion. *Journal of Alternative and Complementary Medicine, 16,* 151–155.

Farley, E., Loup, D., Nelson, M., Mitchell, A., Esplund, G., Macri, C. et al. (1997). Neoplastic transformation of the endocervix associated with down regulation of lactoferrin expression. *Molecular Carcinography, 20,* 240–250.

Fatemi, S. H., & Folsom, T. D. (2009). The neurodevelopmental hypothesis of schizophrenia, revisited. *Schizophrenia Bulletin, 35,* 528–548.

Fattore, L., & Fratta, W. (2011). Beyond THC: The new generation of cannabinoid designer drugs. *Frontiers in Behavioral Neuroscience, 5,* 1–12.

Faust, K. A., & McKibben, J. N. (1999). Marital dissolution: Divorce, separation, annulment, and widowhood. In M. B. Sussman, S. K., Steinmetz, & G. W. Peterson (Eds.), *Handbook of marriage and the family* (pp. 475–502). New York: Plenum Press.

Fava, G. A., Grandi, S., Zielezny, M., & Rafanelli, C. (1996). Four-year outcome for cognitive-behavioral treatment of residual symptoms in major depression. *American Journal of Psychiatry, 153,* 945–947.

Fazio, N. M., & Palm, L. J. (1998). Attributional style, depression, and grade point averages of college students. *Psychological Reports, 83,* 159–162.

FDA Public Health Advisory. (2004, October 15). *Suicidality in children and adolescents being treated with antidepressant medications.* Retrieved from www.fda.gov/cder/drug/antidepressants/SSRIPHA200410.htm

Federal Bureau of Investigation (FBI). (2009). *Uniform Crime Reports: 2008 hate crime statistics.* Retrieved from http://www.fbi.gov/ucr/hc2008/incidents.html

Federal Bureau of Investigation (FBI). (2010). *Uniform Crime Reports.* Retrieved from http://www.fbi.gov/ucr/2009prelimsem/table_4.html

Federal Bureau of Investigation (FBI). (2012a). *Uniform Crime Reports: 2012 hate crime statistics.* Retrieved from http://www.fbi.gov/about-us/cjis/ucr/hate-crime/2012/topic-pages/incidents-and-offenses/incidentsandoffenses_final

Federal Bureau of Investigation (FBI). (2012b). *Uniform Crime Reports: 2012 violent crime statistics.* Retrieved from http://www.fbi.gov/about-us/cjis/ucr/crime-in-the-u.s/2012/crime-in-the-u.s.-2012/violent-crime/violent-crime

Feeley, T., Anker, A. E., & Aloe, A. M. (2012). The door-in-the-face persuasive message strategy: A meta-analysis of the first 35 years. *Communication Monographs, 79,* 316–343. doi:10.1080/03637751.2012.697631

Feeney, E., O'Brien, S., Scannell, A., Markey, A., & Gibney, E. R. (2011). Genetic variation in taste perception: Does it have a role in healthy eating? *Proceedings of the Nutrition Society, 70,* 135–143.

Feinberg, M. E., Button, T. M., Neiderhiser, J. M., Reiss, D., & Hetherington, E. M. (2007). Parenting and adolescent antisocial behavior and depression: Evidence of genotype 3 parenting environment interaction. *Archives of General Psychiatry, 64,* 457–465.

Feingold, A. (1988). Matching for attractiveness in romantic partners and same-sex friends: A meta-analysis and theoretical critique. *Psychological Bulletin, 104,* 226–235.

Feinstein, J. S., Adolphs, R., Damasio, A., & Tranel, D. (2011). The human amygdala and the induction and experience of fear. *Current Biology, 21,* 1–5.

Feldman, N. H., Griffiths, T. L., Goldwater, S., & Morgan, J. L. (2013). A role for the developing lexicon in phonetic category acquisition. *Psychological Review, 120,* 751–778. doi:10.1037/a0034245

Felker, B., Hawkins, E., Dobie, D., Gutierrez, J., & McFall, M. (2008). Characteristics of deployed Operation Iraqi Freedom military personnel who seek mental health care. *Military Medicine, 173,* 155–158.

Felmingham, K., Kemp, A., Williams, L., Das, P., Hughes, G., Peduto, A. et al. (2007). Changes in anterior cingulated and amygdala after cognitive behavior therapy of posttraumatic stress disorder. *Psychological Science, 18,* 127–129.

Fenton, W. S., & McGlashan, T. H. (1994). Antecedents, symptom progression, and long-term outcome of the deficit syndrome in schizophrenia. *American Journal of Psychiatry, 151,* 351–356.

Ferguson, C. P., & Pigott, T. A. (2000). Anorexia and bulimia nervosa: Neurobiology and pharmacotherapy. *Behavior Therapy, 31,* 237–263.

Feroli, K., & Burstein, G. (2003). Adolescent sexually transmitted diseases. *American Journal of Maternal/Child Nursing, 28,* 113–118.

Ferrante, J. (2011). *Sociology: A global perspective* (Enhanced 7th ed.). Belmont, CA: Wadsworth, Cengage Learning.

Ferreira, S. E., de Mello, M. T., Pompeia, S., & de Souza-Formigoni, M. L. (2006). Effects of energy drink ingestion on alcohol intoxication. *Alcoholism, Clinical and Experimental Research, 30,* 598–605.

Ferrucci, R., Brunoni, A. R., Parazzini, M., Vergari, M., Rossi, E., Fumagalli, M. et al. (2013). Modulating human procedural learning by cerebellar transcranial direct current stimulation. *The Cerebellum, 12,* 485–492. doi:10.1007/s12311-012-0436-9

Festinger, L. (1951). Architecture and group membership. *Journal of Social Issues, 1,* 152–163.

Festinger, L. (1957). *A theory of cognitive dissonance.* Evanston, IL: Row, Peterson.

Festinger, L., Schachter, S., & Back, K. (1950). *Social pressures in informal groups: A study of human factors in housing.* Stanford, CA: Stanford University Press.

Fichna, J., Janecka, A., Piestrzeniewicz, M., Costentin, J., & do Rego, J. C. (2007). Antidepressant-like effect of endomorphin-1 and endomorphin-2 in mice. *Neuropsychopharmacology, 32,* 813–821.

Fiedler, K., & Krueger, J. I. (2013). Afterthoughts on precognition: No cogent evidence for anomalous influences of consequent events on preceding cognition. *Theory & Psychology, 23,* 323–333.

Field, A. P. (2006). Is conditioning a useful framework for understanding the development and treatment of phobias? *Clinical Psychology Review, 26,* 857–875.

Field, T. M., Schanberg, S. M., Scafidi, F., Bauer, C. R., Vega-Lahr, N., Garcia, R. et al. (1986). Tactile/kinesthetic stimulation effects of preterm neonates. *Pediatrics, 77,* 654–658.

Fields, D. R. (2007). Sex and the secret nerve. *Scientific American Mind, 18,* 20–27.

Fiellin, D. A., Friedland, G. H., & Gourevitch, M. N. (2006). Opioid dependence: Rationale for and efficacy of existing and new treatments. *Clinical Infectious Diseases, 43*(Suppl.), S173–S177.

Figner, B., & Weber, E. U. (2011). Who takes risks when and why? Determinants of risk takings. *Current Directions in Psychological Science, 20,* 211–216.

Fillmore, K. M., Roach, E. L., & Rice, J. T. (2002). Does caffeine counteract alcohol-induced impairment? The ironic effects of expectancy. *Journal of Studies on Alcohol, 63,* 745–754.

Finch, C. E. (2001). Toward a biology of middle age. In M. E. Lachman (Ed.), *Handbook of midlife development* (pp. 77–108). New York: Wiley.

Finkel, K. J., Searleman, A. C., Tymkew, H., Tanaka, C. Y., Saager, L., Safer-Zadeh, E. et al. (2009). Prevalence of undiagnosed obstructive sleep apnea among adult surgical patients in an academic medical center. *Sleep Medicine, 10,* 753–758.

Finkelstein, D. M., Kubzansky, L. D., Capitman, J., & Goodman, E. (2007). Socioeconomic differences in adolescent stress: The role of psychological resources. *Journal of Adolescent Health, 40,* 127–134.

Finn, R. (2003). Antabuse no panacea for alcoholism. *Clinical Psychiatry News, 31,* 6.

Finn, R. (2004). Functional MRI offers insights into working memory in Alzheimer's (greater whole-brain activation). *Internal Medicine News, 37,* 29.

Fiorentino, L., Marler, M., Stepnowsky, C., Johnson, S., & Ancoli-Israel, S. (2006). Sleep in older African Americans and Caucasians at risk for sleep-disordered breathing. *Behavioral Sleep Medicine, 4,* 164–178.

Fisher, B. S. (2009). The effects of question wording on rape estimates: Evidence from a quasi-experimental design. *Violence Against Women, 15,* 133–147.

Fisher, C. A., Hoffman, K. J., Austin-Lane, J., & Kao, T. C. (2000). The relationship between heavy alcohol use and work productivity loss in active duty military personnel: A secondary analysis of the 1995 Department of Defense Worldwide Survey. *Military Medicine, 165,* 355–361.

Fisher, H. (2000). Lust, attraction, attachment, biology and evolution of the three primary emotional systems of mating, reproduction, and parenting. *Journal of Sex Education and Therapy, 25,* 96–102.

Fisher, H. E. (2004). *Why we love: The nature and chemistry of romantic love.* New York: Holt.

Fisher, S., Kent, T. A., & Bryant, S. G. (1995). Postmarketing surveillance by patient self-monitoring: Preliminary data for sertraline versus fluoxetine. *Journal of Clinical Psychiatry, 56,* 288–296.

Fiske, M. (1980). Tasks and crises of the second half of life: The interrelationship of commitment, coping, and adaptation. In J. E. Birrent & R. B. Sloane (Eds.), *Handbook of mental health and aging* (pp. 337–373). Englewood Cliffs, NJ: Prentice-Hall.

Fiske, S. T., & Taylor, S. E. (2013). *Social cognition* (2nd ed.). Los Angeles: Sage.

Fitzgerald, L. F. (1993). Sexual harassment: Violence against women in the workplace. *American Psychologist, 48,* 1070–1076.

Fitzgerald, P. B., Brown, T. L., Marston, N. A., Daskalakis, Z. J., De Castella, A., & Kulkarni, J. (2003). Transcranial magnetic stimulation in the treatment of depression: A double-blind placebo-controlled trial. *Archives of General Psychiatry, 60,* 1002–1008.

Fitzpatrick, D., & Mooney, R. D. (2012). Vision: The eye. In D. Purves, G. J. Augustine, D. Fitzpatrick, W. C. Hall, A. LaManita, L., & E. White (Eds.), *Neuroscience* (5th ed., pp. 229–256). Sunderland, MA US: Sinauer Associates.

Flanagin, A. J., & Waldeck, J. H. (2004). Technology use and organizational newcomer socialization. *Journal of Business Communication, 41,* 137–165.

Fleeson, W. (2004). Moving personality beyond the person–situation debate. *Current Directions in Psychological Science, 13,* 83–87.

Fletcher, C., & Perry, E. L. (2001). Performance appraisal and feedback: A consideration of national culture and a review of contemporary research and future trends. In N. Anderson, D. S. Ones, H. K. Sinangil, & C. Viswesvaran (Eds.), *Handbook of industrial, work and organizational psychology* (Vol. 1, pp. 127–144). Thousand Oaks, CA: Sage.

Flieller, A. (1999). Comparison of the development of formal thought in adolescent cohorts aged 10 to 15 years (1967–1996 and 1972–1993). *Developmental Psychology, 35,* 1048–1058.

Foa, E. B., McLean, C. P., Capaldi, S., & Rosenfield, D. (2013). Prolonged exposure vs supportive counseling for sexual abuse-related PTSD in adolescent girls: A randomized clinical trial. *Journal of the American Medical Association, 310,* 2650–2657.

Fogel, S. M., & Smith, C. T. (2006). Learning-dependent changes in sleep spindles and stage 2 sleep. *Journal of Sleep Research, 15,* 250–255.

Fogel, S. M., & Smith, C. T. (2011). The function of the sleep spindle: A physiological index of intelligence and a mechanism for sleep-dependent memory consolidation. *Neuroscience and Biobehavioral Reviews, 35,* 1154–1165.

Fogel, S. M., Smith, C. T., & Cote, K. A. (2007). Dissociable learning-dependent changes in REM and non-REM sleep in declarative and procedural memory systems. *Behavior and Brain Research, 180,* 48–61.

Foland-Ross, L. C., Hamilton, J. P., Joormann, J., Berman, M. G., Jonides, J., & Gotlib, I. H. (2013). The neural basis of difficulties disengaging from negative irrelevant material in major depression. *Psychological Science, 24,* 334–344.

Folkman, S., & Lazarus, R. (1988). *Manual for the ways of coping questionnaire.* Palo Alto, CA: Consulting Psychologists Press.

Folkman, S., & Moskowitz, J. T. (2000). Stress, positive emotion, and coping. *Current Directions in Psychological Science, 9,* 115–118.

Follette, W. C., & Hayes, S. C. (2000). Contemporary behavior therapy. In C. R. Snyder & R. E. Ingram (Eds.), *Handbook of psychological change: Psychotherapy processes and practices for the 21st century* (pp. 381–408). New York: Wiley.

Foote, B., Smolin, Y., Neft, D. I., & Lipschitz, D. (2008). Dissociative disorders and suicidality in psychiatric outpatients. *Journal of Nervous and Mental Disease, 196,* 29–36.

Ford, C. S., & Beach, F. A. (1951). *Patterns of sexual behavior.* New York: Harper & Row.

Forehand, R., & McKinney, B. (1993). Historical overview of child discipline in the United States: Implications for mental health clinicians and researchers. *Journal of Child and Family Studies, 2,* 221–228.

Forsyth, D. R., & Corazzini, J. G. (2000). Groups as change agents. In C. R. Snyder & R. E. Ingram (Eds.), *Handbook of psychological change: Psychotherapy processes and practices for the 21st century* (pp. 309–336). New York: Wiley.

Fossum, I. N., Nordnes, L. T., Storemark, S. S., Bjorvatn, B., & Pallesen, S. (2014). The association between use of electronic media in bed before going to sleep and the insomnia symptoms, daytime sleepiness, morningness, and chronotype. *Behavioral Sleep Medicine, 12,* 343–357.

Foster, P. S., Drago, V., Webster, D. G., Harrison, D. W., Crucian, G. P., & Heilman, K. M. (2008). Emotional influences on spatial attention. *Neuropsychology, 22,* 127–135.

Fournier, J. C., Derubeis, R. J., Hollon, S. D., Dimidijian, S. Amsterdam, J. D., Shelton, R. C., & Fawcett, J. (2010). Anti-depressant drug effects and depression severity: A patient-level meta-analysis. *JAMA, 303,* 47–53.

Fowler, J., & Peterson, P. (1981). Increasing reading persistence and altering attributional style of learned helpless children. *Journal of Educational Psychology, 73,* 251–260.

Fowles, D. C., & Dindo, L. (2009). Temperament and psychopathy: A dual-pathway model. *Current Directions in Psychological Science, 18,* 179–183.

Fox, E., Cahill, S., & Zougkou, K. (2010). Preconscious processing biases predict emotional reactivity to stress. *Biological Psychiatry, 67,* 371–377.

Frank, D. A., Jacobs, R. R., Beeghly, M., Augustyn, M., Bellinger, D., Cabral, H. et al. (2002). Level of prenatal cocaine exposure and scores on the Bayley Scales of Infant Development: Modifying effects of caregiver, early intervention, and birth weight. *Pediatrics, 110,* 1143–1152.

Frank, M. C., Amso, D., & Johnson, S.P . (2014). Visual search and attention to faces during early infancy. *Journal of Experimental Child Psychology, 118,* 13–26.

Frankenberger, K. D. (2000). Adolescent egocentrism: A comparison among adolescents and adults. *Journal of Adolescence, 23,* 343–354.

Freedman, J. L., & Fraser, S. C. (1966). Compliance without pressure: The foot-in-the-door technique. *Journal of Experimental Social Psychology, 4,* 195–203.

Freud, A. (1936). *The ego and the mechanisms of defense.* London: Hogarth Press.

Freud, S. (1915). *Repression. In Freud's collected papers* (Vol. 4). London: Hogarth.

Freud, S. (1917). *Mourning and melancholia: Collected works.* London: Hogarth Press.

Freud, S. (1943). *A general introduction to psychoanalysis.* New York: Garden City.

Freud, S. (1949). *An outline of psychoanalysis.* New York: Norton.

Freud, S. (1964). An outline of psycho-analysis. In J. Strachey (Ed. and Trans.), *The standard edition of the complete psychological works of Sigmund Freud* (Vol. 23). London: Hogarth Press. (Original work published 1940)

Freud, S. (1980). *The interpretation of dreams* .(J. Strachey, Ed. and Trans.). New York: Avon. (Original work published 1900)

Freudenmann, R. W., Oxler, F., & Bernschneider-Reif, S. (2006). The origin of MDMA (ecstasy) revisited: The true story reconstructed from the original documents. *Addiction, 101,* 1241–1245.

Frewen, P. A., Dozois, D. J., & Lanius, R. A. (2008). Neuroimaging studies of psychological interventions for mood and anxiety disorders: Empirical and methodological review. *Clinical Psychology Review, 28,* 228–246.

Friedman, M. (1990). Body fat and the metabolic control of food intake. *International Journal of Obesity, 14,* 53–67.

Friedman, M. J. (2009). Phenomenology of posttraumatic stress disorder and acute stress disorder. In M .M. Antony & M. B. Stein (Eds.), *Oxford handbook of anxiety and related disorders* (pp. 65–72). New York: Oxford University Press.

Friedman, M., & Rosenman, R. (1974). *Type A behavior and your heart.* New York: Knopf.

Frielingsdorf, H., Simpson, D. R., Thal, L. J., & Pizzo, D. P. (2007). Nerve growth factor promotes survival of new neurons in the adult hippocampus. *Neurobiology of Disease, 26,* 46–55.

Friesen, C. A., & Kammrath, L. K. (2011). What it pays to know about a close other: The value of if-then personality knowledge in close relationships. *Psychological Science, 22,* 567–571.

Frings, M., Awad, N., Jentzen, W., Dimitrova, A., Kolb., F. P., Diener, H. C. et al. (2006). Involvement of the human cerebellum in short-term and long-term habituation of the acoustic startle response: A serial PET study. *Clinical Neurophysiology, 117,* 1290–1300.

Frost, R. O., Steketee, G., & Tolin, D. F. (2012). Diagnosis and assessment of hoarding disorder. *Annual Review of Clinical Psychology, 8,* 219–242.

Fry, C., & Miller, P. (2002). *Victorian drug trends 2001: Findings from the illicit drug reporting system (IDRS).* National Drug and Alcohol Research Centre (NDARC) Technical Report No. 129. Sydney: NDARC, University of New South Wales.

Fry, R. (2013). *A rising share of young adults live in their parents' home.* Washington, DC: Pew Research Center.

Fu, C. H., Williams, S. C., Cleare, A. J., Brammer, M. J., Walsh, N. D., Kim, J. et al. (2004). Attentuation of the neural response to sad faces in major depression by antidepressant treatment: A prospective, event-related functional magnetic resonance imaging study. *Archives of General Psychiatry, 61,* 877–889.

Fuller-Rowell, T. E., Evans, G. W., & Ong, A. D. (2012). Poverty and health: The mediating role of perceived discrimination. *Psychological Science, 23,* 734–739.

Fulmer, C. A., Gelfand, M. J., Kruglanski, A. W., Kim-Prieto, C., Diener, E., Pierro, A. et al. (2010). On "feeling right" in cultural contexts: How person-culture match affects self-esteem and subjective well-being. *Psychological Science, 21,* 1563–1569.

Fumal, A., & Schoenen, J. (2008). Tension-type headache: Current research and clinical management. *Lancet Neurology, 7,* 70–83.

Funder, D. C. (1993). Explaining traits. *Psychological Inquiry, 5,* 125–127.

Furnham, A., & Paltzer, S. (2010). The portrayal of men and women in television advertisements: An updated review of 30 studies published since 2000. *Scandinavian Journal of Psychology, 51,* 216–236. doi:10.1111; 1–21

Furnham, A., Reeves, E., & Budhani, S. (2002). Parents think their sons are brighter than their daughters: Sex differences in parents' self-estimations and estimations of their children's multiple intelligences. *Journal of Genetic Psychology, 163,* 24–39.

Furnham, A., Wytykowska, A., & Petrides, K. V. (2005). Estimates of multiple intelligences: A study in Poland. *European Psychologist, 10,* 51–59.

Furumoto, L. (1989). The new history of psychology. In I. S. Cohen (Ed.), *The G. Stanley Hall lecture series* (Vol. 9, pp. 5–34). Washington DC: American Psychological Association.

Gael, S. A. (1988). *The job analysis handbook for business, industry, and government* (Vols. 1 and 2). New York: Wiley.

Gaertner, S. L., & Dovidio, J. F. (1986). The aversive form of racism. In J. F. Dovidio & S. L. Gaertner (Eds.), *Prejudice, discrimination, and racism* (pp. 61–89). San Diego, CA: Academic Press.

Gaertner, S. L., & Dovidio, J. F. (2005). Understanding and addressing contemporary racism: From aversive racism to the common ingroup identity model. *Journal of Social Issues, 61,* 615–639.

Gais, S., Lucas, B., & Born, J. (2006). Sleep after learning aids memory recall. *Learning and Memory, 13,* 259–262.

Galensky, T. L., Miltenberger, R. G., Stricker, J. M., & Garlinghouse, M. A. (2001). Functional assessment and treatment of mealtime behavior problems. *Journal of Positive Behavior Interventions, 3,* 211.

Gallerani, M., Manfredini, R., Dal Monte, D., Calo, G., Brunaldi, V., & Simona, C. (2001). Circadian differences in the individual sensitivity to opiate overdose. *Critical Care Medicine, 29,* 96–101.

Galliano, G. (2003). *Gender: Crossing boundaries.* Belmont, CA: Wadsworth.

Gallo, L. C., Troxel, W. M., Kuller, L. H., Sutton-Tyrell, K., Edmundowicz, D., & Matthews, K. A. (2003). Marital status, marital quality, and atherosclerotic burden in postmenopausal women. *Psychosomatic Medicine, 65,* 952–962.

Gallo, L. C., Troxel, W. M., Matthews, K. A., & Kuller, L. H. (2003). Marital status and quality in middle-aged women: Associations with levels and trajectories of cardiovascular risk factors. *Health Psychology, 22,* 453–463.

Gallopin, T., Luppi, P. H., Rambert, F. A., Frydman, A., & Fort, P. (2004). Effect of the wake-promoting agent modafinil on sleep-promoting neurons from the ventrolateral preoptic nucleus: An in vitro pharmacologic study. *Sleep, 27,* 19–25.

Galvan, A. Hare, T., Voss, H., Glover, G., & Casey, B. J. (2007). Risk-taking and the adolescent brain: Who is at risk? *Developmental Science, 10,* F8–F14.

Ganea, P. A., Shutts, K., Spelke, E. S., & DeLoache, J. S. (2007). Thinking of things unseen: Infants' use of language to update mental representations. *Psychological Science, 18,* 734–739.

Gangestad, S. W., Thornhill, R., & Garver-Apgar, C. E. (2005). Adaptations to ovulation: Implications for sexual and social behavior. *Current Directions in Psychological Science, 14,* 312–316.

Gansberg, M. (1964, March 27). 37 who saw murder didn't call the police: Apathy at stabbing of Queens woman shocks inspector. *New York Times,* 1.

Garaulet, M., & Gómez-Abellán, P. (2014). Timing of food intake and obesity: A novel association. *Physiology and Behavior, 134,* 44–50.

Garaulet, M., Esteban, T. A., Lee, Y. C., Smith, C. E., Parnell, L. D., & Ordovás, J. M. (2012). SIRT1 AND CLOCK 3111T>C combined genotype is associated with evening preference and weight loss resistance in a behavioral therapy treatment for obesity. *International Journal of Obesity, 36,* 1436–1441. doi: 10.1038/ijo.2011.270.

Garaulet, M., Gómez-Abellán, P., Alburquerque-Béjar, J. J., Lee, Y. C., Ordovás, J. M., & & Scheer, F. A. (2013). Timing of food intake predicts weight loss effectiveness. *International Journal of Obesity (London), 37,* 604–611. doi: 10.1038/ijo.2012.229.

Garbarino, J. (1997). The role of economic deprivation in the social context of child maltreatment. In M. E. Helfer, R. S. Kempe, & R. D. Krugman (Eds.), *The battered child* (5th ed., pp. 49–60). Chicago: University of Chicago Press.

Garcia, J. (1992). Taste aversion and preference learning in animals. In L. R. Squire, J. H. Byrne, L. Nadel, H. L. Roediger, D. L. Schacter, & R. F. Thompson (Eds.), *Encyclopedia of learning and memory* (pp. 611–613). New York: Macmillan.

Garcia, J., & Koelling, R. A. (1966). Relation of cue to consequence in avoidance learning. *Psychonomic Science, 4,* 123–124.

Garcia, J., Ervin, F. R., & Koelling, R. A. (1966). Learning with prolonged delay of reinforcement. *Psychonomic Science, 5,* 121–122.

Garcia, J., Kimeldorf, D. J., & Koelling, R. A. (1955). Conditioned taste aversion to saccharin resulting from exposure to gamma radiation. *Science, 122,* 157–158. doi:10.1126/science.122.3179.1089

Gardiner, H. W., Mutter, J. D., & Kosmitzki, C. (1998). *Lives across cultures: Cross-cultural human development.* Boston: Allyn & Bacon.

Gardner, H. (1983). *Frames of mind.* New York: Basic Books.

Gardner, H. (1999). *Intelligence reframed: Multiple intelligences for the 21st century.* New York: Basic Books.

Gardner, H. (2004). *Changing minds: The art and science of changing our own and other people's minds.* Boston: Harvard Business School Press.

Garfield, S. L. (1992). Eclectic psychotherapy: A common factors approach. In J. C. Norcross (Ed.), *Handbook of psychotherapy integration* (pp. 169–201). New York: Basic Books.

Garfield, S. L. (1994). Research on client variables in psychotherapy. In A. E. Bergin & S. L. Garfield (Eds.), *Handbook of psychotherapy and behavior change* (4th ed., pp. 190–228). New York: Wiley.

Garlick, D. (2002). Understanding the nature of the general factor of intelligence: The role of individual differences in neural plasticity as an explanatory mechanism. *Psychological Review, 109,* 116–136.

Garlick, D. (2003). Integrating brain science research with intelligence research. *Current Directions in Psychological Science, 12,* 185–189.

Garnock-Jones, K. P., & McCormack, P. L. (2010). Escitalopram: A review of its use in the management of major depressive disorder in adults. *CNS Drugs, 24,* 769–796.

Gartlehner, G., Hansen, R. A., Carey, T. S., Lohr, K. N., Gaynes, B. N., & Randolph, L. C. (2005). Discontinuation rates for selective serotonin reuptake inhibitors and other second-generation antidepressants in outpatients with major depressive disorder: A systematic review and meta-analysis. *International Clinical Psychopharmacology, 20,* 59–69.

Gasbarri, A., Tavares, M. H., Rodrigues, R. C., Tomaz, C., & Pompili, A. (2012). Estrogen, cognitive functions and emotion: An overview on humans, non-human primates and rodents in reproductive years. *Reviews in the Neurosciences, 23,* 587–606. doi:10.1515/revneuro-2012-0051

Gaunt, R. (2006). Couple similarity and marital satisfaction: Are similar spouses happier? *Journal of Personality, 74,* 1401–1420.

Gaval-Cruz, M., & Weinshenker, D. (2009). Mechanisms of disulfiram-induced cocaine abstinence: Antabuse and cocaine relapse. *Molecular Interventions, 9,* 175–187.

Gawin, F. H. (1991). Cocaine addiction: Psychology and neurophysiology. *Science, 251,* 1580–1586.

Gaynes, B. N., Lux, L. J., Lloyd, S. W., Hansen, R. A., Gartlehner, G., Keener, P. et al. (2011). *Nonpharmacologic interventions for treatment-resistant depression in adults.* Comparative Effectiveness Review, No. 33. Rockville, MD: Agency for Healthcare Research and Quality.

Gazzaniga, M. S. (1967). The split brain in man. *Scientific American, 217,* 24–29.

Ge, X., Jin, R., Natsuaki, M. N., Frederick, X., Brody, G. H., Cutrona, C. E. et al. (2006). Pubertal maturation and early substance use risks among African American children. *Psychology of Addictive Behaviors, 20,* 404–414.

Gedo, J. E. (2002). The enduring scientific contributions of Sigmund Freud. *Perspective in Biology and Medicine, 45,* 200–212.

Gehring, W. J., Himle, J., & Nisenson, L. G. (2000). Action-monitoring dysfunction in obsessive-compulsive disorder. *Psychological Science, 11,* 1–6.

Gelade, G. (2002). Creative style, personality, and artistic endeavor. *Genetic, Social and General Psychology Monographs, 128,* 213–234.

Gelfand, S. A. (1981). *Hearing.* New York: Marcel Dekker.

Geller, E. S., Russ, N. W., & Altomari, M. G. (1986). Naturalistic observations of beer drinking among college students. *Journal of Applied Behavior Analysis, 19,* 391–396.

Gelstein, S., Yeshurun, Y., Rozenkrantz, L., Shushan, S., Frumin, I., Roth, Y. et al. (2011). Human tears contain a chemosignal. *Science, 331,* 226–230.

Georgiadis, J. R., Kortekaas, R., Kuipers, R., Nieuwenburg, A., Pruim, J., Reinders, A. A. et al. (2006). Regional cerebral blood flow changes associated with clitorally induced orgasm in healthy women. *European Journal of Neuroscience, 11,* 3305–3316.

Geraerts, E., Lindsay, D. S., Merckelbach, H., Jelicic, M., Raymaekers, L., Arnold, M. M., & Schooler, J. W. (2009). Cognitive mechanisms underlying recovered-memory experiences of childhood sexual abuse. *Psychological Science, 20,* 92–98.

Gerardi, M., Cukor, J., Difede, J., Rizzo, A., & Rothbaum, B. O. (2010). Virtual reality exposure therapy for post-traumatic stress disorder and other anxiety disorders. *Current Psychiatry Reports, 12,* 298–305.

Gergen, K. J., & Gergen, M. M. (1988). Narrative and self as relationship. In L. Berkowitz (Ed.), *Advances in experimental social psychology* (Vol. 21, pp. 17–56). New York: Academic Press.

Gerken, L. (2002). Early sensitivity to linguistic form. *Annual Review of Language Acquisition, 2,* 1–36.

German, C. L., Fleckenstein, A. E., & Hanson, G. R. (2014). Bath salts and synthetic cathinones: An emerging designer drug phenomenon. *Life Sciences, 97,* 2–8.

Germine, L. T., Duchaine, B., & Nakayama, K. (2011). Where cognitive development and aging meet: Face learning ability peaks after age 30. *Cognition, 118,* 201–210. doi:10.1016/j.cognition.2010.11.002

Gernsbacher, M. A. (1985). Surface information and loss in comprehension. *Cognitive Psychology, 17,* 324–363.

Gershoff, E. T. (2002). Corporal punishment by parents and associated child behaviors and experiences: A meta-analytic and theoretical review. *Psychological Bulletin, 128,* 539–579.

Gershoff, E. T. (2010). More harm than good: A summary of scientific research on the intended and unintended effects of corporal punishment on children. *Law and Contemporary Problems, 73,* 31–56.

Geschwind, N. (1975). The apraxias: Neural mechanisms of disorders of learned movements. *American Scientist, 63,* 188–195.

Geschwind, N., & Levitsky, W. (1968). Human brain: Left-right asymmetries in temporal speech region. *Science, 161,* 186–187.

Gheysen, F., Van Opstal, F., Roggeman, C., Van Waelvelde, H., & Fias, W. (2010). Hippocampal contribution to early and later stages of implicit motor sequence learning. *Experimental Brain Research, 202,* 795–807. doi:10.1007/s00221-010-2186-6

Giancola, P. R., Josephs, R. A., Parrott, D. J., & Duke, A. A. (2010). Alcohol myopia revisited: Clarifying aggression and other acts of disinhibition through a distorted lens. *Perspectives on Psychological Science, 5,* 265–278.

Giannotti, F., & Cortesi, F. (2009). Family and cultural influences on sleep development. *Child and Adolescent Psychiatric Clinics of North America, 18,* 849–861.

Gibb, B. E., Alloy, L. B., Abramson, L. Y., Beevers, C. G., & Miller, I. W. (2004). Cognitive vulnerability to depression: A taxometric analysis. *Journal of Abnormal Psychology, 113,* 81–89.

Gibbons, C. J., Fournier, J. C., Stirman, S. W., Derubeis, R. J., Crits-Christoph, P., & Beck, A. T. (2010). The clinical effectiveness of cognitive therapy for depression in an outpatient clinic. *Journal of Affective Disorders, 125,* 169–176.

Gibbons, L. E., Carle, A. C., Mackin, R., Harvey, D., Mukherjee, S., Insel, P. et al. (2012). A composite score for executive functioning, validated in Alzheimer's Disease Neuroimaging Initiative (ADNI) participants with baseline mild cognitive impairment. *Brain Imaging and Behavior, 6,* 517–527. doi:10.1007/s11682-012-9176-1

Gibbs, W. W. (1996). Gaining on fat. *Scientific American, 275,* 88–94.

Gibson, H. B. (1995, April). Recovered memories. *The Psychologist,* pp. 153–154.

Giedd, J. N. (2004). Structural magnetic resonance imaging of the adolescent brain. *Annals of the New York Academy of Sciences, 1021,* 77–85.

Giedd, J. N., Blumentahl, J., Jeffries, N. O., Castellanos, F. X., Liu, H., Zijdenbos, A. et al. (1999). Brain development during childhood and adolescence: A longitudinal MRI study. *Nature Neuroscience, 2,* 861–863.

Gilbert, D. G., Stunkard, M. E., Jensen, R. A., & Detwiler, F. R. J. (1996). Effects of exam stress on mood, cortisol, and immune functioning. *Personality and Individual Differences, 21,* 235–246.

Gilbertson, M. W., Shenton, M. E., Ciszewski, A., Kasai, K., Lasko, N. B., Orr, S. P. et al. (2002). Smaller hippocampal volume predicts pathologic vulnerability to psychological trauma. *Nature Neuroscience, 5,* 1242–1247.

Gildea, K. M., Schneider, T. R., & Shebilske, W. I. (2007). Appraisals and training performance on a complex laboratory task. *Human Factors, 49,* 745–758.

Gillam, B. (1980). Geometrical illusions. *Scientific American, 242,* 102–111.

Gillespie, C. F., & Nemeroff, C. B. (2007). Corticotropin-releasing factor and the psychobiology of early-life stress. *Current Directions in Psychological Science, 16,* 85–89.

Gilligan, C. F. (1982). *In a different voice.* Cambridge, MA: Harvard University Press.

Gillund, G., & Shiffrin, R. M. (1984). A retrieval model for both recognition and recall. *Psychological Review, 91,* 1–67.

Gilson, R. J., & Mindel, A. (2001). Sexually transmitted infections. *British Medical Journal, 322*(729S), 1135–1137.

Girandola, F. (2002). Sequential requests and organ donation. *Journal of Social Psychology, 142,* 171–178.

Girdler, S. S., Jamner, L. D., & Shapiro, D. (1997). Hostility, testosterone and vascular reactivity to stress: Effects of sex. *International Journal of Behavioral Medicine, 4,* 242–263.

Giret, N., Péron, F., Lindová, J., Tichotová, L., Nagle, L., Kreutzer, M. et al. (2010). Referential learning of French and Czech labels in African grey parrots (*Psittacus erithacus*): Different methods yield contrasting results. *Behavioural Processes, 85,* 90–98.

Gitelson, I. B., & McDermott, D. (2006). Parents and their young adult children: Transitions to adulthood. *Child Welfare League of America, 85,* 853–866.

Givens, B. (1995). Low doses of ethanol impair spatial working memory and reduce hippocampal theta activity. *Alcoholism: Clinical and Experimental Research, 19,* 763–767.

Gladwell, M. (2004, September 20). Annals of psychology: Personality plus. *New Yorker,* pp. 42–48.

Glanzer, M., & Cunitz, A. R. (1966). Two storage mechanisms in free recall. *Journal of Verbal Learning and Verbal Behavior, 5,* 351–360.

Glenberg, A. M., Smith, S. M., & Green, C. (1977). Type I rehearsal: Maintenance and more. *Journal of Verbal Learning and Verbal Behavior, 16,* 339–352.

Global Initiative to End All Corporal Punishment of Children. (2013, October 28). *Research in countries which have prohibited all corporal punishment.* Retrieved from the Global Initiative to End All Corporal Punishment of Children website: http://www.endcorporalpunishment.org/pages/frame.html

Glynn, M., & Rhodes, P. (2005). *Estimated HIV prevalence in the United States at the end of 2003.* National HIV Prevention Conference, Atlanta, GA. Abstract T1-Bll01.

Goddard, A. W., Ball, S. G., Martinez, J., Robinson, M. J., Yang, C. R., Russell, J. M. et al. (2010). Current perspectives of the roles of the central norepinephrine system in anxiety and depression. *Depression and Anxiety, 27,* 339–350.

Godden, D. R., & Baddeley, A. D. (1975). Context dependent memory in two natural environments: On land and underwater. *British Journal of Psychology, 66,* 325–332.

Goeders, N. E. (2004). Stress, motivation, and drug addiction. *Current Directions in Psychological Science, 13,* 33–35.

Gold, M. S. (1994). The epidemiology, attitudes, and pharmacology of LSD use in the 1990's. *Psychiatric Annals, 24,* 124–126.

Goldberg, J. F. (2007). What psychotherapists should know about pharmacotherapies for bipolar disorder. *Journal of Clinical Psychology, 63,* 475–490.

Goldsmith, B. (2014, February 4). Scotland becomes the seventeenth country to approve same-sex marriages. Retrieved from http://www.reuters.com/article/2014/02/04/us-britain-scotland-marriage-idUSBREA131N320140204

Goldstein, J. M., & Lewine, R. R. J. (2000). Overview of sex differences in schizophrenia: Where have we been and where do we go from here? In D. J. Castle, J. McGrath, & J. Kulkarni (Eds.), *Women and schizophrenia* (pp. 111–141). Cambridge: Cambridge University Press.

Goleman, D. (1982, March). Staying up: The rebellion against sleep's gentle tyranny. *Psychology Today,* pp. 24–35.

Goleman, D. (1995). *Emotional intelligence.* New York: Bantam.

Goleman, D. (1998). *Working with emotional intelligence.* London: Bloomsbury

Goleman, D., Boyatzis, R. E., & McKee, A. (2002). *Primal leadership: Realizing the power of emotional intelligence.* Boston: Harvard Business School Press.

Gonzalez, H. M., Vega, W. A., Williams, D. R., Tarraf, W., West, B. T., & Neighbors, H. W. (2010). Depression care in the United States: Too little for too few. *Archives of General Psychiatry, 67,* 37–46.

Good, J. J., Woodzicka, J. A., & Wingfield, L. C. (2010). The effects of gender stereotypic and counterstereotypic textbook images on science performance. *Journal of Social Psychology, 150,* 132–147.

Goodnick, P. J. (2000). The use of nimodipine in the treatment of mood disorders. *Bipolar Disorders,* 2(3 Pt. 1), 165–173.

Goodwin, F. K., & Goldstein, M. A. (2003). Optimizing lithium treatment in bipolar disorder: A review of the literature and clinical recommendations. *Journal of Psychiatric Practice, 9,* 333–343.

Goodwin, P. Y., Mosher, W. D., & Chandra, A. (2010). Marriage and cohabitation in the United States: A statistical portrait based on cycle 6 (2002) of the National Survey of Family Growth. *Vital Health Statistics, 23,* 1–45.

Gorchoff, S. M., John, O. P., & Helson, R. (2008). Contextualizing change in marital satisfaction during middle age. *Psychological Science, 19,* 1194–1200.

Gordon, E. F. (2000). *Mockingbird years: A life in and out of therapy.* New York: Basic Books.

Gordon, S. (2008, June 15). Beware the "Blackberry thumb." *U.S. News & World Report.* Retrieved from http://health.usnews.com

Gorman, J. M. (2006). Gender differences in depression and response to psychotropic medication. *Gender Medicine, 3,* 93–109.

Gorsky, R. D., Schwartz, E., & Dennis, D. (1988). The mortality, morbidity, and economic costs of alcohol abuse: New Hampshire. *Preventative Medicine, 17,* 736–745.

Gosling, S. D., & Johnson, A. J. (2010). *Advanced methods for conducting online behavioral research.* Washington, DC: APA Books.

Gotlib, I. H., & Hamilton, J. P. (2008). Neuroimaging and depression: Current status and unresolved issues. *Current Directions in Psychological Science, 17,* 159–163.

Gotlib, I. H., Joormann, J., & Foland-Ross, L. C. (2014). Understanding familial risk for depression: A 25-year perspective. *Perspectives on Psychological Science, 9,* 94–108.

Gottlieb, G., Wahlsten, D., & Lickliter, R. (1998). The significance of biology for human development: A developmental psychobiological systems view. In W. Damon & R. M. Lerner (Eds.), *Handbook of child psychology* (Vol. 1, pp. 233–273). New York: Wiley.

Gottlieb, J., & Carver, C. S. (1980). Anticipation of future interaction and the bystander effect. *Journal of Experimental Social Psychology, 16,* 253–260. doi:10.1016/0022-1031(80)90068-2

Gottman, J. (1999a). *The marriage clinic.* New York: Norton.

Gottman, J. (1999b). *The seven principles of making marriage work.* New York: Crown.

Gotts, S. J., Jo, H., Wallace, G. L., Saad, Z. S., Cox, R. W., & Martin, A. (2013). Two distinct forms of functional lateralization in the human brain. *PNAS: Proceedings of the National Academy of Sciences of the United States of America, 110,* E3435–E3444.

Gouin, K., Murphy, K., & Shah, P. S. (2011). Effects of cocaine use during pregnancy on low birthweight and preterm birth: Systematic review and metaanalyses. *American Journal of Obstetrics and Gynecology, 204,* 340.e1–340.e12.

Gould, R. A., Otto, M. W., Pollack, M. H., & Yap, L. (1997). Cognitive behavioral and pharmacological treatment of generalized anxiety disorder: A preliminary meta-analysis. *Behavior Therapy, 28,* 285–305.

Graber, J. A., Brooks-Gunn, J., & Warren, M. P. (2006). Pubertal effects on adjustment in girls: Moving from demonstrating effects to identifying pathways. *Journal of Youth and Adolescence, 35,* 413–423.

Graber, J. A., Seeley, J. R., Brooks-Gunn, J., & Lewinsohn, P. M. (2004). Is pubertal timing associated with psychopathology in young adulthood? *Journal of the American Academy of Child and Adolescent Psychiatry, 43,* 718–726.

Grace, A. A. (2010). Ventral hippocampus, interneurons, and schizophrenia: A new understanding of the pathophysiology of schizophrenia and its implications for treatment and prevention. *Current Directions in Psychological Science, 19,* 232–237.

Grados, M. A., Walkup, J., & Walford, S. (2003). Genetics of obsessive-compulsive disorders: New findings and challenges. *Brain Development, 25,* S55–S61.

Graf, P., & Schacter, D. L. (1985). Implicit and explicit memory for new associations in normal and amnesiac subjects. *Journal of Experimental Psychology: Learning, Memory, and Cognition, 11,* 501–518.

Graffin, N. F., Ray, W. J., & Lundy, R. (1995). EEG concomitants of hypnosis and hypnotic susceptibility. *Journal of Abnormal Psychology, 104,* 123–131.

Graham, K. S., Simons, J. S., Pratt, K. H., Patterson, K., & Hodges, J. R. (2000). Insights from semantic dementia on the relationship between episodic and semantic memory. *Neurpsychologia, 38,* 313–324.

Graham, R., Devinsky, O., & LaBar, K. S. (2007). Quantifying deficits in the perception of fear and anger in morphed facial expressions after bilateral amygdale damage. *Neuropsychologia, 45,* 42–54.

Grant, B. F., Hasin, D. S., Stinson, F. S., Dawson, D. A., Chou, S. P., Ruan, W. J. et al. (2004). Prevalence, correlates, and disability of personality disorders in the United States: Results from the National Epidemiologic Survey on alcohol and related conditions. *Journal of Clinical Psychiatry, 65,* 948–958.

Grant, B. F., Hasin, D. S., Stinson, F. S., Dawson, D. A., Goldstein, R. B., Smith, S. et al. (2006). The epidemiology of DSM-IV panic disorder and agoraphobia in the United States: Results from the National Epidemiologic Survey on Alcohol and Related Conditions. *Journal of Clinical Psychiatry, 67,* 363–374.

Grant, J. E., & Phillips, K. A. (2004). Is anorexia nervosa a subtype of body dysmorphic disorder? Probably not, but read on. . . . *Harvard Review of Psychiatry, 12,* 123–126.

Green, J. G., McLaughlin, K. A., Berglund, P. A., Gruber, M. J., Sampson, N. A., Zaslavsky, A. M. et al. (2010). Childhood adversities and adult psychiatric disorders in the National Comorbidity Survey Replication I: Associations with first onset of DSM-IV disorders. *Archives of General Psychiatry, 67,* 113–123.

Green, J. P., & Lynn, S. J. (2000). Hypnosis and suggestion-based approaches to smoking cessation: An examination of the evidence. *International Journal of Clinical and Experimental Hypnosis, 48,* 195–224.

Greenberg, L. S., & Johnson, S. M. (1988). *Emotionally focused therapy for couples.* New York: Guilford Press.

Greenberg, L. S., & Rice, L. N. (1997). Humanistic approaches to psychotherapy. In P. L. Wachtel & S. B. Messer (Eds.), *Theories of psychotherapy: Origins and evolution* (pp. 97–129). Washington, DC: American Psychological Association.

Greenberg, L. S., Elliot, R., & Lietaer, G. (1994). Research on humanistic and experiential psychotherapies. In A. Bergin & S. Garfield (Eds.), *Handbook of psychotherapy and behavior change* (4th ed., pp. 509–542). New York: Wiley.

Greenberg, L., Warwar, S., & Malcolm, W. (2010). Emotion-focused couples therapy and the facilitation of forgiveness. *Journal of Marital and Family Therapy, 36,* 28–42.

Greenblatt, D., Harmatz, J., & Shader, R. I. (1993). Plasma alprazolam concentrations: Relation to efficacy and side effects in the treatment of panic disorder. *Archives of General Psychiatry, 50,* 715–732.

Greenfield, P. (1997). You can't take it with you: Why ability assessments don't cross cultures. *American Psychologist, 52,* 1115–1124.

Greenhaus, J. H. (2003). Career dynamics. In W. C. Borman, D. R. Ilgen, & R. J. Klimoski (Eds.), *Handbook of psychology: Industrial and organizational psychology* (Vol. 12, pp. 519–540). New York: Wiley.

Greenough, W. T., Wallace, C. S., Alcantara, A. A., Anderson, B. J., Hawrylak, N., Sirevaag, A. M. et al. (1993). Experience affects the structure of neurons, glia, and blood vessels. In N. J. Anastasiow & S. Harel (Eds.), *At-risk infants: Interventions, family, and research* (pp. 175–185). Baltimore: Paul H. Brookes.

Greenwald, A. G., & Draine, S. C. (1997). Do subliminal stimuli enter the mind unnoticed? Tests with a new method. In J. D. Cohen & J. W. Schooler (Eds.), *Scientific approaches to consciousness: Carnegie Mellon Symposia on cognition* (pp. 83–108). Mahwah, NJ: Erlbaum.

Greer, G. R., & Tolbert, R. (1998). A method of conducting therapeutic sessions with MDMA. *Journal of Psychoactive Drugs, 30,* 371–379.

Gregg, R. A., & Rawls, S. M. (2014). Behavioral pharmacology of designer cathinones: A review of the preclinical literature. *Life Sciences, 97,* 27–30.

Grieger, T. A., Fullerton, C. S., & Ursano, R. J. (2004). Posttraumatic stress disorder, depression, and perceived safety 13 months after September 11th. *Psychiatric Services, 55,* 1061–1063.

Griest, S. E., Folmer, R. L., & Martin, W. H. (2007). Effectiveness of "Dangerous Decibels," a school-based hearing loss prevention program. *American Journal of Audiology, 16,* S165–S181.

Griffey, J. F., & Little, A. C. (2013). Similarities in human visual and declared measures of preference for opposite-sex faces. *Experimental Psychology, 18,* 1–9. doi:10.1027/1618-3169/a000248

Griffiths, K. M., Calear, A. L., & Banfield, M. (2009). Systematic review on Internet Support Groups (ISGs) and depression: Do ISGs reduce depressive symptoms? *Journal of Medical Internet Research, 11,* e40.

Grinspoon, L., & Bakalar, J. B. (1995). Marijuana as medicine: A plea for reconsideration. *Journal of the American Medical Association, 273,* 1875–1876.

Grinspoon, L., Bakalar, J. B., Zimmer, L., & Morgan, J. P. (1997). Marijuana addiction. *Science, 277,* 751–752.

Grivetti, L. E. (2000). Food prejudices and taboos. In K. E. Kipple & K. C. Ornelas (Eds.), *The Cambridge world history of food* (Vol. 1, pp. 1495–1513). Cambridge: Cambridge University Press.

Gropalis, M., Bleichhardt, G., Witthoft, M., & Hiller, W. (2012). Hypochondriasis, somatoform disorders, and anxiety disorders: Sociodemographic variables, general psychopathology, and naturalistic treatment effects. *Journal of Nervous and Mental Disease, 200,* 406–412.

Gross, J. J., Halperin, E., & Porat, R. (2013). Emotion regulation in intractable conflicts. *Current Directions in Psychological Science, 22,* 423–429.

Grossman, L. S., Harrow, M., Rosen, C., Faull, R., & Strauss, G. P. (2008). Sex differences in schizophrenia and other psychotic disorders: A 20-year longitudinal study of psychosis and recovery. *Comprehensive Psychiatry, 49,* 523–529.

Grossman, M. I., & Stein, L. F. (1948). Vagotomy and the hunger-producing action of insulin in man. *Journal of Applied Physiology, 1,* 263–269.

Grossman, P., Niemann, L., Schmidt, S., & Walach, H. (2004). Mindfulness-based stress reduction and health benefits: A meta-analysis. *Journal of Psychosomatic Research, 57,* 35–43.

Grossman, R. P., & Till, B. D. (1998). The persistence of classically conditioned brand attitudes. *Journal of Advertising, 27,* 23–31.

Grossmann, I., Karasawa, M., Izumi, S., Na, J., Varnum, M. E., Kitayama, S., & Nisbett, R. E. (2012). Aging and wisdom: Culture matters. *Psychological Science, 23,* 1059–1066.

Grover, S. (2005). Reification of psychiatric diagnoses as defamatory: Implications for ethical clinical practice. *Ethical Human Psychology and Psychiatry, 7,* 77–86.

Gruen, R. J. (1993). Stress and depression: Toward the development of integrative models. In L. Goldberger & S. Breznitz (Eds.), *Handbook of stress: Theoretical and clinical aspects* (pp. 550–569). New York: Free Press.

Grysman, A., & Hudson, J. A. (2010). Abstracting and extracting: Causal coherence and the development of the life story. *Memory, 18,* 565–580.

Grysman, A., & Hudson, J. A. (2013). Gender differences in autobiographical memory: Developmental and methodological considerations. *Developmental Review, 33,* 239–272. doi:10.1016/j.dr.2013.07.004

Gugger, J. J., & Wagner, M. L. (2007). Rapid eye movement sleep behavior disorder. *Annals of Pharmacotherapy, 41,* 1833–1841.

Guilford, J. P. (1967). *The nature of human intelligence.* New York: McGraw-Hill.

Guilleminault, C., Palombini, L., Pelayo, R., & Chervin, R. D. (2003). Sleepwalking and sleep terrors in prepubertal children: What triggers them? *Pediatrics, 111,* e17–e25.

Guisinger, S. (2003). Adapted to flee famine: Adding an evolutionary perspective on anorexia nervosa. *Psychological Review, 110,* 745–761.

Gurman, A. S., & Jacobson, N. S. (Eds.). (2002). *Clinical handbook of couple therapy* (3rd ed.). New York: Guilford Press.

Gustavson, C. R., & Garcia, J. (1974, August). Pulling a gag on the wily coyote. *Psychology Today,* pp. 68–72.

Guterman, N. B., Tabone, J. K., Bryan, G. M., Taylor, C. A., Napoleon-Hanger, C., & Banman, A. (2013). Examining the effectiveness of home-based parent aide services to reduce risk for physical child abuse and neglect: Six-month findings from a randomized clinical trial. *Child Abuse & Neglect, 37,* 566–577. doi:10.1016/j.chiabu.2013.03.006

Guthrie, J. P., Ash, R. A., & Bendapudi, V. (1995). Additional validity evidence for a measure of morningness. *Journal of Applied Psychology, 80,* 186–190.

Ha, T., Overbeek, G., & Engels, R. C. (2010). Effects of attractiveness and social status on dating desire in heterosexual adolescents: An experimental study. *Archives of Sexual Behavior, 39,* 1063–1071.

Haack, L. J., Metalsky, G. I., Dykman, B. M., & Abramson, L. Y. (1996). Use of current situational information and causal inference: Do dysphoric individuals make "unwarranted" causal inferences? *Cognitive Therapy and Research, 20,* 309–331.

Haber, D. (1994). *Health promotion and aging.* New York: Springer.

Hackett, R. D. (1989). Work attitudes and employee absenteeism: A synthesis of the literature. *Journal of Occupational Psychology, 62,* 235–248.

Hackman, J. R., & Oldham, G. R. (1976). Motivation through the design of work: A test of a theory. *Organizational Behavior and Human Performance, 16,* 250–279.

Hadjikhani, N., Kveraga, K., Naik, P., & Ahlfors, S. P. (2009). Early (M170) activation of face-specific cortex by face-like objects. *Neuroreport, 20,* 403–407.

Haefner, R. (2009, June). More employers screening candidates via social networking sites. Careerbuilder.com

Hagenauer, M. H., & Lee, T. M. (2012). The neuroendocrine control of the circadian system: Adolescent chronotype. *Frontiers in Neuroendocrinology, 33,* 211–229.

Hagenauer, M. H., Perryman, J. I., Lee, T. M., & Carskadon, M. A. (2009). Adolescent changes in the homeostatic and circadian regulation of sleep. *Developmental Neuroscience, 31,* 276–284.

Haidt, J. (2008). Morality. *Perspectives on Psychological Science, 1,* 65–72.

Haie, L., & Do, D. P. (2007). Racial differences in self-reports of sleep duration in a population-based study. *Sleep, 30,* 1096–1103.

Haith, M. M., & Benson, J. B. (1998). Infant cognition. In W. Damon & R. M. Lerner (Eds.), *Handbook of child psychology* (Vol. 1, pp. 235–246). New York: Wiley.

Hakuta, K. (1999). The debate on bilingual education. *Developmental and Behavioral Pediatrics, 20,* 36–37.

Hakuta, K., Bailystok, E., & Wiley, E. (2003). Critical evidence: A test of the critical-period hypothesis for second-language acquisitions. *Psychological Science, 14,* 31–38.

Halaby, A., Haddad, R. S., & Naja, W. J. (in press). Non-antidepressant treatment of social anxiety disorder: A review. *Current Clinical Pharmacology.*

Halim, M. L., Ruble, D., Tamis-LeMonda, C., & Shrout, P. E. (2013). Rigidity in gender-typed behaviors in early childhood: A longitudinal study of ethnic minority children. *Child Development, 84,* 1269–1284.

Hall, D. T., & Nougaim, K. E. (1968). An examination of Maslow's need hierarchy in an organizational setting. *Organizational Behavior and Human Performance, 3,* 12–35.

Halloway, R. L., Anderson, P. J., Defendini, R., & Harper, C. (2007). Sexual dimorphism of the human corpus callosum from three independent samples: Relative size of the corpus callosum. In G. Einstein (Ed.), *Sex and the brain* (pp. 609–621). Cambridge, MA: MIT Press.

Halpern, D. F. (1996). Public policy implications of sex differences in cognitive abilities. *Psychology, Public Policy and Law, 2*(3/4), 564.

Halpern, D. F., & LeMay, M. L. (2000). The smarter sex: A critical review of sex-differences in intelligence. *Educational Psychology Review, 12,* 229–246.

Halpern, D. F., Benbow, C. P., Geary, D. C., Gur, R. C., Hyde, J. S., & Gernsbacher, M. A. (2007). The science of sex differences in science and mathematics. *Psychological Science in the Public Interest, 8,* 1–51.

Halpern, J. H., & Pope, H. G., Jr. (2003). Hallucinogen persisting perception disorder: What do we know after 50 years? *Drug and Alcohol Dependence, 69,* 109–119.

Hamani, C., Mayberg, H., Snyder, B., Giacobbe, P., Kennedy, S., & Lozano, A. M. (2009). Deep brain stimulation of the subcallosal cingulated gyrus for depression: Anatomical location of active contacts in clinical responders and a suggested guideline for targeting. *Journal of Neurosurgery, 111,* 1209–1215.

Hamann, S. (2005). Sex differences in the responses of the human amygdala. *Neuroscientist, 11,* 288–293.

Hamel, R., & Elshout, J. (2000). On the development of knowledge during problem solving. *Journal of Cognitive Psychology, 12,* 289–322.

Hamer, D. (2002). Genetics. Rethinking behavior genetics. *Science, 298,* 71–72.

Hamilton, C. E. (2000). Continuity and discontinuity of attachment from infancy through adolescence. *Child Development, 71,* 690–694.

Hamilton, V. L., Blumenfeld, P. C., Akoh, H., & Miura, K. (1991). Group and gender in Japanese and American elementary classrooms. *Journal of Cross-Cultural Psychology, 22,* 317–346.

Hamlin, J. K. (2013). Moral judgment and action in preverbal infants and toddlers: Evidence for an innate moral core. *Current Directions in Psychological Science, 22,* 186–193.

Hammen, C. (2005). Stress and depression. *Annual Review of Clinical Psychology, 1,* 293–319.

Hammen, C. (2009). Adolescent depression: Stressful interpersonal contexts and risk for recurrence. *Current Directions in Psychological Science, 18,* 200–204.

Hampson, S. E., & Goldberg, L. R. (2006). A first large cohort study of personality trait stability over the 40 years between elementary school and midlife. *Journal of Personality and Social Psychology, 91,* 763–779.

Hanisch, K. A. (1992). The Job Descriptive Index revisited: Questions about the question mark. *Journal of Applied Psychology, 77,* 377–382.

Hanisch, K. A. (1995). Behavioral families and multiple causes: Matching the complexity of responses to the complexity of antecedents. *Current Directions in Psychological Science, 4,* 156–162.

Hanisch, K. A., & Hulin, C. L. (1990). Job attitudes and organizational withdrawal: An examination of retirement and other voluntary withdrawal behaviors. *Journal of Vocational Behavior, 37,* 60–78.

Hanisch, K. A., & Hulin, C. L. (1991). General attitudes and organizational withdrawal: An evaluation of a causal model. *Journal of Vocational Behavior, 39,* 110–128.

Hanisch, K. A., Hulin, C. L., & Roznowski, M. A. (1998). The importance of individuals' repertoires of behaviors: The scientific appropriateness of studying multiple behaviors and general attitudes. *Journal of Organizational Behavior, 19,* 463–480.

Hanna, G. H. (2000). Clinical and family-genetic studies of childhood obsessive-compulsive disorder. In W. K. Goodman, M. V. Rudofer, & J. D. Maser (Eds.), *Obsessive-compulsive disorder: Contemporary issues in treatment* (pp. 87–103). Mahwah, NJ: Erlbaum.

Hanson, G., & Venturelli, P. J. (1998). *Drugs and society* (5th ed.). Boston: Jones and Bartlett.

Hargis, M. (2008, November 5). Social networking sites dos and don'ts. CNN.com. http://www.cnn.com/2008/LIVING/worklife/11/05/cb.social.networking/index.html

Harkins, S. G. (1987). Social loafing and social facilitation. *Journal of Experimental Social Psychology, 23,* 1–18.

Harlow, H. F., & Zimmerman, R. (1959). Affectional responses in the infant monkey. *Science, 130,* 421–432.

Harold, G. T., Fincham, F. D., Osborne, L. N., & Conger, R. D. (1997). Mom and Dad are at it again: Adolescent perceptions of marital conflict and adolescent psychological distress. *Developmental Psychology, 33,* 335–350.

Harris, A., & Seckl, J. (2011). Glucocorticoids, prenatal stress and the programming of disease. *Hormones and Behavior, 59,* 279–289.

Harris, J. D. (1943). Habituatory response decrement in the intact organism. *Psychological Bulletin, 40,* 385–422.

Harris, J. R. (2000). Context-specific learning, personality, and birth order. *Current Directions in Psychological Science, 9,* 174–177.

Harris, S. R., Kemmerling, R. L., & North, M. M. (2002). Brief virtual reality therapy for public speaking. *Cyberpsychology and Behavior, 5,* 543–550.

Harrow, M., Grossman, L. S., Jobe, T. H., & Hernener, E. S. (2005). Do patients with schizophrenia ever show periods of recovery? A 15-year multi-follow-up study. *Schizophrenia Bulletin, 31,* 723–734.

Hart, B. M., Wicherski, M., & Kohout, J. L. (2011) *2010–2011: Faculty in U.S. and Canadian graduate departments of psychology: 2012 graduate study in psychology.* Washington, DC: APA Center for Workforce Studies.

Hartmann, E. (1981, April). The strangest sleep disorder. *Psychology Today,* pp. 14, 16, 18.

Hartmann, U. (2009). Sigmund Freud and his impact on our understanding of male sexual dysfunction. *Journal of Sexual Medicine, 6,* 2332–2339.

Hasin, D., Hatzenbuehler, M. L., Keyes, K., & Ogburn, E. (2006). Substance use disorders: Diagnostic and Statistical Manual of Mental Disorders, fourth edition (DSM-IV) and International Classification of Diseases, tenth edition (ICD-10). *Addiction, 101*(Suppl. 1), 59–75.

Haslam, C., Haslam, S., Knight, C., Gleibs, I., Ysseldyk, R., & McCloskey, L. (2014). We can work it out: Group decision-making builds social identity and enhances the cognitive performance of care residents. *British Journal of Psychology, 105,* 17–34. doi:10.1111/bjop.12012

Hasselmo, M. E. (2010). Consciousness and neural time travel. In E. Perry, D. Collerton, F. LeBeau, & H. Ashton (Eds.), *New horizons in the neuroscience of consciousness* (pp. 73–80). Amsterdam: Benjamins.

Hassett, J. M., Siebert, E. R., & Wallen, K. (2008). Sex differences in rhesus monkey toy preferences parallel those of children. *Hormones and Behavior, 54,* 359–364.

Hastings, E. C., Karas, T. L., Winsler, A., Way, E., Madigan, A., & Tyler, S. (2009). Young children's video/computer game use: Relations with school performance and behavior. *Issues in Mental Health Nursing, 30,* 638–649.

Hatcher, R., Trussell, J., Stewart, F., Stewart, G., Kowal, D., Guest, E. et al. (1994). *Contraceptive technology* (16th ed.). New York: Irvington.

Hatfield, G., & Allred, S. (2012). *Visual experience: Sensation, cognition, and constancy.* New York: Oxford University Press. doi:10.1093/acprof:oso/9780199597277.001.0001

Hatzenbuehler, M. L. (2014). Structural stigma and the health of lesbian, gay, and bisexual populations. *Current Directions in Psychological Science, 23,* 127–132.

Hatzigeorgiadis, A., Zourbanos, N., Galanis, E., & Theodorakis, Y. (2011). Self-talk and sports performance: A meta-analysis. *Psychological Science, 6,* 348–356.

Haus, E., & Smolensky, M. (2006). Biological clocks and shift work: Circadian dysregulation and potential long-term effects. *Cancer Causes and Control, 17,* 489–500.

Hausner, H., Nicklaus, S., Issanchou, S., Mølgaard, C., & Møller, P. (2010). Breastfeeding facilitates acceptance of a novel dietary flavor compound. *Clinical Nutrition, 29,* 141–148.

Havermans, R. C., & Jansen, A. (2007). Increasing children's liking of vegetables through flavour-flavour learning. *Appetite, 48,* 259–262.

Hawco, C., Armony, J. L., & Lepage, M. (2013). Neural activity related to self-initiating elaborative semantic encoding in associative memory. *Neuroimage, 67,* 273–282. doi:10.1016/j.neuroimage.2012.11.004

Hawkley, L. C., & Cacioppo, J. T. (2007). Aging and loneliness: Downhill quickly? *Current Directions in Psychological Science, 16,* 187–191.

Hawkley, L. C., & Cacioppo, J. T. (2010). Loneliness matters: A theoretical and empirical review of consequences and mechanisms. *Annals of Behavioral Medicine, 40,* 218–227.

Hawks, S. R., Hull, M. L., Thalman, R. L., & Richins, P. M. (1995). Review of spiritual health: Definition, role, and intervention strategies in health promotion. *American Journal of Health Promotion, 9,* 371–378.

Hawley, D. F., & Leasure, J. (2012). Region-specific response of the hippocampus to chronic unpredictable stress. *Hippocampus, 22,* 1338–1349. doi:10.1002/hipo.20970

Hayden, E. P., & Nurnberger, J. I., Jr. (2006). Molecular genetics of bipolar disorder. *Genes, Brain and Behavior, 5,* 85–95.

Hayden, E. P., Dougherty, L. R., Maloney, B., Emily Durbin, C., Olino, T. M., Nurnberger, J. I. et al. (2007). Temperamental fearfulness in childhood and the serotonin transporter promoter region polymorphism: A multimethod association study. *Psychiatric Genetics, 17,* 135–142.

Hayden, E. P., Klein, D. N., Dougherty, L. R., Olino, T. M., Dyson, M. W., Durbin, C. E. et al. (2010). The role of brain-derived neurotrophic factor genotype, parental depression, and relationship discord in predicting early-emerging negative emotionality. *Psychological Science, 21,* 1678–1685.

Hayes, E. R., & Plowfield, L. A. (2007). Smoking too young: Students' decisions about tobacco use. *American Journal of Maternal Child Nursing, 32,* 112–116.

Hayes, J. R. (1989). *The complete problem solver* (2nd ed.). Hillsdale, NJ: Erlbaum.

Hayne, H., & Rovee-Collier, C. (1995). The organization of reactivated memory in infancy. *Child Development, 66,* 893–906.

Hays, N. P., & Roberts, S. B. (2008). Aspects of eating behaviors: "Disinhibition" and "restraint" are related to weight gain and BMI in women. *Obesity, 16,* 52–58.

Hayward, M. D., Schaich-Borg, A., Pintar, J. E., & Low, M. J. (2006). Differential involvement of endogenous opioids in sucrose consumption and food reinforcement. *Pharmacology Biochemistry and Behavior, 85,* 601–611.

Heatherton, T. F., & Sargent, J. D. (2009). Does watching smoking in movies promote teenage smoking? *Current Directions in Psychological Science, 18,* 63–67.

Hebb, D. O. (1955). Drives and the C.N.S. (conceptual nervous system). *Psychological Review, 62,* 243–255.

Hedden, T., & Park, D. C. (2003). Contributions of source and inhibitory mechanisms to age-related retroactive interference in verbal working memory. *Journal of Experimental Psychology: General, 132,* 93–122.

Hedden, T., & Yoon, C. (2006). Individual differences in executive processing predict susceptibility to interference in verbal working memory. *Neuropsychology, 20,* 511–528.

Heider, F. (1946). Attitudes and cognitive organization. *Journal of Psychology, 21,* 107–112.

Heider, F. (1958). *The psychology of interpersonal relations.* New York: Wiley.

Heilman, M. E., & Kram, K. E. (1983). Male and female assumptions about colleagues' views of their competence. *Psychology of Women Quarterly, 7,* 329–337.

Heim, C., Bradley, B., Mietzko, T. C., Deveau, T. C., Musselman, D. L., Nemeroff, C. B. et al. (2009). Effect of childhood trauma on adult depression and neuroendocrine function: Sex-specific moderation by CRH receptor 1 gene. *Frontiers in Behavioral Neuroscience, 3,* 41.

Heim, C., Newport, D. J., Mietzko, T., Miller, A. H., & Nemeroff, C. B. (2008). The link between childhood trauma and depression: Insights from HPA axis studies in humans. *Psychoneuroendocrinology, 33,* 693–710.

Heine, S. J. (2008). *Cultural psychology.* New York: Norton.

Heine, S. J., Foster, J. B., & Spina, R. (2009). Do birds of a feather universally flock together? Cultural variation in the similarity-attraction effect. *Asian Journal of Social Psychology, 12,* 247–258.

Heiser, P., Dickhaus, B. Schreiber, W., Clement, H. W., Hasse, C., Hennig, J. et al. (2000). White blood cells and cortisol after sleep deprivation and recovery sleep in humans. *European Archives of Psychiatry and Clinical Neuroscience, 250,* 16–23.

Hejmadi, A., Davidson, R. J., & Rozin, P. (2000). Exploring Hindu Indian emotion expressions. *Psychological Science, 11,* 183–187.

Hélie, S., & Sun, R. (2010). Incubation, insight, and creative problem solving: A unified theory and connectionist model. *Psychological Review, 117,* 994–1024.

Helmholtz, H. L. F. von. (1930). *The sensations of tone* (A. J. Ellis, Trans.). New York: Longmans, Green. (Original work published 1863)

Helmuth, L. (2001). From the mouths (and hands) of babes. *Science, 293,* 1758–1759.

Helwig, C. C. (1997). Making moral cognition respectable (again): A retrospective review of Lawrence Kohlberg. *Contemporary Psychology, 42,* 191–195.

Helzer, J. E., & Canino, G. J. (Eds.). (1992). *Alcoholism in North America, Europe, and Asia.* New York: Oxford University Press.

Hendrick, C., & Hendrick, S. S. (1983). *Liking, loving, and relating.* Pacific Grove, CA: Brooks/Cole.

Hennessy, D. A., & Jakubowski, R. (2007). The impact of perspective and anger on the actor-observer bias among automobile drivers. *Traffic Injury Prevention, 8,* 115–122.

Hennessy, M. B., Schiml-Webb, P. A., & Deak, T. (2009). Separation, sickness, and depression: A new perspective on an old animal model. *Current Directions in Psychological Science, 18,* 227–231.

Henry, B., & Moffitt, T. E. (1997). Neuropsychological and neuroimaging studies of juvenile delinquency and adult criminal behavior. In D. M. Stoff, J. Breiling, & J. D. Maser (Eds.), *Handbook of antisocial personality disorder* (pp. 280–288). New York: Wiley.

Henry, L. A., Messer, D., Luger-Klein, S., & Crane, L. (2012). Phonological, visual, and semantic coding strategies and children's short-term picture memory span. *Quarterly Journal of Experimental Psychology, 65,* 2033–2053. doi: 10.1080/17470218.2012.672997

Henry, W. P., Strupp, H. H., Schacht, T. E., & Gaston, L. (1994). Psychodynamic approaches. In A. E. Bergin & S. L. Garfield (Eds.), *Handbook of psychotherapy and behavior change* (4th ed., pp. 143–189). New York: Wiley.

Herbenick, D., Reece, M., Schick, V., Sanders, S. A., Dodge, B., & Fortenberry, J. D. (2010). Sexual behavior in the United States: Results from a national probability sample of men and women ages 14–94. *Journal of Sexual Medicine, 7*(Suppl. 5), 255–265.

Herbert, B. M., Blechert, J., Hautzinger, M., Matthias, E., & Herbert, C. (2013). Intuitive eating is associated with interoceptive sensitivity: Effects on body mass index. *Appetite, 70,* 22–30. doi:10.1016/j.appet.2013.06.082

Herculano-Houzel, S. (2011). Not all brains are made the same: New views on brain scaling in evolution. *Brain, Behavior and Evolution, 78,* 22–36. doi:10.1159/000327318

Herman, L. M., & Uyeyama, R. J. (1999). The dolphin's grammatical competency: Comments on Kako (1999). *Animal Learning and Behavior, 27,* 18–23.

Herman, L. M., Kuczaj, S. A., II, & Holder, M. D. (1993). Responses to anomalous gestural sequences by a language-trained dolphin: Evidence for processing of semantic relations and syntactical information. *Journal of Experimental Psychology: General, 122,* 184–194.

Heron, M. (2012). Deaths: Leading causes for 2009. *National Vital Statistics Reports,* Vol. 61, No 7. Hyattsville, MD: National Center for Health Statistics.

Heron, M. (2013). Deaths: Leading causes for 2010. *National Vital Statistics Reports, 62,* No. 6. Hyattsville, MD: National Center for Health Statistics.

Heron, M. P., & Smith, B. L. (2007). Deaths: Leading causes for 2003. *National Vital Statistics Reports, 55,* 1–93.

Herrera, N. C., Zajonc, R. B., Wieczorkowska, G., & Cichomski, B. (2003). Beliefs about birth rank and their reflection in reality. *Journal of Personality and Social Psychology, 85,* 142–150.

Herrnstein, R., & Murray, C. (1994). *The bell curve.* New York: Free Press.

Hertel, P. T., & Brozovich, F. (2010). Cognitive habits and memory distortions in anxiety and depression. *Current Directions in Psychological Science, 19,* 155–160.

Hertlein, K. M., & Ricci, R. J. (2004). A systematic research synthesis of EMDR studies: Implementation of the platinum standard. *Trauma, Violence, and Abuse, 5,* 285–300.

Hertzog, C., Kramer, A. F., Wilson, R. S., & Lindenberger, U. (2008). Enrichment effects on adult cognitive development: Can the functional capacity of older adults be preserved and enhanced? *Psychological Science in the Public Interest, 9,* 1–65.

Hesse, E., & Main, M. (2006). Frightened, threatening, and dissociative parental behavior in low-risk samples: Description, discussion, and interpretations. *Development and Psychopathology, 18,* 309–343.

Heston, L. L. (1966). Psychiatric disorders in foster home reared children of schizophrenic mothers. *British Journal of Psychiatry, 112,* 819–825.

Hettema, J. M., Kettenmann, B., Ahluwalia, V. McCarthy, C., Kates, W. R., Schmitt, J. E. et al. (2012). Pilot multimodal twin imaging study of generalized anxiety disorder. *Depression and Anxiety, 29,* 202–209.

Hettema, J. M., Neale, M. C., & Kendler, K. S. (2001). A review and meta-analysis of the genetic epidemiology of anxiety disorders. *American Journal of Psychiatry, 158,* 1568–1578.

Hewlett, W. A. (2000). Benzodiazepines in the treatment of obsessive-compulsive disorder. In W. K. Goodman (Ed.), *Obsessive-compulsive disorder: Contemporary issues in treatment* (pp. 405–429). Mahwah, NJ: Erlbaum.

Hewstone, M., Rubin, M., & Willis, H. (2002). Intergroup bias (social prejudice). *Annual Review of Psychology, 53,* 575–604.

Hicks, B. M., Krueger, R. F., Iacono, W. G., McGue, M., & Patrick, C. J. (2004). Family transmission and heritability of externalizing disorders: A twin-family study. *Archives of General Psychiatry, 61,* 922–928.

Higbee, K. L., & Clay, S. L. (1998). College students' beliefs in the ten-percent myth. *Journal of Psychology, 132,* 469–476.

Higuchi, S., & Saito, T. (2013). Reduction in alcohol consumption: Therapeutic goal in alcohol dependence treatment [Abstract]. *Nihon Arukoru Yakubutsu Igakkai Zasshi, 48,* 17–31.

Hikosaka, O., Nakamura, K., Sakai, K., & Nakamura, H. (2002). Central mechanisms of motor skill learning. *Current Opinion in Neurobiology, 12,* 217–222.

Hilgard, E. R. (1977). *Divided consciousness: Multiple controls in human thought and action.* New York: Wiley.

Hilgard, E. R. (1982). Hypnotic susceptibility and implications for measurement. *International Journal of Clinical and Experimental Hypnosis, 30,* 394–403.

Hilgard, E. R. (1992). Divided consciousness and dissociation. *Consciousness and Cognition, 1,* 16–31.

Hilgard, E. R., Morgan, A. H., & MacDonald, H. (1975). Pain and dissociation in the old pressor test: A study of "hidden reports" through automatic key-pressing and automatic talking. *Journal of Abnormal Psychology, 84,* 280–289.

Hilgart, M., Thorndike, F. P., Pardo, J., & Ritterband, L. M. (2012). Ethical issues of web-based interventions and online therapy. In M. M. Leach, M. J. Stevens, G. Lindsay, A. Ferrero, & Y. Korkut (Eds.), *The Oxford handbook of international psychological ethics* (pp. 426–464). New York: Oxford University Press.

Hill, C. E., & Nakayama, E. Y. (2000). Client-centered therapy: Where has it been and where is it going? A comment on Hathaway (1948). *Journal of Clinical Psychology, 56,* 861–875.

Hill, P. C., & Pargament, K. I. (2003). Advances in the conceptualization and measurement of religion and spirituality. Implications for physical and mental health research. *American Psychologist, 58,* 64–74.

Hill-Soderlund, A. L., & Braungart-Rieker, J. M. (2008). Early individual differences in temperamental reactivity and regulation: Implications for effortful control in early childhood. *Infant Behavior and Development, 31,* 386–397.

Hirai, M., & Clum, G. A. (2005). An Internet-based self-change program for traumatic event related fear, distress, and maladaptive coping. *Journal of Traumatic Stress, 18,* 631–636.

Hiroto, D. S. (1974). Locus of control and learned helplessness. *Journal of Experimental Psychology, 102,* 187–193.

Hirsch, M. S., Conway, B., D'Aquila, R. T., Johnson, V. A., Brun-Vezinet, F., Clotet, B. et al. (1998). Antiretroviral drug resistance testing in adults with HIV infection: Implications for clinical management. *Journal of the American Medical Association, 279,* 1984–1991.

Hirshkowitz, M., Moore, C. A., & Minhoto, G. (1997). The basics of sleep. In M. R. Pressman

& W. C. Orr (Eds.), *Understanding sleep: The evaluation and treatment of sleep disorders* (pp. 11–34). Washington, DC: American Psychological Association.

Hirst, W., Phelps, E. A., Buckner, R. L., Budson, A. E., Cuc, A., Gabrieli, J. E. et al. (2009). Long-term memory for the terrorist attack of September 11: Flashbulb memories, event memories, and the factors that influence their retention. *Journal of Experimental Psychology: General, 138,* 161–176. doi:10.1037/a0015527

Hively, K., & El-Alayli, A. (2014). "You throw like a girl:" The effect of stereotype threat on women's athletic performance and gender stereotypes. *Psychology of Sport and Exercise, 15,* 48–55. doi:10.1016/j.psychsport.2013.09.001

Ho, B.C., Black, D. W., & Andreasen, N. C. (2003). Schizophrenia and other psychotic disorders. In R. E. Hales & S. C. Yudofsky (Eds.), *Textbook of clinical psychiatry* (4th ed., pp. 379–438). Washington DC: American Psychiatric Publishing.

Hobbs, F. B. (with B. L. Damon). (1996). *65+ in the United States.* Washington DC: U.S. Bureau of the Census.

Hobson, J. A., & McCarley, R. W. (1977). The brain as a dream state generator: An activation-synthesis hypothesis of the dream process. *American Journal of Psychiatry, 134,* 1335–1348.

Hobson, J. A., Pace-Schott, E., & Stickgold, R. (2000). Dreaming and the brain: Toward a cognitive neuroscience of conscious states. *Behavioral and Brain Sciences, 23,* 783–842.

Hochberg, L. R., Serruya, M. D., Friehs, G. M., Mukand, J. A., Saleh, M., Caplan, A. H. et al. (2006). Neuronal ensemble control of prosthetic devices by a human with tetraplegia. *Nature, 442,* 164–171.

Hodson, G., Dovidio, J. F., & Gaertner, S. L. (2010). The aversive form of racism. In J. Chin (Ed.), *The psychology of prejudice and discrimination: A revised and condensed edition* (pp. 1–13). Santa Barbara, CA: Praeger/ABC-CLIO.

Hodson, N. A., & Linden, R. W. A. (2006). The effect of monosodium glutamate on parotid salivary flow in comparison to the response to representatives of the other four basic tastes. *Physiology and Behavior, 89,* 711–717.

Hoeft, F., Gabrieli, J. D., Whitfield-Gabrieli, S., Haas, B. W., Bammer, R., Menon, V., & Spiegel, D. (2012). Functional brain basis of hypnotizability. *Archives of General Psychiatry, 69,* 1064–1072.

Hofmann, S. G., & Smits, J. A. (2008). Cognitive-behavioral therapy for adult anxiety disorders: A meta-analysis of randomized placebo-controlled trials. *Journal of Clinical Psychiatry, 69,* 621–632.

Hogben, M. (1998). Factors moderating the effect of televised aggression on viewer behavior. *Communication Research, 25,* 220–247.

Hoge, C. W., Castro, C. A., Messer, S. C., McGurk, D., Cotting, D. I., & Koffman, R. L. (2004). Combat duty in Iraq and Afghanistan, mental health problems, and barriers to care. *New England Journal of Medicine, 351,* 13–22.

Holden, C. (1980, November). Twins reunited. *Science, 80,* 55–59.

Holland, A. J., Sicotte, N., & Treasure, J. (1988). Anorexia nervosa: Evidence of a genetic basis. *Journal of Psychosomatic Research, 32,* 561–571.

Hollon, S. D., & Beck, A. T. (1994). Cognitive and cognitive-behavioral therapies. In A. E. Bergin & S. L. Garfield (Eds.), *Handbook of psychotherapy and behavior change* (4th ed., pp. 447–492). New York: Wiley.

Hollos, M., & Richards, F. A. (1993). Gender-associated development of formal operations in Nigerian adolescents. *Ethos, 21,* 24–52.

Holmans, P., Weissman, M. M., Zubenko, G. S., Scheftner, W. A., Crowe, R. R., Depaulo, J. R. et al. (2007). Genetics of recurrent early-onset major depression (GenRED): Final genome scan report. *American Journal of Psychiatry, 164,* 248–258.

Holmes, D. S. (1987). The influence of meditation versus rest on physiological arousal: A second examination. In M. A. West (Ed.), *The psychology of meditation* (pp. 81–103). Oxford: Clarendon Press.

Holmes, T. H., & Rahe, R. H. (1967). The Social Readjustment Rating Scale. *Journal of Psychosomatic Research, 11,* 213–218.

Holmqvist, J. L., Hill, T., & Lang, A. (2009). Effects of aggression replacement training in young offender institutions. *International Journal of Offender Therapy and Comparative Criminology, 53,* 74–92.

Holroyd, J. (2003). The science of meditation and the state of hypnosis. *American Journal of Clinical Hypnosis, 46,* 109–128.

Holt, E. W., Rung, A. L., Leon, K. A., Firestein, C., & Krousel-Wood, M. (2014). Medication adherence in older adults: A qualitative study. *Educational Gerontology, 40,* 198–211. doi:10.1080/03601277.2013.802186

Holt, S., Brand, J. C., Soveny, C., & Hansky, J. (1992). Relationship of satiety to postprandial glycaemic, insulin and cholecystokinin responses. *Appetite, 18,* 129–141.

Holt-Lunstad, J., Birmingham, W., & Jones, B. Q. (2008). Is there something unique about marriage? The relative impact of marital status, relationship quality, and network social support on ambulatory blood pressure and mental health. *Annals of Behavioral Medicine, 35,* 239–244.

Holt-Lunstad, J., Smith, T. B., & Layton, J. B. (2010). Social relationships and mortality risk: A meta-analytic review. *PLoS Medicine, 7,* e1000316.

Holtzheimer, P. E., III, & Nemeroff, C. B. (2006). Advances in the treatment of depression. *NeuroRx, 3,* 42–56.

Holzel, B. K., Lazar, S. W., Gard, T., Schuman-Olivier, Z., Vago, D. R., & Ott, U. (2011). How does mindfulness meditation work? Proposing mechanisms of action from a conceptual and neural perspective. *Perspectives on Psychological Science, 6,* 537–559.

Hong, R. Y. (2007). Worry and rumination: Differential associations with anxious and depressive symptoms and coping behavior. *Behaviour Research and Therapy, 45,* 277–290.

Hood, D. C., & Finkelstein, M. A. (1986). Sensitivity to light. In K. R. Boff, L. Kaufman, & J. P. Thomas (Eds.), *Handbook of perception and human performance* (pp. 5.1–5.66). New York: Wiley.

Hooley, J. M. (2007). Expressed emotion and relapse of psychopathology. *Annual Review of Clinical Psychology, 3,* 329–352.

Hooley, J. M. (2010). Social factors in schizophrenia. *Current Directions in Psychological Science, 19,* 238–242.

Hooley, J. M., & Hiller, J. B. (1998). Expressed emotion and the pathogenesis of relapse in schizophrenia. In M. F. Lenzenweger & R. H. Dworkin (Eds.), *Origins of the development of schizophrenia* (pp. 447–468). Washington, DC: American Psychological Association.

Horgan, D. D. (1995). *Achieving gender equity: Strategies for the classroom.* Boston: Allyn & Bacon.

Horgan, J. (1996, December). Why Freud isn't dead. *Scientific American,* pp. 106–111.

Horiguchi, H., Winawer, J., Dougherty, R. F., & Wandell, B. A. (2013). Human trichromacy revisited. *PNAS: Proceedings of the National Academy of Sciences of the United States of America, 110,* E260–E269. doi:10.1073/pnas.1214240110

Horn, J. L. (1982). The aging of human abilities. In B. B. Wolman (Ed.), *Handbook of developmental psychology* (pp. 847–870). Englewood Cliffs, NJ: Prentice-Hall.

Horn, J. L., Donaldson, G., & Engstrom, R. (1981). Apprehension, memory, and fluid intelligence decline through the "vital years" of adulthood. *Research on Aging, 3,* 33–84.

Hornboll, B., Macoveanu, J., Rowe, J., Elliott, R., Paulson, O. B., Siebner, H. R., & Knudsen, G. M. (2013). Acute serotonin 2A receptor blocking alters the processing of fearful faces in the orbitofrontal cortex and amygdala. *Journal of Psychopharmacology, 27,* 903–914.

Horne, J. A., & Staff, L. H. E. (1983). Exercise and sleep: Body-heating effects. *Sleep, 6,* 36–46.

Horney, K. (1937). *The neurotic personality of our time.* New York: Norton.

Horney, K. (1939). *New ways in psychoanalysis.* New York: Norton.

Hornyak, M., Feige, B., Riemann, D., & Voderholzer, U. (2006). Periodic leg movements in sleep and periodic limb movement disorder: Prevalence, clinical significance and treatment. *Sleep Medicine Reviews, 10,* 169–177.

Hosking, S. G., Young, K. L., & Regan, M. A. (2009). The effects of text messaging on young drivers. *Human Factors, 51,* 582–592.

Hovey, J. D. (2000). Psychosocial predictors of depression among Central American immigrants. *Psychological Reports, 86,* 1237–1240.

Hovland, C. I., & Weiss, W. (1951). The influence of source credibility on communication effectiveness. *Public Opinion Quarterly, 15,* 635–650.

Howe, M. L. (2000). *The rate of early memories.* Washington, DC: American Psychological Association.

Howe, N., & Strauss, B. (1993). *13th gen: Abort, retry, ignore, fail?* New York: Vintage Press.

Howell, M. R., Kassler, W. J., & Haddix, A. (1997). Partner notification to prevent pelvic inflammatory disease in women: Cost effectiveness of two strategies. *Sexually Transmitted Diseases, 24,* 287–292.

Howes, O. D., & Kapur, S. (2009). The dopamine hypothesis of schizophrenia: Version III—the final common pathway. *Schizophrenia Bulletin, 35,* 549–562.

Howland, J., Rohsenow, D. J., Arnedt, J. T., Bliss, C. A., Hunt, S. K., Calise, T. V. et al. (2011). The acute effects of caffeinated versus non-caffeinated alcoholic beverage on driving performance and attention/reaction time. *Addiction, 106,* 335–341.

Hoyert, D. L., Heron, M. P., Murphy, S. L., & Kung, H. (2006). Deaths: Final data for 2003. *National Vital Statistics Report, 54,* 1–120.

Hoyland, A., Dye, L., & Lawton, C. L. (2009). A systematic review of the effect of breakfast on the cognitive performance of children and adolescents. *Nutrition Research Reviews, 22,* 220–243.

Hsiung, R. C. (2001). Suggested principles of professional ethics for the online provision of mental health services. *Medinfo, 10,* 296–300.

Hu, J., Chiang, L. Y., Koch, M., & Lewin, G. R. (2010). Evidence for a protein tether involved in somatic touch. *EMBO Journal, 29,* 855–867. doi:10.1038/emboj.2009.398

Huang, C. J., Webb, H. E., Zourdos, M. C., & Acevedo, E. O. (2013). Cardiovascular reactivity, stress, and physical activity. *Frontiers in Physiology, 4,* 314.

Huang, Y., Kotov, R., de Girolamo, G., Preti, A., Angermeyer, M., Benjet, C. et al. (2009). DSM-IV personality disorders in the WHO World Mental Health Surveys. *British Journal of Psychiatry, 195,* 46–53.

Hubel, D. H. (1995). *Eye, brain, and vision.* New York: Scientific American Library.

Huber, D., Henrich, G., & Gündel, H. (2005). Psychophysiological response patterns of migraine patients in two habituation tests. *Headache: The Journal of Head and Face Pain, 45,* 1375–1387.

Huddleston, J., & Ge, X. (2003). Boys at puberty: Psychosocial implications. In C. Hayward (Ed.), *Gender differences at puberty* (pp. 113–134). New York: Cambridge University Press.

Hudson, A. J. (2009). Consciousness: Physiological dependence on rapid memory access. *Frontiers in Bioscience, 14,* 2779–2800.

Hudson, S., & Ramsey, J. (2011). The emergence and analysis of synthetic cannabinoids. *Drug Testing & Analysis, 3,* 466–478.

Huesmann, L. R. (Ed.). (1994). *Aggressive behavior: Current perspectives.* New York: Plenum Press.

Huff, N. C., Hernandez, J. A., Blanding, N. Q., & LaBar, K. S. (2009). Delayed extinction attenuates conditioned fear renewal and spontaneous recovery in humans. *Behavioral Neuroscience, 123,* 834–843.

Huff, W., Lenartz, D., Schormann, M., Lee, S. H., Kuhn, J., Koulousakis, A. et al. (2010). Unilateral deep brain stimulation of the nucleus accumbens in patients with treatment-resistant obsessive-compulsive disorder: Outcomes after one year. *Clinical Neurology and Neurosurgery, 112,* 137–143.

Huffcutt, A. I., & Arthur, W., Jr. (1994). Hunter and Hunter (1984) revisited: Interview validity for entry-level jobs. *Journal of Applied Psychology, 79,* 184–190.

Huffziger, S., Reinhard, I., & Kuehner, C. (2009). A longitudinal study of rumination and distraction in formerly depressed inpatients and community controls. *Journal of Abnormal Psychology, 118,* 746–756.

Hughes, D. J., Furnham, A., & Batey, M. (2013). The structure and personality predictors of self-rated creativity. *Thinking Skills and Creativity, 9,* 76–84. doi:10.1016/j.tsc.2012.10.001

Hughes, J., Smith, T. W., Kosterlitz, H. W., Fothergill, L. A., Morgan, B. A., & Morris, H. R. (1975). Identification of two related pentapeptides from the brain with potent opiate agonist activity. *Nature, 258,* 577–579.

Hughes, J. W., Fresco, D. M., Myerscough, R., van Dulmen, M. H., Carlson, L. E., & Josephson, R. (2013). Randomized controlled trial of mindfulness-based stress reduction for prehypertension. *Psychosomatic Medicine, 75,* 721–728.

Hughes, M. E., & Waite, L. J. (2009). Marital biography and health at mid-life. *Journal of Health and Social Behavior, 50,* 344–358.

Hughes, Z. A., Liu, F., Marquis, K., Muniz, L., Pangalos, M. N., Ring, R. H. et al. (2009). Estrogen receptor neurobiology and its potential for translation into broad spectrum therapeutics for CNS Disorders. *Current Molecular Pharmacology, 2,* 215–236.

Hulbert, A. (2003). Colour vision: Primary visual cortex shows its influence. *Current Biology, 13,* R270–R272.

Hull, C. L. (1943). *Principles of behavior.* New York: Appleton-Century-Crofts.

Hummel, M., & Unterwald, E. M. (2002). D1 dopamine receptor: A putative neurochemical and behavioral link to cocaine action. *Journal of Cell Physiology, 191,* 17–27.

Humphreys, K., Winzelberg, A., & Klaw, E. (2000). Psychologists' ethical responsibilities in Internet-based groups: Issues, strategies, and a call for dialogue. *Professional Psychology, Research, and Practice, 31,* 493–496.

Hunt, R. R. (2002). How effective are pharmacologic agents for alcoholism? *Journal of Family Practice, 51,* 577.

Hunter, E. C., Sierra, M., & David, A. S. (2004). The epidemiology of personalization and derealisation: A systematic review. *Social Psychiatry and Psychiatric Epidemiology, 39,* 9–18.

Hupp, J. M., Smith, J. L., Coleman, J. M., & Brunell, A. B. (2010). That's a boy's toy: Gender-typed knowledge in toddlers as a function of mother's marital status. *Journal of Genetic Psychology, 171,* 389–401.

Hurlstone, M. J., Hitch, G. J., & Baddeley, A. D. (2014). Memory for serial order across domains: An overview of the literature and directions for future research. *Psychological Bulletin, 140,* 339–373. doi:10.1037/a0034221

Hurt, H., Brodsky, N. L., Roth, H., Malmud, E., & Giannetta, J. M. (2005). School performance of children with gestational cocaine exposure. *Neurotoxicology and Teratology, 27,* 203–211.

Hurvich, L. M., & Jameson, D. (2000). An opponent-process theory of color vision. In S. Yantis (Ed.), *Visual perception: Essential readings* (pp. 129–144). New York: Psychology Press. (Original work published 1957)

Huston, A. C., & Wright, J. C. (1998). Mass media and children's development. In W. Damon (Series Ed.), *Handbook of child psychology* (Vol. 4, pp. 999–1058). New York: Wiley.

Huttenlocher, P. R. (2002). *Neural plasticity: The effects of environment on the development of the cerebral cortex.* Cambridge, MA: Harvard University Press.

Hyde, J. S., & McKinley, N. M. (1997). Gender differences in cognition: Results from meta-analyses. In P. J. Caplan, M. Crawford, J. S. Hyde, & J. T. E. Richardson (Eds.), *Gender differences in human cognition* (pp. 30–51). New York: Oxford University Press.

Hyde, J. S., Fenneman, E., & Lamon, S. (1990). Gender differences in mathematics performance: A meta-analysis. *Psychological Bulletin, 107,* 139–155.

Hyland, P., Shevlin, M., Adamson, G., & Boduszek, D. (2014). The organization of irrational beliefs in posttraumatic stress symptomology: Testing the predictions of REBT theory using structural equation modelling. *Journal of Clinical Psychology, 70,* 48–59.

Hyman, S. E., & Rudorfer, M. V. (2000). Anxiety disorders. In D. C. Dale & D. D. Federman (Eds.), *Scientific American medicine* (Vol. 3). New York: Healtheon/WebMD Corp.

Iervolino, A. C., Perroud, N., Rullana, M. A., Guipponi, M., Cherkas, L., Collier, D. A., & Mataix-Cols, D. (2009). Prevalence and heritability of compulsive hoarding: A twin study. *American Journal of Psychiatry, 166,* 1156–1161.

Igarashi, H., Hooker, K., Coehlo, & Manoogian, M. M. (2013). "My nest is full": Intergenerational relationships at midlife. *Journal of Aging Studies, 27,* 102–112.

Iidaka, T., Anderson, N. D., Kapur, S., Cabeza, S., & Craik, F. I. M. (2000). The effect of divided attention on encoding and retrieval in episodic memory revealed by positron emission tomography. *Journal of Cognitive Neuroscience, 12,* 267.

Ikonomidou, C., Bittigau, P., Ishimaru, M. J., Wozniak, D. F., Koch, C., Genz, K. et al. (2000). Ethanol-induced apoptotic neurodegeneration and fetal alcohol syndrome. *Science, 287,* 1056–1060.

Ilgen, M. A., & Hutchison, K. E. (2005). A history of major depressive disorder and the response to stress. *Journal of Affective Disorders, 86,* 143–150.

Inciardi, J. A., Surratt, H. L., & Saum, C. A. (1997). *Cocaine-exposed infants: Social legal, and public health issues.* Thousand Oaks, CA: Sage.

Ineichen, B. (1979). The social geography of marriage. In M. Cook & G. Wilson (Eds.), *Love and attraction* (pp. 145–149). New York: Pergamon Press.

Infante-Rivard, C., Fernandez, A., Gauthier, R., David, M., & Rivard, G. E. (1993). Fetal loss associated with caffeine intake before and during pregnancy. *Journal of the American Medical Association, 270,* 2940–2943.

Inglehart, R. Foa, R., Peterson, C., & Welzel, C. (2008). Development, freedom, and rising happiness: A global perspective (1981–2007). *Perspectives on Psychological Science, 3,* 264–285.

Ingram, R. E., Hayes, A., & Scott, W. (2000). Empirically supported treatments: A critical analysis. In C. R. Snyder & R. E. Ingram (Eds.), *Handbook of psychological change: Psychotherapy processes and practices for the 21st century* (pp. 40–60). New York: Wiley.

Innes, C. R., Poudel, G. R., & Jones, R. D. (2013). Efficient and regular patterns of nighttime sleep are related to increased vulnerability to microsleeps following a single night of sleep restriction. *Chronobiology International, 30,* 1187–1196.

Innis, N. K. (1979). Stimulus control of behavior during postreinforcement pause of FI schedules. *Animal Learning and Behavior, 7,* 203–210.

Inostroza, M., & Born, J. (2013). Sleep for preserving and transforming episodic memory. *Annual Review of Neuroscience, 36,* 79–102.

Insel, T., Cuthbert, B., Garvey, M., Heinssen, R., Pine, D., Quinn, K. et al. (2010). Research domain criteria (RDoC): Toward a new classification framework for research on mental disorders. *American Journal of Psychiatry, 167,* 748–751.

Inzlicht , M., & Tullett, A. M. (2010). Reflecting on God: Religious primes can reduce neurophysiological response to errors. *Psychological Science, 21,* 1184–1190.

Inzlicht, M., & Ben-Zeev, T. (2000). A threatening intellectual environment: Why females are susceptible to experiencing problem-solving deficits in the presence of males. *Psychological Science, 11,* 365–371.

Irwin, M., Clark, C., Kennedy, B., Christian Gillin, J., & Ziegler, M. (2003). Nocturnal catecholamines and immune function in insomniacs, depressed patients, and control subjects. *Brain, Behavior, and Immunity, 17,* 365–372.

Irwin, M., McClintick, J., Costlow, C., Fortner, M., White, J., & Gillin, J. C. (1996). Partial night sleep deprivation reduces natural killer and cellular immune responses in humans. *Journal of the Federation of American Societies for Experimental Biology, 10,* 643–653.

Isa, M. R., Moy, F. M., Abdul Razack, A. H., Zainuddin, Z. M., & Zainal, N. Z. (2013). Impact of applied progressive deep muscle relation training on the level of depression, anxiety and stress among prostate cancer patients: A quasi-experimental study. *Asian Pacific Journal of Cancer Research, 14,* 2237–2242.

Isaac, M., & Chand, P. K. (2006). Dissociative and conversion disorders: Defining boundaries. *Current Opinion in Psychiatry, 19,* 61–66.

Isenberg, N., Silbersweig, D., Engelien, A., Emmerich, S., Malavade, K., Beattie, B. et al. (1999). Linguistic threat activates the human amygdala. *Proceedings of the National Academy of Sciences, USA, 96,* 10456–10459.

Iso, H., Simoda, S., & Matsuyama, T. (2006). Environmental change during postnatal development alters behavior, cognitions, and neurogenesis of mice. *Behavioural Brain Research, 179,* 90–98.

Iverson, L. (2003). Cannabis and the brain. *Brain, 126,* 1252–1270.

Izac, S. M. (2006). Basic anatomy and physiology of sleep. *American Journal of Electroneurodiagnostic Technology, 46,* 18–38.

Jablensky, A. (2000). Epidemiology of schizophrenia: The global burden of disease and disability. *European Archives of Psychiatry and Clinical Neuroscience, 250,* 274–285.

Jablensky, A. (2002). The classification of personality disorders: Critical review and need for rethinking. *Psychopathology, 35,* 112–116.

Jablin, F. M. (1982). Organizational communication: An assimilation approach. In M. E. Rolff & C. R. Berger (Eds.), *Social cognition and communication* (pp. 255–286). Beverly Hills, CA: Sage.

Jackson, J. L., Thoemmes, F., Jonkmann, K., Ludtke, O., & Trautwein, U. (2012). Military training and personality trait development: Does the military make the man, or does the man make the military? *Psychological Science, 23,* 270–277.

Jackson, S., & Blake, R. (2010). Neural integration of information specifying human structure from form, motion, and depth. *Journal of Neuroscience, 30,* 838–848.

Jacobs, B. L. (2004). Depression: The brain finally gets into the act. *Current Directions in Psychological Science, 13,* 103–106.

Jacobs, B. L., van Praag, H., & Gage, F. H. (2000). Adult brain neurogenesis and psychiatry: A novel theory of depression. *Molecular Psychiatry, 5,* 262–269.

Jacobs, L. F., & Hyman, J. S. (2013). *The secrets of college success.* 2nd ed. San Francisco: Jossey-Bass.

Jakobsen, J. C., Hansen, J. L., Simonsen, E., & Gluud, C. (2012). The effect of adding psychodynamic therapy to antidepressants in patients with major depressive disorder: A systematic review of randomized clinical trials with meta-analyses and trial sequential analyses. *Journal of Affective Disorders, 137,* 4–14.

Jacobsen, T., & Hofmann, V. (1997). Children's attachment representations: Longitudinal relations to school behavior and academic competency in middle childhood and adolescence. *Developmental Psychology, 33,* 701–710.

Jacoby, L. L., Debner, J. A., & Hay, J. F. (2001). Proactive interference, accessibility bias, and process dissociations: Valid subjective reports of memory. *Journal of Experimental Psychology: Learning, Memory, and Cognition, 27,* 686–700.

Jadack, R. A., Hyde, J. S., Moore, C. F., & Keller, M. L. (1995). Moral reasoning about sexually transmitted diseases. *Child Development, 66,* 167–177.

Jaffari-Bimmel, N., Juffer, F., van Ijzendoorn, M. H., Bakermans-Kranenburg, M. J., & Mooijaart, A. (2006). Social development from infancy to adolescence: Longitudinal and concurrent factors in an adoption sample. *Developmental Psychology, 42,* 1143–1153.

Jaffee, S., & Hyde, J. (2000). Gender differences in moral orientation: A meta-analysis. *Psychological Bulletin, 126,* 703–726.

Jaint, N., Verma, P., Mittal, S., Singh, A. K., & Munjal, S. (2010). Gender based alteration in color perception. *Indian Journal of Physiological Pharmacology, 54,* 366–370.

Jakobsen, J. C., Hansen, J. L., Simonsen, E., & Gluud, C. (2012). The effect of adding psychodynamic therapy to antidepressants in patients with major depressive disorder: A systematic review of randomized clinical trials with meta-analyses and trial sequential analyses. *Journal of Affective Disorders, 137,* 4–14.

James, W. (1884). What is an emotion? *Mind, 9,* 188–205.

James, W. (1890). *The principles of psychology.* New York: Holt.

Jamieson, J. P., Mendes, W. B., & Nock, M. K. (2013). Improving acute stress responses: The power of reappraisal. *Current Directions in Psychological Science, 22,* 51–56.

Jäncke, L., & Steinmetz, H. (2003). Brain size: A possible source of interindividual variability on corpus callosum morphology. In E. Zaidel & M. Iacobini (Eds.), *The parallel brain: The cognitive neuroscience of the corpus callosum* (pp. 51–63). Cambridge, MA: MIT Press.

Jane, J. S., Oltmanns, T. F., South, S. C., & Turkheimer, E. (2007). Gender bias in diagnostic criteria for personality disorders: An item response theory analysis. *Journal of Abnormal Psychology, 116,* 166–175.

Janis, I. L. (1982). *Victims of groupthink* (2nd ed.). Boston: Houghton Mifflin.

Janis, I. L. (1985). Sources of error in strategic decision making. In J. M. Pennings (Ed.), *Organizational strategy and change* (pp. 157–197). San Francisco: Jossey-Bass.

Janis, I. L. (2007). Groupthink. In R. P. Vecchio (Ed.), *Leadership: Understanding the dynamics of power and influence in organizations* (2nd ed., pp. 157–169). Notre Dame, IN: University of Notre Dame Press.

Janoff-Bulman, R. (1992). *Shattered assumptions: Toward a new psychology of trauma.* New York: Maxwell Macmillan International.

Janowitz, H., & Grossman, M. (1950). Hunger and appetite: Some definitions and concepts. *Journal of Mount Sinai Hospital, 16,* 231–240.

Jaremka, L. M., Fagundes, C. P., Peng, J., Bennett, J. M., Glaser, R., Malarkey, W. B., & Kiecolt-Glaser, J. K. (2013). Loneliness promotes inflammation during acute stress. *Psychological Science, 24,* 1089–1097.

Jarrett, R. B., Kraft, D., Doyle, J., Foster, B. M., Eaves, G. G., & Silver, P. C. (2001). Preventing recurrent depression using cognitive therapy with and without a continuation phase. *Archives of General Psychiatry, 58,* 381–388.

Javitt, D. C. (2007). Glutamate and schizophrenia: Phencyclidine, N-Methyl-d-aspartate receptors, and dopamine-glutamate interactions. *International Review of Neurobiology, 78,* 69–108.

Jedrziewski, M. K., Ewbank, D. C., Wang, H., & Trojanowski, J. Q. (2010). Exercise and cognition: Results from the national Long Term Care Survey. *Alzheimer's and Dementia: The Journal of the Alzheimer's Association, 6,* 448–455.

Jemmott, J. B., III, Borysenko, M., McClelland, D. C., Chapman, R., & Benson, H. (1985). Academic stress, power motivation, and decrease in salivary secretory immunoglobulin: A secretion rate. *Lancet, 1,* 1400–1402.

Jenkins, J. M., & Astington, J. W. (1996). Cognitive factors and family structure associated with theory of mind development in young children. *Developmental Psychology, 32,* 70–78.

Jenni, O. G., Achermann, P., & Carskadon, M. A. (2005). Homeostatic sleep regulation in adolescents. *Sleep, 28,* 1446–1454.

Jennings, J. R., Monk, T. H., & van der Molen, M. W. (2003). Sleep deprivation influences some but not all processes of supervisory attention. *Psychological Science, 14,* 473–479.

Jensen, M. P., Ehde, D. M., Gertz, K. J., Stoelb, B. L., Dillworth, T. M., Hirsh, A. T. et al. (2011). Effects of self-hypnosis training and cognitive restructuring on daily pain intensity and catastrophizing in individuals with multiple sclerosis and chronic pain. *International Journal of Clinical and Experimental Hypnosis, 59,* 45–63.

Jeste, D. V. (2004). Tardive dyskinesia rates with atypical antipsychotics in older adults. *Journal of Clinical Psychiatry, 65,* 21–24.

Jiang, J., Schmajuk, N., & Egner, T. (2012). Explaining neural signals in human visual cortex with an associative learning model. *Behavioral Neuroscience, 126,* 575–581. doi:10.1037/a0029029

Jobe, T. H., & Harrow, M. (2010). Schizophrenia course, long-term outcome, recovery, and prognosis. *Current Directions in Psychological Science, 19,* 220–225.

Jobin, J., Wrosch, C., & Scheier, M. F. (2014). Associations between dispositional optimism and diurnal cortisol in a community sample: When stress is perceived as higher than normal. *Health Psychology, 33,* 382–391.

Johnson, B. A. (2008). Update on neuropharmacological treatments for alcoholism: Scientific basis and clinical findings. *Biochemical Pharmacology, 75,* 34–56.

Johnson, J. A. (1997). Units of analysis for the description and explanation of personality. In R. Hogan, J. Johnson, & S. Briggs (Eds.), *Handbook of personality psychology* (pp. 3–93). New York: Academic Press.

Johnson, M. K., Hashtroudi, S., & Lindsay, D. S. (1993). Source monitoring. *Psychological Bulletin, 114,* 3–28.

Johnson, S. M., & Williams-Keeler, L. (1998). Creating healing relationships for couples dealing with trauma: The use of emotionally focused marital therapy. *Journal of Marital and Family Therapy, 24,* 25–40.

Johnson, W., Turkheimer, E., Gottesman, I. I., & Bouchard, T. J., Jr. (2009). Beyond heritability: Twin studies in behavioral research. *Current Directions in Psychological Science, 18,* 217–220.

John-Steiner, V., & Mahn, H. (1996). Sociocultural approaches to learning and development: A Vygotskian framework. *Educational Psychologist, 31,* 191–206.

Johnston, L. D., Bachman, J. G., & O'Malley, P. M. (2013). *Monitoring the future: Questionnaire responses from the nation's high school seniors, 2011.* Ann Arbor, MI: Institute for Social Research.

Johnston, L. D., O'Malley, P. M., Bachman, J. G., & Schulenberg, J. E. (2013). *Monitoring the future: National results on drug use; 2012 overview, key findings on adolescent drug use.* Ann Arbor: Institute for Social Research, University of Michigan.

Johnston, L. D., O'Malley, P. M., Bachman, J. G., & Schulenberg, J. E. (2013, December 18). *American teens more cautious about using synthetic drugs.* University of Michigan News Service: Ann Arbor, MI. Retrieved from http://www.monitoringthefuture.org

Johnston, L. D., O'Malley, P. M., Bachman, J. G., & Schulenberg, J. E. (2009a). *Monitoring the future: National results on adolescent drug use; Overview of key findings, 2008* (NIH Publication No. 09-7401). Bethesda, MD: National Institute on Drug Abuse.

Johnston, L. D., O'Malley, P. M., Bachman, J. G., & Schulenberg, J. E. (2009b, December 14). *Teen marijuana use tilts up, while some drugs decline in use.* Ann Arbor: University of Michigan News Service. Retrieved from www.monitoringthefuture.org

Joiner, T. (2010). *Myths about suicide.* Cambridge, MA: Harvard University Press.

Jolicoeur, P., & Kosslyn, S. M. (1985). Demand characteristics in image scanning experiments. *Journal of Mental Imagery, 9,* 41–49.

Joliot, A. E. (2001). A comparative study of body image satisfaction and attitudes among American, Israeli, Spanish, and Brazilian college women (United States). *Dissertation Abstracts International: B. The Physical Sciences and Engineering, 61,* 55–67.

Jonason, P. K. (2009). The value of physical attractiveness in romantic partners: Modeling biological and social variables. *Journal of Social Psychology, 149,* 229–240.

Jones, E. E. (1979). The rocky road from acts to dispositions. *American Psychologist, 34,* 107–117.

Jones, E. E., & Nesbitt, R. E. (1971). *The actor and the observer: Divergent perceptions of the causes of behavior.* Morristown, NJ: General Learning Press.

Jones, M. C. (1924). A laboratory study of fear: The case of Peter. *Pedagogical Seminary, 31,* 308–315.

Jones, N. P., Papadakis, A. A., Hogan, C. M., & Strauman, T. J. (2009). Over and over again: Rumination, reflection, and promotion goal failure and their interactive effects on depressive symptoms. *Behaviour Research & Therapy, 47,* 254–259.

Jones, S. A., & Wilson, A. E. (2009). The horizon line, linear perspective, interposition, and background brightness as determinants of the magnitude of the pictorial moon illusion. *Attention, Perception, & Psychophysics, 71,* 131–142.

Jones, S., & Dindia, K. (2004). A meta-analytic perspective on sex equity in the classroom. *Review of Educational Research, 74,* 443–471.

Jones, S., Casswell, S., & Zhang, J. F. (1995). The economic costs of alcohol-related absenteeism and reduced productivity among the working population of New Zealand. *Addiction, 90,* 1455–1461.

Jonsson, E. G., Burgert, E., Crocq, M. A., Gustavsson, J. P., Forslund, K., Mattila-Evenden, M. et al. (2003). Association study between dopamine D3 receptor gene variant and personality traits. *American Journal of Medical Genetics, 117B,* 61–65.

Joormann, J. (2010). Cognitive inhibition and emotion regulation in depression. *Current Directions in Psychological Science, 19,* 161–166.

Joormann, J., Levens, S. M., & Gotlib, I. H. (2011). Sticky thoughts: Depressions and rumination are associated with difficulties manipulating emotional material in working memory. *Psychological Science, 22,* 979–983.

Jordan, A. S., & McEvoy, R. D. (2003). Gender differences in sleep apnea: Epidemiology, clinical presentation and pathogenic mechanisms. *Sleep Medical Review, 7,* 377–389.

Jordan, G., Deeb, S. S., Bosten, J. M., & Mollon, J. D. (2010). The dimensionality of color vision in carriers of anomalous trichromacy. *Journal of Vision, 10,* 12. doi: 10.1167/10.8.12

Jordan, K. D., Masters, K. S., Hooker, S. A., Ruiz, J. M., & Smith, T. W. (in press). An interpersonal approach to religiousness and spirituality: Implications for health and well-being. *Journal of Personality.*

Jorgensen, C. H., Pedersen, B., & Tonnesen, H. (2011). The efficacy of disulfiram for the treatment of alcohol use disorder. *Alcoholism, Clinical and Experimental Research, 35,* 1749–1758.

Jorgensen, G. (2006). Kohlberg and Gilligan: Duet or duel? *Journal of Moral Education, 35,* 179–196.

Joseph, J. E., Liu, X., Jiang, Y., Lynam, D., & Kelly, T. H. (2009). Neural correlates of emotional reactivity in sensation seeking. *Psychological Science, 20,* 215–223.

Joule R.-V., & Azdia, T. (2003). Cognitive dissonance, double forced compliance, and commitment. *European Journal of Social Psychology, 33,* 565–571.

Judge, T. A., Thoresen, C. J., Bono, J. E., & Patton, G. K. (2001). The job satisfaction-job performance relationship: A qualitative and quantitative review. *Psychological Bulletin, 127,* 376–407.

Julien, R. M. (1995). *A primer of drug action.* San Francisco: Freeman.

Jung, C. G. (1967). The psychology of the unconscious. In H. Read, M. Fordham, & G. Adler (Eds.), *Collected works of C. G. Jung* (Vol. 7). Princeton, NJ: Princeton University Press. (Original work published 1917)

Junker, A., Hohlfeld, R., & Meinl, E. (2011). The emerging role of microRNAs in multiple sclerosis. *Nature Reviews: Neurology, 7,* 56–59. doi:10.1038/nrneurol.2010.179

Kahn, D. A. (1995). New strategies in bipolar disorder: Part II. Treatment. *Journal of Practical Psychiatry and Behavioral Health, 3,* 148–157.

Kahneman, D., & Tversky, A. (1973). On the psychology of prediction. *Psychological Review, 80,* 237–251.

Kahneman, D., & Tversky, A. (1984). Choices, values, and frames. *American Psychologist, 39,* 341–350.

Kahol, K., Leyba, M. J., Deka, M., Deka, V., Mayes, S., Smith, M. et al. (2008). Effect of fatigue on psychomotor and cognitive skills. *American Journal of Surgery, 195,* 195–204.

Kaiser Family Foundation. (2006). *Media violence and children.* Retrieved from http://actagainstviolence.apa.org/mediaviolence/index.html

Kajantie, E., & Phillips, D. I. (2006). The effects of sex and hormonal status on the physiological response to acute psychosocial stress. *Psychoneuroendocrinology, 31,* 151–178.

Kako, E. (1999). Elements of syntax in the systems of three language-trained animals. *Animal Learning and Behavior, 27,* 1–14.

Kalish, R. A. (1985). The social context of death and dying. In R. H. Binstock & E. Shanas (Eds.), *Handbook of aging and the social sciences* (2nd ed., pp. 149–170). New York: Van Nostrand Reinhold.

Kandel, D. B. (1978). Similarity in real-life adolescent friendship pairs. *Journal of Personality and Social Psychology, 36,* 306–312.

Kanny, D., Liu, Y., & Brewer, R. D. (2011). Binge drinking—United States, 2009. *Morbidity and Mortality Weekly, 60,* 101–104.

Kanoy, K., Ulku-Steiner, B., Cox, M., & Burchinal, M. (2003). Marital relationship and individual psychological characteristics that predict physical punishment of children. *Journal of Family Psychology, 17,* 20–28.

Kanwisher, N. (2003). The ventral visual pathway in humans: Evidence from fMRI. In L. M. Chalupa & J. S. Werner (Eds.), *The visual neuroscience* (pp. 1179–1190). Cambridge, MA: MIT Press.

Kaplan, C. A., & Simon, H. A. (1990). In search of insight. *Cognitive Psychology, 22,* 374–419.

Kaplan, D. A. (2010, January 22). SAS: A new no. 1 best employer. *Fortune.* http://money.cnn.com/2010/01/21/technology/sas_best_companies.fortune

Kaplan, R. E., Drath, W. H., & Kofodimos, J. R. (1991). *Beyond ambition: How driven managers can lead better and live better.* San Francisco: Jossey-Bass.

Kaplan, R. M. (2007). Should Medicare reimburse providers for weight loss interventions? *American Psychologist, 62,* 217–219.

Kaplan, R. M., & Saccuzzo, D. P. (1989). *Psychological testing: Principles, applications, and issues.* Pacific Grove, CA: Brooks/Cole.

Kaplowitz, P. B., Oberfield, S. E., & the Drug and Therapeutics and Executive Committees of the Lawson Wilkins Pediatric Endocrine Society. (1999). Reexamination of the age limit for defining when puberty is precocious in girls in the United States: Implications for evaluation and treatment. *Pediatrics, 104,* 936–941.

Kapur, S., Craik, F. I. M., Tulving, E., Wilson, A. A., Houle, S., & Brown, G. M. (1994). Neuroanatomical correlates of encoding in episodic memory. *Proceedings of the National Academy of Science, USA, 91,* 2008–2011.

Karch, D. L., Dahlberg, L. L., Patel, N., Davis, T. W., Logan, J. E., Hill, H. A. et al. (2009). Surveillance for violent deaths: National violent death reporting system, 16 states, 2006. *Morbidity & Mortality Weekly Reports: Surveillance Summaries, 58,* 1–44.

Karlsgodt, K. H., Sun, D., & Cannon, T. D. (2010). Structural and functional brain abnormalities in schizophrenia. *Current Directions in Psychological Science, 19,* 226–231.

Karney, B. R., & Bradbury, T. N. (2005). Contextual influences on marriage: Implications for policy and intervention. *Current Directions in Psychological Science, 14,* 171–174.

Karni, A., Tanne, D., Rubenstein, B. S., Askenasy, J. J. M., & Sagi, D. (1994). Dependence on REM sleep of overnight improvement of a perceptual skill. *Science, 265,* 679–682.

Kaskutas, L. A. (2009). Alcoholics anonymous effectiveness: Faith meets science. *Journal of Addictive Diseases, 28,* 145–157.

Kaslow, F. W., Hansson, K., & Lundblad, A. (1994). Long-term marriages in Sweden: And some comparisons with similar couples in the United States. *Contemporary Family Therapy, 16,* 521–537.

Katigbak, M. S., Church, A. T., Guanzon-Lapena, M. A., Carlota, A. J., & del Pilar, G. H. (2002). Are indigenous personality dimensions culture specific? Philippine inventories and the Five-Factor model. *Journal of Personality and Social Psychology, 82,* 89–101.

Katz-Wise, S. L., Priess, H. A., & Hyde, J. S. (2010). Gender-role attitudes and behavior across the transition to parenthood. *Developmental Psychology, 46,* 18–28.

Kaufman, A. S., Kaufman, J. C., Liu, X., & Johnson, C. K. (2009). How do educational attainment and gender relate to fluid intelligence, crystallized intelligence, and academic skills at ages 22–90 years? *Archives of Clinical Neuropsychology, 24,* 153–163.

Kaufman, L., & Rock, L. (1989). The moon illusion thirty years later. In M. Hershenson (Ed.), *The moon illusion* (pp. 193–234). Hillsdale, NJ: Erlbaum.

Kavushansky, A., Kritman, M., Maroun, M., Klein, E., Richter-Levin, G., Hui, K., & Ben-Shachar, D. (2013). β-endorphin degradation and the individual reactivity to traumatic stress. *European Neuropsychopharmacology, 23,* 1779–1788. doi:10.1016/j.euroneuro.2012.12.003

Kawakami, N., Takeskima, T., Ono, Y., Uda, H., Hata, Y., Nakane, Y. et al. (2005). Twelve-month prevalence, severity, and treatment of common mental disorders in communities of Japan: Preliminary finding from the World Mental Health Survey 2002–2003. *Psychiatry and Clinical Neuroscience, 59,* 441–452.

Kazdin, A. E. (1977). *The token economy: A review and evaluation.* New York: Plenum Press.

Kazdin, A. E. (2013). *Behavior modification in applied settings.* Long Grove, IL: Waveland Press.

Kazdin, A. E., & Blase, S. L. (2011). Rebooting psychotherapy research and practice to reduce the burden of mental illness. *Perspectives on Psychological Science, 6,* 21–37.

Keck, P. E., Jr., & McElroy, S. L. (2002). Carbamazepine and valproate in the maintenance treatment of bipolar disorder. *Journal of Clinical Psychiatry, 63,* 13–17.

Keck, P. E., Jr., McElroy, S. L., & Arnold, L. M. (2001). Bipolar disorder. *Medical Clinics of North America, 85,* 645–661.

Keel, P. K., & Klump, K. L. (2003). Are eating disorders culture-bound syndromes? Implications for conceptualizing their etiology. *Psychological Bulletin, 129,* 747–769.

Keller, C. (2001). Effect of teachers' stereotyping on students' stereotyping of mathematics as a male domain. *Journal of Social Psychology, 141,* 165–173.

Keller, J. (2007). Stereotype threat in classroom settings: The interactive effect of domain identification, task difficulty and stereotype threat on female students' math performance. *British Journal of Educational Psychology, 77,* 323–338. doi:10.1348/000709906X113662

Keller, J., & Dauenheimer, D. (2003). Stereotype threat in the classroom: Dejection mediates the disrupting threat effect of women's math performance. *Personality and Social Psychology Bulletin, 29,* 371–381.

Kellner, C. H., Knapp, R., Husain, M. M. Rasmussen, K., Sampson, S., Cullum, M., et al. (2010). Bifrontal, bitemporal and right unilateral electrode placement in ECT: A randomised trial. *British Journal of Psychiatry, 196,* 226–234.

Kelly, D. J., Ge, L., Liu, S., Quinn, P. C., Slater, A. M., Lee, K. et al. (2007). Cross-race preferences for same-race faces extend beyond the African versus Caucasian contrast in 3-month-old infants. *Infancy, 11,* 87–95.

Kelly, M. M., & Forsyth, J. P. (2007). Observational fear conditioning in the acquisition and extinction of attentional bias for threat: An experimental evaluation. *Emotion, 7,* 324–335.

Kelman, C. A. (2001). Egocentric language in deaf children. *American Annals of the Deaf, 146,* 276–279.

Kelsch, W., Sim, S., & Lois, C. (2010). Watching synaptogenesis in the adult brain. *Annual Review of Neuroscience, 33,* 131–149.

Kemeny, M. E. (2003). The psychobiology of stress. *Current Directions in Psychological Science, 12,* 124–129.

Kemp, M., Drummond, P., & McDermott, B. (2010). A wait-list controlled pilot study of eye movement desensitization and reprocessing (EMDR) for children with post-traumatic stress disorder (PTSD) symptoms from motor vehicle accidents. *Clinical Child Psychology and Psychiatry, 15,* 5–25.

Kenardy, J. A., Dow, M. G., Johnston, D. W., Newman, M. G., Thompson, A., & Taylor, C. B. (2003). A comparison of delivery methods of cognitive-behavioral therapy for panic disorder: An international multicenter trial. *Journal of Consulting and Clinical Psychology, 71,* 1068–1075.

Kendall, A. P., Kautz, M. A., Russo, M. B., & Killgore, W. D. (2006). Effects of sleep deprivation on lateral visual attention. *International Journal of Neuroscience, 116,* 1125–1138.

Kendler, K. S., McGuire, M., Gruenberg, A. M., & Walsh, D. (1994). Outcome and family study of the subtypes of schizophrenia in the west of Ireland. *American Journal of Psychiatry, 151,* 849–856.

Kennedy, K., & Hellmich, N. (2011). Medicare to pay for obesity prevention, *USA Today,* online http://usatoday30.usatoday.com/news/health/healthcare/story/2011-11-29/Medicare-to-pay-for-obesity-prevention/51478232/1

Kennedy, S. H., Konarski, J. Z., Segal, Z. V., Lau, M. A., Bieling, P. J., McIntyre, R. S. et al. (2007). Differences in brain glucose metabolism between responders to CBT and venlafaxine in a 16-week randomized controlled trial. *American Journal of Psychiatry, 164,* 778–788.

Kenrick, D. T., & Sheets, V. (1993). Homicidal fantasies. *Ethology and Sociobiology, 14,* 231–246.

Kenrick, D. T., Griskevicius, V., Neuberg, S. L., & Schaller, M. (2010). Renovating the pyramid of needs: Contemporary extensions built upon ancient foundations. *Perspectives on Psychological Science, 5,* 292–314.

Kerns, K. A., Abraham, M. M., Schlegelmilch, A., & Morgan, T. A. (2007). Mother-child attachment in later middle childhood: Assessment approaches and associations with mood and emotion regulation. *Attachment and Human Development, 9,* 33–53.

Kesebir, S., Graham, J., & Oishi, S. (2010). A theory of human needs should be human-centered: Commentary on Kenrick et al. (2010). *Perspectives on Psychological Science, 5,* 315–319.

Kessler, R. C., & Wang, P. S. (2009). The epidemiology of depression. In I. H. Gotlib & C. L. Hammen (Eds.), *Handbook of depression* (2nd ed., pp 5–22). New York: Guilford Press.

Kessler, R. C., Berglund, P. A., Demler, O., Jin, R., & Walters, E. E. (2005). Lifetime prevalence and age-of-onset distributions of DSM-IV disorders in the National Comorbidity Survey Replication (NCS-R). *Archives of General Psychiatry, 62,* 593–602.

Kessler, R. C., Berglund, P. A., Demler, O., Jin, R., Koretz, D., Merikangas, K. R. et al. (2003). The epidemiology of major depressive disorder. Results from the National Comorbidity Survey Replication (NCS-R). *Journal of the American Medical Association, 289,* 3095–3105.

Kessler, R. C., Chiu, W. T., Demler, O., & Walters, E. E. (2005). Prevalence, severity, and comorbidity of twelve-month DSM-IV disorders in the National Comorbidity Survey Replication (NCS-R). *Archives of General Psychiatry, 62,* 617–627.

Kessler, R. C., Chiu, W. T., Jin, R., Ruscio, A. M., Shear, K., & Walters, E. E. (2006). The epidemiology of panic attacks, panic disorder, and agoraphobia in the National Comorbidity Survey Replication. *Archives of General Psychiatry, 63,* 415–424.

Kessler, R. C., Ruscio, A. M., Shear, K., & Wittchen, H. U. (2010). Epidemiology of anxiety disorders. *Current Topics in Behavioral Neurosciences, 2,* 21–35.

Kessler, Y., & Meiran, N. (2006). All updateable objects in working memory are updated whenever any of them are modified: Evidence from the memory updating paradigm. *Journal of Experimental Psychology: Learning, Memory, and Cognition, 32,* 570–585.

Kety, S. S., Wender, P. H., Jacobsen, B., Ingraham, L. J., Jansson, L., Faber, B. et al. (1994). Mental illness in the biological and adoptive relative of schizophrenic adoptees: Replication of the Copenhagen study in the rest of Denmark. *Archives of General Psychiatry, 51,* 442–455.

Kibbe, M. M., & Leslie, A. M. (2011). What do infants remember when they forget? Location and identity in 6-month-olds' memory for objects. *Psychological Science, 22,* 1500–1505.

Kiecolt-Glaser, J. K. (2009). Psychoneuroimmunology: Psychology's gateway to the biomedical future. *Perspectives on Psychological Science, 4,* 367–369.

Kiecolt-Glaser, J. K., & Glaser, R. (1992). Psychoneuroimmunology: Can psychological interventions modulate immunity? *Journal of Consulting and Clinical Psychology, 60,* 569–575.

Kiecolt-Glaser, J. K., Bane, C., Glaser, R., & Malarkey, W. B. (2003). Love, marriage, and divorce: Newlywed's stress hormones foreshadow relationship changes. *Journal of Consulting and Clinical Psychology, 71,* 176–188.

Kiecolt-Glaser, J. K., Marucha, P. T., Malarkey, W. B., Mercado, A. M., & Glaser, R. (1995). Slowing of wound healing by psychological stress. *Lancet, 346,* 1194.

Kiecolt-Glaser, J. K., McGuire, L., Robles, T. F., & Glaser, R. (2002). Emotions, morbidity, and mortality: New perspectives from psychoneuroimmunology. *Annual Review of Psychology, 53,* 83–107.

Kiehl, K. A., Bates, A. T., Laurens, K. R., Hare, R. D., & Liddle, P. F. (2006). Brain potentials implicate temporal lobe abnormalities in criminal psychopaths. *Journal of Abnormal Psychology, 115,* 443–453.

Kieseppa, T., Partonen, T., Haukka, J., Kaprio, J., & Lonnqvist, J. (2004). High concordance of bipolar I disorder in a nationwide sample of twins. *American Journal of Psychiatry, 161,* 1814–1821.

Kihlstrom, J. F. (1993). The continuum of consciousness. *Consciousness and Cognition, 2,* 334–354.

Kihlstrom, J. F. (2001). Dissociative disorders. In H. E. Adams & P. B. Sutker (Eds.), *Comprehensive handbook of psychopathology* (pp. 259–276). New York: Academic/Plenum.

Kihlstrom, J. F. (2005). Dissociative disorders. *Annual Review of Clinical Psychology, 1,* 227–253.

Kihlstrom, J. F., Glisky, M. L., & Angiulo, M. J. (1994). Dissociative tendencies and dissociative disorders. *Journal of Abnormal Psychology, 103,* 117–124.

Kilbride, H. W., Castor, C. A., & Fuger, K. L. (2006). School-age outcome of children with prenatal cocaine exposure following early case management. *Journal of Developmental and Behavioral Pediatrics, 27,* 181–187.

Killen, M., Crystal, D. S., & Watanabe, H. (2002). Japanese and American children's evaluations of peer exclusion, tolerance of differences, and prescriptions for conformity. *Child Development, 73,* 1788–1802.

Kilpatrick, D. G., Ruggiero, K. J., Acierno, R., Saunders, B. E., Resnick, H. S., & Best, C. L. (2003). Violence and risk of PTSD, major depression, substance abuse/dependence, and comorbidity: Results from the National Survey of Adolescents. *Journal of Consulting and Clinical Psychology, 71,* 692–700.

Kim, H. S., Sherman, D. K., & Taylor, S. E. (2008). Culture and social support. *American Psychologist, 63,* 518–526.

Kim, H., & Chung, R. H. (2003). Relationship of recalled parenting style to self-perception in Korean American college students. *Journal of Genetic Psychology, 164,* 481–492.

Kim, J. E., & Moen, P. (2001). Moving into retirement: Preparation and transitions in late midlife. In M. E. Lachman (Ed.), *Handbook of midlife development* (pp. 487–527). New York: Wiley.

Kim, J. E., & Moen, P. (2002). Retirement transitions, gender, and psychological well-being: A life-course, ecological model. *Journal of Gerontology, Series B: Psychological Sciences and Social Sciences, 57,* P212–P222.

Kim, N. (2012). Oculomotor effects in the size-distance paradox and the moon illusion. *Ecological Psychology, 24,* 122–138.

Kimura, D. (2000). *Sex and cognition.* Cambridge, MA: MIT Press.

King, B. M. (2006). The rise, fall, and resurrection of the ventromedial hypothalamus in the regulation of feeding behavior and body weight. *Physiology and Behavior, 87,* 221–244.

King, N. H., Gullone, E., Tonge, B. J., & Ollendick, T. H. (1993). Self-reports of panic attacks and manifest anxiety in adolescents. *Behaviour Research and Therapy, 31,* 111–116.

King, P. M., & Kitchener, K. S. (1994). *Developing reflective judgment: Understanding and promoting intellectual growth and critical thinking in adolescents and adults.* San Francisco: Jossey-Bass.

King, S., St-Hilaire, A., & Heidkamp, D. (2010). Prenatal factors in schizophrenia. *Current Directions in Psychological Science, 19,* 209–213.

Kinnish, K. K., Strassberg, D. S., & Turner, C. W. (2005). Sex differences in the flexibility of sexual orientation: A multidimensional retrospective assessment. *Archives of Sexual Behavior, 34,* 173–183.

Kinomura, S., Larsson, J., Gulyas, B., & Roland, P. E. (1996). Activation by attention of the human reticular formation and thalamic intralaminar nuclei. *Science, 271,* 512–515.

Kinsey, A. C., Pomeroy, W. B., & Martin, C. E. (1948). *Sexual behavior in the human male.* Philadelphia: Saunders.

Kinsey, A. C., Pomeroy, W. B., Martin, C. E., & Gebhard, P. H. (1953). *Sexual behavior in the human female.* Philadelphia: Saunders.

Kirkbride, J. B., Morgan, C., Fearon, P., Dazzan, P., Murray, R. M., & Jones, P. B. (2007). Neighborhood-level effects on psychoses: Re-examining the role of context. *Psychological Medicine, 37,* 1413–1425.

Kirkpatrick, S. A., & Locke, E. A. (1991). Leadership: Do traits matter? *Academy of Management Executive, 5,* 48–60.

Kirmayer, L. J., & Looper, K. J. (2007). Somatoform disorders. In M. Hersen, S. M. Turner, & D. C. Beidel (Eds.), *Adult psychopathology and diagnosis* (5th ed., pp. 410–472). Hoboken, NJ: Wiley.

Kirsch, I. (1994). Cognitive-behavioral hypnotherapy. In J. W. Rhue, S. J. Lynn, & I. Kirsch (Eds.), *Handbook of clinical hypnosis* (pp. 151–172). Washington, DC: American Psychological Association.

Kirsch, I. (2000). The response set theory of hypnosis. *American Journal of Clinical Hypnosis, 42,* 274–292.

Kirsch, I., & Lynn, S. J. (1995). The altered state of hypnosis. *American Psychologist, 50,* 846–858.

Kirsch, I., & Lynn, S. J. (1997). Hypnotic involuntariness and the automaticity of everyday life. *American Journal of Clinical Hypnosis, 40,* 329–348.

Kirsch, I., Deacon, B. J., Huedo-medina, T. B., Scoboria, A., Moore, T. J., & Johnson, B. T. (2008). Initial severity and antidepressant benefits: A meta-analysis of data submitted to the Food and Drug Administration. *PLoS Medicine, 5,* e45.

Kirsch, I., Montgomery, G., & Sapirstein, G. (1995). Hypnosis as an adjunct to cognitive behavioral psychotherapy: A meta-analysis. *Journal of Consulting and Clinical Psychology, 63,* 214–220.

Kisilevsky, B. S., Hains, S. M., Lee, K., Xie, X., Huang, H., Ye, H. H. et al. (2003). Effects of experience on fetal voice recognition. *Psychological Science, 14,* 220–224.

Kito, S., Hasegawa, T., & Koga, Y. (2011). Neuroanatomical correlates of therapeutic efficacy of low-frequency right prefrontal transcranial magnetic stimulation in treatment-resistant depression. *Psychiatry and Clinical Neurosciences, 65,* 175–182.

Klass, D. (1993). Solace and immortality: Bereaved parents' continuing bond with their children. *Death Studies, 17,* 343–368.

Kleim, B., Graham, B., Fihosy, S., Stott, R., & Ehlers, A. (2014). Reduced specificity in episodic future thinking in posttraumatic stress disorder. *Clinical Psychological Science, 2,* 165–173.

Klein, B., Mitchell, J., Abbott, J., Shandley, K., Austin, D., Gilson, K. et al. (2010). A therapist-assisted cognitive behavior therapy internet intervention for posttraumatic stress disorder: Pre-, post- and 3-month follow-up results from an open trial. *Journal of Anxiety Disorders, 24,* 635–644.

Klein, D. N., Lewinsohn, P. M., & Seeley, J. R. (2001). A family study of major depressive disorder in a community sample of adolescents. *Archives of General Psychiatry, 58,* 13–21.

Klein, D. N., Shankman, S. A., & Rose, S. (2006). Ten-year prospective follow-up study of the naturalistic course of dysthymic disorder and double depression. *American Journal of Psychiatry, 163,* 872–880.

Klein, S. B. (1987). *Learning.* New York: McGraw-Hill.

Klein, T. W., & Newton, C. A. (2007). Therapeutic potential of cannabinoid-based drugs. *Advances in Experimental Medicine and Biology, 601,* 395–413.

Klemfuss, J. Z., Milojevich, H. M., Yim, I. S., Bush, E. B., & Quas, J. A. (2013). Stress at encoding, context at retrieval, and children's narrative content. *Journal of Experimental Child Psychology, 116,* 693–706.

Klinger, E., Bouchard, S., Legeron, P., Roy, S., Lauer, F., Chemin, I. et al. (2005). Virtual reality therapy versus cognitive behavior therapy for social phobia: A preliminary controlled study. *Cyberpsychology and Behavior, 8,* 76–88.

Klöckener, T., Hess, S., Belgardt, B., Paeger, L., Verhagen, L. W., Husch, A. et al. (2011). High-fat feeding promotes obesity via insulin receptor/PI3K-dependent inhibition of SF-1 VMH neurons. *Nature Neuroscience, 14,* 911–918. doi: 10.1038/nn.2847

Klonoff, E. A., Landrine, H., & Campbell, R. (2000). Sexist discrimination may account for well-known gender differences in psychiatric symptoms. *Psychology of Women Quarterly, 24,* 93–99.

Kluft, R. P. (1999). Current issues in dissociative identity disorder. *Journal of Practical Psychology and Behavioral Health, 5,* 3–19.

Kobasa, S. C. (1982). Commitment and coping in stress resistance among lawyers. *Journal of Personality and Social Psychology, 42,* 707–717.

Kochanska, G. (1995). Children's temperament, mothers' discipline, and security of attachment: Multiple pathways to emerging internalization. *Child Development, 66,* 597–615.

Koff, E., & Rierdan, J. (1995). Early adolescent girls' understanding of menstruation. *Women and Health, 22,* 1–19.

Kogan, A., Impett, E. A., Oveis, C., Hui, B., Gordon, A. M., & Keltner, D. (2010). When giving feels good: The intrinsic benefits of sacrifice in romantic relationships for the communally motivated. *Psychological Science, 21,* 1918–1924.

Kogut, T., & Ritov, I. (2011). The identifiable victim effect: Causes and boundary conditions. In D. M. Oppenheimer & C. Y. Olivola (Eds.), *The science of giving: Experimental approaches to the study of charity* (pp. 133–145). New York: Psychology Press.

Koh, K. B., Choe, E., Song, J. E., & Lee, E. H. (2006). Effect of coping on endocrinoimmune functions in different stress situations. *Psychiatry Research, 143,* 223–234.

Kohlberg, L. (1969). Stage and sequence: The cognitive-developmental approach to socialization. In D. A. Goslin (Ed.), *Handbook of socialization theory and research* (pp. 347–480). Chicago: Rand McNally.

Kohlberg, L., Levine, C., & Hewer, A. (1983). *Moral stages: A current formulation and a response to critics.* Basel, Switzerland: Karger.

Köhler, W. (1925). *The mentality of apes.* New York: Harcourt Brace.

Kohn, P. M., & Macdonald, J. E. (1992). The survey of recent life experiences: A decontaminated hassles scales for adults. *Journal of Behavioral Medicine, 15,* 221–236.

Kohout, J., & Wicherski, M. (2010). *2010 Graduate study in psychology snapshot: Faculty in U.S.*

and Canadian graduate departments of psychology: 2008–2009. Washington, DC: APA Center for Workforce Studies.

Kolassa, I. T., & Elbert, T. (2007). Structural and functional neuroplasticity in relation to traumatic stress. *Current Directions in Psychological Science, 16,* 321–325.

Koles, Z. J., Lind, J. C., & Flor-Henry, P. (2010). Gender differences in brain functional organization during verbal and spatial cognitive challenges. *Brain Topography, 23,* 199–204. doi:10.1007/s10548-009-0119-0

Komisaruk, B. R., & Whipple, B. (2011). Non-genital orgasms. *Sexual and Relationship Therapy, 26,* 356–372. doi: 10.1080/14681994.2011.649252

Komisaruk, B. R., Wise, N., Frangos, E., Birbano, W., & Allen, K. (2011). An fMRI video animation time-course analysis of brain regions activated during self-stimulation to orgasm in women. *Society for Neuroscience,* 495.03.

Konkol, R. J., Murphey, L. J., Ferriero, D. M., Dempsey, D. A., & Olsen, G. D. (1994). Cocaine metabolites in the neonate: Potential for toxicity. *Journal of Child Neurology, 9,* 242–248.

Koob, G. F., & Bloom, F. E. (1988). Cellular and molecular mechanisms of drug dependence. *Science, 242,* 715–723.

Koolschijn, P. C., & Crone, E. A. (2013). Sex differences and structural brain maturation from childhood to early adulthood. *Developmental Cognitive Neuroscience, 5,* 106–118.

Kopelman, P. G. (2000). Obesity as a medical problem. *Nature, 404,* 635–643.

Kopta, S. M., Lueger, R. J., Saunders, S. M., & Howard, K. I. (1999). Individual psychotherapy outcome and process research: Challenges leading to greater turmoil or a positive transition? *Annual Review of Psychology, 50,* 441–469.

Koslowsky, M., & Babkoff, H. (1992). Meta-analysis of the relationship between total sleep deprivation and performance. *Chronobiology International, 9,* 132–136.

Koss, M. P., & Kilpatrick, D. G. (2001). Rape and sexual assault. In E. Gerrity (Ed.), *The mental health consequences of torture* (pp. 177–193). New York: Kluwer Academic/Plenum Press.

Kosslyn, S. M. (1994). *Image and brain: The resolution of the imagery debate.* Cambridge, MA: MIT Press.

Kosslyn, S. M., Ball, T. M., & Reiser, B. J. (2004). Visual images preserve metric spatial information: Evidence from studies of image scanning. In D. A. Balota & E. J. Marsh (Eds.), *Cognitive psychology: Key readings* (pp. 239–253). New York: Psychology Press. (Original work published 1978)

Kosten, T. R., Wu, G., Huang, W., Harding, M. J., Hamon, S. C., Lappalainen, J., & Nielsen, D. A. (2013). Pharmacogenetic randomized trial for cocaine abuse: Disulfiram and dopamine β-hydroxylase. *Biological Psychiatry, 73,* 219–224. doi:10.1016/j.biopsych.2012.07.011

Koughan, M. (1975, February 23). Arthur Friedman's outrage: Employees decide their pay. *Washington Post.*

Kowalski, K. (2003). The emergence of ethnic and racial attitudes in preschool-aged children. *Journal of Social Psychology, 143,* 677–690.

Kozart, M. F. (2002). Understanding efficacy in psychotherapy. *American Journal of Orthopsychiatry, 72,* 217–231.

Kozlowski, S. W., & Bell, B. S. (2003). Work groups and teams in organizations. In W. C. Borman, D. R. Ilgen, & R. J. Klimoski (Eds.), *Handbook of psychology: Industrial and organizational psychology* (Vol. 12, pp. 333–375). New York: Wiley.

Kraft, J. B., Peters, E. J., Slager, S. L., Jenkins, G. D., Reinalda, M. S., McGrath, P. J. et al. (2007). Analysis of association between the serotonin transporter and antidepressant response in a large clinical sample. *Biological Psychiatry, 61,* 734–742.

Kraft, J. M. (1996). Prenatal alcohol consumption and outcomes for children: A review of the literature. In R. L. Parrott & C. M. Condit (Eds.), *Evaluating women's health messages: A resource book* (pp. 175–189). Thousand Oaks, CA: Sage.

Kraft, T. L., & Pressman, S. D. (2012). Grin and bear it: The influence of manipulated facial expression on the stress response. *Psychological Science, 23,* 1372–1378.

Kraha, A., & Boals, A. (2011). Parents and vehicle purchases for their children: A surprising source of weight bias. *Obesity, 19,* 541–545.

Krampe, H., & Ehrenreich, H. (2010). Supervised disulfiram as adjunct to psychotherapy in alcoholism treatment. *Current Pharmaceutical Design, 16,* 2076–2090.

Krantz, D. S., & McCeney, M. K. (2002). Effects of psychological and social factors on organic disease: A critical assessment of research on coronary heart disease. *Annual Reviews of Psychology, 53,* 341–369.

Kraut, R. E. (1982). Social presence, facial feedback, and emotion. *Journal of Personality and Social Psychology, 42,* 853–863.

Kreibig, S. D. (2010). Autonomic nervous system activity in emotion: A review. *Biological Psychology, 84,* 394–421. doi:10.1016/j.biopsycho.2010.03.010

Kreider, R. M. (2005). Number, timing, and duration of marriages and divorces: 2001. *Current Population Reports,* P70–97. Washington, DC: U.S. Census Bureau.

Kremer, I., Bachner-Melman, R., Reshef, A., Broude, L., Nemanov, L., Gritsenko, I. et al. (2005). Association of the serotonin transporter gene with smoking behavior. *American Journal of Psychiatry, 162,* 924–930.

Krijn, M., Emmelkamp, P. M., Olafsson, R. P., & Biemond, R. (2004). Virtual reality exposure therapy of anxiety disorders: A review. *Clinical Psychology Review, 24,* 259–281.

Kristenson, H. H. (1992). Long-term Antabuse treatment of alcohol-dependent patients. *Acta Psychiatrica Scandinavica, 86* (Suppl. 369), 41–45. doi:10.1111/j.1600-0447.1992.tb03314.X

Kropp, P., Siniatchkin, M., & Gerber, W.-D. (2002). On the pathophysiology of migraine—Links for "empirically based treatment" with neurofeedback. *Applied Psychophysiology and Biofeedback, 27,* 203–213.

Krystal, J. H., Staley, J., Mason, G., Petrakis, I. L., Kaufman, J., Harris, R. A. et al. (2006). Gamma-aminobutyric acid type A receptors and alcoholism: Intoxication, dependence, vulnerability, and treatment. *Archives of General Psychiatry, 63,* 957–968.

Kryukov, V. I. (2012). Towards a unified model of Pavlovian conditioning: Short review of trace conditioning models. *Cognitive Neurodynamics, 6,* 377–398. doi: 10.1007/s11571-012-9195-z

Kübler-Ross, E. (1969). *On death and dying.* New York: Macmillan.

Kübler-Ross, E. (1974). *Questions and answers on death and dying.* New York: Macmillan.

Kudielka, B. M., & Kirschbaum, C. (2005). Sex differences in HPA axis responses to stress: A review. *Biological Psychology, 69,* 113–132.

Kuhbandner, C., Lichtenfeld, S., & Pekrun, R. (2011). Always look on the broad side of life: Happiness increases the breadth of sensory memory. *Emotion, 11,* 958–964. doi:10.1037/a0024075

Kuhn, D., & Crowell, A. (2011). Dialogic argumentation as a vehicle for developing young adolescents' thinking. *Psychological Science, 22,* 545–552.

Kumada, T., Jiang, Y., Cameron, D. B., & Komuro, H. (2007). How does alcohol impair neuronal migration? *Journal of Neuroscience Research, 85,* 465–470.

Kumari, V., ffytche, D. H., Williams, S. C., & Gray, J. A. (2004). Personality predicts brain responses to cognitive demands. *Journal of Neuroscience, 24,* 10636–10641.

Kung, H. S., Hoyert, D. L., Xu, J., & Murphy, S. L. (2008). Deaths: Final data for 2005. *National Vital Statistics Reports, 56*(10).

Kunstman, J. W., & Plant, E. A. (2008). Racing to help: Racial bias in high emergency helping situations. *Journal of Personality and Social Psychology, 95,* 1499–1510.

Kunugi, H., Hori, H., Adachi, N., & Numakawa, T. (2010). Interface between hypothalamic-pituitary-adrenal axis and brain-derived neurotrophic factor in depression. *Psychiatry and Clinical Neurosciences, 64,* 447–459.

Kurdek, L. A. (1999). The nature and predictors of the trajectory of change in marital quality for husbands and wives over the first 10 years of marriage. *Developmental Psychology, 35,* 1283–1296.

Kuriyama, K., Stickgold, R., & Walker, M. P. (2004). Sleep-dependent learning and motor-skill complexity. *Learning and Memory, 11,* 705–713.

Kutscher, E. C. (2008). Antipsychotics. In K. T. Mueser & D. V. Jeste (Eds.), *Clinical handbook of schizophrenia* (pp. 159–167). New York: Guilford Press.

Kuyper, L., & Fokkema, T. (2011). Minority stress and mental health among Dutch LGBs: Examination of differences between sex and sexual orientation. *Journal of Counseling Psychology, 58,* 222–233. doi: 10.1037/a0022688

Kuypers, K. P., Wingen, M., & Ramaekers, J. G. (2008). Memory and mood during the night and in the morning after repeated evening doses of MDMA. *Journal of Psychopharmacology, 22,* 895–903.

Kuzelova, H., Ptacek, R., & Milan, M. (2010). The serotonin transporter gene (5-HTT) variant and psychiatric disorders: Review of current literature. *Neuroendocrinology Letters,* 31, 5.

Kwan, B. M., Dimidjian, S., & Rizvi, S. L. (2010). Treatment preference, engagement, and clinical improvement in pharmacotherapy versus psychotherapy for depression. *Behaviour Research and Therapy, 48,* 799–804.

La Greca, A. M., Silverman, W. K., Lai, B., & Jaccard, J. (2010). Hurricane-related exposure experiences and stressors, other life events, and social support: Concurrent and prospective impact on children's persistent posttraumatic stress symptoms. *Journal of Consulting and Clinical Psychology, 78,* 794–805.

LaBar, K. S. (2007). Beyond fear: Emotional memory mechanisms in the human brain. *Current Directions in Psychological Science, 16,* 173–177.

Lacayo, A. (1995). Neurologic and psychiatric complications of cocaine abuse. *Neuropsychiatry, Neuropsychology, and Behavioral Neurology, 8,* 53–60.

Laceulle, O. M., Ormel, J., Aggen, S. H., Neale, M. C., & Kendler, K. S. (2013). Genetic and environmental influences on the longitudinal structure of neuroticism: A trait-state approach. *Psychological Science, 24,* 1780–1790.

Lack, C. W. (2012). Obsessive-compulsive disorder: Evidence-based treatments and future directions for research. *World Journal of Psychiatry, 2,* 86–90.

Lahey, B. B., Pelham, W. E., Loney, J., Kipp, H., Ehrhardt, A., Lee, S. S. et al. (2004). Three-year predictive validity of DSM-IV attention deficit hyperactivity disorder in children diagnosed at 4–6 years of age. *American Journal of Psychiatry, 161,* 2014–2020.

Lambert, M. J., & Bergen, A. E. (1994). The effectiveness of psychotherapy. In A. E. Bergen & S. L. Garfield (Eds.), *Handbook of psychotherapy and behavior change* (4th ed., pp. 143–189). New York: Wiley.

Lambeth, G. S., & Hallett, M. (2002). Promoting healthy decision making in relationships: Developmental interventions with young adults on college and university campuses. In C. L. Atkinson & D. R. Atkinson (Eds.), *Counseling across the lifespan: Prevention and treatment* (pp. 209–226). Thousand Oaks, CA: Sage.

Lancet, D. Ben-Arie, N., Cohen, S., Gat, U., Gross-Isseroff, R., Horn-Saban, S. et al. (1993). Oflactory receptors: Transduction diversity, human psychophysics and genome analysis. In D. Chadwick, J. Marsh, & J. Goode (Eds.), *The molecular basis of smell and taste transduction* (pp. 131–146). New York: Wiley.

Landabaso, M. A., Iraurgi, I., Sanz, J., Calle, R., Ruiz de Apodaka, J., Jimenez-Lerma, J. M. et al. (1999). Naltrexone in the treatment of alcoholism: Two-year follow up results. *European Journal of Psychiatry, 13,* 97–105.

Lang, A. J., & Stein, M. B. (2001). Social phobia: Prevalence and diagnostic threshold. *Journal of Clinical Psychiatry, 62*(Suppl. 1), 5–10.

Lang, R., Mahoney, R., El Zein, F., Delaune, E., & Amidon, M. (2011). Evidence to practice: Treatment of anxiety in individuals with autism spectrum disorders. *Neuropsychiatric Disease and Treatment, 7,* 27–30.

Lange, T., Dimitrov, S., Fehm, H. L., Westermann, J., & Born, J. (2006). Shift of monocyte function toward cellular immunity during sleep. *Archives of Internal Medicine, 166,* 1695–1700.

Langfred, C. (2004). Too much of a good thing? Negative effects of high trust and individual autonomy in self-managing teams. *Academy of Management Journal, 47,* 385–399.

Langlois, J. H., Roggman, L. A., Casey, R. J., Ritter, J. M., Rieser-Danner, L. A., & Jenkins, V. Y. (1987). Infant preferences for attractive faces: Rudiments of a stereotype? *Developmental Psychology, 23,* 363–369.

Langreth, R. (2000, May 1). Every little bit helps: How even moderate exercise can have a big impact on your health. *Wall Street Journal,* p. R5.

Lansford, J. E. (2009). Parental divorce and children's adjustment. *Perspectives on Psychological Science, 4,* 140–152.

Lanska, M., Olds, J. M., & Westerman, D. L. (2014). Fluency effects in recognition memory: Are perceptual fluency and conceptual fluency interchangeable? *Journal Of Experimental Psychology: Learning, Memory, and Cognition, 40,* 1–11. doi:10.1037/a0034309

Largo-Wight, E., Peterson, P. M., & Chen, W. W. (2005). Perceived problem solving, stress, and health among college students. *American Journal of Health Behavior, 29,* 360–370.

Larkin, M. (1998). On the trail of human pheromones. *Lancet, 351,* 809.

Lassman, D. J., McKie, S., Gregory, L. J., Lal, S., D'Amato, M., Steele, I. et al. (2010). Defining the role of cholecystokinin in the lipid-induced human brain activation matrix. *Gastroenterology, 138,* 1514–1524.

Latané, B., & Darley, J. (1969). Bystander "apathy." *American Scientist, 57,* 244–268.

Latané, B., & L'Herrou, T. (1996). Spatial clustering in the conformity game: Dynamic social impact in electronic groups. *Journal of Personality and Social Psychology, 70,* 1218–1230.

Lating, J. M., Sherman, M. F., Everly, G. S., Jr., Lowry, J. L., & Peragine, T. F. (2004). PTSD reactions and functioning of American Airlines flight attendants in the wake of September 11. *Journal of Nervous and Mental Disorders, 192,* 435–441.

Lattal, K., & Lattal, K. A. (2012). Facets of Pavlovian and operant extinction. *Behavioural Processes, 90,* 1–8. doi:10.1016/j.beproc.2012.03.009

Laubmeier, K. K., Zakowski, S. G., & Bair, J. P. (2004). The role of spirituality in the psychological adjustment to cancer. A test of the transactional model of stress and coping. *International Journal of Behavioral Medicine, 11,* 48–55.

Laugharne, J., Janca, A., & Widiger, T. (2007). Posttraumatic stress disorder and terrorism: Five years after 9/11. *Current Opinion in Psychiatry, 20,* 36–41.

Lavner, J. A., & Bradbury, T. N. (2010). Patterns of change in marital satisfaction over the newlywed years. *Journal of Marriage and Family, 72,* 1171–1187.

Lavoie, C., & Desrochers, S. (2002). Visual habituation at five months: Short-term reliability of measures obtained with a new polynomial regression criterion. *Journal of Genetic Psychology, 163,* 261–271.

Laws, D. R. (2001). Olfactory aversion: Notes on procedure, with speculations on its mechanism of effect. *Sex Abuse, 13,* 275–287.

Lazarus, R. S. (1990). Theory-based stress measurement. *Psychological Inquiry, 1,* 3–13.

Lazarus, R. S. (1991). Cognition and motivation in emotion. *American Psychologist, 46,* 352–367.

Lazarus, R. S. (1993). From psychological stress to the emotions: A history of changing outlooks. *Annual Review of Psychology, 44,* 1–21.

Lazarus, R. S. (1995). Vexing research problems inherent in cognitive-mediational theories of emotion—and some solutions. *Psychological Inquiry, 6,* 183–197.

Lazarus, R. S., & Folkman, S. (1984). *Stress, appraisal, and coping.* New York: Springer.

Leaper, C., & Friedman, C. K. (2007). The socialization of gender. In J. E. Grusec & P. D. Hastings (Eds.), *Handbook of socialization: Theory and research* (pp. 561–587). New York: Guilford Press.

Leary, C., Kelley, M., Morrow, J., & Mikulka, P. (2008). Parental use of physical punishment as related to family environment, psychological well-being, and personality in undergraduates. *Journal of Family Violence, 23,* 1–7.

LeBlanc, J., Ducharme, M. B., & Thompson, M. (2004). Study on the correlation of the autonomic nervous system response to a stressor of high discomfort with personality traits. *Physiology of Behavior, 82,* 647–652.

Lebovits, A. (2007). Cognitive-behavioral approaches to chronic pain. *Primary Psychiatry, 14,* 48–54.

Lebow, J. L., & Gurman, A. S. (1995). Research assessing couple and family therapy. *Annual Review of Psychology, 46,* 27–57.

Lebow, J. L., Chambers, A. L., Christensen, A., & Johnson, S. M. (2012). Research on the treatment of couple distress. *Journal of Marital and Family Therapy, 38,* 145–168.

Lecanuet, J.P., Manera, S., & Jacquet, A.Y. (2002, April). *Fetal cardiac responses to maternal sentences, to playback of these sentences, and to their recordings by another woman's voice.* Paper presented at the XIII International Conference on Infant Studies, Toronto, Ontario, Canada.

Lecat, B., Hilton, D. J., & Crano, W. D. (2009). Group status and reciprocity norms: Can the door-in-the-face effect be obtained in an out-group context? *Group Dynamics: Theory, Research, and Practice, 13,* 178–189. doi:10.1037/a0014956

Leckman, J. F., Denys, D., Simpson, H. B., Mataix-Cols, D., Hollander, E., Saxena, S. et al. (2010). Obsessive-compulsive disorder: A review of the diagnostic criteria and possible subtypes and dimensional signifiers for *DSM-V. Depression and Anxiety, 27,* 507–527.

Lee, A. Y. (2001). The mere exposure effect: An uncertainty reduction explanation revisited. *Personality and Social Psychology Bulletin, 27,* 1255–1266.

Lee, D. C., Sui, X., Ortega, F. B., Kim, Y. S., Church, T. S., Winett, R. A. et al. (2011). Comparisons of leisure-time physical activity and cardiorespiratory fitness as predictors of all-cause mortality in men and women. *British Journal of Sports Medicine, 45,* 504–510.

Lee, S. J., Perron, B. E., Taylor, C. A., & Guterman, N. B. (2011). Parental psychosocial characteristics and corporal punishment in their 3-year-old children. *Journal of Interpersonal Violence, 26,* 71–87.

Lefcourt, H. M. (2001). The humor solution. In C. R. Snyder (Ed.), *Coping with stress: Effective people and processes* (pp. 68–92). New York: Oxford University Press.

Lefcourt, H. M., & Davidson-Katz, K. (1991). The role of humor and the self. In C. R. Synder & D. R. Forsyth (Eds.), *Handbook of social and clinical psychology: The health perspective* (pp. 41–56). New York: Pergamon Press.

Lehto, U. S., Ojanen, M., Dyba, T., Aromaa, A., & Kellokumpu-Lehtinen, P. (2006). Baseline psychosocial predictors of survival in localized breast cancer. *British Journal of Cancer, 94,* 1245–1252.

Leibowitz, S. F. (1991). Brain neuropeptide Y: An integrator of endocrine, metabolic, and behavioral processes. *Brain Research Bulletin, 27,* 333–337.

Leichsenring, F., & Leibing, E. (2007). Psychodynamic psychotherapy: A systematic review of techniques, indications and empirical evidence. *Psychology and Psychotherapy, 80*(Pt. 2), 217–228.

Leichsenring, F., Leibing, E., Kruse, J., New, A. S., & Leweke, F. (2011). Borderline personality disorder. *Lancet, 377,* 74–84.

Leigh, B. C. (1989). In search of the seven dwarves: Issues of measurement and meaning in alcohol expectancy research. *Psychological Bulletin, 105,* 361–373.

Lekander, M., Andreasson, A. N., Kecklund, G., Ekman, R., Ingre, M., Akerstedt, T., & Axelsson, J. (2013). Subjective health perception in healthy young men changes in response to experimentally restricted sleep and subsequent recovery sleep. *Brain, Behavior, and Immunity, 34,* 43–46.

Lemay, E. P., Clark, M. S., & Greenberg, A. (2010). What is beautiful is good because what is beautiful is desired: Physical attractiveness stereotyping as projection of interpersonal goals. *Personality and Social Psychology Bulletin, 36,* 339–353.

Lemola, S., Ledermann, T., & Friedman, E. M. (2013). Variability of sleep duration is related to subjective sleep quality and subjective well-being: An actigraphy study. *PLoS One, 8,* e71292.

Lenox, R. H., & Manji, H. K. (1995). Lithium. In A. F. Schatzberg & C. B. Nemeroff (Eds.), *The American Psychiatric Press textbook of psychopharmacology* (pp. 303–349). Washington, DC: American Psychiatric Press.

Lenze, E. J., Rollman, B. L., Shear, M. K., Dew, M. A., Pollock, B. G., Ciliberti, C. et al. (2009). Escitalopram for older adults with generalized anxiety disorder: A randomized controlled trial. *Journal of the American Medical Association, 301,* 295–303.

Lenzenweger, M. F. (2008). Epidemiology of personality disorders. *Psychiatric Clinics of North America, 31,* 395–403.

Lenzenweger, M. F., Lane, M., Loranger, A., & Kessler, R. (2007). DSM-IV personality disorders in the National Comorbidity Survey Replication. *Biological Psychiatry, 62,* 553–564.

Leon, S. C., Kopta, S. M., Howard, K. I., & Lutz, W. (1999). Predicting patients' responses to psychotherapy: Are some more predictable than others? *Journal of Consulting and Clinical Psychology, 67,* 698–704.

Leopold, D. A., & Rhodes, G. (2010). A comparative view of face perception. *Journal of Comparative Psychology, 124,* 233–251.

LePine, J. A., Erez, A., & Johnston, D. E. (2002). The nature and dimensionality of organizational citizenship behavior: A critical review and a meta-analysis. *Journal of Applied Psychology, 87,* 52–65.

Lepper, M. R., Corpus, J. H., & Iyengar, S. S. (2005). Intrinsic and extrinsic motivational orientations in the classroom: Age differences and academic correlates. *Journal of Educational Psychology, 97,* 184–196.

Lessenger, J. E., & Feinberg, S. D. (2008). Abuse of prescription and over-the-counter medications. *Journal of the American Board of Family Medicine, 21,* 175.

Lester, B. M., Andreozzi, L., & Appiah, L. (2004). Substance use during pregnancy: Time for policy to catch up with research. *Harm Reduction Journal, 1,* 5–49.

Lester, B. M., Corwin, M. J., Sepkoski, C., Seifer, R., Peucker, M., McLaughlin, S. et al. (1991). Neurobehavioral syndromes in cocaine-exposed newborn infants. *Child Development, 62,* 694–705.

Leuchter, A. F., Lesser, I. M., Trivedi, M. H., Rush, A. J., Morris, D. W., Warden, D. et al. (2008). An open pilot study of the combination of escitalopram and bupropion-SR for outpatients with major depressive disorder. *Journal of Psychiatric Practice, 14,* 271–280.

LeVay, S. (1996). *Queer science: The use and abuse of research into homosexuality.* Cambridge, MA: MIT Press.

Levenson, R. W., Carstensen, L. L., & Gottman, J. M. (1993). Long-term marriage: Age, gender, and satisfaction. *Psychology and Aging, 8,* 301–313.

Levenson, R. W., Ekman, P., & Friesen, W. V. (1990). Voluntary facial action generates emotion-specific nervous system activity. *Psychophysiology, 27,* 363–384.

Levin, B. E., & Routh, V. H. (1996). Role of the brain in energy balance and obesity. *American Journal of Physiology, 271,* R491–R500.

Levine, B., Turner, G. R., Tisserand, D., Hevenor, S. J., Graham, S. J., & McIntosh, A. R. (2004). The functional neuroanatomy of episodic and semantic autobiographical remembering: A prospective functional MRI study. *Journal of Cognitive Neuroscience, 16,* 1633–1646.

Levine, M. (2006). *The price of privilege: How parental pressure and material advantage are creating a generation of disconnected and unhappy kids.* New York: HarperCollins.

Levine, R. A., & Campbell, D. T. (1972). *Ethnocentrism: Theories of conflict, ethnic attitudes, and group behavior.* New York: Wiley.

Levinson, D. F., Evgrafov, O. V., Knowles, J. A., Potash, J. B., Weissman, M. M., Scheftner, W. A. et al. (2007). Genetics of recurrent early-onset major depression (GenRED): Significant linkage on chromosome 15q25–q26 after fine mapping with single nucleotide polymorphism markers. *American Journal of Psychiatry, 164,* 259–264.

Levitt, A. G., & Utmann, J. G. A. (1992). From babbling towards the sound systems of English and French: A longitudinal two-case study. *Journal of Child Language, 19,* 19–40.

Levy, B. R., & Myers, L. M. (2004). Preventive health behaviors influenced by self-perceptions of aging. *Preventive Medicine, 39,* 625–629.

Levy, B. R., Slade, M. D., Kunkel, S. R., & Kasl, S. V. (2002). Longevity increased by positive self-perceptions of aging. *Journal of Personality and Social Psychology, 83,* 261–270.

Levy, D. L., Coleman, M. J., Sung, H., Ji, F., Matthysse, S., Mendell, N. R. et al. (2010). The genetic basis of thought disorder and language and communication disturbances in schizophrenia. *Journal of Neurolinguistics, 23,* 176.

Levy, G. D., Taylor, M. G., & Gelman, S. A. (1995). Traditional and evaluative aspects of flexibility in gender roles, social conventions, moral rules, and physical laws. *Child Development, 66,* 515–531.

Levy, N. A., & Janicak, P. G. (2000). Calcium channel antagonists for the treatment of bipolar disorder. *Bipolar Disorders, 2,* 108–119.

Levy-Shiff, R. (1994). Individual and contextual correlates of marital change across the transition to parenthood. *Developmental Psychology, 30,* 591–601.

Lewinsohn, P. M., Clark, G. N., Hops, H., & Andrews, J. (1990). Cognitive-behavioral treatment for depressed adolescents. *Behavior Therapy, 21,* 385–401.

Lewinsohn, P. M., Klein, D. N., & Seeley, J. R. (2000). Bipolar disorder during adolescence and young adulthood in a community sample. *Bipolar Disorders, 2,* 281–293.

Lewinsohn, P. M., Rohde, P., & Seeley, J. R. (1994). Psychosocial risk factors for future adolescent suicide attempts. *Journal of Consulting and Clinical Psychology, 62,* 297–305.

Lewis, B. A., Minnes, S., Short, E.J., Min, M. O., Wu, M., Lang, A. et al. (2013). Language outcomes at 12 years for children exposed prenatally to cocaine. *Journal of Speech, Language, and Hearing Research, 56,* 1662–1676.

Lewis, D. O. (1992). From abuse to violence: Psychophysiological consequences of maltreatment. *Journal of the American Academy of Child and Adolescent Psychiatry, 31,* 383–391.

Lewis, D. O., Yeager, C. A., Blake, P., Bard, B., & Strenziok, M. (2004). Ethics questions raised by the neuropsychiatric, neuropsychological, educational, developmental, and family characteristics of 18 juveniles awaiting execution in Texas. *Journal of the American Academy of Psychiatry and the Law, 32,* 408–429.

Lexiteria Corporation. (2011). Alphadictionary.com. Retrieved from http://www.alphadictionary.com/index.shtml

Leyhe, T., Müller, S., Milian, M., Eschweiler, G. W., & Saur, R. (2009). Impairment of episodic and semantic autobiographical memory in patients with mild cognitive impairment and early Alzheimer's disease. *Neuropsychologia, 47,* 2464–2469. doi: 10.1016/j.neuropsychologia.2009.04.018

Li, C. E., DiGiuseppe, R., & Froh, J. (2006). The roles of sex, gender, and coping in adolescent depression. *Adolescence, 41,* 409–415.

Li, K-C., Hsiao, S., & Li, J-S. (2013). Conditioned taste aversion as instrumental punishment. *Journal of Experimental Psychology, 39,* 294–297.

Li, S., Lindenberger, U., Hommel, B., Aschersleben, G., Prinz, W., & Baltes, P. B. (2004). Transformations in the couplings among intellectual abilities and constituent cognitive processes across the life span. *Psychological Science, 15,* 155–163.

Li, Y., Xiao, X., Ma, W., Jiang, J., Qiu, J., & Zhang, Q. (2013). Electrophysiological evidence for emotional valence and competitive arousal effects on insight problem solving. *Brain Research, 153, 8,* 61–72. doi:10.1016/j.brainres.2013.09.021

Libersat, F., & Pflueger, H.-J. (2004). Monoamines and the orchestration of behavior. *BioScience, 54,* 17–25.

Lichter, D. T., Qian, Z., & Mellott, L. M. (2006). Marriage or dissolution? Union transitions among poor cohabiting women. *Demography, 43,* 223–240.

Lick, D. J., Durso, L. E., & Johnson, K. L. (2013). Minority stress and physical health among sexual minorities. *Perspectives on Psychological Science, 8,* 521–548.

Lieberman, J. A., Stroup, T. S., & Perkins, D. O. (2012). *Essentials of schizophrenia.* Arlington, VA: American Psychiatric Publishing.

Lieberman, J., Chakos, M., Wu, H., Alvir, J., Hoffman, E., Robinson, D. et al. (2001). Longitudinal study of brain morphology in first episode schizophrenia. *Biological Psychiatry, 49,* 487–499.

Lieberman, J., Tollefson, G., Tohen, M., Green, A. I., Gur, R. E., Kahn, R. et al. (2003). Comparative efficacy and safety of atypical and conventional antipsychotic drugs in first-episode psychosis: A randomized, double-blind trial of olanzapine versus haloperidol. *American Journal of Psychiatry, 160,* 1396–1404.

Liebert, R. M., & Spiegler, M. D. (1998). *Personality: Strategies and issues* (8th ed.). Pacific Grove, CA: Brooks/Cole.

Lien, Y., Chu, R., Jen, C., & Wu, C. (2006). Do Chinese commit neither fundamental attribution error nor ultimate attribution error? *Chinese Journal of Psychology, 48,* 163–181.

Lilienfeld, S. O., Wood, J. M., & Garb, H. N. (2000). The scientific status of projective techniques. *Psychological Science in the Public Interest, 1,* 27–66.

Lincoln, A. E., Caswell, S. V., Almquist, J. L., Dunn, R. E., Norris, J. B., & Hinton, R. Y. (2011). Trends in concussion incidence in high school sports: A prospective 11-year study. *American Journal of Sports Medicine, 39,* 958–963. doi:10.1177/0363546510392326

Lindau, S. T., Schumm, L. P., Laumann, E. O., Levinson, W., O'Muircheartaigh, C. A., & Waite, L. J. (2007). A study of sexuality and health among older adults in the United States. *New England Journal of Medicine, 357,* 762–774.

Lindenmayer, J. P., Khan, A., Iskander, A., Abad, M. T., & Parker, B. (2007). A randomized controlled trial of olanzapine versus haloperidol in the treatment of primary negative symptoms and neurocognitive deficits in schizophrenia. *Journal of Clinical Psychiatry, 68,* 368–379.

Ling, D., Niu, T., Feng, Y., Xing, H., & Xu, X. (2004). Association between polymorphism of the dopamine transporter gene and early smoking onset: An interaction risk on nicotine dependence. *Journal of Human Genetics, 49,* 35–39.

Linhares, J. M., Pinto, P. D., & Nascimento, S. M. (2008). The number of discernable colors in natural scenes. *Journal of the Optical Society of America, 25,* 2918–2924.

Linville, P. W., Fischer, G. W., & Salovey, P. (1989). Perceived distributions of characteristics on in-group and out-group members: Empirical evidence and a computer simulation. *Journal of Personality and Social Psychology, 57,* 165–188.

Liossi, C., White, P., & Hatira, P. (2006). Randomized clinical trial of local anesthetic versus a combination of local anesthetic with self-hypnosis in the management of pediatric procedure-related pain. *Health Psychology, 25,* 307–315.

Lippa, R. (2003). Handedness, sexual orientation, and gender-related personality traits in men and women. *Archives of Sexual Behavior, 32,* 103–114.

Lipsitt, L. P. (2003). Crib death: A biobehavioral phenomenon? *Current Directions in Psychological Science, 12,* 164–170.

Lissek, S., Rabin, S., Heller, R. E., Lukenbaugh, D., Geraci, M., Pine, D. S. et al. (2010). Overgeneralization of conditioned fear as a pathogenic marker of panic disorder. *American Journal of Psychiatry, 167,* 47–55.

Littleton, H., Horsley, S., John, S., & Nelson, D. V. (2007). Trauma coping strategies and psychological distress: A meta-analysis. *Journal of Trauma and Stress, 20,* 977–988.

Livingston, I. (2010, April 24). Stabbed hero dies as more than 20 people stroll past him. *New York Post.* Retrieved from http://nypost.com/2010/04/24/stabbed-hero-dies-as-more-than-20-people-stroll-past-him/

Llorente, M. D., Currier, M. B., Norman, S. E., & Mellman, T. A. (1992). Night terrors in adults: Phenomenology and relationship to psychopathology. *Journal of Clinical Psychiatry, 53,* 392–394.

Lloyd, G., Alexander, A. A., Rice, D. G., & Greenfield, N. S. (1980). Life events as predictors of academic performance. *Journal of Human Stress, 6,* 15–26.

Loane, C., & Politis, M. (2012). Buspirone: What is it all about? *Brain Research, 1461,* 111–118.

Lockenhoff, C. E., De Fruyt, F., Terracciano, A., McCrae, R. R., De Bolle, M., Costa, P. T., Jr. et al. (2009). Perceptions of aging across 26 cultures and their culture-level associates. *Psychology and Aging, 24,* 941–954.

Lockhart, R. S., & Craik, F. I. M. (1990). Levels of processing: A retrospective commentary on a framework for memory research. *Canadian Journal of Psychology, 44,* 87–112.

Loersch, C., Durso, G. O., & Petty, R. E. (2013). Vicissitudes of desire: A matching mechanism for subliminal persuasion. *Social Psychological and Personality Science, 4,* 624–631. doi:10.1177/1948550612471975

Loewenstein, R. J., & Putnam, F. W. (2004). The dissociative disorders. In B. J. Sadock, & V. A. Sadock (Eds.), *Posttraumatic stress disorder: DSM-IV and beyond* (8th ed., pp. 1844–1901). Baltimore, MD: Williams & Wilkins.

Loewenstein, W. R. (1960). Biological transducers. *Scientific American, 203,* 98–108.

Loftus, E. F. (1979). *Eyewitness testimony.* Cambridge, MA: Harvard University Press.

Loftus, E. F. (2000). Remembering what never happened. In E. Tulving (Ed.), *Memory, consciousness, and the brain* (pp. 106–118). Philadelphia: Psychology Press.

Loftus, E. F., & Davis, D. (2006). Recovered memories. *Annual Review of Clinical Psychology, 2,* 469–498.

Loftus, E. F., & Palmer, J. C. (1974). Reconstruction of automobile destruction: An example of the interaction between language and memory. *Journal of Verbal Learning and Verbal Behavior, 13,* 585–589.

Loftus, E. F., & Zanni, G. (1975). Eyewitness testimony: The influence of the wording of a question. *Bulletin of the Psychonomic Society, 5,* 86–88.

Logie, R. H. (1999). State of the art: Working memory. *Psychologist, 12,* 174–178.

Logie, R. H., Della Sala, S., Wynn, V., & Baddeley, A. D. (2000, November). *Division of attention in Alzheimer's disease.* Paper presented at the Psychonomics Society meeting, Los Angeles.

Logue, A. W. (1979). Taste aversion and the generality of the laws of learning. *Psychological Bulletin, 86,* 276–296.

Lomenick, J. P., Melguizo, M. S., Mitchell, S. L., Summar, M. L., & Anderson, J. W. (2009). Effects of meals high in carbohydrate, protein, and fat on ghrelin and peptide YY secretion in prepubertal children. *Journal of Clinical Endocrinology and Metabolism, 94,* 4463–4471.

Loney, B. R., Taylor, J., Butler, M. A., & Iacono, W. G. (2007). Adolescent psychopathy features: 6-year temporal stability and the prediction of externalizing symptoms during the transition to adulthood. *Aggressive Behavior, 33,* 242–252.

Long, B. C., & van Stavel, R. (1995). Effects of exercise training on anxiety: A meta-analysis. *Journal of Applied Sport Psychology, 7,* 167–189.

Long, N., Readdy, T., & Raabe, J. (2014). What motivates firefighters to exercise? A mixed-methods investigation of self-determination theory constructs and exercise behavior. *Sport, Exercise, and Performance Psychology, 3,* 203–218, doi: 10.1037/spy0000012

Longstreth Jr., W. T., Koepsell, T. D., Ton, T. G., Hendrickson, A. F., & van Belle, G. (2007). The epidemiology of narcolepsy. *Sleep, 30,* 13–26.

Lonsdorf, T. B., Weike, A. I., Nikamo, P., Schalling, M., Hamm, A. O., & Ohman, A. (2009). Genetic gating of human fear learning and extinction: Possible implications for gene-environment interaction in anxiety disorder. *Psychological Science, 20,* 198–206.

Loo, C. K., Mitchell, P. B., Croker, V. M., Malhi, G. S., Wen, W., Gandevia, S. C., & Sachdev, P. S. (2003). Double-blind controlled investigation of bilateral prefrontal transcranial magnetic stimulation for the treatment of resistant major depression. *Psychological Medicine, 33,* 33–40.

Lopez Cascales, J. J., Oliveira Costa, S. D., de Groot, B. L., & Walters, D. E. (2010). Binding of glutamate to the umami receptor. *Biochemical Chemistry, 152,* 139–144.

Lopez, C. M., Driscoll, K. A., & Kistner, J. A. (2009). Sex differences and response styles: Subtypes of rumination and associations with depressive symptoms. *Journal of Clinical Child and Adolescent Psychology, 38,* 27–35.

Lorenz, F. O., Simons, R. L., Conger, R. D., Elder, G. H., Jr., Johnson, C., & Chao, W. (1997). Married and recently divorced mothers' stressful events and distress: Tracing change across time. *Journal of Marriage and Family, 59,* 219–232.

Lorenz, F. O., Wickrama, K. A., Conger, R. D., & Elder, G. H., Jr. (2006). The short-term and decade-long effects of divorce on women's midlife health. *Journal of Health and Social Behavior, 47,* 111–125.

Lorenzo-Luaces, L., Derubeis, R. J., & Webb, C. A. (2014). Client characteristics as moderators of the relation between the therapeutic alliance and outcome in cognitive therapy for depression. *Journal of Consulting and Clinical Psychology, 82,* 368–373.

Loughnan, S., Haslam, N., Sutton, R. M., & Spencer, B. (2014). Dehumanization and social class: Animality in the stereotypes of "white trash," "chavs," and "bogans." *Social Psychology, 45,* 54–61. doi:10.1027/1864-9335/a000159

Lourenco, O., & Machado, A. (1996). In defense of Piaget's theory: A reply to 10 common criticisms. *Psychological Review, 103,* 143–164.

Loveless, A. S., & Holman, T. B. (2007). *The family in the new millennium: The place of family in human society.* Westport, CT: Praeger.

Lowe, S. R., Dillon, C. O., Rhodes, J. E., & Zwiebach, L. (2013). Defining adult experiences: Perspectives of a diverse sample of young adults. *Journal of Adolescent Research, 28,* 31–68.

Lowis, M. J., Edwards, A. C., & Burton, M. (2009). Coping with retirement: Well-being, health, and religion. *Journal of Psychology, 143,* 427–448.

Lu, H., Xu, F., Rodrigue, K. M., Kennedy, K. M., Cheng, Y., Flicker, B. et al. (2011). Alterations in cerebral metabolic rate and blood supply across the adult lifespan. *Cerebral Cortex, 21,* 1426–1434.. doi:10.1093/cercor/bhq224

Lu, N. Z., Eshleman, A. J., Janowsky, A., & Bethea, C. L. (2003). Ovarian steroid regulation of serotonin reuptake transporter (SERT) binding, distribution, and function in female macaques. *Molecular Psychiatry, 8,* 353–360.

Lucas, R. E. (2005). Time does not heal all wounds: A longitudinal study of reaction and adaptation to divorce. *Psychological Science, 16,* 945–950.

Luders, E., Thompson, P. M., Kurth, F., Hong, J., Phillips, O. R., Wang, Y. et al. (2013). Global and regional alterations of hippocampal anatomy in long-term meditation practitioners. *Human Brain Mapping, 34,* 3369–3375. doi:10.1002/hbm.22153

Ludtke, O., Trautwein, U., & Husemann, N. (2009). Goal and personality trait development in a transitional period: Assessing change and stability in personality development. *Personality and Social Psychology Bulletin, 35,* 428–441.

Luecken, L. J., & Compas, B. E. (2002). Stress, coping, and immune function in breast cancer. *Annals of Behavioral Medicine, 24,* 336–344.

Luhmann, M., Hofmann, W., Eid, M., & Lucas, R. E. (2012). Subjective well-being and adaptation to life events: A meta-analysis. *Journal of Personality and Social Psychology, 102,* 592–615.

Lumer, E. D., Friston, K. J., & Rees, G. (1998). Neural correlates of perceptual rivalry in the human brain. *Science, 280,* 1930–1934.

Luo, J. (2012). Mechanisms of ethanol-induced death of cerebellar granule cells. *The Cerebellum, 11,* 145–154. doi:10.1007/s12311-010-0219-0

Luo, S. (2009). What leads to romantic attraction: Similarity, reciprocity, security, or beauty? Evidence from a speed-dating study. *Journal of Personality, 77,* 933–964.

Lykken, D. T., McGue, M., Tellegen, A., & Bouchard, T. J. (1992). Emergenesis. *American Psychologist, 47,* 1565–1567.

Lynn, B., Yoo, G. J., & Levine, E. G. (in press). "Trust in the Lord": Religious and spiritual practices of African American breast cancer survivors. *Journal of Religion and Health.*

Lynn, S. J. (1997). Automaticity and hypnosis: A sociocognitive account. *International Journal of Clinical and Experimental Hypnosis, 45,* 239–250.

Lynn, S. J., & Green, J. P. (2011). The sociocognitive and dissociation theories of hypnosis: Toward a rapprochement. *International Journal of Clinical and Experimental Hypnosis, 59,* 277–293.

Lynn, S. J., Lilienfeld, S. O., Merckelbach, H., Giesbrecht, T., & van der Kloet, D. (2012). Dissociation and dissociative disorders: Challenging conventional wisdom. *Current Directions in Psychological Science, 21,* 48–53.

Lynne-Landsman, S. D., Graber, J. A., Nichols, T. R., & Botvin, G. J. (2011). Is sensation seeking a stable trait or does it change over time? *Journal of Youth and Adolescence, 40,* 48–58. doi:10.1007/s10964-010-9529-2

Lytton, H., & Romney, D. M. (1991). Parents' differential socialization of boys and girls: A meta-analysis. *Psychological Bulletin, 109,* 267–296.

Lyubomirsky, S., & Layous, K. (2013). How do simple positive activities increase well-being? *Current Directions in Psychological Science, 22,* 5762.

Maas, J. B. (1998). *The sleep advantage: Preparing your mind for peak performance.* New York: Villard.

Macan, T. (2009). The employment interview: A review of current studies and directions for future research. *Human Resource Management Review, 19,* 203–218.

Macfadden, W., Bossie C. A., Turkoz, I., & Haskins, J. T. (2010). Risperidone long-acting therapy in stable patients with recently diagnosed schizophrenia. *International Clinical Psychopharmacology, 25,* 75–82.

Macintosh, H. B., & Johnson, S. (2008). Emotionally focused therapy for couples and childhood sexual abuse survivors. *Journal of Marital and Family Therapy, 34,* 298–315.

MacIntyre, G. F. (1998). And what's keeping you from finishing your book? *Writer's Digest, 78,* 6.

Mackay, J. (2000). *The Penguin atlas of human sexual behavior: Sexuality and sexual practices around the world.* New York: Penguin Putnam.

Maddi, S. R. (2005). On hardiness and other pathways to resilience. *American Psychologist, 60,* 261–262.

Maddi, S. R., & Kobasa, S. C. (1984). *The hardy executive: Health under stress.* Homewood, IL: Dorsey Press.

Maddi, S. R., Harvey, R. H., Khoshaba, D. M., Lu, J. L., Persico, M., & Brow, M. (2006). The personality construct of hardiness: III. Relationships with repression, innovativeness, authoritarianism, and performance. *Journal of Personality, 74,* 575–597.

Maguire, E. A., & Mullally, S. L. (2013). The hippocampus: A manifesto for change. *Journal of Experimental Psychology: General, 142,* 1180–1189. doi:10.1037/a0033650

Maguire, E. A., Woollett, K., & Spiers, H. J. (2006). London taxi drivers and bus drivers: A structural MRI and neuropsychological analysis. *Hippocampus, 16,* 1091–1101.

Magura, S., Laudet, A. B., Mahmood, D., Rosenblum, A., & Knight, E. (2002). Adherence to medication regimes and participation in dual-focus self-help groups. *Psychiatric Services, 53,* 310–316.

Mah, K., & Binik, Y. M. (2002). Do all orgasms feel alike? Evaluating the two-dimensional model of the orgasm experience across gender and sexual context. *Journal of Sex Research, 39,* 104–113.

Maher, A. R., & Theodore, G. (2012). Summary of the comparative effectiveness review on off-label use of atypical antipsychotics. *Journal of Managed Care Pharmacy, 18,* S1–S20.

Maillot, P., Perrot, A., & Hartley, A. (2012). Effects of interactive physical-activity video-game training on physical and cognitive function in older adults. *Psychology and Aging, 27,* 589–600.

Main, M., & Solomon, J. (1990). Procedures for identifying infants as disorganized/disoriented during the Ainsworth Strange Situation. In M. Greenberg, D. Cicchetti, & M. Cummings (Eds.), *Attachment in the preschool years: Theory, research, and intervention* (pp. 121–160). Chicago: University of Chicago Press.

Maisonneuve, J., Palmade, G., & Fourment, C. (1952). Selective choices and propinquity. *Sociometry, 15,* 135–140.

Maj, M., Pirozzi, R., Magliano, L., & Bartoli, L. (1997). Long-term outcome of lithium prophylaxis in bipolar disorder: A 5-year prospective study of 402 patients at a lithium clinic. *American Journal of Psychiatry, 155,* 30–55.

Majdandzic, M., & van den Boom, D. C. (2007). Multimethod longitudinal assessment of temperament in early childhood. *Journal of Personality, 75,* 121–168.

Makinen, J. A., & Johnson, S. M. (2006). Resolving attachment injuries in couples using emotionally focused therapy: Steps toward forgiveness and reconciliation. *Journal of Consulting and Clinical Psychology, 74,* 1055–1064.

Makino, H., & Jitsumori, M. (2007). Discrimination of artificial categories structured by family resemblances: A comparative study in people (Homo sapiens) and pigeons (Columba livia). *Journal of Comparative Psychology, 121,* 22–33.

Makris, N., Swaab, D. F., van der Kouwe, A., Abbs, B., Boriel, D., Handa, R. J. et al. (2013). Volumetric parcellation methodology of the human hypothalamus in neuroimaging: Normative data and sex differences. *Neuroimage, 69,* 1–10. doi:10.1016/j.neuroimage.2012.12.008

Malaspina, D., Harlap, S., Fennig, S., Heiman, D., Nahon, D., Feldman, D. et al. (2001). Advancing paternal age and the risk of schizophrenia. *Archives of General Psychiatry, 58,* 361–367.

Malina, R. M. (1990). Physical growth and performance during the transitional years (9–16). In R. Montemayor, G. R. Adams, & T. P. Gullotta (Eds.), *From childhood to adolescence: A transitional period?* (pp. 41–62). Newbury Park, CA: Sage.

Mancini, A. D., Bonanno, G. A., & Clark, G. E. (2011). Stepping off the hedonic treadmill: Individual differences in response to major life events. *Journal of Individual Differences, 32,* 144–152.

Mann, R. D. (1959). A review of the relationships between personality and performance in small groups. *Psychological Bulletin, 56,* 241–270.

Manning, W. D. (2001). Childbearing in cohabiting unions: Racial and ethnic differences. *Family Planning Perspectives, 33,* 217–223.

Marañon, I., Echeburúa, E., & Grijalvo, J. (2004). Prevalence of personality disorders in patients with eating disorders: A pilot study using the IPDE. *European Eating Disorders Review, 12,* 217–222.

Marazzitti, D., Rotondo, A., Presta, S., Pancioloi-Guasagnucci, M. L., Palego, L., & Conti, L. (1993). Role of serotonin in human aggressive behavior. *Aggressive Behavior, 19,* 347–353.

Marchetti, I., Koster, E. H. W., & De Raedt, R. (2013). Rest-related dynamics of risk and protective factors for depression: A behavioral study. *Clinical Psychological Science, 1,* 443–451.

Marcia, J. E. (2002). Identity and psychosocial development in adulthood. *Identity, 2,* 7–28.

Mareschal, D. (2000). Object knowledge in infancy: Current controversies and approaches. *Trends in Cognitive Science, 4,* 408–416.

Mariotti, J. (1997, March 3). Coping with cyber-age lingo. *Industry Week, 246,* 5.

Mariscal, M., Palma, S., Liorca, J., Perez-Iglesias, R., Pardo-Crespo, R., & Delgado-Rodriguez, M. (2006). Pattern of alcohol consumption during pregnancy and risk for low birth weight. *Annals of Epidemiology, 16,* 432–438.

Markman, A. B., & Ross, B. H. (2003). Category use and category learning. *Psychological Bulletin, 129,* 592–613.

Marks, D. F. (2010). IQ variations across time, race, and nationality: An artifact of differences in literacy skills. *Psychological Reports, 106,* 643–664.

Markus, H. R. (2013). Who am I? Race, ethnicity, and identity. In S .J. Ferguson (Ed.), *Race, gender, sexuality, and social class: Dimensions of inequality* (pp. 179–188). Thousand Oaks, CA: Sage.

Markus, H. R., & Kitayama, S. (2010). Culture and selves: A cycle of mutual constitution. *Perspectives on Psychological Science, 5,* 420–430.

Markus, H., Crane, M., Bernstein, S., & Siladi, M. (1982). Self-schemas and gender. *Journal of Personality and Social Psychology, 42,* 38–50.

Marler, P. R., Duffy, A., & Pickert, R. (1986). Vocal communication in the domestic chicken: II. Is a sender sensitive to the presence and nature of a receiver? *Animal Behavior, 34,* 194–198.

Marques, J. F. (2010). The effect of visual deprivation on the organization of conceptual knowledge: Testing the grounded cognition hypothesis. *Experimental Psychology, 57,* 83–88.

Martin, C. L., & Halverson, C. F. (1981). A schematic processing model of sex typing and stereotyping in children. *Child Development, 52,* 1119–1134.

Martin, C. L., & Halverson, C. F. (1987). The role of cognition in sex role acquisition. In D. B. Carter (Ed.), *Current conceptions of sex roles and sex typing: Theory and research* (pp. 123–137). New York: Praeger.

Martin, C. L., & Ruble, D. (2004). Children's search for gender cues: Cognitive perspectives on gender development. *Current Directions in Psychological Science, 13,* 67–70.

Martin, C. L., & Ruble, D. N. (2010). Patterns of gender development. *Annual Review of Psychology, 61,* 353–381.

Martin, D. J., Garske, J. P., & Davis, M. K. (2000). Relation of the therapeutic alliance with outcome and other variables: A meta-analytic review. *Journal of Consulting and Clinical Psychology, 68,* 438–450.

Martin, G., & Pear, J. (2007). *Behavior modification: What it is and how to do it* (8th ed.). Englewood Cliffs, NJ: Prentice Hall.

Martin, G., England, G., Kaprowy, E., Kilgour, K., & Pilek, V. (1968). Operant conditioning of kindergarten-class behavior in autistic children. *Behavior Research and Therapy, 6,* 281–294.

Martinie, M., Milland, L., & Olive, T. (2013). Some theoretical considerations on attitude, arousal and affect during cognitive dissonance. *Social and Personality Psychology Compass, 7,* 680–688. doi:10.1111/spc3.1205

Martinie, M., Olive, T., & Milland, L. (2010). Cognitive dissonance induced by writing a counterattitudinal essay facilitates performance on simple tasks but not on complex tasks that involve working memory. *Journal of Experimental Social Psychology, 46,* 587–594. doi:10.1016/j.jesp.2009.10.018

Martorana, A., Mori, F., Esposito, Z., Kusayanagi, H., Monteleone, F., Codecà, C. et al. (2009). Dopamine modulates cholinergic cortical excitability in Alzheimer's disease patients. *Neuropsychopharmacology, 34,* 2323–2328.

Martuzzi, R., van der Zwaag, W., Farthouat, J., Gruetter, R., & Blanke, O. (2014). Human finger somatotopy in areas 3b, 1, and 2: A 7T fMRI study using a natural stimulus. *Human Brain Mapping, 35,* 213–226. doi:10.1002/hbm.22172

Marzoli, D., Custodero, M., Pagliara, A., & Tommasi, L. (2013). Sun-induced frowning fosters aggressive feelings. *Cognition and Emotion, 27,* 1513–1521. doi:10.1080/02699931.2013.801338

Mashal, N., & Faust, M. (2008). Right hemisphere sensitivity to novel metaphoric relations: Application of the signal detection theory. *Brain and Language, 104,* 103–112.

Maslow, A. (1968). *Toward a psychology of being* (2nd ed.). New York: Van Nostrand.

Maslow, A. (1970). *Motivation and personality* (2nd ed.). New York: Harper & Row.

Maslow, A. (1971). *The farther reaches of human nature.* New York: Viking.

Massaro, D. W., & Loftus, G. R. (1996). Sensory and perceptual storage. In E. L. Bjork & R. A. Bjork (Eds.), *Memory* (pp. 67–99). San Diego: Academic Press.

Masters, K. S., & Hooker, S. A. (2013). Religiousness/spirituality, cardiovascular disease, and cancer: Cultural integration for health research and intervention. *Journal of Consulting and Clinical Psychology, 81,* 206–216.

Masters, W. H., & Johnson, V. E. (1966). *Human sexual response.* Boston: Little, Brown.

Masters, W. H., Johnson, V. E., & Kolodny, R. C. (1993). *Biological foundations of human sexuality.* New York: HarperCollins.

Mathew, R., Wilson, W., Blazer, D., & George, L. (1993). Psychiatric disorders in adult children of alcoholics: Data from the epidemiologic catchment area project. *American Journal of Psychiatry, 150,* 793–796.

Matlin, M. W., & Foley, H. J. (1997). *Sensation and perception.* Boston: Allyn & Bacon.

Matson, J. L., & Boisjoli, J. A. (2009). The token economy for children with intellectual disability and/or autism: A review. *Research in Developmental Disabilities, 30,* 240–248.

Matsuda, L. A., Lolait, S. J., Brownstein, M. J., Young, A. C., & Bonner, T. I. (1990). Structure of a cannabinoid receptor and functional expression of the cloned cDNA. *Nature, 346,* 561–564.

Matsumoto, D. (1994). *People: Psychology from a cross-cultural perspective.* Pacific Grove, CA: Brooks/Cole.

Matud, M. P. (2004). Gender differences in stress and coping styles. *Personality and Individual Differences, 37,* 1401–1415.

Mauss, I. B., Cook, C. L., Cheng, J. Y., & Gross, J. J. (2007). Individual differences in cognitive reappraisal: Experiential and physiological responses to an anger provocation. *International Journal of Psychophysiology, 66,* 116–124.

Maville, J., & Huerta, C. G. (1997). Stress and social support among Hispanic student nurses: Implications for academic achievement. *Journal of Cultural Diversity, 4,* 18–25.

Maxwell, J. C., & Spence, R. T. (2003). Profiles of club drug users in treatment. *Substance Use and Misuse, 40,* 1409–1426.

Mayberg, H. S. (1997). Limbic-cortical dysregulation: A proposed model of depression. *Journal of Neuropsychiatry & Clinical Neuroscience, 9,* 471–481.

Mayberg, H. S., Liotti, M., Brannan, S. K., McGinnis, S., Mahurin, R. K., Jerabek, P. A. et al. (1999). Reciprocal limbic-cortical function and negative mood: Converging PET findings in depression and normal sadness. *American Journal of Psychiatry, 156,* 675–682.

Mayberg, H. S., Lozano, A. M., Voon, V., McNeely, H. E., Seminowicz, D., Hamani, C. et al. (2005). Deep brain stimulation for treatment-resistant depression. *Neuron, 45,* 651–660.

Mayer, J. D., Salovey, P., Caruso, D. R., & Sitarenios, G. (2003). Measuring emotional intelligence with the MSCEIT V2.0. *Emotion, 3,* 97–105.

Mayer, R. E. (1983). *Thinking, problem solving, cognition.* San Francisco: Freeman.

Mayes, L. C., Bornstein, M. H., Chawarska, K., & Haynes, O. M. (1996). Impaired regulation of arousal in 3-month-old infants exposed prenatally to cocaine and other drugs. *Development and Psychopathology, 8,* 29–42.

Mazure, C. M., Keita, G. P., & Blehar, M. C. (2002). *Summit on women and depression: Proceedings and recommendations.* Washington, DC: American Psychological Association.

McAdams, D. P. (2013). The psychological self as actor, agent, and author. *Perspectives on Psychological Science, 8,* 272–295.

McAdams, D. P., & Olson, B. D. (2010). Personality development: Continuity and change over the life course. *Annual Review of Psychology, 61,* 517–542.

McAlpine, D. D., & Mechanic, D. (2000). Utilization of specialty mental health care among persons with severe mental illness: The roles of demographics, need, insurance, and risk. *Health Services Research, 35,* 277–292.

McAndrew, F. (1986). A cross-cultural study of recognition thresholds for facial expressions of emotions. *Journal of Cross-Cultural Psychology, 17,* 211–224.

McCabe, K. O., & Fleeson, W. (2012). What is extraversion for? Integrating trait and motivational perspectives and identifying the purpose of extraversion. *Psychological Science, 23,* 1498–1505.

McCallie, M. S., Blum, C. M., & Hood, C. J. (2006). Progressive muscle relaxation. *Journal of Human Behavior in the Social Environment, 13,* 51, 66.

McCann, U. D., Wilson, M. J., Sgambati, F. P., & Ricaurte, G. A. (2009). Sleep deprivation differentially impairs cognitive performance in abstinent methylenedioxymethamphetamine ("Ecstasy") users. *Journal of Neuroscience, 29,* 14050–14056.

McCarley, R. W. (1998). Dreams: Disguise of forbidden wishes or transparent reflections of a distinct brain state? *Annals of the New York Academy of Sciences, 843,* 116–133.

McClelland, D. C. (1987). *Human motivation.* Cambridge: Cambridge University Press.

McClung, C. A. (2007). Circadian genes, rhythms and the biology of mood disorders. *Pharmacology and Therapeutics, 114,* 222–232.

McClure, H. H., Snodgrass, J. J., Martinez, C. R., Jr., Eddy, J. M., Jimenez, R. A., & Isiordia, L. E. (2010). Discrimination, psychosocial stress, and health among Latin American immigrants in Oregon. *American Journal of Human Biology, 22,* 421–423.

McConkey, K. M. (1995). Hypnosis, memory, and the ethics of uncertainty. *Australian Psychologist, 30,* 1–10.

McCrae, R. R. (2009, June). Cross-cultural research on the five-factor model of personality (Version 2). *Online Readings in Psychology and Culture* (Unit 6, Chapter 1/V2).

McCrae, R. R., & Costa, P. T. (1998). Personality trait structure as a human universal. *American Psychologist, 52,* 509–516.

McCrae, R. R., Costa, P. T., Ostendorf, F., Angleitner, A., Hrebickova, M., Avia, M. D. et al. (2000). Nature over nurture: Temperament, personality, and life span development. *Journal of Personality and Social Psychology, 78,* 173–186.

McCrae, R. R., Costa, P. T., Pedroso de Lima, M., Simoes, A., Ostendorf, F., Angleitner, A. et al. (1999). Age differences in personality across the adult life span: Parallels in five cultures. *Developmental Psychology, 35,* 466–477.

McCrae, R. R., Costa, P. T., Terracciano, A., Parker, W. D., Mills, C. J., De Fruyt, F. et al. (2002). Personality trait development from age 12 to age 18: Longitudinal, cross-sectional, and cross-cultural analyses. *Journal of Personality and Social Psychology, 83,* 1456–1468.

McCullough, M. E., Hoyt, W. T., Larson, D. S., Koenig, H. G., & Thoresen, C. (2000). Religious involvement and mortality: A meta-analytic review. *Health Psychology, 19,* 211–222.

McEvoy, P. M., & Nathan, P. (2007). Effectiveness of cognitive behavior therapy for diagnostically heterogeneous groups: A benchmarking study. *Journal of Consulting and Clinical Psychology, 75,* 344–350.

McFalls, J. A., Jr. (1990). The risks of reproductive impairment in the later years of childbearing. *Annual Review of Sociology, 16,* 491–519.

McGehee, D. S., Heath, M. J. S., Gelber, S., Devay, P., & Role, L. W. (1995). Nicotine enhancement of fast excitation synaptic transmissions in CNS by presynaptic receptors. *Science, 269,* 1692–1696.

McGlashan, T. H., & Hoffman, R. E. (2000). Schizophrenia as a disorder of developmentally reduced synaptic connectivity. *Archives of General Psychiatry, 57,* 637–648.

McGregor, G., Desaga, J. F., Ehlenz, K., Fischer, A., Heese, F., Hegele, A. et al. (1996). Radioimmunological measurement of leptin in plasma of obese and diabetic human subjects. *Endocrinology, 137,* 1501–1504.

McGuffin, P., Rijsdijk, F., Andrew, M., Sham, P., Katz, R., & Cardno, A. (2003). The heritability of bipolar affective disorder and the genetic relationship to unipolar depression. *Archives of General Psychiatry, 60,* 497–502.

McGuigan, N. (2013). The influence of model status on the tendency of young children to over-imitate. *Journal of Experimental Child Psychology, 116,* 962–969. doi:10.1016/j.jecp.2013.05.004

McHolm, A. E., MacMillan, H. L., & Jamieson, E. (2003). The relationship between childhood physical abuse and suicidality among depressed women: Results from a community sample. *American Journal of Psychiatry, 160,* 933–938.

McIntosh, D. N. (1996). Facial feedback hypotheses: Evidence, implications, and directions. *Motivation and Emotion, 20,* 121–147.

McIntosh, D. N., Poulin, M. J., Silver, R. C., & Holman, E. A. (2011). The distinct roles of spirituality and religiosity in physical and mental health after collective trauma: A national longitudinal study of responses to the 9/11 attacks. *Journal of Behavioral Medicine, 34,* 497–507.

McIntosh, E., Gillanders, D., & Rodgers, S. (2010). Rumination, goal linking, daily hassles and life events in major depression. *Clinical Psychology & Psychotherapy, 17,* 33–43.

McKay, A., & Barrett, M. (2010). Trends in teen pregnancy rates from 1996–2006: A comparison of Canada, Sweden, U.S.A., and England/Wales. *Canadian Journal of Human Sexuality, 19,* 43–52.

McKean, K. J. (1994). Using multiple risk factors to assess the behavioral, cognitive, and affective effects of learned helplessness. *Journal of Psychology, 128,* 177–183.

McKenna, M. C., Zevon, M. A., Corn, B., & Rounds, J. (1999). Psychosocial factors and the development of breast cancer: A meta-analysis. *Health Psychology, 18,* 520–531.

McKillip, J., & Reidel, S. L. (1983). External validity of matching on physical attractiveness for same and opposite sex couples. *Journal of Applied Social Psychology, 13,* 328–337.

McKim, W. A. (1997). *Drugs and behavior.* Upper Saddle River, NJ: Prentice Hall.

McKnight-Eily, L. R., Liu, Y., Perry, G. S., Presley-Cantrell, L. R., Strine, T. W., Lu, H. et al. (2009). Perceived insufficient rest or sleep among adults—United States, 2008. *Morbidity and Mortality Weekly Report, 58,* 1175–1179.

McLaughlin Crabtree, V., & Williams, N. A. (2009). Normal sleep in children and adolescents. *Child and Adolescent Psychiatric Clinics of North America, 18,* 799–811.

McLaughlin, K. A., Borkovec, T. D., & Sibrava, N. J. (2007). The effects of worry and rumination on affect states and cognitive activity. *Behavior Therapy, 38,* 23–38.

McLaughlin, K. A., Green, J. G., Gruber, M. J., Sampson, N. A., Zaslavsky, A. M., & Kessler, R. C. (2010). Childhood adversities and adult psychiatric disorders in the National Comorbidity Survey Replication II: Associations with persistence of DSM-IV disorders. *Archives of General Psychiatry, 67,* 124–132.

McLay, R. N., McBrien, C., Wiederhold, M. D., & Wiederhold, B. K. (2010). Exposure therapy with and without virtual reality to treat PTSD while in the combat theater: A parallel case series. *Cyberpsychology, Behavior, and Social Networking, 13,* 37–42.

McLean, C. P., Asnaani, A., Litz, B. T., & Hofmann, S. G. (2011). Gender differences in anxiety disorders: Prevalence, course of illness, comorbidity and burden of illness. *Journal of Psychiatric Research, 45,* 1027–1035.

McManus, M. A., & Baratta, J. E. (1992). *The relationship of recruiting source to performance and survival.* Paper presented at the annual meeting of the Society for Industrial and Organizational Psychology, Montreal.

McMillen, D. L., Smith, S. M., & Wells-Parker, E. (1989). The effects of alcohol, expectancy, and sensation seeking on driving risk taking. *Addictive Behaviors, 14,* 477–483.

McNeil, D. W., & Kyle, B. N. (2009). Exposure strategies. In S. Cormier, P. S. Nurius, & C. J. Osborn (Eds.), *Interviewing and change strategies for helpers: Fundamental skills and cognitive behavioral interventions* (6th ed., pp. 486–516). Belmont, CA: Brooks/Cole.

McNeill, B., Prieto, L., Niemann, Y., Pizarro, M., Vera, E., & Gomez, S. (2001). Current directions in Chicana/o psychology. *Counseling Psychologist, 29,* 5–17.

McRae, K., Ochsner, K. N., Mauss, I. B., Gabrieli, J. J. D., & Gross, J. J. (2008). Gender differences in emotion regulation: An fMRI study of cognitive reappraisal. *Group Processes & Intergroup Relations, 11,* 143–162.

Medicare to fund obesity treatment. (2004, July 16). CBS News. Available online at http://www.cbsnews.com/stories/2004/07/16/health/main630141.shtml?tag=mncol;lst;1

Medina-Mora, M. E., Borges, G., Lara, C., Benjet, C., Blanco, J., Fleiz, C. et al. (2005). Prevalence, service use, and demographic correlates of 12-month DSM-IV psychiatric disorders in Mexico: Results from the Mexican National Comorbidity Survey. *Psychological Medicine, 35,* 1773–1783.

Mega, C., Ronconi, L., & De Beni, R. (2014). What makes a good student? How emotions, self-regulated learning, and motivation contribute to academic achievement. *Journal of Educational Psychology, 106,* 121–131. doi:10.1037/a0033546

Mehl, M. R., Vazire, S., Holleran, S. E., & Clark, C. S. (2010). Eavesdropping on happiness: Well-being is related to having less small talk and more substantive conversations. *Psychological Science, 21,* 539–541.

Meier, A. E., Fryling, M. J., & Wallace, M. D. (2012). Using high-probability foods to increase the acceptance of low-probability foods. *Journal of Applied Behavior Analysis, 45,* 149–153.

Mellman, T. A., Alim, T., Brown, D. D., Gorodetsky, E., Buzas, B., Lawson, W. B. et al. (2009). Serotonin polymorphisms and posttraumatic stress disorder in a trauma exposed African American population. *Depression and Anxiety, 26,* 993–997.

Meltzer, L. J., & Mindell, J. A. (2006). Sleep and sleep disorders in children and adolescents. *Psychiatric Clinics of North America, 29,* 1059–1076.

Mennella, J. A., & Beauchamp, G. K. (1991). Maternal diet alters the sensory qualities of human milk and nursling's behavior. *Pediatrics, 88,* 737–744.

Menz, M. M., Rihm, J. S., Salari, N., Born, J., Kalisch, R., Pape, H. C. et al. (2013). The role of sleep and sleep deprivation in consolidating fear memories. *NeuroImage, 75,* 87–96.

Menzies, H. (2005). *No time: Stress and the crisis of modern life.* Vancouver, Canada: Douglas & McIntyre.

Menzies, R. G., & Clark, J. C. (1993). A comparison of in vivo and vicarious exposure in the treatment of childhood water phobia. *Behaviour Research and Therapy, 31,* 9–15.

Merikangas, K. R., He, J. P., Burstein, M., Swanson, S. A., Avenevoli, S., Cui, L. et al. (2010). Lifetime prevalence of mental disorder in U.S. adolescents: Results from the National Comorbidity Survey Replication—Adolescent Supplement (NCS-A). *Journal of the American Academy of Child and Adolescent Psychiatry, 49,* 980–989.

Merikangas, K. R., Jin, R., He, J. P., Kessler, R. C., Lee, S., Sampson, N. A. et al. (2011). Prevalence and correlates of bipolar spectrum disorder in the World Mental Health Survey Initiative. *Archive of General Psychiatry, 68,* 241–251.

Merkl, A., Heuser, I., & Bajbouj, M. (2009). Antidepressant electroconvulsive therapy: Mechanism of action, recent advances and limitations. *Experimental Neurology, 219,* 20–26.

Messner, M., Reinhard, M., & Sporer, S. L. (2008). Compliance through direct persuasive appeals: The moderating role of communicator's attractiveness in interpersonal persuasion. *Social Influence, 3,* 67–83.

Meyer, D. (2007). Selective serotonin reuptake inhibitors and their effects on relationship satisfaction. *Family Journal, 15,* 392–397.

Meyer, J. P., & Allen, N. J. (1991). A three-component conceptualization of organizational commitment. *Human Resource Management Review, 1,* 61–89.

Meyer, J. P., & Herscovitch, L. (2001). Commitment in the workplace: Toward a general model. *Human Resource Management Review, 11,* 299–326.

Meyer, L. (1999). Hostile classrooms. *The Advocate, 32*(1), 33–35.

Meyerbroeker, K., Morina, N., Kerkhof, G. A., & Emmelkamp, P. M. (2013). Virtual reality exposure therapy does not provide any additional value in agoraphobic patients: A randomized controlled trial. *Psychotherapy and Psychosomatics, 82,* 170–176.

Mezulis, A. H., Abramson, L. Y., Hyde, J. S., & Hankin, B. L. (2004). Is there a universal positivity bias in attributions? A meta-analytic review of individual, developmental, and cultural differences in the self-serving attributional bias. *Psychological Bulletin, 130,* 711–747.

Micco, J. A., Henin, A., Mick, E., Kim, S., Hopkins, C. A., Biederman, J. et al. (2009). Anxiety and depressive disorders in offspring at high risk for anxiety: A meta-analysis. *Journal of Anxiety Disorders, 23,* 1158–1164.

Michael, G. A., Boucart, M., Degreef, J. F., & Goefroy, O. (2001). The thalamus interrupts top-down attentional control for permitting exploratory shiftings to sensory signals. *Neuroreport, 12,* 2041–2048.

Michael, R. T., Gagnon, J. H., Laumann, E. O., & Kolata, G. (1994). *Sex in America: A definitive survey.* Boston: Little, Brown.

Michalski, D., Kohout, J., Wicherski, M., & Hart, B. (2011). *2009 Doctorate Employment Survey.* Washington, DC: APA Center for Workforce Studies.

Michelson, D., Bancroft, J., Targum, S., Kim, Y., & Tepner, R. (2000). Female sexual dysfunction associated with antidepressant administration: A randomized, placebo-controlled study of pharmacological intervention. *American Journal of Psychiatry, 157,* 239–243.

Migliore, M., Novara, G., & Tegolo, D. (2008). Single neuron binding properties and the magical number 7. *Hippocampus, 18,* 1122–1130.

Milad, M. R., & Rauch, S. L. (2012). Obsessive-compulsive disorder: Beyond segregated corticostriatal pathways. *Trends in Cognitive Sciences, 16,* 43–51.

Milgram, S. (1963). Behavioral study of obedience. *Journal of Abnormal and Social Psychology, 67,* 371–378.

Milgram, S. (1965). Some conditions of obedience and disobedience to authority. *Human Relations, 18,* 57–76.

Milgram, S. (1974). *Obedience to authority: An experimental view.* New York: Harper & Row.

Millar, M. (2002). The effectiveness of the door-in-the-face compliance strategy on friends and strangers. *Journal of Social Psychology, 142,* 295–305.

Miller, A. G. (2009). Reflections on "Replicating Milgram." *American Psychologist, 64,* 20–27.

Miller, B. C., & Benson, B. (1999). Romantic and sexual relationship development during adolescence. In W. Furman, B. B. Brown, & C. Feiring (Eds.), *The development of romantic relationships in adolescence* (pp. 99–121). New York: Cambridge University Press.

Miller, D. T., & Ross, M. (1975). Self-serving biases in the attribution of causality: Fact or fiction? *Psychological Bulletin, 82,* 213–225.

Miller, E. (1999). The pheromone androsterol: Evolutionary considerations. *Mankind Quarterly, 39,* 455–466.

Miller, G. A. (1956). The magical number seven, plus or minus two: Some limits on our capacity for processing information. *Psychological Review, 63,* 81–97.

Miller, G. E., & Blackwell, E. (2006). Turning up the heat: Inflammation as a mechanism linking chronic stress, depression, and heart disease. *Current Directions in Psychological Science, 15,* 269–272.

Miller, G. E., Lachman, M. E., Chen, E., Gruenewald, T. L., Karlamangla, A. S., & Seeman, T. E. (2011). Pathways to resilience: Maternal nurturance as a buffer against the effects of childhood poverty on metabolic syndrome at midlife. *Psychological Science, 22,* 1591–1599.,

Miller, I. J., Jr., & Bartoshuk, L. M. (1991). Taste perception, taste bud distribution, and spatial relationships. In T. V. Gethell, R. L. Doty, L. M. Bartoshuk, & J. B. Snow, Jr. (Eds.), *Smell and taste in health and disease* (pp. 205–233). New York: Raven.

Miller, N. S., & Gold, M. S. (1994). LSD and Ecstasy: Pharmacology, phenomenology, and treatment. *Psychiatric Annals, 24,* 131–133.

Miller, S., & Maner, J. K. (2010). Scent of a woman: Men's testosterone responses to olfactory ovulation cues. *Psychological Science, 21,* 276–283.

Miller, T. Q., Smith, T. W., Turner, C. W., Guijarro, M. L., & Hallet, A. J. (1996). A meta-analytic review of research on hostility and physical health. *Psychological Bulletin, 119,* 322–348.

Miller, T. Q., Turner, C. W., Tindale, R. S., Posavac, E. J., & Dugoni, B. L. (1991). Reasons for the trend toward null findings in research on Type A behavior. *Psychological Bulletin, 110,* 469–485.

Miller, W. R., & Seligman, M. E. P. (1975). Depression and learned helplessness in man. *Journal of Abnormal Psychology, 84,* 228–238.

Miller, W. R., & Thoresen, C. E. (2003). Spirituality, religion, and health. An emerging research field. *American Psychologist, 58,* 24–35.

Milliken, C. S., Auchterlonie, J. L., & Hoge, C. W. (2007). Longitudinal assessment of mental health problems among active and reserve component soldiers returning from the Iraq war. *Journal of the American Medical Association, 298,* 2141–2148.

Milling, L. S., Reardon, J. M., & Carosella, G. M. (2006). Mediation and moderation of psychological pain treatments: Response expectancies and hypnotic suggestibility. *Journal of Consulting and Clinical Psychology, 74,* 253–262.

Milner, C. E., & Cote, K. A. (2009). Benefits of napping in healthy adults: Impact of nap length, time of day, age, and experience with napping. *Journal of Sleep Research, 18,* 272–281.

Milton, J., & Wiseman, R. (2001). Does psi exist? Reply to Storm and Ertel (2001). *Psychological Bulletin, 127,* 434–438.

Minda, J. P., & Smith, J. D. (2002). Comparing prototype-based and exemplar-based accounts of category learning and attentional allocation. *Journal of Experimental Psychology: Learning, Memory, and Cognition, 28,* 275–292.

Miranda, R., De Jaegere, E., Restifo, K., & Schaffer, D. (2014). Longitudinal follow-up study of adolescent who report a suicide attempt: Aspects of suicidal behavior that increase risk of a future attempt. *Depression and Anxiety, 31,* 19–26.

Mischel, W., & Shoda, Y. (1995). A cognitive-affective system theory of personality: Reconceptualizing situations, dispositions, dynamics, and invariance of personality structure. *Psychological Review, 102,* 246–268.

Miselis, R. R., & Epstein, A. N. (1970). Feeding induced by 2-deoxy-D-glucose injections into the lateral ventrical of the rat. *Physiologist, 13,* 262.

Miskovic, V., Moscovitch, D. A., Santesso, D. L., McCabe, R. E., Antony, M. M., & Schmidt, L. A. (2011). Changes in EEG cross-frequency coupling during cognitive behavioral therapy for social anxiety disorder. *Psychological Science, 22,* 507–516.

Mitelman, S. A., Buchsbaum, M. S., Brickman, A. M., & Shihabuddin, L. (2005). Cortical intercorrelations of frontal area volumes in schizophrenia. *Neuroimage, 27,* 753–770.

Mithoefer, M. C., Wagner, M. T., Mithoefer, A. T., Jerome, L., & Doblin, R. (2011). The safety and efficacy of {+/-}3,4-methylenedioxymethamphetamine-assisted psychotherapy in subjects with chronic, treatment-resistant posttraumatic stress disorder: The first randomized controlled pilot study. *Journal of Psychopharmacology, 25,* 439–452.

Mithoefer, M. C., Wagner, M. T., Mithoefer, A. T., Jerome, L., Martin, S. F., Yazar-Klosinski, B. et al. (2013). Durability of improvement in post-traumatic stress disorder symptoms and absence of harmful effects or drug dependency after 3, 4-methylenedioxymethamphetamine-assisted psychotherapy: A prospective long-term follow-up study. *Journal of Psychopharmacology, 27,* 28–39.

Miyauchi, S., Misaki, M., Kan, S., Fukunaga, T., & Koike, T. (2009). Human brain activity time-locked to rapid eye movements during REM sleep. *Experimental Brain Research, 192,* 657–667.

Mizushige, T., Inoue, K., & Fushiki, T. (2007). Why is fat so tasty? Chemical reception of fatty acid on the tongue. *Journal of Nutritional Science and Vitaminology, 53,* 1–4.

Mobini, S., Chambers, L. C., & Yeomans, M. R. (2007). Effects of hunger state on flavour pleasantness conditioning at home: Flavour–nutrient learning vs. flavour–flavour learning. *Appetite, 48,* 20–28.

Moffitt, T. E. (2005). The new look of behavioral genetics in developmental psychopathology: Gene-environment interplay in antisocial behaviors. *Psychological Bulletin, 131,* 533–554.

Moffitt, T. E., Brammer, G. L., Caspi, A., Fawcet, J. P., Raleigh, M., Yuwiler, A. et al. (1998). Whole blood serotonin relates to violence in an epidemiological study. *Biological Psychiatry, 43,* 446–457.

Moffitt, T. E., Caspi, A., Taylor, A., Kokaua, J., Milne, B. J., Polanczyk, G., & Poulton, R. (2010). How common are common mental disorders? Evidence that lifetime prevalence rates are doubled by prospective versus retrospective ascertainment. *Psychological Medicine, 40,* 899–909.

Mogilner, C. (2010). The pursuit of happiness: Time, money, and social connection. *Psychological Science, 21,* 1348–1354.

Mohr, B. A., Guay, A. T., O'Donnell, A. B., & McKinlay, J. B. (2005). Normal, bound and nonbound testosterone levels in normally ageing men: Results from the Massachusetts Male Ageing Study. *Clinical Endocrinology, 62,* 64–73.

Mohr, C. (1964, March 28). Apathy is puzzle in Queens killing. *New York Times,* pp. 21, 40.

Mohr, C., Braun, S., Bridler, R., Chmetz, F., Delfino, J. P., Kluckner, V. J. et al. (2014). Insufficient coping behavior under chronic stress and vulnerability to psychiatric disorders. *Psychopathology, 47,* 235–243.

Mohr, D. C., Duffecy, J., Jin, L., Ludman, E. J., Lewis, A., Begale, M., & McCarthy, M. (2010). Multimodal e-mental health treatment for depression: A feasibility trial. *Journal of Medical Internet Research, 12,* e48.

Mojtabai, R. (2007). Americans' attitudes toward mental health treatment seeking: 1990–2003. *Psychiatric Services, 58,* 642–651.

Mojtabai, R. (2009). Americans' attitudes toward psychiatric medications: 1998–2006. *Psychiatric Services, 60,* 1015–1023.

Mokhber, N., Azarpazhooh, M. R., Khajehdaluee, M., Velayati, A., & Hopwood, M. (2010). Randomized, single-blind, trial of sertraline and buspirone for treatment of elderly patients with generalized anxiety disorder. *Psychiatry and Clinical Neurosciences, 64,* 128–133.

Molero, F., Navas, M. S., Gonzalez, J. L., Aleman, P., & Cuadrado, I. (2003). Paupers or riches: The perception of immigrants, tourists and ingroup members in a sample of Spanish children. *Journal of Ethnic and Migration Studies, 29,* 501–517.

Mommersteeg, P. M., & Pouwer, F. (2012). Personality as a risk factor for the metabolic syndrome: A systematic review. *Journal of Psychosomatic Research, 73,* 326–333.

Monaco, M., & Martin, M. (2007). The millennial student: A new generation of learners. *Athletic Training Education Journal, 2,* 42–46.

Mongrain, V., Lavoie, S., Selmaoui, B., Paquet, J., & Dumont, M. (2004). Phase relationships between sleep–wake cycle and underlying circadian rhythms in Morningness–Eveningness. *Journal of Biological Rhythms, 19,* 248–257.

Monroe, S. M., & Reid, M. W. (2009). Life stress and major depression. *Current Directions in Psychological Science, 18,* 68–72.

Monteith, M., & Winters, J. (2002, May–June). Why we hate. *Psychology Today, 35,* 44–51.

Montemayor, R., & Ranganathan, C. (2012). Asian-Indian parents' attributions about the causes of child behavior: A replication and extension with parents from Chennai, India. *Journal of Genetic Psychology: Research and Theory on Hu-*

man Development, 173, 374–392. doi:10.1080/00221325.2011.614649

Monti-Bloch, L., Diaz-Sanchez, V., Jennings-White, C., & Berliner, D. L. (1998). Modulation of serum testosterone and autonomic function through stimuluation of the male human vomeronasal organ (VNO) with pregna-4, 20-diene-3, 6-dione. *Journal of Steroid Biochemistry and Molecular Biology, 65,* 237–242.

Montoya, M. R. (2008). I'm hot, so I'd say you're not: The influence of objective physical attractiveness on mate selection. *Personality and Social Psychology Bulletin, 34,* 1315–1331.

Moore, E. G. J. (1986). Family socialization and the IQ test performance of traditionally and transracially adopted black children. *Developmental Psychology, 22,* 317–326.

Moore, M. T., & Fresco, D. M. (2007). Depressive realism and attributional style: Implications for individuals at risk for depression. *Behavior Therapy, 38,* 144–154.

Moore, S. M. (1995). Girls' understanding and social constructions of menarche. *Journal of Adolescence, 18,* 87–104.

Moreland, R. L., & Topolinski, S. (2010). The mere exposure phenomenon: A lingering melody by Robert Zajonc. *Emotion Review, 2,* 329–339. doi:10.1177/1754073910375479

Moreno-Walton, L., Brunett, P., Akhtar, S., & DeBlieux, P. M. (2009). Teaching across the generation gap: A consensus from the Council of Emergency Medicine Residency Directors 2009 Academic Assembly. *Academic Emergency Medicine: Special Issue: CORD Educational Advances Supplement, 16,* s19–s24.

Morgenstern, H., & Glazer, W. M. (1993). Identifying risk factors for tardive dyskinesia among long-term outpatients maintained with neuroleptic medications: Results of the Yale Tardive Dyskinesia Study. *Archives of General Psychiatry, 50,* 723–733.

Morin, C. M., Vallieres, A., Guay, B., Ivers, H., Savard, J., Merette, C. et al. (2009). Cognitive behavioral therapy, singly and combined with medication, for persistent insomnia: A randomized controlled trial. *Journal of the American Medical Association, 301,* 2005–2015.

Morisse, D., Batra, L., Hess, L., & Silverman, R. (1996). A demonstration of a token economy for the real world. *Applied and Preventive Psychology, 5,* 41–46.

Morland, L. A., Greene, C. J., Grubbs, K., Kloezeman, K., Mackintosh, M. A., Rosen, C. et al. (2011). Therapist adherence to manualized cognitive-behavioral therapy for anger management delivered to veterans with PTSD via videoconferencing. *Journal of Clinical Psychology, 67,* 629–638.

Morland, L. A., Greene, C. J., Rosen, C. S., Foy, D., Reilly, P., Shore, J. et al. (2010). Telemedicine for anger management therapy in a rural population of combat veterans with posttraumatic stress disorder: A randomized noninferiority trial. *Journal of Clinical Psychiatry, 71,* 855–863.

Morlock, R. J., Tan, M., & Mitchell, D. Y. (2006). Patient characteristics and patterns of drug use for sleep complaints in the United States: Analysis of National Ambulatory Medical Survey data, 1997–2002. *Clinical Therapeutics, 28,* 1044–1053.

Morris, M. W., & Peng, K. (1994). Culture and cause: American and Chinese attributions for social and physical events. *Journal of Personality and Social Psychology, 67,* 949–971. doi:10.1037/0022-3514.67.6.949

Morrison, P. D., Zois, V., McKeown, D. A., Lee, T. D., Holt, D. W., Powell, J. F. et al. (2009). The acute effects of synthetic intravenous Delta9-tetrahydrocannabinol on psychosis, mood and cognitive functioning. *Psychological Medicine, 39,* 1607–1616.

Morrow, E. M., Roffman, J. L., Wolf, D. H., & Coyle, J. T. (2008). Psychiatric neuroscience: Incorporating pathophysiology into clinical case formulation. In T. A. Stern, J. F. Rosenbaum, M. Fava, J. Biederman, & S. L. Rauch (Eds.), *Massachusetts General Hospital comprehensive clinical psychiatry.* Philadelphia: Mosby-Elsevier.

Mortensen, M. E., Sever, L. E., & Oakley, G. P. (1991). Teratology and the epidemiology of birth defects. In S. G. Gabbe, J. R. Niebyl, & J. L. Simpson (Eds.), *Obstetrics: Normal and problem pregnancies* (pp. 233–268). New York: Churchill Livingstone.

Mosedeghrad, A., Ferlie, E., & Rosenberg, D. (2008). A study of the relationship between job satisfaction, organizational commitment and turnover intention among hospital employees. *Health Services Management Research, 21,* 211–227.

Mosing, M. A., Gordon, S. D., Medland, S. E., Statham, D. J., Nelson, E. C., Heath, A. C. et al. (2009). Genetic and environmental influences on the co-morbidity between depression, panic disorder, agoraphobia, and social phobia: A twin study. *Depression and Anxiety, 26,* 1004–1011.

Motivala, S. J., & Irwin, M. R. (2007). Sleep and immunity: Cytokine pathways linking sleep and health outcomes. *Current Directions in Psychological Science, 16,* 21–25.

Motraghi, T. E., Seim, R. W., Meyer, E. C., & Morissette, S. B. (2014). Virtual reality exposure therapy for the treatment of posttraumatic stress disorder: A methodological review using CONSORT guidelines. *Journal of Clinical Psychology, 70,* 197–208.

Mottram, L., & Berger-Gross, P. (2004). An intervention to reduce disruptive behaviors in children with brain injury. *Pediatric Rehabilitation, 7,* 133–143.

Moulton, S., & Kosslyn, S. (2008). Using neuroimagining to resolve the psi debate. *Journal of Cognitive Neuroscience, 20,* 182–192.

Mowen, J. C., & Cialdini, R. B. (1980). On implementing the door-in-the-face compliance technique in a business context. *Journal of Marketing Research, 17,* 253–258.

Moy, J., Petrie, T. A., Dockendorff, S., Greenleaf, C., & Martin, S. (2013). Dieting, exercise, and intuitive eating among early adolescents. *Eating Behaviors, 14,* 529–532. doi: 10.1016/j.eatbeh.2013.06.014

Moyer, C. A., Donnelly, M. P. W., Anderson, J. C., Valek, K. C., Huckaby, S. J., Wiederholt, D. A. et al. (2011). Frontal electroencephalographic asymmetry associated with positive emotion is produced by very brief meditation training. *Psychological Science, 22,* 1277–1279.

Mroczek, D. K., & Spiro, A., III. (2003). Modeling intraindividual change in personality traits: Findings from the Normative Aging Study. *Journal of Gerontology: Psychological Sciences, 58B,* P153–P165.

Mrug, S., Elliott, M., Gilliland, M. J., Grunbaum, J. A., Tortolero, S. R., Cuccaro, P. et al. (2008). Positive parenting and early puberty in girls: Protective effects against aggressive behavior. *Archives of Pediatrics and Adolescent Medicine, 162,* 781–786.

Mueller, C. W., Boyer, E. M., Price, J. L., & Iverson, R. D. (1994). Employee attachment and noncoercive conditions of work: The case of dental hygienists. *Work and Occupations, 21,* 179–212.

Mulcahy, R., Reay, E. E., Wilkinson, R. B., & Owen, C. (2010). A randomized control trial for the effectiveness of group interpersonal psychotherapy for postnatal depression. *Archives of Women's Mental Health, 13,* 125–139.

Müller, M. S., Moe, B., & Groothuis, T. G. (2014). Testosterone increases siblicidal aggression in black-legged kittiwake chicks (*Rissa tridactyla*). *Behavioral Ecology and Sociobiology, 68,* 223–232. doi:10.1007/s00265-013-1637-z

Mulligan, N. W., & Besken, M. (2013). Implicit memory. In D. Reisberg (Ed.), *The Oxford handbook of cognitive psychology* (pp. 220–231). New York: Oxford University Press. doi:10.1093/oxfordhb/9780195376746.013.0015

Mulrow, C. D., Willaims, J. W., Jr., Chiquette, E., Aguilar, C., Hitchcock-Noel, P., Lee, S. et al. (2000). Efficacy of newer medications for treating depression in primary care patients. *American Journal of Medicine, 108,* 54–64.

Mumford, M. D. (2003). Where have we been, where are we going? Taking stock in creativity research. *Creativity Research Journal, 15,* 107–120.

Mumme, D. L., & Fernald, A. (2003). The infant as onlooker: Learning from emotional reactions observed in a television scenario. *Child Development, 74,* 221–237.

Munafo, M. R., Yalcin, B., Willis-Owen, S. A., & Flint, J. (2008). Association of the dopamine D4 receptor (DRD4) gene and approach-related personality traits: Meta-analysis and new data. *Biological Psychiatry, 63,* 197–206.

Munch, M., Knoblauch, V., Blatter, K., Schroder, C., Schnitzler, C., Krauchi, K. et al. (2005). Age-related attenuation of the evening circadian arousal signal in humans. *Neurobiology of Aging, 26,* 1307–1319.

Munoz, R. F., Aguilera, A., Schueller, S. M., Leykin, Y., & Perez-Stable, E. J. (2012). From online randomized controlled trials to participant preference studies: Morphing the San Francisco stop smoking site into a worldwide smoking cessation resource. *Journal of Medical Internet Research, 14,* e64.

Munson, C. (2006). *The effects of Leap Pad's text-to-speech support on kindergarten students' independent reading.* Unpublished master's thesis, University of Valdosta, Valdosta, Georgia. Retrieved from http://hdl.handle.net/10428/105

Murdoch, B. B., Jr. (1962). The serial position effect of free recall. *Journal of Experimental Psychology, 64,* 482–488.

Murillo-Rodriquez, E., Arais-Carrion, O., Sanguino-Rodriguez, K., Gonzalez-Arias, M., & Haro, R. (2009). Mechanisms of sleep-wake cycle modulation. *CNS Neurological Disorders Drug Treatment, 8,* 245–253.

Murphy, K., & Delanty, N. (2007). Sleep deprivation: A clinical perspective. *Sleep and Biological Rhythms, 5,* 2–14.

Murphy, S. (2008). The loss of a child: Sudden death and extended illness perspectives. In M. S. Stroebe, R. O. Hansson, H. Schut, & W. Stroebe (Eds.), *Handbook of bereavement research and practice: Advances in theory and intervention* (pp. 375–395). Washington, DC: American Psychological Association.

Murray, A., Faraoni, M., Castro, M., Alza, N., & Cavallaro, V. (2013). Natural AChE inhibitors from plants and their contribution to Alzheimer's disease therapy. *Current Neuropharmacology, 11,* 388–413. doi:10.2174/1570159X11311040004

Murray, H. A. (1938). *Explorations in personality.* New York: Oxford University Press.

Murray, S. B., & Touyz, S. W. (2012). Masculinity, femininity and male body image: A recipe for future research. *International Journal of Men's Health, 11,* 227–239. doi:10.3149/jmh.1103.227

Murray, S. L., Griffin, D. W., Derrick, J. L., Harris, B., Aloni, M., & Leder, S. (2011). Tempting fate or inviting happiness? Unrealistic idealization prevents the decline of marital satisfaction. *Psychological Science, 22,* 619–626.

Murray, S. O., Olshausen, B. A., & Woods, D. L. (2003). Processing shape, motion, and three-dimensional shape-from-motion in the human cortex. *Cerebral Cortex, 13,* 508–516.

Muscari, M. (2002). Media violence: Advice for parents. *Pediatric Nursing, 28,* 585–591.

Muurahainen, N. E., Kisileff, H. R., Lachaussee, J., & Pi-Sunyer, F. X. (1991). Effect of a soup preload on reduction of food intake by cholecystokinin in humans. *American Journal of Physiology, 260,* R672–R680.

Myers, D. G. (2000). The funds, friends, and faith of happy people. *American Psychologist, 55,* 56–67.

Nacke, L. E., Nacke, A., & Lindley, C. A. (2009). Brain training for silver gamers: Effects of age and game form on effectiveness, efficiency, self-assessment, and gameplay experience. *Cyberpsychology and Behavior, 12,* 493–499.

Naegele, B., Thouvard, V., Pepin, J. L., Levy, P., Bonnet, C., Perret, J. E. et al. (1995). Deficits of cognitive functions in patients with sleep apnea syndrome. *Sleep, 18,* 43–52.

Nagandia, K., & De, S. (2013). Restless legs syndrome: Pathophysiology and modern management. *Postgraduate Medical Journal, 89,* 402–410.

Nairne, J. S. (2002). Remembering over the short term: The case against the standard model. *Annual Review of Psychology, 53,* 53–81.

Naish, P. L. (2010). Hypnosis and hemispheric asymmetry. *Consciousness and Cognition, 19,* 230–234.

Nardi, A. E., Freire, R. C., Valenca, A. M., Amrein, R., de Cerqueira, A. C., Lopes, F. L. et al. (2010). Tapering clonazepam in patients with panic disorder after at least 3 years of treatment. *Journal of Clinical Psychopharmacology, 30,* 290–293.

Narvaez, D. (2010). Moral complexity: The fatal attraction of truthiness and the importance of mature moral functioning. *Perspectives on Psychological Science, 5,* 163–181.

NAS. (2012). Employee referrals: Trends in engagement and technology. *NAS Insights.* Retrieved from http://www.nasrecruitment.com/our-thinking/nas-insights.

Nash, J. M., & Thebarge, R. W. (2006). Understanding psychological stress, its biological processes, and impact on primary headache. *Headache, 46,* 1377–1386.

Nash, M. (1987). What, if anything, is regressed about hypnotic age regression? A review of the empirical literature. *Psychological Bulletin, 102,* 42–52.

Nash, M. (2005). Salient findings: A potentially ground-breaking study on the neuroscience of hypnotizability, a critical review of hypnosis' efficacy, and the neurophysiology of conversion disorder. *International Journal of Clinical and Experimental Hypnosis, 53,* 87–93.

Nassif, A., & Gunter, B. (2008). Gender representation in television advertisements in Britain and Saudi Arabia. *Sex Roles, 58,* 752–760.

Nathan, P. E., Stuart, S. P., & Dolan, S. L. (2000). Research on psychotherapy efficacy and effectiveness: Between Scylla and Charybdis? *Psychological Bulletin, 126,* 964–981.

National Center for Health Statistics. (2013). *Health, United States, 2012.* Hyattsville, MD: Author.

National Comorbidity Survey Replication (NCS-R). (2007). http://www.hcp.med.harvard.edu/ncs

National Gay and Lesbian Task Force. (2007). *Hate crime laws in the U.S.* Retrieved from http://www.thetaskforce.org/downloads/reports/issue_maps/hate_crimes_5_07.pdf

National Gay and Lesbian Task Force. (2013). *Hate crime laws in the U. S.* Online http://www.thetaskforce.org/downloads/reports/issue_maps/hate_crimes_06_13_color.pdf

National Highway Traffic Safety Administration (NHTSA). (2008). *Traffic safety facts, 2008.* Washington, DC: U.S. Department of Transportation.

National Highway Traffic Safety Administration (NHTSA). (2009). *Traffic safety facts: An examination of driver distraction as recorded in NHTSA databases.* Washington, DC: NHTSA's Center for Statistics and Analysis.

National Highway Traffic Safety Administration (NHTSA). (2012). *Traffic safety facts 2010: Alcohol-impaired driving.* Washington, DC: Author.

National Highway Traffic Safety Administration (NHTSA). (2013). *Traffic safety facts: Distracted driving 2011.* Washington, DC: NHTSA's National Center for Statistics and Analysis.

National Institute of Alcohol Abuse and Alcoholism. (2004). NIAAA council approves definition of binge drinking. *NIAAA Newsletter, 3,* 3.

National Institute of Mental Health. (2002). *Suicide facts.* Retrieved from http://www.nimh.nih.gov/research/suifact.htm

National Institute of Mental Health. (2007). *Suicide in the U.S.: Statistics and prevention.* NIH Publication No. 06-4594. Washington, DC: National Institutes of Health, U.S. Department of Health and Human Services.

National Institute on Drug Abuse (NIDA). (2001). *Research report series: Hallucinogens and dissociative drugs.* NIH Publication Number 01-4209. Washington, DC: Author.

National Institute on Drug Abuse (NIDA). (2006a). *Research report series: MDMA (Ecstasy) abuse.* NIH Publication Number 06-4728. Washington, DC: Author.

National Institute on Drug Abuse (NIDA). (2006b). *Research report series: Methamphetamine abuse and addiction.* NIH Publication Number 06-4210. Washington, DC: Author.

National Institute on Drug Abuse (NIDA) & University of Michigan. (2006). *Monitoring the Future national survey results on drug use, 1975–2005: Volume 11. College students and adults ages 19–45.* Washington, DC: Author.

National Institutes of Health. (2000). *The practical guide: Identification, evaluation, and treatment of overweight and obesity in adults.* NIH Publication No. 00-4084. Washington, DC: Author.

National Research Council. (2011). *Explaining divergent levels of longevity in high-income countries.* Washington, DC: National Academies Press.

National Safety Council. (2011). *Injury fact book, 2011 edition.* Retrieved from http://www.nsc.org/NSC%20Picture%20Library/News/web_graphics/Injury_Facts_37.pdf

National Science Foundation (NSF). (2006). *U.S. doctorates in the 20th century.* NSF 06-319. Arlington, VA: Author.

National Science Foundation (NSF), Division of Science Resources Statistics. (2009). *Doctorate recipients from U.S. universities: Summary report 2007–08.* Special Report NSF 10-309. Arlington, VA. Available at http://www.nsf.gov/statistics/nsf10309

National Science Foundation (NSF). (2012). *Science and Engineering Indicators 2012.* Arlington, VA: National Center for Science and Engineering Statistics (NCSES).

National Science Foundation (NSF). (2013). *Women, minorities, and persons with disabilities in science and engineering.* Arlington, VA: National Center for Science and Engineering Statistics (NCSES).

National Scientific Council on the Developing Child (NSCDC). (2007). *The timing and qualityof early experiences combine to shape brain architecture: Working Paper No. 5.* Retrieved from www.developingchild.harvard.edu

National Sleep Foundation. (2004). *Summary findings: 2004 Sleep in America poll.* Washington, DC: Author.

National Sleep Foundation. (2005). *Summary findings: 2005 Sleep in America poll.* Washington, DC: Author.

National Sleep Foundation. (2006). *Summary findings: 2006 Sleep in America poll.* Washington, DC: Author.

National Sleep Foundation. (2009). *Summary findings: 2009 Sleep in America poll.* Washington, DC: Author.

National Sleep Foundation. (2010). *Summary findings: 2010 Sleep in America poll.* Washington, DC: Author.

National Sleep Foundation. (2011). *Sleep in America poll: Communications technology and sleep.* Washington, DC: Author.

National Sleep Foundation. (2013). *International bedroom poll.* Arlington, VA: Author.

Navarro, M. (1995, December 9). Drug sold abroad by prescription becomes widely abused in U.S. *New York Times,* pp. 1, 9.

Nave, K. A. (2010). Myelination and support of axonal integrity by glia. *Nature, 468,* 244–252.

Naylor, J. C., Pritchard, R. D., & Ilgen, D. R. (1980). *A theory of behavior in organizations.* New York: Academic Press.

Nazari, H., Momeni, N., Jariani, M., & Tarrahi, M. J. (2011). Comparison of eye movement desensitization and reprocessing with citalopram in treatment of obsessive-compulsive disorder. *International Journal of Psychiatry in Clinical Practice, 15,* 270–274.

Nederhof, E., Ormel, J., & Oldehinkel, A. EJ. (2014). Mismatch or cumulative stress: The pathway to depression is conditional on attention style. *Psychological Science, 25,* 684–692.

Neher, A. (1991). Maslow's theory of motivation: A critique. *Journal of Humanistic Psychology, 31,* 89–112.

Neisewander, J. L., Cheung, T. C., & Pentkowski, N. S. (2014). Dopamine D3 and 5-HT_{1B} receptor dysregulation as a result of psychostimulant intake and forced abstinence: Implications for medications development. *Neuropharmacology, 76* (Part B), 301–319. doi:10.1016/j.neuropharm.2013.08.014

Nelson, S. K., Kushlev, K., Dunn, E. W., & Lyubomirsky, S. (2014). Parents are slightly happier than nonparents, but causality still cannot be inferred: A reply to Bhargava, Kassam, and Loewenstein (2014). *Psychological Science, 25,* 303–304.

Nelson, S. K., Kushlev, K., English, T., Dunn, E. W., & Lyubomirsky, S. (2013). In defense of parenthood: Children are associated with more joy than misery. *Psychological Science, 24,* 3–10.

Nemeroff, C. B. (2007). The burden of severe depression: A review of diagnostic challenges and treatment alternatives. *Journal of Psychiatric Research, 41,* 189–206.

Neria, Y., Nandi, A., & Galea, S. (2008). Post-traumatic stress disorder following disasters: A systematic review. *Psychological Medicine, 38,* 467–480.

Nestler, E. J., & Carlezon, W. A., Jr. (2006). The mesolimbic dopamine reward circuit in depression. *Biological Psychiatry, 59,* 1151–1159.

Nestor, L., Roberts, G., Garavan, H., & Hester, R. (2008). Deficits in learning and memory: Parahippocampal hyperactivity and frontocortical hypoactivity in cannabis users. *NeuroImage, 40,* 1328–1339.

Nevin, J. A. (2012). Resistance to extinction and behavioral momentum. *Behavioural Processes, 90,* 89–97.

Nevin, J. A., & Grace, R. C. (2005). Resistance to extinction in the steady state and in the transition. *Journal of Experimental Psychology: Animal Behavior Processes, 31,* 199–212.

Nevonen, L., & Broberg, A. G. (2006). A comparison of sequenced individual and group psychotherapy for patients with bulimia nervosa. *International Journal of Eating Disorders, 39,* 117–127.

Newcomb, T. M. (1961). *The acquaintance process.* New York: Holt, Rinehart & Winston.

Newland M. C., & Rasmussen, E. B. (2003). Behavior in adulthood and during aging is affected by contaminant exposure in utero. *Current Directions in Psychological Science, 12,* 212–217.

Newman, M. G., Llera, S. J., Erickson, T. M., Przeworski, A., & Castonguay, L. G. (2013). Worry and generalized anxiety disorder: A review and theoretical synthesis of research on its nature, etiology, mechanisms, and treatment. *Annual Review of Clinical Psychology, 9,* 275–297.

Newmark, T. S., & Bogacki, D. F. (2005). The use of relaxation, hypnosis, and imagery in sport psychiatry. *Clinics in Sports Medicine, 24,* 973–977.

Ni, X., Sicard, T., Bulgin, N., Bismil, R., Chan, K., McMain, S. et al. (2007). Monoamine oxidase A gene is associated with borderline personality disorder. *Psychiatric Genetics, 17,* 153–157.

Nicodemus, K. K., Callicott, J. H., Higier, R. G., Luna, A., Nixon, D. C., Lipska, B. K. et al. (2010). Evidence of statistical epistasis between DISC1, CIT and NDEL1 impacting risk for schizophrenia: Biological validation with functional neuroimaging. *Human Genetics, 127,* 441–452.

Nicoletti, A., & Merriman, W. (2007). Teaching millennial generation students. *Momentum, 38,* 28–31.

Nicolini, H., Arnold, P., Nestadt, G., Lanzagorta, N., & Kennedy, J. L. (2009). Overview of genetics and obsessive-compulsive disorder. *Psychiatry Research, 170,* 7–14.

Niedzwienska, A. (2003). Gender differences in vivid memories. *Sex Roles: A Journal of Research, 49,* 321–331.

Nielsen, M., & Day, R. H. (1999). William James and the evolution of consciousness. *Journal of Theoretical and Philosophical Psychology, 19,* 90–113.

Nieuwenhuijsen, K., Verbeek, J. H., de Boer, A. G., Blonk, R. W., & van Dijk, F. J. (2010). Irrational beliefs in employees with an adjustment, a depressive, or an anxiety disorder: A prospective cohort study. *Journal of Rational-Emotive and Cognitive-Behavior Therapy, 28,* 57–72.

Nijdam, M. J., Gersons, B. P., Reitsma, J. B., de Jongh, A., & Olff, M. (2012). Brief eclectic psychotherapy v. eye movement desensitisation and reprocessing therapy for post-traumatic stress disorder: Randomised controlled trial. *British Journal of Psychiatry, 200,* 224–231.

NIMH Genetics Workgroup. (1998). *Genetics and mental disorders.* NIH Publication No. 98-4268. Rockville, MD: National Institute of Mental Health.

Nisbett, R. (1995). Race, IQ, and scientism. In Steven Fraser (Ed.), *The bell curve wars: Race, intelligence, and the future of America* (pp. 36–57). New York: Basic Books.

Nisbett, R. E., Aronson, J., Blair, C., Dickens, W., Flynn, J., Halpern, D. F., & Turkheimer, E. (2012). Intelligence: New findings and theoretical developments. *American Psychologist, 67,* 130–159. doi:10.1037/a0026699

Nishino, S. (2007). Narcolepsy: Pathophysiology and pharmacology. *Journal of Clinical Psychiatry, 68,* 9–15.

Nishino, S., & Okuro, M. (2010). Emerging treatments for narcolepsy and its related disorders. *Expert Opinion on Emerging Drugs, 15,* 139–158.

Nivoli, A. M., Murru, A., & Vieta, E. (2010). Lithium: Still a cornerstone in the long-term treatment in bipolar disorder? *Neuropsychobiology, 62,* 27–35.

Noah, T., & Robinson, L. (1997, March 3). OK, OK, cigarettes do kill. *U.S. News & World Report,* pp. 29, 32.

Noble, M., & Harding, G. E. (1963). Conditioning of rhesus monkeys as a function of the interval between CS and US. *Journal of Comparative and Physiological Psychology, 56,* 220–224.

Nock, M. K., Borges, G., Bromet, E. J., Cha, C. B., Kessler, R. C., & Lee, S. (2008). Suicide and suicidal behavior. *Epidemiologic Reviews, 30,* 133–154.

Nock, M. K., Hwang, I., Sampson, N., Kessler, R. C., Angermeyer, M., Beautrais, A. et al. (2009). Cross-national analysis of the associations among mental disorders and suicidal behavior: Findings from the WHO World Mental Health Surveys. *PLoS Medicine, 6,* e1000123.

Nolan, R. P., Spanos, N. P., Hayward, A. A., & Scott, H. A. (1995). The efficacy of hypnotic and nonhypnotic response-based imagery for self-managing recurrent headache. *Imagination, Cognition, and Personality, 14,* 183–201.

Nolen-Hoeksema, S. (2001). Gender differences in depression. *Current Directions in Psychological Science, 10,* 173–176.

Nolen-Hoeksema, S. (2002). Gender differences in depression. In I. H. Gotlib & C. L. Hammen (Eds.), *Handbook of depression* (pp. 492–509). New York: Guilford Press.

Nolen-Hoeksema, S., & Hilt, L. M. (2013). *Handbook of depression in adolescents.* London: Routledge.

Nolen-Hoeksema, S., Larson, J., & Grayson, C. (1999). Explaining the gender difference in depressive symptoms. *Journal of Personality and Social Psychology, 77,* 1061–1072.

Nolen-Hoeksema, S., Stice, E., Wade, E., & Bohon, C. (2007). Reciprocal relations between rumination and bulimic, substance abuse, and depressive symptoms in female adolescents. *Journal of Abnormal Psychology, 116,* 198–207.

Nolen-Hoeksema, S., Wisco, B. E., & Lyubomirsky, S. (2008). Rethinking rumination. *Perspectives on Psychological Science, 3,* 400–424.

Norcross, J. C., & Wampold, B. E. (2011). Evidence-based therapy relationships: Research conclusions and clinical practices. *Psychotherapy, 48,* 98–102.

Nordin, S., Razani, J. L., Markison, S., & Murphy, C. (2003). Age-associated increases in intensity discrimination for taste. *Experimental Aging Research, 29,* 371–381.

Norman, R. M., & Malla, A. K. (1993). Stressful life events and schizophrenia: II. Conceptual and methodological issues. *British Journal of Psychiatry, 162,* 166–174.

Norton, P. J., & Price, E. C. (2007). A meta-analytic review of adult cognitive-behavioral treatment outcome across the anxiety disorders. *Journal of Nervous and Mental Disease, 195,* 521–531.

Nosofsky, R. M., & Zaki, S. R. (2002). Exemplar and prototype models revisited: Response strategies, selective attention, and stimulus generalization. *Journal of Experimental Psychology: Learning, Memory, and Cognition, 28,* 924–940.

Nottelmann, E. D., Inoff-Germain, G., Susman, E. J., & Chrousos, G. P. (1990). Hormones and behavior at puberty. In J. Bancroft & J. M. Reinisch (Eds.), *Adolescence and puberty* (pp. 88–123). New York: Oxford University Press.

Novakova, M., Sladek, M., & Sumova, A. (2013). Human chronotype is determined in bodily cells under real-life conditions. *Chronobiology International, 30,* 607–617.

Nowicka, A., & Tacikowski, P. (2011). Transcallosal transfer of information and functional asymmetry of the human brain. *Laterality: Asymmetries of Body, Brain and Cognition, 16,* 35–74. doi:10.1080/13576500903154231

Nummenmaa, L., Hietanen, J. K., Santtila, P., & Hyönä, J. (2012). Gender and visibility of sexual cues influence eye movements while viewing faces and bodies. *Archives of Sexual Behavior, 41,* 1439–1451.

Nunes, J., Jean-Louis, G., Zizi, F., Vasimir, G. J., von Gizycki, H., Brown, C. D. et al. (2008). Sleep duration among black and white Americans: Results of the National Health Interview Survey. *Journal of the National Medical Association, 100,* 317–322.

Nusbaum, E. C., & Silvia, P. J. (2011). Are intelligence and creativity really so different? Fluid intelligence, executive processes, and strategy use in divergent thinking. *Intelligence, 39,* 36–45. doi:10.1016/j.intell.2010.11.002

Nyberg, L., Marklund, P., Persson, J., Cabeza, R., Forkstam, C., Petersson, K. M. et al. (2003). Common prefrontal activations during working memory, episodic memory, and semantic memory. *Neuropsychologia, 41,* 371–377.

Nyer, P. U., & Dellande, S. (2010). Public commitment as a motivator for weight loss. *Psychology and Marketing, 27,* 1–12.

O'Brien, A., Terry, D. J., & Jimmieson, N. L. (2008). Negative affectivity and responses to work stressors: An experimental study. *Anxiety, Stress, and Coping, 21,* 55–83.

O'Brien, K. S., Hunter, J. A., Halberstadt, J., & Anderson, J. (2007). Body image and explicit and implicit anti-fat attitudes: The mediating role of physical appearance comparisons. *Body Image, 4,* 249–256. doi: 10.1016/j.bodyim.2007.06.001

O'Brien, M. (1996). Child-rearing difficulties reported by parents of infants and toddlers. *Journal of Pediatric Psychology, 21,* 433–446.

O'Brien, M. C., McCoy, T. P., Rhodes, S. D., Wagoner, A., & Wolfson, M. (2008). Caffeinated cocktails: Energy drink consumption, high-risk drinking, and alcohol-related consequences among college students. *Academic Emergency Medicine, 15,* 453–460.

O'Bryan, M., Fishbein, H. D., & Ritchey, P. N. (2004). Intergenerational transmission of prejudice, sex role stereotyping, and intolerance. *Adolescence, 39,* 407–426.

O'Connor, D. B., Jones, F., Conner, M., McMillan, B., & Ferguson, E. (2008). Effects of daily hassles and eating style on eating behavior. *Health Psychology, 27,* S20–S31.

O'Keefe, D. J., & Figge, M. (1997). A guilt-based explanation of the door-in-the-face influence strategy. *Human Communication Research, 24,* 64–81.

Oehen, P. Traber, R., Widmer, V., & Schnyder, U. (2013). A randomized, controlled pilot study of MDMA (+/− 3,4-methylenedioxymethamphetamine)-assisted psychotherapy for treatment of resistant, chronic post-traumatic stress disorder (PTSD). *Journal of Psychopharmacology, 27,* 40–52.

Oesch, S., Rüegg, C., Fischer, B., Degen, L., & Beglinger, C. (2006). Effect of gastric distension prior to eating on food intake and feelings of satiety in humans. *Physiology & Behavior, 87,* 903–910. doi: 10.1016/j.physbeh.2006.02.003

Offer, S., & Schneider, B. (2011). Revisiting the gender gap in time-use patterns: Multitasking and well-being among mothers and fathers in dual-earner families. *American Sociological Review, 76,* 809–833.

Offidani, E., Guidi, J., Tomba, E., & Fava, G. A. (2013). Efficacy and tolerability of benzodiazepines versus antidepressants in anxiety disorders: A systematic review and meta-analysis. *Psychotherapy and Psychosomatics, 82,* 355–362.

Oginska, H., & Pokorski, J. (2006). Fatigue and mood correlates of sleep length in three age-social groups: School children, students, and employees. *Chronobiology International, 23,* 1317–1328.

Ogle, C. M., Rubin, D. C., Berntsen, D., & Siegler, I. C. (2013). The frequency and impact of exposure to potentially traumatic events over the life course. *Clinical Psychological Science, 1,* 426–434.

Olatunji, B. O., Davis, M. L., Powers, M. B., & Smits, J. A. (2013). Cognitive-behavioral therapy for obsessive-compulsive disorder: A meta-analysis of treatment outcome and moderators. *Journal of Psychiatric Research, 47,* 33–41.

Olff, M., Langeland, W., Draijer, N., & Gersons, B. P. (2007). Gender differences in posttraumatic stress disorder. *Psychological Bulletin, 133,* 183–204.

Olfson, M., & Pincus, H. A. (1996). Outpatient mental health care in nonhospital settings: Distribution of patients across provider groups. *American Journal of Psychiatry, 153,* 1353–1356.

Olson, R. L., Hanowski, R. J., Hickman, J. S., & Bocanegra, J. (2009). *Driver distraction in commercial vehicle operations.* Department of Transportation. Federal Motor Carrier Safety Administration report no. FMCSA-RRR-09-042. Blacksburg, VA: Virginia Tech Transportation Institute.

Omar, H., McElderry, D., & Zakharia, R. (2003). Educating adolescents about puberty: What are we missing? *International Journal of Adolescent Medicine and Health, 15,* 79–83.

Ondersma, S. J., & Walker, C. E. (1998). Elimination disorders. In T. H. Ollendick & M. Hersen (Eds.), *Handbook of child psychopathology* (pp. 355–380). New York: Plenum Press.

Oosthuizen, P. P., Emsley, R. A., Maritz, J. S., Turner, J. A., & Keyter, N. (2003). Incidence of tardive dyskinesia in first-episode psychosis patients treated with low-dose haloperidol. *Journal of Clinical Psychiatry, 64,* 1075–1080.

Oquendo, M. A., Hastings, R. S., Huang, Y. Y., Simpson, N., Ogden, R. T., Hu, X. Z. et al. (2007). Brain serotonin transporter binding in depressed patients with bipolar disorder using positron emission tomography. *Archives of General Psychiatry, 64,* 201–208.

Orina, M. M., Collins, W. A., Simpson, J. A., Salvatore, J. E ., Haydon, K. C., & Kim, J. S. (2011). Developmental and dyadic perspectives on commitment in adult romantic relationships. *Psychological Science, 22,* 908–915.

Ornoy, A., & Ergaz, Z. (2010). Alcohol abuse in pregnant women: Effects on the fetus and newborn, mode of action and maternal treatment. *International Journal of Environmental Research and Public Health, 7,* 364–379.

Ornstein, S., & Isabella, L. (1990). Age vs. stage models of career attitudes of women: A partial replication and extension. *Journal of Vocational Behavior, 36,* 1–19.

Ortega, L. A., & Karch, D. (2010). Precipitating circumstances of suicide among women of reproductive age in 16 U.S. states, 2003–2007. *Journal of Women's Health, 19,* 5–7.

Ortony, A., & Turner, T. J. (1990). What's basic about basic emotions? *Psychological Review, 97,* 315–331.

Osborne, R. H., Sali, A., Aaronson, N. K., Elsworth, G. R., Mdzewski, B., & Sinclair, A. J. (2004). Immune function and adjustment style: Do they predict survival in breast cancer? *Psychooncology, 13,* 199–210.

Ostelo, R. W. J. G., van Tulder, M. W., Vlaeyen, J. W. S., Linton, S. J., Morley, S. J., & Assendelft, W. J. J. (2007). Behavioural treatment for chronic low-back pain. *Cochrane Database of Systematic Reviews,* Cochrane AN: CD002014.

Osterman, K., Bjorkqvist, K., Lagerspertz, K. M. J., Kaukiainen, A., Huesmann, L. R., & Fraczek, A. (1994). Peer and self-estimated aggression and victimization in 8-year-old children from five ethnic groups. *Aggressive Behavior, 20,* 411–428.

Ostroff, C., Kinicki, A. J., & Tamkins, M. M. (2003). Organizational culture and climate. In W. C. Borman, D. R. Ilgen, & R. J. Klimoski (Eds.), *Handbook of psychology: Industrial and organizational psychology* (Vol. 12, pp. 565–593). New York: Wiley.

Oswalt, S. B., & Wyatt, T. J. (2011). Sexual orientation and differences in mental health, stress, and academic performance in a national sample of U.S. college students. *Journal of Homosexuality, 58,* 1255–1280. doi: 10.1080/00918369.2011.605738

Oteri, A., Salvo, F., Caputi, A. P., & Calapai, G. (2007). Intake of energy drinks in association with alcoholic beverages in a cohort of students of the School of Medicine of the University of Messina. *Alcoholism, Clinical, and Experimental Research, 31,* 1677–1680.

Overman, W. H., Bachevalier, J., Schuhmann, E., & Ryan, P. (1996). Cognitive gender differences in very young children parallel biologically based cognitive gender differences in monkeys. *Behavioral Neuroscience, 110,* 673–684.

Overmier, J. B. (2002). On learned helplessness. *Integrative Physiological and Behavioral Science, 37,* 4–8.

Overmier, J. B., & Seligman, M. E. (1967). Effects of inescapable shock upon subsequent escape and avoidance responding. *Journal of Comparative and Physiological Psychology, 63,* 28–33.

Owens, J. A. (2007). Sleep medicine. In R. M. Kliegman, R. E. Behrman, H. B. Jenson, & B. F. Stanton (Eds.), *Nelson textbook of pediatrics* (18th ed., Chap. 18). Philadelphia: Saunders Elsevier.

Ozturk, L., Pelin, Z., Karadeniz, D., Kaynak, H., Cakar, L., & Gozukirmizi, E. (1999). Effects of 48 hours sleep deprivation on human immune profile. *Sleep Research Online, 2,* 107–111.

Packer, D. J. (2009). Avoiding groupthink: Whereas weakly identified members remain silent, strongly identified members dissent about collective problems. *Psychological Science, 20,* 546–548.

Padela, A. I., & Heisler, M. (2010). The association of perceived abuse and discrimination after September 11, 2001, with psychological distress, level of happiness, and health status among Arab Americans. *American Journal of Public Health, 100,* 284–291.

Page, R. A., & Green, J. P. (2007). An update on age, hypnotic suggestibility, and gender: A brief report. *American Journal of Clinical Hypnosis, 49,* 283–287.

Painter, K. (1997, August 15–17). Doctors have prenatal test for 450 genetic diseases. *USA Today.*

Paivio, A. (1982). The empirical case for dual coding. In J. Yuille (Ed.), *Imagery, cognition, and memory* (pp. 307–332). Hillsdale, NJ: Erlbaum.

Paivio, A. (1986). *Mental representations: A dual coding approach.* New York: Oxford University Press.

Pallier, G. (March, 2003). Gender differences in the self-assessment of accuracy on cognitive tasks. *Sex Roles: A Journal of Research, 48*(5/6), 265–276.

Papadakis, A. A., Prince, R. P., Jones, N. P., & Strauman, T. J. (2006). Self-regulation, rumination, and vulnerability to depression in adolescent girls. *Development and Psychopathology, 18,* 815–829.

Parent, A. S., Teilmann, G., Juul, A., Skakkebaek, N. E., Toppari, J., & Bourguignon, J. P. (2003). The timing of normal puberty and the age limits of sexual precocity: Variations around the world, secular trends, and changes after migration. *Endocrine Reviews, 24,* 668–693.

Paris, J. (2002). Chronic suicidality among patients with borderline personality disorder. *Psychiatric Services, 53,* 738–742.

Park, D. C., & McDonough, I. M. (2013). The dynamic aging mind: Revelations from functional neuroimaging research. *Psychological Science, 8,* 62–67.

Park, J. S., & Lee, K. (2012). Modification of severe violent and aggressive behavior among psychiatric inpatients through the use of a short-term token economy. *Journal of Korean Academy of Nursing, 42,* 1062–1069.

Parker, E. S., Birnbaum, I. M., & Noble, E. P. (1976). Alcohol and memory: Storage and state dependency. *Journal of Verbal Learning and Verbal Behavior, 15,* 691–702.

Parker, G. B., & Brotchie, H. L. (2004). From diathesis to dimorphism: The biology of gender differences in depression. *Journal of Nervous and Mental Disorders, 192,* 210–216.

Parker, G. B., & Brotchie, H. L. (2010). Gender differences in depression. *International Review of Psychiatry, 22,* 429–436.

Parker, G. B., Roy, K., Wilhelm, K., & Mitchell, P. (2001). Assessing the comparative effectiveness of antidepressant therapies: A prospective clinical practice study. *Journal of Clinical Psychiatry, 62,* 117–125.

Parker-Pope, T. (2002, August 27). A new reason for teens to avoid sex: It could be harmful to their health. *Wall Street Journal,* D1.

Parkes, C. M. (1986). *Bereavement: Studies of grief in adult life* (2nd ed.). London: Tavistock.

Parkes, C. M. (1991). Attachment, bonding, and psychiatric problems after bereavement in adult life. In C. M. Parkes, J. Stevenson-Hinde, & P. Marris (Eds.), *Attachment across the life cycle* (pp. 268–292). London: Tavistock/Routledge.

Parkin, A. J., & Leng, N. R. C. (1993). *Neuropsychology of the amnesic syndrome.* Hove, UK: Psychology Press.

Parnas, J., Cannon, T., Jacobsen, B., Schulsinger, H., Schulsinger, F., & Mednick, S. (1993). Lifetime DSM-III-R diagnostic outcomes in the offspring of schizophrenic mothers. *Archives of General Psychiatry, 50,* 707–714.

Parr, E. B., Coffey, V. G., & Hawley, J. A. (2013). "Sarcobesity": A metabolic conundrum. *Maturitas, 74,* 109–113. doi: 10.1016/j.maturitas.2012.10.014

Parsons, T. D., & Rizzo, A. A. (2008). Affective outcomes of virtual reality exposure therapy for anxiety and specific phobias: A meta-analysis. *Journal of Behavior Therapy and Experimental Psychiatry, 39,* 250–261.

Partnership Attitude Tracking Study (PATS). (2006). *The Partnership for a Drug-Free America: Teens in grades 7 through 12 2005.* Retrieved from http://www.drugfree.org/Files/Full_Teen_Report

Partnership Attitude Tracking Study (PATS). (2013). *The 2012 Partnership Attitude Tracking Study.* Retrieved from http://www.drugfree.org/wp-content/uploads/2013/04/PATS-2012-FULL-REPORT2.pdf

Pascalis, O., & Kelly, D. J. (2009). The origins of face processing in humans: Phylogeny and ontogeny. *Perspectives on Psychological Science, 4,* 200–209.

Pascual, A., Guéguen, N., Pujos, S., & Felonneau, M. (2013). Foot-in-the-door and problematic requests: A field experiment. *Social Influence, 8,* 46–53. doi:10.1080/15534510.2012.696038

Pasquet, P., Obeerti, B., El Ati, J., & Hladik, C. M. (2002). Relationships between threshold-based PROP sensitivity and food preferences of Tunisians. *Appetite, 39,* 167–173.

Passie, T., Halpern, J. H., Stichtenoth, D. O., Emrich, H. M., & Hintzen, A. (2008). The pharmacology of lysergic acid diethylamide: A review. *CNS Neuroscience & Therapeutics, 14,* 295–314.

Patel, S. R., Aronson, J. P., Sheth, S. A., & Eskandar, E. N. (2013). Lesion procedures in psychiatric neurosurgery. *World Neurosurgery, 80,* S31. e9–16.

Patrick, M. E., & Maggs, J. L. (2009). Does drinking lead to sex? Daily alcohol-sex behaviors and expectancies among college students. *Psychology of Addictive Behaviors, 23,* 472–481.

Patrick, M. E., & Maggs, J. L. (2014). Energy drinks and alcohol: Links to alcohol behaviors consequences across 56 days. *Journal of Adolescent Health, 54,* 454–459.

Patterson, C. J. (2006). Children of lesbian and gay parents. *Current Directions in Psychological Science, 15,* 241–244.

Paul, G., Elam, B., & Verhulst, S. J. (2007). A longitudinal study of students' perceptions of using deep breathing meditation to reduce testing stresses. *Teaching and Learning in Medicine, 19,* 287–292.

Paulson, R. M., Lord, C. G., Taylor, C. A., Brady, S. E., McIntyre, R. B., & Fuller, E. W. (2012). A matching hypothesis for the activity level of actions involved in attitude–behavior consistency. *Social Psychological and Personality Science, 3,* 40–47. doi:10.1177/1948550611408347

Paulson, S. E., & Sputa, C. L. (1996). Patterns of parenting during adolescence: Perceptions of adolescents and parents. *Adolescence, 31,* 369–381.

Paulus, P. B. (Ed.). (1989). *Psychology of group influence* (2nd ed.). Hillsdale, NJ: Erlbaum.

Pause, B. M., Zlomuzica, A., Kinugawa, K., Mariani, J., Pietrowsky, R., & Dere, E. (2013). Perspectives on episodic-like and episodic memory. *Frontiers in Behavioral Neuroscience, 7,* 33. doi:10.3389/fnbeh.2013.00033

Payne, J. D., & Kensinger, E. A. (2010). Sleep's role in the consolidation of emotional episodic memories. *Current Directions in Psychological Science, 19,* 290–295.

Payne, J. D., Stickgold, R., Swanberg, K., & Kensinger, E. A. (2008). Sleep preferentially enhances memory for emotional components of scenes. *Psychological Science, 8,* 781–788.

Payte, J. T. (1997). Methadone maintenance treatment: The first thirty years. *Journal of Psychoactive Drugs, 29,* 149–153.

Pearlin, L. I. (1993). The social contexts of stress. In L. Goldberger & S. Breznitz (Eds.), *Handbook of stress: Theoretical and clinical aspects* (2nd ed., pp. 303–315). New York: Free Press.

Pearsall, M. J., Christian, M. S., & Ellis, A. P. (2010). Motivating interdependent teams: Individual rewards, shared rewards, or something in between? *Journal of Applied Psychology, 95,* 183–191.

Pedersen, D. M., & Wheeler, J. (1983). The Müller-Lyer illusion among Navajos. *Journal of Social Psychology, 121,* 3–6.

Pedersen, P. B. (2002). Ethics, competence, and other professional issues in culture-centered counseling. In P. B. Pedersen, J. G. Draguns, W. J. Lonner, & J. E. Trimble (Eds.), *Counseling across cultures* (5th ed., pp. 3–28). Thousand Oaks, CA: Sage.

Peelen, M. V., Glaser, B., Vuilleumier, P., & Eliez, S. (2009). Differential development of selectivity for faces and bodies in the fusiform gyrus. *Developmental Science, 12,* F16–F25.

Pelleymounter, M. A., Cullen, M. J., Baker, M. B., Hecht, R., Winters, D., Boone, T. et al. (1995). Effects of the obese gene product on body weight regulation in ob/ob mice. *Science, 269,* 540–543.

Penaloza, A. A., & Calvillo, D. P. (2012). Incubation provides relief from artificial fixation in problem solving. *Creativity Research Journal, 24,* 338–344. doi:10.1080/10400419.2012.730329

Peng, S., Du, J., Jiang, H., Fu, Y., Chen, H., Sun, H. et al. (2013). The dopamine receptor D1 gene is associated with the length of interval between first heroin use and onset of dependence in Chinese Han heroin addicts. *Journal of Neural Transmission, 120,* 1591–1598. doi:10.1007/s00702-013-1029-6

Penley, J. A., Tomaka, J., & Wiebe, J. S. (2002). The association of coping to physical and psychological health outcomes: A meta-analytic review. *Journal of Behavioral Medicine, 25,* 551–603.

Pepperberg, I. M. (1991). A communicative approach to animal cognition: A study of conceptual abilities of an African gray parrot. In C. A. Ristau (Ed.), *Cognitive ethology* (pp. 153–186). Hillsdale, NJ: Erlbaum.

Pepperberg, I. M. (1993). Cognition and communication in an African gray parrot (*Psittacus erithacus*): Studies on a nonhuman, nonprimate, nonmammilian, subject. In H. L. Roitblat, L. M. Herman, & P. E. Nachtigall (Eds.), *Language and communication: Comparative perspectives* (pp. 221–248). Hillsdale, NJ: Erlbaum.

Pepperberg, I. M. (1999). Rethinking syntax: A commentary on E. Kako's "Elements of syntax in the systems of three language-trained animals." *Animal Learning and Behavior, 27,* 15–17.

Perez, M., Joiner, T. E., Jr., & Lewisohn, P. M. (2004). Is major depressive disorder or dysthymia more strongly associated with bulimia nervosa? *International Journal of Eating Disorders, 36,* 55–61.

Perina, K. (2002). Hot on the trail of flashbulb memory. *Psychology Today,* 35, 15–16.

Perlini, A. H., Bertolissi, S., & Lind, D. L. (1999). The effects of women's age and physical appearance on evaluations of attractiveness and social desirability. *Journal of Social Psychology, 139,* 343–344.

Perlis, R. H., Brown, E., Baker, R. W., & Nierenberg, A. A. (2006). Clinical features of bipolar depression versus major depressive disorder in large multi-center trials. *American Journal of Psychiatry, 163,* 225–231.

Perry, C. (1997). Admissibility and per se exclusion of hypnotically elicited recall in American courts of law. *International Journal of Clinical and Experimental Hypnosis, 45,* 266–279.

Perry, E., Walker, M., Grace, J., & Perry, R. (1999). Acetylcholine in mind: A neurotransmitter correlate of consciousness? *Trends in Neurosciences, 22,* 273–280.

Perry, W. G., Jr. (1981). Cognitive and ethical growth. In A. Chickering (Ed.), *The modern American college* (pp. 76–116). San Francisco: Jossey-Bass.

Person, E. S. (1990). The influence of values in psychoanalysis: The case of female psychology. In C. Zanardi (Ed.), *Essential papers in psychoanalysis* (pp. 305–325). New York: University Press.

Person, E. S. (2005). As the wheel turns: A centennial reflection on Freud's Three Essays on the Theory of Sexuality. *Journal of the American Psychoanalytic Association, 53,* 1257–1282.

Pesant, N., & Zadra, A. (2004). Working with dreams in therapy: What do we know and what should we do? *Clinical Psychology Review, 24,* 489–512.

Pesant, N., & Zadra, A. (2006). Dream content and psychological well-being: A longitudinal study of the continuity hypothesis. *Journal of Clinical Psychology, 62,* 111–121.

Peterson, B. E., & Duncan, L. E. (2007). Midlife women's generativity and authoritarianism: Marriage, motherhood, and 10 years of aging. *Psychology and Aging, 22,* 411–419.

Peterson, C. (2000). The future of optimism. *American Psychologist, 55,* 44–55.

Peterson, C., & Bossio, L. M. (2001). Optimism and physical well-being. In E. C. Chang (Ed.), *Optimism and pessimism: Implications for theory, research, and practice* (pp. 127–146). Washington, DC: American Psychological Association.

Peterson, C., & Seligman, M. E. (1984). Causal explanations as a risk factor for depression: Theory and evidence. *Psychological Review, 91,* 347–374.

Peterson, C., Maier, S. F., & Seligman, M. E. P. (1993). *Learned helplessness: A theory for the age of personal control.* New York: Oxford University Press.

Peterson, L. R., & Peterson, M. J. (1959). Short-term retention of individual verbal items. *Journal of Experimental Psychology, 58,* 193–198.

Petitto, L. (2009). New discoveries from the bilingual brain and mind across the lifespan: Implications for education. *Mind, Brain, and Education, 3,* 185–197.

Petrides, K. V., Furnham, A., & Martin, G. N. (2004). Estimates of emotional and psychometric intelligence: Evidence for gender-based stereotypes. *Journal of Social Psychology, 144,* 149–162.

Petrovich, G. D. (2013). Forebrain networks and the control of feeding by environmental learned cues. *Physiology & Behavior, 121,* 10–18. doi:10.1016/j.physbeh.2013.03.024

Petry, N. M., Tedford, J., Austin, M., Nich, C., Carroll, K. M., & Rounsaville, B. J. (2004). Prize reinforcement contingency management for treating cocaine users: How low can we go, and with whom? *Addiction, 99,* 349–360.

Pettigrew, T. F., & Tropp, L. R. (2006). A meta-analytic test of intergroup contact theory. *Journal of Personality and Social Psychology, 90,* 751–783.

Petty, R. E., & Briñol, P. (2008). Persuasion: From single to multiple to metacognitive processes. *Perspectives on Psychological Science, 3,* 137–147.

Petty, R. E., & Cacioppo, J. T. (1986). *Communication and persuasion: Central and peripheral routes to attitude change.* New York: Springer.

Petty, R. E., Cacioppo, J. T., & Goldman, R. (1981). Personal involvement as a determinant of argument-based persuasion. *Journal of Personality and Social Psychology, 41,* 847–855.

Petty, R. E., Fabrigar, L. R., & Wegener, D. T. (2003). Emotional factors in attitudes and persuasion. In R. J. Davidson, K. R. Scherer, & H. H. Goldsmith (Eds.), *Handbook of affective sciences* (pp. 752–772). Oxford: Oxford University Press.

Pew Research Center. (2010). *Millennials: A portrait of generation next.* Retrieved from http://pewsocialtrends.org/files/2010/10/millennials-confident-connected-open-to-change.pdf

Pfaus, J. G. (2009). Pathways of sexual desire. *Journal of Sexual Medicine, 6,* 1506–1533.

Phares, E. J. (1991). *Introduction to personality* (3rd ed.). New York: HarperCollins.

Phelan, S., Nallari, M., Daroch, F. E., & Wing, R. R. (2009). What do physicians recommend to their overweight and obese patients? *Journal of the American Board of Family Medicine, 22,* 115–122.

Phillips, M. R., Li, X., & Zhang, Y. (2002). Suicide rates in China, 1995–99. *Lancet, 359,* 835–840.

Piaget, J. (1929). *The child's conception of the world.* New York: Harcourt Brace.

Piaget, J. (1952). *The origins of intelligence in children.* New York: International Universities Press.

Pickering, G. J., Jain, A. K., & Bezawada, R. (2013). Super-tasting gastronomes? Taste phenotype characterization of foodies and wine experts. *Food Quality and Preference, 28,* 85–91. doi:10.1016/j.foodqual.2012.07.005

Pidoplichko, V. I., DeBiasi, M., Williams, J. T., & Dani, J. A. (1997). Nicotine activates and desensitizes midbrain dopamine neurons. *Nature, 390,* 401–404.

Pierce, J. P. (2005). Influence of movie stars on the initiation of adolescent smoking. *Pediatric Dentistry, 27,* 149.

Pietromonaco, P. R., DeBuse, C. J., & Powers, S. I. (2013). Does attachment get under the skin? Adult romantic attachment and cortisol responses to stress. *Current Directions in Psychological Science, 22,* 63–68.

Pike, K. M., Devlin, M. J., & Loeb, C. (2004). Cognitive-behavioral therapy in the treatment of anorexia nervosa, and binge eating disorder. In J. K. Thompson (Ed.), *Handbook of eating disorders and obesity* (pp. 130–162). New York: Wiley.

Pillar, G., & Lavie, P. (2011). Obstructive sleep apnea: Diagnosis, risk factors, and pathophysiology. *Handbook of Clinical Neurology, 98,* 383–399.

Pillemer, D. B., Wink, P., DiDonato, T. E., & Sanborn, R. L. (2003). Gender differences in autobiographical memory styles of older adults. *Memory, 11,* 525–532.

Pinedo, V. A. (2010). *Swinging '60s had nothing on the '90s—Sex study.* Retrieved from http://www.reuters.com/assests/print?aid=USTRE62F23J20100316

Pinker, S. (1994). *The language instinct: How the mind creates language.* New York: Morrow.

Pinnell, C. M., & Covino, N. A. (2000). Empirical findings on the use of hypnosis in medicine: A critical review. *International Journal of Clinical and Experimental Hypnosis, 48,* 170–194.

Pinto da Mota Matos, A., Alves Ferreira, J. G., & Haase, R. F. (2012). Television and aggression: A test of a mediated model with a sample of Portuguese students. *The Journal of Social Psychology, 152,* 75–91. doi:10.1080/00224545.2011.555645

Piper, A., & Merskey, H. (2004). The persistence of folly: A critical examination of dissociative identity disorder: Part I. The excesses of an improbable concept. *Canadian Journal of Psychiatry, 49,* 592–600.

Pirrallo, R. G., Loomis, C. C., Levine, R., & Woodson, B. T. (2012). The prevalence of sleep problems in emergency medical technicians. *Sleep & Breathing, 16,* 149–162.

Plazzi, B., Corsini, R., Provini, R., Pierangeli, G., Martinelli, P., Montagna, P. et al. (1997). REM sleep behavior disorders in multiple system atrophy. *Neurology, 48,* 1094–1097.

Pleis, J. R., & Lethbridge-Ceiku, M. (2007). Summary health statistics for U.S. adults: National health interview survey, 2006. *Vital Health Statistics, 10,* No. 235.

Plomin, R., DeFries, J. C., McClearn, G. E., & Rutter, M. (2008). *Behavioral genetics* (5th ed.). New York: Freeman.

Plutchik, R. (1984). Emotions: A general psychoevolutionary theory. In K. R. Scherer & P. Ekman (Eds.), *Approaches to emotion* (pp. 197–219). Hillsdale, NJ: Erlbaum.

Poe, G. R., Walsh, C. M., & Bjorness, T. E. (2010). Cognitive neuroscience of sleep. *Progress in Brain Research, 185,* 1–19.

Poelman, D., & Smet, P. F. (2010). Photometry in the dark: Time dependent visibility of low intensity light sources. *Optics Express, 18,* 26293–26299.

Pogue-Geile, M. F., & Yokley, J. L. (2010). Current research on the genetic contributors to schizophrenia. *Current Directions in Psychological Science, 19,* 214–219.

Pollack, W. (1998). Mourning, melancholia, and masculinity: Recognizing and treating depression in men. In W. Pollack & R. Levant (Eds.), *New psychotherapy for men* (pp. 147–166). New York: Wiley.

Pollard, R. J., Coyle, J. P., Gilbert, R. L., & Beck, J. E. (2007). Intraoperative awareness in a regional medical system: A review of 3 years' data. *Anesthesiology, 106,* 269–274.

Polmin, R. (1994). The Emanuel Miller Memorial Lecture 1993: Genetic research and identification of environmental influences. *Journal of Child Psychology and Psychiatry, 35,* 817–834.

Poloskov, E., & Tracey, T. G. (2013). Internalization of U.S. female beauty standards as a mediator of the relationship between Mexican American women's acculturation and body dissatisfaction. *Body Image, 10,* 501–508. doi: 10.1016/j.bodyim.2013.05.005

Polotsky, V. Y., & O'Donnell, C. P. (2007). Genomics of sleep-disordered breathing. *Proceedings of the American Thoracic Society, 4,* 121–126.

Pomeroy, A. (2005). 50 best small and medium places to work: Money talks. *HR Magazine, 50,* 44–65.

Pomeroy, W. (1965, May). Why we tolerate lesbians. *Sexology,* 652–654.

Ponniah, K., & Hollon, S. D. (2009). Empirically supported psychological treatments for adult acute stress disorder and posttraumatic stress disorder: A review. *Depression and Anxiety, 26,* 1086–1109.

Ponniah, K., Magiati, I., & Hollon, S. D. (2013). An update on the efficacy of psychological therapies in the treatment of obsessive-compulsive disorder in adults. *Journal of Obsessive- Compulsive and Related Disorders, 2,* 207–218.

Pool, E., Rehme, A. K., Fink, G. R., Eickhoff, S. B., & Grefkes, C. (2013). Network dynamics engaged in the modulation of motor behavior in healthy subjects. *Neuroimage, 82,* 68–76. doi:10.1016/j.neuroimage.2013.05.123

Pool, R. (2005, Fall/Winter). Motherese. *Research in Review Magazine,* Florida State University.

Poore, A. G., Gagne, F., Barlow, K. M., Lydon, J. E., Taylor, D. M., & Wright, S. C. (2002). Contact and the personal/group discrimination discrepancy in an Inuit community. *Journal of Psychology, 136,* 371–382.

Pope, H. D., Jr., Oliva, P. S., Hudson, J. I., Bodkin, J. A., & Gruber, A. J. (1999). Attitudes toward DSM-IV dissociative disorders diagnoses among board-certified American psychiatrists. *American Journal of Psychiatry, 156,* 321–323.

Pope, H. G., & Yurgelun-Todd, D. (1996). The residual cognitive effects of heavy marijuana use in college students. *Journal of the American Medical Association, 275,* 521–527.

Porkka-Heiskanen, T., Strecker, R. E., Thakkar, M., Bjorkum, A. A., Greene, R. W., & McCarley, R. W. (1997). Adenosine: A mediator of the sleep-inducing effects of prolonged wakefulness. *Science, 276,* 1265–1268.

Porte, H. S., & Hobson, J. A. (1996). Physical motion in dreams: One measure of three theories. *Journal of Abnormal Psychology, 105,* 329–335.

Porter, J. N., Collins, P. F., Muetzel, R. L., Lim, K. O., & Luciana, M. (2011). Associations between cortical thickness and verbal fluency in childhood, adolescence, and young adulthood. *NeuroImage, 55,* 1865–1877.

Porter, R. H. (1999). Olfaction and human kin recognition. *Genetica, 104,* 259–263.

Post, R., Frye, M., Denicoff, K. Leverich, G., Kimbrell, T., & Dunn, R. (1998). Beyond lithium in the treatment of bipolar illness. *Neuropsychopharmacology, 19,* 206–219.

Potter, W. J., Warren, R., Vaughan, M., Howley, K., Land, A., & Hagemeyer, J. (1997). Antisocial acts in reality programming on television. *Journal of Broadcasting and Electronic Media, 41,* 69–89.

Powell, L. H., Calvin, J. E., III, & Calvin, J. E., Jr. (2007). Effective obesity treatments. *American Psychologist, 62,* 234–246.

Powell, L. H., Shahabi, L., & Thoresen, C. E. (2003). Religion and spirituality: Linkages to physical health. *American Psychologist, 58,* 36–52.

Powell, T. J., Silk, K. R., & Albeck, J. H. (2000). Psychiatrists' referrals to self-help groups for people with mood disorders. *Psychiatric Services, 51,* 809–811.

Powers, T. L., & Jack, E. P. (2013). The influence of cognitive dissonance on retail product returns. *Psychology & Marketing, 30,* 724–735. doi:10.1002/mar.20640

Pratkanis, A. R. (1992). The cargo-cult science of subliminal persuasion. *The Skeptical Inquirer, 16,* 260–272.

Pratkanis, A. R., Epley, N., Savitsky, K., & Kachelski, R. A. (2007). Issue 12: Is subliminal persuasion a myth? In J. A. Nier (Ed.), *Taking sides: Clashing views in social psychology* (2nd ed., pp. 230–255). New York: McGraw-Hill.

Prentice, A. M. (2009). Obesity in emerging nations: Evolutionary origins and the impact of rapid nutrition transition. *Nestlé Nutrition Workshop Series. Paediatric Programme, 63,* 47–54.

Prescott, C. A., Hewitt, J. K., Truett, K. R., Heath, A. C., Neale, M. C., & Eaves, L. J. (1994). Genetic and environmental influences on alcohol-related problems in a volunteer sample of older twins. *Journal of Studies on Alcohol, 55,* 184–202.

Pressman, S. D., Cohen, S., Miller, G. E., Barkin, A., Rabin, B. S., & Treanor, J. J. (2005). Loneliness, social network size, and immune response to influenza vaccination in college freshman. *Health Psychology, 24,* 297–306.

Preston, J. A. (2005, June). *Delaying a life: The consequences of career development for the Radcliffe class of 1950.* Paper presented at the IWPR's Eighth International Women's Policy Research Conference.

Price, C. A., & Balaswamy, S. (2009). Beyond health and wealth: Predictors of women's retirement satisfaction. *International Journal of Aging and Human Development, 68,* 195–214.

Price, W. F., & Crapo, R. H. (2002). *Cross-cultural perspectives in introductory psychology.* Belmont, CA: Wadsworth.

Prinzmetal, W., & Beck, D. M. (2001). The tilt-consistency theory of visual illusions. *Journal Of Experimental Psychology: Human Perception and Performance, 27,* 206–217. doi:10.1037/0096-1523.27.1.206

Pritchard, M. E., Wilson, G. S., & Yamnitz, B. (2007). What predicts adjustment among college students? A longitudinal panel study. *Journal of American College Health, 56,* 15–21.

ProCon.org. (2014). *Gay marriage.* Retrieved from http://gaymarriage.procon.org/view.resource.php?resourceID=004857

Prosser, I. B. (1933). *Non-academic development of Negro children in mixed and segregated schools.* Unpublished doctoral dissertation, University of Cincinnati.

Prosser, J. M., & Nelson, L. S. (2012). The toxicology of bath salts: A review of synthetic cathinones. *Journal of Medical Toxicology, 8,* 33–42.

Proudfoot, J. G. (2004). Computer-based treatment for anxiety and depression: Is it feasible? Is it effective? *Neuroscience Biobehavior Review, 28,* 353–363.

Prutkin, J., Duffy, V. B., Etter, L., Fast, K., Gardner, E., Lucchina, L. A. et al. (2000). Genetic variation and inferences about perceived taste intensity in mice and men. *Physiology and Behavior, 69,* 161–173.

Pryor, J. H., Hurtado, S., DeAngelo, L., Palucki-Blake, L., & Tran, S. (2010). *The American freshman: National norms fall 2010.* Los Angeles: Higher Education Research Institute, UCLA.

Ptacek, J. T., Smith, R. E., & Dodge, K. L. (1994). Gender differences in coping with stress: When stressor and appraisals do not differ. *Personality & Social Psychology Bulletin, 20,* 421–430.

Public Health England. (2014). *Public Health England (PHE) release local authority adult obesity data.* Retrieved from https://www.gov.uk/government/news/phe-release-local-authority-adult-obesity-data

Purves, D., Augustine, G. J., Fitzpatrick, D., Katz, L., LaMantia, A. S., & McNamara, J. O. (1997). *Neuroscience.* Sunderland, MA: Sinauer.

Putnam, F. W. (2000). Dissociative disorders. In A. Sameroff, M. Lewis, & S. Miller (Eds.), *Handbook of developmental psychopathology* (2nd ed., pp. 739–754). New York: Kluwer Academic/Plenum.

Putnam, F. W., Guroff, J. J., Silberman, E. K., & Barban, L. (1986). The clinical phenomenology of multiple personality disorder: Review of 100 recent cases. *Journal of Clinical Psychiatry, 47,* 285–293.

Pyke, K., & Johnson, D. (2003). Asian American women and racialized femininities: "Doing" gender across cultural worlds. *Gender and Society, 17,* 33–53.

Pylyshyn, Z. W. (2003). Return of the mental image: Are there really pictures in the brain? *Trends in Cognitive Science, 7,* 113–118.

Pylyshyn, Z. W. (2006). *Seeing and visualizing: It's not what you think.* Cambridge, MA: MIT Press.

Pyun, Y. D. (2013). The effective use of hypnosis in schizophrenia: Structure and strategy. *International Journal of Clinical and Experimental Hypnosis, 61,* 388–400.

Qiu, J., Li, H., Jou, J., Liu, J., Luo, Y., Feng, T. et al. (2010). Neural correlates of the "aha" experiences: Evidence from an fMRI study of insight problem solving. *Cortex: A Journal Devoted to the Study of the Nervous System and Behavior, 46,* 397–403.

Quattrone, G. A., & Jones, E. E. (1980). The perception of variability within ingroups and outgroups: Implications for the law of small number. *Journal of Personality and Social Psychology, 38,* 141–152.

Querido, J. G., Warner, T. D., & Eyberg, S. M. (2002). Parenting styles and child behavior in African American families of preschool children. *Journal of Clinical Child and Adolescent Psychology, 31,* 272–277.

Quickfall, J., & Crockford, D. (2006). Brain neuroimaging in cannabis use: A review. *Journal of Neuropsychiatry and Clinical Neurosciences, 18,* 318–332.

Quigley, B. M., & Leonard, K. E. (2000). Alcohol and the continuation of early marital aggression. *Alcoholism: Clinical and Experimental Research, 24,* 1003–1010.

Quinn, P. C., & Tanaka, J. W. (2007). Early development of perceptual expertise: Within-basic-level categorization experience facilitates the formation of subordinate-level category representations in 6- to 7-month-old infants. *Memory & Cognition, 35,* 1422–1431.

Rabkin, S. W., Boyko, E., Shane, F., & Kaufert, J. (1984). A randomized trial comparing smoking cessation programs utilizing behavior modification, health education, or hypnosis. *Addictive Behaviors, 9,* 157–173.

Raby, K. L., Cicchetti, D., Carlson, E. A., Cutuli, J. J., Englund, M. M., & Egeland, B. (2012). Genetic and caregiving-based contributions to infant attachment: Unique associations with distress reactivity and attachment security. *Psychological Science, 23,* 1016–1023.

Racsmany, M., Conway, M. A., & Demeter, G. (2010). Consolidation of episodic memories during sleep: Long-term effects of retrieval practice. *Psychological Science, 21,* 80–85.

Rahman, Q. (2005). The neurodevelopment of human sexual orientation. *Neuroscience and Biobehavioral Reviews, 29,* 1057–1066.

Raine, A. (1997). Antisocial behavior and psychophysiology: A biological perspective. In D. M. Stoff, J. Breiling, & J. D. Maser (Eds.), *Handbook of antisocial personality disorder* (pp. 289–304). New York: Wiley.

Raine, A. (2008). From genes to brain to antisocial behavior. *Current Directions in Psychological Science, 17,* 323–328.

Raine, A., Lencz, T., Bihrle, S., LaCasse, L., & Colletti, P. (2000). Reduced prefrontal gray matter volume and reduced autonomic activity in antisocial personality disorder. *Archives of General Psychiatry, 57,* 119–127.

Raine, A., Yang, Y., Narr, K. L., & Toga, A. W. (2011). Sex differences in orbitofrontal gray as a partial explanation for sex differences in antisocial personality. *Molecular Psychiatry, 16,* 227–236.

Rainville, P., & Price, D. D. (2003). Hypnosis phenomenology and the neurobiology of consciousness. *International Journal of Clinical and Experimental Hypnosis, 51,* 105–129.

Rainville, P., Duncan, G. H., Price, D. D., Carrier, B., & Bushnell, M. C. (1997). Pain affect encoded in human anterior cingulate but not somatosensory cortex. *Science, 277,* 968–971.

Rajecki, D. W. (2012). Psychology baccalaureates at work: Major area subspecializations, earnings, and occupations. *Teaching of Psychology, 39,* 185–189.

Rajecki, D. W., & Borden, V. M. (2011). Psychology degrees: Employment, wage, and career trajectory consequences. *Perspectives on Psychological Science, 6,* 321–335.

Rakic, P. (1991). Plasticity of cortical development. In S. E. Brauth, W. S. Hall, & R. J. Dooling (Eds.), *Plasticity of development* (pp. 127–161). Cambridge, MA: Bradford/MIT Press.

Ram, S., Seirawan, H., Kumar, S. K., & Clark, G. T. (2010). Prevalence and impact of sleep disorders and sleep habits in the United States. *Sleep & Breathing, 14,* 63–70.

Ramsey-Rennels, J. L., & Langlois, J. H. (2006). Infants' differential processing of female and male faces. *Current Directions in Psychological Science, 15,* 59–62.

Randall, S., Johanson, C. E., Tancer, M., & Roehrs, T. (2009). Effects of acute 3, 4 methylenedioxymethamphetamine on sleep and daytime sleepiness in MDMA users: A preliminary study. *Sleep, 32,* 1513–1519.

Rando, T. A. (1995). Grief and mourning: Accommodating to loss. In H. Wass & R. A. Neimeyer (Eds.), *Dying: Facing the facts* (3rd ed., pp. 211–241). Washington DC: Taylor & Francis.

Ranganathan, M., & D'Souza, D. C. (2006). The acute effects of cannabinoids on memory in humans: A review. *Psychopharmacology (Berlin), 188,* 425–444.

Rank, M. R. (2000). Poverty and economic hardship in families. In D. H. Demo, K. R. Allen, & M. A. Fine (Eds.), *Handbook of family diversity* (pp. 293–315). New York: Oxford University Press.

Rao, H., Hillihan, S. J., Wang, J., Korczykowski, M., Sankoorikal, G. M., Kaercher, K. A. et al. (2007). Genetic variation in serotonin transporter alters resting brain function in healthy individuals. *Biological Psychiatry, 62,* 600–606.

Rapoport, J. L., Addington, A. M., Frangou, S., & Psych, M. R. (2005). The neurodevelopmental model of schizophrenia: Update 2005. *Molecular Psychiatry, 10,* 434–449.

Rappaport, V. J. (2008). Prenatal diagnosis and genetic screening: Integration into prenatal care. *Obstetrics and Gynecology Clinics of North America, 35,* 435–458.

Rasch, B., & Born, J. (2008). Reactivation and consolidation of memory during sleep. *Current Directions in Psychological Science, 17,* 188–192.

Rasmussen, C., Soleimani, M., & Pei, J. (2011). Executive functioning and working memory deficits on the CANTAB among children with prenatal alcohol exposure. *Journal of Population Therapeutics and Clinical Pharmacology, 18,* e44–e53.

Rastelli, F., Tallon-Baudry, C., Migliaccio, R., Toba, M. N., Ducorps, A., Pradat-Diehl, P. et al. (2013). Neural dynamics of neglected targets in patients with right hemisphere damage. *Cortex: A Journal Devoted to the Study of the Nervous System and Behavior, 49,* 1989–1996. doi:10.1016/j.cortex.2013.04.001

Rathbone, C. J., Moulin, C. A., Conway, M. A., & Holmes, E. A. (2012). Autobiographical memory and the self. In N. Braisby & A. Gellatly (Eds.), *Cognitive psychology* (2nd ed., pp. 546–576). New York: Oxford University Press.

Rauch, S. L., Savage, C. R., Alpert, N. M., Dougherty, D., Kendrick, A., Curran, T. et al. (1997). Probing striatal function in obsessive-compulsive disorder: A PET study of implicit sequence learning. *Journal of Neuropsychiatry and Clinical Neuroscience, 9,* 568–573.

Rauch, S. L., Shin, L. M., & Phelps, E. A. (2006). Neurocircuitry models of posttraumatic stress disorder and extinction: Human neuroimaging research—past, present, and future. *Biological Psychiatry, 60,* 376–382.

Rauchs, G., Bertran, F., Guillery-Girard, B., Desgranges, B., Kerrouche, N., Denise, P. et al. (2004). Consolidation of strictly episodic memories mainly requires rapid eye movement sleep. *Sleep, 27,* 395–401.

Ravenna, H., Jones, C., & Kwan, V. S. (2002). Personality change over 40 years of adulthood: Hierarchical linear modeling analyses of two longitudinal samples. *Journal of Personality and Social Psychology, 83,* 752–766.

Ray, R. D., Wilhelm, F. H., & Gross, J. J. (2008). All in the mind's eye? Anger rumination and reappraisal. *Journal of Personality and Social Psychology, 94,* 133–145.

Raz, A. (2005). Attention and hypnosis: Neural substrates and genetic associations of two converging processes. *International Journal of Clinical and Experimental Hypnosis, 53,* 237–258.

Raz, A., Fan, J., & Posner, M. I. (2006). Neuroimaging and genetic associations of attentional and hypnotic processes. *Journal of Physiology (Paris), 99,* 483–491.

Raz, N., & Kennedy, K. M. (2009). A systems approach to age-related change: Neuroanatomical changes, their modifiers, and cognitive correlates. In W. Jagust & M. D'Esposito (Eds.), *Imaging the aging brain* (pp. 43–70). New York: Oxford University Press.

Raz, N., Rodrigue, K. M., Kennedy, K. M., & Acker, J. D. (2007). Vascular health and longitudinal changes in brain and cognition in middle-aged and older adults. *Neuropsychology, 21,* 149–157.

Read, C. N., & Greenberg, B. D. (2009). Psychiatric neurosurgery 2009: Review and perspective. *Seminars in Neurology, 29,* 256–265.

Read, S., & Grundy, E. (2011). Mental health among older married couples: The role of gender and family life. *Social Psychiatry and Psychiatric Epidemiology, 46,* 331–341.

Reber, P. J. (2013). The neural basis of implicit learning and memory: A review of neuropsychological and neuroimaging research. *Neuropsychologia, 51,* 2026–2042. doi:10.1016/j.neuropsychologia .2013.06.019

Recio, G., Schacht, A., & Sommer, W. (2013). Classification of dynamic facial expressions of emotion presented briefly. *Cognition and Emotion, 27,* 1486–1494. doi: 10.1080/02699931.2013.794128

Reder, L. M., Park., H., & Kieffaber, P. D. (2009). Memory systems do not divide on consciousness: Reinterpreting memory in terms of activation and binding. *Psychological Bulletin, 135,* 23–49.

Reece, M., Herbenick, D., Schick, V., Sanders, S., Dodge, B., & Fortenberry, J. D. (2010). Condom use rates in a national probability sample of males and females ages 14 to 94 in the United States. *Journal of Sexual Medicine, 7* (Suppl. 5), 266–276.

Rehder, B., & Hoffman, A. B. (2005). Thirty-something categorization results explained: Selective attention, eyetracking, and models of category learning. *Journal of Experimental Psychology: Learning, Memory, and Cognition, 31,* 811–829.

Reid, K. J., Baron, K. G., Lu, B., Naylor, E., Wolfe, L., & Zee, P. C. (2010). Aerobic exercise improves self-reported sleep and quality of life in older adults with insomnia. *Sleep Medicine, 11,* 934–940.

Reid, P., & Bing, V. (2000). Sexual roles of girls and women: An ethnocultural lifespan perspective. In C. Travis & J. White (Eds.), *Sexuality, society, and feminism* (pp. 141–166). Washington, DC: American Psychological Association.

Reinisch, J. M. (1991). *The Kinsey Institute new report on sex: What you must know to be sexually literate.* New York: St. Martin's Press.

Reisenzein, R. (1983). The Schachter theory of emotion: Two decades later. *Psychological Bulletin, 94,* 239–264.

Reiss, D. (2005). The interplay between genotypes and family relationships: Reframing concepts of development and prevention. *Current Directions in Psychological Science, 14,* 139–143.

Reite, M., Sheeder, J., Teale, P., Richardson, D., Adams, M., & Simon, J. (1995). MEG based brain laterality: Sex differences in normal adults. *Neuropsychologia, 33,* 1607–1616.

Reitzes, D. C., & Mutran, E. J. (2004). The transition to retirement: Stages and factors that influence retirement adjustment. *International Journal of Aging and Human Development, 59,* 63–84.

Rempel, D. M., Keir, P. J., & Bach, J. M. (2008). Effect of wrist posture on carpal tunnel pressure while typing. *Journal of Orthopaedic Research, 26,* 1269–1273.

Ren, J., Li, H., Palaniyappan, L., Liu, H., Wang, J., Li, C., & Rossini, P. M. (2014). Repetitive transcranial magnetic stimulation versus electroconvulsive therapy for major depression: A systematic review and meta-analysis. *Progress in Neuropsychopharmacology & Biological Psychiatry, 51,* 181–189.

Renoult, L., Davidson, P. R., Palombo, D. J., Moscovitch, M., & Levine, B. (2012). Personal semantics: At the crossroads of semantic and episodic memory. *Trends in Cognitive Sciences, 16,* 550–558. doi:10.1016/j.tics.2012.09.003

Repetti, R., Wang, S., & Saxbe, D. (2009). Bringing it all back home: How outside stressors shape families' everyday lives. *Current Directions in Psychological Science, 18,* 106–111.

Repovs, G., & Baddeley, A. (2006). The multicomponent model of working memory: Explorations in experimental cognitive psychology. *Neuroscience, 139,* 5–21.

Rescorla, R. A. (1967). Pavlovian conditioning and its proper control procedures. *Psychological Review, 74,* 71–80.

Resick, P. A., Nishith, P., Weaver, T. L., Astin, M. C., & Feuer, C. A. (2002). A comparison of cognitive-processing therapy with prolonged exposure and a waiting condition for the treatment of chronic posttraumatic stress disorder in female rape victims. *Journal of Consulting and Clinical Psychology, 70,* 867–879.

Resta, O., Foschino-Barbaro, M. P., Legari, G., Talamo, S., Bonfitto, P., Palumbo, A. et al. (2001). Sleep-related breathing disorders, loud snoring and excessive daytime sleepiness in obese subjects. *International Journal of Obesity and Related Metabolic Disorders, 25,* 669–675.

Restuccia, D, Vollono, C., Virdis, D., Piero, I. D., Martucci, L., & Zanini, S. (2014). Patterns of habituation and clinical fluctuations in migraine. *Cephalalgia, 34,* 201–210. doi: 10.1177/0333102413508241

Reyna, V. F., & Farley, F. (2006). Risk and rationality in adolescent decision making. *Psychological Science in the Public Interest, 7,* 1–44.

Reyngoudt, H., Paemeleire, K., Dierickx, A., Descamps, B., Vandemaele, P., De Deene, Y. et al. (2011). Does visual cortex lactate increase following photic stimulation in migraine without aura patients? A functional (1)H-MRS study. *Journal of Headache Pain, 12,* 295–302. doi:10.1007/s10194-011-0295-7

Reynolds, C. R., & Brown, R. T. (Eds.). (1984). *Perspectives on bias in mental testing.* New York: Plenum Press.

Reynolds, J. R., & Burge, S. W. (2008). Educational expectations and the rise in women's post-secondary attainments. *Social Science Research, 37,* 485–499.

Reynolds, P., Hurley, S., Torres, M., Jackson, J., Boyd, P., & Chen, V. W. (2000). Use of coping strategies and breast cancer survival: Results from the Black/White Cancer Survival Study. *American Journal of Epidemiology, 152,* 940–949.

Reynolds, R. M. (2013). Glucocorticoid excess and the developmental origins of disease: Two decades of testing the hypothesis. *Psychoneuroendocrinology, 38,* 1–11.

Rhodes, N., & Wood, W. (1992). Self-esteem and intelligence affect influencability: The mediating role of message reception. *Psychological Bulletin, 111,* 156–171.

Ricca, V., Castellini, G., Mannucci, E., Lo Sauro, C., Ravaldi, C., Rotella, C. M. et al. (2010). Comparison of individual and group cognitive behavioral therapy for binge eating disorder: A randomized, three-year follow-up study. *Appetite, 55,* 656–665.

Rice, F. P. (1992). *Intimate relationships, marriages, and families.* Mountain View, CA: Mayfield.

Rice, V. H. (Ed.). (2000). *Handbook of stress, coping and health.* Thousand Oaks, CA: Sage.

Richards, J., Klein, B., & Carlbring, P. (2003). Internet-based treatment for panic disorder. *Cognitive Behaviour Therapy, 32,* 125–135.

Richardson, G. A., Goldschmidt, L., Leech, S., & Willford, J. (2011). Prenatal cocaine exposure: Effects on mother- and teacher-rated behavior problems and growth in school-age children. *Neurotoxicology and Teratology, 33,* 69–77.

Rickels, K., DeMartinis, N., Garcia-Espana, F., Greenblatt, D. J., Mandos, L. A., & Rynn, M. (2000). Imipramine and buspirone in treatment of patients with generalized anxiety disorder who are discontinuing long-term benzodiazepine therapy. *American Journal of Psychiatry, 157,* 1973–1979.

Rieger, G., Gygax, L., & Bailey, J. M. (2008). Sexual orientation and childhood gender non-conformity: Evidence from home videos. *Developmental Psychology, 44,* 46–58.

Riemann, D., & Perlis, M. L. (2009). The treatments of chronic insomnia: A review of benzodiazepine receptor agonists and psychological and behavioral therapies. *Sleep Medicine Reviews, 13,* 205–214.

Rijsman, R. M., Schoolderman, L. F., Rundervoort, R. S., & Louter, M. (2014). Restless legs syndrome in Parkinson's disease. *Parkinsonism & Related Disorders, 20,* S5–S9.

Riketta, M. (2008). The causal relation between job attitudes and performance: A meta-analysis of panel studies. *Journal of Applied Psychology, 93,* 472–481.

Rinaudo, P., & Wang, E. (2012). Fetal programming and metabolic syndrome. *Annual Review of Physiology, 74,* 107–130.

Rinsky, J. R., & Henshaw, S. P. (2011). Linkages between childhood executive functioning and adolescent social functioning and psychopathology in girls with ADHD. *Child Neuropsychology, 4,* 1–23.

Rios Romenets, S., & Postuma, R. B. (2013). Treatment of restless legs syndrome. *Current Treatment Options in Neurology, 15,* 396–409.

Rishi, M. A., Shetty, M., Wolff, A., Amoateng-Adjepong, Y., & Manthous, C. A. (2010). Atypical antipsychotic medications are independently associated with severe obstructive sleep apnea. *Clinical Neuropharmacology, 33,* 109–113.

Riskind, J. H., Williams, N. L., Gessner, T. L., Chrosniak, L. D., & Cortina, J. M. (2000). The looming maladaptive style: Anxiety, danger, and schematic processing. *Journal of Personality and Social Psychology, 79,* 837–852.

Rivers, P. C. (1994). *Alcohol and human behavior.* Englewood Cliffs, NJ: Wiley.

Roberts, A. L., Gilman, S. E., Brelau, J., & Koenen, K. C. (2011). Race/ethnic differences in exposure to traumatic events, development of post-traumatic stress disorder, and treatment-seeking for post-traumatic stress disorder in the United States. *Psychological Medicine, 41,* 71–83.

Roberts, B. W., & DelVecchio, W. F. (2000). The rank-order consistency of personality traits from childhood to old age: A quantitative review of longitudinal studies. *Psychological Bulletin, 126,* 3–25.

Roberts, B. W., & Mroczek, D. (2008). Personality trait change in adulthood. *Current Directions in Psychological Science, 17,* 31–35.

Roberts, B. W., Caspi, A., & Moffitt, T. E. (2001). The kids are alright: Growth and stability in personality development from adolescence to adulthood. *Journal of Personality and Social Psychology, 81,* 670–683.

Roberts, B. W., Edmonds, G., & Grijalva, E. (2010). It is Developmental Me, not Generation Me: Developmental changes are more important than generational changes in narcissism: Commentary on Trzesniewski & Donnellan (2010). *Perspectives on Psychological Science, 5,* 97–102.

Roberts, B. W., Kuncel, N. R., Shiner, R., Caspi, A., & Goldberg, L. R. (2007). The power of personality: The comparative validity of personality traits, socioeconomic status, and cognitive ability for predicting important life outcomes. *Perspectives on Psychological Science, 2,* 313–345.

Roberts, B. W., Walton, K. E., & Viechtbauer, W. (2006). Patterns of mean-level change in personality traits across the life course: A meta-analysis of longitudinal studies. *Psychological Bulletin, 132,* 1–25.

Roberts, R. D., Schulze, R., O'Brien, K., MacCann, C., Reid, J., & Maul, A. (2006). Exploring the validity of the Mayer-Salovey-Caruso emotional intelligence test (MSCEIT) with established emotions measures. *Emotion, 6,* 663–669.

Roberts, R. E., Roberts, C. R., & Chan, W. (2006). Ethnic differences in symptoms of insomnia among adolescents. *Sleep, 29,* 359–365.

Roberts, S. M. (1995). Applicability of the goodness-of-fit hypothesis to coping with daily hassles. *Psychological Reports, 77*(3, Pt. 1), 943–954.

Robins, L. N., & Regier, D. A. (Eds.). (1991). *Psychiatric disorders in America: The Epidemiologic Catchment Area Study.* New York: Free Press.

Robins, R. W., Fraley, R. C., Roberts, B. W., & Trzesniewski, K. H. (2001). A longitudinal study of personality change in young adulthood. *Journal of Personality, 69,* 617–640.

Robinson, L. A., Berman, J. S., & Neimeyer, R. A. (1990). Psychotherapy for the treatment of depression: A comprehensive review of controlled outcome research. *Psychological Bulletin, 109,* 30–49.

Robinson, N. M., Abbott, R. D., Berninger, V. W., & Busse, J. (1996). The structure of abilities in math-precocious young children: Gender similarities and differences. *Journal of Educational Psychology, 88,* 341–352.

Robles, T. F., & Kiecolt-Glaser, J. K. (2003). The physiology of marriage: Pathways to health. *Physiology and Behavior, 79,* 409–416.

Robles, T. F., Glaser, R., Kiecolt-Glaser, J. K. (2005). Out of balance: A new look at chronic stress, depression, and immunity. *Current Directions in Psychological Science, 14,* 111–115.

Rockafellow, B. D., & Saules, K. K. (2006). Substance use by college students: The role of intrinsic versus extrinsic motivation for athletic involvement. *Psychology of Addictive Behavior, 20,* 279–287.

Rodenburg, R., Benjamin, A., de Roos, C., Meijer, A. M., & Stams, G. J. (2009). Efficacy of EMDR in children: A meta-analysis. *Clinical Psychology Review, 29,* 599–606.

Rodewald, F., Wilhelm-Gosling, C., Emrich, H. M., Reddemann, L., & Gast, U. (2011). Axis-I comorbidity in female patients with dissociative identity disorder not otherwise specified. *Journal of Nervous and Mental Disease, 199,* 122–131.

Rogers, C. R. (1942). *Counseling and psychotherapy.* Boston: Houghton Mifflin.

Rogers, C. R. (1951). *Client-centered therapy: Its current practice, implications, and theory.* Boston: Houghton Mifflin

Rogers, C. R. (1961). *On becoming a person.* Boston: Houghton Mifflin.

Rogers, C. R. (1970). *Carl Rogers on encounter groups.* New York: Harper & Row.

Rogers, C. R. (1980). *A way of being.* Boston: Houghton Mifflin.

Rogers, C. R. (1986). Client-centered therapy. In I. L. Kutash & A. Wolf (Eds.), *Psychotherapists' casebook* (pp. 197–208). San Francisco: Jossey-Bass.

Rogers, M. A., Yamasue, H., Abe, O., Yamada, H., Ohtani, T., Iwanami, A. et al. (2009). Smaller amygdala volume and reduced anterior cingulated gray matter density associated with history of post-traumatic stress disorder. *Psychiatry Research, 174,* 210–216.

Rogers, N. L., Szuba, M. P., Staab, J. P., Evans, D. L., & Dinges, D. F. (2001). Neuroimmunologic aspects of sleep and sleep loss. *Seminars in Clinical Neuropsychiatry, 6,* 295–307.

Rogers, T. B. (1995). *The psychological testing enterprise: An introduction.* Pacific Grove, CA: Brooks/Cole.

Rogoff, B., & Chavajah, P. (1995). What's become of research on the cultural basis of cognitive development? *American Psychologist, 50,* 859–873.

Rogol, A. D., Roemmich, J. N., & Clark, P. A. (2002). Growth at puberty. *Journal of Adolescent Health, 31,* 192–200.

Rohan, M. J., & Zanna, M. P. (1996). Value transmission in families. In C. Seligman & J. M. Olson (Eds.), *The psychology of values: The Ontario symposium* (Vol. 8, pp. 253–276). Mahwah, NJ: Erlbaum.

Rohde, P., Lewinsohn, P. M., Klein, D. N., Seeley, J. R., & Gau, J. M. (2013). Key characteristics of major depressive disorder occurring in childhood, adolescence, emerging adulthood, and adulthood. *Clinical Psychological Science, 1,* 41–53.

Rohrbach, L. A., Grana, R., Vernberg, E., Sussman, S., & Sun, P. (2009). Impact of Hurricane Rita on adolescent substance abuse. *Psychiatry, 72,* 222–237.

Roisman, G. I., & Fraley, R. C. (2006). The limits of genetic influence: A behavior-genetic analysis of infant–caregiver relationship quality and temperament. *Child Development, 77,* 1656–1667.

Roisman, G. I., Clausell, E., Holland, A., Fortuna, K., & Elieff, C. (2008). Adult romantic relationships as contexts of human development: A multimethod comparison of same-sex couples with opposite-sex dating, engaged, and married dyads. *Developmental Psychology, 44,* 91–101.

Rolls, E. T. (2000). The representation of umami tastes in the taste cortex. *Journal of Nutrition, 130,* 960–965.

Romanelli, R. J., Wu, F. M., Gamba, R., Mojtabai, R., & Segal, J. B. (2014). Behavioral therapy and serotonin reuptake inhibitor pharmacotherapy in the treatment of obsessive-compulsive disorder: A systematic review and meta-analysis of head-to-head randomized controlled trials. *Depression and Anxiety, 31,* 641–652.

Romano, E., Bell, T., & Norian, R. (2013). Corporal punishment: Examining attitudes toward the law and factors influencing attitude change. *Journal of Family Violence, 28,* 265–275. doi:10.1007/s10896-013-9494-0

Rooney, N. J., Bradshaw, J. W. S., & Robinson, I. H. (2001). Do dogs respond to play signals given by humans? *Animal Behavior, 61,* 715–722.

Rosch, E. (1973). Natural categories. *Cognitive Psychology, 4,* 328–350.

Rosch, E., Mervis, C. B., Gray, W. D., Johnson, D. M., & Boyes-Braem, P. (2004). Basic objects in natural categories. In D. A. Balota & E. J. Marsh (Eds.), *Cognitive psychology: Key readings* (pp. 448–471). New York: Psychology Press.

Rose, A. J., & Smith, R. L. (2009). Sex differences in peer relationships. In K. H. Rubin, W. M. Bukowski, & B. Laursen (Eds.), *Handbook of peer interactions, relationships, and groups* (pp. 379–393). New York: Guilford Press.

Rose, A. J., Carlson, W., & Waller, E. M. (2007). Prospective associations of co-rumination with friendship and emotional adjustment: Considering the socioemotional trade-offs of co-rumination. *Developmental Psychology, 43,* 1019–1031.

Rose, J. E., Behm, F. M., Salley, A. N., Bates, J. E., Coleman, R. E., Hawk, T. C. et al. (2007). Regional brain activity correlates of nicotine dependence. *Neuropsychopharmacology, 32,* 2441–2452.

Rose, R. J. (1995). Genes and human behavior. *Annual Review of Psychology, 46,* 625–654.

Rose, S. A. (1980). Enhancing visual recognition memory in preterm infants. *Developmental Psychology, 16,* 85–92.

Rosen, J. B. (2004). The neurobiology of conditioned and unconditioned fear: A neurobehavioral system analysis of the amygdale. *Behavior and Cognitive Neuroscience Reviews, 3,* 23–41.

Rosen, J. B., & Donley, M. P. (2006). Animal studies of amygdala function in fear and uncertainty: Relevance to human research. *Biological Psychology, 73,* 49–60.

Rosenblatt, P. C. (2008). Grief across cultures: A review and research agenda. In M. S. Stroebe, R . O. Hansson, H. Schut, & W. Stroebe (Eds.), *Handbook of bereavement research and practice: Advances in theory and intervention* (pp. 207–222). Washington, DC: American Psychological Association.

Rosenblith, J. F. (1992). *In the beginning.* Newbury Park, CA: Sage.

Rosenhan, D. L. (1969). Some origins of the concerns for others. In P. Mussen & M. Covington (Eds.), *Trends and issues in developmental psychology* (pp. 134–153). New York: Holt, Rinehart & Winston.

Rosenhan, D. L. (1973). On being sane in insane places. *Science, 179,* 250–258.

Rosenkranz, M. A., Davidson, R. J., Maccoon, D. G., Sheridan, J. F., Kalin, N. H., & Lutz, A. (2013). A comparison of mindfulness-based stress reduction and an active control in modulation of neurogenic inflammation. *Brain, Behavior, and Immunity, 27,* 174–184.

Roshanaei-Moghaddam, B., Pauly, M. C., Atkins, D. C., Baldwin, S. A., Stein, M. B., & Roy- Byrne, P. (2011). Relative effects of CBT and pharmacotherapy in depression versus anxiety: Is medication somewhat better for depression, and CBT somewhat better for anxiety? *Depression and Anxiety, 28,* 560–567.

Ross, C. A., & Ness, L. (2010). Symptom patterns in dissociative identity disorder patients and the general population. *Journal of Trauma and Dissociation, 11,* 458–468.

Ross, M. W. (1980). Retrospective distortion in homosexual research. *Archives of Sexual Behavior, 9,* 523–531.

Rotenberg, K. J., Costa, P., Trueman, M., & Lattimore, P. (2012). An interactional test of the reformulated helplessness theory of depression in women receiving clinical treatment for eating disorders. *Eating Behaviors, 13,* 264–266.

Roth, J., & Steffens, M. C. (2014). When I becomes we: Associative self-anchoring drives implicit intergroup bias in minimal groups. *Social Psychology,* doi:10.1027/1864-9335/a000169

Roth, S., & Cohen, J. L. (1986). Approach, avoidance, and coping with stress. *American Psychologist, 41,* 813–819.

Roth, T. (2005). Prevalence, associated risks, and treatment patterns of insomnia. *Journal of Clinical Psychiatry, 66,* 10–13.

Roth, T., Krystal, A. D., & Lieberman, J. A., III. (2007). Long-term issues in the treatment of sleep disorders. *CNS Spectrum, 12,* 1–13.

Roth, T., Schwartz, J. R., Hirshkowitz, M., Erman, M. K., Dayno, J. M., & Arora, S. (2007). Evaluation of the safety of modafinil for treatment of excessive sleepiness. *Journal of Clinical Sleep Medicine, 3,* 595–602.

Rothbart, M. K., Ahadi, S. A., & Evans, D. E. (2000). Temperament and personality: Origins and outcomes. *Journal of Personality and Social Psychology, 78,* 122–135.

Rothbaum, B. O., Hodges, L. F., Kooper, R., Opdyke, D., & Williford, J. (1995). Effectiveness of computer-generated (virtual reality) graded exposure in the treatment of acrophobia. *American Journal of Psychiatry, 152,* 626–628.

Rothbaum, B. O., Hodges, L., Watson, B. A., Kessler, G. D., & Opdyke, D. (1996). Virtual reality exposure therapy in the treatment of fear of flying: A case report. *Behavior Research and Therapy, 34,* 477–481.

Rothbaum, B. O., Rizzo, A. S., & Difede, J. (2010). Virtual reality exposure therapy for combat-related posttraumatic stress disorder. *Annals of the New York Academy of Sciences, 1208,* 126–132.

Rouch, I., Wild, P., Ansiau, D., & Marquie, J. C. (2005). Shiftwork experience, age, and cognitive performance. *Ergonomics, 48,* 1282–1293.

Rowe, T. (2006). Fertility and a woman's age. *Journal of Reproductive Medicine, 51,* 157–163.

Rowlett, J. K., Cook, J. M., Duke, A. N., & Platt, D. M. (2005). Selective antagonism of GABAA receptor subtypes: An in vivo approach to exploring the therapeutic and side effects of benzodiazepine-type drugs. *CNS Spectrums, 10,* 40–48.

Roy-Byrne, P. (2014). Treatment in nonresponsive patients with social anxiety: Back to the future with benzodiazepines. *American Journal of Psychiatry, 171,* 1–4.

Ruark, J. (2009, August 3). An intellectual movement for the masses: 10 years after its founding, positive psychology struggles with its own success. *Chronicle of Higher Education.*

Rubin, K. H., Lynch, D., Coplan, R., Rose-Krasnor, L., & Booth, C. L. (1994). "Birds of a feather . . .": Behavioral concordances and preferential personal attraction in children. *Child Development, 65,* 1778–1785.

Rubin, M., & Badea, C. (2012). They're all the same!. . . But for several different reasons: A review of the multicausal nature of perceived group variability. *Current Directions in Psychological Science, 21,* 367–372. doi:10.1177/0963721412457363

Rubin, S. S. (1993). The death of a child is forever: The life course impact of child loss. In M. Stroebe, W. Stroebe, & R. O. Hansson (Eds.), *Handbook of bereavement. Theory, research, and intervention* (pp. 285–299). Cambridge: Cambridge University Press.

Ruderman, A. J. (1985). Dysphoric mood and overeating: A test of restraint theory's disinhibition hypothesis. *Journal of Abnormal Psychology, 94,* 78–85.

Rudgley, R. (1998). *The encyclopedia of psychoactive substances.* New York: Little, Brown.

Rudner, M., Karlsson, T., Gunnarsson, J., & Rönnberg, J. (2013). Levels of processing and language modality specificity in working memory. *Neuropsychologia, 51,* 656–666. doi:10.1016/j.neuropsychologia.2012.12.011

Ruffin, C. L. (1993). Stress and health: Little hassles vs. major life events. *Australian Psychologist, 28,* 201–208.

Ruffman, T., Slade, L., & Redman, J. (2005). Young infants' expectations about hidden objects. *Cognition, 97,* B35–B43.

Ruiz, F. S., Andersen, M. L., Martins, R. C., Zager, A., Lopes, J. D., & Tufik, S. (2012). Immune alterations after selective eye movement or total sleep deprivation in healthy male volunteers. *Innate Immunity, 18,* 44–54.

Rumelhart, D. E. (1980). Schemata: The basic building blocks of cognition. In R. Spiro, B. Bruce, & W. Brewer (Eds.), *Theoretical issues in reading comprehension* (pp. 33–58). Hillsdale, NJ: Erlbaum.

Ruscio, A. M., Brown, T. A., Chiu, W. T., Sareen, J., Stein, M. B., & Kessler, R. C. (2008). Social fears and social phobia in the USA: Results from the National Comorbidity Survey Replication. *Psychological Medicine, 38,* 15–28.

Rush, M. C., Schoel, W. A., & Barnard, S. M. (1995). Psychological resiliency in the public sector: "Hardiness" and pressure for change. *Journal of Vocational Behavior, 46,* 17–39.

Rushton, J. (2012). No narrowing in mean Black–White IQ differences—Predicted by heritable g. *American Psychologist, 67,* 500–501. doi:10.1037/a0029614

Rushton, J. P., & Jensen, A. R. (2005). Thirty years of research on race differences in cognitive ability. *Psychology, Public Policy, and Law, 11,* 235–294.

Rushton, W. A. H. (1975). Visual pigments and color blindness. *Scientific American, 232,* 64–74.

Russell, C. J., & Keel, P. K. (2002). Homosexuality as a specific risk factor for eating disorders in men. *International Journal of Eating Disorders, 31,* 300–306.

Russell, V. A., Zigmond, M. J., Dimatelis, J. J., Daniels, W. M., & Mabandia, M. V. (2014). The interaction between stress and exercise, and its impact on brain function. *Metabolic Brain Disease, 29,* 255–260.

Rutherford, W. (1886). A new theory of hearing. *Journal of Anatomy and Physiology, 21,* 166–168.

Ryon, H. S., & Gleason, M. E. (2014). The role of locus of control in daily life. *Personality and Social Psychology Bulletin, 40,* 121–131.

Saadat, H., Drummond-Lewis, J., Maranets, I., Kaplan, D., Saadat, A., Wang, S. M. et al. (2006). Hypnosis reduces preoperative anxiety in adult patients. *Anesthesia and Analgesia, 102,* 1394–1396.

Saalmann, Y. B., & Kastner, S. (2009). Gain control in the visual thalamus during perception and cognition. *Current Opinion in Neurobiology, 19,* 408–414. doi:10.1016/j.conb.2009.05.007

Sachs, G. S., & Rush, A. J. (2003). Response, remission, and recovery in bipolar disorders: What are the realistic treatment goals? *Journal of Clinical Psychiatry, 64*(Suppl. 6), 18–22.

Sackett, P. R., & DeVore, C. J. (2001). Counterproductive behaviors at work. In N. Anderson, D. S. Ones, H. K. Sinangil, & C. Viswesvaran (Eds.), *Handbook of industrial, work and organizational psychology* (Vol. 1, pp. 145–165). Thousand Oaks, CA: Sage.

Sadker, D. (2000). Gender equity: Still knocking at the classroom door. *Equity and Excellence in Education, 33,* 80–83.

Sadler, W. A. (2000). *The third age: Six principles for growth and renewal after forty.* New York: Perseus.

Sah, P., Faber, E. S. L., Lopez De Armentia, M., & Power, J. (2003). The aymgdaloid complex: Anatomy and physiology. *Physiological Reviews, 83,* 803–834.

Sajatovic, M., Valenstein, M., Blow, F., Ganoczy, D., & Ignacio, R. (2007). Treatment adherence with lithium and anticonvulsant medications among patients with bipolar disorder. *Psychiatric Services, 58,* 855–863.

Sakari, M. M. (1975). Small group cohesiveness and detrimental conformity. *Sociometry, 38,* 340–357.

Salend, S. J. (2001). *Creating inclusive classrooms: Effective and reflective practices* (4th ed.). Upper Saddle River, NJ: Prentice Hall.

Salgado, J. F., Viswesvaran, C., & Ones, D. (2003). Predictors used for personnel selection: An overview of constructs, methods and techniques. In N. Anderson, D. S. Ones, H. K. Sinangil, & C. Viswesvaran (Eds.), *Handbook of industrial, work and organizational psychology* (Vol. 1, pp. 166–199). Thousand Oaks, CA: Sage.

Salkovskis, P. M., Westbrook, D., Davis, J., Jeavons, A., & Gledhill, A. (1997). Effects of neutralizing on intrusive thoughts: An experiment investigating the etiology of obsessive-compulsive disorder. *Behaviour Research and Therapy, 35,* 211–219.

Salthouse, T. A. (2004). What and when of cognitive aging. *Current Directions in Psychological Science, 13,* 140–144.

Salthouse, T. A. (2012). Does the level at which cognitive change occurs change with age? *Psychological Science, 23,* 18–23.

Salvatore, J. E., Chun-Kuo, S. I., Steele, R. D., Simpson, J. A., & Collins, W. A. (2011). Recovering from conflict in romantic relationships: A developmental perspective. *Psychological Science, 22,* 376–383.

Samarel, N. (1995). The dying process. In H. Wass & R. A. Neimeyer (Eds.), *Dying: Facing the facts* (3rd ed., pp. 89–116). Washington DC: Taylor & Francis.

Sanada, M., Ikeda, K., Kimura, K., & Hasegawa, T. (2013). Motivation enhances visual working memory capacity through the modulation of central cognitive processes. *Psychophysiology, 50,* 864–871.

Sanaktekin, O. H., & Sunar, D. (2008). Persuasion and relational versus personal self-esteem: Does the message need to be one- or two-sided? *Social Behavior and Personality, 36,* 1315–1332.

Sanchez-de-la-Torre, M., Campos-Rodriguez, F., & Barbe, F. (2013). Obstructive sleep apnea and cardiovascular disease. *The Lancet: Respiratory Medicine, 1,* 61–72.

Sanchez-Hucles, J. V., & Davis, D. D. (2010). Women and women of color in leadership. *American Psychologist, 65,* 171–181.

Sánchez-Martín, J. R., Azurmendi, A., Pascual-Sagastizabal, E., Cardas, J., Braza, F., Braza, P. et al. (2011). Androgen levels and anger and impulsivity measures as predictors of physical, verbal and indirect aggression in boys and girls. *Psychoneuroendocrinology, 36,* 750–760. doi:10.1016/j.psyneuen.2010.10.011

Sanders, J. D., Happe, H. K., Bylund, D. B., & Murrin, L. C. (2005). Development of the norepinephrine transporter in the rat CNS. *Neuroscience, 130,* 107–117.

Sanderson, C. A., & Cantor, N. (1995). Social dating goals in late adolescence: Implications for safer sexual activity. *Journal of Personality and Social Psychology, 68,* 1121–1134.

Sanes, J. N., Dimitrov, B., & Hallett, M. (1990). Motor learning in patients with cerebellar dysfunction. *Brain, 113,* 103–120.

Sangrigoli, S., & de Schonen, S. (2004). Recognition of own-race and other-race faces by three-month-old infants. *Journal of Child Psychology and Psychiatry, 45,* 1219–1227.

Sanislow, C. A., Pine, D. S., Quinn, K. J., Kojak, M. J., Garvey, M. A., Heinssen, R. K. et al. (2010). Developing constructs for psychopathology research: Research domain criteria. *Journal of Abnormal Psychology, 119,* 631–639.

Sansone, R. A., & Sansone, L. A. (2011). Personality pathology and its influence on eating disorders. *Clinical Neuroscience, 8,* 14–18.

Santelli, J. S., Lindberg, L. D., Abma, J., McNeeley, C. S., & Resnick, M. (2000). Adolescent sexual behavior: Estimates and trends from four nationally representative surveys. *Family Planning Perspectives, 32,* 156–165, 194.

Sanyal, S., & vanTol, H. M. (1997). Review the role of dopamine D4 receptors in schizophrenia and anti-psychotic action. *Journal of Psychiatric Research, 31,* 219–232.

Sapolsky, R. M. (2000). The possibility of neurotoxicity in the hippocampus in major depression: A primer on neuron death. *Biological Psychiatry, 48,* 755–765.

Sapolsky, R. M. (2002). Chickens, eggs and hippocampal atrophy. *Nature Neuroscience, 5,* 1111–1113.

Sarker, M. R., Franks, S., & Caffrey, J. (2013). Direction of post-prandial ghrelin response associated with cortisol response, perceived stress and anxiety, and self-reported coping and hunger in obese women. *Behavioural Brain Research, 257,* 197–200. doi: 10.1016/j.bbr.2013.09.046

Saskin, P. (1997). Obstructive sleep apnea: Treatment options, efficacy, and effects. In M. R. Pressman & W. C. Orr (Eds.), *Understanding sleep: The evaluation and treatment of sleep disorders* (pp. 283–297). Washington DC: American Psychological Association.

Saucier, D. A., McManus, J. L., & Smith, S. J. (2010). Discrimination against out-group members in helping situations. In S. Stürmer & M. Snyder (Eds.), *The psychology of prosocial behavior: Group processes, intergroup relations, and helping* (pp. 103–120). New York: Wiley-Blackwell.

Saudino, K. J., McQuire, S., Reiss, D. Heatherington, E. M., & Plomin, R. (1995). Parent ratings of EAS temperaments in twins, full siblings, half siblings, and step siblings. *Journal of Personality and Social Psychology, 68,* 723–733.

Saunders, E. H., Scott, L. J., McInnis, M. G., & Burmeister, M. (2008). Familiality and diagnostic patterns of subphenotypes in the National Institute of Mental Health bipolar sample. *American Journal of Medical Genetics Part B: Neuropsychiatric Genetics, 147B,* 18–26.

Saunders, N. L., & Summers, M. J. (2011). Longitudinal deficits to attention, executive, and working memory in subtypes of mild cognitive impairment. *Neuropsychology, 25,* 237–248.

Sauter, D. A., Eisner, F., Ekman, P., & Scott, S. K. (2010). Cross-cultural recognition of basic emotions through nonverbal emotional vocalizations. *Proceedings of the National Academy of Sciences USA, 107,* 2408–2412.

Sava, F. A., Yates, B. T., Lupu, V., Szentagotai, A., & David, D. (2009). Cost-effectiveness and cost-utility of cognitive therapy, rational emotive behavioral therapy, and fluoxetine (Prozac) in treating depression: A randomized clinical trial. *Journal of Clinical Psychology, 65,* 36–52.

Savage-Rumbaugh, E. S. (1987). Communication, symbolic communication and language: Reply to Seidenberg and Petitto. *Journal of Experimental Psychology: General, 116,* 288–292.

Savage-Rumbaugh, E. S., McDonald, K., Sevcik, R., Hopkins, W., & Rupert, E. (1986). Spontaneous symbol acquisition and communicative use by pygmy chimpanzees (Pan paniscus). *Journal of Experimental Psychology: General, 115,* 211–235.

Saveanu, R. V., & Nemeroff, C. B. (2012). Etiology of depression: Genetic and environmental factors. *Psychiatric Clinics of North America, 35,* 51–71.

Savin-Williams, R. C. (2006). Who's gay? Does it matter? *Current Directions in Psychological Science, 15,* 40–44.

Savin-Williams, R. C., Joyner, K., & Rieger, G. (2012). Prevalence and stability of self-reported sexual orientation identity during young adulthood. *Archives of Sexual Behavior, 41,* 103–110. doi: .1007/s10508-012-9913-y

Sayette, M. A., Creswell, K. G., Dimoff, J. D., Fairbairn, C. E., Cohn, J. F. et al. (2012). Alcohol and group formation: A multimodal investigation of the effects of alcohol on emotion and social bonding. *Psychological Science, 23,* 869–878.

Sayette, M. A., Reichle, E. D., & Schooler, J. W. (2009). Lost in the sauce: The effects of alcohol on mind wandering. *Psychological Science, 20,* 747–752.

Schachter, S. (1951). Deviation, rejection, and communication. *Journal of Abnormal and Social Psychology, 46,* 190–207.

Schachter, S., & Singer, J. E. (1962). Cognitive, social, and physiological determinants of emotional state. *Psychological Review, 69,* 379–399.

Schacter, D. L., & Addis, D. R. (2007). The cognitive neuroscience of constructive memory: Remembering the past and imagining the future. *Philosophical Transactions of the Royal Society of London, Series B: Biological Sciences, 362,* 773–786.

Schacter, D. L., Alpert, N. M., Savage, C. R., Rauch, S. L., & Alpert, M. S. (1996). Conscious recollection and the hippocampal formation: Evidence from positron emission tomography. *Proceedings of the National Academy of Science, USA, 93,* 321–325.

Schaie, K. W. (1983). The Seattle longitudinal study: A 21-year exploration of psychometric intelligence in adulthood. In K. W. Schaie (Ed.), *Longitudinal studies of adult psychological development* (pp. 64–135). New York: Guilford Press.

Schaie, K. W. (1994). The course of adult intellectual development. *American Psychologist, 49,* 304–313.

Schaie, K. W. (1996). *Intellectual development in adulthood: The Seattle longitudinal study.* New York: Cambridge University Press.

Schaie, K. W., & Willis, S. L. (2000). A stage theory model of adult cognitive development revisited. In B. Rubinstein, M. Moss, & M. Kleban (Eds.), *The many dimensions of aging: Essays in honor of M. Powell Lawton* (pp. 173–191). New York: Springer.

Schatz, P., Moser, R. S., Covassin, T., & Karpf, R. (2011). Early indicators of enduring symptoms in high school athletes with multiple previous concussions. *Neurosurgery, 68,* 1562–1567. doi:10.1227/NEU.0b013e31820e382e

Scheele, D., Striepens, N., Güntürkün, O., Deutschländer, S., Maier, W., Kendrick, K. M., & Hurlemann, R. (2012). Oxytocin modulates social distance between males and females. *The Journal of Neuroscience, 32,* 16074–16079. doi:10.1523/JNEUROSCI.2755-12.2012

Scheier, M. F., & Bridges, M. W. (1995). Person variables and health: Personality predispositions and acute psychological states as shared determinants for disease. *Psychosomatic Medicine, 57,* 255–268.

Schein, E. H. (1985). *Organizational leadership and culture: A dynamic view.* San Francisco: Jossey-Bass.

Scheir, M. F., & Carver, C. S. (1992). Effects of optimism on psychological and physical well-being: Theoretical overview and empirical update. *Cognitive Therapy and Research, 16,* 201–228.

Schenk, S. (2011). MDMA ("ecstasy") abuse as an example of dopamine neuroplasticity. *Neuroscience & Biobehavioral Reviews, 35,* 1203–1218. doi:10.1016/j.neubiorev.2010.12.010

Scherf, K. S., Smyth, J. M., & Delgado, M. R. (2013). The amygdala: An agent of change in adolescent neural networks. *Hormones and Behavior, 64,* 298–313.

Schiller, J. S., Lucas, J. W., Ward, B. W., & Peregoy, J. A. (2012). Summary health statistics for U.S. adults: National Health Interview Survey, 2010. *Vital and Health Statistics,* Series 10, *252,* 1–207.

Schinka, J. A., Letsch, E. A., & Crawford, F. C. (2002). DRD4 and novelty seeking: Results of meta-analyses. *American Journal of Medical Genetics, 114,* 643–648.

Schleifer, S. J., Keller, S. E., Camerino, M., Thornton, J. C., & Stein, M. (1983). Suppression of lymphocyte stimulation following bereavement. *Journal of the American Medical Association, 250,* 374–377.

Schlesier-Stropp, B. (1984). Bulimia: A review of the literature. *Psychological Review, 95,* 247–257.

Schlosser, D. A., Zinberg, J. L., Loewy, R L., Casey-Cannon, S., O'Brien, M. P., Bearden, C. E. et al. (2010). Predicting the longitudinal effects of the family environment on prodromal symptoms and functioning in patients at-risk for psychosis. *Schizophrenia Research, 118,* 69–75.

Schmidt, H. D., & Pierce, R. C. (2006). Systematic administration of a dopamine, but not a serotonin or norepinephrine, transporter inhibitor reinstates cocaine seeking in the rat. *Behavioural Brain Research, 175,* 189–194.

Schmidt, U., Lee, S., Beecham, J., Perkins, S., Treasure, J., Yi, I. et al. (2007). A randomized controlled trial of family therapy and cognitive behavior therapy guided self-care for adolescent with bulimia nervosa and related disorders. *American Journal of Psychiatry, 164,* 591–598.

Schmidt-Hieber, C., Jonas, P., & Bischofberger, J. (2004). Enhanced synaptic plasticity in newly generated granule cells of the adult hippocampus. *Nature, 429,* 184–187.

Schmiedek, F., Lovden, M., & Lindenberger, U. (2013). Keeping it steady: Older adults perform more consistently on cognitive tasks than younger adults. *Psychological Science, 24,* 1747–1754.

Schmitt, D. P., Realo, A., Voracek, M., & Allik, J. (2008). Why can't a man be more like a woman? Sex differences in Big Five personality traits across 55 cultures. *Journal of Personality and Social Psychology, 94,* 168–182.

Schmitt, N., Cortina, J. M., Ingerick, M. J., & Wiechmann, D. (2003). Personnel selection and employee performance. In W. C. Borman, D. R. Ilgen, & R. J. Klimoski (Eds.), *Handbook of psychology: Industrial and organizational psychology* (Vol. 12, pp. 77–105). New York: Wiley.

Schoenborn, C. A. (1986). Health habits of U.S. adults, 1985: The "Alameda 7" revisited. *Public Health Reports, 101,* 571–580.

Schoppe-Sullivan, S. J., Mangelsdorf, S. C., Brown, G. L., & Sokolowski, M. S. (2007). Goodness-of-fit in family context: Infant temperament, marital quality, and early coparenting behavior. *Infant Behavior and Development, 30,* 82–96.

Schottenbauer, M. A., Glass, C. R., Arnkoff, D. B., & Gray, S. H. (2008). Contributions of psychodynamic approaches to treatment of PTSD and trauma: A review of the empirical treatment and psychopathology literature. *Psychiatry, 71,* 13–34.

Schredl, M. (2009). Dreams in patients with sleep disorders. *Sleep Medicine Reviews, 13,* 215–221.

Schredl, M., & Erlacher, D. (2008). Relation between waking sport activities, reading, and dream content in sport students and psychology students. *Journal of Psychology, 142,* 267–275.

Schreiber, J. A., & Brockopp, D. Y. (2012). Twenty-five years later—What do we know about religion/spirituality and psychological well-being among breast cancer survivors? A systematic review. *Journal of Cancer Survivorship, 6,* 82–94.

Schreiber, J., & Dixon, M. R. (2001). Temporal characteristics of slot machine play in recreational gamblers. *Psychological Reports, 89,* 67–72.

Schuch, J. J., Roest, A. M., Nolen, W. A., Penninx, B. W., & de Jonge, P. (2014). Gender differences in major depressive disorder: Results from the Netherlands study of depression and anxiety. *Journal of Affective Disorders, 156,* 156–163.

Schuckit, M. A., & Smith, T. L. (1997). Assessing the risk for alcoholism among sons of alcoholics. *Journal of Studies on Alcohol, 58,* 141–145.

Schueller, S. M., Munoz, R. F., & Mohr, D. C. (2013). Realizing the potential of behavioral intervention technologies. *Current Directions in Psychological Science, 22,* 478–483.

Schuh, K. J., & Griffiths, R. R. (1997). Caffeine reinforcement: The role of withdrawal. *Psychopharmacology, 130,* 320–326.

Schultz, D. P., & Schultz, S. E. (2000). *A history of modern psychology* (7th ed.). Fort Worth, TX: Harcourt Brace.

Schultz, D. P., & Schultz, S. E. (2005). *Theories of personality* (8th ed.). Belmont, CA: Wadsworth.

Schultz, D. P., & Schultz, S. E. (2012). *A history of modern psychology* (10th ed.). Belmont, CA: Wadsworth/Cengage Learning.

Schumacher, J. E., Utley, J., Sutton, L., Horton, T., Hamer, T., You, Z., & Klapow, J. C. (2013). Boosting workplace stair utilization: A study of incremental reinforcement. *Rehabilitation Psychology, 58,* 81–86. doi: 10.1037/a0031764.

Schumm, W. R., Webb, F. J., & Bollman, S. R. (1998). Gender and marital satisfaction: Data from the National Survey of Families and Households. *Psychological Reports, 83,* 319–327.

Schwartz, G., Kim, R. M., Kolundzjia, A. B., Rieger, G., & Sanders, A. R. (2010). Biodemographic and physical correlates of sexual orientation in men. *Archives of Sexual Behavior, 39,* 93–109.

Schwartz, M., O'Neal Chambliss, H., Brownell, K., Blair, S., & Billington, C. (2003). Weight bias among health professionals specializing in obesity. *Obesity Research, 11,* 1033–1039.

Schwartz, P. D., Maynard, A. M., & Uzelac, S. M. (2008). Adolescent egocentrism: A contemporary view. *Adolescence, 43,* 441–448.

Schwarzwald, J., Bizman, A., & Raz, M. (1983). The foot-in-the-door paradigm: Effects of second request size on donation probability and donor generosity. *Personality and Social Psychology Bulletin, 9,* 443–450.

Scoboria, A., Mazzoni, G., & Kirsch, I. (2006). Effects of misleading questions and hypnotic memory suggestion on memory reports: A signal-detection analysis. *International Journal of Clinical and Experimental Hypnosis, 54,* 340–359.

Scoboria, A., Mazzoni, G., Kirsch, I., & Milling, L. S. (2002). Immediate and persisting effects of misleading questions and hypnosis on memory reports. *Journal of Experimental Psychology, Applied, 8,* 26–32.

Scollon, C. N., & Diener, E. (2006). Love, work, and changes in extraversion and neuroticism over time. *Journal of Personality and Social Psychology, 91,* 1152–1165.

Scott, T. R., & Plata-Salaman, C. R. (1991). Coding of taste quality. In T. V. Gethell, R. L. Doty, L. M. Bartoshuk, & J. B. Snow, Jr. (Eds.), *Smell and taste in health and disease* (pp. 345–368). New York: Raven.

Scoville, W. B., & Milner, B. (1957). Loss of recent memory after bilateral hippocampal lesions. *Journal of Neurology, Neurosurgery, and Psychiatry, 20,* 11–19.

Scullin, M. K. (2013). Sleep, memory, and aging: The link between slow-wave sleep and episodic memory changes from younger to older adults. *Psychology and Aging, 28,* 105–114.

Scullin, M. K., & McDaniel, M. A. (2010). Remembering to execute a goal: Sleep on it! *Psychological Science, 21,* 1028–1035.

Scully, J. A., Tosi, H., & Banning, K. (2000). Life events checklist: Revisiting the social readjustment rating scale after 30 years. *Educational and Psychological Measurement, 60,* 864–876.

Sebel, P. S., Bowdle, T. A., Ghoneim, M. M., Rampil, I. J., Padilla, R. E., Gan, T. J. et al. (2004). The incidence of awareness during anesthesia: A multicenter United States study. *Anesthesia and Analgesia, 99,* 833–839.

Seeman, M. V. (2008). Gender. In K. T. Mueser & D. V. Jeste (Eds.), *Clinical handbook of schizophrenia* (pp. 575–580). New York: Guilford Press.

Seeman, P. (1999). Brain development, X: Pruning during development. *American Journal of Psychiatry, 156,* 168.

Seeman, P. (2011). All roads to schizophrenia lead to dopamine supersensitivity and elevated dopamine d2(high) receptors. *CNS Neuroscience & Therapeutics, 17,* 118–132. doi:10.1111/j.1755-5949.2010.00162.

Seery, M. D. (2011). Resilience: A silver lining to experiencing adverse life events? *Current Directions in Psychological Science, 20,* 390–394.

Seery, M. D., Leo, R. J., Lupien, S. P., Kondrak, C. L., & Almonte, J. L. (2013). An upside to adversity? Moderate cumulative lifetime adversity is associated with resilient responses in the face of controlled stressors. *Psychological Science, 24,* 1181–1189.

Segal, M. W. (1974). Alphabet and attraction: An unobtrusive measure of the effect of propinquity in a field setting. *Journal of Personality and Social Psychology, 30,* 654–657.

Segerstrom, S. C. (2000). Personality and the immune system: Models, methods, and mechanisms. *Annals of Behavioral Medicine, 22,* 180–190.

Segerstrom, S. C. (2007). Stress, energy, and immunity: An ecological view. *Current Directions in Psychological Science, 16,* 326–330.

Segerstrom, S. C., & Sephton, S. E. (2010). Optimistic expectancies and cell-mediated immunity: The role of positive affect. *Psychological Science, 21,* 448–455.

Segrin, C., & Nabi, R. L. (2002). Does television viewing cultivate unrealistic expectations about marriage? *Journal of Communication, 52,* 247–263.

Seidler, G. H., & Wagner, F. E. (2006). Comparing the efficacy of EMDR and trauma-focused cognitive-behavioral therapy in the treatment of PTSD: A meta-analytic study. *Psychological Medicine, 36,* 1515–1522.

Seidler, R. D., Purushotham, A., Kim, S.-G., Ugurbil, K., Willingham, D., & Ashe, J. (2002). Cerebellum activation associated with performance change but not after motor learning. *Science (Washington), 296,* 2043–2046.

Seiffert, A. E., Somers, D. C., Dale, A. M., & Tootell, R. B. H. (2003). Functional MRI studies of human visual motion perception: Texture, luminance, attention, and after-effects. *Cerebral Cortex, 13,* 340–349.

Sekuler, R., McLaughlin, C., Kahana, M. J., Wingfield, A., & Yotsumoto, Y. (2006). Short-term visual recognition and temporal order memory are both well-preserved in aging. *Psychology and Aging, 21,* 632–637.

Sela, L., & Sobel, N. (2010). Human olfaction: A constant state of change blindness. *Experimental Brain Research, 205,* 13–29.

Seligman, M. E. P. (1970). On the generality of laws of learning. *Psychological Review, 77,* 406–418.

Seligman, M. E. P. (1989). *Helplessness.* New York: Freeman.

Seligman, M. E. P. (1995). The effectiveness of psychotherapy: The Consumer Reports Study. *American Psychologist, 50,* 965–974.

Seligman, M. E. P., & Csikszentmihalyi, M. (2000). Positive psychology: An introduction. *American Psychologist, 55,* 5–14.

Seligman, M. E. P., & Maier, S. F. (1967). Failure to escape traumatic shock. *Journal of Experimental Psychology, 74,* 1–9.

Selmi, P. M., Klein, M. H., Greist, J. H., Sorrell, S. P., & Erdman, H. P. (1990). Computer-administered cognitive-behavioral therapy for depression. *American Journal of Psychiatry, 147,* 51–56.

Seltzer, J. A. (2001). Families formed outside of marriage. In R. M. Milardo (Ed.), *Understanding families into the new millennium: A decade in review* (pp. 466–487). Minneapolis: National Council on Family Relations.

Selye, H. (1976). *The stress of life.* New York: McGraw-Hill.

Sen, S., Burmeister, M., & Ghosh, D. (2004). Meta-analysis of the association between a serotonin transporter promoter polymorphism (5-HT-TLPR) and anxiety related personality traits. *American Journal of Medical Genetics, 127,* 85–89.

Sen, S., Villafuerte, S., Nesse, R., Stoltenberg, S. F., Hopcian, J., Gleiberman, L. et al. (2004). Serotonin transporter and GABA(A) alpha 6 receptor variants are associated with neuroticism. *Biological Psychiatry, 55,* 244–249.

Senghas, A., & Coppola, M. (2001). Children creating language: How Nicaraguan sign language acquired a spatial grammar. *Psychological Science, 12,* 323–328.

Seto, M. C., & Barbaree, H. E. (1995). The role of alcohol in sexual aggression. *Clinical Psychology Review, 15,* 545–566.

Sexton, J. (1995, July 25). Reviving Kitty Genovese case, and its passions. *New York Times,* pp. B1, B5.

Shadish, W. R., Cook, T. D., & Campbell, D. T. (2002). *Experimental and quasi-experimental designs for generalized causal inference.* Boston: Houghton Mifflin.

Shafer, M., & Crichlow, S. (1996). Antecedents of groupthink: A quantitative study. *Journal of Conflict Resolution, 40,* 415–435.

Shah, D. B., Pesiridou, A., Baltuch, G. H., Malone, D. A., & O'Reardon, J. P. (2008). Functional neurosurgery in the treatment of severe obsessive compulsive disorder and major depression: Overview of disease circuits and therapeutic targeting for the clinician. *Psychiatry, 5,* 24–33.

Shallenberger, R. S. (1993). *Taste chemistry.* London: Blackie.

Shamloo, Z. S., & Cox, W. M. (2010). The relationship between motivational structure, sense of control, intrinsic motivation and university students' alcohol consumption. *Addictive Behavior, 35,* 140–146.

Shanker, S. G., Savage-Rumbaugh, E. S., & Taylor, T. J. (1999). Kanzi: A new beginning. *Animal Learning and Behavior, 27,* 24–25.

Shapiro, F. (1991). Eye movement desensitization and reprocessing procedure: From EMD to EMD/R—a new treatment model for anxiety and related traumata. *Behavior Therapist, 14,* 133–135.

Shapiro, F. (2001). *Eye movement desensitization and reprocessing: Basic principles, protocols, and procedures* (2nd ed.). New York: Guilford Press.

Share, D. L., & Silva, P. A. (2003). Gender bias in IQ-discrepancy and post-discrepancy definitions of reading disability. *Journal of Learning Disabilities, 36,* 4–14.

Sharma, B., & Malik, M. (2013). Bollywood madness and shock therapy: A qualitative and comparative analysis of depiction of electroconvulsive therapy in Indian cinema and Hollywood. *International Journal of Culture and Mental Health, 6,* 130–140.

Sharma, L. (2007). Lifestyles, flying and associated health problems in flight attendants. *Journal of the Royal Society of Health, 127,* 268–275.

Shavers, V. L., & Shavers, B. S. (2006). Racism and health inequity among Americans. *Journal of the National Medical Association, 98,* 386–396.

Shavitt, S., Swan, S., Lowrey, T. M., & Wänke, M. (1994). The interaction of endorser attractiveness and involvement in persuasion depends on the goal that guides message processing. *Journal of Consumer Psychology, 3,* 137–162. doi:10.1016/S1057-7408(08)80002-2

Shaw, H., Ramirez, L., Trost, A., Randall, P., & Stice, E. (2004). Body image and eating disturbances across ethnic groups: More similarities than differences. *Psychology of Addictive Behaviors, 18,* 12–18.

Shaw, L. H., & Gant, L. M. (2002). In defense of the Internet: The relationship between Internet communication and depression, loneliness, self-esteem, and perceived social support. *Cyberpsychology & Behavior, 5,* 157–171.

Shea, A. K., & Steiner, M. (2008). Cigarette smoking during pregnancy. *Nicotine & Tobacco Research, 10,* 267–278.

Shedler, J. (2010). The efficacy of psychodynamic psychotherapy. *American Psychologist, 65,* 98–109.

Sheldon, K. M., Arndt, J., & Houser-Marko, L. (2003). In search of the organismic valuing process: The human tendency to move towards beneficial goal choices. *Journal of Personality, 71,* 835–869.

Sheline, Y. I. (2000). 3D MRI studies of neuroanatomic changes in unipolar major depression: The role of stress and medical comorbidity. *Biological Psychiatry, 48,* 791–800.

Shen, B. J., McCreary, C. P., & Myers, H. F. (2004). Independent and mediated contributions of personality, coping, social support, and depressive symptoms to physical functioning outcome among patients in cardiac rehabilitation. *Journal of Behavioral Medicine, 27,* 39–62.

Shepard, G. M. (2006). Smell images and the flavour system in the brain. *Nature, 444,* 316–321.

Shepard, R. N. (1978). The mental image. *American Psychologist, 33,* 125–137.

Sherif, M. (1966). *In common predicament: Social psychology of intergroup conflict and cooperation.* Boston: Houghton Mifflin.

Sherif, M., Harvey, O. J., White, J., Hood, W., & Sherif, C. (1961). *Intergroup conflict and cooperation: The Robber's Cave experiment.* Norman: University of Oklahoma Press.

Sherman, D. K., Kim, H. S., & Taylor, S. E. (2009). Culture and social support: Neural bases and biological impact. *Progress in Brain Research, 178,* 227–237.

Sherwin, B. B., & Gelfand, M. M. (1987). The role of androgen in the maintenance of sexual functioning in oophorectomized women. *Psychosomatic Medicine, 49,* 397–409.

Shi, J., Levinson, D. F., Duan, J., Sanders, A. R., Zheng, Y., Pe'er, I. et al. (2009). Common variants on chromosome 6p22.1 are associated with schizophrenia. *Nature, 460,* 753–757.

Shields, M. (2004). Stress, health and the benefit of social support. *Health Reports, 15,* 9–38.

Shim, R. S., Compton, M. T., Rust, G., Druss, B. G., & Kaslow, N. J. (2009). Race-ethnicity as a predictor of attitudes toward mental health treatment seeking. *Psychiatric Services, 60,* 1336–1341.

Shimoff, E., Catania, A. C., & Matthews, B. A. (1981). Unstructured human responding: Sensitivity of low-rate performance to schedule contingencies. *Journal of Experimental Analysis of Behavior, 36,* 207–220.

Shin, L. M., Bush, G., Milad, M. R., Lasko, N. B., Brohawn, K. H. et al. (2011). Exaggerated activation of dorsal anterior cingulate cortex during cognitive interference: A monozygotic twin study of posttraumatic stress disorder. *American Journal of Psychiatry, 168,* 979–985.

Shin, L. M., Rauch, S. L., & Pitman, R. K. (2006). Amygdala, medial prefrontal cortex, and hippocampal function in PTSD. *Annals of the New York Academy of Sciences, 1071,* 67–79.

Shiner, R. L., Masten, A. S., & Roberts, J. M. (2003). Childhood personality foreshadows adult personality and life outcomes two decades later. *Journal of Personality, 71,* 1145–1170.

Shinskey, J. L., & Munakata, Y. (2005). Familiarity breeds searching: Infants reverse their novelty preferences when reaching for hidden objects. *Psychological Science, 16,* 596–600.

Shintani, T., Hughes, C., Beckham, S., & O'Connor, H. (1991). Obesity and cardiovascular risk intervention through the ad libitum feeding of traditional Hawaiian diet. *American Journal of Clinical Nutrition, 53,* 1647S–1651S.

Shiraev, E., & Levy, D. (2010). *Cross-cultural psychology* (4th ed.). Boston: Allyn & Bacon.

Shneidman, E. S. (1987, March). At the point of no return. *Psychology Today,* 54–58.

Shoham, V., & Insel, T. R. (2011). Rebooting for whom? Portfolios, technology, and personalized intervention. *Perspectives on Psychological Science, 6,* 478–482.

Short, M. A., Gradisar, M., Lack, L. C., & Wright, H. R. (2013). The impact of sleep on adolescent depressed mood, alertness, and academic performance. *Journal of Adolescence, 36,* 1025–1033.

Shreeram, S., He, J., Kalaydjian, A., Brothers, S., & Merikangas, K. R. (2009). Prevalence of enuresis and its association with attention-deficit/hyperactivity disorder among U.S. children: Results from a nationally representative study. *Journal of the American Academy of Child & Adolescent Psychiatry, 48,* 35–41.

Shtyrov, Y., Nikulin, V. V., & Pulvermüller, F. (2010). Rapid cortical plasticity underlying novel word learning. *Journal of Neuroscience, 30,* 16864–16867.

Shulman, S., Scharf, M., Lumer, D., & Maurer, O. (2001). Parental divorce and young adult children's romantic relationships: Resolution of the divorce experience. *American Journal of Orthopsychiatry, 71,* 473–478.

Siegel, J. M. (2001). The REM sleep-memory consolidation hypothesis. *Science, 294,* 1058–1063.

Siegel, J. M., & Boehmer, L. N. (2006). Narcolepsy and the hypocretin system: Where motion meets emotion. *Nature Clinical Practice Neurology, 2,* 548–556.

Siegel, L. S., & Hodkin, B. (1982). The garden path to the understanding of cognitive development: Has Piaget led us into the poison ivy? In S. Modgil & C. Modgil (Eds.), *Jean Piaget: Consensus and controversy* (pp. 57–82). New York: Praeger.

Siegel, S. (2005). Drug tolerance, drug addiction, and drug anticipation. *Current Directions in Psychological Science, 14,* 296–300.

Siegel, S. (2011). The four-loko effect. *Perspectives on Psychological Science, 6,* 357–362.

Siever, L. J., & Koenigsberg, H. W. (2000). The frustrating no-man's-land of borderline personality disorder. *Cerebrum: The Dana Forum on Brain Science, 2*(4).

Signorielli, N., & Bacue, A. (1999). Recognition and respect: A content analysis of prime-time television characters. *Sex Roles, 40,* 527–544.

Silva, C. E., & Kirsch, I. (1992). Interpretive sets, expectancy, fantasy proneness, and dissociation as predictors of hypnotic response. *Journal of Personality and Social Psychology, 63,* 847–856.

Sim, H. (2000). Relationship of daily hassles and social support to depression and antisocial behavior among early adolescents. *Journal of Youth and Adolescence, 29,* 647–659.

Simão, C. P., Justo, M. G., & Martins, A. T. (2008). Recognizing facial expressions of social emotions: Do males and females differ? *Psicologia: Revista da Associação Portuguesa Psicologia, 22,* 71–85.

Simmler, L. D., Rickli, A., Hoener, M. C., & Liechti, M. E. (2013). Monoamine transporter and receptor interaction profiles of a new series of designer cathinones. *Neuropharmacology, 79C,* 152–160.

Simon, H. A. (1974). How big is a chunk? *Science, 183,* 482–488.

Simpson, G., & Yinger, J. M. (1985). *Racial and cultural minorities.* New York: Plenum Press.

Simpson, J. A., Collins, W. A., & Salvatore, J. E. (2011). The impact of early interpersonal experience on adult romantic relationship functioning: Recent findings from the Minnesota Longitudinal Study of Risk and Adaptation. *Current Directions in Psychological Science, 20,* 355–359.

Simpson, J. A., Collins, W. A., Tran, S., & Haydon, K. C. (2007). Attachment and the experience and expression of emotions in romantic relationships: A developmental perspective. *Journal of Personality and Social Psychology, 92,* 355–367.

Sin, N. L., & Lyubomirsky, S. (2009). Enhancing well-being and alleviating depressive symptoms with positive psychology interventions: A practice friendly meta-analysis. *Journal of Clinical Psychology, 65,* 467–487.

Sinclair, S. (1985). *How animals see.* New York: Facts on File Publications.

Sinnott, J. D. (1998). *The development of logic in adulthood: Postformal thought and its applications.* New York: Plenum.

Sio, U. N., & Ormerod, T. C. (2009). Does incubation enhance problem solving? A meta-analytic review. *Psychological Bulletin, 135,* 94–120.

Skelton, C. (2006). Boys and girls in the elementary school. In C. Skelton, B. Francis, & L. Smulyan (Eds.), *The SAGE handbook of gender and education* (pp. 139–151). London: SAGE.

Skinner, B. F. (1938). *The behavior of organisms.* New York: Appleton-Century-Crofts.

Skinner, B. F. (1953). *Science and human behavior.* New York: Macmillan.

Skinner, B. F. (1958). Teaching machines. *Science, 128,* 969–977.

Skinner, M. D., Lahmek, P., Pham, H., & Aubin, H. J. (2014). Disulfiram efficacy in the treatment of alcohol dependence: A meta-analysis. *PLoS One, 9,* e87366.

Skodol, A. E., & Bender, D. S. (2003). Why are women diagnosed borderline more than men? *Psychiatry Quarterly, 74,* 349–360.

Slameka, N. J. (1966). Differentiation versus unlearning of verbal associations. *Journal of Experimental Psychology, 71,* 822–828.

Slattery, M. L., Curtin, K., Wolff, R. K., Herrick, J. S., Caan, B. J., & Samowitz, W. (2010). Diet, physical activity, and body size associations with rectal tumor mutations and epigenetic changes. *Cancer Causes & Control, 21,* 1237–1245.

Slavin-Muldord, J., Hilsenroth, M., Weinberger, J., & Gold, J. (2011). Therapeutic interventions related to outcome in psychodynamic psychotherapy for anxiety disorder patients. *Journal of Nervous and Mental Disease, 199,* 214–221.

Sloan, R. P., & Bagiella, E. (2002). Claims about religious involvement and health outcomes. *Annals of Behavioral Medicine, 24,* 14–21.

Slotema, C. W., Blom, J. D., Hoek, H. W., & Sommer, I. E. (2010). Should we expand the toolbox of psychiatric treatment methods to include repetitive transcranial magnetic stimulation (rTMS)? A meta-analysis of the efficacy of rTMS in psychiatric disorders. *Journal of Clinical Psychiatry, 71,* 873–884.

Slovic, P., Finucane, M., Peters, E., & MacGregor, D. G. (2002). Rational actors or rational fools: Implications of the affect heuristic for behavioral economics. *Journal of Socio-Economics, 31,* 329–342. doi:10.1016/S1053-5357(02)00174-9

Small, B. J., Hertzog, C., Hultsch, D. F., & Dixon, R. A. (2003). Stability and change in adult personality over 6 years: Findings from the Victoria Longitudinal Study. *Journal of Gerontology: Psychological Sciences, 58B,* P166–P176.

Smetana, J. G., Campione-Barr, N., & Metzger, A. (2006). Adolescent development in interpersonal and societal contexts. *Annual Review of Psychology, 57,* 255–284.

Smillie, L. D. (2013). Extraversion and reward processing. *Current Directions in Psychological Science, 22,* 167–172.

Smith, C. (1995). Sleep states and memory processes. *Behavioural Brain Research, 69*(1–2), 137–145.

Smith, C. A., Organ, D. W., & Near, J. P. (1983). Organizational citizenship behavior: Its nature and antecedents. *Journal of Applied Psychology, 68,* 653–663.

Smith, D. E., & Cogswell, C. (1994). A cross-cultural perspective on adolescent girls' body perception. *Perceptual and Motor Skills, 78,* 744–746.

Smith, J. W., Frawley, P. J., & Polissar, N. L. (1997). Six- and twelve-month abstinence rates in inpatient alcoholics treated with either faradic aversion or chemical aversion compared with matched inpatients from a treatment registry. *Journal of Addictive Diseases, 16,* 5–24.

Smith, M. C., & Dust, M. C. (2006). An exploration of the influence of dispositional traits and appraisal on coping strategies in African

American college students. *Journal of Personality, 74,* 145–174.

Smith, M. C., Coleman, S. R., & Gormezano, I. (1969). Classical conditioning of the rabbit's nictitating membrane response at backward, simultaneous, and forward CS–US intervals. *Journal of Comparative and Physiological Psychology, 69,* 226–231.

Smith, P. C., Kendall, L. M., & Hulin, C. L. (1969). *The measurement of satisfaction in work and retirement.* Chicago: Rand McNally.

Smith, S. L., & Cook, C. A. (2008). *Gender stereotypes: An analysis of popular films and TV.* Geena Davis Institute on Gender in Media. Retrieved from www.thegeenadavisinstitute.org

Smith, T. B., Rodriguez, M. D., & Bernal, G. (2011). Culture. *Journal of Clinical Psychology, 67,* 166–175.

Smith, T. W. (2006). Personality as risk and resilience in physical health. *Current Directions in Psychological Science, 15,* 227–231.

Smith, T. W., Glazer, K., Ruiz, J. M., & Gallo, L. C. (2004). Hostility, anger, aggressiveness and coronary heart disease: An interpersonal perspective on personality, emotion, and health. *Journal of Personality, 72,* 1217–1270.

Smyth, J., Litcher, L., Hurewitz, A., & Stone, A. (2001). Relaxation training and cortisol secretion in adult asthmatics. *Journal of Health Psychology, 6,* 217–227.

Snarey, J. (1995). In a communitarian voice: The sociological expansion of Kohlbergian theory, research, and practice. In W. M. Kurtines & J. L. Gewirtz (Eds.), *Moral development: An introduction* (pp. 109–134). Boston: Allyn & Bacon.

Snyder, A. L., Anderson-Hanley, C., & Arciero, P. J. (2012). Virtual and live social facilitation while exergaming: Competitiveness moderates exercise intensity. *Journal of Sport & Exercise Psychology, 34,* 252–259.

Snyder, C. R., Ilardi, S., Michael, S. T., & Cheavens, J. (2000). Hope theory: Updating a common process for psychological change. In C. R. Snyder & R. E. Ingram (Eds.), *Handbook of psychological change: Psychotherapy processes and practices for the 21st century* (pp. 128–153). New York: Wiley.

Sohail, N. (2013). Stress and academic performance among medical students. *Journal of the College of Physicians and Surgeons, 23,* 67–71.

Solberg, E. E., Halvorsen, R., & Holen, A. (2000). Effect of meditation on immune cells. *Stress Medicine, 16,* 185–190.

Solberg, L. (2010). Data mining on Facebook: A free space for researchers or an IRB nightmare? *University of Illinois Journal of Law, Technology & Policy, 2,* 311.

Soloff, P. H., & Chiapetta, L. (2012). Prospective predictors of suicidal behavior in borderline personality disorder at 6-year follow-up. *American Journal of Psychiatry, 169,* 484–490.

Solomon, A., Arnow, B. A., Gotlib, I. H., & Wind, B. (2003). Individualized measurement of irrational beliefs in remitted depressives. *Journal of Clinical Psychology, 59,* 439–455.

Solomon, L. Z., Solomon, H., & Maiorca, J. (1982). The effects of bystander's anonymity, situational ambiguity, and victim's status on helping. *Journal of Social Psychology, 117,* 285–294. doi:10.1080/00224545.1982.9713438

Somers, V. K., Phil, D., Dyken, M. E., Mark, A. L., & Abboud, F. M. (1993). Sympathetic-nerve activity during sleep in normal subjects. *New England Journal of Medicine, 328,* 303–307.

Somerville, L. H. (2013). The teenage brain: Sensitivity to social evaluation. *Current Directions in Psychological Science, 22,* 121–127.

Somerville, L. H., Jones, R. M., Ruberry, E. J., Dyke, J. P., Glover, G., & Casey, B. J. (2013). The medial prefrontal cortex and the emergence of self-conscious emotion in adolescence. *Psychological Science, 24,* 1554–1562.

Song, Q. H., Xu, R. M., Zhang, Q. H., Ma, M., & Zhao, X. P. (2013). Relaxation training during chemotherapy for breast cancer improves mental health and lessens adverse events. *International Journal of Clinical and Experimental Medicine, 6,* 979–984.

Soper, B., Milford, G. E., & Rosenthal, G. T. (1995). Belief when evidence does not support theory. *Psychology and Marketing, 12,* 415–422.

Soussignan, R. (2002). Duchenne smile, emotional experience, and autonomic reactivity: A test of the facial feedback hypothesis. *Emotion, 2,* 52–74.

Sowell, E. R., Thompson, P. M., Tessner, K. D., & Toga, A. W. (2001). Mapping continued brain growth and gray matter density reduction in dorsal frontal cortex: Inverse relationships during postadolescent brain maturation. *Journal of Neuroscience, 21,* 8819–8829.

Soyka, M., Preuss, U. W., Hesselbrock, V., Zill, P., Koller, G., & Bondy, B. (2008). GABA-A2 receptor subunit gene (GABRA2) polymorphisms and risk for alcohol dependence. *Journal of Psychiatric Research, 42,* 184–191.

Spanos, N. P. (1996). *Multiple identities and false memories: A sociocognitive perspective.* Washington, DC: American Psychological Association.

Spanos, N. P., Burnley, M. C. E., & Cross, P. A. (1993). Response expectancies and interpretations as determinants of hypnotic responding. *Journal of Personality and Social Psychology, 65,* 1237–1242.

Spanou, E. E., & Morogiannis, F. F. (2010). The role of family and socio-cultural factors in the development of eating disorders. *Psychiatriki, 21,* 41–53.

Spearman, C. (1904). The proof and measurement of association between two things. *American Journal of Psychology, 15,* 72–101.

Spencer, J. A., & Fremouw, W. J. (1979). Binge eating as a function of restraint and weight classification. *Journal of Abnormal Psychology, 88,* 262–267.

Spengler, M., Gottschling, J., & Spinath, F. M. (2012). Personality in childhood: A longitudinal behavior genetic approach. *Personality and Individual Differences, 53,* 411–416.

Spera, C., Wentzel, K. R., & Matto, H. C. (2009). Parental aspirations for their children's educational attainment: Relations to ethnicity, parental education, children's academic performance, and parental perceptions of school climate. *Journal of Youth and Adolescence, 38,* 1140–1152.

Spiegel, D. (1997). Trauma, dissociation, and memory. *Annals of the New York Academy of Sciences, 821,* 225–237.

Spiegel, D., Loewenstein, R. J., Lewis-Fernandez, R., Sar, V., Simeon, D., Vermetten, E. et al. (2011). Dissociative disorders in DSM-5. *Depression and Anxiety, 28,* 824–852.

Spriggs, M. (2009). Consent in cyberspace: Internet-based research involving young people. *Monash Bioethics Review, 28,* 1–15.

Squire, L. R. (1992). Memory and the hippocampus: A synthesis from findings with rats, monkeys, and humans. *Psychological Review, 99,* 195–232.

Squire, L. R., Knowlton, B., & Musen, G. (1993). The structure and organization of memory. *Annual Review of Psychology, 44,* 453–495.

Squire, L. R., Ojemann, J. G., Miezin, F. M., Petersen, S. E., Videen, T. O., & Raichle, M. E. (1992). Activation of the hippocampus in normal humans: A functional anatomical study of memory. *Proceedings of the National Academy of Science, USA, 89,* 1837–1841.

Srinivasan, L., Eden, U. T., Mitter, S. K., & Brown, E. N. (2007). General-purpose filter design for neural prosthetic devices. *Journal of Neurophysiology, 98,* 2456–2475.

Srivastava, S., John, O. P., Gosling, S. D., & Potter, J. (2003). Development of personality in early and middle adulthood: Set in plaster or persistent change? *Journal of Personality and Social Psychology, 84,* 1041–1053.

Stacey, D., Clarke, T. K., & Schumann, G. (2009). The genetics of alcoholism. *Current Psychiatry Reports, 11,* 364–369.

Stahl, S. M. (1996). *Essential psychopharmacology.* New York: Cambridge University Press.

Stahl, S. M. (1998). Basic psychopharmacology of antidepressants: Part I. Antidepressants have seven distinct mechanisms of action. *Journal of Clinical Psychiatry, 59*(Suppl. 4), 5–14.

Stahl, S. M. (2001a). Dopamine system stabilizers, aripiprazole, and the next generation of antipsychotics: Part I. "Goldilocks" actions at dopamine receptors. *Journal of Clinical Psychiatry, 62,* 841–842.

Stahl, S. M. (2001b). Dopamine system stabilizers, aripiprazole, and the next generation of antipsychotics: Part II. Illustrating their mechanism of action. *Journal of Clinical Psychiatry, 62,* 923–924.

Stahl, S. M. (2007). Beyond the dopamine hypothesis to the NMDA glutamate receptor hypofunction hypothesis of schizophrenia. *CNS Spectrums, 12,* 265–268.

Stalder, D. R. (2012). A role for social psychology instruction in reducing bias and conflict. *Psychology Learning & Teaching, 11,* 245–255.

Stanley, S. M., Whitton, S. W., Sadberry, S. L., Clements, M. L., & Markman, H. J. (2006). Sacrifice as a predictor of marital outcomes. *Family Process, 45,* 289–303.

Stanovich, K. E., & West, R. F. (1998). Individual differences in rational thought. *Journal of Experimental Psychology: General, 127,* 161–188.

Stanton, A. L., & Low, C. A. (2012). Expressing emotions in stressful contexts: Benefits, moderators, and mechanisms. *Current Directions in Psychological Science, 21,* 124–128.

Stanton, J. L. (2004). The end of TV advertising: Technologies allow consumers to miss what once were the bedrock of consumer product advertising. *Food Processing, 65,* 26.

Starr, C., & Taggart, R. (1989). *Biology: The unity and diversity of life* (5th ed.). Pacific Grove, CA: Wadsworth.

Starrels, M. E. (1994). Husbands' involvement in female gender-typed household chores. *Sex Roles, 31,* 473–491.

Statham, D. J., Heath, A. C., Madden, P., Bucholz, K. Bierut, L., Dinwiddie, S. H. et al. (1998). Suicidal behavior: An epidemiological study. *Psychological Medicine, 28,* 839–855.

Stawski, R. S., Almeida, D. M., Sliwinski, M. J., & Smyth, J. M. (2008). Reported exposure and emotional reactivity to daily stressors: The roles of adult age and global perceived stress. *Psychology and Aging, 23,* 52–61.

Stear, S. (2003). Health and fitness: Series 1. The importance of physical activity on health. *Journal of Family Health Care, 13,* 10–13.

Steele, C. M. (1997). A threat in the air: How stereotypes shape the intellectual identities and performance of women and African-Americans. *American Psychologist, 52,* 613–629.

Steele, C. M., & Aronson, J. (1995). Stereotype threat and the intellectual test performance of African Americans. *Journal of Personality and Social Psychology, 69,* 797–811.

Stefflre, V., Castillo-Vales, V., & Morley, L. (1966). Language and cognition in Yucatan: A cross-cultural replication. *Journal of Personality and Social Psychology, 4,* 112–115.

Stein, D. J., Westenberg, H. G. M., Yang, H., Li, D., & Barbato, L. M. (2003). Fluvoxamine CR in the long-term treatment of social anxiety disorder: The 12- to 24-week extension phase of a multicentre, randomized, placebo-controlled trial. *International Journal of Psychopharmacology, 6,* 317–325.

Stein, J. H., & Reiser, L. W. (1994). A study of white middle-class adolescent boys' responses to "semenarche" (the first ejaculation). *Journal of Youth and Adolescence, 23,* 373–384.

Steinberg, L., & Morris, A. S. (2001). Adolescent development. *Annual Reviews of Psychology, 52,* 83–110.

Steinberg, L., Lamborn, S. D., Dornbusch, S. M., & Darling, N. (1992). Impact of parenting practices on adolescent achievement: Authoritative parenting, school involvement, and encouragement to succeed. *Child Development, 63,* 1266–1281.

Steiner, M., & Born, L. (2000). Diagnosis and treatment of premenstrual dysphoric disorder: An update. *International Clinical Psychopharmacology, 15*(Suppl. 3), S5–S17.

Steiner, M., Dunn, E., & Born, L. (2003). Hormones and mood: From menarche to menopause and beyond. *Journal of Affective Disorders, 74,* 67–83.

Steinhausen, H. C., & Vollrath, M. (1993). The self-image of adolescent patients with eating disorders. *International Journal of Eating Disorders, 13,* 221–229.

Stenblom, E., Montelius, C., Östbring, K., Håkansson, M., Nilsson, S., Rehfeld, J. F., & Erlanson-Albertsson, C. (2013). Supplementation by thylakoids to a high carbohydrate meal decreases feelings of hunger, elevates CCK levels and prevents postprandial hypoglycaemia in overweight women. *Appetite, 68,* 118–123. doi: 10.1016/j.appet.2013.04.022

Stephan, K. E., Marshall, J. C., Friston, K. J., Rowe, J. B., Ritzl, A., Zilles, K. et al. (2003). Lateralized cognitive processes and lateralized task control in the human brain. *Science, 301,* 384–386.

Stephens, C. E., Pear, J. J., Wray, L. D., & Jackson, G. C. (1975). Some effects of reinforcement schedules in teaching picture names to retarded children. *Journal of Applied Behavior Analysis, 8,* 435–447.

Stephens, N. M., & Levine, C. S. (2011). Opting out or denying discrimination? How the framework of free choice in American society influences perceptions of gender inequality. *Psychological Science, 22,* 1231–1236. doi:10.1177/0956797611417260

Stephens, R. S., Roffman, R. A., & Simpson, E. E. (1994). Treating adult marijuana dependence: A test of the relapse prevention model. *Journal of Consulting and Clinical Psychology, 62,* 92–99.

Steriade, M., & McCarley, R. W. (1990). *Brainstem control of wakefulness and sleep.* New York: Plenum Press.

Stern, G. S., McCants, T. R., & Pettine, P. W. (1982). Stress and illness: Controllable and uncontrollable life events' relative contributions. *Personality and Social Psychology Bulletin, 8,* 140–143.

Stern, K. N., & McClintock, M. K. (1998). Regulation of ovulation by human pheromones. *Nature, 392,* 177–179.

Stern, S. L., Dhanda, R., & Hazuda, H. P. (2009). Helplessness predicts the development of hypertension in older Mexican and European Americans. *Journal of Psychosomatic Research, 67,* 333–337.

Sternberg, R. J. (1985). *Beyond IQ: A triarchic theory of human intelligence.* New York: Cambridge University Press.

Sternberg, R. J. (1997a). The concept of intelligence and its role in lifelong learning and success. *American Psychologist, 52,* 1030–1037.

Sternberg, R. J. (1997b). *Successful intelligence.* New York: Plume.

Sternberg, R. J. (1999). *Handbook of creativity.* Cambridge: Cambridge University Press.

Sternberg, R. J., Grigorenko, E. L., & Kidd, K. K. (2005). Intelligence, race, and genetics. *American Psychologist, 60,* 46–59.

Stevens, A., & Coupe, P. (1978). Distortions in judged spatial relations. *Cognitive Psychology, 10,* 422–437.

Stewart, G. L., & Manz, C. C. (1995). Leadership for self-managing work teams: A typology and integrative model. *Human Relations, 48,* 347–370.

Stewart, J. A., Deliyannides, D. A., Hellerstein, D. J., McGrath, P. J., & Stewart, J. W. (2012). Can people with nonsevere major depression benefit from antidepressant medication? *Journal of Clinical Psychiatry, 73,* 518–525.

Stickgold, R., & Walker, M. P. (2007). Sleep-dependent memory consolidation and reconsolidation. *Sleep Medicine, 8,* 331–343.

Stiles, W. B., Barkham, M., Mellor-Clark, J., & Connell, J. (2008). Effectiveness of cognitive-behavioural, person-centered, and psychodynamic therapies in UK primary-care routine practice: Replication in a larger sample. *Psychological Medicine, 38,* 677–688.

Stiles, W. B., Barkham, M., Twigg, E., Mellor-Clark, J., & Cooper, M. (2006). Effectiveness of cognitive-behavioural, person-centered, and psychodynamic therapies as practiced in UK National Health Service settings. *Psychological Medicine, 36,* 555–566.

Stine-Morrow, E. A., Parisi, J. M., Morrow, D. G., Greene, J., & Park, D. C. (2007). An engagement model of cognitive optimization through adulthood. *Journals of Gerontology, Series B: Psychological Sciences and Social Sciences, 62,* 62–69.

Stoel-Gammon, C., & Otomo, K. (1986). Babbling development of hearing impaired and normal subjects. *Journal of Speech and Hearing Disorders, 51,* 33–41.

Stone, J. M., Morrison, P., & Pilowsky, L. S. (2007). Glutamate and dopamine dysregulation in schizophrenia: A synthesis and selective review. *Journal of Psychopharmacology, 21,* 440–452.

Storms, G., DeBoeck, P., & Ruts, W. (2001). Categorization of novel stimuli in well-known natural concepts. *Psychonomic Bulletin and Review, 8,* 377–384.

Storms, M. D. (1973). Videotape and the attribution process: Reversing actors' and observers' points of view. *Journal of Personality and Social Psychology, 27,* 165–175.

Stout, M. (2005). *The sociopath next door.* New York: Broadway Books.

Strassberg, Z., Dodge, K., Pettit, G. S., & Bates, J. E. (1994). Spanking in the home and children's subsequent aggression toward kindergarten peers. *Development and Psychopathology, 6,* 445–461.

Straus, M. A. (1991). Discipline and deviance: Physical punishment of children and violence and other crime in adulthood. *Social Problems, 38,* 133–154.

Strayer, D. L., Drews, F. A., & Crouch, D. J. (2006). A comparison of the cell phone driver and the drunk driver. *Human Factors, 48,* 381–391.

Strickland, B. R. (1989). Internal–external control expectancies: From contingency to creativity. *American Psychologist, 44,* 1–12.

Stright, A. D., Gallagher, K. C., & Kelley, K. (2008). Infant temperament moderates relations between maternal parenting in early childhood and children's adjustment in first grade. *Child Development, 79,* 186–200.

Stroebe, M. (2001). Gender differences in adjustment to bereavement: An empirical and theoretical review. *Review of General Psychology, 5,* 62–83.

Stroebe, W., & Stroebe, M. S. (1993). Determinants of adjustment to bereavement in younger widows and widowers. In M. S. Stroebe, W. Stroebe, & R. O. Hansson (Eds.), *Handbook of bereavement* (pp. 208–226). New York: Cambridge University Press.

Stromquist, N. P. (2007). *The gender socialization process in schools: A cross-national comparison.* Paper commissioned for the EFA Global Monitoring Report, 2008, Education for all by 2015: Will we make it? 2008/ED/EFA/MRT/PI/71.

Substance Abuse and Mental Health Services Administration (SAMHSA). (2006). *Results from the 2005 National Survey on Drug Use and Health: National findings.* Rockville, MD: Office of Applied Studies, NSDUH Series H-30, DHHS Publication No. SMA 06-4194.

Substance Abuse and Mental Health Services Administration (SAMHSA). (2009a). *Results from the 2008 National Survey on Drug Use and Health: National findings.* Rockville, MD: Office of Applied Studies, NSDUH Series H-36, DHHS Publication No. SMA 09-4434.

Substance Abuse and Mental Health Services Administration (SAMHSA). (2009b). *The NSDUH Report: Suicidal thoughts and behaviors among adults.* Rockville, MD: Office of Applied Studies.

Substance Abuse and Mental Health Services Administration (SAMHSA). (2009c). *The NSDUH report: Mental health support and self-help groups.* Rockville, MD: Office of Applied Studies.

Substance Abuse and Mental Health Services Administration (SAMHSA). (2010a). *Results from the 2009 National Survey on Drug Use and Health: Volume I. Summary of national findings.* Rockville, MD: Office of Applied Studies, NSDUH Series H-38A, HHS Publication No. SMA 10-4586.

Substance Abuse and Mental Health Services Administration (SAMHSA). (2010b). *The NSDUH Report: State estimates of drunk and drugged driving.* Rockville, MD: Office of Applied Studies.

Substance Abuse and Mental Health Services Administration (SAMHSA). (2011). *The NSDUH report: Sources of payment for mental health treatment for adults.* Rockville, MD: Center for Behavioral Health Statistics and Quality.

Substance Abuse and Mental Health Services Administration (SAMHSA). (2012a). *The NSDUH report: State estimates of drunk and drugged driving.* Rockville, MD: Center for Behavioral Health Statistics and Quality.

Substance Abuse and Mental Health Services Administration (SAMHSA). (2012b). *Results from the 2010 National Survey on Drug Use and Health: Mental health findings*, NSDUH Series H-42, HHS Publication No. (SMA) 11-4667. Rockville, MD: Author.

Substance Abuse and Mental Health Services Administration (SAMHSA). (2012c). *Results from the 2011 National Survey on Drug Use and Health: Summary of national findings*, NSDUH Series H-44, HHS Publication No. (SMA) 12-4713. Rockville, MD: Author.

Substance Abuse and Mental Health Services Administration (SAMHSA). (2013). *Results from the 2012 National Survey on Drug Use and Health: Summary of national findings*, NSDUH Series H-46, HHS

Publication No. (SMA) 13-4795. Rockville, MD: Author.

Suegami, T., & Laeng, B. (2013). A left cerebral hemisphere's superiority in processing spatial-categorical information in a non-verbal semantic format. *Brain and Cognition, 81,* 294–302. doi:10.1016/j.bandc.2012.10.012

Suh, J. J., Pettinati, H. M., Kampman, K. M., & O'Brien, C. P. (2006). The status of disulfiram: A half of a century later. *Journal of Clinical Psychopharmacology, 26,* 290–302.

Sullivan, J. W., & Horowitz, F. D. (1983). The effects of intonation on infant attention: The role of the rising intonation contour. *Journal of Child Language, 10,* 521–534.

Sullivan, M. A., & O'Leary, S. G. (1990). Maintenance following reward and cost token programs. *Behavior Therapy, 21,* 139–149.

Sullivan, P. F., Neale, M. C., & Kendler, S. K. (2000). Genetic epidemiology of major depression: Review and meta-analysis. *American Journal of Psychiatry, 157,* 1552–1562.

Sundin, J., Fear, N. T., Iversen, A., Rona, R. J., & Wessely, S. (2010). PTSD after deployment to Iraq: Conflicting rates, conflicting claims. *Psychological Medicine, 40,* 367–382.

Sundin, J., Herrell, R. K., Hoge, C. W., Fear, N. T., Adler, A. B., Greenberg, N. et al. (2014). Mental health outcomes in U.S. and U.K. military personnel returning from Iraq. *British Journal of Psychiatry, 204,* 200–207.

Super, D. E. (1957). *The psychology of careers.* New York: Harper & Row.

Super, D. E. (1976). *Career education and the meanings of work.* Washington DC: U.S. Office of Education.

Super, D. E. (1980). A life-span, life-space approach to career development. *Journal of Vocational Behavior, 16,* 282–298.

Super, D. E. (1991). A life-span, life-space approach to career development. In D. Brown, L. Brooks, & Associates (Eds.), *Career choice and development: Applying contemporary theories to practice* (2nd ed., pp. 197–261). San Francisco: Jossey-Bass.

Sussman, S. (2010). A review of Alcoholics Anonymous/Narcotics Anonymous programs for teens. *Evaluation and the Health Professions, 33,* 26–55.

Sutin, A. R., Terracciano, A., Milaneschi, Y., An, Y., Ferrucci, L., & Zonderman, A. B. (2013). The effect of birth cohort on well-being: The legacy of economic hard times. *Psychological Science, 24,* 379–385.

Suzuki, K., Simpson, K. A., Minnion, J. S., Shillito, J. C., & Bloom, S. R. (2010). The role of gut hormones and the hypothalamus in appetite regulation. *Endocrine Journal, 57,* 359–372. doi:10.1507/endocrinj.K10E-077

Swain, I. U., Zelazo, P. R., & Clifton, R. K. (1993). Newborn infants' memory for speech sounds retained over 24 hours. *Developmental Psychology, 29,* 312–323.

Swanson, L. M., Arnedt, J. T., Rosekind, M. R., Belenky, G., Balkin, T. J., & Drake, C. (2010). Sleep disorders and work performance: Findings from the 2008 National Sleep Foundation Sleep in America poll. *Journal of Sleep Research, 20,* 487–494. doi:10.1111/j.1365-2869.2010.00890.x

Swartz, C. (1995). Setting the ECT stimulus. *Psychiatric Times, 12*(6).

Swartz, M., Blazer, D., George, L., & Winfield, I. (1990). Estimating the prevalence of borderline personality disorder in the community. *Journal of Personality Disorders, 4,* 257–272.

Swayze, V. W. (1995). Frontal leucotomy and related psychosurgical procedures in the era before antipsychotics (1935–1954): A historical overview. *American Journal of Psychiatry, 152,* 505–515.

Sweet, T., & Welles, S. L. (2012). Associations of sexual identity or same-sex behaviors with history of childhood sexual abuse and HIV/STI risk in the United States. *JAIDS Journal of Acquired Immune Deficiency Syndromes, 59,* 400–408. doi: 10.1097/QAI.0b013e3182400e75

Swinson, J., & Harrop, A. (2009). Teacher talk directed to boys and girls and its relationship to their behaviour. *Educational Studies, 35,* 515–524.

Symons, C. S., & Johnson, B. T. (1997). The self-reference effect in memory: A meta-analysis. *Psychological Bulletin, 121,* 371–394.

Sysoeva, O. V., Kulikova, M. A., Malyuchenko, N. V., Tonevitskii, A. G., & Ivanitskii, A. M. (2010). Genetic and social factors in the development of aggression. *Human Physiology, 36,* 40–46.

Szasz, T. S. (1987). *Insanity: The idea and its consequences.* New York: Wiley.

Szentirmai, E., Yasuda, T., Taishi, P., Wang, M., Churchill, L., Bohnet, S. et al. (2007). Growth hormone-releasing hormone: Cerebral cortical sleep-related EEG actions and expressions. *American Journal of Physiology: Regulatory, Integrative and Comparative Physiology, 293,* R922–R930.

Szkrybalo, J., & Ruble, D. N. (1999). "God made me a girl": Sex-category constancy judgments and explanations revisited. *Developmental Psychology, 35,* 392–402.

Tager-Flusberg, H. (2005). Putting words together: Morphology and syntax in the preschool years. In J. B. Gleason (Ed.), *The development of language* (5th ed., pp. 148–190). Boston: Allyn & Bacon.

Taghavi, M. R., Goodarzi, M. A., Kazemi, H., & Ghorbani, M. (2006). Irrational beliefs in major depression and generalized anxiety disorder in an Iranian sample: A preliminary study. *Perceptual and Motor Skills, 102,* 187–196.

Tajfel, H. (1982). *Social identity and intergroup relations.* Cambridge: Cambridge University Press.

Takano, Y., & Sogon, S. (2008). Are Japanese more collectivistic than Americans? Examining conformity in in-groups and the reference-group effect. *Journal of Cross-Cultural Psychology, 39,* 237–250.

Tamres, L. K., Janicki, D., & Helgeson, V. S. (2002). Sex differences in coping behavior: A meta-analytic review and an examination of relative coping. *Personality and Social Psychology Review, 6,* 2–30.

Tang, Y. Y., Ma, Y., Fan, Y., Feng, H., Wang, J., Feng, S. et al. (2009). Central and autonomic nervous system interaction is altered by short-term meditation. *Proceedings of the National Academy of Sciences of the United States of America, 106,* 8865–8870.

Tanguy, S., Quarck, G., Etard, O., Gauthier, A., & Denise, P. (2008). Vestibulo-ocular reflex and motion sickness in figure skaters. *European Journal of Applied Physiology, 104,* 1031–1037.

Tankova, I., Adan, A., & Buela-Casal, G. (1994). Circadian typology and individual differences: A review. *Personality and Individual Differences, 16,* 671–684.

Tanner-Smith, E. E. (2010). Negotiating the early developing body: Pubertal timing, body weight, and adolescent girls' substance use. *Journal of Youth and Adolescence, 39,* 1402–1416.

Taormina, R. J., & Gao, J. H. (2013). Maslow and the motivation hierarchy: Measuring satisfaction of the needs. *American Journal of Psychology, 126,* 155–177. doi: 10.5406/amerjpsyc.126.2.0155

Tashkin, D. P. (2005). Smoked marijuana as a cause of lung injury. *Monaldi Archives for Chest Disease, 63,* 92–100.

Tashkin, D. P., Baldwin, G. C., Sarafian, T., Dubinett, S., & Roth, M. D. (2002). Respiratory and immunologic consequences of marijuana smoking. *Journal of Clinical Pharmacology, 42,* 71S–81S.

Tata, D. A., & Anderson, B. J. (2009). The effects of chronic glucocorticoid exposure on dendritic length, synapse numbers and glial volume in animal models: Implications for hippocampal volume reductions in depression. *Physiology and Behavior, 99,* 186–193.

Taurah, L., Chandler, C., & Sanders, G. (2014). Depression, impulsiveness, sleep, and memory in past and present polydrug users of 3, 4-methylenedioxymethamphetamine (MDMA, ecstasy). *Psychopharmacology, 231,* 737–751.

Taylor, C. B., & Luce, K. H. (2003). Computer- and Internet-based psychotherapy interventions. *Current Directions in Psychological Science, 12,* 18–22.

Taylor, D. J., Jenni, O. G., Acebo, C., & Carskadon, M. A. (2005). Sleep tendency during extended wakefulness: Insights into adolescent sleep regulation and behavior. *Journal of Sleep Research, 14,* 239–244.

Taylor, E. J., & Outlaw, F. H. (2002). Use of prayer among persons with cancer. *Holistic Nursing Practices, 16,* 46–60.

Taylor, H. (2002). Poor people and African Americans suffer the most stress from the hassles of daily living. *The Harris Poll #66.*

Taylor, S. E. (2003). *Health psychology* (5th ed.). New York: McGraw-Hill.

Taylor, S. E. (2006). Tend and befriend: Biobehavioral bases of affiliation under stress. *Current Directions in Psychological Science, 15,* 273–277.

Taylor, S. E., Klein, L. C., Lewis, B. P., Gruenewald, T. L., Gurung, R. A., & Updegraff, J. A. (2000). Biobehavioral responses to stress in females: Tend-and-befriend, not fight-or-flight. *Psychological Review, 107,* 411–429.

Taylor, S. E., Way, B. M., Welch, W. T., Hilmert, C. J., Lehman, B. J., & Eisenberger, N. I. (2006). Early family environment, current adversity, the serotonin transporter promoter polymorphism, and depressive symptomatology. *Biological Psychiatry, 60,* 671–676.

Taylor, S. M. (2008). Electroconvulsive therapy, brain-derived neurotrophic factor, and possible neurorestorative benefit of the clinical application of electroconvulsive therapy. *Journal of ECT, 24,* 160–165.

Teachman, B. A. (2014). No appointment necessary: Treating mental illness outside the therapist's office. *Perspectives on Psychological Science, 9,* 85–87.

Teachman, J. D., Tedrow, L. M., & Crowder, K. D. (2000). The changing demography of America's families. *Journal of Marriage and Family, 62,* 1234–1246.

Teasdale, J. D., & Russell, M. L. (1983). Differential effects of induced mood on the recall of positive, negative, and neutral words. *British Journal of Clinical Psychology, 22,* 163–171.

Teasdale, J. D., Scott, J., Moore, R. G., Hayhurst, H., Pope, M., & Paykel, E. S. (2001). How does cognitive therapy prevent relapse in residual depression? Evidence from a controlled trial. *Journal of Consulting and Clinical Psychology, 69,* 347–357.

Teicher, M. H. (2002). Scars that won't heal: The neurobiology of child abuse. *Scientific American, 286,* 68–75.

Teitelbaum, P., & Epstein, A. N. (1962). The lateral hypothalamic syndrome: Recovery of feeding and drinking after lateral hypothalamic lesions. *Psychological Review, 69,* 74–90.

Teitelbaum, P., & Stellar, E. (1954). Recovery from failure to eat produced by hypothalamic lesions. *Science, 120,* 894–895.

Teixeira, P. J., Silva, M. N., Coutinho, S. R., Palmeira, A. L., Mata, J., Vieira, P. N. et al. (2010). Mediators of weight loss and weight loss maintenance in middle-aged women. *Obesity, 18,* 725–735.

Temoshok, L. (1992). *The Type C connection: The behavioral links to cancer and your health.* New York: Random House.

Tenenbaum, H. R., & Leaper, C. (2003). Parent-child conversations about science: The socialization of gender inequities? *Developmental Psychology, 39,* 34–47.

Terhune, D. B., Cardena, E., & Lindgren, M. (2010). Dissociative tendencies and individual differences in high hypnotic suggestibility. *Cognitive Neuropsychology, 17,* 1–23.

Terman, L. M. (1916). *The measurement of intelligence.* Boston: Houghton Mifflin.

Terr, L. C. (1983). Chowchilla revisited: The effects of psychic trauma four years after a school-bus kidnapping. *American Journal of Psychiatry, 140,* 1543–1550.

Terracciano, A., Costa, P. T., & McCrae, R. R. (2006). Personality plasticity after age 30. *Personality and Social Psychology Bulletin, 32,* 999–1009.

Tesarz, J, Leisner, S., Gerhardt, A., Janke, S., Seidler, G. H., Eich, W., & Hartmann, M. (2014). Effects of eye movement desensitization and reprocessing (EMDR) treatment in chronic pain patients: A systematic review. *Pain Medicine, 15,* 247–263.

Teyber, E., & McClure, F. (2000). Therapist variables. In C. R. Snyder & R. E. Ingram (Eds.), *Handbook of psychological change: Psychotherapy processes and practices for the 21st century* (pp. 62–87). New York: Wiley.

Thase, M. E. (2003). Effectiveness of antidepressants: Comparative remission rates. *Journal of Clinical Psychiatry, 64*(Suppl. 2), 3–7.

Thase, M. E. (2010). The role of neurobiologic processes in treating depression. *Journal of Clinical Psychiatry, 71,* e28.

Thase, M. E., Jindal, R., & Howland, R. H. (2002). Biological aspects of depression. In I. H. Gotlib & C. L. Hammen (Eds.), *Handbook of depression* (pp. 192–218). New York: Guilford Press.

The American sex survey: A peek beneath the sheets. (2004, October 21). ABC News. Retrieved from http://abcnews.go.com/images/Politics/959a1AmericanSexSurvey.pdf

Thelen, E. (1995). Motor development: A new synthesis. *American Psychologist, 50,* 79–95.

Thies-Flechtner, K., Muller-Oerlinghausen, B., Seibert, W., Walther, A., & Greil, W. (1996). Effect of prophylactic treatment on suicide risk in patients with major affective disorders. Data from a randomized prospective trial. *Pharmacopsychiatry, 29,* 103–107.

Thomas, A. R., Solorzano, L., & Cobb, H. C. (2007). Culturally responsive counseling and psychotherapy with children and adolescents. In H. Thompson Prout & D. T. Brown (Eds.), *Counseling and psychotherapy with children and adolescents* (4th ed., pp. 64–93). Hoboken, NJ: Wiley.

Thomas, A., & Chess, S. (1977). *Temperament and development.* New York: Brunner/Mazel.

Thomas, A., & Chess, S. (1986). The New York longitudinal study: From infancy to early adult life. In R. Plomin & J. Dunn (Eds.), *The study of temperament: Changes, continuities, and challenges* (pp. 39–52). Hillsdale, NJ: Erlbaum.

Thomas, C. P., Fullerton, C. A., Kim, M., Montejano, L., Lyman, D. R., Dougherty, R. H. et al. (2014). Medication-assisted treatment with buprenorphine: Assessing the evidence. *Psychiatric Services, 65,* 158–170.

Thombs, D. L., O'Mara, R. J., Tsukamoto, M., Rossheim, M. E., Weiler, R. M., Merves, M. L. et al. (2010). Event-level analyses of energy drink consumption and alcohol intoxication in bar patrons. *Addictive Behaviors, 35,* 325–330.

Thompson, P. M., Giedd, J. N., Woods, R. P., MacDonald, D., Evans, A. C., & Togo, A. W. (2000, March 9). Growth patterns in the developing human brain detected by using continuum-mechanical tensor maps. *Nature, 404,* 190–193.

Thorndike, E. L. (1898). Animal intelligence: An experimental study of associative process in animals. *Psychological Review Monograph,* No. 8.

Thorndike, E. L. (1905). *The elements of psychology.* New York: Seiler.

Thorpe, G. L., & Olson, S. L. (1997). *Behavior therapy: Concepts, procedures, and applications* (2nd ed.). Boston: Allyn & Bacon.

Thorpy, M. (2007). Therapeutic advances in narcolepsy. *Sleep Medicine, 8,* 427–440.

Thurber, C. A. (1995). The experience and expression of homesickness in preadolescent and adolescent boys. *Child Development, 66,* 1162–1178.

Thurstone, L. L. (1931). The measurement of social attitudes. *Journal of Abnormal and Social Psychology, 26,* 249–269.

Thurstone, L. L. (1938). *Primary mental abilities.* Chicago: University of Chicago Press.

Tiedemann, J. (2002). Teachers' gender stereotypes as determinants of teacher perceptions in elementary school mathematics. *Educational Studies in Mathematics, 50,* 49–62.

Tienari, P., Wahlberg, K. E., & Wynee, L. C. (2006). Finnish Adoption Study of Schizophrenia: Implications for family interventions. *Families, Systems and Health, 24,* 442–451.

Tienari, P., Wynne, L. C., Laksy, K., Moring, J., Nieminen, P., Sorri, A. et al. (2003). Genetic boundaries of the schizophrenia spectrum: Evidence from the Finnish Adoptive Family Study of Schizophrenia. *American Journal of Psychiatry, 160,* 1567–1594.

Till, B. D., Stanley, S. M., & Priluck, R. (2008). Classical conditioning and celebrity endorsers: An examination of belongingness and resistance to extinction. *Psychology & Marketing, 25,* 179–196. doi:10.1002/mar.20205

Tobin, K. E., Davey, M. A., & Latkin, C. A. (2005). Calling emergency medical services during drug overdose: An examination of individual, social and setting correlates. *Addiction, 100,* 397–404. doi:10.1111/j.1360-0443.2005.00975.

Tohidian, I. (2009). Examining linguistic relativity hypothesis as one of the main views on the relationship between language and thought. *Journal of Psycholinguist Research, 38,* 65–74.

Toledo, M. (2009, January 30). *First comes marriage, then comes love.* ABC News/20/20. Retrieved March 13, 2010, from http://abcnews.go.com/2020/story?id=6762309

Tolin, D. F. (2010). Is cognitive-behavioral therapy more effective than other therapies? A meta-analytic review. *Clinical Psychological Review, 30,* 710–720.

Tolin, D. F., & Foa, E. B. (2006). Sex differences in trauma and posttraumatic stress disorder: A quantitative review of 25 years of research. *Psychological Bulletin, 132,* 959–992.

Tolman, E. C., & Honzik, C. H. (1930). "Insight" in rats. *University of California Publications in Psychology, 4,* 215–232.

Tomasello, M. (2000). Culture and cognitive development. *Current Directions in Psychological Science, 9,* 37–40.

Tomasi, D., & Volkow, N. D. (2012). Laterality patterns of brain functional connectivity: Gender effects. *Cerebral Cortex, 22,* 1455–1462. doi:10.1093/cercor/bhr230

Tondo, L., & Baldessarini, R. J. (2009). Long-term lithium treatment in the prevention of suicidal behavior in bipolar disorder patients. *Epidemiologia e Psichiatria Sociale, 18,* 179–183.

Torgersen, S. (2012). Epidemiology. In T. A. Widiger (Ed.), *The Oxford handbook of personality disorders* (pp. 186–205). New York: Oxford University Press.

Tormala, Z. L., Briñol, P., & Petty, R. E. (2007). Multiple roles for sources credibility under high elaboration: It's all in the timing. *Social Cognition, 25,* 536–552.

Torres, L., Driscoll, M. W., & Voell, M. (2012). Discrimination, acculturation, acculturative stress, and Latino psychological distress: A moderated mediational model. *Cultural Diversity and Ethnic Minority Psychology, 18,* 17–25.

Torrey, E. F., Buka, S., Cannon, T. D., Goldstein, J. M., Seidman, L. J., Liu, T. et al. (2009). Paternal age as a risk factor for schizophrenia: How important is it? *Schizophrenia Research, 114,* 1–5.

Trafimow, D., Armendariz, M. L., & Madsen, L. (2004). A test of whether attributions provide for self-enhancement or self-defense. *Journal of Social Psychology, 144,* 453–463.

Tramoni, E., Felician, O., Barbeau, E. J., Guedi, E., Guye, M., Bartolemei, F. et al. (2011). Long-term consolidation of declarative memory: Insight from temporal epilepsy. *Brain, 134,* 816–831.

Tremblay, R. E., Schaal, B., Boulerice, B., Arseneault, L., Soussignan, R. G., Paquette, D. et al. (1998). Testosterone, physical aggression, dominance, and physical development in early adolescence. *International Journal of Behavioral Development, 22,* 753–777.

Triandis, H. C. (1994). *Culture and social behavior.* New York: McGraw-Hill.

Triplett, N. (1898). The dynamogenic factors in pacemaking and competition. *American Journal of Psychology, 9,* 507–533.

Tripp, A., Kota, R. S., Lewis, D. A., & Sibille, E. (2011). Reduced somatostatin in subgenual anterior cingulate cortex in major depression. *Neurobiology of Disease, 42,* 116–124.

Troisi, J. R., II. (2003). Spontaneous recovery during, but not following, extinction of the discriminative stimulus effects of nicotine in rats: Reinstatement of stimulus control. *The Psychological Record, 53,* 579–592.

Troy, A. S., Shallcross, A. J., & Mauss, I. B. (2013). A person-by-situation approach to emotion regulation: Cognitive reappraisal can either help or hurt, depending on the context. *Psychological Science, 24,* 2505–2514.

Troy, A. S., Wilhelm, F. H., Shallcross, A. J., & Mauss, I. B. (2010). Seeing the silver lining: Cognitive reappraisal ability moderates the relationship between stress and depressive symptoms. *Emotion, 10,* 783–795.

Tryon, W. W. (2005). Possible mechanisms for why desensitization and exposure therapy works. *Clinical Psychology Review, 25,* 67–95.

Trzepacz, P. T., Yu, P., Bhamidipati, P. K., Willis, B., Forrester, T., Tabas, L. et al. (2013). Frontolimbic atrophy is associated with agitation and aggression in mild cognitive impairment and Alzheimer's disease. *Alzheimer's & Dementia, 9*(5, Suppl), S95–S104. doi:10.1016/j.jalz.2012.10.005

Trzesniewski, K. H., & Donnellan, M. B. (2010). Rethinking "Generation Me": A study of cohort effects from 1976–2006. *Perspectives on Psychological Science, 5,* 58–75.

Trzesniewski, K. H., Donnellan, M. B., & Robins, R. W. (2008). Do today's young people really think they are so extraordinary? An examination of secular trends in narcissism and self-enhancement. *Psychological Science, 19,* 181–188.

Tsai, G., Gastfriend, D. R., & Coyle, J. T. (1995). The glutamatergic basis of human alcoholism. *American Journal of Psychiatry, 152,* 332–340.

Tsapelas, I., Aron, A., & Orbuch, T. (2009). Marital boredom now predicts less satisfaction 9 years later. *Psychological Science, 20,* 543–545.

Tsuang, M. T., Fleming, J. A., & Simpson, J. C. (1999). Suicide and schizophrenia. In D. G. Jacobs (Ed.), *The Harvard Medical School guide to suicide assessment and intervention* (pp. 287–299). San Francisco: Jossey-Bass.

Tucker, M. A., & Fishbein, W. (2009). The impact of sleep duration and subject intelligence on declarative and motor memory performance: How much is enough? *Journal of Sleep Research, 18,* 304–312.

Tucker-Drob, E. M., Briley, D. A., & Harden, K. P. (2013). Genetic and environmental influences on cognition across development and context. *Current Directions in Psychological Science, 22,* 349–355.

Tuerk, P. W., Yoder, M., Ruggiero, K. J., Gros, D. F., & Acierno, R. (2010). A pilot study of prolonged exposure therapy for posttraumatic stress disorder delivered via telehealth technology. *Journal of Traumatic Stress, 23,* 116–123.

Tullett, A. M., Teper, R., & Inzlicht, M. (2011). Confronting threats to meaning: A new framework for understanding responses to unsettling events. *Perspectives on Psychological Science, 6,* 447–453.

Tulving, E. (1972). Episodic and semantic memory. In E. Tulving & W. Donaldson (Eds.), *Organisation of memory* (pp. 381–403). London: Academic Press.

Tulving, E. (1974). Cue-dependent forgetting. *American Scientist, 62,* 74–82.

Tulving, E. (1983). *Elements of episodic memory.* Oxford: Oxford University Press.

Turati, C. (2004). Why faces are not special to newborns: An alternative account of the face preference. *Current Directions in Psychological Science, 13,* 5–8.

Turati, C., & Simion, F. (2002). Newborns' recognition of changing and unchanging aspects of schematic faces. *Journal of Experimental Child Psychology, 83,* 239–261.

Turk Charles, S., Reynolds, C. A., & Gatz, M. (2001). Age-related differences and change in positive and negative affect over 23 years. *Journal of Personality and Social Psychology, 80,* 136–151.

Turk, C. L., Heimberg, R. G., & Hope, D. A. (2001). Social anxiety disorder. In D. H. Barlow (Ed.), *Clinical handbook of psychological disorders: A step-by-step treatment manual* (3rd ed., pp. 114–153). New York: Guilford Press.

Turner, A. J., & Ortony, A. (1992). Basic emotions: Can conflicting criteria converge? *Psychological Review, 99,* 566–571.

Turner, P. J., & Gervai, J. (1995). A multidimensional study of gender typing in preschool children and their parents: Personality, attitudes, preferences, behavior, and cultural differences. *Developmental Psychology, 31,* 759–772.

Tversky, A., & Kahneman, D. (1974). Judgment under uncertainty: Heuristics and biases, *Science, 185,* 1124–1131.

Tversky, A., & Kahneman, D. (1980). Causal schemas in judgments under uncertainty. In M. Fishbein (Ed.), *Progress in social psychology* (pp. 49–72). Hillsdale, NJ:Erlbaum.

Tversky, A., & Kahneman, D. (2004). The framing of decisions and the psychology of choice. In D. A. Balota & E. J. Marsh (Eds.), *Cognitive psychology: Key readings* (pp. 621–630). New York: Psychology Press.

Tversky, B. (1981). Distortions in memory for maps. *Cognitive Psychology, 13,* 407–433.

Twenge, J. M. (2001). Birth cohort changes in extraversion: A cross-temporal meta-analysis, 1966–1993. *Personality and Individual Differences, 30,* 735–748.

Twenge, J. M. (2006). *Generation me: Why today's young Americans are more confident, assertive, entitled—and more miserable than ever before.* New York: Free Press.

Twenge, J. M. (2009). Change over time in obedience: The jury's still out, but it might be decreasing. *American Psychologist, 64,* 28–31.

Twenge, J. M., & Campbell, W. K. (2001). Age and birth cohort differences in self-esteem: A cross-temporal meta-analysis. *Personality and Social Psychology Review, 5,* 321–344.

Twenge, J. M., & Campbell, W. K. (2009). *The narcissism epidemic: Living in the age of entitlement.* New York: Free Press.

Twenge, J. M., & Foster, J. D. (2008). Mapping the scale of the narcissism epidemic: Increases in narcissism 2002–2007 within ethnic groups. *Journal of Research in Personality, 42,* 1619–1622.

Twenge, J. M., & Foster, J. D. (2010). Birth cohort increases in narcissistic personality traits among American college students, 1982–2009. *Social Psychological and Personality Science, 1,* 99–106.

Twenge, J. M., Konrath, S., Foster, J. D., Campbell, W. K., & Bushman, B. J. (2008a). Egos inflating over time: A cross-temporal meta-analysis of the Narcissistic Personality Inventory. *Journal of Personality, 76,* 875–901.

Twenge, J. M., Konrath, S., Foster, J. D., Campbell, W. K., & Bushman, B. J. (2008b). Further evidence of an increase in narcissism among college students. *Journal of Personality, 76,* 919–927.

Tylka, T. L. (2006). Development and psychometric evaluation of a measure of intuitive eating. *Journal of Counseling Psychology, 53,* 226–240.

U.S. Census Bureau. (2006). Nation's population one-third minority, *U.S. Census Bureau News.* Retrieved from www.census.gov/Press-release/www/releases/archives/population/006808.html

U.S. Census Bureau. (2008). *Current Population Survey, 2008 annual social & economic supplement.* Washington DC: U.S. Department of Commerce.

U.S. Census Bureau. (2010). *Current Population Survey, 2009. Annual Social and Economic Supplement.* Washington, DC: U.S. Department of Commerce.

U.S. Census Bureau. (2012a). *American community survey, 5-year estimates.* Washington, DC: U.S. Department of Commerce.

U.S. Census Bureau. (2012b). *Current Population Survey, 2011: Annual social and economic supplement.* Washington, DC: U.S. Department of Commerce.

U.S. Census Bureau. (2012c). U.S. Census Bureau projections show a slower growing, older, more diverse nation a half century from now. *U.S. Census Bureau Newsroom.* Retrieved from https://www.census.gov/newsroom/releases/archives/population/cb12-243.html

U.S. Department of Agriculture, Center for Nutrition Policy and Promotion. (2013, August). *Expenditures on children by families, 2012.* Miscellaneous Publication Number 1528-2012. Alexandria, VA: United States Department of Agriculture Center.

U.S. Department of Education. (2009). *Condition of education 2009, Indicator 24.* NCES 2009–081. Washington, DC: National Center for Education Statistics.

U.S. Department of Energy. (2007). The Human Genome Project information. Retrieved from http://www.ornl.gov/hgmis

Uchino, B. N. (2009). Understanding the links between social support and physical health: A life-span perspective with emphasis on the separability of perceived and received support. *Perspectives on Psychological Science, 4,* 236–255.

Uchino, B. N., Cacioppo, J. T., & Kiecolt- Glaser, J. K. (1996). The relationship between social support and physiological processes: A review with emphasis on underlying mechanisms and implications for health. *Psychological Bulletin, 119,* 488–531.

Ultan, R. (1969). Some general characteristics of interrogative systems. *Working Papers in Language Universals* (Stanford University), *1,* 41–63.

Umberson, D., Williams, K., Powers, D. A., Meichu, D. C., & Campbell, A. M. (2005). As good as it gets? A lifecourse perspective on marital quality. *Social Forces, 84,* 493–511.

Ünal, A., de Waard, D., Epstude, K., & Steg, L. (2013). Driving with music: Effects on arousal and performance. *Transportation Research Part F: Traffic Psychology and Behaviour, 21,* 52–65. doi: 10.1016/j.trf.2013.09.004

UNICEF (United Nations Children's Fund). (2009). *State of the world's children.* New York: Author.

United Nations. (2003). *World fertility report 2003.* United Nations publication ST/ESA/SER.A/234. New York: Author.

University of Michigan. (2008, April 8). Exactly how much housework does a husband create? *ScienceDaily.* Retrieved from http://www.sciencedaily.com/releases/2008/04/080403191009.htm

Updegraff, J. A., Silver, R. C., & Holman, E. A. (2008). Searching for and finding meaning in collective trauma: Results from a national longitudinal study of the 9/11 terrorist attacks. *Journal of Personality and Social Psychology, 95,* 709–722.

Ursu, S., Stenger, A., Shear, M. K., Jones, M. R., & Carter, C. S. (2003). Overactive action-monitoring in obsessive-compulsive disorder: Evidence from functional magnetic resonance imaging. *Psychological Science, 14,* 347–353.

Vainionpaa, L. K., Rattya, J., Knip, M., Tapanainen, J. S., Pakarinen, A. J., Lanning, P. et al. (1999). Valproate-induced hyperandrogenism during pubertal maturation in girls with epilepsy. *Annals of Neurology, 45,* 444–450.

Valensi, P., Doaré, L., Perret, G., Germack, R., Pariès, J., & Mesangeau, D. (2003). Cardiovascular vagosympathetic activity in rats with ventromedial hypothalamic obesity. *Obesity Research, 11,* 54–64.

Valenza, E., Simion, F., Cassia, V. M., & Umilta, C. (1996). Face preference at birth. *Journal of Experimental Psychology, 33,* 711–723.

Valenzuela, M., & Sachdev, P. (2009). Can cognitive exercise prevent the onset of dementia? Systematic review of randomized clinical trials with longitudinal follow-up. *American Journal of Geriatric Psychiatry, 17,* 179–187.

Valli, K., & Revonsuo, A. (2009). The threat simulation theory in light of recent empirical evidence: A review. *American Journal of Psychology, 122,* 17–38.

Valli, K., Revonsuo, A., Palkas, O., Ismail, K. H., Ali, K. J., & Punamaki, R. L. (2005). The threat simulation theory of the evolutionary function of dreaming: Evidence from dreams of traumatized children. *Consciousness and Cognition, 14,* 188–218.

Van Apeldoorn, F. J., Timmerman, M. E., Mersch, P. P., van Hout, W. J., Visser, S., van Dyck, R. et al. (2010). A randomized trial of cognitive-behavioral therapy or selective serotonin reuptake inhibitor or both combined for panic disorder with or without agoraphobia: Treatment results through 1-year follow-up. *Journal of Clinical Psychiatry, 71,* 574–586.

Van den Bulck, J. (2003). Text messaging as a cause of sleep interruption in adolescents: Evidence from a cross-sectional study. *Journal of Sleep Research, 12,* 263.

Van den Bulck, J. (2007). Adolescent use of mobile phones for calling and for sending text messages after lights out: Results from a prospective cohort study with a one-year follow-up. *Sleep, 30,* 1220–1223.

van der Kloet, D., Merckelbach, H., Giesbrecht, T., & Lynn, S. J. (2012). Fragmented sleep, fragmented mind: The role of sleep in dissociative symptoms. *Perspectives on Psychological Science, 7,* 159–175.

Van der Kolk, B. A., Spinazzola, J., Blaustein, M. E., Hopper, J. W., Hopper, E. K., Korn, D. L. et al. (2007). A randomized clinical trial of eye movement desensitization and reprocessing (EMDR), fluoxetine, and pill placebo in the treatment of posttraumatic stress disorder: Treatment effects and long-term maintenance. *Journal of Clinical Psychiatry, 68,* 37–46.

van Goozen, S. H. M., Fairchild, G., & Harold, G. T. (2008). The role of neurobiological deficits in childhood antisocial behavior. *Current Directions in Psychological Science, 17,* 224–228.

van Goozen, S., Frijda, N., & de Poll, N. V. (1994). Anger and aggression in women: Influence of sports choice and testosterone administration. *Aggressive Behavior, 20,* 213–222.

Van Heteren, C. F., Boekkooi, P. F., Jongsma, H. W., & Nijhuis, J. G. (2000). Fetal learning and memory. *Lancet, 356,* 9236–9237.

van Hooren, S. A., Valentijn, A. M., Bosma, H., Ponds, R. W., van Boxtel, M. P., & Jolles, J. (2007). Cognitive functioning in healthy older adults aged 64–81: A cohort study into the effects of age, sex, and education. *Neuropsychology, Development, and Cognition, Section B: Aging, Neuropsychology, and Cognition, 14,* 40–54.

van Ijzendoom, M. H., & Sagi-Schwartz, A. (2008). Cross-cultural patterns of attachment: Universal and contextual dimensions. In J. Cassidy & P. R. Shaver (Eds.), *Handbook of attachment: Theory, research and clinical applications* (2nd ed., pp. 880–905). New York: Guilford Press.

van Laar, M., Volkerts, E., & Verbaten, M. (2001). Subcronic effects of the GABA-agonist lorazepam and the 5-HT2A/2C antagonist ritanserin on driving performance, slow wave sleep and daytime sleepiness in healthy volunteers. *Psychopharmacology, 154,* 189–197.

van Solinge, H., & Henkens, K. (2005). Couples' adjustment to retirement: A multi-actor panel study. *Journals of Gerontology, Series B: Psychological Sciences and Social Sciences, 60,* S11–S20.

Vance, E. B., & Wagner, N. N. (1976). Written descriptions of orgasms: A study of sex differences. *Archives of Sexual Behavior, 5,* 87–98.

VandeVusse, L., Irland, J., Healthcare, W. F., Berner, M. A., Fuller, S., & Adams, D. (2007). Hypnosis for childbirth: A retrospective comparative analysis of outcomes in one obstetrician's practice. *American Journal of Clinical Hypnosis, 50,* 109–119.

Vandrey, R. G., Budney, A. J., Hughes, J. R., & Liguori, A. (2008). A within-subject comparison of withdrawal symptoms during abstinence from cannabis, tobacco, and both substances. *Drug and Alcohol Dependence, 92,* 48–54.

Vanini, G., & Baghdoyan, H. A. (2013). Extrasynaptic GABAA receptors in rat pontine reticular formation increase wakefulness. *Sleep: Journal of Sleep and Sleep Disorders Research, 36,* 337–343.

vanReekum, C., Johnstone, T., Etter, A., Wehrle, T., & Scherer, K. (2004). Psychophysiological response to appraisal dimensions in a computer game. *Cognition and Emotion, 18,* 663–688.

Varley, C. K., & Smith, C. J. (2003). Anxiety disorders in the child and teen. *Pediatric Clinics of North America, 50,* 1107–1138.

Vartanian, L. R. (2000). Revisiting the imaginary audience and personal fable constructs of adolescent egocentrism: A conceptual review. *Adolescence, 35,* 639–661.

Vartanian, L. R. (2001). Adolescents' reactions to hypothetical peer group conversations: Evidence for an imaginary audience? *Adolescence, 36,* 347–380.

Vartanian, O., Martindale, C., & Kwiatkowski, J. (2003). Creativity and inductive reasoning: The relationship between divergent thinking and performance on Wason's 2-4-6 task. *The Quarterly Journal of Experimental Psychology, 56A,* 641–655.

Vasquez, M. J. (2007). Cultural difference and the therapeutic alliance: An evidence-based analysis. *American Psychologist, 62,* 875–885.

Vassallo, S., Cooper, S. L., & Douglas, J. M. (2009). Visual scanning in the recognition of facial affect: Is there an observer sex difference? *Journal of Vision, 9,* 1–10.

Vaughn, B. E., Stevenson-Hinde, J., Waters, E., Kotsaftis, A., Lefever, G., Shouldice, A. et al. (1992). Attachment security and temperament in infancy and early childhood: Some conceptual clarifications. *Developmental Psychology, 28,* 463–473.

Venkatesh, K., Biswas, J., & Kumarasamy, N. (2008). Impact of highly active antiretroviral therapy on ophthalmic manifestations in human immune deficiency syndrome. *Indian Journal of Ophthalmology, 56,* 391–393.

Ventura, J., Nuechterlein, K. H., Subotnik, K. L., Hardesty, J. P., & Mintz, J. (2000). Life events can trigger depressive exacerbation in the early course of schizophrenia. *Journal of Abnormal Psychology, 109,* 139–144.

Vergne, D. E., & Nemeroff, C. B. (2006). The interaction of serotonin transporter gene polymorphisms and early adverse life events on vulnerability for major depression. *Current Psychiatry Reports, 8,* 452–457.

Vieta, E., & Goikolea, J. M. (2005). Atypical antipsychotics: Newer options for mania and maintenance therapy. *Bipolar Disorders, 7*(Suppl. 4), 21–33.

Vigezzi, P., Guglielmino, L., Marzorati, P., Silenzio, R., De Chiara, M., Corrado, F. et al. (2006). Multimodal drug addiction treatment: A field comparison of methadone and buprenorphine among heroin- and cocaine-dependent patients. *Journal of Substance Abuse and Treatment, 31,* 3–7.

Vignovic, J. A., & Thompson, L. (2010). Computer-mediated cross-cultural collaboration: Attributing communication errors to the person versus the situation. *Journal of Applied Psychology, 95,* 265–276. doi:10.1037/a001862

Villaneuva, A. T., Buchanan, P. R., Yee, B. J., & Grunstein, R. R. (2005). Ethnicity and obstructive sleep apnea. *Sleep Medical Review, 9,* 419–436.

Vitaliano, P. P., Young, H. M., & Zhang, J. (2004). Is caregiving a risk factor for illness? *Current Directions in Psychological Science, 13,* 13–16.

Voderholzer, U., Al-Shajlawi, A., Weske, G., Feige, B., & Riemann, D. (2003). Are there gender differences in objective and subjective sleep measures? A study of insomniacs and healthy controls. *Depression and Anxiety, 17,* 162–172.

Volkow, N. D., Gillespie, H., Mullani, N., & Tancredi, L. (1996). Brain glucose metabolism in chronic marijuana users at baseline and during marijuana intoxication. *Psychiatry Research: Neuroimaging, 67,* 29–38.

Volkow, N. D., Wang, G. J., Fowler, J. S., Leonido-Yee, M., Franceschi, D., Sedler, M. J. et al. (2001). Association of dopamine transporter reduction with psychomotor impairment in methamphetamine abusers. *American Journal of Psychiatry, 158,* 377–382.

Volterra, A., & Steinhauser, C. (2004). Glial modulation of synaptic transmission in the hippocampus. *Glia, 47,* 249–257.

von Allmen, D., Wurmitzer, K., Martin, E., & Klaver, P. (2013). Neural activity in the hippocampus predicts individual visual short-term memory capacity. *Hippocampus, 23,* 606–615.

von Gontard, A., Schaumburg, H., Hollmann, E., Eiberg, H., & Rittig, S. (2001). The genetics of enuresis: A review. *Journal of Urology, 166,* 2438–2443.

Voorspoels, W., Vanpaemel, W., & Storms, G. (2008). Exemplars and prototypes in natural language concepts: A typicality-based evaluation. *Psychonomic Bulletin & Review, 15,* 630–637.

Voorspoels, W., Vanpaemel, W., & Storms, G. (2011). A formal ideal-based account of typicality. *Psychonomic Bulletin & Review, 18,* 1006–1014. doi:10.3758/s13423-011-0122-9

Voss, J. L., Federmeier, K. D., & Paller, K. A. (2012). The potato chip really does look like Elvis! Neural hallmarks of conceptual processing associated with finding novel shapes subjectively meaningful. *Cerebral Cortex, 22,* 2354–2364.

Vygotsky, L. S. (1978). *Mind in society: The development of higher mental process.* Cambridge, MA: Harvard University Press.

Vygotsky, L. S. (1986). *Thought and language.* Cambridge, MA: MIT Press.

Vygotsky, L. S. (1987). Thinking and speech. In R. W. Reiber & A. S. Carton (Eds.), *The collected works of L. S. Vygotsky: Vol. 1I. Problems of general psychology* (pp. 37–285). New York: Plenum Press. (Original work published 1934)

Vytal, K., & Hamann, S. (2010). Neuroimaging support for discrete neural correlates of basic emotions: A voxel-based meta-analysis. *Journal of Cognitive Neuroscience, 22,* 2864–2885. doi:10.1162/jocn.2009.21366

Wadden, T. A., & Stunkard, A. J. (1987). Psychopathology and obesity. *Annals of the New York Academy of Sciences, 499,* 55–65.

Wade, N. J. (2010). Granit's retina. *Cortex: A Journal Devoted to the Study of the Nervous System and Behavior, 46,* 1070–1071.

Wade, T. D. (2007). Epidemiology of eating disorders: Creating opportunities to move the current classification paradigm forward. *International Journal of Eating Disorders, 40,* s27–s30.

Wagner, B., Knaevelsrud, C., & Maercker, A. (2006). Internet-based cognitive-behavioral therapy for complicated grief: A randomized controlled trial. *Death Studies, 30,* 429–453.

Wagner, G. C., Beuving, L. J., & Hutchinson, R. R. (1980). The effects of gonadal hormone manipulations on aggressive target-biting in mice. *Aggressive Behavior, 6,* 1–7.

Wakefield, J. C. (1992). The concept of mental disorder: On the boundary between biological facts and social values. *American Psychologist, 47,* 373–388.

Walak, J., Szczepanik, M., Woszczak, M., & Józefowicz-Korczyńska, M. (2013). Impact of physiotherapy on quality of life improvement in patients with central vestibular system dysfunction [Abstract]. *Otolaryngol Polska, 67,* 11–17. doi: 10.1016/j.otpol.2012.09.001.

Wald, J., & Taylor, S. (2003). Preliminary research on the efficacy of virtual reality exposure therapy to treat driving phobia. *Cyberpsychology and Behavior, 6,* 459–465.

Waldron-Hennessey, R., & Sabatelli, R. M. (1997). The parental comparison level index: A measure for assessing parental rewards and costs relative to expectations. *Journal of Marriage and Family, 59,* 824–833.

Walker, B. R., Diefenbach, K. S., & Parikh, T. N. (2007). Inhibition within the nucleus tractus solitarius (NTS) ameliorates environmental exploration deficits due to cerebellum lesions in an animal model for autism. *Behavioural Brain Research, 176,* 109–120.

Walker, E., & Tessner, K. (2008). Schizophrenia. *Perspectives on Psychological Science, 3,* 30–37.

Walker, E., Shapiro, D., Esterberg, M., & Trotman, H. (2010). Neurodevelopment and schizophrenia: Broadening the focus. *Current Directions in Psychological Science, 19,* 204–208.

Walker, L. J. (1989). A longitudinal study of moral reasoning. *Child Development, 60,* 157–166.

Walker, L. J. (1995). Sexism in Kohlberg's moral psychology? In W. M. Kurtines & J. L. Gewirtz (Eds.), *Moral development: An introduction* (pp. 83–107). Boston: Allyn & Bacon.

Walker, L. J., & Taylor, J. H. (1991). Stage transitions in moral reasoning: A longitudinal study of developmental processes. *Developmental Psychology, 27,* 330–337.

Walker, M. P. (2009). The role of sleep in cognition and emotion. *Annals of the New York Academy of Sciences, 1156,* 168–197.

Walker, M. P., & Stickgold, R. (2004). Sleep-dependent learning and memory consolidation. *Neuron, 44,* 121–133.

Walker, M. P., & van der Helm, E. (2009). Overnight therapy? The role of sleep in emotional brain processing. *Psychological Bulletin, 135,* 731–748.

Wallace, J., Schneider, T., & McGuffin, P. (2002). Genetics of depression. In I. H. Gotlib & C. L. Hammen (Eds.), *Handbook of depression* (pp. 169–191). New York: Guilford Press.

Wallis, C. (2005, January 9). The new science of happiness. *Time.*

Walster, E., Aronson, E., Abrahams, D., & Rottman, L. (1966). Importance of physical attractiveness in dating behavior. *Journal of Personality and Social Psychology, 4,* 508–516.

Walters, S. T., Foy, B. D., & Castro, R. J. (2003). The agony of Ecstasy: Responding to growing MDMA use among college students. *Journal of American College Health, 51,* 139–141.

Wampold, B. E., Minami, T., Baskin, T. W., & Callen Tierney, S. (2002). A meta-(re)analysis of the effects of cognitive therapy versus other therapies for depression. *Journal of Affective Disorders, 68,* 159–165.

Wampold, B. E., Mondin, G. W., Moody, M., Stich, F., Benson, K., & Ahn, H. (1997). A meta-analysis of outcome studies comparing bona fide psychotherapies: Empirically, "All must have prizes." *Psychological Bulletin, 122,* 203–215.

Wang, J., Korczykowski, M., Rao, H., Fan, Y., Pluta, J., Gur, R. C. et al. (2007). Gender difference in neural response to psychological stress. *Social Cognitive and Affective Neuroscience, 2,* 227–239.

Wang, P. S., Lane, M., Olfson, M., Pincus, H. A., Wells, K. B., & Kessler, R. C. (2005). Twelve-month use of mental health services in the United States: Results from the National Comorbidity Survey Replication. *Archives of General Psychiatry, 62,* 629–640.

Wang, S. H., Baillargeon, R., & Brueckner, L. (2004). Young infants' reasoning about hidden objects: Evidence from violation-of-expectation tasks with test trials only. *Cognition, 93,* 167–198.

Wanner, H. E. (1968). *On remembering, forgetting, and understanding sentences: A study of the deep structure hypothesis.* Unpublished doctoral dissertation, Harvard University.

Warburton, D. M. (1995). Effects of caffeine on cognition and mood without caffeine abstinence. *Psychopharmacology, 119,* 66–70.

Ward, E. V., Berry, C. J., & Shanks, D. R. (2013). Age effects on explicit and implicit memory. *Frontiers in Psychology, 4,* 1–11. doi: 10.3389/fpsyg.2013.00639.

Ward, R., Logan, J., & Spitze, G. (1992). The influence of parent and child needs on coresidence in middle and later life. *Journal of Marriage and Family, 54,* 209–221.

Warner, R., & Steel, B. (1999). Child rearing as a mechanism for social change: The relationship of child gender to parents' commitment to gender equity. *Gender and Society, 13,* 503–517.

Warr, P. B. (1994). Age and employment. In M. D. Dunnette, L. Hough, & H. Triandis (Eds.), *Handbook of industrial and organizational psychology* (pp. 485–550). Palo Alto, CA: Consulting Psychologists Press.

Waschbusch, D. A., Sellers, D. P., LeBlanc, M., & Kelley, M. L. (2003). Helpless attributions and depression in adolescents: The roles of anxiety, event valence, and demographics. *Journal of Adolescence, 26,* 169–183.

Wasserman, E. A., & Miller, R. R. (1997). What's elementary about associative learning? *Annual Review of Psychology, 48,* 573–607.

Wasserman, G. S. (1978). *Color vision: An historical introduction.* New York: Wiley.

Watson, J. B., & Rayner, R. (1920). Conditioned emotional reactions. *Journal of Experimental Psychology, 3,* 1–14.

Watson, J. C., Schein, J., & McMullen, E. (2010). An examination of clients' in-session changes and their relationship to the working alliance and outcome. *Psychotherapy Research, 20,* 224–233.

Watts, B. V., Schnurr, P. P., Mayo, L., Young-Xu, Y., Weeks, W. B., & Friedman, M. J. (2013). Meta-analysis of the efficacy of treatments for post-traumatic stress disorder. *Journal of Clinical Psychiatry, 74,* e541–550.

Waylen, A., & Wolke, D. (2004). Sex 'n' drugs 'n' rock 'n' roll: The meaning and social consequences of pubertal timing. *European Journal of Endocrinology, 151,* U151–U159.

Weaver, A. J., Zelenkauskaite, A., & Samson, L. (2012). The (non)violent world of YouTube: Content trends in web video. *Journal of Communication, 62,* 1065–1083. doi:10.1111/j.1460-2466.2012.01675.x doi:10.1080/17542863.2012.669769

Webb, W. B. (1983). Theories in modern sleep research. In A. Mayes (Ed.), *Sleep mechanisms and functions* (pp. 1–17). Wokingham, UK: Van Nostrand Reinhold.

Webb, W. B., & Campbell, S. S. (1983). Relationships in sleep characteristics of identical and fraternal twins. *Archives of General Psychiatry, 40,* 1093–1095.

Webster Marketon, J. I., & Glaser, R. (2008). Stress hormones and immune function. *Cellular Immunology, 252,* 16–26.

Wechsler, D. (1939). *The measurement of adult intelligence.* Baltimore: Williams & Wilkins.

Weems, C. F., Watts, S. E., Marsee, M. A., Taylor, L. K., Costa, N. M., Cannon, M. F. et al. (2007). The psychological impact of Hurricane Katrina: Contextual differences in psychological symptoms, social support, and discrimination. *Behavior Research and Therapy, 45,* 2295–2306.

Weener, E. F. (2012). *Personal flying: How safe do you want to be?* Retrieved from http://www.ntsb.gov/news/press_releases.html

Wegener, D. T., & Carlston, D. E. (2005). Cognitive processes in attitude formation and change. In D. Albarracín, B. T. Johnson, & M. P. Zanna (Eds.), *Handbook of attitudes* (pp. 493–542). Hillsdale, NJ: Erlbaum.

Weidenmayer, C. P., Anderson, G. M., Zhu, H., Amat, J., Whiteman, R., & Peterson, B. S. (2006). Cortisol levels and hippocampus volumes in healthy preadolescent children. *Biological Psychiatry, 60,* 856–861.

Weinrich, J. D. (1994). Homosexuality. In V. L. Bullough & B. Bullough (Eds.), *Human sexuality: An encyclopedia* (pp. 277–283). New York: Garland.

Weinstein, S., Woodward, T. S., & Ngan, E. T. (2007). Brain activation mediates the association between structural abnormality and symptom severity in schizophrenia. *Neuroimage, 36,* 188–193.

Weinstock, H., Berman, S., & Cates, W., Jr. (2004). Sexually transmitted diseases among American youth: Incidence and prevalence estimates, 2000. *Perspectives on Sexual and Reproductive Health, 36,* 6–10.

Weisberg, Y. J., DeYoung, C. G., & Hirsh, J. B. (2011). Gender differences in personality across the ten aspects of the Big Five. *Frontiers in Psychology, 2,* article 178.

Weisner, T. S., & Wilson-Mitchell, J. E. (1990). Nonconventional family lifestyles and sex typing in six-year-olds. *Child Development, 61,* 1915–1933.

Weissman, M. M. (1993). The epidemiology of personality disorders: A 1990 update. NIMH Conference: Personality disorders (1990, Williamsburg, Virginia). *Journal of Personality Disorders* (Spr. Suppl. 1), 44–62.

Weissman, M. M., Bland, R. C., Canino, G. J., Green-wald, S., Hwu, H. G., Joyce, P. R. et al. (1999). Prevalence of suicide ideation and suicide attempts in nine countries. *Psychological Medicine, 29,* 9–17.

Weissman, M. M., Markowitz, J. C., & Klerman, G. I. (2000). *Comprehensive guide to interpersonal psychotherapy.* New York: Basic Books.

Welch, S. S. (2001). A review of the literature on the epidemiology of parasuicide in the general population. *Psychiatric Services, 52,* 368–375.

Welford, A. T. (1987). Ageing. In R. L. Gregory (Ed.), *The Oxford companion to the mind* (pp. 13–14). Oxford: Oxford University Press.

Wellman, H. M., Cross, D., & Watson, J. (2001). Meta-analysis of theory of mind development: The truth about false-belief. *Child Development, 72,* 655–684.

Wells, D. L., & Ott, C. A. (2011). The "new" marijuana. *Annals of Pharmacotherapy, 45,* 414–417.

Wells, G. L., & Olson, E. A. (2003). Eyewitness testimony. *Annual Review of Psychology, 54,* 277–295.

Wertheimer, M. (1923). Principles of perceptual organization (Abridged trans. by M. Wertheimer). In D. S. Beardslee & M. Wertheimer (Eds.), *Readings in perception* (pp. 115–137). Princeton, NJ: Van Nostrand-Reinhold. (Original work published 1923, *Psychologische Forschung, 41,* 301–350)

West, S. G. (2009). Alternatives to randomized experiments. *Current Directions in Psychological Science, 18,* 299–304.

Westen, D. (1999). The scientific status of unconscious processes: Is Freud really dead? *Journal of the American Psychoanalytic Association, 47,* 1061–1106.

Westen, D., & Bradley, R. (2005). Empirically supported complexity: Rethinking evidence-based practice in psychotherapy. *Current Directions in Psychological Science, 14,* 266–271.

Westermeyer, J. F. (2004). Predictors and characteristics of Erikson's life cycle model among men: A 32-year longitudinal study. *International Journal of Aging and Human Development, 58,* 29–48.

Wetter, D. W., Cofta-Gunn, L., Fouladi, R. T., Irvin, J. E., Daza, P., Mazas, C. et al. (2005). Understanding the association among education, employment characteristics, and smoking. *Addictive Behaviors, 30,* 905–914.

Wever, E. G. (1970). *Theory of hearing.* New York: Wiley. (Original work published 1949)

Weyant, J. M. (1996). Application of compliance techniques to direct-mail requests for charitable donations. *Psychology and Marketing, 13,* 157–170.

Wheeler, D. S., & Miller, R. R. (2008). Determinants of cue interactions. *Behavioral Processes, 78,* 191–203.

Wheeler, M. A., Stuss, D. T., & Tulving, E. (1997). Toward a theory of episodic memory: The frontal lobes and autonoetic consciousness. *Psychological Bulletin, 121,* 331–354.

Wheeler, M. D. (1991). Physical changes of puberty. *Endocrinology and Metabolism Clinics of North America, 20,* 1–14.

Whitbourne, S. K. (1996). *The aging individual.* New York: Springer.

Whitbourne, S. K. (2001). The physical aging process in midlife: Interactions with psychological and sociocultural factors. In M. E. Lachman (Ed.), *Handbook of midlife development* (pp. 109–155). New York: Wiley.

White, L. K., & Edwards, J. N. (1990). Emptying the nest and parental well-being: An analysis of national panel data. *American Sociological Review, 55,* 235–242.

White, L. K., & Rogers, S. J. (1997). Strong support but uneasy relationships: Coresidence and adult children's relationships with their parents. *Journal of Marriage and Family, 59,* 62–76.

White, T. M., Gibbons, M. B., & Schamberger, M. (2006). Cultural sensitivity and supportive expressive psychotherapy: An integrative approach to treatment. *American Journal of Psychotherapy, 60,* 299–316.

Whitton, S. W., & Whisman, M. A. (2010). Relationship satisfaction instability and depression. *Journal of Family Psychology, 24,* 791–794.

Whorf, B. L. (1956). *Language, thought, and reality: Selected writings of Benjamin Lee Whorf.* New York: Wiley.

Wicherski, M., Michalski, D., & Kohout, J. (2009). *2007 Doctorate employment survey.* Washington, DC: American Psychological Association.

Wickelgren, I. (1997). Marijuana: Harder than thought? *Science, 276,* 1967–1968.

Widiger, T. A. (2003). Personality disorder and Axis I psychopathology: The problematic boundary of Axis I and Axis II. *Journal of Personality Disorders, 17,* 90–108.

Widiger, T. A., & Chaynes, K. (2003). Current issues in the assessment of personality disorders. *Current Psychiatry Reports, 5,* 28–35.

Widiger, T. A., & Trull, T. J. (2007). Plate tectonics in the classification of personality disorder: Shifting to a dimensional model. *American Psychologist, 62,* 71–83.

Wiebe, D. J., & Smith, T. W. (1997). Personality and health: Progress and problems in psychosomatics. In R. Hogan, J. Johnson, & S. Briggs (Eds.), *Handbook of personal psychology* (pp. 891–918). New York: Academic Press.

Wiechman Askay, S., & Patterson, D. R. (2007). Hypnotic analgesia. *Expert Review of Neurotherapeutics, 7,* 1675–1683.

Wiederhold, B. K., Jang, D. P., Kim, S. I., & Wiederhold, M. D. (2002). Physiological monitoring as an objective tool in virtual reality therapy. *Cyberpsychology and Behavior, 5,* 77–82.

Wiggins, J. S. (1997). In defense of traits. In R. Hogan, J. Johnson, & S. Briggs (Eds.), *Handbook of personality psychology* (pp. 97–115). New York: Academic Press.

Wijdicks, E. F. M., Atkinson, J. L. D., & Okazaki, H. (2001). Isolated medulla oblongata function after severe traumatic brain injury. *Journal of Neurology, Neurosurgery, and Psychiatry, 70,* 127.

Wilhelm, K., Mitchell, P. B., Niven, H., Finch, A., Wedgwood, L., Scimone, A. et al. (2006). Life events, first depression onset and the serotonin transporter gene. *British Journal of Psychiatry, 188,* 210–215.

Williams, D. R., Gonzalez, H. M., Neighbors, H., Neese, R., Abelson, J. M., Sweetman, J. et al. (2007). Prevalence and distribution of major depressive disorder in African Americans, Caribbean Blacks, and non-Hispanic Whites. *Archives of General Psychiatry, 64,* 305–315.

Williams, J. A., Zimmerman, F. J., & Bell J. F (2013). Norms and trends of sleep time among U.S. children and adolescents. *Archives of Pediatric and Adolescent Medicine, 167,* 55–60. doi: 10.1001/jamapediatrics.2013.423.

Williams, J. M., & Galli, A. (2006). The dopamine transporter: A vigilant border control for psychostimulant action. *Handbook of Experimental Pharmacology, 175,* 215–232.

Williams, K. N., & Kemper, S. (2010). Interventions to reduce cognitive decline in aging. *Journal of Psychosocial Nursing and Mental Health Services, 48,* 1–10.

Williams, L. M., Sidis, A., Gordon, E., & Meares, R. A. (2006). "Missing links" in borderline personality disorder: Loss of neural synchrony relates to lack of emotion regulation and impulse control. *Journal of Psychiatry and Neuroscience, 31,* 181–188.

Williams, P. M., Goodie, J., & Motsinger, L. D. (2008). Treating eating disorders in primary care. *American Family Physician, 77,* 187–195.

Willis, S. L., & Schaie, K. W. (1999). Intellectual functioning in midlife. In S. L. Willis & J. D. Reid (Eds.), *Life in the middle: Psychological and social development in middle age* (pp. 233–247). San Diego, CA: Academic Press.

Wills, T. A., & Fegan, M. (2001). Social networks and social support. In A. Baum, T. A. Revenson, & J. E. Singer (Eds.), *Handbook of health psychology* (pp. 209–234). Mahwah, NJ: Erlbaum.

Willyard, C. (2011, January). Men: A growing minority. *gradPSYCH Magazine,* p. 40.

Wilson, G. T., Grilo, C. M., & Vitousek, K. M. (2007). Psychological treatment of eating disorders. *American Psychologist, 62,* 199–216.

Wilson, K. G., Hayes, S. C., & Gifford, E. V. (1997). Cognition in behavior therapy: Agreements and differences. *Journal of Behavior Therapy and Experimental Psychiatry, 28,* 53–63.

Wilson, R. S., & Bennett, D. A. (2003). Cognitive activity and risk of Alzheimer's disease. *Current Directions in Psychological Science, 12,* 87–91.

Wiltink, J., Michal, M., Wild, P. S., Zwiener, I., Blettner, M., Münzel, T. et al. (2013). Associations between depression and different measures of obesity (BMI, WC, WHtR, WHR). *BMC Psychiatry, 13,* 223. doi: 10.1186/1471-244X-13-223

Wingfield, A., & Kahana, M. J. (2002). The dynamics of memory retrieval in older adulthood. *Canadian Journal of Psychology, 56,* 187–199.

Winocur, G., Moscovitch, M., & Sekeres, M. J. (2013). Factors affecting graded and upgraded memory loss following hippocampal lesions. *Neurobiology of Learning and Memory, 106,* 351–364. doi: 10.1016/j.nlm.2013.10.001

Wirtz, D., Chiu, C. Y., Diener, E., & Oishi, S. (2009). What constitutes a good life? Cultural differences in the role of positive and negative affect in subjective well-being. *Journal of Personality, 77,* 1167–1196.

Wise, S. M. (2000). *Rattling the cage: Toward legal rights for animals.* Cambridge, MA: Perseus Books.

Wiseman, S., & Tulving, E. (1976). Encoding specificity: Relations between recall superiority and recognition failure. *Journal of Experimental Psychology: Human Learning and Memory, 2,* 349–361.

Witt, L. A., Kacmar, M., Carlson, D. S., & Zivnuska, S. (2002). Interactive effects of personality and organizational politics on contextual performance. *Journal of Organizational Behavior, 23,* 911–926.

Witt, S. D. (1997). Parental influence on children's socialization to gender roles. *Adolescence, 32,* 253–259.

Wittchen, H. U., Gloster, A. T., Beesdo-Baum, K., Fava, G., & Craske, M. G. (2010). Agoraphobia: A review of the diagnostic classificatory position and criteria. *Depression and Anxiety, 27,* 113–133.

Wolf, D. H., Gur, R. C., Valdez, J. N., Loughead, J., Elliott, M. A., Gur, R. E. et al. (2007). Alterations of fronto-temporal connectivity during word encoding in schizophrenia. *Psychiatry Research, 154,* 221–232.

Wolf, E. J., Miller, M. W., Reardon, A. F., Ryabchenko, K. A., Castillo, D., & Freund, R. (2012). A latent class analysis of dissociation and posttraumatic stress disorder: Evidence for a dissociative subtype. *Archives of General Psychiatry, 69,* 698–705.

Wolfe, J., Erickson, D. J., Sharkansky, R. J., King, D. W., & King, L. A. (1999). Course and predictors of posttraumatic stress disorder among Gulf War veterans: A prospective analysis. *Journal of Consulting and Clinical Psychology, 67,* 520–528.

Wolitzky, D. L. (1995). The theory and practice of traditional psychoanalytic psychotherapy. In A. S. Gurman & S. B. Messer (Eds.), *Essential psychotherapies* (pp. 12–54). New York: Guilford.

Wolpe, J. (1958). *Psychotherapy by reciprocal inhibition.* Stanford, CA: Stanford University Press.

Won, J., Mair, E. A., Bolger, W. E., & Conran, R. M. (2000). The vomeronasal organ: An objective anatomic analysis of its prevalence. *Ear, Nose, and Throat Journal, 79,* 800.

Woo, Y. S., Bahk, W. M., Jung, Y. E., Jeong, J. H., Lee, H. B., Won, S. H. et al. (2014). One-year rehospitalization rates of patients with first-episode bipolar mania receiving lithium or valproate and adjunctive atypical antipsychotics. *Psychiatry and Clinical Neurosciences, 68,* 418–424.

Wood, J. V., Heimpel, S. A., Manwell, L. A., & Whittington, E. J. (2009). This mood is familiar and I don't deserve to feel better anyway: Mechanisms underlying self-esteem differences in motivation to repair sad moods. *Journal of Personality and Social Psychology, 96,* 363–380.

Woods, S. C. (2013). Metabolic signals and food intake. Forty years of progress. *Appetite, 71,* 440–444. doi: 10.1016/j.appet.2012.08.016

Woods-Giscombé, C. L. (2010). Superwoman schema: African American women's beliefs on-stress, strength, and health. *Qualitative Health Research, 20,* 668–683.

Woollet, K., Glensman, J., & Maguire, E. A. (2008). Non-spatial expertise and hippocampal gray matter volume in humans. *Hippocampus, 18,* 981–984.

Woollett, K., & Maguire, E. A. (2012). Exploring anterograde associative memory in London taxi drivers. *Neuroreport: For Rapid Communication of Neuroscience Research, 23,* 885–888. doi:10.1097/WNR.0b013e328359317e

World Health Organization. (2004). *The World Health Report 2004: Changing history.* Annex Table 3: Burden of disease in DALYs by cause, sex, and mortality stratum in WHO regions, estimates for 2002. Geneva: Author.

World Health Organization. (2008). *The global burden of disease: 2004 update.* Geneva: Author.

Worthy, D. A., Gorlick, M. A., Pacheco, J. L., Schnyer, D. M., & Maddox, W. T. (2011). With age comes wisdom: Decision making in younger and older adults. *Psychological Science, 22,* 1375–1380.

Wright, I. C., Rabe-Hesketh,, S., Woodruff, P. W., David, A. S., Murray, R. M., & Bullmore, E. T. (2000). Meta-analysis of regional brain volumes in schizophrenia. *American Journal of Psychiatry, 157,* 16–25.

Wrightsman, L. S. (1988). *Personality development in adulthood.* Newbury Park, CA: Sage.

Wrightsman, L. S. (1994). *Adult personality development: Vol 1. Theories and concepts.* Thousand Oaks, CA: Sage.

Wu, L., & Mo, L. (2011). Re-examining the classifying advantage and basic level effect. *Acta Psychologica Sinica, 43,* 143–151.

Xiao, Y., Wang, Y., & Felleman, D. J. (2003). A spatially organized representation of colour in macaque cortical area V2. *Nature, 421,* 535–539.

Xie, J., Chen, J., & Wei, Q. (2013). Repetitive transcranial magnetic stimulation versus electroconvulsive therapy for major depression: A meta-analysis of stimulus parameter effects. *Neurological Research, 35,* 1084–1091.

Xie, T., Tong, L., McLane, M. W., Hatzidimitriou, G., Yuan, J., McCann, U. et al. (2006). Loss of serotonin transporter protein after MDMA and other ring-substituted amphetamines. *Neuropsychopharmacology, 31,* 2639–2651.

Xiong, G. L., & Doraiswamy, P. M. (2009). Does meditation enhance cognition and brain plasticity? *Annals of the New York Academy of Sciences, 1172,* 63–69.

Xiong, Y., Mahmood, A., & Chopp, M. (2010). Neurorestorative treatments for traumatic brain injury. *Discovery Medicine, 10,* 434–442.

Xu, J., & Roberts, R. E. (2010). The power of positive emotions: It's a matter of life or death: Subjective well-being and longevity over 28 years in a general population. *Healthy Psychology, 29,* 9–19.

Xu, J., Kochanek, K. D., & Tejada-Vera, B. (2009). Deaths: Preliminary data for 2007. *National Vital Statistics Report, 58,* 1–51.

Xu, L., Sun, X., Lu, J., Tang, M., & Chen, J. D. (2008). Effects of gastric electric stimulation on gastric distention responsive neurons and expressions of CCK in rodent hippocampus. *Obesity, 16,* 951–957.

Yackinous, C. A., & Guinard, J. (2002). Relation between PROP (6-n-propylthiouracil) taster status, taste anatomy and dietary intake measures for young men and women. *Appetite, 38,* 201–209.

Yalom, I. D. (1989). *Love's executioner and other tales of psychotherapy.* New York: HarperCollins.

Yalom, I. D., & Leszcz, M. (2005). *The theory and practice of group psychotherapy* (5th ed.). New York: Basic Books.

Yamagata, S., Suzuki, A., Ando, J., Ono, Y., Kijima, N., Yoshimura, K. et al. (2006). Is the genetic structure of human personality universal? A cross-cultural twin study from North America, Europe, and Asia. *Journal of Personality and Social Psychology, 90,* 987–998.

Yang, C. C., Wan, C. S., & Chiou, W. B. (2010). Dialectical thinking and creativity among young adults: A postformal operations perspective. *Psychological Reports, 106,* 79–92.

Yang, F. M., Grigorenko, A., Tommet, D., Farias, S. T., Mungas, D., Bennett, D. A. et al. (2013). AD pathology and cerebral infarctions are associated with memory and executive functioning one and five years before death. *Journal of Clinical and Experimental Neuropsychology, 35,* 24–34. doi:10.1080/13803395.2012.740001

Yang, P. Y., Ho, K. H., Chen, H. C., & Chien, M. Y. (2012). Exercise training improves sleep quality in middle-aged and older adults with sleep problems: A systematic review. *Journal of Physiotherapy, 58,* 157–163.

Yao, M. Z., Mahood, C., & Linz, D. (2010). Sexual priming, gender stereotyping, and likelihood to sexually harass: Examining the cognitive effects of playing a sexually-explicit video game. *Sex Roles, 62,* 77–88.

Yardley, L., & Kirby, S. (2006). Evaluation of booklet self-management of symptoms in Meniere disease: A randomized controlled trial. *Psychosomatic Medicine, 68,* 762–769.

Yatham, L. N., Liddle, P. F., Lam, R. W., Zis, A. P., Stoessl, A. J., Sossi, V. et al. (2010). Effect of electroconvulsive therapy on brain 5-HT(2) receptors in major depression. *British Journal of Psychiatry, 196,* 474–479.

Yau, K. W., & Hardie, R. C. (2009). Phototransduction motifs and variations. *Cell, 139,* 246–264.

Yerkes, R. M., & Dodson, J. D. (1908). The relation of strength of stimulus to rapidity of habit-formation. *Journal of Comparative Neurology and Psychology, 18,* 459–482.

Yingling, D. R., Utter, G., Vengalil, S., & Mason, B. (2002). Calcium channel blocker, nimodipine, for the treatment of bipolar disorder during pregnancy. *American Journal of Obstetrics and Gynecology, 187,* 1711–1712.

York, J. L., & Welte, J. W. (1994). Gender comparisons of alcohol consumption in alcoholic and nonalcoholic populations. *Journal of Studies on Alcohol, 55,* 743–750.

Young, A. H., McElroy, S. L., Bauer, M., Philips, N., Chang, W., Olausson, B. et al. (2010). A double-blind, placebo-controlled study of quetiapine and lithium monotherapy in adults in the acute phase of bipolar depression (EMBOLDEN I). *Journal of Clinical Psychiatry, 71,* 150–162.

Young, E., & Korszun, A. (2010). Sex, trauma, stress hormones, and depression. *Molecular Psychiatry, 15,* 23–28.

Young, J. K. (2010). Anorexia nervosa and estrogen: Current status of the hypothesis. *Neuroscience and Biobehavioral Reviews, 34,* 1195–1200. doi: 10.1016/j.neubiorev.2010.01.015

Young, N. K. (1997). Effects of alcohol and other drugs on children. *Journal of Psychoactive Drugs, 29,* 23–42.

Yu, F., Ryan, L. H., Schaie, K. W., Willis, S. L., & Kolanowski, A. (2009). Factors associated with cognition in adults: The Seattle longitudinal study. *Research in Nursing and Health, 32,* 540–550.

Yunker, G. W., & Yunker, B. D. (2002). Primal leadership (book). *Personnel Psychology, 55,* 1030–1033.

Zaalberg, R., Manstead, A. S. R., & Fischer, A. H. (2004). Relations between emotions, display rules, social motives, and facial behaviors. *Cognition and Emotion, 18,* 183–207.

Zaccaro, S. J., Mumford, M. D., Connelly, M., Marks, M., & Gilbert, J. A. (2000). Assessment of leader abilities. *Leadership Quarterly, 11,* 37–64.

Zack, E., Barr, R., Gerhardstein, P., Dickerson. K., & Meltzoff, A. N. (2009). Infant imitation from television using a novel touch screen technology. *British Journal of Developmental Psychology, 27,* 13–26.

Zadina, J. E., Hackler, L., Ge, L. J., & Kastin, A. J. (1997). A potent and selective endogeneous agonist for the u-opiate receptor. *Nature, 386,* 499–502.

Zadra, A., Desjardins, S., & Marcotte, E. (2006). Evolutionary function of dreams: A test of the threat simulation theory in recurrent dreams. *Consciousness and Cognition, 15,* 450–463.

Zahn-Waxler, C., & Robinson, J. (1995). Empathy and guilt: Early origins of feelings of responsibility. In J. P. Tangney & K. W. Fischer (Eds.), *Self-conscious emotions* (pp. 143–173). New York: Guilford Press.

Zajonc, R. B. (1965). Social facilitation. *Science, 149,* 269–274.

Zajonc, R. B. (1968). Attitudinal effects of mere exposure. *Journal of Personality and Social Psychology, 9,* 1–27.

Zajonc, R. B. (1980). Feeling and thinking: Preferences need no inferences. *American Psychologist, 35,* 151–175.

Zajonc, R. B., Adelmann, P. K., Murphy, S. T., & Neidenthal, P. M. (1987). Convergence in the physical appearance of spouse. *Motivation and Emotion, 11,* 335–346.

Zajonc, R. B., Murphy, S. T., & Inglehart, M. (1989). Feeling and facial efference: Implications of the vascular theory of emotions. *Psychological Review, 96,* 395–416.

Zanarini, M. C. (2000). Childhood experiences associated with the development of borderline personality disorder. *Psychiatric Clinics of North America, 23,* 89–101.

Zanarini, M. C., Frankenburg, F. R., Reich, D. B., & Fitzmaurice, G. (2012). Attainment and stability of sustained symptomatic remission and recovery among patients with borderline personality disorder and axis II comparison subjects: A 16-year prospective follow-up study. *American Journal of Psychiatry, 169,* 476–483.

Zanarini, M. C., Skodol, A. E., Bender, D., Dolan, R., Sanislow, C., Schaefer, E. et al. (2000). The Collaborative Longitudinal Personality Disorders Study: Reliability of Axis I and II diagnoses. *Journal of Personality Disorders, 14,* 291–299.

Zani, B. (1993). Dating and interpersonal relationships in adolescence. In S. Jackson & H. Rodriguez-Tome (Eds.), *Adolescence and its social worlds* (pp. 95–119). Hillsdale, NJ: Erlbaum.

Zeamer, C., & Fox Tree, J. E. (2013). The process of auditory distraction: Disrupted attention and impaired recall in a simulated lecture environment. *Journal of Experimental Psychology: Learning, Memory, and Cognition, 39,* 1463–1472. doi:10.1037/a0032190

Zebrowitz, L. A., White, B., & Wieneke, K. (2008). Mere exposure and racial prejudice: Exposure to other-race faces increases liking for strangers from that race. *Social Cognition, 26,* 259–275.

Zee, P. C., & Manthena, P. (2007). The brain's master circadian clock: Implications and opportunities for therapy of sleep disorders. *Sleep Medicine Reviews, 11,* 59–70.

Zeitzer, J. M., Nishino, S., & Mignot, E. (2006). The neurobiology of hypocretins (orexins), narcolepsy and related therapeutic interventions. *Trends in Pharmacological Sciences, 27,* 368–374.

Zeman, A., Britton, T., Douglas, N., Hansen, A., Hicks, J., Howard, R. et al. (2004). Narcolepsy and excessive daytime sleepiness. *British Medical Journal, 329,* 724–728.

Zhan, W., Cruickshanks, K. J., Klein, B. E., Klein, R., Huang, G.-H., Pankow, J. S. et al. (2009). Generational differences in the prevalence of hearing impairment in older adults. *American Journal of Epidemiology, 171,* 260–266.

Zhang, A. Y., & Snowden, L. R. (1999). Ethnic characteristics of mental disorders in five U.S. communities. *Cultural Diversity and Ethnic Minority Psychology, 5,* 134–146.

Zhang, B., & Wing, Y. K. (2006). Sex differences in insomnia: A meta-analysis. *Sleep, 29,* 85–93.

Ziegler, D. J., & Leslie, Y. M. (2003). A test of the ABC model underlying rational emotive behavior therapy. *Psychological Reports, 92,* 235–240.

Ziegler, D. J., & Smith, P. N. (2004). Anger and the ABC model underlying rational-emotive behavior therapy. *Psychological Reports, 93,* 1009–1014.

Zimbardo, P. G. (1972, April). Psychology of imprisonment. *Transition/Society,* pp. 4–8.

Zimmer, L., & Morgan, J. P. (1997). *Marijuana myths, marijuana fact: A review of scientific evidence.* New York: Lindesmith Center.

Zinzow, H. M., Resnick, H. S., McCauley, J. L., Amstadter, A. B., Ruggiero, K. J., & Kilpatrick, D. G. (2012). Prevalence and risk of psychiatric disorders as a function of variant rape histories: Results from a national survey of women. *Social Psychiatry and Psychiatric Epidemiology, 47,* 893–902.

Zisook, S., Rush, A. J., Haight, B. R., Clines, D. C., & Rockett, C. B. (2006). Use of bupropion in combination with serotonin reuptake inhibitors. *Biological Psychiatry, 59,* 203–210.

Zorrilla, L. T., Cannon, T. D., Kronenberg, S., Mednick, S. A., Schulsinger, F., Parnas, J. et al. (1997). Structural brain abnormalities in schizophrenia: A family study. *Biological Psychiatry, 42,* 1080–1086.

Zottoli, M. A., & Wanous, J. P. (2000). Recruitment source research: Current status and future directions. *Human Resource Management Review, 10,* 435–451.

Zuckerman, M. (1978). The search for high sensation. *Psychology Today, 11,* 38–99.

Zuckerman, M. (1994). *Behavioral expressions and biosocial bases of sensation seeking.* Cambridge: Cambridge University Press.

Zuckerman, M., & Kuhlman, D. M. (2000). Personality and risk-taking: Common biosocial factors. *Journal of Personality, 68,* 999–1029.

Zvolensky, M. J., Vujanovic, A. A., Bernstein, A., & Leyro, T. (2010). Distress tolerance: Theory, measurement, and relations to psychopathology. *Current Directions in Psychological Science, 19,* 406–410.

Name Index

Aamodt, M. G., 652, 658, 660
Abad, M. G., 143
Abar, B., 378
Abbass, A., 598
Abbott, C. C., 625
Abbott, R., 531
ABC News, 200
Abdel-Khalek, A., 470
Abkevich, V., 570
Abramowitz, J. S., 565
Abramson, L. Y., 573
Acebo, C., 135
Acevedo, B. P., 432
ACHA, 506
Achermann, P., 135
Ackerman, J. P., 160, 397
Adachi, T., 147
Adam, E. K., 384
Addington, J., 610
Addis, D. R., 296
Ader, R., 517
Aderibigbe, Y. A., 562
Adler, Alfred, 470
Administration on Aging, 388
Adolph, K. E., 361
Adolphs, R., 64
Afifi, T. O., 253, 583
Aghajanian, G. K., 165
Ahadi, S. A., 478
Aiello, J. R., 438
Ainsworth, M. D., 376
Akert, R. M., 422
Aknin, L. B., 536
Albeck, J. H., 613
Albouy, G., 299
Aldao, A., 572
Aldridge, M. A., 323
Aleman, A., 624
Alexander, G. M., 97
Allebeck, P., 578–579
Allen, L. B., 614
Allen, N. C., 578
Allen, N. J., 663
Allen, T. D., 658
Alloy, L. B., 573
Allport, G. W., 426, 427, 472–473
Allred, S., 112
Almeida, D. M., 509
Aloe, A. M., 441
Alterovitz, S. S., 431
Alves Ferreira, J. G., 260
Aly, M., 137
Amato, P. R., 397, 398
American Association of Advertising Agencies, 415
American College of Obstetricians and Gynecologists, 358
American Psychiatric Association, 143, 150, 191, 192, 193, 555, 556, 557, 563, 564, 565, 566, 567, 570, 576, 577, 581, 583, 615, 619
American Psychological Association, 4, 20, 22, 31, 34, 202, 253, 594
Amoore, J. E., 107
Amorapanth, P. X., 69
Amso, D., 364, 365
Amsterdam, J. D., 622
Anderson, B. J., 66, 74
Anderson, C., 517, 536
Anderson, C. A., 449, 450
Anderson, E. R., 567
Anderson, J. R., 283, 284, 298, 321
Anderson, N., 659
Anderson, P. L., 604
Anderson-Henley, C., 438
Andreasen, N. C., 575
Andreozzi, L., 358
Andresen, G. V., 239
Andrews-Hanna, J. R., 73
Angiulo, M. J., 563
Angold, A., 547
Anker, A. E., 441
ANRED, 191
Antoni, M. H., 522
Appiah, L., 358
Appleby, D., 32
Appley, M., 487
Arciero, P. J., 438
Arendt, J., 134
Arent, S. M., 176
Arias, J. M. C., 583
Armendariz, M. L., 421
Armfield, J. M., 561
Armitage, R., 137
Armony, J. L., 310
Arnett, J. J., 395, 400
Arnold, L. M., 571
Aron, A., 397
Aronson, E., 415, 422, 425, 429
Aronson, J., 424
Arroll, B., 620, 622
Arthur, J. B., 663
Arthur, W., Jr., 653
Asch, Solomon, 435
Ashby, F. G., 313
Ashcan, K., 625
Ashtari, M., 386
Ashwin, C., 64
Ashworth, S. D., 656
Asnis, G. M., 619
Associated Press, 450
Assor, A., 487
Astin, J. A., 522, 523
Astington, J. W., 369
Atas, A., 471
Atkinson, J. L. D., 62
Atkinson, J. W., 174, 177
Atkinson, R. C., 271
Aucoin, D., 382
Augustine, G. J., 56
Augustus-Horvath, C. L., 185
Aussprung, J., 506
Auyeung, B., 381
Avalos, L. C., 185
Avolio, B. J., 660
Azar, B., 105
Azdia, T., 415
Azevedo, F. A., 46

Bach, J. M., 531
Bachman, J. G., 159, 396
Back, K., 430
Bacue, A., 383
Baddeley, A. D., 279, 281, 282, 293
Badea, C., 426
Baghdoyan, H. A., 63
Bagiella, E., 523
Bagshaw, S. M., Jr., 229
Bahk, C., 320
Bahrick, H. P., 292
Bailey, J. M., 204
Baillargeon, R., 367
Bailystok, E., 324
Bair, J. P., 523
Bajbouj, M., 625
Baker, T. B., 151, 605, 610, 614
Balaswamy, S., 401
Baldessarini, R. J., 623
Ball, G. F., 54
Ball, T. M., 308
Balsam, K. F., 203
Baltes, P. B., 388
Balthazart, J., 54
Balzer, W. K., 662
Bandura, A., 252, 259, 260, 380, 381, 449, 450, 482–483
Banfield, M., 617
Bangasser, D. A., 234
Banich, M. T., 69
Banning, K., 506
Banthia, R., 523
Baraas, R. C., 95
Barakat, M., 137
Baratta, J. E., 656
Barbaree, H. E., 156
Barbe, F., 142
Barbee, J. G., 157
Barch, D. M., 580
Bardone, A. M., 191
Barger, L. K., 136
Bargh, J. A., 471
Bar-Haim, Y., 364
Barker, J., 147
Barker, V., 531
Barlow, D. H., 513, 561, 574, 619, 620, 622
Barnard, S. M., 528
Barnes, A., 576
Barnes, J., 147
Baron, R. A., 447
Barrera, T. L., 612
Barres, B. A., 46, 48
Barrett, M., 26
Barsalou, L. W., 310
Barth, K. S., 605
Bartholow, B. D., 450
Bartlett, F. C., 284
Bartoshuk, L. M., 103, 105
Baskin, D. G., 182
Bass, B. M., 659
Bassuk, S. S., 535
Batabyal, A. A., 397
Bates, B. L., 147
Batey, M., 316
Batsell, W. R., Jr., 239
Batson, C., 454
Batty, G. D., 526
Bauby, Jean-Dominique, 42
Bauer, M. A., 536
Baumann, A. E., 552
Baumeister, R. F., 196, 433
Baumrind, D., 22, 377
Beach, F. A., 203
Beardsley, T., 186
Beatty, W. W., 381
Beauchaine, T. P., 203
Beauchamp, G. K., 103, 105
Beauducel, A., 477
Beauregard, M., 615
Beck, A. T., 561, 572, 609
Beck, D. M., 119
Beck, J. G., 604
Beem, E. E., 517
Behme, C., 322
Békésy, Georg von, 101
Bell, A. R., 204
Bell, B. S., 658
Bell, J. F., 132
Bell, T., 252
Belsky, J., 399
Bem, Daryl, 88
Bem, Sandra, 380
Benabid, A. L., 625
Bender, D. S., 552
Bender, E., 604
Benham, G., 146
Benjamin, A. J., 450
Benjamin, L. T., Jr., 31
Bennett, D. A., 392
Bennett, M. P., 524
Bennett, W. I., 99
Benoit, S. C., 182
Benson, J. B., 370
Ben-Zeev, T., 423
Bergen, A. E., 614
Berger, A. M., 136
Berger-Gross, P., 607
Berglund, P. A., 555, 556, 567, 570
Berk, L. E., 371
Berkowitz, L., 449
Berlau, D. J., 343
Bernal, G., 616
Bernschneider-Reif, S., 161
Bernstein, I. L., 239
Bernstein, K. S., 509
Berntsen, D., 561
Berry, A. K., 143
Berry, C. J., 270
Berry, M. S., 250
Berscheid, E., 432
Bertolissi, S., 432
Berwick, R. C., 322
Besken, M., 288
Beuving, L. J., 448
Bezawada, R., 105
Bezchlibnyk-Butler, K. Z., 161
Bhaskara, R. M., 89
Binder, J., 427
Binet, A., 329
Bing, V., 381
Binik, Y. M., 198
Birch, L. L., 239
Birmingham, W., 397
Birnbaum, I. M., 293
Bischofberger, J., 387
Biss, R. K., 293
Bissell, K., 190
Biswas, J., 533
Biswas-Diener, R., 536
Bizman, A., 441
Bjork, R. A., 145, 147
Bjorness, T. E., 131
Black, A. H., 234
Black, D. W., 575, 583
Black, L. S., 364
Black, M. M., 160
Blackwell, E., 515
Blackwell, L. V., 422
Blake, R., 117
Blanchard, B., 46
Blanchard, R., 204
Blane, H. T., 156
Blase, S. L., 617
Blazer, D. G., 573
Blehar, M. C., 573
Blehm, C., 531
Bleidorn, W., 480
Bleiker, E. M., 527
Blevins, J. E., 182
Blincoe, L., 157
Bloch, R. M., 562
Block, J. A., 481
Blomstedt, P., 625
Bloom, F., 48
Bloom, J. W., 617
Blum, C. M., 522
Boals, A., 189
Boden, M., 309
Boehmer, L. N., 141
Boeri, M. W., 161
Bogacki, D. F., 147
Bogels, S. M., 556
Bohnen, N. I., 73
Boiger, M., 212
Boisjoli, J. A., 255, 607
Bojanowski, V., 108
Bolles, R. C., 234
Bollman, S. R., 397
Bolton, M., 532
Bonanno, G. A., 398, 508, 528
Bond, R., 436
Bonne, O., 66
Bonte, M., 120
Booth, A., 398
Booth-Kewley, S., 526
Bor, D., 274
Borden, V. M., 32
Borges, G., 568, 569
Borman, W. C., 664
Born, J., 130, 131, 137, 138
Born, L., 573–574
Bornet, F. R., 182
Bornovalova, M. A., 583
Bornstein, M. H., 97, 454
Borst, G., 308
Bossio, L. M., 524
Bouchard, T. J., 356, 479
Bovin, M. J., 513
Bowden, C. L., 623
Bowen, R., 390
Bower, B., 295
Bower, J. E., 508
Bower, J. F., 517
Bower, T. G. R., 323
Bowlby, J., 403
Boyatzis, R. E., 336
Boyce, C. J., 536
Boycott, B. B., 92
Boysen, G. A., 564
Brackett, M. A., 336
Bradbury, T. N., 397
Bradley, D. B., 567
Bradley, R., 614, 615
Bradley, R. H., 378
Bradshaw, J. W. S., 326
Brainerd, C. J., 294
Branch, M. N., 250
Brannon, L., 502
Brant, A. M., 387
Bratberg, G. H., 385
Braungart, J. M., 478
Braungart-Rieker, J. M., 377
Brehm, S. S., 430, 447
Bremner, A. J., 367
Brende, J. O., 508
Breslau, J., 554, 555, 556, 567
Bresnahan, M., 576
Brewer, M. B., 426, 430
Brewer, R. D., 154
Bridges, M. W., 527
Brief, D. J., 617
Briley, D. A., 356
Briñol, P., 416, 417
Britt, G. C., 157, 161
Broberg, A. G., 612
Broberg, D. J., 239
Brochu, P. M., 190
Brocke, B., 477
Brockopp, D. Y., 523
Brody, A. L., 614
Brody, M. J., 193
Bronstad, P. M., 432
Brookoff, D., 156
Brooks-Gunn, J., 385
Brotchie, H. L., 574
Brotto, L. A., 196
Brown, A. D., 209
Brown, A. S., 580

Brown, B. B., 396
Brown, B. M., 245
Brown, J. A., 275
Brown, J. D., 421
Brown, R., 295
Brown, R. T., 332
Brown, S. L., 397, 522
Brown, T. A., 552
Browne, A., 574
Brownell, K., 188
Browning, J. R., 430
Brozovich, F., 561
Brueckner, L., 367
Bruffaerts, R., 569
Brugman, T., 522
Bryant, P. E., 367
Bryant, S. G., 622
Bryman, A. S., 659
Brzezinski, A., 134
Buckingham-Howes, S., 160
Buckley, K. W., 26
Bucur, B., 391
Budhani, S., 342
Buehler, R., 525
Buehner, R., 282
Bueno-Nava, A., 55
Bulanda, J. R., 397
Bullock, B., 571
Bullock, W. A., 477
Bumpass, L. L., 396
Burdakov, D., 182, 183
Burgard, S. A., 143
Burge, S. W., 381
Burger, J. M., 442, 444, 445, 446–447, 487
Burke, T. M., 134
Burmeister, M., 479
Burnley, M. C. E., 146
Burt, C. D. B., 285
Burton, M., 401
Bush, S. I., 270
Bushman, B. J., 445, 449, 523
Buss, D. M., 24, 479
Bussey, K., 380, 381
Butler, L. D., 564
Butow, P. N., 527
Butt, M., 142
Butts, K., 571
Butts, S. F., 384
Byrd-Craven, J., 574
Byrne, D., 430
Byrne, M., 578–579

Cacioppo, J. T., 388, 415, 416, 436, 522, 523
Caffrey, J., 181
Cahill, S., 561
Cain, A. S., 191
Cain, W. S., 106
Calabrese, J. R., 623
Calamari, J. E., 557
Caldera, Y. M., 378
Calderoni, M. E., 558
Caldwell, J. A., 136
Calear, A. L., 617
Calvert, H., 532
Calvillo, D. P., 317
Calvin, J. E., III, 189
Calvin, J. E., Jr., 189
Campbell, D. T., 18, 426, 430
Campbell, K. L., 293
Campbell, R., 574
Campbell, S. S., 132
Campione-Barr, N., 396
Campos, B., 11
Campos-Rodriguez, F., 142
Canino, G. J., 151, 156
Cannon, D. S., 605
Cannon, T. D., 579
Cannon, W. B., 206
Canova, A., 182
Cantania, A. C., 250
Cantor, N., 396
Canuso, C. M., 576
Cardena, E., 146
Cardno, A. G., 578
Cardozo, B. L., 558
Carducci, B. J., 480
Carey, B., 288
Carey, G., 478
Carlbring, P., 617
Carlisle, N. B., 275
Carlson, P. J., 571
Carlson, W., 574
Carlston, D. E., 415, 421
Carney, C. E., 132
Carosella, G. M., 146
Carpenter, J. C., 88
Carrington, P., 524
Carroll, K. M., 617
Carskadon, M. A., 135
Carter, K. L., 378
Carter, R. C., 358
Carter, R. S., 381
Cartwright, R. D., 139
Caruso, D., 336
Carver, C. S., 454, 517, 524, 528, 570
Casey, B. J., 386, 390
Caspi, A., 479
Casswell, S., 157
Castel, A. D., 279
Castelnuovo, G., 617
Castillo-Vales, V., 328
Castro, R. J., 161
Cates, W., Jr., 533
Cattell, N. R., 322
Cattell, Raymond, 473
Caudle, K., 390
Cavanagh, K., 617
Ceci, S. J., 294
Censor, N., 299
Centers for Disease Control and Prevention (CDC), 140, 159, 288, 530, 532, 533, 558
Cermak, L. S., 288
Cernoch, J., 365
Chaiken, S., 416
Chakos, M. H., 620
Chambers, D., 309
Chambers, L. C., 104
Chambless, D. L., 614, 615
Chamorro-Premuzic, T., 343
Champagne, F. A., 356
Chan, W., 143
Chand, P. K., 562
Chandler, C., 161
Chandra, A., 398
Chandrashekar, J., 104
Chandrashekara, S., 517
Chang, I. J., 253
Chaput, J. P., 183
Charles, S. T., 508–509
Charney, D. S., 558
Chatterjee, A., 69
Chavajay, P., 390
Chaynes, K., 552
Cheah, C. S., 378
Chen, E., 510, 517
Chen, J., 624
Chen, W. W., 519
Chen, Y. L., 142
Cherry, K. E., 283
Chess, S., 375, 378
Chessick, C. A., 619
Cheung, F. M., 422
Cheung, T. C., 54
Chiang, A. A., 142
Chiapetta, L., 569, 583
Chida, Y., 536
Childress, J. E., 66
Childs, L. A., 229
Chiou, W. B., 391
Chipuer, H. M., 340
Chiu, C., 527
Chiu, W. T., 555, 557, 565, 567, 570
Cho, J. R., 141
Choi, I., 420
Choi, J. S., 560
Chollar, S., 138
Chomsky, N., 322
Chopp, M., 361
Chory-Assad, R. M., 422, 450
Chou, R., 516
Chou, S. P., 156
Choy, Y., 603
Chrisman, S. P., 288
Christian, M. S., 438
Christie, W., 524
Chung, R. H., 378
Church, R. M., 234
Cialdini, R. B., 426, 441, 442
Ciao, A., 190
Cin, S. D., 530
Cinnirella, M., 436
Cipriani, A., 620, 623
Citirik, M., 95
Clark, D. A., 561
Clark, G. E., 398
Clark, J. K., 416, 417
Clark, Kenneth, 31
Clark, L. A., 552
Clark, M. S., 397, 432
Clark, Mamie Phipps, 31
Clark, P. A., 384
Clark, R. E., 651
Clarke, A. C., 430
Clarke, T. K., 155
Clay, S. L., 6
Clum, G. A., 617
CNN, 202
Cobb, H. C., 616
Coccaro, E. F., 448
Cochran, S. V., 575
Cocude, M., 308
Coffer, C. N., 487
Coffey, V. G., 189
Cogswell, C., 192
Cohen, C., 532
Cohen, C. I., 577
Cohen, J. L., 518
Cohen, L. G., 299
Cohen, M. X., 477
Cohen, N. J., 287
Cohen, P., 395
Cohen, R., 580
Cohen, S., 510, 515, 517, 522
Cohen, S. G., 659
Colado, M. I., 161
Colbert-White, E. N., 327
Colcombe, S., 392
Coleman, S. R., 234
Colley, A., 285
Collier, G., 248
Collins, A., 535
Collins, A. M., 310
Collins, M. W., 288
Collins, P. F., 477
Collins, W. A., 377, 396
Coltrane, S., 398
Combs, D. R., 576
Compas, B. E., 517
Compton, W. M., 561
Conklin, H. M., 579
Connelly, W. M., 66
Conrad, M. A., 656
Conway, B. R., 95, 96, 117, 285
Conway, M., 285
Conway, M. A., 131
Cook, C. A., 383
Cook, G., 360
Cook, J. L., 360
Cook, T. D., 18
Cooke, R., 414
Cools, J., 189
Coons, P. M., 563
Cooper, S. L., 97
Cooper, Z. D., 163
Copeland, W. E., 554
Copen, C. E., 396
Coppola, M., 323
Coren, S., 109, 119
Corey, G., 604
Corkin, S., 287
Corpus, J. H., 178
Corra, M., 397
Corrada, M. M., 343
Correll, C. U., 620
Corrigan, P., 523
Cortesi, F., 132
Cortina, M., 598
Corwyn, R. F., 378
Cosmides, L., 321
Costa, P. T., 477–478, 479, 480
Costa-Pinto, F. A., 518
Costello, E. J., 547
Cote, K. A., 131, 141
Coupe, P., 309
Cousins, D. A., 571
Coussons-Read, M., 359
Coutinho-Budd, J., 46
Covington, M. A., 327
Cowan, C. P., 399
Cowan, P. A., 399
Cox, W. M., 178
Crabbe, J. C., 154
Craik, Fergus, 276, 277
Crandall, C. S., 189, 435, 506, 507
Crane, M., 380
Cranny, C. J., 662
Crano, W. D., 441
Crapo, R. H., 139
Craske, M. G., 561
Crawford, F. C., 479
Creamer, M., 558
Crews, F., 471
Crichlow, S., 439
Crick, F., 138
Crits-Christoph, P., 614
Crockett, M. J., 448
Crockford, D., 163
Crombag, H. S., 151
Crone, E. A., 386
Crosby, R., 532
Cross, E. S., 117
Cross, P. A., 146
Crosscope-Happel, C. L., 192
Crosswell, A. D., 517
Crowell, A., 390
Crowley, A. E., 416
Crowley, S. J., 135
Croxford, J. L., 163
Croy, I., 108
Crum, N., 533
Crystal, D. S., 436
Csernansky, J. G., 580
Csikszentmihalyi, M., 28
Cui, M., 399
Cukor, J., 558
Cunha, C., 278
Cunitz, A. R., 279
Curhan, J. R., 209
Curry, K., 159
Cutrona, C. E., 573

Dabbs, J. M., Jr., 448
Dalal, R. S., 664
Dalege, J., 425
Dalen, K., 358
Dalman, C., 578–579
Damak, S., 103
Damasio, A. R., 64
Damasio, H., 71
Damjanovic, A. K., 517
Damm, J., 625
Damon, W., 373
Dang-Vu, T. T., 137
Danhauer, J. L., 99
Danielsdottir, S., 190
D'Anna, L. H., 509
Danner, F., 532
Dannlowski, U., 571
Darley, John, 452–453, 454
Darowish, M., 531
Darwin, Charles, 174, 338
Dasen, P. R., 370
Dasgupta, A. M., 146
Dauenheimer, D., 423
D'Augelli, A. R., 203
Davey, M. A., 454
David, A. S., 562
David, D., 608, 610
Davidson, J. R. T., 508
Davidson, R. J., 212
Davidson-Katz, K., 524
Davies, H., 193
Davies, I. R. L., 328
Davis, D., 294
Davis, D. D., 422
Davis, K. C., 154
Davis, M., 227
Davis, O. S., 356
Davis, Penelope, 285
Davis-Coehlo, B., 190
Davis-Coelho, Kristen, 190
Day, R., 658
Day, R. H., 24
Dayan, E., 299
De, S., 142
Deacon, S. H., 322
Deak, G. O., 369
Deak, T., 572
Deakin, J. F., 579
DeAngelis, T., 190
Deary, I. J., 526
Deaux, K., 431
De Benedittis, G., 516
De Beni, R., 205
Debner, J. A., 293
DeBoeck, P., 313
DeBoer, D. D., 398
DeBuse, C. J., 522
de Carvalho, M. R., 604
DeCasper, A. J., 364
de Castro, J. M., 132, 181
Deci, E. L., 177, 487
de Fonseca, F., 163
Degner, J., 425
Degroot, A. B., 56
DeLacoste-Utamsing, C., 69
Delanty, N., 130, 131, 535
De Leersnyder, J., 212
Delgado, M. R., 386
De Lisi, R., 380
Dellande, S., 440
DeLoache, J., 367
Demany, L., 272
De May, J., 452
Dement, W., 137, 138
Dement, W. C., 132
Demers, L. B., 260
Demeter, G., 131
Denis, M., 308
DePalma, M., 454
Department of Housing and Urban Development, 421–422
de Poll, N. V., 448
Depue, R. A., 477
De Raedt, R., 572
Derringer, J., 474
Derubeis, R. J., 616
de Schonen, S., 364
Desjardins, S., 140
Desrochers, S., 227
Desseilles, M., 138
de Tommaso, M., 228
Deutsch, F. M., 399
Deutsch, J. A., 181
DeValois, K. K., 96
DeValois, R. L., 96
Devinsky, O., 64
Devlin, M., 193
DeVore, C. J., 664
DeWall, C. N., 523
Dewaraja, R., 508
DeYoung, C. G., 480
Dhanda, R., 527
Dhont, K., 425
Diamond, A., 365
Díaz-Mataix, L., 234
Dichter, G. S., 615
Dick, D. M., 156
Dickens, W. T., 340
Dickson, N., 201
Diefenbach, K. S., 63
Diekelmann, S., 138
Diener, C., 528
Diener, E., 480, 487, 522, 536
Dies, R. R., 611
Difede, J., 604
DiGiuseppe, R., 574
Digman, J. M., 481
DiLalla, D. L., 478
Dillworth, T. M., 610
Di lorio, C. R., 161
Dimidjian, S., 616
Dimitrov, B., 299
Dindia, K., 382
Dindo, L., 583
Dinges, D. F., 131
Dingfelder, S. F., 114
Dion, K. K., 432
DiPatrizio, N. V., 188
Dishion, T. J., 583
Dixon, J. F., 622
Dixon, M. R., 249
Do, D. P., 144

Do, J., 55
Dobbs, D., 571
Dodge, G., 660
Dodge, K. L., 518
Dodson, John, 176, 423
Dohrenwend, B. P., 558
Dolan, S. L., 614
Dolbier, C. L., 528
Dollard, J., 451
Domjan, M., 22
Donaldson, G., 334
Donnellan, M. B., 399
Donovan, D. M., 613
Doraiswamy, P. M., 524
Doty, R. L., 107
Douglas, J. M., 97
Douthitt, E. A., 438
Dovidio, John, 423
Dovis, S., 281
Dowling, J. E., 92
Downar, J., 624
Doyère, V., 234
Dozois, D. J., 615
Draganova, R., 365
Draguns, J. G., 616
Draine, S. C., 471
Drath, W. H., 659
Drea, C. M., 381
Drevets, W. C., 571
Driessen, E., 598
Driscoll, K. A., 574
Driver, H. S., 137
Druckman, D., 145, 147
Drummond, P., 616
D'Souza, D. C., 163
Duan, X., 212
Duchaine, B., 73
Ducharme, M. B., 477
Duckitt, J., 424
Duckworth, T. S., 111
Duffy, A., 326
Duke, A. A., 448
Duncan, L. E., 394
Dunkel Schetter, C., 509
Dunn, E., 574
Dunn, E. W., 536
Dunne, M., 204
Durand, V. M., 622
Duric, V., 570
Durmer, J. S., 131
Durso, G. O., 87
Durso, L. E., 509
Durston, S., 386
Dust, M. C., 519
Dweck, C., 483
Dweck, C. S., 527
Dye, L., 535
Dziurowicz-Kozlowska, A. H., 186

Eagly, A. H., 356, 416
Eaton, A. H., 448
Eaton, N., 583
Ebbinghaus, H., 23, 276, 292
Ebmeier, K. P., 570
Ebstein, R. P., 479
Eby, L. T., 658
Echeburúa, E., 193
Edelman, B., 186
Edenberg, H. J., 156
Edmonds, G. W., 479
Edmondson, D., 561
Edwards, A. C., 401
Edwards, J. N., 400
Egan, S. J., 193
Egger, H., 547
Egger, M. D., 227
Egner, T., 117, 146
Ehde, D. M., 610
Ehrenreich, H., 605
Eich, J. E., 293
Einarsson, C., 382
Eisen, S. V., 420
Eisenberger, N. I., 522
Eiser, A. S., 139
Ekman, P., 207, 211, 212
El-Alayli, A., 423
Elen, M., 414
Elfenbein, H. A., 212
Elifson, K. W., 161
El Khoury, D., 181
Elkind, D., 389, 390
Ellason, J. W., 563
Ellenbogen, J. M., 131
Elliott, C. E., 435
Ellis, A., 487, 607, 608
Ellis, A. P., 438
El-Matary, A., 196
Elmore, D. K., 181
Elshout, J., 316
Emery, C. F., 392
End, Christian, 275
Endrighi, R., 524
Engels, R. C., 396
Engstrom, R., 334
Enns, J. T., 109
Epel, E., 508
Epley, N., 87
Epping-Jordan, M. P., 159
Epstein, A. N., 183
Epstein, Robert, 316–317
Epstein, S., 481
Equal Employment Opportunity Commission, 654, 657
Erblich, J., 530
Erez, A., 664
Ergaz, Z., 358
Erikson, Erik, 378, 393
Erlacher, D., 139
Eroglu, C., 46, 48
Errington, A. C., 66
Ervin, F. R., 237
Erwin, E., 471
Escobar, J. I., 576
Escobar, M., 604
ESEMed/MHEDEA, 556
Espy, K. A., 359
Essed, N. H., 104
Esses, V. M., 426
Etkin, A., 560
Ettlinger, M., 328
Evans, A. T., 416, 417
Evans, D. E., 478
Evans, P. J., 531
Eyberg, S. M., 378
Eynon, R., 21
Eysenck, H. J., 317, 473, 476
Eysenck, S. B. G., 476

Fabrigar, L. R., 417
Fadiman, James, 178
Fagundes, C. P., 510, 516, 522
Fairchild, G., 583
Falkenburg, K., 664
Falkum, E., 552
Fan, J., 146
Fan, W., 11
Fan, Y., 524
Farley, F., 390
Fatemi, S. H., 580
Fattore, L., 164
Faust, M., 69
Fazio, N. M., 528
Federal Bureau of Investigation (FBI), 203, 421–422, 447, 448
Federmeier, K. D., 364
Feeley, T., 441
Feeney, E., 105
Fein, S., 447
Feinberg, M. E., 583
Feinberg, S. D., 149
Feingold, A., 432
Feinstein, J. S., 64
Feist, J., 502
Felder, J. N., 615
Feldman, H., 399
Feldman, N. H., 323
Felker, B., 558
Felleman, D. J., 117
Felmingham, K., 615
Fennema, E., 341
Ferguson, C. P., 193
Ferguson, S., 522
Ferlie, E., 663
Fernald, Anne, 260
Ferrante, J., 397
Ferreira, S. E., 158
Ferrucci, R., 63
Festinger, L., 414, 415, 430
Feteha, H., 196
Fichna, J., 56
Field, A. P., 560
Field, T. M., 365
Fields, D. R., 107
Fiellin, D. A., 158
Fifer, W. P., 364
Figge, M., 441
Figner, B., 390
Fillmore, K. M., 151
Finch, C. E., 388
Finkel, D., 392
Finkel, K. J., 142
Finkelstein, D. M., 524
Finkelstein, M. A., 93
Finn, R., 239, 297
Fiorentino, L., 144
Fischer, A. H., 205
Fischer, G. W., 426
Fishbein, H. D., 382
Fishbein, W., 137
Fisher, B. S., 13
Fisher, C. A., 157
Fisher, H., 432
Fisher, H. E., 196
Fisher, S., 622
Fiske, M., 480
Fiske, S. T., 418, 422
Fitzgerald, P. B., 624
Fitzpatrick, D., 93
Flanagin, A. J., 657
Fleckenstein, A. E., 162
Fleeson, W., 481
Fletcher, C., 660
Flieller, A., 390
Flor-Henry, P., 69
Flynn, J. R., 340
Foa, E. B., 558, 603
Fogel, S. M., 131, 137
Fokkema, T., 203
Foland-Ross, L. C., 571, 573
Foley, H. J., 93, 100, 101, 105, 107
Folkman, S., 514, 518, 519
Folmer, R. L., 99
Folsom, T. D., 580
Food and Drug Administration Public Health Advisory, 622
Foote, B., 563, 569
Ford, C. S., 203
Foroud, T., 156
Forsyth, J. P., 561
Fossum, I. N., 141
Foster, J. B., 430
Fourment, C., 430
Fournier, J. C., 622
Fowler, J., 528
Fowles, D. C., 583
Fox, E., 561
Fox Tree, J. E., 290
Foy, B. D., 161
Fragaszy, D. M., 327
Frager, Robert D., 178
Fraley, R. C., 378
Francis, D. J., 359
Francis, E. L., 573
Frank, D. A., 359
Frank, M. C., 364
Frankenberger, K. D., 390
Franks, S., 181
Fraser, S. C., 441
Fratta, W., 164
Frawley, P. J., 239
Freedman, J. L., 441
Freeman, M. R., 46
Freire, R. C., 604
Fremouw, W. J., 189
Fresco, D. M., 573
Freud, A., 466
Freud, S., 139, 294, 464, 467, 572, 597
Freudenmann, R. W., 161
Frewen, P. A., 615
Friedland, G. H., 158
Friedman, C. K., 380
Friedman, E. M., 131, 535
Friedman, H. S., 526
Friedman, M., 187
Friedman, M. J., 526, 561
Frielingsdorf, H., 298
Friesen, C. A., 481
Friesen, W. V., 207, 211
Frijda, N., 448
Frings, M., 227
Friston, K. J., 117
Froh, J., 574
Frost, R. O., 557
Fry, C., 161
Fry, J., 21
Fry, R., 400
Fryling, M. J., 238
Fu, C. H., 571
Fu, Y., 477
Fuchs, D. L., 563
Fuller-Rowell, T. E., 509
Fullerton, C. S., 558
Fulmer, C. A., 486
Fumal, A., 522
Furnham, A., 316, 342, 343, 383
Furumoto, L., 30
Fushiki, T., 56
Fyer, A. J., 603

Gabrieli, J. J. D., 210
Gael, S. A., 653
Gaertner, Samuel, 423
Gais, S., 130
Galea, S., 508
Galensky, T. L., 246
Gallagher, A. M., 380
Gallagher, K. C., 378
Gallerani, M., 158
Galli, A., 160
Galliano, G., 341
Gallo, L. C., 397–398
Galvan, A., 386
Ganea, P. A., 367
Gangestad, S. W., 196
Gansberg, M., 452
Gant, L. M., 531
Gao, J. H., 179
Garaulet, M., 187
Garbarino, J., 451
Garcia, J., 236, 237
Gardiner, H. W., 388
Gardner, H., 333, 334, 335, 337, 340
Garlick, D., 360, 361
Garltlehner, G., 622
Garnock-Jones, K. P., 622
Garver-Apgar, C. E., 196
Gasbarri, A., 54
Gaval-Cruz, M., 239
Gawin, F. H., 160
Gaynes, B. N., 624, 625
Gazzaniga, Michael, 70
Ge, X., 385
Geary, N., 182
Gedo, J. E., 471
Geer, J. H., 270
Gelade, G., 316
Gelfand, M. M., 196
Gelfand, S. A., 98
Gelman, S. A., 382
Gelstein, Shani, 107–108
Geraerts, E., 148
Gerardi, M., 604
Gerber, W.-D., 228
Gergen, K. J., 425
Gergen, M. M., 425
Gerken, L., 365
German, C. L., 162
Germine, L. T., 73
Gernsbacher, M. A., 283
Gershoff, Elizabeth, 253
Gervai, J., 382
Geschwind, N., 68
Gheysen, F., 299
Ghosh, D., 479
Giancola, P. R., 154
Giannotti, F., 132
Gibb, B. E., 573
Gibbons, C. J., 610
Gibbons, L. E., 281
Gibbons, M. B., 616
Gibbs, W. W., 183
Gibson, Eleanor, 364
Giedd, J. N., 386
Gilbert, D. G., 517
Gilbertson, M. W., 66
Gildea, K. M., 513
Gillam, B., 119
Gillanders, D., 572
Gillespie, C. F., 571
Gilligan, Carol, 373–374
Gilliland, K., 477
Gillund, G., 291
Girandola, F., 441
Girdler, S. S., 516
Giret, N., 327
Girgis, Z. M., 446–447
Gitelson, I. B., 400
Givens, B., 154
Gladwell, M., 481
Glanzer, M., 279
Glaser, R., 516, 517
Gleason, M. E., 484
Glenberg, A. M., 276, 277
Glensman, J., 65, 298
Glisky, M. L., 563
Goddard, A. W., 558, 570
Godden, D. R., 293
Goeders, N. E., 151
Gold, M. S., 165
Goldberg, J. F., 623
Goldberg, L. R., 479–480
Goldman, R., 416
Goldsmith, B., 202
Goldstein, M. A., 623
Goleman, D., 130, 336, 660
Gonzalez, A., 182
Gonzalez, H. M., 567
Good, J. J., 423
Goodie, J., 191
Goodwin, F. K., 623
Goodwin, P. Y., 398
Gorchoff, S. M., 400
Gordon, E. F., 501, 599, 613
Gordon, S., 531
Gorman, J. M., 573
Gormezano, I., 234
Gosling, S. D., 11
Gotlib, I. H., 571, 572
Gottesman, Irving, 578, 579
Gottlieb, G., 356
Gottlieb, J., 454
Gottman, J., 397
Gotts, S. J., 68
Gottschling, J., 479
Gouin, K., 359
Gourevitch, M. N., 158
Graber, J. A., 385
Grace, A. A., 579
Grace, R. C., 247
Graesch, A. P., 11
Graf, P., 270
Graffin, N. F., 145
Graham, K. S., 286
Graham, R., 64
Granstrom, K., 382
Grant, B. F., 555, 581
Grant, J. E., 191
Grasha, A. F., 475
Grayson, C., 572
Green, A. R., 161
Green, B., 436
Green, C., 276
Green, J. G., 561, 572, 573
Green, J. P., 146, 147
Greenberg, A., 432
Greenberg, B. D., 625–626
Greenberg, L., 613
Greenberg, L. S., 599, 601
Greenfield, P., 333
Greenhaus, J. H., 658
Greenlees, I., 147
Greenwald, A. G., 471
Greenwood, S. J., 74
Greer, G. R., 161
Gregg, R. A., 162
Grieger, T. A., 558
Griest, S. E., 99
Griffey, J. F., 432
Griffin, D., 525
Griffin, D. W., 397
Griffiths, K. M., 617
Griffiths, R. R., 158
Grigorenko, E. L., 340

Grijalvo, J., 193
Grilo, C. M., 191
Grinspoon, L., 163
Grivetti, L. E., 104
Groothuis, T. G., 448
Gropalis, M., 565
Gross, J. J., 210, 520
Grossman, A. H., 203
Grossman, L. S., 524, 576
Grossman, M., 181
Grossman, R. P., 412
Grossmann, I., 391
Grover, S., 552
Gruen, R. J., 506
Grundy, E., 397
Grusec, J. E., 260
Gruzelier, J., 146
Grysman, A., 285, 393
Gugger, J. J., 138
Guilford, J. P., 333
Guilleminault, C., 143
Guinard, J., 105
Guisinger, S., 193
Gündel, H., 228
Gunter, B., 383
Gurman, A. S., 612, 613
Gustavson, C. R., 237
Guterman, N. B., 451
Gygax, L., 204

Ha, T., 396
Haase, R. F., 260
Haber, D., 388
Hackett, R. D., 664
Hackman, J. R., 662
Haddad, R. S., 619
Hadjikhani, N., 364
Haefner, R., 656
Hagenauer, M. H., 135
Haidt, J., 373
Haie, L., 144
Haith, M. M., 370
Hakuta, K., 324
Halaby, A., 619
Halim, M. L., 380
Hall, D. T., 179
Hallett, M., 299, 396
Halloway, R. L., 69
Halperin, E., 520
Halpern, D. F., 341, 342, 382, 422
Halpern, J. H., 165
Halverson, C. F., 380
Halvorsen, R., 524
Hamani, C., 571, 625
Hamann, S., 212, 558
Hamel, R., 316
Hamer, D., 479
Hamer, M., 524
Hamilton, C. E., 377
Hamilton, J. P., 571
Hamlin, J. K., 373
Hamlin, P. H., 248
Hammen, C., 573
Hammersmith, S. K., 204
Hampson, S. E., 479–480
Haney, M., 163
Hanisch, K. A., 661, 662, 664
Hanna, G. H., 560
Hanna, R., 431
Hanson, G., 163
Hanson, G. R., 162
Hansson, K., 397
Harden, K. P., 356
Hardie, R. C., 93
Harding, G. E., 234
Hargis, M., 656
Harkins, S. G., 438
Harlow, H. F., 375
Harold, G. T., 583
Harris, A., 359
Harris, J. D., 227
Harris, R. A., 154
Harrop, A., 382
Harrow, M., 576
Hart, B. M., 31
Hartley, A., 245
Hartmann, E., 143
Hartmann, U., 471
Hasegawa, T., 571
Hasher, L., 293
Hashtroudi, S., 297
Hasin, D., 552
Hasselmo, M. E., 54
Hassett, J. M., 381
Hastings, E. C., 15
Hataira, P., 147
Hatcher, R., 532
Hatfield, G., 112
Hatzenbuehler, M. L., 509
Hatzigeorgiadis, A., 371
Haus, E., 136
Hausner, H., 105
Havermans, R. C., 237
Hawco, C., 310
Hawkley, L. C., 522, 523
Hawley, D. F., 66
Hawley, J. A., 189
Haworth, C. M., 356
Hay, J. F., 293
Hayden, E. P., 479, 570
Hayes, A., 616
Hayes, E. R., 530
Hayes, J. R., 314
Hays, H., 190
Hays, N. P., 14
Hayward, M. D., 56
Hazuda, H. P., 527
Hebb, D. O., 176
Hedden, T., 293
Heider, F., 414, 418, 430
Heidkamp, D., 580
Heilman, M. E., 423
Heim, C., 572, 574
Heine, S. J., 212, 430
Heiser, P., 130
Heisler, M., 509
Hejmadi, A., 212
Helgeson, V. S., 518
Hélie, S., 317
Heller, W., 69
Hellmich, N., 186
Helmholtz, H. L. F. von, 100
Helmuth, L., 322
Helson, R., 400
Helwig, C. C., 373
Helzer, J. E., 151, 156
Hendrick, C., 430
Hendrick, S. S., 430
Henkens, K., 401
Hennessy, D. A., 420
Hennessy, M. B., 572
Henrich, G., 228
Henry, K. D., 31
Henry, W. P., 274, 598
Henshaw, S. P., 281
Herbenick, D., 199–200
Herbert, B. M., 185
Herculano-Houzel, S., 46
Herman, L. M., 327
Heron, M., 547, 568
Herrera, N. C., 470
Herrnstein, R., 339
Herscovitch, L., 663
Hertel, P. T., 561
Hertzog, C., 392
Hesse, E., 376
Hettema, J. M., 560
Heuser, I., 625
Hewer, A., 372
Hewstone, M., 426
Hicks, B. M., 582
Higbee, K. L., 6
Higuchi, S., 239
Hikosaka, O., 63
Hilgard, E. R., 146
Hilgart, M., 617
Hill, C. E., 601
Hill, P. C., 523
Hill, T., 255
Hill-Soderlund, A. L., 377
Hilt, L. M., 573, 574
Hilton, D. J., 441
Hirai, M., 617
Hiroto, D. S., 527
Hirsch, E., 248
Hirsch, M. S., 197
Hirsh, J. B., 480
Hirshkowitz, M., 131, 138
Hirst, W., 295
Hitch, G. J., 279, 281, 282
Hively, K., 423
Ho, B.-C., 575, 576, 577
Hobbs, B. B., 136
Hobson, J. A., 139, 140
Hochberg, L. R., 24
Hodson, G., 423
Hodson, N. A., 103
Hoeft, F., 145, 146
Hoffman, A. B., 313
Hoffman, R. E., 580
Hofmann, S. G., 610
Hogben, M., 450
Hohlfeld, R., 46
Hokin, L. E., 622
Holden, C., 479
Holder, M. D., 327
Holen, A., 524
Holland, A. J., 193
Hollon, S. D., 614, 615, 616
Hollos, M., 390
Holloway, R. L., 69
Holman, E. A., 508
Holman, T. B., 396
Holmans, P., 570
Holmes, Thomas, 504–506
Holmqvist, J. L., 255
Holt, S., 440
Holt-Lunstad, J., 397, 522
Holzel, B. K., 524
Hong, Y., 527
Hood, C. J., 522
Hood, D. C., 93
Hooker, S. A., 523
Hooley, J. M., 576, 580
Hopcroft, R. L., 567
Horgan, D. D., 382
Horgan, J., 471
Horiguchi, H., 95
Horn, J. L., 334
Hornboll, B., 64
Horne, J. A., 133, 137
Horney, Karen, 470
Hornyak, M., 142
Hosking, S. G., 531
Hovey, J. D., 509
Hovland, C. I., 416
Howe, M. L., 294
Howes, O. D., 579
Howland, J., 158
Hoyer, W. D., 416
Hoyland, A., 535
Hsiao, S., 236
Hsiung, R. C., 617
Hu, J., 109
Huang, C. J., 522, 535
Huang, Y., 581
Hubel, D. H., 96
Huber, D., 228
Huddleston, J., 385
Hudson, A. J., 63
Hudson, J. A., 285, 393
Hudson, S., 164
Huerta, C. G., 506
Huesmann, L. R., 447
Huff, N. C., 240
Huff, W., 625
Huffcutt, A. I., 653
Huffziger, S., 572
Hughes, D. J., 316
Hughes, J., 157
Hughes, J. W., 522, 524
Hughes, M. E., 398
Hughes, Z. A., 574
Hulbert, A., 117
Hulin, C. L., 662, 664
Hull, C. L., 174
Hummel, M., 160
Hummel, T., 108
Hunt, R. R., 239
Hunter, E. C., 562
Hupp, J. M., 382
Hurlstone, M. J., 282
Hurvich, L. M., 96
Husemann, N., 480
Huston, A. C., 383
Hutchinson, R. R., 448
Hutchison, K. E., 572, 574
Huttenlocher, P. R., 361
Hyde, J., 374
Hyde, J. S., 341, 399
Hyland, P., 608
Hyman, J. S., 525

Iacono, W. G., 579
Iervolino, A. C., 557
Igarashi, H., 400
Iidaka, T., 290
Ikonomidou, C., 154, 358
Ilgen, D. R., 663
Ilgen, M. A., 572, 574
Ineichen, B., 430
Infante-Rivard, C., 158
Inglehart, M., 208
Inglehart, R., 537
Ingram, R. E., 616
Innes, C. R., 130
Innis, N. K., 250
Inostroza, M., 137
Inoue, K., 56
Insel, T., 546
Insel, T. R., 617
Inzlicht, M., 423, 523
Irwin, M., 130
Irwin, M. R., 130, 535
Isa, M. R., 522
Isaac, M., 562
Isenberg, N., 64
Iso, H., 298
Iverson, L., 163
Iyengar, S. S., 178
Izac, S. M., 63

Jablensky, A., 576
Jablin, F. M., 657
Jack, E. P., 415
Jackson, J. L., 480
Jackson, S., 117
Jacobs, L. F., 525
Jacobson, N. S., 613
Jacoby, L. L., 293
Jacquet, A. Y., 365
Jadack, R. A., 374
Jaffari-Bimmel, N., 478
Jaffee, S., 374
Jain, A. K., 105
Jaint, N., 97
Jakobsen, J. C., 598
Jakubowski, R., 420
James, W., 174, 206
Jameson, D., 96
Jamieson, G., 146
Jamieson, J. P., 520
Jamner, L. D., 516
Janca, A., 558
Jäncke, L., 69
Jane, J. S., 552
Janicki, D., 518
Janicki-Deverts, D., 522
Janis, I. L., 438, 439
Janoff-Bulman, R., 561
Janowitz, H., 181
Jansen, A., 237
Jaremka, L. M., 523
Jarrett, R. B., 610
Javitt, D. C., 579
Jedrziewski, M. K., 74
Jeffries, J. J., 161
Jenkins, J. M., 369
Jenni, O. G., 135
Jennings, J. R., 131
Jensen, A. R., 340
Jensen, M. P., 147
Jeste, D. V., 620
Jiang, J., 117
Jimmieson, N. L., 521
Jitsumori, M., 312
Jobe, T. H., 576
Jobin, J., 524
John, O. P., 400
Johnson, A. J., 11
Johnson, B. A., 605
Johnson, B. T., 291
Johnson, D., 381
Johnson, D. E., 664
Johnson, J. A., 481
Johnson, K. L., 509
Johnson, M. K., 297
Johnson, P. A., 239
Johnson, S., 613
Johnson, S. L., 570
Johnson, S. M., 613
Johnson, S. P., 364
Johnson, V. E., 197, 198
Johnson, W., 479
John-Steiner, V., 370
Johnston, L. D., 159, 396, 530
Joiner, T., 569
Joiner, T. E., Jr., 191
Jolicoeur, P., 308
Joliot, A. E., 192
Jonas, P., 387
Jonason, P. K., 431
Jones, B. Q., 397
Jones, E. E., 419, 420, 426
Jones, M., 147
Jones, Mary Cover, 602
Jones, N. P., 572
Jones, R. D., 130
Jones, S., 157, 382
Jones, S. A., 119
Jonsson, E. G., 479
Joormann, J., 570, 571, 572
Jordan, A. S., 143
Jordan, G., 97
Jorgensen, C. H., 605
Jorgensen, G., 374
Joseph, J. E., 474
Joule, R.-V., 415
Joyner, K., 202
Judge, T. A., 661
Julien, R. M., 158
Jung, C. G., 469–470
Junker, A., 46
Justo, M. G., 212

Kachelski, R. A., 87
Kahai, S. S., 660
Kahana, M. J., 279
Kahneman, D., 319, 320, 321
Kahol, K., 131, 136
Kahout, J. L., 31
Kaiser Family Foundation, 450
Kajantie, E., 516
Kako, E., 327
Kalish, R. A., 403
Kammrath, L. K., 481
Kandel, D. B., 430
Kane, J. M., 620
Kangas, B. D., 250
Kanny, D., 154
Kanoy, K., 253
Kanwisher, N., 117
Kaplan, C. A., 316
Kaplan, D. A., 650, 660, 665
Kaplan, R. E., 659
Kaplan, R. M., 186, 330
Kaplowitz, P. B., 384
Kapur, S., 579
Karasik, L. B., 361
Karch, D., 569
Karlsgodt, K. H., 579
Karnani, M. M., 182
Karney, B. R., 397
Karni, A., 138
Kaskutas, L. A., 613
Kaslwo, F. W., 397
Kassin, S. M., 447
Kastner, S., 66
Katerud, S., 552
Katigbak, M. S., 478
Katsurada, E., 253
Katz-Wise, S. L., 399
Kaufman, A. S., 334
Kaufman, L., 119
Kaul, C., 634, 638
Kavushansky, A., 56
Kawakami, N., 556
Kawamura, N., 508
Kawas, C., 343
Kazdin, A. E., 255, 617
Keck, P. E., Jr., 571
Keel, P. K., 192, 193
Keir, P. J., 531
Keita, G. P., 573
Keller, C., 382
Keller, J., 423, 424
Kelley, K., 378
Kellner, C. H., 625
Kelly, D. J., 364

Kelly, M. M., 561
Kelman, C. A., 371
Kelsch, W., 361
Kemball, G., 196
Kemeny, M. E., 518
Kemp, M., 616
Kemp, S., 285
Kemper, S., 535
Kendall, L. M., 662
Kendler, K. S., 578
Kennedy, K., 186
Kennedy, K. M., 73
Kennedy, S. H., 615
Kenrick, D. T., 448, 485
Kensinger, E. A., 131
Kent, T. A., 622
Kerns, K. A., 377
Kessler, R. C., 554, 555, 556, 557, 565, 567, 570
Kessler, Y., 280
Kibbe, M. M., 367
Kidd, K. K., 340
Kiecolt-Glaser, J. K., 397, 515, 516, 517
Kieffaber, P. D., 270
Kiehl, K. A., 582
Kieseppa, T., 570
Kihlstrom, J. F., 471, 562, 563, 564
Killen, M., 436
Kilpatrick, D. G., 574
Kim, H., 378
Kim, H. S., 522
Kim, N., 118
Kimeldorf, D. J., 236
Kimura, D., 69
King, B. M., 184, 185
King, S., 580
Kinicki, A. J., 658
Kinnish, K. K., 201
Kinomura, S., 63
Kinsey, A. C., 201
Kirby, S., 229
Kirkbride, J. B., 576
Kirkpatrick, S. A., 659, 660
Kirmayer, L. J., 565
Kirsch, I., 145, 146, 147, 148, 622
Kirsch, L., 146
Kirschbaum, C., 516
Kirschenbaum, D. S., 475
Kisilevsky, B. S., 365
Kistner, J. A., 574
Kitayama, S., 486
Kito, S., 571
Kleim, B., 561
Klein, B., 617
Klein, D. N., 567, 570
Klein, S. B., 234
Klein, T. W., 163
Kleitman, N., 137
Klinger, E., 604
Klöckener, T., 185
Klonoff, E. A., 574
Kluft, R. P., 564
Klump, K. L., 193
Knaevelsrud, C., 617
Knowlton, B., 287
Kobasa, S. C., 528
Kochanek, K. D., 568
Kochanska, G., 252
Koelling, R. A., 236, 237
Koenigsberg, H. W., 583
Kofodimos, J. R., 659
Koga, Y., 571
Kogan, A., 397
Kogut, T., 454
Koh, K. B., 520, 522
Kohlberg, L., 372
Köhler, W., 257
Kohout, J., 4
Koles, Z. J., 69
Kolodny, R. C., 198
Komisaruk, B. R., 197
Koob, G. F., 154
Koolschijn, P. C., 386
Kopelman, P. G., 186
Kopta, S. M., 615
Korszun, A., 574
Kosmitzki, C., 388
Koss, M. P., 574
Kosslyn, S., 87–88
Kosslyn, S. M., 308, 310
Kosten, T. R., 239
Koster, E. H. W., 572
Koughan, M., 650, 658
Kowalski, K., 413, 424
Kozart, M. F., 616
Kozlowski, S. W., 658
Kraft, J. B., 571
Kraft, J. M., 358
Kraft, T. L., 524
Kraha, A., 189
Kram, K. E., 423
Kramer, A. F., 392
Krampe, H., 605
Kraut, R. E., 208
Kreider, R. M., 398
Kremer, I., 530
Kristenson, H. H., 239
Kropp, P., 228
Krystal, A. D., 140
Krystal, J. H., 156
Kryukov, V. I., 234
Kübler-Ross, E., 402–403
Kuczaj, S. A., II, 327
Kudielka, B. M., 516
Kuehner, C., 572
Kuhbandner, C., 272
Kuhlman, D. M., 177, 474
Kuhn, D., 390
Kulik, J., 295
Kuller, L. H., 397–398
Kumada, T., 154
Kumarasamy, N., 533
Kumari, V., 477
Kung, H. S., 568
Kunstman, J. W., 423
Kunugi, H., 571
Kurdek, L. A., 399
Kutscher, E. C., 578
Kuyper, L., 203
Kuypers, K. P., 161
Kuzelova, H., 558, 570
Kwan, B. M., 616
Kwiatkowski, J., 316
Kyle, B. N., 604

LaBar, K. S., 64
Lacayo, A., 160
Laceulle, O. M., 479, 480
Lack, C. W., 610
Laeng, B., 69
La Greca, A. M., 561
Lahey, B. B., 552
Lambert, M. J., 614
Lambeth, G. S., 396
Lamon, S., 341
Lancet, D., 106, 107
Landers, D. M., 176
Landrine, H., 574
Lang, A., 255
Lang, A. J., 556
Lang, R., 610
Lange, T., 130, 535
Langfred, C., 659
Langlois, J. H., 364, 432
Langreth, R., 522
Lanius, R. A., 615
Lansford, J. E., 398
Lanska, M., 310
Lanter, J., 328
Largo-Wight, E., 519
Larkin, M., 107
Larson, J., 572
Lassman, D. J., 182
Latané, B., 435, 452–453, 454
Lating, J. M., 558
Latkin, C. A., 454
Lattal, K. A., 246
Laubmeier, K. K., 523
Laugharne, J., 558
Lavie, P., 142
Lavner, J. A., 397
Lavoie, C., 227
Lawton, C. L., 535
Lawton, J. N., 531
Layous, K., 536
Layton, J. B., 522
Lazarus, R. S., 205, 209–210, 509, 513, 514, 518, 519
Lazerson, A., 48
Leaper, C., 380, 381
Leary, C., 253
Leary, M. R., 433
Leasure, J., 66
LeBlanc, J., 477
Lebovits, A., 522
Lebow, J. L., 612, 613
Lecanuet, J.-P., 365
Lecat, B., 441
Leckman, J. F., 557
Ledermann, T., 131, 535
Ledford, G. E., Jr., 659
Lee, A. Y., 430
Lee, D. C., 535
Lee, G. R., 397
Lee, Helie, 350
Lee, K., 607
Lee, S. J., 451
Lee, T. M., 135
Lefcourt, H. M., 524
Lehto, U. S., 517
Leibowitz, S. F., 183
Leichsenring, F., 583
Lekander, M., 130
Lemay, E. P., 432
LeMay, M. L., 341
Lemola, S., 131, 535
Leng, N. R. C., 297
Lentz, E., 658
Lenze, E. J., 622
Lenzenweger, M. F., 581
Leon, S. C., 616
Leonard, K. E., 156
Lepage, M., 310
LePine, J. A., 664
Lepper, M. R., 178
Leslie, A. M., 367
Lessenger, J. E., 149
Lester, B. M., 358
Lester, D., 470
Leszcz, M., 611
Letsch, E. A., 479
Leucht, S., 620
Leuchter, A. F., 622
Leue, A., 477
LeVay, S., 201
Levens, S. M., 572
Levenson, R. W., 207
Levin, B. E., 184
Levine, B., 286
Levine, C., 372
Levine, C. S., 422
Levine, E. G., 523
Levine, R. A., 426
Levinson, D. F., 570
Levitsky, W., 68
Levitt, A. G., 323
Levy, B. R., 388
Levy, D., 380
Levy, D. L., 578
Levy, G. D., 382
Levy-Shiff, R., 399
Lewinsohn, P. M., 567, 569, 570, 608
Lewis, D. O., 160, 449
Lewinsohn, P. M., 191
Leyhe, T., 286
L'Herrou, T., 435
Li, C. E., 574
Li, J-S., 236
Li, K-C., 236
Li, S., 391, 392
Li, X., 568
Li, Y., 316
Libersat, F., 448
Lichtenfeld, S., 272
Lichter, D. T., 396
Lick, D. J., 509
Lickliter, R., 356
Lieberman, J., 579, 620
Lieberman, J. A., 140, 575
Liebert, R. M., 484
Lien, Y., 420
Lincoln, A. E., 288
Lind, D. L., 432
Lind, J. C., 69
Lindau, S. T., 388
Linden, R. W. A., 103
Lindenberger, U., 391
Lindenmayer, J. P., 620
Lindgren, M., 146
Lindley, C. A., 245
Lindsay, D., 297
Lindsey, E. W., 378
Ling, D., 530
Linhares, J. M., 90
Linville, P. W., 426
Linz, D., 245
Liossi, C., 147
Lippa, R., 204
Lipsitt, L. P., 142
Lipsitz, J. D., 603
Lissek, S., 561
Little, A. C., 432
Littleton, H., 521
Liu, Y., 154
Livingston, I., 452
Livingstone, M. S., 96
Llorente, M. D., 143
Loane, C., 619
Locke, E. A., 659, 660
Lockenhoff, C. E., 388
Lockhart, Robert, 276, 277
Loersch, C., 87
Loewenstein, R. J., 563, 564
Loewenstein, W. R., 109
Loftus, E. F., 294, 296, 297
Loftus, G. R., 272
Logie, R. H., 279, 281, 282
Logue, A. W., 237
Lois, C., 361
Lomenick, J. P., 181
Loney, B. R., 581
Long, B. C., 522
Long, N., 177
Longstreth, W. T., Jr., 141
Loo, C. K., 624
Looper, K. J., 565
Lopez, C. M., 574
Lopez Cascales, J. J., 103
Lorenz, F. O., 398
Lorenzetti, A., 516
Lorenzo-Luaces, L., 616
Loughnan, S., 422
Lourenco, O., 370
Lovden, M., 391
Loveless, A. S., 396
Lowe, S. R., 395
Lowis, M. J., 401
Lu, H. H., 396
Lu, N. Z., 574
Lucas, B., 130
Lucas, R. E., 398, 487
Luce, K. H., 617
Luckman, S. M., 183
Luders, E., 66
Ludtke, O., 480
Luecken, L. J., 517
Luhmann, M., 399
Lumer, E. D., 117
Lundblad, A., 397
Lundy, R., 145
Luo, J., 63
Luo, S., 431
Lutgendorf, S., 522
Lykken, D. T., 479
Lynn, B., 523
Lynn, S. J., 145, 146, 147, 563–564
Lynne-Landsman, S. D., 474
Lytton, H., 382
Lyubomirsky, S., 536, 572

Macan, T., 653
MacDonald, H., 146
Macfadden, W., 620
Machado, A., 370
MacIntosh, H. B., 613
MacIntyre, G. F., 42
Madden, D. J., 391
Maddi, Salvatore, 528
Maddox, W. T., 313
Madsen, L., 421
Maercker, A., 617
Maggs, J. L., 154, 159
Magiati, I., 614
Maguire, E. A., 65, 66, 298
Mah, K., 198
Maher, A. R., 620
Mahmmod, A., 361
Mahn, H., 370
Mahood, C., 245
Maier, S. F., 527, 572
Maillot, P., 245
Main, M., 376
Maiorca, J., 454
Maisonneuve, J., 430
Maj, M., 623
Majdandzic, M., 478
Makinen, J. A., 613
Makino, H., 312
Makris, N., 66
Malapsina, D., 578–579
Malcolm, R. J., 605
Malcolm, W., 613
Malik, M., 450
Malina, R. M., 384
Mancini, A. D., 398
Maner, J. K., 196
Manera, S., 365
Mann, R. D., 660
Manning, C. C., 446–447
Manning, W. D., 399
Manson, J. E., 535
Manstead, A. S. R., 205
Manthena, P., 134
Manz, C. C., 659
Marañon, I., 193
Marazzitti, D., 448
Marchetti, I., 572
Marcia, J. E., 394
Marcotte, E., 140
Mareschal, D., 367
Mariscal, M., 358
Markman, A. B., 311
Marks, D. F., 340
Markus, H., 380
Markus, H. R., 381, 486
Marler, P. R., 326
Marques, J. F., 310
Marshall, C., 610
Martin, C., 654
Martin, C. E., 201
Martin, C. L., 380, 381
Martin, G., 252
Martin, N., 204
Martin, W. H., 99
Martindale, C., 316
Martinie, M., 177, 415, 424
Martins, A. T., 212
Martins, R. N., 245
Martorana, A., 54
Martuzzi, R., 109
Marx, B. P., 513
Marzoli, D., 208
Mashal, N., 69
Mashoodh, R., 356
Maslow, A., 178, 485
Massaro, D. W., 272
Masten, A. S., 480
Masters, K. S., 523
Masters, W. H., 197, 198
Mathew, R., 156
Matlin, M. W., 93, 100, 101, 105, 107
Matson, J. L., 255, 607
Matsuda, L. A., 163
Matsumoto, D., 472
Matsuyama, T., 298
Matthews, B. A., 250
Matthews, K. A., 398
Matto, H. C., 381
Matud, M. P., 518
Mauss, I. B., 210, 520
Maville, J., 506
Mavriplis, C., 422
Maxwell, J. C., 161
Mayberg, H. S., 571, 625–626
Mayer, J., 336
Mayer, R. E., 308
Mayes, L. C., 567
Maynard, A. M., 390
Mazure, C. M., 573, 574
Mazzoni, G., 148
McAdams, D. P., 479, 486
McAndrew, F., 212
McCabe, K. O., 481

McCallie, M. S., 522
McCance-Katz, E. F., 157, 161
McCann, U. D., 161
McCarley, R. W., 131, 140
McClelland, D. C., 174
McClintock, M. K., 107, 196
McCloskey, D., 74
McClung, C. A., 571
McClure, F., 616
McClure, H. H., 509
McCormack, P. L., 622
McCrae, Robert, 477–478, 479, 480
McCreary, C. P., 517
McCullough, M. E., 523
McDaniel, M. A., 131
McDermott, B., 616
McDermott, D., 400
McDonough, I. M., 387
McElderry, D., 384
McElroy, S. L., 571
McEvoy, P. M., 610
McEvoy, R. D., 143
McFall, R. M., 610
McFalls, J. A., Jr., 388
McGehee, D. S., 159
McGlashan, T. H., 580
McGregor, G., 182
McGuffin, P., 570
McGuigan, N., 252
McIntosh, D. N., 207, 523
McIntosh, E., 572
McKay, A., 26
McKean, K. J., 528
McKee, A., 336
McKenna, M. C., 527
McKillip, J., 432
McKim, W. A., 157
McKinley, N. M., 341
McKnight-Eily, L. R., 132, 143, 144
McLaughlin, K. A., 561, 572
McLaughlin Crabtree, V., 132
McLay, R. N., 604
McLean, C. P., 554
McMahon, L. R., 31
McManus, J. L., 454
McManus, M. A., 656
McMillen, D. L., 151
McMullen, E., 616
McNally, R. J., 189
McNeil, D. W., 604
McNeill, B., 381
McRae, Kateri, 210
Medina-Mora, M. E., 556
Mega, C., 205
Mehl, M. R., 536
Meier, A. E., 238
Meinl, E., 46
Meiran, N., 280
Mellman, T. A., 558
Mellott, L. M., 396
Meltzer, L. J., 140
Mendelsohn, G. A., 431
Mendes, W. B., 520
Menlove, F. L., 260
Mennella, J. A., 105
Menz, M. M., 138
Menzies, H., 524
Merikangas, K. R., 547, 567, 570
Merkl, A., 625
Merskey, H., 564
Mesquita, B., 212
Messner, M., 416
Metzger, A., 396
Meyer, Dixie, 433
Meyer, J. P., 663
Meyer, L., 203
Meyerbroeker, K., 603
Mezulis, A. H., 421
Micco, J. A., 560
Michael, G. A., 66
Michalski, D., 4, 33
Michelson, D., 622
Migliore, M., 274
Mignot, E., 141
Milad, M. R., 560
Milan, M., 558
Milford, G. E., 179
Milgram, S., 21, 442, 443, 445–446
Milland, L., 177, 415, 424
Millar, M., 441
Miller, A. G., 444
Miller, D. T., 421
Miller, E., 107
Miller, G. E., 510, 515, 517
Miller, I. J., Jr., 103
Miller, N. S., 165
Miller, P., 161
Miller, R. R., 234
Miller, S., 196
Miller, T. Q., 526
Miller, W. R., 523, 527
Milling, L. S., 146
Milner, B., 65
Milner, C. E., 141
Milton, J., 87
Minda, J. P., 312
Mindell, J. A., 140
Minhoto, G., 131
Miranda, R., 569
Mischel, W., 480
Miselis, R. R., 183
Miskovic, V., 610
Mitchell, D. Y., 143
Mitchison, G., 138
Mitelman, S. A., 579
Mithoefer, M. C., 161
Miyauchi, S., 66
Mizushige, T., 56
Mo, L., 311
Mobini, S., 104
Moe, B., 448
Moffitt, T. E., 479, 547, 555, 582
Mogilner, C., 536
Mohr, B. A., 388
Mohr, C., 452, 506
Mohr, D. C., 617
Mojtabai, R., 592
Mokhber, N., 619
Molero, F., 426
Mommersteeg, P. M., 526
Mongrain, V., 132
Monk, T. H., 131
Monroe, S. M., 573
Montgomery, G., 147
Monti, J. M., 117
Monti-Bloch, L., 107
Montoya, M. R., 432
Mooney, R. D., 93
Moore, C., 524
Moore, C. A., 131
Moore, E. G. J., 340
Moore, E. L., 565
Moore, K. L., 359
Moore, M. T., 573
Moreland, R. L., 430
Morgan, A. H., 146
Morin, C. M., 140
Morland, L. A., 617
Morley, L., 328
Morlock, R. J., 143
Morogiannis, F. F., 191
Morris, A. S., 400
Morris, M. W., 420
Morris, R., 448
Morrison, P., 579
Morrison, P. D., 163
Morrow, E. M., 53
Morsella, E., 471
Moscovitch, M., 137, 298
Mosedeghrad, A., 663
Mosher, W. D., 398
Mosing, M. A., 560
Moskowitz, J. T., 508, 519
Motivala, S. J., 130, 535
Motraghi, T. E., 604
Motsinger, L. D., 191
Mottram, L., 607
Moulton, S., 87–88
Mowen, J. C., 441
Moy, J., 185, 189
Moyer, C. A., 524
Mroczek, D. K., 480
Mrug, S., 384
Mueller, C. W., 663
Mueser, K. T., 576
Mulcahy, R., 612
Mullally, S. L., 65
Müller, M. S., 448
Mulligan, N. W., 288
Mumford, M. D., 316
Mumme, Donna, 260
Munafo, M. R., 479
Munakata, Y., 367
Munch, M., 135
Munoz, R. F., 617
Munson, C., 245
Murdoch, B. B., Jr., 278
Murillo-Rodriguez, E., 66
Murphy, K., 130, 131, 535
Murphy, S., 404
Murphy, S. T., 208
Murray, A., 54
Murray, C., 339
Murray, G., 571
Murray, H. A., 176
Murray, S. B., 192
Murray, S. L., 397
Murray, S. O., 117
Murru, A., 622
Muscari, M., 450
Musen, G., 287
Mutran, E. J., 401
Mutter, J. D., 388
Muurahainen, N. E., 182
Muzino, J. N., 132
Myers, D. G., 397
Myers, H. F., 517
Myers, L. M., 388

Nabi, R. L., 450
Nacke, A., 245
Nacke, L. E., 245
Naegele, B., 141
Nagandia, K., 142
Nairne, J. S., 275
Naish, P. L., 146
Naja, W. J., 619
Nakayama, E. Y., 601
Nakayama, K., 73
Nandi, A., 508
Nardi, A. E., 604, 619
Narvaez, D., 373
NAS, 656
Nascimento, S. M., 90
Nash, M., 148, 516
Nassif, A., 383
Nathan, P., 610
Nathan, P. E., 614
National Center for Health Statistics, 568
National Comorbidity Survey Replication (NCS-R), 547, 554, 574
National Gay and Lesbian Task Force, 203
National Highway Transportation Safety Administration (NHTSA), 156, 531
National Institute of Mental Health (NIMH), 569, 578
National Institute on Alcohol Abuse and Alcoholism, 154
National Institute on Drug Abuse, 160, 161, 164, 165
National Institutes of Health, 186
National Research Council, 535
National Safety Council, 320
National Science Foundation, 31
National Scientific Council on the Developing Child, 360
National Sleep Foundation, 132, 143, 144
Nave, K. A., 46
Naylor, J. C., 663
Nazari, H., 616
Near, J. P., 664
Nederhof, E., 572, 573
Neher, A., 485
Neisewander, J. L., 54
Nelson, C. A., 48
Nelson, L. S., 162
Nelson, S. K., 401
Nemeroff, C. B., 570, 571, 572, 625
Neria, Y., 508
Nesbitt, R. E., 420
Ness, L., 563
Nestler, E. J., 160
Nestor, L., 163
Nevin, J. A., 247
Nevonen, L., 612
Newcomb, T. M., 430
Newland, M. C., 359
Newman, M. G., 561
Newmark, T. S., 147
Newton, C. A., 163
Ngan, E. T., 579
Ni, X., 583
Nicodemus, K. K., 578
Nicolini, H., 560
Niedzwienska, A., 285
Nielsen, M., 24
Nieuwenhuijsen, K., 608
Nijdam, M. J., 616
Nikulin, V. V., 66
Nisbett, R. E., 339, 340, 341
Nishino, S., 141
Nivoli, A. M., 622
Noah, T., 159
Noble, E. P., 293
Noble, M., 234
Nock, M. K., 520, 569
Nolen-Hoeksema, S., 572, 573, 574
Norcross, J. C., 616
Nordin, S., 104
Norian, R., 252
Norton, M. I., 536
Norton, P. J., 610
Nosofsky, R. M., 313
Nottelmann, E. D., 384
Nougaim, K. E., 179
Novakova, M., 132
Novara, G., 274
Nowicka, A., 69
Nummenmaa, L., 196
Nunes, J., 144
Nusbaum, E. C., 316
Nyberg, L., 286
Nyer, P. U., 440

O'Brien, A., 521
O'Brien, K. S., 190
O'Brien, M., 399
O'Brien, M. C., 158, 159
O'Bryan, M., 382
Ochsner, K. N., 210
O'Connor, D. B., 509
O'Donnell, C. P., 142
Oehen, P., 161
Oesch, S., 181
Offer, S., 398
Offidani, E., 619
Oginska, H., 130, 143
Ogle, C. M., 561
Oishi, S., 487
Okazaki, H., 62
O'Keefe, D. J., 441
Okuro, M., 141
Olatunji, B. O., 610
Oldehinkel, A. J., 572
Oldham, G. R., 662
Olds, J. M., 310
Olff, M., 558
Olive, T., 177, 415, 424
Ollendick, T. H., 614
Olshausen, B. A., 117
Olson, B. D., 479
Olson, E. A., 111
Olson, R. L., 531
O'Malley, P. M., 159, 396
Omar, H., 384
Ondersma, S. J., 143
Ones, D., 653
Oosthuizen, P. P., 620
Orbuch, T., 397
Organ, D. W., 664
Orina, M. M., 377
Ormel, J., 572
Ormerod, T. C., 317
Ornoy, A., 358
Ortega, L. A., 569
Ortony, A., 211, 212
Osborne, R. H., 517
O'Shea, E., 161
Ostberg, O., 133
Ostelo, R. W. J. G., 522
Osterman, K., 447
Ostroff, C., 658
Oswalt, S. B., 203
Oteri, A., 158
Otomo, K., 323
Ott, C. A., 164
Outlaw, F. H., 523
Overbeek, G., 396
Overman, W. H., 97
Overmier, J. B., 527, 572
Owens, J. A., 143
Oxler, F., 161

Pace-Schott, E., 140
Packer, D. J., 439
Padela, A. I., 509
Page, R. A., 146
Paivio, A., 274, 283
Palermo-Neto, J., 518
Paller, K. A., 364
Pallier, G., 343
Palm, L. J., 528
Palmade, G., 430
Palmer, J. C., 296
Paltzer, S., 383
Pandina, G., 576
Papadakis, A. A., 574
Parent, A. S., 384
Pargament, K. I., 523
Parikh, T. N., 63
Park, D. C., 293, 387
Park, H., 270
Park, J. S., 607
Parker, E. S., 293
Parker, G. B., 574, 621
Parker-Pope, T., 532
Parkes, C. M., 403
Parkin, A. J., 297
Parr, E. B., 189
Parsons, T. D., 604
Partnership Attitude Tracking Study, 149
Pascalis, O., 364
Pascual, A., 441
Pasquet, P., 105
Passie, T., 164
Patel, S. R., 625
Patrick, M. E., 154, 159
Patterson, C. J., 203
Patterson, D. R., 147
Patterson, G. R., 583
Paul, G., 524
Paulson, R. M., 414
Paulson, S. E., 381
Paulus, P. B., 433
Pause, B. M., 285
Pavlov, Ivan, 226
Payne, J. D., 131
Pear, J., 252
Pearlin, L. I., 506
Pearsall, M. J., 438
Pedersen, B., 605
Pedersen, D. M., 120
Pedersen, G., 552
Pedersen, N. L., 392
Pedersen, P. B., 616
Peelen, M. V., 117
Pei, J., 358
Peiffer, J. J., 245
Pekrun, R., 272
Pelleymounter, M. A., 182
Penaloza, A. A., 317
Peng, K., 420
Peng, S., 54
Penley, J. A., 519
Pentkowski, N. S., 54
Pepperberg, I. M., 327
Perez, M., 191
Perina, K., 295
Perkins, D. O., 575
Perlini, A. H., 432
Perlis, M. L., 140
Perlis, R. H., 570
Perrot, A., 245
Perry, E., 54

Perry, E. L., 660
Perry, W. G., Jr., 391
Persaud, T. V. N., 359
Person, E. S., 471
Pesant, N., 139, 597
Peterson, B. E., 394
Peterson, C., 524, 527
Peterson, L. R., 275
Peterson, M. J., 275
Peterson, P., 528
Peterson, P. M., 519
Petitto, L., 324
Petrides, K. V., 343
Petrovich, G. D., 183
Petry, N. M., 607
Pettigrew, T. F., 427
Pettit, R. W., 253
Petty, R. E., 87, 415, 416, 417, 436
Pew Research Center, 13
Pfaus, J. G., 196
Pflueger, H.-J., 448
Phan, Victoria, 316–317
Phares, E. J., 484
Phelan, S., 535
Phillips, D. I., 516
Phillips, K. A., 191
Phillips, M. R., 568
Piaget, J., 365, 366, 389
Pickering, G. J., 105
Pickert, R., 326
Pidoplichko, V. I., 159
Pierce, J. P., 530
Pieri, A., 516
Pietromonaco, P. R., 522
Pigott, T. A., 193
Pillar, G., 142
Pillard, R. C., 204
Pillemer, D. B., 285
Pilowsky, L. S., 579
Pinedo, V. A., 199
Pinto, P. D., 90
Pinto da Mota Matos, A., 260
Piomelli, D., 188
Piper, A., 564
Pirrallo, R. G., 136
Piskulic, D., 610
Plant, E. A., 423
Plata-Salaman, C. R., 103
Plazzi, B., 138
Plomin, R., 356, 478, 479
Plowfield, L. A., 530
Plutchik, R., 212
Poe, G. R., 131, 138
Poelman, D., 94
Pogue-Geile, M. F., 578–579
Pokorski, J., 130, 143
Polissar, N. L., 239
Politis, M., 619
Pollack, W., 575
Polmin, R., 340
Polotsky, V. Y., 142
Pomeroy, A., 656
Pomeroy, W. B., 201, 203
Ponniah, K., 614, 616
Pool, E., 63
Pool, R., 365
Poore, A. G., 427
Pope, H. G., 163
Pope, H. G., Jr., 165
Porat, R., 520
Porkka-Heiskanen, T., 137
Porte, H. S., 139
Porter, J. N., 386
Porter, R. H., 365
Posner, M. I., 146
Postuma, R. B., 142
Potter, W. J., 450
Poudel, G. R., 130
Pouwer, F., 526
Powell, L. H., 189, 523
Powell, T. J., 613
Powers, S. I., 522
Powers, T. L., 415
Pratkanis, A. R., 87
Preisler, J. J., 506
Prentice, A. M., 188
Prescott, C. A., 156
Pressman, S. D., 523, 524
Preston, J. A., 401
Price, C. A., 401
Price, E. C., 610
Price, W. F., 139
Priess, H. A., 399
Priluck, R., 412
Prinzmetal, W., 119
Pritchard, M. E., 524
Pritchard, R. D., 663
ProCon.org, 202
Prosser, I. B., 31
Prosser, J. M., 162
Prutkin, J., 105
Pryor, J. H., 547
Ptacek, J. T., 518
Ptacek, R., 558
Public Health England, 186
Pulvermüller, F., 66
Purdy, J. E., 22
Purves, D., 48
Putnam, F. W., 563, 564
Pyke, K., 381
Pylyshyn, Z. W., 308, 309
Pyun, Y. D., 147

Qian, Z., 396
Quattrone, G. A., 426
Querido, J. G., 378
Quickfall, J., 163
Quigley, B. M., 156
Quillian, M. R., 310
Quinn, P. C., 311

Raabe, J., 177
Rabinowitz, F. E., 575
Rabkin, S. W., 147
Raby, K. L., 378
Rachman, S., 473
Racsmany, M., 131
Rahe, Richard, 504–506
Rahman, Q., 204
Raine, A., 582, 583
Rainville, P., 147
Rajecki, D. W., 32
Ram, S., 142
Ramaekers, J. G., 161
Ramsey, J., 164
Ramsey-Rennels, J. L., 364
Randall, S., 161
Rando, T. A., 403, 404
Ranganathan, M., 163
Rank, M. R., 398
Rapoport, J. L., 580
Rappaport, V. J., 358
Rasch, B., 131
Rasmussen, C., 358
Rasmussen, E. B., 359
Rastelli, F., 68
Rathbone, C. J., 285
Rauch, S. L., 560
Rauchs, G., 138
Rawls, S. M., 162
Ray, R. D., 520
Ray, W. J., 145
Rayner, R., 235, 236
Raz, A., 146
Raz, M., 441
Raz, N., 73, 343
Read, C. N., 625–626
Read, S., 397
Readdy, T., 177
Reardon, J. M., 146
Reber, P. J., 287
Recio, G., 212
Reder, L. M., 270
Redman, J., 367
Reece, M., 201
Rees, G., 117
Reeves, E., 342
Regan, M. A., 531
Regier, D. A., 576
Rehder, B., 313
Reichle, E. D., 154
Reid, K. J., 141
Reid, M. W., 573
Reid, P., 381
Reidel, S. L., 432
Reinhard, I., 572
Reinhard, M., 416
Reinisch, J. M., 196
Reisberg, D., 309
Reisenzein, R., 209
Reiser, B. J., 308
Reiss, D., 378
Reite, M., 69
Reitzes, D. C., 401
Rempel, D. M., 531
Ren, J., 624, 625
Renoult, L., 286
Repetti, R., 11, 509
Repovs, B., 282
Rescorla, R. A., 234
Resko, J. A., 448
Resta, O., 142
Restuccia, D., 228
Revonsuo, A., 140
Reyna, V. F., 294, 390
Reyngoudt, H., 228
Reynolds, C. R., 332
Reynolds, J. R., 381
Reynolds, P., 517
Reynolds, R. M., 359
Rhodes, N., 417
Ricca, V., 610
Rice, J. T., 151
Rice, L. N., 599, 601
Rice, V. H., 515, 517
Richards, F. A., 390
Richardson, D. R., 447
Richardson, G. A., 359
Rieger, G., 202, 204
Riemann, D., 140
Riese, M. L., 359
Riggins, T., 160
Rijsman, R. M., 142
Riketta, M., 664
Rinaudo, P., 359
Rinsky, J. R., 281
Rios Romenets, S., 142
Rishi, M. A., 620
Riskind, J. H., 561
Ritchey, P. N., 382
Ritov, I., 454
Rivers, P. C., 156
Rizvi, S. L., 616
Rizzo, A. A., 604
Rizzo, A. S., 604
Roach, E. L., 151
Roberts, A. L., 557
Roberts, B. W., 479, 480, 526
Roberts, C. R., 143
Roberts, J. M., 480
Roberts, R. D., 336
Roberts, R. E., 143, 536
Roberts, S. B., 14
Robins, L. N., 576
Robins, R. W., 480
Robinson, I. H., 326
Robinson, J., 252
Robinson, L., 159
Robinson, N. M., 341
Robinson, T. E., 151
Robles, T. F., 397, 517
Rock, L., 119
Rockafellow, B. D., 178
Rodenburg, R., 616
Rodewald, F., 563, 564
Rodgers, S., 572
Rodriguez, M. D., 616
Roemmich, J. N., 384
Roets, A., 425
Roffwarg, H. P., 132
Rogers, C. R., 485, 599
Rogers, M. A., 560
Rogers, N. L., 130
Rogers, R. J., 421
Rogers, S. J., 398
Rogoff, B., 390
Rogol, A. D., 384
Rohan, M. J., 413, 425
Rohde, P., 567, 569
Rohrbach, L. A., 151
Roisman, G. I., 203, 378
Rollins, B. C., 399
Rolls, E. T., 103
Romanelli, R. J., 622
Romano, E., 252
Romney, D. M., 382
Ronconi, L., 205
Rooney, N. J., 326
Rosch, E., 311
Rose, A. J., 382, 574
Rose, J. E., 530
Rose, S., 567
Rose, S. A., 227
Rosenberg, D., 663
Rosenberg, M., 491
Rosenblatt, P. C., 404
Rosenhan, D. L., 444, 552
Rosenkranz, M. A., 524
Rosenman, Ray, 526
Rosenthal, G. T., 179
Roshanaei-Moghaddam, B., 614
Ross, B. H., 311
Ross, C. A., 563
Ross, D., 259, 449
Ross, M., 421, 525
Ross, M. W., 204
Ross, S., 259, 449
Rotenberg, K. J., 528
Roth, G., 487
Roth, J., 425
Roth, S., 518
Roth, T., 140, 141
Rothbart, M. K., 478
Rothbaum, B. O., 377, 604
Rothblum, E. D., 203
Rotter, Julian, 483
Routh, V. H., 184
Rovine, M., 399
Rovine, M. J., 340
Rowe, T., 388
Rowlett, J. K., 56
Roy-Byrne, P., 619
Rozin, P., 212
Ruark, J., 28, 529
Rubin, K. H., 430
Rubin, M., 426
Ruble, D., 380, 381
Ruderman, A. J., 189
Rudestam, K. E., 603
Rudgley, R., 164
Rudner, M., 277
Ruffman, T., 367
Ruiz, F. S., 130, 535
Rumelhart, D. E., 284
Ruscio, A. M., 556
Rush, A. J., 623
Rush, M. C., 528
Rushton, J., 340, 341
Rushton, W. A. H., 94
Russell, C. J., 192
Russell, M. L., 293
Russell, R., 432
Russell, V. A., 510
Rutherford, W., 101
Ruts, W., 313
Ryan, R. M., 177
Ryon, H. S., 484

Saadat, H., 147
Saalmann, Y. B., 66
Sabatelli, R. M., 399
Saccuzzo, D. P., 330
Sachdev, P., 245
Sachs, G. S., 623
Sackett, P. R., 664
Sadker, D., 382
Sadler, W. A., 394–395
Sagi-Schwartz, A., 377
Sah, P., 64
Saito, T., 239
Sajatovic, M., 623
Sakari, M. M., 436
Salend, S. J., 255
Salgado, J. F., 653
Salovey, P., 336, 426
Salthouse, T. A., 391, 392
Salvatore, J. E., 377
Samarel, N., 403
Samson, L., 450
Sanada, M., 281
Sanaktekin, O. H., 417
Sanchez-de-la-Torre, M., 142
Sanchez-Hucles, J. V., 422
Sánchez-Martín, J. R., 448
Sanders, G., 161
Sanders, J. D., 55
Sanderson, C. A., 396
Sanes, J. N., 299
Sangrigoli, S., 364
Sanislow, C. A., 546
Sansone, L. A., 193
Sansone, R. A., 193
Santelli, J. S., 13
Sanyal, S., 619
Sapirstein, G., 147
Sapolsky, R. M., 66
Sarker, M. R., 181
Saskin, P., 142
Saucier, D. A., 454
Saudino, K. J., 479
Saules, K. K., 178
Saunders, E. H., 570
Saunders, N. L., 281
Sauter, D. A., 212
Sava, F. A., 608, 610
Savage-Rumbaugh, E. S., 326
Savage-Rumbaugh, S., 327
Saveanu, R. V., 570, 571
Savin-Williams, R. C., 201, 202
Savitsy, K., 87
Savitz, J., 571
Saxbe, D., 509
Sayette, M. A., 154
Schacht, A., 212
Schachter, S., 209, 430, 435
Schacter, D. L., 270, 296, 298, 299
Schaie, K. W., 334, 391, 392
Schamberger, M., 616
Schatz, P., 288
Scheele, D., 433
Scheier, M. F., 524, 527
Schein, E. H., 658
Schein, J., 616
Scheir, M. F., 528
Schenk, S., 55
Scherf, K. S., 386
Schiller, J. S., 159, 530
Schiml-Webb, P. A., 572
Schinka, J. A., 479
Schleifer, S. J., 517
Schlesier-Stropp, B., 191
Schlosser, D. A., 580
Schmajuk, N., 117
Schmidt, U., 610
Schmidt-Hieber, C., 387
Schmiedek, F., 391
Schmitt, D. P., 480
Schmitt, N., 656
Schneider, B., 398
Schneider, T., 570
Schneider, T. R., 513
Schoel, W. A., 528
Schoenborn, C. A., 535
Schoenen, J., 522
Schooler, J. W., 154
Schoppe-Sullivan, S. J., 378, 399
Schotte, D. E., 189
Schottenbauer, M. A., 598
Schredl, M., 139
Schreiber, J., 249
Schreiber, J. A., 523
Schroeder, M., 21
Schuch, J. J., 567
Schuckit, M. A., 156
Schueller, S. M., 617
Schuh, K. J., 158
Schulenberg, J. E., 159
Schultz, D. P., 244, 329, 463, 484
Schultz, S. E., 244, 329, 463, 484
Schumacher, J. E., 255
Schumann, G., 155
Schumm, W. R., 397
Schwartz, G., 204
Schwartz, J. R., 141
Schwartz, M., 190
Schwartz, P. D., 390
Schwarzwald, J., 441
Schweizer, S., 572
Schyns, B., 664
Scoboria, A., 148
Scollon, C. N., 480
Scott, T. R., 103
Scott, W., 616
Scoville, W. B., 65

Scullin, M. K., 131, 137
Scully, J. A., 506
Seckl, J., 359
Seeley, J. R., 567, 569, 570
Seeman, M. V., 576
Seeman, P., 54
Seery, M. D., 510
Segal, M. W., 430
Segerstrom, S. C., 517, 524, 525
Segrin, C., 450
Seidler, G. H., 63
Seifer, D. B., 384
Seiffert, A. E., 117
Sekeres, M. J., 298
Sekuler, R., 279
Sela, L., 106
Seligman, M. E. P., 28, 237, 522, 527, 528, 572
Selye, H., 514
Semal, C., 272
Sen, S., 479
Senghas, A., 323
Sephton, S. E., 524
Seth, A. K., 274
Seto, M. C., 156
Sexton, J., 453
Shadish, W. R., 18
Shafer, M., 439
Shah, D. B., 625–626
Shahabi, L., 523
Shallcross, A. J., 520
Shallenberger, R. S., 104
Shamloo, Z. S., 178
Shanker, S. G., 326, 327
Shankman, S. A., 567
Shanks, D. R., 270
Shapiro, D., 516
Shapiro, F., 615, 616
Share, David, 342
Sharma, B., 450
Sharma, L., 136
Shavitt, S., 416
Shaw, H., 192
Shaw, L. H., 531
Shea, A. K., 358
Shebilske, W. I., 513
Shedler, J., 598
Sheeran, P., 414
Sheets, V., 448
Sheline, Y. I., 571
Shen, B. J., 517, 524
Shepard, G. M., 105
Shepard, R. N., 308, 309
Sherif, M., 426, 427, 428
Sherman, D. K., 522
Sherwin, B. B., 196
Shi, J., 578–579
Shields, M., 522
Shiffrin, R. M., 291
Shiffrin, R. W., 271
Shim, R. S., 592
Shimoff, E., 250
Shin, L. M., 560
Shiner, R. L., 480
Shinskey, J. L., 367
Shintani, T., 188
Shiraev, E., 380
Shneidman, E. S., 569
Shoda, Y., 480
Shoham, V., 610, 617
Short, M. A., 131, 535
Shovar, N., 421
Shreeram, S., 143
Shtyrov, Y., 66
Shulman, S., 398
Shults, J., 622
Sicotte, N., 193
Siebert, E. R., 381
Siegel, J. M., 138, 141
Siegel, S., 151, 159
Sierra, M., 562
Siever, L. J., 583
Signorielli, N., 383
Silk, K. R., 613
Silva, C. E., 146
Silva, P., 342
Silver, R. C., 508
Silvia, P. J., 316
Sim, H., 509
Sim, S., 361
Simão, C. P., 212
Simion, F., 364
Simmler, L. D., 162
Simoda, S., 298
Simon, H. A., 274, 316
Simon, T., 329
Simpson, G., 426
Simpson, J. A., 377
Sin, N. L., 536
Sinclair, S., 89
Singer, Jerome, 209
Siniatchkin, M., 228
Sinnott, J. D., 391
Sio, U. N., 317
Skelton, C., 382
Skinner, B. F., 244, 247, 252, 257
Skinner, M. D., 605
Skodol, A. E., 552
Slade, L., 367
Sladek, M., 132
Slameka, N. J., 293
Slattery, M. L., 535
Slavich, G. M., 517
Slavin-Mulford, J., 598
Sloan, R. P., 523
Slotema, C. W., 624
Slovic, P., 321
Small, B. J., 480
Smet, P. F., 94
Smetana, J. G., 396
Smillie, L. D., 477
Smith, C., 138
Smith, C. A., 664
Smith, C. J., 619
Smith, C. T., 131, 137
Smith, D. E., 192
Smith, J. D., 312
Smith, J. W., 239
Smith, M. C., 234, 519
Smith, P. B., 436
Smith, P. C., 662
Smith, P. N., 608
Smith, R. E., 518
Smith, R. L., 382
Smith, S. J., 454
Smith, S. L., 383
Smith, S. M., 151, 276
Smith, T. B., 522, 616
Smith, T. L., 156
Smith, T. W., 525, 526
Smits, J. A., 610
Smolensky, M., 136
Smoski, M. J., 615
Smyth, J. M., 386
Snarey, J., 373
Snowden, L. R., 576
Snyder, A. L., 438
Snyder, C. R., 616
Snyder, L. A., 422
Sobel, N., 106
Sogon, S., 436
Sohail, N., 506
Solberg, E. E., 524
Solberg, L., 21
Soleimani, M., 358
Soloff, P. H., 569, 583
Solomon, H., 454
Solomon, J., 376
Solomon, L. Z., 454
Solorzano, L., 616
Somers, V. K., 138
Somerville, L. H., 390
Sommer, W., 212
Song, Q. H., 522
Soper, B., 179
Soussignan, R., 208
Sowell, E. R., 386
Soyka, M., 156
Spanos, N. P., 146, 148
Spanou, E. E., 191
Spearman, C., 333
Spence, R. T., 161
Spencer, J. A., 189
Spengler, M., 479
Spera, C., 381
Spiegel, D., 563
Spiegler, M. D., 484
Spiers, H. J., 65, 66
Spina, R., 430
Spinath, F. M., 479
Spiro, A., III, 480
Sporer, S. L., 416
Spriggs, M., 617
Spuhl, S. T., 371
Sputa, C. L., 381
Squire, L. R., 287, 298
Srinivasan, L., 24
Srivastava, S., 480
Stacey, D., 155
Staff, L. H. E., 137
Stahl, S. M., 154, 579, 620, 621
Stalder, D. R., 420
Stanley, S. M., 397, 412
Stanovich, K. E., 321
Stanton, J. L., 415
Starks, M. T., 203
Starr, C., 50
Stasio, M. J., 159
Stawski, R. S., 388
Stear, S., 522
Steel, B., 382
Steele, C. M., 423, 424
Steffens, M. C., 425
Stefflre, V., 328
Stein, M. B., 556
Steinberg, L., 378, 400
Steiner, M., 358, 573–574
Steinhausen, H. C., 193
Steinhauser, C., 46
Steinmetz, H., 69
Steketee, G., 557
Stellar, E., 183
Stenblom, E., 182
Stephan, K. E., 68
Stephens, C. E., 248
Stephens, N. M., 422
Steptoe, A., 524, 536
Steriade, M., 131
Sterk, C. E., 161
Stern, K. N., 107, 196
Stern, S. L., 527
Sternberg, R. J., 316, 333, 335, 340
Stevens, A., 309
Stewart, G. L., 659
Stewart, J. A., 622
Stewart, R., 656
St-Hilaire, A., 580
Stickgold, R., 131, 140
Stiles, W. B., 601
Stillman, R. D., 323
Stine-Morrow, E. A., 392
Stoel-Gammon, C., 323
Stone, E. F., 662
Stone, J. M., 579
Storms, G., 313
Storms, M. D., 420
Stout, M., 582
Strassberg, D. S., 201
Strassberg, Z., 252
Straus, M. A., 253
Strickland, B. R., 484
Stright, A. D., 378
Stroebe, M., 404
Stromquist, N. P., 382
Stroup, T. S., 575
Stuart, S. P., 614
Stunkard, A. J., 187
Stuss, D. T., 285
Substance Abuse and Mental Health Services Administration (SAMHSA), 149, 151, 156, 159, 160, 161, 163, 164, 530, 546, 547, 569, 595, 613
Suegami, T., 69
Summerfield, C., 117
Summers, M. J., 281
Sumova, A., 132
Sun, D., 579
Sun, R., 317
Sunar, D., 417
Sundin, J., 558
Super, D. E., 400
Sussman, S., 613
Sutin, A. R., 536
Suzuki, K., 181, 185
Swanson, L. M., 136
Swartz, C., 625
Sweet, T., 203
Swinson, J., 382
Symons, C. S., 291
Sysoeva, O. V., 448
Szasz, T. S., 552
Szentirmai, E., 130
Szkrybalo, J., 380

Tacikowski, P., 69
Tager-Flusberg, H., 324
Taggart, R., 50
Taghavi, M. R., 608
Tajfel, H., 426
Takano, Y., 436
Tallot, L., 234
Tamborini, R., 422, 450
Tamis-Lemonda, C. S., 361
Tamkins, M. M., 658
Tamres, L. K., 518
Tan, M., 143
Tanaka, J. W., 311
Tang, Y. Y., 524
Tanguy, S., 229
Tanner-Smith, E. E., 385
Taormina, R. J., 179
Tashkin, D. P., 163
Tata, D. A., 66
Taurah, L., 161
Taylor, C. B., 617
Taylor, D. J., 135
Taylor, E. J., 523
Taylor, H., 509
Taylor, J. H., 373
Taylor, M. G., 382
Taylor, S. E., 418, 422, 502, 516, 522, 573
Taylor, S. M., 625
Taylor, S. R., 137
Taylor, T. J., 326
Teachman, B. A., 617
Teachman, J. D., 399
Teasdale, J. D., 293, 610
Tegolo, D., 274
Teicher, M. H., 449
Teitelbaum, P., 183
Teixeira, P. J., 178
Tejada-Vera, B., 568
Tenenbaum, H. R., 381
Terhune, D. B., 146
Terman, L. M., 329
Terracciano, A., 479, 480
Terry, D. J., 521
Tesarz, J., 616
Tessner, K., 578–579
Teyber, E., 616
Thase, M. E., 571
Thebarge, R. W., 516
Theodore, G., 620
Thomas, A., 375, 378
Thomas, A. R., 616
Thomas, C. P., 158
Thomas, H. D. C., 659
Thomas, K. M., 386
Thombs, D. L., 159
Thompson, L., 419
Thompson, M., 477
Thompson, P. M., 360, 386
Thoresen, C. E., 523
Thorndike, E. L., 241, 242
Thornhill, R., 196
Thorpy, M., 141
Thurber, C. A., 376
Thurstone, L. L., 661
Tiedemann, J., 382
Tienari, P., 578
Till, B. D., 412
Tobin, K. E., 454
Tohidian, I., 325
Tolbert, R., 161
Toledo, M., 397
Tolin, D. F., 557, 558, 603
Tomaka, J., 519
Tomasello, M., 371
Tomasi, D., 69
Tondo, L., 623
Tonnesen, H., 605
Tooby, J., 321
Topolinski, S., 430
Torgersen, S., 583
Tormala, Z. L., 416
Torres, L., 509
Torrey, E. F., 578–579
Tosi, H., 506
Touyz, S. W., 192
Town, J., 598
Trafimow, D., 421
Tramoni, E., 286
Tranel, D., 64
Trautwein, U., 480
Treasure, J., 193
Tremblay, A. A., 183
Tremblay, R. E., 448
Triandis, H. C., 420, 444
Trimble, M., 571
Triplett, N., 438
Tripp, A., 571
Troisi, J. R., II, 240
Tropp, L. R., 427
Troxel, W. M., 397–398
Troy, A. S., 520
Trull, T. J., 552
Tryon, W. W., 604
Trzepacz, P. T., 449
Tsapelas, I., 397
Tucker, M. A., 137
Tucker-Drob, E. M., 356
Tuerk, P. W., 617
Tullett, A. M., 523
Tulving, E., 285, 291, 293
Turati, C., 364
Turner, A. J., 211
Turner, C. W., 201
Turner, J. A., 610
Turner, P. J., 382
Turner, T. J., 212
Tversky, A., 319, 320, 321
Twenge, J. M., 444, 547
Tylka, T. L., 185

Uchino, B. N., 522
Ultan, R., 326
Umberson, D., 399
Ünal, A., 177
UNICEF, 395
University of Michigan, 160
Unterwald, E. M., 160
Updegraff, J. A., 508
Ursano, R. J., 558
U.S. Census Bureau, 11, 31, 396, 398, 399
U.S. Department of Agriculture, 399
U.S. Department of Energy, 338
Utmann, J. G. A., 323
Uyeyama, R. J., 327
Uzelac, S. M., 390

Valensi, P., 184
Valenzuela, M., 245
Valli, K., 140
van Apeldoorn, F. J., 622
Vance, E. B., 198
van den Boom, D. C., 478
Van den Bulck, J., 141
van der Helm, E., 138
van der Kloet, D., 564
van der Molen, M. W., 131
van der Straten, A., 532
VandeVusse, L., 147
Vandrey, R. G., 163
van Dulmen, M., 396
Van Goozen, S., 448
van Goozen, S. H. M., 583
Van Heteren, C. F., 227
Van Hiel, A., 425
van Hooren, S. A., 392
van Ijzendoom, M. H., 377
Vanini, G., 63
van Laar, M., 619
Vanpaemel, W., 313
Van Pay, C. K., 328
vanReekum, C., 210
van Solinge, H., 401
van Stavel, R., 522
vanTol, H. M., 619
Varley, C. K., 619
Vartanian, O., 316, 317
Vasquez, M. J., 616
Vassallo, S., 97

Venkatesh, K., 533
Ventura, J., 580
Venturelli, P. J., 163
Verbaten, M., 619
Vergne, D. E., 572
Verkhratsky, A., 183
Viechtbauer, W., 479, 480
Vieta, E., 622
Vigezzi, P., 158
Vignovic, J. A., 419
Villafuerte, S., 479
Viswesvaran, C., 653
Vitaliano, P. P., 517
Vitousek, K. M., 191
Volkerts, E., 619
Volkow, N. D., 69, 160, 163
Vollrath, M., 193
Volterra, A., 46
von Allmen, D., 274
von Gontard, A., 143
Voorspoels, W., 313
Voss, J. L., 364
Vygotsky, L. S., 325, 370
Vytal, K., 212

Wadden, T. A., 187
Wade, N. J., 96
Wade, T. D., 191, 192
Wagner, B., 617
Wagner, G. C., 448
Wagner, M. L., 138
Wagner, N. N., 198
Wahlberg, K. E., 578
Wahlsten, D., 356
Waite, L. J., 398
Walak, J., 229
Waldeck, J. H., 657
Waldron-Hennessey, R., 399
Walk, Richard, 364
Walker, B. R., 63
Walker, C. E., 143
Walker, E., 578–579, 580
Walker, L. J., 373, 374
Walker, M. P., 131, 138
Walker, W. R., 562
Wallace, G., 573
Wallace, J., 570
Wallace, M. D., 238
Wallen, K., 381
Waller, E. M., 574
Wallis, C., 28, 529
Walsh, B. T., 193
Walsh, C. M., 131
Walster, E., 431, 432
Walters, S. T., 161
Walton, K. E., 479, 480
Waltz, J., 190
Wampold, B. E., 616
Wan, C. S., 391
Wang, E., 359
Wang, J., 516
Wang, P. S., 567, 595
Wang, S., 509
Wang, S. H., 367
Wang, Y., 117
Wanner, H. E., 283
Wanous, J. P., 655
Warburton, D. M., 158
Ward, E. V., 270
Ward, L. M., 109
Warner, R., 382
Warner, T. D., 378
Warren, M. P., 385
Warwar, S., 613
Waschbusch, D. A., 528
Wasserman, E. A., 234
Wasserman, G. S., 94
Watanabe, H., 436
Watson, J. B., 235, 236
Watson, J. C., 616
Watts, B. V., 616
Weaver, A. J., 450
Webb, C. A., 616
Webb, F. J., 397
Webb, W. B., 131, 132
Weber, E. U., 390
Webster Marketon, J. I., 516
Wechsler, D., 330
Weems, C. F., 508
Weener, E. F., 320
Wegener, D. T., 415, 417
Wei, Q., 624
Weidenmayer, C. P., 66
Weinberg, M. S., 204
Weinshenker, D., 239
Weinstein, S., 579
Weisberg, Y. J., 480
Weiss, A., 526
Weiss, W., 416
Weissman, M. M., 568
Welch, S. S., 568
Welford, A. T., 99
Welles, S. L., 203
Wells, D. L., 164
Wells, G. L., 111
Wells-Parker, E., 151
Welte, J. W., 155
Wentzel, K. R., 381
Wertheimer, M., 115
Wesner, K. A., 573
West, R. F., 321
West, S. G., 18
Westen, D., 471, 614, 615
Westerman, D. L., 310
Westermeyer, J. F., 394
Wetter, D. W., 530
Wever, E. G., 101
Weyant, J. M., 440
Wheeler, D. S., 234
Wheeler, J., 120
Wheeler, M. A., 285, 286
Whipple, B., 197
Whisman, M. A., 15
Whitbourne, S. K., 387, 388
White, B., 430
White, L. K., 400
White, P., 147
White, T. M., 616
Whitton, S. W., 15
Whorf, B. L., 325
Wicherski, M., 4, 31
Wickelgren, I., 163
Widick, P., 69
Widiger, T. A., 552, 558
Wiebe, J. S., 519
Wiechman Askay, S., 147
Wieneke, K., 430
Wiggins, J. S., 481
Wijdicks, E. F. M., 62
Wilcox, T., 97
Wiley, E., 324
Wilhelm, F. H., 520
Williams, D. R., 567
Williams, J. A., 132
Williams, J. M., 160
Williams, K. N., 535
Williams, L. M., 583
Williams, N. A., 132
Williams, P. M., 191
Williams-Keeler, L., 613
Willis, H., 426
Willis, S. L., 391
Willyard, C., 31
Wilson, A E., 119
Wilson, G. S., 524
Wilson, G. T., 191
Wilson, R. S., 392
Wilson, T. D., 422
Wiltink, J., 187
Wing, Y. K., 143
Wingen, M., 161
Wingfield, A., 279
Wingfield, L. C., 423
Winocur, G., 298
Winsler, A., 378
Wirtz, D., 537
Wisco, B. E., 572
Wise, S. M., 326, 327
Wiseman, R., 87
Wiseman, S., 293
Witt, L. A., 664
Witt, S. D., 382
Wittchen, H. U., 560
Wojkiewicz, R. A., 381
Wolf, D. H., 579
Wolf, E. J., 564
Wolfe, J., 558
Wolpe, J., 602
Won, J., 107
Woo, Y. S., 623
Wood, J. V., 573
Wood, W., 356, 417
Woodman, G. F., 275
Woods, D. L., 117
Woods, R., 97
Woods, S. C., 182
Woods-Giscombé, C. L., 381
Woodward, T. S., 579
Woodzika, J. A., 423
Woollett, K., 65, 66, 298
World Health Organization, 547, 567
Worthy, D. A., 391
Wright, I. C., 579
Wright, J. C., 383
Wrightsman, L. S., 394
Wrosch, C., 524
Wu, L., 311
Wyatt, T. J., 203
Wynne, L. C., 578
Wytykowska, A., 343

Xiao, Y., 117
Xie, J., 624
Xie, T., 55
Xiong, G. L., 524
Xiong, Y., 361
Xu, J., 536, 568
Xu, L., 181

Yackinous, C. A., 105
Yalom, I. D., 600, 611
Yamagata, S., 478
Yamnitz, B., 524
Yan, Z., 11
Yang, C. C., 391
Yang, F. M., 281
Yang, P. Y., 141
Yao, M. Z., 245
Yardley, L., 229
Yatham, L. N., 625
Yau, K. W., 93
Yeomans, M. R., 104
Yerkes, R. M., 176, 423
Yinger, J. M., 426
Yokley, J. L., 578–579
Yoo, G. J., 523
Yoon, C., 293
York, J. L., 155
Young, A. H., 571, 622
Young, E., 574
Young, H. M., 517
Young, J. K., 193
Young, K. L., 531
Yu, F., 73
Yunker, B. D., 336
Yunker, G. W., 336
Yurgelun-Todd, D., 163

Zaalberg, R., 205
Zaccaro, S. J., 660
Zack, E., 260
Zadina, J. E., 157
Zadra, A., 139, 140, 597
Zahn-Waxler, C., 252
Zajonc, R. B., 208, 210–211, 430, 432, 438
Zakharia, R., 384
Zaki, S. R., 313
Zakowski, S. G., 523
Zanarini, M. C., 583
Zanna, M. P., 413, 425
Zanni, G., 296
Zeamer, C., 290
Zebrowitz, L. A., 430
Zee, P. C., 134
Zeitzer, J. M., 141
Zelenkauskaite, A., 450
Zhang, A. Y., 576
Zhang, B., 143
Zhang, J., 517
Zhang, J. F., 157
Zhang, Y., 568
Ziegler, D. J., 608
Zimbardo, P. G., 436–437
Zimmerman, F. J., 132
Zimmerman, R., 375
Zinzow, H. M., 558
Zisook, S., 622
Zottoli, M. A., 655
Zougkou, K., 561
Zuckerman, M., 177, 474, 475
Zvolensky, M. J., 549

Subject Index

Note: Page numbers in **bold** indicate terms defined in the margins.

abnormal behavior, 546–549. *See also* mental health disorders
absolute threshold, 86
abuse
  aggression and, 449
  dissociative identity disorder and, 563
acceptance stage of dying, 403
accommodation, 91, 366
accommodation phase of grief, 403
acculturative stress, 509
acetylcholine, 54, 57
achievement, need for, 176
acquisition, 238, 246–247
action potentials, 50, **51**
activation-synthesis theory, 140
actor/observer bias, 420
actualizing tendency, 485
Adler, Alfred, 470
adolescence and adulthood
  cognitive development in, 389–392
  moral reasoning in, 372, 373
  physical development in, 383–388
  psychosocial development in, 393–401
adrenal androgens, 77
adrenal cortex, 77
adrenal glands, 77, 196
adrenalin, 514
adrenal medulla, 77
adulthood. *See* adolescence and adulthood; aging
adverse life events, 572
aesthetic needs, 179
affect, blunted, in schizophrenia, 578
affective commitment, 663
affective component of emotion, 205
affective heuristic, 321
affiliation, need for, 176
age regression, 147–148
aggression, 252, 447–451
aging
  brain and, 73–75
  death and dying, 402–404
  intelligence and, 343, 391–392
  memory and, 278–279
  personality and, 479–480
  sexuality and, 199–200
  sleep and, 132
  stress and, 509
agoraphobia, 555, 559
agreeableness, 477
Ainsworth, Mary, 376
alarm reaction, 514
alcohol use, 151, 154–157, 239, 530, 634–644
algorithm, 315
all-or-none fashion, 50, **51**
all-or-nothing thinking, 609
Allport, Gordon, 472–473, 478
alogia, 578
alternative hypothesis, 643
altruism, 452
American Psychological Association, 20, 594
amnesia, 65, 287–289
amniotic sac, 357
amphetamines, 160–161
amplitude, 89
amygdala, 64, 386, 558
anal-expulsiveness, 469
anal-retentiveness, 469
anal stage, 467–468
analytical intelligence, 335
anandamide, 163
androgens, 77, 196
androgynous, 480
andropause, 388
anger at terminal illness, 402
anima and animus, 470
animal research
  attachment and, 375
  ethical guidelines for, 22
  use of language, 326–327
anorexia nervosa, 191–192, 194
anterograde amnesia, 65, **287**
antianxiety medications, 618–619, 623
anticonvulsant medications, 623
antidepressant medications, 620–622, 623
antimanic medications, 622–623
antipsychotic medications, 619–620, 623
antisocial personality disorder, 581–583
anvil, 99
anxiety
  basic anxiety, 470
  causes of, 558, 560–562
  components of, 553–554
  defense mechanisms and, 466–467
  medication for, 618–619
  perspectives on, 28
  symptoms of, 559
  systematic desensitization for, 602–604
  types of disorders, 555–558
anxiety hierarchy, 603
APA style format for psychological references, 5
aphasia, 68
apparent distance theory, 118
approach-approach conflict, 510–511
approach-avoidance conflict, 511–512
appropriate interactions, 594, 596
approximations, successive, 251
arbitrary inference, 609
archetypes, 470
aripiprazole, 620
arousal theories
  of motivation, 176–177
  of personality, 477
Asch, Solomon, 435
assessment of stress, 513–514
assimilation, 366
association cortex, 71
Ativan, 618–619
attachment, 375–377, 613
attention, 84, **86,** 260, **270**
attitude-behavior consistency, 413–414
attitudes, 412–417
attitudes at work, 661–663
attraction, 429–433
attribution, 418–421, 573
atypical antipsychotics, 620
audience variables, 416–417
auditory canal, 99
auditory cortex, 73
auditory hallucinations, 577
auditory nerve, 100
authoritarian parents, 377
authoritative parents, 377–378
authority figures, 445
autism spectrum disorders, 64
autobiographical memory, 285
autonomic nervous system, 59–60
autonomous motivation, 177
autonomy versus shame and doubt stage, 379
availability heuristic, 320
aversion therapy, 238, 239, 604–**605**
aversive racism, 423
avoidance-avoidance conflict, 511
avoidant attachment, 376
avoidant personality disorder, 582
avolition, 578
axon, 48
axon bulb, 48

babbling, 323
bacterial infections, 533, 534
Baek, Hongyong, 350–353, 410–411, 462
Bandura, Albert, 259, 449, 482–483
barbiturates, 157
bargaining stage of dying, 403
basal metabolic rate, 187–**188**
basic anxiety, 470
basic emotions, 211
basic level category, 311
basilar membrane, 100
bath salts, 162
battle fatigue, 508
Bauby, Jean-Dominique, 41–42, 84–85, 128–129, 213
Baumrind, Diana, 377
Beck, Aaron, 608–609
behavior. *See also* personality disorders
  abnormal, 546
  attitude-behavior consistency, 413–414
  changing, and punishment, 252
  consequences of, 243
  controlling or changing, as goal of psychology, 8
  disordered, 577
  gender-role, 381–383
  health-defeating, 529–534
  health-promoting, 534–535
  hormones and, 76–77
  sexual, and sexual orientation, 201–202
  at work, 663–665
behavioral genetics, 478
behavioral intervention technologies, 617
behavioral perspective, 26
behaviorism, 25, 257
behavior modification, 601
behavior therapy, 601–607, 610
Békésy, Georg von, 101
belongingness and love needs, 178–179
Bem, Daryl, 88
Bem, Sandra, 380
benefit-finding, 508
benzodiazepines, 157, 618–619
bereavement, 403–404
BFOQs (bona fide occupational qualifications), 654
biases in attribution, 418–421
Binet, Alfred, 329
binge drinking, 154
binge eating disorder, 192, 193, 194
bingeing, 191
binocular depth cues, 112–113
biological perspective, 24. *See also* consciousness; emotion; motivation; neuroscience; perception; sensation
  on aggression, 448–449
  on anxiety disorders, 558, 560
  on lust, love, and romance, 432–433
  on memory, 297–299
  on mental health disorders, 548
  on mood disorders, 570–571
  on psychoactive drugs, 151
  on schizophrenia, 578–580
  on stress response, 514–516
  on temperament, 374–375
biological preparedness, 237
biomedical therapy, 592, 618–626
biopsychology, 29
biopsychosocial approach, 537, 549
bipolar disorder, **567,** 570, 622–623
birth defects, 358
bisexuals, 201
blastocyst, 357
blindspot, 91–92
blood alcohol concentrations, 155
blunted affect, 578
Bobo doll experiments, 259–260, 449
body mass index, 186
body senses, 109–110
bona fide occupational qualifications (BFOQs), 654
boomerang generation, 400
borderline personality disorder, 582, **583**
bottom-up perceptual processing, 111–112
brain. *See also* nervous system
  in adolescence and adulthood, 385–387
  aging and, 73–75
  auditory pathways of, 100–102
  central nervous system, 61–69
  endocrine system, 76–77
  habituation and, 227–228
  hunger regulation in, 183–185
  in infancy and childhood, 360–361
  memory and, 297–299
  mood disorders and structures of, 571
  neurons in, 46–53
  neurotransmitters in, 53–57
  schizophrenia and structures of, 579
  specialization of function in, 71–73
  split, 69–70
  technologies for studying, 74–75
  visual pathways of, 96–98
brainstem, 61
brain stimulation, 75
brightness, 89–**90,** 112
Broca's aphasia, 68
Broca's area, 68
Brodmann's area 25, 571
Brown v. Board of Education of Topeka, 31
bulimia nervosa, 191, 194
buspirone, 619
buyer's remorse, 512
bystander effect, 453

caffeine, 158–159
California Psychological Inventory (CPI), 489–490
Calkins, Mary, 30
cancer and stress, 517
can-do factors, 656
Cannon-Bard theory of emotion, 206, **207**
cardinal traits, 473
career development, 400–401
carpal tunnel syndrome, 531
case study, 12, 19
cataplexy, 141
catastrophes and stress, 508
catatonic excitement, 577
catatonic stupor, 577
categories, organization of concepts into, 311–313
cathinones, 162
CAT scan (computerized axial tomography), 74

Cattell, Raymond, 333–334, 337, 473, 476, 478
causal hypothesis, 10
causes, 7
cell body, 46, 47
central executive, 281
central nervous system (CNS), 58
cortex, 67–75
forebrain, 63–67
hindbrain, 62–63
midbrain, 63
overview, 61–62
central route to persuasion, 415–416
central traits, 473
centration, 368
cerebellum, 62, 63
cerebral cortex, 63, 67–75
cerebral hemispheres, 63
chakras, 23–24
challenge, appraisal of, 513
"chemistry" of attraction, 432–433
chemotherapy and taste aversion, 240
childhood. *See* infancy and childhood
childhood abuse
aggression and, 449
dissociative identity disorder and, 563
chlamydia, 533, 534
chlorpromazine, 619
cholecystokinin, 182
chronotype, 133
chunking, 274
cigarette smoking, 159, 530
circadian rhythm, 134–136, 187
Clark, Kenneth, 31
Clark, Mamie Phipps, 31
classical conditioning, 233
applications of, 234–237
elements of, 230, 232–233
extinction of, 238, 240
factors affecting, 233–234
Pavlov and, 229–230
of prejudice, 424
in therapy, 602–605
US-UR pairs, 231
classrooms
gender bias in, 382
jigsaw, 428–429
client-centered therapy, 599–601
clinical interview, 491–492
clinical psychologist, 593
clinical psychology, 29
closure, 116
clozapine, 579
club drugs, 161
CNS. *See* central nervous system
cocaine, 160
cochlea, 100
cochlear duct, 100
cognition, 27, 220, **308**. *See also* thinking
attitude change and, 415–416
emotion and, 210–211
happiness and, 536
learning and, 256–258
observational learning and, 260–261
cognitive appraisal, 210, 513–514
cognitive-behavior therapy, 610
cognitive consistency, 414–415
cognitive development
in adolescence and adulthood, 389–392
in infancy and childhood, 363–374
cognitive distortions, 572, 608–609
cognitive map, 258
cognitive-mediational theory of emotion, 209–**210**
cognitive misers, 418
cognitive needs, 179
cognitive neoassociation theory, 449–450
cognitive perspective, 27
on anxiety disorders, 561
on mental health disorders, 548
cognitive psychology, 29
cognitive reappraisal, 520
cognitive therapy, 607–610, **608,** 610
cohabitation, 396–397
cohesiveness, 435
collective unconscious, 470
collectivistic culture, 419–420
color blindness, 95
color vision, 94–96
communication of emotions, 211–212
communicator variables, 416
community psychology, 29
comorbid, 554, 615
companionate love, 432
competent treatment, 594
competing responses, 602
compliance, 440–442
compulsion, 556–557
computerized axial tomography (CAT scan), 74
computer vision syndrome, 531
concepts, 284, **310**–313
concern for others, 446–447
conclusions, use of statistics to draw, 643–644
concordance rate, 204
concrete operations stage, 366, **369**–370
concussions, 288–289
conditioned response (CR), 232
conditioned stimulus (CS), 232
cones, 92–93
confederates, 209, 435
confidentiality, 21, 594
conflict, 510–512
conformity, 435–437
confounding variable, 17
confrontation phase of grief, 403
conscientiousness, 477
conscious level of awareness, 464
consciousness, 128, **130, 270**. *See also* psychoactive drugs
circadian rhythm, 134–136
dreaming, 139–140
hypnosis, 145–148
sleep, 130–133, 136–139, 143–144
sleep disorders, 140–143
consequences, 26, 243
conservation, 368, 369
consonance, 415
constructive memory, 296
contact hypothesis, 427–429
context and forgetting, 293
contiguity, 234
contingency, 234
continuance commitment, 663
continuity hypothesis, 139
continuous reinforcement, 247
contralateral, 68
control group, 16
controlled motivation, 177
conventional level of moral reasoning, 372, 373
convergence, 363
conversation, norms governing, 434
conversion disorder, 564
cooing, 323
cooperative contact, 427
coping, 518
emotion-focused, 519–521
problem-focused, 519
stress management for, 522–525
cornea, 90–91
corpus callosum, 69
correlation, 13–15, 19
correlation coefficient, 14, 640–642, **643**
cortex, 67-75
corticosteroids, 514
Costa, Paul, 477–478
counseling psychologist, 593
counseling psychology, 29
counterproductive behaviors, 664
couple therapist, 593
couple therapy, 613
covert sensitization, 605
CPI (California Psychological Inventory), 489–490
CR (conditioned response**), 232**
crack cocaine, 160
creative intelligence, 336
creativity, 316–317
critical thinking, 6
cross-cultural psychology, 29
crystallization phase of career development, 400
crystallized intelligence, 333–334, **392**
CS (conditioned stimulus), **232**
cubital tunnel syndrome, 531
cue-dependent forgetting, 293, 294
cultural bias, 332
culturally sensitive treatment, 594, 616
culture
abnormal behavior and, 546
alcohol effects and, 156
anxiety disorders and, 561–562
attachment and, 377
conformity and, 436
drug use and, 151
eating disorders and, 192
emotional expression and, 211–212
food preferences and, 104–105
function of language in, 325
fundamental attribution error and, 419–420
happiness and, 536–537
homosexuality and, 202, 203
norms of conversation and, 434
obesity and, 188
organizational, 657–658
perception and, 120
personality and, 479–480
psychosocial development and, 378–380
punishment and, 253
sleep and, 144
therapy and, 594, 616
weight-based prejudice and, 190
cybertherapy, 617
cycle, 98
cyclothymic disorder, 570

daily hassles, 508–509
dark adaptation, 93–94
data, 633. *See also* statistics
distribution of, 638–639
visual depictions of, 634–636
date rape drug, 157
dating, 396
death
leading causes of, 529
reactions to, 402–404
by suicide, 568–569
debriefing, 21–22, 436
decay theory, 292, 294
deceleration phase of career development, 401
deception in research, 21
decibels, 98
decision making, 319
declarative memory, 284–285
deductive reasoning, 318–319
deep sleep, 137
defense mechanisms, 466–467, **520**–521
deindividuation, 437
delusions, 566, **577**
dendrites, 46, 47
denial of terminal illness, 402
dependent personality disorder, 582
dependent variable, 15, 615
depressants, 151, 154–157
depressive disorders
death, dying, and, 403
medication for, 620–622
noninvasive brain stimulation procedures for, 624–625
overview, 566–567
depth perception, 112–115, 364
dermis, 108
description, 7
descriptive statistics, 636
despair, 395
destructive obedience, 442–444
development, 350, 354, **356**. *See also* cognitive development; physical development; psychosocial development
nature-nurture debate and, 356–357
prenatal, 357–360
psychosexual stages of, 467–469
schizophrenia and, 580
developmental psychology, 29
diagnosis, 492, 552
Diagnostic and Statistical Manual of Mental Disorders (DSM), 194, 202, **550**–553
Diener, Ed, 28
diet/dieting, 188–189, 535
difficult infants, 375
diffusion of responsibility, 453
direct observation, 490–491
discrimination
hiring process and, 654–655
in operant conditioning, 250–251
social-class, 509
stereotypes, prejudice, and, 422–**423**
dishabituation, 228
disidentification, 424
disordered behavior, 577
disorganized/disoriented attachment, 376–377
disorganized speech, 577
display rules, 212
disqualifying positive, 609
dissociative disorder, 562–564
dissociative identity disorder, 563–564
dissociative-PTSD subtype, 564
dissonance theory, 415
distraction and memory, 275
distress and abnormal behavior, 546
distributed practice, 290
divergent thinking, 317
diversity and personality, 479–480
Diving Bell and the Butterfly, The (Bauby), 42, 43
divorce, 398
DNA, 46
doctoral degrees in psychology, 32
Dodo bird verdict, 614
door-in-the-face compliance, 441
dopamine, 54, 57, 182, 196
dopamine receptor gene, 479
double-blind study, 16
Down syndrome, 358
dream analysis, 139, **597**
dreaming, 139–140
drive, 174
drive reduction theory, 174–176
driving and texting, 531
drugs. *See* medication; psychoactive drugs
DSM (Diagnostic and Statistical Manual of Mental Disorders), 194, 202, **550**–553
dual coding system, 274
dualistic thinking, 391
duplicity theory, 101–**102**
dysfunction and abnormal behavior, 546
dysthymia, 566–567

ear, anatomy and function of, 99–100
eardrum, 99
easy infants, 375
eating
cues for, 185
losing weight, 188–189
obesity epidemic, 186–188
eating disorders, 190–194
echoic memory, 272
eclectic (therapy) approach, 28, 615
Ecstasy (MDMA), 55, 161
ECT (electroconvulsive therapy), **624**–625
educational psychology, 29
education in psychology, 32–33
EEG (electroencephalogram) technology, 75, 136
ego, 465–466
egocentrism, 368, 390
e-health interventions, 617
elaborative rehearsal, 276, 291
Elavil, 620
Electra complex, 468
electroconvulsive therapy (ECT), 624–625
electroencephalogram (EEG) technology, 75, 136
electromagnetic spectrum, 89
Ellis, Albert, 607–608
embryonic stage, 357, 359
EMDR (eye movement desensitization and reprocessing) therapy, **615**–616

emerging adulthood, 395
emotion, 205–212
punishment and, 252–253
reactions to death and dying, 402–403
emotional coping mechanisms, 466
emotional eating, 185, 189
emotional intelligence, 336
emotionally focused therapy, 613
emotional reasoning, 609
emotional responses, classical conditioning of, 235–236
emotional stability, 473, **476**
emotion-focused coping, 519–521
empathy, 600
employees
hiring, 652–656
job satisfaction, 661–665
recruitment of, 655–656
socializing, 657–661
empty nest, 400
encoding, 270
encoding specificity principle, 293
endocannabinoids, 188
endocrine glands, 76
endocrine system, 55, **76**–77
endorphins, 56, 57
enuresis, 143
environment
focus on, 25–26
noise in, 99
personality and, 480–481
schizophrenia and, 580
sleep and, 132
environmental psychology, 29
enzymes, 52
epidermis, 108–109
episodic memory, 137, **284**–286
Erikson, Erik, 378–380, 393–395
erogenous zones, 197, 467
establishment phase of career development, 401
esteem needs, 179
estrogens, 54, **77, 195**
estrus, 195–196
ethical guidelines
for animal research, 22
for participants, 20–22
for psychotherapists, 593–594, 596
ethic of care, 372, 373–374
ethnicity. *See also* culture
depression and, 567
drug use and, 149
eating disorders and, 192
field of psychology and, 30–31
intelligence and, 340–341
mental health service use and, 595
schizophrenia and, 576
sleep and, 144
stress and, 509
suicide and, 568
evolution, 24
evolutionary perspective, 24
excitation, 51
excitement phase, 197
exemplar, 312–313
exercise, 522, 535
exergames, 245
exhaustion stage of GAS, 515–516
experiment, 15–18, 19
experimental group, 15–16
experimental psychology, 29
explanations, 7
explicit memory, 270
external locus of control, 483–484
extinction, 238
of classically conditioned responses, 238, 240
flooding and, 604
learned helplessness and, 527
in operant conditioning, 246–247
in therapy, 606
extinction burst, 246
extrasensory perception, 87–88
extraversion, 470, **473,** 477–478
extrinsic motivation, 177–178
eye
adaptation to light and dark, 93–94
color vision, 94–96
outer, anatomy of, 90–91
retina, 91–93
eye movement desensitization and reprocessing (EMDR) therapy, 615–616
eyewitness memory, 296–297
Eysenck, Hans, 473, 476–477, 478

facial expression of emotion, 211–212
facial feedback hypothesis, 207–208
false memories, 294
family therapist, 593
family therapy, 612–613
feature detection theory, 116–117
fetal alcohol syndrome, 154, 358
fetal stage, 357–358, 359
fight-or-flight response, 60, 227
figure-ground, 115
fine motor skills, 362
first-order classical conditioning, 235
five factor theory, 477–478
fixations, 469
fixed interval schedule, 249–250
fixed ratio schedule, 248
flashbulb memory, 295
flehmen, 107
flooding, 604
fluid intelligence, 73, **333**–334, 343, **391**
fMRI (functional MRI), 75
food preferences, 104–105
foot-in-the-door compliance, 440–441
forebrain, 61, 63–67
forensic psychology, 29
forgetting, 292–294
forgetting curve, 276
form, perception of, 115–117
formal concept, 311–313
formal operations stage, 366, **370,** 389–391
formal thought disorder, 577
framing of problem, 319
fraternal birth order effect, 204
fraternal twins, 339
free association, 25, **597**
frequency, 98
frequency distribution, 635
frequency polygon, 635
frequency theory, 101, 102
Freud, Sigmund
contributions and criticisms of, 471–472
defense mechanisms, 520
interpretation of dreams, 139
levels of awareness, 464
psychoanalysis and, 596–597
psychosexual stages of development, 467–469
structure of personality, 464–467
unconscious and, 24–25
Freudian slips, 466
Friedman, Arthur, 650, 658, 659, 665
frontal lobe, 67, 71, 579
frustration-aggression hypothesis, 451
functional fixedness, 317
functionalism, 24
functional MRI (fMRI), 75
fundamental attribution error, 419–420
fusiform gyrus, 108

g (general intelligence), **333**
GABA (gamma amino butyric acid), **55**–56, 57, 154
GAD (generalized anxiety disorder), **554**–555, 559
Gage, Phineas, 71
Galton, Francis, 328–329
gamma amino butyric acid (GABA), 55–56, 57, 154
ganglion cells, 91
Ganzfeld procedure, 87
Gardner, Howard, 334, 335, 337
GAS (general adaptation syndrome), **514**–516
gastric bypass surgery, 189
gender
anxiety disorders and, 561–562
autobiographical memory and, 285
brain lateralization and, 69
color blindness and, 96
concussions and, 288
coping and, 518
defined, 203
depression and, 567
eating disorders and, 191–192
emotional expression and, 212
emotional regulation and, 210
field of psychology and, 30–31
intelligence and, 341–343
marital satisfaction and, 397–398
mental health disorders and, 547
mood disorders and, 573–575
personality and, 479–480
reproductive capacity and, 388
schizophrenia and, 576
self-image, puberty, and, 385
sexuality and, 199–200
sexual response cycle and, 197–198
sleep and, 143
stress and, 509
stress response and, 516
suicide and, 568–569
taste and, 105
vision and, 97–98
gender bias, 382
gender permanence, 380
gender-role behavior, 381–383
gender roles, 380
gender-schema theory, 380–381
general adaptation syndrome (GAS), 514–516
general intelligence (g), 333
generalizability, 12
generalization, 250–251
generalized anxiety disorder (GAD), 554–555, 559
generativity versus stagnation stage, 394–395
genes, 338
genetics
alcohol effects and, 155–156
anorexia and, 193
anxiety disorders and, 560
intelligence and, 339–340
migraine headache and, 228
mood disorders and, 570
personality and, 478–479
schizophrenia and, 578–579
sleep and, 132
genital herpes, 533, 534
genital stage, 468–469
genital warts, 533
genotype, 338
Genovese murder, 452
genuineness, 600
germinal stage, 357
Gestalt approach, 115–116
ghrelin, 181
Gilligan, Carol, 373–374
glia, 46
Global Initiative to End All Corporal Punishment of Children, 253
glucoreceptors, 183
glucose, 181
glutamate, 56, 57, 164, 579
glycogen, 181
Goleman, Daniel, 336, 337
gonads, 77
gonorrhea, 533, 534
good continuation, 116, 117, **117**
Goodnight, Jim, 659–660
Gordon, Emily Fox, 498–501, 502–503
grammar, 324
grandiose delusions, 577
grand mal seizure, 69
graphs, 634–636
grief, 403–404
gross motor skills, 362
group influence, 433–439
group therapy, 611–613
groupthink, 438–439
guessing, as heuristic, 315
guided imagery, 523
gustation, 103

habituation, 227–229
hair cells, 100
Haldol, 619
hallucinations, 566, **577**
hallucinogen persisting perception disorder, 165
hallucinogens, 163–165
hammer, 99
happiness and well-being, 536–537
haptic memory, 272
hardy personality, 528
Harlow, Harry, 375
harm, appraisal of, 513
hate crimes, 203
health
alcohol use and, 154
lifestyle, well-being, and, 529–537
personality and, 525–528
health-defeating behaviors, 529–534
health-promoting behaviors, 534–535
health psychology, 29, 498, 502, **504.** *See also* personality
hearing, 98–102, 364–365
helping behavior, 452, 453–454
heritability, 339. *See also* genetics
heterosexuals, 201
heuristic, 315
in attributions, 418–421
in judgments, 320–321
hierarchy of needs, 178–179, 485
higher-order classical conditioning, 235
high glycemic foods, 182
Hilgard, Ernest, 146
hindbrain, 61, 62–63
hippocampus, 65
hiring process, 652–656
histogram, 635
histrionic personality disorder, 582
HIV/AIDS, 533, 534
hoarding disorder, 557, 559
Holmes, Thomas, 504–506
homeostasis, 66–67, **175**
homophobia, 203
homosexuals, 201
homunculus, 71
hormones
depression and, 571, 573–574
endocrine system and, **76**–77
puberty and, 384
sexual desire and, 195–196
Horney, Karen, 30, 470–471
hostile aggression, 447
HPV (human papilloma virus), 533, 534
hue, 89–**90**
human development. *See* development
human factors psychology, 30
Human Genome Project, 338
humanism, 27
humanistic perspective, 27
on mental health disorders, 548
on personality, **485**–487
humanistic therapy, 599–601, 610
human papilloma virus (HPV), 533, 534
hunger
cues and, 185
feedback from body, 181–182
losing weight, 188–189
mechanisms of, 184
obesity epidemic, 186–188
origins of, 180
regulation of in brain, 183–185
hypervigilance, 557
hypnosis, 145–148
hypnotic susceptibility, 145
hypochondriasis, 564
hypothalamus, 66–67
hypothesis, 8, 10

iconic memory, 272
id, 465–466
idealism of youth, 389
identical twins, 339
identity versus role confusion stage, 393–394
illness anxiety disorder, 564–565
illogical thinking, 368–369
ill-structured problems, 315–316
imaginary audience, 390
immune system and stress, 516–518

immunosuppression, 516
impact phase of grief, 403
implicit memory, 270
impression formation, 417–421
incentive, 177
incubation, 317
independent variable, 15, 615
individualistic culture, 419–420
individual psychotherapy, 611
inductive reasoning, 318–319
industrial and organizational (I/O) psychology
employee satisfaction, 661–665
hiring process, 652–656
overview, 30, 649–**650**
role of work in life, 651–652
socializing employees, 657–661
types of jobs, 652
industry versus inferiority stage, 379–380
infancy and childhood
cognitive development in, 363–374
language learning in, 323–325
moral reasoning in, 372, 373
motor milestones in, 362
physical development in, 360–363
psychosocial development in, 374–383
inferential statistics, 643
inferiority complex, 470
informational conformity, 436
informed consent, 20, 594
in-group bias, 426
inhibition, 51
initiative versus guilt stage, 379
inner ear, 99
insight, 257, 316, 596
insomnia, 140–141
instincts, 174
Institutional Review Board (IRB), 20
instrumental aggression, 447
insulin, 182
integrity versus despair stage, 395
intelligence, 328
aging and, 391–392
diversity in, 339–343
measuring, 328–333
nature, nurture, and, 337–339
nature of, 333–336
intelligence quotient (IQ), 329
interactionism, 338, 340
intergroup dynamics and prejudice, 425–427
internal locus of control, 483
interneurons, 59
interpersonal therapy, 598
interpretation
of life events, 607–608
in psychoanalysis, **597**
interval schedule of reinforcement, 249–250
intimacy versus isolation stage, 394
intrapsychic conflicts, 467
intrinsic motivation, 177–178
introspection, 23
introversion, 470, **473,** 477–478
intuition, 315–316
intuitive eating, 185, 189
in vivo exposure, 603
I/O psychology. *See* industrial and organizational (I/O) psychology
ions, 49
IQ (intelligence quotient), **329**
IRB (Institutional Review Board), **20**
iris, 90
irrational beliefs and assumptions, 608
isolation, 394

James, William, 24
James-Lange theory of emotion, 206–207
jet lag, 135
jigsaw classroom, 428–429
job analysis, 653
jobs. *See also* work
prestige of, 651
types of, 652
job satisfaction, 661–663
job withdrawal, 664
Jones, Gilbert Haven, 30
Jones, Mary Cover, 602
judgment, 319–321
Jung, Carl, 469–470
just noticeable difference, 86–**87**

kinesthesis, 109
knowledge, 308
Kohlberg, Lawrence, 372–373
Köhler, Wolfgang, 257
Korsakoff's syndrome, 154
K2, 164
Kübler-Ross, Elisabeth, 402

labeling, 609
Ladd-Franklin, Christine, 30
language, 322
acquisition of, 322–325
animals and, 326–327
function of, 325, 328
language acquisition device, 322
latency stage, 468
latent content of dreams, **139,** 597
latent learning, 257–258
lateral hypothalamus, 183
laughter and stress, 524
law of effect, 241–243, **242**
Lazarus **cognitive-mediational theory of emotion,** 209–**210**
leadership, 659–660
learned helplessness, 527–528, **572**
learning, 220, **226**. *See also* classical conditioning; operant conditioning
acquiring attitudes through, 412–413
aggression and, 449–451
alcohol effects and, 156
anxiety disorders and, 560–561
cognition and, 256–258
dishabituation, 228
observational, 258–261
orienting reflexes and habituation, 226–229
of prejudice, 424–425
legal issues in hiring, 654–655
lens, 91
leptin, 182
levels-of-processing model, 277
Lexapro, 622
libido, 195
licensed professional counselor, 593
licensed social worker, 593
life change unit, 504
life events
early adverse, 572
stress and, **504**–507
light
adaptation to, 93–94
colors of, 94
measurement and properties of, 89–90
light adaptation, 93–94
limbic system, 63, 64–66
linguistic relativity hypothesis, 325, 328
lithium, 622–623
Little Albert experiments, 25–26, 235–236
liver, role of in hunger, 181
lock-and-key theory, 107
locked-in syndrome, 41
locomotive ability, 361
locus of control, 483–484
Loftus, Elizabeth, 296–297
long-term memory, 271
amnesia and, 287–289
capacity of, 283
declarative and procedural, 284–287
encoding in, 283
organization in, 284
retrieval and forgetting in, 289–294
transferring information to, 275–276
loss aversion, 319
loudness, 98
low-balling, 442
LSD (lysergic acid diethylamide), 164–165
lust, 432
lysergic acid diethylamide (LSD), 164–165

magnetic resonance imaging (MRI), 74
magnification, 609
maintenance phase of career development, 401
maintenance rehearsal, 275
major depressive disorder, 566
majority group, 435
mania, 567, 570
manifest content of dreams, **139**
MAO (monoamine oxidase), 474
MAO inhibitors, 620–621
margin of safety, 150
marijuana, 163
marriage, 396, 397–398, 399
Maslow's **hierarchy of needs, 178**–179, 485
massed practice, 290
master's degrees in psychology, 32
matching hypothesis, 432
maternal immune hypothesis, 204
Mayberg, Helen, 571
Mayer-Salovey-Caruso Emotional Intelligence Test (MSCEIT), 336
McCrae, Robert, 477–478
MDMA, 55, 161
mean, 636–637
measurement
of intelligence, 328–333
of light, 89–90
of personality, 488–492
of sensation and perception, 86–88
of stress, 504–507
measures of central tendency, 636–638
media
gender portrayals in, 383
portrayals of violence in, 450
median, 637
medical model, 548
medication
antianxiety, 618–619
anticonvulsant, 623
antidepressant, 620–622
antipsychotic, 579, 619–620
for narcolepsy and cataplexy, 141
psychiatric, 592
medicine, influence of field of, 23–24
meditation, 524
medulla, 62
melatonin, 134
Mellaril, 619
memory. *See also* long-term memory; short-term memory
accuracy of, 295–297
acetylcholine and, 54
aging and, 278–279
biology of, 297–299
defined, 220
development of new memories, 271–282
episodic, 137
forgetting and, 292–294
functions of, 270
improving, 290–291
retrieval and, 289–294
as storage, **270**
three-stages model of, 271–274, 282
working memory model, 279–282
memory blackouts, 154
memory consolidation, 297
memory theory, 139
memory traces, 270
menarche, 384
menopause, 388
mental age, 329
mental equilibrium and disequilibrium, 366
mental health disorders, 498, **546**. *See also* therapy
anxiety, 553–562
biological theories of, 548
classification of, 549–553
dissociative and somatic symptoms, 562–565
mood disorders, 565–567, 570–575
neurotransmitters and, 54–55
personality disorders, 581–583
perspectives on, 547–549
prevalence of, 546–547
schizophrenia, 575–580
suicide and, 568–569
mental health professionals, 592–593
mental representation, 308
mental set, 317
mentoring, 658
mere exposure effect, 211, 430
message variables, 417
microsleep, 130
midbrain, 61, 63
middle ear, 99
midlife crisis, 394–395
migraine headache, 228
Milgram, Stanley, 21–22, 442–443, 445, 446
minimization, 609
Minnesota Multiphasic Personality Inventory (MMPI-2), 489–490
minority stress, 203, 509
misinformation effect, 296
MMPI-2 (Minnesota Multiphasic Personality Inventory), **489**–490
mnemonic devices, 291
Mockingbird Years (Gordon), 501
mode, 638
modeling, 258–261
Molly (MDMA), 161
monoamine oxidase (MAO), 474
monoamine oxidase (MAO) inhibitors, 620–621
monocular depth cues, 114–115
mood disorders, 565–566
bipolar-related, 567, 570
causes of, 570–573
depressive disorders, 566–567
gender and, 574–575
moon illusion, 118–119
moral reasoning, 372–374
morpheme, 324
motivation. *See also* hunger
emotion compared to, 205
to forget, 294
observational learning and, 261
sexual, 195–204
theories of, 174–179
motive, 174
motor cortex, 71
motor neurons, 58–59
MRI (magnetic resonance imaging), 74
MSCEIT (Mayer-Salovey-Caruso Emotional Intelligence Test), 336
Müller-Lyer illusion, 119–120
multiple approach-avoidance conflicts, 512
multiple intelligences, 334, 335
multiple personality disorder, **563**
myelin, 46
myelin sheath, 48
Myers-Briggs Personality Inventory, 489

narcissistic personality disorder, 582
narcolepsy, 141
natural concept, 311–313
naturalistic observation, 11–12, 19
natural selection, 24, **338**
nature-nurture debate, 338
development and, **356**–357
gender-role behavior and, 381–383
needs, hierarchy of, 178–179, 485
negative correlation, 14
negative feedback loop, 175, 180
negative punishment, 243
negative reinforcement, 242–243
negative thinking, 572–573
neodissociation theory, 146
neo-Freudians, 469–471
neonate, 360
nervous system, 57–58
autonomic, 59–60
peripheral, 58–59
somatic, 59
neural growth and pruning, 387
neurobiology of extraversion and introversion, 476–477

neurons, 46
anatomy of, 47–49
firing of, 49–51
in reflex, 46
reuptake, 52–53
sensory and motor, 58–59
stimulation of, 624
synaptic transmission, 51–52
neuropeptide Y, 183
neuroplasticity, 65–66
neuroscience, 24, 46. *See also* central nervous system
biomedical therapies, 618–626
endocrine system, 76–77
neurons, 46–52
neurotransmitters, 53–57
structure of nervous system, 57–60
neuroticism, 473, **476,** 477
neurotransmitters, 48
acetylcholine, 54, 57
described, 53–54, 57
dopamine, 54, 57, 182, 196
endorphins, 56, 57
GABA, 55–56, 57, 154
glutamate, 56, 57, 164, 579
mood disorders and, 570–571
norepinephrine, 55, 57
schizophrenia and, 579
serotonin, 55, 57, 448-449
neutral stimulus, 232
nicotine, 159
nightmares, 143
night shift work, 135–136
night terrors, 143
noise and hearing loss, 99
Nolen-Hoeksema, Susan, 572
nonintuitive eating, 185
non-REM sleep, 137
nontasters, 105
norepinephrine, 55, 57
normal distribution, 639–**640**
normative commitment, 663
normative conformity, 436
norming group, 489
norms, 434–435
nose and sense of smell, 106–108
null hypothesis, 643

obedience, 440, 442–447
obesity, 186–**188**
object permanence, 367
observational learning
of aggression, 449
of attitudes, 413
of prejudice, 424
overview, **258**–261
obsession, 556–557
obsessive-compulsive disorder (OCD), 556–557, 559
obsessive-compulsive personality disorder, 582
occipital lobe, 67, 72–73
OCD (obsessive-compulsive disorder), **556**–557
Oedipus complex, 468
olfaction, 106
olfactory bulb, 107
olfactory epithelium, 106–107
olfactory nerve, 107
150-volt solution, 444
openness, 477
operant conditioning, 241, 412
acquisition and extinction, 246–247
attitude acquisition and, 412–413
design of program of, 252–256
discrimination and generalization, 250–251
experimental study of, 244–245
law of effect and, 241–243
of prejudice, 424
schedules of reinforcement, 247–250
shaping new behaviors, 251
in therapy, 605–607
opiates, 56, **157**–158
opponent-process theory, 96
optic chiasm, 97
optic nerve, 91–92
optimism and stress, 524
oral fixation, 469
oral stage, 467
organismic valuing process, 486
organizational citizenship behaviors, 664
organizational climate, 658
organizational commitment, 663
organizational culture, 658
organizational socialization, 657
organizational withdrawal, 664
orgasm phase, 197–198
orienting reflex, 226–227
outcomes and decision making, 319
outer ear, 99
out-group homogeneity, 426
outliers, 637
oval window, 99–100
ovaries, 77, **196**
overextension, 324
overgeneralization, 609
overlearning, 291
overweight, 186, **188**
oxytocin, 196, 432–433

pancreas, 77
panic disorder, 555, 559
papillae, 103
paranoid personality disorder, 582
parasitic infections, 533–534
parasympathetic nervous system, 60
pareidolia, 364
parenting, 377–378, 398–401
parietal lobe, 67, 72
Parkinson's disease, 54–55, 625
partial reinforcement, 247–**248**
participants
ethical guidelines for, 20–22
selecting, 11
Pavlov, Ivan, 25, 229–230, 257
PCP (phencyclidine), 164
Peek, Kim, 221–223, 284, 300, 306–307
PEN model, 473, 476–477
perceived authority figures, 445
perception, 84, **86**
accuracy of, 118–120
cultural factors in, 120
extrasensory, 87–88
hearing, 98–102
in infancy and childhood, 363–365
interpretation of sensory information, 110–117
language and, 325, 328
of pitch, 100–102
subliminal, 87
vision, 88–98
perceptual constancy, 112, 113, 118–119
perceptual contrast, 441
perfect correlation, 14
performance appraisals, 660–661
periodic limb movement in sleep, 142
peripheral nervous system (PNS), 58
peripheral route to persuasion, 416
permissive parents, 378
persecutory delusions, 577
persistent depressive disorder, 566–567
persistent psychosis, 165
persisting strategies, 510
persona (archetype), 470
personal fable, 390
personality, 350, 462, **464**
hardy, 528
health and, 525–528
humanistic approach, 485–487
measurement of, 488–492
psychoanalytic approach, 464–472
social cognitive approach, 482–484
trait approach, 472–481
Type A, B, and C, 525–526
personality disorders, 193, **581**–583
personality inventory, 488–490
personality neuroscience, 479
personality psychology, 30
personalization, 609
personal responsibility, sense of, 446–447
personal semantics, 286
personal unconscious, 470
person-centered therapy, 599–601
person schemas, 284
person-situation interaction, 480–481
persuasion, 415–417
PET scan (positron emission tomography), 74
phallic stage, 466, **468**
Ph.D. programs, 32
phencyclidine (PCP), 164
phenothiazines, 579
phenotype, 338
pheromones, 107
phoneme, 324
phonological loop, 281
photopigments, 93
physical activity, 522, 535
physical attractiveness, 431–432
physical development
in adolescence and adulthood, 383–388
in infancy and childhood, 360–363
physiological needs, 178
Piaget, Jean, 365–370, 389
pineal gland, 77
pinna, 99
pitch, 98–99
pitch perception, 100–102
pituitary gland, 76–77
placebo effect, 16
placenta, 357
place theory, 100–101, 102
plasticity of brain, 361, 387
plateau phase, 197
pleasure principle, 465
pluralistic ignorance, 453
PNS (peripheral nervous system), **58**
polygenetic, intelligence as, 339
pons, 62, 63, 100
Ponzo illusion, 119
population of interest, 11
positive correlation, 14
positive psychology, 27–28, 30, 487
positive punishment, 243
positive reinforcement, 242–243, 606
positron emission tomography (PET scan), 74
postconventional level of moral reasoning, 372, 373
postformal thought, 391
postsynaptic neuron, 48
posttraumatic growth, 508
posttraumatic stress disorder (PTSD), 66, 508, **557**–558, 559
poverty of speech, 578
poverty of stimulus argument, 322
practical intelligence, 335–336
pragmatics, 324–325
preconscious level of awareness, 464
preconventional level of moral reasoning, 372, 373
prediction, 7, **8**
predictive hypothesis, 10
prefrontal lobotomy, 625
prehension, 361
prejudice, 422
intergroup dynamics and, 425–427
overview, 421–422
reducing, 427–429
social transmission of, 424–425
stereotypes, discrimination, and, 422–423
stereotype threat and, 423–424
weight-based, 189–190
prenatal development, 357–360, 580
preoperational stage, 366, **367**–369
presbyopia, 387
presynaptic neuron, 48
prevalence of mental health disorders, 546–547
preverbal gestures, 324
primacy effect, 278
primary appraisal, 513
primary auditory area, 73
primary drive, 175
primary motor area, 71
primary reinforcer, 255
primary somatosensory area, 72
private speech, 370–371
proactive interference, 292, 294
probability and decision making, 319
problem-focused coping, 519
problem solving, 314–317
procedural memory, 286–287
progressive relaxation training, 522, 602
projective test, 490
prosocial behavior, **452**–454
Prosser, Inez, 31
prototype, 312–313
proximity, 116, 430
Prozac, 622
pseudopsychology, 6
psychiatrist, 593
psychiatry, 32
psychoactive drugs, 148–149
alcohol, 151, 154–157
bath salts, 162
depressants, 151, 157
effects of, 151, 152–153
hallucinogens, 163–165
opiates, 157–158
stimulants, 158–161
tolerance of and dependence on, 150–151
variations in use of, 149–150
psychoanalysis, 25, 596–598, **597,** 610
psychoanalytic perspective
on mental health disorders, 548
on personality, **464**–472
psychoanalytic theory, 25
psychodynamic perspective, 25
psychodynamic therapy, 598
psychological distance, 446
psychology, 4
critical thinking and, 6
gender, ethnicity, and, 30–31
goals of, 8
misconceptions about field of, 4–6
perspectives, 23
reference citations in, 5
science of, 7–18
specialty areas in, 29–30
training in, 32–33
psychoneuroimmunology, 516
psychopathology, 548
psychopharmacology, 618
psychophysics, 86–88
psychosexual stages of development, 467–469
psychosocial development
in adolescence and adulthood, 393–401
in infancy and childhood, 374–383
psychosurgery, 625–626
psychotherapy, 592
psychoticism, 476
Psy.D. programs, 32
PTSD (posttraumatic stress disorder), 66, 508, **557**–558, 559
puberty, 384–385
public lice, 533–534
punishment, 26, **242**–243, 252–255, 606
pupil, 90, **91**
purging, 191

quasi-experiment, 18, 19

race. *See also* culture; ethnicity
intelligence and, 340–341
stress and, 509
Rahe, Richard, 504–506
random assignment, 17–18
random sample, 11
range, 638
rape trauma syndrome, 508
rating scales, 490–491
rational-emotive therapy, 607–608
rationalization, 466–467
ratio schedule of reinforcement, 248–249
Rayner, Rosalie, 25, 235
reactivity, 12
realistic-conflict theory, 426–427
reality principle, 465
reality shock, 400
reasoning, 318–319, 372–374
recall, 290
recency effect, 278–279
reciprocal determinism, 482–483

reciprocity, 441
recognition, 291
reconstructive memory, 296
recovered memory, 148
recruitment, 655–656
reference, delusions of, 577
reference citations, 5
reflection, 600
reflex, 46, **361**
refractory period, 50–**51, 198**
reinforcement, 26, **242,** 247–250, 255–256
relapse rates, 619
relativistic thinking, 391
relaxation, 522, 602
reliability, 332, 488
REM behavior disorder, 138
REM rebound, 138
REM sleep, 137–138
replication of study, 9
representativeness heuristic, 320–321
representative sample, 11
repression of memory, 294
reproductive capacity and gender, 388
resilience, 510
resistance in therapy, 597
resistance stage of GAS, 515
resistant attachment, 376
resolution phase, 198
response, 25
response set theory of hypnosis, 146
resting potential, 49
restless legs syndrome, 142
reticular formation, 62, 63
retina, 91–93
retinal disparity, 112–114
retirement phase, 401
retroactive interference, 293, 294
retrograde amnesia, 287
reuptake, 52–53
reward-processing theory, 477
risk aversion, 319
risperidone, 620
Robber's Cave experiment, 426–428
rods, 92–93
Rogers, Carl, 485–487, 599–601
Rohypnol, 157
role confusion, 393–394
romantic attraction, 432
rooting reflex, 361
Rorschach Inkblot Test, 490
Rotter, Julian, 483–484
ruminative coping style, 572, 574

safety needs, 178
same-sex marriage, 202
sample, 11
samples of convenience, 11
sampling bias, 11
SAS case example, 650, 656, 658, 659–660, 663, 665
satiety, 183
saturation, 89–**90**
scabies, 533–534
scaffolding, 371
scapegoat, 426
scatter plot, 635–636
Schachter-Singer **two-factor theory of emotion, 208**–209
schedule of reinforcement, 247–250
schema, 284, 366–367
schizoid personality disorder, 582
schizophrenia, 575–580
schizotypal personality disorder, 582
school psychology, 30
scientific method, 4, 8–10, 19
sclera, 90
scripts, 284
secondary appraisal, 514
secondary drive, 176
secondary reinforcer, 255
secondary traits, 473
secure attachment, 376
sedatives, 157
selective abstraction, 609
selective serotonin reuptake inhibitors (SSRIs), 55, 621, **622**
self-actualization, 179, **485,** 599
self-concept, 486
self-determination theory, 177–178
self-efficacy, 483
self-fulfilling prophecy, 423, 552
self-help groups, 613
self-serving bias, 420–421
self-talk, 371
self theory, 485–487
Seligman, Martin, 27–28
Selye, Hans, 514
semantic encoding, 283
semantic memory, 284–286
sensation, 84, **86**. *See also* perception
  body senses, 109–110
  measurement of, 86–88
  smell, 106–108
  taste, 103–105
  touch, 108–109
sensation seekers, 474–475
sensitive period, 358–359
sensorimotor stage, 366, **367**
sensory memory, 271, 272–274
sensory neurons, 58–59
separation anxiety, 376
serial-position curve, 278–279
serotonin, 55, 57, 448–449
serotonin transporter gene, 479
set point, 180
sex hormones, 384
sexual arousal, 195
sexual desire, 195–197
sexually transmitted infections (STIs), 532–534
sexual orientation, 200–204
sexual response cycle, 197–198
shadow (archetype), 470
shape, perception of, 112
shaping, 251, 606
shell shock, 508
Sherif, Muzafer, 426
shifting strategies, 510
short-term dynamic therapy, 598
short-term memory, 271
  capacity of, 274
  dual coding system, 274
  duration of, 275–276
  elaborative rehearsal, 276
  existence of, 278
  levels-of-processing model, 277
SIDS (sudden infant death syndrome), 142
significant (results), **643**
similarity (Gestalt principle), **116**
similarity and attraction, 430–431
Simon, Théodore, 329
singlehood, 396
situational attribution, 418
6-n-proppylthiocuracil, 105
60-60 rule, 99
size, perception of, 112
skin and sense of touch, 108–109
Skinner, B. F., 26, 244, 257
Skinner box, 244–245, 248
sleep
  circadian rhythm and, 134–136
  disorders of, 140–143
  dreaming, 139–140
  functions of, 130–131
  as health-promoting behavior, 535
  need for, 131–133
  stages of, 136–139
sleep apnea, 141–142
sleep disorder, 140–143
sleep spindles, 137
sleepwalking, 142–143
slippery slope, 446
slow-to-warm-up infants, 375
slow-wave sleep, 137
smell, 105, 106–108, 196–197, 365
smoking, 159, 530
social anxiety disorder, 556, 559
social-class discrimination, 509
social cognition, 412
social cognitive approach to personality, 482–484
social costs of alcohol use, 156–157
social facilitation, 438
social influence, 412
social learning perspective on mental health disorders, 548
social learning theory, 259
social loafing, 438
social psychology, 30, 350, **412**
social smile, 361
social support, 522–523, 536
social transmission of prejudice, 424–425
sociocultural perspective, 26
sociocultural theory, 325, 549
somatic nervous system, 59
somatic symptom disorders, 564–565
somatosensory cortex, 72
sound waves, 99
source traits, 473
Spearman, Charles, 333, 337
specification phase of career development, 400
specific phobia, 555–**556,** 559
Spice, 164
spirituality
  Millennials and, 13
  need for, 179
  stress and, 523
split brain, **69–70**
spontaneous recovery, 240, 604
sports psychology, 30
SQ3R method, 291
SSRIs (selective serotonin reuptake inhibitors), 55, 621, **622**
stages of reaction to death and dying, 402–403
stagnation, 394
standard deviation, 638
standardized test, 329
standard normal distribution, 640
Stanford-Binet, 329–330
Stanford Hypnotic Susceptibility Scale, 145
Stanford prison experiment, 436–437
statistics, 633–**634**
  correlation coefficient, 640–642
  graphs, 634–636
  measures of central tendency, 636–638
  measures of variability, 638–639
  normal and standard normal distributions, 639–640
  using, to draw conclusions, 643–644
stereotype, 284, 342–343, 382, **422**
stereotype threat, 423–424
Sternberg, Robert, 334–335, 337
Still Life with Rice (Lee), 350, 353
stimulants, 158–161
stimulus, 25
stimulus discrimination, 236
stimulus generalization, 236
stirrup, 99
STIs (sexually transmitted infections), **532**–534
storage (memory), 270. *See also* long-term memory; short-term memory
stranger anxiety, 376
stress, 504
  catastrophes and, 508
  conflict and, 510–512
  coping with, 518–525
  daily hassles and, 508–510
  immune system and, 516–518
  life events and, 504–507
  mood disorders and, 573
stress response
  cognitive appraisal, 513–514
  gender and, 516
  general adaptation syndrome, 514–516
  overview, 512
striatum, 299
structuralism, 23
structured interview, 653–654
subgenual cingulate, 571
subjective well-being, 536–537
sublimation, 467
subliminal perception, 87
subordinate category, 311
substance dependence, 150
successful intelligence, 335
sudden infant death syndrome (SIDS), 142
suicide, 568–569
Sumner, Francis, 30–31
sum of squares, 638
superego, 466
superordinate category, 311
superordinate goal, 427
supertasters, 105
suprachiasmatic nucleus, 134
surface traits, 473
survey, 12–13, 19
symbolic thinking, 367
sympathetic nervous system, 60
synapse, 48
synaptic gap, 48
synaptic transmission, 51
synesthesia, 165
synthetic marijuana, 164
syphilis, 533, 534
systematic desensitization, 602–604

tardive dyskinesia, 620
taste, 103–105, 365
taste aversion, 236–237, 239
taste buds, 103–104
teaching machines, 244–245
technology
  behavioral interventions and, 617
  distraction, memory, and, 275
  health effects of, 531
  operant conditioning and, 245
  for studying brain, 74–75
  virtual reality exposure therapy, 603–604
telegraphic speech, 324
television and violence, 450
temperament, 374–**375,** 478, 536
temporal lobe, 67, 73, 579
teratogens, 358–359
Terman, Lewis, 329
test, 653. *See also* measurement
testes, 77, **196**
testosterone, 196
tetrahydrocannabinol (THC), **163**
texting and driving, 531
thalamus, 66–67
that's-not-all technique, 442
THC (tetrahydrocannabinol), **163**
Thematic Apperception Test, 490
theory, 5, 7. *See also specific theories*
therapeutic alliance, 616
therapy, 498, 590, **592**
  approaches to, 610
  behavior, 601–607
  biomedical, 618–626
  cognitive, 607–610
  effectiveness of, 614–617
  ethical guidelines for, 593–594, 596
  group approaches, 611–613
  humanistic, 599–601
  mental health professionals, 592–593
  psychoanalytic, 596–598
  seeking, 595–596
thinking, 308. *See also* cognition
  concepts, 310–313
  critical, and psychology, 6
  illogical, 368–369
  influence of language on, 325, 328
  negative, 572–573
  postformal, 391
  problem solving, 314–317
  visual images, 308–309
Thorndike's **law of effect,** 241–243, **242**
thought control, delusions of, 577
threat, appraisal of, 513
threat simulation theory, 139–140
three-stages model of memory, 271–274, 282
threshold of excitation, 49
Thurstone, L. L., 333, 337
thylakoids, 182
thyroid gland, 77
timbres, 101
time management, 524–525
tip of the tongue phenomenon, 292
Titchener, Edward, 23
Title VII of Civil Rights Act of 1964, 654

TMS (transcranial magnetic stimulation), **624**
Tofranil, 620
token economy, 255–256, **606**–607
tolerance, 150
Tolman, Edward, 257–258
top-down perceptual processing, 110–111, 118, 284
touch, 108–109, 365
traditional psychoanalysis, 597–598
trait approach to personality, 472–481
trait attribution, 418
traits, 472
transcendence, need for, 179
transcranial magnetic stimulation (TMS), 624
transference, 597–598
transformational leadership, 659
treatment resistance, 624
trial and error, as heuristic, 315
triarchic theory of intelligence, 334–336, **335**
trichromatic theory of color vision, 94–95, 96
tricyclic antidepressants, 620, 621
trust versus mistrust stage, 379
twin studies, 204, 339, 479
two-factor theory of emotion, 208–209
tympanic membrane, 99
Type A personality, 525–527
Type B personality, 525–526
Type C personality, 525–527
tyramine, 621

umami, 103
umbilical cord, 357
unconditional positive regard, 486–487, **600**–601
unconditioned response (UR), 230–231
unconditioned stimulus (US), 230–231
unconscious level of awareness, 24–25, **464,** 471
underextension, 324
understanding, need for, 176
unstructured interview, 653–654
UR (unconditioned response), **230**–231
US (unconditioned stimulus), **230**–231

validity, 332, 488
validity scales, 490
Valium, 618–619
Valproate, 623
variability, measures of, 638–639
variable interval schedule, 250
variable ratio schedule, 248–249
variance, 638
ventricles, 182, 579, 580
ventromedial hypothalamus, 183–184
vesicles, 48
vestibular sense, 109–110
viability, 358
viral infections, 533, 534
virtual reality exposure therapy, 603–604
visible spectrum, 89
vision, 88–98, 363–364
visual cortex, 72–73
visual hallucinations, 577
visual images, 308–309
visuospatial sketch pad, 281
volley theory, 101, 102
vomeronasal sense, 107–108
Vygotsky, Lev, 325, 370–371

WAIS-IV (Wechsler Adult Intelligence Scale), 330–331
Washburn, Margaret, 23, 30
Watson, John B., 25, 235, 257
wavelength, 89
wealth and happiness, 536
Weber's law, 86–**87**
Wechsler, David, 330
Wechsler Adult Intelligence Scale (WAIS-IV), 330–331
weekend lag, 135
weight, losing, 188–189
weight-based prejudice, 189–190
Wellbutrin, 622
well-structured problems, 315–316
Wernicke's aphasia, 68
Wernicke's area, 68
Whorfian hypothesis, 325, 328
will-do factors, 656
withdrawal symptoms, 150–151
word salad, 577
work. *See also* employees; industrial and organizational (I/O) psychology; jobs
  attitudes at, 661–663
  behaviors at, 663–664
  career development, 400–401
  in groups, 437–439
  on night shift, 135–136
  settings of psychologists, 33
working memory, 279–282
work teams/groups, 658–659
work withdrawal, 664
Wundt, Wilhelm, 23

Xanax, 618–619

Yerkes-Dodson curve, 176

zero correlation, 14
Zimbardo, Phillip, 436–437
Zoloft, 622
zone of proximal development, 371
z score, 639, **640**
Zyban, 622
zygote, 357